ENCYCLOPEDIA OF

LATIN
AMERICAN
HISTORY
AND CULTURE

W9-BTR-971

ADVISORY BOARD

Margaret E. Crahan
Hunter College, City University of New York

Richard Graham
University of Texas at Austin

Louis A. Pérez, Jr.
University of North Carolina at Chapel Hill

Jaime E. Rodríguez O.
University of California, Irvine

Susan M. Socolow
Emory University

MONTGOMERY COLLEGE
ROCKVILLE CAMPUS LIBRARY
ROCKVILLE, MARYLAND

ENCYCLOPEDIA OF

LATIN AMERICAN HISTORY AND CULTURE

BARBARA A. TENENBAUM

EDITOR IN CHIEF

Georgette Magassy Dorn
Mary Karasch
John Jay TePaske
Ralph Lee Woodward, Jr.
ASSOCIATE EDITORS

VOLUME 3

Charles Scribner's Sons

MACMILLAN LIBRARY REFERENCE USA

SIMON & SCHUSTER MACMILLAN

NEW YORK

SIMON & SCHUSTER AND PRENTICE HALL INTERNATIONAL

LONDON   MEXICO CITY   NEW DELHI   SINGAPORE   SYDNEY   TORONTO

OCT 0 7 1999

205609

Copyright © 1996 Charles Scribner's Sons

All rights reserved. No part of this book may be reproduced in any form or by any means, electronic or mechanical, including photocopying, recording, or by any information storage and retrieval system, without permission in writing from the Publisher.

An imprint of Simon & Schuster Macmillan
866 Third Ave.
New York, NY 10022

Library of Congress Cataloging-in-Publication Data

Encyclopedia of Latin American history and culture / Barbara A.
    Tenenbaum, editor in chief ; associate editors, Georgette M. Dorn
    . . . [et al.].
        p.   cm.
        Includes bibliographical references and index.
        ISBN 0-684-19253-5 (set : alk. paper). — ISBN 0-684-19752-9 (v. 1
: alk. paper). — ISBN 0-684-19753-7 (v. 2 : alk. paper). — ISBN
0-684-19754-5 (v. 3 : alk. paper). — ISBN 0-684-19755-3 (v. 4 :
alk. paper). — ISBN 0-684-80480-8 (v. 5 : alk. paper).
        1. Latin America—Encyclopedias.   I. Tenenbaum, Barbara A.
F1406.E53   1996   95–31042
980'.003—dc20   CIP

5   7   9   11   13   15   17   19   V/C   20   18   16   14   12   10   8   6   4

PRINTED IN THE UNITED STATES OF AMERICA

The paper used in this publication meets the minimum requirements of American National Standard for Information Sciences—Permanence of Paper for Printed Library Materials. ANSI Z3948-1984.

USING THE ENCYCLOPEDIA

This encyclopedia contains nearly 5,300 separate articles. Most topics appear in English alphabetical order, according to the word-by-word system (e.g., Casa Rosada before Casals). Persons and places generally precede things (Roosevelt, Theodore, before Roosevelt Corollary). Certain subjects are clustered together in composite entries, which may comprise several regions, periods, or genres. For example, the "Slavery" and "Mining" entries contain separate articles for Brazil and Spanish America. "Art" embraces separately signed essays on pre-Columbian, colonial, nineteenth-century, and modern art, as well as folk art.

NATIONAL TOPICS are frequently clustered by country, under one or more of the following subheadings:

> *Constitutions*
> *Organizations* (administrative, cultural, economic, labor, etc.)
> *Political Parties* (listed under the English name and including former revolutionary movements that have entered the political system)
> *Revolutionary Movements*
> *Revolutions*

Note that an event with a distinctive name will be found under that term, whereas a generic name will appear under the appropriate country. Thus, the Chibata Revolt appears under *C* and the Pastry War under *P,* but the Revolution of 1964 appears under "Brazil: Revolutions."

MEASUREMENTS appear in the English system according to United States usage. Following are approximate metric equivalents for the most common units:

> 1 foot = 30 centimeters
> 1 mile = 1.6 kilometers
> 1 acre = 0.4 hectares
> 1 square mile = 2.6 square kilometers
> 1 pound = 0.45 kilograms
> 1 gallon = 3.8 liters

BIOGRAPHICAL ENTRIES (numbering nearly 3,000) are listed separately in an appendix in volume 5, where a rough classification is offered according to sex and field(s) of activity.

CROSS-REFERENCES appear in two forms: SMALL CAPITALS in the text highlight significant persons, concepts, and institutions that are treated in their own entries in the encyclopedia. *See also* references at the end of an entry call attention to articles of more general relevance. Cross-referencing is selective: obvious sources of information (such as most country, state, and city entries) are not highlighted. For full cross-referencing consult the index in volume 5.

ENCYCLOPEDIA OF

LATIN
AMERICAN
HISTORY
AND CULTURE

G

GABEIRA, FERNANDO NAGLE (*b.* 1941), Brazilian political activist and a leading participant in covert, often violent opposition to military rule established in Brazil in April 1964. As a member of the 8 October Revolutionary Movement (Movimento Revolucionário 8 de outubro—MR-8) Gabeira participated in the September 1969 kidnapping of Charles Elbrick, U.S. ambassador to Brazil. The military response to the kidnapping included severe repression and counterintelligence, which led to the eventual capture, torture, and exile of many revolutionaries, including Gabeira. Following a general amnesty for all political exiles, Gabeira returned to Brazil in 1979 and reemerged politically as a cofounder and 1986 gubernatorial candidate of the Green Party (PV), a leftist political party dedicated to social justice, the expansion of citizenship rights, and ecological management and preservation. His writings include *O que é isso, companheiro?* (1978) and *Goiânia, Rua 57* (1987).

A. J. LANGGUTH, *Hidden Terrors* (1978), pp. 166–200; ANDY TRUSKIER, "The Politics of Violence: The Urban Guerrilla in Brazil," in *Urban Guerrilla Warfare in Latin America*, edited by James Kohl and John Litt (1974), pp. 136–148.

DARYLE WILLIAMS

GACHUPÍN. *See* **Peninsular.**

GADSDEN PURCHASE. In 1853, Mexico agreed to sell to the United States nearly 30 million acres (45,535 square miles) in present-day southern ARIZONA and NEW MEXICO. The United States sought land in northern Mexico for a proposed southern transcontinental railroad route that would include a port on the Gulf of California. It also wanted to resolve a boundary controversy that had arisen from errors in John Disturnell's map, which, according to the Treaty of GUADALUPE–HIDALGO, was the basis for delineating the southern limits of New Mexico. Factional interests in both the United States and Mexico eventually limited the amount of land that changed hands. In the United States, sectional rivalries linked to the railroad and slavery led the Senate in 1854 to ratify an amended treaty that bought only the Mesilla Valley. James Gadsden, U.S. minister to Mexico, had been empowered to discuss, in addition, mutual claims, trade issues, and U.S. rights in TEHUANTEPEC; yet only one of these issues figured in the final treaty. The United States wanted to be relieved of its obligation in Article XI of the Treaty of Guadalupe–Hidalgo to protect Mexico from Indian incursions originating north of the border. Mexican President Antonio López de SANTA ANNA succumbed to the fiscal exigencies of his beleaguered government as well as to the fear that an expansionist United States, which had done little to discourage FILIBUSTERING expeditions to northern Mexico since the war, would take what it wanted by force. Mexico ceded the Mesilla territory and abrogated Article XI of the 1848 treaty in return for ten million dollars.

PAUL N. GARBER, *The Gadsden Treaty* (1959); JOSEFINA Z. VÁZQUEZ and LORENZO MEYER, *The United States and Mexico* (1985).

SUSAN M. DEEDS

GAGE, THOMAS (*b.* ca. 1602; *d.* early 1656), British Dominican friar and author of the strongly anti-Spanish *The English-American his travail by sea and land; or a new survey of the West India's, containing a journall of three thousand and three hundred miles within the main Land of America* (1648). Gage came from a fiercely devout English Catholic family that suffered persecution by the English government. Educated by the Jesuits in France and Spain, Gage rebelled against Jesuit discipline and joined the Dominican Order at Jerez, Spain, in 1625, causing his ardently pro-Jesuit father to disinherit him. Gage's descriptive *English-American* begins soon thereafter, with his departure for the Americas as a missionary under the name Tomás de Santa María. Gage described his voyage through the Caribbean to Veracruz and on to Guatemala, where he spent nearly a decade before fleeing the Dominicans when his requests for transfer were denied.

After traversing the rest of Central America, Gage returned to England via Spain at the end of 1637. By then ardently anti-Catholic, he converted to the Anglican Church. The 1648 publication of his inflammatory journal was an instant success and became an important part of the BLACK LEGEND (of Spanish misrule in the Indies). Oliver Cromwell ordered the work reprinted in 1655, and many subsequent editions appeared. While it was strongly anti-Catholic and anti-Spanish, this work reflected Gage's keen observations on many aspects of life in Mexico and Central America, including comments on social and economic affairs as well as on crops, natural history, and flora and fauna. As such, it is one of the more important seventeenth-century descriptions of Central America. Oliver Cromwell consulted Gage regarding the 1655 British invasion of the West Indies, and Gage served as a chaplain to the British forces that captured Jamaica in that year. Gage died in Jamaica the following year.

A. P. NEWTON, ed., *Thomas Gage: The English-American* (1946); J. ERIC S. THOMPSON, [Thomas Gage's] *Travels in the New World* (1958); NORMAN NEWTON, *Thomas Gage in Spanish America* (1969); FREDERIC ROSENGARTEN, JR., *Thomas Gage: The English-American Traveler* (1988).

SUE DAWN MCGRADY

GAHONA, GABRIEL VICENTE (Picheta; *b.* 1828; *d.* 1899), Mexican engraver. Gahona's early artistic calling took him from his birthplace of Mérida, Yucatán, to Italy for study. In Italy, probably through magazines and newspapers, he came to know the lithographic work of Doré, Daumier, Gavarni, and Guy, whose work mirrored Gahona's inclinations and temperament and provided the inspiration for his next project.

Gahona returned to Mérida in 1847 and, under the pseudonym of "Picheta," he began publishing *Don Bullebule*, a comical periodical "published for a society of noisy people." Its themes of satire and social criticism were illustrated with eighty-six xylographs. Although it ceased publication later that year, *Don Bullebule* stands out as one of the first examples of journalistic social criticism in Mexico. It is preserved in two volumes, the first consisting of fifteen issues and the second of seventeen, at the National Library of Newspapers and Periodicals in Mexico City.

In 1851, Gahona opened a lithography studio. In 1880 he served as city council president of Mérida, where he died.

MANUEL TOUSSAINT, *La litografía en México en el siglo XIX* (1934); RAQUEL TIBOL, *Historia general del arte mexicano*, vol. 3 (1964).

ESTHER ACEVEDO

GAÍNZA, GABINO (*b.* 26 October 1753; *d.* 1824), acting captain-general of Guatemala (1821–1822). Born in Pamplona, Spain, Gaínza joined the military at the age of sixteen and served in various posts throughout South America for most of his adult life. He commanded the Spanish force that reconquered Chile in 1814.

Gaínza arrived in Central America from Chile in early 1821 amidst the political turmoil of impending independence from Spain to assume the post of army inspector general. That March, the very ill captain-general of Guatemala, Carlos Luis de Urrutia y Montoya (1750–1825), delegated his authority to Gaínza. After independence on 15 September 1821, Gaínza, who had tolerated creole rebellion, remained in office as chief executive. He played an active role in the decision to annex Central America to Agustín de ITURBIDE's Mexican empire, and he often mediated between the polemical political factions of the era. He was relieved of his command on 22 June 1822 by the new captain-general, Vicente FILÍSOLA. Afterward, he went to Mexico to become an aide-de-camp to Emperor Agustín I (Iturbide).

ENRIQUE DEL CID FERNÁNDEZ, *Don Gabino de Gaínza y otros estudios* (1959).

MICHAEL F. FRY

GAINZA PAZ, ALBERTO (*b.* 16 March 1899; *d.* 26 December 1977), Argentine newspaperman. Gainza Paz gained international attention in 1951 when his newspaper, *La Prensa*, was expropriated by the government of Juan Domingo PERÓN. *La Prensa*, founded in 1869 by the Paz family, had always maintained an independent conservative editorial position dedicated to the expression of "true public opinion." Between 1947 and 1951, Gainza

Paz's views clashed with the policies and practices of the Perón government. The paper and its publisher became international beacons of democracy standing firmly against dictatorship. With the paper's expropriation, it was transformed into a trade union tabloid. Gainza Paz fled into exile, where he became a symbol of freedom of the press and received many honors for his battle. With the fall of Perón in 1955, *La Prensa* was returned to the Paz family, resumed publication under Gainza Paz's direction early in 1956, and regained its former stature.

ROBERT A. POTASH, *The Army and Politics in Argentina, 1945–1962: Perón to Frondizi* (1980), pp. 104–105, 122–123; JOSEPH PAGE, *Perón: A Biography* (1983), pp. 212–214.

PAUL GOODWIN

GAITÁN, JORGE ELIÉCER (*b.* 23 January 1898; *d.* 9 April 1948), Colombian political leader. The man who was widely expected to accede to the presidency of Colombia in 1950 was walking out of his law office in downtown Bogotá with a group of friends at 1:05 P.M. on Friday, 9 April 1948, when he was fatally wounded by a lonely drifter. In life Jorge Eliécer Gaitán commanded the attention of his compatriots through fear-inspiring oratory and masterful political performances. In death he incited uprisings in Bogotá and other cities by passionate followers desperate to bring about quick political change.

In part because he died before rising formally to power, Gaitán's legacy is uncertain. Some are convinced that he was a careful man with a profound sense of equanimity who would have brought peace to Colombia. Others describe him as an inveterate rabble-rouser who would have turned La VIOLENCIA bloodier still had he lived. The scholar Richard Sharpless sees him as a left-leaning socialist, while others describe him as a rather conservative man of lower-middle-class values.

Gaitán was born in Bogotá to parents who struggled to keep a hold on the middle class. His father sold books and his mother was a well-known schoolteacher. Both were rank-and-file members of the Liberal Party, and Jorge Eliécer grew up hearing about the heroic exploits of "progressive" Liberals against the "reactionaries" of the Conservative Party. Although Gaitán would antagonize the leaders of his party throughout his life, confounding them and others at every turn, he would never seriously depart from the ideals of the Liberal Party. At the time of his death, many leaders of the party, and many Conservatives as well, felt a sense of relief, for they could never quite be certain of his allegiance, or how they might manage to control him and his many followers, whom he had formed into disciplined urban crowds that seemingly did only his bidding.

Although his parents were always seeking to ease his way by drawing on their meager political connections, Gaitán strove mightily to rise in society through his own merits. In 1924 he obtained his law degree from the Universidad Nacional with an unorthodox thesis titled *Las ideas socialistas en Colombia*. He then went to Italy to study with Enrico Ferri, and while there he became drawn to the closely knit crowds created by the fascists.

On his return to Colombia in 1928 Gaitán toured the nation, making inflammatory speeches with his trademark guttural voice on the massacre of the UNITED FRUIT COMPANY banana workers. This massacre was the same one Gabriel GARCÍA MÁRQUEZ wrote about in the novel *One Hundred Years of Solitude*.

Regardless of what his ideology may have been, Gaitán was in a sense Colombia's first modern politician. Upon election to the House of Representatives, he worked assiduously to reach the masses and elicit their support. He developed basic programs and ideas that he believed even his most uneducated followers could and should understand. Beyond the lofty and abstract rhetoric of Colombia's traditional politicians, Gaitán referred incessantly to detailed aspects of the daily, personal lives of his followers. He traveled extensively throughout the country, moving electoral politics outside the narrow confines of the two traditional parties. He produced his own newspaper, and was the first to use the radio to reach his followers. When he appeared to be stymied by the Liberals in the 1930s, he briefly formed the Unión Nacional Izquierdista Revolucionaria (UNIR). When troubles continued to appear on the horizon, he could always fall back on his own Gaitanista movement. He went in and out of public office, serving briefly first as mayor of Bogotá in 1936 and 1937, then as minister of education and of labor in 1940 and 1943, until he ran unsuccessfully for the presidency in 1945 and 1946 as a Liberal against the official Liberal candidate. Upon his death he was poised to take over the Liberal Party and win the presidential election of 1950.

The huge riot following his death, in which Gaitán's followers destroyed much of downtown Bogotá and caused disturbances in many other cities as well, is known in Colombia as *el nueve de abril* (the ninth of April), and elsewhere as the BOGOTAZO. At the time, the eyes of the world were on Bogotá, for the Ninth Pan-American Conference was being held in the city. U.S. Secretary of State George Marshall was there, and so too was Fidel CASTRO, who had met with Gaitán days earlier and had another meeting scheduled with him for that very afternoon. For a few brief moments Gaitán became well known to the outside world. And during at least the next three decades in Colombia, Jorge Eliécer Gaitán remained a central and enigmatic force in politics, the source of countless passions, untold conversations, and sundry questions about whether his unfulfilled policies would have succeeded, the answers to which few Colombians have found satisfactory.

RICHARD SHARPLESS, *Gaitán of Colombia: A Political Biography* (1978); HERBERT BRAUN, *The Assassination of Gaitán: Public Life and Urban Violence in Colombia* (1985).

HERBERT BRAUN

See also **Colombia: Political Parties.**

GAITÁN DURÁN, JORGE (*b.* 12 February 1924; *d.* 22 June 1962), Colombian poet and essayist. Despite his death at a young age, Gaitán Durán exerted a lasting influence on Colombian letters. A native of Pamplona Kúcuta, he is remembered primarily as a talented poet who published several books of profound metaphysical poetry. They include *Insistencia en la tristeza* (1946), *Presencia del hombre* (1947), and *Si mañana despierto* (1961). Much of this poetry deals with love and death in an existential void. Love emerges in many of the poems as an attempt to forget the flow of time. Poets and critics in Colombia considered him extraordinarily talented, and a mature writer for his age. His most accomplished book was *Si mañana despierto*.

Gaitán Durán is also remembered as the founding director of the prestigious journal *Mito*, which was published from 1955 until his death in an auto accident at Pointe-a-Pitre, Guadeloupe, in 1962. *Mito* was a cosmopolitan periodical that published the best of European, Latin American, and Colombian writing, thus serving as the voice of a generation of intellectuals in Colombia. Latin American writers who later became internationally recognized, such as Octavio PAZ, Julio CORTÁZAR, and Carlos FUENTES, all appeared in *Mito*, as did the Colombian Nobel laureate Gabriel GARCÍA MÁRQUEZ. *Mito*'s most important impact was its modernization of a provincial literary scene in Colombia.

GIUSEPPE BELLINI, *Historia de la literatura hispanoamericana* (1985); GEORGE R. MC MURRAY, *Spanish American Writing Since 1941* (1987); RAYMOND LESLIE WILLIAMS, *The Colombian Novel, 1844–1987* (1991).

RAYMOND LESLIE WILLIAMS

GAITO, CONSTANTINO (*b.* 3 August 1878; *d.* 14 December 1945), Argentine composer and teacher. Born in Buenos Aires, Gaito began his musical studies with his father, a violinist. At age eleven he began to compose. He received a scholarship from the Argentine government and went to Italy, where he enrolled at San Pietro a Maiella in Naples, studying under Pietro Platania (composition) and Simonetti (piano). He traveled to Milan to meet Giuseppe Verdi, who helped the young Gaito in his career by conducting a concert of his music at the Milan Conservatory. Initially influenced by the Italians, Gaito returned toward the nationalist style upon his return to Argentina in 1900. He wrote eleven operas, among them *Flor de nieve* (1922), *Ollantay* (1926), and *Sangre de las guitarras* (1932), all of which premiered at the TEATRO COLÓN in Buenos Aires. He also wrote two ballets, an oratorio, chamber music, and vocal and piano works.

Gaito was the most renowned music professor of his time, and taught a generation of eminent Argentine composers. He founded a conservatory and taught harmony at the National Conservatory in Buenos Aires. He was also director of the Teatro Argentino in La Plata. Gaito died in Buenos Aires.

Composers of the Americas, vol. 12 (1966), pp. 50–54; GÉRARD BÉHAGUE, *Music in Latin America* (1979); *New Grove Dictionary of Music and Musicians*, vol. 7 (1980).

SUSANA SALGADO

GALÁN, JOSÉ ANTONIO. *See* **Comunero Revolt (New Granada).**

GALÁN, JULIO (*b.* 5 December 1959), Mexican painter. Galán, a native of Múzquiz, Coahuila, studied architecture in Monterrey from 1978 to 1982. At that time he abandoned architecture and dedicated himself to painting. In 1980, he had begun exhibiting in Monterrey at the Galería Arte Actual Mexicano. Influences on his work include Frida KAHLO, Andy Warhol, and David Hockney, as well as Mexican popular painting, comic books, and both Mexican and American kitsch. Frida Kahlo was for many of the artists of the 1980s a symbol of freedom from the Mexican artistic status quo, giving young artists license to explore themselves and their *mexicanidad*. The traditional *ex-voto* and *retablo* formats of the nineteenth and twentieth centuries are echoed in Galán's work. His images are often autobiographical and surrealistic, frequently contain sexual references, and make use of unnatural perspectives. The artist often includes his own image in his pictures, sometimes juxtaposed with a female character, suggesting sexual ambiguities and alternatives. Since the mid-1980s Galán has lived in Monterrey, with frequent stays in New York and Europe. His work is collected and exhibited internationally.

EDWARD J. SULLIVAN, *Aspects of Contemporary Mexican Painting* (1990), esp. pp. 59–66; MUSEO DE ARTE CONTEMPORÁNEO DE MONTERREY, *Julio Galán: Exposición Retrospectiva* (1993); WALDO RASMUSSEN, FATIMA BERCHT, and ELIZABETH FERRER, eds., *Latin American Artists of the Twentieth Century* (1993); LUIS MARIO SCHNEIDER et al., *Julio Galán* (1993).

CLAYTON C. KIRKING

GALÁN, LUIS CARLOS (*b.* 29 September 1943; *d.* 18 August 1989), Colombian politician. Born into a middle-class family in Bucaramanga, Galán was educated in Bogotá. In 1971, at the age of twenty-seven, he was named minister of education in the bipartisan administration of Misael Pastrana Borrero. As editor of the magazine *Nueva Frontera* and later as a senator, Galán inherited from former president Carlos LLERAS RESTREPO the banner of reformist opposition to the "officialist" Liberal regimes of the 1974–1982 period. His attacks on human-rights abuses and the vices of clientelist politics won him much admiration but limited electoral success. His New Liberalism movement peaked at 11 percent in the 1982 presidential election; in late 1986 he returned to the official Liberal fold. In the late 1980s Galán spoke out against the growing power of Colombia's drug cartels; he was considered the likely successor to Virgilio BARCO VARGAS in the presidency. His assassination in August 1989, presumably the work of the Medellín cartel, was the most dramatic moment of the Colombian crisis of 1989–1990.

LUIS CARLOS GALÁN, *Ni un pusa atraí, siempre adelante* (1991).

RICHARD J. STOLLER

GALÁPAGOS ISLANDS, a group of nineteen volcanic islands and numerous islets in the eastern Pacific, lying astride the equator, 600 miles west of mainland Ecuador, of which the islands are a province. The island group, officially named the Archipiélago de Colón by Ecuador in 1892 to honor Christopher Columbus, encompasses a land area of 3,075 square miles and is spread out over 36,000 square miles of sea. The population of the Galapagos was listed as 9,785 in the 1990 census.

Each island was named by both Spanish and English explorers and renamed by Ecuador in 1892. The official Ecuadorian names are cited in this article; however, researchers will find the English names in most earlier descriptions of the islands. The largest island is Isabela, approximately 82 miles long, covering an area of 1,700 square miles, over half the land mass of the others combined. Isabela is typical of the islands in its lava composition; it also has the highest peak, Mount Azul, at 5,541 feet. The five other larger islands are Santa Cruz, Fernandina, San Cristóbal, San Salvador, and Santa María.

In 1535, Thomás de Berlanga, bishop of Panama, inadvertently discovered the Galápagos when his ship was blown off course en route to Peru. He named them Las Encantadas (The Enchanted) due to their mist-shrouded otherworldly appearance and the unusual wildlife typified by giant tortoises and iguanas. The islands were a haven for pirates in the seventeenth century and became a regular stop for whaling vessels in the eighteenth and nineteenth centuries. The islands were unclaimed until 1832, when Ecuador took official possession.

In 1835 the English naturalist Charles Darwin visited the islands and chronicled their flora and fauna. His experiences in the Galápagos contributed significantly to his ideas about evolution and natural selection and his account of the islands brought them international acclaim.

In the early twentieth century, Ecuador considered selling the islands to France, Chile, and the United States but decided to retain possession. In World War II, Ecuador permitted the United States to construct an air base on Baltra Island for the purpose of patrolling Pacific approaches to the Panama Canal. The base was turned over to Ecuador in 1946 and today serves as the principal airstrip.

The unique native animals and plants remain the main attraction of the islands. The archipelago's tortoise

Giant tortoise (approximately 400 pounds) from Santa Cruz Island, Galápagos. PHOTO BY GEORGE HOLTON / PHOTO RESEARCHERS INC.

is thought to be the longest-lived animal on earth. While there are only nine mammals, two bats, and seven rodents, no amphibians, few reptiles, and approximately eighty species of birds indigenous to the islands, animal life is nevertheless of extreme scientific importance due to the islands' centuries of isolation from humans in an austere environment that has led to unique adaptive changes. Large parts of the islands are now preserved as national parks and wildlife refuges.

CHARLES DARWIN, *A Naturalist's Voyage Round the World in HMS Beagle* (1839); WILLIAM BEEBE, *Galápagos, World's End* (1924); THEODORE WOLF, *Geography and Geology of Ecuador* (1933); HERMAN MELVILLE, . . . *The Encantadoas or Enchanted Islands,* with an introduction, critical epilogue, and bibliographical notes by Victor Wolfgang von Hagen (1940); VICTOR WOLFGANG VON HAGEN, *Ecuador and the Galápagos Islands* (1949); IAN THORNTON, *Darwin's Islands: A Natural History of the Galápagos* (1971); JOHN HICKHAM, *The Enchanted Islands* (1986).

GEORGE M. LAUDERBAUGH

GALEANA, HERMENEGILDO (*b.* 13 April 1762; *d.* 27 June 1814), Mexican insurgent leader. Like other members of his family, Galeana, born in Tecpan, joined José María MORELOS at La Sabana in January 1811. He proved valiant and able from the outset, and Morelos named him his lieutenant in May 1811. Galeana won victories in numerous important battles. He took Taxco in December 1811, and occupied Tenancingo the following January. From February to May 1812, he participated in the defense of CUAUTLA, where his aid proved to be of great importance. Morelos named him field marshal in September 1812, at Tehuacán. Galeana participated in the capture of Orizaba in October 1812 and in the taking of Oaxaca that November. He played a decisive role in the taking of Acapulco in April 1813, and in the capture of the fortress of San Diego four months later, when he convinced its commander to surrender. In December 1813 Galeana participated in the attack against Valladolid, where the insurgents were defeated. In January 1814, after the defeat at Puruarán, Galeana headed south, pursued by the royalists. After his death in combat at El Salitral, Galeana's head was exhibited in the plaza of Coyuca.

WILBERT H. TIMMONS, *Morelos: Priest, Soldier, Statesman of Mexico* (1970); VIRGINIA GUEDEA, *José María Morelos y Pavón: Cronología* (1981); *Diccionario Porrúa de historia, geografía y biografía de México*, 5th ed. (1986).

VIRGINIA GUEDEA

GALEANO, EDUARDO HUGHES (*b.* 1940), Uruguayan writer. Born in Montevideo, his writing talents found their first expression in the form of articles on literature and culture published in Montevideo's *Marcha*. Between 1971 and 1984—the duration of Uruguay's military dictatorship—he resided primarily in Spain, returning in the last year to assume editorial responsibilities at the newly founded periodical *Brecha*. His early fiction includes *Los días siguientes* (1963) and *Los fantasmas de día del león y otros relatos* (1967). Later fiction, which depicts a personal encounter with the despised military dictatorship, includes *La canción de nosotros* (1975) and *Días y noches de amor y de guerra* (1978). Galeano's most important work is the widely read *Las venas abiertas de América Latina* (1971), with more than thirty editions since its publication. This work, based on the "dependency" theories popular during the 1960s, presents a history of Latin America as an exploited continent from the time of Columbus to the present. Also noteworthy are the three volumes (fifteenth to eighteenth centuries, eighteenth and nineteenth centuries, twentieth century) of *Memoria del fuego* (1982–1986), a chronology of historical and cultural events that provides a unique and comprehensive view of Latin American identity.

Translations of Galeano's works include *Open Veins of Latin America*, translated by Cedric Belfrage (1973); *Days and Nights of Love and War*, translated by Judith Brister (1983); *Memory of Fire*, translated by Cedric Belfrage (1988); and *The Book of Embraces*, translated by Cedric Belfrage and Mark Shafer (1991).

SARA M. SAZ, "Breath, Liberty, and the Word: Eduardo Galeano's Interpretational History," in *SECOLASA* (21 March 1990): 59–70; DIANA PALAVERICH, "Eduardo Galeano's 'Memoria del Fuego' as Alternative History," in *Antípodas* (3 July 1991): 135–150.

WILLIAM H. KATRA

GALEONES, one of two fleets dispatched to convoy merchant vessels to the New World. The FLEET SYSTEM was set up in 1564. One fleet, known as the *flota*, went to New Spain; the other, the *galeones*, went to the mainland of South America, or Tierra Firme. This latter, which returned from the trade fair at PORTOBELO laden with Peruvian silver, was customarily convoyed by six or eight men-of-war (*galeones* in Spanish) and thus came by its name. After trading was finished, the two fleets would usually reunite at Havana for the return voyage to Seville. The crown defrayed the cost of supporting the convoys by levying an ad valorem tax, known as the AVERÍA, in Seville and the Indies.

By the seventeenth century, foreign pirates, shipwrecks, the contraband trade, the diversification of the colonial economy, and Spain's economic decline had all contributed to the decay of this Atlantic trade. Although officials in Spain favored yearly voyages of the fleets, only twenty-nine sailings to Tierra Firme took place between 1600 and 1650. In the second half of the century that number declined to nineteen. The WAR OF THE SPANISH SUCCESSION (1700–1716) further disrupted the system as French traders entered the Pacific and flooded colonial markets with European wares.

The crown tried to revitalize the system of *flotas* and *galeones* in the eighteenth century but had only limited success. Subsequent trade fairs proved disappointing for the participants until in 1740 the crown reluctantly abandoned the convoy system, substituting individual sailings by licensed merchant vessels coming around Cape Horn.

The classic study of the system of *flotas* and *galeones* is CLARENCE HARING, *Trade and Navigation Between Spain and the Indies in the Time of the Habsburgs* (1918). The most detailed quantitative studies remain PIERRE CHAUNU and HUGUETTE CHAUNU, *Séville et l'Atlantique, 1504–1650*, 8 vols. (1955–1959); LUTGARDO GARCÍA FUENTES, *El comercio español con América, 1650–1700* (1980); and ANTONIO GARCÍA-BAQUERO GONZÁLEZ, *Cádiz y el Atlántico (1717–1778)*, 2 vols. (1976). For the collapse of the convoy system see GEOFFREY J. WALKER, *Spanish Politics and Imperial Trade, 1700–1789* (1979).

KENNETH J. ANDRIEN

GALÍNDEZ, JESÚS DE (*b.* 12 October 1915; *d.* 13/15 March 1956), a critic of the Trujillo regime in the Dominican Republic. A native of Amurrio, Spain, Galíndez held a law degree from the University of Madrid. He had fought against Franco in the Spanish Civil War and in 1939 fled to the Dominican Republic, where he taught in the Diplomatic School and worked as a lawyer in the Department of Labor. When some labor disputes he arbitrated were too favorable to the workers, he got in trouble with the dictator Rafael TRUJILLO. He therefore moved to the United States in 1946 and became a political activist among anti-Trujillo exiles. He enrolled in Columbia University's doctoral program and became a leading critic of Trujillo. In addition to writing a number of articles, he produced a dissertation on Trujillo. He was also a part-time instructor. Galíndez defended his dissertation at the end of February 1956 and disappeared after finishing an evening class on 12 March 1956. There is general agreement that Trujillo had him kidnapped and flown, drugged, to the Dominican Republic, where he was killed after being tortured. His degree was awarded in absentia in June. He had left a Spanish draft of his dissertation with a Chilean friend, which was published as *La era de Trujillo: Un estudio casuístico de dictadura hispanoamericano* (1956). In 1973 an English edition appeared, edited by Russell H. Fitzgibbon: *The Era of Trujillo, Dominican Dictator*.

The disappearance of Galíndez became a cause célèbre. The young pilot Gerald Murphy, who had flown the chartered plane from Amityville, Long Island, on the night of 12 March, with a drugged man aboard, had disappeared in the Dominican Republic in the previous December. Murphy was from the state of Oregon; his congressman, Charles Porter, and Senator Wayne Morse put great pressure on the U.S. Justice and State departments to investigate. The Justice Department turned the investigation over to a federal grand jury that indicted a man associated with the plane's rental on Long Island. He was tried and convicted for violation of the Foreign Agents Registration Act. The body of Galíndez was never found. That of Murphy was found months later hanged in a Dominican jail, reported to be a "suicide."

GERMÁN E. ORNES, *Trujillo: Little Caesar of the Caribbean* (1958), chap. 19; ROBERT D. CRASSWELLER, *Trujillo: The Life and Times of a Caribbean Dictator* (1966), chap. 21; HOWARD J. WIARDA, *Dictatorship and Development: The Methods of Control in Trujillo's Dominican Republic* (1968), pp. 58–59, 149–153, 176–177.

LARMAN C. WILSON

GALINDO, ALEJANDRO (*b.* 14 January 1906), Mexican film director. Galindo was born in Monterrey, Nuevo León, and moved at an early age to Mexico City. He studied drama and photography at the University of Southern California and at the Palmer Institute of Photography in Los Angeles, and served as a film director's assistant in Hollywood. In the early 1930s, he returned to Mexico and worked in radio and film as a scriptwriter. He made his directorial debut in 1938 with the feature *Refugiados en Madrid*. Since then, Galindo has directed over eighty feature films and documentaries. Unquestionably one of the most accomplished directors of the "golden age" of Mexican cinema, Galindo focuses in his films upon questions of national identity and the oppressed. Among his most noted films are *Campeón sin corona* (1945), *Una familia de tantas* (1948), *¡Esquina bajan!* (1948), *Doña Perfecta* (1950), *Espaldas mojadas* (1953), and *El juicio de Martín Cortés* (1974).

LUIS REYES DE LA MAZA, *El cine sonoro en México* (1973); E. BRADFORD BURNS, *Latin American Cinema: Film and History* (1975); CARL J. MORA, *Mexican Cinema: Reflections of a Society: 1896–1980* (1982); and JOHN KING, *Magical Reels: A History of Cinema in Latin America* (1990).

DAVID MACIEL

See also **Cinema.**

GALINDO, BLAS (*b.* 3 February 1910), Mexican composer, teacher, and administrator. A Huichol Indian, Galindo came to Mexico City in 1931 from San Gabriel, Jalisco, and began composition study with Carlos CHÁVEZ at the National Conservatory. He affiliated with three other Chávez students, labeled "Los cuatro," a group committed to the creation and performance of a genuine Mexican music, engendering pieces like his picturesque *Sones de mariachi*, which was premiered at a Mexican exhibit in New York's Museum of Modern Art in 1940. In 1941 he studied composition with Aaron Copland at the Berkshire Music Center and returned to Mexico to complete his conservatory training. He taught at the National Conservatory from 1944, and became its director in 1947, the year in which he was also appointed head of the music department of the National Institute of Fine Arts. His output—encompassing works for piano, small ensembles, orchestra, voice, and chorus—ranges from folkloric to neoclassic to boldly dissonant.

GÉRARD BÉHAGUE, *Music in Latin America: An Introduction* (1979).

ROBERT L. PARKER

GALINDO, JUAN (christened John; *b.* spring or summer 1802; *d.* 30 January 1840), émigré Anglo-Irish activist in Central America. The eldest child of Philemon Galindo, an Anglo-Spanish actor–fencing master, and Catherine Gough, an Anglo-Irish actress, Galindo arrived in Guatemala in 1827 after service with Lord Thomas COCHRANE in South American wars of independence. His varied activities brought him distinction as a scientist, Liberal propagandist, military and administrative officer, and amateur diplomat. Duty and travel provided him opportunity to survey topography, examine archaeological sites, and observe native populations and natural history phenomena that he described in articles published in European scholarly journals. Galindo decried encroachments on Central American territory and involved himself in several defensive countercolonization projects, the major one of which ignited the smoldering Belize boundary and sovereignty issue. His diplomatic mission (1835–1836) to secure British recognition of Central American sovereignty over Belize proved futile. He died while fleeing the site of the battle of El Potrero, near Tegucigalpa, Honduras.

IAN GRAHAM, "Juan Galindo, Enthusiast," in *Estudios de cultura Maya* (Mexico City) 3 (1963): 11–35, stresses Galindo's scientific activities and achievements; WILLIAM J. GRIFFITH, "Juan Galindo, Central American Chauvinist," in *Hispanic American Historical Review* 40, no. 1 (1960): 25–52, emphasizes his role in the boundary disputes and territorial encroachment controversies of the region. WILLIAM J. GRIFFITH, *Empires in the Wilderness: Foreign Colonization and Development in Guatemala, 1834–1844* (1965), lays out Galindo's involvement in a number of colonization and development projects.

WILLIAM J. GRIFFITH

GALINDO, SERGIO (*b.* 2 September 1926), Mexican writer. Born in Xalapa, Veracruz, Galindo first published a collection of short stories in 1951, *La máquina vacía* (The Empty Machine), and in the following years produced a sizable corpus of narrative, mainly novels. They include *Polvos de arroz* (Rice Powder, 1958), *Justicia de enero* (Justice in January, 1959), *El bordo* (The Precipice, 1960), and *La comparsa* (Carnival, 1964). Galindo received the 1986 Premio Xavier Villaurrutía for his novel *Otilia Rauda* (1986). In his writing, Galindo explores the tensions in middle-class Mexican families and the dynamics of intimate relationships. In contrast to the predominant emphasis on national identity in Mexican literature, such psychological concerns emphasize widely shared human behaviors. In addition to his literary production, from 1957 to 1964 Galindo edited the journal *La Palabra y el Hombre* (Word and Man) and directed the publishing department of the University of Veracruz, where he inaugurated an influential fiction series. Between 1965 and 1976 Galindo served in a variety of positions for the National Institute of Fine Arts and the Secretariat of Public Education. Since 1975 he has been a member of the Mexican Academy of Language.

JOHN S. BRUSHWOOD, "The Novels of Sergio Galindo: Planes of Human Relationship," in *Hispania* 51 (1968): 812–816, and *The Spanish American Novel: A Twentieth-Century Survey* (1975), pp. 239–241, 275–277, 316; *La Palabra y el Hombre*, nueva época no. 59–60 (1986), a special issue in honor of Sergio Galindo.

DANNY J. ANDERSON

GALLEGO, LAURA (*b.* 9 February 1924), Puerto Rican poet and educator. Closely identified with her native Bayamón, a suburb of San Juan, Laura Gallego taught high-school Spanish and was an education professor at the University of Puerto Rico. Her published books of poetry are *Presencia* (Presence, 1952), *Celajes* (Clouds, 1959), and *Que voy de vuelo* (Flying away, 1980). A 1972 anthology of her work includes the prose poems of *Almejas de tu nombre* (Clams of your name, 1954) and the previously unpublished collections of verse *En carne viva* (In the flesh), *La red* (The net), and *La del alba seria* (The woman of serious dawn). Gallego often speaks of words and silence in her verses, and in poetic dialogue addresses nature, God, an unnamed presence, and love lost. In *Celajes* Gallego writes about the natural beauty of Puerto Rico and of its people. Wounding images of arrows, darts, daggers, knives, and spines yield in her later poetry to meditative contemplations of the world, mankind, life, God, and the past.

LAURA GALLEGO, *Obra poética*, edited by Luis de Arrigoita (1972), pp. 5–15; JOSEFINA RIVERA DE ALVAREZ, *Literatura puertorriqueña: Su proceso en el tiempo* (1983), pp. 577–578.

ESTELLE IRIZARRY

GALLEGOS, RÓMULO (*b.* 21 August 1884; *d.* 7 April 1969), president of Venezuela (1947–1948). Best known as author of *Doña Bárbara* (1929), Gallegos also made major contributions to Venezuela as a secondary teacher and a politician. As a teacher during the 1920s he influenced a significant number of important politicians, including Rómulo BETANCOURT and Raúl LEONI. As a politician he was elected senator from Apure in 1931, but went into voluntary exile until the death of Juan Vicente GÓMEZ, (1935). On his return he served as minister of education under Eleázar López CONTRERAS, won a seat in the House of Deputies in 1947, and in 1941 took part in the organization of the Democratic Action Party (Acción Democrática).

Among his literary accomplishments, in 1909 Gallegos founded a reformist magazine called *La Alborada* (Dawn of Day), which dealt with political as well as literary topics. His novels combined realism with a deep-seated conviction that civilization would overcome barbarism, that goodness would prevail over evil. Gallegos, never polemical or directly critical of the Gómez dictatorship, published his best work while in exile in Spain. *Doña Bárbara* reflected his positivist background, depicting in an optimistic manner the ultimate victory of the educated Santos Luzardo over the backward Doña Bárbara. Two other novels, both written in exile, also portrayed in beautiful language the reality of Venezuelan life. *Cantaclaro* (1931) was a fictional account of the *llaneros* (plainsmen). *Canaíma* (1935) described the life of Marcos Vargas in the jungle of the Orinoco River valley, where the forces of justice fought those of evil. Later novels, such as *Pobre negro* (1937), which treated a slave rebellion of the 1860s, *El forastero* (1942), and *Sobre la misma tierra* (1943), never reached the high quality of Gallegos's earlier work, probably because of his involvement in political activities.

Gallegos was elected president in 1947; after his overthrow in November 1948, he spent time in Cuba and Mexico. He returned to Venezuela in 1958 and received a hero's welcome. He was awarded many prizes for both his political activities in the past and his writing. Two late novels, *La brizna de paja en el viento* (1952) and *La tierra bajo los pies* (1971), dealt with Cuban and Mexican themes, respectively.

HARRISON HOWARD, *Rómulo Gallegos y la revolución burguesa de Venezuela* (1976); JOSÉ VICENTE ABREU, *Rómulo Gallegos: Ideas educativas en* La Alborada (1978); HUGO RODRÍGUEZ-ALCALA, ed., *Nine Essays on Rómulo Gallegos* (1979); RÓMULO GALLEGOS, *Cuentos completos* (1981); JOSÉ AGUSTÍN CATALA, comp., *El golpe contra el presidente Gallegos: Documentos para la historia . . .* (1983); GUILLERMO MORÓN, *Homenaje a Rómulo Gallegos* (1984); RAFAEL FAUQUIE BESCOS, *Rómulo Gallegos: La realidad, la ficción, el símbolo . . .* (1985).

WINTHROP R. WRIGHT

GALLET, LUCIANO (*b.* 28 June 1893; *d.* 29 October 1931), Brazilian composer and musicologist. In 1913 Gallet enrolled in the Instituto Nacional de Música, where he studied piano with Henrique Oswald and harmony with Agnelo França. His first compositions were in a romantic or impressionistic style, but contact with Mário de ANDRADE resulted in serious studies of Brazilian popular and folk music. Some of Gallet's earliest works consisted of harmonizations and arrangements of folk songs. It is significant that Mário de Andrade, the most important figure in the emerging nationalist movement in music, considered Gallet's research and studies sufficiently significant to arrange for the publication of Gallet's *Estudos de folclore*. Although Gallet has never been considered a major composer, except possibly in the area of the art song, his influence on Brazilian musical life has been significant in numerous areas, including concerts, teaching, composition, discography, radio, journalism, and folk music. In each endeavor he gave evidence of keen analytical thought and contributed to the development of the musical life of Brazil.

LUCIANO GALLET, *Estudos de Folclore* (1934); VASCO MARIZ, *A canção brasileira*, 5th ed. (1985).

DAVID P. APPLEBY

GALLINAZO, a culture that flourished on the north coast of Peru from *ca.* 100 B.C. to A.D. 200. The center of the Gallinazo polity was located in the Virú Valley, about twenty-one miles south of the contemporary city of Trujillo. Gallinazo cultural remains are found from the Casma to the Lambayeque valleys, but the culture's contacts and sphere of influence can be seen as far south as the Rimac Valley to as far north as the Piura Valley.

Research suggests that the Gallinazo polity was the first multivalley state in the Andes, and that this state had an urban capital at the Gallinazo Group site in the Virú Valley. The possibility that this polity had a highly organized form of government was first recognized by Gordon Willey, who suggested that during the Gallinazo period the Virú Valley may have attained state-level political organization. This view has been disputed by David Wilson, whose work in the neighboring Santa Valley led him to believe that the succeeding MOCHE culture was the first state in the region.

Characteristic Gallinazo artifacts include negative, or resist, painted pottery, and handmade redware pots that were decorated with incision, triangular punctuations, appliqué, and notched strips of clay. The most characteristic Gallinazo architecture is large apartmentlike complexes that consist of a honeycomb of rooms made of adobe bricks. The structures lack doorways and windows, and were entered through openings in the roof. The architecture that served public functions include adobe pyramids associated with a complex series of rooms including domestic and administrative structures. The administrative architecture has doorways opening onto long corridors. A number of these rooms are decorated with adobe brick mosaics in distinctive geometric designs and/or yellow paint.

During the Gallinazo occupation of Virú, the valley had a highly organized, integrated settlement system, which included a network of fortifications that protected access to the irrigation system and the capital city. The Gallinazo occupation of the Virú Valley marked the largest extension of the irrigation of the valley throughout the prehistory and history of the valley. At the peak of the Gallinazo polity it incorporated the neighboring Moche and Santa Valleys. The Gallinazo occupations of these valleys were also complex settlement systems, with a number of smaller administrative centers that were subordinate to the Gallinazo Group site.

WENDELL C. BENNETT, *The Gallinazo Group Virú Valley, Peru* (1950); GORDON R. WILLEY, *Prehistoric Settlement Patterns in the Virú Valley, Peru* (1955), and *Archaeological Researches in Retrospect* (1974), pp. 149–178; DAVID J. WILSON, *Prehispanic Settlement Patterns in the Lower Santa Valley, Peru: A Regional Perspective on the Origins and Development of Complex North Coast Society* (1988); HEIDY P. FOGEL, "Settlements in Time: A Study of Social and Political Development During the Gallinazo Occupation of the North Coast of Peru" (Ph.D. diss., Yale University, 1993).

HEIDY P. FOGEL

See also **Archaeology.**

GALLINAZO GROUP SITE, archaeological region located in the Virú Valley on the north coast of Peru. The Gallinazo Group was the largest and most complex site in this region during the GALLINAZO period (*ca.* 100 B.C.– A.D. 200). Consisting of some thirty numbered mounds, the site measures five square miles and contains evidence of some 30,000 rooms on its surface. Covering this area is a large variety of architectural types, including pyramids, dwellings, cemeteries, and administrative structures. Between these is a combination of low-lying architecture not visible on the surface, public spaces, and some agricultural plots.

The dating of the standing architecture has revealed that most of these structures were occupied during the Middle and Late Gallinazo phases. It is clear that during these periods the Gallinazo Group site was a city, and thus it constitutes the first known city in the Andes. The Gallinazo Group site was the location of a concentration of wealth and power during the Gallinazo period, and as such it very likely served as the capital of the Gallinazo multivalley polity.

The site was occupied during all three phases of the Gallinazo sequence and was abandoned at the end of the Late Gallinazo period. Evidence for subsequent occupation of the area is scarce, and is confined mostly to a few intrusive burials dating to the succeeding MOCHE culture. This may be due to the fact that the plain upon which the site is located is extremely arid, and its occupation is only possible when a dependable flow of water can be diverted from the upper valley. The sustained occupation of the Gallinazo Group site was made possible through its integration into a unified valley system with well-defended and extensive irrigation works.

WENDELL C. BENNETT, *The Gallinazo Group Virú Valley, Peru* (1959); GORDON R. WILLEY, *Prehistoric Settlement Patterns in the Virú Valley, Peru* (1955); HEIDY P. FOGEL, "Settlements in Time: A Study of Social and Political Development During the Gallinazo Occupation of the North Coast of Peru" (Ph.D. diss., Yale University, 1993).

HEIDY P. FOGEL

See also **Archaeology.**

GALLO GOYENECHEA, PEDRO LEÓN (*b.* 12 February 1830; *d.* 16 December 1877), Chilean politician. Born into a prosperous mining family at Copiapó, Atacama Province, Gallo took a lifelong interest in politics, strongly supporting President Manuel MONTT (to whom he was related by marriage) at the time of his election (1851) but later turning against his authoritarianism. In January 1859 he launched an armed rebellion against Montt (the Constituent Revolution), sinking much of his fortune into the cause. At his base, the mining town of Copiapó, he recruited an army and manufactured weapons, also issuing his own locally minted currency (constituent pesos). Although Gallo staged a brilliant march to capture LA SERENA (March 1859), his army was defeated at the battle of Cerro Grande, just south of the city, two weeks later in April. Gallo fled into exile, returning to Chile in 1863, when, with his friend Manuel Antonio Matta, he founded the Radical Party, often nicknamed *la tienda de los Matta y los Gallo* (The Matta and Gallo store). In his later years he served as a member of the Chamber of Deputies, and in 1876 he was elected to the Senate.

MARIO BAHAMONDE SILVA, *El caudillo de Copiapó: Copiapó, 1859* (1977), and SIMON COLLIER, "Chile from Independence to the War of the Pacific," in *Cambridge History of Latin America*, edited by Leslie Bethell, vol. 3 (1985), pp. 583–613.

SIMON COLLIER

GALTIERI, LEOPOLDO FORTUNATO (*b.* 15 July 1926), military leader and president of Argentina (1981–1982). Born in Caseros, province of Buenos Aires, he graduated in 1945 from the Military Academy (COLEGIO MILITAR), where he studied military engineering. In 1949 he attended the U.S. Basic Engineering Course in the Panama Canal Zone, and in 1958 he became a professor at the Senior War College. The following year Galtieri was in charge of the advanced engineering course at the Engineering School, and in 1960 he took an advanced engineering course in the United States.

On 28 December 1979 Galtieri became the commander in chief of the Argentine Army. When General Roberto VIOLA fell ill, Galtieri had the military junta declare him president of the republic on 29 December 1981. Galtieri also retained the post of commander in chief of the army.

In 1982 Galtieri approved the plan to recapture the Falkland (Malvinas) Islands from Great Britain, last occupied by the Argentines in the early 1830s. The war, which raged from early April to mid-June 1982, was disastrous for Argentina, and Galtieri was forced to resign on 17 June.

In 1985, General Galtieri was tried for human-rights violations during the DIRTY WAR and for incompetence and maladministration during the FALKLANDS/MALVINAS WAR. He was acquitted on the first issue but convicted on the second. Galtieri was sentenced to twelve years imprisonment. In December 1990 he was released under a general amnesty.

OSCAR R. CARDOSO et al., *Falklands—The Secret Plot* (1987); MARTIN EDWIN ANDERSEN, *Dossier Secreto* (1993).

ROBERT SCHEINA

GALVÁN, MANUEL DE JESÚS (*b.* 1834; *d.* 1910), Dominican writer, politician, and jurist. Galván was considered the Dominican Republic's greatest writer for his book *Enriquillo*, which dealt with the confrontation between the indigenous Tainos and Spanish colonizers. Galván was also a member of the Dominican Congress and a justice of the Supreme Court. Considered a masterwork of Spanish literature, *Enriquillo* is a fictionalized account of the struggle of the last Taino cacique, Enrique, who fled his Spanish landlord into the Bahoruco Mountains and organized with his followers a thirteen-year resistance (1520–1533) to Spanish rule. While Enrique and his followers never surrendered, and while a peace agreement that moved the surviving Tainos to reservations was signed, by the 1550s the Taino population had been virtually wiped out. Galván's novel was not published until 1882 and contains considerable embellishment, including the oft-repeated nineteenth-century style of depicting the indigenous Americans as "noble savages." Despite its nostalgia for the vanquished, Galván's novel is considered one of the greatest novels produced by a Dominican.

MANUEL DE JESÚS GALVÁN, *Manuel de Jesús Galván's Enriquillo: The Cross and the Sword*, translated by Robert Graves (1975); LOUISE L. CRIPPS, *The Spanish Caribbean: From Columbus to Castro* (1979).

MICHAEL POWELSON

GALVÁN RIVERA, MARIANO (*b.* 12 September 1791; *d.* 1876), Mexican publisher. After becoming established in Mexico City as a bookseller, Galván, a native of Tepotzotlán, opened a print shop, with Mariano Arévalo as manager, in 1826. That year he began publishing his *Calendario manual*, which continues to appear under the name *Calendario del más antiguo Galván*. From 1827 to 1830 he published *El observador de la República Mexicana*, and from 1833 to 1834, *El indicador de la Federación Mexicana*, edited by José María Luis MORA. From 1838 to 1843 he published the *Calendario de las señoritas mexica-*

nas. Other works that he published include *Sagrada Biblia* in twenty-five volumes; *El periquillo sarmiento; Colección eclesiástica mexicana; Don Quijote; Dicionario razonado de legislación;* Count de Segur's *Historia universal; Nueva colección de leyes y decretos mexicanos;* and *Concilio III provincial mexicano.* His bookstore became a gathering place for literary and political figures. In 1862 Galván was a member of the Assembly of Notables who decided to establish a monarchy in Mexico. Although imprisoned after MAXIMILIAN's fall, he was soon freed. He died in Mexico City.

Diccionario Porrúa de historia, geografía y biografía de México, 5th ed. (1986).

VIRGINIA GUEDEA

GALVARINO (*d.* December 1557), ARAUCANIAN warrior and hero. Nothing is known about Galvarino's life before the events in which he figured during the Spanish invasion of Chile. At the battle of Lagunillas (or Bío-bío) during Governor García HURTADO DE MENDOZA's (1535–1609) advance into Araucanian territory in 1557, he was captured and had both his hands cut off. The fiery speeches he delivered following his mutilation rallied his people to resist the Spaniards. Soon afterward, at the battle of Millarapue (November 1557), Galvarino was again captured and later hanged with other Araucanian prisoners.

The events of Galvarino's demise were witnessed by the poet-soldier Alonso de ERCILLA Y ZÚÑIGA (1533–1594), who recounted them in memorable passages in his epic *La* ARAUCANA. This more than anything else gave Galvarino the legendary status he enjoys in the pantheon of Araucanian heroism. While some of the speeches attributed to Galvarino in this poem must have been invented by Ercilla, the events themselves are confirmed by independent sources.

SIMON COLLIER

GÁLVEZ, BERNARDO DE (*b.* 25 July 1746; *d.* 30 November 1786), Spanish military officer, governor of LOUISIANA (1777–1783), and viceroy of New Spain (1785–1786), Gálvez was born at Macharavialla, near Málaga, to a family that held many important posts under the Spanish Bourbons. He accompanied his uncle, José de GÁLVEZ, to New Spain, where he gained valuable experience against the APACHES on the northern frontier in 1769. After a tour of training with the French Cantabrian Regiment, he served under General Alejandro O'REILLY in a campaign against Algeria (1774), after which King CHARLES III named him commander of the Louisiana Regiment in 1776.

Upon arriving in New Orleans, however, he received orders to relieve Luis de Unzaga as governor of Louisiana, which he did on 1 January 1777. His administration in Louisiana coincided with the American Revolution, in which he played a prominent role. He increased the population and military strength of the colony and promoted its economic growth in accordance with the instructions of his uncle José, who now served as president of the COUNCIL OF THE INDIES. In collaboration with Oliver Pollock, he clandestinely channeled arms to American revolutionaries operating in the Mississippi Valley, significantly aiding George Rogers Clark. Once Spain declared war on England, he launched a successful military campaign, with major victories at BATON ROUGE (21 September 1779), MOBILE (March 1780), and PENSACOLA (8–10 May 1781). His forces were also instrumental in breaking British military power in the northern Mississippi Valley. Gálvez's victories enabled Spain to recover Florida under the Treaty of Paris (1783) and contributed significantly to the achievement of American independence. Promoted to captain-general, Gálvez governed Cuba from 4 February until 20 April 1785, after which he succeeded his father, Matías de GÁLVEZ, as viceroy of New Spain. He died in Mexico City.

JOHN W. CAUGHEY, *Bernardo de Gálvez in Louisiana, 1776–1783* (1934); JACK D. L. HOLMES, *A Guide to Spanish Louisiana, 1762–1806* (1970); JOSÉ R. BOETA, *Bernardo de Gálvez* (1977); BERNARDO DE GÁLVEZ, *Yo solo: The Battle Journal of Bernardo de Gálvez During the American Revolution* (1978); RALPH L. WOODWARD, JR., *Tribute to Don Bernardo de Gálvez* (1979); WILLIAM S. COKER and ROBERT R. REA, eds., *Anglo-Spanish Confrontation on the Gulf Coast During the American Revolution* (1982); CARMEN DE REPARZ, *Yo solo: Bernardo de Gálvez y la toma de Panzacola en 1781* (1986).

RALPH LEE WOODWARD, JR.

GÁLVEZ, JOSÉ DE (*b.* 2 January 1720; *d.* 17 June 1787), a leading Spanish bureaucrat and statesman instrumental in the reform of eighteenth-century colonial administration. Born a poor hidalgo in Macharaviaya, an Andalusian hill village, Gálvez earned a law degree at the University of Salamanca. Later, he conducted a successful practice in Madrid, in which he handled many cases involving parties in the Americas. He attracted the attention of Abbé Béliardi, a French agent, and through him, gained the patronage of the marqués de Esquilache and the marqués de Grimaldi, enlightened ministers of King Charles III of Spain. Their favor secured him the risky opportunity to conduct a VISITA, that is, a thorough inspection and overhaul of the administration of Mexico, where he arrived in July 1765.

Gálvez carried out a speedy and ruthless reorganization of tax collection and accounting procedures. He jailed corrupt officials, changed the tax structure, instituted a highly profitable tobacco monopoly, and shifted the control of trade with Spain from Mexican to Spanish merchants. In so doing, he forced capital into mining, which he aided with tax reductions, cheap mercury, and technical assistance. In this way, he decisively redirected the Mexican economy.

The *visitador* proposed the introduction of the INTENDANCY SYSTEM (provincial governors) and the establishment of the PROVINCIAS INTERNAS, which created a separate government for the northern region of the country. In addition, Gálvez dealt with the expulsion of the JESUITS, Indian revolts in Sonora, raids in Chihuahua, and orders to colonize Alta California all at the same time. He brutally suppressed the uprisings occasioned by the ban, reorganized government in the north, and got the colonization effort under way by 1769.

Then, the strain of work, the responsibility, and the exhausting and indecisive struggle with the Sonoran Indians broke Gálvez's health, and in late 1769 he suffered a physical and mental collapse. He recovered and returned to Spain in 1771, but the end of the *visita* was clouded.

In Spain Gálvez assumed his place on the COUNCIL OF THE INDIES, to which he was appointed in 1767. He was gradually given more important assignments, and when Julián de Arriaga y Rivera died, Charles III made Gálvez minister of the Indies (February 1776).

As minister, Gálvez tried to institute the reforms he had instituted in Mexico throughout the whole Empire. *Visitadores* cast in Gálvez's mold were sent to Peru, New Granada, Venezuela, and Ecuador to increase revenue, establish intendancies, and invigorate government. The situation in Buenos Aires was complicated by the opportunity, offered by Great Britain's preoccupation with the American Revolution, to settle long-pending disputes with the Portuguese regarding boundaries and smuggling. Eventually Spain declared war and sent a military expedition to the area. The result was the establishment of a viceroyalty of Buenos Aires, organized according to Gálvez's program.

When Spain followed France into an alliance with the Americans against Britain in 1779, Gálvez's reforms were again shouldered aside. Moreover, the need for money and the errors and misfortunes of two *visitadores* produced the TÚPAC AMARU rebellion (1780–1781) in Peru and the COMUNERO REVOLT (1781) in New Granada. Gálvez reacted to them with the same fierce repression he had unleashed in Mexico against those who questioned royal authority.

Nevertheless, when Gálvez became marqués de Sonora in 1785, he could claim an important role in winning back Florida and ejecting the British from the MOSQUITO COAST and DARIÉN. Unfortunately, just as Gálvez sought to bring his full authority to bear on the completion of the internal reforms, he died.

The consequent reorganization of the ministry redirected the course of policy, but Sonora's reforms had been too extensive to be abandoned totally. Gálvez was a hard-working and hard-edged administrator, efficient but not noted for accommodation or suppleness. His legacy of a more rational administration and higher revenues was purchased with the political alienation of many Americans and not a few Spaniards, whom he pushed from their traditional places and powers.

José de Gálvez. Reproduced from Lucas Alaman, *Disertaciones sobre la historia de la república mejicana*, vol. 3 (Mexico, 1942). BENSON LATIN AMERICAN COLLECTION, UNIVERSITY OF TEXAS AT AUSTIN.

There is no comprehensive biography of Gálvez. However, the Mexican *visita* is well covered in HERBERT INGRAM PRIESTLY, *José de Gálvez: Visitor-General of New Spain, 1765–1771* (1916; repr. 1980). The Provincias Internas scheme and the intendant system are thoroughly considered by LUIS NAVARRO GARCÍA in *Don José de Gálvez y la comandancia general de las provincias internas del norte de Nueva España* (1964), and *Intendencias en Indias* (1959). MARIO HERNÁNDEZ SÁNCHEZ-BARBA provides an *Annales* approach in *La última expansión española en America* (1957). Gálvez's impact on trade and government is analyzed in D. A. BRADING, *Miners and Merchants in Bourbon Mexico, 1762–1810* (1971). BRADING's "Bourbon Spain and Its American Empire," in Vol. 1, *The Cambridge History of Latin America*, edited by Leslie Bethell, vol. 1 (1984), pp. 389–439, provides a comprehensive view of the whole period. In most works dealing with the so-called Bourbon reforms there is some treatment of Gálvez and his policies. For example see J. R. FISHER, *Government and Society in Colonial Peru: The Intendant System, 1784–1814* (1970), and JOHN LEDDY PHELAN, *The People and the King: The Comunero Revolution in Colombia, 1781* (1978).

GEORGE M. ADDY

See also **Intendancy System.**

GÁLVEZ, JUAN MANUEL (*b.* 1887; *d.* 19 August 1972), president of Honduras, 1949–1954. Gálvez succeeded the long-time dictator, Tiburcio CARÍAS ANDINO, whom he had served as minister of defense. As Carías's hand-picked successor, Gálvez perpetuated National Party dominance and many of his predecessor's policies. He launched a more vigorous program of public works, infrastructure development, economic diversification, and tax reform while also easing restrictions on civil liberties.

The UNITED FRUIT COMPANY workers' strike in 1954 precipitated a political crisis at the end of Gálvez's administration. Gálvez, who had been a United Fruit attorney for many years, showed little sympathy for the strikers and was clearly annoyed by the encouragement that Guatemala's pro-labor government of Jacobo ARBENZ gave the strikers. He actively collaborated with Guatemalan exiles and the U.S. Central Intelligence Agency in the overthrow of the Arbenz government in June 1954. In the November 1954 elections, Carías sought to return to office, but Liberal candidate Ramón VILLEDA MORALES received a plurality of the votes, with no one receiving a majority. Before the Congress could decide the election, Gálvez's vice president, Julio LOZANO DÍAZ, seized power, ending Gálvez's administration. Gálvez, now in ill health, did not contest Lozano's seizure of dictatorial power, and Lozano later appointed Gálvez president of the Supreme Court.

JAMES D. RUDOLPH, ed., *Honduras, a Country Study*, 2d ed. (1983); JAMES A. MORRIS, *Honduras: Caudillo Politics and Military Rulers* (1984); ALISON ACKER, *Honduras: The Making of a Banana Republic* (1988); JAMES DUNKERLEY, *Power in the Isthmus: A Political History of Modern Central America* (1988); and TOM BARRY and KENT NORSWORTHY, *Honduras: A Country Guide* (1990).

RALPH LEE WOODWARD, JR.

GÁLVEZ, MANUEL (*b.* 18 July 1882; *d.* 14 November 1961), Argentine novelist and essayist. Gálvez was born in the provincial capital of Paraná. When he was three years old, his family moved to Santa Fe, where he studied at the Jesuit school La Inmaculada. In 1897, he completed his secondary studies in Buenos Aires at the Colegio del Salvador. He graduated from the University of Buenos Aires with a law degree in 1904, but never practiced his profession. His dissertation on the theme of white SLAVERY, reveals an early interest in social problems that never abated in his long career as a novelist and essayist.

One of Argentina's foremost novelists from 1915 until 1950, Gálvez played an important role in his country's cultural life. He was conservative in his political ideology, although as a young man he espoused a form of anarchism and defended Tolstoy's Christian socialism. In Gálvez's concept of nationalism, certain ideas were dominant: the central role of the church in maintaining the spirit and traditions of Argentina; an adherence to law and order above individual freedom; a distrust of Anglo-Saxon civilizations; and doubts about the advisability of having a totally democratic government. Nowhere was this nationalism more evident than in Gálvez's biography of the dictator Juan Manuel de ROSAS (1829–1852), whom Gálvez defended on the ground that he unified the country and prevented it from succumbing to the economic and political pressures of the French and English. In *El solar de la raza* (The Birthplace of Our Race, 1913), Gálvez underscored the cultural and spiritual affinity between Argentina and Spain. In works like *La sombra del convento* (The Shadow of the Convent, 1917), Gálvez preached a return to the traditional moral and religious values that could still be found in the provinces and opposed the utilitarian values he associated with life in Buenos Aires.

For twenty-five years, Gálvez served as national inspector of secondary and normal schools, an experience he drew on to write *La maestra normal* (The Normal School Teacher, 1914), which many critics interpreted as an attack on the normal schools and secular education. In novels of social protest such as *Nacha regules* (1919), Gálvez became a social reformer, defending the poor and downtrodden against society's indifference to human suffering.

During his career, Gálvez did much to promote Argentine letters and to make the country's writers known throughout Hispanic America. In 1917, he established the Cooperative Publishers of Buenos Aires and in 1919 founded Pax Publishers to introduce European works in translation to Argentine readers.

WILLIAM REX CRAWFORD, "Manuel Gálvez," in *A Century of Latin American Thought* (1944), pp. 149–164; IGNACIO B. ANZOÁTEGUI, *Manuel Gálvez* (1961); NORMA DESINANO, *La novelística de Manuel Gálvez* (1965); MYRON I. LICHTBLAU, *Manuel Gálvez* (1972); DAVID W. FOSTER, "Ideological Ruptures in Manuel Gálvez's *Historia de arrabal:* Linguistic Conventions," *Hispanic Journal* 4, no. 2 (1983): 21–27; JOHN C. WALKER, "Ideología y metafísica en Manuel Gálvez," *Revista Canadiense de Estudios Hispánicos* 10, no. 3 (1986): 475–490.

MYRON I. LICHTBLAU

See also **Literature: Spanish America.**

GÁLVEZ, MARIANO (*b.* 26 May 1794; *d.* 26 May 1862), chief of state of Guatemala (1831–1838). Gálvez was adopted as a foundling by an influential family in Guatemala City and eventually received a royal dispensation from the legal disadvantages of his suspicious birth. He was educated in the law, and his enthusiasm for the Enlightenment ideas of his day led him to a career in politics. He was much involved in the negotiations and turmoil that preceded independence from Spain. Indeed, he voted in favor of independence, but promoted, in fear of instability, political union with the new Mexican empire. After the fall of Agustín de ITURBIDE, emperor of Mexico, in 1823 and the separation of Central America from Mexico that same year, Gálvez held public offices at both the state and federal level, and in 1831,

Mariano Gálvez. BENSON LATIN AMERICAN COLLECTION, UNIVERSITY OF TEXAS AT AUSTIN.

ties to private property. During his term of office, Gálvez instituted the most radical liberal program of reform of nineteenth-century Guatemala.

Gálvez's reforms alienated, offended, and often threatened the livelihood of large sectors of the population, especially the impoverished peasantry. Liberal trade policy damaged native industry. A head tax of two pesos per capita excessively burdened peasants who found themselves landless after the agrarian reforms. The liberal demand for forced labor on public works projects further increased resentment. Peasants also found burdensome the travel that jury duty required. Eventually, profound discontent became outright rebellion. Peasants formed an unlikely alliance with disgruntled conservatives and clergymen that relied on the leadership of a brilliant guerrilla fighter, José Rafael CARRERA. Gálvez tried desperately to amend the errors of his reform program, but his stopgap measures were too late to impede a revolutionary movement that had gained tremendous momentum. When he tried unsuccessfully to stop the growth of a cholera epidemic in 1837 by implementing the most modern controls, his measures were misinterpreted by peasants as deliberate poisonings. For these reasons, Gálvez's liberal program was destined to die. He was overthrown in February 1838 and later forced into exile in Mexico.

ANTONIO BATRES JÁUREGUI, *El Dr. Mariano Gálvez y su época* (1957); JORGE LUIS ARRIOLA, *Gálvez en la encrucijada: Ensayo crítico en torno al humanismo político de un gobernante* (1961); MIRIAM WILLIFORD, "The Reform Program of Dr. Mariano Gálvez," Ph.D. diss., Tulane University, 1963; WILLIAM JOYCE GRIFFITH, *Empires in the Wilderness: Foreign Colonization and Development in Guatemala, 1834–1844* (1965); FRANCIS POLO SIFONTES, *Mariano Gálvez, éxitos y fracaso de su gobierno* (1979).

MICHAEL F. FRY

after a devastating civil war that destroyed conservative power, he was elected chief of state of Guatemala.

With the leading conservatives in exile and with the power to squash opposition, Gálvez fervently sought to set an example in Guatemala that would eventually turn all of Central America into a modern, progressive republic through enlightened social and economic legislation. His attack on the clergy reduced drastically the wealth and power of the church. He proclaimed religious toleration and destroyed the hegemony of the clergy in education by establishing a system of free, public, lay instruction. He began a series of projects for economic development designed to bring new life to sparsely populated and neglected areas of the country, often using foreign colonization to achieve his goals. He attempted to impose a new and alien system of common law, the LIVINGSTON CODES, on a society accustomed to the civil law of Spain. Most important, he sought to promote economic competitiveness and prosperity by reducing the communal lands of municipali-

GÁLVEZ, MATÍAS DE (*b.* 2 July 1717; *d.* 3 November 1784), captain-general of Guatemala and forty-eighth viceroy of New Spain. He was born in Macharaviaya, Málaga, Spain, the eldest of at least five sons. His younger brother José de Gálvez, minister general of the Indies from 1776 to 1787, made possible Matías's success. Matías's son Bernardo Gálvez (1746–1786) succeeded his father as viceroy.

After a military career characterized by devotion to duty, Gálvez was ordered to Central America as inspector general of the Spanish forces. He arrived at San Fernando de Omoa, Honduras, in July 1778. Gálvez's immediate duty was to prepare the defense of Central America against possible British attack. On 15 January 1779, Gálvez was appointed to replace Martín de Mayorga, who was named viceroy of New Spain, as captain-general and governor of Guatemala. His principal responsibilities were to speed implementation of the Bourbon reforms, to drive the British from the Caribbean coast of Central America, and to finish the construction of a new capital city.

Gálvez reformed the militia and led successful attacks against the British in Honduras in 1779 and in Nicaragua in 1781. He also negotiated successful treaties with the MISKITO INDIANS on the coast. His successes earned him the accolades of the Ayuntamiento of Guatemala as a "true father" of the region and a promotion to field marshal.

As a Bourbon reformer Gálvez attempted to encourage the economy of the region by offering economic incentives and by weakening the economic domination by a clique of merchants in Guatemala City. He established a *banco de rescate* in Tegucigalpa, and granted *repartimientos* of Indians to increase mining production in Honduras. To stimulate indigo production, Gálvez created a *monte pío* (fund for widows and orphans) for the growers so they would not have to rely on the credit extended by Guatemalan merchants. Also to weaken the Guatemalan oligopoly over the prices paid at the annual indigo fair, Gálvez instituted a pricing board and moved the fair. To assure an adequate supply of cattle and full collection of taxes, he moved the annual cattle fair deeper into El Salvador. During his tenure, tax collections increased over 20 percent, but control of the local economy was never wrested from Guatemala City. Despite short-term success, within two decades most of the changes wrought by Gálvez, both military and administrative, were completely undone.

As a result of his accomplishments in Central America and his family connections, Gálvez was named interim viceroy of New Spain on 14 August 1782 and assumed that post in April 1783. Four months later he earned a full viceregal appointment. His term in Mexico was marked by the reconstruction of Chapultepec Palace, improvement of the drainage system of Mexico City through the construction of dikes and drainage canals, installation of a lighting system, establishment of a branch of the BANCO DE SAN CARLOS, and tighter administration of the REAL HACIENDA. During his tenure there was a tripling of royal receipts, due more to external factors than to administrative changes by Gálvez. He died in Mexico City.

CAYETANO ALCÁZAR MOLINA, *Los Vírreinatos en el siglo XVIII*, (1945); TROY S. FLOYD, "Guatemalan Merchants, the Government, and the *Provincianos, 1750–1800*," in *Hispanic American Historical Review* 41, no. 1 (1961): 90–110, and *The Anglo-Spanish Struggle for Mosquitia* (1967), esp. pp. 133–162; MARIANA RODRÍGUEZ DEL VALLE and ANGELES CONEJO DÍEZ DE LA CORTINA, "Matías de Gálvez," in *Los virreyes de Nueva España en el reinado de Carlos III*, edited by José Antonio Calderón Quijano, vol. 2 (1968); WILBUR E. MENERAY, *The Kingdom of Guatemala During the Reign of Charles III, 1759–1788* (1975); AGUSTÍN MENCOS FRANCO, *Estudios históricos sobre Centro América* (1982).

WILBUR E. MENERAY

GAMA, JOSÉ BASILIO DA (*b.* 1741; *d.* 31 July 1795), Brazilian poet. Born in Minas Gerais, Gama studied in Rio de Janeiro under the JESUITS and then in Rome after 1759, when the order was banished from Portuguese possessions. Later, while living in Portugal, he was arrested as a Jesuit sympathizer but escaped exile by gaining favor with the marquês of POMBAL, the realm's chief minister. His most famous work, *O Uruguai*, was published in Lisbon in 1769.

A long poem in ten blank-verse cantos, *O Uruguai* is constructed around episodes from the War of the Seven Reductions (1752–1756), which the Portuguese and Spanish waged jointly against the Jesuits and their TUPI-GUARANÍ Indian mission congregations in Uruguay. Sometimes regarded as an epic, it has also been considered a lyrical narrative and a poetic drama. The original version had been openly pro-Jesuit, but the published version criticizes the Jesuits scathingly, in consonance with Pombal's policies.

O Uruguai is considered the most important literary work of Brazil's colonial period. It presents sympathetically the inevitable demise of indigenous culture before the advance of white men. Its Indian heroes contributed to its popularity among the romantics, who also admired the freedom of its blank verse and who viewed its pictures of Indian life and the Brazilian landscape as a precursor of the autonomous national literature they sought to create.

SIR RICHARD F. BURTON published a translation of *O Uruguai, The Uruguay*, in 1878; a modern scholarly edition of the Burton translation, with introduction and notes by Frederick C. H. García and Edward F. Stanton, was published in 1972. DAVID M. DRIVER, *The Indian in Brazilian Literature* (1942), pp. 22–33, contains a discussion of the poem.

NORWOOD ANDREWS, JR.

GAMA, LUÍS (*b.* 21 June 1830; *d.* 24 August 1882), Brazilian poet, lawyer, and abolitionist. The son of a profligate aristocrat and a rebellious free African woman, Gama was born free in Bahia. At the age of ten he was sold into slavery by his father and shipped to São Paulo. In 1847, while serving as a household slave, Gama was befriended by a student and taught to read and write. Soon afterward, having become aware of the illegality of his enslavement, Gama fled his master's house. He served in the militia for six years and later established himself as a journalist, poet, and self-educated lawyer. In 1859, literate for scarcely a dozen years, he published his first and most successful book of verse, *Primeiras trovas burlescas de Getulino*. Ten years later, by then a noted author, he coedited with Rui Barbosa, Joaquim Nabuco, and others the journal *Radical Paulistano*, which supported the reformist program of parliamentary liberals led by José Tomás NABUCO DE ARAÚJO. As a lawyer, Gama specialized in defending persons kept illegally in SLAVERY, especially Africans held in violation of the anti-slave-trade law of 1831. According to his own count, he thereby freed more than five hundred persons. At the time of his death, Gama was the undisputed leader of the antislavery movement in the province of São Paulo.

SUD MENUCCI, *O precursor da abolicionismo no Brasil (Luíz Gama)* (1938); ROBERT BRENT TOPLIN, *The Abolition of Slavery in Brazil* (1972); ROBERT EDGAR CONRAD, *Children of God's Fire: A Documentary History of Black Slavery in Brazil* (1983), and *The Destruction of Brazilian Slavery, 1850–1888*, 2d ed., rev. (1992).

ROBERT EDGAR CONRAD

GAMA, VASCO DA (*b.* 1460s; *d.* 24 or 25 December 1524), Portuguese explorer, discoverer of the maritime route to India. Son of a member of the household of Prince Fernando, da Gama had been a *fidalgo* in the royal household of King JOÃO II and, at the time of his first voyage, a knight and commander in the Order of Santiago. About 1507 he transferred to the Order of Christ, and in 1519 he became first count of Vidigueira.

King Manuel I named da Gama leader of the armada that sailed from the Tagus River on 8 July 1497 in search of a maritime route to India. Two of the four ships, the *São Gabriel* and the *São Rafael*, were commanded, respectively, by Vasco and his brother, Paulo. After more than ninety days at sea—the longest known voyage out of sight of land by a European to date—da Gama dropped anchor in the Bay of Santa Helena, 100 miles north of the Cape of Good Hope. On 22 November 1497, da Gama rounded the cape and on Christmas Day reached what is now known as Natal. On 2 March 1498, he reached the island of Mozambique. After stopping at Mombasa and Malindi, da Gama—with the help of a Muslim pilot from Gujarat—departed across the Indian Ocean on 24 April, and on 20 May he anchored several miles north of Calicut.

Da Gama remained in India for over three months. Early in his stay, he met with Calicut's Hindu leader, whom the Portuguese called the samorim. But relations with him deteriorated, and da Gama sailed northward to Angediva Island, along India's west coast, south of Goa. Beginning the return voyage on 5 October, da Gama rounded the Cape of Good Hope on 20 March 1499. He arrived in Lisbon in very late August or during the first three weeks in September, though one of his ships, the *Berrio*, already had arrived on 10 July. Honored for his efforts, da Gama was made admiral of India, became a member of the king's council, and was given financial rewards.

Made leader of the fourth Portuguese expedition to India, da Gama set sail from Lisbon in February 1502. After exacting reprisals in Calicut from the natives for the massacre of the Portuguese stationed there, da Gama left India on 28 December 1502 and reached Lisbon on 1 September 1503.

In 1524 da Gama returned to India for a third and final time at the behest of King João III. Sent to clean up corruption and restore authority in Portuguese Asia, he was given the post of viceroy of India, the second to receive that title. Sailing from Lisbon on 9 April 1524, da

Gama reached Chaul on 5 September. His administration was an energetic one, but it was also short, as he died in Cochin less than four months after his arrival.

The definitive biography of Vasco da Gama remains to be written. To date, the best book-length account in English of the first voyage of da Gama is ELAINE SANCEAU, *Good Hope: The Voyage of Vasco da Gama* (1967). It is based largely on the sixteenth-century Portuguese chroniclers. The best short study in English is probably the chapter, "The Indian Ocean Crossing," in JOHN H. PARRY, *The Discovery of the Sea* (1974). The most important source for the first voyage is the diary of an anonymous eyewitness. It has been published in Portuguese in a number of editions and is included in JOSÉ PEDRO MACHADO and VIRIATO CAMPOS, *Vasco da Gama e a sua viagem de descobrimento* (1969). The diary has been edited and translated into English by E. G. RAVENSTEIN (with excellent notes, introduction, and accompanying materials) in *A Journal of the First Voyage of Vasco da Gama, 1497–1499* (1898). A judicious summary in English of da Gama's career is found in BAILEY W. DIFFIE and GEORGE D. WINIUS, *Foundations of the Portuguese Empire, 1415–1580* (1977). Two other useful surveys are found in DAMIÃO PERES, *História dos descobrimentos portugueses*, 3d ed. (1983), and LUIS DE ALBUQUERQUE, *Os descobrimentos portugueses* (1983). AUGUSTO C. TEIXEIRA DE ARAGÃO published many documents dealing with Vasco da Gama in *Vasco da Gama e a Vidigueira, Estudo historico*, 3d ed. (1898).

FRANCIS A. DUTRA

See also **Explorers.**

GAMARRA, AGUSTÍN (*b.* 1785; *d.* 1841), quintessential military CAUDILLO of nineteenth-century Peru, born in Cuzco, and twice president of Peru (1829–1833, 1839–1841) during an unstable period in which there were more than thirty presidents in twenty years (1826–1846). Like Andrés de SANTA CRUZ and Ramón CASTILLA, Gamarra was initially trained by the Spanish colonial army. Under CREOLE Generals José Manuel Goyeneche and Pío Tristán, Gamarra fought against independence movements in the regions of Upper and Southern Peru between 1809 and 1820. In 1820, however, the entire royalist Numancia battalion in which Gamarra served passed over to General José de SAN MARTÍN's independence forces, at the time active on the Peruvian coast. Consequently, Gamarra fought in the independence army in the battles of JUNÍN and AYACUCHO that finally removed Spanish colonial presence in Peru.

Soon after independence Gamarra became prefect of Cuzco and military commander of the southern Peruvian armies. Gamarra was a zealous creole-patriot, politically conservative and protectionist in trading matters. He achieved renown in early "national" military campaigns against Colombian influence in Bolivia (1828) and in the dispute over the port of Guayaquil with Colombia (1829). In the middle of the latter, unsuccessful campaign in Ecuador, Gamarra forcibly exiled President José de la MAR to become president of Peru. In his first presidency, Gamarra foiled at least seventeen rebellions with the aid of his belligerent wife Francisca Zubiaga de Gamarra, but was finally defeated in a civil war by General Luis José Orbegoso in 1833.

Gamarra continued to conspire but did not seize power until 1839, after he led the opposition against General Santa Cruz's PERU-BOLIVIA CONFEDERATION (1836–1839). The Chilean army, employing Peruvian dissenters such as Gamarra himself, defeated Santa Cruz in the battle of YUNGAY (1839). Finally, Gamarra's attempt to incorporate Bolivia into Peru was soundly defeated in the battle of Ingaví (1841), in which Gamarra lost his life.

JORGE BASADRE, *Historia de la República del Perú,* vols. 1–2 (1963); CELIA WU, *Generals and Diplomats: Great Britain and Peru 1820–40* (1991).

ALFONSO W. QUIROZ

GAMARRA, FRANCISCA ZUBIAGA BERNALES DE (LA MARISCALA) (*b.* 1803; *d.* 1835), Peruvian first lady and woman-at-arms. Gamarra was born in Cuzco, the daughter of a Basque merchant and a Cuzqueña. She abandoned a monastic career because of ill health and married the prefect of Cuzco, General Agustín GAMARRA, in 1825. While the former commander of Peruvian forces under Simón BOLÍVAR rose to the presidency of the country, the flamboyant Doña Francisca was making a reputation in her own right. Known as La Mariscala (the lady marshal) for her unusual martial skills, particularly precision shooting, use of the sword, and superb equestrianship, she was also known to lead troops into battle in the country's interminable civil wars. Her political acumen and daring were equally renowned, earning her the sobriquet "La Presidenta" while at her husband's side in the National Palace. Her picturesque career and life ended prematurely in exile and impoverishment in Valparaíso, where she died of tuberculosis at the age of thirty-two.

FRANCISCO VEGAS SEMINARIO, *Bajo el signo de la Mariscala* (1960).

PETER F. KLARÉN

GAMARRA, JOSÉ (*b.* 12 February 1934). Uruguayan artist. Gamarra was born in Tacuarembó, Uruguay, and studied at the School of Fine Arts in Montevideo as well as with Vicente Martin (1952–1959). He studied engraving with John Friedlaender and Iberê Camargo in Rio de Janeiro (1959). In 1963 he was selected for the Biennial of Young Artists in Paris, after which he settled in Arcueil, France.

Gamarra's early works were abstractions inspired by pre-Conquest art motifs and Uruguayan vernacular ironwork. After moving to Paris, he began to paint tropical landscapes modeled after nineteenth-century European and North American visions of Central and South America as a primeval and exotic territory. Historical, mythological, and contemporary figures (Indians, conquistadores, guerrillas, nuns, and pre-Conquest idols) coexist in Gamarra's painted rain forests. War vehicles and artifacts disturb his paradisiacal settings. Objects and human figures have been interpreted as suggesting narratives and critical comments about Latin American history, such as the Spanish conquest or North American interventions (*Five Centuries Later*, 1986).

DAWN ADES, *Art in Latin America: The Modern Era, 1820–1980* (1989), pp. 293–296; ORIANA BADDELEY and VALERIE FRASER, *Drawing the Line: Art and Cultural Identity in Contemporary Latin America* (1989), pp. 24–30.

MARTA GARSD

GAMBARO, GRISELDA (*b.* 28 July 1928); Argentine playwright, short-story writer, and novelist. In *El campo* (1967; *The Camp,* 1971), *El desatino* (1965; *The Blunder*), *Los siameses* (1967; *The Siamese Twins,* 1967), and other works, Gambaro uses symbolic constructions to depict the real nature of human beings and of their relationships, to open "an imaginary space that, in turn, discovers, invents or anticipates new dimensions of reality." For her, valid literature must have an anticipatory quality and should question what constitutes reality and reveal what reality could be. Gambaro, in all her works, is preoccupied with the absurdity of the human condition, the schizophrenic nature of man, and the exercise of power by men and women alike. Her theater and, to some degree, her novels are absurdist constructions with elements of the theater of cruelty and black humor. Gambaro herself has related it to the *grotesco criollo,* a parodic genre rooted in the distortion of the traditional bourgeois drama: that of the love triangle. Her characters are isolated, defeated, and devastated in a brutal, hostile world. Her mostly nonverbal language and violent physical images underline a dramatic vision of life and bestow a nightmarish and Kafkaesque quality to her plays.

Although Gambaro's writings deal with universal problems, not limited to a specific place or time, they could be related to the Argentine reality of the recent past. She won the Drama Critics' Prize for best play of 1990 with *Penas sin importancia* (Unimportant Sorrows).

TAMARA HOLZAPFEL, "Griselda Gambaro's Theatre of the Absurd," in *Latin American Theatre Review* 4, no. 1 (1970): 5–11; SANDRA M. CYPESS, "Physical Imagery in the Plays of Griselda Gambaro," in *Modern Drama* 18, no. 4 (1975): 357–364, and "The Plays of Griselda Gambaro," in *Dramatists in Revolt: The New Latin American Theater,* edited by Leon F. Lyday and George W. Woodyard (1976), pp. 95–109; DAVID W. FOSTER, "The Texture of Dramatic Action in the Plays of Griselda Gambaro," in *Hispanic Journal* 1, no. 2 (1979): 57–66; MARGUERITE FEITLOWITZ, "Crisis, Terror, Disappearance: The Theater of Griselda Gambaro," in *Theater* 21, no. 3 (1990): 34–38.

ANGELA B. DELLEPIANE

GAMBOA IGLESIAS, FEDERICO (*b.* 22 December 1864; *d.* 15 August 1930), Mexican public figure and intellectual, a major essayist for Mexican and international newspapers. A multifaceted intellectual whose contributions ranged from fiction to plays, he documented Mexican intellectual life in his major five-volume memoir *Mi diario*. He also supported intellectual activities by providing important leadership to the prestigious Mexican Academy of Language from 1923 to 1939.

Born in the capital, the son of General Manuel Gamboa, the governor of Jalisco, and Lugarda Iglesias, the sister of the leading Liberal politician José María Iglesias, he studied in New York City and then attended the National School of Law. After joining the Foreign Service in 1888, he served in numerous posts in Latin America and the United States. He was a federal deputy from Chihuahua before representing Mexico as minister to the Netherlands (1911–1912). He became undersecretary of foreign relations (1908–1910) and rose to secretary under Victoriano HUERTA in 1913. Discredited as a public official for his service under Huerta, Gamboa was in exile from 1914 to 1919.

ALBERTO MARÍA CARREÑO, *La Academia Mexicana correspondiente de la Española, 1875–1945* (1946); and FEDERICO GAMBOA, *Diario de Federico Gamboa, 1892–1939* (1977).

RODERIC AI CAMP

GAMIO MARTÍNEZ, MANUEL (*b.* 2 March 1883; *d.* 16 July 1960), a Mexican anthropologist considered the initiator of modern INDIGENISMO studies in Mexico and an activist in Latin American and European societies promoting the examination and preservation of indigenous cultures.

The son of Gabriel Gamio and Marina Martínez, wealthy landowners in the Dominican Republic and Mexico, Gamio was educated in private schools and the National Preparatory School before studying archaeology under Nicolás León and Jesús Galindo y Villa in the National Museum in Mexico City. A student of Franz Boas at Columbia University, he obtained his M.A. in 1911 and returned for a Ph.D. in anthropology in 1921.

Returning to Mexico, Gamio undertook the organization of and became director for the department of anthropology in the secretariat of agriculture (1917–1920). From 1917 to 1920 he also led the first comprehensive exploration of the Teotihuacán ruins in the center of Mexico City's commercial district, where he discovered the TEMPLO MAYOR. Before 1925 he led other explorations and restorations of archaeological sites, including ones in Yucatán and Guatemala. He was a leader of educational and government institutions devoted to archaeological research and served briefly as undersecretary of public education in 1925. Thereafter he gave up archaeology to devote himself to protecting contemporary Indian cultures.

While concentrating on his research and academic pursuits, Gamio also held positions in the secretariat of agriculture and at the Institute for Social Research of the National University during the 1930s. In 1942 he became director of the Inter-American Indigenous Institute, a position he held until his death. Francisco Goitia, a noted Mexican painter, was a close collaborator. Gamio left a prolific body of published works.

MANUEL GAMIO, *Forjando patria* (1916); MANUEL GAMIO and JOSÉ VASCONCELOS, *Aspects of Mexican Civilization* (1926); UNIVERSIDAD NACIONAL AUTÓNOMO DE MÉXICO, *Estudios antropológicos publicados en homenaje al Dr. Manuel Gamio* (1956); and ANGELES GONZÁLEZ GAMIO, *Manuel Gamio, una lucha sin final* (1987).

RODERIC AI CAMP

GAMONALISMO, the phenomenon of local political bossism, in the figure of the *gamonal*. The term is Spanish-American rather than peninsular and probably dates from the early nineteenth century; but even the eminent Colombian philologist Rufino José Cuervo was unable to determine its precise origins. The word *gamonal* is largely synonymous with the older CACIQUE, an Arawak term adopted by the Spanish in the sixteenth century to denote indigenous chieftains, but which in the republican period came to denote personalist local political power in rural and small-town settings. *Gamonal* achieved wider currency in Colombia and Peru, while *cacique* was apparently favored in Mexico; where both are found, *gamonal* seems to have implied a more self-made, less traditional-bound mode of bossism than did *cacique*.

The origins and bases of *gamonalismo* remain largely unexplored; to many nineteenth-century commentators local bossism was the political expression of landowner power, but *gamonal* formation also occurred in regions of relatively democratic land tenure. Commerce was a frequent path to *gamonal* status, as was knowledge of the intricacies of the legal and administrative systems of the republican state. (The extreme version of this latter path is the Colombian *tinterillo*.) In highland Peru, *gamonalismo* often had an ethnic dimension as the multifaceted dominance of MESTIZOS over indigenous communities. Apart from local social and economic conditions, an important variable in the historical assessment of *gamonalismo* is its role in national politics: the *gamonal* in firmly entrenched party systems (such as those of Chile or Colombia) was (and is) quite different from his role in more fluid, CAUDILLO-driven polities. Some of the most sensitive depictions of *gamonalismo* are to be found in fiction, such as the novel *El último gamonal* by the Colombian Gustavo Álvarez GARDEAZÁBAL.

ROBERT H. DIX, *Colombia: The Political Dimensions of Change* (1967); JOSÉ CARLOS MARIÁTEGUI, *Seven Interpretive Essays on Peruvian Reality*, translated by Marjory Urquidi (1971); JOSÉ MARÍA SAMPER, "El triunvirato parroquial," in *Museo de cuadros de costumbres*, vol. 1 (1973), pp. 237–249.

RICHARD J. STOLLER

GÁNDARA ENRÍQUEZ, MARCOS (*b.* 1915), ideological leader of the military junta that assumed power in Ecuador in 1963. Born in Latacunga, Colonel (later General) Gándara, former director of the war academy and functional representative of the armed forces in the Senate, justified the military's assumption of power not simply as the product of contemporary conditions, including the military's perception of a rising threat of Communist subversion, but as a product of a long series of mistaken policies. The military assumed the responsibility for establishing new socioeconomic structures that would permit the evolution of democratic structures dedicated to serving the interests of all citizens.

During its first year in office, the junta suppressed political dissent, announced a series of development projects financed by U.S. loans, adopted a ten-year development plan proposed by the National Planning Board, approved an income tax, and issued an agrarian reform program. Although public opinion toward the junta was generally favorable at the end of its first year in office, the junta refused to develop political alliances or mobilize popular sectors to support its moderate reform program. The junta's rejection of partisan politics was rooted in its image of the military as the only truly national institution whose nonpartisan decisions would naturally generate public support.

Mounting economic problems during the second year of military rule quickly translated into growing public opposition expressed as demonstrations, strikes, and antigovernment media campaigns. By early 1966 the government faced daily challenges to its authority, frequently from students. Civilian politicians forged multiparty alliances that pressed for a return to constitutional government. The government's vacillating response to challenges, particularly from coastal economic and political elites, eroded support for continued military rule within the higher officer corps. A national strike and violent confrontations between students and the military at the Central University in Quito resulted in the fall of the government on 29 March 1966. Gándara went to Bolivia but later returned to Ecuador.

REPÚBLICA DEL ECUADOR, *Plan político de la Junta Militar de Gobierno* (1963); *La Junta Militar de Gobierno y la opinión pública* (1964); MARTIN NEEDLER, *Anatomy of a Coup d'État: Ecuador 1963* (1964); JOHN SAMUEL FITCH, *The Military Coup d'État as a Political Process: Ecuador, 1948–1966* (1977), esp. pp. 55–73.

LINDA ALEXANDER RODRÍGUEZ

GANDAVO, PERO DE MAGALHÃES (*d.* 1576), Portuguese historian. In 1576 Gandavo wrote and published the *História da Província de Santa Cruz, a que vulgarmente chamamos Brasil.* His *Tratado da terra do Brasil,* written before 1573, was not published until 1824 by the Royal Academy of Sciences in Lisbon. Gandavo justifies his enterprise in the prologue to his History, on the basis of the fact that although Brazil had been discovered several decades previously, no Portuguese writer had written about its discovery, and on his intention to persuade people in Portugal to emigrate and settle in the rich and healthy new land. His conception of history made him select as relevant the following elements: the description of the captaincies, the form of government, the distribution of land under the traditional Portuguese SESMARIAS (conditional grants), and the need for SLAVES as a labor force. With descriptive and narrative elements, Gandavo adroitly mixes past and present in each chapter. As other sixteenth-century writers, he dedicates part of his History to the description of plants and their uses; he also describes animals, real and mythical. In the last chapter, Gandavo gives the colonists some hope of finding "much gold and precious stones."

JOSÉ HONÓRIO RODRIGUES, *História da história do Brasil*, vol. 1, *Historiografia colonial* (1979); MASSAUD MOISÉS, *História da literatura brasileira*, vol. 1, *Origens, barroco, arcadismo* (1983); MARIA BEATRIZ NIZZA DA SILVA, *Guia de história do Brasil colonial* (1992).

MARIA BEATRIZ NIZZA DA SILVA

GANDINI, GERARDO (*b.* 16 October 1936), Argentine composer, pianist, and conductor. He was born in Buenos Aires. His principal teachers on piano were Pía Sebastiani and Roberto Caamaño and in composition, Alberto GINASTERA. In 1964 Gandini resided in New York City while on a fellowship from the Ford Foundation. In 1966 he obtained a fellowship from the Italian government that permitted him to study under Goffredo Petrassi at the Accadémia Santa Cecilia in Rome.

He was professor of composition at the Catholic University in Buenos Aires (1962–1970) and at the celebrated Latin American Center for Advanced Musical Studies at the Di Tella Institute in Buenos Aires (1963–1970). An eager participant of the avant-garde school as a composer, Gandini became an active organizer of contemporary music series. He became the director of the Experimental Center for Opera and Ballet (CEOB) sponsored by the Teatro Colón in Buenos Aires. At the CEOB, Gandini premiered many staged works and also commissioned a number of mini-operas, most of them by composers from Argentina. Gandini was a founding member of the Agrupación Música Viva (AMV), a Buenos Aires organization devoted to the promotion of new music. Other members included Antonio TAURIELLO, Armando Krieger, Hilda DIANDA, and Alcides LANZA. Besides his career as a composer and promoter of new music, Gandini is a renowned conductor and pianist who performs frequently in Europe and North America.

His early compositions include Concertino for piano and orchestra (1960); *Variaciones* for orchestra (1962); *Per Mauricio Rinaldi* for chamber orchestra (1963); Concertino no. 3 for harpsichord and ensemble (1964); *Hecha sombra y altura* for ensemble (1965); *A Cow in a Mondrian Painting* for flute and instruments (1967); *Fantasía impromptu* for piano and orchestra (1970); *L'adieu* for piano, vibraphone, three percussionists, and conductor

(1967); *Piange e sospira* for flute, violin, clarinet, and piano (1970).

In his more mature style Gandini has written a number of almost impressionistic compositions, always with a strong poetic vein, such as *. . . e sará* for piano (1973); *7 Preludios* for piano (1977); *Concierto* for Viola and Orchestra (1979); *Eusebius* (1984–1985), five nocturnes for orchestra; *Paisaje imaginario* for piano and orchestra (1988), which was commissioned by the BBC for the Welsh Symphony Orchestra.

RODOLFO ARIZAGA, *Enciclopedia de la música argentina* (1971), p. 151; JOHN VINTON, ed., *Dictionary of Contemporary Music* (1974), p. 261; GÉRARD BÉHAGUE, *Music in Latin America: An Introduction* (1979), p. 339; *Octavo festival de música contemporánea de Alicante* (1992), pp. 26, 94–95.

ALCIDES LANZA

GANTE, PEDRO DE (*b.* ca. 1480; *d.* 1572), Franciscan missionary and educational pioneer in Mexico. Gante was originally from Ghent, Belgium, where he absorbed the refined choral style of the Low Countries. One of the first three FRANCISCANS (all Flemish-born) to arrive in Mexico in 1523, he brought this musical foundation with him, later training the Indian singers employed by the cathedral in Mexico City. Although Gante never took holy orders, remaining a lay brother, his accomplishments and example did much to shape the Franciscan missionary enterprise. Like other early friars, Gante combined Christian fervor with Renaissance humanism. He assumed the inferiority of the indigenous cultures but believed the Indians fully capable of mastering European learning, and he made native education his life's work.

In 1526, Gante founded San José de los Naturales to teach Indian boys reading, writing, music, and basic Catholic doctrine. In addition, the school instructed Indians in Spanish artisanal skills, producing a generation of painters and sculptors who embellished the rapidly proliferating Christian churches (many of them built under Gante's supervision), and trained Indian catechists to aid the Franciscans' Christianization efforts. This institution became a model for the Colegio de Santa Cruz de Tlatelolco, whose goal (later abandoned) was to create a native priesthood.

A superb linguist, Gante composed an early and influential Christian doctrine in NAHUATL (1528), the Aztec language. Gante also wrote regularly to the crown, condemning Spanish abuses and advocating reforms to benefit the Indians. Among other things, he successfully urged Charles V to found an Indian hospital in Mexico City.

ROBERT RICARD, *The Spiritual Conquest of Mexico: An Essay on the Apostolate and the Evangelizing Methods of the Mendicant Orders in New Spain: 1523–1572*, translated by Lesley Byrd Simpson (1966); PEGGY K. LISS, *Mexico Under Spain, 1521–1556: Society and the Origins of Nationality* (1975), esp. pp. 69–94; LINO GÓMEZ CANEDO, *La educación de los marginados durante la época colonial:*

Escuelas y colegios para índios y mestizos en la Nueva España (1982); *La música de México,* edited by Julio Estrada, vol. 1, pt. 1, *Período prehispánico* (Mexico City, 1984).

R. DOUGLAS COPE
ROBERT L. PARKER

GAOS, JOSÉ (*b.* 26 December 1900; *d.* 10 June 1969), Spanish-Mexican philosopher. Gaos was born in Gijón, Spain. He lived in Oviedo with his maternal grandparents until he was fifteen, then moved to Valencia where his parents were residing. While reading the philosophy of James Balmes, Gaos discovered the topic that became the focus of his later thought: the radical historicity of philosophy (i.e., the extent to which any philosophy is grounded in the thinker's historical circumstances). Gaos began to study philosophy at the University of Valencia, then transferred to the University of Madrid in 1921, where he studied with Manuel García Morente, Xavier Zubiri, and, most important, José Ortega y Gasset. He earned his bachelor's degree in 1923 and his doctorate in 1928, both from the University of Madrid.

A firm supporter of the Republican cause, Gaos was named rector of the University of Madrid in 1936. Shortly thereafter, he fled the regime of Francisco Franco, living briefly in Cuba before arriving in Mexico in 1938. He declared himself a *transterrado* (transplant) rather than an exile, and spent the rest of his career encouraging research on the history of ideas in Latin America. His teaching at the Colegio de México and the Universidad Nacional Autónoma de México decisively influenced a generation of major Mexican thinkers, including Leopoldo ZEA. His philosophical work, a unique blend of metaphysics and historicism, was published in Mexico between 1940 and 1972. Gaos died in Mexico City.

For Gaos's works, see José Gaos, *Obras completas, VI: Pensamiento de la lengua española,* prologue by José Luis Abellán, edited by Fernando Salmerón (1990); *Obras completas, VII: Filosofía de la historia e historia de la filosofía,* prologue by Raúl Cardiel Reyes, edited by Fernando Salmerón (1987); *Obras completas, XII: De la filosofía,* prologue by Luis Villoro, edited by Fernando Salmerón (1982); and *Obras completas, XVII: Confesiones profesionales,* prologue by Vera Yamuni, edited by Fernando Salmerón (1982). For discussion of his life and thought, see VERA YAMUNI TABUSH, *José Gaos: El hombre y su pensamiento* (1980), and *José Gaos: Su filosofía* (1989).

AMY A. OLIVER

GARAGAY, an archaeological site in the lower Rimac valley. One of the largest centers of pre-Columbian culture on Peru's central coast during the second millennium B.C., Garagay is 5 miles inland from the Pacific shore. The site was constructed and utilized by agriculturists who grew cotton, sweet potato, and other crops using gravity canals. Although much of Garagay has been destroyed by the metropolitan expansion of Lima, some 39.5 acres survive intact. The surviving portion corresponds to monumental architecture that served as the focus of the site.

The most conspicuous remains are those of a U-shaped platform complex embracing a 22-acre open plaza area. In its final form the terraced central pyramid-platform rose some 75.5 feet above the plaza, and access to its atrium and level summit was provided by a broad inset stairway. Corrected radiocarbon measurements from the site range from 1643 B.C. to 897 B.C., and it is evident that Garagay's massive public constructions are the product of a multitude of superimposed fills and buildings erected over many centuries. In its general ground plan and coarse masonry construction, Garagay resembles dozens of other public centers also dating from the same period that have been found from the Lurín valley to the Pativilca valley.

Garagay is best known for fine clay friezes that decorated the walls of its central and lateral mounds. Excavations of Garagay's central atrium in 1974 revealed a mural painted in yellow, white, red, pink, and grayish blue mineral-based pigments. The main theme was a fanged supernatural creature with spider attributes. Among the Incas, spiders were closely associated with predicting the onset of rainfall, so it is likely that the ceremonies conducted at Garagay and other similar centers on the central coast were intended to ensure the necessary conditions for irrigation agriculture in this arid zone. Elaborate votive offerings of figurines and exotic items such as Ecuadorian *Spondylus* shell were found associated with the atrium and a similar atrium that had been superimposed above it.

A summary in English of investigations at Garagay and related central coast sites can be found in RICHARD L. BURGER, *Chavín and the Origins of Andean Civilization* (1992). The Garagay excavations and the analysis of the materials recovered there have been published in the following articles: ROGGER RAVINES and WILLIAM ISBELL, "Garagay: Sitio ceremonial temprano en el valle de Lima," in *Revista del Museo Nacional* 41 (1984): 253–275, and ROGGER RAVINES, "Sobre la formación de Chavín: Imágenes y símbolos," in *Boletín de Lima* 35 (1984): 27–45. A model for interpreting Garagay and other U-shaped complexes is presented by CARLOS WILLIAMS, "A Scheme for the Early Monumental Architecture of the Central Coast of Peru," in *Early Monumental Architecture in the Andes,* edited by Christopher Donnan (1985).

RICHARD L. BURGER

GARAY, BLAS (*b.* 1873; *d.* 19 December 1899), Paraguayan historian. Born in Asunción, Garay was something of a prodigy, publishing scholarly articles in local newspapers while still a teenager. He was one of the first Paraguayan historians to make systematic use of archives and primary documents of all kinds. He was sent to Spain in 1897 to visit Seville's Archive of the Indies in order to fulfill a government commission to substantiate Paraguay's legal claim to the Chaco Boreal

region. While in Europe, Garay held several minor diplomatic posts.

As a member of the governing Partido Colorado, there was little way that Garay could avoid the passionate politics of his day. His newspaper pieces in *La Prensa*, which he founded, freely attacked his opponents, one of whom challenged Garay to a duel at Villa Hayes on 19 December 1899. Garay was shot, dying at the age of twenty-six.

Among his works, all of which are still read today, are *Compendio elemental de historia del Paraguay* (1896), *El comunismo de las misiones* (1897), and *La revolución de la independencia del Paraguay* (1897).

HARRIS G. WARREN, *Rebirth of the Paraguayan Republic: The First Colorado Era, 1878–1904* (1985); CARLOS ZUBIZARRETA, *Cien vidas paraguayas*, 2d ed. (1985), pp. 222–224.

THOMAS L. WHIGHAM

GARAY, CARLOS (*b.* 1 April 1943), Honduran impressionist painter. Born in Tegucigalpa, Garay studied at the Escuela Nacional de Bellas Artes in that city and from an early age became one of Honduras's few internationally recognized painters. In his formative period he often painted the human figure, but he eventually became known for his impressionist scenes of the Honduran countryside, which reflect an unusual mastery of light and color and a strong sensitivity to Honduran folk culture. In 1981 the Venezuelan government awarded him the Andrés BELLO Prize.

J. EVARISTO LÓPEZ R. and LONGINO BECERRA, *Honduras: 40 pintores* (1989); MARÍA LUISA CASTELLANOS DE MEMBREÑO, in *Aboard*, 16, no. 3 (May–June 1992): 61–66.

RALPH LEE WOODWARD, JR.

GARAY, EPIFANIO (*b.* 1849; *d.* 1903), Colombian artist. Born in Bogotá, Garay was the son of the portrait painter and cabinetmaker Narciso Garay. He studied first with his father and then with José Manuel Groot (1800–1878) while also training at the Academia de Música. He became an opera singer as well as the most important portrait painter in Colombian history. In 1865 he sang in a production of *La Traviata* and in Spanish musical comedies. His paintings during this period included genre, nudes, as well as religious subjects. In 1871 he received honorable mention for his painting *Dolor* at the Anniversary of the Independence show.

Thanks to his skill as a singer, Garay was able to travel extensively, giving him a sophistication noticeable in his paintings. From 1871 to 1880 he toured with the Compañía de Zarzuela, performing at the Musical Academy of New York. He returned to Bogotá in 1880 and was appointed director of the Academia Gutiérrez, but two years later he received a grant from the government to study in Paris with Bouguereau, Boulanger, Ferrier, and Bonnat. When civil war in Colombia led to the cancellation of his grant, he went on a singing tour through the capitals of Europe. He returned to Bogotá and, disappointed with the reception of his work, tried farming and cattle ranching before opening an art school in Cartagena. In 1894 he was named acting director of the School of Fine Arts in Bogotá, becoming director in 1898. With the onset of the revolution of 1899, the school closed. He died in Bogotá.

GABRIEL GIRALDO JARAMILLO, *La miniatura, la pintura y el grabado en Colombia* (1980); EDUARDO SERRANO, *Cien años de arte colombiano, 1886–1986* (1986).

BÉLGICA RODRÍGUEZ

GARAY, EUGENIO (*b.* 16 November 1874; *d.* April 1937), Paraguayan politician and military figure. Born in Asunción, Garay spent part of his early years in the interior town of Pirayú. He later attended the Colegio Nacional in Asunción, where he received a bachelor's degree. Shortly thereafter, he received a scholarship to attend the military academy in Chile, from which he graduated with honors in 1898.

Returning to Paraguay in 1902, Garay entered the army with the rank of captain. When the 1904 revolution removed him temporarily from military service, he entered the world of journalism, working as a reporter for *Los succesos*. In 1908 the government sent him to Europe as a diplomat, but within three years he was back in the country acting as a adviser to the war ministry.

The series of interparty conflicts in the 1910s and 1920s gave Garay the opportunity to rise rapidly through the ranks, but this process was frequently interrupted by reverses when the wrong party was in power. He served as commander at Barrero Grande, minister of war, and then ambassador to Bolivia.

When the CHACO WAR broke out in 1932, Garay was recalled to active service. He headed a regiment that opposed the Bolivian forces at Pampa Grande and then at Campo Vía. Suffering from overwork that bordered on combat fatigue, he was relieved from command at his own request in late 1933, only to be recalled once again by President Eusebio AYALA a few months later. Garay, now a full colonel, commanded the principal Paraguayan units at the battles of Carmen and YRENDAGÜE.

With the conclusion of the war, Garay was demobilized and returned to Asunción. His health now seriously deteriorated because of the intensity of the earlier fighting, he survived the end of hostilities by only two years. He died of a heart attack.

LEANDRO APONTE BENÍTEZ, *General Eugenio Garay: Héroe del Chaco*, 2d ed. (1956), esp. pp. 29–151; ROQUE VALLEJOS, *Antología de la prosa paraguaya* (1973), pp. 85–86; CARLOS ZUBIZARRETA, *Cien vidas paraguayas*, 2d ed. (1985), pp. 284–289.

MARTA FERNÁNDEZ WHIGHAM

GARAY, FRANCISCO DE (*d.* 27 December 1523), governor of Jamaica (1515–1523) and rival of the conquistador Hernán CORTÉS. Garay arrived in the Americas in 1493 with the second voyage of Christopher COLUMBUS. On Hispaniola, Garay combined government service, as notary and later chief constable, with economic venture. By the time he became governor of Jamaica in 1515, he was one of the richest men in the islands. In 1519 he sent four ships under the command of Alonso ÁLVAREZ DE PINEDA to search the Mexican coast north of Pánuco for a westward passage. Pineda and his men were the first Europeans to explore the Gulf coast west of Florida, but, badly damaged in conflicts with the indigenous peoples, the expedition limped back to Veracruz, where most of the men joined Cortés's army.

These mixed results notwithstanding, Garay obtained a royal decree making him *adelantado* (royal representative) and governor of this vast stretch of coastline. This created a conflict with Cortés, who also had claims to Pánuco. In 1523 Garay landed there with several hundred men to confront Cortés directly, but he was preempted shortly thereafter, when Cortés received royal recognition as conqueror of Mexico and governor of New Spain. His authority superseded, Garay quickly acknowledged his defeat and traveled to Mexico City, where he died three days after meeting with Cortés. It was rumored that Cortés had poisoned him, but this seems unlikely, since Garay no longer posed a threat to the conquistador.

JOAQUÍN MEADE, *El adelantado Francisco de Garay* (1947); ROBERT S. WEDDLE, *Spanish Sea: The Gulf of Mexico in North American Discovery, 1500–1685* (1985); HERNÁN CORTÉS, *Hernán Cortés: Letters from Mexico,* 2nd ed., translated and edited by Anthony Pagden (1986).

R. DOUGLAS COPE

GARAY, JUAN DE (*b.* 1528; *d.* March 1583), conquistador, explorer, and governor of Río de la Plata (1578–1583). Born in Vizcaya, Garay arrived in Peru at the age of fourteen in the company of his uncle. He soon joined in the conquest of Tucumán (northern Argentina), settling first in Santa Cruz de la Sierra, where he served as one of the city's *regidores* (councilmen). In 1568 he moved to Asunción, where, awaiting the confirmation of his kinsman Ortiz de Zárate as governor, he was named *alguacil mayor* (chief constable). A dynamic, intrepid, and peripatetic leader, Garay founded the city of Santa Fé in 1573. During his lifetime he engaged in several military campaigns against the Charrúa along the lower Río de la Plata and against the Guaraní in Paraguay. He was also involved in putting down uprisings of discontented settlers in Santa Fé and Asunción.

After the death of Zárate in 1576, Garay, as his lieutenant, became acting governor and captain-general of the Río de la Plata. From Asunción, he organized an expedition of approximately sixty families who reestablished the city of Buenos Aires in 1580. He also headed an expeditionary force that explored south to the region of present-day Mar del Plata. Three years later, Garay was killed in a Querandí Indian attack while attempting to return to Buenos Aires to reinforce troops accompanying the newly arrived governor of Chile.

ENRIQUE UDAONDO, *Diccionario biográfico colonial argentino* (1945), pp. 357–365.

SUSAN M. SOCOLOW

GARCÉS, FRANCISCO TOMÁS HERMENEGILDO (*b.* 12 April 1738; *d.* 19 July 1781), Franciscan missionary who traveled extensively in SONORA, Arizona, and California. Born in Morata del Conde, Spain, Garcés entered the FRANCISCAN order at age fifteen. In 1768 he joined the Franciscans in Sonora as a missionary to the Pima and Papago Indians. From his post at San Xavier del Bac, Garcés made several expeditions into the surrounding areas. In 1774 he joined Juan Bautista de ANZA in opening a route from Sonora to Monterey, establishing a vital supply line to the Spanish settlements of California. In 1775 Garcés again joined Anza in a colonizing expedition to San Francisco. On his return from California, Garcés became the first to break a trail from the Pacific Coast to the Hopi pueblos of northeastern Arizona. In 1779 Garcés journeyed to Yuma to establish missions among the Indians on the Colorado River. Two years later, he was beaten to death in an uprising of Yuma Indians.

ELLIOTT COUES, trans., *On the Trail of a Spanish Pioneer: The Diary of Francisco Garcés*, 2 vols. (1900); HERBERT EUGENE BOLTON, *Outpost of Empire* (1931); JOHN GALVIN, trans., *A Record of Travels in Arizona and California 1775–1776*, by Fr. FRANCISCO GARCÉS (1965); JOHN L. KESSELL, "The Making of a Martyr: The Young Francisco Garcés," in *New Mexico Historical Review* 45, no. 3 (1970): 181–196.

SUZANNE B. PASZTOR

GARCÍA, ALEIXO (*d.* 1525), Portuguese-born EXPLORER, the first European in Paraguay. A minor member of the 1515–1516 Juan Díaz de SOLÍS expedition to the Río de la Plata, García witnessed the murder of Solís at the hands of Charrúa Indians in Uruguay in mid-1516. Some months later, García and eighteen other Europeans were shipwrecked on the Brazilian island of Santa Catharina, where he remained several years, gaining a practical use of the local GUARANI language.

In 1524, he and several companions journeyed to the mainland. Traveling west, they discovered the massive IGUAÇÚ FALLS, crossed the Alto Paraná River, and made contact with the substantial Guarani populations of Paraguay. Told of a fabulously wealthy "white king," who lived further west, García enlisted the aid of 2,000 warriors and immediately set off in that direction through the heavily forested Chaco region. Upon reaching the foothills of the Andes, the small army raided a score of Incan communities. García made off with considerable booty, including a quantity of silver, and returned to the

area of the Paraguay River. He sent word of his adventures (along with a portion of the silver) to Santa Catharina. Before he himself could return to the coast, however, he was murdered by his Indian allies, evidently in late 1525. Some of the silver ornaments he had on his person at the time of his death were discovered a decade later by Spanish explorers entering Paraguay from the south.

CHARLES E. NOWELL, "Aleixo García and the White King," in *Hispanic American Historical Review* 26 (November 1946): 450–466; CARLOS ZUBIZARRETA, *Cien vidas paraguayas*, 2d ed. (1985), pp. 13–15.

THOMAS L. WHIGHAM

GARCÍA, CALIXTO (*b.* 4 August 1839; *d.* 11 December 1898), general during Cuba's wars for independence. García rose through the ranks of the liberating army during the first Cuban war of independence, the TEN YEARS' WAR (1868–1878). Captured by the Spaniards and set free at the end of the war, García attempted to reignite the rebellion by launching what came to be known as the Little War (1878–1880). Once again taken prisoner, he was this time deported to Spain, where he lived until returning to Cuba to join the rebel uprising of 24 February 1895. García first became military chief of Oriente Province and was subsequently appointed second in command of the insurgent army. His troops rendered invaluable assistance to the U.S. expeditionary forces in the the SPANISH–AMERICAN WAR, but they were not allowed to march into Santiago de Cuba when the city was surrendered by the Spaniards in 1898. On this occasion García sent the U.S. military commander a letter of protest that is one of the high points of Cuban nationalism.

There are no good studies of Calixto García available in English. See GERARDO CASTELLANOS GARCÍA, *Tierras y glorias de Oriente: Calixto García* (1927), and JUAN J. E. CASASÚS, *Calixto García (el estratega)*, 4th ed. (1981).

JOSÉ M. HERNÁNDEZ

See also **Cuba: War of Independence.**

GARCÍA, DIEGO (*b.* ca. 1471; *d.* ca. 1535), Portuguese navigator in Spanish service. After participating in Ferdinand MAGELLAN's circumnavigation of the globe, García returned to Spain in 1522, organizing an expedition to the Río de la Plata in 1526. He explored Uruguay and established a shipyard near Colonia. During his expedition up the Paraná, he encountered and then joined forces with Sebastián CABOT in 1528. After returning to Spain in 1530, García and his caravel *Concepción* joined the expedition of Pedro de MENDOZA, *adelantado* (royal provincial governor) of Río de la Plata, departing Spain in August 1535. While in the Canary Islands, García fell ill and died at Gomera.

IONE S. WRIGHT and LISA M. NEKHOM, *Historical Dictionary of Argentina* (1978), p. 341; J. H. PARRY, *The Discovery of South America* (1979), pp. 249–252.

CHRISTEL K. CONVERSE

See also **Explorers.**

GARCÍA, GENARO (*b.* 17 August 1867; *d.* 26 November 1920), Mexican politician, women's rights advocate, and historian. Born in Fresnillo, Zacatecas, García first attended school in San Luis Potosí but continued his studies in the capital, where he received a degree in law. He served as a congressional deputy for several terms; as governor of Zacatecas (1900–1904); as director of the National Museum of Archaeology, History, and Ethnology; and as director of the National Preparatory School.

García published many didactic works. From his *Desigualdad de la mujer* (1891) and *Apuntes sobre la condición de la mujer* (1891), arguing for greater rights for women, to his *Carácter de la conquista española en América y en México* (1901), presenting a pro-Indian perspective, García consistently was ahead of his time. However, he is best known as the editor of the thirty-six-volume *Documentos inéditos o muy raros para la historia de México* (1905–1911), and seven-volume *Documentos históricos mexicanos* (1901–1911), and *Documentos inéditos del siglo XVI para la historia de México* (1914). His library of twenty-five-thousand volumes and manuscripts forms the heart of the Mexican holdings of the Benson Latin American Collection at the University of Texas in Austin.

RODERIC A. CAMP, *Mexican Political Biographies, 1884–1935* (1991).

CARMEN RAMOS-ESCANDÓN

GARCÍA, JOSÉ MAURÍCIO NUNES (*b.* 20/22 September 1767; *d.* 18 April 1830), the most notable Brazilian composer of the early nineteenth century. Son of Lieutenant Apolinário Nunes García and Victoria Maria de Cruz, a black woman, José Maurício (as he is called in Brazil) learned to play the harpsichord and viola and studied *solfeggio* with Salvador José, a local teacher. Religious brotherhoods played a significant cultural role in nineteenth-century Brazilian society, and in 1784 José Maurício was one of the founders of the Brotherhood of St. Cecilia. Having entered the Brotherhood of São Pedro dos Clérigos in 1791, he was ordained a priest the following year on 3 March. In July 1798 José Maurício was appointed to the most important musical position in the city, *mestre de capela* of the cathedral of Rio de Janeiro, where his duties consisted of serving as organist, conductor, composer, and music teacher. For twenty-eight years he taught a music course that was open to the public free of charge, in which he trained some of the most important composers and musicians of the following generation, including Francisco Manuel da SILVA, composer of the Brazilian national anthem.

The arrival of dom JOÃO VI in Rio de Janeiro in 1808 had a decisive influence on the professional career of Padre José Maurício. A member of the BRAGANÇA family, which had a remarkable history of musical patronage, dom João was soon informed of José Maurício's talents and appointed him on 15 June 1808 *mestre de capela* of the royal chapel, where his official duties included acting as organist, conductor, and professor of music. He also composed music for numerous official occasions, thirty-nine musical works in 1809, a year in which dom João decorated him with the Order of Christ.

In 1811 Marcos PORTUGAL, the best-known Portuguese composer of his day, arrived in Rio and was appointed *mestre de capela* of the royal chapel, for practical purposes replacing José Maurício. Thereafter, José Maurício's standing in the royal musical establishment declined. However, his best-known and most significant work, a requiem mass, was written in 1816 after the death of Queen Maria. On 19 December 1819 José Maurício conducted the first performance of the Mozart *Requiem* in Brazil.

Portrait of José Maurício Nunes García. Reproduced from his *Matinas do Natal* (Rio de Janeiro, 1978). COURTESY OF HARVARD COLLEGE LIBRARY.

Accustomed to music composed and performed by Europe's best musicians, dom João was amazed at the abilities of the relatively unknown, native-born mulatto. In a period when musical excellence was judged by adherence to European styles, José Maurício, a devoted admirer of Haydn, made no attempt to deviate from European models.

After dom PEDRO I returned to Portugal in 1821, many of his splendid musical reforms languished from lack of funds. José Maurício's lifelong pension was discontinued, leaving him in difficult financial circumstances until his death in 1830.

CLEOFE PERSON DE MATTOS, *Catálogo temático das obras do Padre José Maurício Nunes Garcia* (1970); STANLEY SADIE, ed., *The New Grove Dictionary of Music and Musicians* (1980); DAVID P. APPLEBY, *The Music of Brazil* (1983); MAURO GAMA, *José Maurício, o padre-compositor* (1983), Portuguese and English text.

DAVID P. APPLEBY

GARCÍA, SARA (*b.* 8 September 1895; *d.* 21 November 1980), Mexican actress. García began her acting career on the stage in 1913. She made her cinematic debut in 1933 in the film *El pulpo humano* and went on to star in over 300 films. Noted for her work as a leading lady, in *Los tres García* (1936) she was cast in the role of the grandmother; from that moment on, García was the film world's perpetual *abuelita*. In 1970 she parodied her familiar screen role in Luis ALCORIZA's *Mecánica nacional*. She is regarded as a national treasure and a leading member of the Mexican cinema.

LUIS REYES DE LA MAZA, *El cine sonoro en México* (1973); E. BRADFORD BURNS, *Latin American Cinema: Film and History* (1975); CARL J. MORA, *Mexican Cinema: Reflections of a Society: 1896–1980* (1982); and JOHN KING, *Magical Reels: A History of Cinema in Latin America* (1990).

DAVID MACIEL

GARCÍA CALDERÓN, FRANCISCO (*b.* 1834; *d.* 1905), a Peruvian lawyer and legal historian. Author of a compilation of nineteenth-century Peruvian law, he was forced to resign as minister of finance in the administration of José BALTA when he could not end Peru's financial dependence on its guano consignees. He achieved prominence and notoriety during the WAR OF THE PACIFIC (1879–1883). A committee of wealthy Limeños elected him president in early 1881, when they anticipated high Chilean occupation taxes. He began the negotiations that eventually led to the Treaty of ANCÓN (1883) that ended the war. During the negotiations, García Calderón adamantly refused to cede the southern departments of Tacna and Arica to Chile. Yet he underwent severe criticism from former president Nicolás de PIÉROLA, who resisted the Chileans from his position in Ayacucho, and from General Andrés A. Cáceres, who fought on in the central highlands. Fearing a rally of resistance among Peruvians and interference from the United States on the issue of cession of territory, the Chileans seized the president and imprisoned him in Santiago until the end of the war.

DAVID WERLICH, *Peru: A Short History* (1978); WILLIAM F. SATER, *Chile and the War of the Pacific* (1986), esp. pp. 206–217.

VINCENT PELOSO

GARCÍA CATURLA, ALEJANDRO (*b.* 7 March 1906; *d.* 12 November 1940) Cuban composer, considered the most talented musical artist of Cuba. Born in Remedios, Caturla was a lawyer by profession and became a judge. He studied music with Pedro Sanjuán in Havana (1926–1927) and attended Nadia Boulanger's classes in Paris (1928). He was founder and first conductor of the Orquesta de Conciertos Caibarién, a chamber ensemble. Together with composer Amadeo ROLDÁN, Caturla became the leader of *Afrocubanismo*, a nationalist musical trend, which mixed elements of white and black culture, incorporating Afro-Cuban songs, rhythms, and dances. Later on he used advanced techniques and French Impressionist styles combined with primitive tunes; as a result, some of his works show surprising juxtapositions of chords and moods. He composed *Concierto de cámara*, *Obertura cubana*, *Danzas cubanas*, and a suite for orchestra (1938). Many vocal works were inspired by Cuban poets such as Alejo CARPENTIER and Nicolás GUILLÉN; other works include one string quartet (1927), *Bembé*, for fourteen instruments, and *Primera suite cubana* (1930) among others. He produced numerous piano works, among them *Danza lucumí* (1928) and *Sonata* (1939). Murdered by a criminal tried in his court, he left unfinished one opera, a ballet, his *Primera sinfonía*, one concerto for piano and orchestra, and several piano and vocal works.

ALEJANDRO GARCÍA CATURLA, "The Development of Cuban Music," in *American Composers on American Music*, edited by Henry Cowell, (1933); A. SALAZAR, "La obra musical de Alejandro García Caturla," in *Revista Cubana* (January 1938): 5–43; *Composers of the Americas*, vol. 3 (1957); GÉRARD BÉHAGUE, *Music in Latin America* (1979); STANLEY SADIE, ed., *The New Grove Dictionary of Music and Musicians*, vol. 4 (1980).

SUSANA SALGADO

GARCÍA CONDE, PEDRO (*b.* 8 February 1806; *d.* 19 December 1851), Mexican soldier. Born in Arizpe, Sonora, he began his military career as a cadet in the presidio company of Cerro Gordo and later served as director of the Military College from 1838 to 1844. In 1842 he was deputy to the national legislature and Secretary of War from 1844 to 1845 in the José Joaquín de HERRERA (1792–1854) government. An ardent patriot, he helped plan and fought in the Battle of Sacramento (1847) against the invading U.S. forces.

An accomplished geographer, García participated in the first geographic survey of the state of Chihuahua in 1833 and in 1842 published *Ensayo estadístico sobre el estado de Chihuahua.* In 1848 he received appointment to the presidency of the Mexican Boundary Commission, which was charged with mapping the new border between Mexico and the United States. He held this position twice but died in Arizpe before finishing the survey.

FLORENCE C. LISTER and ROBERT H. LISTER, *Chihuahua: Storehouse of Storms* (1966), pp. 126, 139.

AARON PAINE MAHR

GARCÍA DE CASTRO, LOPE (*d.* 1576), governor and captain-general of Peru (1564–1569). Born in the district of Astorga, in northwest Spain, García de Castro studied at the University of Salamanca (1534). He received the licenciate in law and taught at Salamanca until his appointment as *oidor* (justice) of the Audiencia of Valladolid (1541). In 1558, Philip II transferred him to the COUNCIL OF THE INDIES.

In response to complaints against Viceroy Diego López de Zúñiga, conde de Nieva, the king sent García de Castro to Peru to investigate and replace the errant official. When García de Castro reached American shores, he learned the viceroy had been assassinated (20 February 1564).

In October 1564 he arrived in Lima, where he began five years of honest, effective, and dedicated administration. In 1565 he established the Casa de Moneda (Mint Office) of Lima. (It was transferred to Potosí in 1572.) Ordered to increase royal revenues and cut expenses, he began the following year to collect the *almojarifazgo* (import duty) and undertook to organize effective exploitation of the mercury mines at HUANCAVELICA. He divided Peru into provinces and established the *corregimiento* system for the local administration of Indians. In 1567 he founded an audiencia at Concepción, in Chile. (Suppressed in 1573, it was reestablished in 1609 at Santiago.)

García de Castro faced continued pressure from the ARAUCANIANS on the Chilean frontier and the CHIRIGUANOS in lowland Bolivia, opposition from the neo-Inca state at Vilcabamba, northwest of Cuzco, and a bothersome uprising in the central Peruvian highlands associated with the Taki Onqoy movement. For more effective administration of Lima, he created El Cercado, an Indian town. During his rule the Tridentine reforms were announced in Lima (1565) and the Second Lima Church Council (1567–1568), which improved the administration of Indian *doctrinas,* was convened. At this time, also, the JESUITS began their work in Peru. García de Castro provided support for Captain Juan Álvarez Maldonado's exploration of the Mojos territory in the upper Amazon basin and, under his nephew Álvaro de Mendaña, also organized a voyage of exploration in the Pacific (1567–1568) that led to the discovery of the Solomon Islands. García de Castro returned to Spain in November 1569, shortly after welcoming the new viceroy, Francisco de TOLEDO Y FIGUEROA.

MANUEL DE MENDIBURU, *Diccionario histórico-biográfico del Perú,* vol. 5 (1933), pp. 345–350; RUBÉN VARGAS UGARTE, *Historia del Perú: Virreinato (1551–1600)* (1949), pp. 151–211; *Historia general del Perú,* vol. 2 (1966–1984).

NOBLE DAVID COOK

GARCÍA DIEGO Y MORENO, FRANCISCO (*b.* 1785; *d.* 19 November 1846), bishop of California (1840–1846). The Mexican-born Franciscan was the first Catholic bishop of the CALIFORNIAS. Associated with the apostolic college of Guadalupe in Zacatecas, he arrived to serve in the Alta California missions in January 1833 with a contingent of Zacatecan FRANCISCANS sent to replace their brethren from the college of San Fernando in the MISSIONS of southern Alta California.

The bishopric of the Californias was established by a Mexican law (19 September 1836) authorizing the president to negotiate with the papacy to establish the new bishopric. This initiative also allocated 6,000 pesos from public funds for the support of the new bishop and transferred the administration of the so-called Pious Fund, an endowment organized by the JESUITS to finance their activities in BAJA CALIFORNIA, to his jurisdiction, although the Mexican government later resumed control of the fund. The papacy approved the new bishopric on 27 April 1840.

President Antastasio BUSTAMANTE selected Diego y Moreno from a list of three candidates submitted by the papacy. After having sworn an oath of loyalty to the president of Mexico, Diego y Moreno was consecrated as bishop at the shrine of the Virgin of Guadalupe outside Mexico City on 4 October 1841. He served in Alta California for six years and died in Santa Barbara.

ZEPHYRIN ENGELHARDT, O.F.M., *Missions and Missionaries of California,* 4 vols. (1929–1930); MAYNARD J. GEIGER, O.F.M., *Franciscan Missionaries in Hispanic California, 1769–1848* (1968).

ROBERT H. JACKSON

See also **Obras Pías.**

GARCÍA GODOY, HÉCTOR (*b.* 1921; *d.* 1970), Dominican provisional president (1965–1966). Born into one of the Dominican Republic's old elite families, García Godoy distinguished himself as a career diplomat whose skill, tact, and moderation prepared him for his role as provisional president after the overthrow of Juan BOSCH (1963) and subsequent U.S. military invasion of his country (1965). Offered the position of president by U.S. Ambassador Ellsworth Bunker, García faced the difficult task of reconciling opposing forces, the left-leaning Constitutionalists and the right-wing military elements, who had kept the country in a chaotic civil war since Bosch's fall. During his nine months in office, he faced pressures from both factions as well as the United States. He rose to the occasion by eliminating the most troublesome military leaders who had refused to negotiate. His presidency smoothed the way for elections in June 1966 and for the birth of a new Dominican government led by Joaquín BALAGUER. Afterward, García served as Dominican ambassador to Washington. Many Dominicans hoped that, upon his return, he would run for president. In 1970, García founded the Movimiento de Conciliación Nacional (MCN) in preparation for the 1974 presidential campaign. Soon thereafter, however, he died of a heart attack.

HOWARD WIARDA, *The Dominican Republic: A Nation in Transition* (1969); IAN BELL, *The Dominican Republic* (1981).

PAMELA MURRAY

GARCÍA GRANADOS, MIGUEL (*b.* 29 September 1809; *d.* 8 September 1878), a leader in the Guatemalan liberal revolution of 1871. Born in Cádiz, Spain, García Granados went to Guatemala with his parents as an infant. While he was still a young man he became interested in military affairs and in liberal political philosophy, especially that of Voltaire and Rousseau. As Spaniards, his family was not involved in the independence movement, but they shared many of the new ideals. García Granados traveled to New York with his older brothers in 1823. He studied there and in Philadelphia and London before returning to Guatemala in 1826. When conflicts began developing with El Salvador, he followed his older brothers into military service.

García Granados participated in two invasions of El Salvador, where he was captured, held prisoner, and exiled to Mexico, not returning to Guatemala until 1840.

Miguel García Granados. Reproduced from *Memoria del General Miguel García Granados* (Guatemala, 1978). COURTESY OF HARVARD COLLEGE LIBRARY.

During the following thirty years he became a leader in the movements for political change, a free press, public education, fiscal reform, and restrictions on the power of the church. He served as a leader of the liberal cause in the conservative-controlled National Assembly during the long dictatorship of Rafael CARRERA. While in exile in Mexico he had met Justo Rufino BARRIOS. Together they planned the overthrow of the conservative government. They invaded Guatemala in May 1871 and, after a series of battles, entered Guatemala City victorious on June 30. García Granados became interim president and served until 1873, when Barrios succeeded him as the constitutionally elected president. The revolution of 1871 led to the expulsion of religious orders, to professionalization of the military, to expanded public education and public works throughout the country, and to a concept of the state as a positive force for introducing change in the society and the economy.

MIGUEL GARCÍA GRANADOS, *Memorias* (1952); JOSÉ SANTACRUZ NORIEGA, *Gobierno del Capitán General D. Miguel García Granados* (1979).

DAVID L. JICKLING

GARCÍA ICAZBALCETA, JOAQUÍN (*b.* 21 August 1825; *d.* 26 November 1894), Mexican historian and bibliographer. One of the most recognized historians of Mexico, Joaquín García Icazbalceta dedicated a lifetime to collecting, editing, and publishing documents that centered on the Europeanization of Mexico in the sixteenth century. Born in Mexico City to a Spanish father and Mexican mother, he left with his family for exile in Spain, where they remained seven years (1829–1836). Though he received no formal education outside of tutoring in the home, early in life he showed a strong interest in literature. He joined the family business in Mexico City, where he successfully balanced a career in commerce with his literary interests.

In 1848, after participating in the war against the United States, García Icazbalceta began in earnest to collect original manuscripts of historical and linguistic value. He spent the remainder of his life compiling bibliographies, writing numerous books and articles, and publishing documents for use by future historians. Most notable among his works are the *Bibliografía mexicana del siglo XVI* (1954), the two-volume *Colección de documentos para la historia de México* (1971), and a four-volume biography of Juan de ZUMÁRRAGA, first archbishop of Mexico. At the time of his death, García Icazbalceta served as director of the Mexican Academy of Language.

HENRY R. WAGNER, *Joaquín García Icazbalceta* (1935); MANUEL G. MARTÍNEZ, "Don Joaquín García Icazbalceta: His Place in Mexican Historiography," in *Studies in Hispanic American History*, vol. 4 (1947); HOWARD F. CLINE, "Selected Nineteenth-Century Mexican Writers on Ethnohistory," in *Handbook of Middle American Indians*, vol. 13 (1973), pp. 370–427.

BRIAN C. BELANGER

GARCÍA MÁRQUEZ, GABRIEL (*b.* 6 March 1927), Colombian novelist and short-story writer. The two most important years of García Márquez's career are 1967, when his masterpiece *Cien años de soledad* (1967; *One Hundred Years of Solitude,* 1970) brought him overnight fame, and 1982, when he was awarded the Nobel Prize.

García Márquez was born in Aracataca, a town near the Atlantic coast, where he spent the first eight years of his life. His law studies at the National University in Bogotá were interrupted in 1948 by El BOGOTAZO, an outburst of violence triggered by the assassination of a popular politician. The university was closed, and García Márquez returned to the Atlantic coast, where he worked for several years as a journalist. The symbiotic relationship between his journalism and his fiction is the hallmark of much of his work. An early example is the novella *Relato de un náufrago* (1970; *The Story of a Shipwrecked Sailor,* 1986), which is the result of interviews he held with a young Colombian sailor who spent ten days on a raft after being swept overboard in the Caribbean. Although the youth's narration, which reads like a novel, appeared in the press in 1954, it was not printed in book form until 1970.

In 1955 García Márquez published his first novel, *La hojarasca* (Leaf Storm, 1972), whose plot and style recall Faulkner's *As I Lay Dying* (1930). Six years later, having lived as a journalist in Europe, Caracas, and New York, he published his novelette *El coronel no tiene quien le escriba* (1961; No One Writes to the Colonel, 1986). It is the masterful portrait of an aging, poverty-stricken ex-military officer who waits for his pension while hoping that his fighting cock will win a fortune in an upcoming contest. This sparsely written volume (one detects Hemingway's influence) is enhanced by veiled allusions to a bloody civil conflict (La VIOLENCIA) and by the good-humored but tenacious protagonist, who embodies the Colombian people's struggle against oppression.

García Márquez moved to Mexico in 1961 and the next year published *Los funerales de la Mamá Grande* (Big Mama's Funeral), a collection of eight tales dramatizing the political and social realities of Colombia. In 1965, after several years of writer's block, the author was driving to Acapulco when he envisioned the fictional world he had endeavored to create for more than a decade. Eighteen months later he emerged from his study with the manuscript of *One Hundred Years of Solitude.* This novel, perhaps the second best (after *Don Quijote*) ever to be written in Spanish, tells the story of Macondo (the author's native Aracataca) from Genesis to Apocalypse. Seven generations of the Buendía family, the leading characters of the saga, find themselves caught up in the totality of human experience, ranging from the historical and the mythical to the everyday, the fantastic, the tragic, the comic, and the absurd. Major sections of the novel, which has been seen as a rewriting of history designed to refute official lies, deal with Colombia's nineteenth-century civil wars, the banana boom, and gringo imperialism.

Soon after the publication of *One Hundred Years of Solitude,* García Márquez moved to Barcelona to write *El otoño del patriarca* (1975; *The Autumn of the Patriarch,* 1976). This portrait of a prototypical Latin American dictator represents a daring experiment in the use of poetic language and literary technique, which explains in part why it is often considered the author's most significant achievement to date. The protagonist embodies all the evils of despotism, but equally important is the solitude imposed on him by the absolute power he wields. Like its predecessor, *The Autumn of the Patriarch* is sprinkled with humor and fantasy, but its rambling style and shifting points of view make it far more demanding of the reader.

Since 1975 García Márquez has maintained residences in both Mexico and Colombia. *Crónica de una muerte anunciada* (1981; *Chronicle of a Death Foretold,* 1982) records the testimony of witnesses to the murder of Santiago Nasar, the youth accused of seducing Ángela Vicario prior to her marriage. When, on her wedding night, Ángela's husband discovers that she is not a virgin, he returns her to her parents. The following morning, her twin brothers kill Nasar on the doorstep of his home. A riveting mélange of journalism and detective story, the novel implicitly condemns not only the Catholic church but also the primitive code of honor endorsed by the town citizens.

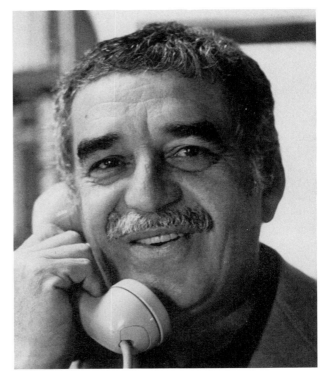

Gabriel García Márquez after learning he has been awarded the Nobel Prize for literature, 21 October 1982. UPI / BETTMANN ARCHIVE.

Both of García Márquez's most recent novels rely on historical and geographical documentation to enrich setting and plot. *El amor en los tiempos del cólera* (1985; *Love in the Time of Cholera,* 1988) describes Cartagena between 1870 and 1930, a time when the decaying, historic city was plagued by a series of epidemics. The action focuses on the aging process of the protagonists, two of whom, Fermina Daza and Florentino Ariza, are patterned after the author's parents. Reviewers have described this novel as one of the best love stories ever written. The protagonist of *El general en su laberinto* (1989; *The General in His Labyrinth,* 1990) is Simón BOLÍVAR, the liberator of much of South America. In May 1830, mortally ill and disillusioned by his fruitless efforts to unite the continent under a single leader, Bolívar traveled down the Magdalena River from Santa Fe de Bogotá to the Atlantic coast, hoping to spend his remaining years in Europe. He died shortly after arriving in the port city of Santa Marta. Although the foreground action is a lineal account of Bolívar's arduous journey to his grave, numerous flashbacks evoke remnants of his life, molding an intricate labyrinth of memories, dreams, and hallucinations.

García Márquez's most recent works are *Doce cuentos peregrinos* (1992; *Strange Pilgrims,* 1993) and *Del amor y otros demonios* (1994; *Of Love and Other Demons,* 1995). The former is a collection of short stories about Latin Americans living in Europe; the latter, a novel, is set in a Colombian coastal city during the eighteenth century. Based on a legend, it narrates the strange tale of a young girl, Sierva María de Todos los Angeles, who is bitten by a rabid dog, falls in love with a priest, and ultimately dies in a convent during the exorcism mandated by the Inquisition. This final episode, in addition to the vivid descriptions of decadence and poverty, dramatizes the negative impact of Spanish colonialism.

With his broad literary canvases laced with myths and fantasy, García Márquez has rescued the contemporary novel from its rigid laws of logic. In its totality, his oeuvre depicts the stark reality of an underdeveloped, strife-torn continent universalized by the humanistic elements of unfettered imagination and aesthetic perception. García Márquez is one of the world's most widely admired writers of fiction today. The end result of his prodigious enterprise is an original, comprehensive vision of human experience.

ROBERT LEWIS SIMS, *The Evolution of Myth in García Márquez from "La hojarasca" to "Cien años de soledad"* (1970); GEORGE R. MC MURRAY, *Gabriel García Márquez* (1977); HARLEY D. OBERHELMAN, *The Presence of Faulkner in the Writings of García Márquez* (1980); REGINA JANES, *Gabriel García Márquez: Revolutions in Wonderland* (1981); PLINIO APULEYO MENDOZA, *The Fragrance of Guava* (interview with García Márquez), translated by Ann Wright (1983); RAYMOND L. WILLIAMS, *Gabriel García Márquez* (1984); GEORGE R. MC MURRAY, ed., *Critical Essays on Gabriel García Márquez* (1987); STEPHEN MINTA, *García Márquez: Writer of Colombia* (1987); KATHLEEN MC NERNEY, *Understanding Gabriel García Márquez* (1989); KENRICK MOSE, *Defamiliarization in the Work of Gabriel García Márquez* (1989); GENE H. BELL-VILLADA, *García Márquez: The Man and His Work* (1990); HARLEY D. OBERHELMAN, *Gabriel García Márquez: A Study of the Short Fiction* (1991).

GEORGE R. MCMURRAY

See also **Literature: Spanish America.**

GARCÍA MEZA, LUIS, army officer and Bolivian dictator (1980–1981). Following the coup d'état by General Alberto Natusch Busch in November 1979, García Meza—a professional army officer—was named commander in chief of the armed forces of Bolivia. After Natusch's overthrow a few weeks later, his successor, President Lidia GUEILER TEJADA, demanded García Meza's resignation. After first refusing to resign, García Meza was finally removed, but he continued to control the armed forces. On 17 July 1980, he led an insurrection that overthrew Gueiler.

García Meza's regime was one of the most brutal dictatorships in the country's history. Political parties, labor unions, and many other organizations were suppressed and their headquarters destroyed. Several important political leaders were murdered. Leading figures in the García Meza government, including his ministers of interior and education, were involved in the international cocaine trade. Because of this involvement the United States refused to extend diplomatic recognition to the García Meza government, and the television program *60 Minutes* twice aired a segment devoted to the Bolivian "drug smugglers' government."

In August 1981, García Meza was forced to resign. He fled abroad and was convicted in absentia of serious crimes. In 1994, the Bolivian government was still trying to have García Meza extradited to Bolivia from São Paulo, Brazil.

ROBERT J. ALEXANDER, *Bolivia: Past, Present, and Future of Its Politics* (1982).

ROBERT J. ALEXANDER

GARCÍA MORENO, GABRIEL (*b.* 24 December 1821; *d.* 6 August 1875), president of Ecuador (1861–1865, 1869–1875). Born in Guayaquil into a family of modest means, Gabriel García Moreno completed his early studies at home before going to Quito for his secondary and university studies. He received a doctorate in law at the University of Quito, and in 1846 married the aristocratic Rosa Ascásubi Matheu. In 1855–1856 he took courses in the natural sciences in France at the Sorbonne.

García Moreno entered politics as a liberal, an opponent of General Juan José FLORES, and an admirer of the enlightened Vicente ROCAFUERTE. He gained notoriety as a publisher of three polemical newspapers: *El Zurriago* (1845), *El Vengador* (1846–1847), and *La Nación* (1853). His vehement opposition to the government forced him into exile three times between 1850 and 1856.

Life abroad induced him to turn conservative, to become a francophile, and to champion the cause of the Catholic church.

Upon completing scientific studies in Paris in 1856, he returned to Ecuador and was named rector of the University of Quito. Soon afterward he won a seat in the Senate. When the government became mired in a grave crisis with Peru, García Moreno took part in a campaign that toppled the government and precipitated a period of anarchy in Ecuador.

In May 1859 a *junta de notables* named García Moreno a member of a triumvirate. He quickly emerged as the dominant leader but soon suffered a military defeat that caused him to flee to Peru. After securing support from the Peruvian president, he managed in a few months to return to Quito and to take charge there. Desperate to pacify the nation, he secretly proposed to establish a French protectorate over Ecuador. France did not respond to the proposal.

By early 1861 the nation was sufficiently pacified for a national convention to elect García Moreno president for four years. He completed his term of office, bullied two successors for the next four years, and then seized power by force. He remained president until his violent death in 1875.

During his first administration García Moreno held power by ruthless repression of the opposition. He reformed the treasury, increased revenues, turned public schools over to the clergy, allowed the JESUITS to return to Ecuador, and defended his nation from the aggressive intentions of Colombia and Peru. His efforts to modernize the university and improve the transportation system gave the impression of continued liberalism, but his repression of criticism and his espousal of unabashed clericalism revealed a shift to authoritarian conservatism. Most revealing was the negotiation in 1862 of a controversial concordat with the Vatican that surrendered the *patronato* (government authority over clerical appointments and revenues), permitted church censorship of school texts, and called for reform of corrupt religious orders. A subsequent campaign to spiritualize the clergy helped turn the church into a strong pillar of the state.

The authoritarian Constitution of 1869 allowed García Moreno to become a legal dictator and to press his religious fervor to surprising extremes. Non-Catholics were denied civil rights, substantial sums of money were donated to the Vatican, and in 1873 the nation was dedicated to the Sacred Heart of Jesus. In secular affairs, García Moreno founded an astronomical observatory, a new military academy, and a polytechnic school. Public works included many new roads, especially a good cart road from Quito to Guayaquil, initiation of railroad lines, and a large prison in Quito.

While García Moreno was arranging his own reelection in 1875, copies of Juan MONTALVO's *La dictadura perpetua,* an inflammatory indictment of the Ecuadorian dictator, arrived in Quito. Soon afterward a group of young liberals, probably incited by Montalvo's words, cut down the president with machete blows. This bloody act ended the dictatorship but turned García Moreno into a martyr of conservatism.

GEORGE HOWE, "García Moreno's Efforts to Unite Ecuador and France," in *Hispanic American Historical Review* 16, no. 2 (1936): 257–262; LUIS ROBALINO DÁVILA, *García Moreno* (1948); SEVERO GOMEZJURADO, *Vida de García Moreno,* 10 vols. (1954–1971); BENJAMÍN CARRIÓN, *García Moreno: El santo del patíbulo* (1959); RICHARD PATTEE, *Gabriel García Moreno y el Ecuador de su tiempo,* 3d ed. (1962).

MARK J. VAN AKEN

GARCÍA MORILLO, ROBERTO (*b.* 22 January 1911), Argentine composer and critic. He was born in Buenos Aires and studied at the National Conservatory of Music and Theater Arts under the guidance of Floro Ugarte, José GIL, José André, and Constantino GAITO. Garcia Morillo is noted for the absence of nationalistic elements in his music. His style evolved as atonal music, with modernistic, dissonant harmonies, and very contrapuntal lines but without harshly clashing sounds. Garcia Morillo evoked the Hispanic origins of his ancestors, using renovated archaic forms and textures in his works such as his cantata Marín (1948–1950). The municipality of Buenos Aires awarded a composition prize for his *Poema para orquesta* (1932) and for *Las pinturas negras de Goya* (1939). His ballets *Harrild* (1941) and *Usher* (1940–1941) were awarded distinctions from the National Commission on culture and the Wagnerian Society, as was his music for the film *Juvenilia,* which received the Municipal Prize for film music in 1943. In 1938 he began writing music criticism for the newspaper *La Nación* in Buenos Aires, and he has written other articles for *Modern Music, Musical Courier,* and the *Revista ARS.* He is the author of several books: *Mussorgsky* (1943), *Rimsky Korsakoff* (1945), *Estudios sobre la danza* (1948), with Dora Kriner, *Siete músicos europeos* (1949), and *Carlos Chávez* (1960).

Some of Garcia Morillo's earlier compositions contain traces of neoclassicism, like his Piano Sonata no. 3, op. 14 (1944–1945). Other works of the same period demonstrate his dexterity with rhythms and the use of engaging and intriguing melodies. Among his important works are *Tres pinturas de Paul Klee* (1944); *El tamarit* (1953), a chamber cantata for soprano, baritone, and orchestra; *Romances del amor y de la muerte* for bass (1959); *Música para oboe y orquesta* (1962); *Cantata de los caballeros* for soprano (1965); *Música para violin y cuerdas* (1967); Symphony no. 1 (1946–1948); *Obertura para un drama romántico* (1954); Symphony no. 2 (1954–1955); Symphony no. 3 (1961); *Divertimento sobre temas de Paul Klee* (1967); *Ciclo de Dante Alighieri* for chamber orchestra (1970); and *Variaciones apolíneas* for piano (1958–1959).

Cuarto Inter-American Music Festival (1968), pp. 44, 47, 70; *Primer festival internacional de música contemporánea* (1970), p. 29; RODOLFO ARIZAGA, *Enciclopedia de la música argentina* (1971), pp. 153–155; GÉRARD BÉHAGUE, *Music in Latin America: An Introduction* (1979), pp. 276–277; *New Grove Dictionary of Music and Musicians* (1980).

ALCIDES LANZA

GARCÍA PELÁEZ, FRANCISCO DE PAULA (*b.* 2 April 1785; *d.* 25 January 1867), archbishop of Guatemala, with jurisdiction over all of Central America (1846–1867). Born into a ladino family of modest means in San Juan Sacatepéquez, Guatemala, García Peláez studied law and theology at the University of San Carlos, where he received his doctorate in 1819. Although regarded as somewhat liberal in the late colonial period, as archbishop during the long, conservative dictatorship of José Rafael CARRERA, he became known as an ultraconservative. He had offered the first course in political economy at the University of San Carlos in 1814.

In 1842 Pope Gregory XVI named García archbishop coadjutor, to succeed the archbishopric upon the death of Archbishop Ramón CASÁUS, after it was clear that Casáus would not return to Guatemala from his exile in Havana. Following Casáus's death in late 1845, García was formally installed as archbishop, although he had been acting archbishop since 1844. García's appointment was a setback for the Guatemalan elite and particularly for Juan José de AYCINENA, who had expected to be named. Jorge VITERI Y UNGO was especially influential in arranging García's appointment as part of a compromise to get papal approval of a separate diocese of El Salvador, of which Viteri was named bishop. In 1861 Pope Pius IX named García Peláez domestic prelate and attending bishop to the pontifical throne, essentially a step below cardinal.

García Peláez wrote a three-volume history of the colonial Kingdom of Guatemala, *Memorias para la historia del antiguo reino de Guatemala*, a work commissioned by Governor Mariano GÁLVEZ.

There is a detailed biographical sketch in *Gaceta de Guatemala* (27 June–25 August 1867). See also FRANCISCO FERNÁNDEZ HALL, "Historiadores de Guatemala posteriores a la independencia nacional: El Doctor Don Francisco de Paula García Peláez," in *Anales de la Sociedad de Geografía e Historia* 15, no. 3 (1939): 261–278; and three articles in *Anales de la Sociedad de Geografía e Historia* 40, no. 1/2 (1967): 15–36, commemorating the centenary of the death of García Peláez: FRANCISCO GALL, "En el centenario del fallecimiento de García Peláez"; VALENTÍN SOLÓRZANO FERNÁNDEZ, "García Peláez: Cátedra prima de economía política en el Reino de Guatemala"; and JORGE LUIS ARRIOLA, "García Peláez, uno de los precursores del liberalismo económico en Guatemala."

RALPH LEE WOODWARD, JR.

GARCÍA PÉREZ, ALAN (*b.* 23 May 1949), president of Peru (1985–1990). García, born in Lima to middle-class parents active in the American Popular Revolutionary Alliance (APRA), was seven years old when his father was released from political detention. He earned a law degree from San Marcos University and pursued graduate work in Madrid and at the Sorbonne, where he received a doctorate in sociology. He won election to the Constituent Assembly in 1978 and outpolled all APRA candidates in 1980 to gain a seat in the Chamber of Deputies. In 1985 he led APRA to its first presidential victory and at thirty-six became Latin America's youngest chief executive.

García's reformist policies limited foreign debt repayment to 10 percent of national export earnings, thereby stimulating economic growth through 1987. His efforts to provide economic resources to rural areas affected by the Shining Path insurgency and his strong human rights stand contributed to reductions in violence during the first months of his term. But García's reforms foundered after a prison massacre in which more than 270 Shining Path inmates were killed by the military and police in June 1986, while García was hosting the Socialist International convention in a bid for a leadership position. Garcías's bank nationalization program failed in June 1987. The last three years of his term were marked by four-digit inflation, an economic decline of over 20 percent, and an escalation of violence and human rights abuses related to the Shining Path insurgency.

Upon leaving office in 1990, García assumed his seat in the Senate as a former president and regained leadership of APRA in party elections in early 1992. After the self-coup (*autogolpe*) of April 1992 by his successor, Alberto FUJIMORI, he evaded arrest and obtained asylum in Colombia. Allegations of corruption contributed to his expulsion from APRA in 1994.

DAVID P. WERLICH, "Debt, Democracy, and Terrorism in Peru," in *Current History* 86 (January 1987): 29–34ff; REX HUDSON, ed., *Peru: A Country Study*, 4th ed. (1993).

DAVID SCOTT PALMER

See also **Peru: Political parties; Peru: Revolutionary Movements.**

GARCÍA ROBLES, ALFONSO (*b.* 20 March 1911), Mexican foreign service officer and disarmament specialist. A native of Zamora, Michoacán, García Robles completed his studies in law at the University of Paris, where he was one of two laureates at the Institute of International Studies in 1936. He also received a diploma from the International Law Academy at the Hague (1938). He joined the diplomatic corps in 1939, serving in a number of foreign assignments and posts within the secretariat of foreign relations. He is considered to have been largely responsible for the Nuclear Arms Treaty of TLATELOLCO in 1967, later serving as Mexico's permanent representative to the United Nations Committee on Disarmament. For his efforts in regional disarmament, he was awarded the Nobel Prize for peace in 1982. He culminated his professional career in 1975 as secretary for foreign relations, receiving the rank of ambassador emeritus (1981). He is the author of numerous books and articles.

Excélsior, 30 December 1975, p. 11; *New York Times,* 14 October 1982, p. 10; *Hispano Americano* 25 (October 1982): 9–10.

RODERIC AI CAMP

GARCÍA SALINAS, FRANCISCO (*b.* 1786; *d.* 1841),

Mexican cabinet minister and governor of the state of Zacatecas. García was born on a hacienda in the state of Zacatecas. As a young man he was involved in the mining business in Zacatecas. In 1821, he was the *regidor* (president) of the *ayuntamiento* (city council) of Zacatecas and was elected to represent the state in the First Constituent Congress of Mexico in 1822. García continued to serve in the Congress as deputy and then as senator from Zacatecas from 1823 to 1827, taking a special interest in financial matters and helping to reestablish Mexico's foreign credit. President Guadalupe VICTORIA selected García as his minister of the treasury, a post he held for only a few months (2 November 1827 to 15 February 1828) prior to his election as governor of the state of Zacatecas in 1828.

García's administration of Zacatecas was a model of liberal reform that made the state, with its strong militia, one of the bulwarks of the federal system. García attempted to use church property to create a bank for agricultural credit and to use state funds to redistribute agricultural land by dividing large properties for sale. His administration also sought to develop the mining industry and the manufacture of cotton, silk, and woolen textiles. The state of Zacatecas opened new schools under the Lancasterian system of ''utilitarian'' education and vaccinated thousands of children against smallpox. The defeat of the Zacatecas militia by conservative and centralist forces in 1832 and 1835 marked a turning point in the early republican history of Mexico. After stepping down as governor in 1834, García continued in command of the state's militia. He retired to his hacienda, where he died.

JESÚS ROMERO FLORES, *Historia de los estados de la República mexicana* (1964); CHARLES A. HALE, *Mexican Liberalism in the Age of Mora* (1968); *Diccionario Porrúa de historia, biografía y geografía de México,* 5th ed. (1986).

D. F. STEVENS

GARCÍA Y GONZÁLEZ, VICENTE (*b.* 23 January 1833; *d.* 4 March 1886), Cuban general. General García was one of the regional military caudillos who emerged in Cuba during the TEN YEARS' WAR (1868–1878). A native of the district of Las Tunas, Oriente Province, he was something of a feudal lord. He led his guerrilla troops to some brilliant victories over the Spanish army, but he was unruly and inconsistent, and his ambition prompted him to launch seditious movements against the insurgent pro-

visional government, finally contributing to its collapse and the ultimate failure of the insurgent effort. García participated in some obscure way in the negotiations with the Spanish that culminated in the end of the war. Afterward he sought refuge in Venezuela, where he spent the rest of his life. He died in Río Chico, Venezuela.

There are no sources in English. His grandson wrote a book-length biography: FLORENCIO GARCÍA CISNEROS, *El león de Santa Rita: El general Vicente García y la guerra de los diez años, Cuba, 1868–1878* (1988). García's military career is discussed in FERNANDO FIGUEREDO, *La revolución de Yara* (1969).

JOSÉ M. HERNÁNDEZ

GARCILASO DE LA VEGA, EL INCA (*b.* 12 April 1539; *d.* 22/23 April 1616), Peruvian author and historian. Born in Cuzco, son of Captain Sebastián Garcilaso de la Vega and INCA princess Chimpu Oello, his original name was Gómez Suárez de Figueroa. He studied, along with other MESTIZO children, under the cathedral canon

Garcilaso de la Vega. LIBRARY OF CONGRESS.

Juan de Cuellar. About 1552 his father married a wealthy Spaniard, and Garcilaso's Inca mother and siblings were forced to leave the household. His father died in 1559, and the following year the young Garcilaso set sail for Spain, planning to live and study with the support of a small stipend provided by his father's will. He would never return to Peru.

After settling in Montilla, in southern Spain, under the patronage of his uncle, Alonso de Vargas, Garcilaso fought briefly (1570–1571) in Granada during the uprising of the Moriscos of Alpujarras. About 1591 he moved to nearby Córdoba and devoted much of the remainder of his life to writing. His first literary effort was the translation of the *Diálogos de amor* (Dialogues of Love) of Leon Hebreo (Madrid, 1590), which served as a model of stylistic accomplishment. His first history, *La Florida del Inca* (1605), tells the story of the famous Hernando de SOTO expedition to what became the southeastern part of the United States. Based on published sources and the oral account of soldier Gonzalo Silvestre, Garcilaso was able to weave a detailed and compelling picture of the trials and tribulations of the Spanish exploration of Florida. When facts were lacking, he created with vivid ingenuity. His next history, the *First Part of the Royal Commentaries of the Incas,* appeared in Lisbon in 1609. Based on recollections of what he learned as a youth in Peru and on written sources, including the chronicle of Blas Valera, this is an articulate and compelling, if not always accurate, account of Inca civilization. With a brilliant prose style, and with the authority of speaking in the native American voice, he attempted to bring Inca institutions and history to the Europeans.

Continued reliance on Garcilaso as a primary source clouds and blurs an authentic vision of TAHUANTINSUYU (The Land of the Four Quarters), even in the twentieth century. Indeed, Marcelino Menéndez y Pelayo, in his *Historia de la poesía hispano-americana,* wrote that the *Royal Commentaries* was not really history but might best be classified as a utopian novel. The second part of Garcilaso's commentaries, published one year after his death under the title of *Historia general del Perú* (1617), outlines the Spanish conquest of the Incas to the execution of TÚPAC AMARU I during the administration of Viceroy Francisco de TOLEDO (1567–1581). That Garcilaso was the first native American writer to be widely read in Europe, and continues to be read with pleasure and profit in spite of lapses into historical fantasy, is a lasting testament to his superb literary skills.

JOHN GRIER VARNER, *El Inca: The Life and Times of Garcilaso de la Vega* (1968); DONALD G. CASTANIEN, *El Inca Garcilaso de la Vega* (1969); MARGARITA ZAMORA, *Language, Authority, and Indigenous History in the "Comentarios reales de los Incas"* (1988).

NOBLE DAVID COOK

GARDEL, CARLOS (*b.* 11 December 1890; *d.* 24 June 1935), arguably Latin America's greatest twentieth-century popular singer and the supreme figure in the

Carlos Gardel, ca. 1930. ARCHIVO GENERAL DE LA NACIÓN, BUENOS AIRES.

story of the Argentine TANGO. Born in Toulouse, France, he was taken at the age of two by his unmarried mother to Buenos Aires, where he grew up in tenement rooms and on the streets. A naturally gifted baritone, he won local renown in the modest barrios of Buenos Aires before forming a celebrated folk duo with a Uruguayan friend, José Razzano (1887–1960), that lasted from 1913 to 1925.

In the early 1920s, with the development of the TANGO as a form of popular song, a movement Gardel himself strongly pioneered, he concentrated mostly on the new genre, making hundreds of recordings. Successful visits to Spain in 1925–1926 and 1927–1928 were followed by spectacular triumphs in the cabarets and music halls of Paris in 1928–1929. By now a superstar in Argentina and Uruguay, Gardel went on to gain unrivaled popularity all over Latin America by starring in seven movies, shot in Paris (1931–1932) and New York (1934–1935). These were mediocre, low-budget productions that nonetheless memorably projected Gardel's exceptional vocal talent and winning personality.

While undertaking a tour of countries around the Caribbean in 1935, the star was tragically killed in an airplane collision at Medellín, Colombia. His repatriated remains were accorded a solemn funeral attended by enormous crowds in Buenos Aires. Gardel's memory has been the focus of an assiduously cultivated popular cult. The centennial of his birth, December 1990, was extensively celebrated throughout Latin America.

SIMON COLLIER, *The Life, Music, and Times of Carlos Gardel* (1986); JOSÉ GOBELLO, *Tres estudios gardelianos* (1991); MIGUEL ÁNGEL MORENA, *Historia artística de Carlos Gardel: Estudio cronológico* (1991).

SIMON COLLIER

GARIBALDI, GIUSEPPE (*b.* 4 July 1807; *d.* 2 June 1882), Italian revolutionary and patriot. Garibaldi was born in Nice (then in Italy), son of Domenico Garibaldi, a sailor, and Rosa Ragiundo. A member of Giuseppe Mazzini's Young Italy, he was forced to flee the country because of his revolutionary activities. After arriving in Rio de Janeiro in 1836, he supported the revolutionary movement in Rio Grande do Sul as a privateer. Garibaldi was wounded during a naval engagement with Uruguayan lighters. After obtaining medical treatment at Gualeguay, Argentina, he returned to Rio Grande to fight alongside the rebels.

In 1841 Garibaldi and Ana María Ribeiro da Silva, a native of Santa Catarina, arrived in Montevideo, with their son Menotti. There they were married (16 June 1842) and had two more children, Riccioti and Teresita. For a few months Garibaldi was a business agent and a history and mathematics instructor; then he assumed command of President Fructuoso RIVERA's small navy of five ships. His attempt to challenge Buenos Aires's control of the rivers failed when his ships were destroyed at Costa Bravo by Admiral William BROWN on 15 August 1842, marking the end of Rivera's naval power. Garibaldi escaped overland to Montevideo.

During Manuel ORIBE's siege of Montevideo, Garibaldi, who held the rank of colonel, organized the Italian Legion of 600 men and a small fleet to protect the port. He successfully kept the bay of Montevideo free of the enemy. In 1844 he commanded one of the three columns that General José María PAZ led in an assault on Oribe's position in Cerrito. In 1845 he commanded a fleet of three ships with a landing force of 700 men of the Italian Legion, 200 Montevideo infantrymen under Colonel Lorenzo BATLLE, and 100 cavalrymen. Escorted by an Anglo-French squadron, he took and sacked Gualeguaychú, Colonia, and Salto.

Upon returning to Montevideo, Garibaldi was promoted to general (16 February 1846), and briefly commanded the forces defending the city. In August 1847 he returned to Europe to resume his fight for Italian unification. After his defeat in Rome by French forces (1849), he lived in Tangier, New York, Sardinia, and finally Caprera. He resumed his struggle for Italian unification in 1856. Four years later, after the death of Ana María, he married the Marchioness Giuseppina Raimondi. That year, encouraged by the Sardinian minister Camillo Cavour, he went to the aid of the Sicilian revolutionaries. Garibaldi landed at Marsala, and from there went on to capture Palermo and Messina and to establish a provisional government. His dream finally was realized when Italian troops entered Rome in 1870.

His *I Mille* (1874) is an account of his campaigns. Garibaldi and his sons fought for France in the Franco-Prussian War. After a brief term as national deputy, he returned to Caprera, where he wrote two novels and his *Memorie Autobiografiche* (*Garibaldi: An Autobiography*, 1860). He married Francisca Armorino in 1880 and died at Caprera.

JACINTO R. YABEN, "Garibaldi, G." in *Biografiás argentinas y sudamericanas*, vol. 2 (1938), pp. 747–751; VICENTE O. CUTOLO, "Garibaldi," in *Nuevo diccionario biográfico argentino, 1750–1930*, vol. 3 (1971), pp. 263–265; FERNANDO DEL CORRO, *El Diario* (Paraná), 23 September 1980. In English see THEODORE DWIGHT, *The Life of General Garibaldi, Translated from His Private Papers; with the History of His Splendid Exploits in Rome, Lombardy, Sicily, and Naples, to the Present Time.* (1877); *Autobiography of Giuseppe Garibaldi*, translated by A. Warner, with a supplement by Jessie White Mario, 3 vols. (1889); *The Memoirs of Garibaldi*, edited by Alexandre Dumas, translated with an introduction by R. S. Garnett, with contributions by George Sand and Victor Hugo. (1931); PETER DE POLNAY, *Garibaldi: The Man and the Legend.* (1961); DAVID GLASS LARG, *Giuseppe Garibaldi* (1934); JOHN LYNCH, *Argentine Dictator: Juan Manuel de Rosas, 1829–1852* (1981), pp. 193, 275, 280; YSABEL F. RENNIE, *The Argentine Republic* (1945), p. 60.

JOSEPH T. CRISCENTI

GARIBAY, PEDRO (*b.* 1729; *d.* 1815), viceroy of Mexico (16 September 1808–19 July 1809). A Madrid-born military officer, Garibay arrived in New Spain after service in Europe and the Caribbean, eventually being promoted to the rank of field marshal before he retired. When Napoleon intervened in Spain in 1808, José de ITURRIGARAY, viceroy of Mexico, was overthrown because of his pro-Mexican sentiments in a coup led by Spanish merchants and supported by the Mexico City AUDIENCIA (royal court). As senior military figure in the colony, and thought by the conservatives to be easily manipulatable, the elderly, infirm Garibay was appointed viceroy and eventually recognized by the caretaker government in Spain. Though his emasculated government lasted only ten months, he was honored in retirement and granted a large annual pension.

MANUEL RIVERA CAMBAS, *Los gobernantes de México*, vol. 3 (1964), pp. 243–255; CHRISTON I. ARCHER, *The Army in Bourbon Mexico, 1760–1810* (1977); TIMOTHY E. ANNA, *The Fall of the Royal Government in Mexico City* (1978).

ERIC VAN YOUNG

GARIBAY KINTANA, ÁNGEL MARÍA (*b.* 18 June 1892; *d.* 19 October 1967), Mexican scholar and priest who pioneered in the study and translation of the literary traditions of the ancient Mexicans. Garibay was born in Toluca. While at the Seminario Conciliar de México (1906–1917), he learned Latin and Greek (and later published works on Greek philosophers) and became interested in Nahuatl language and culture. In subsequent years Garibay added Hebrew, French, Italian, German,

English, and Otomí, as well as Nahuatl, to his language repertoire. He was ordained in 1917; later (especially 1924–1941) he served as a missionary and became more and more focused on his Nahua and Otomí studies. In 1941 Garibay was named prebendary canon of the Basilica of Guadalupe. From 1956 he served as director of the Seminario de Cultura Nahuatl at the Universidad Nacional. In 1952 he was named extraordinary professor at the Faculty of Philosophy and Letters at the Universidad Nacional. Although he began publishing articles in 1913, his major works appeared from 1940 through 1965; they included *Poesía indígena de la altiplanicie*, *Llave del Nahuatl* (1940), *Historia de la literatura Nahuatl* (2 vols, 1940), and three important volumes on the songs and poetry of the ancient Mexicans. His numerous translations of Nahuatl prose, historical texts, epic hymns, religious and lyric poetry, *pláticas* (short lectures), and other texts opened new doors to understanding the pre-Hispanic cultures of Mexico, and stimulated intense scholarly and humanistic interest in these arenas. Garibay died in Mexico City.

MIGUEL LEÓN-PORTILLA, "Ángel Ma. Garibay K. (1892–1992), en el centenario de su nacimiento," in *Estudios de cultura Nahuatl* 22 (1992):167–180.

FRANCES F. BERDAN

GARIFUNA. *See* **Caribs.**

GARIMPO, a small-scale, informal gold, diamond, and tin placer mining camp. *Garimpos* have been part of the penetration of the Brazilian interior since the first arrival of Europeans. *Garimpagem* (the mining activity itself) has involved primarily the poorer sectors of society, including escaped slaves who, during the colonial period, lived in runaway-slave communities (*quilombos*). *Garimpeiro* (miner) exploration led to major gold and diamond strikes at the beginning of the eighteenth century. Despite sporadic attempts by formal MINING companies to mine gold in Brazil since that time, Brazilian gold mining remained dominated by *garimpos* until the 1960s.

In the 1970s, substantial gold deposits were discovered in the Amazon Basin, stimulating an extensive GOLD RUSH. Most of the *garimpos* that proliferated throughout the Amazon were run by independent operators; others were financed by wealthy entrepreneurs based in the mining areas or in Brazil's major cities. Though *garimpagem* remained largely within the INFORMAL ECONOMY, it maintained strong links to the formal economy through the market and purchase of manufactured items. In the late 1980s, *garimpos* contributed up to $1 billion annually to the Brazilian economy.

Garimpo technology has been rudimentary, involving the use of shovels, picks, carrying bags, sieves, and pans, and more recently small pump engines to control water. Mercury also has been employed to amalgamate with gold, causing severe ecological degradation of water-

ways and health problems for *garimpeiros*. Reflecting the widespread competition for resources in Brazil, *garimpos* have been in conflict at times with government and police authorities, large mining companies, native peoples, and the environment.

JOSÉ VERÍSSIMO DA COSTA PEREIRA, "Faiscadores" and "Garimpeiros," in *Tipos e aspectos do Brasil*, 10th ed. (1975), pp. 163–168, 324–326; G. ROCHA, ed., *Em busca de ouro: Garimpos e garimpeiros no Brasil* (1984); MARIANNE SCHMINK, "Social Change in the Garimpo," in *Change in the Amazon Basin: The Frontier After a Decade of Colonization,* edited by John Hemming, vol. 2 (1985), pp. 185–199; David Cleary, *Anatomy of the Amazon Gold Rush* (1990).

ROBERT WILCOX

GARMENDIA, FRANCISCO, nineteenth-century capitalist and early industrialist, Peruvian born in Argentina. In 1861, Garmendia established one of the first factories in Latin America, a TEXTILE factory in Lucre; he imported industrial machines from France and, in an impressive feat of entrepreneurship, transported them by mule across the southern Andes of Peru to the town of Quispicanchis, near Cuzco. The factory replaced the old colonial textile mills (OBRAJES) of that region. The woolen textile it produced was of a coarse quality targeted for purchase by the Indian population. The factory had chronic financial and technical problems and faced increasing competition by export-import commercial firms based in Arequipa, but remained in business as the only factory in Cuzco Department up to 1898.

ALBERTO FLORES GALINDO, *Arequipa y el sur andino: Ensayo de historia regional (siglos XVIII–XX)* (1977).

ALFONSO W. QUIROZ

GARMENDIA, SALVADOR (*b.* 1928), Venezuelan novelist and short-story writer. One of Venezuela's major fiction writers of the century, Garmendia has published more than a dozen books since the late 1950s. Although he is recognized by writers and critics alike, Garmendia has never been included among the writers of the Boom of Latin American literature in the 1960s and 1970s. Consequently, his fiction is far better known in the Hispanic world than in the United States, particularly his novels *Los pequeños seres* (1959), *Día de cenizas* (1963), *Los habitantes* (1968), and *El Capitán Kid* (1988).

The masterly use of a precise point of view makes Garmendia one of Latin America's best exponents of the narrative technique of the French *nouveau roman*. In his early novels, he portrays alienated characters in urban environments. The protagonist in *Los pequeños seres* becomes so desperate with his circumstances that he commits suicide. Protagonists in his other early fiction include such characters as an unemployed truck driver and a frustrated writer. In his later fiction, such as *El Capitán Kid* (1988), *Crónicas sádicas* (1990), and *Cuentos cómicos* (1991), Garmendia's tone is less anguished and often ironic and quite humorous.

JOHN S. BRUSHWOOD, *The Spanish American Novel: A Twentieth-Century Survey* (1975); GIUSEPPE BELLINI, *Historia de la literatura hispanoamericana* (1985); GEORGE MC MURRAY, *Spanish American Writing Since 1941* (1987).

RAYMOND LESLIE WILLIAMS

GARRIDO CANABAL, TOMÁS (*b.* 20 September 1891; *d.* 1943), radical Mexican provincial politician who dominated political life in the Gulf state of Tabasco in the 1920s and early 1930s. He is most remembered for his fanatical persecution of Catholic priests during the church-state conflict in the 1920s.

Born in Catazajá, Chiapas, Garrido studied law in Campeche and Mérida before serving as interim governor in 1919. He was governor of Tabasco from 1923 to 1926, senator (1927–1930), and governor once again from 1931 to 1934. With the support of his own Red Shirt movement, he took such extreme steps against priests as to prompt an investigation by the English Roman Catholic novelist Graham Greene, which resulted in Greene's famous 1940 work *The Power and the Glory.*

Garrido joined General Lazaro CÁRDENAS's first cabinet as secretary of agriculture (1934–1935). He refused Cárdenas's offer of a continued post in the cabinet, shortly after which his mentor, General Plutarco CALLES, was forced to leave Mexico. Garrido went into voluntary exile in Costa Rica, from which he returned to Mexico in 1940.

BALTASAR DROMUNDO, *Tomás Garrido, su vida y su leyenda* (1953); GRAHAM GREENE, *The Lawless Roads* (1955, repr. 1992); ALAN M. KIRSHNER, ''Tomás Garrido Canabal and the Mexican Red Shirt Movement'' (Master's thesis, New York University, 1970); and PEPE BULNES, *Gobernantes de Tabasco* (1979).

RODERIC AI CAMP

GARRIDO-LECCA SEMINARIO, CELSO (*b.* 9 March 1926), Peruvian composer. Born in Piura, Peru, Garrido-Lecca was a student of Rodolfo HOLZMANN's until moving to Chile, where he studied under Free Focke and Domingo Santa Cruz. He also studied orchestration with Aaron Copland in the United States. Later, at the Theater Institute of the University of Chile, he served as musical adviser, composition teacher, and composer. After the fall of the government of President Salvador Allende in 1973, he returned to Peru. He has taught at the National Conservatory in Lima and has represented Peru at various international events, including the Second Encuentros de Música Latinoamericana (Cuba, 1972) and the First International Rostrum of Latin American Music (TRIMALCA) International Music Council (IMC; Colombia, 1979). The music of Garrido-Lecca is often aleatoric, and utilizes modern signs and methods of notation. Garrido-Lecca has composed works for orches-

tra, string quartet, and piano, as well as chamber music and incidental music for theater and films.

JOHN VINTON, ed., *Dictionary of Contemporary Music* (1971); SAMUEL CLARO VALDÉS, *Historia de la música en Chile* (1973); GÉRARD BÉHAGUE, *Music in Latin America: An Introduction* (1979).

SERGIO BARROSO

GARRO, ELENA (*b.* 11 December 1920), Mexican novelist, short-story writer, and playwright. Although Garro has spent much of her adult life in Spain and France, her writing reflects Mexican society, which she views pessimistically. Her coupling of detailed realistic descriptions and nightmarish fantasies places her among the magical realists. In her first book, *Los recuerdos del porvenir* (1963), she re-creates her hometown, Iguala, which she sees as a microcosm of Mexican society: desperate, defeated, and doomed. Garro actually wrote the book in the 1950s and published it later, with the encouragement of Octavio Paz, her husband from 1937 to 1959. Her first collection of stories, *La semana en colores* (1964), draws on Indian beliefs. Her second, *Andamos huyendo Lola* (1980), combines childhood memories with fantasy to create a kind of hell in which characters are constantly fleeing and scrounging for food. *Testimonios sobre Mariana* (1981) captures the anguish of modern society and parodies the bourgeois intellectual. *Reencuentro de personajes* (1982) examines the sober themes of violence, sexual manipulation, and psychological torture. In *La casa junto al río* (1983), Garro returns to her childhood village, still steeped in pettiness and mediocrity. *Y matarazo no llamó*, written in 1960 but published in 1991, is a kind of political thriller with existential undercurrents: the main character, an alienated loner, is lured into a political snare that drives him mad and leads him to an absurd end. Garro wrote a number of one-act as well as full-length plays featuring avant-garde techniques. *Felipe Angeles* (1979) is a three-act work that presents a negative view of the Mexican Revolution.

FRANK DAUSTER, ''El teatro de Elena Garro: Evasión e ilusión,'' in *Ensayos sobre el teatro hispanoamericano* (1975), pp. 66–77; BETH MILLER and A. GONZÁLEZ, ''Elena Garro,'' in *26 autoras del México actual* (1978), pp. 199–219; MONIQUE LEMAITRE, ''El deseo de la muerte y la muerte del deseo en la obra de Elena Garro: Hacia una definición de la escritura femenina en su obra,'' *Revista Iberoamericana* 55 (1989): 1005–1017; ROBERT K. ANDERSON, ''Recurrent Themes in Two Novels by Elena Garro,'' *Selecta* 11 (1990): 83–86; ANITA K. STOLL, ed., *A Different Reality: Studies on the Work of Elena Garro* (1990); ANITA K. STOLL, ''The Old World vs. the New: Cultural Conflict in Four Works of Elena Garro,'' *Letras Peninsulares* 5 (1991): 95–106.

BARBARA MUJICA

GARRO, JOSÉ DE (*d.* ca. 1702), governor of Buenos Aires (1678–1682). Garro was born in Guipúzcoa, in the Basque country of northern Spain. He saw intense action in the wars in Portugal and Catalonia. In 1671 he came to America to govern Tucumán, where he was outstanding for his role in public works and in Indian fighting. As governor of Buenos Aires, Garro was responsible for confronting the advance of the Portuguese, who in 1680 had founded the colony of Sacramento in the eastern territory. Garro stormed the colony and took its founder, Manuel Lobo, prisoner. Later he served for ten years as governor of Chile (1682–1691), where his rule was particularly notable for the conversion of Indians. He went on to become military commander of Gibraltar (1693–1702) and finally of his homeland, Guipúzcoa (1702), where he died.

MONTANER Y SIMÓN, ed., *Diccionario enciclopédico hispano-americano* (1938); ENRIQUE UDAONDO, *Diccionario biográfico colonial Argentino* (1945).

JOSÉ DE TORRES WILSON

GARVEY, MARCUS (*b.* 17 August 1887; *d.* 10 June 1940), Pan-African nationalist. Garvey was born in Saint Ann's Bay, Jamaica, to a comfortable family, possibly descendants of maroons. He attended school until the age of fourteen, when a financial crisis in his family obliged him to go to work as a printer's apprentice. By the age of nineteen, he had mastered the skills of this trade, which he was able to use later in his career as a publicist and propagandist in the cause of black nationalism. Between 1910 and 1914 he traveled in the Caribbean and Central America and resided in London. It was during this period that his political ideas took shape. In 1914 he returned to Jamaica and founded the Universal Negro Improvement Association (UNIA), which was received with little enthusiasm. In 1916, Garvey decided to travel to the United States, where his ideas gave rise to an important mass movement for the dignity and independence of blacks. In 1918 he formed a branch of UNIA in New York City and began the publication of the weekly *Negro World,* which quickly attained a large, international circulation. With the hope of aiding communication between African Americans and Africans, and to help further his "Back to Africa" vision, he founded the Black Star shipping line in 1919.

In 1920 UNIA reached its high point when it held its first international convention in New York. As the organization grew in size and importance, it faced increasing repression from U.S. authorities and from the European colonial powers that controlled Africa and the West Indies. Moreover, problems within UNIA derailed Garvey's plans. By 1921 the Black Star Line was a fiasco, as were efforts to colonize Africa and other projects begun in the United States. In 1923 the U.S. government accused Garvey of fraud, and he was sent to prison in 1925. In 1927 his sentence was commuted and he was deported to Jamaica. Although he continued his fight there and in London, where he relocated in 1935, he never regained the international influence he had had at the beginning of the 1920s. By the time of his death in London, he was forgotten.

The importance of Garveyism is that it was the first movement of the black masses based on black pride and dignity. Its international character also was significant. UNIA had branches in the countries of the Caribbean and Central America and was well received by the migrant plantation workers of the West Indies and Jamaica. Garvey is remembered as the forerunner of black nationalism in Africa and in America.

DAVID CRONON, *Black Moses: The Story of Marcus Garvey and the Universal Negro Improvement Association* (1955); THEODORE G. VINCENT, *Black Power and the Garvey Movement* (1971); JUDITH STEIN, *The World of Marcus Garvey: Race and Class in Modern Society* (1986).

VÍCTOR ACUÑA

GARZA SADA FAMILY, major Mexican entrepreneurial family. The original head of probably the single most influential and extensive capitalist family in Mexico was Isaac Garza Garza, the son of Juan de la Garza Martínez, mayor of Monterrey, and Manuela Garza, Jewish immigrants from Spain who had settled in the region of Monterrey, Nuevo León. After studying merchandizing in Santander, Spain, he went into the grocery business with José Calderón, who married his aunt. Isaac married Consuelo Sada Muguerza, daughter of Francisco Sada Gómez, and in 1899 founded with his father-in-law Fábrica de Vidrios y Cristales de Monterrey, of which he became president. With other partners, he established a number of major firms at the turn of the century, including Cervecería Cuauhtémoc (1890), whose partners, often related by marriage, included José A. Muguerza and Francisco Sada, and the Fundidora de Fierro y Acero, with Vicente Ferrara.

His union with Consuelo produced numerous children, among them Eugenio Garza Sada, Isaac Garza Sada, and Roberto Garza Sada. Eugenio, the oldest of this generation, took over the leadership of a major group of interlocking corporations, which became known popularly as the "Monterrey Group." These included the original brewery, Cervecería Cuauhtémoc; a bottling company, Hojalata y Lámina; and Empaques de Cartón Titán, a packaging firm. Another son, Isaac, took over another set of firms, and also developed his own businesses. These children, in turn, intermarried with other prominent Monterrey families, including the Laguera and Sepúlveda families.

The untimely death of Eugenio Garza Sada, who was murdered in September 1973, served as a catalyst in breaking up the beer, glass, and steel empire into four separate, but complementary, holding companies. All of these conglomerates rank among the top fifty companies in Mexico. The most famous of these groups, the ALFA industrial group, the largest in Latin America in the early 1980s, was founded by Bernardo Garza Sada, grandson of Isaac and son of Roberto. The other components are led by VITRO, VISA, controlled by the Garza Laguera family, and the CYDSA group, presided over by the Sada Zambrano family. The Garza Sadas continue to be a dominant force among Mexican capitalists, as shareholders and board members of leading industrial firms, as members of entrepreneurial interest groups, as leaders of business organizations, and as managers of major industrial holding groups.

ISIDRO VIZCAYA CANALES, *Los orígenes de la industrialización de Monterrey* (1971); MENNO VELLINGA, *Economic Development and the Dynamics of Class: Industrialization, Power and Control in Monterrey, Mexico* (1979); ALEX SARAGOZA, *The Monterrey Elite and the Mexican State, 1880–1940* (1988); RODERIC AI CAMP, *Entrepreneurs and Politics in Twentieth Century Mexico* (1989).

RODERIC AI CAMP

See also **Mexico: Organizations.**

GASCA, PEDRO DE LA (*b.* August 1493; *d.* 10 November 1567), president of the Audiencia of Lima and bishop of Palencia and Sigüenza. Born in a hamlet in Ávila, Spain, Gasca briefly attended the University of Salamanca before leaving in 1508 to attend the recently founded University of Alcalá de Henares, where he received a master of theology. He continued in Alcalá as *colegial* in the Colegio Mayor of San Ildefonso. In 1522 he returned to Salamanca to complete a study of law and in 1528 served briefly as rector of Salamanca.

In 1531, Gasca became affiliated with the Colegio Mayor de San Bartolomé, where he assumed the duties of rector for two terms. He received a prebend in Salamanca's cathedral (1531) and was named *maestrescuela* (teacher of divinity). Returning to Alcalá in 1537 as *vicario* (vicar), he was placed under the tutelage of Francisco de los COBOS, secretary of Holy Roman Emperor Charles V. Shortly thereafter he became general inspector of Valencia and, in 1540, justice of the Council of the Inquisition. Gasca served well in both capacities, impressing Cobos, who saw in him the qualities necessary to pacify Peru, then in the throes of rebellion. In late 1545 Gasca accepted the royal commission naming him president of the Audiencia of Lima and giving him power to offer pardons and make grants. He also was empowered to revoke the onerous chapter 30 of the NEW LAWS, which prohibited inheritance of *encomiendas*, and to authorize new *entradas*. In addition he had general power to grant all types of office and to conduct any business in the name of the monarch.

Gasca left Spain in April 1546. When he reached Santa Marta, Colombia, on 10 July he learned of the execution of Viceroy Blasco NÚÑEZ VELA after the battle of Añaquito (18 January 1546). In Panama he entered into negotiations with Pizarrists, convincing many to abandon the rebels. By April 1547, when he headed south, he had gained the support of the Pacific fleet under Admiral Hinojosa. When they first landed, they discovered that several important cities in the north already had declared for the royalist cause. On 30 June Gasca reached

Tumbes, on Peru's north coast, with a substantial force. During their one-and-a-half month's stay, Lima declared for the royalists, and the Pizarrists left for the highlands.

Gasca established military headquarters at Jauja, by which time he had collected 700 harquebusiers, 500 pikemen, and 400 horsemen. News of a stunning defeat of the royalist force (20 October 1547) under Diego de Centeno at Huarina, to the south, failed to discourage Gasca's forces. The final battle between Gonzalo PIZARRO and Gasca (9 April 1548) on the plain of Jaquijahuana, not far west of Cuzco, ended in royalist triumph; most Pizarrists threw down their arms and surrendered. Gonzalo Pizarro and his leading commander Francisco de Carvajal, along with some 48 principal leaders, were executed; 350 rebels were sent to labor in the galleys; and 700 were exiled from Peru.

In July 1548, Gasca retired with his secretary and Archbishop Loaysa to the hamlet of Guaynarima to distribute the spoils (Indian *encomiendas*) to the victors. He then departed for Lima, leaving the archbishop to announce the awards in Cuzco. The results shocked most royalists, two-thirds of whom received no grants, while some rebels who returned to the crown at the last moment were well rewarded. In May 1548 Gasca ordered a general inspection and tribute assessment for the *encomiendas*. The first systematic census to be undertaken and largely completed, it began in March 1549, with two inspectors for each district. Gasca's purpose was to increase yet stabilize tribute collection and to protect the Native Americans as much as possible.

Gasca restored the administration of justice under firm royal authority. He licensed new expeditions, one of which led to the foundation of the city of La Paz, Bolivia. He also named Pedro de VALDIVIA governor and captain-general of Chile, thus recognizing him as conqueror of that land. Most important for the crown, he carried back an enormous treasure. Shipment of the king's fifth had long been delayed as a result of Peru's civil wars. Gasca left Lima in January 1550 and reached Seville in September. In November he reported to the COUNCIL OF THE INDIES in Valladolid, where he was ordered to inform directly Charles V, who was then in Flanders. On 6 April, while he was in Barcelona preparing to travel to Germany, Gasca became bishop of Palencia. He sailed to Genoa, then north to Mantua, where he met Prince Philip in June. Passing through Trent, where the church council was in session, Gasca finally met Charles V (CHARLES I of Spain) at Augsburg on 2 July 1551. The emperor received him with gratitude, for Gasca had restored a rebellious colony and provided the treasure that would allow Charles V to continue his imperial religious and political policies in the heart of Europe.

Gasca returned to Spain early in 1553 and assumed his post at Palencia on 6 March. He was asked to report to the Council of the Indies several times in following years, and in 1556 he was called on by Charles V to escort his sisters, Queen Leonor of France and Queen Maria of Hungary, to interview the Infanta Maria of Portugal in

Badajoz. Named Bishop of Sigüenza in 1561, he served there until his death at the age of seventy-four.

Pedro de la Gasca is buried in a beautiful stone coffin bearing his effigy in the center of the church of Santa María Magdalena, which he built in Valladolid.

JUAN CRISTÓBAL CALVETE DE ESTRELLA, *Rebelión de Pizarro en el Perú y vida de don Pedro Gasca* (1963–1965); TEODORO HAMPE MARTÍNEZ, *Don Pedro de la Gasca* (1493–1567), *su obra política en España y América* (1989).

NOBLE DAVID COOK

GASOHOL INDUSTRY. *Gasohol* is the term for varying blends of gasoline and ethyl alcohol (ethanol) and can also describe any mixture of other petroleum fuels containing ethanol or methanol. In the United States, ethanol obtained from corn was used after the fuel shortage in the aftermath of the Arab oil embargo (1973–1974). The real story of gasohol as an industry, however, dates back to World War I in Brazil, with the production of ethanol from sugarcane for use in gasohol. Another spurt of mandated gasohol use occurred during the worldwide depression of the 1930s and again during World War II, because of uncertain oil supplies, but gasohol use evaporated in the 1950s with the availability of low-cost oil from the Middle East. It was not until the October 1973 oil price explosion coincidental with war in the Middle East that renewed attention was paid to renewable fuels. Brazil had to respond to balance-of-payments problems due to rising costs of oil imports, which significantly constrained economic development. In 1975 the country launched the largest initiative in the world to produce ethanol. The National Alcohol Program—Proálcool—had technical, economic, and social consequences. It created new technology in refining, agriculture, and transportation. It saved hard currency by reducing oil imports while creating new jobs and improving workers' incomes overall.

The oil crisis had been the catalyst for Proálcool, but developments in the SUGAR INDUSTRY were also seminal. In that period, traditional cane sugar exports were declining with falling world prices. The replacement of sugar with ethanol production displaced imported oil and reduced world sugar supplies. Moreover, sugarcane has a highly favorable energy balance when ethanol is produced. Processing is self-sufficient because the caloric value of generated bagasse is sufficient to provide more than the fuel for refinery operations. The Brazilian Ethanol Producers' Special Committee reported that solar energy on one acre of sugarcane yields an average of 602 gallons of ethanol, while the same energy on one acre of corn yields only 375 gallons.

After the first decade, Proálcool, though remaining controversial, created over 2 million jobs directly and indirectly. Wages increased throughout Brazil; rural migration into urban centers was stemmed; higher-yield sugarcane varieties were developed; better management improved soil use and distillery processes and gave a higher yield of fermentation.

Gasohol in Brazil contains as much as 80% ethanol; undiluted ethanol is also used in vehicles with specially adapted engines. In its various forms in Brazil, it is a national achievement. It has increased the domestic content of fuels, displaced imported oil (saving an estimated $8.5 billion on oil imports with subsequent annual savings exceeding $1 billion), and provided benefits for workers and industry. Ethanol is a renewable, but expensive fuel; government subsidies to offset high production costs are required to make gasohol competitive in established gasoline markets. The required subsidy depends on the price of petroleum. The oil price collapse in 1986 made the gasohol subsidy an economic catastrophe for the Brazilian government. Yet given the existing large investment in Proálcool, the industrial expertise developed, and its strategic value, abandoning the program would be a disaster. Thus, gasohol in national markets has to be politically justified as a "national security" issue. In the global energy markets gasohol must continue to rely on public subsidies while being virtually economically irrelevant.

DARIO SCUKA, *The Economics of Gasohol* (1979); STEVEN J. WINSTON, *Ethanol Fuels: Use, Production and Economics* (1981); THE ROYAL SOCIETY OF CANADA, *International Symposium on Ethanol from Biomass*, Winnipeg, Canada, 13–15 October 1982; HARRY ROTHMAN, ROD GREENSHIELDS, and FRANCISCO ROSILLO CALLE, *The Alcohol Economy: Fuel Ethanol and the Brazilian Experience* (1983); WORLD BANK, *Economic Aspects of the Alcohol Programme* (1984); R. SERÔA DA MOTTA, *A Social–Cost Benefit Study of Ethanol Production in Brazil*, Department of Economics, University College London, Discussion Paper No. 86.02 (1986); MICHAEL R. LEBLANC, *Ethanol: Economic and Policy Tradeoffs* (1988); COMISSÃO NACIONAL DE ENERGIA, *Política de combustíveis líquidos automotivos* (1988); DARIO SCUKA, *Ethanol Imports and the "Gasohol" Connection: Historical Background and Analysis in an International Perspective, 1978–1989* (1990).

DARIO SCUKA

GASTÃO D'ORLÉANS (Luís Filipe Maria Fernando, Conde d'Eu; *b.* 28 April 1842; *d.* 28 August 1922), husband to ISABEL, heir to the Brazilian throne. A member of the French royal family, the Conde d'Eu spent his early years in exile, first in England and then in Spain, where he trained as an army officer, fighting in Morocco. Family connections—his uncle married PEDRO II's sister—and personal qualities led to his marriage in 1864 to Isabel. Hard working, cultured, and liberal in political outlook, Conde d'Eu at first sought an active role in Brazilian affairs, which Pedro II denied him. In 1869 he was named commander in chief of Brazil's forces in the WAR OF THE TRIPLE ALLIANCE, and he secured total victory in 1870. His war experience left him psychologically insecure and subject to recurring depression, and he restricted himself thereafter to family affairs and to chairing a few army commissions. Despite his considerable talents, he did not shine in public life, in part owing to growing deafness. His lack of charisma and his erratic treatment of subordinates meant that he did not command support or sympathy. The Conde d'Eu never ceased to be an outsider in Brazil. After the empire's fall in 1889, he spent his final years in contented privacy in France.

ALBERTO RANGEL, *Gastão de Orléans (o ultimo conde d'Eu)* (São Paulo, 1935); ALFREDO D'ESCRAGNAROLLE TAUNAY, VISCONDE DE TAUNAY, *Memórias* (Rio de Janeiro, 1960), pp. 308–314.

RODERICK J. BARMAN

GATÓN ARCE, FREDDY (*b.* 27 March 1920), Dominican poet. Born in San Pedro de Macoris, Gatón is the last surviving champion of La Poesía Sorprendida, a movement that in the 1940s set out to reform Dominican poetry by transcending the local reality and embracing new and regenerative influences from European and American literatures. His enigmatic prose poem *Vlía* (1944), a text credited with introducing to the country the poetic form of automatic writing, which makes no concessions to the reader's understanding, highlights the kinship of Gatón Arce to the poets of Dada and surrealism. Despite the hermetism of his early work, his subsequent texts are more accessible to the uninitiated reader, with themes that manifest a concern with love, the downtrodden, and the relationship between the matter and spirit. His poetry, partly collected in *Retiro hacia la luz: poesía 1944–1979* (1980), has continued to evolve; a dozen volumes have appeared in print since 1980. A lawyer by profession, Gatón Arce has also been a professor, an administrator at the Autonomous University of Santo Domingo, and, since 1980, the director of the newspaper *El Nacional.* He is acclaimed for having enriched journalistic prose in the Dominican Republic.

ALBERTO BAEZA FLORES, *La poesía dominicana en el siglo XX: 1943–1947* (1977); JOSÉ ALCÁNTARA ALMÁNZAR, *Estudios de poesía dominicana* (1979); MARÍA DEL C. PROSDOCIMI DE RIVERA, *La poesía de Freddy Gatón Arce: Una interpretación* (1983).

SILVIO TORRES-SAILLANT

GAUCHESCA LITERATURE, a literary form invented by writers living in the city of Buenos Aires who recreated the speech characteristics of the GAUCHO and his octosyllabic verses, although with differences in rhymes and strophic distribution. It appeared toward the end of the eighteenth century in the littoral region of Argentina, in the province of Buenos Aires, and on the plains of Uruguay, and it is considered a literary genre within Argentine letters. Gauchesca literature was conceived, developed, and endured on the fringes of established Argentine literature; that is, it existed as a parallel literary genre. It was a dissident literature whose authors were considered rebels pitting the new, popular, and native against the established peninsular and cultured. It continued as marginal literature until its artistic worth was finally recognized in the first quarter of the twentieth century.

Gauchesca literature is composed of works written in verse by sophisticated, urban authors. The protagonist is the historical gaucho, from his appearance during the seventeenth century until his assimilation into sedentary life at the end of the nineteenth century, emphasizing his characteristic as an equestrian peasant without specific occupation. These works are set in the PAMPAS and reproduce the unique linguistic features of the gaucho, which include an archaic rural dialect rich in unique comparisons and metaphors. They are very graphic and humorous, and generally employ proverbial sentences, idiolects, and a lack of logical sequence in many parts of the discourse, with a resulting effect of intense laconism. The thematic repertoire is generally limited to injustice, poverty, the fight against the establishment (the local magistrate or justice of peace, the police, the military), life on the ESTANCIA, the horse, and the mate (friendship), revealing the particular world and world view of the gaucho. Gauchesca works rely on the *cantar opinando* (singing, but giving an opinion) and usually adopt the form of dialogue and autobiographical narrative, and they are designed to attract the sympathy and the adherence of the reader to causes defended by the gaucho.

Although there were some timid expressions of gauchesca literature at the end of the eighteenth century, the genre formally begins with Bartolomé HIDALGO (1788–1822) and his *Diálogos* (1820–1822) and *Relación* (1822). Hidalgo is credited with consciously selecting the socially marginal gaucho and building around him a literature with a sociopolitical message that the masses could understand. Although Hilario ASCASUBI and Estanislao del CAMPO are other writers associated with gauchesca literature, the towering figure of the genre is José HERNÁNDEZ, author of the Argentine national poem, MARTÍN FIERRO (1872–1879), which represents the highest point of the genre. This poem, together with some of Hidalgo's texts, entered the folkloric oral tradition, which contributed to the idealization or mythicization of the figure of the gaucho. In this respect, the *folletines gauchescos* (gauchesco feuilletons) of Eduardo Gutiérrez, produced in the last quarter of the nineteenth century, should be cited, as well as the dramatization of one of them, *Juan Moreira,* which marks the beginnings of the Argentine theater. This process of mythicization reached its summit in 1926 with the novel of Ricardo GÜIRALDES, *Don Segundo Sombra.* From that time on, the gaucho is transfigured into an archetype, a symbol of the true Argentine and the Argentine nationality. As such, it can be found in poems, novels, short stories, the theater, and on the radio.

Gauchesca literature should be understood as one of the two specifically Spanish-American literary genres, the other being the Afro-Antillean poetry of Puerto Rico and Cuba. Gauchesca literature is unique in its semiconversational, semiliterary intonation obtained by using the octosyllabic verse and by adopting a careless syntax, which is almost always narrated by a person who either evokes old times (always arcadian) or is furiously propagandistic and critical of the present political times. Gauchesca is also original because of its nonliterary character, its introduction of rusticity into a cultured literary tradition. Confronted with a literature of illustrious men performing heroic deeds, gauchesca presented antiheroes, poor peasants who were scorned and hopeless. Finally, gauchesca literature is significant because it represents the first appearance of an indigenous Argentine literary art form.

JORGE L. BORGES, ''La poesía gauchesca,'' in his *Discusión* (1964), pp. 11–38; RICARDO RODRÍGUEZ MOLAS, *Historia social del gaucho* (1968); FÉLIX WEINBERG, ''Una etapa poco conocida de la poesía gauchesca: De Hidalgo a Ascasubi (1823–1851),'' in *Revista Iberoamericana* 40, nos. 87–88 (1974): 353–391; HORACIO J. BECCO et al., *Trayectoria de la poesía gauchesca* (1977); RICHARD W. SLATTA, ''Man to Myth: Literary and Symbolic Images,'' in his *Gauchos and the Vanishing Frontier* (1983), pp. 180–192; JOSEFINA LUDMER, *El género gauchesco: Un tratado sobre la patria* (1988); RODOLFO A. BORELLO, ''El *Martín Fierro* y la poesía gauchesca,'' in *Boletín de la Academia Argentina de Letras* 54, nos. 211–212 (1989): 97–129.

ANGELA B. DELLEPIANE

GAUCHO, the cowboy of Argentina and Uruguay. Gauchos played an important historical role in the Río de la Plata and remain important cultural and political symbols. Gauchos, first called *gauderios*, emerged as a distinct social group of wild-cattle hunters during the early eighteenth century.

Gauchos believed in common access to the pampa's resources: land, water, and livestock. During the colonial era the vast herds of wild cattle and horses on the plains seemed inexhaustible. Gauchos scorned or were ignorant of remote government officials who tried to monopolize the killing of cattle. They fled from or resisted official attempts to dominate, direct, and draft them.

The gaucho adopted much of his equestrian subculture from Indians of the PAMPAS. He customarily wore a poncho, a CHIRIPÁ (baggy, diaperlike pants) held up by a stout leather belt (*tirador*), and on his feet homemade boots (BOTAS DE POTRO) and iron spurs. He armed himself with the BOLEADORAS and a swordlike knife (FACÓN).

Colonial and early-national-period officials viewed the gaucho as an unlettered, uncivilized barbarian, not significantly superior to the Indians of the pampas. Only a shallow, superstitious acquaintance with the symbols of Catholicism separated the gaucho, in the official eye, from the ''savages'' of the plains. Gauchos became the targets of vagrancy and military conscription laws designed to end their free-riding life-style.

Conscripted gauchos fought against Indians on the frontier, the British who invaded Buenos Aires and Montevideo in 1806 and 1807, and the Spanish royalist forces during the independence wars. José Gervasio ARTIGAS ably led his gaucho army in Uruguay. His military service somewhat improved the gaucho's image and gave him a reputation for valor and patriotism. The word ''gaucho'' became less an epithet than a description of the ranch worker who rode horses and tended cattle.

Gauchos worked seasonally on ranches (ESTANCIAS), rounding up and branding cattle. Some gauchos, such

Gauchos wrangling cattle in Buenos Aires Province, Argentina. PHOTO COURTESY OF H. HOFFENBERG AND THE INSTITUTO AUTÓNOMO BIBLIOTECA NACIONAL, CARACAS, VENEZUELA.

as the DOMADOR (broncobuster) or BAQUIANO (scout), earned higher wages because of their special skills.

As the nineteenth century progressed, the landed elite and Europeanized politicians gradually subdued the gaucho and radically changed his life. More restrictive laws, new technology, and a diversified rural economy marginalized the gaucho.

Beginning in the late nineteenth century, the gaucho began a transition from the realm of history into folklore and literature. Many important writers of Argentina and Uruguay made the gaucho the focus of their work. Following the pioneering poetry of Bartolomé HIDALGO and Hilario ASCASUBI, writers including José HERNÁNDEZ, Benito LYNCH, Leopoldo LUGONES, and Ricardo GÜIRALDES honored the gaucho in poetry and prose. Today calling someone or something ''very gaucho'' remains a compliment.

FERNANDO ASSUNÇÃO, *El gaucho* (1963); RICARDO RODRÍGUEZ MOLAS, *Historia social del gaucho* (1968); MADALINE WALLIS NICHOLS, *The Gaucho* (1968); DOMINGO F. SARMIENTO, *Life in the Argentine Republic in the Days of the Tyrants*, translated by Mary Mann (1971); RICHARD W. SLATTA, *Gauchos and the Vanishing Frontier* (1983); RICHARD W. SLATTA, *Cowboys of the Americas* (1990).

RICHARD W. SLATTA

GAÚCHO. During the nineteenth and early twentieth centuries, the Brazilian gaúcho, cousin of the Argentine and Uruguayan cowboy, was the cowboy of the RIO GRANDE DO SUL. The term also refers to a native of that region. Gaúchos roamed the open plain hunting semiferal cattle for their hides. They dressed in baggy *bombacha* pants and a poncho and wore a long knife. Gaúchos participated as cavalry soldiers in the nineteenth-century wars and rebellions of the border region. Twentieth-century modernization forced them into employment on newly fenced ESTANCIAS (ranches), ending their seminomadic way of life. Gaúcho life-style and customs have been preserved in music and dance, outdoor barbecues, and *chimarrão* (YERBA MATÉ).

JOSEPH LOVE, *Rio Grande do Sul and Brazilian Regionalism, 1882–1930* (1971); SPENCER L. LEITMAN, ''Socio-Economic Roots of the Ragamuffin War: A Chapter in Early Brazilian History'' (Ph.D. diss., Univ. of Texas, 1972); LINDALVO BEZERRA DOS SANTOS, ''O Gaúcho,'' in *Tipos e aspectos do Brasil*, 10th ed. (1975), pp. 425–26; RICHARD W. SLATTA, *Cowboys of the Americas* (1990), pp. 56–57, 199.

ROBERT WILCOX

See also **Vaqueiros.**

GAVIDIA, FRANCISCO ANTONIO (*b.* 29 December 1864; *d.* 23 September 1955), Salvadoran romantic poet and writer, one of the originators of modernism in Spanish America. Gavidia was born in San Miguel. His *Versos* (1884) brought him great notice for their innovations in meter and imagery, and he is believed to have

been an important influence on his friend Rubén DARÍO. A long career as leading literary figure in San Salvador followed, with perhaps his most significant poetic work being the epic and dramatic *Sóteer o tierra de preseas* (1920). Gavidia's classic ode *A Centroamérica* (1945) reflected his strong democratic conviction and belief in Central American union. His literary versatility was also reflected in dramatic works, critical essays, and historical works, among which his two-volume *Historia moderna de El Salvador* (1917–1918), focusing on the Salvadoran independence movements of 1811 and 1814, was the most important. Gavidia died in San Salvador.

Boletín de la Academi salvadoreña 1, honoring Gavidia (August 1940); ROBERTO ARMIJO and JOSÉ NAPOLEON RODRÍGUEZ RUIZ, *Francisco Gavidia: La odisea de su genio*, 2 vols. (1965); JOSÉ SALVADOR GUADIQUE, *Gavidia, el amigo de Darío*, 2 vols. (1965); MARIO HERNÁNDEZ-AGUIRRE, *Gavidia: Poesía, literatura, humanismo* (1968); CRISTÓBAL HUMBERTO IBARRA, *Francisco Gavidia y Rubén Darío, semilla y floración del modernismo*, 2d ed. (1976); LUIS GALLEGOS VALDÉS, *Panorama de la literatura salvadoreña del período precolombino a 1980*, 3d ed. (1989); JOHN BEVERLEY and MARC ZIMMERMAN, *Literature and Politics in the Central American Revolutions* (1990), pp. 118–119.

RALPH LEE WOODWARD, JR.

GAVIRIA TRUJILLO, CÉSAR AUGUSTO (*b.* 31 March 1947), president of Colombia (1990–1994). Born in Pereira, Gaviria studied economics at the Universidad de Los Andes. At the age of twenty-three he began his political career with election to the Pereira Municipal Council in 1970. He was appointed mayor of Pereira in 1974 and later served as vice minister of development in the administration of President César TURBAY AYALA (1978). Gaviria combined his political activities with those of a journalist, first with the newspaper *La* Tarde in Pereira, of which he became editor in 1982, and then as political and economic correspondent for the newspaper *El Tiempo*. He was appointed deputy director of the Liberal Party in 1986 and then served as minister of the treasury and minister of the interior in the administration of President Virgilio BARCO. In 1989 he became the campaign director of presidential candidate Luis Carlos GALÁN SARMIENTO. After Galán's assassination in August of that year, Gaviria was selected to be the presidential candidate of the Liberal Party. He was elected president of Colombia in 1990, with 47 percent of the votes.

Gaviria's election marked a generational and, to a lesser extent, an ideological shift in Colombian politics. He was the first of the post-VIOLENCIA generation to become president, elected with the support of a coalition of traditional Liberal Party bosses and the followers of the reform-minded Galán. Gaviria confronted the problems of narcotics-linked terrorism and a general lack of confidence in the political system with youthful energy and a neoliberal vision. He was the youngest elected president of Colombia in the twentieth century, and many of those who were appointed to serve in his government were younger than he. Continuing the process of reintegration of guerrilla groups into the political life of the country, which Gaviria had directed as a member of the administration of President Barco, he appointed M-16 leader Antonio NAVARRO WOLF to his cabinet.

Perhaps the crowning achievement of the Gaviria presidency was constitutional reform, the first since 1886, which modernized the state structure and the judicial system. The Constitution of 1991 was generally viewed as opening the political arena to more than the two traditional parties and as guaranteeing democratic participation. The Gaviria administration also promoted a more open economy, with an emphasis on privatization and deregulation. Trade barriers were lowered, regional economic integration (particularly with Venezuela) was supported, foreign investment was encouraged, labor legislation was modernized, and the role of private enterprise was emphasized. For these reasons and for Gaviria's cooperation in the effort to suppress the drug traffic, his administration was lauded by the U.S. government. By the end of his term, Gaviria was seen as an ''efficiency-seeking technocrat'' who had effectively initiated political and economic reforms that enabled Colombia to break out of the cycle of political and drug-related violence, slow economic growth, and political dissatisfaction that had characterized it in the 1980s.

In March 1994 Gaviria was elected to a five-year term as secretary general of the Organization of American States (OAS), and upon completion of his presidential term, in September 1994, he assumed that position.

DAVID BUSHNELL, *The Making of Modern Colombia: A Nation in Spite of Itself* (1993).

JAMES PATRICK KIERNAN

See also **Colombia: Constitutions.**

GAY, CLAUDIO (*b.* 1800, *d.* 1873), botanist, traveler, draftsman, whose research, drawings, and watercolors contributed to European knowledge of South America. Born in Draguignan, France, Gay lived for twelve years in Chile. Under the auspices of the Chilean government he traveled throughout the country between 1843 and 1851, studying and recording material for his *Historia física y política de Chile*. The results of his research were published in twenty-four volumes, with two accompanying volumes of lithographs, in 1854. Of a total 289 lithographs, 103 describe plant life and 134 are devoted to fauna. Published under the general title of *History*, the remaining illustrations recorded various trades, costumes, pastimes, *tertulias* (social gatherings), views of cities, gauchos, and customs of the Araucanian Indians. The lithographs were based on Gay's own sketches and on drawings by various artists, such as the renowned German traveler and painter Johann Moritz RUGENDAS.

The lithographic work was executed by Lehnert, Dupressoir, and Van Der Burch. Gay published several botanical studies of South America in European scientific journals. He died in France.

DIEGO BARROS ARANA, *Don Claudio Gay: Su vida y sus obras* (1876); DAWN ADES, *Art in Latin America: The Modern Era, 1820–1980* (1989), p. 68.

MARTA GARSD

GAZETA DE GUATEMALA, Guatemalan periodical published 1729–1731 and 1797–1816. First published on 1 November 1729, *La Gazeta de Guatemala* (The Guatemala Gazette) arose from a dispute between civil and religious authorities over the best way to confront piracy. It was the second periodical published in Latin America and the third on the American continent. The first was the *Boston News-Letter* in 1704 (which followed the 1690 single edition of *Publick Occurrences* in Boston). The second was *La Gazeta de México* in 1722. The first edition of *La Gazeta de Guatemala* consisted of a calendar of religious feasts, notices of arrivals of ships and merchandise, items about tribute-paying Indians who belonged to religious orders, and other news. It continued as a monthly until 1731.

The periodical began its second life on 13 February 1797, when the Spanish Bourbons were attempting to implement reforms in America. This time it published the views of groups advocating the reform of the colonial system, through which it made known the profound problems in the captaincy general of Guatemala. Its writers were prominent members of the Economic Society of Friends of the Country, an organization whose members espoused the reformist ideas of the period. This time *La Gazeta de Guatemala* was published weekly. It was widely distributed throughout Central America and beyond.

The paper's publication was suspended in 1816. It was followed by PEDRO MOLINA's *El Editor Constitucional* and José Cecilio del VALLE's *El Amigo de la Patria*, both in 1820. Thereafter a series of official newspapers were published under various titles, including *Gaceta del Gobierno, Boletín de Noticias, Boletín Oficial, El Tiempo, La Gaceta, Gaceta de Guatemala, El Guatemalteco*, and *Diario de Centroamérica*.

LEÓN DE GANDARIAS, ''Jornadas periodísticas,'' in *Etapas notables de la prensa guatemalteca* (1959); RIGOBERTO BRAN AZMITIA, *Panorama del periodismo guatemalteco y centroamericano* (1967); CARLOS C. HAEUSSLER YELA, *Diccionario general de Guatemala* (1983), vol. 3, pp. 1224–1231.

OSCAR G. PELÁEZ ALMENGOR

See also **Guatemala: Organizations; Journalism.**

GAZETA DE LIMA, Peruvian periodical of the mid-eighteenth century. The *Gazeta* (or *Gaceta*) *de Lima* was published on an irregular basis beginning in 1743 and continuing until the early nineteenth century. There were often about six issues a year. Initially the *Gazeta* contained reprints of material taken from European publications, especially the *Gazeta de Madrid*, but it also included some local news, such as appointments to office, the arrival and departure of ships at Callao, and deaths of local dignitaries. Beginning in 1793, it appeared as a government publication designed to present the official version of events in revolutionary France and Europe.

ELLA DUNBAR TEMPLE, *La Gaceta de Lima del siglo XVIII. Facsímiles de seis ejemplares raros de este periódico* (1965).

MARK A. BURKHOLDER

See also **Gazetas; Journalism.**

GAZETAS, newspapers published primarily from the 1760s on. Although the first *gazeta* appeared in New Spain in 1722 and a longer-lived successor lasted from 1728 to 1742, it was only in the late eighteenth century that these short newspapers, usually published on a biweekly or weekly basis, began to appear widely. Typically these later *gazetas* served as vehicles to present not only local news but also, and more important, enlightened thought and approaches to practical, everyday problems for the edification of their readers.

The best-known newspaper in Peru was the MERCURIO PERUANO, published from 1791 to 1795 as the expression of a group of self-styled "enlightened" intellectuals. Through the *Mercurio,* the supporters of progress tried to provide Peruvians with "useful knowledge" of their region and information relevant to their daily lives. Thus it published articles that, among other things, advocated burial outside churches for reasons of health, supported more efficient mining techniques, and analyzed the viceroyalty's commerce.

As in Peru, periodicals reached a broader audience in New Spain than did formal schooling. The foremost Mexican publicist was the cleric José Antonio ALZATE Y RAMÍREZ (1729–1799), an enlightened advocate of scientific knowledge and its application to contemporary problems. His *Gaceta de literatura de México* (1788–1795) provided a stream of informative articles on medicine, applied science, agronomy, and a host of other scientific topics. A daily paper, *Diario de México,* originally edited by Carlos María BUSTAMANTE, appeared from 1805 to 1817.

In Guatemala the *Gazeta de Guatemala* (whose modern series began in 1797) reflected the curiosity of intellectuals in Guatemala City at the time. Published by Ignacio Beteta, the *Gazeta* sought to provide "useful knowledge" through articles on the economy, medicine, and commerce, and campaigned vigorously to end Latin's sway as the language of university instruction.

Newspapers also appeared in Havana, Bogotá, and Buenos Aires prior to 1808. After that date, the number of publications increased rapidly.

BAILEY W. DIFFIE, *Latin-American Civilization: Colonial Period* (1945; repr. 1967), pp. 553–561; JOHN TATE LANNING, *The Eighteenth-Century Enlightenment in the University of San Carlos de Guatemala* (1956), esp. pp. 83–91.

MARK A. BURKHOLDER

See also **Journalism.**

GÊ (also Jê), the name of linguistically and culturally related Amerindian peoples located in what is now central and southern Brazil. Gê is one of the principal language families of native lowland South America. Based on linguistic affiliation, Gê peoples are divided into northern, central, and southern branches, which are the three branches of the Gê linguistic family. Varying degrees of mutual intelligibility obtain among speakers of the languages of any given branch; there is, however, little or no mutual intelligibility between speakers of different branches. The Northern Gê consist of the Eastern Timbira (Apaniekra, Ramkokamekra, Krĩkatí, and Krahó), Western Timbira (Apinayé), Kayapó (Gorotire, Xikrin, Kokraimôro, Kubenkrankegn, Kubenkrangnoti, Mekrangnoti, Txukamhamãe), and Suyá groups. The Shavante and Sherente peoples make up the central branch, and the Shokleng and Kaingang groups form the southern branch. Linguists also consider the Gê languages to be related to a wider network of lowland Amerindian languages and families known as Macro-Gê, which includes, among others, Maxacalí, Botocudo, Karajá, Fulniô, and possibly even TUPÍ. Today, the Gê groups span a large area stretching from the states of Maranhão and Pará in the north to the southern state of Santa Catarina.

Although reports of what appear to be Gê-speaking peoples date from the mid-seventeenth century, and eighteenth-century colonial records that document *aldeiamentos* (settlements) of Gê-speaking groups, little was known of the Gê until the middle of the present century. The linguistic and cultural similarities of the various geographically dispersed Gê peoples were only formally recognized in 1867, when Karl von Martius named the family in his preliminary classification of the peoples and languages of central Brazil. The first descriptive accounts of Gê peoples did not, however, appear until the 1940s, when Curt NIMUENDAJÚ published his ethnographic accounts of the Apinayé (1939), the Sherente (1942), and the Eastern Timbira (1946). During this same period the Salesian missionaries Antonio Colbacchini and Caesar Albisetti published their monograph of the neighboring Bororo (1942). Their descriptions detail many aspects of a people who, despite significant differences, share many similarities with the Gê. The relationship between the Gê and Bororo continues to baffle specialists to the present day.

Although the Gê and Bororo had previously been classified by Julian Steward (1946) as marginal peoples, a category characterized by rudimentary technology and simple patterns of social organization (defined, in fact, in terms of traits they were reported to lack), both Nimuendajú's accounts and that of the Salesians depict societies possessing simple technologies yet characterized by extremely complex social systems. These descriptions presented social theorists with an apparent anomaly: How did peoples with such rudimentary technologies have such complex patterns of social organization?

Discarding speculations that attempt to explain the paradox by suggesting that the Gê and Bororo are the degenerate remnants of some higher civilization or that the reported complex social divisions are simply native mystifications, a group of scholars led by David Maybury-Lewis set out to unravel the puzzles of central Brazilian social organization through further ethnographic study within a comparative framework. This ambitious effort, known as the Harvard Central Brazil Project, has revised anthropological thinking concerning the basis of social organization among Gê and Bororo societies. Because a hypothesis pertaining to any one of the groups can be tested in other closely related societies, Gê peoples continue to be particularly appealing for the study of comparative social behavior. Subsequent studies have broadened the comparative picture along various dimensions, including material and expressive culture, and have contributed to knowledge of the Gê.

In the 1990s many Gê peoples are actively involved in struggles to preserve their lands and cultural traditions. For example, the Kayapó are actively fighting against a series of proposed dams that, if completed, will inundate lands they traditionally inhabit. The Shavante and others are seeking to achieve economic independence from FUNAI. All the Gê are bent on preserving their heritage, thereby continuing a theme that has distinguished them since colonial times.

IRVINE DAVIS, "Comparative Jê Phonology," *Estudos Lingüisticos* 1, no. 2 (1966): 10–24, and "Some Macro-Jê relationships," *International Journal of American Linguistics* 34 (1968): 42–47; DAVID MAYBURY-LEWIS, *Dialectical Societies: The Gê and Bororo of Central Brazil* (1979), pp. ix–13.

LAURA GRAHAM

See also **Indians.**

GEFFRARD, FABRE NICOLAS (*b.* 1803; *d.* 31 December 1878), Haitian general and president (1859–1867). Geffrard rose to the rank of general under Emperor Faustin SOULOUQUE (1785–1867). He was one of the few to emerge with credit from Soulouque's disastrous last invasion of the Dominican Republic (1856). As head of the army, Geffrard led a revolt against Soulouque in 1858 and restored the republican constitution. He became president the following year and sought to improve Haiti's international image, which had deteriorated under Soulouque's harsh and nationalistic regime. He signed a concordat with the Holy See in 1860,

and he obtained U.S. recognition of the Haitian state in 1862. President Abraham Lincoln and Congress had proposed settling U.S. blacks in Haiti, but in spite of some cooperation from Geffrard, the scheme failed.

Internally, Geffrard favored the Catholic church and attacked VODUN, which had grown under Soulouque. He also favored the mulatto class, which had suffered under the regimes since 1844. Early in his term he attempted to install a more open and less authoritarian government, but assassination attempts against him and his family and a revolt led by Sylvain SALNAVE (1827–1870) at Cap Haïtien in 1865 pushed him to the familiar pattern of repression and executions. Geffrard was overthrown by Salnave in 1867, and he left for exile in Jamaica, where he died.

MURDO J. MACLEOD

GEGO (Gertrude Goldschmidt; *b.* 1 August 1912; *d.* 17 September 1994), Venezuelan artist. Trained as an architect, Gego emigrated to Venezuela from her native Germany in 1939. In the latter half of the 1950s, she began to create a geometric sculpture that explored perceptual aspects of planes and volumes. She taught at the Universidad Central de Venezuela from 1958 to 1967 and at the Instituto Nacional de Cooperación Educativa (INCE) from 1964 to 1977. Gego is best known for her innovative abstract works that extend a systematic approach to three-dimensional art into a poetic ineffability. Her *Reticuláreas* (1969), for example, comprise webs of wire segments that have been hooked together and hung from the ceiling; filling a room, the *Reticuláreas* confront the viewer with a quasi-geometric and semimobile linear articulation of space. Gego's architectural projects have included sculptures at the Banco Industrial de Venezuela, Caracas, in 1962 and (in collaboration with her husband, Gerd Leufert) on the facades of the Sede del INCE in 1969. Her one-woman exhibitions include those in Caracas at the Museo de Bellas Artes in 1961, 1964, 1968, 1969, and 1984; at the Museo de Arte Contemporáneo in 1977; and at the Galería de Arte Nacional in 1982. Gego died in Caracas.

HANNI OSSOTT, *Gego* (1977); MARTA TRABA, *Gego* (1977); RUTH AUERBACH, *Gego: Entre la estructura y el objeto* (1988).

JOSEPH R. WOLIN

GEISEL, ERNESTO (*b.* 3 August 1908), president of Brazil (1974–1979). A career army officer of German Protestant parentage from Rio Grande do Sul, Geisel entered the army on 31 March 1925. After graduating from the military college of Realengo in Rio de Janeiro, he served with the BRAZILIAN EXPEDITIONARY FORCE (FEB) during World War II. He attended the U.S. Army Command and General Staff College at Fort Leavenworth, Kansas, and went on to fill various command and general staff positions. As a colonel he directed the

Brazilian National Petroleum (Petrobrás) Refinery at Cubatão, São Paulo, in 1955–1956, and the next year he joined the National Petroleum Council. After his promotion to general on 25 March 1961, he served a series of military presidents as chief of military household (1964–1967), minister of the superior military tribunal (1967–1969), and president of Petrobrás (1969–1973).

Geisel's presidential candidacy was initiated by the military high command (his brother, Orlando, held the post of army minister from 1969 to 1974), confirmed by the National Renovating Alliance (Arena), the government party, and certified by 400 out of 503 members of the electoral college. Once inaugurated (March 1974), Geisel was confronted with the collapse of the "ECONOMIC MIRACLE," brought on by the oil crisis of 1973. His administration launched a series of petroleum-substitution plans, including hydroelectric projects such as Itaipú and gasohol refineries to convert sugar to fuel. His initial efforts to come to terms with socially active elements of the Catholic church failed, but tentative attempts at relaxation (DISTENSÃO) of the political process restricted after the 1964 coup were evident by the end of his term.

Also taking place during the Geisel years was the end of the "unwritten alliance" between the United States and Brazil that had endured for three quarters of a century. The U.S. defeat in Southeast Asia, Cuban military intervention in Angola, Communist involvement in Mozambique, U.S.–USSR détente, and U.S. economic decline were capped by U.S. allegations of human-rights abuses. Geisel responded by canceling the defense agreement with the United States and redirecting Brazilian foreign policy to encompass more productive partners who were also interested in containing Soviet expansion. These included Japan, West Germany, and, briefly, Iran, along with the outcast quartet of South Korea, Taiwan, Israel, and South Africa. Investments from these members of the New Inter-Oceanic Alliance were encouraged. Concurrently, Brazil launched a cultural and commercial campaign in Lusophone Africa—Angola, Mozambique, and Guinea-Bissau—then proceeded to initiate development (since canceled) of its own nuclear weapons under Project Solimões (1977–1991).

Geisel's efforts at a democratic opening domestically (ABERTURA) and reorientation in foreign policy precipitated a crisis in the hard-line military that was not resolved by the closure of congress in April 1977. It resurfaced in October 1977, when Geisel fired army minister General Sélvio Frota and other officers who contested the new directions.

As his successor Geisel selected General João Baptista FIGUEIREDO, who promised to proceed with the democratic opening up of the country. After retiring from public office on 15 March 1979, Geisel dedicated himself to private entrepreneurial activities.

WILLIAM PERRY, *Contemporary Brazilian Foreign Policy: The International Strategy of an Emerging Power* (1976); RIORDAN ROETT, ed., *Brazil in the Seventies* (1976); WALDER DE GOES, *O Brasil do General Geisel* (1978); JAN KNIPPERS BLACK, "The Military and Political Decompression in Brazil," in *Armed Forces and Society* 6, no. 4 (1980): 625–637; ROBERT LEVINE, "Brazil: Democracy Without Adjective," in *Current History* 78 (1980): 49–52.

LEWIS A. TAMBS

GELLY, JUAN ANDRÉS (*b.* 1790; *d.* 1856), Paraguayan diplomat and author. Born in Asunción, Gelly left at an early age to complete his education at the Real Colegio de San Carlos in Buenos Aires. After the Platine states gained their independence, he became involved in the Argentine civil wars as a partisan of Manuel Dorrego and the Unitario Party. With the defeat of that party in the late 1820s, Gelly left Argentina. Instead of returning to Paraguay, where the dictator José Gaspar Rodríguez de FRANCIA had already persecuted his family, Gelly went to Montevideo to continue his legal studies. He soon became a well-known figure in expatriate circles.

Gelly made his way back to Paraguay after Francia's death in 1840. Overcoming his initial suspicion of Gelly's intentions, President Carlos Antonio LÓPEZ decided to call him into government service. Gelly's considerable experience in Uruguayan journalism made him an obvious choice for editor of the new state newspaper *El Paraguayo Independiente*.

In 1846 Gelly was dispatched to Rio de Janeiro to negotiate a boundary and trade agreement with the Brazilian Empire. Though this agreement was stillborn, he remained in Brazil as agent and publicist for the Paraguayan government. During his stay, he wrote a laudatory account of Paraguay's progress under López, entitled *El Paraguay, lo que fue, lo que es, y lo que será* (1848). Acting as delegation secretary, he later accompanied the president's son, Francisco Solano López, on a mission to Europe (1853–1854). He died in Asunción two years later.

R. ANTONIO RAMOS, *Juan Andrés Gelly* (1972); CARLOS ZUBIZARRETA, *Cien vidas paraguayas*, 2d ed. (1985), pp. 139–140.

THOMAS L. WHIGHAM

GELLY Y OBES, JUAN ANDRÉS (*b.* 20 May 1815; *d.* 19 September 1904), Argentine general. Born in Buenos Aires, Gelly y Obes took exile in Montevideo with the rest of his family during the dictatorship of Juan Manuel de ROSAS. In 1839 he joined the UNITARIO forces fighting against Rosas. Returning to Argentina after the fall of Rosas, he held both military and political offices in the separatist government of Buenos Aires Province and in 1861 became minister of war for a united Argentina in the cabinet of Bartolomé MITRE. He became chief of staff of the Argentine army of operations during the WAR OF THE TRIPLE ALLIANCE as well as personally taking part in many of the battles.

After the war Gelly y Obes fought against rebellious *caudillos* of the interior, yet took part himself in Mitre's unsuccessful 1874 uprising and in the porteño rebellion of 1880 over the federalization of Buenos Aires. He continued to hold various political and military positions until his death.

ARTURO CAPDEVILA, ed., *Vidas de grandes argentinos*, vol. 2 (1966), pp. 9–12; JOSÉ S. CAMPOBASSI, *Mitre y su época* (1980).

DAVID BUSHNELL

See also **Argentina: Revolutionary Movements.**

GELVES, MARQUÉS DE (Diego Carrillo de Mendoza y Pimentel; *b.* 1500s; *d.* 1600s), fourteenth viceroy of New Spain (1621–1624). The Gelves administration is an excellent example of the limitations of colonial reform in the seventeenth century. Gelves arrived in Mexico under orders to improve government efficiency, crack down on the widespread corruption in public administration, and increase tax revenue. He enjoyed some success, particularly in the last endeavor. But he also managed to offend nearly every important sector of colonial society, partly because of his high-handed and autocratic manner and partly because his reforms threatened the financial interests of merchants, the creole elite, and many government officials.

The viceroy's most serious feud, however, was with the equally proud and unbending archbishop of Mexico, Juan Pérez de la Serna. Their dispute quickly evolved into a contest between civil and ecclesiastical authority. Pérez de la Serna excommunicated Gelves; Gelves exiled the archbishop. En route to the coast, the archbishop placed Mexico City under interdict, which was to begin on the morning of 15 January 1624. The populace, already angry at the viceroy over high maize prices, sided with the archbishop. A riot broke out in the central plaza, and soon a crowd of some thirty thousand was shouting for the viceroy's blood. The rioters stormed the palace, but Gelves escaped, disguised in servant's clothing, and fled to the Monastery of San Francisco. The *audiencia,* claiming that Gelves had abandoned his post, assumed viceregal authority. Although the crown briefly reinstated Gelves before replacing him, the marqués was in effect the first Mexican viceroy overthrown in a popular revolt.

CHESTER L. GUTHRIE, ''Riots in Seventeenth-Century Mexico City: A Study of Social and Economic Conditions,'' in *Greater America: Essays in Honor of Herbert Eugene Bolton* (1945), pp. 243–258; JONATHAN I. ISRAEL, *Race, Class, and Politics in Colonial Mexico, 1610–1670* (1975); RICHARD E. BOYER, ''Mexico in the Seventeenth Century: Transition of a Colonial Society,'' in *Hispanic American History Review* 57, no. 3 (1977): 455–478.

R. DOUGLAS COPE

GEMS AND GEMSTONES have been important to both the early development and the present-day economy in several key areas of South America. Brazil now has the leading gemstone industry in Latin America, including mining, cutting, polishing, setting, marketing, and exporting.

EMERALDS

Archaeological discoveries in Colombia have revealed the use of emeralds in pre-Columbian jewelry. Early accounts of the ceremonies that took place at Lake Guatavita, high in the Andes Mountains of Colombia, describe the use of both gold and emeralds as offerings thrown into the sacred lake. Soon after the arrival of the Spanish CONQUISTADORES, emeralds were being traded as far north as Mexico and as far south as Chile. Emeralds were soon discovered in the areas of Muzo and Chivor, located north and northeast of Bogotá. Chivor was particularly well known to the early Spaniards, who employed thousands of local Indians as slave labor. In the early seventeenth century, word of the brutal working conditions at Chivor resulted in both royal and papal decrees prohibiting the use of Indian slave labor, and the mines were forced to close. Both Muzo and Chivor have had a violent and checkered history since colonial times. Both mines are known to produce among the finest emeralds in the world, yet the mines have rarely been worked at a profit. In the 1970s, however, the government opened Muzo to private mining ventures, the operations of which have been relatively successful. Chivor remains less developed. Both areas retain an unfortunate reputation for violence because of anarchy among the independent miners. In 1976, an estimated 50,000 people were killed. Economic statistics are difficult to maintain, largely because of significant production from the independent miners, (*guaqueros*) of the area. It is certain, however, that emeralds are a very important part of the Colombian economy.

Today, Colombian emeralds can be seen in the crown jewels of the world as well as in the finest jewelry stores. Particularly important historic collections of Colombian emeralds are among the treasures of the Topkapi Museum in Istanbul, Turkey, and in the crown jewels of Iran. Many of these fine, historic emeralds made their way around the world. In the late sixteenth century, the Spanish brought back from the New World large quantities of emeralds, with which they reportedly flooded the emerald markets in Europe. Europeans, in turn, found a willing market with the Mogul rulers of India. The Moguls were particularly fond of carving large gems and attaching them to clothing. In 1739, however, invading Persian armies sacked the Mogul treasuries of Delhi and brought enormous quantities of emeralds back to the Middle East, where many remain today. Additional deposits of emeralds were discovered in Brazil in the 1960s, and are currently mined in Goiás and Bahia.

DIAMONDS

Diamonds became an important part of the Brazilian economy in the mid-eighteenth century, after they were discovered in the river gravels around the town of Diamantina in the state of Minas Gerais in 1725. The world's production had previously come from the famous mines around Golconda in India. By the eighteenth century, however, these Indian mines were nearing depletion. The discovery of the Brazilian deposits shifted world attention on Brazil. The Portuguese explorer Sebastino Leme do Prado, who had previously lived in India, is credited with the first identification of diamonds in Brazil. It is reported that the diamonds were being used by local gold miners as chips in card games. These "chips" were sent off to Amsterdam for appraisal and the diamond-bearing area was immediately declared crown property. In its height of production in 1851, as many as 300,000 carats were mined annually from the Diamantina area as well as from a new find in the state of Bahia. The diamonds were recovered from the alluvial river gravels solely by panning. Gold commonly accompanied the diamonds. Several important diamonds were recovered from these river gravels, including the 726.6-carat Presidente Vargas Diamond, which was discovered in 1938.

By the 1880s, however, Brazil could not keep up with the world demand for diamonds. At the same time, the huge diamond deposits of southern Africa were discovered, and attention shifted away from Brazil. There is no doubt that diamonds had a significant impact on the Brazilian economy of the late eighteenth and early nineteenth centuries. Today, huge dredges still mine the gravels around Diamantina for gold and diamonds, although on a world scale, production is insignificant.

OTHER GEMS

No other gem materials could be considered of importance until the outbreak of World War II. The great demand for "strategic" minerals such as quartz and tourmaline prompted a massive exploration program throughout South America. Success, however, was focused on the state of Minas Gerais in Brazil. Minas Gerais is rich in granite geologic formations known as pegmatites. These pegmatites are sometimes called "nature's jewel box" because of the vast array of gemstones that they may contain. In addition to the strategically important quartz and tourmaline, pegmatites are home to topaz, aquamarine and morganite beryl, kunzite, and many different species of garnet. While most of these gems were overlooked in favor of the relatively more important strategic minerals for the war effort, the end of the war brought on massive gem-mining programs. Today, the majority of the world's supply of quartz, tourmaline, topaz, garnet, kunzite, and beryl come from Brazil.

Other areas of South America that can be considered of importance to today's gem market, but that have had little if any importance historically, include the great agate and amethyst deposits near Artigas, Uruguay, and bordering Rio Grande do Sul, Brazil. Huge quantities are mined from the basaltic lava flows to supply the gem markets around the world. Amethyst is also mined in Minas Gerais and Bahia. Opals that rival those from Australia come from Piauí, Brazil. Argentina is known for small quantities of "stalactitic" rhodochrosite, sometimes known as "Inca Rose." Venezuela is a minor producer of diamonds, and Chile of lapis lazuli.

Central America has produced a limited variety of gem materials historically, though some have been recovered in significant amounts. Most notable are the jade deposits near the Palmilla River in Guatemala, which were worked in pre-Columbian times. Artifacts made of jade from this region have surfaced throughout Mexico to the north and into Colombia to the south. In recent times, the Dominican Republic has supplied a good portion of the world's amber market.

Mexico has produced significant supplies of opal. This opal tends to have an orange body color with or without fire, or play of color. It can also be red and is sometimes called fire opal. Fire opals have been produced only since the late nineteenth century, although they may have been known to the Aztecs. Most of the opals come from the mines near Querétaro.

s. h. ball, "Historical Notes on Gem Mining," in *Economic Geology* 26 (1931): 681–738; peter w. rainier, *Green Fire* (1942); r. maillard, *Diamonds: Myth, Magic, and Reality* (1980); peter c. keller, "Emeralds of Colombia," in *Gems and Gemology* 17 (1981): 80–92; k. proctor, "Gem Pegmatites of Minas Gerais, Brazil," in *Gems and Gemology* 20 (1984): 78–100.

Peter C. Keller

GENDER AND SEXUALITY. In Latin America gender-laden terms designated the social worth and status of women and men. *Hembrismo, machismo, marianismo, feminismo,* and *patria potestad* describe and prescribe gender relations. As *hembra,* for example, women are identified by their biological nature and reproductive capacity. *Hembrismo* implies that women are physically vulnerable, pregnancy proves the virility of men, and sex is the medium of communication and the functional link between women and men.

Machismo is a convention that affords men respect and power. Manliness is measured by men's ability to head traditional families, produce children, protect the virginity of female relatives, and defend against other men. The *machista* is brave, forceful, insubordinate, and sexually aggressive but never sensitive. To display soft or effeminate traits invites ridicule or harassment for homosexual behavior.

Women are, then, both objects and proof of men's power and authority. Yet female purity, *marianismo,* arrogates to women moral superiority that men cannot attain. Wives and mothers are expected to suffer the sexual infidelities of their husbands, and for their pain they earn respect from their communities. Their families, and especially their sons, esteem their chastity and emotional restraint. *Maternidad,* or motherhood, is essential to women's public and private images. With the Virgin Mary, the mother of Christ, as their symbol of perfect womanhood, faithful, all-suffering women may gain a modicum of power as men's moral superiors. These traditional patterns are changing in urban Latin America.

Under the *patria potestad*, men/fathers have power over females in their family. Brought to Spain by the Romans, the *patria potestad* laws of the thirteenth-century were codified in the SIETE PARTIDAS, introduced to the American colonies and adapted to local circumstances in the RECOPILACIÓN DE LEYES DE LAS INDIAS of 1681, and conservatively reformed in the Spanish Napoleonic Code. These laws deemed men responsible for the economic survival of the family unit and the civil authority over all family members. Within the church family, men were religious leaders whose authority over moral covenants and institutionalized belief systems enshrined a patriarchal faith. Empowered by both civil and canon law, men arrogated to themselves all formal positions of authority, and they created laws and sanctions to protect and preserve a patriarchal social order.

Traditionally women's places were within the home, where their primary functions were to have children and to ensure the survival of the young. Prescriptive separate spheres, male domination, and homophobic attitudes notwithstanding, gender roles have always been complex and transitional. Attitudes set by an aggressive, masculine Iberian conquest of the region, by tenets of Roman Catholicism, and by Amerindian and African cultures have been challenged by survival needs. From the colonial period onward, widows and spinsters have acquired and maintained wealth and sought their own liberation. Only marriage, not gender per se, limited women's legal authority. In the modern period, technology has allowed women and men to control the sizes of families, to share in the financial support of the family unit, and to compete in politics and work. While it is unclear whether the power of patriarchy has been affected significantly over time, it is certain that new theories of government, industrial work structures, individual rights, sexuality consciousness, and modern gender standards have offered alternatives to old social and gender orderings.

COLONIALIZATION (1492–1810)
Outnumbered by millions, Iberians of necessity carried out conquest and domination by brute force and absolute authority. Upon contact, Iberian men formed legitimate and illegitimate unions with native women. Both the church and crown encouraged sanctioned marriage, but Iberian obsession with *pureza de sangre* (racial purity) caused the crown to accept unsanctioned unions between Iberians and Indians. The church, however, faithfully defended marriage, even between people of different racial backgrounds. At the Council of Trent (1545–1563), the church passed legislation regularizing marital union and imposed European standards of Catholic morality on citizens of the New World.

Initially Spaniards married Indian women, but by 1550 they preferred marriage with immigrant Spanish women and concubinage with women of color. To arrest legal interbreeding among people of different races and social status, the crown in 1728 decreed that men in the military, members of nobility, and bureaucrats needed official permission to marry people outside their class and caste. In 1778, the church, too, limited mixed marriages in the Real Pragmática, giving parents the right to guide their children in the selection of mates. Beginning in 1805, interracial marriages could take place only with the dispensation of civil authorities. Despite concern with *pureza de sangre*, MESTIZOS—often the issuance of unsanctioned unions—outnumbered Iberians and creoles. Their social positions, however, were ambiguous, since they were neither Indian nor Iberian.

SLAVERY, too, had a sexual dimension that reflected the dominance of the Iberian. Almost immediately, Spaniards and Portuguese traders brought Africans to the Americas to work on sugar plantations. In Brazil and the Caribbean, black men toiled and died, many without marrying. African women worked in homes as well as in fields, and they were prey to sexual advances of Iberian males. Like Indian women, they could not expect to marry their Iberian masters, but they might attain improved living standards for themselves and their offspring, though even that was not guaranteed. The African male was powerless to protect the women of his race, and thus slavery also meant sexual domination of African women and the emasculation of African men.

From sexual associations formed during the Conquest came the predominant social customs. Iberians dominated Indians and Africans, powerful men could be sexually aggressive and promiscuous, Iberian blood was preferred, mestizos and mulattoes composed a new race that was despised, and women of all races assumed a subordinate status to Iberian men and to men within their own classes and castes.

Religious rituals reinforced, instructed, and prescribed behavior and beliefs associated with gender roles. Catholic conversion of non-Europeans, an essential aspect of conquest and colonization, suppressed and subsumed Indian and African polytheisms, rendering them undercurrents and folkways in a prevailing Catholic society. Church ritual and advice from the confessional box taught parishioners chastity and monogamy. At the Council of Trent, the church took moral issue with free and unsanctioned unions common to some Indian communities and practiced by Iberian colonists, despite church disapproval. At stake was preserving women's virginity until marriage. Those who deviated from church dictates were branded sinners. Furthermore, instruction in proper sexual conduct became a means of acculturating Indians and Africans to Iberian culture, since sex, marriage, and cultural mingling fell under the jurisdiction of the church.

Unlike Catholicism, practical Indian and African beliefs resolved everyday gender problems such as impotence, unfaithfulness, attracting a love partner, and unwanted pregnancies. Catholic discouragement of folk religions came in the form of persecuting offenders before inquisitional tribunals. The persistence of these belief systems suggests that SANTERÍA, VOODOO, CANDOMBLÉ, and Indian *curanderas* (healers) allowed people to assert control over their sexuality. Since women more than men practiced witchcraft, it might also be assumed that women sought surreptitious ways of protecting their sex from domination by men, the church, and the state.

Class and caste created deep divisions between people of the same gender, divisions that may have been more important than the cleavage between women and men. Spanish and creole women, for example, tended to marry later, have fewer children, and work within the home more often than Indian or mestizo women. They also remained single and did not remarry when widowed with the same frequency as lower-class women of color did. Upper-class white women, when they worked, managed properties or loaned money. But for the most part, women clustered more at the unskilled-service levels, although some few Spanish and creole women were moneylenders and estate managers. The remaining professions were left for women of color in the lower classes, who worked in the cottage textile industry and as domestics, street vendors, pieceworkers, midwives, healers, prostitutes, and slaves.

Men, too, had careers, professions, or jobs according to their social status, but they reached professional levels women could never attain. Mestizo and mulatto men were artisans and skilled laborers, even teachers. Indian and black men were unskilled and skilled laborers, farmers, and slaves.

The power of the patriarch extended to nearly all aspects of life, but it was curtailed somewhat in convents. Though priests confessed the nuns and saw to their religious purity, in some convents nuns such as Sor JUANA INÉS DE LA CRUZ studied and wrote. Convents not only shielded women from worldly realities, they also served as lending institutions. In Brazil, for example, entering novices paid a dowry, which the convent invested. Families contributing dowries could borrow money as long as their relative remained in the nunnery. Asunción Lavrin reminds us, however, that most nuns were pious women who devoted their lives to poverty, charity, chastity, and prayer. Though their associations with men differed from those of women outside the convent, their vows were not an attempt at liberation from patriarchal rule, for they were ultimately subordinates in a patriarchal faith.

The BOURBON REFORMS (1764–1804) placed particular emphasis upon efficient, systematic production and introduced new governmental agencies and scientific procedures to extract New World wealth. Imposed Bourbon trade regulations threatened some of the cottage industries, such as textile production, which had been run by women. The reforms also created new opportunities in teaching for women.

The Bourbon Reforms notwithstanding, the century

of enlightenment in Latin America left most women with limited work opportunities and divided along class and caste lines. Only women of the well-to-do classes were no longer cloistered and condemned to lives of idleness in the same numbers as before. But all women benefited from an enhanced notion of motherhood: they were viewed as fundamental conduits of modern values to their children and as leaders in philanthropy, which gave their historic private occupations a public importance.

GENDER ASSOCIATIONS IN THE NINETEENTH CENTURY
Napoleon Bonaparte's removal of the Spanish kings (1808) provoked wars of independence beginning in 1810. Women of all classes were affected by war, with many fleeing—some in carriages and others on foot—before advancing armies. Before it was all over, gender lines had blurred, as the focus on victory overcame the restrictions of sex. Left to survive outside the walls of their homes and spurred on by their devotion to the men in their families and to ideals of national independence, women served as soldiers, conspirators, nurses, arms smugglers, writers, and money solicitors. In most countries, especially after independence had been won early in the nineteenth century, women's efforts were all but forgotten in societies insensitive to gender inequities. An exception to this rule was Cuba (independent in 1898), where women's contributions were legendary and served to drive men to equal their sacrifices. José MARTÍ remarked about *mambisa* bravery, "With women such as these, it is easy to be heroes."

Independence pitted ideals of greater individual freedom, federalist government, the separation of church and state, and laissez-faire capitalism against the more familiar corporate state with community allegiance, central government, the union of church and government, and a controlled economy. Nineteenth-century leaders fought civil wars over rules of government and over national boundaries. Women moved with the troops as soldiers, cooks, and nurses, and they entered professions vacated by men. Destruction caused economic decline in agriculture but opened up work in light industry for both women and men. Economic and political instability forced women into new roles, and as that happened, nationalism and motherhood became inextricably intertwined. Mothers sacrificing themselves and their children for independence became a symbol of militant patriotism.

The end of the nineteenth century brought relative peace, but as the troops returned, men replaced women at work. Decades of struggle toward modern statehood made some women want to redefine gender roles. In some countries, male politicians modernized legal codes, which subsequently opened the way for demands that democratic rights be extended to all citizens, including women and men from the dominated classes. Educated women from the elite and professional classes came forward with petitions for suffrage, equal education, and new civil legislation. In a few instances, such as in the Tobacco Stemmers' Guild in Cuba, working women organized in unions and guilds for protective legislation and equal rights. These early reform efforts, which were rooted in nineteenth-century liberal notions of democracy, universal suffrage, and scientific government fueled the nascent labor movement.

GENDER ASSOCIATIONS IN THE TWENTIETH CENTURY
The twentieth century brought ideals of class struggle that involved women and men in revolutionary, sometimes Marxist, movements against old forms of rule. In the nineteenth century, new values and nascent capitalism emphasized individualism. The closed family unit opened to the public as women and children became wage earners and members of the informal labor force. Women organized reform movements that focused on political authority, legal reforms, and access to education and jobs.

The promise of prosperity and order did not materialize for most Latin Americans. Women and men were pushed off the land. Men migrated from farm to city in search of work, often leaving women unwed mothers and heads of impoverished households. Women migrated, too, leaving their families behind and finding work primarily as domestic servants or prostitutes in urban centers.

Between 1880 and 1940 social activists, both feminist and Marxist, rallied to defend the poor. In Chile, Argentina, Uruguay, Brazil, and Cuba, women's movements formed and demanded new rights and protection for women and children. These early women's groups grew out of nineteenth-century philanthropic associations, but they broadened their goals by viewing patriarchy as an impediment to female self-determination. Yet these early activists were slow to attack *machismo* directly as the root of repression. Instead, Latin Americans attempted to empower women as mothers and as the creators of a new social order based on moral responsibility. When forced to confront misogyny, they chided men and even objected to men's right to kill adulterous wives, to commit adultery with impunity, and to ignore their illegitimate children.

That Latin American feminists were loath to confront total and arbitrary male authority could imply female weakness and the absence of committed feminism. It is also explained by the multiple fronts where issues of social justice were addressed. They joined revolutionary movements that opposed illegitimate governments, repressive police action, foreign intervention, poverty, and social injustice. Thus, women sided with men when men fought for changing the social order, and they were against men when men repressed women. They were never purely feminists in the U.S. sense.

Early women's organizations were diverse, some seeking only suffrage, others general social reform, and still others socialist feminism. Conservative women activists, such as members of the LIGA PATRIÓTICA in Ar-

gentina, supported liberal reforms for women in their quest to shore up power for the Conservative Party. Moderates formed the majority in the feminist movement. They approved of extensive social and labor reforms under a capitalist regime. Cuba, Brazil, and Argentina were the three countries with strong socialist feminist groups whose members, unlike other feminists, looked to political centralization and community guarantees, not autonomy and individual rights, to aid poor women. As a result of women's activism, nations passed progressive legislation that improved gender equity. Ecuador granted women suffrage in 1929, and by 1933 Uruguay, Brazil, and Cuba had followed. Surprisingly Argentina and Mexico, two nations where women had organized early, did not grant voting rights to women until 1947 and 1953, respectively.

To men, women's liberation was only a minor side effect of a larger effort to establish a new ruling order. The outcome of this effort was progressive labor, penal, and civil laws in Argentina, Chile, Uruguay, Brazil, and Cuba that granted women divorce rights, labor protection and equality, maternity codes, and civil equality. Some of these reforms granted individual women authority and independence vis à vis individual men, but ultimately authority lay with the state.

Latin American women joined international feminist movements as early as 1889. At the 1928 Pan-American Union (PAU) meeting in Havana, Cuban feminists from a variety of organizations marched with Doris Stevens and the U.S. National Women's Party, spoke at special meetings, and succeeded in forming the Inter-American Commission on Women within the PAU to oversee women's rights throughout the hemisphere. This was the first international feminist organization, out of a spirit of Pan-Americanism. This effort did not, however, draw support from socialist feminists who viewed North American involvement as another form of imperialism.

From 1940 to 1960, rebelliousness in Latin America either languished or was suppressed by dictatorships. With the Cuban Revolution of 1959, however, social nationalism sent rebels to arms to challenge internal colonialism and U.S. hegemony. Women, confident of their place in a new socialist world, fought alongside men. Many, however, were disenchanted by the unliberated attitudes of their *compañeros,* who, on the personal level, relegated them to secondary positions within the movement and dominated them sexually. Neofeminists, convinced by national revolution as well as by notions of gender equality coming from the radical feminist movement in the United States, inspired Latin American women to restate their own principles of liberation. The tone of Latin American feminism became more militant than forty years earlier. Activists attacked the patriarchy directly but resisted lesbian feminism, which they associated with the North American movement. Latin American feminists sought ways to organize the poor, and to explain violence and sexual harassment. Theorists began

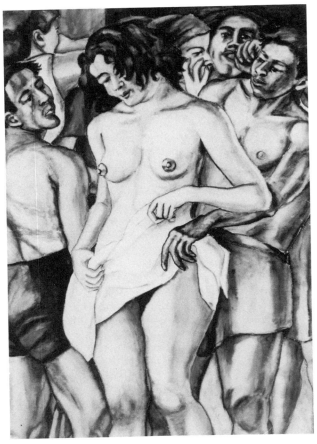

Frine o Trata de Blancas. Watercolor by Debra Arango, ca. 1942–1944. MUSEO DE ARTE MODERNO DE MEDELLÍN; PHOTO BY CARLOS TOBON.

deconstructing the language as a root cause of exaggerated gender separation and evaluation.

The split between North American and Latin American feminists was clearly articulated at the United Nations International Women's Year meeting in Mexico City in 1975. Mexican feminists, in particular, decried the irrelevance of the U.S. movement for Latin American women. They accused North Americans of concentrating on legal equality, redefinitions of gender, sexuality, political power, and birth control when Latin American women were intent on rescuing their families from poverty, military repression, and lack of economic development. Subsequently, many economic development projects in Latin America contained components for women, and in time notions of appropriate technology and appreciation for the social contributions of all members of communities informed development plans.

FORBIDDEN SEXUALITY

Prostitution, long considered a "necessary evil," was and is the logical consequence of female economic and educational destitution, the commercial value attached to sex, the social dominance of men, and strictly taught morals regarding the bonds of marriage. Men's presumed appetite for sex and women's presumed weaker physical drive have excused men's search for sexual satisfaction outside the home. Taboos placed on respectable women seeking sexual gratification have, on the surface, discouraged expectations of sexual fulfillment between wives and husbands.

Prostitutes have been despised by society for selling themselves. Most prostitutes have been among the poorest and the most defiled members of society. More often than not, general condemnations of commercial sex have overwhelmed objective knowledge about the social and economic arrangements that have made prostitution a reasonable choice for some women. Male prostitution, often ignored by public authorities unless it included homosexual relations, has rarely incited the condemnations that female prostitution has.

During the colonial period, matters of prostitution were handled by ecclesiastical courts. In the eighteenth century, the church established *casas de correción* or *casas de sanidad* (correctional houses) to rehabilitate women, usually nonwhites. Priests, bishops, and inquisitional tribunals heard accusations of prostitution, and all discouraged the practice. Most reprehensible was the offer by parents to sell their daughters to brothels and by husbands to prostitute their wives. Consenting adult women were reprimanded with increasing severity as connections between venereal disease and promiscuous sex became clear.

In the nineteenth century, prostitution came under the aegis of the state, and justifications for controlling it included deterring the spread of venereal disease and collecting taxes. During the second half of the nineteenth century, as governments began to stabilize and modernization challenged old moral codes, prostitution came to be understood as an economic, social, and political problem. Modern concepts of the state held that the family formed the basis of society. The values, belief systems, behavior, and relationships that were formed within the family projected patriotic images.

Argentina serves as an example of how and why the rules regarding prostitution changed. The government's legalization of prostitution by an 1875 ordinance was a means of controlling an already viable business. Under the ordinance, officials collected revenues, set up health clinics, and formally designated parts of the city for prostitution, thus isolating prostitutes from the rest of society. Moreover, in response to international and national accusations of white slavery (the importing of white prostitutes), the government increasingly limited the operations of brothels and passed antisolicitation laws.

In 1934, after 58 years of legalized prostitution, Argentine officials began outlawing bordellos, claiming that prostitutes did not register with health clinics, that venereal disease was spreading, and that prostitutes engaged in scandalous behavior. They were also responding to Buenos Aires's reputation as a center of white slave trade. Moreover, industrialization offered employment alternatives. Municipality after municipality abolished their licensed houses and incorporated new legislation, most notably the Law of Social Profilaxis (1936), that provided medical care, repatriation, and employment for reformed prostitutes.

With the advent of Juan PERÓN in 1944, governing values changed once again. Women had been working at respectable jobs in increased numbers since the turn of the century, and by 1947 they could vote. Women, thus, were supportive of the pro-labor administration. At the same time, homosexuals were beginning to demand a place in Argentina's moral ordering. Old sex-burdened folkways were disappearing. The tango, originally danced in bordellos between sexually commanding men and alluring women, was replaced by soccer (an all-male player and spectator sport) as the activity of national passion. Homosexuality was beginning to find some expression in literature and art, despite the fact that many Argentines were scandalized by gay relationships. In response Perón promised conservative morality and a return to family values. Part of his plan involved legalizing prostitution, and in 1954 the law was changed so that prostitutes again could practice their trade legally as part of a patriotic defense against illness and unspeakable perversion.

After the Cuban Revolution in 1959, Fidel CASTRO's government tried to end prostitution through rehabilitation programs, respectable jobs, and distribution of wealth. The Federation of Cuban Women, founded in 1960, educated women. Literacy programs were set up to rehabilitate former prostitutes, and vocational schools trained women to work in textile factories. The Cubans concentrated on the economic and political causes of prostitution, believing that by eliminating poverty and a sense of marginalization, prostitution would disappear.

Public soliciting was prohibited, but clandestine commerce continued. The source of inequality came from tourists, who were allowed to shop in "dollar stores" (where only foreign currency was accepted). Avoiding the surveillance of tourist police, young women approached tourists, exchanging sex for clothing and food bought in tourist and diplomatic stores. Until 1989 this sort of commerce was light, but the *período especial* (economic crisis caused by the dissolution of the Soviet Union) created such hardship in Cuba that prostitutes began plying their trade as openly as in the pre-1959 period.

Homosexual acts have been considered social aberrations and deviant behavior in every Latin American country. Yet the history of homosexuality in Latin America is complicated by the unification of Amerindian, Iberian, and African cultures, each of which has had a different perception of homosexuality.

According to some scholars, homosexuality was acceptable behavior among a few Indian groups. Archaeological evidence shows that Zunis in New Mexico, the ARAUCANIANS of Chile and southern Peru, and the INCAS practiced male homosexuality. The most graphic evidence is in Peruvian Moche pottery, with its explicit depictions of men engaged in homosexual lovemaking. Furthermore, no source suggests that homosexual intercourse was punished or discouraged.

The Iberian conquerors, repulsed by native homosexual acts, called the mystified Indians sodomites, and the clergy condemned the accused to be eaten alive by dogs. Yet there is some evidence that the conquerors also practiced homosexual intercourse. During the colonial period, Iberian homosexuals were brought before inquisitional tribunals, where their sin was known as the "ultimate crime against morality" and the "abominable or unspeakable crime," and they were punished by the *auto-da-fé*. During periods of leniency or neglect, homosexuals in cities were forced to reside in the same poor areas where prostitutes lived. Individual freedoms did not extend to this marginalized group, as gay men could not belong to the military, seek public office, or hold government jobs. Their sexual behavior was also a crime for which individuals could be imprisoned.

Controlling vice proved increasingly difficult in the nineteenth century as Latin American ports opened to international trade and foreign immigration. Port cities were overpopulated with prostitutes. Police records note the arrests of purse snatchers who dressed as women, perhaps to disguise their criminal intent or, alternatively, to express their sexual preference.

Gays and lesbians have felt the greatest repression from authoritarian and totalitarian regimes, which direct police raids even against members of the ruling class. In post-1959 revolutionary Cuba, measures against homosexuals were especially repressive. Under liberal governments, homosexuals have been ignored and neglected but never accepted. Only in the middle- to late-twentieth century have homosexuals organized to protect themselves from arbitrary repression. As early as 1969 in Argentina, but generally in the early 1980s, gays and lesbians formed their own organizations. In 1983 the Fifth March for Gay Pride, which included thirteen homosexual groups, took place in Mexico City.

Venezuela, Colombia, Puerto Rico, and Brazil all have active gay movements. Formed in 1969, the Argentine El Grupo Nuestro Mundo attracted homosexuals with divergent political affiliations. In 1971, the organization renamed itself the Frente de Liberación Homosexual de la Argentina. What united members was a commitment to fighting *machismo*, the convention of male domination that affected all women and gay men. Members believed that by ending male domination, they would cause a profound revolution, a psychological transformation that would alter the fundamental tenets of Argentine culture.

Although the gay movement gathered force during a period of radical mobilization and revolt against military rule, gays found leftist groups as repressive as the right-wing military government. Only feminists appreciated the benefits to be gained by stopping male domination, but even they were often unwilling to support gay rights. Still, the Frente persisted and in 1973 published a manifesto that demanded the immediate cessation of police repression of homosexuals, the abrogation of an antihomosexual edict, and the freeing of homosexual prisoners. Homosexual activists, more than political dissidents, had to work clandestinely, which impeded the other great objective of creating a gay consciousness and identity. These early dissenters actively engaged in theoretical and cultural analyses that explained their social marginalization and planned confrontations with their oppressors.

Juan Perón's third presidency (1973–1974) proved as repressive of gays as the military government it replaced. Despite the fact that gay organizations had gone to the streets in support of Perón, the right wing of the Peronist Party assailed homosexuals while the party as a whole ignored their manifestos. Disillusioned gays found no comfort among the leftist Montoneros, who denied them membership in their organization. Still with no political home, homosexuals were despised and alone in their struggle. When gay activists declared their opposition to Perón in 1973, they became the victims of police repression. To survive, they had to go underground, where they remained until the fall of the military regime in 1982.

Since then, Argentine gay organizations have grown, especially as a result of their joining the chorus of protesters demanding information on the victims of the DIRTY WAR (1976–1981). Activists counted at least seventy of the missing from among their ranks. Under the new democratic governments of presidents Raúl ALFONSÍN and Carlos MENEM, gay organizations established official headquarters in downtown Buenos Aires, where they began publishing news journals and political pamphlets.

Latin American societies continue to be patriarchal ones in which relations of gender and sex have changed only slightly. Pressure for reform has come from international women's and gay rights movements, which Latin American reformists have adapted to the various and complex Latin American settings.

EVELYN STEVENS, "Marianismo, the Other Face of Machismo in Latin America," in Female and Male in Latin America, edited by Ann Pescatello (1973), pp. 89–101; VERENA MARTÍNEZ ALIER, Marriage, Class, and Colour in Nineteenth-Century Cuba (1974); JEAN G. PERISTIANY, Honour and Shame: The Values of Mediterranean Society (1974); ASUNCIÓN LAVRIN, ed., Latin American Women: Historical Perspectives (1978); ELSA CHANEY, Supermadre: Women in Politics in Latin America (1979); DORIS M. LADD, Mexican Women in Anahuac and New Spain: Aztec Roles, Spanish Notary Revelations, Creole Genius (1979); ASUNCIÓN LAVRIN and EDITH COUTURIER, "Dowries and Wills: A View of Women's Socio-Economic Role in Colonial Guadalajara and Puebla, 1640–1790," in Hispanic American Historical Review 59, no. 2 (May 1979): 280–304; JUNE NASH and HELEN I. SAFA, eds., Sex and Class in Latin America: Women's Perspectives on Politics, Economics, and the Family in the Third World (1980); SUSAN SOCOLOW, "Women and Crime: Buenos Aires, 1757–1797," in Journal of Latin American Studies 12 (May 1980): 39–54; SUSAN SOCOLOW, "Marriage, Birth, and Inheritance: The Merchants of Eighteenth-Century Buenos Aires," in American Historical Review 60, no. 3 (August 1980): 387–406; FONDO DE CULTURA ECONÓMICA, Familia y sexualidad en Nueva España (1982); MARYSSA NAVARRO, "Evita's Charismatic Leadership," in Latin American Populism in Comparative Perspective, edited by Michael L. Coniff (1982), pp. 47–66; MARIA PATRICIA FERNÁNDEZ KELLY, For We Are Sold, I and My People: Women and Industry in Mexico's Frontier (1983); LUIS MARTIN, Daughters of the Conquistadores: Women of the Viceroyalty of Peru (1983); JOHN TUTINO, "Power, Class, and Family: Men and Women in the Mexican Elite, 1750–1810," in The Americas 39 (1983): 359–381; ALEJANDRO JOCKL, Ahora, los gay (1984); SANDRA F. MCGEE, "Right-Wing Female Activists in Buenos Aires, 1900–1932," in Women and the Structure of Society, edited by Barbara J. Harris and Joann McNamara (1984), pp. 85–97; RIGOBERTA MENCHÚ, I . . . Rigoberta Menchú: An Indian Woman in Guatemala (1984); ZELMAR ACEVEDO, Homosexualidad: Hacia la destrucción de mitos (1985); SILVIA ARROM, Women of Mexico City, 1790–1857 (1985); EDITH COUTURIER, "Women and the Family in Eighteenth-Century Mexico: Law and Practice," in Journal of Family History 10, no. 3 (Autumn 1985): 294–304; SUSAN KELLOGG, "Aztec Inheritance in Sixteenth-Century Mexico City: Colonial Patterns, Prehispanic Influences," in Ethnohistory 23, no. 3 (Summer 1986): 313–330; ELIZABETH ANNE KUZNESOF, Household Economy and Urban Development: São Paulo, 1765 to 1836 (1986); ELEANOR L. LEACOCK and HELEN I. SAFA, eds., Women's Work: Development and the Division of Labor by Gender (1986); ALIDA METCALF, "Fathers and Sons: The Politics of Inheritance in a Colonial Brazilian Township," in Hispanic American Historical Review 66, no. 3 (August 1986): 455–484; JUNE NASH and HELEN I. SAFA, eds., Women and Change in Latin America (1986); RONALDO VAINFAZ ed., Historia e sexualidade no Brasil (1986); RUTH BEHAR, "Sex and Sin, Witchcraft and the Devil in Late-Colonial Mexico," in American Ethnologist 14, no. 1 (February 1987): 34–54; IRENE SILVERBLATT, Moon, Sun, and Witches: Gender, Ideologies, and Class in Inca and Colonial Peru (1987); SUSAN KELLOGG, "Households in Late Prehispanic and Early Colonial Mexico: Their Structure and Its Implications for the Study of Historical Demography," in The Americas 44 (April 1988): 483–494; DAPHNE PATAI, Brazilian Women Speak: Contemporary Life Stories (1988); OCTAVIO PAZ, Sor Juana: Or, the Traps of Faith, translated by Margaret Peden (1988); PATRICIA SEED, To Love, Honor, and Obey in Colonial Mexico (1988); ELECTA ARENAL and STACEY SCHLAU, Untold Sisters: Hispanic Nuns in Their Own Works, translated by Amanda Powell (1989); SUSAN C. BOURQUE, "Gender and the State: Perspectives from Latin America," in Women, the State, and Development, edited by Sue Ellen Charlton, Jana Everett, and Kathleen Staudt (1989), pp. 114–129; JANE S. JAQUETTE, ed., The Women's Movement in Latin America: Feminism and the Transition to Democracy (1989); ALEXANDRA PARMA COOK and NOBEL DAVID COOK, Good Faith and Truthful Ignorance: A Case of Transatlantic Bigamy (1990); EDITH COUTURIER, " 'For the Greater Service of God': Opulent Foundations and Women's Philanthropy in Colonial Mexico," in Lady Bountiful Revisited: Women, Philanthropy, and Power, edited by Kathleen D. McCarthy (1990), pp. 119–141; ELIZABETH SALAS, Soldaderas in the Mexican Military: Myth and History (1990); SANDRA MESSINGER CYPRESS, La Malinche in Mexican Literature: From History to Myth (1991); DAVID WILLIAM FOSTER, Gay and Lesbian Themes in Latin American Writing (1991); RAMÓN GUTIÉRREZ, When Jesus Came, the Corn Mothers Went Away: Marriage, Sexuality, and Power in New Mexico, 1500–1846 (1991);

DONNA J. GUY, *Sex and Danger in Buenos Aires: Prostitution, Family, and Nation in Argentina* (1991); SANDRA F. MCGEE, "Gender and Sociopolitical Change in Twentieth-Century Latin America," in *Hispanic American Historical Review* 71 (1991): 259–306; FRANCESCA MILLER, *Latin American Women and the Search for Social Justice* (1991); MURIEL NAZZARI, *Disappearance of the Dowry: Women, Families, and Social Change in São Paulo, Brazil (1600–1900)* (1991); LYNN STEPHEN, *Zapotec Women* (1991); K. LYNN STONER, *From the House to the Streets: The Cuban Woman's Movement for Legal Reform, 1898–1940* (1991); K. LYNN STONER, "On Men Reforming the Rights of Men: The Abrogation of the Cuban Adultery Law, 1930," in *Cuban Studies/Estudios Cubanos* 21 (1991): 83–99.

K. LYNN STONER

See also **Interamerican Congress of Women (1947); Women in Latin America; Women in Paraguay.**

GENÍZARO, an eighteenth- and nineteenth-century New Mexican identification given initially to Plains Indian women and children (rarely adult men) captured in intertribal warfare and sold or ransomed to Spanish authorities who assigned them to Christian settlers for "civilizing" and service as domestics and herders. The term is most appropriately applied to the offspring of the captives. Intermarriage among the descendants of former members of different Plains tribes who had been reared in the Spanish milieu created a subpopulation that was biologically Indian, yet different from both Plains and PUEBLO peoples, and culturally Hispanic. The *genízaro* population filled significant political, economic, and social niches as settlers of strategic frontier villages, as members of the militia (where their reputation as fearless combatants was recognized), as emissaries to Plains tribes, and as farmers and other types of workers.

GILBERTO BENITO CÓRDOBA, *Abiquiu and Don Cacahuate: A Folk History of a New Mexican Village* (1973); FRANCES LEON SWADESH, *Los Primeros Pobladores: Hispanic Americans of the Ute Frontier* (1974); ANGÉLICO CHÁVEZ, "Genízaros," in *Handbook of North American Indians*, vol. 9, edited by Alfonso Ortiz (1979); ADRIAN BUSTAMANTE, "The Matter Was Never Resolved: The *Casta* System in Colonial New Mexico, 1693–1823," in *New Mexico Historical Review* 66, no. 2 (1991): 143–163.

ROBERT HIMMERICH Y VALENCIA

GERCHUNOFF, ALBERTO (*b.* 1 January 1884; *d.* 2 March 1950), writer and journalist, born in Proskuroff (Khmelnitski) Russia; he emigrated with his family to Argentina in 1889, settling in Moisés Ville, Santa Fe Province. After his father's murder, the family moved to Rajil in Entre Ríos Province. In his classic *Los gauchos judíos* (1910; *The Jewish Gauchos of the Pampas*, 1955), Gerchunoff envisioned the promised land based on the agricultural colonies founded by Baron Hirsch as a haven for JEWS fleeing from pogroms in czarist Russia. He moved to Buenos Aires in 1895, where he met Enrique DICKMANN and Alfredo L. PALACIOS—the major figures

of the Socialist Party—and writer Leopoldo LUGONES and Robert J. Payró. He began writing for the journal *Caras y Caretas,* where he developed a following for his sharp wit and satirical portrayals. Gerchunoff would later serve as a model for Abrahan Orloff in Manuel GÁLVEZ's *El mal metafísico* (1916). In 1909 Gerchunoff joined the staff of *La Nación,* which for a young Jewish immigrant signaled acceptance into the literary establishment.

His most acclaimed work, *Los gauchos judíos,* was published during the centennial of Argentine independence. Gerchunoff considered Argentina a "new Zion" where Jews could become fully integrated and therefore forgo the notion of a return to Palestine. The impact of the Holocaust, however, about which he wrote in *El problema judío* (1945), persuaded him to advocate the establishment of the state of Israel. His faith in Argentina led him to dismiss as deviations anti-Semitic acts such as those that occurred during the SEMANA TRÁGICA ("tragic week") in Buenos Aires in January 1919.

Gerchunoff achieved his own integration into Argentine culture through his assimilation of Spanish literary classics, such as *Don Quixote.* A superb prose fiction writer of twenty-six books, he was also an acclaimed journalist and lecturer: *Retorno a Don Quijote* (1951), *Enrique Heine: El poeta de nuestra intimidad* (1927), *Las imágenes del país* (1931), and *El pino y la palmera* (1952) demonstrate the broad range of his literary production.

MANUEL KANTOR, *Alberto Gerchunoff* (1969); MYRIAM E. GROVER DE NASATSKY, *Bibliografía de Alberto Gerchunoff* (1976); LEONARDO SENKMAN, *La identidad judía en la literatura argentina* (1983); BEATRIZ MARQUIS STAMBLER, *Vida y obra de Alberto Gerchunoff* (1985).

SAÚL SOSNOWSKI

GERMAN–LATIN AMERICAN RELATIONS. Although the Hansa cities and Prussia had earlier maintained consulates in independent Latin America, formal German–Latin American relations began only in 1871 with the founding of the German Empire. Diplomatic representation was accompanied by improved transatlantic communications, an upsurge in trade and investment, and modest increases in German immigration. By 1914, Germans held important mining concessions in Mexico, Peru, and Chile; Argentina was Germany's second most important trading partner outside Europe; German investments rivaled those of France and the United States, if not of Great Britain. German migration to South America, particularly to the temperate Southern Cone, increased, though it never equaled the massive movement to the United States. The emigrants included educators, scientists, and technicians; many made important contributions to the cultural and economic development of their new homelands.

Following the lead of Chile, which welcomed a Prussian military training mission in the 1870s, several nations contracted with German military training missions

55

before World War I; sales of German weapons also increased. Germany's colonial ambitions stimulated theorists of empire to dreams of expansion into South and Central America. Richard Tannenberg's 1914 plan, a publicist's vision of a reorganized South America under German tutelage, caused alarm in London, Paris, and Washington, but it is improbable that German strategists considered implementing it. It is, however, certain that those strategists did not consider the Monroe Doctrine a hindrance to German projects in the Western Hemisphere. From December 1902 to March 1903 a serious confrontation with the United States resulted when Venezuela defaulted on European debts. A German-led naval force threatened intervention, provoking President Theodore Roosevelt to threaten the Europeans with U.S. naval might (the dispute was adjudicated in 1904 by the Hague Court). Germany also fished in the troubled waters of the MEXICAN REVOLUTION (1910–1917) and overreached itself in the ZIMMERMANN TELEGRAM affair of 1917, an immediate cause of U.S. entry into WORLD WAR I.

Brazil and six small Central American and Caribbean nations also declared war on Germany and the other Central Powers; during the war German economic interests almost everywhere lost ground to competitors, especially the United States. With restored economic and diplomatic relations after 1918, German industrialists established branch plants in a number of countries; German-speaking immigrants—including noteworthy contingents from old areas of German settlement in Russia and Eastern Europe—resumed their move to the Southern Cone.

In the drive for economic self-sufficiency in the 1930s, Germany sought assured Latin American sources of foodstuffs and raw materials. The search culminated in 1934 in a trade policy of strict bilateralism, embodied in treaties with Brazil, Argentina, and other countries, which produced gains at British and North American expense. The economic offensive was accompanied after 1933 by strident propaganda and by strengthened relations between the Third Reich and the poorly assimilated German-speaking communities of the area; NAZIS labored to organize these communities for purposes that were never clarified. The expansion of German-controlled airlines, particularly near the Panama Canal, worried the North American military. In the United States belief grew in a vast German strategic project to create—through subversion of undemocratic political elites and perhaps with the aid of German-speaking "fifth columns"—a congeries of Latin American client states of the Third Reich within the Western Hemisphere. Fears were aggravated in 1938 and 1939 by armed uprisings in Brazil and Chile that appeared to implicate German elements, by German negotiations for Mexican oil in the aftermath of the nationalization controversy of 1938, and by exposés of alleged German plots in Argentina and Uruguay.

In the late 1930s German rearmament reduced the amount of civilian goods available to trade for Latin American raw materials, and the economic offensive lost its impetus. Nevertheless, Hitler's military victories from 1939 to 1941 lent credibility to German promises to integrate Latin America into a reorganized European economy under German hegemony. Therefore, in 1940 the United States undertook a costly program of pre-emptive buying of Latin American commodities. (It should be noted that since 1945 historians have found no evidence of the widely believed-in "German master plan" for the Americas.)

German–Latin American communications and trade were interrupted by the outbreak of WORLD WAR II in September 1939. At the foreign ministers' conference held in Rio de Janeiro early in 1942, the Latin American states, except Argentina and Chile, followed the United States in declaring war on the Axis powers (Germany, Italy, and Japan). Apart from Brazil and Mexico, Latin America's war effort was limited to increased production of raw materials for the Allies, closure of Axis embassies, seizures of Axis property, and expulsion of Axis nationals deemed dangerous. German espionage networks, continental in scope but centered in Argentina, were not suppressed until 1944. The threat of invasion—which proved ephemeral—caused Latin American governments to request and receive U.S. lend-lease arms; the result was increased military collaboration under U.S. leadership.

As the war ended, Washington, ostensibly out of concern that Axis war criminals would escape to Latin America, pressed Latin American governments to suppress German-language institutions and to close their doors to refugees. These pressures offended Latin American sovereignty and were unsuccessful: thousands of Axis nationals migrated to Latin America after 1945. Many were scientists and technicians; some were fugitives. Some were both. Normal relations were restored between the Federal Republic of Germany and the Latin American nations in the 1950s.

BARBARA W. TUCHMAN, *The Zimmermann Telegram* (1966); JÜRGEN SCHAEFER, *Deutsche Militärhilfe in Südamerika: Militär- und Rüstungsinteressen in Argentinien, Bolivien und Chile vor 1914* (1974); HOLGER W. HERWIG, *Politics of Frustration: The United States in German Naval Planning, 1889–1941* (1976); REINER POMMERIN, *Das Dritte Reich und Lateinamerika* (1977); STANLEY E. HILTON, *Hitler's Secret War in South America, 1939–1945: German Military Espionage and Allied Counterespionage in Brazil* (1981); FRIEDRICH KATZ, *The Secret War in Mexico: Europe, the United States, and the Mexican Revolution* (1981); LESLIE B. ROUT, JR. and JOHN F. BRATZEL, *The Shadow War: German Espionage and United States Counterespionage in Latin America During World War II* (1986); FREDERICK C. LUEBKE, *Germans in Brazil: A Comparative History of Cultural Conflict During World War I* (1987); RONALD C. NEWTON, *The "Nazi Menace" in Argentina, 1931–1947* (1991).

RONALD C. NEWTON

GERMANS IN LATIN AMERICA. German beginnings in Latin America were modest. In 1528 Emperor Charles

V awarded a concession in present-day Venezuela to the Welser bank of Augsburg, from which he had borrowed heavily; in 1529 Germans settled at Coro. German governance of native peoples proved no more adept or humane than that of the Spanish; the colony failed to prosper, and the concession was revoked in 1548. From Coro, Nikolaus Federmann explored to the area of Bogotá in 1539 but found he had been preceded by Gonzalo Jiménez de QUESADA. Ulrich Schmidl of Ulm, representing German bankers, chronicled the Mendoza expedition that in 1535–1536 founded Buenos Aires. In the seventeenth and eighteenth centuries German Jesuits—Martin DOBRIZHOFFER is the best known—were active in Paraguay and the Río de la Plata.

During the Wars of Independence Hansa traders provided rebels with arms and shipping. In the following years German merchants settled in Latin American port cities; not a few married local women, became landowners, and joined local oligarchies. German mercenary soldiers served in Brazil and fought elsewhere in the civil wars of the period. In the 1830s the Brazilian government brought German peasants to colonize the southern frontier in Santa Catarina, Rio Grande do Sul, and, later, Paraná. Ascending the rivers, Germans formed rural and small-town communities that retained a Germanic imprint for more than a century. Chile brought Hessian colonists to the southern frontier in the 1850s and 1860s. There, isolated from centers of Chilean population, they created a similar Germanic zone. Bernhard Forster (Friedrich Nietzsche's brother-in-law) headed a utopian colony in Paraguay in the 1880s. Well into the twentieth century, Germans continued to found or join agricultural colonies, particularly in southern Brazil, Chile, Argentina, Uruguay, and Paraguay. They played a major role, for example, in the opening of Argentina's Misiones Territory between the two world wars. In Guatemala they were prominent in the coffee industry.

However, North America remained the destination of the majority of German emigrants. As Germany rose to world power after 1871, German communities in Latin America remained small and typically comprised well-to-do merchants; bankers; managers and technicians of German electrical, chemical, metallurgical, and pharmaceutical firms; and educators and public service professionals under contract to Latin American governments. German military advisers were influential in Chile, Argentina, and Bolivia. Germans proved adaptable to Latin American business and social conditions, and—sheltered by insular, status-conscious, and largely Protestant communities—slow to assimilate.

In WORLD WAR I, Allied blockades brought hardship; in Argentina and more notably Brazil (which declared war on Germany in 1917) nationalist riots destroyed property and terrorized individuals. German immigration resumed after 1918, now including war veterans and political irreconcilables, young people without prospects, businessmen ruined by inflation, and ethnic

Germans driven from Russia and eastern Europe by war and Slavic nationalism. In the 1930s the NAZI government proselytized in German collectivities overseas, stimulating pan-German nationalism and creating the illusion of a resurgent worldwide German cultural community. Nazi publicists reckoned "racial" Germans to number 900,000 in Brazil, 240,000 in Argentina, and 50,000 to 80,000 in Chile. As war approached in Europe, Nazi activities provoked fear that German communities represented potential "fifth columns." Armed uprisings in Brazil and Chile in 1938 that appeared to implicate Nazis, and rumored plots in Argentina and Uruguay, caused Latin American governments, particularly Getúlio VARGAS's dictatorship in Brazil, to restrict sharply the autonomy of German (and other ethnic) schools, churches, newspapers, and social institutions.

WORLD WAR II brought further restrictions, as under U.S. urging all hemisphere governments except Argentina and Chile declared war on the Axis. Pressed by Allied blockades and blacklists, German businesses adopted local cover or closed. Intrigues involving clandestine German agents and Allied intelligence agencies kept alarm alive; Axis property was seized; "dangerous" individuals were deported. The U.S. State Department considered a program of forced assimilation of Germans and the dissolution of all German-language institutions in the Western Hemisphere; the program, however—impractical and violating Latin American sovereignty—was not implemented except (partly) in Argentina. After 1945 the United States also sought to prevent Germans from migrating to Latin America; nevertheless, many thousands of veterans, war criminals, political irreconcilables, and scientists and technicians valuable to Latin American industrialization succeeded in doing so. Since 1945, apart from remote MENNONITE colonies in Paraguay and Uruguay, and Colonia Libertad in Chile, German-speaking collectivities have fragmented and declined. Many, unable to resist assimilation, have virtually disappeared, although some still exist in Brazil.

EMILIO WILLEMS, *A aculturação dos alemães no Brasil: Estudo antropológico dos imigrantes alemães e seus descendentes no Brasil* (1946); JEAN ROCHE, *La colonisation allemande et le Rio Grande do Sul* (1959); KÄTHE HARMS-BALZER, *Die Nationalisierung der deutschen Einwanderer und ihrer Nachkommen in Brasilien als Problem der deutsch-brasilianischer Beziehunger, 1930–1938* (1970); JEAN-PIERRE BLANCPAIN, *Les allemands au Chili, 1816–1945* (1974); GEORGE F. W. YOUNG, *Germans in Chile: Immigration and Colonization, 1849–1914* (1974); DONALD M. MC KALE, *The Swastika Outside Germany* (1977); RONALD C. NEWTON, *German Buenos Aires, 1900–1933: Social Change and Cultural Conflict* (1977); HARTMUT FRÖSCHLE, ed., *Die Deutschen in Lateinamerika* (1979); ALFREDO M. SEIFERHELD, *Nazismo y fascismo en el Paraguay: Vísperas de la II guerra mundial, 1936–1939* (1983); FREDERICK C. LUEBKE, *Germans in Brazil: A Comparative History of Cultural Conflict During World War I* (1987); RONALD C. NEWTON, *The "Nazi Menace" in Argentina, 1931–1947* (1991).

RONALD C. NEWTON

GERZSO, GUNTHER (*b.* 17 June 1915), Mexican painter. Born in Mexico City, Gerzso considers himself a self-taught artist. From 1941 to 1962, while painting, he designed sets for the Mexican cinema. In 1974 he studied lithography at the Tamarind Institute, University of New Mexico. His works have been shown since 1955 in exhibitions such as "Latin American Art Since Independence" at the Yale University Art Gallery (1966). He represented Mexico at the eighth biennial exhibition in São Paulo (1965). The University of Texas Art Museum in Austin in 1976 and the Museum of Modern Art in Mexico City in 1977 organized major retrospectives of his work. In 1978 he was awarded the national Fine Arts Prize by the Mexican government.

BÉLGICA RODRÍGUEZ

GESTIDO, OSCAR DANIEL (*b.* 28 November 1901; *d.* 6 December 1967), Uruguayan military leader and president (1967). Gestido was born to a middle-class family in Montevideo. He began his military career in 1917 in the artillery. Beginning in 1923, he played an active role in organizing the Uruguayan Air Force. Between 1951 and 1955 he held the post of inspector general of the army. He later retired from the military, beginning his political career at a time of profound crisis in Uruguay. During the nationalist governments, Gestido had demonstrated skill in the administration of public bodies such as PLUNA, the state airline (1949–1951), and AFE, the state railroad (1957–1959). From 1963 to 1966 he was a member of the National Council of Government.

Gestido's image was one of honesty, which contrasted with the ever-more tarnished reputations of most politicians at the time. In 1966, the Colorado Front of Unity (List 515) was formed to support Gestido's successful presidential campaign. However, he died only nine months into his term, which was completed by his vice president, Jorge PACHECO ARECO.

Boletín del Estado Mayor del Ejército, nos. 112–115; JUAN CARLOS PEDEMONTE, *Los presidentes del Uruguay* (1984).

JOSÉ DE TORRES WILSON

GHIOLDI, AMÉRICO (*b.* 23 May 1899; *d.* ca. 1979/80), Argentine Socialist councilman, congressman, and party leader. Born in Buenos Aires, Ghioldi was a secondary school teacher, university professor, and prominent figure in Argentina's Socialist Party. He had joined the party by the early 1920s, and was elected, at the age of twenty-five, to the city council of Buenos Aires, where he served for five years. Following the course of a number of his council colleagues, he served three terms as national deputy from Buenos Aires (1932–1936, 1936–1940, 1940–1943). In Congress, Ghioldi was a leading member of the Socialist opposition to the conservative majority, noted especially for spearheading the struggle against what was considered undue concessions to foreign capital and interests in the 1930s.

Like most Socialist congressmen, Ghioldi concurrently held important positions in the party hierarchy, including editor of the Socialists' main newspaper, *La Vanguardia,* as well as of other publications. In the 1940s and thereafter, Ghioldi became one of the loudest Socialist voices in opposition to the regime of Juan PERÓN (1946–1955), publishing a number of books critical of Peronism. In the late 1970s, in a controversial decision, he accepted appointment from the military government of General Jorge VIDELA (1976–1980) as Argentina's ambassador to Portugal.

RICHARD J. WALTER

See also **Argentina: Political Parties.**

GHIOLDI, RODOLFO (*b.* 21 January 1897; *d.* 3 July 1985), Argentine political leader, born in Buenos Aires, brother of Américo GHIOLDI. In 1918, he helped establish the Internationalist Socialist Party (PSI), which was renamed the Communist Party (PC) in 1920. Ghioldi traveled several times to the Soviet Union in the 1920s and 1930s and was one of only two Latin Americans to sit as an alternate delegate on the Comintern's executive committee. He served as the Argentine party's president in 1930–1931 and, along with Victorio Codovilla, dominated the Argentine Communists for most of their history. Ghioldi was his party's unsuccessful senatorial candidate in 1946 and a presidential candidate in the 1951 elections, but he never held public office.

As with most Argentine communists, he was a strict disciple of the party's often slavishly pro-Soviet line. Ideologically, Ghioldi adhered to orthodox positions on the role of the party and the necessity of passing through historical stages in the movement toward socialism.

ROLLIE POPPINO, *International Communism in Latin America: A History of the Movement, 1917–1963* (1964); JORGE ABELARDO RAMOS, *Historia del stalinismo en la Argentina* (1969); SHELDON B. LISS, *Marxist Thought in Latin America* (1984).

JAMES P. BRENNAN

See also **Argentina: Political Parties.**

GIBBS AND SONS, ANTONY, a British merchant house that began operating in Peru shortly after independence in 1822. It was designated by the Peruvian state as the principal contractor or supplier of GUANO to Great Britain between 1842 and 1861. As such, Gibbs became a major financier to the Peruvian state during the so-called guano boom between 1840 and 1880. In a major economic and political shift, Gibbs was then deposed as consignee in 1862 by a group of native contractors, which included future president Manuel PARDO, who held the contract until 1869. Later, in a similar arrangement, Gibbs became the sole supplier of nitrates from southern Peru after the expropriation of the industry by the Pardo administration in 1875. The company continued to do business in Peru long after both the guano and nitrate booms ended in Peru in the late 1870s.

W. M. MATHEW, *The House of Gibbs and the Peruvian Guano Monopoly* (1981).

PETER F. KLARÉN

GIL, GILBERTO (*b.* 3 March 1942), prominent and innovative Brazilian composer and musician. Gil, along with Caetano VELOSO and others, was a major figure in the late-1960s cultural and musical movement known as TROPICALISMO, and continues to be one of the nation's most influential performers, especially as an articulator of a distinctly black idiom in popular music. Through the utilization in the 1960s of highly stylized versions of folk forms in compositions such as "Louvação" (1967; Homage) and "Procissão" (1965; Processional), the cinematographic construction of lyrics, and the original use of folk instruments in "Domingo no parque" (1967; Sunday in the Park), the introduction of electric instruments in "Questão de ordem" (1968; Question of Order), and the parodic use of advertising jargon in "Geléia geral" (1968; General Jelly), this last written with Torquato Neto. Gil was largely responsible for redefining the parameters of MÚSICA POPULAR BRASILEIRA (Brazilian popular music).

Born and raised in the state of Bahia, like his contemporary Veloso, Gil was influenced by backlands *forro* singer Luís GONZAGA, *samba canção* composer Dorival CAYMMI, and especially the major figure of BOSSA NOVA, João GILBERTO. He also incorporated popular styles from Spanish America and consciously adapted the British rhythm-and-blues style of the Beatles to a Brazilian mode, most notably in "O sonho acabou" (1972; The Dream Is Over), released after his forced exile in England from 1969 to 1972 (presumably because he was a visible proponent of *tropicalismo*).

Two formal and thematic preoccupations that recur in Gil's numerous songs from the 1970s and 1980s are mysticism and the music and culture of the African diaspora. Of the latter type, the most significant work can perhaps be found on the albums *Refavela* (1977; an invented word meaning to "re-ghetto"), which prefigures the shift of primary identification among many young Brazilian blacks from being Brazilian to being of African descent, and *Raça humana* (1984; Human Race). This second album, which was partly recorded with the Wailers in Jamaica and popularized reggae as a style to be utilized in Brazilian popular music, simultaneously portrays the African diaspora as the epitome of a universal historical experience and implies that Gilberto Gil, as the logical heir to the legacy of Jamaican singer Bob Marley, is the bard of this diaspora.

FRED DE GOES, ed., *Gilberto Gil: Literatura comentada* (1982); ANTÔNIO RISÉRIO, ed., *Gilberto Gil: Expresso 2222* (1982); CHARLES A. PERRONE, *Masters of Contemporary Brazilian Song* (1989).

ROBERT MYERS

GIL, JERÓNIMO ANTONIO (*b.* 1732; *d.* 18 April 1798), engraver. Trained in painting and engraving at the Academia de San Fernando in Madrid, Gil arrived in New Spain in 1778 to take charge of the Royal Mint in Mexico City and was entrusted with establishing a school of engraving there. His efforts in artistic education eventually resulted in the ACADEMIA DE SAN CARLOS, formally established in 1785, of which he was director until his death. His works include medals, coins, and illustrations. Especially noteworthy is the commemorative medal of Manuel TOLSÁ's equestrian statue of CHARLES IV.

JEAN CHARLOT, *Mexican Art and the Academy of San Carlos: 1785–1915* (1962); THOMAS A. BROWN, *La Academia de San Carlos de la Nueva España* (1976).

CLARA BARGELLINI

GIL DE TABOADA Y LEMOS, FRANCISCO (*b.* 1733; *d.* 1810), viceroy of Peru (1790–1796). A native of Santa María de Sotolongo (Galicia), Gil pursued a naval career before serving briefly as viceroy, first, of New Granada (1789) and, soon thereafter, of Peru. Despite the increasing political confusion in Madrid in the early 1790s, Peru experienced considerable cultural development during his term of office: the progressive journal MERCURIO PERUANO appeared regularly, and the Society of Friends of the Country of Lima, which published the journal, sought, with viceregal support, to promote economic growth. Gil oversaw the production of a detailed census of the population in 1791, and a program of public works, and sought to restore the prestige of viceregal authority at the expense of the provincial intendants (first appointed in 1784).

On his return to Spain, Gil joined the Supreme Council of War, becoming commander of the navy in 1799, minister of marine in 1805, and a member of FERDINAND VII's Junta de Gobierno by means of which the latter forced his father to abdicate and assumed the throne in March 1808. Following Ferdinand's own abdication several months later, Gil refused to recognize Joseph Bonaparte as king of Spain and retired from office.

MANUEL A. FUENTES, ed., *Memorias de los virreyes que han gobernado el Perú*, vol. 6 (1859), pp. 1–353; CARLOS DEUSTÚA PIMENTEL, *Las intendencias en el Perú, 1790–1796* (1965).

JOHN R. FISHER

GIL FORTOUL, JOSÉ (*b.* November 1861; *d.* 15 June 1943), Venezuelan historian, writer, and politician. Gil Fortoul obtained his early education in El Tocuyo. After his early training in philosophy at the Colegio La Concordia, he left for Caracas in 1880 to study law, but eventually earned a doctorate in political science from the Universidad Central de Venezuela in 1885. He came in contact with the intellectual elements of the city and quickly gravitated toward positivist circles. Gil Fortoul traveled to Europe to fill various diplomatic posts for the government and remained there for ten years, during which he was intensely active intellectually.

Returning to Venezuela in 1897, Gil Fortoul collaborated on *El Cojo Ilustrado,* an important cultural magazine of the era. By government order he was given the task of writing a history of Venezuela. In 1902 he was dispatched to Europe, again on a diplomatic mission, and there wrote *Historia constitucional de Venezuela* (2 vols., 1907–1909). Upon his return to Venezuela in 1910, he joined a circle of intellectuals close to General Juan Vicente GÓMEZ, and subsequently became engaged in important public duties. Over the next several years, he served as senator, minister of public education, and chargé d'affaires for the presidency. As plenipotentiary minister of Venezuela (1917–1924), he was responsible for, among other things, negotiating the border conflicts between Venezuela and Colombia. In 1932 Gil Fortoul became director of *El Nuevo Diario,* a government publication. He also served as president of the Venezuelan Society of International Law.

Gil Fortoul is the author of a dense intellectual opus. Among his most outstanding books are *El hombre y la historia* (1890), *Filosofía constitucional* (1890), *Cartas a Pascual* (1894), *El humo de mi pipa* (1891), and *Historia constitucional de Venezuela* (2 vols., 1907–1909).

JUAN PENZINI HERNÁNDEZ, *Vida y obra de José Gil Fortoul (1861–1943)* (1972); TOMÁS POLANCO ALCÁNTARA, *Gil Fortoul: Una luz en la sombra* (1979); and ELENA PLAZA, *José Gil Fortoul: Los nuevos caminos de la razón, la historia como ciencia* (1985).

INÉS QUINTERO

See also **Positivism.**

GILARDI, GILARDO (*b.* 25 May 1889; *d.* 16 January 1963) Argentine composer and teacher. Born in San Fernando, Gilardi began his musical studies with his father; later he studied with the composer Pablo Berutti. He was a founding member of the Grupo Renovación (1929), an adviser to the Argentine National Orchestra and the National Cultural Commission, and a member of the Argentine Cinematography Academy. In his early works, Gilardi composed in the nationalist style, but as he matured he turned to more sophisticated compositional languages, as evidenced by the universalist style of his religious works, which include *Misa de requiem* (1914/1918), *Te Deum* (1936), *Misa de Gloria* (1936), and *Stabat Mater* (1952) all for organ, orchestra, and chorus. He composed two operas, as well as symphonic music, chamber works, music for children's chorus, vocal and piano works, and film and stage music. His opera *Ilse* (1919) premiered at the TEATRO COLÓN in Buenos Aires, 13 July 1923, and *El gaucho con botas nuevas* (1936), a symphonic humorous piece, premiered in the United States under the baton of José Iturbi. Gilardi was a music critic and lecturer, and an excellent teacher. He was professor of harmony, counterpoint, and composition at the National Conservatory in Buenos Aires and at the School of Fine Arts of the National University of La Plata, and a juror in musical competitions. He died in Buenos Aires.

Composers of the Americas, vol. 12 (1966); JORGE OSCAR PICKENHAYN, *Gilardo Gilardi* (1966); *New Grove Dictionary of Music and Musicians,* vol. 7 (1980).

SUSANA SALGADO

GILBERTO, JOÃO (*b.* 1932), Brazilian singer and guitarist. Along with Antônio Carlos JOBIM, Vinícius de Moraes, and Carlos Lyra, João Gilberto launched the bossa-nova musical movement in Brazil in the late 1950s. Born in Joazeiro, a small town in the interior of Bahia State, Gilberto moved in 1949 to Rio de Janeiro, where he performed initially with vocal groups such as Garotos da Lua. Gilberto's highly syncopated style of playing the acoustic guitar, which distilled complex samba rhythms into a simplified form while utilizing harmonically progressive chords, provided the basic beat of the emerging BOSSA-NOVA style. Meanwhile, he also mastered a low-key, precise, subtle, and highly rhythmic vocal style that would also mark the genre.

Gilberto's guitar playing was first heard on Elizeth Cardoso's 1958 album "Canção do amor demais"; his debut as a recording artist came later that year, when Odeon released his singles "Chega de saudade" and "Desafinado" (each cowritten by Antônio Carlos Jobim). In 1959, Gilberto launched his debut album, "Chega de saudade," considered the first bossa-nova album. He recorded several more bossa LPs in the next few years in Brazil and the United States, including the highly successful album "Getz-Gilberto," with American saxophonist Stan Getz in 1964. On it, João's then-wife Astrud dueted with him on "The Girl from Ipanema," one of the world's best-known songs of the late twentieth century.

Gilberto had a profound influence on the next generation of Brazilian musicians, but from the late 1960s on João has led a reclusive life, with only sporadic concert appearances and record releases. He recorded only a handful of records in the 1970s and 1980s, among them: "Brasil" (1981), "João Gilberto Interpreta Tom Jobim" (1985), "João Gilberto: Live in Montreux" (1987), and "João" (1991).

JOSÉ EDUARDO HOMEM DE MELLO, *Música popular brasileira* (1976); AUGUSTO DE CAMPOS, *Balanço da bossa e outras bossas* (1978); RUY CASTRO, *Chega de saudade* (1991); CHRIS MC GOWAN and RICARDO PESSANHA, *The Brazilian Sound: Samba, Bossa Nova, and the Popular Music of Brazil* (1991).

CHRIS MCGOWAN

GILDEMEISTER FAMILY, owners of sugar plantations in the Chicama Valley on the northern coast of Peru. In the early twentieth century they built a vast network of lands around Hacienda Casa Grande. Their successes led them to expand operations, and in the early 1920s they purchased Hacienda Roma, owned by the Larco family. The purchase signaled a trend toward centralization of land ownership that characterized the Peruvian SUGAR INDUSTRY in the late nineteenth and early twentieth centuries. Centralization and heavy investment in technical improvements were accompanied by a search for cheap labor. Asian indenture had ended, and to expand the labor force with indigenous people, the Gildemeisters, Peruvians with strong German ties, sent labor agents to the highland villages, where they advanced money to young men. The highlanders became heavily indebted peons on the plantations. Later, this same labor force was set free through total conversion to wage labor. Proletarianization of the indebted workers signified that by World War I, Peruvian sugar had reached a period of major expansion. That is because the replacement of sharecroppers and tenants with a mobile labor force meant sugar agriculture was flexible enough to meet market fluctuations. Some scholars see the process as the beginning point in establishing links between anti-imperialism and anticapitalism in Peruvian politics. At this time the American Popular Revolutionary Alliance (APRA) emerged as a major political force in the sugar valleys of coastal Peru. Many of the party's earliest rank and file, formerly small sugar producers, were driven off the land and into artisanry and technical work for the big producers.

PETER KLARÉN, *Modernization, Dislocation, and Aprismo: Origins of the Peruvian Aprista Party, 1870–1932* (1973); PETER BLANCHARD, *The Origins of the Peruvian Labor Movement, 1883–1919* (1982).

VINCENT PELOSO

See also **Peru: Political Parties.**

GILL, JUAN BAUTISTA (*b.* 1840; *d.* 12 April 1877), president of Paraguay (1874–1877). Born into a well-connected Asunción family, Gill spent his earliest years in the Paraguayan capital, where, for a time, he worked as apprentice to his father, a high official of the Carlos Antonio LÓPEZ government. In 1854 the younger Gill journeyed to Buenos Aires, where he spent several years studying medicine. He returned to Paraguay just before the beginning of the WAR OF THE TRIPLE ALLIANCE in 1864. During the fighting he distinguished himself as a medical orderly and participated in several battles before being captured at Angostura in 1868.

Upon his release one year later, Gill immediately involved himself in the turbulent politics of the postwar period. His vociferous support for Conservatives Cirilo Antonio RIVAROLA and Cándido BAREIRO gave him some prominence on the Paraguayan scene, as did his friendly connections with the Brazilians, whose army occupied the country. These same connections, however, earned Gill many enemies in the liberal camp.

Between 1872 and 1874 Bareiro masterminded a series of revolts aimed at toppling the government of Salvador Jovellanos. Although Gill played only a minor part in these actions, he stood the most to gain when the Brazilians dropped their support of Jovellanos. With their help, he became president in 1874.

Gill has often been portrayed as a Brazilian puppet, but he sincerely wished to see foreign troops leave Paraguay and worked tirelessly to that end. In 1876 he signed the Machaín-Irigoyen treaty with Argentina, an agreement that provided for the arbitration of the border dispute involving the Gran Chaco territory and thereby hastened the evacuation of the remaining Brazilian troops.

Gill had little opportunity to enjoy his laurels. In April 1877, a band of assassins led by Juan Silvano Godoi murdered the president on his way to government house.

HARRIS G. WARREN, *Paraguay and the Triple Alliance: The Postwar Decade, 1869–1878* (1978), pp. 195–274 and *passim*; CARLOS ZUBIZARRETA, *Cien vidas paraguayas*, 2d ed. (1985), pp. 192–195.

THOMAS L. WHIGHAM

GINASTERA, ALBERTO EVARISTO (*b.* 11 April 1916; *d.* 25 June 1983), Argentine musician. Born in Buenos Aires, Ginastera began his studies at age twelve, at the Alberto Williams Conservatory, graduating in 1935 with a gold medal in composition. In 1936 he entered the National Conservatory of Music to study with Athos Palma (harmony), José Gil (counterpoint), and José André (composition). His career as a composer began in the early 1930s, while he was a student at the Conservatory. His first significant work in the Argentine national idiom was the ballet *Panambí* (1936), which premiered at the TEATRO COLÓN, 12 July 1940; it later won both the Municipal and the National Prize for Music. The turning point of his career came with a commission from the American Ballet Caravan for which he wrote *Estancia* (1941), which earned him a place of distinction among young Argentine composers. That same year he was named professor of composition at the National Conservatory. In 1942 he received a Guggenheim fellowship, but he did not go to the United States until after World War II. He lived in New York from 1945 to 1947 and attended Aaron Copland's classes at Tanglewood.

In 1948 Ginastera returned to Buenos Aires, where he founded the Argentine chapter of the International Society for Contemporary Music (ISCM). He was appointed director of the Conservatory of the Province of Buenos Aires in La Plata. Over the years he attended concerts of his works in Frankfurt, Oslo, Rome, Stockholm, Paris, and London. He participated in the Latin American Music Festival of Caracas (1957), acting as juror for the composition competition. The following year he went to the United States to attend the premiere

Alberto Ginastera. ORGANIZATION OF AMERICAN STATES.

JOHN VINTON, ed., *Dictionary of Contemporary Music* (1974); *New Grove Dictionary of Music and Musicians* (1980); *New Grove Dictionary of Opera*, vol. 7 (1992).

SUSANA SALGADO

GIRIBALDI, (VICENTE) TOMÁS E. (*b.* 18 October 1847; *d.* 11 April 1930), Uruguayan composer. Giribaldi was born in Montevideo, where he began his studies with Giuseppe Strigelli and the celebrated Italian bass player Giovanni Bottesini. Later, he studied with the Spaniard Carmelo Calvo and the Italian Giuseppe Giuffra, European composers who had settled in Montevideo. As a member of a family of musicians of Italian origin, Giribaldi became an active participant in the musical life of Montevideo at an early age. His first compositions were piano and vocal pieces; as he matured, he became attracted to the operatic forms. As the first opera written by a Uruguayan composer, *La Parisina*, which premiered at the TEATRO SOLÍS in Montevideo on 14 September 1878, earned for Giribaldi a place of honor in the music history of his country. The Italian libretto by Felice Romani was sung by the artists of the Italian Lyric Company Nazarino under the baton of maestro Leopoldo Montenegro. Giribaldi composed three additional operas: *Manfredi di Svevia, Inés de Castro,* and *Magda,* none of which achieved the success of *La Parisina.* In addition, he composed works for orchestra, band, and piano, as well as chamber music, including the symphonic poem *El Athenaeum,* and the suite *Scènes militaires.* He died in Montevideo.

SUSANA SALGADO, *Breve historia de la música culta en el Uruguay,* 2d ed. (1980); *New Grove Dictionary of Opera*, vol. 2 (1992); SUSANA SALGADO, *The Teatro Solís of Montevideo* (forthcoming).

SUSANA SALGADO

of his *Segundo Cuarteto* by the Juilliard Quartet at the First Inter-American Music Festival in Washington, D.C. During the Second Inter-American Music Festival (1961), Ginastera achieved world recognition with the premiere of the *Cantata para América Mágica* and the Piano Concerto No. 1, commissioned by the Fromm and Koussevitzky foundations, respectively. His opera *Don Rodrigo,* based on a libretto by Alejandro Casona, premiered at the Teatro Colón in July 1964. Soon there followed two additional operas, both commissioned by the Opera Society of Washington: *Bomarzo* (May 1967) and *Beatrix Cenci,* performed on 10 September 1971 during the inauguration of the Kennedy Center for the Performing Arts.

Ginastera was one of the most prominent Latin American composers of the twentieth century and much of his music has entered the international repertory. His works have an exuberant, dramatic quality, and they range in style from a subjective nationalism to a more objective, abstract mode, using advanced techniques: polytonality, microtonality, aleatory procedures, and twelve-tone writing. All of his compositions retain a lyrical, expressionistic aspect, involving the use of *Sprechstimme* (speech song) in the vocal works. He died in Geneva.

GIRÓN, FRANCISCO HERNÁNDEZ (*d.* 7 December 1554), leader of the last major uprising against royal authority during the Peruvian civil wars. Born in Cáceres, he probably participated in the conquest of Veragua in 1535, before continuing to Peru. A relative of Captain Lorenzo de Aldana, he marched under orders of Francisco PIZARRO to remove Sebastián de BELALCÁZAR from the north in 1538. Largely successful, he became a *vecino* of Pasto. He was a supporter of Viceroy Blasco NÚÑEZ VELA during the uprising of Gonzalo PIZARRO, and was named a captain of a company of infantry pikemen. He served the viceroy as well, particularly in defense of the rear guard.

During the battle of Añaquito (January 1546), Girón was in charge of a group of harquebusiers but fell wounded and was captured by Gonzalo Pizarro. Pizarro forced the prisoner to negotiate with Benalcázar to gain his support. But with the arrival of Pedro de la GASCA (ca. 1547), both Benalcázar and Girón traveled to Andahuaylas to join the royal cause. Girón received substantial reward: la Gasca extended him the *encomienda* of Jaquijahuana. He was, nevertheless, dissatisfied. Realizing his disaffection, and hoping to rid himself of the malcontent, La Gasca appointed him leader of an expedition to conquer the fierce Chunchos Indians. At this juncture, however, Girón's disagreements with the *corregidor* of Cuzco got him charged and brought to the Audiencia of Lima for trial. Freed on bond, he returned to Cuzco, where on 12 November 1553 he organized another uprising, this time directed against authorities of the Audiencia of Lima, which had ordered a new tribute assessment and the end to personal service of the Indians. He and his forces left Cuzco on 4 January 1554.

Meanwhile, after learning of the uprising, Marshall Alonso de Alvarado amassed an army of 700 Spaniards and 7,000 native Americans in the name of the king. (In late December 1553 the *oidores* in Lima had revoked the order ending personal service and created a military force in Lima.) Both forces met and fought at Chuquinga on 21 May 1554. Victorious, Girón traveled to Cuzco; at the same time, royal forces were reorganized. The final battle took place 8 October 1554 at the Inca site of PUCARÁ. There, Girón's fortunes ended. The majority of his soldiers deserted, but the rebel escaped capture and fled to Acarí, hoping to take flight to freedom. Unfortunately, the ship sailed out of the harbor as his weary soldiers arrived, so he marched northward to CHINCHA, then entered the highlands, taking refuge in Hatun-Jauja. It was there he was captured after a final skirmish. He was transported to Lima and beheaded as a traitor in the Plaza de Armas on 7 December 1554.

JOSÉ ANTONIO DEL BUSTO DUTHURBURU, *Historia general del Perú*, vol. 2, *Descubrimiento y conquista* (1978); ALEXANDRA PARMA COOK and NOBLE DAVID COOK, *Good Faith and Truthful Ignorance: A Case of Transatlantic Bigamy* (1992).

NOBLE DAVID COOK

GIRÓN DE LEÓN, ANDRÉS DE JESÚS (*b*. 14 February 1946), Guatemalan priest and peasant leader. Girón was born in Santa Cruz del Quiché and was raised in the municipality of Tecpán in Chimaltenango. He received religious training at the seminary of Santiago de Guatemala and later in the United States.

Girón became an important national political figure when he founded the National Peasants' Association for Land (Asociación Nacional Campesina Pro-Tierra) in 1986. He received widespread media attention by leading 16,000 peasants on an 88-mile march from Escuintla to Guatemala City in May of 1986. His organization acquired several large landholdings for campesinos to farm cooperatively, but the movement lost membership and importance after 1989.

JULIO CASTELLANOS CAMBRANES, *Agrarismo en Guatemala* (Guatemala and Madrid, 1986).

RACHEL A. MAY

GIRONELLA, ALBERTO (*b*. 26 September 1929), Mexican painter and illustrator. Born in Mexico City, Gironella considers himself a self-taught artist. He is a very talented draftsman and sensitive colorist. In 1959 he received a prize in the Paris Biennial of young painters. Since that time, his work has appeared in many individual and group exhibitions in the United States, Latin America, Europe, and Japan. His most noted individual shows have been at the Galería Prisse in Mexico City (1959), the offices of the Organization of American States in Washington, D.C. (1959), the Galería Juan Martín in Mexico City (1963, 1964, 1968, 1977, and 1979), the Sala Nacional of the Palacio de Bellas Artes in Mexico City (1972), and the Museo de Arte Moderno in Mexico City (1977). Gironella tempers crude naturalism with formal elements derived from Spanish painters, resulting in sarcastic reinterpretations of seventeenth-century court life. He also draws on familiar figures in Mexican folk art, such as the skeleton.

BÉLGICA RODRÍGUEZ

GIRRI, ALBERTO (*b*. 1919), Argentine poet. Born in Buenos Aires, Girri may best be described as one of the last of the prominent male modernist poetic voices of the turbulent mid-twentieth century in Argentina. Girri wrote against the backdrop of some of the most violent and unstable times in his country's history, and his poetry evinces the firm conviction that a humanistic cultural tradition is the best refuge from and bulwark against the insecurities of life. Girri's modernist aesthetic put him outside the sphere of committed literature that was central at the time, and his poetry is marked by an emphasis on the solitude of the poetic voice and by extensive elaborations on the hermetic surrealism of the period, often with an impressive sense of the terror of existential anguish. Girri also published many translations of English-language poets.

JORGE A. PAITA, "La poesía de Alberto Girri: Rigor de un intelecto exasperado," in *Sur*, no. 285 (1963): 92–99; SANTIAGO KOVADLOFF, "Alberto Girri: La poesía es el corazón de la literatura," in *Crisis* no. 40 (1976): 40–44; SAÚL YURKIEVICH, "Alberto Girri: Fases de su creciente," *Hispamérica* 10, no. 29 (1981): 99–105; ALICIA BORINSKY, "Interlocución y aporia: Notas a propósito de Alberto Girri y Juan Gelman," in *Revista Iberoamericana* 49, no. 125 (1983): 879–887.

DAVID WILLIAM FOSTER

GISMONTI, EGBERTO (*b*. 5 December 1944), Brazilian composer, guitarist, and pianist. Born into a musical family with many professional musicians, including a band-director grandfather and a band-director uncle, Egberto Gismonti enrolled for his first music lessons in the musical conservatory of NOVA FRIBURGO in the state of Rio de Janeiro at age five. He studied fifteen years with Jacques Klein and Aurelio Silveira, and then was awarded a grant for study in Vienna. An arrangement of one of his compositions, *O sonho*, written for an orchestra of one hundred performers, was performed in Rio in 1968. Shortly thereafter he went to France, where he continued his musical studies and worked as a professional accompanist.

Gismonti is best known for his startlingly vivid settings of songs recorded on compact discs released in France, Germany, and Brazil. His use of electronic instruments, traditional percussion instruments, Brazilian percussion instruments, and Indian flutes have made recordings such as *Agua e vinho* (1972) and other song settings powerful expressions of Brazilian popular culture. He has also been active as a composer of film music in *A penúltima donzela* (1969), *Em familia* (1971), and *Confissões do frei Abóbora* (1971).

MARCOS ANTÔNIO MARCONDES, ed., *Enciclopédia da música brasileira: Erudita, folclórica e popular* (1977).

DAVID P. APPLEBY

GLANTZ, MARGO (*b.* 28 January 1930), Mexican writer and critic. A professor of philosophy and letters at the National University of Mexico, Glantz was for a time director of the university's creative journal *Punto de Partida* and head of the department of literature at the National Institute of Fine Arts (1982–1986). Her work includes creative prose, literary and cultural criticism, and translations. Her memoir *Las genealogías* (1981), about her family of Ukrainian Jewish origin, won the Magda Donato Literary Prize in 1982. This was followed by the Xavier Villarrutia Prize for the prose poem *Síndrome de naufragios* in 1984. As a feminist, Glantz has defied the conventional "male" genres to render postmodern, innovative, and experimental texts where a woman's perspective necessarily alters the traditional forms. As a critic, she is recognized for her controversial critique of "la generación de la Onda" (wave), a group of young writers influenced by the U.S. counterculture of the early 1970s. Glantz has also translated the works of Georges Bataille, Jerzy Grotowski, and Thomas Kyd.

MAGDALENA GARCÍA-PINTO, "Margo Glantz" in *Women Writers of Latin America: Intimate Histories* (1988), pp. 105–122; NORA PASTERNAC, "Margo Glantz: La escritura fragmentaria," in *Mujer y Literatura Mexicana y Chicana: Culturas en contacto*, vol. 1 (1988), pp. 205–210; MAGDALENA GARCÍA-PINTO, "La problemática de la sexualidad en la escritura de Margo Glantz," in *Coloquio internacional: Escritura y sexualidad en la literatura hispanoamericana*, edited by Alain Sicard and Fernando Moreno (1990), pp. 31–47; NAOMI LINDSTROM, "No pronunciarás de Margo Glantz: Los nombres como señas de la imaginación cultural," *Revista Iberoamericana* 56, no. 150 (1990): 275–287.

NORMA KLAHN

GLISSANT, ÉDOUARD (*b.* 21 September 1928), writer and teacher of Martinique. Aimé CÉSAIRE was Glissant's professor at the Lycée Schoelcher in Fort-de-France, Martinique. With the group Franc-Jeu, Glissant and Frantz Fanon worked for Aimé Césaire's election to the Constituent Assembly in 1945. Glissant went to France on a scholarship in 1946. Active in the Front Antillo-Guyanais pour l'Indépendance, Glissant was barred (1961) from returning to Martinique or traveling to Algeria. After the French government finally allowed Glissant to return to Martinique in 1965, he founded the Institut Martiniquais d'Études and the journal *Acoma* in an effort to develop cultural consciousness among young Martinicans. Glissant later accepted a chair in Francophone literature at Louisiana State University.

Édouard Glissant has become the major proponent of "creolization," a concept that underscores acceptance of a decentered position in the world, the willingness to encounter the other rather than take one's own standpoint as central, and the will to take cross-breeding (*métissage*) as normal rather than exceptional and reprehensible. Purists are shocked by the contagious mixing of cultures in the language of the young. "Alert to the intermingling of world cultures," poets, according to Glissant, "are delighted." Glissant wants to build the Tower of Babel "in all languages."

Works by Édouard Glissant include: *Un champ d'îles* (poetry, 1953); *La lézarde* (novel, 1958); translated by J. Michael Dash as *The Ripening* (1985); *Monsieur Toussaint* (play, 1961), translated by Joseph G. Foster and Barbara Franklin (1981); *Le sang rivé* (poetry, 1961); *Le quatrième siècle* (novel, 1962), Prix Charles-Vallon; *Poèmes . . .* (poetry, 1965); *Malemort* (novel, 1975); *La case du commandeur* (novel, 1981); *Le discours antillais* (essays, 1981), translated by J. Michael Dash as *Caribbean Discourse: Selected Essays* (1989); *Le sel noir* (rev. ed., 1983); *Les Indes; Un champ d'îles; La terre inquiète* (collected poems, 1985); *Pays rêvé, pays réel* (poems, 1985); *Mahagony* (novel, 1987); *Poétique de la relation* (essays, 1990); *Fastes* (poems, 1991).

BERNADETTE CAILLER, *Conquérants de la nuit nue: Édouard Glissant et l'histoire antillaise* (1988). J. MICHAEL DASH, *Caribbean Discourse: World Literature Today* 63, no. 4 (1989), special issue devoted to Glissant: bibliography, texts, critical articles; PATRICK CHAMOISEAU and RAPHAËL CONFIANT, *Lettres créoles: Tracées antillaises et continentales de la littérature, 1635–1975* (1991), pp. 185–202.

CARROL F. COATES

GOA AND PORTUGUESE ASIA. Goa, Daman, and Diu—all located in India—Malacca, the Moluccas, Macau, and Timor were the most important Portuguese areas in Asia. Portugal was the major European commercial power east of the Cape of Good Hope during the sixteenth century. After 1650 Portugal maintained only a minor position in Asia.

Goa A Portuguese possession from 1510 to 1961, then a territory of India until 1987, Goa is now an Indian state. Located on the Arabian Sea about 250 miles south of Bombay, Goa has two distinct areas: the Old Conquests, with a strong Catholic presence, includes Ilhas, Bardes, and Salcette; and the New Conquests, with a Hindu majority, includes the outlying districts taken from the Marathas between 1746 and 1782. Goa is about

60 miles in length and 40 miles in width at its widest point, with a total area of some 1,400 square miles. The highest elevations, about 3,400 feet, occur in the Western Ghats, on the border with Karnataka. Three distinct climates mark the seasons: hot in April and May, at 84°F; monsoon from June to September, at 81°F; and cool and dry from October to March, at 77°F. The soils, though below average for fertility, are well watered: Goa receives about 92 inches of rain each year. The major crops are rice, cashews, areca, mangoes, and coconuts. Cattle raising and fishing have also been important in the area. In the twentieth century, iron ore and manganese have been mined and exported on a large scale. Since independence, tourism also contributes significantly to Goa's economy.

Hindu Saraswat Brahmans, who were granted exclusive control of both internal and external state monopolies by the Portuguese in the sixteenth century, have dominated Goan commercial life ever since. Catholic Saraswat Brahmans have been important landowners since the sixteenth century. Catholic Goans can be found living throughout the world; reportedly there are more Catholic Goans in Bombay than in Goa itself. Konkani is the state's official language; other languages spoken in Goa include English, Portuguese, Marathi, and Urdu.

The population of Goa totaled 266,000 in 1810, and had reached more than 1 million by 1990. Approximately 67 percent of Goans are Hindu, 30 percent are Catholic, and 3 percent are Islamic or Protestant. Goans enjoy the highest per capita income in India.

Daman Daman is a port city 23 square miles in extent, located on the Gulf of Cambay in Gujarat State, about 100 miles north of Bombay and 50 miles south of Surat (the major port in India in 1700). Daman was conquered by the Portuguese in 1559. The nearby districts of Dadra and Nagar Haveli were taken from the Marathas in 1780 and thereafter administered from Daman until 1954, the year in which the Indians ousted the Portuguese from the inland areas. A flourishing port until Portuguese sea power declined in the seventeenth century, Daman continued to be a major exporter of cotton textiles to an area extending from Goa to Hormuz and Mozambique until 1820. The city enjoyed a brief boom from 1815 to 1840 while exporting Malwa opium to the Far East. The city's population was 32,000 in 1810 and approximately 50,000 in 1985.

Diu About 17 square miles in total area, Diu consists of a fortified island, a larger island, and a narrow strip of land at the end of the Kathiawar Peninsula on the Saurashtra coast of Gujarat State, about 165 miles northwest of Bombay. After seizing the area in 1534, the Portuguese constructed a fort at Diu, which thereafter served as a critical link in their control of the Indian Ocean. Diu's commercial ties extended from the Gulf of Cambay to the Red Sea area and East Africa. Cotton textiles were the major export in an economy dominated by banyans. In the 1820s and 1830s Diu shared in the export trade of Malwa opium to the Far East. Few

Portuguese ever resided in Diu. The city's population was 9,500 in 1810 and approximately 35,000 in 1985.

Malacca A port city in present-day Malaysia on the Straits of Malacca, Malacca is located about 120 miles northwest of Singapore. Prior to 1500, Chinese, Indian, and Arab merchants made Malacca the major commercial center for spices in the Far Eastern trade. Alfonso d'Albuquerque conquered the city for Portugal in 1511, after which the Portuguese made huge profits in the spice trade. The Dutch expelled the Portuguese from Malacca in 1641.

The Moluccas The Moluccas are a group of islands, comprising about 28,000 square miles of land, located east of Celebes, west of New Guinea, north of Timor, and south of the Philippines. Also known as the Spice Islands, the Moluccas are a rich agricultural zone famous for abundant spices such as cloves, nutmeg, mace, and pepper. Christopher COLUMBUS was seeking a quicker way to voyage to the Moluccas when he "discovered" the New World. The Portuguese established a presence in the Moluccas in 1511 and thereafter fought almost continuously with the Spanish, the English, and the Dutch to maintain control of the area's spice riches. The Dutch finally succeeded in expelling the Portuguese in 1612.

Macau Macau (also spelled Macao) consists of the islands of Taipa and Coloane and a small, narrow peninsula projecting from the Chinese mainland on the western side of the Pearl River estuary, about 40 miles southeast of Hong Kong. Macau has a total area of about 6.5 square miles. The southwest monsoon dominates the area's climate from April to September; rainfall ranges from 40 to 100 inches annually. July and August are the warmest months, at 84°F, and December is the coolest, at 51°F.

Like Hong Kong, Macau owes its existence to its proximity to the key Chinese port of Guangdong (Canton). The Portuguese established Macau as an outpost for trade with China in 1557, and thereafter paid tribute to the Chinese emperor until 1849. From Macau, Portuguese merchants also developed links with Japan, the Philippines, Timor, Indonesia, and Southeast Asia. The Portuguese built a new customhouse to handle increasing trade in 1784. From 1770 to 1840 Macau enjoyed an economic boom due to its middleman role in the opium trade from India to Guangdong and other areas of China. As the opium trade declined in importance, Macau prospered anew from shipping Chinese coolies to Peru, Cuba, and elswhere. During World War II Macau served as a refuge from the Japanese, who did not attempt to seize the city (Portugal was a neutral state during the war). Gambling casinos, tourism, manufacturing, and the reexport of Chinese products have been the mainstays of Macau's economy since the 1950s. On 20 December 1999 Macau will revert to China; however, Macau will retain its autonomy for the following fifty years.

Timor Timor is the easternmost island in the Lesser Sunda chain, and is situated about 500 miles east of Bali and about 400 miles northwest of Australia. The island is about 300 miles long and 40 miles wide, with a total area of some 12,000 square miles. Timor has a mountainous terrain, with its highest elevation nearing 10,000 feet. Timor has a long dry season and an irregular monsoon season from December to April.

The Portuguese began to trade with Timor between 1513 and 1520, seeking sandalwood, honey, and beeswax. Missionaries arrived between 1562 and 1585, with permanent Portuguese settlers following in 1586. The Portuguese lost Malacca to the Dutch in 1641 and the western half of Timor to the Dutch in 1651. Thereafter Macau dominated the Portuguese trade with Timor. Dili, the major port and capital of the Portuguese eastern half of Timor, sent sandalwood and slaves to Macau from 1769 to perhaps as late as the early 1900s. Opium, imported from Macau, was introduced into western Indonesia via Timor in exchange for agricultural products. Slavery still existed in Timor in the nineteenth century and was not phased out until after the abolition decree for Portuguese Asia in 1875. Slavery existed in Timor until the eve of World War I. Coffee has been the major export since the 1860s.

The Japanese occupied Timor during World War II. Destruction was widespread, including the loss of the island's archives. Oil exploration in the Timor Sea has continued since the 1970s. The Portuguese revolution of 1974 led to East Timor's unilateral declaration of independence from Portuguese rule. But Indonesia invaded Timor that same year and annexed the entire island. Guerrilla warfare and human rights abuses have characterized the island's history ever since, as the people of Timor, having thrown off the yoke of Portuguese and Dutch rule, now attempt to oust the Indonesians.

The population of East Timor was slightly over 900,000 in the 1850s, and stood at about 550,000 in 1980.

CHARLES R. BOXER, *Fidalgos in the Far East: 1550–1770* (1968), and *The Portuguese Seaborne Empire, 1425–1825* (1969); ARTUR TEODORE DE MATOS, *Timor português: 1515–1769* (1974); ANTHONY R. DISNEY, *Twilight of the Pepper Empire: Portuguese Trade in Southwest India in the Early Seventeenth Century* (1978); TEOTONIO R. DE SOUZA, *Medieval Goa: A Socio-Economic History* (1979); CHARLES R. BOXER, *Portuguese India in the Mid-Seventeenth Century* (1980); MICHAEL R. PEARSON, *Coastal Western India* (1981); RUDY BAUSS, "A Legacy of British Free Trade Policies: The End of Trade and Commerce between India and the Portuguese Empire, 1780–1830," in *Calcutta Historical Journal* 6 (1982); GERVASE CLARENCE-SMITH, *The Third Portuguese Empire, 1825–1975* (1985); MICHAEL N. PEARSON, *The Portuguese in India.* Vol. I.1, *The New Cambridge History of India* (1988); ANTHONY REID, *Southeast Asia in the Age of Commerce, 1450–1680* (1988); SANJAY SUBRAHMANYAM, *The Political Economy of Commerce: Southern India, 1500–1650* (1990) and *The Portuguese Empire in Asia, 1500–1700: A Political and Economic History* (1993).

RUDY BAUSS

GOBERNADOR. In Spanish America the *gobernador* (governor) ranked behind the VICEROY, CAPTAIN-GENERAL, and president in the hierarchy of colonial administrators. Like so many colonial institutions, the governorship had its origins in medieval Spain when the monarchs of Castile and Aragon appointed *procuradores* to represent royal interests and enforce royal laws in areas where they could not rule personally. (Such officials became the viceroys in areas of Spain taken from the Moors.)

The first governor in the New World was Christopher COLUMBUS, who received the title Governor of the Indies in the Capitulations of Santa Fe in April 1492. Soon after, however, Ferdinand and Isabella replaced him as governor of Española with two loyal subjects, first with Francisco de BOBADILLA and then with Nicolás de OVANDO, thus firmly establishing the governorship in the Indies. As the Spanish presence in the Caribbean increased, the crown appointed governors for the newly conquered islands, the best known of whom were Juan Ponce de LEÓN in Puerto Rico and Diego de VELÁSQUEZ in Cuba.

Extension of the Spanish conquest into Mexico and South America ultimately led CHARLES I to establish viceroys in New Spain (Mexico) and Peru and captain-generals in areas of the Spanish Indies far removed from the viceregal capitals such as Chile, Guatemala, and Venezuela. Governors served in less important areas such as Florida, Nicaragua, and Panama and in some of the key cities such as Cartagena, Huancavelica, and Veracruz. For most of these gubernatorial posts, the appointee had to have the military rank of colonel and to have been born in Spain, but the crown occasionally ignored one or both of these requirements if a would-be governor had demonstrated his fitness for office in other ways.

Recopilación de leyes de los Reynos de las Indias, 4 vols. (1681; repr. 1973), libro V, título II; JOHN JAY TE PASKE, *The Governorship of Spanish Florida, 1700–1763* (1964).

JOHN JAY TePASKE

GODOI, JUAN SILVANO (*b.* 12 November 1850; *d.* 27 January 1926), Paraguayan historian, bibliophile, and political figure. Though born in Asunción, Godoi spent his early years in Buenos Aires, where he studied law. He interrupted his studies in 1869 to return to Paraguay to participate, at age nineteen, in the drafting of his country's first democratic constitution.

The defeat of Marshal Francisco Solano LÓPEZ a year later initiated a period of great political instability and foreign intervention in Paraguay; various factions vied for power. Godoi joined actively in a number of political intrigues, including the 1877 assassination of President Juan Bautista GILL, a Brazilian puppet. As a result of these activities, Godoi was forced into exile and went to Argentina, where he stayed eighteen years. While there, he remained active in emigré politics, however, and on several occasions helped to arm rebel groups who sought to invade Paraguay.

In the mid-1890s Godoi accepted a government compromise that permitted him to return to Asunción. While in exile, he had amassed a prize-winning library of 20,000 volumes, which he now used to form the nucleus of a new national library. From 1902 until his death, Godoi was director of the National Library, Museum, and Archive. He was also a historian of note, having written a dozen studies, including *Monografías históricas* (1893), *Últimas operaciones de guerra del General José Eduvigis Díaz* (1897), *Mi misión a Río de Janeiro* (1897), *La muerte del Mariscal López* (1905), *El baron de Río Branco* (1912), and *El Asalto a los acorazados* (1919). Godoi's personal diaries and manuscripts are now held in the Special Collections Library of the University of California, Riverside.

WILLIAM BELMONT PARKER, *Paraguayans of To-Day* (repr. 1967), pp. 15–17; JACK RAY THOMAS, *Biographical Dictionary of Latin American Historians and Historiography* (1984); CARLOS ZUBIZARRETA, *Cien vidas paraguayas*, 2d ed. (1985), pp. 218–222.

THOMAS L. WHIGHAM

GODOY, MANUEL (*b.* 12 May 1767; *d.* 4 October 1851), first minister and favorite of Charles IV of Spain. Godoy was born into a modest hidalgo family in Estremadura. He obtained an adequate education in the liberal arts and, at the age of nineteen, entered the royal bodyguards. From this position he rose to power rapidly amid rumors that he was Queen María Luisa's lover. The titles he acquired included duke of Alcudia, prime minister (1792), admiral general of Spain and the Indies, and Prince of the Peace (after negotiating the Peace of Basel with France in 1795). The unprecedented princely title set him above all other grandees in Spain.

Circumstances as well as favoritism played a role in Godoy's ascent. Previous ministers had failed to appease the revolutionaries in France, and CHARLES IV's change in policy toward France required someone not identified with the policies of the past.

In domestic policy, Godoy attempted to carry on the reforming spirit of the reign of CHARLES III, but his lack of experience led to a series of ad hoc policies and his most radical proposals were based on the royal need for revenue. His colonial policy, like those of his ministerial predecessors, also sought to increase revenue. Suspecting that he was treating with enemies of the Revolution, the Directory in France urged his dismissal and Godoy resigned his post on 28 March 1798.

Godoy returned to power in 1801 with the blessing of Charles IV and María Luisa. Although without formal office, Godoy enjoyed a powerful influence in policy making. Thereafter he became a pawn of NAPOLEON and, believing he had a future as the prince of the Algarve, was instrumental in allowing French troops to enter Spain.

Contemporaries despised Godoy as a young, inexperienced upstart, and although he tried to win the political support of moderate reformists, his foreign policy had disastrous results that fed his opponents' ire. Godoy was despised in the colonies as well as in Spain and the news of the riot at Aranjuez (1808) that led to his dismissal and Charles's abdication was joyously received in Spain and throughout the empire.

JACQUES CHASTENET, *Godoy, Master of Spain, 1792–1808* (1953); RICHARD HERR, *The Eighteenth-Century Revolution in Spain* (1958), esp. pp. 348–444; CARLOS SECO SERRANO, *Godoy, el hombre y el político* (1978); DOUGLAS HILT, *The Troubled Trinity* (1987).

SUZANNE HILES BURKHOLDER

GODOY CRUZ, TOMÁS (*b.* 6 March 1791; *d.* 15 May 1852), Argentine businessman, educator, and politician. Born in MENDOZA to a patrician family, Godoy Cruz earned degrees in philosophy and law from the University of San Felipe, Chile, in 1810 and 1813. When Facundo QUIROGA invaded Mendoza in 1831, José Videla Castillo, de facto governor of the province, and his allies, of whom Godoy Cruz was one, were exiled to Chile. In exile during the 1830s, Godoy Cruz published a *Manual* (1838) on textiles, taught extensively in related fields, and invested in Argentine commerce, mining, and textiles. Aware of Godoy Cruz's expertise, Governor José Félix Aldao asked him back from exile and in 1846 appointed him to direct governmental policies regarding textile industries in the province. His most notable contribution, however, was in politics. A contemporary viewed him as someone "accustomed to the admiration and even respect of San Martín and O'Higgins, having a great appreciation for his own person and the conviction of his opinions." Godoy Cruz, a close collaborator of SAN MARTÍN and a suppporter of Platine independence who donated his homestead to the cause early in the conflict, displayed this self-confidence in the Congress of TUCUMÁN (1816–1819) and as governor of Mendoza (1820–1822), where he died.

PEDRO ISIDRO CARAFFA, *Hombres notables de Cuyo* (1912); ENRIQUE UDAONDO, *Diccionario biográfico argentino* (1938), pp. 459–460; BENITO MARIANETTI, *Un mendocino en el Congreso de Tucumán* (1966).

FIDEL IGLESIAS

GOERITZ, MATHIAS (*b.* 4 April 1915; *d.* 1990?), Mexican painter, sculptor, and teacher. Born in Danzig, Goeritz studied medicine, art, art history, and philosophy in Berlin. He arrived in Mexico in 1949 and began an active life in the arts as a teacher, artist, and founder of four art galleries between 1950 and 1952 in Guadalajara, Jalisco. He is primarily known for his experimental museum El Eco, constructed in Mexico City in 1953, and his great Plaza of the Five Towers, constructed in 1957–1958 in Satellite City, a suburb of Mexico City. The monumental size of the towers and the spatial integration of a sculpture with the floor and walls of El Eco influenced primary structure and minimalist sculptors of the United States and Mexico in the 1960s and 1970s.

In 1960 Goeritz distributed "Please Stop," a printed leaflet, in front of the Museum of Modern Art in New York City to protest the exhibition of Jean Tinguely's *Homage to New York,* a self-destructing machine, because it exemplified the loss of spirituality in art. In 1961 a manifesto by Goeritz inspired Petro Friedeberg, José Luis CUEVAS, and others to form a group in Mexico City called Los Hartos (Fed Up). Goertiz's other major works include Pyramid of Mixcose (1970) for a housing project in Mexico City; Centro del Espacio Escultorico (1979), sixty-four modules with sculpture near the ancient site of Cuicuilco; and Laberinto de Jerusalem (1973–1980), a community center in Jerusalem that is a wonderful example of sculpture combined with architecture.

GREGORY BATTCOCK, *Minimal Art: A Critical Anthology* (1968); FREDERICO MORAIS, *Mathias Goeritz* (1982).

JACINTO QUIRARTE

GOETHALS, GEORGE WASHINGTON (*b.* 29 June 1858; *d.* 21 January 1928), U.S. Army officer and engineer. After graduating from the United States Military Academy in 1880, Goethals studied engineering at Willetts Point, New York; taught for four years at West Point; and supervised improvement work on the Ohio and Tennessee rivers. He was chief of engineers with the First Army Corps during the Spanish-American War in 1898; supervised river and harbor works in New England from 1900 to 1903; and served on the U.S. Army's general staff from 1903 to 1907. Following the resignation of two civilian engineers, President Theodore Roosevelt in 1907 appointed Goethals chief of the army engineers supervising the construction of the PANAMA CANAL. Goethals brought the project to completion in early 1914 after overcoming problems in engineering, supply, climate, disease, and living conditions. At that time President Woodrow Wilson appointed Goethals the first governor of the Canal Zone. During World War I, Goethals served as director of purchase, storage, and traffic for the War Department. He retired from the military after the war to establish his own engineering consulting firm.

GEORGE W. GOETHALS, ed., *The Panama Canal: An Engineering Treatise,* 2 vols. (1916); JOSEPH B. BISHOP, *Goethals: Genius of the Panama Canal* (1930); DAVID MC CULLOUGH, *The Path Between the Seas: The Creation of the Panama Canal, 1870–1914* (1977).

THOMAS M. LEONARD

GOIÁS, a Brazilian state that had an area of 248,000 square miles until 1989, when the new state of TOCANTINS was created out of a portion of it. Goiás now covers 137,000 square miles and has a population of 4 million (1990 est.). The geographical center of Brazil, Goiás encompasses the Federal District and the new capital of BRASÍLIA. The name *Goiás* comes from one of the tribes of Indians who used to be very numerous throughout the territory. The first chronicler, Silva e Souza, counted seventeen tribes in existence at the beginning of the nineteenth century. Today they are nearly all extinct.

During the sixteenth and seventeenth centuries, Goiás was only occasionally reached by explorers and raiders who came from São Paulo to hunt Indians. It was officially discovered during the gold rush by Bartolomeu Bueno de Silva's ("The Anhanguera") expedition (1722–1725). The discovery of gold brought about the first colonization and the characteristics typical of a gold rush: violence, instability, a rapid boom, and a sudden decline. This period lasted about sixty years (1726–1785) and left behind a town and three dozen frontier settlements with a total population of about sixty thousand.

The gold gone, the population became sedentary, spreading out over the plains and sierras and dedicating themselves to subsistence farming and the raising of cattle. Throughout the entire nineteenth century and into the first decades of the twentieth, the export of livestock constituted the area's only commercial relationship with the rest of the country. The population grew slowly, aided by constant immigration from the neighboring states of São Paulo, Minas Gerais, Bahia, and Maranhão. The 1920 census registered 500,000 inhabitants living throughout the vast open spaces.

The third phase of colonization began with the Revolution of 1930 and the so-called "march to the west." This initiated a very dynamic period for the population of the Goiás area that was still going strong in the mid-1990s. In 1933 construction was begun on the new capital of Goiás, Goiânia, both symbolizing and stimulating the drive toward modernization and progress. Its establishment should have marked the fall of the old oligarchies and the beginning of economic progress. In both cases, however, the road proved longer than anticipated. The triumph of Goiânia was not the hoped for industrial modernization, but the great impulse given to the agricultural colonization of the east central region of the country.

By 1990, the population of Goiâna had reached over a million. The construction of BRASÍLIA begun in 1960 (as a political commitment to the development of Brazil's interior) and the completion of great nationalized railroads—especially the one from Belém to Brasília—promoted the occupation of the last open spaces: the valleys of the ARAGUAIA and the TOCANTINS rivers in the extreme north. In recent decades, government projects have aided the growth of the livestock industry and of exportable crops (soy, corn, and rice).

LUIS PALACIN, *Goiás, 1722–1822: Estrutura e conjuntura numa Capitania de Minas* (1972); F. ITAMI CAMPOS, *Coronelismo em Goiás* (1983); LUIS PALACIN and MARIA AUGUSTA DE SANT'ANNA MORAES, *História de Goiás,* 4th ed. (1986); NASR N. FAYAD CHAUL, *A construção de Goiânia e a transferência da capital* (1988).

LUIS PALACÍN

See also **Bandeirantes.**

GOICURÍA Y CABRERA, DOMINGO (*b.* 23 June 1804; *d.* 6 May 1870), Cuban independence figure. Goicuría, a native of Havana, was a rich merchant who became even richer during the U.S. Civil War running supplies from Mexico to Texas. He favored slavery and the colonization of Cuba by whites. A tenacious opponent of Spanish colonial rule, at first he advocated the annexation of the island to the United States, and in 1855 he supported a U.S.-backed expedition to Cuba that failed. This led him to embrace the idea of independence, and a year later he joined forces with the American filibuster William WALKER for the invasion of Nicaragua. He expected that after taking over Nicaragua, Walker would invade Cuba. But Walker wanted to conquer the rest of Central America rather than Cuba, and the two men quarreled. Afterward Goicuría intensified his anti-Spanish activities until he finally succeeded in invading Cuba after the 1868 outbreak of the TEN YEARS' WAR. He was captured in February 1870 by the Spaniards and three months later was publicly executed by garrote in Havana.

GERALD E. POYO makes some references to Goicuría's activities in *"With All and for the Good of All"* (1989). See also VIDAL MORALES, *Iniciadores y primeros mártires de la revolución cubana* (1963), vol 3.

JOSÉ M. HERNÁNDEZ

See also **Filibustering.**

GOLBERY DO COUTO E SILVA (*b.* 21 August 1911; *d.* 18 September 1987), Brazilian military officer and political figure. Born in Rio Grande do Sul, Golbery graduated from the military command college. He attended the U.S. Army Command and General Staff College at Fort Leavenworth in 1944 before serving in the BRAZILIAN EXPEDITIONARY FORCE (FEB) in Italy in 1944–1945. In 1952 he began teaching at the recently formed Higher War College (Escola Superior de Guerra—ESG). Through his writings and work in the ESG, he exerted enormous influence on the formation of the National Security Doctrine. Golbery became the head of the National Security Council under Jânio QUADROS in 1961 but resigned when João GOULART became president in the same year. Between 1961 and 1964 he headed the IPES (Instituto de Pesquisas e Estudos Sociais), a privately funded think tank and intelligence-gathering operation that played a notorious role in working for the overthrow of Goulart.

After the military coup of 1964, President Humberto CASTELLO BRANCO created the SNI (Serviço Nacional de Informações) and named Golbery to head the agency with cabinet-level status. Along with other "moderates," Golbery lost influence with the "election" of Artur COSTA E SILVA (1967–1969) and then Emílio MÉDICI (1969–1974) to the presidency. He served as the head of the civilian presidential staff during the administration of Ernesto GEISEL (1974–1979) and in the first two years of the presidency of João Baptista FIGUEIREDO (1979–1985).

Along with Geisel, Golbery was one of the principal figures in the shaky and tentative process of ABERTURA (political opening). He resigned from the government in 1981 when he was unable to persuade the president to press an investigation of a political scandal implicating the hardliners in the government and the SNI.

GOLBERY DO COUTO E SILVA, *Aspectos geopolíticos do Brasil* (1957), and *Geopolítica do Brasil* (1967); PLÍNIO DE ABREU RAMOS and CID BENJAMIN, "Golberi do Couto e Silva," in *Dicionário histórico biográfico* (1983); MARIA HELENA MOREIRA ALVES, *State and Opposition in Military Brazil* (1985); THOMAS E. SKIDMORE, *The Politics of Military Rule in Brazil, 1964–85* (1988).

MARSHALL C. EAKIN

See also **Military Dictatorships.**

GOLD. *See* **Goldwork; Mining.**

GOLD RUSHES, BRAZIL. The quest for gold has been a significant part of Brazilian history, driving much of Portuguese and Brazilian penetration into the interior of the country. Large deposits of gold were discovered at the beginning of the eighteenth century in Minas Gerais, Mato Grosso, Goiás, and Bahia. The subsequent gold rush transformed the Portuguese colony, stimulating extensive immigration from Portugal, further exploration of the remote interior, and a substantial increase in African slave importations. Extracted primarily by slave labor, gold became the principal Brazilian export for over half a century, supporting the Portuguese Empire worldwide and probably financing the foundations of the industrial revolution in Britain. Perhaps as much as one-half of production left the colony illegally. With the subsequent exhaustion of these deposits, gold's share of the Brazilian economy declined precipitously, even with the entry of foreign MINING engineers and technology in the mid-nineteenth century. Gold mining came to be dominated by small-scale, informal placer operations (GARIMPOS).

The discovery of substantial gold deposits in the Amazon Basin in the 1960s and 1970s dynamized the mining sector, provoking the most extensive gold rush of the twentieth century in the Americas. Throughout the Amazon, hundreds of *garimpos* have competed with large mining companies for access to deposits. Gold mined in the late 1980s contributed over $1 billion annually to the legal Brazilian economy, as well as fueling a lucrative black market. Nearly 90 percent was supplied by *garimpos*. At the same time, deforestation, burning, the use of mercury to amalgamate with gold, and the invasion of aboriginal lands have caused severe environmental and social disruption. This conflictive situation has provoked both international and Brazilian condemnation of the unregulated nature of the gold rush, an issue only partially addressed by Brazilian governments to date.

CHARLES BOXER, *The Golden Age of Brazil, 1695–1750* (1962); G. ROCHA, ed., *Em busca de ouro: Garimpos e garimpeiros no Brasil* (1984); MARSHALL EAKIN, "The Role of British Capital in the Development of Brazilian Gold Mining," in *Miners and Mining in the Americas*, edited by W. C. Greaves and Thomas Greaves (1985), pp. 10–28; DAVID CLEARY, *Anatomy of the Amazon Gold Rush* (1990).

ROBERT WILCOX

GOLDEMBERG, ISAAC (*b.* 15 November 1945), Peruvian author. Goldemberg was born in the small town of Chepén. His father and his family, Russian Jews, had immigrated to Peru in the 1930s. His maternal grandmother, a mestiza medicine woman, was from Cajamarca. Goldemberg received a Catholic education under the supervision of the local parish priest and was unaware of his Jewish heritage for a number of years. Learning of his mixed religious background reinforced his sense of being different from both Catholics and Jews. It is not surprising that the question of identity and a sense of exile pervade his works.

Completely bilingual in Spanish and English, Goldemberg helped produce the English translation of *Hombre de paso*, which was published in a bilingual edition. Among authors and critics who have praised his work are José Miguel Oviedo, Severo SARDUY, Marco Martos, and Mario VARGAS LLOSA.

Since 1984 Goldemberg has lived in New York City, where he is a director of the Latin American Writers Institute/Instituto de Escritores Latinoamericanos, which organizes exhibitions of Latin American fiction and criticism. He is also on the staff of *Brújula/Compass*, a bimonthly magazine of bilingual Latino and Latin American literature written in the United States.

Goldemberg's published works are *Tiempo de silencio* (1969), poetry; *De Chepén a La Habana* (1973), poetry; *The Fragmented Life of Don Jacobo Lerner*, translated by Robert Picciotto (1976); *La vida a plazos de don Jacobo Lerner*, 2d ed. (1980); *Hombre de paso/Just Passing Through*, translated by David Unger and Isaac Goldemberg (1981); *Tiempo al tiempo* (1984); *Play by Play*, translated by Hardie St. Martin (1985); *La vida al contado* (1989), poetry, with a preface by Marco Martos and a sketchy and selective autobiographical account by Goldemberg.

GUIDO A. PODESTÁ

GOLDEN LAW, which was passed by the Brazilian Senate and sanctioned by Princess ISABEL on 13 May 1888, freed all remaining slaves (approximately 600,000) and abolished the institution of SLAVERY. Despite the desperate resistance of some planters (especially those whose properties were heavily mortgaged against the value of their slaves), the law recognized what had become fact. Slaves had fled plantations in increasing numbers, causing many planters to free their remaining slaves in hopes of retaining their services as wage workers or sharecroppers. Planters who had already begun to hire indentured immigrant laborers, notably in the SÃO PAULO zone, found their economic position strengthened. In the cities slave populations had dwindled so dramatically that by 1888 in Rio de Janeiro only about 7,000 slaves remained of an estimated 100,000 slaves living there in the 1860s. Contemporary abolitionists—particularly Joaquim NABUCO and André Rebouças—were outspoken critics of what they regarded as only a partial abolition that had failed to include land reform, necessary in their view if Brazil was to realize its potential as a producing nation on a footing with the industrializing societies of Europe. Questions remain regarding the post-emancipation lives of former slaves and blacks as we seek to understand more precisely what changed and what persisted.

ROBERT CONRAD, *The Destruction of Brazilian Slavery, 1850–1888* (1972), esp. pp. 239–277; JOAQUIM NABUCO, *Abolitionism: The Brazilian Antislavery Struggle*, translated and edited by Robert Conrad (1977).

SANDRA LAUDERDALE GRAHAM

See also **Free Birth Law; Queirós Law; Sexagenarian Law.**

GOLDSCHMIDT, GERTRUDE. *See* **Gego.**

GOLDWORK, PRE-COLUMBIAN. Gold and items made from it continue to fascinate now as they did 500 years ago when conquistadores first landed on the shores of the Americas. The metal was used by the natives of most cultures in the Americas, from Mexico south to Argentina. Although the level of craftsmanship varied considerably, techniques used in the New World were virtually the same as those utilized by craftsmen in the Old World, with the exception of vitreous enameling. The reasons for these parallels in cultural technologies are basic.

Gold, silver, and copper are easily worked with very simple technology. In fact, gold and silver are the two most malleable metals on earth. Pre-Hispanic goldsmiths utilized extremely dense, hard stone hammers (e.g. of magnetite) without handles; stone anvils; chisels; and chasing tools made of gold/copper alloys to cut and chase the gold. These tools no doubt were augmented by tools made of wood, bone, and leather.

With the addition of braziers to hold charcoal fires—and the use of long bamboo tubes, with ceramic tips, blown through to make the fires much hotter—metalworkers were able to make binary and ternary alloys, and to melt them into ingots from which they could forge sheet and wire—the raw stock necessary to manufacture some of the pieces that we see today in museums and that dazzled the conquistadores when they arrived.

Less important metals were platinum and lead. Platinum occurred in the southern Colombia/northern Ecuador borderland. Its extremely high melting point limited its use to what could be termed small experimental pieces. Lead was employed for ore extraction, probably of silver, in the southern half of Peru and northern Bolivia; other uses of lead have not been well documented.

The need to adorn the body with gold nuggets gathered from streams may well have been the earliest use of gold by Brazilian tribes and other South American cultures, although much additional research remains to be done. It is certain that humankind's fascination with gold promotes its use as soon as it is introduced into a culture.

Sophisticated sheetmetal pieces were being made on the South American continent as early as 1500–1000 B.C. in the north coast culture known as Cupisnique. North coast Peru has also yielded evidence of gold fabricated into very complex pieces as early as 700–800 B.C. The La Tolita area of Ecuador/Colombia has yielded dates from 400 B.C.–A.D. 200. It would seem likely from these dates that from about the time of Christ, gold working was moving northward in Colombia into Panama and thence Mexico, since reliable dating gets later as one moves north.

There were two loci of gold working in South America. One was the direct working characterized by Peruvian smiths. The other was indirect working of the gold

Pre-Columbian goldwork of Quimbaya Indians. Colombia, ca. 1500. MUSEO DE AMÉRICA, MADRID; LAURIE PLATT WINFREY, INC.

characterized by the refined and intricate lost-wax cast designs of the goldsmiths in Colombia.

In Peru, the goldsmiths' industry tended to make mainly sheet and wire. The Peruvian cultures inclined toward large ceremonial or showy pieces (e.g., large ceremonial masks and very large raised gold vessels), with only small quantities of personal body adornment. Nowhere else on the continent were the technically more difficult direct metalworking techniques carried to such advanced extremes as in Peru.

Direct working of the metal involved forming by hammering and cutting individual parts that were then assembled with mechanical (e.g., strap and slot, tab and slot) or thermal joins. This is called fabrication. The major fabrication techniques used by pre-Hispanic goldsmiths were forging sheet and wire, raising vessels, chasing and repoussé, real filigree, granulation, protobrazing, and depletion gilding. The cultures most associated with these techniques were on the north coast of Peru (e.g., Mochica and SICÁN).

The Colombian smiths seemed to respond artistically to the indirect approach of fashioning the work in wax, to be cast in gold. It allowed them to fashion lovely small-scale cast pieces. Though the indirect approach certainly yielded some very large cast pieces, there was more preoccupation with personal, decorative body adornment such as necklaces, earrings, nose rings, and labrets. Many examples abound to show that Colombian goldsmiths knew direct metalworking techniques. However, their fascination with lost-wax casting, and the plenteous supply of beeswax available, certainly allowed them to master the indirect approach to metalwork; this skill was carried up into Mexico.

Indirect working of gold by lost-wax casting was done by making the piece in wax and then coating it with a liquid refractory material composed of caliche, powdered charcoal, and lime. When the refractory hardened, like plaster, the mold was placed in a heat source, the wax is eliminated; then molten metal could be poured in. After cooling, the refractory was broken away, revealing the casting piece. It could then be finished and polished. The cultures most associated with this technique are Costa Rica (Diquis), Panama (Coclé, Chiriqui'), and Colombia (Sinu', Muisca).

Studies of pre-Hispanic metalwork have been hampered by the conquistadores' massive looting, which virtually eliminated metalwork from Mexico, and grave robbing, which still occurs despite efforts to control it. This has affected efforts to locate workshop sites and undisturbed tombs so they may be scientifically excavated and the maximum information gleaned from their contents to aid in the understanding of the work and life of these ancient peoples.

Surveys of ancient and modern techniques are in OPPI UNTRACHT, *Jewelry Concepts and Technology* (1982). A more complete discussion of Peruvian goldsmithing techniques is in HEATHER LECHTMAN, "Traditions and Styles in Central Andean Metalworking," in *The Beginning of the Use of Metals and Alloys,* edited by Robert Madden (1988), pp. 344–378, and IZUMI SHI-MADA and JO ANN GRIFFIN, "Precious Metal Objects of the Middle Sican," in *Scientific American,* 270 (April 1994): 82–89. See also JULIE JONES, ed., *The Art of Precolumbian Gold* (1985).

JO ANN GRIFFIN

GÓLGOTAS, the younger, more radical wing of the Colombian Liberal Party in the first half of the 1850s. The label Gólgotas apparently came from a Conservative editorialist's criticism of José María SAMPER's positive comparison of socialism with the ideals of the martyr of Golgotha at a meeting of the Republican School. These men supported the separation of church and state, the elimination of clerical privilege, extreme federalism, the reduction of the power of the executive and military, universal manhood suffrage, the expulsion of the Jesuits, the abolition of slavery, absolute freedom of the press and of speech, and laissez-faire economics—principles that they helped incorporate into the Constitution of 1853. The more moderate, Santanderista wing of the Liberal Party, labeled Draconianos, so opposed the 1853 constitution that many assisted José María MELO's 1854 coup. Leading Gólgotas, including Manuel MURILLO TORO, Rafael NÚÑEZ, Salvador CAMACHO ROLDÁN, Francisco J. ZALDÚA, and Aquileo PARRA, dominated the 1863–1885 Liberal era.

GERARDO MOLINA, *Las ideas liberales en Colombia: 1849–1914* (1970); HELEN DELPAR, *Red Against Blue: The Liberal Party in Colombian Politics, 1863–1899* (1981); *Los radicales del siglo XIX: Escritos políticos* (1984).

DAVID SOWELL

See also **Colombia: Political Parties.**

GOMES, ANTÔNIO CARLOS (*b.* 11 July 1836; *d.* 16 September 1896), the first Brazilian musician to achieve considerable success in Italy as a composer of operas. Son of a bandmaster whose most notable achievement appears to have been fathering twenty-six children, Tonico (as Antônio Carlos was called as a boy) learned the fundamentals of music and an elementary knowledge of several instruments from his father at an early age. His *Hino acadêmico,* an early composition, was well received, and he went to Rio de Janeiro in order to enroll in the Imperial Conservatory of Music. His conservatory studies in composition with Joaquim Giannini reinforced his interest in opera, and two works, *A noite do castelo,* produced in 1861, and *Joana de Flandres,* in 1863, met considerable success, resulting in a government subsidy for study in Italy. The greatest success of Gomes's career was the performance of his opera *Il Guarany* at La Scala, in Milan, on 19 March 1870. *Il Guarany* was followed by *Fosca, Salvator Rosa, Maria Tudor, Lo schiavo,* and *Condor,* his last opera, but none of the later works achieved the success of *Il Guarany.*

Gomes chose Brazilian subjects for some of his operas, but his style of writing and approach was Italian at a time of rising musical nationalism in Brazil. Expecting unqualified and enthusiastic acceptance in his native country during a time of rising republican sentiments, he was instead considered an aristocrat out of touch with political realities. The fact that his family sought to forbid performances of his operas in the Portuguese language, insisting on Italian, did nothing to allay the suspicions of adherents of the new nationalist sentiments.

Revista brasileira de música, vol. 3 (1936); LUIS HEITOR CORREA DE AZEVEDO, *150 anos de música no Brasil (1800–1950)* (1956).

DAVID P. APPLEBY

GOMES, EDUARDO (*b.* 20 September 1896; *d.* 13 June 1981), Brazilian Air Force officer and political leader. Born in Petrópolis, Rio de Janeiro, Gomes enlisted in the army in 1916. He was commissioned in 1919, and three years later he became a national hero as one of the *tenente* defenders and survivors of the Revolt of Fort COPACABANA. Imprisoned for his role as an air observer during the revolt of 1924, he returned to active duty in 1927. His assignment to the army air corps included the task, in 1930, of establishing the Brazilian military air mail systems. With the creation of the Brazilian air force in 1941, Gomes served as commander of the First and Second Air Zones in the northeastern section of the country during World War II.

In 1945, Gomes helped to organize the anti-Vargas National Democratic Union (União Democrática Nacional—UDN) and ran unsuccessfully against General Eurico DUTRA as its presidential candidate that year, and in 1950 against Getúlio VARGAS. He was an official and elder statesman of the party until its dissolution in 1965. Appointed minister of the air force by President João CAFÉ FILHO in 1954, Gomes retired from active service in 1961 with the rank of air marshal. President Humberto CASTELO BRANCO recalled him to serve as air minister after the revolution of 1964. He died in Rio de Janeiro.

RONALD M. SCHNEIDER, *Order and Progress: A Political History of Brazil* (1991); E. BRADFORD BURNS, *A History of Brazil* (1993).

MICHAEL L. JAMES

See also **Brazil: Political Parties.**

GÓMEZ, BENIGNO (*b.* 1934), Honduran painter and sculptor. Gómez is a native of the department of Santa Barbara, Honduras. His woodcarvings of doves won him a scholarship in 1950 to study at the Escuela Nacional de Bellas Artes in Tegucigalpa, where he was strongly influenced by Max EUCEDA. In 1960 he won another scholarship to study in Rome, where he remained until 1966, when he returned to Tegucigalpa as a professor at the Escuela Nacional de Bellas Artes. By now his neorealist paintings of the human figure had won him much recognition, particularly for his innovative use of color, but later he became more noted for his surrealist paintings. A trademark of his work is the presence of doves in virtually all his paintings, symbols of Gómez's optimistic spirit.

J. EVARISTO LÓPEZ R. and LONGINO BECERRA, *Honduras: 40 pintores* (1989).

RALPH LEE WOODWARD, JR.

GÓMEZ, EUGENIO (*b.* 1890; *d.* 1963), leader of the Uruguayan Communist party. As a barber in Montevideo he came into contact with the labor movement and joined the port workers' Federación Obrera Marítima (Maritime Workers Federation) and the Partido Socialista del Uruguay (Socialist Party—PSU), led by Emílio FRUGONI. During the debate about PSU membership in the Third International and subscription to its twenty-one conditions (1920), Gómez, Celestino Mibelli, and Rodríguez Saraillé led the majority faction favoring acceptance. After a special party conference held on 16–18 April 1921, the PSU changed its name to Partido Comunista del Uruguay (PCU). Frugoni and his minority faction reestablished the PSU in 1923.

From 1921 to 1955 Gómez headed the party executive committee, serving as its general secretary from the time of party proscription during the dictatorship of Gabriel TERRA (1937). Under his leadership the PCU became one of the most active promoters of Uruguayan solidarity with the Spanish Republic and the Anti-Nazi Action, and achieved its best election results in 1946.

Gómez was deputy from 1942 to 1946 and was a member of the parliamentary Special Commission on Working Conditions in Uruguay. After 1946 his leadership was characterized by an increasing loss of popularity due to personality cult and power abuse. In 1955 PCU membership stood at about 5,000.

EUGENIO GÓMEZ, *Los intelectuales del Partido Comunista* (1945), *Historia del Partido Comunista del Uruguay hasta 1951* (1951), and *Historia de una traición* (1960); PHILIP B. TAYLOR, *Government and Politics of Uruguay* (1966); RODNEY ARISMENDI, *Ocho corazones latiendo* (1987); RODNEY ARISMENDI et al. *El partido: 68 aniversario del PCU* (1955).

DIETER SCHONEBOHM

GÓMEZ, INDALECIO (*b.* 1851; *d.* 18 August 1920), Argentine statesman and author. Born in Salta and trained as a lawyer at the University of Buenos Aires, Gómez began his political career as a national deputy representing Salta Province. He gained national prominence as director of the National Bank of Argentina during the administration of Carlos PELLEGRINI (1890–1892). He remained active in national politics, serving as Argentina's ambassador to Germany under President Manuel QUINTANA (1904–1906) and as the interior minister under President Roque SÁENZ PEÑA (1910–1913). As interior minister, he orchestrated the passage of the SÁENZ PEÑA LAW (1911), which granted universal male suffrage and established a

secret ballot for elections. Gómez supervised its implementation in the national congressional elections of April 1912. In numerous books and articles, including *El episcopado y la paz* (1895), he established his reputation as a political and social traditionalist who defended the elite values of Argentina's Generation of 1880 during an era of turmoil and reform.

NATALIO R. BOTANA, ''La reforma política del 1912,'' in *El régimen oligárquico: Materiales para el estudio de la realidad argentina (hasta 1930)*, edited by G. Giménez Zapiola (1975), pp. 232–245; and *El orden conservador: La política argentina entre 1880 y 1916*, 2d ed. (1985), esp. pp. 217–291.

DANIEL LEWIS

GÓMEZ, JOSÉ MIGUEL (*b.* ca. 1720; *d.* 1805), best-known colonial painter of Honduras. Born in Tegucigalpa, Gómez painted mostly religious themes. He began his studies in Comayagua but later studied in Guatemala City. He returned to Comayagua, where his painting of San José de Calasanz for the Araque family brought him to the attention of Bishop Rodríguez de Rivera, who commissioned a series of works from him for the cathedral of Comayagua. Gómez's paintings were characterized by their natural realism. He later painted many religious canvases for churches in and around Tegucigalpa. His painting of Father José Simón Zelaya is especially notable, as was his final painting, in 1805, of *La Divina Pastora*, depicting the Virgin with Child and a lamb, a vivid painting that reflected the influence of his Spanish and Guatemalan teachers.

J. EVARISTO LÓPEZ R. and LONGINO BECERRA, *Honduras: 40 pintores* (1989).

RALPH LEE WOODWARD, JR.

GÓMEZ, JOSÉ MIGUEL (*b.* 1858; *d.* 1921), president of Cuba (1909–1913). General Gómez began his rise to prominence during the TEN YEARS' WAR and was governor of Santa Clara during the U.S. occupation under General Leonard WOOD. An astute and clever politician, Gómez switched from the Conservative to the Liberal Party in 1906 when the former failed to support his bid for the presidency. He was also active in the insurrection against President Tomás ESTRADA PALMA in 1906.

Running again on the Liberal Party ticket in 1908, Gómez won. During his presidency, the government was accused of corruption, patronage, and suspending duties on the exports of SUGAR and other products. The administration is perhaps better known for its expenditures that approached $140 million and for the 1912 military campaign against a black military force and its supporters, the Independent Party of Color.

Gómez was defeated in 1912 but remained in the political limelight. In 1920, opposed to Liberal policies and increasing internal strife, he plotted an unsuccessful revolution.

WILLIAM FLETCHER JOHNSON, *The History of Cuba* (1920); LOUIS A. PÉREZ, *Cuba: Between Reform and Revolution* (1988).

ALLAN S. R. SUMNALL

GOMÉZ, JOSÉ VALENTÍN (*b.* 8 November 1774; *d.* 20 September 1833), Argentine educator and diplomat. Born in Buenos Aires and educated as a cleric at the University of Córdoba, Goméz became an ardent supporter of the revolution and subsequently a diplomat of the new government. In 1813 he was elected to the National Assembly and thereafter was sent on several diplomatic missions. One of his most interesting illustrates the monarchist tendencies of the government he represented. Under Juan Martín de PUEYRREDÓN in 1819 he went on a secret mission to France in order to persuade the French minister of foreign affairs, the Baron Dessolle, to establish a monarchy in La Plata under a European dynastic family. The duke of Lucca was the favored candidate, but Dessolle changed his mind and the scheme was abandoned. Gómez became the rector of the University of Buenos Aires in 1823 and was responsible for introducing the Lancastrian system of education and attempting other educational reforms. He died in Buenos Aires.

NICHOLAS P. CUSHNER

GÓMEZ, JUAN CARLOS (*b.* 1820; *d.* 1884), Uruguayan journalist and poet. The long siege of Montevideo by Blanco Party forces under Manuel ORIBE, who was supported by Argentina's dictator, Juan Manuel de ROSAS, provided Gómez with an incentive to move to Chile in 1843. While there he joined Argentines and fellow liberals Domingo SARMIENTO and Bartolomé MITRE in the struggle against Rosas, and then in the task of implementing a liberal program of institutional renovation. His defense of freedom of the press in Valparaíso's *El Mercurio* in the 1840s and his promotion of liberal reforms in Buenos Aires's *El Orden, La Tribuna,* and *El Nacional* in the 1850s—and for a brief period in Montevideo's *El Nacional*—earned him wide respect.

Between 1852 and 1863 Gómez divided his time between Montevideo and Buenos Aires. In Montevideo he served as a representative in the national legislature and as minister of foreign relations. In Buenos Aires he supported Mitre's Nationalist Party. His principled opinions often sparked angry polemic: he stridently promoted the union of Uruguay and Argentina in a "United States of the Plata," and he was an outspoken critic, beginning in 1869, of Argentina's role in the WAR OF THE TRIPLE ALLIANCE. Following Juan Bautista ALBERDI, he argued that the war "against the people" had weakened the Spanish-speaking countries of the Plata relative to their historical rival, Brazil. Gómez promoted the liberal ideas of the period, including the need to attract a European population to the regions of the Plata, to combat the retrograde rural

society that joined despotic caudillos with illiterate gauchos, and to modernize at whatever cost. Gómez also wrote poetry. His "La libertad" is one of the finest in Uruguay's romantic canon.

JULIO MARÍA ISOSA, *Juan Carlos Gómez* (1905).

WILLIAM H. KATRA

See also **Uruguay: Political Parties.**

GÓMEZ, JUAN GUALBERTO (*b.* 12 July 1854; *d.* 5 March 1933), Cuban independence figure, journalist, and politician. Gómez was born in a sugar mill in Matanzas Province, the son of black slaves who managed to purchase his freedom upon his birth. When Cuba's struggle for independence began, his parents sent him in 1869 to study in Paris, where he became a journalist. Afterward he traveled through the Caribbean and Mexico, returning to Cuba in 1878 when the TEN YEARS' WAR ended. At this time he met José MARTÍ, who would become his close friend and with whom he immediately began to conspire against Spain. Deported from Cuba on account of these activities, Gómez settled in Madrid, where he spent the next ten years working on various daily newspapers. He also became the secretary of the Madrid abolitionist society. When he finally was allowed to return to Cuba (1890), Gómez again worked as Martí's secret agent on the island, and when the 1895–1898 war of independence broke out, he was imprisoned and once more deported to Spain. Returning in 1898, he participated in the Cuban constituent assembly of 1900–1901, where he was one of the strongest opponents of the PLATT AMENDMENT. Afterward he became one of the editors of the daily *La Lucha,* and was elected to the Cuban Senate in the 1910s. Gómez died in Havana.

There are no English sources on Gómez. See OCTAVIO R. COSTA, *Juan Gualberto Gómez: Una vida sin sombra* (1984); and GUSTAVO DUPLESSIS, *Un hombre, sus ideas y un paraguas: Evocación de Juan Gualberto Gómez y su ideario* (1959).

JOSÉ M. HERNÁNDEZ

GÓMEZ, JUAN VICENTE (*b.* 24 July 1857; *d.* 17 December 1935), president and dictator of Venezuela (1908–1935). During his twenty-seven-year dictatorship, Gómez created the modern Venezuelan nation-state. Like Porfirio Díaz of Mexico (1876–1911), Gómez brought an end to internecine struggles for power, established a strong central government, began the construction of a nationwide transportation and communication system, and put the economy on a stable basis through the judicious use of petroleum revenues. Along with Rómulo BETANCOURT, he is one of Venezuela's major twentieth-century political figures.

Gómez achieved power at midlife. A former butcher and cattle rancher from Táchira, he became involved in politics in 1892 when he joined Cipriano CASTRO in an abortive political movement. Forced into exile in Colombia following the failure of that struggle, Gómez returned in 1899 as an officer in Castro's small Army of the Liberal Restoration. At the age of forty-two, he entered Caracas for the first time. There he served Castro as a loyal and trusted associate, and played an instrumental role in defeating the many groups who rose up against Castro's regime. Gómez risked his life on numerous occasions to put down major revolts. In so doing, he won support from the Venezuelan military establishment, which considered him both brave and honest. He also gained allies among the civilian elites, who saw Gómez as an efficient, if ruthless, military leader. Like most caudillos, he also had a large following among the nation's campesinos, who revered him, in part because they believed he possessed supernatural powers.

In 1908, Castro named Gómez as acting president while he sought medical treatment in Europe. Gómez took advantage of his chief's absence to proclaim himself president of Venezuela. His pronouncement met with immediate success, both at home and abroad. Castro's enemies thought that Gómez was an individual they could control. Foreign powers, which had suffered through the Castro years, also believed they could trust Gómez. Within weeks of his coup, the United States recognized the new government, and European powers quickly followed suit. As a result, Gómez enjoyed good relations with the United States and European nations, all of whom played an important role in the development of Venezuela's oil resources.

Recently, Venezuelan scholars have begun to revise part of the Gómez legacy. While continuing to condemn him for the torture and imprisonment of opponents; his monopolization of land and concessions for himself, his family, and his friends; his high-handed use of censorship and police violence to silence his critics; and his seeming surrender of Venezuelan petroleum to foreign economic interests, they now recognize Gómez and his associates as important contributors to Venezuela's modernization. Without the Gómez administration, they argue, Venezuela would have continued as a wartorn nation, with a predominantly agricultural economy that depended on the vagaries of international demand for its chief export crops, coffee and cacao. Under Gómez, the nation enjoyed unprecedented economic stability and growth, as well as political calm. A close alliance with bankers, financiers, businessmen, and representatives of the United States assured the former. Constitutions of 1914, 1922, 1925, 1928, 1929, and 1931 guaranteed the latter.

From the outset of his administration, Gómez gave generous concessions to foreign interests. His oil policy followed a moderate course based on his desire to develop the industry rapidly, with the aid of foreign investment. Under the direction of Development Minister Gumersindo Torres (1918–1922), a mining law of 1918 and a petroleum code of 1920 limited the freedom of companies. But under pressure from the U.S. State Department, Gómez had Congress remove some of the most restrictive measures from the 1920 code. In 1922, a new law gave foreign oil companies what they wanted: low taxes and royalty payments to Venezuela, slow exploitation rates, and no restriction on the amount of land the companies held.

Gómez also made important changes in the organization of the national armed forces. In 1910, the first inspector general of the army, Félix Galavís, opened the Military Academy, which trained the next generation of professional officers. Military professionalization assured Gómez of an armed force that could defend the nation as well as put down domestic revolts. Since the officers often received higher salaries than their civilian counterparts, Gómez attracted candidates to the armed forces who had closer ties to the Caracas elites than did the older officers. Until his death, his brothers and fellow Tachiran officers comprised a separate and more powerful part of the officers, whereas the younger generation trained during his rule comprised the backbone of the post-Gómez generation of military leaders.

Juan Vicente Gómez at the burial of his brother, Juan Crisóstomo (Juancho) Gómez 1923. INSTITUTO AUTÓNOMO BIBLIOTECA; PHOTO BY LUIS FELIPE TORO.

Perhaps as important as his reform of the military, his fiscal policies also had a long-term impact upon Venezuela. Gómez often showed his rancher background when it came to budgets. Like his minister of the Treasury, Román Cárdenas (1913–1922), he believed firmly in a balanced budget. Cárdenas's centralization of tax collection helped raise monies needed to run the government efficiently. Cuts in salaries and expenditures, along with amortization of foreign debts, turned Venezuela into a nation with no public debt by the mid-1920s. Vicente Lecuna [Salbach], who served as director of the Bank of Venezuela, also worked with Gómez on the national budget. His mastery of international monetary exchange placed Venezuela on a firm footing as the nation entered its oil boom. Gómez died in Maracay, Venezuela.

DANIEL JOSEPH CLINTON [writing as Thomas Rourke], *Gómez, Tyrant of the Andes* (1936); LUIS CORDERO VELÁSQUEZ, *Gómez y las fuerzas vivas* (1971); DOMINGO ALBERTO RANGEL, *Gomez, el amo del poder* (1975); ELÍAS PINO ITURRIETA, *Positivismo y gomecismo* (1978); ANGEL ZIEMS, *El gomecismo y la formación del ejército nacional* (1979); STEPHEN G. RABE, *The Road to OPEC: United States Relations with Venezuela, 1919–1979* (1982); BRIAN STUART MC BETH, *Juan Vicente Gómez and the Oil Companies in Venezuela, 1908–1935* (1983).

WINTHROP R. WRIGHT

See also **Colombia.**

GOMÉZ, MIGUEL MARIANO (*b.* 1890; *d.* 1951), Cuba's sixth constitutionally elected president (May–December 1936) and the son of José Miguel Gómez, the second president. Gómez's term lasted for less than a year because he was the first president to be removed from office by Congress. A conservative member of Cuba's traditional ruling elite, he served in the House of Representatives for twelve years. Gómez was elected mayor of Havana during the Gerardo MACHADO Y MORALES administration. However, he attacked the repressive measures of the Machado regime. In January 1936, backed by the Liberal Party and army chief Fulgencio BATISTA Y ZALDÍVAR, he was elected president.

Gómez's biggest political shortcoming was his refusal to acknowledge the paramount position of General Batista. Inaugurated in May 1936, his first mistake was to choose his cabinet without consulting the general. His downfall came in December, when he vetoed a bill, supported by Batista, to set up a system of rural schools operated by the military. Gomez was adamant about reasserting civilian control over the government, and he believed that army control over rural education would erode constitutional and civilian power. Three days after the veto, General Batista had him impeached by the Senate.

HUGH THOMAS, *Cuba; or, the Pursuit of Freedom* (1971); IRWIN F. GELLMAN, *Roosevelt and Batista: Good Neighbor Diplomacy in Cuba, 1933–1945* (1973); ROBERT J. ALEXANDER, ed., *Biographical Dictionary of Latin American and Caribbean Political Leaders* (1988).

DAVID CAREY, JR.

GÓMEZ CARRILLO, ENRIQUE (*b.* 27 February 1873; *d.* 29 November 1927), Guatemalan chronicler, novelist, and pioneer of modern journalistic reporting. As a child, Gómez Carrillo traveled with his parents to Spain, returning first to San Salvador and then to his birthplace of Guatemala City, where he studied. His mother taught him French at home. As a youth, he wrote for the local papers, praising modernism and severely criticizing the style of such revered Guatemalan writers as José MILLA. Rubén DARÍO helped him travel to Spain, where he published his work in various literary magazines and edited the Madrid daily newspaper *El Liberal*, helping to modernize the Spanish press. In Paris, where he would reside until his death, he worked as a correspondent for several Latin American and Spanish periodicals. He befriended Paul Verlaine and was Mata Hari's lover. He published *Esquisses* (1892), *Sensaciones de arte* (1893), and *Del amor, del dolor y del vicio* (1898). Gómez Carrillo's legacy is his exquisite prose, the cosmopolitan vision which liberated him from provincialism, and especially the journalistic style of his literary stories.

JUAN MANUEL MENDOZA, *Enrique Gómez Carrillo, estudio crítico-biográfico: Su vida, su obra y su época*, 2 vols. (1946); ALFONSO E. BARRIENTOS, *Enrique Gómez Carrillo* (1973); VÍCTOR CASTILLO LÓPEZ, *Bibliografía de Enrique Gómez Carrillo* (1984).

FERNANDO GONZÁLEZ DAVISON

GÓMEZ CASTRO, LAUREANO (*b.* 20 February 1889; *d.* 13 July 1965), president of Colombia (1950–1953). Born in Bogotá to middle-class parents from Ocaña, Norte de Santander, Gómez attended the Colegio de San Bartolomé and studied engineering at the Universidad Nacional (1905–1909). He was drawn, however, to politics. At twenty, he became editor of *La Unidad*, a Conservative paper, and remained at its helm until its demise in 1916. In the same period, he was elected to Congress and to Cundinamarca's Chamber of Deputies (1911–1916). His oratory was usually vehement and often wounding. President Marco Fidel SUÁREZ resigned in 1921 rather than suffer Gómez's taunts. After serving as minister plenipotentiary to Chile and Argentina (1923–1925), Gómez returned home in 1925 to become public works minister. His ambitious infrastructure program was rejected by the Congress, and he left public service until 1931, when he was appointed envoy to Germany. Some months later he was elected senator, remaining in office until removed—for calumny—in 1943.

A Liberal victory in 1930 left a power vacuum among Conservatives that Gómez, through his editorials in Bogotá's *El País* (1932–1934) and *El Siglo* (1936–1948), sought to fill. He unremittingly opposed the regimes of Enrique OLAYA HERRERA, Alfonso LÓPEZ PUMAREJO, and Eduardo SANTOS. Gómez's enthusiasm for Franco's Spain reflected his authoritarianism. The collapse, in 1945–1946, of Liberal unity brought in Gómez's choice, Mariano OSPINA PÉREZ, a Conservative, as president (1946). The increasing political violence led to Liberal withdrawal from the cabinet, and as a result Gómez became foreign minister in 1948. Nearly lynched in the BOGOTAZO of 9 April 1948, he fled to Spain. Gómez returned in 1949, ran unopposed (the Liberals abstained from voting), and won the presidency. His term was marked by repression, extreme partisanship, and violence. Some infrastructural improvements were achieved, however, including stadia in Bogotá and Medellín, roads, and oil pipelines. With no Congress to answer to, Gómez sent a Colombian battalion to join United Nations forces in Korea (1951–1953). On 13 June 1953, he was overthrown by General Gustavo ROJAS PINILLA and exiled to Spain. In 1956, joined by Liberal politicians at Sitges, Spain, Gómez founded the National Front. He died in Bogotá.

JOSÉ FRANCISCO SOCORRÁS, *Laureano Gómez, psicoanálisis de un resentido* (1942); ALBERTO BERMÚDEZ, *El buen gobierno . . . Laureano Gómez* (1974); JAMES D. HENDERSON, *Conservative Thought in Latin America: The Ideas of Laureano Gómez* (1988).

J. LEÓN HELGUERA

See also **Violencia, La.**

GÓMEZ-CRUZ, ERNESTO (*b.* 7 November 1933), Mexican stage and screen actor. Born in Veracruz, Gómez-Cruz studied theater at his hometown university. In 1967 he debuted in the acclaimed film *Los caifanes,* and since then has starred or costarred in over eighty features. He has received more best actor or supporting actor awards than any other actor in Mexican cinema. Gómez-Cruz is known for his ability to play a wide range of roles. His noted films include *Actas de Marusia* (1975), *Cadena perpetua; La venida del Rey Olmos; La vispera; Auandar Anapu, El imperio de la fortuna* (1986), *El norte; Lo que importa es vivir* (1988), and *Barroco.* Gómez-Cruz has also had a successful television and stage career.

LUIS REYES DE LA MAZA, *El cine sonoro en México* (1973); E. BRADFORD BURNS, *Latin American Cinema: Film and History* (1975); CARL J. MORA, *Mexican Cinema: Reflections of a Society: 1896–1980* (1982); and JOHN KING, *Magical Reels: A History of Cinema in Latin America* (1990).

DAVID MACIEL

GÓMEZ DE AVELLANEDA Y ARTEAGA, GERTRUDIS (*b.* 23 March 1814; *d.* 1 February 1873), Cuban poet, novelist and playwright. Gómez de Avellaneda has the rare distinction of being claimed by the literatures of two countries, Cuba and Spain. Born in the city of Puerto Príncipe (now Camagüey) to a Spanish father and a Cuban mother, she spent her childhood and youth in Cuba. In 1836 she left Cuba with her mother and stepfather and settled in Spain, where she embarked on a literary career and what was for the times a scandalous personal life: she had several love affairs and bore a child out of wedlock, who died a few months after birth.

Gertrudis Gómez de Avellaneda. ORGANIZATION OF AMERICAN STATES.

Gómez de Avellaneda was a friend and peer of several of the most distinguished Spanish poets, writers, and politicians of the day. In June of 1845 she was the winner of the two top prizes given by the Liceo de Madrid (she submitted one of the entries using her brother's name). In 1846 she married but three months later was widowed. Afterward, she retired to a convent briefly, only to return with fervor to literary life. Between 1844 and 1858, several of her plays were staged in Madrid, some with great success. In 1852 she was denied membership in the Royal Spanish Academy because she was a woman.

In 1854 Gómez de Avellaneda married a powerful, well-known politician, Colonel Domingo Verdugo, who was later given an official post in Cuba. In 1859, she returned with him to her native land where she was warmly welcomed and awarded the highest official honors from the literary community, including coronation by Luisa Pérez de Zambrana, a renowned Cuban poet. She remained in Cuba until the death of her husband in 1863. In 1865 thereafter she left Cuba with her brother, and after touring the United States, London, and Paris, she settled in Madrid in 1864; she remaind there until her death.

Gómez de Avellaneda is regarded as one of the most important Cuban poets and a notable novelist. Many critics consider her a feminist, and her ideas about slavery, as depicted in her best-known novel, *Sab* (1841), were revolutionary at the time.

Many distinguished writers have written about the life and works of Gómez de Avellaneda: Gastón Baquero, Regino Eladio Boti y Barreivo, Belkis Cuza Malé, Marcelino Menéndez y Pelayo, Enrique José Varona, Pedro Henríquez Ureña, Dulce María Loynaz, José Lezama Lima among them. A compilation of her best works is *Sus mejores poesías* (1953). See also *Complete Works* (1961), which contains criticism and a biobibliography. Studies in English include EDWIN BUCHER WILLIAMS, *The Life and Dramatic Works of Gertrudis Gómez de Avellaneda* (1924).

ROBERTO VALERO

GÓMEZ FARÍAS, VALENTÍN, (*b.* 1781; *d.* 1858), liberal reformer, vice president and acting president of Mexico (1833–1834 and 1846–1847) during two of Antonio López de SANTA ANNA's presidencies. Born in Guadalajara, Gómez Farías received his degree in 1807 and practiced medicine in Aguascalientes. He began his political career as *regidor* (president) of the *ayuntamiento* (city council) of Aguascalientes and was later elected to the Spanish Cortes. After independence, the state of Zacatecas elected him to the First Constituent Congress (1822), and during the 1820s he served repeatedly in the national legislature. In early 1833 he was finance minister before serving as acting president during the absences of Santa Anna in 1833–1834.

During this period, Gómez Farías attempted to carry out radical changes in the social and political structure of Mexico. His government first advised the clergy to restrict themselves to religious matters when speaking from the pulpit. Prompted by Gómez Farías and his allies José María Luis MORA and Lorenzo de ZAVALA, Congress voted to end the monopoly of the Catholic church over education and founded the Directorate of Public Instruction to organize public education in the Federal District and the national territories. Gómez Farías's government asserted its authority over the church hierarchy as well, claiming the right under the PATRONATO REAL to name bishops and archbishops. Congress also abolished mandatory payment of the tithe and gave priests and members of religious orders the freedom to renounce their vows.

But these liberal reforms did not include toleration of other religions. Anticlerical legislation was combined with official "protection" for the Catholic church. Although some church property was confiscated to pay for educational reforms, Gómez Farías supported Mora's plan to sell all nonessential church property and collect a 4 percent tax on the sales. The proceeds of the tax would be divided between the federal government and the states, and the proceeds of the sales would be used to pay the expenses of the church. Gómez Farías also sponsored reforms to limit the power of the national army by reducing its size and abolishing its *fuero*, thus requiring military officers to stand trial in civil courts. These reforms were aborted when the army, the church, and wealthy conservatives supported a rebellion for "Religion and Fueros," forcing Santa Anna to remove Gómez Farías from office in 1834.

Gómez Farías, his pregnant wife, and his three small children fled into exile with few resources, since Gómez Farías was unable to collect the pay due him. He returned to Mexico in 1838 and in 1840 supported an unsuccessful rebellion by General José de URREA. Exiled again, he spent time in New York, Yucatán, and New Orleans before returning to Mexico in 1845.

Gómez Farías exercised presidential power as vice president under Santa Anna during the war with the United States in 1846–1847. When he sought to nationalize church property to pay for the war, the militia of Mexico City launched the "Rebellion of the Polkos" (1847), and Santa Anna reassumed the presidency. Gómez Farías was a member of the national legislature, where he opposed the Treaty of GUADALUPE HIDALGO and supported the Revolution of AYUTLA. He was elected to the Constitutional Congress of 1856–1857 and died in Mexico City.

CHARLES A. HALE, *Mexican Liberalism in the Age of Mora, 1821–1853* (1968), pp. 108–147, 165–175, 218–221; MICHAEL P. COSTELOE, *La primera república federal en México (1824–1835): Un estudio de los partidos políticos en el México independiente* (1975), pp. 371–436; MICHAEL P. COSTELOE, *Church and State in Independent Mexico—A Study of the Patronage Debate, 1821–1857* (1978); BARBARA A. TENENBAUM, *The Politics of Penury: Debt and Taxes in Mexico, 1821–1856* (1986), pp. 38–39, 80; MICHAEL P. COSTELOE, "A Pronunciamiento in Nineteenth-Century Mexico: '15 de julio de 1840,'" in *Mexican Studies/Estudios Mexicanos* 4 (Summer 1988): 245–264.

D. F. STEVENS

See also **Anticlericalism.**

GÓMEZ HURTADO, ALVARO (*b.* 8 May 1919), leader of Colombia's National Salvation Movement, a splinter of the Social Conservative Party. Gómez, a native of Bogotá, was editor-in-chief and remains an owner of the Bogotá newspaper *El Siglo* (later *El Nuevo Siglo*). A candidate for president in 1974, 1986, and 1990, he has been active in national politics since the 1940s. He was elected to the House of Representatives twice in the 1940s and to the Senate six times from the 1950s through the 1980s. Gómez inherited leadership of the "doctrinaire" wing of Colombia's Conservative Party following the death in 1965 of his father, former Colombian president Laureano GÓMEZ CASTRO (1950–1953). A staunch anti-Communist in his youth, and a close collaborator of his father during Colombia's politically turbulent 1940s and 1950s, Gómez later advocated redistributive economic programs within a setting of economic liberalism.

Gómez has consistently defended traditional conservative social values, as defined in Roman Catholic doctrine. Kidnapped by members of the M-19 guerrilla organization in June 1988, he was released unharmed after six weeks. In June 1990, he joined his kidnappers, by then elected delegates of the newly formed M-19 Party, to participate in drafting Colombia's progressive Constitution of 1991.

ALVARO GÓMEZ HURTADO, *El pensamiento económico-social de Alvaro Gómez* (1985); JONATHAN HARTLYN, *The Politics of Coalition Rule in Colombia* (1988).

JAMES D. HENDERSON

See also **Colombia: Constitutions; Colombia: Political Parties; Colombia: Revolutionary Movements.**

GÓMEZ MORÍN, MANUEL (*b.* 27 February 1897; *d.* 18 April 1972), Mexican financial figure, intellectual, and opposition leader. Born in Batopilas, Chihuahua, the son of a miner, he completed a course of studies at the National Preparatory School (1913–1915) and legal studies at the National School of Law (1915–1918). He maintained close friendships with the ''Seven Wise Men,'' including Alfonso CASO, Vicente LOMBARDO TOLEDANO, and Narciso BASSOLS. Appointed a professor in 1918, he went on to influence a generation of prominent political figures.

Gómez Morín quickly entered public life, serving as *oficial mayor* and undersecretary of the treasury (1919–1921), and as founder and first director (1925–1929) of the board of the federal reserve Bank of Mexico. In 1923 he secretly gave financial support to the rebellion of Adolfo de la HUERTA and later served as unofficial treasurer of José VASCONCELOS's presidential campaign. Following that, he retired from public life (1929), but in 1931 he was the author of the first reform of credit institutions.

Meanwhile, he maintained his academic career as director of the National Law School from 1922 to 1924 and rector of the National University in 1933 and 1934. He subsequently went into private law practice and invested wisely in many major corporations at their founding. In 1939, disenchanted with the direction of the state, he and Efraín González Luna founded the National Action Party (PAN), which became Mexico's major opposition party until 1988. He spent his last thirty years as an investor and practitioner of law.

JAMES WALLACE WILKIE and EDNA MONZÓN DE WILKIE, *México visto en el siglo XX* (1969), and *Testimonio en la muerte de Manuel Gómez Morín* (1973); and ENRIQUE KRAUZE, *Caudillos culturales en la revolución mexicana* (1976).

RODERIC AI CAMP

See also **Mexico: Political Parties.**

GÓMEZ PEDRAZA, MANUEL (*b.* 1789?; *d.* 14 May 1851), Mexican politician and general. Born in Queré-

taro to a prominent family, he fought for the royalist cause in the War of Independence and then supported the ITURBIDE empire. Gómez successfully managed the ideological switch to federalism in 1824 and held several government posts, civil and military, during the Guadalupe VICTORIA presidency (1824–1829). A Scottish Rite Mason, he was elected president of Mexico in 1828 but was prevented from taking office by the revolt of the ACORDADE. After returning from exile, he served the final three months of his presidential term in 1833. He was elected to later congresses and held various ministerial posts. Known for his oratory and personal eccentricity—he forgot his own wedding day—he became a prominent member of the social elite in the capital. As one of the leaders of the moderate liberal federalists, Gómez was a presidential candidate on more than one occasion.

MANUEL RIVERA CAMBAS, *Los gobernantes de México,* rev. ed. by Leonardo Pasquel, vol. 4 (1964), pp. 359–374; STANLEY C. GREEN, *The Mexican Republic: The First Decade* (1987), pp. 88, 156–160, 229.

MICHAEL P. COSTELOE

GÓMEZ Y BÁEZ, MÁXIMO (*b.* 18 November 1836; *d.* 17 June 1905), major military leader in the wars for Cuban independence (1868–1878, 1895–1898). Born in Baní, Santo Domingo, into a middle-class family, he attended a local elementary school and a religious seminary. He began his military career at age sixteen, in the war against the Haitians and later served as a lieutenant in the Dominican army. After the 1866 civil war in Santo Domingo resulted in the loss of all his property, Gómez fled to Cuba. Settling in Bayamó, he became a fervent advocate of independence. When Carlos Manuel de CÉSPEDES's EL GRITO DE YARA (The Shout of Yara) inaugurated the TEN YEARS' WAR (1868–1878), he joined Céspedes, quickly proving himself to be an invaluable military strategist and leader. With his promotion to the rank of general, he began a close association with the rebel leaders Antonio MACEO and Calixto GARCÍA.

Gómez and Maceo came to believe that success in the war was unlikely without an expansion into the prosperous western provinces. They advocated the mass disruption of sugar production and the liberation of slaves, hoping that the damage to Cuba's economic base would bring a quick rebel victory. The revolution's civilian leaders opposed the plan, but in 1872 fear of defeat made them consent to a modified version of it. Gómez and Maceo marched west, burning sugar plantations and freeing slaves. After several months, heavy casualties and low provisions necessitated their return, but changes in the political climate made a renewal of the campaign impossible. Disillusioned and frustrated with the lack of progress, Gómez pressed for a truce with the Spanish. In 1878 the Pact of ZANJÓN ended the Ten Years' War, and the rebel leaders who were unwilling to accept the truce went into exile.

During his years in exile, Gómez joined Maceo and the poet José MARTÍ and began preparations for a second revolution against Spain. Gómez and Martí had frequent disputes over strategy, resulting in a brief break in 1884; nevertheless, by 1893 their differences had been put aside and Martí named Gómez military commander of the Cuban Revolutionary Party. On 25 March 1895, he and Maceo issued the Manifesto of Monte Christi, renewing the CUBAN REVOLUTION.

When Martí died in a skirmish on 19 May 1895, Gómez assumed the mantle of leadership, becoming the commander in chief of the movement. Under his leadership, the war was immediately extended into the western provinces. He issued a moratorium on sugar production, promising death and destruction of property to anyone in violation of his decree. Although these tactics seriously endangered Cuba's economic future, they proved effective in the war. By 1897 the rebels had moved into Matanzas and Havana.

A year later, a Spanish counteroffensive left the rebels struggling to maintain their positions, but U.S. entry into the war (1898) put an end to Spanish resistance. Following a four-year occupation, during which time the rebel leaders were all but totally ignored, the United States withdrew. As the Republic of Cuba was being established (20 May 1902), Gómez was urged to run for president, but he declined to do so, saying, "Men of war for war, and those of peace for peace."

CHARLES E. CHAPMAN, *A History of the Cuban Republic* (1969); HUGH THOMAS, *Cuba: The Pursuit of Freedom* (1971) and *Mayor General Máximo Gómez Báez: Sus campañas militares*, 2 vols. (1986); TOMÁS BÁEZ DÍAZ, *Máximo Gómez: El Libertador* (1986); JUAN BOSCH, *Máximo Gómez: De Monte Christi a la Gloria, tres años de guerra en Cuba* (1986); GENERAL MÁXIMO GÓMEZ Y BÁEZ, *Revoluciones . . . Cuba y hogar*, edited by Bernardo Gómez Toro (1986).

SARA FLEMING

See also **Spanish-American War.**

GONDRA, MANUEL (*b.* 1 January 1871; *d.* 8 March 1927), Paraguayan scholar, statesman, and president (1910–1911, 1920–1921). Manuel E. Gondra's varied and distinguished career in education, the military, diplomacy, and politics established him as one of Paraguay's leading public figures of the twentieth century. Born of an Argentine father and Paraguayan mother, Gondra was educated in the schools of Asunción and the Colegio Nacional. It was at the Colegio Nacional that Gondra later built a reputation as a highly effective educational reformer. Entering public life in 1902, he served as Paraguay's minister to Brazil (1905–1908) before being elected president in 1920. Confronting escalating political violence, Gondra resigned within a year of assuming the presidency.

During the ensuing decade, Gondra served as minister of war, reorganizing Paraguay's army and clarifying his nation's legal claim to the disputed Chaco region. While serving as Paraguay's minister in Washington in 1920, Gondra was again elected to the presidency. He fell victim to civil strife once again, however, and resigned his office after only fifteen months. Achieving more as a statesman than as a politician, Gondra was awarded his greatest recognition for his sponsorship of a treaty to prevent war among the American states at the Fifth International Conference of American States at Santiago, Chile, in 1923. For this initiative, Gondra was lauded by the Pan-American Union soon after his death in 1927. An accomplished scholar, Gondra owned one of the finest libraries in South America. His collection, containing 7,283 books, 2,633 pamphlets, 20,000 pages of manuscripts, and 270 maps, is now housed in the Benson Collection at the University of Texas.

C.E. CASTAÑEDA and J. AUTREY DABBS, "The Manuel Gondra Collection," in *Handbook of Latin American Studies* 6 (1940): 505–517; ARTURO BRAY, *Hombres y épocas del Paraguay* (1943), esp. pp. 152–159; HARRIS GAYLORD WARREN, *Paraguay: An Informal History* (1949), esp. pp. 265–278; MICHAEL GROW, *The Good Neighbor Policy and Authoritarianism in Paraguay: United States Economic Expansion and Great-Power Rivalry in Latin America During World War II* (1981).

DANIEL M. MASTERSON

See also **Gondra Treaty; Pan-American Conferences.**

GONDRA TREATY (1923), an agreement that is now viewed as the inspiration for the present-day peacekeeping mechanisms of the ORGANIZATION OF AMERICAN STATES, it was named for the Paraguayan statesman Manuel GONDRA, who sponsored the initiative at the Fifth International Conference of American States in Santiago, Chile, in May 1923. The treaty's seven articles detail procedures for the settlement of disputes between the American republics through an impartial investigation of the facts relating to the controversy. Disputes that couldn't be resolved through normal diplomatic means would be submitted to a commission of inquiry composed of five members, all nationals of American states, who would then render a final report within one year. The report would not have the force of arbitral awards and would be binding on the parties involved for only six months after its issuance. The treaty called for the establishment of permanent commissions in Washington, D.C., and Montevideo, Uruguay, to receive requests for inquiries and to notify the other parties involved. The Gondra Treaty mirrored the outlines of the February 1923 Washington Conference treaty between the United States and the Central American republics, which established similar procedures for commissions of inquiry to resolve disputes. Significantly, the Gondra Treaty called for disputes in the hemisphere to be resolved by the American republics themselves.

L. S. ROWE, "The Fifth International Conference of American States," in *Bulletin of the Pan American Union* 57, no. 2 (1923):

109–113, see also pp. 114–173; ARTHUR P. WHITAKER, *The Western Hemisphere Idea: Its Rise and Decline* (1954), esp. pp. 108–131; ROBERT N. BURR and ROLAND D. HUSSEY, eds., *Documents on Inter-American Cooperation*, vol. 2 (1955), esp. pp. 87–89; SAMUEL GUY INMAN, *Inter-American Conferences, 1826–1954: History and Problems* (1965), esp. pp. 88–106.

DANIEL M. MASTERSON

GONZAGA, FRANCISCA HEDWIGES (Chiquinha; *b.* 17 October 1847; *d.* 28 February 1935), a colorful key figure in the early history of Brazilian musical nationalism. Daughter of an imperial field marshall, José Basileu Neves Gonzaga, Francisca Gonzaga was married at the age of thirteen to an officer in the Merchant Marine at the insistence of her parents. She divorced her husband at the age of eighteen and left home with her children, whom she supported by giving music lessons. She was befriended by composer Joaquim Antônio da Silva CALLADO JUNIOR, who, in spite of her basically classical training, introduced her to the *chorões*, popular musicians composing in an improvisational style. Gonzaga proved to be such an apt apprentice that she soon improvised a polka, "Atraente," at a party honoring composer Henrique Alves de Mesquita. This song achieved widespread popularity and was followed by a flood of popular pieces called *valsas*, polkas, tangos, *maxixes, lundus, quadrilhas, fados, gavotas,* mazurkas, *barcarolas, habaneras,* and *serenatas.* She is best known, however, as composer of seventy-seven pieces for theater, which consisted of comedies, operettas, and incidental music for plays that captured the imagination of the public and defined popular styles in a manner that influenced composers of art music. Her independent spirit and disregard for convention made her a sensation in her day. In addition to being the first woman in Brazil to conduct a theater orchestra and military band, Gonzaga also was extremely active in antislavery and republican causes, even selling manuscripts and using royalty funds to contribute to these causes.

ARY VASCONCELOS, *Panorama da música popular brasileira* (1964); DAVID P. APPLEBY, *The Music of Brazil* (1983).

DAVID P. APPLEBY

GONZAGA, LUIZ (*b.* 13 Dec. 1912; *d.* 2 Aug. 1989), Brazilian singer, composer, and accordionist. Gonzaga transformed the rural folk music of the Northeast into a national urban popular music in the late 1940s and early 1950s. Born in the state of Pernambuco, he learned the traditional music of the Northeastern backlands and distinguished himself as an accordionist. After a stint in the military he moved south to Rio de Janeiro in the late 1930s and began performing contemporary popular music in clubs and on radio shows. Success came in the mid-1940s, when he teamed up with Humberto Teixeira, a poet from the state of Ceará, and incorporated Northeastern music into his repertoire. Together they adapted

syncopated rhythmic figures used by Northeastern folk guitarists to create a new song-and-dance genre they called *baião*. In 1946 the pair co-authored the song entitled "Baião," which became a commercial success and ushered in a Northeastern phase in the history of Brazilian popular music. During the late 1940s and early 1950s, Gonzaga and his co-writers, Teixeira and Zé Dantas, released a string of hit recordings based on the *baião* and other Northeastern genres, such as *chamego, xote, xaxado,* and *forró.* The songs spoke of the culture, history, and physical beauty of the Northeast, and Gonzaga became a spokesman for Northeastern culture. He was crowned "King of the Baião."

When the national *baião* craze waned in the late 1950s, Gonzaga returned to the Northeast to spend his time performing throughout the interior. In the late 1960s, Gonzaga's music found a new generation of Brazilian listeners when the contemporary popular musicians Caetano VELOSO and Gilberto GIL popularized new versions of his songs. During the 1970s and 1980s, Gonzaga performed with numerous Brazilian popular musicians, such as Gal Costa, Milton NASCIMENTO, Fagner, Elba Ramalho, and his own son, Gonzaguinha. At the time of his death Gonzaga had made more than 200 recordings.

JOSÉ RAMOS TINHORÃO, *Pequena história da música popular: da modinha ao tropicalismo*, 5th ed. (1986); MUNDICARMO MARIA ROCHA FERRETTI, *Baião dos dois: Zedantas e Luiz Gonzaga* (1988); CHRIS MC GOWAN and RICARDO PESSANHA, *The Brazilian Sound: Samba, Bossa Nova, and the Popular Music of Brazil* (1991).

LARRY N. CROOK

See also **Music: Popular Music and Dance.**

GONZAGA, TOMÁS ANTÔNIO (*b.* 1744; *d.* 1810), Brazilian poet. Born in Portugal to a Brazilian father from Rio de Janeiro and a mother of English background, Gonzaga went to Brazil as a child, where he studied in the Jesuit school in Bahia. After completing his law degree at Coimbra, Portugal, in 1768, he became a magistrate in Beja, Portugal, and later in gold-driven Vila Rica, in Minas Gerais province in Brazil. There, as both a *reinol* (that is, one born in Portugal and living in colonial Brazil) and a poet, he became involved in political and intellectual societies. Cláudio Manuel da COSTA (1729–1789) and Inácio José de Alvarenga Peixoto (1744–1793) were among his closest friends and conspirators in the failed INCONFIDÊNCIA MINEIRA, the Mineiran Conspiracy of 1789. Gonzaga's judicial career in Brazil suffered because of a bitter political feud with the governor of Minas Gerais, Luís da Cunha e Meneses, who accused him of opportunism and corruption. Tried as a participant in the Mineiran Conspiracy, Gonzaga was sent into exile in Mozambique, where he married a rich widow, gradually regained his official position, and, at his death, was the Mozambican customs magistrate.

Gonzaga's poetry belongs to the Arcadian school, which flourished in late-eighteenth-century Minas

Gerais. Using the name "Dirceu," he dedicated his lyrics to his beloved Marília, a sixteen-year-old girl he had intended to marry. He continued to write love poems throughout his exile in Mozambique, even when all hope of this marriage had already been dashed. Because his work was published on two continents and in several volumes (1792, 1799, 1812), the exact corpus of his poetry, published under the title *Marília de Dirceu*, has yet to be definitively established.

Perhaps more significant than his poems are the *Cartas chilenas* (1863), now attributed to Gonzaga. A veiled attack on Cunha e Meneses's government, these thirteen free-verse satirical letters offer a fascinating view of life in colonial Minas, in particular of the societal conflicts that surfaced among government officials, nobles, merchants, gold prospectors, and slaves.

Gonzaga's life and writings have inspired works by many other Brazilian writers down to the present, including Casimiro de Abreu, CASTRO ALVES, and Drummond de ANDRADE.

WILSON MARTINS, *História da inteligência brasileira* (1976–1983).

IRWIN STERN

GONZÁLEZ, ABRAHAM (*b.* 7 June 1864; *d.* 7 March 1913), governor of Chihuahua, Mexico (1911–1913), minister of internal affairs (1911–1912). González was a gunrunner for the insurgency of Francisco I. MADERO (1909–1910). As governor he instituted a number of political reforms, including the abolition of company towns and the hated office of *jefe político* (district boss). After an interlude in Madero's cabinet, González returned to Chihuahua to confront growing unrest that erupted in the rebellion of Pascual OROZCO, Jr., in 1912. He defeated the Orozquistas, only to die at the hands of the reactionary forces that overthrew Madero. González typified the Maderista, middle-class political reformers caught between the radical demands of their present and worker followers and the reactionary Porfirian oligarchy.

There are two important biographies of González: FRANCISCO R. ALMADA, *Vida, proceso y muerte de Abraham González* (1967), and WILLIAM H. BEEZLEY, *Insurgent Governor: Abraham González and the Mexican Revolution* (1973).

MARK WASSERMAN

GONZÁLEZ, BEATRIZ (*b.* 1938), Colombian artist. González studied fine arts at the Universidad de los Andes in Bogotá (1959–1962) and printmaking at the Academia van Beeldende Kunsten in Rotterdam (1966). Her first individual exhibition was held at the Museo de Arte Moderno in Bogotá in 1964. González employs both popular imagery and well-known artworks as departure points, taking images from such European masterpieces as Leonardo da Vinci's *Mona Lisa* and Jan Vermeer's *The Lacemaker* and placing them within the context of Colombian daily life. She is also known for her satirical portraits of prominent Colombian figures. Her works of the 1960s and 1970s are generally characterized by strong colors and a sense of irony, thus bearing a relationship to pop art. González now explores social themes: questions of identity, the history of her culture, and the impact of these issues on the lives of contemporary Colombians. González was included in the Bienal de São Paulo (1971) and the Biennale di Venezia (1978). Retrospectives were held at the Museo de Arte Moderno La Tertulia in Cali (1976) and the Museo de Arte Moderno in Bogotá (1984).

JUDITH GLUCK STEINBERG

GONZÁLEZ, CARLOS (*b.* 1 December 1905), Uruguayan artist, who specialized in woodcut. Born in Melo, in the department of Cerro Largo, González studied with Andrés Etchebarne Bidart. In his youth, he traveled throughout the Uruguayan countryside selling his family's wheatmill products; later he devoted himself to forestry. It was not until 1938 that he began to make woodcuts. He received gold medals from the National Salon of Fine Arts in Montevideo in 1943 and 1944. His subjects were local legends, traditional countryside scenes, and socially concerned testimonies to the poverty-stricken rural areas. In a typical González woodcut, the central scene is surrounded by a printed border filled with written messages and symbols representing rural work, leisure, and culture. The figurative elements on the margins complement the central scene. Together, both marginal and central illustrations narrate events from Latin American and Uruguayan history. His printing style was harsh and sketchy, often the result of carving wood with a common knife.

González wanted his art to have a didactic function, specifically, to tell the history and social reality of Uruguay as he interpreted it. This task, he believed, required a collective (or cooperative) effort. Feeling isolated, he abandoned artistic practice at the prime of his career, in 1944. In 1970 he was credited with the invention of Uruguayan printmaking at the Fourth American Biennial of Printmaking in Santiago, Chile.

ANGEL KALENBERG, *Carlos González o la invención del grabado uruguayo* (1970); ALICIA HABER, "Vernacular Culture in Uruguayan Art: An Analysis of the Documentary Function of the Works of Pedro Figari, Carlos González and Luis Solari," in *Latin American and Caribbean Center, Florida University, Occasional Paper Series* (Spring 1982):9–15, and *Carlos González: El grabado como puente visual* (1988).

MARTA GARSD

GONZÁLEZ, FLORENTINO (*b.* 1805; *d.* ca. 1875), Colombian political figure of the Liberal Party. Born in Cincelada, Santander, González studied at the College of San Bartolomé, obtaining the degree of doctor of jurisprudence in 1825. One of the participants in the attempt against Simón BOLÍVAR's life in 1828, González barely escaped the firing squad. He went to Europe in 1841, remaining there until 1846.

González's claim to historical notoriety rests on his being widely credited as the foremost proponent of free trade, a position based on ideas he had picked up in Great Britain in the early 1840s. As minister of finance in the first administration of Tomás Cipriano de MOSQUERA (1845–1849), he implemented policies that reflected his ideas. In the ensuing Liberal Party split between an elite faction (the *gólgotas*) and a more "popular" faction (the *draconianos*), González attacked the *draconianos* as dangerous socialist levelers. As he became ideologically closer to the Conservatives and because he favored annexation to the United States to avoid political instability, he broke with his party and faded away from the political stage. In 1860 he left Colombia never to return. He died in Argentina.

GUSTAVO OTERO MUÑOZ, *Semblanzas Colombianas* (1938); GERARDO MOLINA, *Las ideas liberales en Colombia, 1849–1914* (1970); JAIME DUARTE FRENCH, *Florentino González: Razón y sinrazón de una lucha política* (1982).

JOSÉ ESCORCIA

GONZÁLEZ, JOAQUÍN VÍCTOR (*b.* 6 March 1863; *d.* 21 December 1923), Argentine author, educator, diplomat, and statesman. Born in Chilecito, La Rioja Province, he received his law degree from the University of Córdoba in 1886. He began his political career in 1886, when he was elected as a deputy representing La Rioja. He then served as the province's governor (1889–1891) and senator (1907–1923). President Julio ROCA (1898–1904) appointed him interior minister (1901) and later foreign relations minister (1903). He continued his service under President Manuel QUINTANA (1904–1906), heading the Ministry of Justice and Public Instruction. He concluded his public service by representing Argentina in the League of Nations.

An authority on law and politics as well as education, he is best known for his literary and historical works, including *La tradición nacional* (1888) and *Mis montañas* (1893). He taught law at the University of Córdoba (1894), served on the National Education Council (1896), and became the first rector of the National University of La Plata (1906).

JOAQUÍN V. GONZÁLEZ, *Obras completas de Joaquín V. González*, 25 vols. (1935–1937); ARTURO MARASSO, *Joaquín V. González, el artista y el hombre* (1937).

DANIEL LEWIS

GONZÁLEZ, JUAN NATALICIO (*b.* 8 September 1897; *d.* 6 December 1966), Paraguayan poet, historian, journalist, statesman, and president (1948–1949). González was born in Villerrica and studied at the Colegio Nacional in Asunción. He began his literary career under the guidance of Juan O'LEARY, with whom he shared many stylistic and thematic traits. González later became associated with many other Paraguayan apologists in the task of reconstructing the image of their country. In 1920, he founded the journal *Guaranía*, which went through several stages as a vital cultural vehicle and continued to be published into the 1940s. In 1925 González lived in Paris, where he was active in publishing. The dominant Colorado Party supported him in his bid for president and he assumed office on 15 August 1948. His own party quickly disagreed with some of his policies and had him removed in February 1949, after which he resided in Mexico.

Throughout his life he dedicated himself to national themes. His *Solano López y otros ensayos* (1926) is his best-known work, followed by *Proceso y formación de la cultura paraguaya* (1938).

J. NATALICIO GONZÁLEZ, *Motivos de la tierra escarlata* (1952), and *Ideología guaraní* (1958); HUGO RODRÍGUEZ-ALCALÁ, *Historia de la literatura paraguaya* (1971), pp. 80–81; 98–99.

CATALINA SEGOVIA-CASE

GONZÁLEZ, JUAN VICENTE (*b.* 28 May 1810; *d.* 1 October 1866), Venezuelan politician, writer, and journalist. Associated with the Liberals in 1840, González subsequently distanced himself from them to the extent that by 1845 he had become one of their most radical opponents, promulgating his politics through various newspapers: *Cicerón y Catilina, Diario de la Tarde,* and *La Prensa.*

González ceased political activity during the regime of José Tadeo MONAGAS, founded the El Salvador del Mundo school (The Savior of the World School) in 1849, and did an extensive and varied amount of literary and historiographic work. His *Biografía de José Felix Ribas* (1858) is representative of what is known in Venezuela as romantic historiography. Later on he opposed profederation propaganda and, together with defenders of civilian rule during the FEDERAL WAR (1859–1863), opposed the dictatorship of José Antonio PÁEZ. In 1863 González supported the regime of Juan Crisóstomo FALCÓN, and then left his public activities to dedicate himself primarily to literary work, founding the *Revista Literaria* in 1865.

See MARCO ANTONIO SALUZZO, *Juan Vicente González* (1901); HÉCTOR CUENCA, *Juan Vicente González (1811–1866)* (1953); and LUIS CORREA, *Tres ensayos sobre Juan Vicente González, 1810–1866* (1987). A selection of his most important political and literary writings can be found in *Pensamiento político Venezolano del siglo XIX*, vols. 2 and 3 (1961).

INÉS QUINTERO

GONZÁLEZ, MANUEL (*b.* 18 June 1833; *d.* 8 May 1893), president of Mexico (1880–1884). Born in the state of Tamaulipas, González began his career as a professional soldier in 1847. During the War of the REFORM (1857–

1860), González fought on the losing Conservative side, but during the FRENCH INTERVENTION (1862–1867), he served with Liberal general PORFIRIO DÍAZ and eventually became Díaz's chief of staff. Promoted to brigadier general in 1867, González served as governor of the National Palace and military commander of the Federal District (1871–1873).

After supporting Díaz's unsuccessful PLAN OF LA NORIA in 1871, González played a prominent military role in Díaz's triumph under the PLAN OF TUXTEPEC in 1876. In March 1878 González was appointed minister of war by President Díaz. Ineligible for reelection in 1880, Díaz worked secretly for the election of González, who took office in December 1880.

As president, González adopted a policy of conciliation toward the national congress, the state governments, the Roman Catholic church, and the military. In foreign relations, he eased long-standing border problems with the United States by agreeing to permit reciprocal crossing of troops and settled a lingering boundary dispute with Guatemala. Relations with Great Britain, broken in 1867, were renewed in 1884.

González accelerated government promotion of economic development, especially in the areas of transportation and communications. Federal lands were opened for settlement, and efforts were made to promote colonization and immigration. In 1884, the government issued a new mining code permitting private ownership of subsoil resources for the first time. Unfortunately for González, who had inherited an empty treasury, his spending for economic development only exacerbated the country's ongoing financial problems. The introduction of new nickel coinage in 1882 provoked inflation and devaluation. Negotiations aimed at settling the long-standing debt owed to British creditors also discredited González.

González completed his term of office amid mounting political crisis; he returned the presidency to Díaz in 1884. González later served three terms as governor of Guanajuato.

DANIEL COSÍO VILLEGAS, *Historia moderna de México*, vol. 8 (1970), pp. 575–798; DON M. COERVER, *The Porfirian Interregnum: The Presidency of Manuel González of Mexico, 1880–1884* (1979).

DON M. COERVER

GONZÁLEZ, PABLO (*b.* 5 May 1879; *d.* 4 March 1950), Mexican general and revolutionary. González is best known for his military exploits in the Constitutionalist army of revolutionary chief Venustiano CARRANZA and his role in the death of agrarian leader and revolutionary Emiliano ZAPATA.

González was born in Lampazos, Nuevo León, and orphaned at age five. He attended primary school in Nadadores, Coahuila, and then tried to enter the National Military College, but was turned down. He worked in a flour mill in Lampazos (1893), served as a laborer and later foreman on the Santa Fe Railroad

(1902), and worked in California (1903). He joined the liberal political movement headed by Ricardo FLORES MAGÓN (1873–1922) and in 1907 edited the Mexican Liberal Party (PLM) newspaper *Revolución*. Later he joined the Anti-Reelectionist Party and supported Francisco I. MADERO against long-time dictator Porfirio DÍAZ. He commanded Madero's forces in Coahuila, rising to the rank of colonel (1911). In 1912 he fought against the anti-Madero rebellion led by Pascual OROZCO.

After joining the forces of Carranza in 1913, González rose to the rank of general and commander-in-chief of the armies of the Northeast and West. He participated in the Convention of AGUASCALIENTES (1914–1915); became the zone commander of Morelos, Puebla, Oaxaca, and Tlaxcala; and served as the governor of Morelos (1916, 1919). While commander in Morelos he carried out an especially vicious military campaign against the Zapatistas and is considered to be the perpetrator of Emiliano Zapata's assassination (1919). In 1920 González ran unsuccessfully for the presidency and, upon Álvaro Obregón's overthrow of Carranza, rebelled against the new regime in July 1920. Captured and sentenced to death, González was allowed to seek asylum in San Antonio, Texas, where he remained until 1940. He died in Monterrey, Nuevo León.

JOSÉ MORALES HESSE, *El General Pablo González: Datos para la historia, 1910–1916* (1916); JOHN W. F. DULLES, *Yesterday in Mexico: A Chronicle of the Revolution, 1919–1936* (1961); CHARLES C. CUMBERLAND, *Mexico: The Constitutionalist Years* (1972); RAMÓN EDUARDO RUÍZ, *The Great Rebellion: Mexico, 1905–1924* (1980); ALAN KNIGHT, *The Mexican Revolution*, 2 vols. (1986), esp. vol. 2.

DAVID LaFRANCE

GONZÁLEZ ÁVILA, JORGE (*b.* 10 December 1925), Mexican composer. Born in Mérida, Yucatán, González Ávila was a pupil of the Spanish composer Rodolfo HALFFTER at the National Conservatory of Mexico. Like a number of Halffter's pupils, González Ávila became a true believer in the twelve-tone and avant-garde serial techniques that the Spanish master had been promoting in Mexico City's musical circles since his arrival in 1939. No dogmatist, González Ávila, who was predominately a composer of piano works, did not follow Halffter's style strictly but took an independent approach to the use of serial elements. Between 1961 and 1964 he wrote a collection of twenty-four inventions for piano; he was also the author of several collections of piano études, some of which demonstrate dodecaphonic writing.

MARIO KURI-ALDANA, *Jóvenes compositores mexicanos* (1974); GÉRARD BÉHAGUE, *Music in Latin America* (1979).

SUSANA SALGADO

GONZÁLEZ CAMARENA, JORGE (*b.* 1908; *d.* 24 May 1980), Mexican artist. González Camarena is known for his murals and sculptures. He invented a system of geometric harmonies by fusing precise painting with subdued but vibrant color and textures. Among his public murals are *The Formation of Mexico* (1950), in the Instituto Mexicano del Seguro Social (in front of whose entrance stand his sculptures of *Man* and *Woman*); *Belisario Dominguez* (1956), in the Cámara de Senadores; and *Liberation* (1958), in the Palacio de Bellas Artes—all in Mexico City. Many of his other murals were commercial commissions.

BERNARD S. MYERS, *Mexican Painting in Our Time* (1956); ANTONIO RODRÍGUEZ, *A History of Mexican Mural Painting,* translated by Marina Corby (1969).

SHIFRA M. GOLDMAN

GONZÁLEZ CASANOVA, PABLO (*b.* 11 February 1922), Mexican social scientist and academic administrator. A rigorous scholar and theorist of internal colonialism, dependency, and other conceptual models of analysis of the Latin American historical and contemporary reality, González Casanova has authored and edited over 200 books and published nearly as many scholarly articles. His most important studies include the classic *La democracía en México* (1965) and *El estado y los partidos políticos en México* (1981). He has also held important academic-administrative positions, including director of the Escuela de Ciencias Políticas y Sociales (1957–1965) and president of the National Autonomous University of Mexico (UNAM) (1970–1972). In 1984, González Casanova was awarded the National Prize in Mexico for Social Sciences and Humanities.

DAVID MACIEL

GONZÁLEZ DÁVILA, GIL (*b.* 1490; *d.* 1550), Spanish conqueror and explorer of Nicaragua. While still a young man, González achieved renown for his military exploits in Europe and won permission from the Spanish king to explore Central America. He left Spain in 1518, passed through Cuba, and reached Panama in 1519. Although holding a commission from the king himself, González fell afoul of the tyrannical governor of Panama, Pedro Arias de ÁVILA (Pedrarias), a circumstance that delayed his expedition for three years. These intervening years, however, enabled González to familiarize himself with New World conditions and gather information of use to his mission.

In 1522 González set out by sea with the fleet of the recently executed Vasco Núñez de Balboa and reached Costa Rica. Finding no easy riches there, González's interest in lands northward was aroused by a Costa Rican *cacique*. Abandoning his worm-eaten fleet, he continued inland on foot. Using his Costa Rican contacts, González obtained an introduction to Chief NICARAO, leader of a large settlement of Indians, and spent eight days with him in the area now known as Rivas. González subsequently claimed the entire region for the king

of Spain and named it Nicaragua, a derivation of the chief's name. The Spaniards did not have much time to exploit their new acquisition, however; on 17 April 1522 a rival chief, Diriangen, attacked their group, forcing the would-be conquerors to withdraw.

Arriving in Panama, González recounted his accomplishments for the governor: the discovery of Lake Nicaragua, the addition of 224 leagues of land to the king's empire, the purported baptism of some 32,000 Indians, and the seizure of riches. González also claimed Nicaragua as his separate and independent authority, granted under the king's commission, something Pedrarias found unacceptable. A bitter competition for jurisdiction followed—a common occurrence among the Spanish conquerors—until Pedrarias stripped González of his right to primacy in the area and replaced him with Francisco FERNÁNDEZ DE CÓRDOBA. González managed to flee Panama with 112,524 gold pesos obtained during his Nicaraguan expedition. He remained in Santo Domingo for several years, all the while pressing his claims and plotting a military counterattack.

In 1525 González and his supporters defeated a detachment of Fernández's men and encouraged Fernández to rebel against Pedrarias. The three-way struggle for Nicaragua prompted a year-long civil war ending in 1526 and culminating in Fernández's execution when Pedrarias moved northward to assume the governorship himself.

González remained in exile and returned to Panama in 1532, the year after the death of his arch rival, Pedrarias. He continued to fight for his claims and formed an alliance with Hernán CORTÉS against Cristóbal de OLID, who was attempting to set up his own authority in Honduras. González was found guilty of the assassination of Olid. But he had won the gratitude of Cortés, who permitted him to return to Spain, where he spent the remainder of his days enjoying his reputation and his riches.

HARVEY K. MEYER, *Historical Dictionary of Nicaragua* (1972); ERNESTO CHINCHILLA AGUILAR, *Historia de Centroamérica*, 3 vols. (1974–1977); and RALPH LEE WOODWARD, JR., *Central America: A Nation Divided* (1985).

KAREN RACINE

GONZÁLEZ DE ESLAVA, FERNÁN (ca. 1534–ca. 1601), Spanish playwright in New Spain. González de Eslava was born in Spain, probably León, but his precise birthplace, along with many other details concerning his life, remain unknown. He arrived in Mexico around 1558, and within five years there were notices of his poetic activities. As a playwright he is known primarily for his *coloquios*, the first of which dates from about 1567. By 1572 he was preparing to be a cleric, but two years later he was jailed for seventeen days when his writing produced a conflict between the Viceroy Martín ENRÍQUEZ DE ALMANSA and Archbishop Pedro MOYA DE CONTRERAS. He became a priest, probably by 1575 or 1576, and wrote his last *coloquio* in 1600.

As a playwright in the New World González de Eslava is neither first (Juan Pérez Ramírez deserves that honor) nor American (having been born in Spain). His theater is religious with didactic aims. In the second half of the sixteenth century, theater was designed for the new, primarily creole, society being formed. His dramatic works consist of sixteen *coloquios*, four *entremeses*, and nine *loas*. The works tended to be light and facile, and to give a clear and honest vision of life in the colony. Without pretensions, they communicated a religious message (at least eleven of the *coloquios* are considered "sacramental") that was easily accessible to a wide public. González de Eslava had a gift for versification, and his plays are marked by a delightful use of language that incorporated New World structures. He is particularly known for an engaging sense of humor that pervades his language, his characters, and the situations. His *simple* is a likely precursor of the Siglo de Oro *gracioso*. On occasion González de Eslava revealed his disdain for the indigenous population, but for all his defects, he is still the major writer of Mexico who anticipated Sor JUANA INÉS DE LA CRUZ by a full century.

AMADO ALONSO, "Biografía de Fernán González de Eslava," in *Revista de filología hispánica* 2, no. 3 (n.d.): 213–321; FRIDA WEBER VON KURLAT, "El teatro anterior a Lope de Vega y la novela picaresca (A propósito de los *Coloquios espirituales y sacramentales* de Hernán González de Eslava)," in *Filología* 6 (1960): 1–27, and *Lo cómico en el teatro de Fernán González de Esclava* (1963); JULIE GREER JOHNSON, "Three Celestina Figures of Colonial Spanish American Literature," in *Celestinesca,* 5, no. 1 (May 1981): 41–46.

GEORGE WOODYARD

GONZÁLEZ DE SANTA CRUZ, ROQUE (*b.* 1576; *d.* 15 November 1628), Paraguayan Jesuit who founded many of the Jesuit missions (*reducciones*) in his native land, as well as in present-day Argentina and Uruguay. Born of Spanish parents in Asunción, he learned GUARANÍ as a child. He was ordained a priest around 1589 and worked among the Indians in the region of Jejuí, north of Asunción. In 1603 he was named rector of the cathedral in Asunción, and in 1609 he entered the Society of Jesus. As a Jesuit he returned to work with the Indians. He helped build the first of the *reducciones*, San Ignacio Guazú, south of Asunción. In 1614 he wrote a letter to his brother Francisco, the lieutenant governor of Asunción, in which he denounced the *encomenderos* for their mistreatment of the Indians. He went on to found many other *reducciones* in southern Paraguay, in the province of Misiones in present-day Argentina, and in Uruguay. In 1627 he was appointed superior of all of the *reducciones* in Uruguay. At Caaró, in modern Rio Grande do Sul, Brazil, he and two other JESUITS were killed by Indian shamans who were hostile to his efforts to Christianize the Indians in their region.

González was a skilled builder, leader, and organizer. Although he died at the hands of hostile Indians, he was greatly esteemed by the Indians in general, who appreciated his efforts to organize them in defense of their land and culture against Spanish exploiters. The first Paraguayan to be a missionary in his own land, he was also the first martyr born in the New World. He was canonized in 1988.

CLEMENT J. MC NASPY, *Conquistador Without Sword: The Life of Roque González, S.J.* (1984); PHILIP CARAMAN, *The Lost Paradise,* 2d ed. (1990); SILVIO PALACIOS and ENA ZOFFOLI, *Gloria y tragedia de las misiones guaraníes* (1991).

JEFFREY KLAIBER

See also **Missions, Jesuit.**

GONZÁLEZ FLORES, ALFREDO (*b.* 15 June 1877; *d.* 28 December 1962), president of Costa Rica (1914–1917). Born in Heredia, González Flores received a law degree in 1902. The Costa Rican Congress chose him to be president of the Republic in 1914. Ironically, Costa Ricans were supposed to elect their president directly for the first time that year, but none of the three candidates received a majority, sending the matter to Congress, which selected González Flores, who had not even been on the original ballot.

González Flores became president at a time when Costa Rica's population was growing dramatically and the price for its principal export, coffee, was falling precipitously. Costa Rica was beginning to experience the effects of monoculture, wherin its "golden bean" was leaving a bitter taste. González Flores courageously proposed an income tax to try to alleviate the suffering of the poor, but he was too weak politically for such bold action.

The outbreak of World War I compounded his difficulties. With exports curtailed and imported goods scarce, Costa Rica experienced inflation and declining revenues. Though González Flores attempted progressive economic measures by imposing exchange regulations, levying export taxes, and cutting salaries of public employees, he had little support. The minister of defense, General Federico TINOCO GRANADOS took advantage of the president's unpopularity to stage a coup on 27 January 1917, which established the second dictatorship in Costa Rican history.

González Flores persuaded President Woodrow WILSON not to recognize the Tinoco dictatorship. In recent years biographers have viewed him more favorably as a precursor of Costa Rican reform movements. He gave a lifetime of service to his native city, Heredia, and Costa Rica awarded him the Benemérito de la Patria in 1954.

EDUARDO OCONITRILLO GARCÍA, *Alfredo González Flores* (1980); CHARLES D. AMERINGER, *Democracy in Costa Rica* (1982); HAROLD D. NELSON, ed., *Costa Rica: A Country Study,* 2d ed. (1983); MARC EDELMAN AND JOANNE KENEN, eds., *The Costa Rica Reader* (1989).

CHARLES D. AMERINGER

GONZÁLEZ GOYRI, ROBERTO (*b.* 1924), Guatemalan artist, inspired by pre-Conquest cultures. He studied with Rafael Yela Günther at the Academy of Fine Arts in Guatemala City, where he received academic training, and worked as a draftsman at the National Museum of Archeology. On a grant from the Guatemalan government, he studied in New York from 1948 to 1952. International recognition came in 1951, when he won a prize for a sculpture of the unknown political prisoner in a contest sponsored by the London Institute of Contemporary Arts. The Museum of Modern Art in New York acquired his semiabstract sculpture *The Wolf* (1951) in 1955. He was director of the National School of Plastic Arts in Guatemala City (1957–1958).

As a sculptor, González Goyri worked with terracotta, concrete, and metals combining an expressionist, symbolic style with abstract motifs. His mural and sculptural projects for public buildings, such as the Social Security Institute in Guatemala City (1959), and his monumental sculpture of the Guatemalan Indian hero TECÚN-UMÁN (1963) symbolically depict Guatemalan history from the dawn of Maya civilization to independence. As a painter, he has worked primarily in a post-cubist style, inspired by the strong colors found in Guatemalan crafts. His mural *Religion in Guatemala: Its Pre-Hispanic, Colonial, and Contemporary Roots* (1992) is a monumental interpretation of Guatemalan religious life, from the *Popol Vuh*, the sacred Maya book, to the present.

GILBERT CHASE, *Contemporary Art in Latin America* (1970), pp. 46–48, 247–248; JOSÉ GÓMEZ SICRE, *Roberto González Goyri* (1986); DELIA QUIÑONEZ, *Mural "La religión en Guatemala, sus raíces prehispánicas, coloniales y sincréticas contemporáneas"* (1992).

MARTA GARSD

GONZÁLEZ LEÓN, ADRIANO (*b.* 1931), Venezuelan fiction writer. One of Venezuela's most innovative and demanding writers, González León is the author of one of the most accomplished Venezuelan novels of the century, *País portátil* (1969). He also published the novel *Asfalto-infierno* (1963) and several volumes of short fiction. His first set of stories, *Las hogueras más altas* (1957), portrays solitary and violent characters. González León used Faulknerian narrative techniques to construct his historical and political novel *País portátil,* which tells the story of the Barazarte family through the mind of one of its members, a young revolutionary. At the same time, *País portátil* also recounts Venezuelan history since the nineteenth century. The young revolutionary, Andrés, carries a bomb on a bus through the city of Caracas. The reader is bombarded with images of modern urban chaos in the city and the conscious and subconscious thoughts of Andrés. González León has published short fiction in the 1970s and 1980s, but no other novels.

JOHN S. BRUSHWOOD, *The Spanish American Novel: A Twentieth-Century Survey* (1975); GIUSEPPE BELLINI, *Historia de la literatura hispanoamericana* (1985); GEORGE MC MURRAY, *Spanish American Writing Since 1941* (1987).

RAYMOND LESLIE WILLIAMS

GONZÁLEZ MARTÍNEZ, ENRIQUE (*b.* 13 April 1871; *d.* 19 February 1952), Mexican poet. A central figure in the literary life of the nation from the beginning of the Revolution until his death at mid-century, González Martínez was trained as a physician but spent most of his career in public service. His early poetry reflects the turn-of-the-century *modernista* techniques, and in the 1920s there are traces of *vanguardista* influences; he is noted, however, for his consistent, profound exploration of personal experience and metaphysical searching through his art. He is a master of traditional forms, especially of the sonnet; his language evolves toward simplicity; biblical and classical allusions are common, but never recondite. The condition of solitude, a certain pantheistic urging, a longing for lucidity and transcendent vision, the "resplendent moment," give shape to much of his work. An occasional trace of didacticism may also be found.

The early period culminates in the definition of his voice in *Silénter* (1909) and *Los senderos ocultos* (1911). The latter collection includes the sonnet "Tuércele el cuello al cisne" ("Wring the Swan's Neck"), his most anthologized poem, often misread as marking the end of *modernismo*. González Martínez is best understood as one of the most important exponents of the symbolist strain in *modernismo* as it has subsequently evolved. *Parábolas y otros poemas* (1918), *El romero alucinado* (1923), and *Las señales furtivas* (1925) are major collections of his middle period. His later poetry is marked by the death of his wife and of his son, Enrique González Rojo (1899–1939), also a poet. These works include *Ausencia y canto* (1937), *El diluvio de fuego* (1938), *Bajo el signo mortal* (1942), and *El nuevo Narciso y otros poemas* (1952). The "Estancias," twenty-one octaves and a concluding sonnet that open this last collection, are an exceptionally beautiful summing up of his life and art. He wrote an autobiography published in two parts, *El hombre del buho* (1944) and *La apacible locura* (1951). He was a fine translator of French poetry. In 1911 he was elected to the Mexican Academy, and he was a member of the ATENEO DE LA JUVENTUD and a founding member of the Colegio Nacional (1943).

ANTONIO CASTRO LEAL edited a fine edition of the *Obras completas* (1971). The fundamental study of the poet is JOHN S. BRUSHWOOD, *Enrique González Martínez* (1969). Many important critical articles were collected by JOSÉ LUIS MARTÍNEZ in *La obra de Enrique González Martínez* (1951). See also JOSÉ MANUEL TOPETE, *El mundo poético de Enrique González Martínez* (1967), and HARRY L. ROSSER, "Enrique González Martínez: 'Matacisnes' y concepción estética," in *Cuadernos Americanos* 243 (1982): 181–188.

MICHAEL J. DOUDOROFF

GONZÁLEZ ORTEGA, JESÚS (*b.* 1822; *d.* 1881), Mexican military officer and cabinet minister. Born on a hacienda near Teúl, Zacatecas, and educated in Guadalajara, Ortega held an office job in Teúl until the War of the REFORM. Of liberal ideas, he was elected to the legislature of the state of Zacatecas in 1858 and soon after was designated the state's governor. Ortega began his military career by organizing and leading the Zacatecas militia. One of the most successful liberal generals, he was appointed by President Benito JUÁREZ to succeed Santos DEGOLLADO. After a series of victories over the Conservatives, Ortega led the victorious liberal army into Mexico City on 1 January 1861, ending the War of the Reform.

After Juárez named him minister of war on 20 January, Ortega resigned three months later over political differences with the president. Under the Constitution of 1857, as the congressionally elected interim president of the Supreme Court, Ortega was first in line of succession to the presidency of the republic. During the French Intervention, President Juárez reluctantly turned to Ortega to take command of the Army of the East. After the siege of Puebla in 1863, Ortega was forced to surrender, but he escaped his captors and fled to the United States. Juárez decreed the extension of his own presidential term and announced that Ortega had renounced his claim to the presidency by remaining in a foreign country without permission. When Ortega returned to Mexico in 1866, he was arrested and held without trial. He was released in August 1868 with the stipulation that the government reserved the right to prosecute him. Ortega resigned as president of the Court and retired from politics.

IVIE E. CADENHEAD, JR., *Jesús González Ortega and Mexican National Politics* (1972); LAURENS B. PERRY, *Juárez and Díaz: Machine Politics in Mexico* (1978); RICHARD N. SINKIN, *The Mexican Reform, 1855–1876: A Study in Liberal Nation-Building* (1979); *Diccionario Porrúa de historia, biografía y geografía de México*, 5th ed. (1986).

D. F. STEVENS

GONZÁLEZ PRADA, MANUEL (*b.* 5 January 1844; *d.* 22 July 1918), Peruvian writer. González Prada was born in Lima and studied law there. A cofounder of the Unión Nacional, a short-lived liberal party, in 1891, and author of twenty-one books and three pamphlets, he was the first ideological agitator of modern Peru. In his sociopolitical essays, written with cutting sentences and satirical in tone, his witty mordancy is softened by an expert application of literary devices that reveals a powerful will and a firm determination to invent, adapt, transform, and re-create a literary language to be used as a comfortable, swift, efficient, and suitable linguistic vehicle. His best-known books are *Pájinas libres* (1894) and *Horas de lucha* (1908).

LUIS ALBERTO SÁNCHEZ, *Mito y realidad de Gojnzález Prada* (1976); MANUEL GONZÁLEZ PRADA, *Obras* (1985); EUGENIO CHANG-RODRÍGUEZ, "Manuel González Prada," in *Latin American Writers* (1989), vol. 1, pp. 283–288.

EUGENIO CHANG-RODRÍGUEZ

GONZÁLEZ PRADA POPULAR UNIVERSITIES, politicized educational efforts in Peru during the early 1920s that were inspired by the student leader and politician Víctor Raúl HAYA DE LA TORRE. These popular universities offered free evening courses for workers while the Peruvian university under the regime of Augusto B. LEGUÍA (1919–1930) was disrupted. Moreover, they were effective, practical means by which a growing populist movement, led by Haya de la Torre, won large sectors of labor away from earlier ANARCHIST influences. Haya emphasized some of the anarchist elements of his own ideology among the universities' participants. The young Haya had been influenced in Lima by the eminent anarchist intellectual Manuel GONZÁLEZ PRADA. Socialist leader José Carlos MARIÁTEGUI collaborated with Haya until 1928 in the organization of the popular universities, which later were the basis of Aprista unions.

STEVE STEIN, *Populism in Peru: The Emergence of the Masses and the Politics of Social Control* (1980).

ALFONSO W. QUIROZ

GONZÁLEZ SUÁREZ, (MANUEL MARÍA) FEDERICO (*b.* 12 April 1844; *d.* 1 December 1917), noted Ecuadoran historian and archbishop of Quito (1906–1917). González Suárez, a native of Quito, is most remembered for his multivolume *Historia general de la República del Ecuador* (1890–1903), based on extensive research in local archives and in Spain. González Suárez's goal had been to write a general history of America, but he completed only the eight volumes that dealt with Ecuador's pre-Columbian and colonial eras. He devoted most of his attention to the ecclesiastical history of the city of Quito, giving scant notice to Guayaquil or to economic matters. González Suárez's mild criticism of the colonial Ecuadorian clergy evoked bitter attacks from the church and from conservatives. Other works by González Suárez are *Estudio histórico sobre las Canaris* (1878), *Historia eclesiástica del Ecuador* (1881), *Nueva miscelanea o colección de opusculos publicados* (1910), and *Defensa de mi criterio histórico* (1937).

During the terms of the Liberal president Eloy Alfaro y Arosemena (1895–1901, 1906–1911) and the drive to secularize Ecuadorian society (principally through measures for civil marriage and divorce), Archbishop González Suárez played a critical role in depoliticizing the clergy. A peacemaker, he provided a calm voice for moderation in the clergy. His publications inspired a group of young disciples, most notably Jacinto Jijón y Caamaño.

For a discussion of González Suárez's contribution to Ecuadorian historical scholarship, see ADAM SZÁSZDI, "The Historiography of the Republic of Ecuador," in *Hispanic American Historical Review* 44, 4 (1964): 503–550; and GEORGE A. BRUBAKER,

"Federico González Suárez, Historian of Ecuador," in *Journal of Inter-American Studies* 5, 2 (1963): 235–248. See also NICOLÁS JIMÉNEZ, *Biografía del ilustrísimo Federico González Suárez* (1936).

RONN F. PINEO

GONZÁLEZ VIDELA, GABRIEL (*b.* 22 November 1898; *d.* 22 August 1980), president of Chile (1946–1952). A lawyer who was born in the provinces, González Videla served as a diplomat before ruling Chile during the turbulent post–World War II era. As a member of the Radical Party's left wing, he promised to revive many of Pedro Aguirre Cerda's policies. Unable to win the popular vote in the 1946 election, he entered into a political alliance with the Liberal and Communist parties. When it became clear that he could not reconcile these two ideological foes, González Videla dismissed the Communists from his cabinet. The Communists retaliated by launching a series of violent strikes that paralyzed the nation, eventually forcing González Videla to use the military to restore order. Claiming to have discovered a leftist plot, he outlawed the Communist Party and broke off diplomatic relations with Eastern bloc nations.

As president, González Videla encountered substantial economic problems. A decline in world copper prices and the onset of powerful inflation—33 percent in 1947 alone—devastated the Chilean economy. When the government imposed an austerity program, it precipitated a series of violent public demonstrations.

While it was beset by economic and political problems, the González Videla government was not without its accomplishments: the state built a steel plant, organized a government oil company, encouraged hydroelectric projects, founded the Technical University, and enfranchised women.

FEDERICO G. GIL, *The Political System of Chile* (1966), pp. 72–76, 227, 277; PAUL W. DRAKE, *Socialism and Populism in Chile: 1932–52* (1978), pp. 281–291.

WILLIAM F. SATER

GONZÁLEZ VIGIL, FRANCISCO DE PAULA. *See* Vigil, Francisco de Paula González.

GONZÁLEZ VÍQUEZ, CLETO (*b.* 13 October 1858; *d.* 23 September 1937), president of Costa Rica (1906–1910, 1928–1932). González Víquez was born in Barba de Heredia, Costa Rica, to an aristocratic family. He was an eminent attorney, distinguished politician, and one of the most illustrious historians of his country. With his colleague, friend, and adversary Ricardo JIMÉNEZ, he dominated national politics for four decades in an era characterized by CAUDILLISMO. He published numerous works on law and history, most notable of which are his investigations into historical geography and genealogy and his interesting studies of protocol, from which we can learn about colonial life in Costa Rica. He studied

law at the University of St. Thomas, where his performance was outstanding. He took part in the commission that drew up the civil, penal, and legal codes.

González Víquez had an important political career, in which he served twice as a representative to the national Congress and once as minister of Government. He defended liberal principles and opposed the reformist movements of the era. In 1906, after a controversial election in which his rivals were expelled from the country, he was elected president of Costa Rica, an office he held until 1910. In Congress he led the opposition to President Alfredo GONZÁLEZ FLORES from 1916 to 1917 and supported the coup d'état that drove Flores from power. In the 1920s he maintained his liberal stance and continued to be influential in the National Republican Party. He was again elected president in 1928 in the last years of the liberal republic, and he was forced to face the effects of the economic crisis beginning in 1929.

RALPH LEE WOODWARD, JR., *Central America: A Nation Divided*, 2d ed. (1985); CARLOS ARAYA POCHET, *Historia de los partidos politicos: Liberacíon nacional* (1968).

JORGE MARIO SALAZAR

GOOD NEIGHBOR POLICY, a general description of the efforts of the United States to improve relations with Latin America in the 1930s and 1940s. The policy is most often associated with the administration of Franklin D. ROOSEVELT (1933–1945).

Because the Good Neighbor pledged nonintervention and noninterference in Latin America's domestic affairs, its most visible impact was political. In the Cuban crisis of 1933, Roosevelt intervened not with troops but with a special emissary, Assistant Secretary of State Sumner WELLES, who ultimately negotiated the arrangement whereby Fulgencio BATISTA gained effective power. Roosevelt graciously received the new Panamanian president, Harmadio ARIAS, in 1933 and the following year dispatched Welles to thrash out a new canal treaty, which mollified Panamanian critics yet preserved U.S. interests. In the Mexican oil crisis of 1938, Roosevelt hesitated in joining the oil companies in their denunciation of Mexican President Lázaro CÁRDENAS's expropriation decree. Four years later, Mexico and the United States created a wartime economic alliance.

The Good Neighbor policy restored U.S. trade with Latin America and created a hemispheric bloc against the Axis powers. Neither was easily achieved, for German economic and cultural endeavors in Latin America in the 1930s appeared more compatible with the Latin corporatist political tradition. At the eighth inter-American conference at Lima (1938) and the special meetings of foreign ministers at Panama (1939), Havana (1940), and Rio de Janeiro (1942), Latin America's commitment to a united hemisphere steadily increased.

After Pearl Harbor, the efforts to create a united hemisphere intensified. The State Department created the post of coordinator of inter-American affairs to promote inter-American cultural understanding. As Latin American governments joined the war effort, the U.S. military, economic, and cultural presence expanded. By the end of the war, the Latin American economies were virtually intertwined with the U.S. economy. Regrettably, at war's end, much of the goodwill built through Good Neighbor cultural understanding dissipated under U.S. determination to fashion a solid anticommunist Latin American bloc.

BRYCE WOOD, *The Making of the Good Neighbor Policy* (1961); DAVID GREEN, *The Containment of Latin America* (1971); DICK STEWARD, *Trade and Hemisphere: The Good Neighbor Policy and Reciprocal Trade* (1975); IRWIN F. GELLMAN, *Good Neighbor Diplomacy: United States Policies in Latin America, 1933–1945* (1979).

LESTER D. LANGLEY

See also **United States–Latin American Relations.**

GORODISCHER, ANGÉLICA (*b.* 28 July 1928), Argentine writer. Born in Buenos Aires to an upper-middle-class Spanish family, Gorodischer began writing late in life in the port town of Rosario, where she settled with her husband and children. *Opus dos* (1967), her first novel, the short stories contained in *Bajo las jubeas en flor* (1973; Under the Jubeas in Bloom) and in *Casta luna electrónica* (1977; Chaste Electronic Moon), and particularly her tales of the intergalactic trips of a traveling salesman from Rosario, Trafalgar Medrano (*Trafalgar,* 1979), would permit classifying her as a writer of speculative science fiction. On the other hand, these stories, together with some others, constitute what could be labeled as "fantastic." Some could even be classed as thrillers, whodunits, and Gothic tales. She is interested in the absurd, monstrosities, dreams, myths; in the great themes that are a pretext for human beings to continue fighting to live; in the relationship between man and the universe, man and God, and power and death; in all that man does not know.

For Gorodischer, literature is a way of "unmasking" reality. In her works there is a counterpoint between the imaginary and the real worlds that gives transcendental meaning to her stories, so they end by being allegories, metaphors, or symbolic chronicles of the contemporary world and of the human condition, generally presented in a humorous vein.

M. PATRICIA MOSIER, "Communicating Transcendence in Angélica Gorodischer's *Trafalgar,*" in *Chasqui* 12, no. 2–3 (1983): 63–71; ANGELA B. DELLEPIANE, "Contar = mester de fantasía o la narrativa de Angélica Gorodischer," in *Revista Iberoamericana* 51, no. 132–133 (1985): 627–640, and "Narrativa fantástica y narrativa de ciencia-ficción," in *Plural* (Mexico), 188 (May 1987): 48–50.

ANGELA B. DELLEPIANE

GOROSTIZA, MANUEL EDUARDO DE (*b.* 1789; *d.* 1851), Mexican military officer, diplomat, cabinet min-

ister, and dramatist. Gorostiza was born in Veracruz, but his family returned to Spain after the death of his father, a colonial governor, when he was five. Because of his liberalism, Gorostiza was forced to flee from Spain to Mexico in 1822. He served as a Mexican representative in London, where he kept the British Parliament and public well informed about U.S. designs on Texas in the late 1820s. In 1830 he was named Mexico's minister plenipotentiary in London and minister to all the European countries. In 1933 Gorostiza was recalled to Mexico, where he served on Gómez Farías's commission on educational reform and was named the first director of the National Library and the National Theater.

After the fall of Gómez Farías, Gorostiza wrote and produced plays to support himself, reviving the theater in Mexico and becoming famous for his comedies in Spain as well. He later served as Mexican minister in Washington (1836), treasury minister (1838, 1842–1843, 1846), and foreign relations minister (1838–1839). During the U.S. invasion of Mexico in 1847, Gorostiza organized and paid for a battalion, which he led at the Battle of Churubusco.

CARLOS GONZÁLEZ PEÑA, *History of Mexican Literature*, translated by Gusta Barfield Nance and Florence Johnson Dunstan, 3d ed. (1968); *Diccionario Porrúa de historia, biografía y geografía de México*, 5th ed. (1986).

D. F. STEVENS

GOROSTIZA ACALÁ, JOSÉ (*b.* 10 November 1901; *d.* 16 March 1973), Mexican poet and diplomat. He and his brother Celestino were major intellectual figures in Mexico and were members of the Contemporáneos intellectual circle with Jaime TORRES BODET. Octavio PAZ considered Gorostiza to be a major Latin American poet.

A native of Villahermosa, Tabasco, Gorostiza began teaching at the National Preparatory School in 1921 and published his first book of poems in 1925. Joining the foreign service, he became first chancellor in London in 1927, after which he served as head of the fine arts department in public education. He returned to the foreign service where, in the 1930s and 1940s, he held a series of posts abroad, including ones in Italy, Guatemala, and Cuba. In 1950 he became ambassador to Greece and, a year later, permanent representative to the United Nations. He culminated his career as undersecretary of foreign relations (1953–1964), serving briefly as secretary in 1964. He won the National Literary Prize in 1968.

MERLIN H. FORSTER, "The *Contemporáneos*, 1915–1932: A Study in Twentieth-Century Mexican Letters" (Ph.D. diss., University of Illinois, 1960); ANDREW P. DEBICKI, *La poesía de José Gorostiza* (1962); JOSÉ GOROSTIZA, *Death Without End*, translated by Laura Villaseñor (1969); and JUAN GELPÍ, *Enunciación y dependencia en José Gorostiza* (1984).

RODERIC AI CAMP

GORRITI, JUAN IGNACIO DE (*b.* June 1766; *d.* 25 May 1842), Argentine priest and independence leader. Born in Los Horcones, Gorriti's early education in Latin and philosophy was directed by the FRANCISCANS in Jujuy. From 1781 to 1789 he studied theology and literature at the Colegio Nusetra Señora de Monserrat in Córdoba, and he obtained a doctorate in sacred theology from the University in Charcas in 1791. He briefly worked as a parish priest in Cochinoca and Casabindo, small villages in the altiplano of Jujuy, earning distinction for his sermons. He participated in Argentina's independence movement, arguing that the authority of the viceroys and other Spanish officials had expired when the French deposed the legitimate king of Spain. In September 1810, he was named representative of Jujuy to the revolutionary Junta de Buenos Aires. He remained in politics as Salta's representative to the Congress in 1824 but was exiled to Bolivia by political enemies in 1831. There he wrote "Reflexiones sobre las causas morales de las convulsiones interiores de los nuevos estados americanos y examen de los medios eficaces para remediarlas" (Valparaíso, 1836), an early attempt to solve the problems facing the newly formed nations of South America. Gorriti died in Sucre, Bolivia.

EMILIO A. BIDONDO and SUSAN M. RAMÍREZ, *Juan Ignacio de Gorriti: Sacerdote y patricio* (Buenos Aires, 1987); JUAN IGNACIO DE GORRITI, *Papeles* (Jujuy, 1936); ABEL CHÁNETON, *Historia de Vélez Sarsfield* (Buenos Aires, 1969).

J. DAVID DRESSING

GOULART, JOÃO BELCHIOR MARQUES (*b.* 1 March 1919; *d.* 6 December 1976), Brazilian Labor Party (PTB) leader and president of Brazil (1961–1964), whose overthrow led to two decades of military rule.

João "Jango" Goulart was born in São Borja, Rio Grande do Sul. His family was allied politically and economically with that of Getúlio VARGAS. Jango, the eldest boy of eight children, spent his early years on the family ranches that produced cattle, sheep, and horses. From the age of nine, he attended schools in larger cities, finally receiving a law degree in 1939. He soon took over the family businesses and became a millionaire.

Jango befriended Getúlio Vargas when the latter returned to São Borja in 1945. A popular figure, Jango formed district chapters of Vargas's PTB. Eventually he became a confidant, aide, and spokesman for Vargas during his 1950 campaign for president. At about that time his sister married Leonel BRIZOLA, who would become his closest political ally.

After leading the PTB in Pôrto Alegre for a year, Jango transferred to Rio to help Vargas manage national labor politics, for which he was appointed labor minister in 1953. He showed great skill in handling workers, whom he favored with a 100-percent wage hike in 1954. The furor resulting from this decision forced Jango's resignation, but he continued to exercise great influence in labor matters through his leadership of the PTB.

In many ways Vargas's heir, Jango rode the PTB into the vice presidency in 1956 and again in 1961, allying with Juscelino KUBITSCHEK and Jânio QUADROS, respectively. He continued to use his position to help labor, and the PTB grew rapidly in Congress and the states—the only major party to do so.

Jango was in China when Quadros resigned in August 1961, creating a succession crisis. His many supporters—especially Brizola in Rio Grande—threatened civil war should the military attempt to deny the presidency to Jango. A compromise between Congress and the military chiefs allowed Jango to be titular president in a parliamentary system. The arrangement proved cumbersome, and when put to a plebiscite in early 1963, it was abandoned.

Goulart took the restored presidential powers as a vote of confidence, yet his tenure proved controversial and stormy. Although he continued to enjoy popularity among the working class, he never captured (as Vargas had) the support of the middle and upper classes. The U.S. government treated him with aloofness, especially after Brizola nationalized a subsidiary of International Telephone and Telegraph. U.S. businessmen, abetted by increasingly cool diplomatic relations, worked to discredit Goulart, while Washington disallowed financial assistance. The country plunged into a depression, exacerbated by Goulart's erratic policies and mismanagement. Politics became dangerously polarized, and Goulart failed in several attempts to conciliate opposing groups. Finally, in March 1964 he decided to make a bold appeal to the workers, rural poor, and leftists by announcing a major reforms package, including redistribution of land near federal installations. This effort, as well as his mishandling of two military revolts, led the army to overthrow him on 1 April 1964 in order to rid the country of a leftist president and restore economic order. Goulart flew into exile and lived in Uruguay and Argentina until his death from a heart attack.

THOMAS E. SKIDMORE, *Politics in Brazil, 1930–1964* (1967); JOHN W. F. DULLES, *Unrest in Brazil* (1970); LUÍS ALBERTO MONIZ BANDEIRA, *O governo João Goulart* (1977); JAN KNIPPERS BLACK, *United States Penetration of Brazil* (1977); ISRAEL BELOCH and ALZIRA ALVES DE ABREU, comps., *Dicionário histórico-biográfico brasileiro, 1930–1983* (1984); EDGARD CARONE, *A república liberal* (1985).

MICHAEL L. CONNIFF

GRAÇA ARANHA, JOSÉ PEREIRA DA (*b.* 21 June 1868; *d.* 26 January 1931), Brazilian writer of the premodernist social novel. Graça Aranha was born to an aristocratic Maranhão family and graduated from law school in Recife. While municipal judge in the German settlement of Porto do Cachoeiro in 1890, his observations of the immigrants' struggle inspired the plot for his first and most famous novel, *Canaã* (1902; *Canaan*, 1920). Previous to its publication he was elected to a seat on the BRAZILIAN ACADEMY OF LETTERS. From 1900 to 1920 he held diplomatic offices and traveled through many parts of Europe. Upon his return to Brazil he published *A estética da vida* (1920). Graça Aranha's thesis novels are sociological studies of the contemporary Brazilian problem of assimilation of races and cultures, and philosophical explorations of his theory of universalism and humanitarian evolutionism. His documentary prose contains brilliant descriptions and abstract characters.

Aside from a modest literary production, Graça Aranha's most important contribution is his role in initiating the modernist movement in Brazil. He organized MODERN ART WEEK in 1922 to promote among Brazilian artists a reformation of national thought and sensibility, launching the modernist movement in the arts, which sought to rediscover Brazil in its native elements. He broke with the Academy of Letters in 1924, calling on its members to create a national literature.

GRAÇA ARANHA, *Trechos escolhidos por Renato Almeida* (1958), esp. pp. 4–19; JOÃO CRUZ COSTA, "Graça Aranha," in *A History of Ideas in Brazil* (1964); GRAÇA ARANHA, *Obra completa,* edited by Afrânio Coutinho (1969), esp. pp. 17–36.

LORI MADDEN

GRACE, W. R., AND COMPANY, a major U.S. industrial company that played an influential role in the history of Latin America from the 1850s to the 1950s. It was the first multinational in Latin America, and through its multifaceted commercial and industrial activities was long associated with the development and modernization of the region, but, by contrast, its critics linked it with the negative concomitants of IMPERIALISM and capitalism, such as exploitation of nonrenewable resources, creation of enclave economies, preferential treatment of foreigners, repatriation of profits, interference in host country politics, and numerous other activities they considered detrimental in the economic development of a region.

The company was founded in 1854 by a young Irish immigrant to Peru. William Russell Grace began working in the booming business of exporting guano from Peru to North America and Europe and then branched out into other aspects of the growing trade between the west coast of South America and the United States. He moved the headquarters of his fledgling company to New York City after the Civil War, but kept his connections with South America close and dependable by bringing in brothers, cousins, and other relatives to operate Grace trading houses in Valparaiso, Callao, and other South American ports and cities.

By the early twentieth century, W. R. Grace was the major presence in trade and commerce between North America and South America. The first steamship line between the Americas, the Grace Line, dominated shipping between New York City and South America, and the company diversified into activities as varied as owning and operating sugar plantations in Peru, buying and marketing tin from Bolivia, mining nitrates in Chile, financing railroads in Ecuador, and operating Panagra, the premier air carrier between the Americas from the 1930s to the 1950s. In the 1950s the company decided to focus its investments on the U.S. chemical industry and divested itself of its Latin American interests. By the 1970s the company that was known as Casa Grace along the west coast of South America no longer had any significant Latin American presence.

JONATHAN V. LEVIN, *The Export Economies: Their Pattern of Development in Historical Perspective* (1960); MIRA WILKINS, *The Maturing of Multinational Enterprise: American Business Abroad from 1914 to 1970* (1974); LAWRENCE A. CLAYTON, *Grace: W. R. Grace & Co.: The Formative Years, 1850–1930* (1985); MARQUIS JAMES, *Merchant Adventurer: The Story of W. R. Grace* (1993).

LAWRENCE A. CLAYTON

GRACIAS, seat of Lempira Department in Honduras and first capital city in Central America. Founded, according to some accounts, in 1536 by Gonzalo de Arredondo y Alvarado, and on 14 January 1539 by Juan de Montejo, according to others, Gracias a Dios in western Honduras became the seat of the AUDIENCIA DE LOS CONFINES as well as of the subsequent Audiencia of Guatemala. Its early economy was based upon gold and silver mining. However, the town began an economic decline by the end of the seventeenth century. In 1855 the forces of Guatemalan General Rafael CARRERA defeated Honduran General Trinidad CABAÑAS there. In 1915 an earthquake devastated the town, which has since been rebuilt.

LUIS MARIÑAS OTERO, *Honduras,* 2d ed. (1983); RALPH LEE WOODWARD, JR., *Central America: A Nation Divided,* 2d ed. (1985).

JEFFREY D. SAMUELS

GRAEF FERNÁNDEZ, CARLOS (*b.* 25 February 1911), Mexican mathematician and educator. A disciple of Manuel SANDOVAL VALLARTA, Graef Fernández graduated from the National University with a degree in engineering before completing a Ph.D. at the Massachusetts Institute of Technology in 1940. He began teaching relativity at the National School of Science in Mexico in 1941 and then at Harvard from 1944 to 1945. He devoted many decades to teaching at the National University, serving as dean of the National School of Sciences (1957–1959) and director of the Institute of Physics. A leader in Mexico's efforts to harness nuclear energy, he coordinated its national commission in the 1960s, and served as a governor of the International Organization of Atomic Energy (1960–1961). Mexico awarded him its National Prize in Sciences in 1970.

Enciclopedia de México, vol. 5 (1976), pp. 493–494.

RODERIC AI CAMP

GRAF SPEE, German pocket battleship sunk in December 1939 off the coast of Uruguay. The *Graf Spee* had been sinking British merchant vessels almost from the outset of World War II. From 30 September to 7 December it sank nine merchant vessels. The *Graf Spee* was being hunted down by the British and French navies and on 13 December 1939, 250 miles east of Montevideo, the battleship was engaged in battle by the British cruisers *Achilles*, *Ajax*, and *Exeter*. At the end of the engagement, the damaged *Graf Spee* steered toward neutral Montevideo pursued by the British ships. The vessel was allowed to remain in Montevideo until 17 December. Captain Hans Langsdorff knew that his ship was not completely seaworthy, let alone battleworthy, and that the British were waiting to engage him again. So, on 17 December, he took the ship out of Montevideo and when it was a mile outside territorial waters, scuttled it.

DUDLEY POPE, *"Graf Spee": The Life and Death of a Raider* (1957); GEOFFREY MARTIN BENNETT, *Battle of the River Plate* (1972); RONY ALMEIDA, *Historia del acorazado de bolsillo Almirante "Graf Spee"* (1977).

JUAN MANUEL PÉREZ

GRAN COLOMBIA. The union of all the Spanish Viceroyalty of New Granada—Venezuela, New Granada, and Quito (Ecuador)—in a single independent nation was proclaimed the Republic of Colombia by the Congress of ANGOSTURA in December 1819. It later came to be known as Gran Colombia, to distinguish it from the smaller Colombia of today. It received a formal constitution at the Congress of CÚCUTA in 1821, when the liberation of Ecuador had only begun and no Ecuadorans were present. But Ecuador was successfully incorporated in 1822, after the forces of Simón Bolívar prevailed in its struggle for independence.

The creation of Gran Colombia was mainly a result of the personal influence of BOLÍVAR and the manner in which independence was achieved: by armies composed of Venezuelans and New Granadans (and eventually Ecuadorans) that moved back and forth between sections under Bolívar's leadership. However, the union was fragile because of the great distances covered, the primitive state of transportation, and the lack of strong social, cultural, and economic ties among regions. Once the war was over, regionalist sentiments were expressed more forcefully, especially in Venezuela, which staged a first revolt in 1826. The union disintegrated completely in 1830, when Venezuela and Ecuador became separate republics, leaving the central core (present-day Colombia and Panama) to reconstitute itself as the Republic of New Granada. Even then, the separate nations continued to observe Gran Colombian legislation until it was repealed or revised; retained the same colors (yellow, blue, red) in their flags; and retained a common cult of Bolívar.

JOSÉ MANUEL RESTREPO, *Historia de la revolución de la República de Colombia en la América meridional*, 3d ed., 8 vols. (1942–1951); DAVID BUSHNELL, *The Santander Regime in Gran Colombia* (1954; repr. 1970).

DAVID BUSHNELL

GRAN MINERÍA, a massive Chilean copper complex encompassing three mines: El Teniente, Chuquicamata, and Potrerillos. Although Chile was a substantial copper producer in the mid-nineteenth century, its output began to flag in the late 1870s. Modernizing the mines, which would have increased their productivity, would have required massive infusions of expensive technology. Although Chilean capitalists had the funds, they preferred to invest either in the booming NITRATE INDUSTRY, which brought in a high rate of return, or in ventures abroad.

In 1904 the American capitalist William Braden purchased El Teniente, a mine located near Santiago, where he introduced techniques that permitted the exploitation of low-grade copper ore. Braden subsequently sold El Teniente to the Guggenheim mining interests, which in turn transferred it to the KENNECOTT COPPER COMPANY. Then in 1911 the Guggenheims acquired what became the world's largest open-pit mine, Chuquicamata, located in Chile's Norte Chico. With the infusion of large sums of money to upgrade it, this mine quickly matched El Teniente's production levels. After restructuring their holdings, in 1915, the Guggenheims turned over Chuquicamata to Kennecott. In 1923, Kennecott sold Chuquicamata to the Anaconda Copper Mining Company, which named it the Chile Exploration Company. This corporation also developed the third part of the Gran Minería, Los Andes, in Potrerillos, for which it is now named.

These mines became classic examples of company towns where the mines owned the housing, the store, and the social facilities. These isolated copper mines did not consume much in the way of locally produced goods, largely because Chile did not manufacture what the mining companies needed. The work force, though well paid by Chilean standards, was never large. Consequently, the huge profits resulting from low labor costs and minimal taxation were remitted abroad.

In the twentieth century this situation slowly began to change. For one thing, improvements in working conditions and increased social benefits mandated by the 1925 Constitution increased the cost of labor. More significantly, during the Great Depression the Chilean government shifted the main tax burden from nitrates to copper. The Moneda, or executive branch, accomplished this in two ways: by imposing a direct levy on revenues and by setting up exchange controls, thus forcing those copper companies that wished to remit their profits to the United States to purchase the dollars from the Chilean state. The creation of CORFO (Corporación de Fomento, or Development Corporation) increased the burden on the copper companies, because the Moneda levied a special tax on the mines to finance the diversification of the Chilean economy. By 1939 the tax rate on American mining corporations had risen to 33 percent.

Copper sales boomed during World War II, when the U.S. government agreed to pay a special rate of 12 cents per pound and abolished the import tax on Chilean copper. The Moneda increased the tax on the COPPER INDUSTRY, raising it to 65 percent of the companies' profits at the same time the mines were paying a premium of 60 percent to purchase dollars. Chileans would subsequently complain that since the world market price was higher than the 12 cents per pound the United States paid, Washington had cheated Santiago.

Prices did rise after the war, encouraging the owners of the Chuquicamata mine to expand its facilities, but the owners of the other two, because of sagging profits, did not. When the onset of the Korean War brought another surge in copper prices, the United States again negotiated a treaty with U.S.-owned copper companies, setting the price at 24.5 cents per pound. Vowing not to be cheated twice, the Chilean government nullified this agreement and reopened the negotiations. The result was the Washington Treaty of 1951, which fixed the price at 27.5 cents per pound. Not only would the Chilean government reap the extra 3 cents, but it would have the right to market directly 20 percent of the copper mined in Chile. The following year the Chilean government declared that it would purchase the mines' output and sell it directly, in order to benefit from the higher prices.

Taxes then became so prohibitive—in some cases 90 percent—that companies became reluctant to modernize their mines, particularly after 1953, when copper prices fell at the end of the Korean War. This failure to invest reduced Chile's share of the world market. Clearly, the government had to do something to increase production and raise its revenues.

In 1955, the Carlos IBÁÑEZ administration instituted a new policy called *El nuevo trato*, the new deal, that set the tax rate on the copper companies at 50 percent. To encourage production the government also levied a 25 percent surcharge, which it offered to forgo if the mines increased their output. Most of the copper companies complied, but the results proved disappointing: mechanization reduced their work forces, and even though Anaconda opened a new mine, El Salvador, Chile's share of world copper declined. This dismal performance disappointed those who had expected more from *El nuevo trato*.

Eduardo FREI, a Christian Democrat, drastically altered the status of the Gran Minería companies. Frei wanted the state to purchase an interest in the copper corporations so that henceforth it would participate in all aspects of mining, from extraction to its ultimate sale. Under his direction, in 1965 the Chilean government purchased 51 percent of the El Teniente mine from Kennecott, which remained a junior partner.

Frei's "Chileanization" program failed to appease the nationalists, who argued that the copper companies had cheated the government. When, in 1969, the price of copper increased on the world market, Frei's critics demanded that he renegotiate his earlier agreement with the U.S.-owned copper companies. Anaconda subsequently agreed to sell 51 percent of its holdings in Chuquicamata and El Salvador.

After his 1970 election, President Salvador ALLENDE announced that he would purchase the remaining 49 percent of Kennecott and Anaconda. Although he promised to pay compensation, he stipulated that he would deduct from that award all profits he considered excessive, meaning any amount over 12 percent. In September 1971 he declared that since Anaconda and Kennecott had made excess profits of approximately $770 million, these companies owed the Chilean government approximately $380 million. Clearly, politics, not international law, had motivated Allende's desire to end what he considered a cycle of dependency on the United States. Regrettably, politics often dictated the policies of the nationalized mines: worker discipline declined, and it became difficult to obtain spare parts. The mines, their work forces swollen, simply became less productive, and hence less profitable.

The PINOCHET government (1973–1990), which returned stability to the mines, moved to seek an accommodation with Kennecott and Anaconda. In 1974 it agreed to pay them for their shares in their respective former holdings. Finally, after decades, the Gran Minería became completely Chilean.

CLARK REYNOLDS, "Development Problems of an Export Economy: The Case of Chile and Copper," in Markos Mamalakis and Clark W. Reynolds, *Essays on The Chilean Economy* (1965) pp. 203–298; LELAND PEDERSON, *The Mining Industry of the Norte Chico, Chile* (1966); MARKOS MAMALAKIS, "The Contribution of Copper to Chilean Economic Development, 1920–1967," in RAYMOND FRECH MIKESELL, *Foreign Investment in the Petroleum and Mineral Industries: Case Studies of Investor–Host Country Relations* (1971), pp. 387–420; ERIC N. BAKLANOFF, *Expropriation of U.S. Investments in Cuba, Mexico, and Chile* (1975); THEODORE H. MORAN, *Multinational Corporations and the Politics of Dependence: Copper in Chile* (1975); JOANNE F. PRZEWORSKI, *The Decline of the Copper Industry in Chile and the Entrance of North American Capital, 1870 to 1916* (1980); PAUL E. SIGMUND, *Multinationals in Latin America: The Politics of Nationalization* (1980); FRANCISCO ZAPATA, "Nationalization, Copper Miners and the Military Government in Chile," in THOMAS C. GREAVES and WILLIAM CULVER, *Miners and Mining in the Americas* (1985), pp. 256–276.

WILLIAM F. SATER

See also **Chile: Organizations.**

GRANADA, the earliest Spanish settlement in Nicaragua and the oldest continuously inhabited city in Central America. Located on the western end of Lake Nicaragua, Granada was founded in 1524 by Francisco Hernández de Córdoba. Built on the site of the ancient Indian town of Jaltepa, it became an important trading center and a major port for the new colony. Spanish seagoing ships sailed directly to Granada until an earthquake created shallows in the San Juan River, which connects Lake Nicaragua with the Atlantic coast. Access to the sea also made Granada a target for buccaneers in the seventeenth century. After independence it became the center of the Conservative Party. Followers of the opposition Liberal Party, led by the American filibuster William WALKER, burned the city in 1856. Rebuilt, Granada has maintained its colonial appearance. It is the principal port on the lake and serves as the terminus for the railroad to Corinto. It is currently the third-largest city in the country, after Managua and León. Its estimated population is 45,000 (1990).

ALEJANDRO BARBARENA PÉREZ, *Granada, Nicaragua* (1971).

DAVID L. JICKLING

GRANADA, Spain, province in Andalusia and its capital city. Located at the foot of the Sierra Nevada mountains, Granada was historically known as a silk manufacturing center. The province included the city of Granada, one of the three largest cities in Castile in the fifteenth century, and a large concentration of Spain's Moorish population. The last refuge of the Moors during the Reconquest, Granada surrendered to FERDINAND and ISABELLA on 2 January 1492. In 1499, Cardinal Francisco Jiménez de CISNEROS introduced forcible conversion of the Moors, an action that led to the revolt of the Alpujarras in 1500. After the revolt was crushed, the Moors were given the choice to convert or emigrate. After another revolt (1568–1570), the Moorish population was scattered and resettled throughout the rest of Spain.

ANTONIO DOMÍNGUEZ ORTIZ and BERNARD VINCENT, *Historia de los Moriscos* (1978); HENRI LAPEYRE, *Geografía de la España morisca* (1986).

SUZANNE HILES BURKHOLDER

GRANADEROS A CABALLO, Argentine elite regiment created by José de SAN MARTÍN. On his return to Argentina from Spain in 1812, San Martín obtained from the revolutionary government authorization to raise and command a regiment of mounted grenadiers (*granaderos a caballo*) who would be both carefully selected and rigorously trained. The unit first saw service under San Martín in early 1813 at the battle of SAN LORENZO. It later fought in Chile and Peru (serving with the forces of BOLÍVAR after San Martín's departure) and produced numerous officers who went on to command other units. It was dissolved in 1826 but restored in 1903 as a permanent unit whose duties include that of serving as ceremonial escort to the president of Argentina.

RICARDO ROJAS, *San Martín; Knight of the Andes,* translated by Herschel Brickel (1967), pp. 28–33; LUIS ALBERTO LEONI, *Regimiento Granaderos a Caballo de los Andes: Historia de una epopeya* (1968).

DAVID BUSHNELL

GRANDJEAN DE MONTIGNY, AUGUSTE HENRI VICTOR (*b.* 15 July 1776; *d.* 2 March 1850), French architect. Grandjean de Montigny studied at the École des Beaux-Arts in Paris. He arrived in Rio de Janeiro with the FRENCH ARTISTIC MISSION, which was organized by Joaquim Lebreton (1760–1819) at the invitation of the Portuguese crown. After his arrival on 26 March 1816, he was asked to design the future Academy of Fine Arts, and he was nominated professor of ARCHITECTURE and given two assistants. The construction of the academy began, but financial difficulties delayed its completion.

Meanwhile Grandjean de Montigny looked for other jobs, such as the Praça do Comércio (1820), a structure in which merchants conducted business. He was also responsible for the old market of Candelária (1836) and for several private houses. Grandjean de Montigny and other French artists were in charge of decorating Rio de Janeiro's Palace Square with ephemeral structures for the coronation of JOÃO VI (6 February 1818). Greek temples, Roman arches, and obelisks were the fashion for this kind of urban decoration in public festivities, after which they were destroyed. Montigny operated a private school of architecture until 1824, when Emperor PEDRO I finally ordered that the construction of the Academy of Fine Arts, where Montigny held his lectures, be concluded.

ADOLFO MORALES DE LOS RIOS, FILHO, *Grandjean de Montigny e a evolução da arte brasileira* (1941); AFFONSO DE ESCRAGNOLLE TAUNAY, *A missão artística de 1816* (1956).

MARIA BEATRIZ NIZZA DA SILVA

GRAU, ENRIQUE (*b.* 18 December 1920), Colombian painter. Grau was born to a prominent family from Cartagena that encouraged his creative talents. His first exhibition, in 1940, preceded formal art studies, which he began at the Art Students League in New York City (1941–1942). Grau has worked in many media, including set design, costumes, and films. However, his reputation as one of the most important Colombian artists—along with Fernando BOTERO, Alejandro OBREGÓN, Edgar Negret, and Eduardo Ramírez VILLAMIZAR—was established in the early 1960s by his paintings. Although he was always a figurative artist, Grau's works of 1955–1962 show the influence of abstract geometry; his images—in painting, drawing, and sculpture from 1962—demonstrate the development of a style that combines refined mimetic skills with satire.

Retrospectives of Grau's work have been organized in Colombia by the Universidad Nacional, Bogotá (1963); the Museo de Arte Moderno, Bogotá (1973), and the Fundación Da Vinci, Manizales (graphic work, 1988). Grau's work also has been featured in international exhibitions focusing on contemporary Colombian and Latin American art: Latin American Art Since Independence (Yale University Art Gallery and University of Texas Art Museum, 1966); Lateinamerikanisch Kunstausstellung (Kunsthalle, Berlin, 1964); El Arte Colombiano a Través de los Siglos (Petit Palais, Paris, 1975); Perspective on the

Present: Contemporary Latin America and the Caribbean (Nagoya City Art Museum, 1991).

GERMÁN RUBIANO CABALLERO, ed., *Enrique Grau* (1983); STANTON L. CATLIN et al., *Enrique Grau, Colombian Artist* (1991).

FATIMA BERCHT

GRAU, MIGUEL (*b.* 1834; *d.* 1879), Peru's greatest naval hero, renowned for his prowess as admiral of the Peruvian navy in command of the ironclad *Huáscar* during the WAR OF THE PACIFIC (1879–1883). Born in Piura, Grau started his career as a sailor on whaling ships. In 1856 he obtained the rank of lieutenant. He participated in the CAUDILLO struggles of the time in support of General Manuel Ignacio VIVANCO against Ramón CASTILLA, a political decision that led to his ouster from the war navy in 1858. At the end of Castilla's second presidential term, however, Grau was back in the navy on a mission to Europe under Admiral Aurelio García y García to buy badly needed warships. In 1865, Grau supported Colonel Manuel Ignacio PRADO's uprising against compliance with a forced treaty with Spain, and in 1866 he fought the bellicose Spanish fleet in the battle of Abtao.

In 1868, Grau was appointed commander of the *Huáscar*. He opposed the coup attempt by the GUTIÉRREZ BROTHERS in 1872, after which he became commander in chief of the Peruvian navy as well as deputy for Paita (1876–1878). At the start of the War of the Pacific in 1879, Grau returned to the command of the *Huáscar*, one of two ironclads Peru sent against the far more numerous Chilean fleet. Grau performed legendary feats against Chilean vessels and ports trying to buy time for new warship purchases. He died in the naval battle of Angamos, which secured decisive naval superiority for Chile.

JORGE BASADRE, *Historia de la República del Perú*, vol. 5 (1963).

ALFONSO W. QUIROZ

GRAU SAN MARTÍN, RAMÓN (*b.* 13 September 1887; *d.* 28 July 1969), Cuban physician and politician, president of Cuba (1933–1934, 1944–1948). Born into a privileged and well-known family, Grau San Martín received a first-class education in both the sciences and the humanities. He earned a medical degree and began a lifetime involvement with the University of Havana, where he served on many committees. Beginning in 1927, Grau actively and consistently opposed the dictatorship of Gerardo MACHADO; indeed, he was the only faculty member who refused to sign the edict authorizing Machado's honorary doctorate from the university. For his efforts, Grau was jailed and exiled from Cuba in the late 1920s.

In the early 1930s, the tide of anti-Machado sentiment in Cuba was swelled by the Depression and growing anti-American feeling. Progressive elements of the military and civilian groups banded together to force out Machado, who resigned through the mediation of U.S. representative Sumner WELLES. A provisional government, headed by Carlos Manuel de CÉSPEDES, was itself quickly overthrown on 4 September 1933. This revolt brought to the forefront Sergeant Fulgencio BATISTA Y ZALDÍVAR as its chief and Grau as the most prominent member of a civilian pentarchy.

Events unfolded rapidly and, backed by his faithful students, Grau and Antonio Guiteras became the principals of a brief but extremely important political experiment. On 10 September, Grau abrogated the hated PLATT AMENDMENT, which had kept Cuba in a state of dependence on the United States. The revolutionary government effected other dramatic changes, including the requirement that at least 50 percent of a business's employees had to be Cuban, the granting of autonomy to the University of Havana and removal of restrictions for enrollment, the extension of the vote to women, compulsory trade unionization and the creation of professional associations, and an agrarian reform designed to benefit peasants. Not surprisingly, the government's activism spurred demonstrations for more radical reforms, earning it the enmity of the political Right and hostility from the United States. Furthermore, as the demands of the Left began to outpace the reforms, another potential support base for the Grau–Guiteras team was alienated. In January 1934 a military coup led by Batista, by then the army chief, toppled the government, although the legacy of the experiment lived on.

Grau remained active in politics and university life for the next decade. He founded the Authentic Party and won the presidential election in 1944. During his four-year term, Grau returned to many of his previous policies. This time, in the years of euphoria after World War II, Grau found a more fertile and sophisticated political climate for his ideas. Although he was an opportunist with a keen sense of symbolism and ceremony, Grau held to his basic principles of anti-imperialism, nationalism, and non-Marxist socialism throughout his life.

EMMA PÉREZ, *La política educacional del Dr. Grau San Martín* (1948); LUIS AGUILAR, *Cuba 1933: Prologue to Revolution* (1972); SAMUEL FARBER, *Revolution and Reaction in Cuba, 1933–1960* (1976); ANTONIO LANCÍS Y SÁNCHEZ, *Grau, estadista y político* (1985); and LOUIS A. PÉREZ, JR., *Cuba: Between Reform and Revolution* (1988).

KAREN RACINE

GREMIOS. *See* **Guilds.**

GRENADA, Caribbean nation-state located in the southern part of the Windward Islands. Consisting of 133 square miles and 101,000 inhabitants, Grenada is composed of three islands: Grenada proper and the smaller islands of Carriacou and Petit-Martinique. The islands were populated by Carib Indians who offered fierce resistance to European settlers until 1654, when the last Caribs committed suicide to avoid capture by the French colonizers.

French rule lasted for over a century and resulted in the importation of African slaves whose descendants make up the majority of Grenada's population today. The French introduced Roman Catholicism, which is still Grenada's predominant religion. The establishment of British control in 1783 brought an increase in the number of slaves, a worsening of their treatment, and the attempt to suppress the Roman Catholic faith. In 1795 a Grenadian mulatto, Julien Fedon, launched a revolt in order to restore French rule. His rebellion turned into a massive slave insurrection that took the British fifteen months to crush.

Facing competition from larger sugar producers as well as the abolition of slavery (1838), Grenada's plantation owners switched from sugar to the production of cocoa and spices (particularly nutmeg) by the second half of the nineteenth century. During the same period, the development of commerce produced a native bourgeoisie that resented the monopoly of power held by the British crown and the plantocracy, and demanded a voice in the political life of Grenada. Theophilus Albert Marryshow became the leader of this rising class, which he represented in Grenada's Legislative Council during the first half of the twentieth century. Also influential in Grenada's working-class politics was Tubal Uriah ''Buzz'' Butler.

Trade unions were legalized on Grenada in 1933, but they organized only the urban workers. The agricultural laborers continued to live in abject poverty until 1950, when they found a champion in Eric M. Gairy, who organized them in his Grenada Manual and Mental Workers' Union (GMMWU) and the Grenada United Labour Party (GULP). During 1951, Gairy was able to wring concessions from the landlords by violent strikes and demonstrations in the countryside. He dominated Grenadian politics until 1979.

It became apparent that Gairy was neglecting his constituents when he entered into questionable business ventures and tried to ingratiate himself with the British colonial authorities and Grenada's elite. Given that the only political opposition, Herbert A. Blaize's Grenadian National Party, championed the upper class, it is not surprising that the majority of Grenadians preferred the corrupt Gairy to the elitist Blaize. It was not until 1973 that Gairy met the real challenge of the NEW JEWEL MOVEMENT (NJM), which appealed to the same social strata as he did. Gairy responded by dispatching his terrorist Mongoose Gang. With the granting of independence to Grenada on 7 February 1974, now Prime Minister Gairy cast off all restraints and established a quasi-dictatorship that was despised throughout the Caribbean. On 13 March 1979, the New Jewel Movement toppled Gairy, who was in New York City at the time, in a bloodless coup. Grenadians hailed his ouster.

It was soon evident, however, that Grenada had exchanged one dictator for another. While Maurice Bishop's party (the People's Revolutionary Government) introduced educational and health reforms and began construction of a needed international airport, the elections that the NJM had promised never materialized. Instead, all opposition newspapers and organizations were prohibited and critics of the new regime found themselves incarcerated. In the autumn of 1983, tensions within the revolutionary leadership led to fratricidal strife between Bishop and his deputy, Bernard Coard. Bishop and some of his closest advisers were executed on 19 October 1983. The subsequent Revolutionary Military Council was deposed on 25 October, when troops from the United States and various Caribbean islands invaded Grenada.

The first postinvasion national elections were held in December 1984. Herbert Blaize, representing the New National Party (NNP), became prime minister, an office he held until his death in December 1989. His tenure was marked by close friendship with the Reagan administration, large contributions of U.S. aid, the expansion of tourism as the country's major industry, and reprisals against former supporters of the Bishop regime.

The government of Nicholas Brathwaite, who was elected prime minister on 13 March 1990, has proven to be more conciliatory, more popular, and less conservative. It promises to close the deep fissures within Grenadian society that were produced by the era of Gairy and the subsequent Grenadian revolution.

RAYMUND P. DEVAS, *The Island of Grenada, 1650–1950* (1964); PATRICK EMMANUEL, *Crown Colony Politics in Grenada, 1917–1951* (1978); TONY THORNDIKE, *Grenada* (1985); STEVE CLARK, ''The Second Assassination of Maurice Bishop,'' in *New International* 6 (1987): 11–96; KAI P. SCHOENHALS, *Grenada* (1990).

KAI P. SCHOENHALS

GRENADINES, hundreds of islets, rocks, and reefs that comprise the top of a volcanic ridge between SAINT VINCENT and GRENADA in the WINDWARD ISLANDS of the eastern Caribbean. Collectively they cover about 35 square miles. Ten are populated, having a population of about 12,000 in 1980. The Grenadines are dependencies of two independent nation-states: Saint Vincent and the Grenadines, and Grenada. Those between Grenada and Carriacou are dependencies of Grenada; the largest is Carriacou (pop. 7,000). The remainder are integral parts of Saint Vincent, the largest being Bequia (pop. 2,600).

Archaeologists surmise that the aboriginal Ciboney were followed and perhaps displaced by migrations of Arawak and CARIB peoples from the South American mainland. Strong Carib resistance made European occupation a difficult process until late in the eighteenth century. The Caribs named these islands Begos; the Grenadines later were renamed by either the Spanish or the French, although Bequia and Canouan are linguistic corruptions of Carib names. The French claimed the

Grenadines in 1664 as extensions of their holding of Grenada. In 1675 a slave ship sank in the Bequia–Saint Vincent channel. Surviving slaves swam to both islands, where Caribs took them in—the origins of the "Black Caribs," the descendants of the mixing of these two peoples.

These small islands changed hands often from the seventeenth through the nineteenth centuries as European conflicts spilled over into the West Indies, and the Caribs strenuously fought all comers. As a result of the SEVEN YEARS' WAR, Saint Vincent, Grenada, DOMINICA, and the Grenadines were ceded to Britain and formed into a Windward Islands Federation. For easier administration, the Grenadines were divided between Grenada and Saint Vincent. In 1770 the British made concerted efforts to colonize these islands by surveying and distributing land. The Windward Federation ended by 1776. Between 1779 and 1783 Saint Vincent and its Grenadines were under French rule, after which they returned to British control; colonists began to plant sugarcane, using African slave labor on large plantations. The Caribs rebelled one last time in 1795; their defeat led to their deportation to British Honduras.

The postemancipation period in the Grenadines was a difficult one. For all the efforts of British planters, final emancipation in 1838 effectively marked the steady decline of both COTTON and SUGAR production, and the latter ultimately ended. The emigration of whites and blacks in the postslavery period was both a cause and a consequence of a decline of all cash crops for export. The resident population was left relatively free to develop its own creole culture without many elite whites, and the small island economies were redirected to livestock raising for export, whaling, fishing, and subsistence agriculture. Somewhat isolated, Grenadine populations developed strong separate identities and customs that fueled suspicion of the larger, dominant islands of which they were political dependencies.

The first half of the twentieth century brought additional problems from a large eruption of Soufrière on Saint Vincent, trade disruptions from two world wars, and social unrest during the mid-1930s. During the post–World War II period, there was some economic development as a result of money sent home by those who had emigrated to look for work. Many Grenadine men found work as sailors as world trade recovered. In recent years, some of the Grenadines have become popular with tourists arriving by yacht, and the foreign exchange earned from TOURISM has increased, supplementing more traditional agriculture, fishing, whaling, and boat building.

In general, Grenadine inhabitants are descended from African slaves, from indentured European labor imported in the early period of European colonization, and from a mix of these two groups (ethnic proportions and economic activities vary depending on the island). Portuguese Madeirans and East Indian immigrants are also represented.

MICHAEL G. SMITH, *Kinship and Community in Carriacou* (1962); CLIVE A. FRANK, *History of Begos: The Grenadines from Columbus to Today* (1976); DANA JINKINS and JILL BOBROW, *St. Vincent and the Grenadines: A Plural Country* (1985); ROBERT B. POTTER, comp., *St. Vincent and the Grenadines* (1992).

ROSEMARY BRANA-SHUTE

GREYTOWN (SAN JUAN DEL NORTE), a small trading settlement in Nicaragua where the San Juan River enters the Caribbean. The port has served various nations—Spain, Nicaragua, Costa Rica, Great Britain, and the United States—for trade and transit since the sixteenth century. In the late colonial era, San Juan del Norte, as it originally was named, became an outlet for Costa Rican gold and other contraband goods that were exchanged for trade goods from Jamaica. The British and the MOSQUITO Indians claimed the port in 1841, but the British sent a naval force to drive away the Nicaraguan authorities in February 1848. They renamed the village Greytown, in honor of Charles Grey, governor of Jamaica.

Great competition for power made Greytown a place of considerable activity from 1848 until the 1880s. In 1848, the Royal West India Mail Steam Packet Company initiated monthly service between San Juan and Southampton, England. From 1849 to 1869, Cornelius Vanderbilt's Accessory Transit Company exercised transit rights up the San Juan River and across Lake Nicaragua with steamer connection to California. During the 1850s, Greytown served as a lifeline for reinforcements and supplies during U.S. FILIBUSTERING. In mid-1854, the competition between Britain and the United States heated up to the point that the U.S.S. *Cyane* destroyed the town.

In 1860, Great Britain and Nicaragua signed a treaty that made San Juan del Norte a free port. In the 1860s, silting created sandbars in the estuary of the river that rendered the port of little use for ocean vessels. The British moved their commercial operations north to BLUEFIELDS, but U.S. promoters of a Nicaraguan canal attempted to keep the port as one terminal of the canal until bankruptcy ended the canal project during the depression of the 1890s. Since the 1890s, San Juan del Norte has shriveled into an isolated village of several hundred people, surrounded by decaying buildings and rusting equipment.

MARIO RODRÍGUEZ, *A Palmerstonian Diplomat in Central America, Frederick Chatfield, Esq.* (1964); MURDO MAC LEOD, *Spanish Central America: A Socioeconomic History, 1520–1720* (1973); CRAIG L. DOZIER, *Nicaragua's Mosquito Shore* (1985); RALPH LEE WOODWARD, JR., *Central America: A Nation Divided* (1985).

THOMAS SCHOONOVER

See also **Panama Canal.**

GRIJALVA, JUAN DE (*b.* ca. 1489; *d.* 1527), conquistador who first learned of the Aztec Empire and a nephew of

Pánfilo de NARVÁEZ. Grijalva was born in Cuéllar and came to the Caribbean as a youth. He accompanied Diego VELÁZQUEZ, and later his uncle, on their first expeditions to Cuba in 1511, and subsequently resided in prominence on the island. In 1518, Governor Velázquez dispatched him to expand upon the discoveries made by Francisco FERNÁNDEZ DE CÓRDOBA along the coast of Yucatán. His fleet discovered Cozumel, the Grijalva and Banderas rivers, and San Juan de Ulúa. After his force was attacked at the latter site by a number of natives in canoes, he decided not to attempt to colonize and returned to Cuba, an action that greatly displeased Velázquez. The first Spaniard to learn of the Aztec Empire, Grijalva reported its existence to Velázquez, but he did not accompany CORTÉS. He was killed in battle against natives near Villahermosa.

HUGH THOMAS, *Conquest of Mexico* (1993).

JOHN E. KICZA

GRILO, SARAH (*b.* 1919), Argentine painter. Born in Buenos Aires, Grilo lived in Madrid and Paris (1948–1950) and traveled throughout Europe and the United States (1957–1958). According to Damián Bayón, among the Buenos Aires group comprising José Fernández Muro, Clorindo Testa, Kasuya Sakai, and Miguel Ocampo, Grilo "always represented the extreme sensibility to color." From 1960 she evidenced this sensibility in compositions whose right-angled structures were permanently altered by the inclusion of circular forms. Her chromatic modulations are suggestive of the tonal values

Sarah Grilo at Galería Bonino, Buenos Aires, with one of her paintings, 1961. LA NACIÓN.

of Pierre Bonnard and his concept of color as a continuous state of exaltation in which form loses all importance. Later Grilo introduced tachiste effects (graphic signs). Her right-angled structures disappeared, giving way to a surface freely dotted with spots of paint and sprinkled with texts, words, letters, and numbers backed by radiant color, which created imaginary codices of great enchantment. Grilo has exhibited throughout North and South America as well as in Europe. She has received several awards, including the Wertheim Prize (Buenos Aires, 1961) and a Guggenheim Foundation Fellowship (New York, 1962).

Museum of Modern Art of Latin America (1985); LILY SOSA DE NEWTON, *Diccionario biográfico de mujeres argentinas*, 3d ed. (1986); VICENTE GESUALDO, ALDO BIGLIONE, and RODOLFO SANTOS, *Diccionario de artistas plásticos en la Argentina* (1988).

AMALIA CORTINA ARAVENA

GRIMARD, LUC (pseudonyms, Lin Dege; Marie Gérard; *b.* 30 January 1886; *d.* 24 October 1954), Haitian writer, educator, and diplomat. Luc Grimard finished a law degree at age nineteen. He taught classics, philosophy, and social science before serving as Haitian consul in Le Havre (1922–1927). During his directorship of the Lycée Philippe Guerrier in Cap Haïtien (1927–1932), Grimard's resistance to the American occupation (1915–1934) was exemplary to his students. In 1932 he went to Port-au-Prince as inspector of the École Normale des Instituteurs. He was named director of *Le Temps* (1938) and later of the Catholic daily, *La Phalange* (1941–1950). President Elie Lescot appointed him conservator of the Musée Sténio Vincent (1941). Grimard also served as rector of the University of Haiti (1951–1954) and was a member of the Cuban Academy of Arts and Letters.

His first volumes of poetry were published in France in 1927. His early verse has been compared to that of Paul Verlaine. Later he turned to Haitian history, nature, and women for inspiration. From his early poetry through his stories there runs a thread of fascination with mystery and the supernatural.

Among his other works are *Jours de gloire* (theater, with Dominique Hippolyte, 1917; *Ritournelles* (poetry, 1927); *Sur ma flûte de bambou* (poetry, 1927); *Du sable entre les doigts* (novellas, 1941); *Bakoulou* (novellas, with André F. Chevallier, 1950); and *L'offrande du laurier* (poetry, 1950). See also F. RAPHAËL BERROU and PRADEL POMPILUS, *Histoire de la littérature haïtienne illustrée par les textes*, vol. 2 (1975), pp. 437–452.

CARROL F. COATES

GRINGO, a slang, usually derogatory term used in Mexico for Anglo-Americans or English speakers. Elsewhere in Latin America it can also refer to someone who speaks Spanish badly.

The origin of this term is veiled in mystery. According to folk legend, the term may have developed during the MEXICAN WAR, when the Mexican population heard

U.S. soldiers singing a popular song, "Green Grow the Lilacs." Another possibility is that it is a corruption of the Spanish word *griego* (Greek), meaning strange or foreign words that are not understood.

DON H. RADLER, *El Gringo: The Yankee Image in Latin America* (1962); *Diccionario manual ilustrado de la lengua española*, 4th ed. (1989).

RICHARD GRISWOLD DEL CASTILLO

GRIPPO, VÍCTOR (*b.* 10 May 1936), Argentine artist. Born in the town of Junín, in the province of Buenos Aires, Grippo studied chemistry and design at the University of La Plata. In 1971, he became a leading member of a group of thirteen artists (known as *Grupo de los Trece*). Named GRUPO DE CAYC (for the Centro de Arte y Comunicación where they met), these painters wanted to generate radical changes in the practice of art through the exploration of the relation of art to science and the use of massive communication techniques and inexpensive materials.

In his installation *Analogy 1* (1971), sprouting potatoes were strung together with zinc and copper electrodes and connected with a voltmeter. By means of written descriptions, Grippo drew parallels between the germinating tubers' energetic power and the awakening of human consciousness: the potato, a staple food native to South America, symbolizes the potential of autochthonous resources. Manual labor, in its most rudimentary forms, was the subject of his installation *Crafts* (1976). Since the 1980s his work has consisted of assemblages of quasi-geometric forms that resemble spheres, artificer's lead pencils, and *crusets*.

JORGE GLUSBERG, *Del pop-art a la nueva imagen* (1985), pp. 167–176, and *Víctor Grippo: Obras de 1965 a 1987* (1988); and WALDO RASMUSSEN ET AL., *Latin American Artists of the Twentieth Century* (1993).

MARTA GARSD

GRITO DE ASENCIO, popular uprising in Uruguay that took place on 28 February 1811 on the banks of the Asencio River, near Mercedes, in the present-day department of Soriano. Inspired by José ARTIGAS, who was in Entre Ríos, Argentina, at the time, two inhabitants of the area, Pedro Viera and Venancio Benavídez, led the revolt. Although the uprising was against the government in Montevideo and in support of the junta in Buenos Aires, with the problem of independence from Spain yet to be addressed, the Grito de Asencio is traditionally taken to signify the starting of the revolution in the BANDA ORIENTAL.

JOHN STREET, *Artigas and the Emancipation of Uruguay* (1959); WASHINGTON REYES ABADIE and ANDRÉS VÁZQUEZ ROMERO, *Crónica general del Uruguay,* vol. 2 (1984).

JOSÉ DE TORRES WILSON

GRITO DE BAIRE, the declaration proclaimed at the village of Baire, near Santiago de Cuba, that began the Cuban War of Independence on 24 February 1895. Immediately, the Cuban forces in the western part of the island were defeated by the Spaniards. The main complaints against the Spanish crown were excessive taxation; a huge Cuban foreign debt; discrimination against Cubans for government positions; royal absolutism; and the lack of the basic freedoms of speech, press, and assembly. The Spanish crown was not singled out as the only enemy. Elite landowners were also recognized as an oppressive ruling class.

Led by José MARTÍ and other veterans of the TEN YEARS' WAR, the insurrection appealed to oppressed groups such as poor blacks, whites, workers, and peasants as its main base of support. The goal was to create a truly sovereign nation and end the role played by Cuba as a bridgehead for further Spanish intervention in Latin America.

HUGH THOMAS, *Cuba; or, the Pursuit of Freedom* (1971); JAMES D. RUDOLPH, *Cuba: A Country Study* (1985); JAIME SUCHLICKI, *Cuba from Columbus to Castro,* 3d ed. (1990).

DAVID CAREY, JR.

See also **Cuba: War of Independence.**

GRITO DE DOLORES. *See* **Mexico: 1810–1910.**

GRITO DE LARES (23–24 September 1868), Puerto Rico's first armed uprising against Spanish colonial rule. Organized by the physician Ramón Emeterio BETANCES, the lawyer Segundo Ruíz Belvis, and a dozen coffee planters from western Puerto Rico, the conspiracy sought to liberate the island from Spain, free the slaves, and end the peonage that kept free laborers in virtual servitude. Although parts of the plan were carried out the night of 23 September, following the rebels' occupation of Lares the movement was summarily crushed by the Spanish troops on the island. More than 500 of the suspected conspirators were sent to prison, where eighty of them died of disease. The rest were freed by an amnesty decree issued in January 1869 by a revolutionary government that had just deposed Queen Isabella II in Madrid. The revolt is believed to have pushed Spain to implement social and political reforms, among them the abolition of SLAVERY and the creation of political parties in Puerto Rico.

The most complete account of the Grito de Lares is in OLGA JIMÉNEZ DE WAGENHEIM, *Puerto Rico's Revolt for Independence: El Grito de Lares* (1985, 1993). Brief accounts are also found in most general histories of Puerto Rico.

OLGA JIMÉNEZ DE WAGENHEIM

GRITO DE YARA, declaration of Cuban independence made in the eastern region of Yara (10 October 1868).

Efforts at reform having failed, Carlos Manuel CÉSPEDES led the organization of eastern Cuban planters in a conspiracy against continued Spanish rule in Cuba. On 10 October 1868, at his plantation of La Demajagua, near Bayamo, he proclaimed Cuban independence, universal suffrage, and an end to SLAVERY. Freeing his thirty slaves, who then joined his rebel army, his "grito de Yara" thus launched the TEN YEARS' WAR (1868–1878). It became the rallying cry for the rapid expansion of the rebellion across eastern Cuba. The rebels enjoyed substantial early success, but the revolt eventually succumbed to internal divisions and Spanish repression. Although declaring his opposition to slavery, Céspedes called only for "the gradual, indemnified emancipation of the slaves." He later modified his position even more to reassure slaveholders of western Cuba whom he hoped to attract to the movement. This ambiguity contributed to the division within the independence movement among the CREOLES.

FERNANDO FIGUEREDO, *La revolución de Yara* (1902; repr. 1969); HUGH THOMAS, *Cuba, the Pursuit of Freedom* (1971); LOUIS A. PÉREZ, *Cuba, Between Reform and Revolution* (1988).

RALPH LEE WOODWARD, JR.

GRITO DE YPIRANGA. *See* **Brazil: Independence Movements.**

GROUSSAC, PAUL (*b.* 15 February 1848; *d.* 27 June 1929), Argentine essayist, philosopher, and historian. François Paul Groussac was born in Toulouse, France, and finished secondary school in Brest. He settled in Argentina in 1866, during the WAR OF THE TRIPLE ALLIANCE (Paraguayan War), and went on to became a leading intellectual in his adopted country. Groussac taught mathematics at the COLEGIO NACIONAL in Buenos Aires and spent many hours in the national library broadening his intellectual horizons. He lived in San Miguel de Tucumán in northwestern Argentina, taught at the Colegio Nacional in Tucumán (1871–1874), became superintendent of education in that province (1874–1878), and was appointed director of the Teachers' College in 1878.

Keenly interested in Argentine history and Latin American thought, Groussac wrote for Argentine newspapers and authored important books in the field. His works include: *Los jesuítas en Tucumán* (The Jesuits in Tucuman [1873]), *Les îles Malouines* (The Malvinas [1910]), *Viaje intelectual* (Intellectual Voyage [1904]), *El pensamiento de América* (American, i.e., Latin American, Thought [1989]), *El Congreso de Tucumán* (1916), *Los que pasaban* (Some Who Passed Through [1919]), and *Del Plata al Niágara* (1897). Combative in his newspaper articles, Groussac was befriended by such influential intellectuals and politicians as Nicolás AVELLANEDA, José Manuel ESTRADA, Eduardo WILDE, Lucio V. MANSILLA, Aristóbulo DEL VALLE, and Carlos PELLEGRINI. Groussac's lasting contributions included the reorganization

of the National Library, of which he became director in 1885; the publication of the scholarly journal *La Biblioteca* (1896), which became *Anales de la Biblioteca* in 1900 (it ceased publication in 1915); and participation in the founding of *El Sud Americano* and *La Nación*. He belonged to the influential group of educators and writers at the turn of the century who shaped modern Argentina. He died in Buenos Aires.

ALFONSO DE LAFERRÈRE, "Noticia preliminar," in *Páginas de Groussac* (1928), pp. 7–41; JOAQUÍN G. MARTÍNEZ, *François Paul Groussac: Su vida, su obra* (1948); PAUL GROUSSAC, *Jorge Luis Borges selecciona lo mejor de Paul Groussac* (1981).

GEORGETTE MAGASSY DORN

GROVE VALLEJO, MARMADUKE (*b.* 6 July 1878; *d.* 15 May 1954), Chilean army officer and Socialist Party leader. Grove was born in Copiapó. He enrolled at the Escuela Naval in 1892, was dismissed in 1894, but two years later entered the Escuela Militar. Upon graduation in 1898, Second Lieutenant Grove entered the artillery. In 1901 he became a first lieutenant and was assigned to the staff of the Escuela Militar. Four years later he was sent to Germany and spent time in an artillery regiment and at the Charlottenburg Artillery Training School, where he received a diploma. In 1910 he returned to Chile a captain. He studied at the Academia de Guerra (staff school) from 1912 to 1914. He married Rebeca Valenzuela in 1915.

As a young officer, Grove was known for his advanced social and political ideas. In 1918 he was promoted to major, served on the Division I staff, then on the general staff, and the next year was appointed subdirector of the Escuela Militar in Santiago. For his outspoken criticism of war ministry activities in 1920, Grove was transferred out of Santiago, but he moved back to the Escuela Militar in 1921. He was a key figure in the military-political activities of 1924–1925. Then after quarreling with army strongman Carlos IBÁÑEZ DEL CAMPO (president, 1927–1931), he was posted to Europe on a mission for Chile's fledgling air corps, which he had helped found. There he plotted against Ibáñez and tried unsuccessfully to overthrow him, for which he was exiled to Easter Island. He escaped and, following Ibáñez's ouster in 1931, was appointed air commodore. Grove became a key figure in the 1932 Socialist Republic, was exiled again, and was elected to the Senate (while in jail) soon after his return, serving from 1934 to 1949. He was an early leader of the Socialist Party, and the party's contender for the Popular Front presidential candidacy in 1938, before giving way to Radical Pedro Aguirre Cerda.

JORGE GROVE V., *Descorriendo el velo: Episodio de los doce días de la República Socialista* (1933); JACK RAY THOMAS, "The Evolution of a Chilean Socialist: Marmaduke Grove," in *Hispanic American Historical Review* (February 1967): 22–37; WILLIAM H. BEEZLEY and JUDITH EWELL, *The Human Tradition in Latin America: The Twentieth Century* (1987), pp. 41–57.

FREDERICK M. NUNN

101

GRUPO DE CAYC, a group of Argentine artists, based at the Centro de Arte y Comunicación (CAYC) in Buenos Aires, who pioneered the development of "systems art" in Argentina in the 1970s. The CAYC was founded in 1969 during the so-called Revolución Argentina of 1966–1973, which established General Juan Carlos Ongania's repressive military dictatorship. Its purpose is to unite artists and theorists from various disciplines—primarily art, architecture, and communications—and to encourage the integration of art, science, and social concerns through experimental projects in these fields. It has sponsored courses, exhibitions, symposia, and other events that have attracted intellectuals from throughout the world. The Grupo de CAYC, known occasionally as the Grupo de 13, was founded in 1971 by the art critic Jorge Glusberg. Inspired by a talk at the CAYC by the avant-garde Polish director Jerzy Grotowski, Glusberg invited twenty-five artists to establish a "laboratory" similar to Grotowski's Laboratory Theater in Warsaw. Twelve accepted: Jacques Bedel, Luis Benedit, Gregorio Dujovny, Carlos Ginzberg, Víctor GRIPPO, Jorge González Mir, Vicente Marotta, Luis Pazos, Alfredo Portillos, Juan Carlos Romero, Julio Teich, and Horacio Zabala.

These artists subsequently invited the English psychoanalyst David Cooper to analyze the group's internal dynamics. By 1975 it was formally constituted as the Grupo de CAYC with these members: Bedel, Benedit, Glusberg, Grippo, González Mir, Marotta, Pazos, and Portillos, as well as Leopoldo Maler and the architect Clorindo Testa. Since the early 1970s, these artists have pursued what Glusberg has called "systems art"—a nexus of nontraditional modes of art deriving from the tradition of Marcel Duchamp, including conceptual, ecological, body, and performance art. Their work is notable for its experimental quality, its commitment to affirming the inextricable relationship between art and society at large, and its ability to address simultaneously the Latin American condition and universal concerns. The Grupo de CAYC has exhibited widely in Latin America and Europe. In 1977 it received the Premio Itamaraty at the XIV Bienal de São Paulo.

The Group of Thirteen at the XIV Bienal de São Paulo, exhibition catalog (1977); *CAYC Group at the Bank of Ireland, Dublin, in Association with ROSC '80,* exhibition catalog (1980); JORGE GLUSBERG, *Art in Argentina* (1986); SALLY BAKER, ed., *Art of the Americas: The Argentine Project* (1992).

JOHN ALAN FARMER

GRUPO MADÍ AND ASOCIACIÓN ARTE CONCRETO-INVENCIÓN, Argentine abstract art movements. Both the Grupo Madí and the Asociación Arte Concreto-Invención emerged in Buenos Aires in the latter half of the 1940s. Each comprised a like-minded group of painters and sculptors working in more-or-less constructivist and geometric modes of nonrepresentational art. These artists came together for the purposes of exhibiting and supporting rival, although closely related, theoretical platforms, which were expressed in manifestos, publications, and "happenings." The art of both groups appeared radical by virtue of its experimentation with new and often industrial materials, and its break with conventional sculptural and pictorial formats; sculptures and reliefs often employed movable components that invited the spectator's participation.

Arte Concreto-Invención and Madí had a common point of origin in the magazine *Arturo,* published as a single issue in 1944, which had espoused the cause of abstract art in Argentina. Its contributors included Carmelo ARDEN QUIN, Gyula KOSICE, Tomás Maldonado, Lidy Prati, Rhod Rothfuss, and the poet Edgar Bayley. Maldonado, along with Prati, Alfredo Hlito, Manuel Espinosa, Enio IOMMI, Claudio Girola, Raúl LOZZA, Alberto Molenberg, and others officially inaugurated the Asociación Arte Concreto-Invención with a manifesto and an exhibition at the Salón Peuser in March 1946. That August, the Grupo Madí was launched with an exhibition at the Instituto Francés de Estudios Superiores that included Arden Quin, Kosice, Rothfuss, Diyi Laañ, and Martín Blaszko. The origin of the name "Madí" is contested; its meaning, depending on the source, is either nonexistent or an acronym, most convincingly of *"movimento arte de invención."* Madí, too, had its manifesto, but the group soon splintered when Arden Quin and Blaszko broke away in 1947 to found a parallel group with the same name.

That same year, Lozza, Molenberg, and Lozza's two brothers left the Asociación Arte Concreto-Invención and started yet another constructivism-based abstract group they called Perceptismo. The various factions of the Argentine avant-garde were invited to participate in the *Salon des réalités nouvelles* at the Palais des Beaux-Arts in Paris in the summer of 1948. In September, a similarly multilateral exhibition was held in Buenos Aires at the Van Riel Galería de Arte. Shortly thereafter, the Asociación Arte Concreto-Invención dissolved when Maldonado left for Europe at the end of the year. The Perceptismo group lasted until 1953, when its eponymous review ceased publication. Members of the Grupo Madí continued to exhibit together as a group until at least the early 1960s.

NELLY PERAZZO, *El arte concreto en la Argentina en la década del 40* (1983); DAWN ADES, "Arte Madí/Arte Concreto-Invención," in her *Art in Latin America: The Modern Era, 1820–1980* (1989); pp. 241–251; FATIMA BERCHT and JOSEPH R. WOLIN, "Asociación Arte Concreto-Invención, Arte Madí y Perceptisimo," and ARACY AMARAL, "Abstract Constructivist Trends in Argentina, Brazil, Venezuela, and Colombia," in Waldo Rasmussen et al., eds., *Latin American Artists of the Twentieth Century* (1993), pp. 321–324, 86–99.

JOSEPH R. WOLIN

GUADALAJARA, capital of the state of Jalisco and the major industrial, marketing, and transportation center of western Mexico. With a population approaching 4 mil-

Avenida Morelos, Plaza de la Liberación, and Cathedral, Guadalajara, Mexico. PHOTO BY MARTIN LITTON / PHOTO RESEARCHERS INC.

lion in 1990, it is the second largest city in the Republic. It is located about 285 miles west of Mexico City at an altitude of about 5,150 feet. At the northern edge of Mesoamerica during pre-Columbian times, the area of the present city was occupied by a series of small city-states whose economies were based on farming and limited irrigation. Initially Guadalajara stood at the present-day site of Nochistlán, and later at two other locations, before it was established in the Atemajac Valley in 1542.

The discovery of silver in ZACATECAS drew the focus of Spanish settlement in western Mexico toward Guadalajara: in 1548 the bishop located his residence there, and in 1560 it became the capital of Nueva Galicia when the *audiencia* moved from Compostela. By the early 1600s, however, the city still was small, with a population of only 500 Spaniards. The recovery of the Indian population after 1650 and the rapid growth of the overall population in the eighteenth century, resulting from its flourishing agriculture (grain, meat, and other foodstuffs) and industry (textiles, soap, and leather), were instrumental in making Guadalajara a small city of about 20,000 inhabitants in 1803. Spurred by an expand-

ing textile industry and the arrival of the railroad in the 1890s, Guadalajara grew rapidly during the last half of the nineteenth century, and new railway construction strengthened the city's economic dominance of western Mexico. Guadalajara eclipsed PUEBLA as Mexico's second largest city in the 1870s, and its population reached 100,000 before 1900.

The *tapatíos*, as the residents of Guadalajara are called, have been characterized as politically conservative and staunchly Catholic, a heritage that frequently has placed them at odds with the more liberal secularism of the central government. Guadalajara is typified by a strong regional pride and is the home of MARIACHI music and tequila, both of which practically have become national symbols. The city has maintained its colonial core, but it suffers also from an increasing urban blight and growing traffic problems. It has large, modern shopping malls and underwent a downtown redevelopment in the late 1970s and early 1980s.

ERIC VAN YOUNG, *Hacienda and Market in Eighteenth-Century Mexico: The Rural Economy of the Guadalajara Region, 1675–1820* (1981); LINDA GREENOW, *Credit and Socioeconomic Change in Co-*

lonial Mexico: Loans and Mortgages in Guadalajara, 1720–1820 (1983); KATHLEEN LOGAN, *Haciendo Pueblo: The Development of a Guadalajaran Suburb* (1984).

JOHN J. WINBERRY

GUADALUPE, BASILICA OF, the church near Mexico City built to shelter the image of the Virgin of GUADA-LUPE. Over the centuries several buildings have housed the famous image of the vision which is said to have appeared in 1531. The first sanctuary was modest, but a larger church was finished in 1622 when the cult had begun to acquire fame. A grander building in *tezontle* and limestone was erected between 1695 and 1709 by Pedro de ARRIETA. However, an undated plan signed by José Durán may represent a first or an alternative project. In it the church has a central plan, as is appropriate for a sanctuary, and a tower at each corner. What was built by Arrieta and still exists is a Latin cross with a nave, side aisles, and a dome over the crossing—a building that was basically rectangular and retained the four towers. The considerable protrusion of the apse area, like the decoration of the interior, is due to exten-

Basilica of Our Lady of Guadalupe. ORGANIZATION OF AMERICAN STATES.

sive late-nineteenth-century restoration and remodeling. The facade portal with sober Corinthian columns, a narrative relief, and many angular elements is notable for its projection onto the plaza.

In 1904 the church was elevated to the rank of basilica. Despite repeated restorations, uneven settling of the ground under Arrieta's church provoked fears that it would collapse, and it was closed in 1976. Between 1974 and 1976, a new basilica with a tentlike silhouette was built by Pedro RAMÍREZ VÁZQUEZ and his associates to house the image.

GEORGE KUBLER, *Art and Architecture in Spain and Portugal and Their American Dominions, 1500 to 1800* (1959); *Álbum del 450 aniversario de las apariciones de Nuestra Señora de Guadalupe* (1981), pp. 284–289.

CLARA BARGELLINI

See also **Architecture.**

GUADALUPE, CONVENIO DE (11 March 1844). Early in March 1844 José Rafael CARRERA forced the resignation of a Guatemalan government dominated by the conservative elite of the capital. An army uprising followed, undoubtedly engineered by Carrera himself. Carrera and the army quickly agreed to the Convenio of Guadalupe, which barred the clergy from political office and dissolved the assembly, its authority to be replaced by a popularly elected council of state with one native representative from each department—a sharp break with earlier legislatures, which had been dominated by Guatemala City members. It also provided for clear executive authority over the legislative branch and expanded the authority of the military.

While the Convenio de Guadalupe immediately favored the liberals by checking the conservative elite of Guatemala City, its real significance was the increase of military power over civil government and the reduction of legislative and judicial power. The assembly obediently ratified the *convenio* on 13 March and dissolved itself on the next day, thus laying the foundation for Rafael Carrera to take over the presidency in December 1844 and reinforcing a pattern of military superiority over the civil government that has characterized Guatemalan government ever since.

Gaceta oficial (Guatemala City), 18 March 1844; RALPH LEE WOODWARD, JR., *Rafael Carrera and the Emergence of the Republic of Guatemala, 1821–1871* (1993).

RALPH LEE WOODWARD, JR.

See also **Guatemala.**

GUADALUPE, VIRGIN OF, preeminent devotion of Mexico, also popular throughout Latin America. The Virgin Mary is said to have appeared to JUAN DIEGO, a Nahua peasant, in December 1531, at Tepeyac, a hill north of Mexico City. The Virgin commanded the build-

Virgin of Guadalupe. A representation in mother-of-pearl inlay. MUSEO FRANZ MAYER, MEXICO CITY.

dalupe as early as 1556, there is no incontrovertible evidence of the apparitions before 1648, when the story was first popularized by Miguel Sánchez. He made only the vaguest references to his sources. In 1649 Luis Lasso de la Vega published a Nahuatl account, now usually called the *Nican mopohua*. This is frequently accepted as the authentic account, in part because its authorship has been attributed to the noted native scholar Antonio Valeriano. This attribution is demonstrably mistaken. Most likely the story was a cult legend dating from the early seventeenth century, perhaps an offshoot of the story of the Virgin of Remedios, that was embellished and popularized by Sánchez. Other than the name, the Mexican Guadalupe has no connection with the Guadalupe of Estremadura. Similarly, the existence of a pre-Hispanic native devotion at Tepeyac is questionable, and there was no conscious substitution of the Virgin of Guadalupe for a native deity.

In addition to its religious significance, the image and cult of Guadalupe have had a profound social, cultural, and political impact on Mexico. In the period from 1648 until 1736, the devotion was confined to the criollos of New Spain, who viewed it as a sign of special divine favor. After the success attributed to the Virgin of Guadalupe in stopping an epidemic in 1736–1737, the cult spread to other parts of the Spanish Empire and was granted a proper feast by the papacy (1754). It also grew in popularity among the Indians, partly as the result of a deliberate evangelization by the church. Eventually, it became the only devotion that transcended regional boundaries and racial differences. Guadalupe has been viewed as a symbol of liberation (as in its use by Miguel HIDALGO Y COSTILLA and Emiliano ZAPATA) and of submission (as by some preachers of the eighteenth and nineteenth centuries). It was also closely entwined with criollo consciousness in the colonial period and Mexican nationalism in the independence period. "Mexico was born at Tepeyac" is how it is often phrased. The Virgin of Guadalupe was proclaimed patroness of all Latin America in 1910 and of the Philippines in 1935. In 1945 Pope Pius XII called her the Queen of Mexico and Empress of the Americas.

MIGUEL SÁNCHEZ, *Imagen de la Virgen Maria, Madre de Dios de Guadalupe* (1648); JACQUES LAFAYE, *Quetzalcoatl and Guadalupe: The Formation of Mexican National Consciousness 1531–1813*, translated by Benjamin Keen (1976); PRIMO FELICIANO VALÁZQUEZ, *La aparición de Santa María de Guadalupe* (1931, 1981); ERNESTO DE LA TORRE VILLAR and RAMIRO NAVARRO DE ANDA, eds., *Testimonios históricos guadalupanos* (1982); ERNEST J. BURRUS, S.J., *The Basic Bibliography of the Guadalupan Apparitions (1531–1723)* (1983); WILLIAM B. TAYLOR, "The Virgin of Guadalupe: An Inquiry into the Social History of Marian Devotion," *American Ethnologist* 14 (1987): 9–33; STAFFORD POOLE, C.M., *Our Lady of Guadalupe: The Origins and Sources of a Mexican National Symbol, 1531–1797* (1994).

STAFFORD POOLE, C.M.

See also **Catholic Church; O'Gorman, Edmundo.**

ing of a church on the site. When the bishop-elect of Mexico, Juan de ZUMÁRRAGA, asked for a sign, she directed Juan Diego to gather roses from the top of the hill and take them in his mantle (*tilma*) to the bishop-elect. When Juan Diego opened the mantle before Zumárraga, the Virgin's image was imprinted on it. It is popularly believed to be the same image venerated today at the basilica of Guadalupe.

The historical substratum for the apparition account is weak. Although a chapel of ease (*ermita*), without a resident priest, existed at Tepeyac under the name Gua-

GUADALUPE HIDALGO, TREATY OF (1848),

the agreement that ended the war between the United States and Mexico. Signed on 2 February and entered into force on 30 May, it transferred to the United States more than half of Mexico's national territory, over 500,000 square miles, including the present states of California, Nevada, Arizona, New Mexico, and Colorado, in return for an indemnity payment of $15 million to compensate for losses inflicted on Mexicans by the Americans during the war. In Article V, the treaty established the Rio Grande as the boundary between the two countries. Articles VIII and IX promised protection of the civil and property rights of former Mexican citizens within the newly acquired territories. Article X, which specifically guaranteed the protection of land grants, was deleted by the U.S. Congress. Article XI provided guarantees that the U.S. government would police its side of the border to prevent Indian raids on Mexican settlements. Article XXI provided, for the first time in any treaty signed by the United States, for compulsory arbitration of future disputes between the two countries.

Mexican and Chicano scholars generally agree that the United States has violated most of the provisions dealing with civil rights and land. Some contemporary Southwestern American Indian tribes, such as the Hopis and Papagos, however, regard the treaty as a document that can be interpreted to protect them.

JOSÉ MARÍA ROA BARCENA, *Recuerdos de la invasión norteamericana, 1846–1848* (1883; repr. 1947); DAVID M. PLETCHER, *The Diplomacy of Annexation: Texas, Oregon, and the Mexican War* (1973); RICHARD GRISWOLD DEL CASTILLO, *The Treaty of Guadalupe Hidalgo: A Legacy of Conflict* (1990).

RICHARD GRISWOLD DEL CASTILLO

See also **United States–Latin American Relations.**

GUADALUPES, LOS,

one of the first secret political societies established in New Spain. (The other was the SOCIEDAD DE CABALLEROS RACIONALES.) Los Guadalupes was founded in Mexico City in 1811 by a group of autonomists and persons disaffected with the colonial regime who were convinced that aiding the insurgent movement by establishing an alternative organ of government was the best way to foster their interests. They were devoted to the Virgin of Guadalupe, whose image the insurgents placed on their banner. The society first aided the insurgents Ignacio RAYÓN and later José María MORELOS, with whom they corresponded and to whom they sent information, arms, money, men, and a press. Based on a small group of leaders, and composed at the beginning of lawyers united by professional ties, friendship, and COMPADRAZGO (tie between a godfather and a father), the society expanded to include nobles, property owners, clergymen, merchants, several women, and even an Indian official. Besides aiding the insurgents, the Guadalupes took advantage of opportunities for political action within the system. Thus, they participated in the constitutional elections of 1812–1813, in which they joined forces with other autonomists to secure the victory of their candidates. The society's existence was discovered by the authorities in 1814, and several of its members were prosecuted and exiled. Shortly thereafter, the society ceased to function, but many of its former members continued their efforts to promote Mexican autonomy.

WILBERT H. TIMMONS, "Los Guadalupes," in *Hispanic American Historical Review* 30 (Nov. 1950): 453–479; ERNESTO DE LA TORRE VILLAR, *Los Guadalupes y la independencia, con una selección de documentos inéditos* (1985); and VIRGINIA GUEDEA, *En busca de un gobierno alterno: Los Guadalupes de México* (1992).

VIRGINIA GUEDEA

GUADELOUPE. *See* **Martinique and Guadeloupe.**

GUAIRÁ FALLS,

waterfall system known in Portuguese as Sete Quedas (Seven Falls), located not far from the town of Guairá in the Brazilian state of PARANÁ. In 1982 these waterfalls were "drowned" in the lake that was collected behind the ITAIPÚ dam.

ANÍBAL MIRANDA, *Paraguay y las obras hidroeléctricas binacionales* (Asunción, 1988).

CÉSAR N. CAVIEDES

GUALE,

Spanish province in the state of Georgia. The Guales were a semiagricultural Muskogean people, organized politically into paired chiefdoms, who lived in southeastern North America. At the time of their first contact with Europeans, their territory stretched from Saint Andrews Sound to Edisto Island on the coast, and their language was understood for 200 leagues inland. Sapelo Sound, which may hold the site of Lucas VÁSQUEZ DE AYLLÓN's 1526 settlement of San Miguel de Gualdape, was an area of dense Guale population.

Pedro MENÉNDEZ DE AVILÉS visited the "Island of Guale" (Saint Catherines Island) in 1566 and was received as a rainmaker, but early Jesuit and Franciscan efforts at conversion were hindered by the demands of the Spanish garrison at Santa Elena on Parris Island and competition from French corsair traders. The Guale Rebellion of 1597, with its five Franciscan martyrs, was a civil war between Spanish and French factions that ended in the conquest by Spain of coastal Guale and its rebirth as a mission province.

In the seventeenth century the Christian towns of Guale served the presidio of SAINT AUGUSTINE as buffer zone, breadbasket, and labor enclave. The extent of population loss in the province due to disease and fugitivism was concealed by an influx of Yamasees, whom the Guales sent to do their labor service. In the 1680s the trade rivalry of Charleston and assaults by pirates and by Indians with English firearms caused the province to shrink: the northern border retreated from Saint Catherines Island to Sapelo, then to Amelia. After Amelia Island was overrun by the forces of Colonel James Moore of Carolina in 1702, the last of the Guales fled to the presidio. Their few descendants were evacuated to Cuba in 1763, under the terms that ended the SEVEN YEARS' WAR.

JOHN TATE LANNING, *The Spanish Missions of Georgia* (1935); MAYNARD J. GEIGER, *The Franciscan Conquest of Florida (1573–1618)* (1937); GRANT D. JONES, ''The Ethnohistory of the Guale Coast Through 1684,'' in David H. Thomas et al., *The Anthropology of St. Catherines Island: (1) Natural and Cultural History, Anthropological Papers of the American Museum of Natural History*, vol. 55, pt. 2 (1978), pp. 178–210, 241–243; PAUL E. HOFFMAN, *A New Andalucia and a Way to the Orient: The American Southeast During the Sixteenth Century* (1990).

AMY TURNER BUSHNELL

GUAMAN POMA DE AYALA, FELIPE (*b.* ca. 1535; *d. ca.* 1615), one of the most polemic and most admired native authors of the colonial period. Guaman Poma wrote *Primer nueva corónica y bien gobierno* (ca. 1615), a long, illustrated history (1,188 pages with 398 pen-and-ink drawings) of ancient Andean times, Inca rule, and Spanish rule. The book was discovered in 1908 in the Royal Danish Library in Copenhagen and was first published in 1936. An abridged version, *Letter to a King*, translated by Christopher Dilke, appeared in 1978. Anthropologists consider the book a primary source of information on the pre-Columbian Andean world and on the first decades of Spanish colonization. Literary scholars, after ignoring the document for years, now regard it as a symbolic representation in which the author criticizes colonial rule while submitting a plan for ''good government'' to the Spanish king, PHILIP III, to whom the chronicle is addressed. Traditionally, historians have pointed out inaccuracies in Guaman Poma's work; however, recent research has explained how and why the author took advantage of information available from native and European sources to present an Andean version of history.

With the exception of what Guaman Poma says about himself in *Primer nueva corónica*, there is very little documentary evidence about his life. It is believed that he was born about 1535 in San Cristóbal de Suntunto (a small village in what is today the province of Ayacucho in Peru), lived for several years in Cuzco, and later moved (about 1562) to the city of Guamanga, now known as Ayacucho. According to Guaman Poma, his father was an ethnic lord of the Yarovilcas, a group conquered by the Incas and later incorporated into their empire; his mother was the daughter of the powerful Inca ruler Túpac Yupanqui. The historical evidence does not support Guaman Poma's claim to this distinguished lineage.

Educated in the Spanish language and culture, perhaps by missionaries, and well versed in Quechua, his native tongue, Guaman Poma became an interpreter in

Self-portrait of Guaman Poma de Ayala. Reproduced from *El primer nueva corónica y buen gobierno* (ca. 1615). COURTESY OF THE ROYAL LIBRARY, COPENHAGEN.

the campaigns against idol worship in the Andes (ca. 1568–1571). It is very probable that he also served as interpreter in the Third Council of Lima (1583–1584). In this regard, it has been speculated that it was through the library of the church inspector Cristóbal de Albornoz, as well as through books belonging to missionaries, that Guaman Poma became familiar with the writings of key religious, historical, and juridical authors and with engravings and illustrations of saints and biblical themes. These books and iconography, together with the Andean oral tradition and Guaman Poma's own experiences, became the sources of *Primer nueva corónica*.

Legal documents show that Guaman Poma served again as interpreter (1594) and, in addition, was the witness in a land claim presented by native Andeans (1595). He was later expelled from Guamanga (1600) and San Cristóbal de Suntunto (1611) for his defense of the native population and for claiming ancestral lands. Guaman Poma returned to Lima in 1601, to complain

107

about the poor treatment that he and other Indians were receiving from colonial administrators, and in 1613, to present the manuscript of *Primer nueva corónica* to the viceroy. Even though he failed in this attempt, in a letter (Guamanga, 14 February 1615) to Philip III he states that his chronicle has been completed. After this date we lose all track of him.

Guaman Poma's encyclopedic work is the living and angry testimony of how a native Andean experienced and interpreted the cultural clash brought about by the Conquest and colonization. *Primer nueva corónica* exhibits the talents of an indigenous historian who took up the pen, thus bringing together European and Andean traditions, Spanish and Quechua, writing and painting, to praise the past, condemn colonial administrators, and demand a better society for his people.

JOHN V. MURRA, "Guaman Poma de Ayala: A Seventeenth-Century Indian's Account of Andean Civilization," in *Natural History* 70 (1961): 25–63; FRANKLIN PEASE, "Prólogo," in FELIPE GUAMAN POMA DE AYALA, *Nueva corónica y buen gobierno* (1980); ROLENA ADORNO, *Guaman Poma: Writing and Resistance in Colonial Peru* (1986); RAQUEL CHANG-RODRÍGUEZ, *La apropiación del signo: Tres cronistas indígenas del Perú* (1988); MERCEDES LÓPEZ BARALT, *Icono y conquista: Guaman Poma de Ayala* (1988); ROGER A. ZAPATA, *Guaman Poma: Indigenismo y estética de la dependencia en la cultura peruana* (1989); ROLENA ADORNO et al., *Guaman Poma de Ayala: The Colonial Art of an Andean Author* (1992).

RAQUEL CHANG-RODRÍGUEZ

GUANABARA BAY, Brazil's second-largest bay, located in the state of Rio de Janeiro. Its area is 165 square miles, and it measures 18 miles north to south. When the Portuguese navigator André Gonçalves first entered the bay on what is widely believed to be 1 January 1502, he thought he had discovered the outlet of an immense river, which he named the Rio de Janeiro, after the month of his arrival. The land on the bay's western shore adopted the name when the city of Rio de Janeiro was founded in 1567. Famous for its natural beauty, Guanabara Bay has one of the world's best locations for port facilities. Protection from wind and surf is insured by the small size of its entrance (1,650 yards), the depth of its water, and the surrounding mountains. Since the mid-nineteenth century the bay has held one of the busiest ports of Brazil's central–south coast. At the beginning of the 1990s it was a focal point for ecological campaigns to detoxify its polluted waters.

SUEANN CAULFIELD

GUANABARA STATE. When Brazil's capital was transferred from the city of Rio de Janeiro to Brasília in 1960, the old municipal region that had included the capital of colonial Brazil (1763–1808), the seat of the Portuguese crown (1808–1822), the Brazilian Empire (1822–1889), and the capital of the Federal Republic (1889–1960) became the nation's smallest state and was given the name Guanabara. The creation of Guanabara State, and the transfer of the capital had been determined by the constitutions of 1891, 1934, and 1946.

Soon after these measures were implemented, however, it became clear that both Guanabara State and neighboring Rio de Janeiro were at a political and economic disadvantage compared with the bigger, more economically diverse Minas Gerais and São Paulo. Lack of capital and infrastructure in Rio de Janeiro and of natural resources in Guanabara, which depended upon its neighbor for water and electricity, together with the migration of urban industries from Guanabara to Rio de Janeiro, convinced most of the politicians of both states, including their two governors, that there should be a merger. In 1975 the national Congress decided that the two states would join, and named the new state Rio de Janeiro. The area that had been Guanabara State became the municipal district of Rio de Janeiro.

Fatos e Fotos, May 2, 1967, pp. 14–16; Feb. 12, 1970, pp. 4–7; June 10, 1974, pp. 14–17; *Grande enciclopedia Larousse* (1978).

SUEANN CAULFIELD

GUANACASTE, the northwesternmost province of Costa Rica, bordering NICARAGUA. Today it includes both the Nicoya Peninsula and the area from the volcanic mountain chain (Cordillera de Guanacaste) down to the Tempisque River basin. In colonial times Guanacaste referred only to the Tempisque plains or the settlement of Liberia, today the provincial capital but barely a collection of huts as late as the early nineteenth century.

Prior to independence both Nicoya and Costa Rica had been politically dependent upon Nicaragua, with the Costa Rican jurisdiction extending to just south of Liberia on the plain and the Partido de Nicoya controlling both the peninsula and the northern plains. During the CORTES OF CÁDIZ era (1812–1814) all of Nicoya was added to Costa Rica for electoral purposes to reach the minimum figure of 60,000 inhabitants needed to elect one deputy. In a CABILDO ABIERTO of 25 July 1824, Nicoya allegedly chose to remain with Costa Rica rather than Nicaragua, a choice the Central American Federation provisionally approved on 9 December 1825. Nicaragua and Costa Rica argued repeatedly over this issue in a number of agreements signed during the nineteenth century, especially the Cañas–Jerez Treaty of 15 April 1858. This was upheld, from the Costa Rican point of view, by the arbitration of U.S. President Grover Cleveland in 1888. The entire province was briefly renamed Moracia (1854–1860), in honor of President Juan Rafael MORA's defeat of William WALKER in Nicaragua.

Guanacaste was traditionally ruled by absentee landlords from Nicaragua and highland Costa Rica. Until the early twentieth century most settlement was in the Indian towns of Nicoya and Santa Cruz on the Nicoya Peninsula, with open-range cattle ranches on the plains. In the early twentieth century a substantial gold mining region opened up in the mountains at the southern end of the province, and by mid-century major improvements in cattle breeding and pasture were rapidly modernizing the plains areas. Some of the most violent and bitter agrarian conflicts in Cosa Rican history came out of these processes.

Since the 1960s Guanacaste has developed a mechanized farming economy in rice, corn, and beans. It has also benefited from a large-scale TOURIST industry based on the province's beaches and national parks. However, much of the laboring population has been forced to migrate in search of better opportunities in the Central Valley region and farm work along the Atlantic and southern Pacific coasts.

On Guanacaste, see LOWELL GUDMUNDSON, *Hacendados, precaristas y políticos: La ganadería y el latifundismo guanacasteco, 1800–1950* (1980); MARC EDELMAN, *The Logic of the Latifundio* (1993). On boundaries, see LUIS FERNANDO SIBAJA CHACÓN, *Nuestro límite con nicaragua* (1974). For firsthand descriptions, see CARLOS MELÉNDEZ CHAVERRI, ed., *Viajeros por Guanacaste* (1974).

LOWELL GUDMUNDSON

GUANACO. See **Llama.**

GUANAJUATO, a city in Mexico best known as the leading producer of silver in New Spain and the world in the second half of the eighteenth century. Guanajuato was founded as a small mining camp in the northern Bajío about 1554. Alexander von HUMBOLDT, a German traveler who visited the city in 1803, deemed the veins in Guanajuato (La Valenciana) to be the richest in the world. He also reported an estimated "5,000 miners and workmen" were occupied with mining operations there.

Guanajuato was not surrounded by primordial indigenous communities, but by only a few settler pueblos of Otomí and Tarascans. Nevertheless, it represented an attractive lure to Indians seeking work. Owing to both immigration and natural increase, its population jumped from 156,140 to 397,924 between 1742 and 1793. Compared to the central highlands, the region was much more urban and ethnically mixed, features that created a considerable internal market for the agricultural and manufactured goods of the Bajío.

Resistance to governmental controls and Jesuit expulsion prompted uprisings in Guanajuato in the 1760s. But it was the Hidalgo revolt of 1810 that endowed Guanajuato with even greater notoriety. Home to some three hundred peninsular-born Spaniards and the silver jewel in the crown, the city represented a prize conquest for the insurgents, who took it by storm in September of that year. Its capture was achieved largely through the defeat of the city's elite at the municipal granary, or *alhóndiga*, where many Spaniards sought refuge. The memory of bloody independence pursuits at Guanajuato stayed with Mexico's establishment for a long time

afterward. Mining activity picked up again at the end of the nineteenth century and, along with agriculture, stock-raising, and tourism, sustains Guanajuato today.

ERIC R. WOLF, "The Mexican Bajío in the Eighteenth Century," in *Synoptic Studies of Mexican Culture*, no. 17, edited by Robert Wauchope (1957), pp. 177–198; HUGH M. HAMILL, JR., *The Hidalgo Revolt* (1966), pp. 51–52, 91–93, 124, 137–141, 149; D. A. BRADING, *Miners and Merchants in Bourbon Mexico, 1763–1810* (1971), pp. 223–339; ALEXANDER VON HUMBOLDT, *Political Essay on the Kingdom of New Spain,* translated by John Black and edited by Mary Maples Dunn (1972), pp. 151–156.

STEPHANIE WOOD

GUANGALA, an archaeological culture or ceramic phase defined for the southwest coast of Ecuador and dated from 100 B.C. to A.D. 800. First identified at the village of Guangala by G. H. S. Bushnell, Guangala cultural remains are distributed along the coast of Guayas Province from PUNÁ ISLAND north to southern Manabí Province; in the east the territorial limits of Guangala are unknown, but sites do not extend as far as the Guayas River. The Guangala way of life has been reconstructed from artifacts, human burials, and other remains excavated from a few sites on and near the Santa Elena Peninsula, a semiarid zone considered to have less agricultural potential than other portions of Ecuador.

Guangala ceramics are known primarily from artifacts without provenience. The style represents one of several regional variants that developed out of the preceding, geographically widespread CHORRERA tradition. The Guangala style is characterized by innovative ceramic features which suggest that there was significant evolution also in other aspects of Guangala society and economy. Guangala society has been interpreted as less differentiated and hierarchical than some of the neighboring ethnic groups in the Regional Developmental period.

The earliest Guangala pottery is found in small sites scattered extensively along small rivers over the entire region—evidence of a large and expanding population. By middle Guangala times, people were numerous and lived in large and small permanent villages as well as in dispersed homesteads. One large site on the Bay of Santa Elena had "mounds" which, according to the excavator, may have supported houses. Some communities maintained water catchment structures. Many sites were located adjacent to beaches, river mouths, and mangrove estuaries, where people practiced a mixed economy of farming, fishing, gathering, hunting, craft production, and trade for exotic raw materials. Smaller, "rural" sites were often oriented to small parcels of fertile river bottom land, where farmers cultivated cotton, corn, squash, sweet potatoes, beans, peppers, and fruit. Some sites show domestic craft specialization such as the production of grinding stones or shell beads.

The Guangala people buried their dead, legs extended, in tombs beneath their habitation sites and accompanied by offerings, some of which were preserved: ceramic vessels, obsidian blades, lime containers made of shell (used during coca leaf chewing rituals), fishhooks, beads and ornaments, stone tools, sets of three stones, or three shark teeth, and copper artifacts.

The largest Guangala sites, presumably once occupied by the more powerful local shamans who used a variety of exotic and luxury goods, were located inland in the more well-watered valleys where the agricultural potential is high even today. These sites, several of which have been heavily looted, have produced the finest Guangala pottery and ceramic figurines. Artifacts such as clay seats, associated with shamanistic power, and elaborate figurines and musical instruments suggest that the people at these sites were socially complex and had elaborate rituals. Guangala material culture shows elegant pottery types, handsome figurines, whistles and ocarinas, and personal ornaments, all suggestive of the complexity of social life.

The Guangala people practiced local economic specialties such as fishing at coastal locations, agriculture at inland locations, manufacture of goods such as copper needles and fishhooks and shell artifacts. They no doubt engaged in both local and long-distance exchange, the latter perhaps involving sea voyaging by elites which brought into the region obsidian (volcanic glass for stone tool making), serpentine, rock crystal, and copper, possibly in exchange for export commodities like mother-of-pearl and *Spondylus*—much appreciated outside of the region. Exotic imports found their way into most Guangala sites, indicating that political leaders circulated rather than concentrated the wealth.

G. H. S. BUSHNELL, *The Archaeology of the Santa Elena Peninsula in South-West Ecuador* (1951); EMILIO ESTRADA, *Prehistoria de Manabí* (1957); BETTY J. MEGGERS, *Ecuador* (1966); ALLISON C. PAULSEN, ''Patterns of Maritime Trade Between South Coastal Ecuador and Western Mesoamerica, 1500 B.C.–A.D. 600,'' in *The Sea in the Pre-Columbian World*, edited by Elizabeth B. Benson (1974), pp. 141–166; MARIA ANN MASUCCI, *Ceramic Change in the Guangala Phase, Southwest Ecuador: A Typology and Chronology* (Ph.D. diss., Southern Methodist University, 1992); KAREN E. STOTHERT, *Un sitio de Guangala Temprano en el suroeste del Ecuador* (Guayaquil, 1993).

KAREN E. STOTHERT

See also **Bahia; Jama-Coaque.**

GUANO INDUSTRY. Guano, a superb natural fertilizer, was the dominant export of nineteenth-century Peru; the guano industry constitutes a classic example of a Latin American boom-and-bust export experience. Guano is the dried excrement of seabirds (from Quechua, *huanu*, ''dung''). On small islands astride the southern Peruvian coast, favorable meteorological conditions of the HUMBOLDT CURRENT led, over the centuries, to unparalleled accumulations of unleached guano—sometimes hundreds of feet thick in the CHINCHA ISLANDS. Rich in nitrogen and phosphates, guano was used extensively by pre-Columbian agriculturalists but sparingly by Spanish colonists. In the early 1840s, guano suddenly became an international export commodity, as Europe, undergoing an agricultural revolution, discovered its powerful chemical, productive, and economic properties.

Thus guano emerged, between 1841 and 1879, as Peru's critical export, in one of the busiest commodity trades of the nineteenth-century world. Peru entered its legendary Age of Guano. Over four decades, roughly 11.5 million tons of bird manure made its way to Britain, France, the southern United States, and a host of minor markets; at prices fluctuating between $25 and $50 a ton, the aggregate market value of the trade reached about $750 million. Peru's long-suffering state swiftly grasped the opportunity, declaring a national monopoly over the fertilizer in 1841, and deflecting over the years the inevitable foreign pressures to liberalize the guano trade. Innovatively led by General Ramón CASTILLA, Peru commercialized its deposits mainly through profit-sharing consignment sales, dominated during the initial two decades by the British firm of Antony GIBBS and Sons. By the 1860s, the state had turned to marketing contracts with emerging national

A living carpet of *aves guaneras*. Peru, 1980. ORGANIZATION OF AMERICAN STATES.

merchants, Hijos del País (native sons) such as Manuel PARDO. In the 1870s this approach was replaced with a direct-sales policy linked to foreign-debt servicing and exemplified by the controversial DREYFUS CONTRACT of 1869, signed by the government of Peru and the French company of Dreyfus Brothers. If its international marketing, finance, and politics proved complex, extraction of guano remained a primitive if oppressive affair. Modest numbers of convicts, coolies, and other hapless laborers funneled the unprocessed and toxic dung into the bowels of awaiting ships.

Abroad, guano use helped boost productivity of crops such as turnips, grains, and tobacco; within Peru, the staggering revenue injections revitalized national finance and a sagging postcolonial economy and polity in Lima. Overall, the Peruvian state deftly managed to capture an impressive 60 percent of final sales, or nearly $500 million. The boom, climaxing in the 1860s with annual sales of over $20 million, brought coastal Peru squarely into the world economy.

Guano, and the country's relatively easy access to London bond markets, activated a new commercial-entrepreneurial class, centered around the dramatic expansion of public finance and state activities (real estate spending grew fivefold between 1850 and 1870). In politics, such wealth allowed Peru finally to consolidate its shaky caudillo-style central state and smooth over political conflicts among the elite, eventually spawning the reformist politics of the Partido Civil, which superseded military rule in 1872. The social impact of guano was mixed; benefits were largely confined to connected *Limeño* families while popular groups (such as artisans) suffered the effects of intensified manufactured imports, inflation, and political neglect.

The singular economic fact is that Peru's guano industry led to little sustained, diversified, or nationwide development. In many respects, mounting dependence on bird dung heightened the vulnerability of the Peruvian economy. Apart from the urban commercial bonanza, a burgeoning banking system in the 1860s, and rising modern coastal sugar and cotton plantations in the 1870s, guano worked slowly on the private sector and on the economy and peoples of Peru's vast Andean interior. By the 1860s, official Peru, with its reduced tax base, resorted to ever larger issues on European capital markets. In part, this borrowing was to realize the schemes of visionary politicians who grasped the impending problems of guano exhaustion and the country's low level of national integration. For example, a mammoth railroad construction project, directed by the North American Henry MEIGGS, absorbed fully one-fifth of all guano profits. After its frenetic start in the mid-1860s, Peru's national rail network lay largely uncompleted. Meanwhile, by 1875 Peru's foreign debt had soared to £35 million—by far Latin America's largest on record.

As quickly as it appeared, the Age of Guano evaporated in the mid-1870s. The collapse struck all facets of a Peruvian economy and polity built upon the so-called fictitious prosperity. In a few short years, quality reserves dwindled, substitution and nitrates competition intensified, and European lenders retrenched. The result was Peru's world-shattering default on its foreign debt in 1876 and a broad political and social crisis. In the coup de grace of 1879, Peru and Chile went to war for control of the world's next natural fertilizer, the ATACAMA DESERT nitrates. Peru's smashing defeat in the WAR OF THE PACIFIC, which exposed the frailty of her national development, ended in the loss of assets and accomplishments remaining from the export era. Peru today retains a modest guano industry for local needs.

Economic historians have long pondered the meaning of Peru's experience with guano. While all agree it was a "lost opportunity" for development, explanations widely differ. Traditionally, guano is seen as an adverse "enclave" economy. In this view, export-sector revenues and demand filtered abroad to foreign capitalists, merchants, and luxury imports, leaving little impulse for the backward domestic economy. The quantitative studies of Shane Hunt overturned this view by showing how guano produced significant demand effects for the Peruvian economy and a potential for competent public investment. However, cost-price pressures still led to a dangerously overspecialized and productively stagnant rentier economy. Some historians stress, in the absence of wide-ranging social reforms, the limited ability of guano to strengthen national markets and promote cogent national consciousness among national elites; guano exemplifies a tragic "dependency" experience. Other historians explore Peru's historical dynamics of integration with the world economy, which display a paradoxical blend of import liberalism and autocratic statism that stifled prospects for growth. Whatever the cause, the guano age left a legacy of superficial urban modernization and fragmented Andean society—persisting dilemmas for modern Peru.

JONATHAN V. LEVIN, *The Export Economies: Their Patterns of Development in Historical Perspective* (1960), esp. ch. 2; HERACLIO BONILLA, *Guano y burguesía en el Perú* (1974); W. M. MATHEW, *The House of Gibbs and the Peruvian Guano Monopoly* (1981); SHANE J. HUNT, "Growth and Guano in Nineteenth-Century Peru," in *The Latin American Economies: Growth and the Export Sector, 1830–1930*, edited by Roberto Cortés and Shane J. Hunt (1985), pp. 255–319; ALFONSO W. QUIRÓZ, *La deuda defraudada: Consolidación de 1850 y dominio económico en el Perú* (1987); PAUL GOOTENBERG, *Between Silver and Guano: Commercial Policy and the State in Postindependence Peru* (1989) and *Imagining Development: Economic Ideas in Peru's Fictitious Prosperity of Guano, 1840–1880* (1993).

PAUL GOOTENBERG

See also **Agriculture; Foreign Trade.**

GUANTÁNAMO BAY, an inlet on the extreme southeast coast of Cuba. The bay makes an excellent harbor because it is sheltered from storms, has deep waters, and lies near the Windward Passage. After the U.S.

Guantanamo Bay, Cuba. F. LEE CORKRAN / SYGMA.

Navy found it useful in the SPANISH-AMERICAN WAR (1898), the U.S. government decided to acquire the bay for a naval base. The right to do so was provided for in the PLATT AMENDMENT, which was appended to the Cuban constitution of 1901 and incorporated in a treaty between the United States and Cuba on 22 May 1903. On 2 July 1903, the United States leased the bay and its outer shoreline for $2,000 annually. Although the United States abrogated the Platt Amendment in 1934, it retained the right to the naval base in Guantánamo Bay. After coming to power in 1959, Fidel CASTRO unsuccessfully attempted to force the United States from the facility but continued to permit Cuban nationals to work for the U.S. Navy.

EMILIO ROIG DE LEUCHSENRING, *Historia de la Enmienda Platt*, 2 vols. (1935); DAVID F. HEALY, *The United States in Cuba, 1898–1902: Generals, Politicians, and the Search for Policy* (1963); GARY L. MARIS, "International Law and Guantánamo," *Journal of Politics* 29 (1967): 261–286; WALTER J. RAYMOND, "The Feasibility of Rapprochement Between the Republic of Cuba and the United States: The Case of the Guantánamo Naval Base," *Caribbean Quarterly* 21 (1975): 35–46.

THOMAS M. LEONARD

GUAPORE. *See* **Rondônia.**

GUARANÁ INDUSTRY, the production of a range of products, including a popular Brazilian beverage, based on *guaraná* seeds. *Guaraná* (hilea) seeds are found on small climbing plants (*Paullinia cupana*) that grow in the Maués Valley in the state of Pará or that grow wild in the tropical rain forest. Amazonian Indians invented the process of turning them into a drink. After removing the almondlike seeds from their black shell, Indians roasted and pounded them into powder. They pressed the powder into chocolate-colored disks or ten- to twelve-inch-long sticks, which they either traded or consumed in drinks. Before drinking it, Indians used the rasplike tongue bone of the *pirarucu* fish to file some of the pressed powder into a cup of hot or cold water.

Guaraná has grown in popularity among Brazilians in the twentieth century. They believe it cures ailments such as fevers, headaches, and stomach cramps. It is now sold in powdered or liquid extract form. Now the base for many other drinks, Maués Valley workers produce *guaraná* powder for bottlers in Rio and São Paulo, where they heavily sweeten and carbonate it before marketing it as a soft drink. Indians also work its paste into ornamental shapes, such as alligators, snakes, or birds, to sell in curio shops. By 1990, 300 tons a year were being produced for internal and external markets, but that was not nearly enough to keep up with the ever-increasing demand, especially from health-food stores in Brazil and abroad.

ROBERT SOUTHEY, *History of Brazil* (1822); JOHN HEMMING, *Amazon Frontier* (1987).

CAROLYN JOSTOCK

GUARANI INDIANS, a branch of the TUPI-GUARANI linguistic family of east-central South America. A semisedentary people, they lived south of the Amazon between the Brazilian coast and the Río Paraná and Río Paraguay. Immediately before contact with Spaniards in the early 1500s, they were concentrated in the upper Platine region east of the Paraná and Paraguay rivers, when their population of perhaps 300,000 was divided into fourteen subgroups, or Guarás, of which the Carios of central Paraguay are best known. They moved frequently to find fertile land because they supported themselves by swidden agriculture, cultivating manioc, sweet potatoes, maize, and other crops, which they supplemented with hunting and fishing.

In the 1530s, Guaranis sought an alliance with Spanish expeditionaries to strengthen their efforts against their PAYAGUÁ enemies, who dominated the Río Paraguay. Guarani chiefs gave daughters and nieces to Spaniards as wives or concubines, which was their way of establishing a relationship of equals. Spaniards were supposed to reciprocate but looked down on Guaranis. Guaranis labored for Spaniards to obtain the iron tools that revolutionized aboriginal work habits.

Iron tools and new allies, Guaranis thought, would make their lives more secure. When they realized that Spaniards regarded them not as allies but as inferiors, some Guaranis in 1545 rose in revolt. Several other Indian rebellions followed but were unsuccessful, partly because many other Guaranis allied themselves with Spaniards. In 1556, to avoid uncontrolled exploitation of Guaranis, Govenor Domingo Martínez de IRALA founded the Paraguayan ENCOMIENDA, the dominant institution of Guarani labor in the early colony; declining numbers of Guaranis labored for elite colonists to the end of the colonial period.

Unions between Guarani women and Spanish men in the early years initiated a process of ethnogenesis. This fusion of Native Americans and Europeans continued to produce mestizo children and a distinctive Paraguayan culture based on nearly universal understanding of the Guarani language.

Guaranis at the margins of settler-controlled land along the Paranapanema in Guairá (now Parána in Brazil), Itaty (in northern Paraguay), and south of the Tebicuari River in Paraguay and Argentina joined Catholic MISSIONS staffed by JESUITS after 1610. Guaranis chose missions in order to obtain steady supplies of Spanish artifacts and food and to gain the security from Brazilian slave raiders that Jesuits promised. From such *encomienda* towns as Yaguarón and Tobatí, Guarani men and women throughout the colonial period escaped the degraded status of "Indian" and moved into Spanish society. Lesser members of Guaranis who left Jesuit missions did the same, but after the departure of Jesuits in

1767 and 1768, mission Guaranis also slowly dispersed into northern Argentina, Uruguay, and western Brazil and became ancestors of the popular classes of those republics. Their descendants in Paraguay form the Guarani-speaking rural population of today.

Guaranis in Paraguay numbered about 40,000 people, or a tenth of the population of the young republic in 1848, when the government of Carlos Antonio LÓPEZ liberated them from their discriminatory status. They officially became Paraguayans. They then were obligated to serve in the military, and their formerly protected lands were available for sale. In the twentieth century, isolated bands of Guaranis provided anthropologists with opportunities to explore their culture, but the lasting influence of the Guaranis lies in the everyday language of Paraguayans. Most of the people of the modern republic are descendants of Guaranis.

ALFRED MÉTRAUX, "The Guarani," in *Handbook of South American Indians*, vol. 3, edited by Julian H. Steward (1948); ELMAN R. SERVICE, "The *Encomienda* in Paraguay," in *Hispanic American Historical Review* 31, no. 2 (1951): 230–252, and *Spanish-Guarani Relations in Early Colonial Paraguay* (1954; repr. 1971); GUILLERMO FÚRLONG [CÁRDIFF], *Misiones y sus pueblos Guaraníes* (1962); JOHN HEMMING, *Red Gold: The Conquest of the Brazilian Indians* (1978); JAMES SCHOFIELD SAEGER, "Survival and Abolition: The Eighteenth-Century Paraguayan Encomienda," in *The Americas: A Quarterly Review of Inter-American Cultural History* 38, no. 1 (1981): 59–85; BRANISLAVA SUSNIK, *El rol de los indígenas en la formación y en la vivencia del Paraguay* (1982–1983).

JAMES SCHOFIELD SAEGER

See also **Indians.**

Guarani Indian vintners by Jean-Baptiste Debret. Province of São Pedro do Rio Grande do Sul, ca. 1834–1839. ICONOGRAPHIA.

GUARANI WAR (1753–1756). A series of armed engagements between a joint Spanish-Portuguese force and a group of GUARANI Indians who actively resisted Spanish cession of their lands to the Portuguese. In 1750 a treaty was signed in Madrid that transferred the Portuguese settlement of Colonia to Spain in exchange for a several-hundred-mile wedge of Spanish territory east of the Uruguay River. Within this territory, however, were several Guarani MISSIONS under the control of the Society of Jesus (JESUITS). The Indians of these missions adamantly rejected the idea of their lands being given to the Portuguese, their age-old enemies. Despite the orders of the Spanish governor, and of their Jesuit administrators, the Indians of the seven missions refused to evacuate their communities and instead organized a spirited military defense under a Guarani *corregidor* named Sepé Tiarayú.

Sepé met in February 1753 with Spanish and Portuguese commissioners but declined to make any concessions. The sixty-eight men under his command never constituted much of a threat, but the joint European force decided to withdraw anyway to avoid bloodshed. This act in fact made matters worse, for when news of the incident reached Madrid and Lisbon, it was made to look like cowardice in the face of Jesuit machinations. The Europeans thereafter began to fight in earnest and rarely offered quarter. For their part, the Guarani had prepared well for war, fashioning every piece of scrap metal into arrowheads and increasing the size of their rustic army to over a thousand.

In February 1754 the Indians besieged Santo Amaro, a small Portuguese fort they finally captured after a month's combat. In July an allied army of 3,000 men advanced from two directions to capture San Borja in order to cut off the flow of supplies from missions west of the Uruguay. Four months later several Guarani *caciques* surrendered after bloody resistance.

Switching tactics, Sepé forged an alliance with savage Charrúa Indians, a move that until that point had been unthinkable. Toward the end of 1755 a new European army began a merciless campaign. The Spanish and Portuguese faced a force of 1,600 Indians, armed mostly with bows and, according to one account, several rudimentary cannons fashioned from bamboo.

Sepé was killed at this time in a minor skirmish and his place taken by Nicolás Ñeenguirú, a minor *correquidor* who failed to inspire the same kind of loyalty as his predecessor. On 10 February 1756 a major battle took place at Caaybaté, in the hill country south of the Yacuí River. The Indians found themselves surrounded, and although Nicolás attempted to negotiate terms, the Indians ended up fighting hand-to-hand. The slaughter lasted more than an hour, with the trenches dug by the Guarani now serving as their burial pits.

Caaybaté broke the main Indian resistance, though guerrilla activities continued for a number of months afterwards. Some Indians fled into the jungles and swamps where they lived in isolation for decades. Ironically, in the 1760s, these same territories for which so many Indians had died were restored to the Spanish crown. The power and prestige of the Jesuits in that part of South America, however, was dramatically diminished.

MAGNUS MÖRNER, *The Expulsion of the Jesuits from Latin America* (1965); PHILIP CARAMAN, *The Lost Paradise: The Jesuit Republic in South America* (1990), pp. 235–255.

THOMAS L. WHIGHAM

GUARDIA, RICARDO ADOLFO DE LA (*b.* 14 June 1899; *d.* 29 December 1970), president of Panama (1941–1945). Minister of government and justice under president Arnulfo ARIAS MADRID, Guardia organized a movement to depose the dictator. He assumed the office of president with the support of the National Guard, the oligarchy, and much of the Panamanian populace. The attack on Pearl Harbor brought fear that the Panama Canal would become a target, and Guardia endorsed controversial plans for the construction of U.S. bases in Panama. In 1944 the National Assembly rebelled against Guardia's authority, insisting that he name a constitu-

tional successor. In response, he dissolved the assembly and abrogated the 1941 constitution. He called elections in 1945 that established a new assembly and installed Enrique A. JIMÉNEZ as provisional president. Arias returned to power in 1949, forcing Guardia to flee to the Canal Zone, where he remained until 1951.

MANUEL MARÍA ALBA C., *Cronología de los gobernantes de Panamá, 1510–1967* (1967), pp. 329–333; ERNESTO J. CASTILLERO R., *Historia de Panamá* (1982), pp. 253–255.

SARA FLEMING

GUARDIA GUTIÉRREZ, TOMÁS (*b.* 16 December 1831; *d.* 6 July 1882), president and dictator of Costa Rica (1870–1882). Guardia is often seen as the expression of triumphant liberalism in Costa Rica with his dictatorial style, the rewriting of the Constitution of 1871, and the hegemony of an entire generation of elitist Liberals in the 1880s and 1890s. However, Guardia was not the first to champion liberal policies, and his reign was more a reflection of severe intra-elite tensions within a liberal framework than of liberalism's ascendancy for the first time. Indeed, the Constitution of 1871 proved to be a highly presidentialist document, with Guardia and his relatives rigidly controlling political power for some twenty years while pursuing liberal economic transformation of the country.

Guardia, born in Bagaces, was the son of leading ranching families in Guanacaste and Alajuela provinces. Nevertheless, his power transcended particular regions. His father's family was originally from Panama, and the family remained active in the politics of that nation as well. As a colonel in the Costa Rican army, Guardia led a revolt against the government, taking the artillery barracks in San José on 27 April 1870. He became general commandant of an interim government headed by Bruno Carranza Ramírez. He was elected president in 1872 under a system that centralized the election procedures in the executive branch. He engineered the election of an ally, Aniceto Esquivel Sáenz, in 1876, but soon thereafter (1877) he reassumed the presidency as virtual dictator. He convened yet another Constituent Assembly in 1880 and reestablished the Constitution of 1871 by decree in 1882. Guardia died of natural causes in 1882, prior to the scheduled presidential election.

Guardia was something of an outsider in mid-nineteenth-century Costa Rican politics. He was not a leading member of the coffee oligarchy, dominated by the Mora and MONTEALEGRE clans, which had ruled for over twenty years before his coup. Many of his policies can best be seen as designed to wrest political power from the family-based cliques of the coffee barons of the Central Valley. He exiled former President José María Montealegre Fernández to the United States for life in 1872, and, although his own family would benefit enormously, much of his regime's support came from non-oligarchic forces in the coffee economy. Coffee elite members who were more ideologically and institutionally than personally oriented, as well as liberals of more modest social origins, tended to support Guardia, while the "old money" families more often felt his wrath.

Guardia's regime was most highly identified with the long-lasting (until 1949) Constitution of 1871 and the building of the RAILROAD to the Atlantic coast. The latter endeavor was contracted with Minor KEITH and led to both the first serious foreign debt and to the UNITED FRUIT COMPANY dominance of much of the Atlantic coast province of Limón. Other major achievements included the abolition of the death penalty in 1882, the beginning of a major effort at mass primary education, and, curiously for an avowedly presidentialist regime, the strengthening of both the legislative branch and legal norms in public affairs. A substantial group of ideologically committed liberal deputies and magistrates came to power during Guardia's reign, as is suggested by the reformulation of the Civil Code in 1886.

In foreign affairs Guardia was able to deter Central American unification efforts led by the Guatemalan strongman Justo Rufino BARRIOS, preserving local independence and a special commercial relationship with Great Britain. Perhaps the overzealous pursuit of British loan capital and investment, brokered by Keith, is today seen as the most negative aspect of Guardia's admittedly authoritarian form of liberalism.

For Guardia the most basic source is DONNA COTTON, "Costa Rica and the Era of Tomás Guardia" (Ph.D. diss., George Washington University, 1972). See also EUGENIO RODRÍGUEZ, *Don Tomás Guardia y el estado liberal* (1989); JOSÉ LUIS VEGA CARBALLO, *Orden y progreso: La formacíon del estado nacional en Costa Rica* (1981); CARLOS MELÉNDEZ CHAVERRI, comp., *Documentos fundamentales del siglo xix* (1978); EUGENIO RODRÍGUEZ, *El pensamiento liberal: Antología* (1979); and RAFAEL OBREGÓN LORÍA, *Conflictos militares y políticos de Costa Rica* (1951)

LOWELL GUDMUNDSON

GUARDIA NAVARRO, ERNESTO DE LA

GUARDIA NAVARRO, ERNESTO DE LA (*b.* 30 May 1904; *d.* 2 May 1983), president of Panama (1956–1960). Born in Panama City, Guardia Navarro, a conservative businessman with a degree from Dartmouth, was the first Panamanian president since World War II to complete his term in office. Elected to the presidency in 1956 as a candidate of the National Patriotic Coalition, he furthered programs begun by President José Antonio REMÓN CANTERA (1952–1955). He created a minimum wage, sponsored housing projects, undertook minor educational reforms, and lowered unemployment levels. In 1958 he began negotiations with U.S. President Eisenhower over the fine points of the Remón–Eisenhower Treaty, seeking an equal status for the Spanish language and the Panamanian flag in the Canal Zone.

In April 1959 a group of Cubans intending to overthrow Guardia Navarro's government landed in Colón. The conflict was quickly resolved and the invaders de-

ported. In November of the same year, violence erupted when protesters marched into the Canal Zone carrying Panamanian flags. Eisenhower conceded, and the Panamanian flag was raised in the zone. In 1960, Guardia Navarro's term ended peacefully with the election of a member of the opposition.

MANUEL MARÍA ALBA C., *Cronología de los gobernantes de Panamá, 1510–1967* (1967), pp. 360–364; ERNESTO J. CASTILLERO R., *Historia de Panamá* (1982), pp. 267–270.

SARA FLEMING

See also **Panama Canal Zone: Flag Riots.**

GUARDIOLA, SANTOS

GUARDIOLA, SANTOS (*b.* 1812; *d.* 11 January 1862), military figure and president of Honduras (1856–1862). Guardiola established himself as a prominent Conservative and military leader during the NATIONAL WAR against William WALKER's invasions. Known as "the butcher," Guardiola was considered a particularly ruthless and cruel commander. His forces defeated Walker and the latter's small force of fifty-five men at Rivas on 29 June 1855. Guatemalan Conservatives helped establish Guardiola as president of Honduras on 17 February 1856. He assumed a second term on 2 July 1860 and ruled until his assassination.

Guardiola's presidency had certain measurable successes at first but in the end was marred by violence and economic stagnation. After signing an alliance with Guatemala and El Salvador against Walker, Guardiola set out to assert Honduran sovereignty over the BAY ISLANDS and MOSQUITO COAST, areas of permanent British incursions and long-standing dispute. British citizens were allowed to remain as inhabitants of the Bay Islands and were exempt from taxation. The Dallas-Clarendon Convention of 17 October 1856 removed the British protectorate over the Mosquito Coast but at the same time restricted Honduran sovereignty. Plans were made in January 1853 for an interoceanic railway with the founding of Ferrocarril Interoceánico de Honduras (Interoceanic Railway Company) on 28 April 1854, organized in Honduras with offices in New York and London. Walker's eventual capture and execution at Trujillo in 1860 represented the pinnacle of Guardiola's presidency.

Difficulties with Miguel del Cid, head of the diocese of Honduras, resulted in Guardiola's excommunication on 26 December 1860. Guardiola's rebuke and anticlericalism erupted in the *Guerra de los padres,* which pitted the church against its former Conservative ally in April 1861. The same month, Guardiola was forced by deteriorating economic conditions to authorize the issue of copper coins. The deteriorating economy, coupled with the violence of Guardiola's presidency, led to his assassination in early 1862 and, after several Conservative administrations, to the consolidation of power by the Liberal Party in 1876.

LORENZO MONTÚFAR, *Reseña historica de Centro-América*, 7 vols. (1878–1888); LUIS MARIÑAS OTERO, *Honduras*, 3d ed. (1983); PABLO YANKELEVICH, *Honduras: una historia breve* (1988).

JEFFREY D. SAMUELS

GUARNIERI, GIANFRANCESCO (*b.* 6 August 1934), Brazilian dramatist and actor. Guarnieri has been a central figure in modern Brazilian theater and is particularly associated with the Arena Theater of São Paulo. His political orientation is Marxist, and his Brechtian theatrical technique requires the audience's direct emotional participation in the action to achieve a type of classical catharsis. *Eles não usam black-tie* (1958), his most celebrated play, presents the inevitable personal tragedy resulting from disunity in workers' struggles. Other dramas question the accepted truths of Brazilian history and the nation's contemporary reality. His *Ponto de partida* (1976) is an allegorical protest against the military regime's murder of journalist Vladimir HERZOG.

LESLIE DAMASCENO, "Theater History," in *Dictionary of Brazilian Literature* (1988); IRWIN STERN, "Guarnieri, Gianfrancesco," in *Dictionary of Brazilian Literature* (1988).

IRWIN STERN

GUARNIERI, M[OZART] CAMARGO (*b.* 1 February 1907), Brazilian composer, conductor, teacher, and leader of the nationalist school of composers. Guarnieri was the son of a Sicilian immigrant remotely related to the Guarneri family of violin makers (the name was accidentally changed due to the mistake of an immigration official) and a Brazilian mother. His father, Miguel Guarnieri, an amateur musician, played the piano, flute, and string bass. He had a lifelong passion for opera and named his four sons Mozart, Rossini, Bellini, and Verdi. When Guarnieri became aware of the significance of the name Mozart, he dropped it and signed his name M. Camargo Guarnieri, feeling that it was presumptuous to be called by the name of the great master. Aware that his son had musical talent, and that educational opportunities were limited in the town of Tieté, Miguel Guarnieri moved to the city of São Paulo in 1922. In São Paulo, Camargo was placed under the tutelage of two teachers who exercised a decisive influence on his artistic and intellectual development: the Italian conductor and teacher Lamberto Baldi and Mário de ANDRADE, philosopher, teacher, and leader of the modernist movement in Brazil. Guarnieri studied with both teachers during the same period. Andrade undertook the direction of Guarnieri's studies in aesthetics and literature, and Baldi taught him counterpoint, fugue, and orchestration, while also gently guiding his efforts in composition. Guarnieri's first successful composition to exhibit obvious national characteristics was a sonatina for piano written in 1928. This work exhibited several characteristics of Guarnieri's mature style of composition: melodies that sounded folklike while avoiding direct quotations of folk melodies, use of typically Brazilian tempo and expression markings in Portuguese—*Molengamente* (indolently) and *Ponteado e bem dengoso* (with a plucked sound, coyly), contrapuntal writing, and use of layers of syncopated voices.

Guarnieri had a major influence on Brazilian music by his teaching of composition, by establishing a high level of craftsmanship in his own musical writing, and by providing a model of tonal and nontonal works with convincing national elements. Although Guarnieri did some writing in an atonal style, he soon came to the conviction that his style of writing was incompatible with what he regarded as the straitjacket of dodecaphony. He believed so strongly that atonality was incompatible with the development of national elements that he conducted a vigorous debate in Brazilian newspapers against what he regarded as the pernicious influence of atonality in the works of Brazilian composers.

Camargo Guarnieri wrote over six hundred musical works, many unpublished. The fifty *Ponteios* for piano are one of the most significant contributions to piano literature from any Brazilian composer and are a treasure of elements uniquely and distinctively Brazilian. Several orchestral works have won international acclaim, and his fourth and fifth sonatas for violin are masterpieces of the genre.

MARION VERHAALEN, "The Solo Piano Music of Francisco Mignone and Camargo Guarnieri" (Ed.D. diss., Columbia Univ., 1971); DAVID P. APPLEBY, *The Music of Brazil* (1983).

DAVID P. APPLEBY

GUATEMALA. [Coverage begins with a survey of the political history. There follow a variety of entries on specialized topics: **Constitutions; Organizations; Political Parties;** and **Terrorist Organizations.** The **Audiencia of Guatemala** follows thereafter.]

The modern republic of Guatemala occupies but a small part of what was the Spanish dominion of that name from the early sixteenth century to the beginning of the nineteenth. (See GUATEMALA, AUDIENCIA OF, with map.) The colonial Kingdom of Guatemala included several diverse provinces that were often remote from and resentful toward the commercial and bureaucratic elites of the capital. The destruction by earthquake of the capital city (Antigua Guatemala) toward the end of the colonial period (1773) and the establishment of a new capital some 25 miles away coincided with the emergence of new economic and political forces that would characterize independent Guatemala.

The fragmentation that occurred with independence left the state of Guatemala with boundaries approximating the present-day republic, bounded on the west by Mexico, on the south by the Pacific Ocean, on the east by El Salvador and Honduras, and on the north by Mexico, Belize, and the Caribbean Sea.

From a population of less than a million at the time of independence, Guatemalan population grew at the rate of about 1.3 percent annually during the nineteenth century, and then at rates between 2 and 3 percent annually during the twentieth century. By 1990 its population was more than 9 million. Its population has always been ethnically diverse, with a very large percentage of Indians, especially MAYAS, who have generally been reported to represent about 60 percent of the total during the second half of the twentieth century. Fifty-six percent of the population have Spanish as their first language, while for 44 percent it is an Indian language. Recently, careful demographic research has suggested that the indigenous population has been undercounted in modern Guatemalan censuses, and that in the twentieth century the Indian population has been growing somewhat more rapidly than the MESTIZO (LADINO) population.

Guatemala is third in area (42,042 square miles) among the five Central American states, but it has always been the most populous. It is estimated that its population will reach 11,656,000 by the year 2000. It has a population density of about 233 inhabitants per square mile with an annual population growth rate of 2.3 percent. In 1990 nearly 45 percent of the population was under age fourteen. The literacy rate was about 50 percent, urban population was 32.7 percent, and annual per capita gross national product was about $920.

INDEPENDENCE TO 1850

Guatemala remained loyal to the Spanish crown throughout the difficult years of the Napoleonic wars and their aftermath. The Spanish CONSTITUTION OF 1812, which allowed more political participation by the creoles of Guatemala City, paved the way for independence. The repressive ruler Captain General José de BUSTAMANTE Y GUERRA (1811–1818) sought to insulate the Kingdom of Guatemala from the war for independence in neighboring Mexico, but a pro-independence sentiment became more open after the restoration of the constitution in 1820. The fiery Pedro MOLINA led those favoring independence, and when news arrived of the Mexican Plan of IGUALA, a council of notables in Guatemala City declared the independence of the kingdom on 15 September 1821. Guatemalan conservatives then succeeded in incorporating Guatemala and the other Central American states within Agustín de ITURBIDE's Mexican Empire in January 1822. When that empire fell little more than a year later, however, a Central American congress meeting in Guatemala declared its independence and established the UNITED PROVINCES OF CENTRAL AMERICA. In this turbulent period, however, the province of El Salvador had separated itself from Guatemala, and the state of Chiapas decided to remain with Mexico, leaving the state of Guatemala with approximately its present territorial configuration. (There would be a number of subsequent minor adjustments to its boundaries, most notably the loss of Soconusco to Mexico.)

As the largest province, Guatemala played a leading role in the Central American federation. It became embroiled in a bitter civil war (1826–1829) when the federal

president, Manuel José ARCE, intervened in the Guatemalan state government, removing its liberal governor, Juan BARRUNDIA, and replacing him with the conservative Mariano AYCINENA. When Aycinena usurped the power of the federal government (1827), Arce resigned and was succeeded by Vice President Mariano Beltranena, a Guatemalan and a kinsman of Aycinena. The civil war especially pitted Guatemala against El Salvador, but in the end liberal forces under Honduran General Francisco MORAZÁN triumphed and dealt vindictively with the conservative Guatemalans, exiling most of the leading figures. Barrundia was restored to the governorship of Guatemala. He was succeeded by Mariano GÁLVEZ (1831–1838), who, more than any other individual, established the liberal agenda for nineteenth-century Guatemala.

Morazán moved the federal capital to San Salvador in 1834. Under Gálvez the state of Guatemala launched major liberal reforms consistent with Morazán's policy against the conservative creole elite of the Guatemalan capital that had inherited much of the economic and social power of the Spanish colony. Strong anticlerical measures reduced the power of the clergy, and much of the church's land was auctioned off by the state to encourage more rapid export-led economic development. COCHINEAL (a crimson dye derived from insects that thrive on the nopal cactus), produced mainly around Antigua and Amatitlán, was the leading export, as the British demand for imports for its growing textile industry tied the Guatemalan economy closely to Belize and England. Gálvez also encouraged immigration, and his friendly policy toward northern Europeans, including a massive land grant for an English colonization scheme, caused opponents to charge that he was more sympathetic to foreign than to national interests. Political and judicial reform, notably the adoption of the LIVINGSTON civil and penal codes (1834) in a misguided attempt to replace the traditional Spanish legal system with a modern, English-based system, brought further opposition from lawyers and others. These reforms had created widespread opposition among both the Guatemala City elite and country people by 1836, when a serious cholera epidemic swept the country.

The government's well-intentioned efforts to control the cholera epidemic aroused the rural population, already aggrieved by the liberal reforms and encouraged by an irate clergy. Under the leadership of José Rafael CARRERA, a ladino from Guatemala City who had settled in Mataquescuintla after the civil war, isolated armed uprisings were united into a powerful guerrilla insurgency that brought down the Gálvez government on 1 February 1838. Divisions between the liberals hastened the downfall of Gálvez, and when the successor government—strongly influenced by the more radical liberals José Francisco BARRUNDIA and Pedro MOLINA—failed to meet the expectations of Carrera and his peasant guerrillas, it, too, fell. Carrera imposed a conservative government under Mariano RIVERA PAZ, who ruled most of the time between 1839 and 1844 and presided over a strong conservative reaction against the liberalism that had followed independence.

Carrera, meanwhile, supported by much of the conservative clergy, built a strong army. He was the real master of the country from 1839 until his death in 1865. While generally insisting on conservative policy, during the 1840s he trusted neither the liberal nor the conservative elite of the capital and tried to rule by using politicians from both factions. He became president of the state of Guatemala in December 1844, and in March 1847, strongly influenced by both conservative states' rights interests and British interests represented by Frederick CHATFIELD, he established the Republic of Guatemala. Guatemala was thus the first Central American state to declare its absolute independence from the now defunct Central American federation; the other states soon followed.

Liberal ascendancy in the legislature, however, combined with growing popular resistance, forced Carrera from office and into exile in Chiapas in August 1848. Unable to provide effective government or to quell the rural insurgency, the liberals soon turned power over to the military under Colonel Mariano PAREDES. Carrera then returned to highland Guatemala with a military force composed mainly of Indians. He quickly regained control of the country and on 3 August 1849 became commander in chief of the Guatemalan army. He consolidated his power in Guatemala with the unequivocal support of the conservatives while pursuing an aggressive policy against other Central American liberals, an effort that culminated in his stunning military victory over the "National Army"—composed of liberals from all of the states, but in which José Francisco Barrundia was highly instrumental—at San José la Arada on 2 February 1851. On 6 November 1851 he resumed the presidency and on 21 October 1854 formally became president for life, a virtual monarch with few restrictions on his power.

1850 TO 1900

Although strongly conservative and characterized by the active participation of the clergy in the government and legislature, after 1850 Guatemala accelerated its dependence on agroexports and began to pay more attention to infrastructure development. Coffee replaced cochineal as the principal export, and by the end of the conservative era it amounted to 50 percent of all Guatemalan exports. Until his death in 1865, however, Carrera prevented large-scale alienation of Indian lands for the coffee expansion.

Carrera also had a heavy hand in the affairs of his Central American neighbors, intervening directly in Honduras and El Salvador to maintain governments friendly to Guatemalan interests. In 1856–1857 Guatemala sent the largest number of troops to the NATIONAL WAR, a campaign in which Guatemala and the other Central American states combined forces to oust the North American filibuster William WALKER from Nicaragua. In Carrera's final military adventure, in 1863, Guatemala put down the rising Gerardo BARRIOS and restored more conservative rule in El Salvador. By 1865 Guatemala had achieved considerable stability and prosperity, but military repression and dictatorial rule had become characteristic of its government.

General Vicente CERNA (1865–1871) succeeded Carrera. He continued Carrera's conservative rule but was less concerned about protecting Indian land and labor from exploitation by coffee and other producers. Thus, the Cerna administration was a transition—especially in economic and social terms—to the Liberal Reforma that began in 1871.

Liberal opposition to the conservative dictatorship had been largely driven into exile under Carrera except for the presence of Miguel GARCÍA GRANADOS in the weak Guatemalan legislature. García Granados came from a prominent capital family, so the government tolerated his eloquent liberal oratory, but he could not rally much support in the otherwise repressive environment of Carrera's Guatemala. After Carrera's death, however, more violent opposition began to emerge, especially from Serapio CRUZ, who had expected to succeed Carrera, and from coffee planters and liberals in the populous highlands of western Guatemala. After the death of Cruz in 1870, Justo Rufino BARRIOS emerged as the military leader of the rebellion and Miguel García Granados finally joined it to form a provisional government in March 1871. The rebels defeated Cerna's army at San Lucas Sacatepéquez on 29 June 1871 and marched into the capital on the following day. García Granados became president, but his close ties to the elite of the capital led to a break with Barrios and other highlanders who wanted more sweeping reforms. In the election of 1873 Barrios won the presidency and became the first of a series of strong liberal dictators.

Barrios emphasized economic growth and courted foreign investment to begin the development of railroads and modern ports while greatly expanding the COFFEE INDUSTRY. He began the modernization of Guatemala City and Quetzaltenango and represented the coming to power in Guatemala of the liberal-positivist philosophy that would remain dominant until at least 1944. Barrios promoted strongly anticlerical legislation, suppressed the tithe, abolished the regular orders, expropriated church property, and vastly reduced the number of priests in the country; he also established religious liberty, civil marriage and divorce, and state collection of vital statistics. He launched a public education system at all levels and took the University of San Carlos out of the control of the church, making it the state university and establishing other secondary and normal schools. His educational reforms, however, benefited primarily the upper and middle sectors of Guatemala City and Quetzaltenango. Most rural Guatemalans continued to have little access to education and often now lost their village priests, who formerly had provided some education to parishioners. His restructuring of the university emphasized professional and technical education at the expense of the humanities and liberal arts, another reflection of positivist thinking.

Coffee exports soared as Barrios encouraged the encroachment of ladino planters on Indian communal lands and made their labor more accessible to planters. He notably improved the transportation infrastructure for overseas trade and facilitated formation of banks and other financial institutions to provide credit for economic development and modernization. New ministries of agriculture, development, and education reflected his emphasis on economic growth as well as the increased role of the state. He attracted foreign immigration and investment as German and U.S. influence increased notably. His administration also codified the laws and promulgated a new constitution in 1879, under which he was reelected in 1880.

In foreign affairs Barrios played an important role in the neighboring states of El Salvador and Honduras, and he settled differences with Mexico at the cost of giving up Guatemalan claims to SOCONUSCO and other parts of Chiapas. He renewed the Guatemalan claim to Belize, however, repudiating the WYKE–AYCINENA TREATY of 1859 with Great Britain. He also tried to revive the unionist spirit of Francisco Morazán and to reestablish the Central American federation by means of Guatemalan military power. That effort, however, ended abruptly in 1885, when Salvadoran forces defeated the Guatemalan army at CHALCHUAPA, where Barrios died in battle.

Barrios established a new "coffee elite," whose economic base was centered in the western highlands around Quetzaltenango, reducing the power of the Guatemala City merchant elite that had dominated the country since the late colonial period. At the same time, he greatly accelerated exploitation of the indigenous population and moved Guatemala more rapidly into an export-led economy dependent on foreign markets and investment. Although celebrated in Guatemalan history as the "Reformer" who ended the long conservative dictatorships of Rafael Carrera and Vicente Cerna, his own dictatorial rule and strengthening of the military established a pattern for subsequent liberal governments that made repression a characteristic of government in Guatemala extending to the present. Barrios's personal wealth increased enormously during his rule, especially in comparison with earlier Guatemalan presidents. In this, too, he set a pattern that many of his successors would emulate.

General Manuel Lisandro BARILLAS, a political favorite from Quetzaltenango, succeeded Barrios (1885–1892) and continued most of his development policies. Barrios's nephew, José María REYNA BARRIOS, succeeded to the presidency in 1892. When he was assassinated in 1898, another Quetzaltenango liberal, Manuel ESTRADA CABRERA, came to power and remained in office until 1920, his twenty-two-year rule being the longest uninterrupted presidency in Guatemalan history.

1900 TO 1950

Under Estrada Cabrera the liberal emphasis on economic development surged forward, while the political idealism of earlier liberals all but disappeared. Coffee exports continued to expand, but the most notable economic development was the rise of the UNITED FRUIT COMPANY (UFCO), which developed the banana industry in Guatemala's lowlands. Its subsidiary, the INTERNATIONAL RAILWAYS OF CENTRAL AMERICA, completed the railway from Guatemala City to the Caribbean, as well as other lines, and developed PUERTO BARRIOS as Guatemala's leading port. UFCO, with its transport subsidiaries, thus achieved the dominant position not only in banana production but also in Guatemala's internal and external transportation systems. While UFCO gave Guatemala much of the material progress that liberals had advocated since the 1820s, its enormous economic strength, its abuses of its power, its virtual monopoly over Guatemalan overseas transport, and its obvious foreign character made many Guatemalans resentful throughout the first half of the twentieth century.

Despite great economic advancement, the harsh repression, uneven economic gains, and corrupt government under Estrada Cabrera exposed his regime to growing opposition. His mental deterioration after 1918 contributed to the success of a plot that forced him from office in April 1920. The new Unionist Party took power under the presidency of a leading businessman, Carlos HERRERA, but in 1921 that government fell and Liberal Party generals José María ORELLANA (1921–1926) and Lázaro T. CHACÓN (1926–1930) ruled Guatemala for the remainder of the decade.

Despite their military appearance, the governments of the 1920s were more open and democratic than the Estrada Cabrera dictatorship that preceded them. For the most part, political participation was limited to rivalry among different segments of the elite, but labor unions and leftist parties, although not free from some repression, began to organize and gain some adherents. There was also continued economic growth, although most rural Guatemalans saw little of it, and as coffee and other agroexports expanded along with a more rapidly rising population, there began to be shortages of land for food production in some areas. The coffee elite retained strong control through alliance with the military, and fear of the major revolution taking place in adjacent Mexico kept them on guard against any genuine transfer of political power from the elite to the middle or working classes.

The Great Depression sharply arrested the modest progress of the 1920s. The value of coffee exports plummeted from $34 million in 1927 to $9.3 million in 1932.

By 1931 there were serious economic and social problems arising from declining exports and insufficient attention to subsistence agriculture. President Chacón became gravely ill, and upon his death in December 1930 the Assembly designated a civilian, Baudilio Palma, to succeed him. Palma served only four days, however, before a military coup replaced him with General Manuel Orellana on 16 December. In an effort to restore at least a semblance of constitutional government, however, Orellana resigned on 2 January 1931, turning the office over to José María Reina Andrade, who had been one of Estrada Cabrera's ministers and was now serving as president of the Assembly. Reina Andrade served until a pro forma election could be held; the Liberal Party candidate General Jorge UBICO Y CASTAÑEDA was overwhelmingly elected and took office on 14 February 1931.

Ubico built a strong political machine based not only on his military command but also on close alliance with the giant UFCO and with German coffee interests, at least until the outbreak of WORLD WAR II, when he quickly abandoned his pro-German stance and made Guatemala the first Latin American country to join the United States in declaring war against Germany. He began this regime with a strong crackdown on Communist and other leftist labor and political groups, assuring the elite that he was protecting them from the kind of revolution that was occurring in Mexico or the brief Communist uprising that had occurred in El Salvador in January 1932. A ruthless purge of these leftists left labor unions and opposition political parties impotent during Ubico's thirteen-year rule as their leaders were executed or exiled. Ubico also strongly supported the system of ensuring the coffee planters an adequate supply of cheap Indian labor for their harvests. He abolished debt peonage in 1934 but replaced it with a system based on a vagrancy law that required the peasants to work on the coffee FINCAS in a system resembling the colonial REPARTIMIENTO, which also provided workers for Ubico's ambitious road-building program. He reduced Indian autonomy by a new system of municipal government that replaced the Indian mayors with presidential appointees.

Opposition to the dictatorship began to surface during World War II. A strong anti-Fascist U.S. propaganda program attacking antidemocratic regimes, although directed against the Axis powers, had the effect of undermining the Ubico dictatorship in Guatemala. In addition, Ubico's expropriation of German-owned property in collaboration with the United States, although applauded by many Guatemalans who benefited by acquiring those properties and who had found the German "gringos" overbearing, nevertheless cost Ubico the support of a significant part of the coffee elite and resulted in a decline in Guatemalan coffee production. Moreover, wartime inflation hit the middle class hard. It was from this class, especially in the capital, that the most vocal opposition came, as university students began to stage demonstrations against the regime.

Opposition from students and intellectuals and other middle-class interests in the capital began to appear in 1942. After some street violence, Ubico, in ill health, stepped down on 1 July 1944 and turned power over to a loyal military junta, a member of which, General Federico Ponce Vaides, was subsequently elected provisional president by the Congress. When Ponce could not check the rising opposition, a coalition of civilians and middle-grade military officers forced the downfall of the regime on 20 October 1944. Major Francisco ARANA, Captain Jacobo ARBENZ GUZMÁN, and a civilian, Jorge Toriello, formed a junta that presided over the country until the inauguration of the new president, elected in December 1944. In the meantime, a constituent assembly wrote a modern constitution that codified the ideals of the Guatemalan Revolution of 1944.

In the late Ubico years, in the more complex Guatemalan socioeconomic environment that the Liberal economic growth had fostered, several new political parties representing disgruntled elite as well as middle-class and working-class interests formed underground. Most of these parties agreed on the candidacy of Juan José ARÉVALO, a young philosophy professor who had left Guatemala in protest against the Ubico dictatorship in 1934, soon after receiving his doctorate in Argentina. He had returned to Argentina and spent little of his adult life in Guatemala, but he had established a reputation as a learned man and one who had broken with Ubico. He won the 1944 presidential election in a landslide and began a five-year term dedicated to reforms that reflected both his Argentine experience and some obvious influence from the MEXICAN REVOLUTION.

As had been the case of Mexico, the Guatemalan revolution called for a return to the more idealistic liberalism of the early nineteenth century. It emphasized broader political participation, particularly of the middle and working classes, and was therefore friendly to renewed labor organization and a broad spectrum of political parties. It emphasized constitutional government, and the Constitution of 1945 was a twentieth-century charter that included many of the earlier liberal political guarantees while adding substantial social guarantees drawn from the Mexican Constitution of 1917. No reelection of a president and popular suffrage were important principles in reaction to the practice of CONTINUISMO under Estrada Cabrera and Ubico. Its strong support of labor required implementation of a modern labor code. There was also a hint of anticlericalism, bringing the opposition of the Roman Catholic hierarchy, which had begun to enjoy something of a rapprochement with the state under Ubico. The church would become one of the most important opponents of the revolutionary governments of Arévalo and Arbenz.

Arévalo idealistically described his ideology as "spiritual socialism." Opponents railed against the revolutionary government as "Communist," but more accurately it was an attempt to encourage enlightened capitalism in Guatemala with adequate provision for social justice and a healthier distribution of wealth. Its duration under Arévalo (1945–1950) and his successor, Jacobo Arbenz (1951–1954), nevertheless represented a revolution in the sense of challenging the exclusive power of the coffee and military elites that had ruled since 1871. The phrase "ten years of Spring" has been used by some who have written on the period to reflect the emphasis on popular participation and social benefits in comparison with the period both before and after.

Labor especially benefited from the revolution. The assembly abolished the vagrancy law of 1934 and the labor code provided a broad range of progressive rights to workers and their unions, but tangible benefits were much greater for urban than for rural workers. Marxists were in the vanguard of urban labor unions. Although Arévalo tolerated them, he made it clear that he was not their leader as he resisted Marxist attempts to establish a formal Communist Party. Arévalo, in fact, was one of a number of non-Communist social democratic leaders in the Caribbean region after World War II who represented what was often called the "democratic Left" in attempting to bring the emerging middle classes into more active participation in government and to provide a better distribution of wealth in their countries. Other notable members of this generation included José FIGUERES of Costa Rica, Juan BOSCH of the Dominican Republic, and Rómulo BETANCOURT of Venezuela.

THE ARBENZ PERIOD

A struggle over succession in the election of 1950 moved Guatemala more sharply to the left and led ultimately to the downfall of the revolution. Rivals for the presidency were the two military leaders of the 1944 revolt, Francisco Arana and Jacobo Arbenz. The more conservative Arana commanded the army and had protected the revolution by putting down a score of attempted coups. Arbenz, more to the left, was minister of defense and closer to Arévalo. When Arévalo and Arbenz suspected Arana of plotting a coup of his own, the assassination of Arana at Amatitlán in July 1949 paved the way for Arbenz's easy victory in the 1950 election. But Arana's murder triggered the most serious military coup attempt of Arévalo's administration. The growth of organized labor played a significant role here as a general strike in support of the government contributed to the coup's failure. In the election, Arbenz defeated General Miguel YDÍGORAS FUENTES, Ubico's minister of public works, who felt forced to flee the country in the face of rising violence during the election campaign.

Arbenz's election shifted the revolution markedly toward the left, especially with his strong rhetoric against UFCO and his talk of land reform. UFCO had responded to the threat with an active public relations campaign that marshaled U.S. public and government opposition to the Arbenz administration. Arbenz, much influenced by his wife, María Christina Vilanova de Arbenz, played into the hands of those opposing him by allowing Communists openly to organize a party and

by establishing a close relationship with the Marxist labor unions. The Guatemalan Communist newspaper, *Octubre,* added fuel to the fire with its blatant pro-Soviet and Marxist reporting. All this coincided with the election to the U.S. presidency of General Dwight D. Eisenhower, who appointed the zealous anti-Communist John Foster DULLES as secretary of state.

Arbenz's agrarian reform act, Decree 900 of 27 June 1952, laid the foundation for an expropriation of large landholdings that seemed to be aimed especially at UFCO, although it focused primarily on distributing public lands. Virtually no land in the highlands was touched by the act. Only 15 percent of the 650,000 acres owned by UFCO was marked for expropriation, but there was immediately a major dispute over Guatemalan compensation for this land, the government offering little more than $600,000 and the company claiming a value of almost $16 million.

The United States launched a diplomatic offensive against the Arbenz government in 1953, followed by a covert scheme of the CENTRAL INTELLIGENCE AGENCY to overthrow the regime in 1954 through its support of a small Guatemalan exile force commanded by Colonel Carlos CASTILLO ARMAS. Opposition to Arbenz within Guatemala was on the rise, although he still enjoyed wide popularity among urban labor and some elements of the middle class despite his resort to widespread repression of opponents after 1953. Success of the CIA scheme, however, depended on the refusal of the Guatemalan army to defend the Arbenz regime. The army thus remained the arbiter of Guatemalan politics, as it had been since the 1840s, but in this case it was strongly supported by the agroexport and commercial elite and the Roman Catholic hierarchy.

THE 1960s

The overthrow of Arbenz marked the beginning of one of the darkest periods in Guatemalan history, as a strong reaction against the revolutionary reforms under the presidency of Castillo Armas (1954–1957) resulted in the suppression of the labor movement and the repeal of nonenforcement of much of the social reform legislation, including the agrarian reform. With strong U.S. backing, Castillo Armas and his National Democratic Movement (MDN) set the tone for the next thirty years of military rule. The Communists and other leftists, to some degree united in the Guatemalan Labor Party (PGT), were outlawed and went underground. Divisions among the military, however, hindered the stability that might have been expected. After Castillo Armas was assassinated in July 1957, intense rivalry among the various military factions was accompanied by considerable corruption, but finally Miguel Ydígoras Fuentes emerged triumphant with his Rendención Party in the election of 1958. Ydígoras served until his overthrow in 1963 by another military faction led by Colonel Enrique PERALTA AZURDIA, who formed the Democratic Institutional Party (PID).

Ydígoras attempted to restore the traditional Liberal Party oligarchy—now greatly expanded with new agricultural and industrial enterprises resulting from large-scale U.S. investment encouraged by the Eisenhower and Kennedy administrations—while paying lip service to the middle-class and working-class interests stimulated by the Arévalo-Arbenz years. He cooperated in the establishment of the CENTRAL AMERICAN COMMON MARKET, which served the Guatemalan economy well. Less repressive than Castillo Armas, Ydígoras ran into difficulty when the Cuban Revolution alarmed right-wing Guatemalans. Ydígoras personally led the troops in putting down a Cuban-supported revolt in November 1960, but remnants of those insurgents escaped into the hills of eastern Guatemala, organized the Rebel Armed Forces (FAR), and launched a guerrilla war that continued into the 1990s. This activity, combined with Ydígoras's apparent willingness to allow Arévalo's candidacy in the approaching 1963 presidential election, led to his overthrow by Peralta, who ruled the country from 1963 to 1966.

Peralta attempted to create a broader base of support for his PID, which he compared to the corporate Mexican Institutional Revolutionary Party (PRI). He also intensified the anticommunism campaign and became heavily involved in efforts to suppress the leftist guerrillas. Peralta's Constitution of 1965 provided a framework for cooperation between the PID and Mario Sandoval Alarcón's National Liberation Movement (MLN)—successor to Castillo Armas's MDN—on the right and the Revolutionary Party (PR)—successor to Arévalo's Revolutionary Action Party (PAR)—on the moderate left. Out of this arrangement came a relatively free election, although it was restricted to those three parties. Violence soared as right-wing death squads murdered labor and leftist leaders and the guerrillas stepped up their campaign against government forces.

Not long before the election, the PR candidate, Mario MÉNDEZ MONTENEGRO, was probably assassinated (though his death appeared to be a suicide). His brother, Julio César MÉNDEZ MONTENEGRO, succeeded him as the candidate and with strong reformist support won the election, threatening widespread popular demonstrations if he were not allowed to take office. The PID accepted his presidency after Méndez's secret assurance that the army leaders would retain their power, thereby precluding any real change. Thus the repression continued, with strong U.S. counterinsurgency support, in an effort to stop the guerrillas, who were gaining support in the countryside although they controlled relatively little territory. A campaign of calculated terror led by Colonel Carlos ARANA OSORIO spread violence and lack of respect for human rights over the land as the army murdered thousands of people suspected of aiding the guerrillas. While Méndez enjoyed the distinction of completing his four-year term as the only civilian president of Guatemala between 1950 and 1985, he was unable to change the basic pattern of military rule and growing violations of human rights.

The FAR, led by Luis TURCIOS LIMA until his death in a car accident in 1966, was the principal guerrilla group, but in 1965 it divided, with Marco Antonio YON SOSA breaking away to form the MR-13. Yon Sosa died in a clash with Mexican troops in 1970, but both groups continued to harass the army. Some believed the army would not completely destroy the guerrillas because their presence justified continued high appropriations and other benefits for the military. In the 1970s two new guerrilla groups emerged—the Guerrilla Army of the Poor (EGP), which tended to replace the FAR, especially in the western highlands, where it tried to mobilize the Indians, and the Organization of the People in Arms (OPRA).

1970–1990

Arana Osorio, the PID candidate in 1970, campaigned openly on an anti-Communist platform that promised more repression. With the PR discredited, the rising Christian Democratic Party became the principal legal opposition to the military but was still too weak to have much of a chance; the PID easily won a controlled election in which fewer than half the registered voters participated. In the 1974 election General Kjell LAUGERUD continued PID domination of the country but faced a stiff challenge from a Christian Democrat (DCG)–led coalition that nominated a conservative military officer, General Efraín RÍOS MONTT. Confronted with obvious and widespread electoral fraud, the DCG claimed to have won, but the official results gave Laugerud the victory.

Laugerud, the son of a Norwegian immigrant, had served as Arana's chief of staff. He moderated the repressive appearance of the previous administration somewhat, although it remained a military dictatorship. There was some increase in labor union organization and opposition political activity, allowing the Christian Democrats in particular to gain ground. A devastating earthquake in February 1976 created special problems for his administration and stimulated opposition political activities, which were met with new repressive tactics.

In 1978 General Romeo LUCAS GARCÍA of the PID succeeded to the presidency in another fraudulent election in which voter abstention reached new heights (table 1).

Although by the early 1970s the expanding population and increased agroexport production were contributing to rising poverty in Guatemala, the economy also made impressive gains owing to diversification of agroexport production and industrial expansion. In Guatemala City business continued to expand and the growing middle class enjoyed affluence despite serious inflation. The petroleum crisis of the 1970s was less damaging to Guatemala than to many other Latin American states because of the exploitation of small but significant oil reserves in the Petén.

TABLE 1   Voter Abstention in Guatemalan Elections, 1944–1978

Year	Eligible Voters	Votes	Percent Abstention	Votes for Winning Candidate	% of Eligible Votes for Winning Candidate
1944	310,000	296,200	4.5	255,700	82.5
1950	583,300	407,500	31.1	266,800	45.7
1958	736,400	492,300	33.1	191,000	25.9
1966	944,200	531,300	43.7	209,400	22.2
1970	1,190,500	640,700	46.2	251,100	21.1
1974	1,568,700	727,876	53.6	298,953	19.1
1978	1,785,876	651,817	63.5	269,973	15.1

SOURCE: Adapted from Julio Castellanos Cambranes, "Origins of the Crisis of the Established Order in Guatemala," translated by David O. Wise, in Steve C. Ropp and James A. Morris, eds., *Central America: Crisis and Adaptation* (1984), p. 136.

The military elite had begun to enter the economy in a major way. Not only did the generals receive enormous salaries when they served as president, but they used their position to acquire private companies, large land-holdings, and monopolistic concessions. They established their own bank (Banco del Ejército) as another institutional base for their economic interests. The cor-ruption associated with this economic expansion and the wealth of these military officers reached obscene proportions in a country beset with staggering poverty among the majority of its population. Combined with the earthquake, the general downturn in the international economy had by the early 1980s caused falling prices for Guatemalan coffee, cotton, and sugar exports, while domestic inflation increased. Guatemala's trade deficit rose from $63 million in 1980 to $409 million in 1981.

Meanwhile, Lucas and the right-wing death squads launched a brutal policy of genocide against Indians suspected of supporting or joining the guerrillas, as Guatemala became notorious for its human rights violations. As the generals continued to seize large tracts of land, thousands of Indians fled into Chiapas, where large refugee camps sprang up. All this focused unfavorable attention on Guatemala and damaged the important tourist revenues. Under President Jimmy Carter, U.S. policy sought to distance itself from the Guatemalan military, ending official military aid altogether. Yet Carter's human rights policy only hardened the resolve of the Guatemalan officers to deal violently with the Left and even with moderate progressives such as the Christian Democrats. Guatemala simply made up a partial cutoff of U.S. arms sales with arms and advisers from Israel. Terror and assassination took a horrifying toll among labor leaders and University of San Carlos students and faculty. Meanwhile, the general economic level of the population worsened (table 2).

Following the 1982 rigged election of another PID general, Angel Aníbal Guevara, several younger officers, supported by elements in both the extreme right-wing MLN and the DCG, engineered a coup that prevented him from taking office, ousting Lucas during the last days of his term and replacing him with a junta headed by General RÍOS MONTT. The elevation of Ríos Montt to the presidency reflected not only an end to the long domination by the PID but also the phenomenal rise of evangelical Protestantism in Guatemala, for Gen-

Women weaving in Guatemala, 1980. LATIN AMERICAN LIBRARY, TULANE UNIVERSITY.

TABLE 2   Income Distribution in Guatemala, 1981

Percent of Population	Monthly Income (US$)
51.3	Less than $150
27.6	$151 to $300
8.4	$301 to $400
5.9	$401 to $900
3.5	$601 to $1,200
2.0	$901 to $1,200
1.3	More than $1,200

SOURCE: Inforpress Centroamericano, *Centroamérica, 1982, análisis económicos y políticos sobre la región* (1982), p. 131.

eral Ríos Montt was a minister of the California-based Evangelical Church of the Word (Iglesia del Verbo). Evangelical Protestantism had grown remarkably since about 1960, and an estimated 20 percent of Guatemala's population were Protestants by 1980. In contrast to the new Catholic evangelism in the country, which has been often associated with "liberation theology" and the political Left, most of the Protestants were conservative and identified with pro-U.S. policies.

Ríos Montt's brief presidency served as a transition away from direct military rule. Superficially there was a noticeable effort to curb corruption and to encourage a higher degree of ethics in government. More impressive was the decline of death-squad activities and the restoration of security and peace in the central highlands. Political assassinations in the cities virtually ceased and the decline of tourism, to which the violence had contributed, was reversed for a time.

The economic and military strength of the powerful generals who had ruled the country since 1954 could not be easily turned back, however, nor was Ríos Montt in any sense sympathetic to leftist interests. He and the officers he represented were concerned with preserving the privileged position of the military and perceived that military abuses and corruption threatened the institution. In the countryside, Ríos Montt stepped up efforts to defeat the guerrillas. Massacres of Indian communities continued, as did the flow of refugees into Mexico. His government inaugurated a system of civil patrols, requiring Indians to serve, usually without firearms, as guardians against the guerrillas. Those who refused were killed. Ríos also suspended the constitution, restricted labor unions, and prohibited the functioning of political parties in his effort to maintain order. In response, the leftists united in the Guatemalan National Revolutionary Union (URNG), an umbrella organization for the Guatemalan Labor Party (PGT), FAR, EGP, and OPRA.

Ríos's challenge to the military oligarchy, his constant moralistic preaching, the excessively large role of North American Protestants in his advisory councils, the imposition of a sales tax, and his meddling with powerful economic interests ensured that his regime was short-

lived. In August 1983 another coup replaced him with Defense Minister General Oscar Humberto MEJÍA VICTORES. Cynicism, corruption, and anticommunism were the most conspicuous characteristics of the Mejía government, with commitment to the same neoliberal policies on behalf of the elites that had characterized Guatemalan governments since 1954. However, concerned over their image and dismayed at their failure to manage the complex economic and social problems besetting the country, the officers decided to turn the government over to civilians. International pressure from human rights activists, a sharp decline in tourism, falling coffee prices, and the military government's inability to solve Guatemala's severe economic problems contributed to the army's decision to permit a free election and to turn over the presidency to a civilian.

Elections for a constitutional convention on 1 July 1984 again reflected widespread voter apathy, despite the participation of seventeen political parties. Under the resulting 1985 constitution, a free election was held and Guatemala was hailed for its "conversion" to civilian democracy after some three decades of military domination. A multitude of political parties ranging from extreme right to center vied for the presidency, while the left remained outside the legal political spectrum. A runoff between the top contenders resulted in the victory of a center-right and U.S.-backed Christian Democrat, Vinicio CEREZO. Popular participation in the election surged upward after years of declining voter turnout under the military regimes. A wave of optimism accompanied Cerezo's inauguration in January 1986, even though it was understood that he was strictly limited in his approach to the state's socioeconomic problems by the ultimate authority of the army.

Cerezo achieved some foreign policy successes as he established himself as a leader in the Central American peace process in alliance with Costa Rican President Oscar ARIAS. These efforts helped to end Nicaragua's civil war and bring about a free election there in 1990, opened talks between the governments and guerrillas in El Salvador and Guatemala, and laid the foundations for the Central American Parliament and a Central American summit conference to foster greater economic and political integration of the isthmus. Cerezo also moved toward resolution of Guatemala's long-smoldering dispute over sovereignty in neighboring Belize.

In domestic affairs, however, Cerezo ran into formidable obstacles. The new constitution emphasized open political dialogue and freedom of the press, yet the real power remained with the military. Furthermore, Cerezo not only failed to solve serious socioeconomic ills but saw them worsen considerably. During his administration labor and peasant participation in the political process remained weak, and as a result, at least in part, of the deteriorating economy, there was an increase in the level of violence not only from the guerrillas but also from right-wing death squads, the military, personal vendettas, and rising common crime. The economic decline was exacerbated by declining prices for Guatemalan exports, especially coffee, until a freeze in Brazil reversed the downward trend. The heavy foreign debt made balancing the budget impossible, especially when the government expanded the bureaucracy and appeared to tolerate widespread corruption and scandal.

Devaluation of the currency contributed to greater poverty during Cerezo's administration as inflation outran wages. Strikes and other work stoppages, especially in the public sector, seriously damaged government services. The Christian Democrats had appealed to middle-class and lower-class voters with promises of more social and economic benefits, but Cerezo's government carefully catered more to business interests, the military, and U.S. and international banking interests regarding the debt. Although it refused to turn over as much of the national resources to private ownership as U.S. advisers recommended, it privatized the national airline, Aviateca, and generally pursued conservative austerity programs in which the gap between rich and poor widened without reducing the debt significantly.

Ineligible for reelection (a legacy of the 1944 reaction to long dictatorships of the past), Cerezo left office in 1991, but popular rejection of his Christian Democratic administration was obvious when the DCG gained only a tiny minority of the popular vote in the November 1990 election. In a runoff between two conservative candidates on 6 January 1991, Jorge SERRANO ELÍAS won in a landslide, defeating newspaper editor Jorge CARPIO by a two-to-one majority. Serrano, of the relatively unknown Solidary Action Movement (MAS) before the election, gained many votes from those supporting Ríos Montt, who had been ruled ineligible. A born-again Christian, like Ríos Montt, Serrano became the first Protestant elected president in Latin American history. He promised to establish a ''social pact'' involving business, government, and labor. Voter apathy was again high, however, with 44 percent of the 3.2 million registered voters refusing to cast ballots in the November election and 54 percent abstaining in the runoff.

Serrano was careful not to antagonize the military, but as violence rose from both left and right, there was growing pessimism about his chances for success. Serrano, a forty-five-year-old industrial engineer, pursued neoliberal economic policies and was more acceptable to the conservative power structure than Cerezo. Like Cerezo, however, he failed to hold the real power, and disillusionment with the new democracy had become widespread by 1992.

No adequate general history of Guatemala exists in English. CHESTER LLOYD JONES, *Guatemala, Past and Present* (1940), is badly out of date, although it provides a useful summary of the earlier standard Guatemalan sources. It has been generally replaced by JIM HANDY, *Gift of the Devil: A History of Guatemala* (1984), a work which is best on the post-World War II period but includes a passable summary of earlier periods. Several general and period histories of Central America contain considerable coverage of Guatemala, including MURDO J. MAC-LEOD, *Spanish Central America: A Socioeconomic History, 1520–1720* (1973); RALPH LEE WOODWARD, JR., *Central America: A Nation Divided*, 2d ed. (1985); MILES WORTMAN, *Government and Society in Central America, 1680–1840* (1982); JAMES DUNKERLEY, *Power in the Isthmus: A Political History of Modern America* (1988); and LESLIE BETHELL, ed., *Central America Since Independence* (1991).

There is a larger body of more specialized works that provide better coverage on certain topics or periods, among which the following are representative: RICHARD N. ADAMS, *Crucifixion by Power: Essays on Guatemalan Social Structure, 1944–1966* (1970); KENNETH GRIEB's study of Jorge Ubico, *Guatemalan Caudillo* (1979); DAVID J. MC CREERY, *Development and the State in Reforma Guatemala, 1871–1885* (1983) and his *Rural Guatemala, 1760–1940* (forthcoming); CAROL A. SMITH, ed., *Guatemalan Indians and the State: 1540 to 1988* (1990); PIERO GLEIJESES, *Shattered Hope: The Guatemalan Revolution and the United States, 1944–1954* (1991); and RALPH LEE WOODWARD, JR., *Rafael Carrera and the Emergence of the Republic of Guatemala* (1992). A useful interpretation of contemporary Guatemala is VICTOR PERERA, *Guatemala: The Unfinished Conquest* (1993). In Spanish there are numerous works on Guatemalan history. Much of this work, as well as that of a number of foreign authors, will be included in the forthcoming multivolume *Historia general de Guatemala*, edited by JORGE LUJÁN MUÑOZ.

RALPH LEE WOODWARD, JR.

See also **Central America.**

GUATEMALA: CONSTITUTIONS. The 15 September 1821 Declaration of Independence for Central America led to the drafting of a Magna Carta by Central American delegates, including those from CHIAPAS. After a brief annexation of the isthmus by Mexico until 1823, the delegates convened again to reaffirm Central American independence. Chiapas, however, remained under Mexican authority. Influenced by the Spanish liberalism of the CORTES OF CÁDIZ and the U.S. Constitution, the representatives drafted the Constitution of the United Provinces of CENTRAL AMERICA, promulgated 24 November 1824. Within the following year, each of the member states (Guatemala, Honduras, El Salvador, Nicaragua, and Costa Rica) drafted its own constitution, under the same terms. These constitutions, including the 1825 Constitution of the State of Guatemala, incorporated the three classic branches of legislative, executive, and judiciary. They provided the states with important powers, including those of tax collection and the creation of armed militias, which would lead to the eventual deterioration of federal power.

At the outset of a period dominated by conservatives, the Guatemalan authorities declared secession from the federation on 17 April 1839. May of that year saw the installation of a new constituent assembly, which drafted various temporary constitutional laws, including the Law of Guarantees, aimed at supporting the basic management of the Guatemalan state. There were various conflicts with the liberals, and other constituent assemblies convened in 1844 and 1845, but they were dissolved because the documents they drafted did not entirely reflect conservative thought. In 1847 the central government officially declared the Republic of Guatemala, but in 1848 another constituent assembly was dissolved after drafting a new constitution that failed to be ratified.

After the battle of La Arada in 1851, when President Rafael Carrera attained absolute power in the area, a new, conservative assembly convened. In October of that year, the group issued a Constitutional Act consisting of eighteen Articles. Afterward Carrera became President for Life, a dictatorship that was endorsed by both the Church and the elite.

In 1871 the so-called Liberal Revolution broke out. A constituent assembly was formed in 1872, but its sessions were suspended a year later. In 1876 the assembly met again, but only to ratify the dictatorship of Justo Rufino BARRIOS. Another constituent assembly met in 1879 and put into effect in December of that year the Constitution which, except for a few changes, remained in place until 1944. It contained the liberal principles of the Constitution of 1824, including an article that limited the term of office. However, the vote was reserved only for literates and conducted by voice under the supervision of an official delegate, whom no one would dare to go against. Thus the elected representatives met two or three months out of the year in order to ratify whatever the president had mandated. Except during the presidencies between 1885 and 1898, this formalism supported what was in fact a dictatorship. After that year it was routine for the Congress to modify the Constitutional Article that limited the term of office, in order to permit the president to remain in power. Manuel Estrada Cabrera made use of this practice, maintaining a dictatorship that lasted from 1898 to 1920.

After Estrada Cabrera's ouster and the brief conservative administration that lasted until 1921, some constitutional amendments were made. In that year the liberals returned to power, and despite some conflicts, continued to govern. Jorge UBICO made use of the same practice as Estrada Cabrera, ignoring the limit which the Constitution placed on his term of office. The Revolutionary Junta of November 1944 put an end to the "liberal" Constitution. The new Assembly ratified a new Constitution in March 1945 that assured democracy. It guaranteed the free organization of employers' groups, unions and political parties which was previously denied, and allowed for freedom of opinion and of the press. It created a Social Security program and workers' tribunals. Its articles also established the principle of the "social function of private property," which would be the focus of great conflict. Finally, members of the oligarchy, both liberal and conservative, met to confront social reform, especially when it affected landholdings.

With the Washington-assisted ouster of the reformist administration in 1954, the Constitution of 1945 was thrown out and a new one promulgated in 1956. Without changing the state administrative structure outlined in the previous constitution, this one restricted the partic-

ipation of political parties and eliminated the concept of "the social function of private property." In 1963 the army took charge of the state and abolished the Constitution. Members of a new constituent assembly were chosen from among sympathizers with the authorities and from among the heirs of the liberals and conservatives. A new constitution, very much like the preceding one, was promulgated in September 1965. Authorized political parties remained subject to the State. The limit on the term of the presidency was respected, although military presidents predominated until the military coup in 1982.

Following the coup, differences among military leaders, and between the army and important landowners, were overwhelmed by a general insurgency that led to a violent civil war. Domestic and international opinion pressed for a new constitution that would expand democratic rights. A new constituent assembly, elected in a transparent manner, labored from 1984 to 1985, with little influence from the military. The new constitution and new electoral law contained important differences from their predecessors. Political parties are now free to operate and the rights of indigenous communities have been recognized. The Constitution calls for the creation of a Constitutional Court and a Human Rights Prosecutor designated by the Congress—both founded to confront violations of individual rights. It strengthens the role of Congress. A constitutional reform to restrict the army's activities in civil life is being considered.

LUIS MARINAS OTERO, *Las constituciones de Guatemala* (1958).

FERNANDO GONZÁLEZ DAVISON

GUATEMALA: ORGANIZATIONS

Economic Society of Guatemala
Sociedad Económica de Amigos del País de Guatemala

First established in 1795, the Sociedad Económica de Amigos del País de Guatemala was inspired by similar institutions in Europe and the New World that sought to spread the "new science" of the Enlightenment. Working in conjunction with the GAZETA DE GUATEMALA, a liberal news daily, the society sought to improve the economy of colonial Guatemala by encouraging free trade, establishing trade and technical schools, improving agricultural techniques, and challenging established economic interests. After independence, some of Guatemala's most prominent citizens, including José Cecilio del VALLE, played an active role in the society. With the failure of union in Central America, the society ceased to be an advocate of free-trade liberalism but continued to work to improve Guatemala's economy under the conservative guidelines established by Rafael CARRERA and his successors. It continued in operation until 1881, when Liberal President Justo Rufino BARRIOS disbanded it.

The society was established by royal decree in 1795,

with José Antonio de LIENDO Y GOICOECHEA, Alejandro RAMÍREZ, Jacobo VILLAURRUTIA, and Antonio Muró among the founding members. A school was established to teach arithmetic, hydraulics, optics, geography, and civil engineering. Through the *Gazeta*, articles were published by such Enlightenment writers as Buffon, Descartes, Locke, and Montesquieu. The society also presented scientific, historical, and social papers, one of which led to its suppression. In 1799, the society published a paper by Muró that argued that Indians be allowed to wear Spanish-style clothing, in essence defying a long-established practice in Spanish America. In 1800 the crown ordered the suppression of the society for this and other violations of the laws as recorded in the RECOPILACIÓN, the Laws of the Indies.

The Society was reestablished in 1810, at least partly to appease the growing voices of liberalism in the colony. Captain-General José BUSTAMANTE Y GUERRA was openly hostile to the society, and in the confusion of independence and its aftermath, it ceased to operate in 1821. In 1829 the Legislative Assembly reestablished the society, and José Cecilio del Valle was named its director. After an initial period of activity, the society again declined, then revived in 1840, this time under control of the Conservatives.

Throughout the nineteenth century, the Society worked to promote literacy, especially among the Indians; training in marketable skills, such as weaving, horticulture, and engineering; and the cultivation of cash crops such as coffee and cochineal. But its efforts were poorly organized and haphazard, and the advancement of the economy and education likely would have continued even had the society not existed. Its inability to significantly improve the education and economy of Guatemala only underscored the backward nature of the country in the late colonial, independence, and postindependence periods. Guatemala today still suffers from many of the ills first identified in the 1790s: a low literacy rate, overdependence on a single cash crop, and an Indian population that has yet to be integrated into the national political, economic, and social structures.

JOSÉ LUIS REYES MONROY, *Apuntes para una monografía de la Sociedad Económia de Amigos del País* (1954); ROBERT JONES SHAFER, *The Economic Societies in the Spanish World, 1763–1821* (1958); ELISA LUQUE-ALCALDE, *La Sociedad Económica de Amigos del País de Guatemala* (1962); RALPH LEE WOODWARD, JR., *Class, Privilege, and Economic Development: The Consulado de Comercio of Guatemala, 1793–1871* (1966).

MICHAEL POWELSON

GUATEMALA: POLITICAL PARTIES

Guatemalan Labor Party
Partido Guatemalteco del Trabajo—PGT

The PGT is a communist political party founded by José Manuel FORTUNY. The party evolved from the secretive Democratic Vanguard created in 1947, which changed its name to the Guatemalan Communist Party and gained legal recognition from President Jacobo ARBENZ in 1951. To avoid constitutional restrictions on political parties with international affiliations, the party dropped the word "communist" from its title and became the Partido Guatemalteco del Trabajo (PGT) in 1952. Attacked by opponents of the Guatemalan Revolution as a dangerous communist threat, in actuality the party had only modest political power. Party ranks never surpassed 4,000 members. PGT candidates failed to win more than four of the fifty-six seats in Congress. Party activists obtained subcabinet posts, but none achieved the level of cabinet minister. Party affiliates did, however, play important roles in agrarian reform and in labor organizations.

Banned after the fall of the Arbenz regime in 1954, the PGT went underground and operated clandestinely despite government persecution. The outlawed party sponsored guerrilla fronts in the early 1960s and in the 1970s. The PGT and three other rebel groups united to form the Guatemalan National Revolutionary Unity (URNG) in January 1982 to coordinate their antigovernment campaigns.

ROBERT J. ALEXANDER, *Communism in Latin America* (1957), esp. pp. 350–364; RICHARD GOTT, *Guerrilla Movements in Latin America* (1971), esp. pp. 31–90; GEORGE BLACK, with MILTON JAMAIL and NORMA STOLTZ CHINCHILLA, *Garrison Guatemala* (1984).

STEVEN S. GILLICK

National Guatemalan Revolutionary Unity
Unidad Revolucionaria Nacional
Guatemalteca—URNG

The National Guatemalan Revolutionary Unity was organized in January 1982 as a front for the four Guatemalan leftist guerrilla movements: the Guatemalan Labor Party—PGT (1949), the Rebel Armed Forces—FAR (1962), the Organization of the People in Arms—ORPA (1971), and the Guerrilla Army of the Poor—EGP (1972). It sought to stop repression and bring an end to the long Guatemalan civil war through negotiations with the governments of Marco Vinicio CEREZO (1986–1991), Jorge SERRANO ELÍAS (1991–1993), and Ramiro de León Carpio (1993–   ), but the government and the guerrillas failed to reach an accord.

JAMES DUNKERLEY, *Power in the Isthmus: A Political History of Modern Central America* (1988); PHIL GUNSON and GREG CHAMBERLAIN, *The Dictionary of Contemporary Politics of Central America and the Caribbean* (1991); VICTOR PERERA, *Unfinished Conquest: The Guatemalan Tragedy* (1993).

RALPH LEE WOODWARD, JR.

Revolutionary Action Party
Partido de Acción Revolucionaria—PAR

PAR, the major electoral vehicle of both presidents Juan José ARÉVALO (1945–1951) and Jacobo ARBENZ (1951–1954) during the revolutionary decade in Guatemala, was founded in 1945 by a merger of the two main parties of the October Revolution (1944), the Popular Liberation Front (Frente Popular Libertador—FPL) and the National Renovation Party (Renovación Nacional—RN). The party's ideological position was that of moderate socialism.

When the communist José Manuel FORTUNY was chosen secretary general in November 1946, the more moderate wing of the party left to reconstitute the FPL. In late 1947 Fortuny and his followers secretly formed a communist party, the Vanguardia Democrática Guatemalteca, but continued to use the PAR to legitimize their political activities. However, a coalition of socialists and noncommunist Marxists led by Augusto Charnaud MacDonald recaptured the party leadership in March 1949.

PAR was the major party in the coalition backing Arbenz in the 1950 elections. Shortly thereafter the Fortuny faction split from the PAR, and the democratic socialist faction of Charnaud MacDonald formed the Socialist Party (PS) in 1951. The PAR then joined the FPL, RN, and PS in creating the Party of the Guatemalan Revolution (PRG) in 1952 to support Arbenz's agrarian reform program, but it later withdrew. The PAR was dissolved after the overthrow of Arbenz in 1954.

RONALD M. SCHNEIDER, *Communism in Guatemala, 1944–1954* (1958); ASIES, *El rol de los partidos políticos en Guatemala* (1985).

ROLAND H. EBEL

Unionist Party
Partido Unionista

On 25 December 1919, thirty-one prominent citizens of the republic of Guatemala gathered with eighteen representatives of the capital's organized laborers to found a new political party, the Unionist Party. Created under the banner of Central American unity, the party announced in a pamphlet that its primary concern was the creation of a Central American republic. Despite the denials of party founders, all Guatemalans soon realized that the real purpose of the organization was to oppose the outdated and repressive government of Manuel ESTRADA CABRERA (1898–1920). The active participation in the establishment of the Unionist Party by distinguished members of the Guatemalan business community and prominent labor activists indicated the deep sense of disillusionment almost a half decade of Liberal POSITIVISM—with its consolidation of power in the presidency, absence of political democracy, and emphasis on economic development—had fostered.

In the early weeks of 1920 support for the Unionist Party grew rapidly and soon became extremely widespread. Even Estrada Cabrera's close relationship with the United States was not sufficient to impede the development of a unified opposition of students, urban workers, military officers, and a large proportion of the disgruntled elite under the Unionist banner. In response to a number of government arrests, the Unionists, with the support of the Guatemalan legislative body, the National Assembly, chose to attempt the removal of Estrada Cabrera on 5 April. The Assembly responded decisively on 8 April 1920 by declaring President Estrada Cabrera insane and electing Carlos HERRERA as the new president.

Unfortunately for Herrera and the Unionist Party, an economic crisis and the revival of traditional political animosities first weakened and ultimately destroyed the fragile Unionist government. Herrera's inability or unwillingness to heed the advice of his ministers and govern with authority and vigor when irresponsible journalism, labor unrest, or peasant discontent arose, was a major factor in his removal. However, most significant were the fears expressed by members of Guatemala's military and coffee elite, who accused the president and the Unionists of promoting unrest, failing to quell labor radicalism, and permitting outbreaks of peasant insurrections. By late 1921, it was obvious that Herrera had failed to satisfy the demands of the republic's coffee elite for stability and profitability. On the evening of 5 December 1921, three senior army officers led a successful military coup that forced Herrera to resign and effectively ended the Unionists' brief term in government.

RAFAEL ARÉVALO MARTINEZ, *¡Ecce Pericles! La tiranía de Manuel Estrada Cabrera en Guatemala* (1983), pp. 463–478; WADE KIT, "Precursor of Change: Failed Reform and the Guatemalan Coffee Elite, 1918–1926" (Master's thesis, Univ. of Saskatchewan, 1989).

WADE A. KIT

GUATEMALA: TERRORIST ORGANIZATIONS

Mano Blanca
White Hand

Formed in 1966 by landowners and politicians associated with the National Liberation Movement (MLN), this right-wing Guatemalan DEATH SQUAD justified its terrorist operations as a necessary part of the global struggle against communist subversion. Backed by the military and unrestrained by the police, it was one of several death squads that tortured, killed, and kidnapped reformists. The most notorious act of the vigilantes was the kidnapping of the reactionary Archbishop Mario Casariego in March 1968 in an effort to embarrass civilian president Julio César MÉNDEZ MONTENEGRO (1966–1970). Its terrorist actions supplemented the military's brutal counterinsurgency against the guerrilla movements of eastern Guatemala. In the early 1970s, the Mano Blanca disappeared as the military severed its long-standing connections to the MLN.

SUSANNE JONAS and DAVID TOBIS, eds., *Guatemala* (1974), esp. pp. 176–203; JAMES DUNKERLEY, *Power in the Isthmus* (1988), esp. pp. 456–461.

PAUL J. DOSAL

Ojo Por Ojo

Eye for an Eye, a right-wing terrorist group in Guatemala, emerged from the escalating violence of the late 1960s. Although it formally initiated operations in April 1970, some of its members were linked to the Mano Blanca, a terrorist group that had been operating since 1966. Like the other paramilitary groups, it was formed to check the success of the guerrilla movement in eastern Guatemala. Organized and supported by wealthy landowners and the military, Ojo por Ojo likely received assistance and encouragement from high-ranking government officials. One of its alleged leaders, Mario Sandoval Alarcón, was a prominent right-wing politician involved in the 1954 "liberation" and the subsequent purging of alleged Communists. Sandoval invoked the biblical injunction to take an eye for an eye to justify terrorist attacks on suspected leftist sympathizers. Ojo por Ojo targeted the "brains behind the guerrillas" at the University of San Carlos in Guatemala City.

MILTON HENRY JAMAIL, "Guatemala 1944–1972: The Politics of Aborted Revolution" (Ph.D. diss., University of Arizona, 1972); SUSANNE JONAS and DAVID TOBIS, eds., *Guatemala* (1974), esp. pp. 176–203; JAMES DUNKERLEY, *Power in the Isthmus* (1988), esp. pp. 456–461.

PAUL J. DOSAL

GUATEMALA, AUDIENCIA OF, an administrative unit of the Spanish colonial empire corresponding roughly to modern CENTRAL AMERICA. Properly, the term refers both to the territorial jurisdiction and to the highest royal tribunal located in it. The territorial unit was known also as the Kingdom of Guatemala, and for most of the colonial period it included what is today Guatemala, El Salvador, Honduras, Nicaragua, and Costa Rica as well as Belize and the Mexican state of Chiapas. Except for brief periods in the sixteenth century, it did not include Panama. The tribunal was known initially as the Audiencia of Los Confines (because its original seat was between the frontiers of Guatemala and Nicaragua), but it came later to be called simply the Audiencia of Guatemala.

EARLY HISTORY

The earliest Spanish governors in Central America were powerful, personalistic dictators whose claims to rule were rooted in the Conquest or in the defeat of rival Spaniards. These men, who included Pedro de ALVARADO in Guatemala and Pedro Arias de ÁVILA in Nicaragua and Panama, held royal commissions, but in practice they were only nominally subject to outside authority. The discovery of gold in Honduras and continuing abuses against the Indian population pointed to the need for a stronger royal presence in Central America proper.

In the NEW LAWS OF 1542, the Spanish crown created the *Audiencia de los Confines,* whose jurisdiction stretched from the Yucatán peninsula south to the isthmus of Panama. The new tribunal consisted of a president, Alonso de Maldonado (1542–1548), and three *oidores* (judges). In 1544, it established itself at Gracias a Dios, a gold-mining center in western Honduras. Gracias a Dios was isolated and a poor location for an administrative center. When its mines began to decline, it lost its early economic importance. In 1548, the crown ordered the transfer of the audiencia to SANTIAGO DE LOS CABALLEROS (modern Antigua), in the more populous and accessible central valley of Guatemala. Maldonado's successor, Alonso LÓPEZ DE CERRATO (1548–1555), supervised the move in 1549 and became known for his energetic enforcement of those parts of the New Laws designed to protect the Indians and restrict the *encomienda.*

The sixteenth century saw many adjustments and readjustments to the audiencia's jurisdiction. In 1550, the crown separated Panama from it and attached it to the Audiencia of Lima, which had also been created by the New Laws. In 1556, Guatemala gained jurisdiction over the Pacific Coast province of Soconusco, which had previously belonged to the Audiencia of Mexico, but four years later it lost the Yucatán peninsula to the same tribunal. The most radical change came in 1563, when the crown ordered the transfer of the audiencia seat from Santiago to Panama City. Although the audiencia regained jurisdiction over Panama, it lost Guatemala and part of Honduras, which were assigned to the Audiencia of Mexico. This arrangement proved unsatisfactory, however, and the crown soon reversed it. The audiencia returned to Santiago in 1570, with its previous jurisdiction restored. Panama's own audiencia, which the New Laws had dissolved, was reestablished, and this province thereafter remained independent of Guatemalan jurisdiction.

The Audiencia of Guatemala remained at Santiago for more than 200 years, until severe earthquakes in 1773 caused its relocation to newly founded GUATEMALA CITY, which would be its home until the region gained independence from Spain in 1821.

POLITICAL INSTITUTIONS AND SUBDIVISIONS

Spanish colonial audiencias embodied powers and functions that we would today separate into the modern categories of executive, legislative, and judicial. The president and *oidores* sat both collectively and individually as legislators and as appellate and first-instance judges. In Guatemala, initially, they also functioned as a collegial executive, but in 1560, President Juan Núñez de Landecho (1559–1563) received a separate commission as governor general, with powers equivalent to those of the viceroy of New Spain. Although technically subordinate to the Viceroyalty of New Spain, the president-governors of Guatemala governed autonomously and reported directly to the COUNCIL OF THE INDIES in Spain. The presidency itself evolved into a separate executive increasingly distinct from the audiencia, a development

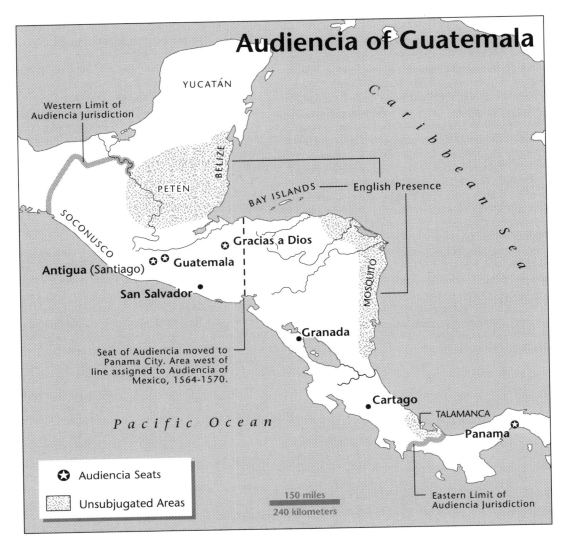

Audiencia of Guatemala

YUCATÁN

Western Limit of
Audiencia Jurisdiction

BELIZE

PETEN

SOCONUSCO

Caribbean Sea

BAY ISLANDS —— English Presence

✪ **Gracias a Dios**

✪✪ **Guatemala**

Antigua (Santiago)

San Salvador

MOSQUITO

Seat of Audiencia moved to
Panama City. Area west of
line assigned to Audiencia of
Mexico, 1564-1570.

Granada

Pacific Ocean

Cartago

TALAMANCA

Panama ✪

✪ Audiencia Seats

⬚ Unsubjugated Areas

150 miles
240 kilometers

Eastern Limit of
Audiencia Jurisdiction

favored by the need for a centralized military command, which resulted from the growing foreign threat in the Caribbean. Early presidents were all *letrados* (university-trained lawyers), but in the seventeenth century the crown began to occasionally appoint military officers, with the additional title of captain-general. The first military president was the Conde de la Gómera (1611–1626). Especially after the mid-seventeenth century, most presidents came from military, rather than legal, backgrounds.

At the local level, the audiencia's jurisdiction was divided into district magistracies, governed by officials known variously as CORREGIDORES, ALCALDES MAYORES, and GOBERNADORES (governors, but not to be confused with the early post-Conquest governors or with the presidents in their function as governors-general). Although their titles differed, in accordance with perceived differences in the importance of their jurisdictions, these magistrates were identical in powers and responsibilities, if not in pay and prestige. They governed independently of

each other and answered directly to the president and audiencia.

Salaries for all local magistrates were low, but opportunities to supplement one's income through corruption and abuse were great. Indeed, the crown expected its appointees to extract additional compensation from their Indian and MESTIZO charges. Such appointments provided a means of cultivating elite loyalty at minimal cost to the treasury.

ECONOMICS AND SOCIETY

Central America was a poor colony. Honduran mines continued to produce after the early boom played out, but their output was negligible. Cacao became a major export in the second half of the sixteenth century, but export peaked by the beginning of the seventeenth. IN-DIGO gained importance in the seventeenth and eighteenth centuries, and it transformed society and the landscape in what is today eastern Guatemala and El Salvador. Competition was stiff, however, and the most profitable world markets were closed to Central American producers because of mercantilist trade regulations.

Money was scarce in the colony, but Santiago, San Salvador, Granada, Cartago, and other cities and towns provided domestic markets for artisanries and foodstuffs. Much of this production was in the hands of Indian and mestizo communal and smallholders, but some prominent CREOLE families built substantial fortunes and large landholdings based on wheat, sugar, and cattle production, especially in the central valley of Guatemala. Also, the colonial economy was able to support a small but powerful clique of peninsular merchants, who allied themselves by marriage with landed creole families, controlled strategic sectors of the economy, and dominated the influential *cabildo* (city council) of Santiago.

WAR AND POLITICS

Despite the region's poverty, its strategic location between the Caribbean Sea and the Pacific Ocean made its security essential to the Spanish crown. Foreign incursions, which became more frequent throughout the seventeenth and eighteenth centuries, represented a chronic threat. Pirate raids were common on the Caribbean coasts, and buccaneers sacked Granada in 1665 and 1670. English interlopers established themselves in the Bay Islands (Islas de la Bahia) in the 1640s and at Belize in the 1660s; from these beachheads, they expanded their control to much of the Mosquito Coast during the following century. The colonial wars of the eighteenth century interfered with trade and placed a large financial burden on the colony as well.

The first priority of audiencia presidents throughout the colonial period was to maintain domestic order and to mobilize sufficient resources to pay for the fortifications, garrisons, and ships necessary to defend the province against foreign enemies. To this end, they made accommodations with local elites, who generally declined to be taxed, except on their own terms. The greatest financial burden fell upon the Indian population in the form of the tribute, or head tax. Indeed, the importance of Indian labor and production in general to the economic well-being of the colony was reflected in the fact that the attempts of the crown to prohibit exploitative and abusive practices by the colonial elite generally came to little. For example, the *repartimiento* (labor draft) for agriculture, which was abolished in New Spain in 1633, survived in the Audiencia of Guatemala until the end of the colonial period. Presidents found it expedient to wink at smuggling activities, both out of fear of provoking creole discontent and because illegal trade provided the needed specie to convert tribute payments in kind into cash, to pay other taxes, and to service the increasingly frequent "voluntary donations," *composiciones*, and other payments called for by the financially strapped crown.

Collusion with the entrenched colonial elite weakened Spanish government in Central America. Military presidents, such as Martín Carlos de Mencos (1659–1668) and Jacinto de Barrios Leal (1688–1695), frequently split with their lawyer colleagues on the audiencia and sided with local interests on questions that pitted them against royal policy. By the close of the seventeenth century, the colony had become factionalized and crisis-ridden. In an effort to maintain some control, the crown, between 1670 and 1702, commissioned no fewer than four general *visitas* of the province, none of which produced significant results, and at least two of which nearly provoked rebellions. The royal decision during the WAR OF THE SPANISH SUCCESSION (1702–1713) to raise funds by selling audiencia positions further weakened Spanish authority in the region.

BOURBON REFORMS

The energetic Bourbon monarchy attempted later in the eighteenth century to tighten its control over Central America and to extract greater revenues from it. Some reform measures undertaken were long overdue. The crown created a mint in Guatemala in 1733 in an attempt to stimulate mining production and to increase the amount of money in circulation. Measures to liberalize the commercial system, especially the Free Trade Decree of 1778, opened up economic opportunities for colonial exports. In 1793, Guatemalan merchants finally received permission to organize their own guild, or CONSULADO, independent of that of Mexico. The Bourbons also sought to reform the complicated and corrupt system of colonial administration. Peninsulars were favored over creoles for bureaucratic appointments, and a new office (regent of the audiencia, introduced in 1776) was designed to counterbalance the power of the president. A major restructuring of local administration occurred with the intendancy reform of 1786, which consolidated several smaller jurisdictions into four larger ones: Chiapas, Honduras, Nicaragua, and El Salvador. Guatemala remained separate, but the loss of control over the indigo-rich Salvadoran jurisdiction was a blow to the power of its merchant elite and contributed significantly to the development of a separatist tradition in Central America.

Although admirable from the point of view of efficiency, honest administration, and economic development, the BOURBON REFORMS undermined traditional accommodations and alienated established elites by closing them out of employment opportunities. Their economic benefits were largely undermined by the cost of ongoing warfare and by the earthquakes that devastated the capital city in 1773. Dissatisfaction with Spanish rule grew among the colonial elites, and although the strong-arm tactics of President José de BUSTAMANTE Y GUERRA (1811–1818) kept the colony quiet while wars of rebellion were raging elsewhere in the Americas, Central American creoles were receptive to independence when confronted with the collapse of royal authority in neighboring Mexico in 1821.

Two standard general works in English on colonial Central America are MURDO J. MAC LEOD, *Spanish Central America: A*

Socioeconomic History, 1520–1720 (1973), and MILES L. WORTMAN, *Government and Society in Central America, 1680–1840* (1982). A useful institutional study is CARLOS MOLINA ARGÜELLO, "Gobernaciones, alcaldías mayores y corregimientos en el Reino de Guatemala," in *Anuario de estudios americanos* 17 (1960): 105–132. On the impact of war and international rivalry, see TROY S. FLOYD, *The Anglo-Spanish Struggle for Mosquitia* (1967). Studies of political issues and conflicts in the sixteenth and seventeenth centuries include WILLIAM L. SHERMAN, *Forced Native Labor in Sixteenth-Century Central America* (1979); MURDO J. MAC LEOD, "The Primitive Nation State, Delegation of Functions, and Results: Some Examples from Early Colonial Central America," in *Essays in the Political, Economic, and Social History of Colonial Latin America*, edited by Karen Spalding (1982); and STEPHEN WEBRE, "Política y comercio en la Guatemala del siglo XVII," in *Revista de historia* 15 (January–June 1987): 27–41, and "El trabajo forzoso de los indígenas en la política colonial guatemalteca, siglo XVII," in *Anuario de estudios centroamericanos* 13, no. 2 (1987): 49–61. On the Bourbon period, see TROY S. FLOYD, "The Guatemalan Merchants, the Government, and the *Provincianos*, 1750–1800," in *Hispanic American Historical Review* 41, no. 1 (1961): 90–110; and RALPH LEE WOODWARD, JR., "Economic and Social Origins of the Guatemalan Political Parties, 1773–1823," in *Hispanic American Historical Review* 45, no. 4 (1965): 544–566, and *Class Privilege and Economic Development: The Consulado de Comercio of Guatemala, 1793–1871* (1966).

STEPHEN WEBRE

See also **Audiencia** and individual countries.

GUATEMALA CITY, the capital of Guatemala, whose 1991 population was estimated at 1.1 million. The New Guatemala of the Assumption, better known as Guatemala City, was founded officially in Ermita Valley on 2 January 1776 as the seat of the Realm of Guatemala. The former capital city of Antigua (Old Guatemala), situated 25 miles from the present capital, was destroyed by a series of earthquakes in 1773. The cooperation of all levels of society was needed to move the capital. One notable aspect of the move was the forced relocation of seventeen Indian settlements to the new city in order to provide it with a labor force and essential products. The landless mestizos rapidly populated the new city, and as of 1778 the city had a population of 10,841. In order to assist the development of an adequate infrastructure, the Spanish Crown halted the collection of taxes from the new city for ten years. One of the principal tasks was to provide drinking water.

The rebuilding of the Guatemalan capital during the last days of the colonial era was motivated not only by the earthquakes that devastated the original city but also by Bourbon political reforms of the last half of the eighteenth century. However, because of strong church as well as popular opposition to the relocation and the lack of resources, the new city did not achieve the physical stature or population size of Santiago until well after independence. In its physical as well as social structure it imitated the urban centers of Spain. Political independence in 1821 brought no significant improvement in living conditions for the city's population. On the contrary, in 1829 the wars of the UNITED PROVINCES OF CENTRAL AMERICA were waged in its streets, and in 1834 the president of the United Provinces, Francisco MORAZÁN, moved the seat to the city of San Salvador.

With the triumph of Rafael CARRERA in 1838–1840, the city experienced a second period of modest growth and stability as capital, first of the state of Guatemala, and after 1847, of the republic of Guatemala. The cultivation of kermes and the export of cochineal and coffee had a favorable impact on the city's economy. Projects begun in colonial days, such as the cathedral, were finally completed. The national theater (Teatro Carrera) was also inaugurated during this period.

With the arrival of the Liberals to power in 1871 and the impetus of a thriving coffee economy, the number of public projects grew as the functions of the state administration were expanded to meet the demands of the country's growing industry. New methods of transportation in the city were introduced, such as the horse-drawn tramway and the urban rail system. President José María REYNA BARRIOS backed efforts to beautify the city through the construction of new buildings and avenues.

During the dictatorship of Manuel ESTRADA CABRERA (1898–1920), Guatemala City experienced one of its worst disasters. In 1917–1918 it was almost totally destroyed by earthquakes. The poor were obliged to live in camps until the end of the 1920s. The ruin of the city was one of the factors contributing to the overthrow of Estrada Cabrera in April 1920. Subsequent governments applied themselves with little success to the task of rebuilding. The dictatorship of Jorge UBICO (1931–1944) initiated some of the most important infrastructural projects for the city, such as underground sewers. The present government palace was also built under Ubico.

The revolution of October 1944 brought about infrastructural development focused on athletic activities as well as new laws that encouraged people to rent houses in the city. Perhaps one of the most important urban reforms attempted in Guatemala in the twentieth century, the tenant law was stopped short by the counterrevolution of 1954. The earthquake of 4 February 1976, like the previous earthquakes, brought about changes and alterations in the city. Neighborhoods of low-cost housing grew due to the government's policy of selling inexpensive lots on which the victims of the disaster could build new homes. Since then the growth of the city has been augmented by the concentration of industrial and state administrative centers. The original city occupied an area of approximately 3.5 square miles. As of the early 1990s it encompassed between 35 and 40 square miles. Besides its agreeable climate, one of the Guatemalan capital's strongest attractions is the natural beauty of the valley in which it is situated. However, as is the case with many cities of Latin America, Guatemala City's deficiencies in public services are appreciable.

View of cathedral in Guatemala City. BENSON LATIN AMERICAN COLLECTION, UNIVERSITY OF TEXAS AT AUSTIN.

A comprehensive history of Guatemala City remains to be written, but GISELA GELLERT and J. C. PINTO SORIA, *Ciudad de Guatemala: Dos estudios sobre su evolución urbana (1524–1950)* (1992), is a useful beginning. On the movement of the city from Antigua to its present location, see INGE LANGENBERG, *Urbanisation und Bevölkerungsstruktur der Stadt Guatemala in der ausgehenden Kolonialzeit: Eine sozialhistorische Analyse der Stadtverlegung und ihrer Auswirkungen auf die demographische, berufliche, und soziale Gliederung der Bevölkerung (1773–1824)* (1981), and her briefer summary, "La estructura urbana y el cambio social en la ciudad de Guatemala a fines de la época colonial (1773–1824)," in STEPHEN A. WEBRE, ed., *La sociedad colonial en Guatemala: estudios regionales y locales* (1989), pp. 221–249. See also MARÍA CRISTINA ZILBERMANN DE LUJÁN, *Aspectos socioeconómicos del traslado de la Ciudad de Guatemala (1773–1783)* (1987); and PEDRO PÉREZ VALENZUELA, *La nueva Guatemala de la Asunción: Terremoto de Santa Marta, fundación en el Llano de la Virgen*, 2 vols. (1964).

Oscar Peláez Almengor
Gisela Gellert

GUATEMALA COMPANY, a trading company (sometimes known as the Pacific Company) formed in 1748 by a group of Guatemalan merchants in the wake of the Bourbon reform of the Sevilla–Cádiz monopoly over colonial trade. The reforms opened commerce to a wider number of Spaniards and colonists both to stimulate trade and to discourage smuggling. Inspired by the success of the Real Compañía Guizpuzcoana in the production and trade of cacao in Venezuela, the Guatemalans petitioned the crown in 1741 for the right to trade with Mexico, Peru, and Spain. The company was finally formed in 1748, and its merchants were especially interested in supplying the Honduran mining areas with Peruvian mercury and other goods, and in acting as the middlemen in the Pacific trade with Peru. Within a decade, however, the Peru trade had lost its importance for Central America, while the export of indigo to Spain, generally ignored by the Guatemalan merchants, had become lucrative. When the Guatemala Company finally turned its sights on the indigo trade, competition from Spanish merchants and Spanish capital prohibited the fledgling company from successfully entering this market. The company never got off the ground; Ramón de Lupategui exhausted the company's financial resources in Realejo, building only one of the two boats needed to launch the endeavor. This, combined with the decline of the Peruvian trade and competition from Spaniards, spelled the end of the Guatemala Company.

ROLAND DENNIS HUSSEY, *The Caracas Company, 1728–1784: A Study in the History of Spanish Monopolistic Trade* (1977); MILES L. WORTMAN, *Government and Society in Central America, 1680–1840* (1982); RAQUEL RICO LINAGE, *Las reales compañías de comercio con América* (1983).

J. David Dressing

See also **Bourbon Reforms.**

GUAYAQUIL, largest city in Ecuador (1992 population est. 1.6 million–2.3 million) and capital of Guayas Province. Located thirty miles upriver from the Gulf of Guayaquil, Guayaquil is situated on one of the best natural harbors of the Pacific coast of the Americas. It lies at the mouth of the Guayas River basin, a zone of approximately 25,000 square miles of exceptionally fertile land with countless navigable rivers. These geographic advantages have helped make Guayaquil the commercial heart of Ecuador.

Founded in 1531 (or 1535–1536) by Spanish conquistador Sebastian de BELALCÁZAR, the city enjoyed during the colonial period a modest prosperity as an important contraband entrepôt and the major shipbuilding center on the Pacific. In 1820 Guayaquil grew weary of the burden of Spanish war taxes and declared its independence, becoming a free city. However, in 1822 Simón BOLÍVAR attached the district of Guayaquil to Gran Colombia.

Agricultural exports have typically provided the mainstay of Guayaquil's economy. CACAO, grown in the adjacent lowlands, became an increasingly important export from the late colonial era forward, and from the 1870s to the 1920s cacao dominated Ecuador's economy. During this period Ecuador emerged as the world's leading producer of cacao. Following the 1920s price collapse brought on by African competition, exports from the region lagged. In the 1950s, however, exports of BANANAS brought a new period of prosperity to the city. Beginning in the 1970s Amazonian oil became the nation's chief export, eclipsing coastal products. Nevertheless, Guaya-

quil continues to serve as Ecuador's commercial center. The city is today home to what little light industry the nation has.

Until the early twentieth century, Guayaquil had a special notoriety as a disease-infested port. Recent research seems to affirm this judgment. Beyond a high incidence of lethal endemic respiratory and digestive afflictions, epidemics—yellow fever, bubonic plague, cholera, typhoid, and smallpox—repeatedly haunted the city.

Culturally, Guayaquil is distinct from Quito, the nation's other leading city. Indeed, the cities may be viewed as hostile competitors, two separate regional power bases in a nation profoundly divided by geography. Racism informs this contentiousness, with many white Quiteños regarding Guayaquil as uncommonly ugly, irreligious, and crass, peopled by racially "inferior" and illegitimate mixed-blood *montuvios*. At the same time, many Guayaquileños consider Quiteños to be prideful and sanctimonious, their ostentatious piety wrought with hypocrisy. If Guayaquileños are prone to a certain defensiveness (uncritically accepting the capital's claims to be the sole Ecuadorian bastion of "superior" European culture), they do tend to be more cosmopolitan, tolerant, and open than their sometimes reserved, provincial, and stern *serrano* counterparts.

This feud has punctuated Ecuadorian politics. For Guayaquil, the principal difficulty historically has been financial. Taxes on its commerce nearly always have

Anonymous painting of the wharf at Guayaquil, 1884. Reproduced from *América pintoresca*, 3d ed. (Bogotá, 1987). COURTESY OF EL ANCORA EDITORES.

been the most important source of government revenue, but these funds are controlled by the national government in Quito. This has led to recurrent clashes between the cities. Because Quito and the SIERRA are more populous than Guayaquil and the coast, the capital has prevailed in the struggles; Quito and the rest of the economically isolated sierra have continually claimed the largest share of government outlays. Battles between regionally based caudillos, sometimes representing the elite in each region, have traditionally vexed Ecuador. During the cacao years the prosperity of Guayaquil and the coast brought the two regions into closer balance, but after the collapse of cacao the advantage shifted back to Quito. After World War II the rise of mass urbanization in Guayaquil, coupled with the export boom in bananas, began a reconfiguration of regional political power, a development reflected in the emergence of coastal-based populist leader José María VELASCO IBARRA (president 1934–1935, 1944–1947, 1960–1961). But in the late twentieth century the flood of tax revenues from the export of ORIENTE oil has freed Quito from its fiscal dependence on Guayaquil, reducing coastal influence.

See LOIS CRAWFORD DE ROBERTS's pathbreaking study, *El Ecuador en la época del cacaotera* (1980), also available in English as LOIS JOHNSON WEINMAN, "Ecuador and Cacao: Domestic Responses to the Boom-Collapse Monoexport Cycle" (Ph.D. diss., University of California, Los Angeles, 1970). MICHAEL T. HAMERLY, *Historia social y económica de la antigua provincia de Guayaquil 1763–1842* (1973), also available in English as "A Social and Economic History of the City and District of Guayaquil During the Late Colonial and Independence Periods" (Ph.D. diss., University of Florida, 1970), provides some of the numbers. See also RONN F. PINEO, "Misery and Death in the Pearl of the Pacific: Public Health Care in Guayaquil, Ecuador, 1870–1925," in *Hispanic American Historical Review* 70, no. 4 (1990): 609–638; and *Economy, Society, and the Politics of Urban Reform: Guayaquil, Ecuador, 1870–1925* (forthcoming). JULIO ESTRADA YCAZA has written innumerable books and articles in Spanish on Guayaquil, including *El hospital de Guayaquil* (1974).

RONN F. PINEO

See also **Diseases; Public Health.**

GUAYAQUIL

General Strike of 1922

The collapse of international prices for Ecuador's monocultural export, CACAO beans, led to deteriorating economic conditions. Popular frustration increased as the government proved unable to remedy the situation. Inspired by an earlier successful railroad workers' strike, Guayaquil trolley and power company workers walked out, soon followed by nearly all worker groups in the city. Growing in strength, workers called for aggressive government action to maintain the slipping value of the sucre (Ecuador's national currency). On 15 November

1922, workers and their families held a mass downtown rally. Police and the military opened fire, killing at least three hundred. Eyewitnesses agreed that the attack was unprovoked. For Ecuadorian labor, the victims stand as martyrs to the union movement. Historical interpretations of the general strike vary: standard accounts depict events as another example of anarchist-led protest; recent work sees the uprising as more spontaneous, and not effectively led by any single group.

RONN F. PINEO, "Reinterpreting Labor Militancy: The Collapse of the Cacao Economy and the General Strike of 1922 in Guayaquil, Ecuador," in *Hispanic American Historical Review* 68, no. 4 (1988): 707–736. For a concise overview of the evolution of the labor movement, see RICHARD LEE MILK, "Ecuador," in *Latin American Labor Organizations,* edited by Gerald Michael Greenfield and Sheldon L. Maram (1987), pp. 289–305. Also worthwhile is PATRICIO YCAZA, *Historia del movimiento obrero ecuatoriano,* 2d ed. (1984). For the broader political economic context, see OSVALDO HURTADO, *Political Power in Ecuador,* translated by NICK D. MILLS, JR. (1985).

RONN F. PINEO

GUAYAQUIL: SHIPBUILDING INDUSTRY. Shipbuilding in Guayaquil, Ecuador, during the colonial period became one of the leading maritime and naval enterprises in the Viceroyalty of Peru. Virtually isolated from the Atlantic world, the Pacific colonies of the Spanish Empire early on had to develop shipbuilding independently to meet the needs of an empire that grew to stretch along the Pacific coast from Mexico to Chile.

The small port city of Guayaquil, located along the lower reaches of the broad Guayas River in modern Ecuador, possessed excellent access to a hinterland rich in shipbuilding timbers, especially the resistant and durable wood from the *guachapeli* tree. As traffic continued to grow between the Viceroyalty of Peru and Spain via the Isthmus of Panama, especially after the discovery of silver at Potosí in modern Bolivia in 1545, the shipyards at Guayaquil expanded to meet the needs of transporting silver north and European merchandise south.

The creation and expansion of the ARMADA DEL MAR DEL SUR in the wake of English and Dutch attacks on the viceroyalty in the 1570s and 1580s further stimulated the industry. All of the large royal galleons built in the sixteenth and seventeenth centuries to transport silver and protect the viceroyalty were constructed at Guayaquil, endowing the port with a strategic importance of considerable value in the defense of the Spanish Empire in the Pacific.

Commercially, the ships built at Guayaquil supported the development of a lively inter- and intra-viceregal trade that moved the colonies toward a greater self-sufficiency in the seventeenth century. Olive oil, wheat, sugar, cacao, tobacco, wine, textiles, wood, and myriad other products grown and produced along the west coast were carried on ship bottoms launched from the shipyards of Guayaquil. In 1590 there were about thirty-five to forty ships and barks in the merchant marine; a century later, at least seventy-two large seagoing vessels plied the waters of the Viceroyalty of Peru, most of them built in Guayaquil.

The earliest shipbuilders were Spaniards, caulkers and carpenters who brought their knowledge of shipbuilding to the New World. As time passed, increasingly larger numbers of blacks (slave and free) and mulattoes joined, and then supplanted, the original Spanish artisans and craftsmen. Indians and mestizos rounded out the work force in a typical seventeenth-century shipyard. For a major royal job (two large galleons were occasionally built at the same time), it was not unusual for virtually all citizens to be involved in the shipbuilding, from the Indian laborers felling trees in the interior to the master mulatto craftsmen overseeing the design.

By the eighteenth century, the industry was challenged by better ships from Europe, especially from France, which more and more frequently sailed into the Pacific to trade, navigate, and compete with ships built in the Viceroyalty of Peru. But the shipyards of Guayaquil proved the Spanish and colonials to have been an inventive and flexible lot, adapting to the necessities of trade and war at sea in a new environment with immense versatility and success.

The book that deals most directly with the subject is LAWRENCE A. CLAYTON, *Caulkers and Carpenters in a New World: The Shipyards of Colonial Guayaquil* (1980). A classic study of trade and navigation is WOODROW WILSON BORAH, *Early Colonial Trade and Navigation Between Mexico and Peru* (1954). For an economic history of the seventeenth-century viceroyalty as a whole, see KENNETH J. ANDRIEN, *Crisis and Decline: The Viceroyalty of Peru in the Seventeenth Century* (1985). On the defense of the viceroyalty, see CARLA RAHN PHILLIPS, *Six Galleons for the King of Spain: Imperial Defense in the Early Seventeenth Century* (1986); and PETER T. BRADLEY, *The Lure of Peru: Maritime Intrusion into the South Sea, 1598–1701* (1989).

LAWRENCE A. CLAYTON

See also **Mining.**

GUAYAQUIL CONFERENCE (1822), a meeting between the two revolutionaries SAN MARTÍN and BOLÍVAR. As an independent republic, the port city and province of Guayaquil in present-day Ecuador was of great interest both to José de San Martín in Peru and Simón Bolívar in Colombia. After annexing Quito following the Battle of PICHINCHA (24 May 1822), Bolívar rushed down to Guayaquil with a large contingent of Colombian troops to ensure that the port also "joined" the Colombian republic. He entered the city on 11 July 1822. Two days later he abolished the government, annexing Guayaquil on 31 July.

General José de San Martín landed in Guayaquil on 26 July to discuss the status of the port and the province as well as the future of the struggle for independence.

Although the province had not as yet been formally annexed to Colombia, it was totally in the control of that nation's troops. Thus, it was evident that the "question" of Guayaquil had been resolved in favor of Colombia. Although the two great liberators met several times during the next two days, the details of their conversations remain obscure. Apparently realizing that he could not complete the liberation of Peru without Colombian help, San Martín suggested that the two leaders collaborate. That proved impossible. San Martín then returned to Lima and resigned, leaving the field open for Bolívar, to whom ultimately fell the honor of completing the liberation of South America.

Subsequently, the nature of the Guayaquil meeting has generated much heat and little light as historians of Venezuela and Argentina have taken up their pens in support of national paladins.

WILLIAM H. GRAY, "Bolívar's Conquest of Guayaquil," in *Hispanic American Historical Review* 27, pt. 4 (November 1947): 603–622; GERHARD MASUR, "The Conference of Guayaquil," in *Hispanic American Historical Review* 31, pt. 2 (May 1951): 189–229; JULIO ESTRADA YCAZA, *La lucha de Guayaquil por el Estado de Quito*, vol. 2 (1984), esp. pp. 513–575.

JAIME E. RODRÍGUEZ O.

See also **Wars of Independence.**

GUAYAQUIL, GROUP OF, a circle of twentieth-century social protest authors. This literary movement began in 1930 with the publication of a collection of short stories, *Los que se van: Cuentos del cholo y del montuvio* (*Those Who Go Away: Stories of the Mestizos and Country People*), by Demetrio AGUILERA MALTA, Joaquín Gallegos Lara, and Enrique Gil Gilberto. The authors angrily denounced the racial and class inequities of modern Ecuador. The group, all young novelists from Guayaquil, sought in their work to offer a realistic depiction of life in Ecuador. As with others in the *indianista* tradition in Latin American literature, the Group of Guayaquil took the side of the exploited—the Indians, *montuvios*, blacks, mulattoes, CHOLOS, peasants, and workers—and attacked the exploiters—the elite, the overseers, the priests, and the local police. Two particularly influential novels focused on the government massacre of Guayaquil workers in 1922: Gallegos Lara's *Las cruces sobre el agua* (1946); and Alfredo PAREJA Y DIEZ CANSECO's *Baldomera* (1938). Other Ecuadorian authors who followed in this tradition were José de la Cuadra, Ángel Felicisimo Rojas, Pablo Palacio, Pedro Jorge Vera, Humberto Salvador, and, most notably, Jorge ICAZA CORONEL, author of the classic *Huasipungo* (1934).

For a discussion of Ecuadorian literature, see ANGEL F. ROJAS, *La novela ecuatoriana* (1948). For the political context, consult DAVID W. SCHODT, *Ecuador: An Andean Enigma* (1987).

RONN F. PINEO

See also **Huasipungo.**

GUAYAQUIL, REPUBLIC OF (1820–1822). The city of Guayaquil moved toward independence in 1820 as a result of growing local dismay over ever more burdensome imperial war taxes and the weakening of Spanish sea power on the Pacific coast. Guayaquil city leaders declared independence on 9 October, followed by a *cabildo abierto* to ratify the action. José Joaquín OLMEDO, poet, lawyer, *cabildo* member, and delegate at the Spanish Cortes in Cadiz, was the first governor of the republic. For Guayaquil several options but no clear consensus emerged: independence; joining Peru or Gran Colombia; or rejoining Spain. Given the continuing royalist military presence in the sierra, Olmedo sought the help of both José de SAN MARTÍN and Simón BOLÍVAR, hoping to avoid surrendering Guayaquil's independence to either. San Martín promised Guayaquil self-determination; Bolívar, however, saw Guayaquil as already comprising part of Gran Colombia. In May 1822 rebel general Antonio José de SUCRE defeated the last royalist resistance in the sierra, forcing a decision on the disposition of Guayaquil. Quito quickly joined Gran Colombia and pressured Guayaquil to do likewise, fearing that the latter might become independent or, worse, might join Peru. Bolívar flatly rejected Olmedo's repeated assertions of a Guayaquileño right to self-determination. His liberation army entered Guayaquil in July 1822, and he placed the city under his authority. Three thousand troops surrounded the city. Given the uncertain loyalties of the greatly outnumbered city militia, Olmedo saw no choice but capitulation. San Martín met with Bolívar at Guayaquil in July 1822 and accepted Bolívar's deeds as a fait accompli. To some Guayaquileños, Bolívar's coup brought "the last day of despotism and the first day of the same." Guayaquil's brief experience as an independent state reflected a long-coveted autonomy and continues to inform the region's sense of separateness.

ROGER DAVIS's Ph.D. dissertation, "Ecuador Under Gran Colombia, 1820–1830: Regionalism, Localism, and Legitimacy in the Emergence of an Andean Republic" (University of Arizona, 1983), provides an excellent extended discussion. For an overview of the period, see FREDRICK B. PIKE, *The United States and the Andean Republics* (1977).

RONN F. PINEO

See also **Flores, Juan José.**

GUAYAQUIL–QUITO RAILWAY. During the late nineteenth century Ecuador sought to emulate the success of other nations that had used RAILROADS to create commercial opportunities and to spread modernity. However, railroads are a technology poorly suited to Ecuador's rugged Andean topography. Under the initiative of President Gabriel GARCÍA MORENO (1861–1865, 1869–1875), in the 1860s Ecuador began construction of a rail line from the port of Guayaquil to the mountain capital in Quito. Work went forward haltingly. The line, completed in 1908, proved an astonishing engineering feat, rising some 10,000 feet in but 50 miles, crossing the Chan Chan River some twenty-six times. The 281-mile line reduced travel time between the coast and the capital from two weeks to about twelve hours. Unfortunately, the railway proved as expensive to operate as it had been to build, and the enterprise almost never showed a profit. The high hopes for it proved unrealistic: the sierra remained economically isolated. Worse, servicing the foreign debt incurred in building the railroad became a bitterly contentious issue.

Ecuadorian railway workers, as was frequently the case elsewhere in Latin America, spearheaded the nation's small labor movement. In October 1922 the railwaymen of Durán (near Guayaquil) won a stunning victory over the U.S. company that operated the line. Support for the workers' position by President José Luis Tamayo (1920–1924) proved decisive. Guayaquil workers soon followed the railwaymen's lead, launching a general strike in November 1922. This popular movement, however, was not successful, ending in a government massacre of the strikers.

DAWN ANN WILES, "Land Transportation Within Ecuador, 1822–1954" (Ph.D. diss., Louisiana State University, 1971), provides extended treatment of this topic. On financing, see the enormously valuable study by LINDA ALEXANDER RODRÍGUEZ, *The Search for Public Policy: Regional Politics and Government Finances in Ecuador, 1830–1940* (1985). On the labor movement, see RICHARD LEE MILK, "Growth and Development of Ecuador's Worker Organizations, 1895–1944" (Ph.D. diss., Indiana University, 1977). On events in 1922, see RONN F. PINEO, "Reinterpreting Labor Militancy: The Collapse of the Cacao Economy and the General Strike of 1922 in Guayaquil, Ecuador," in *Hispanic American Historical Review* 68, no. 4 (1988): 707–736.

RONN F. PINEO

See also **Alfaro Delgado, José Eloy.**

GUAYASAMÍN, OSWALDO (*b.* July 1919), Ecuadoran painter. Born in Quito, to a humble Indian family, Guayasamín demonstrated his artistic talents at an early age. In 1932 he began studies at Quito's National School of Fine Arts, graduating with honors in 1941. In the following year he had his first solo exhibitions, in Quito and Guayaquil. In 1943, Guayasamín received an invitation through Nelson ROCKEFELLER, who worked for the State Department, to visit the United States. This gave him the opportunity to study firsthand the works of masters like El Greco, Francisco Goya, and Pablo Picasso. The Mexican muralist José Clemente OROZCO, whom Guayasamín met and worked with for a brief period in 1943, had a major impact on the development of his painting, especially on the expressive distortions of the human figure. In fact, throughout decades of prolific work—in painting, drawing, and printmaking—Guayasamín's main pictorial subject has been the human figure, rendered in isolation or as a part of epic scenes, a symbolic carrier of the artist's quest for social and political justice.

137

From the late 1940s, the ideological and humanitarian appeal of his images, inspired by past and current struggles in Latin America, won Guayasamín commissions for large murals, created for public spaces like the Casa de la Cultura Ecuatoriana, Quito (1948); Centro Bolívar, Caracas (1954); Palacio del Gobierno, Quito (1958); and Barajas Airport, Madrid (1982). Exhibitions of his work outside Ecuador include those at the Museo de Bellas Artes, Caracas (1954); Pan-American Union, Washington, D.C. (1955); IV Bienal de São Paulo (1957); Palacio de Bellas Artes, Mexico City (1968); Museo Español de Arte Contemporáneo, Madrid (1972); Musée d'Art Moderne de la Ville de Paris (1973); the Hermitage, Saint Petersburg, Russia (1982); Museo Nacional Palacio de Bellas Artes, Havana (1985).

OSWALDO GUAYASAMÍN, *De orbe novo decades* (1989); RÉGIS DEBRAY, "Guayasamín et les hommes de maïs," in *Le Nouvel Observateur*, December 1973, reprinted in *Art d'Amérique Latine 1911–1968* (1992), 228–230; ANNICK SANJURJO, ed., *Contemporary Latin American Artists* (1993).

FATIMA BERCHT

GUAYCURUANS. *See* **Paraguay.**

GUDIÑO KIEFFER, EDUARDO (*b.* 2 November 1935), Argentine writer. Born in Esperanza, he was the son of Luis Gudiño Kramer, who wrote on the legendary gaucho Judíos in Entre Ríos at the turn of the century. Gudiño Kieffer never emerged as a major novelist in Argentina, but he attracted some attention in the 1960s and 1970s for his trenchant satiric characterizations of the mentalities and personalities that emerged from the cultural effervescence before the military coup of 1966 and the resistant countercultures it fueled. The effective destruction of this milieu by the DIRTY WAR in the 1970s, the concomitant pessimism the latter engendered, and the sober (if not postmodern) attitudes that accompanied the return to constitutional democracy in 1983 appear to have left Gudiño Kieffer without much material. Yet his most significant work, *Guía de pecadores en la cual se contiene una larga y copiosa exhortación a la virtud y guarda de los mandamientos divinos* (1972), with all of its baroque counterreformation intertextualities, is both an acerbic denunciation of the moral righteousness of the Argentine neofascism of the period and a biting characterization of individuals more marked by libertinism than libertarianism. Published at the pivotal time of the brief and ultimately failed transition to a Peronista-led democracy (the 1973–1976 parenthesis between almost two decades of military rule), *Guía* can be read as a parable of the irresolvable ideological dilemmas of urban Argentine society at that time. Gudiño Kieffer's narrative style is also notable for the incorporation of multiple colloquial registers of urban, multimedia-oriented life. *Carta abierta Buenos Aires violento* (1970) is an essay denouncing the violence in Argentine social life, a recurring emphasis in contemporary Argentine fiction.

RAÚL H. CASTAGNINO, "*Para comerte mejor* y la crítica social," in *Nueva Narrativa Hispanoamericana* 3, no. 2 (1973): 121–130; AUGUSTO TAMAYO VARGAS, "Lo antiguo y lo novísimo en la picaresca de Eduardo Gudiño," in *Cuadernos Hispanoamericanos*, no. 295 (1975): 199–203; JUAN EPPLE, "Entrevista: Eduardo Gudiño Kieffer," in *Hispamérica* 6, no. 18 (1977): 47–61.

DAVID WILLIAM FOSTER

GÜEGÜENCE, central character in a famous Nicaraguan folk dance. Although it was performed until well into the twentieth century, the *Baile del Güegüence* (Güegüence's Dance) dates from the sixteenth century. Through their performance the dancers portray the clash of two peoples and the ability of indigenous cultures to survive such assault, through passive resistance and syncretism. The cast of characters includes Spanish and CREOLE officials who make demands on Güegüence, representing the Indians and LADINOS. The dance itself, though highly comical and entertaining, contains a clear message as Güegüence evades the authorities' orders by feigning deafness and ignorance. Although Güegüence is portrayed as the more clever and resilient of the combatants, the dance ends in accommodation when the son of Güegüence marries the governor's daughter. Symbolically, such a union implies the merging of the two to create a new people, but Güegüence continues to lament the new conditions. The persistence and continued popularity of the *Baile del Güegüence* indicates its relevance for the indigenous elements of Nicaraguan and Central American society that continue to struggle with authority and a foreign culture.

DANIEL G. BRINTON, ed., *The Güegüence: A Comedy in the Nahuatl-Spanish Dialect of Nicaragua* (1883); ENRIQUE PEÑA HERNÁNDEZ, *Folklore de Nicaragua* (1968); FRANCISCO PÉREZ HERNÁNDEZ, *Estudios del folklore nicaragüense* (1968); EMILIO ÁLVAREZ LEJARZA, *El Güegüence: Comedia-bailete de la época colonial* (1977).

KAREN RACINE

See also **Music.**

GUEILER TEJADA, LIDIA (*b.* 1926), president of Bolivia (16 November 1979–17 July 1980). Born in Cochabamba, Gueiler, a graduate of the American Institute in La Paz, was trained as an accountant. She served as a deputy in Congress on two separate occasions and as ambassador to the Federal Republic of Germany, Colombia, and Venezuela. Her *La mujer y la revolución* (1957) was about the role of women in the 1952 Bolivian national revolution. She joined the Nationalist Revolutionary Movement (MNR) in the 1940s but went on to join the leftist Revolutionary Workers Party (POR) in the 1950s. In November 1979, Gueiler emerged as the compromise candidate between Walter GUEVARA ARZE and General

Alberto Natusch Busch, who had ended the former's short-lived interim government on 2 November. On 16 November, she became the first woman ever to be elected president of Bolivia.

Gueiler presided over a particularly difficult time in Bolivian history when relations between the armed forces and civilians were at their lowest level. Her mission was mainly to hold power until a new round of elections on 29 June 1980 could determine the next constitutional president. The elections went off as scheduled, but Gueiler could do little to prevent disgruntled sectors of the armed forces tied to drug traffickers from launching a coup on 17 July 1980 that ended Bolivia's return to democracy. Gueiler spent the next two years in exile. When democracy returned to Bolivia in October 1982, Lidia Gueiler was named ambassador to Colombia and later served as ambassador to Venezuela.

JAMES DUNKERLEY, *Rebellion in the Veins: Political Struggle in Bolivia, 1952–1982* (1984); RAÚL RIVADENEIRA PRADA, *El laberinto politico de Bolivia* (1984).

EDUARDO A. GAMARRA

See also **Bolivia: Political Parties.**

GÜEMES, MARTÍN (*b.* 7 February 1785; *d.* 17 June 1821), ruler of Argentina's northwestern province of Salta (1815–1821). Argentina's deep political divisions and Salta's peripheral location have combined to shroud Güemes in controversial, often erroneous images. No one, however, denies his forceful military leadership in ejecting Spanish royalists from the north. *Salteños* revere him as a patriot and defender of provincial autonomy against centralist political forces. Born and educated in Salta, Güemes joined the military as a cadet in 1799, at the age of fourteen. He first saw action during the English invasion of Buenos Aires in 1806. An aide to Santiago LINIERS, he received a promotion to the rank of lieutenant and later to general.

Güemes joined the independence forces after the revolution of May 1810. He led a military unit into Upper Peru that gained intelligence on royalist movements and disrupted their communications. Güemes then served in Montevideo and Buenos Aires. In March 1814, General José de SAN MARTÍN appointed him general commander of forces in Salta. The success of Güemes's GAUCHO cavalrymen in expelling the royalists from Salta created great popular support. Thanks to his kinship ties to the *salteño* landed elite, he was elected governor of the province in May 1815.

Like Juan Manuel de ROSAS in Buenos Aires Province, Güemes drew support from both the gaucho masses and elements of the landed elite. But he aroused strong opposition from political rivals and from some wealthy *salteños* with his taxation and land-reform proposals. He died ten days after being wounded by a royalist supporter, possibly with the complicity of local opponents. The anti-Güemes PATRIA NUEVA movement condemned

him as a tyrant. Yet he effectively held royalist forces at bay and led his province through a period of brutal warfare and political conflict.

ATILIO CORNEJO, *Historia de Güemes* (1946); ROGER M. HAIGH, *Martín Güemes: Tyrant or Tool?* (1968).

RICHARD W. SLATTA

GÜEMES-PACHECO Y PADILLA, JUAN VICENTE DE. *See* **Revillagigedo, Conde de.**

GUERRA, RAMÓN (*b.* 1841; *d.* 1922), Venezuelan caudillo. Guerra began his political and military career during the FEDERAL WAR (1859–1863), becoming a key figure in the Venezuelan political alliances of the era. He was an opponent of Juan Crisóstomo FALCÓN; both an enemy and temporary ally of Antonio GUZMÁN BLANCO; a successful military commander (1892) and later member of the Consejo Militar (1893) in the regime of General Joaquín CRESPO; and a crucial figure behind the victory of Cipriano CASTRO, whom he later opposed in LA LIBERTADORA REVOLUTION of 1901–1903. He supported the accession to power of Juan Vicente GÓMEZ and was part of the Council of Government. When that body dissolved in 1914, Guerra retired permanently from public life.

RAMÓN J. VELÁSQUEZ, *La caída del liberalismo amarillo: Tiempo y drama de Antonio Paredes* (1977); INÉS QUINTERO, *El ocaso de una estirpe: la centralización restauradora y el fin de los caudillos histórico* (1989).

INÉS QUINTERO

GUERRA-PEIXE, CÉSAR. *See* **Peixe, César Guerra.**

GUERRA Y SÁNCHEZ, RAMIRO (*b.* 31 January 1880; *d.* 30 October 1970), Cuban historian. Because of the intrinsic value and influence of his writings, Guerra, a native of Batabanó, Havana Province, is arguably Cuba's foremost historian of the twentieth century. Starting as a teacher in a modest rural school, he rose to become professor and director of Havana's Normal School, school superintendent of Pinar del Río Province, and national school superintendent. In 1932–1933 he held the position of secretary to the president's cabinet. He also represented Cuba as technical adviser to numerous missions abroad. In his books Guerra severely criticized U.S. policies toward Cuba and Spanish America. Many of them are still classic studies, such as his *Guerra de los diez años, 1868–1878*, 2 vols. (1950). None, however, has had the impact of *Azúcar y población en las Antillas* (1927), originally a series of newspaper articles; many editions of it have appeared, including an abridged English translation as *Sugar and Society in the Caribbean* (1964). This volume, a sober indictment of the dangers of latifundism in

Cuba, contributed greatly to shaping the views of the 1933 Cuban revolutionaries.

For a review in English of Guerra's work in the context of Cuban historiography, see ROBERT FREEMAN SMITH, "Twentieth-Century Cuban Historiography," *Hispanic American Historical Review* 44 (February 1964): 44–73.

JOSÉ M. HERNÁNDEZ

See also **Latifundia.**

GUERRA DOS FARRAPOS. *See* **Farroupilha Revolt.**

GUERRA GRANDE, Uruguayan civil war fought from 1839 to 1851. It was the longest and hardest fought in the country's history—hence the name "Great War."

The struggle originated in the rivalry between the Colorado and Blanco parties and their respective leaders, Fructuoso RIVERA and Manuel ORIBE. On 1 March 1839 Rivera became president for a second time, after overthrowing Oribe with the help of UNITARIO exiles from Argentina. Ten days later, under pressure from the Unitarios, Rivera declared war on the Argentine dictator Juan Manuel de ROSAS (himself allied to Oribe and the Blancos), an act that marked the beginning of the Guerra Grande.

Rivera defeated a first invasion from Argentina, but from 1842 to 1845 he suffered a series of defeats. With the help of Rosas, Oribe and the Blancos drove Rivera into exile in Brazil and confined the Colorado government to Montevideo, which for nine years remained under siege. Rivera returned to the struggle in the Uruguayan interior in 1846, but was removed from his command the following year. On each side, in fact, the war was marked by dissension among members of the respective Uruguayan parties and between those parties and their foreign allies.

Dissension was particularly severe on the Colorado side, pitting civilian party leaders against Rivera, and Colorados against foreign collaborators. The latter included not just the Unitarios, whose only interest was to overthrow Rosas, but the French and British, who in 1845 began a joint intervention in the RÍO DE LA PLATA over questions of river navigation and the interests of their own subjects. The outsiders' interests coincided with those of the Colorados only in that both groups opposed the apparent intent of Rosas to convert Uruguay into an Argentine satellite. Tensions also arose simply from the crowding of thousands of foreigners—from Argentine enemies of Rosas to such European volunteers as the future champion of Italian unification, Giuseppe Garibaldi—into besieged Montevideo.

The stalemate ended when Governor Justo José de URQUIZA of Entre Ríos Province, Argentina, broke with Rosas in May 1851. The Colorados quickly reached an agreement with Urquiza, whose subsequent advance into Uruguay caused Oribe and the Blancos to make

peace in October of the same year. The siege of Montevideo was lifted, the Guerra Grande was over, and Rosas himself was overthrown in February 1852.

Uruguayan Blancos would later look back on Oribe as having bravely defended national values against foreign intruders, whereas the Colorado version of history extols the heroic defense of Montevideo against the dictator Rosas and his Uruguayan lackeys. Both versions ignore the lack of clear policy differences between the parties and the fact that their leaders were often engaged in negotiations in the very midst of the struggle. But the legacy of the war was an intensification of Uruguayan partisan alignments that lasted into the twentieth century.

JOHN F. CADY, *Foreign Intervention in the Río de la Plata* (1929); JUAN E. PIVEL DEVOTO and ALCIRA RANIERI DE PIVEL DEVOTO, *La Guerra Grande 1839–1851* (1971); JOSÉ PEDRO BARRÁN, *Apogeo y crisis del Uruguay pastoral y caudillesco 1838–1875* (1974); JOHN LYNCH, *Argentine Dictator: Juan Manuel de Rosas, 1829–1852* (1981).

DAVID BUSHNELL

See also **Uruguay: Political Parties.**

GUERRERO, state of southern Mexico (pop. 2,174,162 in 1980) formed in 1849 from portions of the states of México, Michoacán, and Puebla. Guerrero is perhaps best known as the site of violent social movements from Mexico's 1810–1821 War of Independence to the leftist guerrilla campaigns of the 1970s. The capital of the state is Chilpancingo; its largest city is Acapulco (pop. 409,335 in 1980). The state encompasses 24,631 square miles of extremely diverse topography and climate, from warm and humid coastal plains to rugged and arid mountain ranges.

In the colonial period mulatto sharecroppers cultivated cotton on the coast for Mexico's domestic TEXTILE INDUSTRY, and Indian peasants and creole landowners produced food in the mountains and northern valleys for the silver mining center of TAXCO. Beginning in 1810, these social groups joined forces in the War of Independence, first under José María MORELOS Y PAVÓN and then Vicente GUERRERO. Fighting in the area ended when Guerrero and royalist commander Agustín de ITURBIDE issued the PLAN OF IGUALA in 1821. After independence Guerrero was largely an economic backwater, although it benefited briefly from the demand for cotton generated by Mexico's first protectionist industrial experiments. Federalist movements based on alliances between peasants and local elites led to the creation of the state in 1849 and to the Revolution of Ayutla in 1854–1855. The latter, led by former insurgent Juan ÁLVAREZ, began the period of Mexican national history known as the REFORM.

Subsequently Guerrero faded from prominence. Although peasant rebellions continued, they no longer were strengthened by alliances with local elites. The rapid economic development of the PORFIRIATO largely bypassed the area. Railroad construction reached only northern Guerrero. However, population growth and the legal assault on peasant village landholdings increased agrarian tensions. During the MEXICAN REVOLUTION local political activity was intense and confused. A rapidly successful movement against Porfirio DÍAZ later created a split along class lines, with most peasants eventually supporting Emiliano ZAPATA and his PLAN OF AYALA.

Guerrero has experienced little industrial development. TOURISM in Acapulco and other coastal sites became the largest generator of income in the 1960s, followed by remittances from those who had migrated to Mexico City and the United States. The area's continuing poverty fueled 1970s guerrilla movements led by Lucio Cabanas and Genaro Vázquez. Although these movements were repressed, opposition to the ruling Revolutionary Institutional Party (PRI) remains strong.

MOISÉS OCHOA CAMPOS, *Breve historia del Estado de Guerrero* (1968); FRANCISCO GOMEZ-JARA, *Bonapartismo y lucha campesina en la Costa Grande de Guerrero* (1979); IAN JACOBS, *Ranchero Revolt: The Mexican Revolution in Guerrero* (1982); *Ensayos para la historia del Estado de Guerrero* (1985); *Historia de la cuestión agraria mexicana: Estado de Guerrero 1867–1940* (1987); MOISÉS SANTOS CARRERA and JESÚS ÁLVAREZ HERNÁNDEZ, *Historia de la cuestión agraria mexicana, Estado de Guerrero: Épocas prehispánica y colonial* (1988).

PETER GUARDINO

See also **Mexico: War of Independence.**

GUERRERO, VICENTE (*b.* 10 August 1783; *d.* 14 February 1831), Mexican independence leader and politician. Born in Tixtla in the present state that bears his name, he joined the insurgent Hermenegildo GALEANA in 1810 under José María MORELOS. He continued the struggle after Morelos's defeat and death in 1815. In 1821 he joined Agustín de ITURBIDE's movement, emerging as one of the major military leaders after independence, but soon broke with Iturbide.

In the 1820s Guerrero, now a prominent populist, became the Grand Master of the YORKINOS (York rite Masons) in 1826. After losing the bitterly contested presidential election of 1828, he joined his supporters in the Revolt of ACORDADA, and became president in 1829. Guerrero attempted to introduce democratic programs as well as to address the nation's fiscal crisis. While dealing with the emotional issue of the expulsion of the Spaniards and mass politics, he also faced a Spanish attempt to reconquer Mexico in the summer of 1829. Although victorious against the invaders, the president faced a revolt by conservatives led by his own vice president, Anastasio BUSTAMANTE. He abandoned office in December 1830. But the Bustamante administration proved to be repressive and threatened the autonomy of the states. As a result, Guerrero was enticed to lead a revolt against the government that had driven him from office. Unable to defeat him on the field of battle, the Bustamante administration managed to capture him by treachery, then to court-martial and execute him.

WILLIAM F. SPRAGUE, *Vicente Guerrero, Mexican Liberator: A Study in Patriotism* (1939); ROMEO R. FLORES CABALLERO, *Counterrevolution: The Role of the Spaniards in the Independence of Mexico, 1804–38* (1974), pp. 47–142; MICHAEL P. COSTELOE, *La Primera República Federal de México, 1824–1835* (1975), pp. 178–274; JAIME E RODRÍGUEZ O., *The Emergence of Spanish America: Vicente Rocafuerte and Spanish Americanism, 1808–1832* (1975), esp. pp. 210–228; STANLEY C. GREEN, *The Mexican Republic: The First Decade, 1823–1832* (1987), pp. 140–209.

JAIME E. RODRÍGUEZ O.

GUERRERO, XAVIER (*b.* 3 December 1896; *d.* 1975), Mexican artist. Xavier Guerrero learned painting from his house-decorator father. In 1921, he collaborated with Roberto MONTENEGRO on murals in the old Colegio de San Pedro y San Pablo and with Diego RIVERA in 1922–1923 on his mural in the Anfiteatro Bolívar in the National Preparatory School in Mexico City. Later he assisted Rivera with murals in the Secretaria de Educación, where he used a fresco technique. When David ALFARO SIQUEIROS was commissioned by the Mexican government to paint a mural for the Mexican-donated Escuela Mexicana in Chillán, Chile (1941), Guerrero joined him and painted murals in Chillán and Santiago. He also did murals in Chapingo, Cuernavaca, and Guadalajara.

BERNARD S. MYERS, *Mexican Painting in Our Time* (1956); ANTONIO RODRÍGUEZ, *A History of Mexican Mural Painting*, translated by Marina Corby (1969).

SHIFRA M. GOLDMAN

GUERRERO Y TORRES, FRANCISCO ANTONIO (*b.* February 1727; *d.* 20 December 1792), Mexican architect. Guerrero y Torres, born in Guadalupe, is the most famous of the last architects of New Spain to achieve maturity and success before the establishment of the ACADEMIA DE SAN CARLOS and the subsequent adoption of academic neoclassicism. After he passed the examination for master architect in 1767, he designed buildings in a neoclassical style proper to New Spain (generally called *neostilo*), retaining the materials, taste for color, and many of the motifs of *estípite* baroque (or Churrigueresque). Favored by wealthy criollos of Mexico City, he designed and built palaces, notably those of ITURBIDE and of the counts of Santiago de Calimaya. Criticized by the Academia toward the end of his life, Guerrero y Torres nevertheless built, at his own expense and in his characteristic manner, the Chapel of the Pocito near the Basilica of GUADALUPE, between 1777 and 1791. It is generally considered his masterpiece.

HEINRICH BERLIN, "Three Master Architects in New Spain," in *Hispanic American Historical Review* 27 (1947): 375–383. IGNAcio f. gonzález-polo, *El palacio de los condes de Santiago de Calimaya* (1983).

Clara Bargellini

See also **Architecture.**

GUERRILLA ARMY OF THE POOR. *See* **Guatemala: Political Parties: National Guatemalan Revolutionary Unity.**

GUERRILLA MOVEMENTS. In Latin America, guerrilla movements can be divided into several periods. The pre-Marxist period includes colonial resistance movements, early independence revolts, and revolutionary movements of the late nineteenth and early twentieth centuries, typified by the Cuban independence movement, the mexican revolution, and the movement led by Augusto C. sandino in Nicaragua. They are the prelude to the *foco* guerrilla movements of the 1960s and 1970s, spawned by the victory of Fidel castro's cuban revolution in 1959. By the 1980s, other tactics had superseded the guerrilla cadre, such as the Indian focus of Guatemala's National Guatemalan Revolutionary Union (URNG) and Peru's Sendero Luminoso. All Latin American guerrilla movements, although they borrow from other groups, are primarily products of local rebel traditions.

These traditions began in the resistance to European colonization. Renegade bands (cimarrones, or Maroons) in inaccessible mountainous areas throughout Latin America offered sanctuaries for runaway slaves and Indians, who raided the European settlements. The sierra maestra in Cuba, the mountainous frontier areas of Nicaragua and El Salvador, the jungles of Petén and Yucatán, the Andes of Peru and Bolivia, the plains of Venezuela and Argentina, and coastal Brazil were all places that nurtured revolt.

In the eighteenth and nineteenth centuries, major guerrilla-style Indian revolts had temporary successes: those of José túpac amaru and Julián túpac catari in the Andes, and the caste war of yucatán. After independence, guerrilla-style armies were successful in Guatemala (José Rafael carrera), Cuba (José martí and Máximo gómez y báez), and Mexico (Benito juárez, Pancho villa, Emiliano zapata); in the 1920s and 1930s the anti-imperialist struggles of Sandino in Nicaragua and Agustín Farabundo martí in El Salvador inspired later guerrillas.

The modern guerrilla era began with Castro's successful revolution against Cuban dictator Fulgencio batista, launched in late 1958. Castro's twenty-sixth of july movement was inspired by radical Christian Democracy, not the Communist Party. Purposely invoking nationalism, Castro made the headquarters of his army the Sierra Maestra, in Cuba's easternmost province. This had been the sanctuary of Martí and Gómez y Báez.

There Castro, under the Marxist influence of his brother Raúl castro and Argentine professional revolutionary Ernesto (Che) guevara, developed the guerrilla tactics used later throughout Latin America. The main elements were a strong caudillist leader; revolutionary symbolism and myths utilizing movement leaders and past nationalist heroes; and a guerrilla nucleus (*foco*) inspiring national insurrection that was attached to, but not dependent on, local peasantry. After the Cuban triumph, Guevara proselytized this mixture (*focoismo*) as the winning revolutionary strategy for Latin America. He added the concept of the guerrilla as the revolutionary "new man," who, through the *foco* strategy, would make the "subjective" conditions necessary for revolutionary success. As articulated by Raúl Castro: "The *foco* is the little motor that sets in motion the big motor of the revolution."

With this formula, Guevara and Castro immediately started to urge other Latin revolutionaries to follow the example of the Cuban revolution, until then the only successful Marxist revolution in the hemisphere. Guevara's philosophy reached the masses through the articulate writings of the French intellectual Régis debray. The heyday of *focoismo* was the 1960s and 1970s. Historian Donald Hodges sees Guevara's philosophy developing in four "insurrectionary waves." The first was against Caribbean-style dictators; the second, starting in 1962, expanded the struggle to "pseudo-democratic" regimes in Central and South America; the third, called "many Vietnams," was launched against U.S. neocolonialism; and the fourth, after Guevara's death in Bolivia, was the urban *foco* struggle in Uruguay and Argentina.

The first wave, immediately after Castro's triumph, was a series of abortive attempts to land *foco* units in Panama, Nicaragua, the Dominican Republic, and Haiti. The second was more serious: Guevara saw the Andes as the Sierra Maestra of Central and South America; this period featured struggles in Guatemala, Venezuela, and Colombia, and a rising competition with orthodox communism over the viability of *focoismo*.

Colombia had the earliest Communist-backed guerrilla movement. The Colombian Communist Party (PCC) admitted in 1965 that it had undertaken guerrilla warfare as a secondary struggle in a prerevolutionary situation. This was necessitated by the 1964 government action to wipe out the independent peasant republics formed during La violencia (1948–1957). The partisans regrouped as the Southern Guerrilla Bloc, and at the PCC's tenth congress (1965) they united with other units to become the Revolutionary Armed Forces of Colombia (FARC). In 1964, tired of the defensive strategy of the Communist guerrillas (decried by Debray), the radical student Fabio Vásquez Castaño had formed an independent Guevarist guerrilla group, the Army of National Liberation (ELN). The radical priest Camilo torres restrepo joined it shortly before his death in 1965. Because the Communist Party always reverted to a noninsurrectionary strategy, the guerrilla movement in Colombia became just another player in the national anarchy.

As in Colombia, the Communist Party of Venezuela (PCV) gave ambivalent support to the guerrilla movement Armed Forces of National Liberation/National Liberation Front (FALN/FLN), led by a former army officer, Douglas Bravo. The PCV was originally pushed into supporting guerrilla action by the increasingly anticommunist stance of the populist president Rómulo BETANCOURT (1960–1962). However, legalization of the party in 1963 led to disavowal of guerrilla action and removal of Bravo and other guerrilla leaders from party leadership. This precipitated the major breach between *focoismo* and orthodox communism; Castro and Guevara (in absentia) supported Bravo and openly criticized the party. The conflict between young, revolution-prone New Leftists and older Communist Party functionaries had by then spread throughout Latin America.

At that stage, the third insurrectionary wave was in full swing. This consisted of a "Bolivarian/continental" strategy, using Bolivia as a central jumping-off point to encourage moribund guerrilla movements in Peru, Argentina, Chile, Uruguay, and Brazil. Guevara reasoned that the Cuban success had alerted the United States and its local bourgeois allies (thus rationalizing the lack of success for *foco* exports). Any revolutionary success would have to come through a prolonged "people's war." Vietnam, not Cuba, was the right model, and by 1967 Guevara hoped to spark "many Vietnams" in Latin America. The objective revolutionary conditions in Bolivia seemed perfect: peasant disillusion with a bourgeois land reform, low GNP, government reneging on mine labor reform, and increased encroachment by the United States into local politics. However, the preparations, strategy, and personnel were all faulty, and Guevara was captured and executed just months after establishing a guerrilla training camp in the Alto Beni area of southeastern Bolivia.

In Brazil, a variant of *focoismo* existed in Carlos MARIGHELA's (also Marighella) Action for National Liberation (ALN), which criticized Guevarism for depending on one *foco* location (impractical for the continental dimension of Brazil). Instead, ALN opted to organize urban masses indirectly and from the rural areas. Due to failure to find satisfactory rural sanctuaries, ALN's urban organizing attempts were ended faster by the police than those of guerrilla groups in Argentina and Uruguay.

The death of Guevara ushered in Hodges's fourth insurrectionary period of urban struggle, which Debray, along with Hodges, saw as the future hope. The essential aspect of Uruguay's Tupamarus was a political-military *foco*, revolutionary nationalism easily identifiable by the urban masses. Raúl SENDIC, a former student and union organizer, and Pedro GUILLÉN were the founders. An escalating series of spectacular robberies, kidnappings of prominent individuals, and reprisals against mounting

death squad activity ended in the brutal repression of September 1971; nearly 2,000 activists were captured and 29 were known dead.

Argentina's MONTONEROS, an independent urban guerrilla nucleus directed by Trotskyites, outlasted the Tupamarus by eight years. In 1959–1962, Cuban-style training camps were started by the Armed Forces of Liberation (FAL), a dissident Communist Party youth faction implementing Guevara's call to resist "pseudo-democratic" regimes. In 1969 the FAL evolved into the Montoneros, founded by Fernando Abal Medino and named after gaucho cavalry units in the 1810 War of Independence. The Montoneros were part of the radical Peronist wing, but after a series of urban disruptions (most famous the 1969 Corodobazo), kidnappings, and other urban actions, President Juan PERÓN officially broke with the Montoneros in May 1974. The military consequently cracked down on the Montoneros' rural *foco* in the city of Tucumán, and the Montoneros reciprocated by storming the army barracks at Monte Chingola. In 1977, the Treaty of Rome united the Montoneros and the Authentic Peronist Party (PPA) into the Montonero Peronist Movement. However, a month later the army effectively destroyed the People's Revolutionary Army (ERP), a Montonero army; and in 1979 a Montonero counteroffensive to the escalating DIRTY WAR of the military regime collapsed, ending the movement's effectiveness.

Mexico also had urban guerrillas in the 1970s. In 1974, the Fuerzas Revolucionarias Armadas del Pueblo (FRAP) kidnapped President Luis ECHEVERRÍA's father-in-law, the governor of Jalisco. In the mountains of Guerrero, 10,000 army troops took over a year to eliminate former schoolteacher Lucio Cabañas and his guerrilla army, after they had kidnapped a gubernatorial candidate, Senator Rubén Figueroa, and assassinated the Acapulco chief of police. Later in the 1990s, a guerrilla movement calling itself the Zapatista Liberation Front emerged in Chiapas. Just before his assassination the presidential candidate of Mexico's Institutional Revolutionary Party, Luis Donaldo Colosio, made a spectacular peace accord with the Zapatistas. However, as of early 1995, the Zapatistas were still active, and several political assassinations were attributed to them.

In 1979, as the Montonero downfall signaled the end of South American *focoismo*, two Central American guerrilla movements took the spotlight. The Sandinista National Liberation Front (FSLN) was founded in 1961 by Carlos FONSECA AMADOR and others who had gone into exile after the abortive attempt to oust Luis SOMOZA DEBAYLE during Guevara's "Caribbean dictators" stage of insurrection. Fonseca learned from the Cuban Revolution the need to fuse Marxism with local national and anti-imperialistic traditions. He thus studied the guerrilla campaign of Augusto César SANDINO, who led the Army for Defense of the National Sovereignty (EDSN) against a combination of the U.S. Marines and Nicaraguan National Guard from 1927 through 1933.

In contrast with the Cuban scenario, it was a coalition of middle-class and working-class urban mass organizations that provided the impetus that overthrew Anastasio SOMOZA DEBAYLE; the crucial battles were, therefore, fought by urban groups in Nicaragua's cities and towns, under guerrilla leadership. After triumph in 1979, the FSLN was attacked by a right-wing guerrilla force, the CONTRAS. On the Honduran frontier, it was composed of former Somoza National Guard members and peasants disaffected with Sandinista Marxism, and was supplied and trained by the CIA. On the Costa Rican border, a guerrilla group independent of CIA control, and led by former Sandinista "Captain Zero" (Edén PASTORA), fought a more modest campaign. The election in 1990 of Conservative President Violeta BARRIOS DE CHAMORRO ended both the active contra conflict and the Sandinista attempt to build a hybrid socialist society. Since then, various informal remnants of the contra movement, known as recontras, have kept up hostilities against both the government and former Sandinista opponents.

The history of the El Salvador guerrilla movement is more complicated than that of Nicaragua. The 1969 "Soccer War" with Honduras generated a crisis within the Salvadoran Communist Party (PCS), leading the party secretary, Salvador Cayetano Carpio, to found the guerrilla Popular Liberation Front-Farabundo Martí (FLP), named for Agustín Farabundo Martí, the popular Communist and former aide to Sandino who led the disastrous 1932 revolt that culminated in the MATANZA massacre of 10,000 to 30,000 Indian peasants. Carpio did not adhere to the *foco* theory, opting for the "prolonged people's war" concept of Vietnam and posited by Guevara in Bolivia. In 1972, however, a more middle-class group of Christian Democratic Party (PDC) deserters formed the *foco*-style Revolutionary Army of the People (ERP). Internal disputes in the guerrilla camps led to the assassination of the writer Roque DALTON and the suicide of Carpio. In 1980, the stalling of reforms by the new provisional government led to the formation of the umbrella opposition body, the Democratic Revolutionary Front (FDR), and to the establishment of a united guerrilla command (FMLN) as the military arm of the FDR in the same year brought on a decade-long civil war. In 1991, as a result of the collapse of Soviet support and U.S. impatience with the prolonged conflict, the FMLN and the government signed a demilitarization pact in exchange for political recognition of the Left.

In the 1980s and early 1990s, three other guerrilla groups took center stage, none of them *foco*-oriented. They claimed to represent Indian interests in Guatemala, Peru, and Chiapas, Mexico.

Marxist guerrilla activity started in Guatemala in 1960, when two army refugees from a barracks uprising, Marco Antonio YON SOSA and Luis Agusto TURCIOS LIMA, formed the 13 November Revolutionary Movement (MR-13). As in Colombia and Venezuela, the Communist Guatemalan Workers Party (PGT) initially spoke for all guerrilla groups, which united in the Communist-backed Rebel Armed Forces (FAR). The FAR broke up when the PGT dropped insurrection to back populist presidential candidate Julio César MÉNDEZ MONTENEGRO, who, upon election, allowed the counterguerrilla offensive that by August 1967 reduced the FAR, with a rural support unequaled in Latin America, to a handful of survivors hiding in Guatemala City.

By the 1980s, Guatemala's guerrillas were making a comeback under the umbrella organization National Guatemalan Revolutionary Union (URNG). Major new leftist guerrilla groups included the Guerrilla Army of the Poor (EGP) and the Organization of People in Arms (OPRA). The government's scorched-earth policy, "frijoles y fusiles" (beans and bullets), plus URNG's refusal to cater to Mayan interests, led to a guerrilla decline. The rebels made a comeback starting in 1985, but despite an Indian–guerrilla fusion group, the failure of the white-led Marxist guerrillas to endorse specific Indian issues (such as an autonomous Indian state) leaves the movement's future uncertain.

In Peru, the effort to rouse the Indian majority to insurrection was temporarily successful. Peru's long history of rebellion goes back to the first known guerrilla campaign: the INCA pretender MANCO CAPAC launched raids against the Spanish invaders from his Andes hideouts. The same tactic was repeated in the 1740s by Juan Santos ATAHUALPA. A century after the revolts of José Túpac Amaru and Julián Túpac Catari, Indian guerrillas in central Peru and Bolivia fought hacienda encroachment on lands of traditional Andean communities (AYLLUS). In 1963, Trotskyite peasant organizer Hugo BLANCO led an abortive uprising near the Inca capital of Cuzco, followed by *foco* guerrilla groups in south-central Peru. The most famous was the Movement of the Revolutionary Left (MIR), a radical APRA offshoot (APRA-Rebelde). These guerrilla groups of the 1960s and 1970s, although they spoke the Indian language and were integrated into Indian society, were co-opted by government agriculture reform, the basis of Indian discontent. However, by the 1980s reforms either did not work or were not implemented, creating a disillusionment receptive to the most extreme of all Latin American guerrilla groups, the Sendero Luminoso, named after the first nationalist Marxist philosopher José Carlos MARIÁTEGUI's allusion to a "shining path" (*sendero luminoso*) for Peruvian national aspirations.

Officially known as the Communist Party of Peru, a Maoist splinter of the Moscow-oriented Peruvian Communist Party, the Sendero was organized in the 1970s in Peru's most backward province, Ayacucho, where its claim that feudalism is the main obstacle still makes sense. Sendero has a hierarchical military structure topped by "President Gonzalo" (Abimael Guzmán); a strategy, opposite to the selectivity of *focoismo*, that has every party member also a soldier; and the prominence of women in intermediate leadership as well as the rank and file.

Victim of Sendero Luminoso, Ayacucho, Peru, 1984.
SYGMA.

However, as in Guatemala, no serious integration of Indian programs appears in Sendero's strictly Marxist communiqués. The surprise capture of Guzmán, on 12 September 1992 at least temporarily disoriented the organization.

On pre-Marxist guerrilla movements, see STEVE STERN, ed., *Resistance, Rebellion, and Consciousness in the Andean Peasant World, 18th to 20th Centuries* (1987), especially FLORENCIO MALLON, "Nationalist and Anti-state Coalitions in the War of the Pacific: Junin and Cajamarca, 1879–1902" and pt. 1 of the book, "From Resistance to Insurrection: Crisis of the Colonial Order." DONALD HODGES, *Intellectual Foundations of the Nicaraguan Revolution* (1986), provides detailed insights.

Works by guerrilla leaders or their theoreticians include FIDEL CASTRO, *Revolutionary Struggle 1947–1958*, edited by Rolando E. Bonachea and Nelson P. Valdes, vol. 1 of his *Selected Works* (1972). ERNESTO (CHE) GUEVARA published selected works (1970). The most notorious is *Handbook of Revolution*. The most erudite defense of *focoismo* is offered by RÉGIS DEBRAY, *Revolution in the Revolution?*, translated by Bobbye Ortiz (1967).

The tactics of Uruguay's Tupamarus are explained by that group's leading ideologue: ABRAHAM GUILLÉN, *Estrategia de la guerrilla urbana* (1965). Other works by guerrilla leaders include HUGO BLANCO, *Land or Death: The Peasant Struggle in Peru* (1972); CARLOS MARIGHELA, *For the Liberation of Brazil*, translated by John Butt and Rosemary Sheed (1971); CAMILO TORRES, *Revolutionary Priest: The Complete Writings and Messages of Camilo Torres*, translated by June de Cipriano Alcantara (1971), and *Douglas Bravo Speaks: Interview with Venezuelan Guerrilla Leader* (1970). First-hand accounts of life in guerrilla camps include CHARLES CLEMENTS, *Witness to War* (1984); and OMAR CABEZAS, *Fire from the Mountain*, translated by Kathleen Weaver (1985).

DONALD HODGES, *The Latin American Revolution: Politics and Strategy from Apro-Marxism to Guevarism* (1974), focuses on the fact that contemporary New Left movements sprang from earlier nationalism. His *Argentina, 1943–1987* (1988), is the main work on the Montoneros. RICHARD GOTT, *Guerrilla Movements in Latin America* (1971), focuses on Guevarism up to Che's death.

Works presenting negative appraisals of guerrilla movements include CARLOS IVAN DEGREGORI, *Que difícil es ser Dios* (1989), a Marxist criticism of the Sendero Luminoso; ROBERT MOSS, *Terrorism Versus Democracy* (1971), on the Tupamarus; THEODORE DRAPER, *Castroism: Theory and Practice* (1965); and TAD SZULC, *Fidel* (1986).

Other analyses of guerrilla movements are JOHN A. BOOTH, *The End and the Beginning: the Nicaraguan Revolution* (1982); JAMES DUNKERLEY, *Power in the Isthmus* (1988); and CAROL SMITH, *Indians and the State in Guatemala* (1990).

EDMOND KONRAD

See also **Communism; Political Parties; Revolutionary Movements** (under individual countries).

GUEVARA, ERNESTO "CHE" (*b.* 14 June 1928; *d.* 9 October 1967), Marxist revolutionary and guerrilla. Guevara was born into a middle-class family in Rosario, Argentina. He attended medical school in Buenos Aires and received a medical degree in 1953. Guevara traveled widely throughout Latin America and arrived in December 1953 in Guatemala, where he became active in the Guatemalan revolution and met exiled Cuban revolutionaries. When U.S.-backed forces toppled the Guatemalan government in 1954, Guevara fled to Mexico.

Guevara's Cuban friends introduced him to Raúl and Fidel CASTRO in Mexico City during the summer of 1955. Guevara joined Castro's rebel group as one of the eighty-two revolutionaries who landed on the coast of Cuba on 2 December 1956. When Castro created a second rebel column in 1957, he promoted Guevara to commander. Guevara and his troops were among the rebel forces that entered Havana on 2 January 1959.

Guevara championed insurrection against dictatorship and U.S. imperialism throughout Latin America. His book *Guerrilla Warfare*, published in 1960, offered a practical guide for aspiring revolutionaries. Guevara recommended the creation of guerrilla *focos* in the countryside to serve as bases of operations. From the *foco* guerrillas would serve as a vanguard and eventually create an invincible people's army. Guevara stressed that there was no need to wait for revolutionary condi-

145

Ernesto "Che" Guevara in Havana, Cuba, 1963. Reproduced from Lee Lockwood, *Castro's Cuba, Cuba's Fidel* (New York, 1969). LEE LOCKWOOD.

tions to develop; the insurrection itself would create such conditions. Guerrilla fronts, inspired by the Cuban model and Guevara's call to arms, emerged throughout Latin America in the 1960s, but these groups had limited impact.

Guevara played a central role in the early government of revolutionary Cuba. As director of the Industrial Department of the National Institute of Agrarian Reform (INRA), president of the National Bank of Cuba, and Minister of Industry, Guevara shaped the early economic policy of the revolution. He favored extensive state ownership of productive enterprises and central economic planning. Guevara sought to create a "new socialist man" dedicated to the revolution and motivated by moral rather than material incentives. He hoped ultimately to abolish money altogether. Castro sided with Guevara against opponents who favored reliance on market forces within a socialist framework, and Guevara's economic policies enjoyed official sanction until the late 1960s. Guevara also carried out numerous diplomatic missions abroad.

Eventually Guevara's influence in Cuban government waned. In 1965 he resigned his post as minister of industry. The reasons are obscure. Some scholars suggest

a falling out between Guevara and Castro, while others claim Guevara left to engage in guerrilla activity. Guevara planned to use Bolivia as a base for continental revolution, and he set up a guerrilla *foco* there in 1966. They launched their first military action in March 1967. The movement, however, suffered numerous difficulties, including failure to win the trust of local peasants, inhospitable terrain, internal divisions, and poor relations with the Bolivian Communist Party. Bolivian troops, assisted by U.S. military advisers, inflicted serious losses on Guevara's forces. A Bolivian army unit captured Guevara and his last followers on 8 October 1967. These same troops murdered Guevara the next day. His image and political theory, however, have remained an inspiration for Latin American leftists into the 1990s.

ERNESTO GUEVARA, *Guerrilla Warfare*, translated by J. P. Morray (1961); ANDREW SINCLAIR, *Che Guevara* (1970); MICHAEL LOWY, *The Marxism of Che Guevara: Philosophy, Economics, and Revolutionary Warfare*, translated by Brian Pearce (1973); ERNESTO GUEVARA, *Che Guevara and the Cuban Revolution: Writings and Speeches of Ernesto Che Guevara*, edited by David Deutschmann (1987); GARY PRADO SALMÓN, *The Defeat of Che Guevara: Military response to Guerrilla Challenge in Bolivia*, translated by John Deredita (1990).

STEVEN S. GILLICK

See also **Cuban Revolution.**

GUEVARA ARZE, WALTER (*b.* 11 March 1911), interim president of Bolivia (August 1979–November 1979). As a young lawyer, Guevara formed part of the post–CHACO WAR generation that founded the Nationalist Revolutionary Movement (MNR) in 1941. Guevara was the author of the 1944 *Ayopaya Thesis*, a manifesto that advocated sociopolitical rights for Bolivia's indigenous masses. He joined Víctor PAZ ESTENSSORO, Hernán SILES ZUAZO, and others in leading the MNR revolution of 1952. In 1959, owing mainly to the MNR's refusal to recognize his claim to the presidency, Guevara split with the party and founded the Authentic Revolutionary Party (Partido Revolucionario Auténtico—PRA). Several years later, in 1964, Guevara joined General René BARRIENTOS ORTUÑO to topple Paz Estenssoro and the MNR.

Guevara served several terms in Congress, was a cabinet officer for numerous governments between 1952 and 1974, and was Bolivia's ambassador to the Organization of American States, the United Nations, and France. The pinnacle of his career came in August 1979, when he was elected interim president of Bolivia following the failure of the nation's principal political parties to elect a head of state among the top three vote getters in the national elections.

Guevara was one of the principal opponents of military rule after the coup that toppled him on 2 November 1979. When democracy was reestablished in 1982, Guevara reclaimed his senatorship and played an important role as a frequent critic of the Siles Zuazo government. In the late 1980s, Guevara led a successful campaign to unite factions that had split away from the MNR. As a reward for his efforts, the MNR named him its vice-presidential candidate for the 1989 elections. His race was unsuccessful, however. In late 1993, he fell ill and ended most public appearances.

JAMES DUNKERLEY, *Rebellion in the Veins: Political Struggle in Bolivia, 1952–1982* (1984); and HORACIO TRUJILLO, *Los partidos politicos en América Latina: Partidos politicos y sistema de partidos en Bolivia* (1991).

EDUARDO A. GAMARRA

See also **Bolivia: Political Parties.**

GUGGIARI, JOSÉ PATRICIO (*b.* 17 March 1884; *d.* 1957), Paraguayan statesman and president (1928–1932). The son of Italian immigrants, Guggiari was born in Asunción, but as a young child moved to the interior town of Villarrica, where he received his early education. He returned to Paraguay to pursue legal studies and received a doctorate in law from the National University in 1910.

Guggiari began his political career by affiliating with the Liberal Party as early as 1903. At that time the Liberals were divided into various bickering factions unable to reach a consensus on overall policy for the country. Guggiari worked hard to reconcile these various groups. Though he was only partly successful, he gained a reputation as a level-headed and efficient democrat. He rose to the highest ranks within the party, as well as within the legislative branch of government. He was elected deputy in 1912, and in 1918 was chosen president of the Chamber of Deputies. Two years later, President Manuel GONDRA chose him to become interior minister.

The 1928 presidential election in which Guggiari defeated Eduardo Fleitas was widely regarded as the most honest up to that time. As president, he dedicated himself to the consolidation of Paraguay's democratic institutions after years of instability. These efforts, however, were eclipsed by the worsening dispute with Bolivia over the Gran Chaco region. The ensuing tensions indirectly brought about Guggiari's downfall. On 23 October 1931, university students protested his government's cautious response to Bolivian incursions by staging a rally in front of the National Palace. The police fired upon the assemblage, killing eight and wounding thirty. Mortified by these events, Guggiari resigned the presidency two days later. He died in Buenos Aires after a long exile.

WILLIAM BELMONT PARKER, *Paraguayans of To-Day* (repr. 1967), pp. 199–200; EFRAÍM CARDOZO, *Efermérides de la historia del Paraguay* (1967), pp. 401–402; CHARLES J. KOLINSKI, *Historical Dictionary of Paraguay* (1973), p. 117.

THOMAS L. WHIGHAM

GUIANA HIGHLANDS, the region in northern South America where Brazil, Guyana, and Venezuela meet at Mount Roraima at 9,094 feet. Most scholars mark the eastern boundary as the Essequibo River, but others extend the massif along northern Brazil and southern Guyana, Suriname, and French Guiana. The Highlands occupy almost half of Venezuela. Their waters drain into the Orinoco River on the west and north, into the Essequibo River on the east, and into the Negro and Branco rivers on the south. With elevations from 1,640 to 2,600 feet in most places but from 2,600 to 4,900 feet in others, the Highlands contain commercial amounts of manganese, nickel, bauxite, diamonds, gold, and iron. With some of the largest deposits of high-grade iron ore in the world, they explain Venezuela's development of its most underpopulated and underdeveloped state, Bolívar, and the location of Venezuela's hydroelectric power and iron and steel industries at Ciudad Guayana.

These resources are responsible for the ongoing boundary dispute between Venezuela and Guyana (British Guiana before its independence in 1966). The dispute, only over the easternmost part of the Highlands, but three-fifths of Guyana's territory, dates to the 1840s, when British agents pushed into the zone west of the Essequibo River. The Venezuelan claim rests on the string of missions that were planted in the eighteenth century along the major rivers and streams of the area but were destroyed as the result of the wars of independence and anticlerical measures of republican governments. Guyana's claim and current possession, not recognized by Venezuela, arise from a British presence there since the 1840s and an 1899 arbitration decision in its favor. In 1962 Venezuela presented historical documents with the "inside story" of why it would not abide by this decision.

For the Venezuelan point of view, see the excellent survey by JOHN V. LOMBARDI, *Venezuela: The Search for Order, the Dream for Progress* (1982). For Guyana's side, consult CHAITRAM SINGH, *Guyana: Politics in a Plantation Society* (1988).

MAURICE P. BRUNGARDT

GUIDO, BEATRIZ (*b.* 1925; *d.* 4 March 1988), Argentine writer. Guido's fiction exemplifies the literary production of Argentina during the 1950s, which was deeply influenced by a postwar European sensibility of ethical despair and the imperative to manifest a social commitment, especially in the creation of fictional characters obliged to participate as fully conscious individuals in the dirty business of life. Many Argentine writers, including Guido, manifested their adherence to this imperative by addressing the historical upheaval produced in their country first by Peronism and then by the rabid reaction to it by the traditionalist oligarchy. A Rosario native, Guido was superbly skillful in portraying the alternately oblivious and cynical moral corruption at the core of the power elite (more the landed gentry than the nouveaux-riches capitalists who at-

147

tracted the attention of a subsequent generation). Perhaps her two best works are her first, *La casa del ángel* (1954; *The House of the Angel*, 1957), of interest from a feminist perspective because of the dominant motif of the psychosexual abuse of the young female protagonist, Ana, and *El incendio y las vísperas* (1964; *End of a Day*, 1966), which centers on the torching in April 1953 by Peronista hoodlums of the Jockey Club, a legendary oligarchic bastion in Buenos Aires. The novel uses this event as an axis to portray the intersecting conflicts of two Peronista opponents: the decadent oligarchy and the emerging revolutionary left. Guido, whose novels provoked many outraged responses, saw several of her works filmed by her husband, Leopoldo Torre Nilsson, with whom she collaborated on numerous cinematographic projects.

ARTURO JAURETCHE, *El medio pelo en la sociedad argentina* (1966), pp. 193–216; FERNANDO PEDRO ALONSO and ARTURO REZZANO, *Novela y sociedad argentinas* (1971), pp. 184–193; BEATRIZ GUIDO, *¿Quién le teme a mis temas?* (1977); NORA DE MARVAL DE MCNAIR, "Adolescencia y hechizo en el mundo literario de Beatriz Guido: Tres variaciones en torno a un mismo tema," in *Círculo* 10 (1981): 29–40; JOSÉ A. MAHIEU, "Beatriz Guido: Las dos escrituras," in *Cuadernos Hispanoamericanos*, no. 437 (1986): 153–168.

DAVID WILLIAM FOSTER

GUIDO, JOSÉ MARÍA (*b.* 1910; *d.* 1975), provisional president of Argentina (1962–1963). Born in Buenos Aires, Guido worked as a lawyer in Viedma, Río Negro Province. He became active in politics as a member of the Radical Party. In 1958, he was elected senator from Río Negro. In the Argentine Senate he served as president pro tempore. When economic and political conditions led to a military coup against President Arturo FRONDIZI in March 1962, the Azul (Blue) faction of the Argentine army convinced him to accept the office of president in accordance with the Argentine Constitution.

Guido served briefly as a figurehead for the military leadership. Not surprisingly, with Congress dissolved and the majority PERONIST PARTY banned, his administration accomplished little. In accordance with the military's wishes, he issued an amnesty decree for rebellious officers of the army's hard-line Colorado faction in 1963. In July of that year, after the military approved new elections to maintain the semblance of civilian rule, he turned power over to Arturo ILLÍA (1963–1966).

MARVIN GOLDWERT, *Democracy, Militarism, and Nationalism in Argentina, 1930–1966: An Interpretation* (1972), pp. 188–197; GARY W. WYNIA, *Argentina in the Postwar Era: Politics and Economic Policy-Making in a Divided Society* (1978), pp. 122–125.

DANIEL LEWIS

GUILDS (GREMIOS), self-governing organizations that established and enforced rules for the production and sale of specialized goods. Members were artisans such as shoemakers, silversmiths, carpenters, and harness makers. Guilds flourished chiefly in the colonial era.

At the time of European exploration and conquest of the New World, the artisan trades of Spain and Portugal were organized in guilds, which dealt with economic life, and COFRADÍAS (lay brotherhoods), which supervised religious activities and social welfare for members. In the New World, migrant European craftsmen organized guilds initially to improve their social status and limit competition from indigenous producers. During the period 1545–1560, guilds were first established in the major cities of the viceroyalties of Mexico and Peru. Before the end of the century, guilds were sanctioned in secondary cities such as Guatemala City, Potosí, Guadalajara, and Puebla. Eventually, rudimentary craft organizations, if not recognized guilds, were formed in most Spanish colonial cities.

The self-interested initiatives of guild founders were supported by city governments, which sought to protect consumers from exorbitant prices and goods of shoddy quality. Municipal governments delegated a broad range of regulatory powers to guild authorities. Each guild maintained an effective monopoly of its market. It also determined membership and training criteria, the products that could be produced, prices, wages, and working conditions. From early times, religious, racial, and ethnic characteristics were used to limit access to guild membership.

Guilds were organized hierarchically in three ranks: masters, journeymen, and apprentices. Only masters could own shops and sell directly to the public. Masters also controlled all guild offices and the examination system that permitted younger craftsmen to achieve higher rank. In effect, these powers allowed masters to limit competition and favor the advancement of their own children and kinsmen.

Once guilds were in place, elected officers set prices and maintained quality control through inspections. They could assess fines, seize goods, and even close shops. Guild officers also served as judges and mediators when disputes arose among guild members or between guild members and customers.

There were fewer guilds organized in Brazilian cities. Those that were created lacked both the social status and independent economic power of the guilds in the Spanish colonies. In Brazil, the rapid development of SLAVERY and the integration of large numbers of slaves in artisan trades proved to be a major obstacle to the delegation of self-governing powers.

Essential elements of the European craft tradition were common even where guilds were not formally organized. Nearly everywhere, apprenticeship was regulated by contract. Parents, guardians, or the state placed young boys with master artisans for set periods. Contracts stipulated living conditions in the master's house and the skills that would be taught, and explicitly sanctioned the master's authority to discipline his apprentice. Recognized masters were also granted the right to supervise the promotion of journeymen to the rank of master. Most commonly an aspiring journeyman was required to demonstrate theoretical and practical knowledge and then produce a master work selected at random from a book of designs sanctioned by a European guild.

Colonial guilds were weaker than those in Iberia because they reflected colonial social relations that were forged by the Conquest and the Atlantic SLAVE TRADE. Although European artisans often recruited and trained apprentices among Amerindian, African, and mixed-race populations, efforts to exclude nonwhites from the rank of master or from guild offices led to racial divisions that undermined solidarity. Colonial authorities and powerful commercial interests also worked to limit the ability of artisans to restrict imports or eliminate competing production by indigenous groups.

By the eighteenth century, guilds were increasingly viewed as corrupt obstacles to economic progress. In Europe and Latin America, reformers associated with the ideas of economic liberalism sought to reform drastically or eliminate guilds. With the achievement of independence, the economic powers of guilds were nearly universally eliminated. Nevertheless, in many artisan trades a training regime based on apprenticeship was retained well into the modern period.

RAUL CARRANCO Y TRUJILLO, *Las ordeñanzas de gremios de Nueva Espana* (1932); MANUEL CARRERA STAMPA, *Los gremios mexicanos* (1954); LYMAN L. JOHNSON, "The Artisans of Buenos Aires during the Viceroyalty, 1776–1810" (Ph.D. diss., University of Connecticut, 1974).

LYMAN L. JOHNSON

GUILLÉN, NICOLÁS (*b.* 10 July 1902; *d.* 16 July 1989), Cuban poet. A contender for the Nobel Prize for literature, Nicolás Guillén was Cuba's national poet. He developed an early interest in poetry and published his first poems in *Camagüey Gráfico* in 1920. That same year he enrolled in the University of Havana to pursue a degree in law. For lack of interest and for financial reasons, Guillén left the university a few weeks later and returned to his native city, where he earned a living as a printer, a trade he learned from his father. With Vicente Menéndez Roque he edited the literary section of the newspaper *Las Dos Repúblicas* and contributed to *Orto* and *Castalia*, both literary reviews.

Guillén made a second attempt to continue his studies in Havana in 1921 but, as before and for similar reasons, he returned to Camagüey. That same year he gathered his poems under the title "Cerebro y corazón," which remained unpublished as a book until 1965. He also published his sonnets in *Alma Mater*, published the magazine *Lis*, and edited *El Camagüeyano*.

In 1926 Guillén went to work as a typist for the Ministry of the Interior in Havana, but continued to write and publish poetry. It was through Gustavo E. Urrutia, who invited the poet to write for a section he edited,

"Ideales de una raza," in the *Diario de la Marina*, that Guillén began to compose poems about Afro-Cubans, which resulted in the publication of *Motivos de son* in 1930. These poems, along with others by José Zacarías TALLET, Ramón GUIRAO, and Emilio BALLAGAS, became part of the Negrista movement of the 1920s and 1930s. In his poems Guillén explored the exoticism and rhythm of the other poets, but also added a social and cultural dimension about the lives of Cuban people of African descent.

After the *Diario de la Marina* ceased to publish Urrutia's column, Guillén continued to explore Afro-Cuban themes in Lino Dou's "La marcha de una raza," in the newspaper *El Mundo*. Subsequently, he published *Sóngoro cosongo* (1931) and *West Indies, Ltd.* (1934), which were more expressive about the subordinate conditions of blacks and their need to develop self pride not only in Cuba but throughout the Caribbean. During this period, Guillén was editor of the newspaper *Información* and the weekly *El Loco*.

Guillén's political life and literary activities began to merge. In 1935, as a result of his political activities, he was forced from his job at the Department of Culture. He became a member of the editorial boards of *Resumen*, a publication of the Communist Party, and *Mediodía*, which he edited when it was transformed into a politico-literary weekly. In 1937, with other Cuban and Latin American notables, he attended the Congress of Writers and Artists in Mexico and the Second International Congress of Writers for the Defense of Culture in Barcelona, Valencia, and Madrid. That same year he joined the Cuban Communist Party and the following year two of his poems were published in its newspaper *Hoy*. Guillén's *Cantos para soldados y sones para turistas* (1937) and *España: Poema en cuatro angustias y una esperanza* (1937), completed before his trip to Spain, address conditions mainly in Cuba and Spain, respectively, and belong to a period of ideological commitment.

For Guillén, the 1940s were characterized by an internationalist consciousness and extensive travel throughout the world. After an unsuccessful candidacy for mayor of Camagüey in 1940, he traveled to Haiti in 1942 and Venezuela in 1945, and later to Colombia, Peru, Chile, Argentina, Uruguay, and Brazil. *El son entero: Suma poética, 1929–1946*, published while he was in Buenos Aires in 1947, gathers poems written both prior to and following his travels. Following an unsuccessful run in 1948 as senatorial candidate for the Cuban Communist Party he returned to Havana. Other trips included attending the World Peace conference in New York City and meetings in Paris, Prague, and Mexico; he later traveled extensively throughout Eastern Europe and the Soviet Union. Between 1948 and 1958, he wrote and compiled his *Elegías*.

An active opponent of the BATISTA dictatorship, after 1953 Guillén lived in exile for six years and continued to travel in Latin America and Europe, where he received the Lenin International Peace Prize in 1954. Guillén lived in Paris from 1955 to 1958 and then moved to Buenos Aires, where he resided until Fidel CASTRO's revolutionary triumph. *La paloma del vuelo popular*, which contains six elegies, is a product of this period and was published in Buenos Aires in 1958. Guillén returned to Cuba on 23 January 1959 as a hero of sorts. In 1961 he became a member of the National Council of Education and was named president of the National Union of Writers and Artists of Cuba; he later joined the Central Committee of the Communist Party. *Tengo* (1964), *El gran zoo* (1967), *La rueda dentada* (1972), *El diario que a diario* (1972), and *Sol de domingo* (1982) draw upon Guillén's social and political concerns as well as his inventiveness and creativity in developing further his poetic talents, particularly so with *El diario que a diario,* but these later collections do not reach the levels of literary quality, innovation, or importance he attained in his early work. *Prosa de prisa, 1929–1972,* a three-volume collection of newspaper articles, was published in 1975–1976. Guillén is buried in the Colón Cemetery in Havana.

Nancy Morejón, Keith Ellis, Ángel Augier, and others have suggested that Guillén's poetry is limited to an ideological or revolutionary perspective. Other critics, however, such as Vera Kutzinski, Roberto González Echevarría, Antonio Benítez Rojo, and Gustavo Pérez Firmat place Guillén within a broader literary framework. For example, Pérez Firmat points to Guillén's interest in writing Italian sonnets and madrigals, González Echevarría to his fascination for Baroque poetry, and Benítez Rojo to the different stages in his career, shifting from Communist, to controversial, to subversive, and to philosophical positions. This more recent reading of Guillén confirms his greatness as a truly outstanding poet who appeals to a variety of readers.

NANCY MOREJÓN, ed., *Recopilación de textos sobre Nicolás Guillén* (1974) and *Nación y mestizaje en Nicolás Guillén* (1982); LORNA WILLIAMS, *Self and Society in the Poetry of Nicolás Guillén* (1982); KEITH ELLIS, *Cuba's Nicolás Guillén: Poetry and Ideology* (1983); ÁNGEL AUGIER, *Nicolás Guillén: Estudio biográfico-crítico* (1984); VERA M. KUTZINSKI, *Against the American Grain* (1987), pp. 133–235; VERA M. KUTZINSKI, ed., "Nicolás Guillén," in *Callaloo* 10 (1987); IAN I. SMART, *Nicolás Guillén: Popular Poet of the Caribbean* (1990).

WILLIAM LUIS

GUIMARÃES, ULYSSES SILVEIRA (*b.* 6 October 1916; *d.* 12 October 1992), Brazilian politician. Until his death in a helicopter crash off the coast of Rio de Janeiro, Ulysses Guimarães was one of Brazil's most prominent federal legislators. Although Guimarães suffered numerous setbacks during his lengthy career, including political repression, endemic legislative gridlock, and unsuccessful presidential bids in 1974 and 1989, his political persona symbolized a devout dedication to democratic principles in public service and national life.

As the long-standing president of the Brazilian Democratic Movement (MDB), which existed from 1966 to 1979, and its successor, the Brazilian Democratic Movement Party (PMDB), Guimarães led the party's legislative opposition to military rule and support of the restoration and extension of democracy. Guimarães played an instrumental role in the 1985 campaign for direct presidential elections, the 1987–1988 Constituent Assembly, and the 1992 impeachment proceedings against Fernando COLLOR DE MELLO. Toward the end of his political career, Guimarães's political influence faltered somewhat with the splintering of the PMDB into competing leftist and centrist parties.

A native of the state of São Paulo, Guimarães received a law degree from the University of São Paulo in 1940 and entered national politics in 1950 as a federal legislator for the Social Democratic Party (PSD). He served briefly as minister of industry and commerce (1961–1962) and represented the PSD in the Chamber of Deputies until 1966, when he joined the MDB. In 1974 Guimarães was the MDB "anticandidate" for president, running on a platform of opposition to repressive military rule. Although handily defeated by the military candidate, he remained a power broker throughout the 1970s and 1980s. Guimarães also represented Brazil in numerous international conventions.

"Ulisses Guimarães," in *Dicionário histórico-biográfico brasileiro* (1984), pp. 1,571–1,574; THOMAS SKIDMORE, *The Politics of Military Rule in Brazil, 1964–85* (1988); *Veja* (21 October 1992), pp. 16–31.

DARYLE WILLIAMS

See also **Brazil: Political Parties.**

GUINÉ, GUINEA, an imprecise European term for western Africa since the fifteenth century. To the Portuguese, "Guiné" indicated a large part of coastal West Africa to the south of Cape Bojador. To other Europeans, "Guinea" defined all of western Africa from the Senegal River to the Orange River in South Africa, with a further division into Upper and Lower Guinea. Guinea-Bissau was the site of a Portuguese fort and trading factory, which supplied many enslaved Africans to Latin America. Guinea-Bissau and the former French colony of Guinea are now independent countries in West Africa.

PHILIP D. CURTIN, *The Atlantic Slave Trade* (1969); JOEL SERRÃO, "Guiné," in *Pequeno dicionário de história de Portugal* (1987).

MARY KARASCH

See also **Africa, Portuguese; Slavery; Slave Trade.**

GÜIRALDES, RICARDO (*b.* 13 February 1886; *d.* 8 October 1927), Argentine writer. Born in Buenos Aires into a patrician family of ESTANCIA owners, he spent the first three years of his life in Paris, speaking French before he learned his native language; an experience that permitted him to enrich his Spanish writings with bold transplants. His devotion to everything French and to his own land engendered a deep symbiosis of the European and Argentine heritages. A sophisticated European as well as a GAUCHO, skillful at tasks practiced by the cowboys of the PAMPA, he was also a refined Argentine gentleman who helped to popularize the TANGO in Paris's café society. The First World War caused him to retreat into spiritualistic, existentialist, and oriental philosophies. In his yearly pilgrimages to Paris, he established deep friendships with the French writer Valéry Larbaud and the most important "decadent" poets of the time, who greatly influenced his literature. A man of authentic nationalistic feelings for Argentina, like many of his countrymen at the time, Güiraldes wanted to idealize his native roots while enriching them with the best European contributions. He had an ecumenical outlook and eagerness, although deeply rooted in his country and in his time. Güiraldes served as a board member of the influential literary magazines *Martín Fierro* and *Proa*, exercising a guiding role among younger writers. He published three volumes of poetry, two of short stories, and four novels; not a large body of work, but one of high quality and very avant garde. In 1926, a few months before his death in Paris, he won the National Prize for Literature for his novel *Don Segundo Sombra*, a classic of Argentine literature. Güiraldes found his voice, at once "gaucha," full of peasant imagery, but also very French. The book was innovative in the very personal style of his narrative; in being a bildungsroman, in which Güiraldes proposed a model for the education of his people with its hyperbolized figure of the gaucho; and in its depiction of a free, stoic, lonely, and silent life.

P. R. BEARDSELL, "French Influences in Güiraldes's Early Experiments," in *Bulletin of Hispanic Studies* 16 (1969): 331–344; WILLIAM W. MEGENNEY, ed., *Four Essays on Ricardo Güiraldes (1886–1927)* (1977); GIOVANNI PREVITALI, *Ricardo Güiraldes and "Don Segundo Sombra": Life and Works* (1963); NINA M. SCOTT, "Language, Humor, and Myth in the Frontier Novels of the Americas: Wister, Güiraldes, and Amado," in Program in Latin American Studies (Amherst, Mass.), *Occasional Papers*, no. 16 (1983): 1–34.

ANGELA B. DELLEPIANE

GUIRAO, RAMÓN (*b.* 1908; *d.* 17 March 1949), Cuban poet. A founding member of the *Sociedad de Estudios Afrocubanos*, Guirao first gained national attention with his poem "La bailadora de rumba," which appeared in the literary supplement of Havana's *Diario de la Marina* in 1928. From 1933 to 1940 he lived in Mexico, where he worked as a journalist. In 1937 he gained recognition for an essay on Cuba, which he presented to the secretary of education. He was the editor of the journal *Grafos*. Guirao played an instrumental role in the development of literature devoted to Afro-Cuban themes, as exemplified by such works as "Poetas negros y mestizos de la época esclavista," which appeared in *Bohemia* in 1934.

He worked until the end of his life editing *Advance y Alerta*, and contributed to several other literary journals.

PEDRO BARREDA, *The Black Protagonist in the Cuban Novel* (1979), pp. 15, 27, and 29; *Diccionario de la Literatura Cubana*, vol. 1, edited by Marina García (1980), p. 416; WILLIAM LUIS, *Literary Bondage* (1990), pp. 7 and 178.

MICHAEL A. POLUSHIN

See also **Literature.**

GUIRIOR, MANUEL (*b.* 23 March 1708; *d.* 25 November 1788), viceroy of Peru (1776–1780). Born into a noble family in Aoiz (Navarre), Guirior pursued a distinguished naval career, primarily in the Mediterranean, before taking up in 1772 his appointment as viceroy of New Granada. During this first period of office, which ended in 1776 with his transfer to Lima, he acquired a reputation for firmness in dealing with frontier Indians, for progressive economic policies, and for the expansion and reorganization of university education. His service in Peru, by contrast, was blighted by the loss of Upper Peru (present-day Bolivia), high defense costs occasioned by the outbreak of war between Spain and Great Britain, and a prolonged conflict with the *visitador general* (inspector general), José Antonio de Areche, who arrived in Lima in 1777 to undertake a radical program of administrative, judicial, and fiscal reform. Although recalled to Spain in disgrace in 1780, Guirior was rehabilitated by the COUNCIL OF THE INDIES in 1785 and given the title Marqués de Guirior.

EUNICE J. GATES, "Don José Antonio de Areche: His Own Defense," in *Hispanic American Historical Review* 8 (1928): 14–42; VICENTE PALACIO ATARD, *Areche y Guirior. Observaciones sobre el fracaso de una visita al Perú* (1946); JOSÉ MANUEL PÉREZ AYALA, "Aspectos desconocidos de la vida del Virrey don Manuel de Guirior, co-fundador de la Biblioteca Nacional de Bogotá," in *Boletín de Historia y Antigüedades* 43 (1956): 156–182.

JOHN R. FISHER

GUTIÉRREZ, EULALIO (*b.* 1880; *d.* 12 August 1939), Mexican revolutionary and convention president. Gutiérrez was born of a peasant family on the Hacienda Santo Domingo in the village of Ramos Arizpe, Coahuila, and was a shepherd in his youth. He later became a miner for the Mazapil Copper Company of Concepción del Oro, in Zacatecas.

Gutiérrez became a member of Ricardo FLORES MAGÓN's Liberal Party in 1906, and in 1909 he joined the group opposing the reelection of Porfirio DÍAZ to the presidency. With his brother Luis Gutiérrez, he supported Francisco MADERO in 1910. In 1913 he joined the Constitutionalists, rising to military commander of San Luis Potosí in 1914. On November 3 of that year, at the Convention of Aguascalientes, he was selected by the representatives of the leading military commanders to serve as their president, a post he held until 16 January 1915.

The Convention failed, however, to obtain the support of all the victorious revolutionaries, and the Constitutionalists split their support between Venustiano CARRANZA on the one hand and Francisco VILLA and Emiliano ZAPATA on the other. Gutiérrez opposed both Carranza and Villa during 1915, and the following year went into exile. After returning to Mexico, he served as a senator from Coahuila in the 1920s, but left Mexico again after supporting the unsuccessful Escobar rebellion of 1929 by followers of the recently assassinated Álvaro OBREGÓN. He retired permanently from politics thereafter.

MANUEL GARCÍA PURÓN, *México y su gobernantes, biografías* (1964); and ROBERT E. QUIRK, *The Mexican Revolution, 1914–1915* (1981).

RODERIC AI CAMP

GUTIÉRREZ, GUSTAVO (*b.* 8 June 1928), Peruvian priest and founder of LIBERATION THEOLOGY. His attempt to interpret the meaning of Christianity within the context of the struggle for justice unleashed a revolution in Latin American theological inquiry. After training for the priesthood in Europe in the 1950s, Gutiérrez became part of a South and Central American network of Catholic church reformers seeking to apply the teachings of the Second Vatican Council (1962–1965) to Latin American conditions. Influenced by radicalized students, the Peruvian Marxist José Carlos MARIÁTEGUI, the author José María ARGUEDAS, and DEPENDENCY THEORY, Gutiérrez came to champion the liberation of the Latin American poor. In 1968 he coauthored the central texts of the famous Medellín Latin American bishops' conference that denounced social and economic inequality. In his 1971 foundational text *Teología de la liberación: Perspectivas,* he proposed the new theological method of theology as reflection on the commitment of Christians to construct a just society.

The liberation theology movement that his ideas spawned committed some members of the Catholic church to defend the rights of the marginalized. Because of his use of certain aspects of Marxist theory, Gutiérrez's theology has attracted Vatican and conservative criticism. Nevertheless, he has continued to refine his ideas through conferences, international theological networks, and contact with the poor. In later works Gutiérrez has developed a spirituality of suffering.

GUSTAVO GUTIÉRREZ, *A Theology of Liberation,* rev. ed. (1988); *The Future of Liberation Theology,* edited by Marc H. Ellis and Otto Maduro (1989), esp. part II; PENNY LERNOUX, *People of God* (1989); CHRISTIAN SMITH, *The Emergence of Liberation Theology* (1991).

MATTHEW J. O'MEAGHER

See also **Catholic Church; Conference of Latin American Bishops.**

GUTIÉRREZ, JOSÉ MARÍA (*b.* 20 June 1831; *d.* 26 December 1903), lawyer, journalist, and public figure deeply involved in issues concerning the character of Argentine nationhood, constitutionality, and administration. Gutiérrez served in numerous government positions, beginning in 1852 in the Ministry of Government of Buenos Aires Province, and as secretary of the Chamber of Representatives (1854–1857). He participated in the first Battle of CEPEDA (1859) and in the Battle of PAVÓN, where the Confederation of Provinces was defeated in 1861. From 1862, Gutiérrez founded and edited *La Nación,* a paper devoted to defending Bartolomé MITRE, who became the first constitutional president of Argentina in 1862; in 1878, Gutiérrez founded another paper, *La Patria Argentina.* He was minister of justice and public instruction in 1877, was minister of state from 1890 to 1892, and from 1895 until his death, served on the National Council of Education.

VICENTE OSVALDO CUTOLO, ed., *Nuevo diccionario biográfico argentino,* vol. 3 (1971); TULIO HALPERÍN DONGHI, ed., *Proyecto y construcción de una nación: Argentina, 1846–1880* (1980); JOHN LYNCH, *Argentine Dictator: Juan Manuel de Rosas, 1829–1852* (1981).

HILARY BURGER

GUTIÉRREZ BROTHERS, Peruvian insurrectionists. Persistent military rule of Peru since 1821 had spawned widespread antimilitarism, especially in Lima, in the late nineteenth century. Popular sentiment in the election of 1872 therefore lay with Manuel PARDO, the wealthy merchant who promised a severely reduced military budget and weakening of the military's grip on public offices. Most of the military agreed to stay clear of the election, but the minister of war, Colonel Tomás Gutiérrez, considered the election a direct challenge to the rightful preeminence of the military in Peruvian politics. Gutiérrez organized his brothers, fellow military officers Silvestre, Marceliano, and Marcelino, to seize President José BALTA and declared himself president of the republic on July 22, a week before the inauguration of Pardo. Local military garrisons received widespread public support to actively oppose the coup d'etat. The Gutiérrez brothers tried to organize a defense against the popular rejection of their actions, but armed civilians shot Silvestre in downtown Lima and beheaded him. When enraged mobs learned that the rebels had authorized the murder of Balta, they became uncontrollable. A mob killed Tomás and mutilated his body. The bodies of Tomás and Silvestre were then hung from the facade of the cathedral of Lima. Marceliano died fighting in Callao, and Marcelino escaped unharmed. The Gutiérrez uprising marked a nadir in the popular view of the military and may have undermined the confidence of the army and navy in preparing for the upcoming war with Chile.

DAVID P. WERLICH, *Peru: A Short History* (1978), esp. pp. 95–96; MARGARITA GIESECKE, *Masas urbanas y rebelión en la historia. Golpe de estado: Lima 1872* (1978).

VINCENT PELOSO

See also **Military Dictatorships.**

GUTIÉRREZ DE LARA, JOSÉ BERNARDO (*b.* 20 August 1774; *d.* 13 May 1841), revolutionary during the MEXICAN WAR OF INDEPENDENCE. Born in San Ignacio de Loyola, Tamaulipas, Gutiérrez de Lara was a blacksmith, merchant, and property owner, who participated in the independence struggle in Tamaulipas, served as an envoy from Miguel HIDALGO to the government of the United States, and led an invasion of Texas in 1812–1813. He later became involved in other military activities, including the expeditions of Francisco Javier MINA and James Long.

Following Mexican independence, Gutiérrez de Lara returned to Tamaulipas, where he was elected governor in 1824. He served until late 1825, when he became commandant general of the eastern Provincias Internas. Resigning the post in 1826, he did not again become involved in politics until 1839, when he opposed Antonio Canales's efforts to organize a Republic of the Río Grande.

JULIA KATHRYN GARRETT, *Green Flag over Texas* (1939); RIE JARRATT, *Gutiérrez de Lara, Mexican-Texan* (1949).

JESÚS F. DE LA TEJA

GUTIÉRREZ DE PADILLA, JUAN (*b.* ca. 1590; *d.* April 1664), Spanish-born Mexican composer. Educated at the cathedral choir school in his native city of Málaga, Gutiérrez served as music director in Jérez de la Frontera and at the Cádiz cathedral in Spain before emigrating to New Spain around 1622. He was employed as a musician in the Puebla cathedral and in 1629 became its *maestro de capilla*. This post, held until his death, placed him in charge of all music activities, including instruction of the choirboys at the Colegio de San Pedro. The position was considerably enhanced by the support of the wealthy Bishop Palafox y Mendoza. His Latin sacred music bears the early baroque traits of chromaticism and double choir antiphony that prevailed in Europe, but he also wrote popular, dancelike *chanzonettas* and *villancicos* in the vernacular to be used on special feast days.

ROBERT STEVENSON, *Music in Mexico: A Historical Survey* (1952).

ROBERT L. PARKER

GUTIÉRREZ DE PIÑERES, JUAN FRANCISCO (*b.* 25 August 1732; *d.* 7 October 1802), regent-visitor of New Granada (1776–1783). Born in Lebeña, León, Spain, Gutiérrez studied law in Seville, was appointed to the Audiencia of Valladolid in 1774, and two years later became OIDOR of the CASA DE CONTRATACIÓN. In December 1776, José de GÁLVEZ named him visitor-general of NEW GRANADA and regent of the Audiencia of Santa Fe, bearing instructions to improve the administration of royal revenues.

With the outbreak of war in 1779 came authorization to raise taxes and royal monopoly prices. A technocrat lacking political skills, Gutiérrez pursued his mission with such zeal that Viceroy Manuel FLORES MALDONADO Martínez y Bodquín urged caution, but to no avail. When Flores assumed military command on the coast, he relinquished his civil powers to Gutiérrez. The COMUNERO REVOLT of 1781, protesting his measures, forced the regent-visitor to flee Santa Fe for Cartagena. Thereafter, Gutiérrez saw his effective powers diminished, although he returned to the viceregal capital in 1782. Recalled to Spain in 1783, he assumed a position on the COUNCIL OF THE INDIES, where he remained until his death.

JOSÉ MARÍA RESTREPO SÁENZ, *Biografías de los mandatarios y ministros de la Real Audiencia, 1671–1819* (1952), especially pp. 509–514; ALLAN J. KUETHE, *Military Reform and Society in New Granada, 1773–1808* (1977); and JOHN LEDDY PHELAN, *The People and the King: The Comunero Revolution in Colombia, 1781* (1978).

ALLAN J. KUETHE

GUTIÉRREZ ESTRADA, JOSÉ MARÍA (*b.* 1800; *d.* 1867), Mexican diplomat and politician. Born in the city of Campeche, Gutiérrez Estrada moved to Mexico City with his family when he was young. He was appointed minister of foreign relations by President Antonio López de SANTA ANNA (1834–1835) and later served as Mexico's diplomatic representative in several European countries. Upon his return to Mexico in 1840, Gutiérrez Estrada published an open letter to the president in which he called for free discussion of a liberal constitutional monarchy in Mexico, arguing that the monarchical form of government was more consistent with the traditions, needs, and interests of the Mexican people. He warned of the need for a strong government to defend Mexico against U.S. aggression, saying "If we do not change our ways, perhaps twenty years will not pass before we see the flag of the United States waving above our National Palace."

The pamphlet caused a sensation, and Gutiérrez Estrada was denounced by both liberals and conservatives. Although he was forced to flee to Europe, he continued his campaign for a Mexican monarchy. His fears were realized in 1847, when the U.S. army conquered Mexico and raised the Stars and Stripes above the National Palace, after which his proposal gained greater support among Mexican conservatives. Gutiérrez Estrada received various diplomatic commissions and was president of the commission that offered the crown of Mexico to Maximilian at Miramar. Each of his three wives was from a noble family.

ALFRED JACKSON HANNA and KATHRYN ABBEY HANNA, *Napoleon III and Mexico: American Triumph over Monarchy* (1971); *Diccionario Porrúa de historia, biografía y geografía de México*, 5th ed. (1986).

D. F. STEVENS

GUTIÉRREZ GARBÍN, VÍCTOR MANUEL (*b.* 10 January 1922; *d.* March 1966), Guatemalan educator and labor leader. Gutiérrez was born in the rural Guatemalan department of Santa Rosa. He was educated as a primary school teacher in Guatemala and taught at the National Boys' Institute in the western province of Chiquimula. After a short teaching stint in the capital, Gutiérrez was made the subdirector of the Industrial Institute for Boys in 1944.

During the revolutionary period (1944–1954), Gutiérrez became the most important and influential labor leader in the history of the country. His career as a labor leader began when he founded the Guatemalan Union of Educational Workers (Sindicato de Trabajadores en Educación de Guatemala, STEG) in 1944. After 1946, as president of the largest national workers' union, later the Confederation of Guatemalan Workers (Confederación de Trabajadores de Guatemala) and later the General Confederation of Guatemalan Workers (Confederación General de Trabajadores de Guatemala), he organized over 100,000 workers. He was known as a particularly honest and dedicated organizer who always maintained close ties to the rank-and-file of the labor movement. Gutiérrez was elected to Congress in 1950, and became first secretary of the Congress in 1954.

Because of his involvement with the Communist Party, Gutiérrez fled Guatemala in 1954. In March 1966, while attempting to return to Guatemala from Mexico, he disappeared, allegedly dropped from an airplane over the Pacific Ocean by Guatemalan security forces. His body was never found.

RONALD SCHNEIDER, *Communism in Guatemala: 1944–1954* (1958); MARIO LÓPEZ LARRAVE, *Breve historia del movimiento sindical guatemalteco*, 2d ed. (1979); JIM HANDY, *Gift of the Devil* (1984).

RACHEL A. MAY

GUTIÉRREZ GONZÁLEZ, GREGORIO (*b.* 9 May 1826; *d.* 6 July 1872), Colombian poet considered the bard of his native Antioquia. After studying law in Bogotá, Gutiérrez held various judicial and legislative posts in Antioquia and represented the province in Congress. As a poet he is remembered partly for his romantic lyrics, such as the two poems entitled "A Julia" and the nostalgic and melancholy "Aures." His major literary achievement, however, is the *Memoria científica sobre el cultivo del maíz en Antioquia*, first published in 1866. A celebration of rural life in Antioquia, this long poem traces the cycle of corn cultivation from preparation of the field to the gathering of the crop. It also contrasts the delicious dishes made of corn with the "vile potato." The poem's bucolic imagery reveals the author's romantic roots yet its homely details impart a realistic flavor, as does the use of local dialect by Gutiérrez, who said that he wrote in *antioqueño*, not in Spanish.

GREGORIO GUTIÉRREZ GONZÁLEZ, *Obras completas*, edited by Rafael Montoya y Montoya (1958); JAVIER ARANGO FERRER, *Raíz y desarrollo de la literatura* (1965), pp. 255–263.

HELEN DELPAR

GUTIÉRREZ GUERRA, JOSÉ (*b.* 5 September 1869; *d.* 3 February 1929), president of Bolivia (1917–1920). Born in Sucre, Gutiérrez Guerra was the last president of the period of Liberal Party domination (1899–1920). His administration was marked by rigged elections and government scandals. Gutiérrez Guerra initially included the main opposition party, the Republicans, in a cabinet of "national concentration" in an effort to sidestep a surge of nationalist fervor over recouping the Pacific coastal area lost during the WAR OF THE PACIFIC (1879–1884) with Chile. However, by 1919 party politics again turned acrimonious. The Liberal Party split over whether to fine Simón Iturri PATIÑO, the most important Bolivian TIN-mine owner and important supporter of the party, who brought 80,000 cans of alcohol into the country after his contract to do so had expired. As a result, the Republican Party was able to organize an almost bloodless coup in July 1920 that toppled the government and ended twenty years of Liberal Party hegemony.

The best treatment of the Gutiérrez Guerra government is contained in HERBERT S. KLEIN, *Parties and Political Change in Bolivia: 1880–1952* (1969), pp. 53–61. For the position of an opposition politician, see DAVID ALVÉSTEGUI, *Salamanca, su gravitación sobre el destino de Bolivia*, vol. 2 (1958), pp. 179–255.

ERICK D. LANGER

See also: **Bolivia: Political Parties.**

GUTIÉRREZ NÁJERA, MANUEL (*b.* 22 December 1859; *d.* 3 February 1895), Mexican writer. Gutiérrez Nájera was born in Mexico City. His father was a journalist and writer and his mother a devout Catholic. The middle-class family privately educated him and he developed a strong interest in reading classic literature and contemporary French works. He worked as a journalist and in 1888 was appointed to a political post. Gutiérrez Nájera was one of the progenitors of Spanish American *modernista* writing in Mexico. Through his poetry, essays, short stories, and journalistic chronicles, he explored in Spanish the stylistic and linguistic potentials associated with the French Parnassian and Symbolist movements. He wrote under pseudonyms such as Mr. Can-Can, El Duque Job, Puck, and many others. Together with Carlos Díaz Dufoo, he founded *Revista*

Azul (1894–1896; Blue Review), one of the principal *modernista* publications in Spanish America. He is frequently known only as a poet, but his prose writing in both the short story and chronicle genres is equally innovative and represents his aesthetic concerns and French cultural influences. His short stories include the collections *Cuentos frágiles* (1883; Fragile Stories) and *Cuentos color de humo* (1898; Smoke-Colored Stories). His chronicles appear in series such as *Crónicas color de rosa* (Rose-Colored Chronicles), *Crónicas color de lluvia* (Rain-Colored Chronicles), *Crónicas color de oro* (Gold-Colored Chronicles), and *Crónicas de mil colores* (Myriad-Colored Chronicles). Gutiérrez Nájera died in Mexico City at the height of his career.

MARINA GÁLVEZ, "Manuel Gutiérrez Nájera," in *Historia de la Literatura Hispanoamericana*. Vol. 2, *Del neoclasicismo al modernismo*, edited by Luis Íñigo Madrigal (1987), pp. 583–590; IVAN A. SCHULMAN, "Manuel Gutiérrez Nájera," in *Latin American Writers*, edited by Carlos A. Solé and María Isabel Abreu, vol. 1 (1989), pp. 351–357.

DANNY J. ANDERSON

GUTIÉRREZ Y ESPINOSA, FELIPE (*b.* 26 May 1825; *d.* 27 November 1899), Puerto Rican composer. Gutiérrez is considered the best Puerto Rican composer of the nineteenth century and the main figure of Puerto Rico's musical life during that period. Born in San Juan, Gutiérrez received music lessons from his father when very young; thereafter he was self-taught. Starting as a battalion musician, he won the position of maestro de capilla of the San Juan Cathedral in 1858. Later he conducted the orchestra of the Teatro Municipal (later the Teatro Tapia). Around 1873 he traveled to Europe, studying in Paris for one year. Gutiérrez composed sacred music: masses, one oratorio, eight Salve Reginas, and other minor religious works. Of his three operas, *Guarionex*, *El bearnés*, and *Macías*, the last is the only extant opera of the nineteenth century in Puerto Rico. It was awarded a gold medal in 1871, but went unperformed in the twentieth century until 19 August 1977 at the Teatro Tapia, because its manuscript had been lost. Gutiérrez also composed one zarzuela and other orchestral and chamber music.

FEDERICO ASENJO, *Las fiestas de San Juan* (1868); R. STEVENSON, *A Guide to Caribbean Music History* (1975); D. THOMPSON, "Musical Archaeology, Fine Talent Bring *Macías* to Life," *San Juan Star*, 7 June 1978; *New Grove Dictionary of Music and Musicians*, vol. 7 (1980); *New Grove Dictionary of Opera*, vols. 2 and 4 (1992).

SUSANA SALGADO

GUYANA, the only English-speaking country in South America, independent since 1966. It is bordered by Venezuela, Suriname, Brazil, and the Atlantic Ocean. Two-thirds of Guyana's 83,000 square miles are covered with lush rain forests that yield valuable timber, especially greenheart. The country is also endowed with rich resources of gold, diamonds, and high-grade BAUXITE ore, as well as extensive areas of fertile coastland on which SUGAR and RICE are grown. The Land of Many Waters, as it is called, boasts a plethora of rivers. The four major ones are the Demerara, on which Georgetown, the capital and chief port, is located; the Essequibo, the largest; the Berbice; and the Corentyne. There are innumerable rapids and waterfalls along the rivers. Kaieteur Falls on the Potaro River thunders into a gorge at the height of 741 feet. Mount Roraima (9,094 feet), on the borders with Venezuela and Brazil, was the setting for Arthur Conan Doyle's fictional *The Lost World* (1912).

The population of this Land of Six Peoples was approximately 750,000 in the 1980 census and was composed of Amerindians; Africans and East Indians, comprising the majority; and smaller groups of Europeans and Chinese, with varying mixtures. The culture and religion of the country reflect these ethnic groups. Hindu temples, Muslim mosques, and Christian churches of several denominations are located throughout. The Guyanese are bound together by a common language—English, a legacy of English colonialism—international foods, and a passion for cricket.

The Dutch were the first Europeans to colonize the Wild Coast of Guyana, which extended from the mouth of the Amazon to the Orinoco. The early colonies began in the late sixteenth century, establishing friendly relations with the Amerindians and carrying on trade in dyes and letterwood. By 1675 they had established sugar, COFFEE, TOBACCO, and COTTON plantations worked by African slaves. In 1763 there was a massive slave revolt against the Dutch, which was quelled with the help of the Amerindians. At the end of the eighteenth century, there were short intervals of British and French control before Dutch rule was superseded by British control in 1803. The Dutch heritage remains in many place-names, such as Stabroek, Vlissengen, Beterverwagting, in the *kokers* or sluice gates, and in the famous Sea Wall.

The main developments in nineteenth-century British Guiana were the emancipation of nearly 83,000 slaves in 1834, the establishment of villages along the coastlands by former slaves, and the importation of indentured workers from Africa, Madeira, India, and China to meet the labor shortage. Two outstanding events marked the end of the nineteenth century: the promulgation of the new Constitution of 1891 and the 1899 Paris settlement, which awarded the Orinoco River to Venezuela, supposedly ending the fifty-five-year-old border dispute. The 1970 Protocol of Port-of-Spain, which established a twelve-year moratorium on the resuscitated boundary question, was not renewed in 1982.

In 1917 East Indian immigration to the colony was stopped, and in 1928 British Guiana became a crown colony. The Court of Policy and the Combined Court, legacies of Dutch government, were replaced by a Legislative and Executive Council. The 1940s, 1950s, and 1960s were years of much political agitation and many strikes as the leading political parties, the People's Progressive Party (PPP), the People's National Congress (PNC), and the United Force (UF) jockeyed for power. The 1953 and 1957 elections were won by the PPP under its leader, Dr. Cheddi Jagan.

On 26 May 1966, Guyana gained independence under a coalition government headed by the PNC leader, Forbes Burnham. On 23 February 1970, Guyana became the first Cooperative Republic within the Commonwealth to be governed by an elected president rather than a British-appointed governor-general. The dual control system of education (controlled by both church and state) was abolished in 1976, and free education from nursery school to university was initiated. The University of Guyana, established in 1963, was engaged on a cost recovery program in the early 1990s. The standard of education in Guyana, which once boasted the highest literacy rate in the Caribbean, has dropped considerably since the 1970s, exacerbated by the migration of many teachers to the Caribbean, North America, and the United Kingdom.

After a twenty-six-year period of PNC government, the PPP won the 1992 elections under Dr. Cheddi Jagan, who became president for a five-year term. The economy began experiencing a more open investment climate in 1990; as a consequence, many private business enterprises have sprung up. International funding, through the International Monetary Fund and the INTER-AMERICAN DEVELOPMENT BANK, among others, is supporting improvements and the rehabilitation of the country's infrastructure. The immense interior resources, especially gold, are attracting foreign and local investments. Eco-tourism is making marked strides and has much potential, but the country is sensitive to ecological exploitation. A large tract of forest—IWOKRAMA—has been dedicated to an experimental project for the study of rain-forest resources and their careful development. The building of roads is seen as a sine qua non for the development of the interior. The 220-mile road from Georgetown to Brazil has yet to be completed.

Timehri, Guyana's only international airport, 25 miles south of Georgetown, is served by a number of regional airlines with international connections to all major destinations. Guyana Airways Corporation (GAC) connects the country with North America and with a number of locations within the mining and interior areas of Guyana.

Guyana is a member of the United Nations, and in the mid-1990s maintained diplomatic relations with over ninety countries, of which fourteen had missions to the country. Its respected role in international affairs was illustrated by the election of its ambassador to the United Nations as the president of the General Assembly for 1993–1994.

For an understanding of early Dutch and British relationships with, and policy toward, the Amerindians, see M. NOEL MENEZES, British Policy Towards the Amerindians in British Guiana, 1803–1873 (1977). Major works on political and constitutional developments are HAROLD ALEXANDER LUTCHMAN, From Colonialism to Co-operative Republic: Aspects of Political Development in Guyana (1974), and M. SHAHABUDDEEN, Constitutional Development in Guyana, 1621–1978 (1978). Economic and social relationships among the Guyanese are discussed in WALTER RODNEY, A History of the Guyanese Working People (1981), as well as in THOMAS J. SPINNER, JR., A Political and Social History of Guyana, 1945–1983 (1984). For the evolution of the Venezuela–Guyana border conflict since the 1960s, see JACQUELINE ANNE BRAVEBOY-WAGNER, The Venezuela–Guyana Border Dispute: Britain's Colonial Legacy in Latin America (1984). Recent works in religious and cultural history are DALE BISNAUTH, History of Religions in the Caribbean, 2d ed. (1993), and MARY NOEL MENEZES, The Portuguese of Guyana: A Study of Culture and Conflict (1994).

SISTER M. NOEL MENEZES, R.S.M.

GUZMÁN, ANTONIO LEOCADIO (b. 14 November 1801; d. 13 November 1884), Venezuelan politician and publicist. In 1825, Guzmán founded the newspaper El Argos. In 1830, he served as minister of interior, justice, and police. He helped organize the Liberal Party in 1840 and edited the party's newspaper, El Venezolano, which called for universal suffrage for males, emancipation of slaves, and the end of capital punishment. Guzmán served José Tadeo MONAGAS as minister of interior and justice and as vice president. In 1853, he went to Peru as ambassador. He joined the Junta Patriótica de Venezuela, led by Ezequiel Zamora, in 1858, and served as a propagandist. Guzmán's son Antonio GUZMÁN BLANCO became president in 1870.

FRANCISCO GONZÁLEZ GUINÁN, Historia contemporánea de Venezuela, vols. 2–4 (1954); JOHN V. LOMBARDI, Venezuela: The Search for Order, the Dream of Progress (1982); HECTOR MUJICA, La historia en una silla (1982); ANTONIO LEOCADIO GUZMÁN, Antonio Leocadio Guzmán, 2 vols. (1983).

WINTHROP R. WRIGHT

GUZMÁN, AUGUSTO (b. 1 September 1903) Bolivian writer and historian. Guzmán was a prolific and diverse intellectual whose literary production includes novels, short stories, biographies, criticism, and literary history. He has centered his historical work on the region of COCHABAMBA. His novel Prisionero de guerra, based on his own experience as a soldier, is an important testimony of the CHACO WAR (1932–1935). Another major theme in his work is the condition of Indians and mestizos (those of mixed blood) in the countryside of Bolivia. His most popular work, "La cruel Martina" ("The Cruel Martina") is a short story that was made into a film in 1989. His literary criticism is a valuable source of information on Bolivian literature, while the biographies he wrote serve as a point of intersection between his literary and historical interests and are his best contribution to Bolivian studies. With the years, Guzmán has become one of the most respected representatives of Bolivian intellectual life.

LEONARDO GARCÍA PABÓN

GUZMÁN, ENRIQUE (*b.* 2 August 1843; *d.* 23 May 1911), Nicaraguan intellectual and politician. Guzmán is renowned throughout Central America as a writer and a politician. In 1862 he published his first satirical essays. As a youth he was a member of the Liberal Party, but from 1886 to 1911 he was affiliated with the Conservatives. Guzmán first became politically active during his father's run for the presidency in 1867. In 1879 he served as a deputy in Congress. Among his friends was President Joaquín ZAVALA (1879–1883; 1893). Guzmán encouraged Zavala to maintain good relations with neighboring states in order to preserve Nicaraguan neutrality and peace. Under Zavala, he served as minister to Chile and Peru. During the ZELAYA dictatorship, he conspired against the government.

PEDRO JOAQUÍN CHAMORRO ZELAYA, *Enrique Guzmán y su tiempo* (1965); ENRIQUE GUZMÁN SELVA, *Escritos biográficos de Enrique Guzmán* (1976).

SHANNON BELLAMY

GUZMÁN, MARTÍN LUÍS (*b.* 6 October 1887; *d.* 22 December 1976), Mexican literary figure and cultural entrepreneur best remembered for his post-Revolutionary novels *El águila y la serpiente* (1928) and *La sombra del caudillo* (1929). Based on personal experience, these works provide some of the best insights into the Revolution as well as a condemnation of the leading post-Revolutionary figures of the 1920s. Although he was part of the El Ateneo literary group in 1911, Guzmán largely abandoned his literary career in the 1930s, instead pursuing journalism and publishing.

The son of an army officer who died in combat during the Revolution, Guzmán joined the Constitutionalists. After founding many newspapers, he spent five years (1915–1920) of self-imposed exile in Spain and the United States. When his daily, *El Mundo*, was confiscated by the Obregón administration, he again exiled himself to Spain (ca. 1923–1936), where he directed several newspapers. In the 1940s he founded a number of publishing companies as well as the weekly magazine *El Tiempo* (modeled after *Time* magazine), which he directed until his death. He received the National Prize for Literature in 1958.

RUTH STANTON, "Martín Luís Guzmán's Place in Modern Mexican Literature," in *Hispania* 26 (1943): 136–138; MARTÍN LUÍS GUZMÁN, *Apunte sobre una personalidad* (1955); *Tiempo* (3 January 1977): 5–23; and WILLIAM MEGENNEY, ed., *Five Essays on Martín Luís Guzmán* (1978).

RODERIC AI CAMP

GUZMÁN, NUÑO BELTRÁN DE (*b.* ca. 1485; *d.* 26 October 1558), governor of Pánuco (1527), president of New Spain's first AUDIENCIA (1528–1531), conqueror of Nueva Galicia (1529), and founder of GUADALAJARA (1531). Of the lower nobility of Guadalajara, Spain,

Guzmán became noted for his corruption and brutality toward indigenous people. In Pánuco he earned the enmity of Hernán CORTÉS and other first conquerors by aggressively trying to expand his jurisdiction at their expense and, as *audiencia* president, by profiteering from the confiscation of their properties. Relations were not improved when in 1530 he tortured and then executed Cazonci, the Tarascan ruler of MICHOACÁN, an ally of Cortés. In 1531, while Guzmán was still in Nueva Galicia, the first *audiencia* and its president were replaced, in part because of the complaints of such prominent figures as Bishop Juan de ZUMÁRRAGA. Guzmán continued as governor of New Galicia until January 1537, when he was arrested. After languishing in jail for eighteen months, he left Mexico in mid-1538, arriving in Spain in December (or perhaps in early 1539). He remained with the royal court under a kind of house arrest until his death in Valladolid.

The overwhelmingly negative picture of Guzmán that has come down to us is partly the result of his conflict with Cortés; with the exception of Guzmán's own correspondence, most of the primary information comes from the pens and testimony of Cortés's adherents, such as Francisco López de Gómara, who wrote that if "Nuño de Guzmán had been as good a governor as he was a warrior, he would have had the best place in the Indies; but he behaved badly both to Indians and Spaniards" (*Life of the Conqueror*, p. 394).

The most complete biography of Guzmán remains DONALD E. CHIPMAN, *Nuño de Guzmán and the Province of Pánuco in New Spain, 1518–1533* (1967). J. BENEDICT WARREN, *The Conquest of Michoacán* (1985), focuses on Guzmán's later career, especially his exploits among the Tarascans of Michoacán. See also FRANCISCO LÓPEZ DE GÓMARA, *Cortés: The Life of the Conqueror by His Secretary*, translated and edited by Lesley Byrd Simpson (1964).

ROBERT HASKETT

GUZMÁN BLANCO, ANTONIO LEOCADIO (*b.* 1829; *d.* 1899), president of Venezuela (1870–1877, 1879–1884, 1886–1888). The son of Antonio Leocadio GUZMÁN, founder of the Liberal Party, Antonio Guzmán Blanco came to power as head of state upon taking Caracas by force on 27 April 1870. After more than a decade of civil war, he enforced order for almost two decades. Under his leadership, Venezuela made educational advancements, built many public works, and experienced economic progress.

Guzmán Blanco was not the typical nineteenth-century CAUDILLO. He studied law and medicine, and lived and traveled abroad. In the 1840s, he served as consul in New York and Philadelphia, and as secretary of the Venezuelan embassy in Washington, D.C.

When General Juan Crisóstomo FALCÓN declared in 1859 in favor of a federal system, Guzmán Blanco joined him. As an agent of Falcón, he succeeded in ending the five years of civil war and anarchy when he negotiated the Treaty of Coche on 24 April 1863. The treaty called for

157

Antonio Leocadio Guzmán Blanco. ORGANIZATION OF AMERICAN STATES.

the convening of a National Assembly, which appointed Falcón president and Guzmán Blanco vice president.

The peace thus established was short lived. Falcón governed from 1863 to 1868 amid constant political challenges and economic difficulties. Having inherited a nation which had experienced many years of civil conflict and economic disruptions, Falcón found that one of his most pressing problems was to negotiate with European creditors to reestablish Venezuela's credit and obtain a new loan.

This task was entrusted to Guzmán Blanco, who left for London in August 1863. He successfully contracted for a loan of £1.5 million, which was expected to raise 4.5 million pesos, but because of Venezuela's poor credit rating, only 1.5 million pesos were realized. Establishing a pattern he was to repeat often over the next three decades, Guzmán Blanco personally profited from this transaction.

The reign of Falcón saw a continuation of political anarchy, and, by 1867, Venezuela was again in flames. In 1868, José Tadeo MONAGAS captured Caracas; he died that November, leaving his son José Ruperto in control. Guzmán Blanco fled to Curaçao and established himself as leader of the Liberals. On 14 February 1870, he landed in Venezuela, marched to Caracas, and took the capital on 27 April. He assumed control of his nation and dominated it for the next eighteen years. Thus began one of the few extended periods of peace Venezuela was to enjoy in the nineteenth century.

Elections were held on 15 April 1873, and Guzmán Blanco arranged to win all but eighteen of the more than two hundred thousand votes cast. It was at this point that congress bestowed on him the title "Illustrious American and Regenerator of Venezuela." The president enjoyed his many titles and had numerous streets, boulevards, and plazas named for himself. Early in his rule his picture was placed in all public buildings, and many parks were adorned with a statue honoring him.

Guzmán Blanco was aided in his efforts to improve the Venezuelan economy by his appointing able economic and financial advisers. One of the more challenging tasks was the ever-present public debt. Benefiting from the years of peace, Venezuela enjoyed a period of economic growth which contributed to an improvement in its credit rating. Agriculture in particular benefited from the president's attention, and WHEAT and COFFEE became the principal items of export.

The national economy also benefited from the extensive construction of highways, as communications between leading cities were improved. The main ports of La Guaira and Puerto Cabello were improved, and telegraph communication was established between Caracas and the state capitals. A rail link between Caracas and La Guaira was begun. Other public works included construction of a capitol, a federal court building, and a national theater, and expansion of the university. Education benefited under Guzmán Blanco's leadership. He instituted an extensive building program with the goal of making education free and available to all students for the first time in Venezuela.

One of the early challenges to Guzmán Blanco came from the Roman Catholic church. He and his party were seen as anticlerical and were opposed by the archbishop of Caracas. When asked for a *Te Deum* to celebrate the new government, Archbishop Silvestre Guevara y Lira refused, and was exiled. Soon after, Guzmán Blanco established civil marriages, prohibited the church from holding tracts of uncultivated land, and ended the practice, dating from the colonial period, of the state contributing to the church. An active Mason, the president saw to the building of the Masonic Temple in Caracas. After 1876, Guzmán Blanco made peace with the church but ensured that he kept it in its place.

In 1876, with a handpicked successor, Francisco LINARES ALCÁNTARA, as president, Guzmán Blanco left for Europe as Venezuela's representative to six governments. When Linares died in 1878, loyal Guzmancistas, Joaquín CRESPO and Pablo ROJAS PAÚL, took charge and recalled their patron from Europe. Guzmán Blanco stayed in Caracas from 1879 until 1884, when he returned to his luxurious life in Paris. Before leaving Venezuela, however, he oversaw the election of Crespo as president. The economy deteriorated, and congress called him home. He arrived in August 1886 to genuine demonstrations of support but, within a year, expressions of discontent began to surface. As some editors wrote about alternatives to Guzmán Blanco, their papers were confiscated and they were jailed, a practice followed earlier in his rule whenever it was felt necessary.

Rojas Pául was selected by Guzmán Blanco to take over when he again returned to the comforts of Paris in 1888. This time, however, the puppet did not follow the master, and Rojas Pául established himself as the real ruler of the nation. Since there was widespread anti-Guzmán Blanco sentiment, this was not so diffi-cult to accomplish. The former president never returned to his native land. He died in Europe a decade later.

GUILLERMO MORÓN, *A History of Venezuela,* edited and translated by John Street (1963), esp. pp. 170–181; GEORGE S. WISE, *Caudillo: A Portrait of Antonio Guzmán Blanco* (1951; repr. 1970).

CHARLES CARRERAS

H

HACIENDA. In its most general sense, this word means "estate" or "all worldly possessions of an individual." In Latin America the word is used most commonly as a generic term for all types of large rural properties ranging in size from a few hundred hectares (1 hectare equals 2.47 acres) to hundreds of square kilometers (1 square kilometer equals .04 square miles). Large rural estates and the individuals and institutions who control them have dominated the peoples, politics, and economies of Latin America since the sixteenth century and still do in many places in the late twentieth century.

The origins of the great estate in Latin America can be traced back to two or three decades after the Conquest, when the first land grants (*mercedes*) were given to Spanish conquerors and to later immigrants. Other holdings were acquired less auspiciously by usurping unoccupied Indian land. These squatters' holdings were subsequently legalized and titled by payments to the crown (*composiciones*). Regardless of their legal or illegal origins, haciendas grew by later donations, sales, usurpations, and *composiciones*.

Most haciendas developed independently of the *encomienda*. Early *encomenderos*, using positions on the municipal councils in nearby Spanish towns, sometimes granted themselves one or more plots of land from among the parcels that had been used by their Indian charges. As more and more of the Indians died or moved away, however, their abandoned parcels were granted to other later-arriving Spanish immigrants in an effort to further colonization and settlement of the land, increase the quantity of needed foodstuffs and draft animals and reward individuals who had served the king. These *mercedes* far outnumbered those granted to *encomenderos*. Nevertheless, *mercedes* of both the *encomendero* and non-*encomendero* types became the nuclei of individual farms and stock-raising enterprises that later grew into the large estates that dominated both countryside and city.

Large estates or haciendas can be grouped into three main types. One is the ranch, which developed from the *estancia* (*fazenda,* in Portuguese). The *estancia* was an early and popular type of enterprise because its establishment required relatively little capital and small numbers of laborers. Transportation costs were insignificant because cattle could be driven to market. Before the eighteenth century, however, an *estancia* was not the large ranch, in the legal sense, that we envision today. Typically, its owner (the *estanciero*) had legal title to only a few units of land, on which he usually built a house for himself or his steward (*mayordomo*), a storage shed or building, and one or more corrals. This became

El Cortijo plantation and brown sugar mill, ca. 1880. BENSON LATIN AMERICAN COLLECTION, UNIVERSITY OF TEXAS AT AUSTIN.

his operational headquarters. The *estancia,* in other words, was no more than a cattle station. Pastures were common domain. In the eighteenth century the crown, in need of money, sold the pastures to the highest bidder. It was only then that the *estanciero* consolidated control over a large area of pasturelands and the ranch was legally born.

A mixed farm was the second type of hacienda. Some *estancias* became haciendas when part of the land, usually that near the headquarters, was planted in crops. The mixed farm required more capital and more labor than the *estancia* but less than a specialized farm.

The third type of hacienda was the specialized farm, usually dedicated to producing only one crop for a distant market. The typical crops grown—sugar cane, rice, cacao, and wheat—required processing. During colonial times these specialized farms, the forerunners of modern plantations, took their names from the type of mill or processing facilities installed on the premises. An *ingenio* referred to a water-powered mill. A *trapiche* was an animal-powered mill. Both of these terms usually referred to sugar estates. A *molino* could be either water or animal powered and usually referred to a wheat- or rice-producing enterprise.

All three types of estate relied on a dependent labor force: Indians who had left their communities and become personal retainers (*naborías* and *yanaconas*); community members working on a temporary basis to earn money to pay their tribute; and wage-earning or salaried Spaniards, creoles, mestizos, and mulattoes who worked on haciendas in various capacities from peon to *mayordomo,* or steward, over the years. In tropical areas, where haciendas produced sugar or cacao, owners sometimes purchased large numbers of black slaves to do much of the work. These laborers lived in huts or

houses near the operational center of the estate, which, in some cases, grew to the size and complexity of small towns, complete with church and jail.

In contrast to earlier stereotypes of the self-sufficient hacienda, more recent studies have shown that most haciendas, however remote, produced for a market. The hacienda, while not always profitable, did generate revenues and, in some cases, became the basis of considerable fortunes. In the process it became the measure of a person's or a family's power and prestige.

Thus, land in Latin America became the hallmark of elite standing. It achieved this status because landowners, or *hacendados,* were wealthy. They controlled the means of production and as such provided employment for agricultural workers (plowing, herding, planting, harvesting, etc.), skilled craftsmen (carpenters, metal smiths, etc.), and urban professionals (scribes, lawyers, bankers). They also wielded political power, directly or indirectly, on the municipal council and often at higher levels of government as well.

The *hacendados* were, then, the epitome of success and as such were imitated. Mine owners, merchants, and professionals who achieved wealth bought land. Miners might acquire a hacienda to raise foodstuffs or mules needed in mining and thus vertically integrate their enterprises. But the prestige of owning vast tracks of land was also an incentive. Given the early prejudices against commerce, merchants too were attracted to landownership as a means of shedding their tainted image and validating their status. One reason nineteenth-century urban professionals were often politically liberal, and thus anticlerical, was their hope of wresting control of the church's vast landholdings. When the church lost hold of its properties, they were often sold, giving professionals and other monied segments of society the opportunity to acquire the one item that marked their ascension into, or established their permanent standing in, the elite.

In modern times, the issues of land concentration and land reform have become serious political matters, and increasing pressure for redistribution sometimes has erupted into revolts and guerrilla wars. Emiliano ZAPATA's demands for land reform and restitution during the Mexican Revolution brought the issue to world attention, since Mexico was not the only country where a small minority owned and controlled great proportions of arable land while the vast majority of rural inhabitants were landless and poor. President Lázaro CÁRDENAS (1934–1940) became an immortalized folk hero by redistributing land to Mexican peasants in the 1930s.

Bolivian peasants did not wait for governmental action. They began invading haciendas soon after the Bolivian Revolution of 1952. The Movimiento Nacionalista Revolucionario (Nationalist Revolutionary Movement), or MNR, subsequently issued a land reform law to legalize their seizures, thereby securing the peasants' allegiance and making this party of middle-class origins look more "revolutionary" than it in fact was.

Meanwhile, peasants everywhere were organizing. In the late 1950s in the southern Andes near Cuzco, Peru, Hugo Blanco, a young Trotskyist agronomist, organized a peasant federation, sparking a series of tenant strikes and land seizures. Peasant syndicates formed in northeastern Brazil, where "Land to the Tiller" became a rallying cry.

The ALLIANCE FOR PROGRESS (1961) challenged the governing elites throughout the hemisphere to redistribute property. Several countries passed land reform laws in the 1960s and 1970s, but few of them proved effective. Perhaps the greatest progress in redistributing land occurred during the short tenure of President Salvador ALLENDE (1970–1973) in Chile while General Juan VELASCO ALVARADO (1968–1975) occupied the presidential palace in Peru, and under the Sandinistas in Nicaragua (1979–1990). After these regimes lost power, however, many of the expropriated properties were returned to their former owners. Thus, large estates and their owners still dominate the economy in many areas of Latin America. However, the efforts of peasants to protect the land they retain to recover those already lost promise continuing struggles over this issue.

FRANÇOIS CHEVALIER, *La formation des grands domaines au Mexique: Terre et société aux XVIe–XVIIe siècles* (1952); ERIC R. WOLF and SIDNEY W. MINTZ, "Haciendas and Plantations in Middle America and the Antilles," in *Social and Economic Studies* 6, no. 3 (1957):380–412; JAMES M. LOCKHART, "Encomienda and *Hacienda*: The Evolution of the Great Estate in the Spanish Indies," in *Hispanic American Historical Review* 49, no. 3 (1969):411–29; ESPINOZA R. GUSTAVO and CARLOS MALPICA, *El problema de la tierra* (1970); ROBERT G. KEITH, *Conquest and Agrarian Change: The Emergence of the Hacienda System on the Peruvian Coast* (1976); HENRY PEASE GARCÍA et al., *Estado y política agraria:* *Cuatro ensayos* (1977); and HERMAN W. KONRAD, *A Jesuit Hacienda in Colonial Mexico: Santa Lucía, 1576–1767* (1980).

SUSAN E. RAMÍREZ

HAITI

ABORIGINAL QUISQUEYA AND COLONIAL SANTO DOMINGO AND SAINT-DOMINGUE

Haiti, a tropical mountainous country, occupies the western third of the major Antillean island of Quisqueya, the aboriginal name for Hispaniola. It has been the stage for some of history's most dramatic ethnic and cultural changes. Europeans completely displaced the aboriginal Amerindian populations and, in their turn, were pushed out by Africans—all within a space of three hundred years.

The colonial divisions between French Saint-Domingue and Spanish Santo Domingo, and between the Republic of Haiti and the Dominican Republic, are relatively modern, and histories of the island as it was before the European invasions have tended to treat it as one whole.

Beginning about 5000 B.C. successive waves of Amerindian migrations reached Hispaniola via Central America or via the Caribbean island chain from South America. Sedentary horticulturists arrived in the Greater Antilles about 300 B.C. or later. By A.D. 1000 complex chiefdoms headed by CACIQUES had developed and the local peoples, of mainly Arawak origins, seem to have called themselves TAINOS. The chiefdoms in Hispaniola may have been fewer, larger, and more powerful than those in neighboring Puerto Rico, and they engaged in inter-island, and possibly circum-Caribbean, trade.

The population on Hispaniola gradually increased, notably after about A.D. 600. This growth was related to *conuco* agriculture, intensive cultivation of carefully prepared mounds which produced staggered, year-round supplies of starches of the manioc-cassava family. Requiring constant horticulture, this system, while productive, was fragile and easily disrupted. The population totals maintained by these *conucos* around 1490 or so are a subject of dispute, with estimates ranging from 100,000 to 8 million.

In early December 1492, Christopher Columbus's ships, on his first voyage to America, reached the north coast of the island, and after a brief initial period of minimal intrusion, the Spanish invaders secretly disrupted the ethnic and economic structures of the island. Disease, destruction of the fragile *conuco* system, massive forced and voluntary movements of slave and laboring populations, Spanish internecine strife, and an imposed tributary system based on gold reduced the aboriginal population to about 30,000 by 1514, and this remnant died out soon afterwards. The Spaniards attempted unsuccessfully to fill the demographic vacuum by importing Amerindian captives from the Bahamas and other Caribbean areas, which caused severe losses in those places.

By 1550 or so Hispaniola had witnessed a dramatic social and agricultural revolution. Its dense starch-consuming population had disappeared and had been replaced by a sparse meat-consuming group of Spaniards, a few other Europeans, and African slaves. The island had become a political dependency of distant power centers in Europe, having exported perhaps as much as fifty tons of gold to these centers in its first half century or more as a colony. Vast herds of semiferal cattle, horses, and pigs roamed the abandoned *conucos* and the forests, and as alluvial gold in the rivers became exhausted, the Spanish population, much of it in the capital city of Santo Domingo, emigrated to Cuba and Mexico or turned to transatlantic exports of hides. Hispaniola, originally the center of Spain's American colonies, had become peripheral, and the Spanish part of the island would so remain throughout the colonial period.

French pirates began to infest the coasts in the 1550s. In 1553, for example, François Leclerc destroyed the small settlement of Yaguana, later the site of the Haitian capital of Port-au-Prince. For the rest of the century the countryside was left to herds of grazing animals. By the 1620s French and English pirates and outlaws, some of them exiled French Huguenots, began to settle on La Tortue (Tortuga), an island off the north coast of what is now Haiti. From this base they camped and hunted on the "mainland." These buccaneers (from the French *bocaner*, "to smoke") dried and smoked meat from the abundant cattle. As their settlements became more numerous and permanent settlers began to live on the north coast, the few remaining Spaniards withdrew to the eastern part of the island. The arrival in 1665 of a French governor, Bernard d'Ogeron, in La Tortue, brought stability, and by the time of his death in 1675 an early planter society had emerged and the English pirates had been expelled. By the Treaty of Ryswick (1697), Spain ceded the western third of Hispaniola to France, and the official colony of Saint-Domingue (Haiti) began.

The new colony underwent dramatic economic and ethnic transformations, becoming France's richest colony and the wealthiest in the Caribbean. By the late eighteenth century it was exporting great quantities of tropical produce, especially SUGAR, INDIGO, and COFFEE. This plantation agriculture depended on the rich soils of the plains, and, above all, on the importation and labor of large numbers of West African slaves, many of whom died of disease, overwork, and abuse. Slaves and free blacks made up the majority of the colonial population. By 1789, the year of the French Revolution, the colony was composed of some 450,000 black slaves, 30,000 or more free blacks and mulattoes, and about 40,000 whites. The city of Cap Français (now Cap Haitien) was prosperous and the leading port, although Port-au-Prince, in spite of disastrous earthquakes, fires, and epidemics, was to surpass "Le Cap" after independence.

This flourishing colony was, however, inherently un-stable. Fugitive slaves (MAROONS) in the mountains, or across the border in Santo Domingo, harassed plantations and travelers, and repulsed several expeditions sent against them. In 1784 the government agreed not to pursue them if they refrained from attacks. Riots in the cities and slave resistance on the plantations continued to cause violent reactions from the authorities. Absentee landlords, epidemics, and a constant export of wealth distracted the colony. Above all, the inherent exploitation and racial discrimination of chattel SLAVERY created a divided society and a caste system based on ethnic categories. The three castes, their status confirmed and reinforced by colonial law, were the whites, the *affranchis*, or free coloreds—many of them the result of sexual relations between white masters and black slaves, and other manumitted slaves and their offspring—and the slaves, who vastly outnumbered the others.

Whites had almost all political power, although the governor general and the intendant were often at odds with the *grands blancs* (elite whites), who feared and opposed French interests. Forming a sort of middle class were the *petits blancs,* many of them artisans or tradesmen, mulatto landowners and merchants, and some free blacks, who resented the *grands blancs* yet aspired to their station, and feared the despised slave masses. Some of the *affranchis* had become prosperous landowners. There was a further division within the slave population itself between the creoles, born in Saint-Domingue or elsewhere in the Caribbean, and the *bossals,* born in Africa. It was believed, and is still argued, that the creoles were more Europeanized, while the *bossals* were inherently more alienated and rebellious and stricter adherents to VODUN (or voodoo), a religious cult, largely African in origin.

THE HAITIAN REVOLUTION

In spite of these tensions and divisions it was a push from the metropolis that drove the colony toward its years of violent conflict, foreign intervention, and final independence. The events leading to 1789, and the French Revolution itself, meant different things to the different castes and subcastes of Saint-Domingue. The *grands blancs,* who found themselves in the paradoxical position of advocating both the ideas of the European Enlightenment and the continuation of slavery sought greater autonomy from both the radical nature of the revolutionary mother country and from what they perceived as their bondage to the interests of its merchants and markets. Those below the *grands blancs,* including some *petits blancs* and many *affranchis,* saw in liberty, equality, and fraternity a chance to defeat, or at least join, the colonial aristocracy. Many argued for the principles of equality while glancing nervously over their shoulders, or while ignoring the slave masses.

The society *Les Amis des Noirs,* founded in Paris the year before the Revolution to advocate a gradual abolition of slavery, took up the cause of mulatto equality and supported Jacques Vincent OGÉ, one of the *affranchis* commissioners to the National Assembly in Paris, Jean-Baptiste Chavannes, and other mulattoes. When Ogé returned to Saint-Domingue, he and Chavannes led a mulatto revolt. Defeated, they fled to Santo Domingo and, after extradition, were condemned and broken on the wheel in February 1791. Mulattoes in the south continued to resist, and, led by André RIGAUD, obtained a provisional understanding from the whites that they would not oppose acts of the French National Assembly on behalf of freedmen. On 14 August 1791, following a voodoo ceremony at Bois-Caiman, a founding myth of Haitian nationalism, slaves on the northern plain revolted, burning plantations and killing whites. Forty thousand laid siege to Le Cap, where many whites with slaves of dubious loyalty had taken refuge. In the south and around Port-au-Prince a three-caste war continued, with mulattoes shifting sides as it became expedient.

The English in Jamaica, fearful of slave revolts, began to help the whites. Spain, hoping to expel the French and regain their lost colony, sided with the rebels, denouncing the French as republican atheists. The United States feared the infection of revolution would cause slave uprisings in its southern states but also wished to continue the lucrative trade with Saint-Domingue, under either white or black rule. The French republicans sent a commission to bring peace, but both sides dismissed it.

Léger Félicité SONTHONAX, a Jacobin member of *Les Amis des Noirs*, was then sent by the National Assembly with two other new commissioners to Saint-Domingue to renew peace negotiations. At first Sonthonax favored the mulattoes and made no concessions on slavery. He suspected the whites, whom he considered to be royalists. On 29 August 1793 he proclaimed the abolition of slavery to obtain black support. The local whites were not his only problem. By late August a Spanish invading army reached Le Cap, and the following month an English army disembarked, as part of a plan by William Pitt the Younger to conquer the French West Indies.

Among the black rebels who joined the Spanish army in the north was a former slave, Toussaint L'OUVERTURE, who rose rapidly to a high rank and proved to be a skilled military and political leader. His able subordinates included a radical black, Jean-Jacques DESSALINES. By May 1794 Toussaint had responded to the French National Convention's abolition of slavery by deserting the Spanish side. Yellow fever, disagreements with French planters, and poor leadership soon reduced both Spanish and British expeditions to defensive remnants. In July 1795 Spain withdrew from the conflict and ceded Santo Domingo to France.

Toussaint proved to be a master of military tactics and political maneuverings. He gradually eliminated all internal and external opponents, and in 1798 the English also withdrew. Toussaint now turned his attention to Rigaud and the mulatto armies of the south. Rigaud attacked Toussaint's forces on 16 June 1799, and a race war, the War of Knives, further devastated the country.

During the siege of the southern port of Jacmel, two more rebels came to the fore. Henri CHRISTOPHE led Toussaint's besieging forces, and Dessalines went to terrorize the mulattoes of the south. After an easy conquest of the Spanish province of Santo Domingo, Toussaint, still nominally loyal to France, was in fact the ruler of the whole island. In February 1801 he appointed a group of seven whites and three mulattoes to draw up a constitution. As could have been predicted, the new constitution appointed Toussaint governor for life, abolished slavery, and maintained the fiction of French rule.

Toussaint's projects to rebuild the shattered economy and to oblige the former slaves to return to their plantations were halted by a Napoleonic invasion in January 1802. Bonaparte had officially recognized Toussaint as captain-general of the colony in March 1801, but after his defeat in Egypt his attention turned to the West Indies, where his attempt to restore French colonialism met with the approval of England and the United States. He sent French forces in January 1802 but miscalculated the skill and fervor of the black revolutionaries. The leader of the expedition, General Charles LECLERC, Napoleon's brother-in-law, shared his optimism as well as his ignorance of the island. At first Leclerc met with success, seizing all the main ports, but Toussaint, Dessalines, and Christophe continued to lead a guerrilla war from the interior. Then, in actions which still remain inexplicable, Christophe surrendered and Toussaint came to terms with Leclerc. Dessalines came over to Leclerc soon after. Lesser guerrilla generals continued to resist, but Leclerc seemed to have won the island for Napoleon.

Where black resistance had waned, yellow fever took over and cut down the French soldiery. Leclerc seized Toussaint and sent him to France, where he died in prison on 7 April 1803. He then tried to disarm the black population. These actions led many former slaves to realize that a return to plantation slavery was imminent, and they fled to the interior to join the guerrillas, although Christophe, Dessalines, and other major black leaders continued to fight for Leclerc.

The brutalities and massacres on both sides increased in August and September 1802, and the war became widespread. By October the tide had turned, and Dessalines, Christophe, and Alexandre PÉTION abandoned the doomed Leclerc and rejoined the rebels. Leclerc died of yellow fever at Le Cap soon afterwards. General Donatien ROCHAMBEAU, a soldier experienced in the Caribbean, took over, added a new contingent of 10,000 troops, and proved to be even more brutal than Leclerc. One can only conclude that he believed in the extermination of all the former black slaves and their replacement by new *bossals*. All the evidence indicates that Napoleon approved of these methods. The war became one of dreadful atrocities.

External forces settled the issue. England went to war against France in May 1803 and by June was attacking French port garrisons in Saint-Domingue. Dessalines took the opportunity to counterattack, burning plantations and executing whites. Many survivors fled the island. A mass evacuation of local whites and French soldiers from Le Cap in late November 1803 ended French rule in Saint-Domingue, although Santo Domingo remained under French authority.

The rebels named the new republic Haiti, an Arawak name, and Dessalines became leader of the nation for life, a precedent for many later Haitian rulers. On 1 January 1804 independence was declared and a convention at Gonaives, firmly controlled by Dessalines, set about writing the laws that would govern the infant state.

The Haitian Revolution has received little scholarly attention, yet it was an event of importance both within Haiti and in the world outside. Accounts have tended to emphasize the carnage and destruction and the inability of this once rich colony and its early leaders to restore prosperity. While some have attempted rudimentary analyses of this failure, others have resorted to brief fatalistic or racist conclusions. In fact the fifteen or so years of the Haitian Revolution were the focal point of some long-term changes, and the scene of other more dramatic ones, all in a complex weave yet to be untangled.

From the demographic point of view, the Haitian Revolution and the massacres perpetrated against whites by Dessalines in March 1804 were not new but rather the culmination of the region's second great demographic switch. Whites had replaced Native Americans in the early sixteenth century. By the time of the outbreak of the fighting in 1789, imported black slaves vastly outnumbered whites, and the rebel blacks completed the change by driving out or killing most of the white population and many of the mixed bloods. These expulsions, the carnage on both sides, and the epidemics and other hardships of the revolutionary years, lowered the remaining population by as much as 50 percent, according to some estimates. (Of the half million inhabitants before the revolt began, only 250,000 or so remained.) Gender imbalance had always been pronounced among the slaves, especially in the *bossal* group. By 1804 war casualties among slaves had apparently brought parity.

In 1804, the sugar plantation complex lay in ruins, and despite efforts to revive it, failed to recover. Several factors were at play. One of them was the labor shortage arising from the disappearance of half of the population, a drop in numbers which was especially severe among black field workers. Another factor was the lack of capital. Sugar, far more than coffee, tobacco, or indigo, required large capital investments, but most local accumulations had been destroyed and, for obvious reasons, there were no foreign lenders. Former slaves, moreover, obviously loathed sugar plantations—attacks on them were a major feature of the wars—and resisted all attempts after peace returned to recruit them for sugar plantation labor. Such factors, and above all the end of slavery, one of the great aims and accomplishments of

the Haitian Revolution, led to radical changes in soil use during and after the Revolution. Such changes did not necessarily mean a collapse of production, as many writers have assumed, and as will be discussed further below. Agriculture was forced to become less labor and capital intensive, but the peasantry and export merchants adjusted, and foreign trade and domestic food supplies revived rapidly after 1804.

In the political arena the Haitian Revolution brought to power a new elite of black and mulatto generals. Military prowess created the new legitimacy, and the foreign models that impressed the liberators—as they had in Gran Colombia and Mexico—were those which stressed the stability to be found in life presidencies, or even those which glorified Napoleonic imperial rule. This centralizing militarism was reinforced by the perception among the new elite that they and their infant nation were beleaguered. France did not relinquish its claims until later, the white North Atlantic nations mocked the new leadership and deplored its existence, and slavery continued to be the fate of most Caribbean people, causing Haitians to dread its return. Given this fearful climate, Dessalines became governor-general for life in September 1803 and proclaimed himself Emperor Jacques I on 8 October 1804. He was assassinated by unknowns on 17 October 1806.

Both England and Spain, while happy to see France defeated, were obsessed with the possible impact of the slave uprising on Cuba, Santo Domingo (which had reverted to Spain in 1809), and Jamaica. Haitian fears of Santo Domingo were equally strong because of its potential use as a base for reconquest by European powers. In slave societies in general the success of the Haitian Revolution may have delayed political independence. In both Cuba and Brazil the planter class reinforced its ties to the mother country. France's attitudes had varied wildly. Under the Jacobins and Sonthonax, the government had ended slavery and had supported independence. Under Napoleonic rule Leclerc and the sadistic Rochambeau had tried to destroy the Haitian Revolution and reimpose the *ancien régime*. French fears continued because of the proximity of the slave societies in Guadeloupe and Martinique. The United States was ambivalent. Southern slaveholders tried to exclude all news and people who could spread sedition to slaves, but U.S. trade with Haiti had increased before the Revolution, indeed had passed that of France, and commercial interests were keen to replace France as a trading partner.

FROM INDEPENDENCE TO U.S. INVASION, 1804–1915
When Dessalines's tyrannical empire ended with his murder, Haiti split apart. Alexandre Pétion, a mulatto who had supported Rigaud against Toussaint, declared a republic and defied Henri Christophe, a black who had fought with Toussaint and Dessalines. Meanwhile, Christophe declared himself king. A truce divided the country into north and south, although for a while André

Rigaud, once imprisoned in France with Toussaint, set up a third state in the southern peninsula when he escaped and returned to Haiti in 1810. (He died the following year.)

In the north, Christophe, copying Toussaint, attempted to restore the sugar plantations by work discipline and obligatory labor. Although he established friendly relations with foreign powers, he was also aware of the threat of invasion and built the mountaintop fortress of La Ferrière. Pétion in the south was more moderate, and many large estates were broken up and distributed to veterans of the wars. On his death in 1818, Jean-Pierre BOYER, a mulatto supporter of Rigaud, became president. He reunited the nation when Christophe's harsh rule in the north caused a revolt. Christophe committed suicide in 1820.

Boyer's long presidency (1818–1843) was a formative period for Haiti. He conquered Santo Domingo in 1822, thus ending slavery throughout Hispaniola, and opened negotiations with France. The French were adamant in their insistence that they were still the legal power in Haiti, and Boyer, worried about the precarious position of the small mulatto ruling class, appeared to be willing to accept some form of French allegiance. Popular hatred of the idea of French domination was such, however, that Boyer finally bargained for French recognition in return for Haitian payment of an indemnity of 150 million francs and favorable tariffs on French goods. The indemnity has been heavily criticized because it forced Haiti into foreign borrowing and internal taxation, and obviously lessened opportunities for local investment. It also allowed foreign economic manipulation. But from Boyer's point of view, recognition from France, which ended the threat of invasion, was worth the price.

Boyer reversed Pétion's *laissez-faire* attitude toward the land question. Like Toussaint and Christophe he dreamed of a plantation economy geared to exports. His efforts to stop the alienation of public lands, and his famous *Code Rurale* (1826), which attempted to restrict movement and force people to work, were clearly designed to create a stable labor force for the few large landowners. His rural policies, however, failed to reverse the trend toward small peasant subsistence holdings. Sugar production continued to fall, although small-holder crops such as coffee and cacao took up some of the slack. Unfortunately for the country's ecological future, timber, including valuable stands of hardwoods, became a valuable export. Commerce with the United States flourished.

The president continued Toussaint's opposition to the popular religion, Vodun, and although somewhat antireligious, he made serious efforts to win international "respectability" by negotiating a concordat with the Holy See. Elite culture revived, much of it, in Port-au-Prince at least, European in derivation.

Boyer's regime failed to halt the trend toward a small-holding peasantry, and his overthrow in 1843 showed that certain other characteristics of elite politics and Haitian life were becoming ingrained. Boyer's government was dominated by mulattoes who enriched themselves through government office or favors. Excluded mulattoes and elite blacks, especially from the south, agitated for more democracy, although they gave little thought to the inclusion of the rural black masses. The division between the tiny mulatto minority and a small black elite, a division that had been strengthened by the Ogé revolt, the civil war between Toussaint and Rigaud, the split between Christophe and Pétion, and by the Boyer regime, was to become a major feature of elite politics.

The implications of this ethnic politics were often more proclaimed than real. In general, at this time, mulattoes were wealthier than blacks, but there were many exceptions, especially when blacks were able to seize power in the military and the presidency, two of the main sources of wealth when exports declined in the 1840s and later. Mulattoes, moreover, tended to be more cosmopolitan, more connected to outside power centers, while blacks, in general, were more local and nationalistic. Blacks also were more prone to call in rural peasant insurgents, whether *piquets* or CACOS, to tip the political balance in their favor in Cap Haitien and especially Port-au-Prince. Hardly more than political shadings, these differences meant less once a leader was in office. Conduct and policy reflect race and politics in some presidencies, but more often they do not. Legislation that showed any interest in or benefit to the rural masses was rare indeed in nineteenth-century Haiti.

A pattern that evolved after the exile of Boyer—who fled to Jamaica, the haven for deposed Haitian presidents throughout the nineteenth century—was the oscillation between long periods of dictatorial stability and unstable interregnums, with brief tenures in the presidency and turbulent politics. The quarter century of Boyer's rule was followed by four brief presidencies, none of which lasted for even one year. These interludes in office illustrate another feature of Haitian elite politics, the so-called *politique de doublure* (understudy politics) by which elite politicians or merchants, usually mulattoes, governed behind a black puppet, often a figurehead army general with some peasant support. The four elderly generals who followed Boyer to the presidency—Guerrier was eighty-seven when he took office—showed little initiative, but with the fifth selection, an obscure black from the presidential guard, Faustin SOULOUQUE, another long reign began.

Soulouque turned on his sponsors, set up an urban terror squad, the *zinglins*, used the southern *piquets* adroitly to frighten the merchants of Port-au-Prince, but then executed the *piquet* leader, Pierre Noir, when he threatened to become too powerful. Soulouque massacred many mulattoes, although several mulattoes served in his cabinet. After a year or so in office he arranged his elevation to emperor, and his tenure in office lasted almost twelve years (1847–1859). Although terror and bribery were among his weapons, there is no doubt that he created a form of legitimacy for his rule among significant sectors of the population. He tolerated, perhaps even encouraged, voodoo. The parallels with the regimes of Dessalines and Duvalier *père* are striking.

The last former slave to rule Haiti, Soulouque was preoccupied with national territorial integrity, and twice invaded the Dominican Republic, which had broken away after the fall of Boyer. These incursions were for the purpose of self-aggrandizement, no doubt, but also arose from the old concern that the neighbor state would become a base for foreign intrusion. His defeats in the Dominican Republic led to his overthrow by General Fabre GEFFRARD, a dark mulatto (*griffe*), who, as if to validate the stereotypes of mulatto elite behavior, spent much of his presidency gaining international respectability and favor. He detested voodoo as barbarism and signed another concordat with the Holy See in 1860. Two years later, President Abraham Lincoln finally gave U.S. diplomatic recognition to Haiti, and Geffrard encouraged the immigration of black U.S. citizens, with little success. Geffrard was overthrown by another mulatto general, Silvain SALNAVE (6 May 1867), and fled to Jamaica.

Salnave, who also declared himself president for life, was unusual in that he was a mulatto who had support from some black factions. He seems to have enjoyed some popularity among the poor of Port-au-Prince. Such was not the case, however, with the *cacos,* the successors to the southern *piquets* of the 1840s. These bands of middling peasants, or *habitants,* opposed Salnave, and played a large if intermittent role in politics until after the U.S. occupation (1915–1934). Their goals were often obscure. They gave their support, first to one general then to another, on the basis of promises of short-term advantages. Perhaps what they sought in general was benign neglect—promises that peasant land tenure or political arrangements in the rural areas would not be disturbed. Once their man was installed in the presidency these rural groups usually disbanded, as subsistence agriculturists often must, thus failing to keep up pressure on their leader. Then, when a later generation saw new possibilities, they would rise again.

Between Salnave's execution in January 1870 and the chaotic politics that began in August 1911 and ended in the U.S. invasion of 1915, the Liberal Party, often the representative of the mulatto elite, faced opposition from the National Party, the organ of the black elites. With a few exceptions these political struggles were violent.

Selected by the National Assembly after a provisional government, President Nissage Saget completed his term of office (1870–1874) and stepped down voluntarily. President Boisrond Canal resigned in disgust in July 1879 because he could not make his constitutional relationship work with a hostile legislature. Apart from these exceptions presidencies began and ended by force or the threat of it. Once in office a president was faced with the need to implement policies and collect money to run the government and to pay off political creditors and hungry, potentially hostile officeholders. Peasants were hard to tax, unless the president could find a way to tax or seize their export produce—by this time almost all coffee—as it passed through the ports. Interfering with exports or imports alienated the small but important bourgeoisie, mainly in Port-au-Prince, which could be intimidated by politically strategic attacks on offices and shops, a judiciously timed massacre, or the threat of armed soldiery or *cacos.* Presidents needed the merchants and business community, especially when the *politique de doublure* was in force.

Foreign interference was another factor. The British and the French still held colonies in the Caribbean and insisted on the payment of loans. The tendency of deposed presidents to flee to Jamaica, or of invading armies to come from the Dominican Republic, presented additional opportunities for foreign meddling. Of growing importance was the United States. An exporter of capital by the 1890s, and a power that increasingly considered the Caribbean as its private backyard lake, the U.S. government and business community found the sporadic unrest in Haiti to be a threat to U.S. citizens and their interests. The United States found Haiti's black nationalism to be an affront and many of its policies, such as the constitutional provision against ownership of land by foreign whites, to be an obstacle to investment. Moreover, Haiti's geographical position athwart the entrances to the northern Caribbean (notably its natural harbor at Môle St. Nicolas on the northeast coast) also provoked interference from the United States and other powers.

The need for money, the relationship with the national bourgeoisie, and fear of foreign power, faced each president, whatever his ethnic politics and proclamations. The welfare of the majority was forgotten, and several presidents found themselves appeasing foreign governments, negotiating new loans with them, or even negotiating leases of national territory. Such was the rivalry for the presidency and the precariousness of tenure once in office that some Haitian leaders treacherously called in foreign military support against their compatriot opponents.

President Louis Étienne Lysius Félicité SALOMON (1879–1888) had served in Soulouque's cabinet and was a noted black nationalist. He survived an invasion from Jamaica backed by the British, suppressed dissidence, and claimed to fight for national integrity. Yet he found it expedient to support the concordat with the Holy See in spite of the anticlerical, pro-voodoo opinions of many of his followers. He negotiated with the United States for the lease of national territory, founded the Banque Nationale backed by French capital, and, in return for the liquidation of the French indemnity, accepted a French military mission. He even permitted foreign companies to own Haitian land.

Between 1911 and 1915 there were six presidents. The last of them, Vilbrun Guillaume Sam, who had ordered the execution of jailed opponents, was dragged out of the French embassy and torn to pieces by an enraged mob. The U.S. Marines landed that same day, 28 July 1915.

FROM THE U.S. OCCUPATION TO THE DUVALIERS AND THEIR LEGACY

Explanations of the reasons for the invasion have varied. The pretext was the rioting preceding the murder of President Sam, which the United States considered a threat to U.S. citizens and property in Haiti. There may have been a wish to forestall the French, whose embassy had been violated. There was certainly U.S. concern over Germany, which, with World War I raging, had designs on Môle St. Nicolas on the northeast coast of Haiti. Germany had at various times asserted its right to protect the sizable German merchant community in Port-au-Prince. The U.S. investors, moreover, had bought out the French interest in the Banque Nationale. The British, for their part, often acted as protectors of the increasingly important Syrian-Lebanese merchant group that dominated much of Haiti's commercial life. Interests in the United States had long been frustrated at the difficulties in penetrating the Haitian economy. The combination of these fears and frustrations, when added to the strategic hegemony that the United States was establishing in the Caribbean, gave enough impetus to justify the invasion and the occupation, which lasted nineteen years.

Those who defend the U.S. occupation refer to the political and financial stability that it brought. There were also material gains. Health conditions improved; roads, hospitals, and schools were built; and more foreign investment flowed in. U.S. interests came first, however, and the reversal of the old policy prohibiting foreign ownership of land—a reversal that led to land purchase by U.S. capital—was resented. Provoking even more resentment was the U.S. policy of favoring the mulatto elite, evidenced by the installation in the presidency of a series of mulattoes. Rural anger at the imposition of the *corvée*, a system of obligatory labor drafts, caused a *cacos* revolt in 1918 led by *habitants* such as Charlemagne PÉRALTE, who was killed after a violent campaign by the U.S. Marines. Nationalistic fervor increased after the revolt, and President Franklin D. Roosevelt finally withdrew U.S. troops in 1934.

Much has been made of the ethnological and nationalistic movement that began as a reaction to the foreign occupation. A group of intellectuals strove to emphasize the African part of Haiti's heritage, stressing *négritude,* voodoo, and indigenous creole culture. These tendencies were exacerbated by the killing of thousands of Haitians in the Dominican Republic by the government of Rafael TRUJILLO. The *Griot* movement, one of whose founders was François DUVALIER, demanded a revolution that would throw off all European attachments; he rewrote Haitian political history emphasizing the black past even more than the National Party had

done. In 1941–1942 the Catholic church, with the support of President Elie LESCOT, led an "anti-superstitious campaign" in an attempt to eradicate voodoo, and further aroused the new revolutionaries.

Dumarsais ESTIMÉ, a black nationalist, won an army-supervised election in 1946, displacing the mulatto elites. The Estimé regime proved to be ineffectual. Personal ambitions led many black politicians to desert him, the elite bourgeoisie found him too radical, and the Left complained of inaction. When the army overthrew him in 1950 and Paul MAGLOIRE became president, there was little opposition, although in retrospect Estimé was considered a hero. Magloire was welcomed by the elites, the Catholic church, and the Port-au-Prince business community. There was a brief burst of prosperity, at least in the city, under Magloire. His minority politics were dated, however.

Magloire's overthrow in 1956 brought another interregnum while the blacks who had followed Estimé struggled for power. Gradually, François Duvalier, a black physician, gained the lukewarm support of the army and a majority among the electorate. He won the presidential election of 1957, presenting himself as the culmination of the Estimé presidency, as a *Griot,* and a black, but also as a moderate reformer who favored business and the Catholic church.

Duvalier ruled Haiti as "president for life" for almost fourteen years (1957–1971). Like Soulouque, he quickly threw off those who had believed that the amenable tone of his campaign speeches could lead to his manipulation. He also astutely survived a series of attempted coups and assassinations in the early years of his regime; from then on he never relaxed terroristic vigilance and authoritarian rule. By the mid-1960s Duvalier reigned supreme. All his leading opponents were dead or in exile.

Duvalier had elaborated his philosophy of government in many books and articles, but his rule failed to develop much of it. After the elimination of his rivals, his regime was fraught with revolutionary rhetoric and symbols, but his policies were conservative. He succeeded in replacing foreign priests with Haitian nationals. He also ferociously dismantled some sectors of the elites and thereby won the support of parts of the new black urban middle class, the voodoo hierarchy, and the political leaders of the villages. Under both his presidency and the even longer one of his son Jean-Claude DUVALIER (1971–1986), however, little was done or even attempted to solve the dreadful economic and social ills of Haiti. The peasantry found his support of voodoo and his nationalism to their liking and, at the very least, did not oppose him, but their standard of living began to deteriorate more rapidly than before because of an increasing population and the resulting division and subdivision of land holding. Much has been made of the elites who fled into exile because of the repression under Duvalier's secret police and the *tontons macoutes.* Since his regime many of the rural poor have emigrated to the

Dominican Republic, the Bahamas, and the United States.

The regime of Duvalier *fils* was less violent than that of his father, but became increasingly associated with the old elites and with spectacular corruption. When his support disappeared, he was flown to exile in France by the U.S. government. Haiti then entered another of its interregnums. Elections were canceled and presidencies were ephemeral. The army reasserted itself in national politics. If anything was new in the late 1980s and early 1990s it was the acceleration of the ecological and Malthusian crisis, plus the more vigorous participation of the rapidly growing urban masses in decision making. The election of Jean-Bertrand ARISTIDE to the presidency in 1990 by a large popular vote did not, however, prevent his overthrow and exile soon afterward. Aristide, unpopular among many leaders in the U.S. because of his radical rhetoric, nevertheless received U.S. and U.N. help in his struggle to regain power. By 1994 blockades against Haiti were in force, and repression within the country was harsh. U.S. diplomatic and military pressure effected Aristide's restoration in October 1994, but the problems facing Haiti remained overwhelming.

JEAN-BAPTISTE LABAT, *Voyage aux isles de l'Amérique* (*Antilles*): *1693–1705*, 2 vols. (1931); M. L. E. MOREAU DE SAINT-MÉRY, *Description topographique, physique, civile, politique et historique de la partie française de l'Ile de Saint Dominique*, 3 vols., 3d ed. (1958); GABRIEL DEBIEN, *Plantations et esclaves à Saint-Domingue* (1962); C. L. R. JAMES, *The Black Jacobins: Toussaint L'Ouverture and the San Domingo Revolution* (1963); JOACHIM BENOIT, "La bourgeoisie d'affaires haïtienne au 19ème siècle," in *Nouvelle Optique* I, no. 4 (1971): 50–70; HANS R. SCHMIDT, JR., *The United States Occupation of Haiti: 1915–1934* (1971); FRANÇOIS GIROD, *La vie quotidienne de la société créole: Saint-Domingue au XVIIᵉ siècle* (1972); FRANK MOYA PONS, *La dominación haitiana, 1822–1844* (1972); THOMAS O. OTT, *The Haitian Revolution, 1789–1804* (1973); DAVID NICHOLLS, *From Dessalines to Duvalier: Race, Colour, and National Independence in Haiti* (1979); PAUL BUTEL, *Les Caraïbes au temps des flibustiers* (1982); DAVID P. GEGGUS, *Slavery, War, and Revolution: The British Occupation of Saint Domingue, 1793–1798* (1982); BRENDA G. PLUMMER, *Haiti and the Great Powers, 1902–1915* (1988); ALEX DUPUY, *Haiti in the World Economy, Class, Race, and Underdevelopment since 1700* (1989); MICHEL-ROLPH TROUILLOT, *Haiti, State Against Nation: The Origins and Legacy of Duvalierism* (1990); SAMUEL M. WILSON, *Hispaniola: Caribbean Chiefdoms in the Age of Columbus* (1990).

MURDO J. MACLEOD

See also **Caste and Class Structure; Slave Revolts.**

HAITI: CONSTITUTIONS. Haiti has had about twenty constitutions, both real and nominal, many illustrating the apt creole proverb: "A constitution is paper; a bayonet is steel." A common characteristic of most of them has been a strong president and a weak legislature.

The first constitution, Autonomy and Independence (TOUSSAINT, 1801), written ten years after independence from France, gave France suzerainty and provided for forced labor. The second (DESSALINES, 1805) abolished

slavery "forever," separated church and state, applied the word "black" to all Haitians, and prohibited foreign ownership of land. The third (PÉTION's first, 1806) is modeled after that of the United States. The fourth (CHRISTOPHE, 1811) created a nobility. The fifth (Pétion's second, 1816) granted the president his office for life. The sixth (Riché, 1846) empowered the joint chambers to elect the president. The seventh (Domingue, 1874) concentrated all power in the presidency. That of 1889 (HYPPOLITE) revised the previous constitution of 1879 (Salomon) and served as the basis of government until the U.S. occupation.

The Constitution of 1918, written during the U.S. occupation by Assistant Navy Secretary Franklin D. ROOSEVELT, cancelled the prohibition of foreign ownership of land and added individual democratic rights. The eleventh constitution (1927) increased the powers of the president, as did that of 1932 (Vincent).

The constitutions of the postoccupation and Duvalier era were the thirteenth (MAGLOIRE, 1950), a liberal one written by the scholar-diplomat Dantès Bellegarde that provided for female suffrage beginning in 1957, and the fourteenth (DUVALIER, 1957), which increased the powers of the president and excluded foreigners from retail trade. Duvalier's second constitution (1961) reduced the legislature to one chamber and increased the powers of the president. Duvalier's third, which was the sixteenth constitution, made Duvalier president for life, authorized him to choose his successor, and changed the flag's colors.

"Baby Doc" Duvalier's first constitution, the seventeenth (1983), combined a set of progressive social goals with new presidential powers of appointment and new power over the legislature. Baby Doc's second (1985) provided the legislature with new powers, created the position of prime minister, and permitted political parties (a public-relations response to U.S. pressure, approved by a fraudulent referendum).

The first constitution of the post-Duvalier era, that of 1987, restored the two-chamber legislature, reduced the powers of the president by dividing the executive authority between president and prime minister, created a permanent electoral council, removed the new *force publique* from direct control of the president and minister of the interior, prohibited for ten years the participation in government of "any person well known for having been . . . one of the architects of the dictatorship and of its maintenance during the last twenty-nine years," provided many basic human rights, recognized Creole (Kreyol) as the national language, legalized VODUN, and recognized no state religion. It was approved by a free and popular referendum.

President Leslie François Manigat was removed by General Henri Namphy, who became president, dissolved the legislature, and abolished all constitutions. Namphy in turn was removed by General Prosper Avril, who restored the nineteenth constitution, except for thirty-eight articles.

General Avril was forced out in 1989 and he was replaced by supreme court judge Ertha PASCAL-TROUILLOT, who became provisional president in 1990 under article 149 of the constitution. (This article provides that if the office of president is vacant, the chief justice or a member will become acting president until elections are held.) In free elections, Jean-Bertrand ARISTIDE, a leftist priest, was elected president; he was inaugurated in February 1991. While president, Aristide took advantage of article 295 of the constitution, which authorized him for a six-month period "to proceed to carry out any reforms deemed necessary in the Government Administration . . . and in the Judiciary." He gave some provocative speeches threatening the elite "bourgeoisie" and the military; the latter overthrew him in late September. The ORGANIZATION OF AMERICAN STATES (OAS) responded by approving economic sanctions against the military government of General Raoul Cédras to bring about Aristide's restoration. The United Nations joined the OAS in 1993 and joint efforts were made to negotiate a settlement. An accord was reached in July, providing for the selection of a prime minister (Robert Malval), lifting of sanctions, political amnesty, and Aristide's return. The accord could not be implemented once the military reneged although sanctions were strengthened. In June 1994, the military government, acting under article 149, inaugurated Supreme Court Chief Justice Émile Jonassaint as provisional president. President Aristide was restored to power in late 1994.

JAMES G. LEYBURN, *The Haitian People* (1941), esp. chap. 13; DAVID NICHOLLS, *From Dessalines to Duvalier: Race, Colour, and National Independence in Haiti* (1979), esp. chap. 2; BRIAN WEINSTEIN and AARON SEGAL, *Haiti: Political Failures, Cultural Successes* (1984), pp. 51–54; JAMES FERGUSON, *Papa Doc, Baby Doc: Haiti and the Duvaliers* (1987), esp. pp. 80, 83–85, 156–158; PATRICK BELLEGARDE-SMITH, *Haiti: The Breached Citadel* (1989), pp. 44–46, 123–126, 139–140.

LARMAN C. WILSON

HALFFTER, RODOLFO (*b.* 20 October 1900; *d.* 14 October 1987), Spanish composer. Mainly self-taught, Halffter in 1929 sought advice from the eminent composer Manuel de Falla with whose spare, neoclassic style his music is frequently compared. He gained recognition in Europe in the mid-1930s but moved to Mexico in 1939. A permanent resident and citizen of Mexico from 1940, he held posts as professor at the National Conservatory (from 1940) and director of the composers' cooperative publishing firm, Ediciones Mexicanas de Música (from 1946). In 1969 Halffter was inducted into the Mexican Academy of Arts. He wrote some twelve-tone serial music, the first in Mexico, but his style retained its characteristic clarity and melodiousness with tinges of dissonance and without any Mexican influences. His students include Héctor QUINTANAR and Eduardo MATA.

DAN MALMSTRÖM, *Twentieth-Century Mexican Music* (1974); GÉRARD BÉHAGUE, *Music in Latin America: An Introduction* (1979).

ROBERT L. PARKER

HALLUCINOGENS. *See* **Drugs and Drug Trade.**

HALPERÍN-DONGHI, TULIO (*b.* 27 October 1926), Argentine historian. Born and educated in Argentina, Halperín-Donghi received his doctorate from the University of Buenos Aires in 1955. He taught at the universities of Rosario and Buenos Aires from 1955 until the military coup led by Juan Carlos ONGANÍA in 1966. Since then, he taught at Harvard, Oxford, and the University of California at Berkeley. Halperín-Donghi's work covers a wide range of topics in political history, economic and fiscal history, and social and intellectual history. His contributions on the crisis of independence, the fledgling efforts at national organization, and the social and economic continuities from the Bourbon to the post-Independence periods are particularly strong. His most important work is *Revolución y guerra: Formación de una elite dirigente en la Argentina criolla* (1972), which details the breakdown of the colonial order and the emergence of new elites in a context of social and political crisis. Other works include *Tradición política española e ideología revolucionaria de Mayo* (1961), *Guerra y finanzas en los orígenes del estado argentino* (1982), and *José Hernández y sus mundos* (1985). He has also written such comprehensive histories as *Historia contemporánea de América Latina* (1969), *Hispanoamérica después de la independencia* (1972), and *El espejo de la historia: Problemas argentinos y perspectivas latinoamericanas* (1987). This last volume places Argentina in a Latin American context and reveals how Halperín's view of the region has been deepened by his years of life abroad. He retired from the University of California at Berkeley in 1994.

JOHN V. LOMBARDI, "Detail and the Grand Design in History," in *Latin American Research Review* 14, no. 2 (1979): 223–226; FRANK SAFFORD, "History, 1750–1850," in *Latin America and the Caribbean: A Critical Guide to Research Sources*, edited by Paula H. Covington (1992).

IVÁN JAKSIĆ

HAMBURG-AMERICA LINE, a shipping company founded in 1847 by Hamburg shipowners to provide a "regular connection between Hamburg and North America by means of sailing ships under Hamburg flags." Originally the Hamburg-Amerikanische-Packetfahrt-Actien Gesellschaft, it was called HAPAG even after the line changed its name in 1893 to Hamburg-Amerika Line. The company slogan was "Mein Feld ist die Welt" (My field is the world). It began operations in Latin America in the 1850s, but entered that region most seriously when it reached an agreement with the KOSMOS

LINE in 1901 and purchased the Atlas line. These two steps conceded HAPAG major European influence in freight service with Latin America.

About 1905, a serious conflict between HAPAG and the UNITED FRUIT COMPANY arose when one of HAPAG's acquisitions, Atlas Steamship Company, entered into a profitable relationship with American Fruit and other banana exporters that competed with United Fruit. In 1913 United Fruit opposition and poor reception of the bananas in Europe persuaded HAPAG to sell Atlas to United Fruit and to terminate its ties to American Fruit.

HAPAG service to Latin America was disrupted in World War I and reestablished through a shared steamer service, the Deutsche Westküsten-Dienst (Germany West Coast Service). This service was disrupted again in 1939 and resumed its functions in 1953.

OTTO MATHIES, *Hamburgs Reederei 1814–1914* (1924); PETER FRANZ STUBMANN, *Mein Feld ist die Welt: Albert Ballin: Sein Leben* (repr. 1926; 1960); WARREN ARMSTRONG, *Atlantic Highway* (1962); LAMAR CECIL, *Albert Ballin: Business and Politics in Imperial Germany, 1888–1918* (1967).

THOMAS SCHOONOVER

HAMMOCK, a woven portable bed hung from posts or hooks, originally produced by indigenous peoples from crude cotton or palm fibers, also known as *hamaca* in Spanish and *rede* in Portuguese. The use of the hammock in Latin America was first recorded by Pero Vaz da Caminha in 1500 in his description of a Tupiniquin home. He used the word *rede*, or fishing net, for its similarity in appearance. Europeans soon discovered the advantages of a portable, washable, ventilated bed that elevated the user above the rodents, insects, and floodwaters of the tropics.

Hammocks flourished throughout most of Mexico, the Caribbean, and Central and South America (especially within the Amazon Basin), with the exception of Chile and Argentina (where their use was limited) and Bolivia. They were not documented elsewhere in the world by the earliest explorers. Scholars are still undecided as to the place of origin of the hammock. The foremost Brazilian authority, Luís da Câmara Cascudo, believes that they were invented by the Arawaks (though many scholars favor the CARIBS), who passed them on to the TUPI.

Particularly in colonial Brazil, beautifully woven linen or silk hammocks with floor-sweeping overhangs became symbols of wealth and prestige. The Portuguese employed hammocks of many sizes as delivery tables and cradles, nuptial and trysting beds, porch rockers, offices, and coffins for the dead. Hammocks called *taboca* or *palanquíns* carried by two slaves were also used as transportation. They are now used principally by the poor of the North and Northeast, where they are produced manually and industrially.

LUÍS DA CÂMARA CASCUDO, *Rêde-de-dormir: Uma pesquisa etnográfica* (1959), and *Dicionário do folclore brasileiro*, 3d ed. (1972).

GAYLE WAGGONER LOPES

HANDELMANN, GOTTFRIED HEINRICH (*b.* 9 August 1827; *d.* 26 April 1891), German historian of Hispaniola and Brazil. Son of a prosperous saddle maker of Altona, Hamburg, Handelmann studied history at the universities of Heidelberg, Berlin, Göttingen, and Kiel under some distinguished scholars, including Leopold von Ranke. As a student in Kiel, Handelmann was active in the German population's struggle against Danish authority in Schleswig-Holstein. In 1854 the University of Kiel accepted his doctoral dissertation on relations between the German Hanseatic League and the Scandinavian powers. In 1866, after Schleswig-Holstein's incorporation into Prussia, Handelmann was named curator of Schleswig-Holstein antiquities and professor of history at the University of Kiel, positions he held until his death.

Concerned by the rising tide of German immigration to the Western Hemisphere, Handelmann in the 1850s turned to the study of the history of colonization in the Americas. In short order he produced *Geschichte der Vereinigten Staaten* (History of the United States, 1856), *Geschichte der insel Hayti* (History of the Island of Hispaniola, 1856), and *Geschichte von Brasilien* (History of Brazil, 1860). The last is by far the most important and, with nearly a thousand pages, longer than the other two combined. The first history of Brazil by an academically trained historian, it takes a regional approach to the colonization of Portuguese America and lacks a unifying theme. The final section of the book, dealing with the 1808–1844 period, is most useful for its coverage of Brazilian immigration policy, which is compared unfavorably with that of the United States.

JOHN HYSLOP, ''Heinrich Handelmann and Brazilian History,'' in *Teaching Latin American History*, edited by E. Bradford Burns et al. (1977), pp. 40–50.

NEILL MACAULAY

HANKE, LEWIS ULYSSES (*b.* 2 January 1905; *d.* 26 March 1993), pioneering historian and educator. In 1935, as a Harvard instructor, Hanke became the first editor of the multidisciplinary annotated bibliography, *Handbook of Latin American Studies*, which was begun following a meeting of Latin American historians who decided that such a bibliography would play a pivotal role in advancing the field. Still appearing yearly, the *Handbook* is now also available on the Internet.

Born in Oregon City, Oregon, Hanke graduated from Northwestern University. He then became an instructor at the University of Hawaii (1926–1927), taught at the

American University of Beirut, Lebanon (1927–1930), and in 1936 received a doctorate in history from Harvard, where he remained teaching until 1939. From 1939 to 1951 he was the first director of the Hispanic Foundation (now Hispanic Division) of the Library of Congress. Hanke brought the *Handbook* to the Library, where he edited it and where it remained after he left. In his books *The Spanish Struggle for Justice in the Conquest of America* (1949) and *Aristotle and the American Indians: A Study in Race Prejudice in the Modern World* (1959), Hanke ushered in a new era in examining human-rights issues in Latin American history. After leaving the Library of Congress he taught at the University of Texas (1951–1961), Columbia University (1961–1967), the University of California at Irvine (1967–1969), and the University of Massachusetts (1969–1975).

Hanke also strove to preserve Latin American and Caribbean archives and initiated many guides to archival holdings. He was editor of the *Hispanic American Historical Review* from 1954 to 1960, edited the *History of Latin American Civilization* (2d ed.; 1973), and coedited *Historia de la Villa Imperial de Potosí por Bartolomé Arzáns de Orsúa y Vela* (3 vols.; 1965) and *Los virreyes españoles en América durante el gobierno de la casa de Austria* (12 vols.; 1976–1980). Another remarkable publication coedited by Hanke is the *Guide to the Study of United States History Outside the U.S.* (5 vols.; 1945–1980). Hanke's wife, Kate, collaborated on most of his books. In 1974 Hanke became the first Latin Americanist to be elected president of the American Historical Association. Other high honors bestowed on him include membership in the Hispanic Society of America; the Gulbenkian, Rosenbach, and numerous other fellowships; and in 1992 Spain's prestigious Antonio Nebrija Prize.

RICHARD GRAHAM and PETER H. SMITH, eds., *New Approaches to Latin American History* (1974); DAN HAZEN, "The *Handbook of Latin American Studies* at (Volume) Fifty: Area Studies Bibliography in a Context of Change," in *Inter-American Review of Bibliography* 41, no. 2 (1991): 195–202.

GEORGETTE MAGASSY DORN

HARO BARRAZA, GUILLERMO (*b.* 21 March 1913), Mexican astronomer and physicist. Born in Mexico City, the son of José Haro and Leonor Barraza, Haro graduated from the National University and did postgraduate work at the Harvard University Observatory (1943–1944). A full-time researcher at the National University, he initiated an extensive fellowship program to train future Mexican scientists. He directed the National Astronomical Observatory for two decades (1948–1968) as well as the Tonantzintla Astrophysics Observatory. With Samuel RAMOS and Elí de Gortari, he cofounded the Seminar of Scientific and Philosophical Problems, which published dozens of works. His own work has appeared in English, and he has edited several scientific journals. He became a member of the National College

in 1953, and Mexico awarded him its National Prize in Sciences (1963).

Enciclopedia de México, vol. 6 (1977), p. 365.

RODERIC AI CAMP

HARO Y TAMARIZ, ANTONIO DE (*b.* 1811; *d.* 1869), Mexican politician. Born in the city of Puebla, Haro y Tamariz studied law in Rome. He served as finance minister in 1844, 1846, and 1853 and was elected to the Senate in 1850 and 1852. During the war with the United States in 1846, Haro y Tamariz proposed that church property be sold and that the government collect taxes on the sales. Prices would be set on the assumption that annual rents represented 5 percent of the value of the property. Renters would have first preference in purchasing their homes. The church delayed implementation of the plan, and the government's desperate need for funds forced it to drop the disentailment plan, but it later served as a model for the Liberal reforms of 1856.

A lifelong associate of Antonio López de SANTA ANNA, Haro y Tamariz himself became more conservative, collaborating with Lucas ALAMÁN and serving in Santa Anna's cabinet in 1853. Unable to convince the church to make any further loans to the government and unwilling to borrow from *agiotistas* (moneylenders), Haro y Tamariz resigned only three months later. After the liberal Revolution of AYUTLA overthrew Santa Anna, Haro y Tamariz launched a conservative rebellion in Puebla in December 1855 with the support of the army and the clergy. His Plan of Zacapoaxtla (1855) called for a restoration of the privileges of the church and the army and a return to the conservative Constitution of 1842. After a ferocious battle for the streets of Puebla, Haro y Tamariz was forced to surrender but managed to escape his captors. He supported the Conservative cause during the War of the REFORM and the empire of MAXIMILIAN.

JAN BAZANT, *Antonio Haro y Tamariz y sus aventuras políticas, 1811–1869* (1985); BARBARA A. TENENBAUM, *The Politics of Penury: Debt and Taxes in Mexico, 1821–1856* (1986), pp. 78–79, 121–126, 150–153; *Diccionario Porrúa de historia, biografía y geografía de México*, 5th ed. (1986).

D. F. STEVENS

HAVANA, Cuba's capital and principal seaport of slightly more than two million inhabitants (1990). Founded by Diego de VELÁZQUEZ in 1514 on the island's southern coast, San Cristóbal de la Habana was transplanted in 1519 to its present location because of both the magnificent natural harbor and the proximity to the Gulf Stream. Becoming the colonial capital in 1553, the city lay on the western side of the bay, which bottlenecked into an easily defended passage at its mouth. Eventually, the massive Morro castle was erected at the entrance's eastern shore.

Engraved view of Havana. LIBRARY OF CONGRESS.

Known as the "Key to the New World," Havana commanded the exit from the Caribbean Sea and the route to and from Veracruz, Mexico. As the imperial commercial system evolved during the sixteenth century, Havana's bay harbored the Mexican treasure fleet returning to Seville and the southern fleet on its return voyage from Cartagena. Service industries enriched the city, and its immediate hinterland enjoyed a periodic market for foodstuffs, although the economy generally remained underdeveloped until the eighteenth century.

When Spanish mercantilist strategy broadened to emphasize tropical agricultural products as well as precious metals, Havana's hinterland responded, and the city assumed the role of exporter. In 1717 the royal TOBACCO MONOPOLY began its century-long existence, emphasizing the importance of the Cuban leaf. The HAVANA COMPANY, established in 1740, promoted the marketing of SUGAR in Spain. The 1765 Regulation of Free Trade for the Caribbean Islands permitted Havana access to nine Spanish ports and enhanced marketing flexibility. The FREE TRADE ACT of 1778, especially when broadened to include Veracruz in 1788, afforded Havana the additional role of entrepôt for important portions of the Mexican and Caribbean trade. Although the Havana Company quickly faded from importance after 1765, local entrepreneurs plunged Havana's hinterland into the sugar revolution of the late eighteenth century. Thus, as deregulation dismantled the historic convoy system that had assigned Havana central importance, it simultaneously provided the port with new, larger opportunities.

During the early nineteenth century, after revolution had destroyed the sugar economy of Saint-Domingue,

Cuban production assumed world leadership. Although the collapse of Spain's continental empire diminished Havana's function as entrepôt, the city, now permitted international free trade, emerged as a major commercial center owing to continuing demand for its sugar and tobacco, a role set to endure into modern times. The population of Havana, counted at 41,000 in 1778, had climbed to 94,000 by 1827, and some 240,000 at century's end.

Heavily fortified and stoutly garrisoned, strategic Havana ranked as the most important strongpoint of the Spanish Empire. A major naval base, Havana also developed into a primary shipbuilding center during the eighteenth century. Following Havana's capture in 1762 and the subsequent eleven-month British occupation, Spain invested huge quantities of Mexican SILVER to enhance its military. Defense waned as a major industry following Spain's loss of its continental colonies, but Havana regained its historic role as a strategic military base after Cuban independence, during the United States' protectorate. Although this role diminished following WORLD WAR II, it reappeared forcefully when Cuba fell under SOVIET influence during the CASTRO dictatorship, again earning its capital massive outside subsidies. Nevertheless, Havana, once one of the world's most beautiful, vibrant cities, experienced hard times under the Castro regime and its commercial isolation from its American economic base.

HUGH THOMAS, *Cuba: The Pursuit of Freedom* (1971); LEVÍ MARRERO, *Cuba: Economía y sociedad*, 15 vols. (1972–1992), especially vols. 1–2, 7–10, and 12; JOHN ROBERT MC NEILL, *Atlantic Empires of France and Spain: Louisbourg and Havana, 1700–1763* (1985); JAIME SUCHLICKI, *Cuba: From Columbus to Castro*, 3d ed.

(1990); ALLAN J. KUETHE, "Havana in the Eighteenth Century," in *Atlantic Port Cities: Economy, Culture, and Society in the Atlantic World, 1650–1850,* edited by Franklin W. Knight and Peggy K. Liss (1991).

ALLAN J. KUETHE

HAVANA COMPANY (La Real Compañía de Comercio de la Habana), established by the CÉDULA of 18 December 1740, was intended to guarantee its royal, metropolitan, and (majority) Cuban investors a "monopoly" of the trade between Spain and Cuba, as well as to stimulate ship construction in Havana, supply troops stationed there, and provide coast-guarding services against smugglers and pirates. Over the next twenty years, the company introduced approximately 5,000 slaves into the island, while dominating the exportation of tobacco and sugar and the importation and sale of provisions and European goods. The Havana Company was reorganized in 1760 and suffered severe losses with the fall of Havana to the British two years later, although it continued in existence until the end of the century.

JULIO LE RIVEREND, *Economic History of Cuba* (1967); VICENTE BÁEZ, ed., *La enciclopedia de Cuba: Historia,* vol. 5 (1974), pp. 170–171; LEVÍ MARRERO, *Cuba: Economía y sociedad,* vol. 7 (1978), pp. 102–165.

LINDA K. SALVUCCI

HAVANA CONFERENCES (1928, 1940). *See* **Pan-American Conferences.**

HAWKINS, JOHN (*b.* 1532; *d.* 12 November 1595), an Englishman active in the West Indies from 1562 to 1600 who was primarily interested in trading. In the early 1560s, a new group of interlopers, the English, were led by the ingenious John Hawkins of Plymouth, who organized four trading voyages to the Indies from 1562 to 1568, personally leading three of them. His purpose was trade: to exchange cloth and merchandise from England and slaves from Africa with the Spanish in return for sugar, hides, and silver. Hawkins wanted to legitimize his activities with the Spanish government by securing a license to trade freely. Even though he vowed to fight privateers if the Spanish would grant him the license he desired, the Spanish refused to do so, wishing to avoid setting a precedent.

Hawkins's earliest venture was successful in business terms, although his overall plan failed. The first voyage embarked in October 1562 and prospered greatly, as he traveled among the Caribbean islands trading English goods and African slaves for hides and sugar, returning to England in September 1563. Hawkins's first effort succeeded in the midst of relative peace between the English and Spanish. Relations between the two nations soured quickly, however, as the peace between England

and Spain that was based on common opposition to France broke down when France weakened from internal religious wars.

Thus, Hawkins's second and third voyages faced greater difficulties as Spain clamped down on its colonies and fervently attempted to prohibit foreign trade. Meanwhile, by the time of the second voyage (October 1564–September 1565), Hawkins had received more direct support from the English government. Nevertheless, the second and third voyages proved relatively unsuccessful in terms of trade, though each had its own accomplishments.

On his third and final voyage (October 1567–January 1569), Hawkins was bound for home in September 1568 when bad weather forced his fleet to dock at SAN JUAN DE ULÚA, the port of Veracruz. Later that month, a Spanish *flota* encountered his fleet there and destroyed most of it. In early 1569, after great hardships, he and fifteen remaining companions reached England. The Spanish, in fact, had proved unwilling to allow open trading, treating foreigners like Hawkins as pirates.

After aiding in the English defeat of the Spanish Armada in 1588, Hawkins and Francis DRAKE returned to the Caribbean in 1595 with a large fleet, attempting an Indies Voyage, a plan intended to break the territorial power of the Spanish in the New World. The well-prepared Spanish defeated this ill-fated effort at San Juan, Puerto Rico, and at Cartagena, Colombia. They also defeated the English on the Isthmus of Panama at PORTO BELLO. John Hawkins's career thus came to an ignominious end.

SIR JULIAN S. CORBETT, *Drake and the Tudor Navy,* 2 vols. (1898, repr. 1988); C. H. HARING, *The Buccaneers in the West Indies in the XVII Century* (1910); J. A. WILLIAMSON, *Sir John Hawkins: The Time and the Man* (1927) and *Hawkins of Plymouth* (1949); KENNETH R. ANDREWS, *The Last Voyage of Drake and Hawkins* (1972); J. H. PARRY et al., *A Short History of the West Indies,* 4th ed. (1987).

BLAKE D. PATTRIDGE

See also **Piracy.**

HAY–BUNAU-VARILLA TREATY (1903), an agreement between Panama and the United States providing the legal basis for U.S. construction of the PANAMA CANAL and the creation of the Canal Zone. It was signed on 18 November by U.S. Secretary of State John Hay and Philippe Bunau-Varilla two weeks after the Panamanian revolution against Colombia. Early in 1903, the United States had negotiated a canal treaty with Colombia, but opposition within the Colombian National Assembly to concessions made by the Colombian negotiator (Tomás Herrán) and concerns that Colombia would not receive sufficient economic benefits from the sale of the French canal company's properties to the U.S. led to its defeat. In the U.S. Senate, those who favored a Nicaraguan canal were heartened. As a French national with a strong commitment to a canal in Panama, Bunau-Varilla lobbied for the Panama route and served as intermediary between dissident Panamanians, French canal interests, and important U.S. officials who favored the Panama route. Through his contacts, Bunau-Varilla knew that the U.S. government would guarantee the revolution's success once the Panamanians had acted. As Panama's first representative to the United States, Bunau-Varilla granted virtually every right and privilege the United States had asked for in the earlier HAY–HERRÁN TREATY with Colombia. These included the right to construct a canal, fortify it, and to "act as if it were sovereign" in the Canal Zone, for $10 million and a $250,000 annual rental. The treaty expired in 1979.

WALTER LA FEBER, *The Panama Canal: The Crisis in Historical Perspective* (1978); RICHARD H. COLLIN, *Theodore Roosevelt's Caribbean: The Panama Canal, the Monroe Doctrine, and the Latin American Context* (1990); MICHAEL CONNIFF, *Panama and the United States: The Forced Alliance* (1991).

LESTER D. LANGLEY

See also **Good Neighbor Policy; Roosevelt, Theodore; Taft Agreement; United States–Latin American Relations.**

HAY–HERRÁN TREATY (1903), the agreement of 22 January which, had it been ratified, would have authorized the United States to build a canal through Colombia's province of Panama. The agreement, negotiated by John Hay, U.S. secretary of state, and Tomás Herrán, Colombian chargé d'affaires in Washington, was rejected by the Colombian Senate. That prompted President Theodore ROOSEVELT and other canal promoters to endorse Panama's separation from Colombia. After independence, the treaty served as a draft for rights ceded by the new republic to the United States.

The treaty empowered the United States to purchase the machinery and works of the French Compagnie Nouvelle in Panama and to build a canal along the route worked by the French. Colombia would grant to the U.S. government a zone six miles wide (excluding the terminal cities of Panamá and Colón) for construction, operation, maintenance, and defense of the canal. Colombia, in exchange, would retain sovereignty over the zone. The United States would pay $10 million upon ratification and $25,000 per year upon completion of the canal. The treaty would remain in effect for one hundred years and was renewable at the sole discretion of the United States. Finally, the United States would operate all administrative services in the zone except the police.

On 12 August 1903 the Colombian Senate unanimously rejected the treaty, which had become hugely unpopular in Bogotá. The main reasons were insufficient compensation, threat to sovereignty, and perpetuity. At this point, agents of the Compagnie Nouvelle and Panamanian conservatives conspired to declare

Panama independent, with the blessing of the U.S. government.

E. TAYLOR PARKS, *Colombia and the United States, 1765–1934* (1935); EDUARDO LEMAITRE ROMÁN, *Panamá y su separación de Colombia*, 2d ed. (1972); JAMES M. SKINNER, *France and Panama: The Unknown Years, 1894–1908* (1989); JOHN MAJOR, *Prize Possession: The United States and the Panama Canal, 1903–1977* (1993).

MICHAEL L. CONNIFF

HAY–PAUNCEFOTE TREATIES (1901), the agreements between the United States and Great Britain that permitted the former to build a canal in Central America, thereby clearing the way for U.S. construction of the Panama Canal. The first version, signed on 5 February 1901, envisioned a waterway like the Suez Canal, without fortifications. When U.S. public opinion disputed the neutrality clauses and the Senate amended the treaty to include military protection, U.S. secretary of state John Hay was obliged to renegotiate it with British ambassador Julian Pauncefote. The second treaty, signed on 18 November 1901, did not mention fortifications, implicitly allowing the United States to defend the canal with military installations. It was approved by the newly inaugurated president, Theodore ROOSEVELT (who aspired to build a canal in Central America), and won easy ratification in the Senate.

Roosevelt and congressional leaders believed that the canal had to be wholly owned and operated by the United States. Simultaneously with the Hay–Pauncefote treaties, the U.S. State Department negotiated a treaty with Nicaragua permitting construction of the canal there. Later events, however, led to selection of the present site in Panama.

These treaties nullified portions of the controversial CLAYTON–BULWER TREATY of 1850, which committed the United States and Britain to a jointly run canal with no fortifications. This treaty had elicited severe criticism ever since its approval and was a definite irritant in Anglo-American relations. British acquiescence to its modification signaled recognition of a U.S. sphere of influence in the Caribbean basin and foreshadowed the country's rise to world power status.

GERSTLE MACK, *The Land Divided* (1944); MARY WILHELMINE WILLIAMS, *Anglo-American Isthmian Diplomacy, 1815–1915*, 2d ed. (1965); DAVID MC CULLOUGH, *The Path Between the Seas* (1977); ROBERT A. NAYLOR, *Penny Ante Imperialism: The Mosquito Shore and the Bay of Honduras, 1600–1914* (1989).

MICHAEL L. CONNIFF

HAYA DE LA TORRE, VÍCTOR RAÚL (*b.* 22 February 1895; *d.* 2 August 1979), pivotal politician in Peruvian politics of the twentieth century, founder in 1924 of the Popular Revolutionary Alliance of America (APRA), a movement with continental ambitions, and in 1931 the local Peruvian Aprista Party (PAP). Haya developed an

Víctor Raúl Haya de la Torre at political rally in 1931. LATIN AMERICAN LIBRARY, TULANE UNIVERSITY.

ideology that was initially anti-imperialist but gradually turned conciliatory. He was supported mainly by the lower middle classes of Peru, who were attracted by his charisma, his populist-nationalist views, and his syncretic-Indianist appeal.

Haya was born in Trujillo to a family of provincial distinction. However, his father, Raúl Edmundo, had to rely on his professional income as a journalist to support his family. Peter Klarén proposes that Haya's initial ideological positions were possibly minted in reaction to the expansior of land property by foreign companies in La Libertad at the turn of the century. Haya studied law in Trujillo (1915) and Lima (1917). After meeting the intellectual Manuel GONZÁLEZ PRADA in the Peruvian capital, Haya added anarchistic elements to his provincial bohemian stance.

In 1919, Peruvian workers were fighting for the eight-hour workday. Haya's policy of solidarity with the workers allowed him to surface as student leader. He was president of the Student Federation in 1919 and 1920, leading a student congress in Cuzco, fighting for the reform of the university, and establishing the "popular universities" that constituted the bases of the future PAP. Haya was initially a fellow traveler of the rising socialist movement and collaborated in journalistic activities with socialist intellectual José Carlos MARIÁTEGUI.

By 1924, Haya had developed a strong opposition to President Augusto B. LEGUÍA and was imprisoned and exiled. Haya was invited by Mexican indigenist and minister of education José VASCONCELOS to Mexico, where he started his continental ideological movement.

He broke politically with Mariátegui and became a stern opponent of COMMUNISM.

After extensive travel and study in Europe he returned to Peru when Leguía fell in 1930. In the 1931 elections, Haya lost to the nationalist colonel Luis SÁNCHEZ CERRO. Apristas claimed fraud and organized an uprising in Trujillo in 1932 which was brutally repressed by the army. Haya was imprisoned but then freed after Sánchez Cerro's death in 1933. Thereafter he engaged in clandestine politics, and did not return to open campaigning until 1945, with the election of APRA-supported Luis José BUSTAMANTE Y RIVERO. In 1948, however, another Aprista uprising, this time in Callao, led to repression by General Manuel ODRÍA and Haya's political asylum in the Colombian embassy in Lima (1949–1954).

By 1956 a more subdued Haya established with President Manuel PRADO a pact whose objective was an Aprista victory in the 1962 elections. However, once again Haya's presidential ambitions were thwarted by a military coup against Prado. Elections in 1963 resulted in the defeat of Haya by Fernando BELAÚNDE. During Belaúnde's regime, Haya's party formed a coalition of opposition with his former enemy Odría. The military coup of 1968 against Belaúnde further delayed Haya's ambitions. Only in 1978–1979 was Haya able to occupy the largely honorary post of president of the Constituent Assembly.

HARRY KANTOR, *The Ideology and Program of the Peruvian Aprista Movement* (1966); VÍCTOR RAÚL HAYA DE LA TORRE, *Obras completas*, 7 vols. (1976–1977); STEVE STEIN, *Populism in Peru* (1980); FREDRICK PIKE, *The Politics of the Miraculous in Peru: Haya de la Torre and the Spiritualist Tradition* (1986).

ALFONSO W. QUIROZ

HEIREMANS, LUIS ALBERTO (*b.* 14 July 1928; *d.* 25 October 1964), Chilean dramatist and writer. With the Chileans Egon WOLFF and Jorge DÍAZ, Heiremans shares international renown as a dramatist. He is an outstanding writer of his country's Generation of '50. He was an active member of the movement that began in the 1940s to reform drama in the university, which has had a great effect on the Latin American stage.

Aside from his highly praised brief narratives, collected in *Los mejores cuentos de Luis Alberto Heiremans* (1966), the critical world has identified three phases of his work. Outstanding in the initial phase is *Moscas sobre el mármol* (1958). The transitional phase includes *Los güenos versos* (1958), *Sigue la estrella* (1958), and *La ronda de la buena nueva* (1961), and the mature phase includes *Buenaventura* (1961), and his exceptional trilogy *Versos de ciego* (1961), *El abanderado* (1962), and *El Tony chico* (1964). His sensibility tended toward the existentialist, and he went beyond traditional literary realism. His works developed a poetic theater that symbolically codifies, sometimes through certain biblical correlations, the elements of custom and folklore in Chile, with the effect of making them universal.

GRINOR ROJO, "Luis Alberto Heiremans," in *Latin American Writers,* edited by Carlos A. Solé and Maria Isabel Abreu, (1989).

LUIS CORREA-DÍAZ

See also **Theater.**

HENEQUEN INDUSTRY. Located primarily in YU-CATÁN, the extraction of raw fiber from the henequen agave and the production of rope and twine therefrom was at one time a thriving industry. Henequen rope was used by the ancient Maya and then by the Spaniards as rigging. Extraction of the fiber was so labor-intensive that production was limited. In the 1850s, however, when the Yucatecan invention of the steam-powered decorticator to remove the fiber made mass production possible, the hacienda owners of northwestern Yucatán began planting large quantities of henequen. Demand abroad was stimulated by the invention in 1878 of the McCormick reaper, which required large quantities of binder twine.

The economy of Yucatán came to be based on henequen exports, especially to the United States, and the state became the wealthiest and most opulent in Porfirian Mexico. Profits at first went mostly to the landowning elite; the workers—Maya Indians, many of whom were debt peons—received few benefits. However, with the creation in 1902 of the International Harvester Corporation—a U.S. trust that established almost complete control over the purchase of henequen on the world market—a large part of the profits went to the United States. This situation continued until the breakup of the trust in 1915.

The MEXICAN REVOLUTION brought about the abolition of peonage and the emergence of free labor on the haciendas, while competition from other producers changed the world market for twine and led to declining prices. Agrarian reforms in the 1930s resulted ultimately in the destruction of the landowning class, but mismanagement and corruption in the state-run economy led to the impoverishment of the peasants. Foreign competition also cut into profitability, and by 1990 henequen production was no longer a significant segment of the economy of Yucatán.

NARCISA TRUJILLO, "Las primeras máquinas desfibradoras de henequén," *Enciclopedia yucatanese,* vol. 3 (1947), pp. 627–656; GONZALO CAMARA ZAVALA, "Historia de la industria henequenera hasta 1919," *Enciclopedia yucatanese,* vol. 3 (1947), pp. 657–725; ENRIQUE AZNAR MENDOZA, "Historia de la industria henequenera desde 1919 hasta nuestros días," *Enciclopedia yucatanese,* vol. 3 (1947), pp. 727–787; MOISÉS GONZÁLEZ NAVARRO, *Raza y tierra: La Guerra de Castas y el henequén* (1970); ALLEN WELLS, *Yucatán's Gilded Age: Haciendas, Henequen, and International Harvester, 1860–1915* (1985); JEFFREY BRANNON and ERIC N. BAKLANOFF, *Agrarian Reform and Public Enterprise in Mexico: The Political Economy of Yucatán's Henequen Industry* (1987).

ROBERT W. PATCH

HENRÍQUEZ, CAMILO (*b.* 20 July 1769; *d.* 16 May 1825), Chilean patriot, revolutionary, and propagandist, "the

Henequen in the Yucatán. ARCHIVO GENERAL DE LA NACIÓN, MEXICO.

father of Chilean journalism." Henríquez was born in Valdivia, but in 1784 he was sent for his education to Lima, where he lived for the next quarter century, entering a minor religious order in 1787. He was three times investigated by the INQUISITION because of his interest in prohibited books, such as those of Jean-Jacques Rousseau (1712–1778), Guillaume-Thomas-François de Raynal (1713–1796), and Louis-Sébastien Mercier (1740–1814).

Henríquez returned to his native Chile at the end of 1810 and threw himself into politics with enthusiasm. When the patriot government acquired its first printing press (from the United States), he was given the task of editing the first Chilean newspaper, La Aurora de Chile (13 February 1812 to 1 April 1813). The prospectus he issued prior to the first issue made a resonant claim: "After the sad and intolerable silence of three centuries—centuries of infamy and lamentation!—the voice of reason and truth will be heard amongst us." The newspaper contained many articles by its editor. On 6 April 1813 La Aurora was replaced by a second newspaper, El Monitor Araucano, which ran until the eve of the battle of RANCAGUA (1–2 October 1814) and the downfall of patriot Chile. Henríquez used these newssheets to spread his own revolutionary ideas. Between 1814 and 1822 he lived in exile in Buenos Aires, once again publishing newspapers for a time. In 1822 he returned to Chile at the invitation of Bernardo o'HIGGINS and played a minor role in public affairs for what remained of his life.

Henríquez's place as a publicist of patriot and revolutionary ideas during the PATRIA VIEJA in Chile was unrivaled. His writing is always clear and direct. A brief flirtation with monarchism during his Argentine exile was no more than a temporary aberration from his liberal, democratic, and republican ideas.

RAÚL SILVA CASTRO, ed., Escritos políticos de Camilo Henríquez (1960), SIMON COLLIER, Ideas and Politics of Chilean Independence, 1808–1833 (1967), chap. 3.

SIMON COLLIER

See also **Journalism.**

HENRÍQUEZ UREÑA, MAX (b. 16 November 1885; d. 23 January 1968), Dominican educator, writer, and diplomat. Henríquez Ureña, born in Santo Domingo, was the son of Francisco HENRÍQUEZ Y CARVAJAL, president of the Dominican Republic (1916), and the Dominican poetess and educator Salomé UREÑA DE HENRÍQUEZ. After receiving a law doctorate in 1913, he began his public career in 1916, as secretary to his father. This appointment was followed by twenty years of diplomatic service as his country's representative in various European capitals, the League of Nations, and the United Nations. During the first year of Rafael L. TRUJILLO's reign (1930–1931), Henríquez Ureña was in charge of Dominican public education. Along with other

Dominican intellectuals, he established the Dominican Academy of History. In Cuba, he founded the journals Cuba Literaria and Archipiélago. Henríquez Ureña contributed to important Hispanic magazines, such as El Cojo Ilustrado (Venezuela), Cuba Contemporánea and El Fígaro (Cuba), and Caras y Caretas (Argentina). He taught at various universities in the Dominican Republic and abroad, including the Universidad Nacional Pedro Henríquez Ureña (UNPHU). Henríquez Ureña's most famous literary work is Los Estados Unidos y la República Dominicana (published in Cuba in 1919), in which he denounced the armed intervention by the United States in the Dominican Republic during 1916. Another well-known work is Panorama histórico de la literatura dominicana, a survey of Dominican literature published in Rio de Janeiro in 1945. Henríquez Ureña died in Santo Domingo.

HENRÍQUEZ UREÑA's writings include Cuentos insulares (1947); Breve historia del modernismo (1954); Garra de luz (1958); De Rimbaud a Pasternak y Quasimodo (1960); El retorno de los galeones, 2d ed., rev. and enlarged (1963); La independencia efímera, 3d ed. (1967); "Mi padre": Perfil biográfico de Francisco Henríquez y Carvajal (1988). See also Enciclopedia dominicana, vol. 3 (1978), p. 264.

KAI P. SCHOENHALS

HENRÍQUEZ UREÑA, PEDRO (b. 29 June 1884; d. 11 May 1946), Dominican and Spanish American intellectual, educator, philologist, and literary critic. Born in Santo Domingo of a prominent family, he spent most of his lifetime outside his native country. His early schooling was in the Dominican Republic and in the United States (1902–1904), and he began his literary activities during a first residence in Cuba (1904–1905). He lived in Mexico from 1906 through 1914, where he completed a law degree, taught at the Preparatory School of the University of Mexico, and together with Alfonso REYES, Antonio CASO, and other young intellectuals took part in the founding of the ATENEO DE LA JUVENTUD. He traveled to the United States again in 1914, and between 1916 and 1921 he both taught and did postgraduate work in Spanish literature at the University of Minnesota (his doctoral thesis, defended in 1918, was on versification in Hispanic poetry). In a second and shorter Mexican residence (1921–1924) he undertook a number of teaching and administrative responsibilities. In mid-1924 he left Mexico for Argentina, and for more than twenty years held secondary and university teaching positions in both Buenos Aires and nearby La Plata. He also carried on wideranging intellectual activities: a steady stream of books and articles on linguistics and literature, lectures, and consultations with journals and publishing houses. In 1931–1933 he served for a short time as General Superintendent of Education in the Dominican Republic, and in 1940–1941 he was invited to deliver the Charles Eliot Norton lectures at Harvard University.

Henríquez Ureña's influence was evident in several

generations of well-trained students, but clearly his most significant contribution as a thinker and scholar has come in the expansiveness and persuasive clarity of his own writings. His publications are voluminous and contribute brilliantly to the study of language, literature, and culture in the Spanish-speaking world. As a linguist, Henríquez Ureña's best contributions are probably his *Gramática castellana* (1938–1939), his much reprinted grammar done with Amado Alonso, and his dialectal studies on American Spanish: *El español en México, los Estados Unidos y la América Central* (1938) and *El español en Santo Domingo* (1940). His most influential literary studies are the published doctoral thesis on versification, *La versificación irregular en la poesía castellana* (1920), and the Norton lectures from Harvard, *Literary Currents in Hispanic America* (1945; translated by Joaquín Díez Canedo and published in 1949 as *Las corrientes literarias en la América Hispánica*). As a cultural observer, his best-known work is *Seis ensayos en busca de nuestra expresión* (1928), a series of six persuasive essays on the possibilities of expressing an authentic American culture in Spanish.

The most useful general commentary on Henríquez Ureña and his work is JUAN JACOBO DE LARA, *Pedro Henríquez Ureña: Su vida y su obra* (1975). For another general article, see ENRIQUE ANDERSON IMBERT, "Pedro Henríquez Ureña," in *Latin American Writers*, edited by Carlos A. Solé and Maria Isabel Abreu, vol. 2 (1989). Henríquez Ureña's published works are available in JUAN JACOBO DE LARA, ed., *Obras completas*, 10 vols. (1976–1980). See also several anthologies: EMMA SUSANA SPERATTI PIÑERO, *Obra crítica* (1960); JOSÉ ALCÁNTARA ALMÁNZAR, *Ensayos* (1976); and ANGEL RAMA and RAFAEL GUTIÉRREZ GIRARDOT, *La utopía de América* (1978). The most detailed bibliographic listing of Henríquez Ureña's publications is still EMMA SUSANA SPERATTI PIÑERO, "Crono-bibliografía de Pedro Henríquez Ureña," in *Obra crítica*, pp. 751–793. For detailed accounts of the years spent in the United States and Mexico, see ALFREDO A. ROGGIANO, ed., *Pedro Henríquez Ureña en los Estados Unidos* (1961), and *Pedro Henríquez Ureña en México* (1989).

MERLIN H. FORSTER

See also **Ureña de Henríquez, Salomé.**

HENRÍQUEZ Y CARVAJAL, FRANCISCO (*b.* 14 January 1859; *d.* 1935), provisional president of the Dominican Republic (1916). After the U.S. Marines invaded the Dominican Republic in 1916, Washington was unwilling to allow direct rule. The Dominican Congress reacted by meeting in secrecy and selecting Francisco Henríquez y Carvajal as provisional president. The United States was willing to allow Henríquez y Carvajal to take power under the conditions it determined. Unwilling to become a puppet of the United States, Henríquez y Carvajal resigned and left the country in November 1916. The Dominican Congress was dissolved and the United States imposed martial law by the occupying marines. These conditions prevailed until the marines were withdrawn in 1924.

SELDEN RODMAN, *Quisqueya: A History of the Dominican Republic* (1964); HOWARD J. WIARDA, *The Dominican Republic: Nation in Transition* (1969); IAN BELL, *The Dominican Republic* (1981); HOWARD J. WIARDA and M. J. KRYZANEK, *The Dominican Republic: A Caribbean Crucible* (1982).

HEATHER K. THIESSEN

HENRY THE NAVIGATOR (*b.* 4 March 1394; *d.* 13 November 1460), Portuguese prince noted for promoting the voyages of discovery that led to Portugal's creation of an overseas empire. Third son of King John I and Philippa of Lancaster, daughter of John of Gaunt of England, Prince Henry (Infante Dom Henrique) was duke of Viseu, governor of the city of Ceuta (captured in 1415 by the Portuguese from the Moroccans in an expedition in which Henry played a key role), the governor of the Algarve, Portugal's southernmost province, where Henry established his own court at Sagres in 1419.

Prince Henry is one of the most controversial figures in Portuguese historiography, for historians differ widely in their assessments of the extent and motives of his leadership role in Portugal's voyages of discovery. In the *Crónica da Guiné*, Gomes Eanes de Azurara, a contemporary chronicler of the discoveries, portrays Prince Henry as a model crusader: a tireless fighter, a pious man, and a chaste saint who never married. Azurara's portrait does not, however, match other evidence concerning Henry's character, which suggests that he was a skilled politician with an acute sense of *raison d'état*, that he was a crafty courtier who knew how to employ court intrigue for his own advantage; or that he was a practical man of affairs whose preoccupation with overseas expansion reflected his purpose of serving both God and Mammon.

On several occasions Henry's actions put the lives of his own brothers or half brothers in peril. For example, his unsuccessful expedition to Tangiers in 1437 resulted in the capture of his younger brother, Dom Fernando, by the Moors. The Moors demanded the return of Ceuta as the price of Fernando's release. Hardliners in the Portuguese court, including Henry, opposed giving up Ceuta, and as a result Fernando died in captivity in Fez in 1443. Henry also supported the war against Dom Afonso, duke of Bragança, and his half brother, who was involved in a power struggle with Dom Pedro, his older brother. At the battle of Alfarrobeira in 1449 Dom Pedro was killed. Many Portuguese historians blame Dom Pedro's death on Henry's intrigues.

Concerning his role in overseas expansion, Azurar notes that João de Alenquer, the "vedor da fazenda," had convinced Prince Henry of the economic advantages of capturing Ceuta, then believed to be a bridgehead to the gold-producing lands south of the Sahara. Similarly, Diogo Gomes, one of the sea captains Henry supported, confided to Martin Behaim of Nürnburg that Prince Henry had been told about Saharan gold by the

Moors of Ceuta and that he had vowed to find it by land or sea. This view of Henry's thirst for gold has been developed by a school of Portuguese historians led by Alexandre Herculano and presently is reflected in the writings of Vitorino Magalhães Godinho and others, who contend that the economic motive and maintaining the security of Portugal were the main reasons for the overseas expansion.

Nevertheless, in 1960 the Portuguese marked the five-hundred-year anniversary of Prince Henry's death by honoring him as the "saint of the Promontory of Sagres," a heroic visionary who initiated Portugal's overseas discoveries and was the fountainhead of its empire.

A. H. DE CARVALHO E ARAUJO HERCULANO, "Cogitações soltas de um homem obscuro," in *Opusculos*, vol. 6 (1897); JOAQUIM PEDRO DE OLIVEIRA MARTINS, *Os filhos de D. João I* (1936); DU-ARTE LEITE, *História dos descobrimentos*, edited by Vitorino Magalhães Godinho (1960); VITORINO MAGALHÃES GODINHO, *Os descobrimentos e a economia mundial*, 2 vols. (1965–1968); C. R. BOXER, *The Portuguese Seaborne Empire* (1969); BAILEY W. DIFFIE and GEORGE D. WINIUS, *Foundations of the Portuguese Empire: Europe and the World in the Age of Expansion* (1972); JOAQUIM VERÍSSIMO SERRÃO, *História de Portugal*, 12 vols. (1978–1990); A. H. DE OLIVEIRA MARQUES, *História de Portugal*, 3 vols. (1981–1983); GERVASE CLARENCE-SMITH, *The Third Portuguese Empire, 1825–1975* (1985).

TOMÉ N. MBUIA JOÃO

See also **Explorers and Exploration; Portuguese Empire.**

HERBS. *See* **Spices and Herbs.**

HEREDIA, one of the four provinces in the Central Valley of Costa Rica. Heredia was settled in the eighteenth century by Spanish and Creole farmers. Although it had rich volcanic soil, like the rest of Costa Rica, it had a minuscule indigenous labor force, and thus remained only sparsely settled. By 1824, the town of Heredia had still fewer than four thousand inhabitants. It became the provincial capital of Heredia Province in 1848, when the boundaries of the region were extended northward to include the Sarapiquí Valley.

During the twentieth century, Heredia became more closely tied to metropolitan San José, although the provincial capital still retains its legal identity. In 1972, Costa Rica established its second national university in Heredia.

CAROLYN HALL, *Costa Rica: A Geographical Interpretation in Historical Perspective* (1985); HÉCTOR PÉREZ-BRIGNOLI, *Las variables demográficas en las economías de exportación: El ejemplo del Valle Central de Costa Rica* (1978); RALPH LEE WOODWARD, JR., *Central America: A Nation Divided* (1985).

VIRGINIA GARRARD-BURNETT

HEREDIA Y HEREDIA, JOSÉ M. (*b.* 31 December 1803; *d.* 7 May 1839), Cuban Romantic poet. Heredia, born in Santiago de Cuba, was the most important literary figure of Latin American romanticism. His early education was directed by his father, José Francisco Heredia y Mieses, an important politician who traveled extensively in the colonies. Heredia graduated from the University of Havana Law School in 1823 and became an important member of the anti-Spanish movement on the island.

The Spanish authorities transferred Heredia's father to the Audiencia of Mexico in 1819. That year José followed him there and published his first book of poems, *Ensayos poéticos*, in Mexico. In 1821 he returned to Cuba, married, and published three books: *La inconstancia, Misantropía*, and *El desamor*. Also in 1822 Heredia was appointed rector of the Pontífica Universidad de la Habana. The following year he embarked for the United States, where in Boston he met Felix Varela and José Saco, Cuban liberals and advocates of independence. In 1824, he visited Niagara Falls, which inspired one of this best-known poems, "El Niágara." In December 1824 the Cuban government condemned him to perpetual exile for his involvement in revolutionary activities. Heredia died in Toluca, Mexico.

For the complete works of Heredia, see *Poesías completas* (1970); *Diccionario de la literatura cubana*, vol. 1 (1980), pp. 430–438; EMILIO DÍAZ ECHANI and JOSÉ MARÍA ROCA FRANQUESA, *Historia de la literatura española e hispanoamericana*, 3d ed., vol. 1 (1982), pp. 741–746.

DARIÉN DAVIS

HERMOSILLO, JAIME-HUMBERTO (*b.* 1942), Mexican film director. Born in Aguascalientes, Hermosillo studied film direction at the Center of Film Studies of the National Autonomous University of Mexico (UNAM). He began his career by producing short narrative films and documentaries. His first full-length film was *La verdadera vocación de Magdalena* (1971). Since that debut, Hermosillo has been one of the most consistent and dedicated directors of contemporary Mexican cinema. His main themes are the changing middle-class family, sexuality and alternative life-styles, and the demise of tradition and values. Many of his leading characters are women or gay men. Among his most critically praised films are *La pasión según Berenice* (1976), *Matine* (1977), *Naufragio* (1977), *Amor libre* (1979), *María de mi corazón* (1979), and *La tarea* (1991). Hermosillo was awarded the Ariel for best direction by the Mexican film academy for *La pasión según Berenice* and *Naufragio*.

LUIS REYES DE LA MAZA, *El cine sonoro en México* (1973); E. BRADFORD BURNS, *Latin American Cinema: Film and History* (1975); CARL J. MORA, *Mexican Cinema: Reflections of a Society: 1896–1980* (1982); and JOHN KING, *Magical Reels: A History of Cinema in Latin America* (1990).

DAVID MACIEL

See also **Cinema.**

HERNÁNDEZ, FELISBERTO (*b.* 20 October 1902; *d.* 1964), Uruguayan writer. During his adolescence he studied music and performed as a concert pianist. Along with the Argentine Jorge Luis BORGES, he is considered one of the foremost writers of fantasy literature in the Río de la Plata countries. Hernández's lifelong commitment to music can be seen in his work. In the short story "El balcón" ("The Balcony," 1947), the narrator is a concert pianist. The narrative exemplifies the author's deceptively simple but ingenuous prose style, which he uses to analyze sensations, turning them into metaphors.

Early works such as *Libro sin tapas* (1929), *La cara de Ana* (1930), and *La envenenada* (1931) are characterized by humor, the writer's power of observation, and an exuberance in the construction of fantasies. His most acclaimed works begin with *Por los tiempos de Clemente Colling* (1942) and *Nadie encendía las lámparas* (1947), novels of "evocation" in which the anecdotal takes second place to poetic reconstruction of reality and real people, on the basis of memory. *Las hortensias* (1949), *La casa inundada* (1960), and *El cocodrilo* (1962) mark the culmination of his fictional narrative, in which memory and fantasy constitute the dual pillars of narrative discourse.

Additional works by Hernández include *El caballo perdido* (1943); *Tierras de memoria* (1965); and *Obras completas*, 3 vols. (1983).

NORAH GIRALDI DE DEI CAS, *Felisberto Hernández: Del creador al hombre* (1975); WALTER RELA, *Felisberto Hernández: Bibliografía anotada* (1979); ROBERTO ECHAVARREN WELKER, *El espacio de la verdad: Práctica del texto en Felisberto Hernández* (1981); RICARDO PALLARES and REINA REYES, *¿Otro Felisberto?* (1983); ROSARIO FERRÉ, *El acomodador* (1986).

WILLIAM H. KATRA

HERNÁNDEZ, FRANCISCO (*b.* ca. 1517; *d.* 1587), medical doctor and botanist from Puebla de Montalbán, Toledo, Spain. While studying at Alcalá de Henares, Hernández learned of Erasmus of Rotterdam's doctrines and those of the most outstanding humanists of his time. He practiced medicine in Toledo and Seville and was King Philip II's court physician. Upon his appointment as *Protomédico de Indias* in 1570, he went to New Spain, where he became deeply interested in Nahuatl medicine, the therapeutic uses of American flora and fauna, and the Nahuatl cultural approaches to diseases.

Antagonized by the Mexican viceroy, Hernández returned to Spain in 1577. He was then dismissed as court physician and replaced by Nardo Antonio Recco, who severely abbreviated Hernández's written works, many of which were destroyed by fire in 1671. Nevertheless, a large number of Hernández's botanical and medical writings are extant. They include *Rerum medicarum Novae Hispaniae* (Rome, 1628), *Quatro libros de la naturaleza y virtudes medicinales de las plantas y animales de la Nueva España* (Mexico, 1615), and *De antiquitatibus Novae Hispaniae* (Mexico, 1926).

GERMÁN SOMOLINOS D'ARDOIS, *Vida y obra de Francisco Hernández* (1960); GUENTER B. RISSE, "Medicine in New Spain," in *Medicine in the New World: New Spain, New France, and New England*, edited by Ronald L. Numbers (1987); BERNARD ORTIZ DE MONTELLANO, *Aztec Medicine, Health, and Nutrition* (1990).

CARMEN BENITO-VESSELS

HERNÁNDEZ, JOSÉ (*b.* 10 November 1834; *d.* 21 October 1886), Argentine poet, legislator, journalist, politician, soldier, and author of MARTÍN FIERRO. He exemplified the dual personality typical of the Argentine writer of the nineteenth century: a man of action and of thought. Paradoxically, although he created the most celebrated piece of Argentine literature, he was mostly a man of action. Endowed with great physical dexterity and well acquainted with the life-style of GAUCHOS, Hernández enrolled in the army at age nineteen, fighting in the internecine wars between the central government and the provinces. He retired as assistant captain and in 1858 emigrated to the province of Entre Ríos, where he participated in the revolutions in that part of the country. There, Hernández began his journalistic career, but in 1859 he was back in the army as assistant to General Justo José de URQUIZA, taking part in the battles of CEPEDA (1859) and PAVÓN (1861). An opponent of General Bartolomé MITRE and of President Domingo F. SARMIENTO, Hernández returned to Buenos Aires to found the newspaper *El Río de la Plata*, where he defended the gauchos and attacked Sarmiento. After participating in the Ricardo LÓPEZ JORDÁN rebellion, Hernández escaped to Brazil.

In 1872, back in Buenos Aires, he published the first part of *Martín Fierro*; the second appeared in 1879. He became a legislator (representative and senator) and was instrumental in founding the city of La Plata. His very active life illustrates his commitment to serve his country politically and militarily. It explains also the ideology of the heroic poem he created. Hernández wrote *Instrucción del estanciero* (1881; Education of the Rancher), and political and journalistic pieces that reflected his views as a public persona, citizen, and politician. In his ideology and language, Hernández epitomized the "interior" (provinces) of Argentina. His major work, the poem *Martín Fierro*, is a combative denunciation of social injustice and the virtual genocide of a social strata of the population, that of the gaucho. He adhered to the ARGENTINE CONFEDERATION, a political alliance that confronted the Buenos Aires *estancieros* (ranchers) and defended the right of the provinces to share power with the domineering city. He defended the rights of the gauchos, unjustly and cruelly repressed by a government that reduced them to pariahs, without rights to possess land, real freedom, or a hopeful future.

HORACIO ZORRAQUÍN BECÚ, *Tiempo y vida de José Hernández* (1972); RODOLFO A. BORELLO, *Hernández: Poesía y política* (1973); OLGA FERNÁNDEZ LATOUR DE BOTAS, *José Hernández* (1973); JUAN CARLOS GHIANO, "Hernández, en el centenario de su muerte," in *Boletín de la Academia Argentina de Letras* 51, no. 201–202 (1986): 293–301; ANTONIO PAGÉS LARRAYA, "José Hernández," in *Latin American Writers,* edited by Carlos A. Solé and Maria Isabel Abreu, vol. 1 (1989) pp. 235–245.

ANGELA B. DELLEPIANE

HERNÁNDEZ, JOSÉ MANUEL (*b.* ca. 1853; *d.* 1919), Venezuelan caudillo and politician. A native of Caracas and a perennial revolutionary, Hernández was injured in battle in 1870. After extensive travel in the West Indies and throughout Venezuela, and engaging in various business ventures, "El Mocho" (the maimed) became the president of Bolívar State, where he opposed attempts at centralization by the authorities in Caracas, and also served in Congress. One of three candidates in the 1987 presidential election, Hernández gained enormous popularity by waging Venezuela's first modern political campaign through appealing directly to the masses and campaigning throughout the country under the banner of the Liberal Nationalist Party. Losing in a grossly fraudulent election, the idealistic populist then led an unsuccessful rebellion against the new government of the official candidate, Ignacio Andrade. Hernández was imprisoned and later exiled, but returned to Venezuela in 1908 to accept a high post in the regime of Juan Vicente GÓMEZ.

ROBERT L. GILMORE, *Caudillism and Militarism in Venezuela, 1810–1910* (1964); RAMÓN J. VELÁSQUEZ, *La caída del liberalismo amarillo* (1972); JUDITH EWELL, *Venezuela: A Century of Change* (1984).

WINFIELD J. BURGGRAAFF

HERNÁNDEZ, LUISA JOSEFINA (*b.* 2 November 1928), Mexican writer. Born in México City, Luisa Josefina Hernández is the most important woman author as well as one of the most innovative playwrights in Mexico. She has distinguished herself not only as a dramatist but as a novelist, translator, critic, and essayist. Her fictional works are noted for the range of their subject matter, their stylistic and structural variety, and their ironic tone and assiduous avoidance of sentimentality.

Hernández studied drama under Rodolfo USIGLI at the University of Mexico and was later appointed to the Rudolfo Usigli chair in dramatic composition there. She earned her doctorate with a study of the religious iconography of the colonial period and became the first woman to be awarded emeritus status by the University of Mexico. She has taught in the United States and in several other countries.

Hernández is known for her feminist critique of the "macho" mythologies of Mexican culture, and for her trenchant yet sympathetic portrayal of the plight of Mexican men. She has written approximately forty plays and twenty novels. Her most celebrated stage works are *La calle de la gran ocasión I* and *II* (1962; 1985); *El órden de los factores* (1983), *Escándalo en Puerto Santo*

(1962), and *Los huéspedes reales* (1958). She translates from German, English, French, Latin, and Greek authors ranging from Shakespeare to Euripides to Arthur Miller to Brecht. She has won most of the major prizes for literature in Mexico, including the Villaurutía Prize (1983) for her novel *Apocalypsis cum figuris* (1982). Her most recent works are a novel, *Almeida* (1989), and a dramatic adaptation of this novel by the same name.

For a thorough bibliography see Hernández's *La calle de la gran ocasión,* 2d ed. (1985).

WILLIAM I. OLIVER

HERNÁNDEZ COLÓN, RAFAEL (*b.* 24 October 1936), president of Puerto Rico's Popular Democratic Party and twice governor of Puerto Rico. As the son of Rafael Hernández Matos, associate justice of the supreme court of Puerto Rico, Hernández Colón began his education in local schools in Ponce and continued at the Valley Forge Military Academy in Pennsylvania. He graduated from Johns Hopkins University and received his law degree from the University of Puerto Rico, where he taught law from 1961 until 1966.

Hernández Colón entered politics in 1965 by appointment to the post of secretary of justice, where he wrote the Political Code, the Mortgage Code, and the Plebiscite Act of 1967. In 1968 Hernández Colón was elected senator-at-large and served as president of the Senate from 1969 to 1972.

At age thirty-six he was the youngest person to fill the post of governor when first elected in 1972. His inability to deal with growing economic problems led to his defeat in a 1978 reelection bid, but he won the office again in 1984.

KENNETH R. FARR, *Historical Dictionary of Puerto Rico and the U.S. Virgin Islands* (1973); *Personalities Caribbean,* 7th ed. (1983); ROBERT J. ALEXANDER, ed., *Biographical Dictionary of Latin American and Caribbean Political Leaders* (1988).

DAVID CAREY, JR.

See also **Puerto Rico: Political Parties.**

HERNÁNDEZ (FERNÁNDEZ) DE CÓRDOBA, FRANCISCO (*d.* 1518), Spanish navigator and CONQUISTADOR from the province of Córdoba. (He is not to be confused with Francisco FERNÁNDEZ DE CÓRDOBA [*d.* 1526], the conqueror of Nicaragua.) A leading settler of Cuba under Governor Diego Velásquez, Hernández agreed to lead the first major effort to conquer the MAYAS on the YUCATÁN Peninsula (1517). The Mayas defeated him, however, killing more than half his expedition. Hernández suffered thirty-three wounds, from which he died soon after his return to his home at Villa de Sancti-Spiritus. Although it failed, this expedition stimulated new interest in Mexico, which led eventually to the expedition of CORTÉS in 1519. News of the expedition also reached and worried the AZTEC emperor, MOTECUH-ZOMA II.

BERNAL DÍAZ DEL CASTILLO, *The True History of the Conquest of New Spain,* translated by Alfred P. Maudslay, vol. 1, (1908–1916), pp. 14–26; JOHN H. PARRY and ROBERT G. KEITH, *New Iberian World: A Documentary History of the Discovery and Settlement of Latin America to the Early Seventeenth Century,* vol. 3, (1984), pp. 131–143.

RALPH LEE WOODWARD, JR.

See also **Explorers.**

HERNÁNDEZ MARTÍNEZ, MAXIMILIANO (*b.* 1882; *d.* May 1966), career army officer and politician, president of El Salvador (1931–1934 and 1935–1944).

Born in San Salvador and educated at the Guatemalan military academy, Martínez entered the army in 1899. Rising rapidly during the 1906 border war with Guatemala, he reached the rank of major three years after receiving his commission. By 1919 he held the rank of brigadier general. Highly regarded by his colleagues for his ability as a planner and strategist, Martínez spent most of his army career as a professor at the Salvadoran Military Academy and in the office of the chief of staff. His features were both Indian and boyish, and he always appeared considerably younger than his age. Despite a calm exterior, he was regarded as a stern commander and a strong-willed, ambitious man.

Martínez's political rise began in 1930. One of six candidates for the presidency, Martínez withdrew to become the vice-presidential candidate of Arturo ARAÚJO, a wealthy landowner who enjoyed labor-movement support. Receiving only a plurality of the votes in the January 1931 election, the pair was elected by the National Assembly. General Martínez was appointed minister of war in addition to his vice presidency. The regime proved controversial and was confronted with the economic and financial crises caused by the global depression.

The maneuvering resulting from a military coup on 2 December 1931 brought Martínez to power. Although Martínez was not directly involved in the coup and was apparently held prisoner by the junior officers who led the revolt during its initial stages, he was suspected of complicity. After several days of confusion, Martínez was released by the military directorate and installed as provisional president (5 December) in accordance with the constitutional provisions. While the junior officers apparently intended that he be a figurehead, he eventually outmaneuvered them to take full control.

Martínez's consolidation of power was facilitated by a leftist-led peasant uprising during January 1932. The bloody rebellion, which reflected peasant discontent, numbered Communists among its leadership. Attacks on landowners and towns in many areas of the country greatly alarmed the elite, which turned to the army for protection. The army put down the revolt after incur-ring extensive casualties, variously numbered from 10,000 to 30,000, in what became known as the MA-TANZA (massacre). The result changed the nation's political climate, solidifying the power of General Martínez, creating support for a military regime, and leaving the entire isthmus frightened of communism.

Initially other Central American governments, in particular that of General Jorge UBICO in Guatemala, supported the United States in opposing Martínez. Contending that the WASHINGTON TREATIES of 1923 precluded recognition of anyone who came to power as the result of a coup, the United States insisted on Martínez's resignation. Martínez and Ubico became rivals in a diplomatic contest for support throughout the isthmus. When nonrecognition failed to topple Martínez because of his control of the internal government security apparatus and U.S. reluctance to intervene militarily, the United States recognized the Martínez regime in January 1934. The general arranged his own reelection in violation of the Salvadoran constitution in 1934, beginning his second term in March 1935. After a prolonged stalemate, the Central American Conference of 1934 was convened to modify the Washington treaties of 1923.

Martínez held the nation in the tight grip of a harsh dictatorship until 1944. A theosophist and spiritualist who believed in the transmigration of human souls into other persons, he was rumored to be involved in rituals and was often regarded as a witch doctor. The security apparatus controlled all aspects of Salvadoran life, including the press, ruthlessly suppressing dissent.

The general did stamp out corruption, cease foreign borrowing, and stabilize the currency. His regime was best known for its public works program, which though not as extensive as that of his Guatemalan contemporary, changed the face of the nation. His efforts included extensive road building as well as the construction of many government buildings. He was periodically reelected, save for a brief interim regime.

After a few years of continued rivalry, Martínez and Ubico joined the leaders of Honduras and Nicaragua in a détente in which each agreed to prevent rebel movements against his neighbors, thereby acknowledging that none could gain ascendancy. This agreement gave rise to the myth of a Central American DICTATORS LEAGUE, which seemed to gain further credence when both Guatemala and El Salvador became the first governments to recognize the new Spanish regime of Generalíssimo Francisco Franco in Spain. In fact, however, there was no formal agreement and certainly no linkage to the Axis powers. Rather, the respective Central American military presidents merely adopted a mutual nonintervention policy.

Martínez was forced from office on 8 May 1944 by a general strike protesting a new effort to extend his tenure yet again. The revolution proved short-lived, but though the military regained control, Martínez's hour had passed, and he remained in exile in Honduras until his death.

THOMAS P. ANDERSON, *Matanza: El Salvador's Communist Revolt of 1932* (1971); KENNETH J. GRIEB, "The United States and the Rise of General Maximiliano Hernández Martínez," in *Journal of Latin American Studies* 3, no. 2 (1971): 151–172; PATRICIA PARKMAN, *Nonviolent Insurrection in El Salvador* (1988).

KENNETH J. GRIEB

HERNÁNDEZ MONCADA, EDUARDO (*b.* 24 September 1899), Mexican composer and conductor trained in the National Conservatory under Rafael Tello. He was Carlos CHÁVEZ's assistant conductor with the Mexican Symphony Orchestra from 1929 to 1935 and was named director of the new National Symphony Orchestra of the Conservatory, formed in 1947. He assisted Carlos Chávez's composition workshop briefly in 1960 and was well-known for his work as choirmaster of the National Opera Chorus. Mexican folk elements moderately imbue his music, such as the ballet *Ixtepec* and his only opera, *Elena.*

DAN MALMSTRÖM, *Twentieth-Century Mexican Music* (1974).

ROBERT L. PARKER

HERRÁN, PEDRO ALCÁNTARA (*b.* 19 October 1800; *d.* 26 April 1872), president of New Granada (1841–1845). Born to gentry in Bogotá, Herrán served with the patriots from 1814 to 1816 and the royalists from 1816 to 1820, rising from private to captain. In the service of New Granada from 1821, he became a general by 1828. A partisan of BOLÍVAR, he left Colombia in mid-1830 for Europe, where he lived until 1834. During that sojourn, he forged ties to generals Francisco de Paula SANTANDER and Tomás Cipriano de MOSQUERA, and he married the latter's daughter in 1842. Back in Colombia, Herrán served as minister of interior and foreign affairs (1838–1839), and commanded the army during the WAR OF THE SUPREMES (1839–1842). During his presidency, the regime sponsored education, recalled the Jesuits (1842), and centralized government via the 1843 Constitution. Herrán was minister to the United States from 1846 to 1848. He later worked for Mosquera and Company (1851–1854) in New York, then returned to Colombia to lead the constitutionalist army against General José María MELO (1954). He was Colombian envoy in Washington from 1855 to 1859. The following year he returned home; he was fired by Mosquera (1862). Again in Washington, he was Guatemalan minister to Peru (1863) and Salvadoran minister to Peru (1865). After being restored to Colombian military service (1866–1867) by Mosquera, Herrán returned to Colombia, where he was elected senator from ANTIOQUIA (1870–1872). He died in Bogotá.

EDUARDO POSADA and PEDRO MARÍA IBÁÑEZ, *Vida de Herrán* (1903); ROBERT H. DAVIS, "Apuntes biográficos e interpretativos sobre el General Pedro Alcántara Herrán," in *Archivo epistolar del General Mosquera . . . Correspondencia con . . . Herrán,* vol. 1, edited by J. León Helguera and Robert H. Davis (1972).

J. LEÓN HELGUERA

HERRÁN, SATURNINO (*b.* 9 July 1887; *d.* 8 October 1918), Mexican artist. Born in Aguascalientes, Herrán was one of the pioneers of the modern Mexican movement and is known primarily for a mural project for the National Theater, *Our Gods,* for which he did numerous studies from 1914 to 1918. It was never completed, but his focus on issues of Mexican identity have assured him a place in the history of Mexican art. He emphasized the dual nature of Mexican identity by using the Aztec earth goddess Coatlicue as the central motif, on which he superimposed an image of the crucified Christ. The Aztec deity symbolizes the indigenous character of Mexico and the Christ figure its European aspect. Figures making offerings are shown on each side of the central motif, Indians on the left and Spaniards on the right. Easel paintings by Herrán on Mexican subjects (people at work, fiestas, traditions, and history) inspired the artists of the Mexican School of the 1920s through 1940s. In portraits and a series of paintings he called "the creoles," he used distinctive colonial churches in the background to identify the sitters as Mexican and the location as Mexico. Each of the criollas portrays a beautiful woman as a symbol of Mexico. In his early paintings of 1912 and 1914, Herrán placed elderly figures in thematic contexts that emphasized their hopeless condition, exhausted by a life of toil and suffering. In his later works of 1917, the elderly figures have a serenity and peace that reflects a spirituality or intense religiosity.

La Ofrenda by Saturnino Herrán, 1913. CENIDIAP / INBA.

FAUSTO RAMÍREZ, "Notas para una nueva lectura de la obra de Saturnino Herrán," in *Saturnino Herrán, 1887–1987,* of Museo de Aguascalientes (Mexico, 1987); SATURNINO HERRÁN, *Saturnino Herrán,* edited by Felipe Garrido, with texts by Ramon Lopez Velarde (1988); JACINTO QUIRARTE, *Mexico: Splendors of Thirty Centuries* (1990), pp. 579–584.

JACINTO QUIRARTE

HERRÁN Y ZALDÚA, ANTONIO SATURNINO (*b.* 11 February 1797; *d.* 7 February 1868), Colombian prelate. Born in Honda, Tolima, Herrán studied in Bogotá, where he received his doctorate in law. He was ordained in 1821, then served in various parishes around and in Bogotá until 1830, when he became a canon of the Bogotá cathedral. In 1833 he assisted in the escape of General José María SARDÁ, a conspirator against President Francisco de Paula SANTANDER. By 1840 Herrán was vicar general of Bogotá and a close associate of Archbishop Manuel José MOSQUERA. As second in command of the archdiocese, he became enmeshed in the church–state conflict during the presidency of José Hilario LÓPEZ (1849–1853). In October 1852 he was imprisoned by the government. The exile of Mosquera left him in charge of the archdiocese from 1853 to 1854, and he was elected its archbishop in January 1856. Herrán devoted his time (unsuccessfully) to re-creating his predecessor's reforms and to forming groups to aid the needy. The virulence of Tomás Cipriano de MOSQUERA's anticlericalism (1861–1863) brought rupture with the church. Herrán was exiled to Cartagena (1861–1864), was back in favor (1864–1866) during Manuel MURILLO TORO's presidency, then had to deal again with Mosquera's ill will (1866–1867). He died in Villeta, about forty miles from Bogotá.

JOSÉ MARÍA SAMPER, *Galería nacional de hombres ilustres o notables, o sea colección de bocetos biográficos* (1879), pp. 227–240; GONZALO URIBE VILLEGAS, *Los arzobispos y obispos colombianos desde la colonia hasta nuestros días* (1918), pp. 266–289; JOSÉ RESTREPO POSADA, "Illmo. Señor Don Antonio Herrán y Zaldúa . . . ," in *Arquidiócesis de Bogotá: Datos biográficos de sus prelados,* vol. 2 (1963), pp. 325–525.

J. LEÓN HELGUERA

HERRERA, BARTOLOMÉ (*b.* 1808; *d.* 10 August 1864), one of a group of Roman Catholic church leaders at the time of independence in Peru who sought to retain for the church the same privileged position it had held in colonial society. He was the leading advocate of the continuation of Rome's dominance over the Peruvian church. A man of humble origins who became an orphan at the age of five, Herrera later studied and taught philosophy. But he did his best work as a priest, among people in poor parishes. Basically he believed in leadership of republics by intelligent, moral elites, be they Inca or Spanish, and respect for faith and legitimate authority. He served the government of José Rufino

ECHENIQUE (1851–1855) at the head of two ministries, and later he acted as Peru's ambassador to Rome. In 1860 he presided over a constitutional convention and was disappointed that the delegates did not restore to the church the privileges it had lost in 1855. He then served as bishop of Arequipa until his death.

JEFFREY L. KLAIBER, *Religion and Revolution in Peru, 1824–1976* (1977) and *The Catholic Church in Peru, 1821–1985: A Social History* (1992), esp. pp. 64–70.

VINCENT PELOSO

See also **Anticlericalism.**

HERRERA, BENJAMÍN (*b.* 1850, *d.* 29 February 1924), Colombian Liberal Party leader. Herrera was born in Cali of northern Colombian parents. He fought for the Liberal government in the revolution of 1876–1877 and was an officer in the Colombian army until the Liberals lost power in the mid-1880s. During the WAR OF THE THOUSAND DAYS (1899–1902), Herrera emerged along with Rafael URIBE URIBE as a top Liberal military leader. By late 1902 Herrera controlled most of Panama, but he was urged to make peace by Uribe Uribe, who himself took this step in October. When U.S. officials warned that they would not permit fighting near Panama City or Colón, Herrera signed a treaty with the Colombian government on 21 November 1902 that virtually ended the war.

In the postwar period Herrera often differed with Uribe Uribe regarding Liberal policy in the face of Conservative hegemony in government, but he remained a proponent of peaceful opposition. In 1922 he was the Liberal presidential candidate but was defeated by Conservative Pedro Nel OSPINA by a vote of 413,619 to 256,231 in what Liberals claimed was a fraudulent election.

LUCAS CABALLERO, *Memorias de la guerra de los mil días* (1939); J. A. OSORIO LIZARAZO, "Biografía de un caudillo: Benjamín Herrera," in *Revista de América* 10 (April 1947):36–63; CHARLES W. BERGQUIST, *Coffee and Conflict in Colombia, 1886–1910* (1978).

HELEN DELPAR

See also **Colombia: Political Parties.**

HERRERA, CARLOS (*b.* 1856; *d.* 6 July 1930), interim president of Guatemala. Herrera assumed the Guatemalan presidency as leader of the Guatemalan Unionist Party on 8 April 1920 after the removal of the nation's longest reigning dictator, Manuel ESTRADA CABRERA. A member of one of Guatemala's premier families, and the owner of large sugar and coffee plantations, Herrera supposedly possessed no strong political ambitions. But in the wake of Estrada Cabrera's ouster, he acknowledged the nation's need for a fair and competent interim leader. Herrera was considered by his peers to be a cultured and learned gentleman. Of distinguished seventeenth-century Spanish heritage, he was widely respected for his qualities of honesty, incorruptibility, and administrative prowess.

After only twenty months in office, however, political instability and a severe economic crisis had overwhelmed Herrera's ill-prepared Unionist government. On the evening of 5 December 1921 a group of senior army officers headed by generals José María ORELLANA, José María Lima, and Miguel Larrave entered the residence of the president and demanded his resignation. He promptly complied with their request.

Although a member of the coffee elite himself, Herrera chose to govern in a manner that often disregarded the concerns of the dominant political and economic sector of the country. Although willing to suppress peasant unrest as severely as previous Liberal regimes, he occasionally permitted the lower classes to voice their concerns. Because of this, coffee growers, merchants, army officers, and some urban professionals were convinced that his administration jeopardized their interests and so they acted to undermine his authority.

JOSEPH A. PITTI, "Jorge Ubico and Guatemalan Politics in the 1920's" (Ph.D. diss., University of New Mexico, 1975); WADE KIT, "The Unionist Experiment in Guatemala, 1920–1921: Conciliation, Disintegration, and the Liberal Junta," in *Americas* (July 1993).

WADE A. KIT

HERRERA, DIONISIO DE (*b.* 9 October 1781; *d.* 13 June 1850), chief of state of Honduras (1823–1827) and Nicaragua (1830–1833). Born to a wealthy creole family in Choluteca, Honduras, Herrera obtained a law degree in 1820. After serving as secretary to the municipal council of Tegucigalpa, Honduras, he became representative to the Cortes from Comayagua Province. He wrote the 28 September 1821 Declaration of Independence of Tegucigalpa and later represented Honduras in the Imperial Congress of Mexico (1822). After Central America separated from Mexico and formed the UNITED PROVINCES OF CENTRAL AMERICA in 1824, he became chief of state of Honduras and defended the country unsuccessfully against Federal president Manuel ARCE. Herrera was imprisoned in Guatemala until 1829, when the Liberal forces under Francisco MORAZÁN overthrew the Arce regime after a three-year civil war.

Herrera returned to politics and was elected president of the assembly of Honduras while also representing Choluteca. Later the government sent him as an envoy to Nicaragua, where he became chief of state from 1830 to 1833. He was elected by the Salvadoran assembly in 1834 to serve as chief of state in El Salvador, but he abandoned politics, except for a brief term as vice president of the Constituent Assembly of Honduras in 1839. He died in San Salvador.

RAFAEL HELIODORO VALLE, "Dionisio de Herrera, 1783–1850: A Centennial Tribute," in *Hispanic American Historical Review*

30 (November 1950): 554–558; RÓMULO DURÓN Y GAMERO, *Historia de Honduras* (1956); JOSÉ REINA VALENZUELA, *El prócer Dionisio de Herrera* (1965).

JEFFREY D. SAMUELS

HERRERA, FLAVIO (*b.* 19 February 1895; *d.* 31 January 1968), noted Guatemalan romantic author and poet. Born in Guatemala City, Herrera graduated in law from the national university. He traveled widely in Europe, Asia, Africa, and America. His first major collection of stories, *La lente opaca*, was published in Germany in 1921 while he lived there. Herrera served as ambassador for his country to Uruguay, Brazil, and Argentina. He established the first school of journalism in Guatemala at San Carlos University, where he also was a professor of law. His novels include *El tigre* (1934), *La tempestad* (1935), and *Caos* (1949). His poems were published in *Solera* (1962). An owner of coffee farms, he lived the last years of his life in Guatemala City with an elderly uncle.

ENRIQUE ANDERSON-IMBERT, *Spanish-American Literature: A History*, 2d ed. (1969); EPAMINONDAS QUINTANA, ed., *La generación de 1920* (1971).

DAVID L. JICKLING

HERRERA, JOSÉ JOAQUÍN ANTONIO FLORENCIO (*b.* 23 February 1792; *d.* 10 February 1854), Mexican general and politician. Born at Jalapa, Herrera was twice president of Mexico (1844–1845 and 1848–1851) and had a distinguished career in both the army and in political life. He fought for the royalists in the War of Independence, retiring in 1820 with the rank of lieutenant-colonel to Perote, where he opened a drugstore. After the publication of the PLAN OF IGUALA, he joined the insurgency and was promoted to brigadier-general. A member of the first independent congress, he opposed Agustín de ITURBIDE and was jailed. His subsequent career alternated between senior military commands and political posts as minister of war, member of congress, and governor of the Federal District. Known as a moderate liberal federalist, he was elected interim president in 1844 and president in 1845. Forced to resign as the result of a military revolt, he was accused of being willing to negotiate the surrender of Texas to the United States. He was elected to congress in 1846–1847 and was military commander of Mexico City during the U.S. invasion. In 1848, he was again elected president, and served until the completion of his term in 1851, only the second Mexican head of state up to that time to do so. Herrera was director of the national pawn shop (Monte de Piedad) after he left the presidency, and retired in 1853.

THOMAS EWING COTNER, *The Military and Political Career of José Joaquín de Herrera (1792–1854)* (1969).

MICHAEL P. COSTELOE

HERRERA, LUIS ALBERTO DE (*b.* 22 July 1873; *d.* 8 April 1959), political leader of the Blancos (National Party) in Uruguay for much of the first six decades of the twentieth century. The only politician whose stature could be considered equal to that of the Colorado leader José BATLLE Y ORDÓÑEZ, Herrera was a political caudillo of enormous staying power, even though he was never elected president.

Herrera served as a deputy in Congress from 1905 to 1909 and from 1914 to 1918. He was a senator from 1938 to 1942 and from 1955 to 1959 and a candidate for president six times. A chief architect of the 1933 coup and of the 1934 and 1952 constitutions, Herrera engineered the Blanco electoral victory in 1958, which gave the party control of the executive (a plural executive at the time) for the first time in the century.

A conservative nationalist, Herrera founded in 1933 the newspaper *El Debate*, from which he expounded his opposition to much of the liberal, welfare-state agenda of the Colorado followers of José Batlle. Herrera opposed Uruguay's collaboration with and support for the Allies in World War II. By the 1950s, he had become a strident conservative anticommunist.

Herrera wrote volumes on Uruguayan history and foreign policy. His grandson, Luis LACALLE, was elected president of Uruguay in 1989.

EDUARDO VÍCTOR HAEDO, *Herrera: Caudillo oriental* (1969); LUIS LACALLE, *Herrera: Un nacionalismo oriental* (1978).

MARTIN WEINSTEIN

HERRERA, TOMÁS (*b.* 21 December 1804; *d.* 5 December 1854), army officer and governor of Panama (1831–1840; 1845–1849). Born in Panama City, Herrera participated in the WARS OF INDEPENDENCE, serving under Simón Bolívar. After rising to the rank of colonel in the armed forces of NEW GRANADA, he was named governor of Panama in 1831.

In the midst of the political chaos created by the liberal revolt in New Granada in 1839–1840, a Panamanian popular assembly declared its independence on 18 November 1840 and persuaded Herrera to assume the presidency. In 1841, however, discussions with negotiators from New Granada convinced Herrera to denounce Panamanian autonomy, and in December he signed an agreement that provided for the reintegration of Panama.

As a result of his participation in the act of secession, Herrera was forced into exile in 1841. But by 1845, Herrera was rehabilitated and that year was appointed as governor of Panama by the president of New Granada, Tomás MOSQUERA. After Herrera's term ended in 1849, he became minister of war in the cabinet of New Granada's liberal president José Hilario LÓPEZ. In 1854 Herrera took a leading role in the defense of New Granada against the dictator José María MELO (1854) and was mortally wounded in battle near Bogotá on 4 December.

CONCHA PEÑA, *Tomás Herrera* (1954); JUAN CRISTÓBAL ZÚÑIGA, *El General Tomás Herrera, Hoy* (1986).

WADE A. KIT

HERRERA CAMPINS, LUIS (*b.* 1925), Venezuelan president (1979–1984). A long-time leader of the Social Christian COPEI (Comité de Organización Política Electoral Independiente) Party of Venezuela, Herrera Campins began his political career as president of the (Catholic) National Union of Students in the 1940s and later became the head of COPEI's youth organization. While in exile during the military dictatorship (1948–1958), he received a law degree in Spain. In 1958 Herrera Campins returned to Venezuela and was elected first to the Chamber of Deputies and subsequently to the Senate on the COPEI ticket. During the 1960s and 1970s he served as president of COPEI, president of the party's congressional delegation, and secretary-general of the Latin American Congress of Christian Democratic Organizations. After a bitter primary battle Herrera Campins won COPEI's nomination for president in 1978 and was victorious in the general election. His presidency was marked by falling oil prices, rising foreign debt, and economic crisis. His leadership was regarded by many as weak and ineffective.

ALFREDO PEÑA, *Conversaciones con Luis Herrera Campins* (1978); DONALD L. HERMAN, *Christian Democracy in Venezuela* (1980); DAVID E. BLANK, *Venezuela: Politics in a Petroleum Republic* (1984).

WINFIELD J. BURGGRAAFF

HERRERA LANE, FELIPE (*b.* 17 June 1922), Chilean economist, lawyer, author, and leader of international organizations. Born in Valparaiso, Herrera studied law and philosophy at the University of Chile and then economics at the London School of Economics. He returned to teach economics and political economy at the University of Chile from 1947 to 1958, spending 1950–1951 teaching at the London School of Economics. At the same time, he served in various Chilean ministries, acted as a general director of the Chilean Central Bank from 1953 to 1958, and was a member of the boards of governors of the World Bank and the International Monetary Fund, where he acted as executive director from 1958 to 1960. Herrera's most important achievement was his involvement as one of the principal figures in the conception and establishment of the INTER-AMERICAN DEVELOPMENT BANK in 1959. He was elected first president of the new institution in 1960 and continued in that position until 1971. As one in charge of implementing the high ideals conceived for the bank, Herrera played the instrumental role in determining the initial thrust of development programs for Latin America. After his resignation, he returned to Chile to pursue his academic career. He briefly became involved in the

Socialist politics of his past (he was defeated in a bid to become rector of the University of Chile in 1972), but ultimately rejected a cabinet position in the Salvador ALLENDE government in 1973. During much of the 1970s and 1980s, Herrera acted as executive of various international organizations, promoted international and Latin American development programs, and authored numerous books.

FELIPE HERRERA LANE, *Vigencia del Banco Interamericano de Desarrollo: Antecedentes y perspectivas* (1982) and *El Banco Interamericano de Desarrollo: Experiencias y reflexiones* (1989).

J. DAVID DRESSING

HERRERA Y OBES, JULIO (*b.* 9 January 1841; *d.* 6 August 1912), Uruguayan politician and journalist, president of Uruguay (1890–1894). Herrera y Obes came from a prestigious family of professionals affiliated with the Colorado Party. He served as secretary to General Venancio FLORES in the WAR OF THE TRIPLE ALLIANCE in 1865. He was minister of foreign affairs in 1872, representative to the national Parliament (*diputado*) from 1873 to 1875, and minister of government from 1886 to 1887 in the constitutional government of General Máximo TAJES. He was the principal inspiration behind the transition to civilian democracy from the militarism of Colonel Lorenzo LATORRE and General Máximo Santos. Elected president in 1890, Herrera y Obes immediately faced a serious financial crisis during which various banks failed, including the National Bank. He overcame the crisis by a consolidation of debts arranged in Great Britain and by maintaining the gold standard in Uruguay. These moves later brought enormous advantages for Urugayan public finance. A man of refined culture and from a wealthy landowning family, he represented an era of civil elitism in which little faith was placed in the idea of people governing themselves. He brought before the Parliament the notion of "directive influence," in which the president would be involved in all the actions of his administration.

Herrera y Obes was a romantic personality, for decades the beau of Elvira Reyes. He began visiting her by carriage in his days of splendor and ended as an old man taking the tramway to see her in her Prado villa. He retained his prestige among elite members of his party until the end of his days, but when he died, President José BATLLE Y ORDÓÑEZ denied him funerary honors. The term "oligarchic democracy" is used when referring to this period because the idea of "directive influence" implied the involvement of the president in the designation of his own successor.

LUIS MELIÁN LAFINOR, *Apuntes para la biografía del doctor Julio Herrera y Obes* (1920); RAÚL MONTERO BUSTAMANTE, *Estampas* (1942); ENRIQUE MÉNDEZ VIVES, *El Uruguay de la modernización* (1975); WASHINGTON REYES ABADIE, *Julio Herrera y Obes, el primer jefe civil* (1977).

JOSÉ DE TORRES WILSON

Dr. Julio Herrera y Obes, ca. 1890. MUSEO HISTÓRICO NACIONAL, URUGUAY.

HERRERA Y REISSIG, JULIO (*b.* 9 January 1875; *d.* 18 March 1910), poet and essayist who belonged to the Uruguayan Generation of 1900. Herrera was born in Montevideo into a prominent family; he was the nephew of Julio HERRERA Y OBES, president of Uruguay (1890–1894). Suffering from a heart condition, his education was sporadic in private schools and from relatives. He resigned for health reasons from his job as clerk in the Customs Office and later from his position as assistant inspector-general of the National Board of Elementary Schools. Herrera flirted briefly with politics, but grew disenchanted. For the most part financially dependent on his family, after 1897 he devoted his life to literature and in 1899–1900 published the literary journal *La Revista*. A follower of modernism, Herrera stressed ideals of beauty and harmony and opposed the prevailing materialism of his age. Herrera was an important part of a brilliant decade in Uruguayan literature—the first decade of the twentieth century. After his worst heart attack in 1900, he wrote "La vida," first published in 1906, and "Las pascuas del tiempo," written in 1900 but not published until 1913. There followed *Los peregrinos de piedra* (1909), *Ópalos: Poemas en prosa* (1919), *Los parques abandonados* (1919), and *Las lunas de oro* (1924). Herrera's poetry was imbued with aestheticism, imagination, inventiveness, and irony. He also wrote essays and newspaper articles. His prose writings include *Epílogo wagneriano a la "política de fusión"* (1902) and *Prosas: Críticas, cuentos, comentarios* (1918). Important editions of his collected works are *Poesías completas* (1942), *Obras poéticas* (1966), with a prologue by Alberto Zum Felde, and *Poesía completa y prosa selecta* (1978), with an introduction by Idea Vilariño.

ANTONIO SELUJA, *Julio Herrera y Reissig: vida y obra* (1984); GWEN KIRKPATRICK, *The Dissonant Legacy of Modernismo: Lugones, Herrera y Reissig, and the Voices of Modern Spanish American Poetry* (1989).

GEORGETTE MAGASSY DORN

HERRERA Y TORDESILLAS, ANTONIO DE (*b.* 1549; *d.* 1625), Spanish colonial historian and official chronicler of the Indies. Antonio de Herrera had a long and distinguished career in which he wrote one of the most encyclopedic accounts of Spanish activities in the New World. In his early years, he was appointed as secretary to Vespasiano Gonzaga, viceroy of Naples, where he began his history of the reign of Philip II. Herrera's loyalty to the cause of the crown attracted the attention of the court, and in 1596 he was appointed the official historian of the Indies, with the task of providing a favorable account of the Conquest and settlement of the New World to combat the negative versions being written by BLACK LEGEND partisans in England and northern Europe.

Herrera's most famous work, the eight-volume *Historia general de los hechos de los castellanos en las islas y tierra firme del mar océano*, was published in Madrid from 1601 to 1615. As official historian, Herrera had access to persons and documents not available to other contemporary writers. He had never set foot in the New World and therefore relied upon information contained in the *relaciones geográficas* and other state-sponsored informational surveys and reports, the writings of Bartolomé de las CASAS, Diego de LANDA, Gonzalo Fernández OVIEDO, and Francisco López de Gómara. Like others of his time, Herrera was obsessed with chronology and inclusiveness; his synthesis is remarkable, but the wealth of information renders his *Historia general* difficult for the modern reader.

Herrera's mission was to glorify the work of Ferdinand and Isabella by emphasizing their Christianizing mission and true concern for the Indians. As an imperialist historian, he sought to justify the empire as a unit and accordingly deemphasized the accomplishments of individual conquerors. Nevertheless, unlike Gómara and Oviedo, Herrera gave Columbus credit for his unique achievement. The chronicle is told from a clearly European perspective; it opens with a description of the Spanish Empire and continues with a discussion of official activities in the New World from 1492 to 1546. Herrera was intellectually honest enough to admit to some of the abuses that had occurred, but he refused to condemn the process of the Conquest in general. He did

incorporate many of Las Casas's ideas and did much to restore his good name, but on the question of official policy toward Indians, Herrera took the side of Oviedo and Sepúlveda. Herrera's *Historia general* is a substantial and informative work, and it is a major example of the sophistication of the late imperialist school of colonial historiography.

C. PÉREZ BUSTAMENTE, "El cronista Antonio de Herrera y la historia de Alejandro Farnesio," in *Boletín de la Universidad de Santiago de Compostela* 6, no. 21 (1934): 35–76; MANUEL BALLESTEROS GAIBROIS, "Antonio de Herrera, 1549–1625," in *Handbook of Middle American Indians*. Vol 13, *Guide to Ethnohistorical Sources*, edited by Howard F. Cline (1973), pp. 240–255; and DAVID A. BRADING, *The First America: The Spanish Monarchy, Creole Patriots, and the Liberal State, 1492–1867* (1991).

KAREN RACINE

HERRERABARRÍA, ADRIANO (*b.* 28 Dec. 1928), Panamanian painter. After completing a master of fine arts at the San Carlos Academy in Mexico City (1955), Herrerabarría returned to Panama, where he was an art professor and later director of the Escuela Nacional de Artes Plásticas.

Herrerabarría's early work reflected the influence of social realism and Mexican muralism. In his mature style, which can be described as a surrealism of organic forms, he combined sociopolitical and racial issues with a visionary mysticism, as in *Posesión* (1981). Unorthodox and rebellious, he published his radical views in numerous articles. In addition to his easel paintings, he created numerous murals.

RODRIGO MIRÓ, *4 artistas panameños contemporáneos* (1981); ERIK WOLFSCHOON, *Las manifestaciones artísticas en Panamá* (1983).

MONICA E. KUPFER

HERRERISMO, a political movement of Uruguay's Blanco (National) Party, organized around the figure of Luis Alberto de HERRERA (1873–1959). The movement was distinguished by conservative and populist paternalism, devotion to its hero, and nationalism. It was the most important political force in the Blanco Party between 1920 and 1960.

Herrera fought in the country's civil wars in 1897 and 1904. With Aparicio SARAVIA's defeat in 1904, the Blanco Party made its definitive entrance into electoral politics. Herrera was the architect of this transition, in which the old party exchanged "swords for votes." Herrerismo played a key role in the plebiscite that defeated BATLLISMO in 1916 and was the principal force opposing the ruling Colorado Party in 1922, 1926, 1930, 1942, 1946, and 1950.

In 1933 the movement supported Gabriel TERRA's coup and was a principal ally of his regime. Herrerismo symbolized the existence of a popular conservative party and the system of COPARTICIPACIÓN between Blancos and Colorados. Allied with the RURALISTA leader Benito NARDONE, the movement triumphed in the general elections of 1958. The following year Herrera died while openly opposing his former ally Nardone. Not until 1989 did Herrerismo regroup under Herrera's grandnephew Alberto LACALLE DE HERRERA, whose neoconservative/neoliberal views won over the majority of his party and triumphed in the national elections.

CARLOS REAL DE AZÚA, "Herrera: El colegiado en el Uruguay," in *Historia de América en el siglo XX* (1972); WASHINGTON REYES ABADIE, *Breve historia del Partido Nacional* (1989); RICARDO ROCHA IMAZ, *Los Blancos: De Oribe a Lacalle, 1836–1990* (1990).

FERNANDO FILGUEIRA

HERTZOG GARAIZABAL, ENRIQUE (*b.* 10 November 1897; *d.* 31 July 1981), Bolivian physician and politician, president of Bolivia (March 1947–October 1949). Hertzog, a native of La Paz, served as cabinet minister three times during the presidency of Daniel SALAMANCA. In the 1947 election Hertzog and his vice president, Mamerto URRIOLAGOITÍA, served as standard-bearers of the reconstituted Partido Unión Republicana Socialista. From the beginning of his administration, Hertzog faced severe labor unrest and a vocal political opposition. Concluding that his astute and tough-minded vice president was more adept in achieving results, Hertzog voluntarily left the office to Urriolagoitía, who completed the term in May 1951. Yet during Hertzog's two years in office, his government achieved improvements in education, social services, and communications. Hertzog returned to private life with the reputation of a dedicated citizen. He died in Buenos Aires.

HERBERT S. KLEIN, *Parties and Political Change in Bolivia 1880–1952* (1969); CARLOS D. MESA GISBERT, *Presidentes de Bolivia: Entre urnas y fusiles*, 2d ed. (1990).

CHARLES W. ARNADE

HERZOG, VLADIMIR (*b.* 1937; *d.* 24 October 1975), a prominent victim of torture under Brazil's repressive military regime. Herzog was a widely respected São Paulo journalist who had worked for the newspaper *O Estado de São Paulo,* for the British Broadcasting Company, and in films. Herzog earned his degree from the University of São Paulo and later taught in its School of Communications. At the time of his death he was the news director of São Paulo's television station TV Cultura.

Brazilian security forces considered Herzog, a Yugoslavian Jew who had emigrated with his family to Brazil, a communist. In September 1975 he voluntarily presented himself for questioning to the local Center for Internal Defense–Department of Internal Order at the headquarters of the Second Army. The following day Herzog's body was returned to his wife with the explanation that he had hanged himself in his cell. Herzog's wife received the body in a sealed coffin and was warned not to open it. Military guards kept a watchful eye over the burial services to ensure that the coffin remained closed.

Herzog's death caused a swift, angry public reaction and became a symbol for supporters of the human rights movement to end state-sanctioned violence in Brazil. Despite government efforts to cover up the incident, Herzog's murder created a national and international scandal for the administration of Ernesto GEISEL because of its brutality and anti-Semitic undertones. Geisel, who was already in the process of moving the state apparatus away from brutal repression (*distensão*), took advantage of the scandal prompted by Herzog's death to neutralize the most repressive elements in São Paulo who were resisting *distensão*.

FERNANDO JORDÃO, *Dossiê Herzog-Prisão: Tortura e morte no Brasil* (1979); MARIA HELENA MOREIRA ALVES, *State and Opposition in Military Brazil* (1985); REPORT OF THE ARCHDIOCESE OF SÃO PAULO, *Torture in Brazil* (1986); LAWRENCE WESCHLER, *A Miracle, A Universe: Settling Accounts with Torturers* (1991).

SONNY B. DAVIS

HEUREAUX, ULISES (*b.* 21 October 1845; *d.* 26 July 1889), Dominican military officer and dictator (1882–1889). Known as Lilís, Heureaux was born at Puerto Plata to a Haitian father and a mother from the Lesser Antilles. Although raised in poverty, Heureaux acquired a good knowledge of economics, public finance, French, and English. He distinguished himself in the War of Restoration (1863–1865), during which he became the close friend of the leader of the insurrection against Spain, General Gregorio LUPERÓN.

After the restoration of Dominican independence, Heureaux became one of the outstanding leaders of the Partido Azul (Blue Party), on whose behalf he fought the Partido Rojo (Red Party) of the Dominican caudillo Buenaventura BÁEZ. During Báez's notorious Regime of the Six Years (1868–1874), Heureaux successfully opposed the caudillo's forces in the south of the country. In 1876 he defended militarily the presidency of Ulises ESPAILLAT. On orders of Luperón, Heureaux terminated the presidency of Cesareo Guillermo in 1879. He became minister of the interior and the police during the presidency of Archbishop Fernando Arturo de Meriño (1880–1882), whom he succeeded as president (1882–1884).

Heureaux became president again in 1887 and ruled the Dominican Republic as an iron-fisted dictator until his assassination on 26 July 1899 at Moca. The establishment of his dictatorship led to his complete break with Luperón, who was driven into exile in Puerto Rico. After decades of chaotic political strife, civil war, and fiscal irresponsibility, Heureaux's dictatorship provided the necessary climate for a great influx of foreign (especially U.S.) capital to the Dominican Republic and for the rapid development of the sugar industry. Heureaux's dictatorship served as a model for that of Rafael Leónidas Trujillo.

JAIME DE JESÚS DOMÍNGUEZ, *La dictadura de Heureaux* (1986); MU-KIEN A. SANG, *Ulises Heureaux* (1987).

KAI P. SCHOENHALS

HICKENLOOPER AMENDMENT, an amendment to the Foreign Assistance Act of 1962. Named after its sponsor, Senator Bourke B. Hickenlooper (Republican of Iowa), the amendment provided for a cutoff of economic assistance from the United States to any government that failed to take adequate steps for the compensation of expropriated U.S. companies. Following a military coup in 1968, the Peruvian government sought to reduce its economic dependency on the United States by nationalizing the International Petroleum Company. In an effort to secure adequate compensation for IPC, the Nixon administration threatened to terminate Peru's economic assistance and its access to international credit institutions. By the mid-1970s, Congress had dropped the amendment from its foreign assistance legislation.

FRANK CHURCH, "Toward a New Policy for Latin America," in *Latin America and the United States in the 1970s,* edited by Richard B. Gray (1971); ADELBERTO J. PINELO, *The Multinational Corporation as a Force in Latin American Politics: A Case Study of the International Petroleum Company in Peru* (1973); ERIC N. BAKLANOFF, "The Expropriation of United States Investments in Latin America, 1959–1974," *SECOLAS Annals* 8 (1977): 48–60.

THOMAS M. LEONARD

HIDALGO, a Spanish term that originally meant "son of some means" (*hijo d'algo*) and over time became shortened to "hidalgo." As its origin suggests, the term indicated a person of some means, but not an heir to a great fortune or nobility. The term applied to some of the leaders of expeditions of the Conquest who were members of the lesser nobility seeking their fortune in the Americas.

In the sixteenth century, Spanish hidalgos were identified by the title "Don," as in Don Hernán Cortés, and women were identified by the feminine "Doña." Spanish leaders also flattered native elites who collaborated with them by addressing them as "Don." In the conquest of Mexico, the lord of TETZCOCO, who provided critical support against the NAHUAS, was called Don Fernando de Alva Ixtlilxóchitl. Cortés's female companion and interpreter was called "Doña Marina." After the Conquest, Spaniards continued to use "Don" in addressing native political leaders.

Over the course of the colonial era, the European identification of "Don" or "Doña" with the lesser Spanish nobility ended, and it became a general term of respect used for an older person, a master craftsman, an employer, or someone in a position of authority.

LYLE MC ALISTER, "Social Structure and Social Change in New Spain," *Hispanic American Historical Review* 43, no. 3 (1963): 349–370.

PATRICIA SEED

HIDALGO, BARTOLOMÉ (*b.* 24 August 1788; *d.* 28 November 1822), Uruguayan gauchesco poet, fervent defender of the independence of his native country, and a close friend of its liberator, José ARTIGAS. Hidalgo attended a Friars Franciscan school. He became a bookkeeper in the ministry of the royal public treasury in 1806 and then joined the militia. Hidalgo fought the English and the Portuguese and was declared *Benemérito de la Patria* (National Hero) for his *Himno oriental* (Oriental [Uruguayan] Anthem). He carried out a series of political functions in the newly liberated Uruguay, including administrator of the general post office, interim finance minister, and censor at the Casa de Comedias. In 1818 he went to live in Argentina, where he died in the village of Morón. He wrote "militant" poetry (*Cielitos y Diálogos patrióticos,* 1820–1822), inspired by his fervid participation in the civil movement for independence.

Hidalgo was the initiator of GAUCHESCA LITERATURE, poetic compositions written from the point of view of the GAUCHOS, recreating also their speech, an archaic form of Spanish (see the *Diálogos* as well as *Relación de las fiestas mayas de 1822*). A neoclassic poet, Hidalgo nevertheless was very successful in creating this form of *rioplatense* (Argentine and Uruguayan) popular poetry, which attracted the mass of the citizenry at a moment when it was necessary to impress on them the need for independence. His passion for freedom and concern for subjects that inspired the people ensured the success of this new kind of authentically American sociopolitical poetry.

MARTINIANO LEGUIZAMÓN, *El primer poeta criollo del Río de la Plata,* 2d ed. (1944); NICOLÁS FUSCO SANSONE, ed., *Vida y obras de Bartolomé Hidalgo, primer poeta uruguayo* (1952); RODOLFO BORELLO, "Hidalgo, iniciador de la poesía gauchesca," in *Cuadernos Hispanoamericanos* 204 (December 1966): 619–646.

ANGELA B. DELLEPIANE

HIDALGO, ENRIQUE AGUSTÍN (*b.* 28 August 1876; *d.* 27 September 1915), Guatemalan satirical writer. Born in Guatemala City, Hidalgo did not finish secondary school owing to family financial problems. He worked as a newspaper writer, businessman, and teacher. As a writer he used the pseudonym "Felipillo," the name of an Indian interpreter who had accompanied the Spanish conquistadores. His most famous work of humor, the poem *Latas y latones,* was published posthumously in 1916.

ENRIQUE A. HIDALGO, *Latas y latones,* 2d ed. (1961); HUMBERTO PORTA MENCOS, *Parnaso Guatemalteco,* new ed. (1977).

DAVID L. JICKLING

HIDALGO DE CISNEROS, BALTASAR. *See* **Cisneros, Baltasar Hidalgo.**

HIDALGO Y COSTILLA, MIGUEL (*b.* 8 May 1753; *d.* 30 July 1811), leader of the MEXICAN INDEPENDENCE movement (1810–1811). Born near Pénjamo, Guanajuato, the son of a HACIENDA administrator, Hidalgo distinguished himself as a philosophy and theology student at the Colegio de San Nicolás Obispo in Valladolid, Morelia, and at the Royal and Pontifical University in Mexico City. In 1778 he was ordained a priest. He gained recognition for his innovative thought and in 1791 became rector of the Colegio de San Nicolás. In 1792, however, his fortunes changed and he was appointed curate of the distant provincial town of Colima. Although the causes of Hidalgo's removal are not known, historians speculate that financial mismanagement, gambling, heterodox thinking, or his well-known affairs with women were responsible. He is known to have fathered several children.

Hidalgo was transferred to San Felipe near Guanajuato, and in 1803 to the prosperous town of Dolores. A landowner, educator, and restless reformer, Hidalgo devoted much of his time to stimulating industrial development at Dolores, introducing a pottery works, a brick factory, mulberry trees for silkworms, a tannery, an olive grove, apiaries, and vineyards. He knew the French language, which was unusual for a Mexican cleric, read modern philosophy, learned Indian languages, and loved music. He spent much of his time in the nearby city of Guanajuato, where he was highly respected in intellectual circles. Some of Hidalgo's activities brought him into conflict with colonial administrators, and he was investigated on several occasions by the INQUISITION.

Although it is not known exactly where Hidalgo began to support the idea of independence, he knew Ignacio ALLENDE before 1810, had many contacts with the 1809 conspirators of Valladolid, and probably attended secret meetings of disgruntled CREOLES at Guanajuato and Querétaro. Many creoles in the Bajío region would not forgive the Spaniards for the 1808 overthrow of Viceroy José de ITURRIGARAY. As with the 1809 conspiracy in Valladolid and other plots, the creole leaders planned to achieve their goals by mobilizing the Indian and mestizo populations. The denunciation of the Querétaro conspiracy by some of its participants caught Hidalgo, Allende, and the other leaders by surprise. Although Hidalgo had manufactured some lances at Dolores and developed ties with members of the local provincial militia units, the exposure of the plot forced him to initiate the revolt prematurely.

The revolt commenced on 16 September 1810 with Hidalgo leading his brother Mariano, Ignacio Allende, Juan ALDAMA, and a few others to free prisoners held at the local jail and to arrest the district subdelegate and seventeen Spanish residents. After gathering some militiamen and others who possessed arms, Hidalgo marched on San Miguel el Grande and Celaya, arresting European Spaniards and threatening to execute them if there was armed resistance. Under the banner of the Virgin of GUADALUPE, the rebellion recruited large numbers of Indian and MESTIZO villagers and residents of haciendas armed with lances, machetes, slings, bows, agricultural implements, sticks, or stones. They joined what became a triumphant if anarchic progress from town to town.

Hidalgo's revolutionary program remained unclear, but he sanctioned the confiscation of Spanish wealth at the same time he claimed to support King FERDINAND VII. The *ayuntamiento* of Celaya and the rebel chiefs named Hidalgo supreme commander. At GUANAJUATO on 28 September 1810, armed resistance by Intendant Juan Antonio RIAÑO at the fortified ALHÓNDIGA led to the massacre of royalists and looting of the city by Hidalgo's followers and local plebeian elements. After taking some preliminary steps toward creating a new government, an organized army, a cannon foundry, and a mint, Hidalgo and his enormous force—estimated to be 60,000 strong—moved to the city of Valladolid, Morelia, which was occupied without resistance.

Declared generalíssimo, Hidalgo marched toward Mexico City by way of Toluca. On 30 October 1810, the inchoate rebel masses confronted a fairly well-disciplined royalist force commanded by Torcuato Trujillo. Following the battle of Monte de las Cruces, the royalists withdrew, granting a theoretical victory to the insurgents, but the green rebel troops had suffered such heavy casualties that many deserted. Hidalgo hesitated until 2 November before abandoning his plan to occupy the capital, realizing that his forces needed better military discipline, munitions, and weaponry. From this point, Hidalgo and Allende led a peripatetic march to disastrous rebel defeats by the royalist Army of the Center, commanded by Félix CALLEJA, at Aculco (7 November), Guanajuato (25 November), and Puente de Calderón, near Guadalajara (17 January 1811). After each battlefield defeat, the rebel forces dispersed, abandoning artillery, equipment, and transport.

Hidalgo did not fully formulate his ideas about independence or the form of government that was to replace the colonial regime, and he failed to develop a strategic plan to fight the war. At Guadalajara, however, he appointed ministers of justice and state, and he named a plenipotentiary to the United States. He abolished SLAVERY, ended the unpopular tribute tax for Indians, and suspended the state monopolies of paper and gunpowder. The availability of a press at Guadalajara permitted the insurgents to publish a paper, *El Despertador Americano,* in which they disseminated their ideas and responded to royalist propaganda. Despite these advances, Hidalgo's dependence upon the lower classes and willingness to condone the cold-blooded slaughter of Spanish prisoners polarized the population and compelled the great majority of creoles to espouse the royalist cause.

Portrait of Miguel Hidalgo y Costilla. Oil on canvas by José Ines Tovilla, 1912. MUSEO NACIONAL DE HISTORIA, MEXICO.

Notwithstanding the continued popularity of Hidalgo and the rebellion, by the beginning of 1811 it was obvious that the military advantage rested with the royalist armies of Calleja and José de la Cruz. At Guadalajara, Allende opposed a definitive battlefield confrontation and proposed the division of the poorly armed and inexperienced rebel forces into several groups. This proposal was quite logical, but Hidalgo believed that the enormous numbers in the rebel force at Guadalajara— estimated by some historians at over 100,000 men— would overrun the royalists. However, in the six-hour battle at Puente de Calderón, the royalists annihilated the main force of the rebel army, freeing Calleja and other royalist commanders to pursue remaining rebel concentrations.

The senior insurgent leaders fled north with Hidalgo to Zacatecas. Differences between Hidalgo and the more moderate Allende had broken out previously, but even stronger denunciations followed in the wake of the disastrous military defeats. At the hacienda of Pabellón, near Aguascalientes, Allende replaced Hidalgo as the senior political and military chief of the rebellion. In the march across Coahuila to seek assistance in the United States, Hidalgo and his senior commanders were surprised and captured. Sent to Chihuahua for trial, Hidalgo was defrocked and executed by firing squad. His head was sent with those of Allende, Aldama, and Mariano JIMÉNEZ to be displayed in iron cages at the four corners of the Alhóndiga of Guanajuato. Following independence, Hidalgo's remains were reinterred in Mexico City.

The best study on Hidalgo in English is HUGH M. HAMILL, *The Hidalgo Revolt: Prelude to Mexican Independence* (1966). For detail on the nature of the Hidalgo insurgency, see BRIAN R. HAMNETT, *Roots of Insurgency: Mexican Regions, 1750–1824* (1986); and JOHN TUTINO, *From Insurrection to Revolution in Mexico: Social Bases of Agrarian Violence, 1750–1940* (1986). There is useful material on the agrarian roots of the Hidalgo rebellion in DAVID A BRADING, *Haciendas and Ranchos in the Mexican Bajío: León, 1700–1860* (1978); and ERIC VAN YOUNG, "Moving Toward Revolt: Agrarian Origins of the Hidalgo Rebellion in the Guadalajara Region," in *Riot, Rebellion, and Revolution: Rural Social Conflict in Mexico*, edited by Friedrich Katz (1988). For the religious aspects, see NANCY M. FARRISS, *Crown and Clergy in Colonial Mexico, 1759–1821: The Crisis of Ecclesiastical Privilege* (1968). Although critical of Hidalgo, LUCAS ALAMÁN, *Historia de México desde los primeros movimientos que prepararon su independencia en el año de 1808 hasta la época presente*, 5 vols. (1849–1852; repr. 1942), offers complte detail and views that appear in all subsequent studies. Also see CARLOS MARÍA DE BUSTAMANTE, *Cuadro histórico de la Revolución Mexicana*, 3 vols. (1961); and JOSÉ MARÍA LUIS MORA, *Mexico y sus revoluciones*, 2d ed., 3 vols. (1965).

CHRISTON I. ARCHER

HIDES INDUSTRY, a major economic activity of colonial Latin America. LIVESTOCK accompanied the early Spanish explorers to the Río de la Plata. During the seventeenth century, rapidly growing herds of wild cattle and horses grazed the fertile pampas. Enterprising Indians developed a significant livestock trade through Andean passes with ARAUCANIANS (Aucas) in Chile.

Conflict among Spaniards, mestizos, and Indians over plains resources worsened during the eighteenth century. Municipal officials in Buenos Aires and elsewhere tried to regulate the rapidly expanding traffic in hides. On a month-long VAQUERÍA (wild-cattle hunt), GAUCHOS might harvest thousands of hides. Legally, wild-cattle hunters had to obtain a special permit (*acción*). Many gauchos, however, engaged in illegal, freelance wild-cattle hunts and sold the animals they killed to unscrupulous merchants.

The early colonial hides trade was crude but profitable. Gauchos used hocking blades attached to long lances to hamstring and thus disable the animals. The riders then returned to kill and flay them. The hides were then staked out on the PAMPA to dry in the sun.

Drying hides, Frigorífico de Rio Gallejos, Argentina, 1968. ORGANIZATION OF AMERICAN STATES.

Hides were sold in both internal and external markets, but exports to Europe boomed during the eighteenth century. Buenos Aires exported about 185,000 hides from 1726 to 1738. City officials, concerned over the diminishing herds, took sterner measures to limit unsanctioned hunting by Indians and gauchos. By the mid-1700s, *estancieros* began laying claim to well-watered sections of the pampas and to the animals that grazed there. *Mataderos* (slaughterhouses) appeared on some ESTANCIAS.

Buenos Aires exported more than 500,000 cattle hides during the 1810s; the figure rose to 2.3 million during the 1840s. Hides accounted for 65 percent of total exports in 1822. By the 1890s, however, they accounted for 26 percent. Other products, notably refrigerated beef, wool, and grains, marginalized the hides industry. Nevertheless, Argentina remains a leading producer of leather clothing and shoes.

JONATHAN BROWN, *A Socioeconomic History of Argentina, 1776–1860* (1979); BAILEY W. DIFFIE, *History of Colonial Brazil, 1500–1792* (1987).

RICHARD W. SLATTA

See also **Meat Industry.**

HIGHWAYS. Geography and culture have made highways important in Latin America since the earliest civilizations. Vast spaces and lack of navigable rivers put a premium on good roads in much of Latin America, yet until the twentieth century highway networks expanded very little. Throughout most of their history, many Latin American highways could hardly be called roads—they were defined more by the traffic that used them than by any physical features. Yet highways have always served as vital links between otherwise isolated and distinct regions, connecting centers of power with the periphery and producers with their markets, communicating information and ideas, acting as axes of change and growth, and, in the twentieth century especially, promoting the development of previously unexploited areas.

Both the AZTEC and the INCA empires expanded along roads necessary for the movement of their armies. Rugged mountain territories made such passage difficult, however, and each state devised appropriate strategies for moving its forces. In Aztec Mexico, cross-country roads were merely unsurfaced trails, wide enough only for single-file traffic. Heavy *tameme* traffic linked principal towns in the Valley of Mexico with the tributary towns outside it via many complementary routes that ran both north-south and east-west. A primary east-west route linked the gulf coastal trading villages with the Valley of Mexico—the route followed by Cortés—and then down the western slopes of the sierra to the Pacific at the village of Huatalco near Acapulco. North-south routes went in many directions from the valley, funneling tribute into the center and Aztec armies outward on marches of conquest. In Mexico's rough terrain

the armies were limited to established roads, but because of their size they often had to use more than one route to deliver their forces efficiently. Control of roads was critical and proved one of the first objectives of conquest and warfare. At the height of Aztec power their highways reached as far south as Central America and north into the lands of the CHICHIMECS, and were to be used by the Spaniards during their own marches.

Cuzco was the center of the Inca empire and hub of its sophisticated highway network, described in glowing terms by the Spanish chronicler Pedro de CIEZA DE LEÓN:

This road which passes over deep valleys and lofty mountains, by snowy heights and waterfalls, through living rock and along the edges of torturous currents. In all these places, the road is well constructed, on the inclining mountains well terraced, . . . in the snowy heights well built with steps and resting places, and along its entire length swept cleanly and kept clear of debris—with post stations and storehouses and Temples of the Sun at appointed intervals along its length.

Inca administration of their roads was strict and efficient, enforcing local maintenance of road beds as well as *tambos*, or rest houses. In the Andes, importantly, roads were traveled by packs of llamas hauling goods.

The Inca network consisted of four primary trunks radiating from Cuzco. The northern route, the Camino de Chinchasuyu, ran into what is today Ecuador, linking the towns of Vilcas, Cajamarca, Quito, and, at the far north, Huaca. The main southern route, the Camino de Collasuyu, ran to Lake Titicaca and into modern Bolivia. Two branches took the Camino de Collasuyu farther south; one went down out of the Andes into modern Argentina, and the other continued south from Bolivia into Chile as far south as Santiago. The Camino de Cuntisuyu led west from Cuzco, providing access to Pacific coastal regions, and a fourth, less significant route, the Camino de Antisuyu, led east from Cuzco.

During the colonial period, indigenous highway networks changed little or fell into disrepair. Roads were still defined more by the traffic that used them than by actual tracks that marked their route. Lyle N. McAlister notes that while Spaniards may have extended and supplemented some existing roads, efforts concentrated on easing access to new mining areas. Most colonial roads were nothing more than trails, especially in the highlands, and were vulnerable to slides, erosion, and flooding. The development of livestock breeding, however, began to change the face of highways. Beasts replaced human bearers in Mexico and augmented llamas in the Andes. A carting industry developed on Iberian tradition developed in suitable regions such as northern Mexico and in Argentina.

In colonial Mexico, the main routes included the Veracruz–Mexico City–Acapulco road, linking the Atlantic with the Pacific and Europe with Asia. Another main trade route led north from Mexico City to Santa Fe de Nuevo México, passing through the mining towns of Querétaro, Guanajuato, Zacatecas, Durango, and Chi-

Pan-American Highway in El Salvador, 1930s. LIBRARY OF CONGRESS.

huahua to Santa Fe and Taos. A similar southern route to Guatemala, through Oaxaca, linked the cities of Puebla, Tepeaca, and Tuxtla with Guatemala City and passed through many distinct ethnic regions. Secondary routes, still of some significance, linked Mexico City with San Luis Potosí and Monterrey, with Toluca and Valladolid (Morelia), and with León and Guadalajara. These roads not only served the silver economies and regional trade of New Spain, but they also brought Iberian culture to the farthest and most isolated outposts of the empire. The European institutions represented by such settlements hastened the acculturation of many native peoples.

There was no primary land route running the length of Central America, but the transisthmian route across Panama was among the most important in the Indies. The difficult mountain trail channeled Peruvian silver from Panama City to Nombre de Dios and later Portobelo, then on to Europe. A much longer, equally important silver road traversed a large part of the Andes in South America, serving the mines of Upper Peru.

Peruvian roads were built on the Inca system linking the capital of Lima with the mines of Potosí and then through the South American interior to the Atlantic ports of Buenos Aires and Montevideo. The dominant trade and communication route in South America, it connected all the major cities. From Potosí, the northern route passed through La Plata (or La Paz), Cuzco, Huamanga (Ayacucho), Huancavelica and its mercury mines, and finally Lima and its port of Callao. South from Potosí, the route ran down out of the Andes through the Argentine settlements of Jujuy, Salta, San Miguel de Tucumán, and Córdoba before reaching the Río de la Plata. Spaniards also developed some important secondary routes in South America, such as one connecting Potosí with the closer port of Arica and another crossing the pampas from Buenos Aires to Mendoza, then over the Andes into Santiago, Chile. As in New Spain, South American roads hastened the consolidation of empire.

There was little change in the highway systems of Latin America through the colonial period, except for the volume of traffic dictated by economic prosperity. Several late-eighteenth-century efforts to improve the main routes, mainly through bridge construction and some paving, proved costly and difficult, and most fell through with the advent of the independence wars.

An exception, however, was Brazil. By 1800 coffee was a major export crop from the area of Rio de Janeiro and São Paulo, and ever-increasing production was being successfully hauled from plantation to port via a dynamic, adaptive transport sector that included mule trains, slave labor, and new roads. Brazil's first RAILROADS replaced this complex, which had shown that it could support sustained economic growth.

The damage and crisis occasioned by war and its aftermath stifled road development in most of Latin America in the early nineteenth century, and railroads precluded their development in the second half. Roads certainly would have encouraged economic progress in many areas, but patterns of development favored export-oriented economies and the primacy of export-oriented infrastructures. Modern, efficient railroads serving producing regions and ports expanded at the expense of internal highway development. Significant highway construction awaited the appearance of automobiles and trucks.

Motor transportation made possible the exploitation

of previously unsettled lands. Most Latin American nations began comprehensive highway construction programs in the first decades of the twentieth century, with varying degrees of success. Argentina, riding a wave of prosperity through the 1920s, improved its system significantly. In Mexico, despite the widespread destruction of the Revolution, highway construction increased dramatically after 1925. From 1925 to 1950, with the first phases of a national program, some 13,600 miles of paved road were completed; in the next ten years this number doubled. By 1975 Mexico had completed 115,000 miles of paved highway reaching into all regions of the country. In general, most Latin American nations saw important expansion in the years after World War II with the emergence of nationalist governments and import-substitution development strategies. By the 1970s and 1980s, however, difficulties in financing slowed many programs and brought others to a virtual standstill.

The PAN-AMERICAN HIGHWAY system is an international project linking the Northern and Southern Hemispheres. Sponsored by the ORGANIZATION OF AMERICAN STATES (OAS) and largely funded by the United States, the Pan-American system was first proposed in 1925 with the purpose of establishing a physical link among the capital cities of the American states. This concept was soon replaced by a more extensive highway system that included other routes between countries. The Pan-American system is generally regarded as a success, often serving as a major route in the areas through which it passes, and it is also recognized as a unifying link between American countries.

Perhaps the most ambitious road construction program has occurred in Brazil, with the TRANSAMAZON HIGHWAY. Part of a long-term plan to populate and develop Brazil's "backlands," it has been constructed in several phases. The first route completed was the Belém-Brasília highway, built between 1957 and 1967, linking the capital with the eastern edge of the Amazon Basin and much of Goiás Province. The second route, the Cuiabá-Santarém highway, was started several years after the first. This road leads from the state of Mato Grosso into the northwest and the state of Rondônia, and it too triggered significant internal migration and an economic boom based on the extraction of forest resources. The third major link, the Transamazonica, links the Northeast with the far west, through the provinces of Pará and Amazonas. This major stretch was intended to integrate these isolated regions with the rest of the country, free the Amazon Basin from dependence on the river for transport, provide an emigration route for land-poor Northeasterners, facilitate the discovery of mineral wealth, and promote the economic growth of unexploited regions. All the aims, it is argued, were intended to strengthen the hand of the military governments that planned and began the network. Similar projects, although on a much smaller scale, in Colombia, Ecuador, Peru, and Bolivia have also attempted to penetrate parts of the Amazon, often with similar social and economic results.

ALBERTO REGAL, Los caminos del Inca en el antiguo Perú (1936); PEDRO DE CIEZA DE LEÓN, The Incas, translated by Harriet de Onís, edited by Victor Wolfgang von Hagen (1959); JOSÉ JOAQUÍN REAL DÍAZ and MANUEL CARRERA STAMPA, Las ferias comerciales de Nueva España (1959); CONCOLORCORVO, El Lazarillo: A Guide for Inexperienced Travelers Between Buenos Aires and Lima, 1773, translated by Walter D. Kline (1965); DAVID RINGROSE, "Carting in the Hispanic World: An Example of Divergent Development," in Hispanic American Historical Review 50, no. 1 (1970): 30–51; SECRETARIA DE OBRAS PÚBLICAS, Caminos y desarrollo: México, 1925–1975 (1975); KENNETH LEDERMAN, Modern Frontier Expansion in Brazil and Adjacent Amazonian Lands (1981); LYLE N. MC ALISTER, Spain and Portugal in the New World, 1492–1700 (1984); ROSS HASSIG, Aztec Warfare: Imperial Expansion and Political Control (1988).

JEREMY STAHL

HIPPOLYTE, DOMINIQUE, (pseudonym, Pierre Breville; b. 4 August 1889; d. 8 April 1967), Haitian writer and lawyer. Hippolyte anticipated the themes of the Indigenist School. Besides nature and love, he demonstrated close knowledge of peasant beliefs. As a student, he acted in a play by Massillon COICOU and was deeply affected by the execution of the Coicou brothers in 1908. Patriotic disapproval of the U.S. occupation of Haiti (1915–1934) is to be found both in his poetry and in the drama Le forçat (1933). Hippolyte early introduced the poetry of the black American Countee Cullen in La revue indigène, helping to make the Harlem Renaissance known among Haitian intellectuals. He is the outstanding Haitian playwright of the first half of the twentieth century.

Hippolyte was trained in law and eventually was named bâtonnier of the attorneys in Port-au-Prince. He served at one time as a commissaire in the civil court. He headed the Haitian Commission of Intellectual Cooperation and the Alliance Française of Port-au-Prince. Laval University awarded him an honorary doctorate.

Jours de gloire (theater; with Luc Grimard, 1917); Quand elle aime (theater, 1918); Le baiser de l'aïeul (theater, 1924); La route ensoleillée (poetry, 1927); Tocaye (theater, 1940); Anacaona (theater, with Frédéric Burr-Reynaud, 1941); and Le torrent (theater, with Placide David, 1965).

See also NAOMI M. GARRET, The Renaissance of Haitian Poetry (1963), pp. 47–48; ROBERT CORNEVIN, Le théâtre haïtien des origines à nos jours (1973), pp. 132–135; F. RAPHAËL BERROU and PRADEL POMPILUS, Histoire de la littérature haïtienne illustrée par les textes, vol. 2 (1975), pp. 460–469, and vol. 3 (1977), pp. 424–441.

CARROL F. COATES

HIRSCH, MAURICE VON (b. 9 December 1831; d. 21 April 1896), European-born philanthropist and founder of the Jewish Colonization Association. Baron Maurice von Hirsch established himself as a generous benefactor in Jewish affairs in Europe and as an important leader in efforts to resettle European JEWS in Latin America.

Born in Munich to a wealthy and influential banking

family, Hirsch likewise pursued a banking career, first in his family's business, than later with the firm of Bischoffsheim and Goldschmidt. Hirsch further increased his personal fortune by investing in the railroad and sugar industries.

The Hirsch family had long been involved in assisting persecuted Jews in Europe, a tradition Hirsch continued with efforts to provide relief in Russia. Pessimistic about the future in Europe, Hirsch looked to colonization in the Americas as a new beginning for persecuted Jews. He founded the Jewish Colonization Association in London in 1891 with precisely this goal in mind.

During the late nineteenth century, Argentina welcomed the prospect of IMMIGRATION from Europe, particularly to its rural agricultural areas. Thus, in 1892 the Jewish Colonization Association chose Buenos Aires as the location for its headquarters in Latin America and established colonies throughout Argentina. These colonies organized around agricultural development and livestock, provided homes for nearly thirty thousand Jews by the start of World War II, by which time the majority of new settlers had emigrated, to escape the rise of Nazism in Germany.

As his legacy, Maurice von Hirsch left not only a tremendous personal fortune but also an association which after his death became one of the world's largest charitable organizations.

THEODORE NORMAN, *An Outstretched Arm: A History of the Jewish Colonization Association* (1985).

JOHN DUDLEY

HISE–SELVA TREATY (1849), an agreement between the United States and Nicaragua that was signed on 21 June 1849 but never presented to the U.S. Senate. It was negotiated by U.S. chargé Elijah Hise and Buenaventura Selva, a Nicaraguan special agent sent to Guatemala to collaborate with Hise. Although he had not been given specific instructions, Hise was aware that he was to advance U.S. transit possibilities and stop British encroachments, which undermined U.S. transit options. The U.S. government supported the Nicaraguan claim to GREYTOWN (San Juan del Norte) and the whole Mosquito coast.

The Hise–Selva treaty granted the U.S. government and its citizens the right of transit and fortification of transit routes. In return, the United States pledged to protect Nicaraguan soil from foreign incursions. U.S. Secretary of State John Clayton used this and a treaty by Ephraim George SQUIER with Honduras to persuade the British to negotiate the CLAYTON–BULWER TREATY in 1850.

MARIO RODRÍQUEZ, *A Palmerstonian Diplomat in Central America: Frederick Chatfield, Esq.* (1964); WILBUR DEVEREAU JONES, *The American Problem in British Diplomacy, 1841–1861* (1974); KARL BERMAN, *Under the Big Stick: Nicaragua and the United States Since 1848* (1986).

THOMAS SCHOONOVER

HISPANIOLA (also Española), the island, named by COLUMBUS, between Cuba and Puerto Rico; its western half became HAITI and eastern half the DOMINICAN REPUBLIC. The island may have been called Bohío by its native Taino inhabitants, the same name the exploring

Urbs Domingo in Hispaniola (Santo Domingo, Dominican Republic). Engraving in Montanus, *De Niewe en Onbekende Weerld* (1671). LIBRARY OF CONGRESS.

Spaniards attributed to house compounds occupied by extended families throughout the West Indies. After his first voyage, Columbus left behind on Hispaniola a group of men who settled a garrison town known as Navidad. Upon returning to Hispaniola, late in November 1493, Columbus found the settlers dead and Navidad in ruins. So ended the first recorded colonization by Europeans of the Americas.

Undeterred, Columbus sailed back eastward along the coast of Hispaniola and on 1 January 1494 laid out the town of Isabela, named in honor of his patron queen. Other settlements, for the most part as ephemeral if not as unfortunate as Navidad, were established throughout the island, but it was not until the founding of Santo Domingo, in August 1496, that the Spaniards secured a permanent, functional base of operation. For the next two decades Santo Domingo served as a strategic port from which to explore, conquer, and colonize the surrounding islands and mainland. It was from Santo Domingo that Ponce de León set out for Puerto Rico, Velásquez and del Campo for Cuba, Esquivel for Jamaica, Balboa for Panama and the Pacific, and Pizarro for Peru.

If Santo Domingo was successful as a point of embarkation, it had a far less distinguished role in putting its own house in order. Hispaniola's woes began early. The relatively peaceful TAINOS, unlike their Carib neighbors, at first offered no great resistance to Spanish intrusion. They were so abused and exploited, however, that an uprising took place in 1494. Mismanagement by Columbus in his fever for gold set a crippling trend no reforms could reverse. Within scarcely a generation Hispaniola was gutted, its inhabitants depopulated to extinction in a tragedy that would be enacted again and again elsewhere, if not always to the same fatal degree. Spanish interest in Hispaniola dwindled as fast as its native groups perished, to such an extent that a rival European power (France) was able to establish a colony on its western perimeter, while other imperial nations (the British and Dutch foremost among them) filled in the surrounding islands' vacuum.

The best account of initial exploration and settlement is CARL O. SAUER, *The Early Spanish Main* (1966; 2d ed. 1992). A definitive synthesis of native culture at the time of first contact is IRVING ROUSE, *The Tainos: Rise and Decline of the People who Greeted Columbus* (1992). Controversy over the magnitude and rapidity of native population demise still abounds, best represented by SHERBURNE F. COOK and WOODROW BORAH, in "The Aboriginal Population of Hispaniola," *Essays in Population History* 1 (1971): 376–410 and DAVID HENIGE, "On the Contact Population of Hispaniola: History as Higher Mathematics," in *Hispanic American Historical Review* 58:2 (1978): 217–237. On the French forging of Haiti, see ROBERT D. HEINL and NANCY G. HEINL, *Written in Blood: The Story of the Haitian People, 1492–1971* (1978).

W. GEORGE LOVELL

See also **Explorers.**

HOCHSCHILD, MAURICIO (*b.* 17 February 1881; *d.* 1965), Bolivian tin magnate. A naturalized Argentine citizen of Jewish ancestry who was born in Biblis, Germany, Hochschild emigrated to Chile in 1911. Twenty years later he was one of three tin barons of the Bolivian oligarchy (the Rosca) whose economic, social, and political privilege dominated the country until 1952. His mines, the second-largest tin producers, averaged 25 percent of Bolivia's total tin output after World War II and provided most of the ore sold to the United States. Hochschild influenced public opinion through his La Paz newspaper, *Última Hora.*

A mining engineer educated at Freiburg University, Hochschild was a metals broker until depressed tin prices after World War I enabled him to buy up bankrupt mines. By 1911 he had acquired the Minera Unificada del Cerro de Potosí; subsequently he consolidated the Compañía Minera de Oruro and the San José, Itos, Colquiri, and Matilde mines into the Hochschild Group. He narrowly escaped the animosity of the military socialist governments of Germán BUSCH, who ordered him shot for opposing the 1939 mining law, and of Gualberto VILLARROEL, who had him kidnapped. The 1952 revolution nationalized his mining properties.

VÍCTOR ANDRADE, *My Missions for Revolutionary Bolivia, 1944–1962,* edited by Cole Blasier (1976) pp. 69–70, 114–121, 123–124; EDUARDO ARZE CUADROS, *La economía de Bolivia* (1979), pp. 259–261; ALFONSO CRESPO, *Los Aramayo de Chichas, tres generaciones de mineros bolivianos* (1981), pp. 249–250, 311–316, 325–335.

WALTRAUD QUEISER MORALES

See also **Aramayo Family; Tin Industry.**

HOLANDA, SÉRGIO BUARQUE DE (*b.* 11 July 1902; *d.* 24 April 1982), Brazilian historian. Born in São Paulo, Holanda was the son of a civil servant who had migrated there from the former Dutch colony of Pernambuco, a fact reflected by his surname. After completing his secondary education in São Paulo, Holanda left for Rio de Janeiro in 1921 to attend law school. In Rio he abandoned his legal studies for a precarious career as an essayist, literary critic, and free-lance journalist. He became part of the "modernist" movement, which rejected Portuguese formalism and exalted Brazilian popular culture. Holanda's writings attracted the attention of São Paulo press lord Assis Chateaubriand, who sent him to Germany as correspondent for his newspaper *O Jornal.* In Berlin in 1929–1930 Holanda familiarized himself with the main trends of German historiography and social science and developed a taste for the works of Max Weber. In Germany, Holanda felt the call to write a history of Brazil, to explain his country to the world. The result was *Raízes do Brasil* (Roots of Brazil) published in Brazil in 1936, after his return from Europe.

In *Raízes do Brasil* Holanda introduces the concept of the "cordial man"—the predominant Brazilian political type, the leader who prefers conciliation to confrontation. The cordial interaction of its leaders, according to Holanda, enabled Brazil to survive and expand on a fragmented continent, but thwarted necessary social change. The book launched Holanda on an academic career that culminated with his tenure as professor of the history of Brazilian civilization at the University of São Paulo from 1957 to 1969. His other major works include *Monções* (Monsoons [1945]), a study of westward movement from São Paulo; *Caminhos e Fronteiras* (Roads and Frontiers [1957]), a cultural interpretation of Brazilian colonial expansion; and *Visão do paraíso* (Vision of Paradise [1959]), an analysis of the images that drew colonists to the frontiers of Brazil. Holanda is the general editor of the first six volumes of the *História geral da civilização brasileira* (General History of Brazilian Civilization [1960–1971]) and the sole author of volume seven, *Do império à república* (From the Empire to the Republic [1972]).

RICHARD GRAHAM, "An Interview with Sérgio Buarque de Holanda," in *Hispanic American Historical Review* 62, no. 1 (1982):3–17; RICHARD M. MORSE, "Sérgio Buarque de Holanda (1902–82)," in *Hispanic American Historical Review* 63, no. 1 (1983):147–150.

NEILL MACAULAY

HOLGUÍN, JORGE (*b.* 30 October 1848; *d.* 2 March 1928), Colombian statesman who twice served as acting president (1909 and 1921–1922). Born in Cali, Holguín was well connected socially and politically. He was a nephew of Manuel María Mallarino (1808–1872), who was president from 1855 to 1857, and the younger brother of Carlos Holguín, who served as chief executive from 1888 to 1892. His wife, Cecilia, was the daughter of Conservative paladin Julio ARBOLEDA.

Like his kinsmen, Jorge became involved in Conservative politics, fighting in the revolution of 1876–1877 and serving as a party director in the 1880s. During the Conservative-dominated regeneration, he served in the senate and in the cabinets of Miguel Antonio CARO and Manuel A. Sanclemente. A long-time supporter of Rafael REYES, Holguín was a member of the commission headed by Reyes that unsuccessfully sought redress from the United States after the secession of Panama in 1903. During Reyes's presidency, Holguín negotiated an agreement with foreign bondholders (1905) that revived Colombia's international credit. When Reyes was forced from power in mid-1909, he designated Holguín to serve as president until a successor was chosen. Holguín again served as chief executive upon the resignation of Marco Fidel SUÁREZ in 1921.

JORGE HOLGUÍN, *Desde cerca: Asuntos colombianos* (1908); JULIO HOLGUÍN ARBOLEDA, *Mucho en serio y algo en broma* (1959).

HELEN DELPAR

HOLY ALLIANCE, an agreement among the monarchs of Russia, Austria, and Prussia made in Paris on 26 September 1815 after the Congress of Vienna tried to rearrange Europe in the aftermath of the Napoleonic Wars. The alliance consisted of a philosophical pledge to carry out foreign relations on the basis of Christian morals. Eventually it was signed by all European rulers except the king of Britain and the pope. The United States feared that the European powers would use the alliance as a pretext to attempt to restore Spanish dominion over South America by force. Seeing the agreement as a threat to liberal regimes, the United States announced the MONROE DOCTRINE on 2 December 1823, arguing that any attempt by the European monarchies to impose absolutism in the Western Hemisphere would be interpreted as a threat to the security of the United States.

ARTHUR PRESTON WHITAKER, *The United States and the Independence of Latin America, 1800–1830* (1941); DANA GARDNER MUNRO, *The Latin American Republics: A History,* 3d ed. (1960); DONALD MARQUAND DOZER, *Latin America: An Interpretive History* (1962).

HILARY BURGER

HOLZMANN, RODOLFO (*b.* 27 November 1910; *d.* 4 April 1992), Peruvian composer and ethnomusicologist. Born in Breslau, Germany, Holzmann began his music studies at age six and moved to Berlin in 1931 to study with Wladimir Vogel (composition), Winfried Wolf (piano), and Robert Robitschek (conducting). In 1933 he participated in the Session of Musical Studies organized by Hermann Scherchen in Strasbourg, taking conducting lessons with Scherchen. He later moved to Paris to study with Karol Rathaus (1934) and attended the twelfth festival of the International Society of Contemporary Music in Florence, Italy. He also studied oboe at the Zurich Conservatory. In 1938 Holzmann moved to Lima, where he was professor of oboe at the Alzedo Academy of Music as well as the violinist for the National Symphony. In 1945 he became professor of composition at the National Conservatory of Music in Lima, later becoming professor of orchestral conducting. He also taught at the University of Texas at Austin (1957–1958). His ethnomusicological studies of Peruvian music are among the most important in the twentieth century and have received worldwide praise. Among his compositions are orchestral works, choral music, chamber music, and an extensive collection of songs based on Spanish and Peruvian melodies. He died in Lima.

Composers of the Americas, vol. 4 (1958), pp. 96–104; ENRIQUE PINILLA, "Rodolfo Holzmann y su panorama de la música tradicional del Perú," in *Revista peruana de cultura* 7–8 (1966): 274; *New Grove Dictionary of Music and Musicians,* vol. 8 (1980).

SUSANA SALGADO

HOMAR, LORENZO (*b.* 1913), Puerto Rican graphic artist. Homer, a native of San Juan, migrated to New

York with his family in 1928. His early training was in design; he worked for Cartier from 1937 until 1950. He took courses at the Art Students' League (1931) and Pratt Institute (1940). In 1946, after military service, Homar attended the Brooklyn Museum Art School, where he studied with RUFINO TAMAYO and Arthur Osver and came into contact with Ben Shahn. Returning to Puerto Rico in 1950, Homar founded the Center for Puerto Rican Art (CAP) with Rafael Tufiño and José A. Torres Martinó. CAP was part of a movement to create a national art that was both accessible and contemporary.

In 1951 Homar began working with the Division of Community Education, which produced educational materials, including silk-screen posters, books, and films, for Puerto Rico's rural population. He became the director of its graphics workshop in 1952. Awarded a Guggenheim fellowship in 1956, Homar returned to New York. From 1957 to 1973, he headed the graphic arts workshop at the Institute for Puerto Rican Culture and trained many of the island's most prominent printmakers in xylography, silk screen, and other techniques. In 1970 Homar was one of the organizers of the first Bienal de San Juan del Grabado Latinoamericano. He established his own workshop in 1973. He has been awarded numerous prizes, and his work has been shown internationally.

MUSEO DE ARTE DE PONCE, *Exposición retrospectiva de la obra de Lorenzo Homar* (1978); THE SQUIBB GALLERY (Princeton, N.J.), *Puerto Rican Painting: Between Past and Present* (1987); BRONX MUSEUM OF THE ARTS (Bronx, N.Y.), *The Latin American Spirit: Art and Artists in the United States, 1920–1970* (1988).

MIRIAM BASILIO

HONDURAS

THE INDEPENDENCE ERA (1823–1838)

In 1823 the short-lived Mexican Empire, which had enveloped CENTRAL AMERICA after the rupture with Spain, collapsed. The failure of the Spanish and Mexican empires in rapid succsssion prompted Honduras, in many ways the poorest of American provinces, to join the United Provinces of Central America. With fewer than 150,000 inhabitants widely dispersed in "hermit" villages tucked away in isolated mountain valleys, Honduras seemed more an administrative designation than a nation in gestation. Cattlemen running large herds on the savannas of Olancho in the east and on the coastal plains of Choluteca in the south of the country had little in common or contact with the Amerindian and mestizo peasant smallholders in the western borderlands with El Salvador and Guatemala or with the gangs of mahogany cutters on the North Coast. Treacherous mule tracks winding over mountains and through rivers comprised the only link between these diverse zones. Municipal rivalry between COMAYAGUA, the run-down seat of provincial government during the colonial era, and

TEGUCIGALPA, an insurgent mining and commercial town thirty miles to the south, further divided the province. Nevertheless, a sufficient sense of national identity clearly had taken root; in time the province became the nation of Honduras.

As Spanish, Mexican, and, somewhat later, Central American dominions successively fell away due to circumstances not of their making and largely beyond their control, the prospect of national independence, ready or not, reverberated across Honduras. These events inflamed the long-standing rivalry between Comayagua and Tegucigalpa. Men of means in both these two dusty towns and throughout Honduras generally—government bureaucrats, soldiers, lawyers, church officials, mine operators, retail merchants linked to mercantile houses in Guatemala and Belize, and cattle ranchers and exporters—tried to discern the implications of this devolution of power to the province and took whatever steps they deemed expedient to protect their interests. For instance, elites in Tegucigalpa briefly tried to end their subordination to Comayagua by becoming a separate province within the Central American confederation.

Straightaway, however, events in the neighboring provinces—Guatemala, El Salvador, and Nicaragua—began to dictate the Honduran political agenda. Two native sons, José Cecilio del VALLE, a poor but ambitious lawyer and self-taught philosopher originally from Choluteca, and Francisco MORAZÁN, an equally ambitious military and political man of humble Tegucigalpa origins, quickly emerged as leaders, respectively, of the conservatives and liberals in the confederation. Both were elected president of Central America: Morazán in 1830 and again in 1834 after del Valle, elected earlier that same year, died before taking office.

These early struggles between Liberals and Conservatives kept the provincial government at Comayagua in a constant uproar as one provisional head of state succeeded another, but the rest of Honduras was generally spared serious upheaval. Morazán's supporters in Comayagua sought to impose the variant of liberalism then in vogue in Guatemala and El Salvador—especially the disestablishment of the Roman Catholic church—on Honduras. Such "enlightened" iconoclasm goaded conservatives to revolt. As Morazán's pending defeat became evident in 1838, conservatives took control and helped dismantle the Federation by declaring Honduras an independent republic on 26 October 1838.

ERA OF CONSERVATIVE HEGEMONY (1838–1875)

During the subsequent forty years, Conservatives, such as Francisco FERRERA (1840–1847), Juan LINDO ZELAYA (1847–1852), Santos GUARDIOLA (1885–1862), and José María Medina (1864–1871) elaborated a republican facsimile of the colonial regime. These resurrected and renovated colonial institutions were familiar to, and aptly suited, the mestizo and Indian peasant majority in Honduras. Nonetheless, unreconstructed Liberals, such as

View of downtown Tegucigalpa. © 1990 PETER MENZEL / STOCK, BOSTON.

Trinidad CABAÑAS (1852–1855) intransigently refused to abandon the liberal agenda. All too often, the ideological struggles degenerated into personal feuds between rival CAUDILLOS (warlords) and their small, poorly armed bands of retainers. As a result, endemic civil anarchy and widespread social banditry persisted year after year.

That these conflicts were often succored by partisans in Guatemala, El Salvador, and Nicaragua certainly helped to perpetuate them; and that diplomats from beyond the isthmus meddled as well exacerbated them. Frederick CHATFIELD, the first British consul to Central America (1834–1852), made a career of gunboat diplomacy to advance what he deemed to be Britain's interests. The British repeatedly took and abandoned the BAY ISLANDS until 1859, and they bombarded and occupied North Coast ports in 1849 and again in 1873 to compel loan repayments. At mid-century, the United States, in the person of amateur archaeologist Ephraim George SQUIER, briefly challenged Chatfield over, among other things, coaling rights to Tigre Island in the Gulf of FONSECA. Even private filibusters contributed to the domestic turmoil in Honduras: most nobably the Tennessee soldier of fortune William WALKER, who in the aftermath of his astonishing saga in Nicaragua, tried to recoup his dream of empire in Honduras but ended up before a firing squad instead.

Meanwhile, the ''forty-niners'' seeking passage to California inspired E. G. SQUIER to promote an interoceanic railway across Honduras from Puerto Cortés to the Gulf of Fonseca. Conflicting survey reports, wildly varying estimates of costs, and a soft financial market led Squier to abandon the project. Alternate routes across Panama and the continental United States soon made a Honduran interoceanic railway virtually irrelevant to the needs of world trade. Honduran elites, however, had been beguiled by the dream of opening up their nation's undeveloped hinterland by means of an interoceanic railroad. In the 1860s, President José María Medina borrowed enough money from London bankers to construct a sixty-mile section of narrow-gauge track from Puerto Cortés through and beyond San Pedro Sula. This short spur of track did little to alter the primary means of transportation for most Hondurans from what it had been since the earliest colonial days—feet, horses, and mules—but the enormous foreign debt Honduras incurred hovered over the country for almost a century and thwarted almost every bid to coax foreign capital there.

Despite the impediments of political turmoil, rural isolation, and the lack of modern means of transportation, the ordinary Honduran CAMPESINO, though poor, may actually have fared better than his counterparts elsewhere in Central America. The Honduran elites, on the other hand, were much poorer than their Central American peers. Because the peasants lived in widely scattered villages isolated by rugged mountain ranges, the elites found it impossible to mobilize them for export agricultural production. Moreover, the widespread folk participation in the diversified exports—livestock, hides and pelts, precious metals, logwood, INDIGO, sarsaparilla, rum, and TOBACCO—supplemented peasants' subsistence but did little to provide a surplus for the elite.

ERA OF NEOLIBERALISM (1875–1903)
In the early 1870s, a new kind of liberalism dedicated to order as well as to progress had replaced the Conservatives in Guatemala and El Salvador. The new Guatemalan strongman, Justo Rufino BARRIOS, in order to secure his eastern flank from cross-border raids from sanctuaries in Honduras, masterminded the overthrow of Conservative President Medina and his replacement by a handpicked fellow neo-Liberal. Barrios initially chose Céleo Arias (1872–1874), but when Arias was unable to maintain order, he backed Ponciano Leiva. When Leiva (1874–1876) also failed to quell dissent, Barrios replaced him too.

The third replacement, Marco Aurelio SOTO (1876–1883), although a Honduran, had risen to high office in Guatemala under Barrios. As Barrios's disciple, Soto espoused the neoliberal gospel of rapid economic progress and absolute social and political obedience. Soto and his chief adviser, Ramón ROSA, quickly restored order, wrote a new constitution, and drafted numerous legal codes. With order restored, they turned their attention to progress. By 1880, Soto had tied all the important towns and many small villages into a telegraph grid and connected it to international cable networks in the United States and Europe. He also began construction of the Southern Highway, a cart road designed to link TEGUCIGALPA, the newly designated capital of Honduras, to SAN LORENZO, the mainland Pacific port on the Gulf of Fonseca.

In 1880, Soto and a New York export-import merchant established the New York and Honduras Rosario Mining Company to work an abandoned silver mine the president owned. The merchant's son, Washington S. Valentine, took charge of the company's operation at San Juancito, a few miles northeast of Tegucigalpa. The Rosario turned out to be the richest silver mine between Mexico and Bolivia, and a MINING boom soon gripped the Honduran Pacific Slope. Foreign capitalists, primarily North American, formed more than one hundred companies to rework abandoned colonial silver and gold mines using modern techniques and imported machinery. Despite staunch support from Soto and his successor, Luis Bográn (1883–1891), almost all of the concerns failed before they produced any bullion—Rosario being a singular exception. Anemic capitalization, incompetent management, inappropriate technology, and steadily falling silver prices conspired to snuff the boom. Although mining failed to realize the Hondurans' high expectations, it did stimulate highway construction, wholesale and retail commerce, and a range of small-scale industries.

Much of what was accomplished during the decade and a half of sustained peace under Soto and Bográn was undone during a bloody civil war that erupted soon after Bográn left office. Near the end of his first term in 1887, Bográn had organized the Progressive party to withstand former president Céleo Arias's challenge to his reelection later that year. In the next election, former president Ponciano Leiva, the Progressive Party's candidate, was challenged by Doctor Policarpo BONILLA, leader of the Liberal Party since Céleo Arias's death. Leiva won the openly rigged election, but after a little more than a year in office (1891–1893), Leiva was edged out of office and eventually replaced by his minister of war, Domingo Vásquez (1893–1894).

Vásquez's heavy-handed tyranny soon provoked rebellion by Liberal exiles in Nicaragua headed by Doctor Policarpo Bonilla, General Manuel BONILLA (no relation to Policarpo), and General Terencio Sierra—all future presidents of Honduras. Although Vásquez destroyed the initial invasion force, a second assault, generously supported by fellow Nicaraguan liberal, José Santos ZELAYA, dislodged Vásquez.

The victorious invaders, at Policarpo Bonilla's insistence, immediately convened a constituent assembly to rewrite the Honduran constitution according to Liberal precepts. With his personal prestige at an all-time high, don Policarpo easily won election as president. During his term (1895–1899), he relentlessly centralized power in the executive branch, embedded his surprisingly advanced ideas of public administration and jurisprudence in revisions of the country's legal codes, did what he could to heal the ravages of the civil war that had brought him to power, and tried to put the country's economy on a sound footing. Policarpo was a fanatical proponent of disciplined political parties that offered voters clearly distinct ideological choices. He also believed that regularly held democratic elections for single-term presidents would solve the bulk of Honduras's political problems. Near the end of his term, he attempted unsuccessfully to revive the long-standing liberal dream of reuniting Central America.

In keeping with his convictions, Doctor Bonilla refused to run for a second term. Unfortunately, his popularly elected successor, General Terencio Sierra (1899–1903), shared little of Bonilla's vision for Honduras. Instead, he spent the bulk of his administration laying the groundwork for perpetuating his power.

THE BANANA REPUBLIC (1903–1950)
By 1900, BANANAS had already emerged as the nation's most important export product. Schooner and tramp steamer captains had begun to visit North Coast ports to purchase bananas for sale in New Orleans and other Gulf Coast cities. Although exports gradually rose during the late nineteenth century, large-scale commercial banana production lagged until a complex set of technological innovations could be developed. After 1900 North American banana pioneers—the most prominent in Honduras being the VACARRO BROTHERS of New Orleans, founders of Standard Fruit Company at La Ceiba, and Samuel ("the Banana Man") ZEMURRAY, founder of CUYAMEL FRUIT COMPANY and a later director of UNITED FRUIT COMPANY—parlayed their entrepreneurial skills and access to large funds of investment capital into banana empires featuring vast banana plantations, fleets

of cargo ships, precision marketing networks, and state-of-the-art radio communication systems. By 1930 United Fruit and Standard Fruit had made Honduras the leading banana exporter in the world, at 30 million bunches a year. Large numbers of Hondurans left their highland villages to work on the banana plantations, thus shifting the population center from the Pacific Slope to the North Coast. By 1940, however, the Great Depression, World War II, and Sigatoka and Panama banana plant diseases pushed Honduras behind Ecuador in production.

This dynamic banana "enclave" further destabilized an already precarious political system. Because the banana companies needed land grants, favorable labor laws, and permission to build railroads and other facilities from the government, they increasingly meddled in Honduran political affairs. At first, however, they received spontaneous support from the government. The 1903 election, which ended with General Manuel Bonilla getting the largest number of votes but not a majority, threw the election into the National Congress. When the Congress gave the election to a rival, General Bonilla revolted and took power. During his first term (1903–1907), he awarded generous concessions of every stripe to the fledgling banana companies, but his repression of opposition politicos and closure of the National Congress in 1904 ultimately led to his ouster by militant Liberals led by General Miguel R. DÁVILA.

President Dávila (1907–1911), despite the timorous protection of the 1907 Central American Peace Treaties and the attendant Court of Justice, was plagued by repeated cross-border raids by political foes. His downfall, however, came when Samuel Zemurray financed an invasion by former president Manuel Bonilla in order to prevent Dávila from adopting a debt settlement plan that would have given vast power to mining magnate Washington S. Valentine and financier J. P. Morgan. General Bonilla's term (1911–1913) was cut short by his death; he was succeeded by his vice president, Francisco BERTRAND (1913–1919).

Bertrand was acceptable to both his fellow countrymen and the banana companies until he tried to engineer the election of his brother-in-law as president in 1919. The most popular opposition leader, General Rafael López Gutiérrez, led the resistance and ultimately won the presidency (1920–1924). The seventeen uprisings that occurred during President López Gutiérrez's term were a prelude to the civil war that erupted when General Tiburcio CARÍAS ANDINO won the 1923 election without a majority. Despite the presence of U.S. ships on both coasts and marines in North Coast towns and in the capital, much blood flowed before U.S. State Department special envoy Sumner WELLES finally persuaded the rival factions to meet aboard the U.S.S. Milwaukee anchored off Amapala in the Gulf of Fonseca.

New elections were held, and Doctor Miguel PAZ BARAONA, General Carías's running mate in 1923, was voted in. President Paz Baraona (1925–1929) temporarily reduced political tensions, managed to reschedule

the massive Honduran foreign debt by negotiating the Lyall Plan with Great Britain, and held free elections at the end of his term in 1928, in which the opposition Liberal candidate Doctor Vincent Mejia Colindres (1928–1932) won. Mejia Colindres, in turn, also held free elections, in which General Carías emerged victorious, retaining power by various stratagems until 1948.

By 1924, the year of the last major political upheaval before mid-century, the United Fruit and Standard Fruit Companies had absorbed their lesser competition and had acquired virtually every concession they might need for the foreseeable future. Moreover, because of large profits, they were able to substitute economic pressure for strong-arm tactics. Still, the sharp plunge in employment and revenues that accompanied the Great Depresssion, the ravages of banana diseases, and World War II produced severe strains that would have automatically led to political disorder in earlier times. General Tiburcio Carías Andino (1933–1948), however, was able to surmount these difficulties (even while meticulously repaying the British bondholders on the Lyall Plan's schedule). He even brought a modicum of prosperity to his country, got the national budget in the black, built many new roads in rural areas, and inaugurated air transport service to many otherwise isolated towns and villages. The cost, however, was also high. The Carías dictatorship shelved democratic practices for the duration, reduced the National Congress to a rubber stamp, strengthened the institutional foundations of the military establishment, especially the air force (begun in 1934), and harshly repressed labor organizations on behalf of the banana and mining companies.

CONTEMPORARY HONDURAS (1950–1990)
By the mid-1940s, Honduras had clearly changed, but the outside world had changed even more. University students, taking their cue from the successful student-led coups in neighboring dictatorships, began agitating for a return to democracy; women protested outside the presidential palace seeking release of political prisoners. Carías, finally bowing to these and to pressures from the United States, announced that he would not run again in 1948. He did, however, handpick his successor, Juan Manuel GÁLVEZ DURÓN (1949–1954).

Despite his long association with Carías, Gálvez granted opposition parties and labor unions considerable latitude to organize and mobilize support. On the eve of the 1954 elections, U.S. CENTRAL INTELLIGENCE AGENCY agents in Honduras launched a covert operation against the allegedly communistic government of Guatemala, and more than fifty thousand North Coast workers went on strike against United Fruit and Standard Fruit Companies. In these unsettled conditions, none of the three candidates—General Carías for the National Party, Abraham William Calderón for the Movimiento Nacional Reformista, and Dr. Ramón VILLEDA MORALES for the Liberal Party—received a majority, although Villeda Morales lacked only some eight

205

thousand votes. Gálvez, meanwhile, had suffered a heart attack and turned the government over to his vice president, Julio LOZANO DÍAZ. Lozano declared himself chief of state and cobbled together a "unity" government with initial support from all three candidates in the 1954 election. But when it became increasingly clear by 1956–1957 that Lozano intended to prolong his stay, the military took the initiative and ejected Lozano on 21 October 1957.

The military junta, increasingly dominated by the head of the air force, Colonel Oswaldo LÓPEZ ARELLANO, negotiated a peace accord between the Liberals and Nationalists in preparation for calling a constituent assembly to elect a civilian president for a six-year term. The assembly elected the Liberal Dr. Villeda Morales, the candidate with the largest vote total in 1954. During his term (1957–1962), Villeda Morales worked to implement the Alliance for Progress—the Kennedy administration's plan for modernization and economic growth in Latin America. Labor unions began to prosper, and peasants began to acquire land through government-sponsored agrarian reform—which made the banana companies and the traditional landed elite nervous. When the Liberal Party unwisely chose a firebrand, Modesto RODAS ALVARADO, as its candidate for the 1963 elections, Colonel López Arellano, claiming that a Communist takeover threatened, seized power on 3 October and sent Villeda into exile. The military, in one guise or another, retained power until 1978.

More than twenty-five years earlier, the Central American nations had formed a common market to circumvent the obstacles to economic development inherent in their small, individual domestic markets. As the most primitive of the five economies, Honduras benefited the least from the free trade arrangements. Shortly after Colonel López Arellano had himself named to a six-year term (1965–1971), acute economic problems were blamed on the 300,000 Salvadoran immigrants. The continuing economic crisis and rising tensions with El Salvador over Honduran mistreatment of its citizens began to erode López's support within the military and the Nationalist Party. His fall from favor was postponed when the so-called FOOTBALL WAR erupted in mid 1969. The Honduran air force acquitted itself with distinction, but the ORGANIZATION OF AMERICAN STATES intervened before the superior Salvadoran ground forces could make serious inroads into Honduras. For a short time, the military regime enjoyed genuine popular support, but the war only aggravated the deteriorating economic conditions.

By 1970, a coalition of businessmen, peasants, and union leaders had managed to mount a request that President López Arellano form a unity government and hold elections; when the two major parties also reached a unity pact, the president acquiesced. National party candidate, Ramón Ernesto CRUZ, won the election but proved ineffective in controlling the increasingly militant labor unions and peasant syndicates; his two-year term (1971–1972) ended with a coup, led once again by Colonel López Arellano.

For a brief moment during López Arellano's third administration (1972–1975), the military toyed with the notion of mobilizing popular support for deep social and economic reforms. Tentative steps in this direction, in combination with the final phase of the Sandinista rebellion in Nicaragua and the devastation of hurricane Fifi, consolidated an alliance of conservative landowners, businessmen, and elements of the army. These forces took advantage of the "Bananagate" scandal, in which Colonel López Arellano was accused of taking bribes from United Brands, to install a military technocrat, Colonel Juan Alberto Melgar Castro, as chief of state (1975–1978). When he too was discredited several years later, General Policarpo PAZ GARCÍA, the new head of the armed forces, took over control of the government (1978–1982) and slowly returned it to civilian politicians. Liberals won both the constitutional and presidential elections of 1980–1981. Doctor Roberto SUAZO CÓRDOBA (1982–1986) and his Liberal successor José Azcoma de Hoya (1986–1990) presided over a steadily worsening economy and the rapid buildup of U.S. military forces to combat Marxists in Nicaragua, El Salvador, and Guatemala.

WILLIAM S. STOKES, *Honduras: An Area Study in Government* (1950); LUCAS PAREDES, *Drama político de Honduras* (1958); RALPH LEE WOODWARD, JR., *Central America: A Nation Divided* (1976); THOMAS L. KARNES, *Tropical Enterprise: The Standard Fruit and Steamship Company in Latin America* (1978); JAMES D. RUDOLPH, *Honduras: A Country Study* (2d ed. 1984); JAMES A. MORRIS, *Honduras: Caudillo Politics and Military Rulers* (1984); VICTOR BULMER-THOMAS, *The Political Economy of Central America Since 1920* (1987); KENNETH V. FINNEY, *In Quest of El Dorado: Precious Metal Mining and the Modernization of Honduras, 1880–1900* (1987); JAMES DUNKERLEY, *Power in the Isthmus: A Political History of Modern Central America* (1988); KENNETH J. GRIEB, *Central America in the Nineteenth and Twentieth Centuries: An Annotated Bibliography* (1988).

KENNETH V. FINNEY

HONDURAS: CONSTITUTIONS. Honduras has been governed under many constitutions, beginning with the Spanish Constitution of Cádiz (1812). Other constitutions were promulgated in 1825, 1839, 1848, 1852, 1865, 1873, 1874 (putting the Constitution of 1865 back in force), 1880, 1894, 1936, 1957, 1965, and 1982. In general, these constitutions produced in the nineteenth century alternated between reflecting the tenets of the Liberal and the Conservative parties. Of the myriad documents, those which have impacted Honduran political development more thoroughly include the constitutions of 1812, 1824, and 1965.

The Constitution of Cádiz was produced by the CORTES OF CÁDIZ during the Napoleonic occupation of Spain (1808–1814) by Spanish and American representatives. The Kingdom of Guatemala was allotted twelve deputies to the parliament in Spain and regional *diputaciones provinciales* were set up in León, Nicaragua; Ciudad Real, Spain; and Guatemala City. Although this constitution was nullified by King FERDINAND VII upon his return to the Spanish throne in 1814, it was restored in 1820 and served as the basis for subsequent constitutions. It provided a division of powers among legislative, judicial, and executive branches, as well as constitutional restrictions on royal (executive) powers vis-à-vis legislative powers.

The Constitution of 1824 was promulgated throughout Central America upon the dissolution of the Mexican Empire and Central American secession. The five states of Honduras, Guatemala, El Salvador, Nicaragua, and Costa Rica formed the UNITED PROVINCES OF CENTRAL AMERICA, a federal system that ultimately failed to hold together the five states. Yet, this same constitution set the framework for unification sentiments that have permeated the histories of all five, especially during the remainder of the nineteenth century. The Constitution of 1824 drew heavily on the Constitution of Cádiz and on the U.S. Constitution of 1789, as well as on the French legal tradition. The chamber of deputies held most of the political power and was elected by proportional representation of the eligible electorate. The electorate was limited by gender, literacy, and property qualifications. The legislative branch controlled the judicial and executive branches; and executive functions were divided between the executive and a senate. Provisions granting the "freedom and independence" of the states led to a struggle between the advocates of centralism and federalism and correlated directly with Liberal-Conservative divisions. After the dissolution of the United Provinces in 1839, Honduras was governed under a series of constitutions that alternated between Liberal ideals of free education, foreign investment, free trade, religious tolerance, and Conservative ideals of trade restrictions and protection of the church and indigenous peoples. The structure and balance of power did not alter as greatly on paper as it did in practice.

A Constituent Assembly, elected in 1963 following the overthrow of President José Ramón VILLEDA MORALES, promulgated the Constitution of 1965. The Constitution of 1957 had already made significant changes in social policies, education, the family, electoral procedures, the role of the armed forces, and labor. Human rights had also been guaranteed under the Villeda administration. Dominated by National Party members (more a Liberal splinter group than a successor to the Conservative Party), the Constituent Assembly of 1965 designated Colonel Oswaldo LÓPEZ ARELLANO as the new president, to serve for six years. The assembly also declared itself the first Congress under the new constitution. The document divided the government into the same three branches and specified that the president be the commander of the armed forces. The legislature was unicameral and proportionally representative. The Supreme Court of Honduras consisted of seven justices serving limited terms.

The constitution is divided into fourteen "titles," which, despite hinting at the restoration of union, produce a very centralized government with a strong executive and a relatively weaker legislative branch. Over time, Honduran constitutions showed a political evolution from colony to state to republic, and from a strong legislative branch to a strong military and executive branch. However, the Constitution of 1965 reminded Hondurans that they were still part of "the Federal Republic of Central America" and, while assuring Honduran sovereignty, left open the possibility of Central American reunification in the future.

RAMÓN ROSA, "Social Constitution of Honduras," in RALPH LEE WOODWARD, JR., ed., *Positivism in Latin America, 1850–1900: Are Order and Progress Reconcilable?* (1971); HARVEY K. MEYER, *Historical Dictionary of Honduras* (1976); MARIO RODRÍGUEZ, *The Cádiz Experiment* (1978); LUIS MARIÑAS OTERO, *Las constituciones de Honduras* (1982); and *Honduras*, 2d ed. (1983); JAMES A. MORRIS, *Honduras: Caudillo Politics and Military Rulers* (1984).

JEFFREY D. SAMUELS

HONDURAS: POLITICAL PARTIES

National Party
Partido Nacional de Honduras—PNH

The National Party of Honduras emerged in the early twentieth century as the principal opposition to the Liberal Party, which had dominated the country since the 1870s. Made up of both disgruntled Liberals and former Conservative Party members, it formally organized in 1916 under the leadership of Francisco BERTRAND, although it did not become a cohesive organization until Tiburcio CARÍAS ANDINO took over its leadership in the 1920s. Despite lip service to nationalism, the party became closely allied to the U.S.-owned UNITED FRUIT COMPANY. Carías failed in efforts to unseat the Liberals in 1923 and 1928. However, he finally won the election of 1932 and ruled Honduras from 1933 to 1948, firmly establishing the National Party in Honduran politics.

Ideologically, the party was much influenced in its formative years by Dr. Paulino Valladares and has tended to be somewhat to the right of the Liberal Party. Personalism, however, has always been more important than ideology in the party. In the post-Carías period, the party developed close ties with the Honduran army, although not to the exclusion of the Liberal influence there. The Liberals ended the long National Party rule in 1957. Beginning in 1956, however, the army established itself as the principal political power in the country, and in 1963 it restored the National Party to power. Since then the National and Liberal parties have often joined in unity pacts to share power.

Civilian government was restored in 1981. The National Party, led by Rafael Leonardo CALLEJAS, lost to the Liberals that year and again in 1985. But in 1990 Callejas returned to power on a strongly neoliberal economic platform. Deteriorating economic conditions, however, led to another Liberal victory in the 1993 presidential election.

JAMES D. RUDOLPH, ed., *Honduras, A Country Study*, 2d ed. (1983); ALISON ACKER, *Honduras: The Making of a Banana Republic* (1988); JAMES DUNKERLEY, *Power in the Isthmus: A Political History of Modern Central America* (1988); TOM BARRY and KENT NORSWORTHY, *Honduras: A Country Guide* (1990).

RALPH LEE WOODWARD, JR.

HONDURAS COMPANY, a trading enterprise established by the Spanish monarchy. The Honduras Company (La Compañia de Comercio de Honduras) was chartered by the Spanish king, PHILIP V on 25 January 1714, as one of the earliest of the BOURBON REFORMS. It granted the marquis of Montesacro an exclusive license to trade with Honduras; but only one trading expedition, from Cádiz, was ever made, and the Honduras Company ceased to exist after its return to Spain in 1717. It launched, however, a pattern of more liberal trade policies to follow, notably with the establishment of the CARACAS COMPANY in 1728, the HAVANA COMPANY in 1740, two Guatemalan companies in 1750–1756, and the passage of the FREE TRADE ACT of 1778. Such trading companies were established to engage in officially regulated commerce with limited geographic regions, thus beginning the breakdown of the Seville-Cádiz merchant monopoly.

ROLAND HUSSEY, *The Caracas Company, 1728–1784: A Study in the History of Spanish Monopolistic Trade* (1934); CARMELO SÁENZ DE SANTAMARÍA, "La Compañia de Comercio de Honduras, 1714–1717," *Revista de Indias* 40 (1980): 129–157; LUIS MARIÑAS OTERO, *Honduras*, 2d ed. (1983).

JEFFREY D. SAMUELS

HOPKINS, EDWARD AUGUSTUS (b. 1822; d. 10 June 1891), U.S. diplomat and entrepreneur active in Paraguay and Argentina. The son of an Episcopalian bishop in Vermont, Hopkins was twenty-two years old when he decided to abandon a faltering career in the U.S. Navy and try his luck as an entrepreneur in South America. He obtained a commission as U.S. agent to Paraguay in 1845.

President Carlos Antonio LÓPEZ welcomed the young man as though he were a full-fledged ambassador. Hopkins actually encouraged this attitude by exaggerating his own authority, claiming that he was empowered to mediate between the Paraguayan government and the *porteño* dictator Juan Manuel de ROSAS. Eventually, the U.S. State Department had to repudiate the grandiose claims of its agent and order his return to Washington.

Hopkins refused to give up. Over the next few years, he returned to Paraguay five times. He explored its rivers and gained a comprehensive knowledge of its commercial potential. Though somewhat chastened by his earlier experience, López agreed to extend a series of trade privileges to Hopkins if the United States were to recognize Paraguayan independence.

In 1853, when the U.S. recognized Paraguay, Hopkins returned to Asunción as consul and quickly moved to take advantage of López's offer. He had already organized a corporation—the United States and Paraguay Navigation Company—and with the capital it provided, set up a half-dozen enterprises in Paraguay. These included a cigar factory, a brick factory, a sawmill, and a distillery, all of which operated under license from López. The Paraguayan president even extended loans to Hopkins as well as the labor of state prisoners for the various projects.

Things did not go as planned. Hopkins's blustering personal style had always irked the punctilious López, but the North American's open-ended promises had always caused him to ignore his instincts. López, however, revoked the concessions granted Hopkins and, in 1854, expelled him from the republic.

By this time, the bad feelings between the two men had grown into a diplomatic incident that ultimately resulted in an abortive U.S. naval intervention. López reluctantly agreed to mediation to settle the dispute.

After his Paraguayan fiasco, Hopkins stayed on in the Platine region. He lived for another thirty-seven years in and around Buenos Aires, where he made a name for himself promoting telegraph companies, steamships, and railroads. Throughout this time he maintained a quasi-official position within the Argentine government and was a personal friend of many highly placed Argentine politicians. In the early 1890s, he returned to the United States as secretary of the Argentine delegation to an international railway conference, and there died in Washington, D.C.

HAROLD F. PETERSON, "Edward A. Hopkins: A Pioneer Promoter in Paraguay," in *Hispanic American Historical Review* 22, no. 2 (1942): 245–261; ROBERT D. WOOD, *The Voyage of Water Witch* (1985); THOMAS L. WHIGHAM, *The Politics of River Trade: Tradition and Development in the Upper Plata, 1780–1870* (1991), pp. 145–147.

THOMAS L. WHIGHAM

See also **Water Witch Incident.**

HORN, CAPE. The Cabo de Hornos is a promontory located on the Isla Hornos in Chile at 55 degrees south and 67 degrees west latitudes, considered the southernmost tip of the continent. Discovered by the Dutch corsairs W. C. Schouten and J. Le Maire on 29 January 1611, it was named Hoorn, for the birthplace of Schouten. The discovery dispelled the belief that TIERRA DEL FUEGO was the northern margin of a large southern continent, Terra Australis, and established a second passage from the Atlantic Ocean to the Pacific Ocean. Sailing ships preferred the open oceanic passage to the narrow and treacherous Strait of MAGELLAN, although heavy storms and the strong westerlies would sometimes paralyze vessels for weeks. Steam navigation dealt a blow to the Cape Horn route by making navigation along the Strait of Magellan safer.

WEBB CHILES, *Storm Passage: Alone Around Cape Horn* (1977); ERROLL BRUCE, *Cape Horn to Port* (1978); and HAL ROTH, *Two Against Cape Horn* (1978).

CÉSAR N. CAVIEDES

HORNERO BIRD, a songbird species native to the flat eastern PAMPAS of Argentina. The hornero bird is known for its ovenlike mud nests, which it builds on fence posts and other likely spots on the flat, treeless grasslands. Its sweet songs and blithe spirit are mythologized in popular gaucho poetry and song.

WILLIAM H. HUDSON, *Far Away and Long Ago* (1918); GERALD M. DURRELL, *The Drunken Forest* (1956).

KRISTINE L. JONES

HORSES. *See* **Livestock.**

HOSTOS Y BONILLA, EUGENIO MARÍA DE (*b.* 11 January 1839; *d.* 11 August 1903), Puerto Rican philosopher, sociologist, educator, patriot, and man of letters. Born in Río Cañas, Hostos attended elementary school in San Juan, secondary school at the Institute of Balboa in Spain, and enrolled in law school in Madrid. He joined the Spanish republican movement and gained their promise of independence for Puerto Rico and Cuba. When the republicans abandoned that promise, Hostos moved to the United States in 1869.

In New York, he joined the Cuban Revolutionary Junta and became managing editor of its official periodical. Realizing that Cuban independence could not be fought from New York, he began a four-year journey in 1870 that would take him throughout South America to win support for the independence cause. Long an advocate of abolition of SLAVERY and of Antillean federation after independence, Hostos involved himself during his travels with various social injustices. In Lima, his writings proved instrumental in turning public opinion against the mistreatment of Chinese laborers and against the Oroya railway project, despite the fact that its builders offered to donate $200,000 to the movement. In 1872, he taught at the University of Chile in Santiago, where his writings helped gain women the right of admission to professional programs. While in Argentina in 1873, he became a spokesman for a transandean railroad to Chile. In honor of his efforts, the first locomotive to complete the journey was named the *Eugenio María de Hostos*.

In 1875, he settled in Santo Domingo, where he founded a newspaper that echoed one of his strongest dreams, a federation of the Hispanic West Indies. After a brief trip to Venezuela where he married, he returned to Santo Domingo and revamped the education system,

Eugenio María de Hostos y Bonilla. LIBRARY OF CONGRESS.

introducing the scientific method to the curriculum. He stated that the only revolution that had not taken place in Latin America was in education and he added the reformation of educational systems to his political agenda. After a disagreement with the Dominican dictator, Ulises HEUREAUX in 1888, he accepted an invitation from officials to return to Chile and reform its educational system.

Hostos returned to New York in 1898 and for two years unsuccessfully agitated for a plebiscite to determine the future status of Puerto Rico, even participating in a delegation that presented demands to President William McKinley. After the assassination of Heureaux, he returned to the Dominican Republic as inspector general of schools.

Hostos wrote fifty books and numerous essays. The impact of his novel, *La peregrinación de Bayoán*, is said to be as profound for Cuban independence as *Uncle Tom's Cabin* was for the abolitionist movement in the United States. His treatise on the scientific education of women made him a precursor of later feminist causes and his political writings made him a forerunner of the doctrine of self-determination in his homeland. It is said that no national literature evolved in the Dominican Republic until after his service to that country. His educational endeavors included founding schools, writing textbooks, and authoring the laws governing education. He wrote best of his own beliefs when he said in *La peregrinación,* "I wish that they will say: In that Island [Puerto Rico] a man was born who loved truth, desired justice, and worked for the good of men."

Hostos's own works can be found in his twenty-volume *Obras Completas.* For general information on his life, see EUGENIO CARLOS DE HOSTOS, ed., *Eugenio María de Hostos: Promoter of Pan-Americanism* (1954). For his time in the Dominican Republic, see EMILIO RODRÍGUEZ DEMORIZI, *Luperón y Hostos* (1975), and for Cuba, EMILIO ROIG DE LEUCHSENRING, *Hostos y Cuba,* 2d ed. (1974). On Hostos's participation in Puerto Rican concerns, see ARTURO MORALES CARRIÓN, *Puerto Rico: A Political and Cultural History* (1983). For discussions on his works, see LOIDA FIGUEROA, *Hostos, el angustiado* (1988); JUAN BOSCH, *Hostos, el sembrador* (1976); and ADELAIDA LUGO GUERNELLI, *Eugenio María de Hostos, ensayista y crítico literario* (1970).

JACQUELYN BRIGGS KENT

HOUSSAY, BERNARDO A. (*b.* 10 April 1887; *d.* 21 September 1971), Argentine physiologist, teacher, and researcher, Latin America's first Nobel laureate in science. Born to a French family in Buenos Aires, Houssay studied and, beginning in 1910, taught medicine at the University of Buenos Aires. In 1919 he was named professor of physiology and director of the Institute of Physiology. In 1933, at the initiative of the "Houssay group," the Asociación Argentina para el Progreso de las Ciencias was founded; it played a commanding role in obtaining and disbursing funding for Argentine scientific research. With his associates and hundreds of other intellectuals, Houssay was dismissed by the military government in 1943; he later clashed with President Juan PERÓN. Out of official favor, he continued his research under private auspices. By the late 1940s his writings on endocrinology, nutrition, physiology, pharmacology, diabetes, and medical education gained him an international reputation. Honors and awards culminated in 1947 in the Nobel Prize in physiology or medicine (shared with Carl F. and Gerty T. Cori), awarded to him in recognition of his research on the role of the pituitary gland in carbohydrate metabolism—research that pointed the way toward alternatives to insulin. Houssay served as president of the National Council for Scientific and Technical Research and remained professionally active until his death. His works include *Concepto de la universidad* (1940), *La crisis actual y bases para el adelanto de la universidad* (1943), *Human Physiology* (1965), and *La emigración de científicos, profesionales, y técnicos de la Argentina* (1966).

CARL F. CORI et al., eds., *Perspectives in Biology* (1963); SIR FRANK YOUNG and V. G. FOGLIA, "Bernard A. Houssay," in *Biographical Memoirs of Fellows of the Royal Society,* vol. 20 (1974), pp. 247–270; GUENTER B. RISSE, "Houssay, Bernardo A.," in *Dictionary of Scientific Biography,* vol. 15 (1978), pp. 228–229; MARCELINO CEREIJIDO, *La nuca de Houssay: Las ciencia argentina entre Billiken y el exilio* (1990).

RONALD C. NEWTON

HOUSTON, SAM (*b.* 2 March 1793; *d.* 26 July 1863), president of the Republic of Texas (1836–1838, 1841–1844). Born near Timber Ridge Church, Rockbridge County, Virginia, Houston received little formal schooling and spent three years among the Cherokee Indians. In 1813, he enlisted in the U.S. Army and was wounded in an engagement with the Creek Indians at Horseshoe Bend. He left the army in 1818 to study law in Nashville. His popularity led to a variety of elected and appointed offices, including two terms in Congress (1823, 1825) and election as governor of Tennessee (1827). He resigned the governorship in 1829 and spent the next six years establishing diplomatic and trade relations with the Indians.

Houston moved to Texas in 1832 and was caught up in the turmoil between the Mexican government and the Anglo-American population. He was elected a delegate to the Consultation of all Texas communities in 1835, and the revolutionary government awarded him a commission as major general. He signed the Declaration of Independence on 2 March 1836, and two days later he was selected to command the Texas Army, which he led to victory at the battle of SAN JACINTO on 21 April of that year. On 5 September 1836, Houston was elected president of the Republic of Texas, an office he held twice during that nation's nine-year history. When Texas joined the United States, Houston was sent to the U.S. Senate, where he served for fourteen years. On 21 December 1859 he was inaugurated governor of Texas, but his opposition to secession and his refusal to swear allegiance to the Confederate government forced him to relinquish the office in 1861. He spent the last years of his life at his home in Huntsville, Texas.

AMELIA W. WILLIAMS and EUGENE. C. BARKER, *The Writings of Sam Houston,* 8 vols. (1938–1943); SAM HOUSTON, *The Autobiography of Sam Houston,* edited by Donald Day and Harry Herbert Ullom (1954); MARION KARL WISEHART, *Sam Houston, American Giant* (1962); LLERENA FRIEND, *Sam Houston, the Great Designer* (1969).

MICHAEL R. GREEN

See also **Texas Revolution.**

HOWARD, JENNIE ELIZA (*b.* 24 July 1845; *d.* 29 July 1931), North American schoolteacher and educator. Born in Coldbrook Springs, Massachusetts, Howard studied at the Framingham Normal School and taught in Boston and Worcester, where she became an assistant principal in a boys' school. Howard was an experienced teacher by 1883, when she joined Domingo Faustino SARMIENTO's program that brought North American teachers to Argentina. She is the best remembered of the more than eighty-eight teachers who worked in Argentina from 1867 to the turn of the century because she wrote a book about her experiences: *In Distant Climes and Other Years* (1931). Howard taught or ran schools in Paraná; in Corrientes, where she established a normal school; and in San Nicolás de los Arroyos, at the eastern limit of the pampa. There she was assistant principal of the normal school and head of the model grade school, both of which she established.

Howard retired in 1903, when she lost her voice, but she remained in Argentina where she became the mainstay of the English-speaking community in Buenos Aires. When the government cut all pensions, more than one hundred of Howard's former students organized to get hers restored, and they feted her on her eighty-fifth birthday in a public hall. Her portrait still hangs in the public school she founded in San Nicolás. Howard died in Buenos Aires.

ALICE HOUSTON LUIGGI, *65 Valiants* (1965).

GEORGETTE MAGASSY DORN

HUACA, the generic name for supernatural powers or spirits worshiped by the INCAS as well as by modern Andean Indians as a manifestation of their animistic beliefs. According to John Rowe, the name *huaca* derives from the QUECHUA word for "shrine." Huacas, places or objects of local importance, are extremely numerous throughout the Andean region. As a type they include geographical features such as springs, rivers, stone outcrops, boulders of unusual shape, caves, quarries, hills, and mountains (especially snow-capped ones). Natural phenomena such as deformed animals, plants, or humans, or human or animal twins, as well as people,

animals, or objects struck by lightning, are also considered *huacas*. Ruins of ancient sites are another class of *huacas*, and the Incas made offerings at such sites as Tiahuanaco in Bolivia and Pikillacta in the Cuzco valley. In modern times, the term *huaca* has become a synonym for archaeological ruins on the coast of Peru. Yet another class of *huacas* is that of agricultural field guardian spirits, which are usually said to reside in small, irregularly shaped stones found in the fields.

The principal source on Inca huacas is JOHN H. ROWE, "Inca Culture at the Time of the Spanish Conquest," in *Handbook of South American Indians*, vol. 2 (1946), pp. 183–330. For a description of modern native cults in the Cuzco region see MICHAEL J. SALLNOW, *Pilgrims of the Andes* (1987).

GORDON F. McEWAN

HUANCAVELICA, city and department of Peru made famous by colonial mercury mines. Located 150 miles southeast of Lima, the city lies in a steep mountain valley along the Icho River, 11,895 feet above sea level. The famous Santa Bárbara mine of colonial times lay atop cliffs south of the city at an altitude of 14,300 feet.

Indians worked the quicksilver deposits during pre-Hispanic times, but the district became economically important only when the Spaniards began to refine silver through amalgamation. In 1563 Amador Cabrera, an *encomendero* (agent) from Huamanga, learned about the site from the *kuraka* (Indian headman) Gonzalo Ñavincopa. Miners and operators founded the Villa Rica de Oropesa, named for Viceroy Francisco de TOLEDO's home in Spain, on 4 August 1571. (After Toledo's departure the city gradually reverted to the name of Huancavelica.) Toledo expropriated the district for the crown in 1572. He then contracted with mine operators to pro-

The city of Huancavelica, 1984. ARCHIVO CARETAS.

duce mercury at a set price and agreed to provide them with cheap, forced Indian labor known as the MITA.

The Huancavelica mine quickly became a deathtrap for the Indian laborers. In its greed and inexperience the mining guild neglected to dig a ventilation shaft, and the mercury dust poisoned many. Indian villages subject to the *mita* looked upon the labor draft as a death sentence and were encouraged in their opposition by governors, priests, *hacendados,* and *kurakas* who wanted to exploit the workers themselves. As Indians died or fled, population in the *mita* provinces declined dramatically. Conditions improved in 1642 with completion of the Our Lady of Belén adit, which ventilated the mine. Thereafter more Indians were willing to work as wage laborers at the mine.

Huancavelica was the only American mercury mine of any significance, and until the 1770s it provided nearly all the quicksilver used by Peruvian silver refiners. It also made occasional shipments to Mexico, but the crown generally supplied the northern viceroyalty from its mines at Almadén, Spain. With the Peruvian mining expansion of the eighteenth century, Huancavelica struggled to meet mercury demand, its richest ores exhausted. Production costs were five times higher than at Almadén.

Blaming Huancavelica's problems on corruption and primitive technology, the royal inspector (*visitador*) José Antonio de Areche abolished the guild in 1779 and turned the Santa Bárbara mine over to Nicolás de Saravia, who agreed to produce greater quantities at a much lower price. When Saravia died unexpectedly the following year, Areche decided to turn the mine over to government administration, which had been very successful at Almadén. In 1784, because of the mercury mine, Huancavelica became a small intendancy, independent of the intendant of Huamanga's jurisdiction.

Nevertheless, Fernando Márquez de la Plata, the intendant, knew little about mining and allowed his unscrupulous mine director to extract the ore-laden natural supports of the mine to increase mercury output. On 25 September 1786 the top half of the mine collapsed. As head of a royal technological mission to Peru, Baron Thaddeus von Nordenflicht made comprehensive recommendations to renovate the mine in 1792, but his proposal died from lack of money and xenophobic resistance. Perhaps as important, Spanish authorities decided to halt Huancavelica production and supply Peru from Almadén in order to make the colonists dependent upon Spain for mercury.

Despite those imperial intentions, Almadén was unable to provide secure and adequate supplies, and Huancavelica intendants permitted private interests to work deposits outside the Santa Bárbara mine, where huge quantities of low-grade ore were available. Some production at Huancavelica continued after Peruvian independence, along with periodic attempts to reopen the great mine itself. The low price for mercury on the world market crippled those attempts, however, and Huan-

cavelica stagnated in modern times, a colonial city dependent on grazing and wool for its scant existence.

ARTHUR P. WHITAKER, *The Huancavelica Mercury Mine: A Contribution to the History of the Bourbon Renaissance in the Spanish Empire* (1941); GUILLERMO LOHMANN VILLENA, *Las minas de Huancavelica en los siglos XVI y XVII* (1949); ROBERT G. YATES, DEAN F. KENT, and JAIME FERNÁNDEZ CONCHA, *Geology of the Huancavelica Quicksilver District, Peru* (1951); HENRI FAVRE, "Caracteres sociales fundamentales de la aglomeración urbana de Huancavelica," in *Cuadernos de antropología* 8 (1965): 25–30; GWENDOLIN COBB, *Potosí y Huancavelica: Bases económicas del Peru, 1545–1640* (1977); CARLOS CONTRERAS, *La ciudad del mercurio: Huancavelica, 1570–1700* (1982); MERVYN LANG, "El derrumbe de Huancavelica en 1786: Fracaso de una reforma borbónica," in *Histórica* 10, no. 2 (1986): 213–226; and KENDALL W. BROWN, "La crisis financiera peruana al comienzo del siglo XVIII, la minería de plata y la mina de azogues de Huancavelica," in *Revista de Indias* 40, no. 182–183 (1988): 349–383.

KENDALL W. BROWN

See also **Mining.**

HUANCAYO, province in the central highlands of Peru encompassing primarily the area of the fertile Mantaro Valley. Its capital city, also named Huancayo (1990 population 252,000), developed into an important commercial center in the mid-nineteenth century. Prior to the arrival of the Spanish colonizers, the Huancas, an ethnic group initially hostile to Incan expansion, inhabited the area. Just north of today's Huancayo province, Francisco PIZARRO founded the town of Jauja as the initial center of his Peruvian conquests, but later opted for the city of Lima on the coast for defensive purposes. The city of Huancayo was founded in the eighteenth century. In the nineteenth century the city hosted the Constitutional Congress of 1839 and the declaration of the abolition of SLAVERY. During the WAR OF THE PACIFIC it was a center of the resistance led by General Andrés Avelino CÁCERES against the Chilean occupation.

The major productive activities of the region are agriculture (potatoes, cereals), livestock, and light manufacturing (in the city). A variety of produce is sold in the city of Huancayo in picturesque weekly fairs, which were originally a way of exchanging regional rural products for manufactures and cash. A branch of the central highland RAILWAY system arrived in Huancayo in 1908 to enhance the city's commercial character. The main communication route with Lima today is the Central Highway, which displaced the railway in importance in the 1930s and 1940s.

FLORENCIA MALLON, *The Defense of Community in Peru's Central Highlands* (1983); FIONA WILSON, "The Conflict Between Indigenous and Immigrant Commercial Systems in the Peruvian Central Sierra, 1900–1940," in *Region and Class in Modern Peruvian History,* edited by Rory Miller (1987).

ALFONSO W. QUIROZ

HUÁNUCO, department in the north-central highlands of Peru. At an altitude of 6,273 feet, its capital city of Huánuco (1990 population 61,812) is a commercial center and traditionally the gateway to the colonization of the jungle region to the east. The canyons and valleys of the Huallaga and Pachitea rivers, tributaries of the Marañón and Ucayali, which eventually form the Amazon River, provide two of the few access routes to the jungle, connecting with the easternmost towns of Tingo María and Pucallpa.

Prior to the founding of Huánuco Viejo, the first Spanish settlement and missionary post not far from contemporary Huánuco, the INCA state controlled the administrative center of Huánuco Pampa, just north of the city of Huánuco. Recent archaeological studies have determined that Huánuco Pampa was part of an infrastructural system that facilitated ritual reciprocities between the state and the local ethnic groups. Prior to the Incas, a CHAVÍN-influenced culture built what are today known as the ruins of KOTOSH. In 1742–1753 the region and the city were the scene of the Indian messianic rebellion led by Juan Santos ATAHUALPA.

CRAIG MORRIS, "The Infrastructure of Inka Control in the Peruvian Central Highlands," in *The Inca and Aztec States, 1400–1800,* edited by George Collier et al. (1982).

ALFONSO W. QUIROZ

HUARAZ, the capital city of the province of the same name in the highland department of Ancash, Peru. Created by decree on 25 July 1857, the department is bounded on the north by the province of Huaylas, on the south by Cajatambo province, on the east by Pomabamba and Huari provinces at the top of the Cordillera Nevada mountain range, and on the west by Santa province. Its origins can be traced back to a community of Indians that was given in *encomienda* to Sebastián de Torres. During the next two centuries, the town became an increasingly important economic and religious center. In 1788 its citizens were granted the right to elect a municipal council (*cabildo*), and the settlement was officially given the title of *villa.*

During the next century, military leaders such as Simón BOLÍVAR and Agustín GAMARRA used Huaraz as a base, as much for its rich agricultural hinterland, which produced wheat, barley, potatoes, corn, and cotton for cloth, as for its strategic position *vis à vis* Lima to its southwest. In the twentieth century, Huaraz was the scene of an Aprist uprising against the government of Luis Sánchez Cerro in 1932. In 1970 Huaraz was 90 percent destroyed as a result of an EARTHQUAKE that was labeled the worst natural disaster recorded in the Western Hemisphere.

MARIANO FELIPE PAZ SOLDÁN, *Diccionario geográfico estadístico del Perú* (1877); RUBEN VARGAS UGARTE, *Historia general del Perú,* 10 vols. (1971); DAVID P. WERLICH, *Peru: A Short History* (1978).

SUSAN E. RAMÍREZ

HUARI (Wari), the earliest recognized pre-Columbian empire in Peru and the name assigned to a large Middle Horizon (ca. A.D. 650–1000) city located in the eastern Ayacucho Valley that is recognized as its capital. The size and complexity of Huari remained unrecognized because it was overshadowed by early colonial descriptions of the Bolivian site of TIWANAKU in the Lake Titicaca Basin, to which the INCAS refer in their origin myths. However, recent research indicates that the Incas most likely inherited an imperial tradition that was first developed by the Huari during the Middle Horizon. In the absence of any known form of writing, QUIPUS (colored, knotted strings) were developed and used to record state transactions, an information system also later adopted by the Incas. A road system was built to connect the capital of Huari with its hinterland, some parts of which now lie below the Inca highway system.

Several construction phases are evident in the city. Within the urban center, a Huari building plan consisting of a pattern of regularly arranged rooms of standardized shapes can be detected. One of the dominant architectural components in this style is the repetition of square (sometimes trapezoidal) ground plans with a central courtyard or patio surrounded by narrow two- or three-story galleries or corridors. The provincial Huari towns share similarities in architectural layout, which suggests a central decision-making body was responsible for their plan, while construction efforts probably relied on local masons and workers.

Huari officials gained control of distant territories to the north, south, and west through religious proselytization and military force. These expansion efforts are inferred from changes in regional Middle Horizon settlement patterns that coincide with the appearance of Huari architectural compounds and pottery. Ceramic styles and votive offerings of oversized vessels with Huari figural iconography occur at the capital and within provincial centers and smaller communities as part of the religious images that were propagated throughout the empire. The city of Huari as the seat of imperial power reached its demise in the mid-ninth century. PACHACAMAC, on the central coast, was a principal Huari oracle and pilgrimage center.

LUIS LUMBRERAS, "La cultura Wari," in *Etnología y arqueología* 1, no. 1 (1960): 130–227, *Las fundaciones de Huamanga* (1974), and *The Peoples and Cultures of Ancient Peru* (1974); WILLIAM ISBELL and KATHARINA SCHREIBER, "Was Huari a State?" in *American Antiquity* 43, no. 3 (1978): 372–389; ANITA G. COOK, "The Middle Horizon Ceramic Offerings from Conchopata," in *Ñawpa Pacha* 22–23 (1984–1985): 49–90; WILLIAM ISBELL and GORDON MC EWAN, eds., *Huari Administrative Structure: Prehistoric Monumental Architecture and State Government* (1991); KATHERINA SCHREIBER, *Wari Imperialism in Middle Horizon Peru,* Anthropological Papers, no. 87 (Museum of Anthropology, University of Michigan, 1992); CRAIG MORRIS and ADRIANA VON HAGEN, *The Inca Empire and its Andean Origins* (1993).

ANITA COOK

See also **Huarpa.**

HUARPA, one of several Early Intermediate Period (A.D. 1–600) cultures of the Ayacucho Basin in the highlands of Peru. Ceramics that are now associated with Huarpa settlements were first recognized by Julio C. TELLO in 1931 from a small number of rather simple but large pottery ladles and vessels. The name was initially given to ceramics with black or black and red on white decoration. Survey work and excavations in the regions of the Huanta and Ayacucho basins were conducted by Peruvian and North American projects between 1967 and 1982. The results of surface collections at Ayacucho sites indicate that Huarpa architecture and artifacts are found at 300 of the more than 500 sites recorded in the region. Huarpa remains have been found stratigraphically beneath later Middle Horizon HUARI occupations. Consequently, Huarpa immediately precedes and lays the foundations for the emergence of the Huari state (A.D. 650–1000) in the Ayacucho Valley.

Huarpa architecture includes both circular and rectangular buildings, many covered in coarse stucco, with indications that some circular buildings may have been painted in red or pink. Evidence of stone canals has been identified at several excavated sites in the Ayacucho area and within Huarpa levels at the site of Huari.

Within the urban perimeters of Huari at least four localities have been identified with Huarpa remains, and the result of excavations at the site confirms that Middle Horizon Huari architecture overlies several Huarpa communities. It is unclear whether Huari emerged on the foundations of a unified earlier confederacy of Huarpa sites or whether, as Luis Lumbreras argues, Huarpa had already achieved statehood with its capital at Ñawinpukio on the southern extremity of the Ayacucho Valley.

Radiocarbon dates range between 200 B.C. and A.D. 200 for the greater Ayacucho area and a date of A.D. 285, plus or minus 120 years (Libby half-life), was obtained from the Moraduchayoq sector of Huari, where excavations identified one of the earlier Huarpa communities.

ALFRED KROEBER, "Peruvian Archaeology in 1942," in *Viking Fund Publications in Anthropology*, no. 4 (1944); JOHN H. ROWE et al., "Reconnaissance Notes on the Site of Huari, near Ayacucho, Peru," in *American Antiquity* 16, no. 2 (1950): 120–137; WENDELL C. BENNETT, *Excavations at Wari, Ayacucho, Peru* (1953); LUIS LUMBRERAS, *Las fundaciones de Huamanga* (1974), *The Peoples and Cultures of Ancient Peru* (1974), and "The Stratigraphy of the Open Sites," in *Prehistory of the Ayacucho Basin, Peru*, Vol. II: *Excavations and Chronology*, edited by Richard MacNeish et al. (1981); PATRICIA KNOBLOCH, "A Study of the Andean Huari Ceramics from the Early Intermediate Period to the Middle Horizon Epoch I" (Ph.D. diss., SUNY at Binghamton, 1983); ALLISON PAULSEN, "Huaca del Loro Revisited: The Nasca-Huarpa Connection," in *Investigations of the Andean Past*, Daniel H. Sandweiss, ed. (1983); WILLIAM ISBELL and GORDON MC EWAN, eds., *Huari Administrative Structure: Prehistoric Monumental Architecture and State Government* (1991), esp. pp. 55–69.

ANITA COOK

HUASCAR (*b*. ca. 1495; *d*. 1532), son of Inca HUAYNA CAPAC. Huascar, born near Cuzco, had one of the most legitimate claims to leadership of TAHUANTINSUYU at the time of the death (1525) of his father, for his mother was the primary wife Ragua Ocllo. In accordance with their customs, the INCA elite in Cuzco quickly performed the religious ceremonies acknowledging the assumption of power of the new ruler.

Half brother ATAHUALPA, who according to some had been named as one of the successors during the fevered last days of Huayna Capac, refused to come to Cuzco for the celebrations, preferring instead to remain in the Quito district with the large military force that had helped subjugate the area. The ill-treatment accorded the emissaries Atahualpa sent to Huascar led to open hostilities between the two factions. Atahualpa's army, under capable leaders Quizquiz and Chalicuchima, moved southward, and finally Chalicuchima succeeded in capturing Huascar outside Cuzco. By then the Cañaris, a northern ethnic group who strongly supported the Huascar faction, had been thoroughly beaten. General Quizquiz went on to march into the capital of Cuzco and attempt to destroy completely Huascar's supporters.

It was at this juncture that the Europeans under Francisco PIZARRO entered the Andean highlands and captured Atahualpa at CAJAMARCA on 16 November 1532. Atahualpa, fearing that the Spaniards might attempt to supplant him and rule through Huascar, ordered the execution of his half brother. The escort that was accompanying Huascar from Cuzco to Cajamarca carried out the orders at Andamarca, between Huamachuco and Huaylas. Huascar's demise was followed within months by the Spanish execution of Atahualpa on 26 July 1533, thus bringing to an end the effective independence of Tahuantinsuyu.

JOHN HEMMING, *The Conquest of the Incas* (1970); FRANKLIN PEASE, *Los últimos Incas del Perú* (1972).

NOBLE DAVID COOK

HUASIPUNGO, a forced labor system of the Ecuadorian sierra. The word was derived from the Quechua language (*huasi*, "house," and *pungo/pungu*, "door"). Most Indians submitted to variations of this system from the colonial period until recently. In order to obtain access to a small parcel of land (a *huasipungo*), Indian families would consent to provide agricultural labor and to serve as domestic servants for a HACIENDA owner. The Indians had the right to collect wood and straw from the owner's land or to graze animals upon it. The owner paid wages for labor and typically supplied Indians with food, clothing, animals, and cash.

Most Indian families quickly lapsed into debt, losing their freedom of movement until they retired their obligations. This seldom happened. Thus restricted, the Indians suffered various abuses, either at the hands of the hacienda owner or, more commonly, from foremen, police, or the local clergy. Legislative decrees designed to end this system of DEBT PEONAGE, such as the ban on *concertaje* in 1918, did little to halt the practice. However, the Agrarian Reform Law of 1964 finally turned the *huasipungos* over to the Indian families that worked them. Jorge ICAZA's Indianist novel *Huasipungo* (1934) provided a vivid depiction of the oppression of Indians under this forced labor arrangement and increased the attention given to the problem.

On sierra relations of production, consult MAGNUS MÖRNER, *The Andean Past: Land, Societies, and Conflicts* (1985); OSVALDO HURTADO, *Political Power in Ecuador*, translated by Nick D. Mills, Jr. (1985); and ENRIQUE AYALA MORA, ed., *Nueva historia del Ecuador: Época republicana I*, vol. 7 (1983).

RONN F. PINEO

See also **Guayaquil, Group of; Slavery: Indian.**

HUASTECA, THE, a huge and historically important region of northeastern Mexico once inhabited by the Huastec Indians. Today this topographically and climatically diverse area is divided among the states of Veracruz, San Luis Potosí, Hidalgo, Querétaro, and Tamaulipas. Beginning in the arid eastern reaches of the elevated central plateau, and stretching through the abrupt Sierra Madre Oriental, the Huasteca expands in the humid, tropical lowlands of the Gulf of Mexico. Soils, rainfall, and vegetation vary widely in this broad expanse and have fostered many forms of adaptation by both the ancient Huastec inhabitants and the largely mestizo population that has extensively replaced them since Spanish contact.

Archaeological evidence suggests that the Huasteca had fluctuating borders that once extended far southward down the Gulf coastal plain in the direction of the Maya Indians, who are linguistically and culturally related to the Huastecs. The conflictive migrations of other pre-Hispanic groups, as well as Aztec conquests, produced enclaves at some points and a strong regional tradition of warfare.

Spanish seaborne expeditions to the Huasteca began from Cuba in 1518 and Jamaica in 1519 and were followed by a difficult overland conquest by Hernán CORTÉS in 1522. Between 1526 and 1533 Nuño de GUZMÁN brutally crushed numerous revolts when the province, then called Pánuco, was governed separately from New Spain. In modern times much of the once forested coastal zone has become man-made savannah for cattle ranching. The discovery of major oil deposits at the turn of the century has brought roads and industrial concentration at the port of Tampico.

Long-term ethnographic studies have been undertaken by GUY STRESSER-PEAN, ''Les indiens Huastèques'' in *Huastecos, Totonacos y sus vecinos* (1953). Recent archaeological and historical interpretations are in S. JEFFREY K. WILKERSON, *Ethnogenesis of the Huastecs and Totonacs* (1973); and ''Presencia huasteca y cronología cultural en el norte de Veracruz Central,'' in *Huax-*

tecos y Totonacos, edited by Lorenzo Ochoa (1989), pp. 257–279. Two major studies of early colonial history are MANUEL TOUSSAINT, *La conquista de Pánuco* (1948); and DONALD E. CHIPMAN, *Nuño de Guzmán and the Province of Pánuco in New Spain, 1518–1533* (1967). The principal study of regional flora is HENRI PUIG, *Végétation de la Huasteca, Méxique* (1976).

S. JEFFREY K. WILKERSON

HUAYNA CAPAC (*b.* ca. 1488; *d.* ca. 1527), Inca emperor (ca. 1493–1527), the last undisputed ruler of the Inca empire. The son of the emperor Topa Inca and the grandson of the great PACHACUTI, he ruled during the time of the first Spanish contact with Andean South America. During his reign the empire was extended northward to the Ancasmayo River, the present boundary between modern Colombia and Ecuador. Although the extent of Huayna Capac's conquests were substantially less than those of his father and grandfather, they took much longer; he was absent from the capital at Cuzco for nearly twenty years. His prolonged absence and his preference for maintaining his royal court in the city of Quito, far to the north of the imperial capital, eventually generated a schism within the Inca state.

Huayna Capac died suddenly during one of the great plagues brought to the New World by the Europeans. His presumptive heir, Ninan Cuyochi, also died about the same time, leaving the succession unclear. As a result, two of Huayna Capac's sons, HUASCAR, who was in Cuzco, and Atahualpa, who had been with his father in the north, initiated the civil war that greatly weakened the empire just prior to its conquest by Francisco PIZARRO.

Principal sources on Huayna Capac include JOHN H. ROWE, ''Inca Culture at the Time of the Spanish Conquest,'' in *Handbook of South American Indians*, vol. 2 (1946), pp. 183–330; BURR CARTWRIGHT BRUNDAGE, *The Empire of the Inca* (1963) and *The Lords of Cuzco: A History and Description of the Inca People in Their Final Days* (1967); *The Incas of Pedro de Cieza de León*, translated by Harriet de Onis (1959); and BERNABE COBO, *History of the Inca Empire*, translated by Roland Hamilton (1979).

GORDON F. MCEWAN

See also **Incas.**

HUDSON, WILLIAM HENRY (*b.* 4 August 1841; *d.* 18 August 1922), British naturalist and writer. Born on a farm near Buenos Aires to American parents, William Henry Hudson spent the majority of his youth on the Argentine pampas before emigrating to England in the late 1860s. He lived a good part of his life in poverty and obscurity until the publication in 1885 of his first novel, *The Purple Land that England Lost*. This book, characteristic of his early work, was a romantic fiction set in Latin America, filled with detailed descriptions of the natural beauty of the region. Hudson's ideas were apparently shaped largely by his reading of Darwin and a belief in the ultimate authority of nature.

Although Hudson's writing had not gained a wide audience, he established friendships with several influential literary figures of the late nineteenth and early twentieth centuries, including Joseph Conrad and Ford Madox Ford. He followed his early romances with several works of fiction as well collections of essays and studies of the natural sciences. Among Hudson's most acclaimed works are *A Hind in Richmond Park* (1922), *Green Mansions* (1904), *Birds of La Plata* (1920), and his autobiographical writings, *Idle Days in Patagonia* (1893) and *Far Away and Long Ago* (1918).

Commercial success eluded Hudson until late in life, when, in the years before and after World War I, he wrote stories of English rural life expressing his philosophy of acquiescence to nature, a philosophy which would gain influence as the naturalistic movements of the twentieth century progressed.

AMY D. RONNER, *W. H. Hudson: the Man, the Novelist, the Naturalist* (1986); DAVID MILLER, *W. H. Hudson and the Elusive Paradise* (1990).

JOHN DUDLEY

HUERTA, ADOLFO DE LA. *See* de la Huerta, Adolfo.

HUERTA, VICTORIANO (*b.* 23 March 1845; *d.* 13 January 1916), general and president of Mexico (1913–1914). Huerta is best known for his role in the overthrow and death of President Francisco I. MADERO (1873–1913).

He was born in Colotlán, Jalisco, the son of a cavalry soldier and a Huichol Indian. He studied in the state capital, Guadalajara, before graduating from the National Military College as a construction engineer in 1876. As a career army officer he gained the rank of colonel in 1894, was promoted to brigadier general in 1901, and became division general in 1912. He headed the Third Infantry Battalion (1894–1901); fought Mayas in Yucatán under General Ignacio A. Bravo (1835–1918) in 1903; served as head of public works in the state government of General Bernardo Reyes (1850–1913) in Monterrey, Nuevo León (1905–1909); battled Zapatistas in Morelos and Guerrero in 1911; escorted President Porfirio DÍAZ into exile at Veracruz in 1911; and defeated the Pascual OROZCO rebellion in 1912.

In February 1913, upon the outbreak in Mexico City of the antigovernment rebellion led by Félix DÍAZ, Manuel Mondragón, and Bernardo Reyes, President Francisco Madero named Huerta military commander in charge of all progovernment forces. During the ensuing events, including the battle that devastated large portions of central Mexico City, known as the DECENA TRÁGICA, or tragic ten days (9–19 February 1913), Huerta conspired against Madero. With U.S. Ambassador Henry Lane WILSON acting as mediator, Huerta made a pact (El Pacto de la Embajada [Pact of the Embassy]) with the rebels in which he agreed to join forces with them in return for the provisional presidency. Sub-

sequently, Huerta forced Madero and Vice President José María PINO SUÁREZ to resign. Although there is no direct evidence to substantiate it, he apparently ordered them shot on 22 February 1913.

Huerta's call for recognition of his government met with three important opponents. One was Emiliano ZAPATA, whose followers continued their antigovernment struggle for land begun during the Madero administration. The second was the governor of Coahuila, Venustiano CARRANZA, who on 26 March 1913 issued his Plan de Guadalupe condemning Huerta's illegitimate rise to power and calling for his overthrow. Soon the Carrancistas and Zapatistas posed a significant challenge to Huerta in the north and south of the country, respectively. Huerta's third opponent was the newly elected U.S. president, Woodrow WILSON, who took office in early March 1913. He immediately removed pro-Huerta Ambassador Henry Lane Wilson and refused to grant diplomatic recognition to the Huerta government.

The brutal and authoritarian nature of Huerta's rule undermined what support he had, except among hardcore conservatives and the Catholic church. His closing of the national congress, his persecution and killing of opponents, his manipulation of the October 1913 vote to elect himself constitutional president, and his militarization of society to combat Carrancistas and Zapatistas all took their toll. In April 1914 Woodrow Wilson ordered U.S. forces to occupy the port of Veracruz, thus substantially reducing Huerta's income and ability to import arms.

On 15 July 1914, with opposing armies led by Zapata, Álvaro OBREGÓN, Francisco "Pancho" VILLA, and Pablo GONZÁLEZ bearing down on Mexico City, Huerta fled the country. He lived in London, England, and Barcelona, Spain, before sailing for New York in March 1915. With the backing of anti-Carrancista Mexicans and the German government, Huerta hoped to raise a force in the United States that would return him to power. While traveling by train to El Paso, Texas, on 27 June 1915, U.S. agents arrested Huerta and fellow conspirator Pascual Orozco in Newman, New Mexico. Huerta was then incarcerated at Fort Bliss, Texas, where he died of cirrhosis of the liver.

Twentieth-century Mexican historiography generally portrays Huerta as the demon of the MEXICAN REVOLUTION of 1910. His brutality, cynicism, and abuse of alcohol and allegedly of drugs are constantly cited. He is accused of ending the nation's experiment in democracy and of attempting to return it to the dark days of the Porfirio Díaz dictatorship (1876–1911). All revolutionaries and their actions are measured against Huerta's regime. In this way, Huerta has served as an important counterpoint, allowing for diverse political and socioeconomic factions to join under the banner of the Revolution. Nevertheless, at least one important study claims that Huerta's administration was not as conservative as the Díaz regime in several areas, including agrarian reform, labor, church policy, and foreign relations, and even more progressive in some of these areas than subsequent, so-called revolutionary governments.

GEORGE J. RAUSCH, JR., "Victoriano Huerta: A Political Biography" (Ph.D. diss., University of Illinois, 1960); MICHAEL C. MEYER, *Huerta: A Political Portrait* (1972); ALAN KNIGHT, *The Mexican Revolution*, 2 vols. (1986), esp. vol. 1, pp. 481–490, vol. 2, pp. 1–162; MICHAEL C. MEYER and WILLIAM L. SHERMAN, *The Course of Mexican History*, 3d ed. (1987), esp. pp. 523–534.

DAVID LaFRANCE

HUERTAS, ESTEBAN (*b.* 1876; *d.* 1943), Panamanian general and a key figure in the independence of Panama. He was born in Umbita, Boyacá, Columbia, and went into the army at an early age. He was sent to Panama and participated in the WAR OF THE THOUSAND DAYS, fighting in the province of Coclé. In October 1903 the Columbian government, nervous about the revolutionary activities in Panama, sent the Tiradores battalion, under the command of Generals Juan B. Tobar and Ramón G. Amaya, to relieve Huertas as military commander because they believed that he was conspiring with the revolutionaries. When General Tobar arrived in Panama City with his officers on 3 November, Huertas had them arrested. Once the news of the arrests reached the revolutionaries, they declared for independence. When the army was abolished after independence, Huertas was given the title of Hero of the Fatherland.

ERNESTO DE JESÚS CASTILLERO REYES, *Historia de Panamá*, 7th ed. (1962); JORGE CONTE PORRAS, *Diccionario biográfico ilustrado de Panamá*, 2d ed. (1986).

JUAN MANUEL PÉREZ

HUGUENOTS. *See* **French in Colonial Brazil.**

HUICHOLS, a Mexican Indian group largely concentrated in the rugged mountains of the Sierra Madre Occidental, mainly in the states of Jalisco and Nayarit. They are by far the largest Indian group in Mexico to have maintained relatively intact its indigenous religion and ritual, without significant Catholic modification.

A young Huichol signals with a horn to announce the return of peyote pilgrims. Sierra Madre in Jalisco, Mexico. © KAL MULLER / WOODFIN CAMP & ASSOCIATES.

The Huichols bear a stronger resemblance to other northwestern Mexican Indians than to those of central Mexico. Their language has a close relationship to Cora, both of which belong to the Aztecoidan branch of the Greater Nahua (Uto-Aztecan) language family. Their own name for themselves is Wixárika, or Wixarite; "Huichol" is a Spanish corruption, perhaps of Guisole or Guachichil, a now-extinct population of desert hunter-gatherers.

The Huichol settlement pattern is one of scattered extended-family farmsteads, most with their own *xiriki* ("god-house"). There are no villages as such, and until recently the ceremonial and governmental centers in the five indigenous communities were virtually deserted except during community-wide celebrations of Spanish colonial origin. Large circular temples (*tuki*), with adjacent god-houses, are located in the ceremonial centers and in a few other sacred places in the mountains; the *tuki* and its ceremonies are in the charge of graded religious functionaries with fixed terms of office. There are also many shrines within and outside the Huichol territory.

The Huichols have a long and well-developed tradition of sacred art and, more recently, of folk art for sale, especially colorful wool yarn "paintings" of mythological subjects. The native deities are mainly those of nature: fire, sun, earth and growth, deer, maize, rain, terrestrial water, and mountains. All are addressed by kinship terms. Among the most important are Tatewarí (Our Grandfather), the old fire god; Tayaupá (Our Father Sun); Takutsi Nakawé, the old earth and creator goddess; and Great-grandfather Maxa Kwaxi (Deer Tail). The culture hero-cum-trickster and Deer Person Kauyumari is the intermediary between mortals and gods and the principal assistant to the *mara'akáte* (sing. *mara'akáme*), the numerous shaman-priests who conduct the many ceremonies, some community-wide, others pertaining to the family. Deer, maize, and the sacred hallucinogenic peyote cactus, which is collected on annual pilgrimages to the north-central desert in San Luis Potosí, are conceptually merged.

Precise population figures for the Huichols are hard to come by; a 1959 estimate gives the total as just over 7,000, but this was probably low. The latest census (1990) gives them a population of 19,000 over the age of five, of whom about half reside within the five indigenous communities in the Sierra. There is a sizable colony on the lower Río Lerma, in Nayarit, dating from the 1920s and 1930s, when some communities were virtually depopulated during the so-called CRISTERO REBELLION (1926–1929). Huichols have also settled in or near such cities as Tepic, Guadalajara, Durango, and Zacatecas, and even as far away as Mexico City. Most, easily recognizable by their distinctive native costume, continue to maintain ties to their old homeland and religion.

CARL LUMHOLTZ, *Symbolism of the Huichol Indians* (1900); BARBARA G. MYERHOFF, *Peyote Hunt: The Sacred Journey of the Huichol Indians* (1974); KATHLEEN BERRIN, *Art of the Huichol Indians* (1978).

PETER T. FURST

HUIDOBRO FERNÁNDEZ, VICENTE (*b.* 10 January 1893; *d.* 2 January 1948), Chilean poet. The principal figure of the avant-garde movement in Latin American LITERATURE, Huidobro was born in Santiago to an aristocratic family; his privileged upbringing included education in Chilean private schools. In 1916 Huidobro moved to Paris, where he started publishing the most innovative poetry in the Spanish language. He was a cofounder, with the French poets Guillaume Apollinaire and Pierre Reverdy, of the literary review *Nord-Sud* (1917–1918), and along with Max Jacob, Paul Dermée, and the cubist painters Juan Gris and Pablo Picasso, helped design a new spatial poetry that used calligrammatic and ideogrammatic forms. His personal poetic style, which he called creationism, was a modality that emphasized the autonomy of poetic expression, a result of the transformation of external referents and of laws of grammar and "sense," and created its own images, descriptions, and concepts. In 1918 he brought fresh air to Spanish poetry with four volumes published in Madrid, *Poemas árticos, Ecuatorial, Tour Eiffel*, and *Hallali.*

The Spanish poets Gerardo Diego and Juan LARREA were his most faithful and direct disciples, but many other young poets imitated his creationist poetry. As a consequence of his influence, the literary movement Ultra was developed by Rafael Cansinos-Asséns and Guillermo de Torre. Ultraism was developed also in Buenos Aires by Jorge Luis BORGES, and Imagism arose in Chile, Simplicism in Peru, and Estridentism in Mexico. During the 1920s, Huidobro published three books in French: *Saisons choisies* (1921), *Tout à coup* (1925), and *Automne régulier* (1924). The most genial poetic expression of Huidobro is *Altazor; o, El viaje en paracaídas* (1931), a poem in seven cantos, which narrates a simultaneous flight and fall through seven regions, equating death with mystical experience. The work constitutes a poetic Babel, employing a variety of poetic languages that intimates both a plenitude of meaning and the gradual destruction of language. *Altazor* stands as an extraordinary example of the poetic avant garde. *Temblor de cielo* (1931), a prose poem written simultaneously with *Altazor*, deals with the meaning of life under the Nietzschean concept of the death of God. Huidobro's later poetic works include *Ver y palpar* (1941) and *El ciudadano del olvido* (1941). In these books his creative ingenuity manifests itself in whimsical as well as tragic visions of life and world. His last poems were collected in *Últimos poemas* (1948), published posthumously.

Huidobro's life in Paris, Madrid, and Santiago touched in various ways the literary cultures of these cities. Contacts with cubist poets and painters and with dadaists in Paris, with ultraists in Madrid, with the younger groups of Runrunists and Mandrágora in Santiago, all speak of his wide-ranging ability to disseminate the forms and concepts of the new poetry. The general content of *Nord-Sud, Índice de poesía americana nueva* (1926), and *Antología de poesía chilena nueva* (1935) marks the breadth and significance of his influence. In 1925 he published *Manifestes,* a collection of essays on creationism and poetic theory. Huidobro also contributed significantly to the renewal of narrative forms with his *hazaña* (heroic feat) *Mío Cid Campeador* (1929), his film-novel *Cagliostro* (1934), *Papá; o, El diario de Alicia Mir* (1934), *La próxima: Historia que pasó en un tiempo más* (1934), *Sátiro; o, El poder de las palabras* (1938) (*Satyr; or, The Power of Words,* [1939]), and *Tres inmensas novelas* (1935) in collaboration with the German poet Hans Arp. His collections of essays include *Pasando y pasando* (1914), *Finis Britannia!* (1923), and *Vientos contrarios* (1926). Huidobro also wrote two plays, *Gilles de Raíz* (1932), in French, and *En la luna* (1934).

CEDOMIL GOIC, *La poesía de Vicente Huidobro,* 2d ed. (1974); GEORGE YÚDICE, *Vicente Huidobro y la motivación del lenguaje* (1978); RENÉ DE COSTA, *Vicente Huidobro: The Careers of a Poet* (1984); MERLIN H. FORSTER, "Vicente Huidobro," in *Latin American Writers,* edited by Carlos A. Solé and Maria Isabel Abreu, vol. 2 (1989), pp. 755–764.

CEDOMIL GOIC

HUINCAS, ARAUCANIAN/MAPUCHE word used to refer to non-Mapuche (also said to mean "thief"). Mapuche oral tradition and the construction of the word (*pu,* from, and *Inca*) suggest that the term for "outsider" came into use during the decades of Mapuche resistance to the expansion of the INCA Empire in the fifteenth century. The word came into common usage among Spanish speakers in Chile and Argentina in the eighteenth and nineteenth centuries, when CREOLE settlement in the southern frontier zones intensified intercultural contact.

RODOLFO LENZ, *Diccionario etimológico* (1910).

KRISTINE L. JONES

HUITZILOPOCHTLI, AZTEC deity of war, patron of the Mexica. According to native histories, the Mexica brought Huitzilopochtli from their original home at AZTLAN to the site of TENOCHTITLÁN, the center of their future empire. The deity guided their journey and their subsequent rise to military power. His cult was a major focus of Aztec state ritual, especially the heart sacrifice of prisoners of war. He was one of the four TEZCATLIPOCAS, gods responsible for cosmic creation and destruction; he was also associated with the sun of the winter dry season. He shared the Great Temple of Tenochtitlán with the rain god TLALOC, patron of the rainy season. The name Huitzilopochtli, "Hummingbird-Left," alludes to the winter sun's passage through the southern sky (seen as being on the sun's left hand); hummingbirds were also associated with the sun and

with the souls of those who died in war and in sacrifice. Huitzilopochtli's birthplace was the mythical Coatepec, "Serpent Mountain," where his mother, the earth goddess COATLICUE, was magically impregnated while sweeping the mountaintop temple. Huitzilopochtli foiled a plot by his elder sister and brothers by emerging from the womb fully grown and armed with the Fire Serpent that encircles the Mesoamerican cosmos.

DIEGO DURÁN, *Book of the Gods and Rites and the Ancient Calendar,* translated and edited by Fernando Horcasitas and Doris Heyden (1971); EVA HUNT, *The Transformation of the Hummingbird* (1977); ELIZABETH H. BOONE, "Incarnations of the Aztec Supernatural: The Image of Huitzilopochtli in Mexico and Europe," in *Transactions of the American Philosophical Society* 79, pt. 2 (1989).

LOUISE M. BURKHART

HULL, CORDELL (*b.* 2 October 1871; *d.* 23 July 1955), U.S. secretary of state (1933–1944) during the administration of Franklin D. ROOSEVELT. Although Roosevelt bypassed his secretary of state on many matters, Hull played an active role in Latin American affairs. Along with Roosevelt and Assistant Secretary of State Sumner WELLES, Hull formulated the GOOD NEIGHBOR POLICY, which sought to improve relations between the United States and the nations of Latin America. Hull's principal contributions to the Good Neighbor Policy were threefold. First, in 1933, at the PAN-AMERICAN CONFERENCE in Montevideo, he surprised and pleased fellow delegates by endorsing the principle of nonintervention in the affairs of Latin American nations. Second, Hull was the principal architect of the reciprocal trade agreements that increased commerce between the United States and its hemispheric neighbors. Finally, as World War II approached, he helped negotiate mutual defense agreements among nations of the Western Hemisphere.

Works on Hull include *The Memoirs of Cordell Hull,* 2 vols. (1948), and JULIUS W. PRATT, *Cordell Hull, 1933–1944,* 2 vols. (1964). See also IRWIN F. GELLMAN, *Good Neighbor Diplomacy: United States Policies in Latin America, 1933–1945* (1979).

PATRICK J. MANEY

See also **United States–Latin American Relations.**

HULL–ALFARO TREATY (1936), an agreement signed on 2 March by the United States and Panama that made certain concessions regarding the operation of the Panama Canal in keeping with Franklin Roosevelt's GOOD NEIGHBOR POLICY. It did not, however, alter the relationship of great power–client state established in the HAY–BUNAU-VARILLA TREATY of 1903. The treaty, ratified reluctantly by the U.S. Senate only in 1939, did not mollify Panamanian nationalists for long.

Initiative for reforming canal operating policies came in 1933, when Panama's president, Harmodio

ARIAS, visited Washington to explain his country's economic problems stemming from the Depression. Between 1933 and 1936, Roosevelt's secretary of state, Cordell Hull, and Arias's foreign minister, Ricardo Alfaro, labored to produce several treaties and agreements that would make good neighbors of the two countries. The United States gave up its protectorate role and powers of territorial acquisition, and it raised the annuity payment to $436,000 to compensate for the devaluation of the dollar. Hull also agreed to curtail commissary sales to those not employed by the canal, to curb contraband, to give Panamanian merchants access to passing ships, and to allow Panamanians free transit across the Canal Zone. Finally, an ancillary note promised equal employment treatment of Panamanian and U.S. nationals.

The armed services opposed most of these measures and fought ratification by the Senate. The main elements were approved only upon a special appeal by Roosevelt to set the stage for an inter-American defense conference in Panama. The outbreak of World War II, meanwhile, made the canal a major security concern and postponed effective implementation of many parts of the treaty.

WILLIAM D. MC CAIN, *The United States and the Republic of Panama* (1937; repr. 1966); JOHN MAJOR, *Prize Possession: The United States and the Panama Canal, 1903–1977* (1993).

MICHAEL L. CONNIFF

HUMAITÁ, a strategic point on the left bank of the Paraguay River some 20 miles north of its confluence with the Paraná. At this spot the Paraguayans constructed a fortress that prevented the advance of the Brazilians and Argentines during the WAR OF THE TRIPLE ALLIANCE (1864–1870). A guardpost had been established near Humaitá in the late colonial era to discourage smuggling. Yet, it was only during the 1850s, when Brazilian vessels began to freely transit the river to Mato Grosso, that the government of Carlos Antonio LÓPEZ decided to build a solid structure with the help of British military engineers. This "Sevastopol of South America" eventually grew to massive size and boasted some 380 cannon of various calibers.

During the war, Humaitá provided Paraguay with its principal defensive bastion; it warded off a thirteen-month Allied siege that started in June 1867. During this period a series of bloody engagements was fought along the periphery of the fort, leaving perhaps as many as 100,000 dead. The Allied navies regularly pounded the earthworks, leaving the defenders with little hope of relief. They, nonetheless, held on until July 1868, when the last starving remnants of the garrison evacuated the fort. This capitulation left open the way to the Paraguayan capital of Asunción, enabling the Allies to move in that direction a few months later. Today, the ruins of Humaitá, especially those of the small church at its center, have been partially restored as a national monument.

Church of San Carlos ruins, Humaitá, Paraguay. LIBRARY OF CONGRESS.

GEORGE THOMPSON, *The War in Paraguay* (1869); CHARLES J. KOLINSKI, *Independence or Death! The Story of the Paraguayan War* (1965).

THOMAS L. WHIGHAM

HUMAN RIGHTS. Human rights violations in Latin America became a major issue in the second half of the twentieth century. This development was due not only to the frequency and severity of violations, but also to the resulting proliferation of human rights organizations, which numbered several hundred by the 1990s. Many were created in countries in which authoritarian military regimes replaced civilian governments in the 1960s and 1970s. Others emerged as a result of increased mobilization of sectors of society historically denied their rights such as Native Americans, African Americans, peasants, women, and children. Still others were created because of the increased political space that the erosion of long-term dictatorships afforded. Regional organizations appeared facilitating the sharing of resources and expertise, particularly to document violations, publicize them, and call the perpetrators to account.

The roots of the Latin American human rights movements can be traced back to the early sixteenth century. Activists frequently cite the Dominican friar Bartolomé de LAS CASAS, who defended Native Americans during the Spanish conquest of America, as the inspiration for their work. Las Casas insisted on the humanity of the indigenes and hence the obligation to respect their rights. Nevertheless, the realities of colonial exploitation of land and labor undercut his and others' efforts. Ironically, Las Casas initially suggested the utilization of African SLAVE labor in order to protect Native Americans, a position he later abandoned.

The evolution of human rights in Latin America was strongly influenced by the concepts of state and society that Spain and Portugal transmitted to the Americas. State power was theoretically concentrated in the monarch, yet there was substantial devolution of authority, particularly in the far-flung colonies. In an attempt to maintain royal authority, the crown tended to create overlapping jurisdictions, which gave rise to frequent conflicts among royal representatives and weakened the rule of law. Substantial inequalities were accepted in society and the enjoyment of civil and political rights was generally related to socioeconomic status.

During the colonial period, fear of uprisings contributed to the incorporation of Native and African Americans into society in a restricted fashion without the same rights, privileges, and obligations as white subjects. The indigenes enjoyed more rights than the African slaves, as they were legally considered to constitute a separate commonwealth that had its own laws and magistrates. While this status provided Native Americans some degree of protection, the economic objectives of metropolitan and colonial elites frequently undercut it. Furthermore, the social legacy of the degradation of the labor force as a result of slavery and DEBT PEONAGE reinforced unequal status. As a result, the colonial period ended with highly stratified societies in which the majority were deprived of the benefits of citizenry as well as access to land and other sources of wealth that they could have used as an economic base to assert their rights.

In the nineteenth century the adoption of republican forms of government and constitutions guaranteeing rights did not overcome the colonial legacy of authoritarianism, paternalism, personalism, and unequal application of the law. Civil and political rights were enjoyed largely by elites, who were expected to assume responsibility for the body politic, including the masses, who had limited rights commensurate with what was understood to be their lesser capacity. This not only encouraged acceptance of inferior status, but of patriarchalism and paternalism, which in the nineteenth and twentieth centuries were reflected in the prevalence of CAUDILLISM, clientelism, and racial and sexual discrimination.

Beginning in the latter part of the nineteenth century pressures generated by ECONOMIC DEVELOPMENT, urbanization, IMMIGRATION, and the expansion of education and suffrage resulted in increased enjoyment of rights, particularly civil and political ones, by the ordinary citizen. Expansion of the enjoyment of socioeconomic rights was more limited. Overall the benefits of economic development were distributed unequally with the majority in most countries living in poverty. The failure of many elected civilian governments from the 1920s to the 1960s to satisfy mounting popular pressures for economic improvement helped bring to power the national security states of the 1960s and 1970s, which promised strong economic growth as well as an end to political and labor conflicts and subversion.

Mothers of the Plaza de Mayo protest human rights abuses by the government. Buenos Aires, ca. 1981. PHOTO BY ALICIA D'AMICO.

NATIONAL SECURITY STATES

Unlike most earlier military governments the national security regimes that took power in Brazil (1964–1985), Uruguay (1973–1985), Chile (1973–1990), and Argentina (1976–1983) aimed at a complete transformation of state and society. They sought to unleash the nation's potential for economic growth in order for the country to assume a prominent place in the international community. The thoroughgoing restructuring that the military proposed required substantial coercion, thereby giving rise to massive violations of rights. Political parties and labor unions, as well as civic, popular, professional, and student associations were restricted or repressed. Congresses were marginalized or suppressed. Press CENSORSHIP was imposed and freedom of association limited. Due process was often ignored. Torture, executions, and disappearances carried out by the police and military stimulated the creation of a wide variety of national and international human rights organizations.

Many of these were based in religious institutions, such as the Justice and Peace Commission of the Archdiocese of São Paulo, Brazil (Comissão de Justiça e Paz—CPJ). Founded by Monsignor Paulo Evaristo ARNS in 1972 and run by a Protestant minister, Jaime Wright, it became a model for similar organizations throughout the country which documented violations and provided legal and other assistance. As repression grew, particularly from 1968 to 1972, the CPJs increasingly cooperated with secular organizations, such as the Brazilian Bar Association (Ordem de Advogados do Brasil—OAB) and the Bahian based Center for Research and Social Action (Centro de Estudos e Ação Social—CEAS). As state terror declined in the mid-1970s these, and other groups, refocused their attention on such ongoing problems as urban and rural working conditions, particularly of landless peasants, slum dwellers, and indigenous peoples. In the Amazon region, as well as in urban industrial areas, environmental rights sometimes appeared to be in conflict with the expansion of the job market and intense debates were precipitated over how best to promote workers' rights at the same time as environmental preservation. In recent years human rights organizations in Brazil have increasingly focused on the rights of landless peasants (e.g., Pastoral Commission on Land/Comissão Pastoral da Terra—CPT), African Brazilians (e.g., Group for Black Consciousness and Unity/Grupo União e Consciência Negra), Native Americans (e.g., Center for Legal Assistance to Indians/Centro de Assistência Jurídica ao Indio—CAJI), Women (e.g., Women's Network/Rede Mulher), and street children (e.g., National Movement for Street Children/Movimento Nacional de Meninos e Meninas de Rua).

Torture and other gross violations of human rights did not disappear with the return to civilian government in 1985. Such wrongs led to the revamping of existing groups and the establishment of new ones, including the Center for the Study of Violence at the University of São Paulo (Nucleo de Estudos da Violência) and Torture—Never Again! (Grupo Tortuar Nunca Mas!). Of particular concern to these organizations is the reduction of military and police violence and the improvement of jail conditions.

In Chile, where a national security state was established as a result of a military coup led by General Augusto PINOCHET in September 1973, the Catholic, Methodist, Lutheran, and Jewish communities responded quickly by establishing the Committee for Peace (Comité para la Paz). Transformed in 1975 into the Vicariate of Solidarity (Vicaría de la Solidaridad), it provided legal, medical, psychological, and socioeconomic services for the victims of human rights violations and their families. Research into the theoretical and legal bases of national security regimes, as well as into a wide range of public policy issues, was undertaken by the associated Academy of Christian Humanism (Academia de Humanismo Cristiano), whose publications circulated in Chile and abroad. With traditional avenues of political participation restricted, such human rights organizations became refuges for democrats representing a wide spectrum of political and ideological positions. The gravity of the human rights violations tended to override preexisting political divisions, some of which would reemerge once repression diminished.

Among the most notable human rights groups of this period were organizations of relatives of victims, such as the mothers of the disappeared in Argentina (Madres de La Plaza de Mayo). They gathered every Thursday afternoon to silently circle the plaza in front of the presidential palace holding aloft pictures of their disappeared children. Similar associations began appearing in other countries eventually forming in 1981 a network known as the Latin American Federation of Associations of Relatives of the Detained-Disappeared (Federación Latinoamericana de Asociaciones de Familiares de Detenidos-Desaparecidos—FEDEFAM). Other international groups, such as the SERVICE FOR PEACE AND JUSTICE (Servicio Paz y Justicia—SERPAJ), promoted the utilization of nonviolent mechanisms of resistance in the face of gross violations of human rights citing the examples of Mohandas Ghandhi and Martin Luther King, Jr. For his work with SERPAJ the Argentine sculptor, Adolfo PÉREZ ESQUIVEL, was awarded the 1980 Nobel Peace Prize. SERPAJ emerged as a leader of the human rights community in Uruguay in the 1970s and 1980s not only documenting violations, but also analyzing their ideological and structural causes, as well as the consequences of the creation of a culture of fear.

DICTATORSHIPS AND FRAGILE DEMOCRACIES

Human rights organizations also appeared in countries where traditional dictatorships had long held sway, as in Nicaragua and Paraguay, or where the military controlled civilian regimes, as in El Salvador and Guatemala. National and international pressures for greater democratization helped create increased political space for such groups, which contributed to a decrease in gross violations by the late 1980s, whereupon the human rights community turned their attention to more systemic problems involving civil and socioeconomic rights.

Nicaragua exemplifies the evolving role of human rights organizations and the cooperation between national and international groups. Beginning in the 1950s and 1960s politicians, students, workers, peasants, small businesspeople, priests, nuns, and alienated elites began challenging the SOMOZA regime which had ruled Nicaragua since the 1930s with U.S. cooperation. Embezzlement of humanitarian assistance sent in response to a devastating earthquake in 1972 revealed the extent of government corruption and lack of concern for basic rights. National and international human rights groups, including Nicaragua's Permanent Commission for Human Rights (Comisión Permanente de Derechos Humanos—CPDH) and the Washington Office on Latin America (WOLA) challenged the legitimacy of the government thereby encouraging support for the Sandinista National Liberation Front (Frente Sandinista de Liberación Nacional—FSLN). When the latter took power in July 1979 it committed itself to making human rights a cornerstone of its government. There were some improvements, but there were also serious violations, particularly of civil and political rights, which the CPDH, WOLA, and others, such as the Inter-American Commission of Human Rights, criticized. The situation worsened as the U.S.-supported CONTRAS precipitated internal warfare that lasted until 1989. Neither the overthrow of Somoza nor the election in 1990 of Violeta BARRIOS DE CHAMORRO resulted in an end to violations as their causes are deeply rooted in substantial socioeconomic inequalities and facilitated by the historical weakness of the rule of law in the country.

In Paraguay, the dictatorship of Alfredo STROESSNER (1954–1989) was toppled by a coalition of civilian-military elites who concluded that the government had lost its legitimacy in large measure because of chronic rights violations. The fact-finding and popular educational work of the Committee of Churches for Emergency Assistance (Comité de Iglesias para Ayudas de Emergencia), Women for Democracy (Mujeres por la Democracia), and organizations such as the Bar Association (Colegio de Abogados) were essential to Stroessner's downfall. They also played a major role in the 1993 national elections in which a civilian was elected president for the first time in 39 years. While human rights violations continue, the veil of secrecy and impunity that historically shrouded them began to lift.

From the 1930s on military dominated governments ruled in El Salvador and Guatemala where state terror was used to eliminate opposition and suppress democratic sectors. In both countries by the 1970s broad-based social movements, political and labor organizations, as well as human rights groups had begun to sharply challenge the governments, which responded with intense repression. Assassinations and disappearances of human rights advocates, religious and labor leaders, as well as politicians escalated. During the 1980s, it is estimated by international human rights organizations, 70,000 civilians were killed in El Salvador and over 100,000 in Guatemala, many by the police and military or as a result of civil war. Included among them was the Archbishop of San Salvador, Oscar ROMERO, who had supported an archdiocesan legal aid office (Socorro Jurídico), the principal mechanism for documenting human rights violations in the country. In Guatemala Myrna Mack Chang, a scholar at the think tank AVANSCO (Associación para el Avance de las Ciencias Sociales), which assisted refugees and indigenous communities via analyses of their situation, was assassinated because of her work. International attention was focused on violations of Native Americans' rights by the awarding of the 1992 Nobel Peace Prize to the activist, Rigoberta MENCHÚ. In 1987 a peace agreement approved by the Central American presidents facilitated human rights accords being reached which resulted in UN rights monitors operating in both countries. While they contributed to a decline in violations, serious problems continued.

In the 1980s conflict in Peru also resulted in high levels of violations as the guerrilla movements known as Shining Path (Sendero Luminoso) and Túpac Amaru attempted to topple the government. The former adopted a strategy of fomenting chaos within society through bombing civilians, massacres, and assassinations of community leaders. The Peruvian military and police response violated not only the rights of the guerrillas, but also of civilians. In addition, the presence of international DRUG traffickers resulted in many residents of rural communities being forced to abandon their homes and livelihoods. By the early 1990s GUERRILLA warfare had subsided, but violence continued exacerbated by the weakness of legal guarantees of rights. In Peru, as well as in neighboring countries, the Andean Commission of Jurists (Comisión Andina de Juristas) took the lead in documenting and analyzing new sources of rights violations.

The complexity of the human rights situation in Peru is equalled by those in Colombia, Mexico, Cuba, and Haiti. Colombia shares some of the same problems as Peru including guerrilla warfare, violence generated by drug trafficking, widespread socioeconomic dislocation, and military and police impunity. The latter is also a factor in the persistence of violations in Mexico, where a 1985 earthquake revealed the graves of disappeared citizens under a police headquarters. Abuses of state power, together with violations of socioeconomic rights, contributed to a peasant uprising in CHIAPAS in January 1994. Widespread national and international recognition of the extent of serious violations in the area helped pressure the government of Carlos SALINAS DE GORTARI (1988–1994) and his successor Ernesto Zedillo (1994–)

to negotiate. Among the principal demands of the guerrillas were greater respect on the part of the government for the full spectrum of human rights, including fairer elections in a country where one party had dominated since the 1920s.

Cuba also has a one-party system led since 1959 by Fidel CASTRO. He, too, justified the overthrow of a dictatorship on the grounds that his government would promote and defend human rights. While some progress was made, particularly with respect to socioeconomic rights in the early years of the Cuban revolution, the end of Soviet economic aid and a U.S.-instigated economic embargo undermined early advances. Civil and political rights have not fared well under the Castro regime with restrictions on political and labor organizing, freedom of speech and association, as well as competitive elections. Freedom of religion has also been restricted. Small human rights groups emerged in the 1970s and 1980s and became targets for state security, including the Cuban Committee for Human Rights (Comité Cubano Pro Derechos Humanos) and the Martí Committee for Human Rights (Comité Martí por los Derechos Humanos). In addition, there is an extensive network of Cuban human rights groups abroad, although cooperation is sometimes limited by political and ideological differences. Since 1959 Cuba has been the frequent subject of reports by international rights agencies including the Organization of American States's Inter-American Commission on Human Rights, Americas Watch, and Amnesty International.

Cuba's neighbor Haiti has also suffered from serious human rights violations. Acute socioeconomic inequalities and the political marginalization of the vast majority of the population dating from the colonial period have contributed to gross violations of both civil/political and socioeconomic rights. Repression became systematized during the reigns of François DUVALIER (1957–1971) and his son Jean-Claude Duvalier (1971–1986). The 1990 election of the Roman Catholic priest Jean-Bertrand ARISTIDE with widespread popular support heartened human rights activists, but this victory threatened entrenched interests and prompted a military coup in September 1991. Domestic opposition resulted in escalating repression and an exodus of Haitians seeking refuge in neighboring countries, including the United States. The latter, via the United Nations and the Organization of American States (OAS), together with other nations, strongly pressured for a return of Aristide. His return was not accomplished until late 1994. During Aristide's absence, Haitian human rights organizations both on the island and abroad fought for democratic government and socioeconomic justice. Leaders of such organizations often became targets of assassination, such as Lafontant Joseph, founder of the Center for the Promotion of Human Rights (Centre de Promotion des Droits Humaines), or imprisonment, such as George Gourgue of

the Haitian League for Human Rights (Ligue Haitienne des Droits Humaines). In the United States, the Miami-based Haitian Refugee Center and the National Coalition for Haitian Refugees lobbied for changes in U.S. immigration legislation and greater rights' protections for Haitians. The fact that over four-fifths of the population of Haiti lives in poverty has impeded substantial rights progress.

CONCLUSION

One result of the emergence of strong human rights movements in Latin America was the initiation of a sharp debate over what to do about violators after repression ceased. Truth commissions were established in several countries, including Argentina, Chile, and El Salvador, following the return to civilian government. Charged with establishing responsibility for gross violations, particularly disappearances and executions, these commissions contributed to the transition to democracy and to greater respect for rights and the rule of law. Few attempts were made to prosecute violators, the emphasis being placed on truth telling and reconciliation rather than on justice in legal terms. In Brazil, where no official truth commission was established, the Archdiocese of São Paulo produced a multivolume study, *Nunca Mais,* that documented the nature, extent, and impact of gross violations of human rights under the military government (1964–1985). SERPAJ-Uruguay published a similar work entitled *Nunca Más,* which included an analysis of the experiences of victims who survived. In all these countries impunity for the military and police generally prevailed, with a few exceptions.

The 1980s witnessed changes in the nature of human rights violations and in the emphases of human rights organizations. This was, in part, a result of a substantial reduction in the number of authoritarian regimes in Latin America which, given the end of the Cold War, could no longer justify repression on the grounds of the alleged threat of international Communist subversion. The emergence of fragile democracies did not, however, guarantee substantially increased human rights enjoyment. Indeed, many Latin Americans still suffered serious violations. This situation was exacerbated by increased violence resulting from such factors as the growth in common criminality, drug trafficking, guerrilla conflicts, and the traditional weakness of judiciaries and the rule of law.

A prime impediment to the widespread enjoyment of human rights has been the frequent use of states of exception or emergency by which governments suspend certain laws and constitutional protections on the grounds of a serious threat to the state. According to the American Convention of Human Rights, certain rights, including life, physical integrity, due process, and freedom of thought, conscience, and religion, are guaranteed even during states of emergency or exception. Nevertheless, such rights are often denied. In the face of the traditional weakness of the courts and magistrates in Latin America, such situations further diminish the confidence of the citizenry in the rule of law and the judiciary. This limits the possibilities for consolidating more democratic systems.

The weaknesses of legal institutions in Latin America, as well as increased human rights activism, have led more Latin Americans to turn to international organizations to defend their rights. Chief among these are such non-governmental groups as Amnesty International, Human Rights Watch, and the Washington Office on Latin America, as well as such multilateral agencies as the Inter-American Commission of Human Rights, the Inter-American Court of Human Rights, and the Inter-American Institute of Human Rights.

Six months prior to the adoption of the Universal Declaration of Human Rights in 1948 by the member states of the United Nations, an American Declaration of the Rights and Duties of Man was adopted by Western Hemisphere nations. Thirty years later the American Convention of Human Rights came into force thereby binding the countries that ratified it to accept the jurisdiction of the Inter-American Commission of Human Rights. The latter was charged with promoting human rights in the member states of the Organization of American States, assisting in the drafting of human rights documents, advising member states on human rights issues, producing country reports, mediating human rights disputes between nations, initiating cases against signatories of the Convention, and recommending cases to the Inter-American Court of Human Rights.

The court has contentious jurisdiction in cases brought against those states that accept its jurisdiction. It has advisory jurisdiction in cases involving any member of the OAS. The court also has authority in the interpretation and application of the convention, as well as treaties relating to the protection of human rights. In addition, it has jurisdiction in the resolution of conflicts between national law and the convention or related treaties. Since 1990 the number of cases brought before the court has increased.

The Inter-American Institute of Human Rights, created in 1981, is charged with the promotion of human rights principally through education, research, training, and technical assistance. It provides courses for human rights advocates and government officials, as well as groups of individuals whose rights have been violated. Research has focused on a broad spectrum of rights issues including facilitating transitions from authoritarian to democratic governments, empowering minorities, and penal reform. Via its Center for Electoral Assistance and Promotion (Centro de Asesoría y Promoción Electoral—CAPEL) it has assisted in organizing and evaluating elections, as well as analyzing their potential for strengthening democratic processes and enhancing human rights.

While human rights abuses throughout Latin America in the latter part of the twentieth century were common, they also gave rise to some of the most effective rights organizations worldwide. These groups were particularly innovative in devising new strategies and tactics for the defense of human rights. The transfer of expertise from one organization to another occurred not only within countries but among countries. Human rights organizations in other parts of the world have called upon their Latin American counterparts for advice, technical assistance, and training. The achievements of the Latin American rights movements suggest that the mechanisms for defense of human rights have been greatly strengthened in the face of ongoing challenges.

TOM J. FARER, "Human Rights and Human Wrongs: Is the Liberal Model Sufficient?" in Human Rights Quarterly 7, no. 2 (May 1985): 189–204; E. A. CEBOTAREV, "Women, Human Rights, and the Family in Development Theory and Practice," in Revue canadienne d'études du développement 9, no. 2 (1988): 187–200; CECILIA MEDINA, "The Inter-American Commission on Human Rights and the Inter-American Court of Human Rights: Reflections on a Joint Venture," in Human Rights Quarterly 12 (1990): 439–464; LYNDA E. FROST, "The Evolution of the Inter-American Court of Human Rights: Reflections of Present and Former Judges," in Human Rights Quarterly 14 (1992): 171–205; JACK DONNELLY, International Human Rights (1993); HUGO E. FRÜHLING, "Human Rights in Constitutional Order and in Political Practice in Latin America," in Constitutionalism and Democracy: Transitions in the Contemporary World, edited by Douglas Greenberg et al. (1993), pp. 85–104.

MARGARET E. CRAHAN

See also **Asylum; Brazil: Organizations; Chile: Organizations; Nicaragua: Political Parties; Peru: Revolutionary Movements.**

HUMBOLDT, ALEXANDER VON (*b.* 14 September 1769; *d.* 6 May 1859), German scientist and traveler to the New World. Humboldt was born in Berlin into a wealthy family. He attended several German universities and by 1790 had developed a keen interest in botany and obtained a solid introduction to physics and chemistry. A trip to England that year confirmed his interest in nature and a love for foreign travel. Named assistant inspector in the Department of Mines in 1792, Humboldt embarked upon a short-lived bureaucratic career that led him through eastern Europe. The death of his mother in 1796, however, freed him from the necessity of working for a living and allowed him to travel as he chose.

Humboldt was the most illustrious of a number of foreigners who went to the New World in the closing decades of the colonial era. With the permission and recommendation of the Spanish crown, in 1799 he and his traveling companion, the French botanist Aimé BONPLAND, reached Venezuela and began their five-year voyage through Spanish America. Laden with scientific instruments, they were able, in good Enlightenment fashion, to measure such things as latitude, longitude, temperature, and air pressure, and to illustrate their findings. The volume of data collected was enormous and established Humboldt as a major scholar of international reputation.

Humboldt's journey took him into the interior of Venezuela, to New Granada, Quito, Lima, Cuba, and finally, to New Spain. A keen observer of the landscape and the political, economic, and social conditions of its inhabitants, Humboldt also mingled with the elites in the cities and gained access from royal officials to numerous government documents containing demographic and economic information. Because he was well educated and familiar with current intellectual trends, Humboldt was able to share modern ideas and techniques from Europe with colonial intellectuals and bureaucrats, and thus helped disseminate European knowledge and the belief in material progress throughout the New World. He also commented on hindrances to progress resulting from Spanish fiscal and commercial policy and stimulated creoles to believe that improvement in government was necessary. At the same time, Humboldt accurately observed the state of science in the New World at the end of the colonial period. His conclusions emphasized that modern scientific thought was more widespread in New Spain than in Peru and other parts of South America—and, not surprisingly, that it was more widespread in urban centers than in the provinces.

After returning to Europe, Humboldt wrote about his voyage in major works treasured by both contemporaries and historians. His writings include the *Voyage aux régions équinoxiales du nouveau continent ...* (34 vols., 1805–1834); *Essai politique sur le royaume de la Nouvelle-Espagne* (3 vols., 1811–1812; a part of the *Voyage*); *Essai politique sur l'île de Cuba* (2 vols., 1826); and publications devoted to scientific topics.

The *Essai politique ... Nouvelle-Espagne* included considerable official data made available as a result of Humboldt's royal introduction to colonial officials in New Spain. More important, it had profound political implications because the creole elite believed its descriptions of Mexican wealth and progress meant that Mexico had the resources necessary for an existence independent from Spain.

ALEXANDER VON HUMBOLDT, *Political Essay on the Kingdom of New Spain*, (abridged), translated by John Black, edited by Mary Maples Dunn (1972; repr. 1988); PEGGY K. LISS, *Atlantic Empires* (1983), esp. pp. 182–183; D. A. BRADING, *The First America: The Spanish Monarchy, Creole Patriots, and the Liberal State 1492–1867* (1991), chap. 23.

MARK A. BURKHOLDER

See also **Science**.

HUMBOLDT CURRENT (Peruvian Current), ocean current flowing from high Pacific latitudes into temperate western South America, along the coasts of Chile and Peru. It was named after Alexander von HUMBOLDT by European cartographers to honor his monograph entitled *Memoir About Ocean Currents* (1837), but is traditionally known among Spanish conquerors and travellers as the Peruvian Current. The southern tip appears at about 41 degrees south latitude; the current turns away from the continent at Punta Pariñas and heads to the GALÁPAGOS ISLANDS. Its width varies between 145 and 220 miles; several subsystems are created by eddies and upwelling foci. At the southern extreme the annual mean water temperature is 14°C; at Punta Pariñas it reached 21°C. However, numerous upwellings of even lower temperatures appear where the outline of the coast is altered by promontories and capes.

The section of the current that runs closest to the mainland carries the coldest water, very rich in oxygen and carbon. As the deeper water approaches the coast, it begins to warm, creating a zone rich in marine life (zooplankton and phytoplankton). Plankton feed fish, especially anchovies, which in turn feed birds, whose guano covers the CHINCHA ISLANDS, off the coast of central Peru. Coastal peoples of ancient and colonial Peru depended on the marine riches of the current for their livelihood. In the twentieth century, the abundance of fish enabled Peru to emerge as the largest exporter of fish meal in the world.

At intervals varying between 7 and 11 years, the current is destabilized by a warm oceanic anomaly called EL NIÑO, which causes widespread death of fish and the sea mammals and birds that feed on them.

ROBERT CUSHMAN MURPHY, "The Humboldt Current," in his *Bird Islands of Peru* (1925); ERWIN SCHWEIGGER, *El litoral peruano* (Lima, 1964); EMILIO ROMERO, *Perú: Una nueva geografía*, 2 vols. (1973); and D. PAULY, M. MUCK, J. MENDO, and I. TSUKAYAMA, eds., *The Peruvian Upwelling Ecosystem: Dynamics and Interactions* (Manila, 1989).

CÉSAR N. CAVIEDES
JOHN C. SUPER

HUNDRED HOUR WAR. *See* **Football War.**

HURRICANES. With considerable luck Columbus explored portions of the Caribbean in the late summer and fall of 1492 without encountering the characteristic storms of those latitudes in that season—the hurricanes. The Spaniards probably experienced their first hurricane when a storm struck the settlement at Isabela on Hispaniola and two ships were lost. Thereafter, Spaniards and other Europeans who sailed or settled on Caribbean coasts and islands came to know and fear the hurricanes. A colonial official in Puerto Rico complained in 1765 that the local people counted time by the coming and going of governors and fleets, visits of the bishops, and the hurricanes.

Of course, the indigenous peoples of the Caribbean region had known the great storms. There is considerable debate over the etymology of the word "hurricane," some believing it is a Maya term that was somehow introduced into the Caribbean prior to 1492 and others seeing its origins in the TAINO word *hurakán*. Peter MARTYR used the term *furacanes* in his *Decadas* (1511). The Arawaks of the Bahamas counted hurricanes, along with fire, sickness, and enemy raids, as a chief danger. The Taino seem to have recognized the circulatory nature of these storms; their curved, legged symbol for a hurricane is much like that used by modern meteorologists, a rather remarkable fact because not until William Reid's *Law of Storms* (1838) were the rotary circulation and progressive motion of hurricanes generally recognized.

Modern meteorology defines a hurricane as a tropical cyclone with winds exceeding 65 knots (73 miles) per hour, although winds exceeding 175 knots (200 mph) have been recorded. The storms usually include heavy rainfall and are accompanied in coastal regions by high tides or storm waves that often are their most destructive features. Hurricanes usually originate in the Caribbean or in the eastern Atlantic. The latter, "Cape Verdean" hurricanes have been among the most destructive. Although hurricanes can occur throughout the year, the traditional season is June to November, with highest incidence in August and September. The force of hurricanes has been felt from Central America (Belize was badly damaged in 1787 and again in 1931) to New England, but the islands of the Lesser and Greater Antilles from Barbados to Cuba and the Gulf coasts of Mexico and the North American mainland have suffered the most in terms of numbers of hurricanes and levels of damage.

Hurricanes have been a constant threat to populations, property, and commerce in the region. In the colonial era, the Spanish fleet was organized around the hurricane season, with departure of the homeward-bound fleet from Havana scheduled to precede the beginning of the hurricane season in June. Delays and mishaps, however, often resulted in shipwrecks and other disasters following hurricanes. The sinking of silver-bearing galleons in 1622, 1624, and 1630 contributed to a financial crisis in Spain. In the Caribbean, hurricanes brought severe destruction of property and crops. The town of Santo Domingo was virtually destroyed in 1508 and again in 1509. Havana lost over 1,000 people and thousands of homes in the hurricane of 1768. The "Great Hurricane" of 1780 killed some 9,000 in Martinique and 4,000 in Barbados, and wreaked havoc on British, French, and Spanish fleets. The Cuban town of Santa Cruz del Sur was devastated by a 1932 hurricane.

Agricultural losses also result from the storms. In Puerto Rico (where hurricanes are named for the saint on whose feast day they occur) San Narciso (1867) resulted in major agricultural losses, San Ciriaco (1899) wreaked havoc on the coffee areas in the center of the island, and San Felipe (1928) essentially ended Puerto Rico's coffee exports. Cuban sugar production declined by half after devastating hurricanes from 1844 to 1846. The production of bananas in Cuba was wrecked by a hurricane in 1898. In more recent times hurricanes Gilbert (1988) in Jamaica and Hugo (1989) in Puerto Rico have demonstrated the continued vulnerability of societies and economies to hurricanes.

Given the impact of the hurricanes on the economy and life-style of the Greater Antilles, it is not surprising that Spanish and Caribbean scientists have been important in the study of these storms. Andrés Poëy y Aguirre published a chronology of 400 Caribbean hurricanes, accompanied by an extensive bibliography, in 1855. He became the first director of the Observatorio Fisicometerológico of Havana in 1860. The Spanish meteorologist Father Benito VIÑES, director of the College of Belén observatory in Havana (1870–1893), concentrated on meteorological observations of hurricane formation and tracks. He made the first successful hurricane forecast in 1875. He later published important scientific works on hurricane structure and behavior.

Although scientific and communication advances such as the barometer in the seventeenth century, the telegraph in the nineteenth century, and satellite observation in the twentieth century have enabled better prediction and preparation for hurricanes, human and property losses have intensified with the growth of population and the settlement of areas of higher risk. These losses are often suffered disproportionately by poorer nations and by poorer segments of the population.

LUIS A. SALIVIA, *Historia de los temporales de Puerto Rico* (1950); DAVID M. LUDLUM, *Early American Hurricanes, 1492–1870* (1963); JOSÉ CARLOS MILLÁS, *Hurricanes of the Caribbean and Adjacent Regions* (1968); FERNANDO ORTIZ, *El huracán: Su mitología y sus símbolos*, 2d ed. (1984).

STUART B. SCHWARTZ

HURTADO DE MENDOZA, ANDRÉS (marquis of Cañete), viceroy of Peru (ca. 1556–1561). The marquis of Cañete arrived in Peru with the express purpose of strengthening royal authority, which had been lessened by four years of rule by the AUDIENCIA, the high court of Lima that held executive power within the colony in the absence of a viceroy. As part of this effort, a rival *audiencia* and administrative network for Upper Peru were established in Charcas in 1559. Committed to solidifying the crown's power over Peru's Indian population, Cañete sought to claim lands and reclaim labor service that had been granted to local elites through *encomiendas* (grants of Indian labor). The opening of the mercury mines of HUANCAVELICA in 1560 increased the demand for Indian labor, and Cañete became the first viceroy responsible for the production and transportation of Huancavelica mercury to the colony's silver mines, particularly Potosí.

For an account of the establishment of royal authority in Peru see HENRY F. DOBYNS and PAUL L. DOUGHTY, *Peru: A Cultural History* (1976), esp. pp. 59–87. For information on Huancavelica see ARTHUR P. WHITAKER, *The Huancavelica Mercury Mine* (1941); STEVE J. STERN, *Peru's Indian Peoples and the Challenge of Spanish Conquest: Huamanga to 1640* (1982).

ANN M. WIGHTMAN

See also **Encomienda.**

HURTADO DE MENDOZA, GARCÍA (*b.* 1535; *d.* 1609), Spanish conquistador, governor of Chile, and viceroy of Peru. Hurtado de Mendoza was the second son of the marqués de Cañete (a title he eventually inherited). His father, then viceroy of Peru, appointed him governor of Chile. He arrived there in 1557 and almost immediately launched offensives against the ARAUCANIANS of the south, whom he defeated in the battles of Lagunillas (Bío-bío) and Millarapue. After founding the new settlement of Cañete, he ventured further south, where he discovered the archipelago of CHILOÉ and founded Osorno (1558). In December 1558 he won another victory over the Araucanians at Quiapo. The governor also sent ships to explore the STRAIT OF MAGELLAN and an expedition across the Andes to conquer CUYO: the Argentine city of MENDOZA (founded in 1561) is named after him.

Dismissed from the governorship by King PHILIP II (1527–1528) (his father was concurrently stripped of office), Hurtado de Mendoza left Chile in February 1561. The king later restored him to favor and made him viceroy of Peru (1588–1596). Hurtado de Mendoza was a celebrated figure in his own time: two plays were written to eulogize his exploits, one of them, *El Arauco domado,* by Lope de Vega.

FERNANDO CAMPOS HARRIET, *Don García Hurtado de Mendoza en la historia americana* (1969).

SIMON COLLIER

HURTADO LARREA, OSVALDO (*b.* 26 June 1939), president of Ecuador (1981–1983). After completing secondary education in Riobamba, Hurtado entered the Catholic University in Quito, where he became a political activist, eventually emerging as a leader of the Christian Democratic Party (PDC). After completing a doctorate, he taught political sociology at the Catholic University in Quito and published widely on the need for structural reform. In 1971 he drafted a detailed party program that emphasized structural and social reforms to promote national development and integration. In 1978 the military government appointed Hurtado chairman of the commission charged with revising electoral legislation in preparation for a return to civilian rule.

In the 1978–1979 presidential election, Hurtado, whose coalition was not allowed on the ballot, ran as the vice presidential candidate on the Concentración de Fuerzas Populares (CFP) ticket with Jaime ROLDÓS AGUILERA. Their successful issue-oriented campaign in-

augurated a new phase in Ecuadorian electoral politics. They represented a new generation of political leaders, whose desire to expand the electorate, strengthen democratic institutions, and implement planned national development, threatened traditional political and economic elites.

When Jaime Roldós died in a plane crash on 24 May 1981, Hurtado became president. He inherited a severe budgetary crisis precipitated by the decline of the world price of petroleum and by growing opposition from organized labor—who opposed the government's commitment to fiscal restraint—and from business groups—who opposed the expansion of the state and its growing autonomy in economic policy-making. Although the domestic and international economic situation prevented Hurtado from achieving most of his reform program, he was able to complete his term and peacefully transfer power to a democratically elected successor.

HOWARD HANDELMAN, "The Dilemma of Ecuadorian Democracy. Part II, Hurtado and the Debt Trap," in *UFSI Reports* 35 (1984); and "The Dilemma of Ecuadorian Democracy. Part III, The 1983–1984 Presidential Elections," in *UFSI Reports* 36 (1984); DAVID W. SCHODT, *Ecuador: An Andean Enigma* (1987), esp. pp. 144–153; JOHN D. MARTZ, *Politics and Petroleum in Ecuador* (1987), esp. pp. 302–368; OSVALDO HURTADO, *Democracia y crisis* (1984), and *Política democrática, testimonios: 1964–1989* (1990).

LINDA ALEXANDER RODRÍGUEZ

See also **Ecuador: Political Parties.**

HYPPOLITE, HECTOR (*b.* 16 September 1894; *d.* 1948), Haitian painter and VODUN priest. Hyppolite led a simple, hard life in rural Haiti until he was discovered in 1944 by the European surrealist poet and art connoisseur André Breton and the Haitian art patron DeWitt Peters. Hyppolite's primitive paintings brought him immediate international attention and introduced the world to Haitian folk culture. His works were exhibited at a UNESCO show in Paris in 1947 and have spawned many imitators. The paintings of Hector Hyppolite are noted for their free, bold colors, their technical naïvete, and themes drawn from Haiti's unique, syncretic religion and vodun customs. Today his work hangs in many of the world's finest galleries.

SELDEN RODMAN, *The Miracle of Haitian Art* (1974); ELEANOR INGALLS CHRISTENSEN, *The Art of Haiti* (1975); UTE STEBICH, ed., *Haitian Art* (1978).

KAREN RACINE

HYPPOLITE, LOUIS MODESTIN FLORVILLE (*b.* ca. 1827; *d.* 24 March 1896), president of Haiti (1889–1896). On 9 October 1889 the Haitian Constituent Assembly elected Florville Hyppolite to the Haitian presidency following his successful revolt against the government of François Denys Légitime. The United States had supplied weapons in support of Hyppolite against his French-backed opponent and expected the new president to reward its generosity with a naval station in Haiti. But Haitian national pride more than the resistance of Hyppolite blocked U.S. acquisition of the harbor at Môle Saint-Nicholas. Many U.S. newspapers of the time blamed U.S. Ambassador to Haiti Frederick Douglass rather than recognize this fact.

Hyppolite, though a black and from the north, had leanings toward the mulatto-dominated Liberal Party. On the domestic scene, his greatest achievements were public-works projects, especially those involving communication and transportation. Hyppolite's biggest domestic problems, however, were heavy internal debt and French infringements on Haitian sovereignty. He found no solutions. He forced the French embassy to cease its practices of granting French citizenship to Hai-

tians of proven Gallic ancestry. This had been a mulatto ploy to dodge Haitian law, but it became a Pyrrhic victory when Hyppolite borrowed 50 million francs from France to redeem his internal debt.

In 1893 Hyppolite scored a diplomatic triumph by appointing Frederick Douglass to represent Haiti at the World's Columbian Exposition of 1893 in Chicago. The old abolitionist had frequently expressed pride in Haiti but never to the extent that it confused his ambassadorial duties (1889–1891). Three years later Hyppolite died during a coup against his government.

JACQUES N. LEGER, *Haiti: Her History and Her Detractors* (1907); JAMES LEYBURN, *The Haitian People* (1941); RAYFORD W. LOGAN, *The Diplomatic Relations of the United States with Haiti, 1776–1891* (1941); DAVID NICHOLLS, *From Dessalines to Duvalier: Race, Colour, and National Independence in Haiti* (1979).

THOMAS O. OTT

IANNI, OCTAVIO (*b.* 13 October 1926), Brazilian sociologist. Ianni, a native of Itu, São Paulo, taught at the university of São Paulo. In 1950 he worked with Florestan Fernandes and Fernando Henrique Cardoso, doing research on race relations sponsored by UNESCO. After teaching in the United States (1967), England (1969), and Mexico (1968–1973), Ianni returned to Brazil in 1977. He then taught at the Pontifical Catholic University of São Paulo and the State University of Campinas.

Ianni's writings include *Estado e capitalismo no Brasil* (1965), *Raças e classes sociais no Brasil* (1966), *Sociologia da sociologia latino-americana* (1971), *Sociologia e sociedade no Brasil* (1975), *Escravidão e racismo* (1978), *O ABC da classe operária* (1980), *A ditadura do grande capital* (1981), and *Origens agrárias do estado brasileiro* (1984).

THOMAS E. SKIDMORE, *Politics in Brazil, 1930–1964; An Experiment in Democracy* (1968); JOHN KENNETH GALBRAITH, *The New Industrial State* (1967).

ELIANA MARIA REA GOLDSCHMIDT

IBÁÑEZ, ROBERTO (*b.* 1902), Uruguayan poet, writer, literary critic, politician, educator, and husband of Sara de IBÁÑEZ. Among his important positions were director of the National Institute of Literary Investigations and Archives and editor of *Anden*. Although his poetry was published as early as 1925, in the work *Olas*, it is his 1939 collection, *Mitología de la sangre,* that is the most memorable, with its controlled technical virtuosity and vivid representation of psychological suffering, nostalgia for infancy, and horror of existence. In other collections Ibáñez treats the creative process and the sense of his own totality: ''La poesía es el testimonio de mi ser'' (Poetry is the testimony of my being). *La frontera* (1966) won the prestigious prize of Cuba's Casa de las Américas.

Other major works by Ibáñez are *La danza de los horizontes* (1927), *La leyenda patria y su contorno histórico* (1959), and *Americanismo y modernismo* (1968). With Esther de CÁCERES and Fernando de Pereda, Ibáñez is a major representative of the Ultraist school of literature.

FRANCISCO AGUILERA and GEORGETTE MAGASSY DORN, *The Archive of Hispanic Literature on Tape: A Descriptive Guide* (1974); *Diccionario de autores iberoamericanos* (1982).

WILLIAM H. KATRA

IBÁÑEZ, SARA DE (*b.* 1905; *d.* 1971), Uruguayan poet, literary critic, and educator. Born Sara Iglesias Casadei in Tacuarembó, she married Roberto IBÁÑEZ in 1928. In 1940 she produced her most important collection of poetry, *Canto.* With a prologue by Pablo NERUDA, it won the top prize in a Montevideo poetry competition in 1941 because of its wide range of vocabulary and its classical purity of form. Most distinguished among Ibáñez's eight other poetry publications is the epic poem *Canto a Artigas* (1952), which won a prestigious prize from Uruguay's National Academy of Letters.

Some of Ibáñez's poems reveal nature and the inner soul as sources of inspiration. A poet's poet, Ibáñez in much of her work allows often dark symbolism, ornate expression, and attention to lyrical technique to predominate over human issues. A key theme of her verses is the anguished rift between physical and spiritual love. Additional sources of inspiration are historical themes and nature.

Ibáñez's major works include *Canto a Montevideo* (1941), *La batalla* (1967), and *Canto póstumo* (1973). She was acclaimed as a major poet by Gabriela MISTRAL, Carlos Drummond de ANDRADE, Manuel BANDEIRA, and Cecilia MEIRELES.

LIDICE GÓMEZ MANGO, *Homenaje a Sara de Ibáñez* (1971); A. GEYSSE, *Diccionario universal de las letras* (1973); FRANCISCO AGUILERA and GEORGETTE MAGASSY DORN, *The Archive of Hispanic Literature on Tape: A Descriptive Guide* (1974).

WILLIAM H. KATRA

IBÁÑEZ DEL CAMPO, CARLOS (*b.* 3 November 1877; *d.* 28 April 1960), Chilean army officer and president (1927–1931 and 1952–1958). Born in Linares, Ibáñez entered the Escuela Militar in Santiago in 1896. Two years later he was commissioned a second lieutenant and in 1900 he was promoted to first lieutenant. While a student at the Academia de Guerra, he was selected for the first El Salvador mission (1903) directed by Captain Juan Pablo Bennett. There he took charge of the new military school and formed the tiny nation's cavalry corps. Ibáñez won acclaim in the Central American country for his horsemanship and for taking part (against orders) in a minor battle between Salvadoran and Guatemalan forces in 1906, an adventure that made him the only Chilean officer to participate in a real war after 1883. He held the rank of colonel in El Salvador and made an advantageous marriage there to a young Salvadoran woman, Doña Rosa Quiroz Avila, with whom he returned to Chile in 1909.

Ibáñez served with the Cazadores cavalry regiment and then returned to the Academia de Guerra to complete his staff training. In 1914 he was on the staff of Division I, Tacna, and in 1919, now a major, was named police prefect in Iquique.

In 1921 President Arturo ALESSANDRI PALMA named Ibáñez director of the Cavalry School, where he came to know a number of political figures in the capital professionally and socially. He became involved with political affairs culminating in the military movements of 1924–1925 that resulted first in Alessandri's resignation and then his return. In 1925 Ibáñez became war minister, rising quickly from colonel to general. He quarreled

Carlos Ibáñez del Campo. PHOTOGRAPHIC ARCHIVE, UNIVERSIDAD DE CHILE.

frequently with Alessandri. In 1927, after brief stints as interior minister and vice president, he was elected president under the new 1925 Constitution. Then a widower, he married his second wife, Graciela Letellier, during his presidency.

Ibáñez's authoritarian administration (1927–1931) borrowed heavily from abroad to finance public works projects. He manipulated a spuriously elected Congress, brooked no political opposition, and applied the new constitution selectively, thus enhancing the powers of the executive branch. He involved the state in public health, communications, education, economic development, welfare, social security, and transportation more than ever before. His administration's economic policies made Chile vulnerable to the worldwide economic collapse, thus weakening his position and undermining his popularity by 1930.

Ibáñez resigned the presidency in 1931 during a general strike. He lived for a time in Argentina, returned to Chile, and was a contender for the Popular Front presidential candidacy of 1938 until his association with Chilean fascists became an embarrassment. He remained politically active in the 1940s and served as senator before being elected to a second term as president (1952–1958), as the candidate of a broad coalition of independent groups, small parties, and the corporativist Agrarian Labor Party. His repeated attempts to manipulate the army did not help him in any way and restored democratic processes precluded any return to the "good old days" of strong executive leadership. He died two years after turning the presidency over to Jorge Alessandri Rodríguez, son of his old nemesis.

RENÉ MONTERO MORENO, *La verdad sobre Ibáñez* (1952); ERNESTO WÜRTH ROJAS, *Ibáñez: Caudillo enigmático* (1958); LUIS CORREA PRIETO, *El presidente Ibáñez, la política, y los políticos: Apuntes para la historia* (1962); FREDERICK M. NUNN, *Chilean Politics, 1920–1931: The Honorable Mission of the Armed Forces* (1970), and *The Military in Chilean History: Essays on Civil-Military Relations, 1810–1973* (1976).

FREDERICK M. NUNN

IBARBOUROU, JUANA DE (Juana Fernández Morales; *b.* 8 March 1892; *d.* 1979), Uruguayan poet and fiction writer. Born in Melo, she was educated in a convent and later in the public-school system. In 1914 she married Captain Lucas Ibarbourou, with whom she had a child. In 1918 they moved to Montevideo, where she began to publish her poems in the literary section of *La Razón*. Her poems were so well received that the prestigious Argentine magazine *Caras y Caretas* dedicated an issue to her. *Las lenguas de diamante* was published in 1919 by the Argentine writer Manuel GÁLVEZ, then director of Editorial Buenos Aires.

Her poetry was first conceived within the modernist aesthetic, but with less ornamental language. *Raíz salvaje* (Wild Root, 1922) and *El cántaro fresco* (Fresh Pitcher, 1920) offer a more intimate tone, with themes of love, life, and the sensual pleasure of being alive. In 1929 the title of "Juana de America" was officially bestowed upon her by the Uruguayan public in a ceremony presided over by Juan ZORRILLA DE SAN MARTÍN, José Santos CHOCANO, and Alfonso REYES and attended by delegations from twenty Spanish American countries.

In *La rosa de los vientos* (Compass, 1930) Ibarbourou experiments with the language of earlier avant-garde writers. In 1934, two years after her father died, she published a volume of lyric prose with religious themes, *Loores de Nuestra Señora* (Praise to Our Lady), and another volume of works with similar concerns, *Estampas de la biblia* (Scenes from the Bible). She continued to be hailed throughout the continent. In 1944 she published *Chico Carlo*, a book of "memoirs" of her childhood, and in 1945 she wrote a children's play (*Los sueños de Natacha*). In 1947, Ibarbourou became a member of the Uruguayan Academy of Letters. *Perdida*, whose title came from D'Annunzio's chosen name for dancer Eleonore Duse, appeared in 1950. In this book, she renewed her seemingly diminished interest in poetry, and from then on she did not cease to write.

Juana de Ibarbourou. Reproduced from Juana de Ibarbourou, *Estampas de la Biblia* (Montevideo, 1934). COURTESY OF HARVARD COLLEGE LIBRARY.

When her mother died, Ibarbourou became ill and depressed, a condition that lasted for some years and was a theme reflected in her poetry. At the same time, as Angel Rama has pointed out, she also continued to insist on frozen imagery, enabling the poetic voice to retain the past in an idealized construction, as shown in *Azor* (1953), *Romances del destino* (1955), *Oro y tormenta* (Gold and Storm, 1956), and *Elegía* (1967).

In 1957 a plenary session of UNESCO was organized in Montevideo to honor Ibarbourou. Attending as a representative of the poetry of Uruguay and of America, she presented her *Autobiografía lírica*, a recollection of some thirty-five years as a poet. Her *Obras completas* were first published in Spain in 1953 by Editorial Aguilar. Her other works are *La pasajera* (The Passenger, 1967) and *Juan Soldado* (Johnny Soldier, 1971).

Ibarbourou, who had enjoyed fame and a comfortable life, experienced considerable hardship in her later years. She died in Montevideo, poor and mostly forgotten by the very public that acclaimed her.

JORGE ARBELECHE, *Juana de Ibarbourou* (1978); ETHEL DUTRA VIEYTO, *Aproximación a Juana de Ibarbourou* (1979); JORGE OSCAR PICKENHAYN, *Vida y obra de Juana de Ibarbourou* (1980); ISABEL SESTO GILARDONI, *Juana de Ibarbourou* (1981); ESTHER FELICIANO MENDOZA, *Juana de Ibarbourou* (1981); SYLVIA PUENTES DE OYENARD, *Juana de Ibarbourou: Bibliografía* (1988).

MAGDALENA GARCÍA PINTO

IBARGÜENGOITIA, JORGE (*b.* 22 February 1928; *d.* 27 November 1983), Mexican novelist, playwright, and journalist. Ibargüengoitia was born in Guanajuato, studied engineering and drama at the National Autonomous University of Mexico (UNAM), and won scholarships from the Sociedad Mexicana de Escritors (1954, 1955) and the Rockefeller (1955) and Gusseheim (1969) foundations. Among his works are the imaginative novels *Los relámpagos de agosto* (1964), *La ley de Herodes* (1967), and *Maten al león* (1969). His farcical comedies resemble those by Samuel Beckett and Harold Pinter: *Susana y los jóvenes* (1954), *Clotilde en su casa* (1955), and *Llegó Margo* and *Ante varias esfinges*, both in 1956. Later a disagreement with his mentor Rodolfo Usigli and some unfortunate stage productions alienated Ibargüengoitia from the theater. His last play, *El atentado* (1962), a historical farce about a presidential assassination, received the Casa de las Américas Prize in 1963. Two of his books are available in English translation: *Muertas* (*The Dead Girls*, 1983) and *Dos crímenes* (*Two Crimes*, 1984).

His sardonic sense of humor and imaginative techniques made him one of the best writers of his generation. He died in a plane crash in Spain.

WILLIS KNAPP JONES, *Behind Spanish American Footlights* (1966); WALTER M. LANGFORD, *The Mexican Novel Comes of Age* (1971); VICENTE LEÑERO, *Los pasos de Jorge* (1989).

GUILLERMO SCHMIDHUBER

IBARGUREN, CARLOS (*b.* 18 April 1877; *d.* 3 April 1956), Argentine statesman and nationalist intellectual. A distinguished lawyer, Ibarguren served as under secretary of finance and under secretary of agriculture during President Julio Argentino ROCA's second administration (1898–1904). He subsequently became secretary of the Federal Supreme Court (1906–1912) and minister of justice and education, under President Roque SÁENZ PEÑA (1912–1913). One of the founders of the Democratic Progressive Party in 1914, he was a candidate for the presidency in 1922. As a historian, he was awarded a national prize for his work *Juan Manuel de Rosas: Su vida, su tiempo, su drama* (1930). He supported General José Félix URIBURU's 1930 military coup and that same year was appointed *interventor* (delegate of the federal government) in the province of Córdoba, where he made it clear he shared Uriburu's belief in the need for a corporatist reorganization of the country's economic and political institutions. The corporatist leanings of the "nationalist revolution" were made even more explicit in Ibarguren's *La inquietud de esta hora* (1934), clearly inspired by the corporatist experiments of Italy, Germany, Austria, and Portugal, and by Pope Pius XI's encyclical *Quadragesimo anno* (1934). Although plans for a constitutional reform along those lines did not prosper, Ibarguren became one of the leading intellectuals of the nationalist reaction against the classical model of liberal democracy.

CARLOS IBARGUREN, *La historia que he vivido,* 2d ed. (1969), provides an illustrative account of the intellectual roots of Argentine nationalism. See also SANDRA MC GEE DEUTSCH, *Counterrevolution in Argentina, 1900–1932: The Argentine Patriotic League* (1986); and DAVID ROCK, "Intellectual Precursors of Conservative Nationalism in Argentina, 1900–1927," in *Hispanic American Historical Review* 67, no. 2 (1987): 271–300.

EDUARDO A. ZIMMERMANN

IBARRA, DIEGO (*b.* ca. 1510; *d.* 1600), Mexican miner. A HIDALGO from Guipúzcoa and a knight of Santiago, Ibarra came to New Spain in 1540 during the time of Viceroy Antonio de MENDOZA and participated in the wars against the Chichimec tribes and the Caxcanes in Jalisco. Ibarra, Juan de Tolosa, Cristóbal de Oñate (1504/1505–c. 1570), and Baltazar de Temiño de Bañuelos (1530–1600) are credited with discovering and opening the great silver mines of Zacatecas and founding that city on 1 January 1548. After amassing a great fortune in the mines, Ibarra married Ana de Valasco y Castilla, a daughter of Viceroy Luis de VELASCO. In 1561 he loaned his nephew Francisco Ibarra 200,000 pesos to explore Nueva Galicia and Nueva Vizcaya. In 1576, Ibarra succeeded Francisco (*d.* 1575) as governor of Nueva Vizcaya. Ibarra organized an expedition of conquest into Sinaloa in 1583. He dedicated some of his fortune to constructing parish churches, the most notable of which being the parochial church at Pánuco. Ibarra moved to Mexico City later in life and finally to Tultitlán, where he died in 1600.

PHILLIP WAYNE POWELL, *Soldiers, Indians, and Silver: The Northward Advance of New Spain, 1550–1600* (1952), pp. 11–14; PETER BAKEWELL, *Silver Mining and Society in Colonial Mexico: Zacatecas, 1546–1700* (1971), pp. 11–12.

AARON PAINE MAHR

See also **Mixtón War.**

IBARRA, JOSÉ DE PINEDA (*b.* 1629; *d.* 1680), first master printer of Guatemala. Ibarra was born in Mexico City to Diego de Ibarra and Juana Muñiz de Pineda. After a period of collaboration with noted printers of the metropolis, Ibarra moved to Puebla, where he married María Montez Ramírez. With the financial assistance of Payo Enríquez de Rivera, Bishop of Guatemala, he purchased a printing press and related equipment. Under contract with Enríquez, Ibarra set out for the

Kingdom of Guatemala, arriving in the capital, Santiago de los Caballeros, in July 1660. In Santiago (present-day Antigua) he established a printing shop, the first of its kind in the country. Ibarra's only son, Antonio, who took over the business after his father's death, was born in 1661. Though granted a monopoly by Captain General Martín Carlos Mencos on the printing of religious and school materials, he was forced to engage in a variety of business ventures in order to supplement his meager earnings as a printer. He died, debt ridden, in Antigua.

JOSÉ TORIBIO MEDINA, *La imprenta en Guatemala (1660–1821)* (1910; rep. 1964); VÍCTOR MIGUEL DÍAZ, *Historia de imprenta en Guatemala desde los tiempos de la colonia hasta la época actual* (1930); ALEXANDER A. M. STOLS, *La introducción de la imprenta en Guatemala* (1960); DAVID VELA, *La imprenta en Guatemala colonial* (1960); LAWRENCE S. THOMPSON, *Printing in Colonial Spanish America* (1962; rev. ed. 1976).

JORGE H. GONZÁLEZ

IBARRA, JUAN FELIPE (*b*. 1 May 1787; *d*. 15 July 1851), Argentine military leader and Federalist governor of the province of Santiago del Estero (1831–1851). A native of Santiago del Estero, Argentina, Ibarra studied briefly for the priesthood before he began his military career in 1810. During the WARS OF INDEPENDENCE, he served with distinction on the staffs of SAN MARTÍN and BELGRANO, rising to the high rank of graduate sergeant major in 1817. In 1820, in response to an appeal by the local autonomists, he used the urban Abipone garrison to expel from the province of Santiago del Estero occupying forces of Governor Bernabé Aráoz of Mendoza and subsequently was elected political and military governor by a *cabildo abierto* (open town council). He encouraged economic development by protecting local industries from competition with imports and by authorizing the minting of real and half-real coins. A Federalist, Ibarra admired the state system and the internal economic organization of the United States. He survived a plot by the UNITARISTOS to have the poet Hilario ASCASUBI assassinate him, but the Unitarists finally overthrew him. Other Federalists restored him to power, and in 1831 the legislature elected him governor and brigadier general, a post he held until his death.

A paternalistic ruler, Ibarra encouraged education, built churches, exercised the PATRONATO REAL, banned imports that threatened the local economy, and condemned gambling, alcoholism, and other vices. Some see him as a barbarian, ignorant and cruel; others, as a popular caudillo and Federalist.

TULIO HALPERÍN-DONGHI, *Politics, Economics, and Society in Argentina in the Revolutionary Period*, translated by Richard Southern (1975); JOHN LYNCH, *Argentine Dictator: Juan Manuel de Rosas, 1829–1852* (1981), pp. 67, 226; JOSEPH T. CRISCENTI, ed., *Sarmiento and His Argentina* (1993), pp. 105, 156.

JOSEPH T. CRISCENTI

ICA, central coastal Peruvian department and city. Located approximately 170 miles southeast of the capital of Lima, the department has a surface area of 8,205 square miles and a population of 542,900 (1990 estimate). The city of Ica has 152,300 residents (1990 estimate). The Ica River, flowing into the Pacific from January to April, when rainfall is sufficient on the upper western slopes of the Andes, provides water for irrigation of fertile coastal fields. The valley is extremely dry, with less than one-half inch of rainfall yearly. In the winter (May through August) there are dense mists (*garúa*). Cacti will grow on slopes above 2,300 feet, but it is only by irrigation that the coastal desert bears crops.

Under the INCAS numerous agricultural crops were cultivated in the region, and various marine resources were exploited. With European contact following the 1530s, the native population fell sharply, by over 90 percent, the consequence of disease, the breakdown of hydraulic systems, exploitation, and the introduction of Old World crops and animals that changed the ecological balance. Wheat and vegetables were grown and transported to the Lima market. Grapes were quickly introduced, as the soil and climate seemed perfect for viticulture. By the 1590s wine and subsequently brandy (PISCO) supplied growing urban markets in Lima and highland mining centers. In the sixteenth century, African SLAVES were imported to replace the declining number of Indians, and by the mid-nineteenth century Chinese workers came to play an important role in the local labor market. During the twentieth century, cotton replaced grapes as the primary agricultural commodity, although Ica continued to be a major supplier of fresh vegetables for Lima.

ALBERTO ROSSEL CASTRO, *Historia regional de Ica* (1964); EUGENE A. HAMMEL, *Power in Ica: The Structural History of a Peruvian Community* (1969); ROBERT G. KEITH, *Conquest and Agrarian Change: The Emergence of the Hacienda System on the Peruvian Coast* (1976).

NOBLE DAVID COOK

ICA, PRE-COLUMBIAN. The Ica Valley of the Peruvian south coast has been continuously inhabited for more than four thousand years. The Ica pottery-making tradition, which began about 2500 B.C., has been studied more intensively than that of any other part of the Andes. It provides a chronological yardstick, divided into three periods and three horizons, against which other local pottery-style sequences can be measured in a system of relative chronology. From earliest to latest are the Initial Period, Early Horizon, Early Intermediate Period, Middle Horizon, Late Intermediate Period, and Late Horizon.

Ica was occasionally subjected to outside influence: from CHAVÍN in the Early Horizon, from MOCHE near the end of the Early Intermediate Period, from HUARI in the Middle Horizon, and finally as a result of the INCA conquest in the Late Horizon. Such influence is reflected

ICAZA CORONEL

in pottery form and decoration as well as other aspects of culture. Changes in the pottery of Ica are used to mark the beginnings of the periods and horizons.

New religious elements from Chavín reached Ica around 1500 B.C., perhaps brought by missionaries. Moche influence, arriving around A.D. 100, was weaker but also involved religious elements. The Huari state, which conquered Ica around A.D. 600, also brought religious changes, which are reflected in the art; but after the fall of Huari, around A.D. 800, Ica potters abandoned these foreign symbols, creating geometric decoration executed in red, black, and white on an unpolished surface.

The Ica style of pottery began some hundred years later when Ica artists revived some of the colors and designs from Huari art, including mythical birds and animals. The interpretation of these designs suggests that they were copied from older objects with no understanding of their earlier meanings. Such archaism, or copying from earlier art styles, was not uncommon in pre-Columbian Peru. From this archaized base, then, the Ica style developed and changed throughout the Late Intermediate Period and beyond. The animal figures were soon dropped, as were the additional colors, but the bird figures changed and multiplied, and to them were added fishes, indicating the importance of the sea to these people. Combined with geometric designs, these figures were applied to elegantly shaped and highly polished vessels, which acquired considerable prestige outside the valley. The wide distribution of Ica-style pottery indicates far-flung contacts and the possibility of a growing influence of the Ica Valley polities in the Late Intermediate Period, an influence cut short by the Inca conquest of Ica and the rest of the south coast about 1476.

The Incas involved some of the Ica nobility in the local administrative organization, and Inca shapes and designs were mingled with those of the local art style. Nevertheless, when the Inca Empire fell, Ica artists again rejected the foreign elements and returned to their own pre-Conquest trends. Their persistence in abolishing the symbols of conquest provides us with a key to the nature of the proud and independent people of Ica before their culture was destroyed by the Europeans.

DOROTHY MENZEL et al., *The Paracas Pottery of Ica: A Study in Style and Time*, University of California Publications in American Archaeology and Ethnology, 50 (1964); PATRICIA J. LYON, "Innovation Through Archaism: The Origins of the Ica Pottery Style," in *Nawpa Pacha* 4 (1966): 31–62; DONALD A. PROULX, *Local Differences and Time Differences in Nasca Pottery*, University of California Publications in Anthropology, 5 (1968); DOROTHY MENZEL, *Pottery Style and Society in Ancient Peru: Art as a Mirror of History in the Ica Valley, 1350–1570* (1976) and *The Archaeology of Ancient Peru and the Work of Max Uhle* (1977).

PATRICIA J. LYON

ICAZA CORONEL, JORGE (*b.* 10 July 1906; *d.* 26 May 1979), Ecuadorian novelist, playwright, and short-story writer. In general, Icaza's fiction has become linked to the regionalist movement of social protest of the 1930s; his best-known novel, *Huasipungo* (1934), attacks the exploitation of Indians in Ecuador. Written from the point of view of the dominant urban class in Ecuador, the novel highlights the ethnic and class gulf between Indians and whites by following, on the one hand, an idyllic love relationship between two young Indians and, on the other, the encroachment of foreign capitalism on an Indian community that is eventually destroyed. Grotesque, sordid descriptions of harsh living conditions and exploitation are meant to create a better awareness of the plight of the Ecuadorian Indians, most of whom lack the bare necessities of life in the novel.

In similar fashion, *En las calles* (1935) narrates a historical event in which an Indian soldier, assigned to quell a battle between rival political factions, ends up firing upon his own community. Icaza's next novels, *Cholos* (1937) and *Huairapamushcas* (1948), take a more complicated view of the struggle between Indians and whites. The CHOLO, or half-breed, works for the exploiter against the Indians until he realizes that his people are being oppressed. While no one survives the massacre in *Huasipungo*, in *Huairapamushcas*, an allusion to the survival of the *cholo* suggests the creation of a symbiotic relationship between Indians and whites. While not as well known as Icaza's first novel, by far his best is *El chulla Romero y Flores* (1958), a masterly recreation of the trials and tribulations of a marginalized *cholo* as he moves from a rural to an urban environment, thus complicating his life even more as he comes to grips with his mixed racial heritage. Icaza's last novel, *Atrapados* (1972), is more artistically rendered and contains autobiographical elements that portray the concerns of a writer whose creativity is vastly limited to the confines of the sociopolitical world in which he lives.

ENRIQUE OJEDA CASTILLO, *Cuatro obras de Jorge Icaza* (1961); THEODORE A. SACKETT, *El arte en la novelística de Jorge Icaza* (1974); MANUEL CORRALES PASCUAL, *Jorge Icaza: Frontera del relato indigenista* (1974); ANTHONY J. VETRANO, *La problemática psico-social y su correlación lingüística en las novelas de Jorge Icaza* (1974).

DICK GERDES

IGLESIAS, JOSÉ MARÍA (*b.* 1823; *d.* 1891), Mexican jurist and politician. Born in Mexico City and educated at El Colegio de San Gregorio, Iglesias began his political career in 1846 as a Mexico City councilman. As editor of *El Siglo XX* (1847–1850), he opposed the administration of SANTA ANNA and the Treaty of GUADALUPE HIDALGO (1848). After the triumph of the Liberal Revolution of Ayutla in 1854, Iglesias served in the ministries of treasury and justice and was later elected to the Supreme Court. The War of the REFORM (1857–1860) forced his return to private life, but he filled a variety of positions between 1863 and 1871 during the Benito JUÁREZ presidency: minister of justice (twice), minister of the trea-

236

sury (twice), and minister of government. He was elected president of the Supreme Court in 1873.

As head of the Supreme Court, Iglesias fought against presidential-gubernational control of elections. He became part of a three-way contest for power in 1876, when President Sebastián LERDO DE TEJADA (1827–1889) ran for reelection. Iglesias maintained that the 1876 elections were fraudulent and that presidential power had devolved upon him as the constitutional successor to the president. Earlier, PORFIRIO DÍAZ had pronounced against Lerdo de Tejada in the PLAN OF TUXTEPEC (1876). Repeated efforts to bring Díaz and Iglesias together failed. After Díaz dealt Lerdo's troops a major defeat at the battle of Tecoac on 16 November 1876, he turned on Iglesias.

As a professional soldier, Díaz's ability to attract military support proved crucial. Although supporters of Iglesias controlled over one-half of the country in December 1876, defections and military defeats forced Iglesias into exile in the United States in January 1877. He returned to Mexico in October 1877, but he did not resume his public career.

JOSÉ MARÍA IGLESIAS, *Autobiografía* (1893); FRANK A. KNAPP, JR., *The Life of Sebastián Lerdo de Tejada, 1823–1889* (1951); LAURENS BALLARD PERRY, *Juárez and Díaz: Machine Politics in Mexico* (1978).

DON M. COERVER

IGLESIAS, MIGUEL (*b.* 11 June 1830; *d.* 7 November 1909), provisional president of Peru (1884–1885). A wealthy landowner from the northern Peruvian department of Cajamarca, Iglesias was commander of Peruvian forces in the WAR OF THE PACIFIC (1879–1883). In August 1882, with Peru occupied by the Chilean army and beset by internal political divisions, Iglesias issued the Cry of Montán, in which he advocated pursuing peace with Chile even if it meant the loss of some Peruvian territory. In October 1882, he convened an assembly of northern Peruvian departments that proclaimed him supreme leader of the country.

Recognized as president of Peru by the Chilean government, Iglesias signed the Treaty of ANCÓN (October 1883), which ended the war between the two nations. Iglesias convened a constituent assembly in Lima that ratified the treaty and designated him provisional president of Peru (1 March 1884). General Andrés Avelino CÁCERES immediately opposed the Iglesias government, and after a long and bloody civil war, his forces occupied Lima in December 1885. Iglesias renounced his claims to the presidency and left the country. He died in Lima.

Iglesias's significance in Peruvian history is best presented in JORGE BASADRE, *Historia de la República del Perú* (1964), vol. 6, pp. 2619–2620. See also FREDRICK B. PIKE, *The Modern History of Peru* (1967), esp. pp. 146–152.

WILLIAM E. SKUBAN

IGLESIAS CASTRO, RAFAEL (*b.* 18 April 1861; *d.* 11 April 1924), president of Costa Rica (1894–1898, 1898–1902). After graduating from the Colegio de Cartago, Iglesias studied law at the University of Santo Tomás but left before obtaining his law degree. His first significant political experience came in 1889 when he supported the presidential candidacy of José Joaquín Rodríguez. When Rodríguez assumed the presidency in 1890, he named Iglesias minister of war. In 1893 Iglesias became minister of finance and commerce, and also married the president's daughter. As a presidential candidate in 1894 he enjoyed the support of the incumbent administration and took power after the government had suppressed his political opposition. In 1897 Iglesias secured congressional passage of a constitutional amendment that permitted his reelection and subsequently won a second presidential term when his opponents withdrew from the electoral process. During his two terms Iglesias placed the nation on the gold standard; inaugurated the National Theater; promoted railroads, highways, and port facilities; and oversaw the construction of a number of schools and hospitals. An authoritarian figure who often abused the political rights of the opposition, Iglesias nonetheless allowed freedom of the press. He stepped down from power in 1902 and ran unsuccessfully for the presidency in 1910 and again in 1914.

HAROLD H. BONILLA, *Nuestros presidentes* (1942); JAMES L. BUSEY, "The Presidents of Costa Rica," in *Americas* 18 (1961): 55–70; THEODORE S. CREEDMAN, *Historical Dictionary of Costa Rica* (1977).

RICHARD V. SALISBURY

IGLESIAS PANTIN, SANTIAGO (*b.* 22 February 1872; *d.* 5 December 1939), Puerto Rican labor leader. Born in La Coruña, Spain, Iglesias Pantin arrived in Cuba in 1886 as a stowaway and remained there until sailing for Puerto Rico in 1896. He began his political activities in 1898, being arrested for attempting to raise the "cost of labor." In 1900, he traveled to New York because of ill-health. While in New York, he became acquainted with members of the American Federation of Labor. The following year he was appointed union organizer for Puerto Rico and Cuba. In 1918, Iglesias Pantin organized the Pan American Federation of Labor and continued to participate and promote labor concerns until his death from malaria in 1939.

CLARENCE OLLSON SENIOR, *Santiago Iglesias: Labor Crusader* (1972); GONZALO F. CORDOVA, *Santiago Iglesias: Creador del Movimiento Obrero de Puerto Rico* (1980).

ALLAN S. R. SUMNALL

IGUAÇÚ. Formerly a part of the states of Amazonas and Mato Grosso in Brazil, the Federal Territory of Iguaçú was formed at the meeting point of Brazil, Argentina, and Paraguay as a result of the Constitution of 1946. This constitution allowed the military government to establish new states in the interior in order to improve its position in the Senate, and to minimize the influence of larger, more populated states such as São Paulo and Minas Gerais. In the early seventeenth century this area was central to the struggle between the frontier slave raiders and European missionaries. Not until the middle of that century were the Jesuits able to maintain some security against Paulista resistance to Indian protection.

ROLLIE E. POPPINO, *Brazil: The Land and People* (1968); ROBERT WESSON and DAVID V. FLEISHER, *Fleisher, Brazil in Transition* (1983).

CAROLYN E. VIEIRA

See also **Brazil: Constitutions.**

IGUAÇÚ FALLS, a series of 275 cataracts between Brazil and Argentina that form a horseshoe 2.5 miles wide across the Iguaçú River, and include the fifth highest falls in the world. The area was transformed through the construction of the Itaipú hydroelectric facility and today includes a population of roughly a quarter of a million near the mouth of the Iguaçú where it flows into the Paraná River. Previously the city of Foz do Iguaçú, seventeen miles from the falls, was a military outpost and center for YERBA MATÉ production and trade.

CAROLYN E. VIEIRA

IGUANA, warm-climate lizard that has a long body covered with scales, a crest along its back, and short limbs ending in five digits. The common iguana (*Iguana iguana*), found in tropical America, is green. It may reach 6½ feet in length, including its tail. Extensively hunted for its chickenlike meat, it is very popular in Central American markets. An excellent swimmer, it drops into water if threatened by danger. The Rhinoceros iguana (*Cyclura cornuta*), extremely rare, inhabits the island of Hispaniola. It is so named for the three horns on its snout.

The Galápagos marine iguana (*Amblyrhynchus cristatus*) is black. The Hood's Island iguana, which has reddish spots, is the only lizard known to feed in the surf, mainly on seaweed. During the mating season, each iguana has a carefully marked territory. If one male invades the territory of another, a long, nonfatal fight ensues. If a female iguana trespasses on the territory of another female, there is a bloody battle. An excellent swimmer, the Galápagos marine iguana spends time underwater and basking in the sun.

The Galápagos land iguana (*Conolophus subcristatus*) is a brown, quiet, inoffensive leaf eater that lives in dry, sparsely vegetated areas. It has a heavy body and strong limbs. The total length averages 43 inches, including a 24-inch tail. During the mating season, males fight ritual battles. This species is threatened with extinction due to hunting by humans, birds of prey, and introduced wild animals. It is strictly protected in the Galápagos Na-

View of Iguaçú Falls from Argentina. CARL FRANK / PHOTO RESEARCHERS, INC.

tional Park; eggs are collected and iguanas are raised at the Charles Darwin Research Station on Santa Cruz Island.

MARSTON BATES, *The Land and Wildlife of South America* (1964), pp. 132–133; ERWIN PATZELT, *Fauna del Ecuador* (1989), p. 212; FRANCESCO B. SALVATORI, *Rare Animals of the World* (1990), p. 151.

RAÚL CUCALÓN

ILLAPA, the Inca thunder god, was believed to control the weather. The INCAS prayed to Illapa for rain and protection from drought. He was envisioned as a warrior in the sky who held a sling and was dressed in shining garments. The lightning was believed to be the flashing of his clothing, and the thunder was the crack of his sling. His sling stone was the lightning bolt that broke his sister's water jug, causing the rain to fall. In a land of frequent drought, where the people depended on agriculture to sustain them, the god of rain was of paramount importance.

JOHN H. ROWE, "Inca Culture at the Time of the Spanish Conquest," in *Handbook of South American Indians*, vol. 2 (1946), pp. 183–330. Additional sources include BURR CARTWRIGHT BRUNDAGE, *The Empire of the Inca* (1963) and *The Lords of Cuzco: A History and Description of the Inca People in Their Final Days* (1967).

GORDON F. McEWAN

ILLESCAS, CARLOS (*b.* 19 May 1918), Guatemalan poet, considered one of the best in the "Generation of the 1940s" and the *Acento* literary circle. During the presidency of Jacobo ARBENZ GUZMÁN (1951–1954), he was the president's personal secretary. As a result, Illescas was forced into exile after the 1954 invasion of the country that led to the overthrow of the Arbenz government. He has lived in Mexico City ever since. Illescas is renowned not only as a poet but also as a radio and television scriptwriter, and as a distinguished professor of creative writing. His poetry is characterized by its mixture of classical Castilian language and powerful surrealist metaphor and imagery. His books are *Friso de otoño* (1958); *Ejercicios* (1960); *Réquiem del obsceno* (1963); *Los cuentos de Marsias* (1973); *Manual de simios y otros poemas* (1977); *El mar es una llaga* (1980); and *Usted es la culpable* (1983).

FRANCISCO ALBIZÚREZ PALMA and CATALINA BARRIOS Y BARRIOS, *Historia de la literatura guatemalteca*, vol. 3 (1987), p. 136.

ARTURO ARIAS

ILLIA, ARTURO UMBERTO (*b.* 4 August 1900; *d.* 1 January 1983), president of Argentina (1963–1966). A country doctor from Córdoba, Illia was born in Pergamino and entered Radical Party politics as a follower of Governor Amadeo Sabattini (1935–1940). Throughout his political career Illia adhered to the nationalist principles that *sabattinismo* had resuscitated in the Radical Civic Union (UCR). He was elected president in 1963 on the Radical Civic Union of the People (UCRP) ticket with only 26 percent of the vote. His administration marked the first serious return to the economic nationalism of the 1946–1955 Peronist government. Illia rescinded the exploration agreements reached by his predecessor, Arturo FRONDIZI, with the foreign oil companies and undertook expansionary policies by liberalizing credit, increasing wages, and redistributing income to the working class. Price and exchange controls were also established. Despite his economic program, Illia's relations with the Peronist trade union movement were antagonistic and general strikes by the General Confederation of Workers (CGT) undermined the government and its policies. After Illia went on the offensive and attempted to oust the entrenched labor bureaucracy through a series of labor reform laws, including supervised union elections and tighter control of union monies, the labor movement began to openly encourage a coup d'état, which finally occurred in June 1966.

GARY W. WYNIA, *Argentina in the Postwar Era: Politics and Economic Policy Making in a Divided Society* (1978); CÉSAR TCACH, *Sabattinismo y peronismo: Partidos políticos en Córdoba, 1943–1955* (1991).

JAMES P. BRENNAN

See also **Argentina: Political Parties.**

IMMIGRATION. All human groups in the Western Hemisphere are the result of migration at greater or lesser remove. The ancestors of aboriginal populations arrived in several stages via the Asian land bridge between 25,000 and 12,000 years ago, by most reckonings. During the colonial era over 1 million people emigrated from Spain to its American possessions, and a similar number of Portuguese went to Brazil. The largest intercontinental population transfer involved the approximately 12 million Africans who were forced across the Atlantic to what is now Latin America and the Caribbean in the slave trade, which lasted for more than 350 years. All Latin American nations have received at least some foreign immigrants since independence, including political expatriates and resident merchant or entrepreneurial groups from Europe, the Middle East, Asia, and North America. Earlier in the nineteenth century, the national governments in several countries promoted colonization schemes intended to populate border areas and encourage new economic activities, but demographically significant population transfers took place only after mid-century. All statistics on historical migration are to some extent problematic, and those given here are rounded approximations for purposes of comparison.

This entry will focus on the large-scale voluntary intercontinental migrations of the period from the 1870s

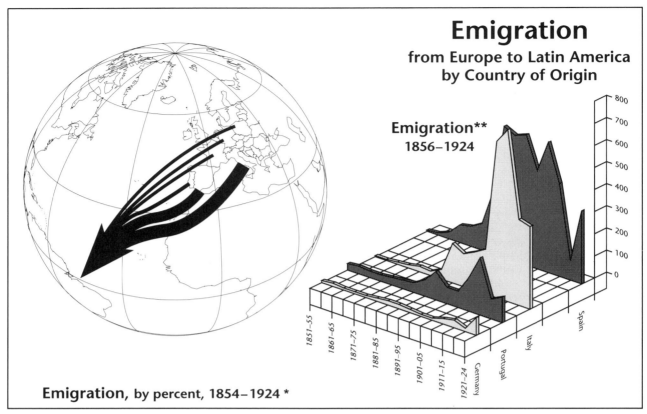

Emigration
from Europe to Latin America
by Country of Origin

Emigration**
1856–1924

Emigration, by percent, 1854–1924 *

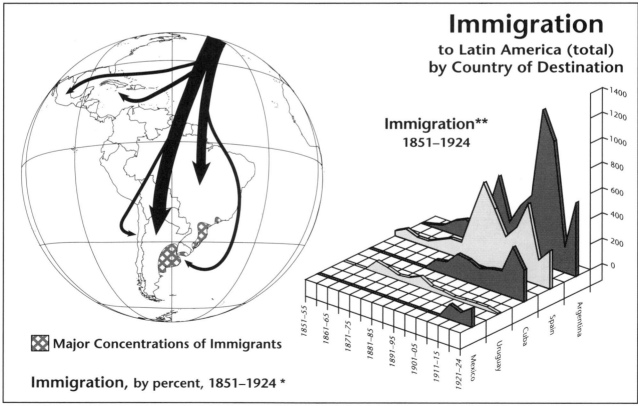

Immigration
to Latin America (total)
by Country of Destination

Immigration**
1851–1924

Major Concentrations of Immigrants

Immigration, by percent, 1851–1924 *

* SOURCE: M. MÖRNER, *Adventurers and Proletarians: The Story of Migrants in Latin America* (University of Pittsburgh Press, 1985).

** SOURCE: FERENCZI and WILCOX, *International Migrations*, vols. 1 and 2 (New York: National Bureau of Economic Research, 1929).

to 1930, which involved primarily immigrants from southern Europe, whose main destinations, in proportional terms, were Argentina, Uruguay, and Brazil. Changes in the international economy in the second half of the nineteenth century, particularly the social dislocation attending industrialization and urbanization in Europe, along with population growth following a general decline in mortality rates, contributed to the "push" factors causing people to leave their homelands. The same general phenomena led to the emergence of dynamic centers of export-oriented economic activity in southern South America, the "pull" factors making certain areas of Latin America likely destinations for international migrants. Similarly, the global economic depression of the 1930s signaled the end of the era of mass immigration.

In Argentina beginning in the 1830s, a group of political leaders and intellectuals, including Juan Bautista ALBERDI and Domingo Faustino SARMIENTO, advocated European immigration as a force for modernization and nation building. From the 1860s, with the expansion of the European market for wheat and chilled beef (the shipping of which was facilitated by the development of refrigerated steamships), labor demand expanded rapidly in the port of Buenos Aires and the surrounding pampas region. Seasonal migrants, young men nicknamed *golondrinas* (swallows), typically spent three or four months of the year in Argentina working on the wheat harvest. Many others stayed to become tenant farmers, or filled a range of occupational niches in the urban activities of meat packing, transportation, artisanal and industrial pursuits, and commerce. Net immigration totaled 3.4 million by the 1930s, about half of which was from Italy and another quarter from Spain. By 1895 about one-quarter of the Argentine population of 4 million was foreign born, a proportion that rose to 30 percent by 1914 (2.4 million of 7.9 million). In the

latter year, 44 percent of the population of Buenos Aires Province was foreign born.

Uruguay has mirrored Argentina in many aspects of immigration, if on a reduced scale. With a total population of 132,000 in the mid-nineteenth century, Uruguay received a net influx of about 640,000 immigrants from the 1880s to the 1930s, also primarily from Italy and Spain, accompanying a period of economic growth based on wool, beef, and wheat exports. Montevideo, like Buenos Aires, grew explosively, and by 1900 some 29 percent of the country's population (268,000 of 936,000) was located in the capital city, where half the population was foreign born.

In Brazil mass immigration is associated with three distinct if geographically adjacent areas of the southeastern part of the country. As of 1872 just 4 percent of Brazil's population was nonslave foreign-born (388,000 of 9.9 million). In the succeeding half-century net immigration totaled 3.3 million, of which more than half (1.7 million) went to São Paulo State. The rest were concentrated in the city of Rio de Janeiro and in the three states south of São Paulo (Paraná, Santa Catarina, and Rio Grande do Sul). Following long-standing patterns, the largest immigrant group in the city of Rio was Portuguese, concentrated in small-scale commerce and later in the industrial labor force. In the three southernmost states many immigrants entered officially sponsored semi-isolated farming colonies in which a single ethnic group (commonly German or Italian) predominated and retained its distinctive cultural identity. By 1920 the foreign-born still made up only 5 percent of the total population of Brazil (1.6 million of 30.6 million), but they were concentrated in the southeast, where they were 13 percent of the population. Immigrants were present in São Paulo's population in proportions (18 percent in 1920) similar to those of Argentina.

In the 1880s São Paulo coffee planters, anticipating

Immigrants disembarking in Buenos Aires, 1890s. ARCHIVO GENERAL DE LA NACIÓN, BUENOS AIRES.

241

final abolition in 1888, began to promote and recruit Europeans as a replacement for slave labor on plantations in the expanding western part of the state. The state government subsidized the passage of more than a million people from that period to the late 1920s. Of the total immigration to São Paulo, just over 1 million were Italian, followed by Portuguese (404,000) and Spanish (388,000). The majority worked as field hands on coffee plantations, at least for a time, and a significant number eventually managed to become coffee farmers themselves, if typically on a smaller scale than on Brazilian-owned plantations. As in Argentina and Uruguay, immigrants eventually filled a wide range of rural and urban occupations in the dynamic economic environment of São Paulo, fueled by export agriculture. Beginning in 1908, but particularly from the late 1910s, more than 100,000 Japanese arrived, creating the base for the largest concentration of people of Japanese descent outside the islands themselves.

Between 1870 and 1930, 10 million immigrants arrived at South American ports along the coast from Rio de Janeiro to Buenos Aires, resulting in a net population inflow of perhaps 7 million. (Chile, next after Argentina, Brazil, and Uruguay as a destination for immigrants, received less than 100,000 in the same period.) In addition to the predominant groups from Italy and Spain (and from Portugal and Japan to Brazil), people from France, Germany, and Eastern Europe and Christians from the Syria-Lebanon area (mislabeled ''Turks'' due to the passports by which most were seeking respite from Ottoman dominion) constituted numerically significant groups. As in other cases of mass immigration, the influx transformed the demographic composition of that part of South America, with immense social, cultural, economic, and political consequences. There were high and varying rates of return to homelands, and considerable geographic and social mobility within the receiving areas, even as elements of the native lower classes were marginalized by the influx from abroad and local elites for the most part maintained political control.

CARL SOLBERG, *Immigration and Nationalism, Argentina and Chile, 1890–1914* (1970); NICOLÁS SÁNCHEZ-ALBORNOZ, *The Population of Latin America* (1974), esp. pp. 146–181; THOMAS MERRICK and DOUGLAS GRAHAM, *Population and Economic Development in Brazil* (1979), esp. pp. 80–117; THOMAS H. HOLLOWAY, *Immigrants on the Land: Coffee and Society in São Paulo, 1886–1934* (1980); MAGNUS MÖRNER, with the collaboration of HAROLD SIMS, *Adventurers and Proletarians: The Story of Migrants in Latin America* (1985); THOMAS H. HOLLOWAY, ''Immigration and the Rural South,'' in *Modern Brazil: Elites and Masses in Historical Perspective*, edited by Michael Conniff and Frank D. McCann (1989), pp. 140–160.

THOMAS H. HOLLOWAY

IMMIGRATION, PARAGUAY. Though many countries in Latin America have been shaped by their immigrant populations, Paraguay is unusual in that most of its immigrants have settled in rural agricultural colonies that have been homogeneous ethnic, religious, or ideological enclaves. This pattern was established as early as 1855, when Francisco Solano LÓPEZ, son of the Paraguayan president, arranged for the transport of 400 French colonists to the Gran CHACO region directly across from Asunción. There they expected to receive government help in founding a farming community to be called Nueva Burdeos. In fact, little help was forthcoming, and the colonization effort was abandoned almost at the moment it began.

The WAR OF THE TRIPLE ALLIANCE (1864–1870) brought not only the defeat of López's armies but also a significant demographic dislocation in Paraguay. (Some sources claim the country lost nearly half its population of 400,000, and perhaps as much as 80 percent of its men.) This loss gave a sense of urgency to new state-sponsored and private programs of immigration, which cropped up in considerable number over the last decades of the nineteenth century. The first such project, which came to fruition in 1872–1873, involved a party of 900 immigrants from England, the so-called Lincolnshire Farmers, who had received encouragement from unscrupulous recruiters on the streets of London but who were utterly unprepared for the rigors of life in rural Paraguay. Government officials were in no position to help these settlers other than to grant them control over small plots of public land at Itapé and Itá. Utterly destitute, the great majority of the ''farmers'' drifted into Asunción, where the British consul raised the funds necessary for their passage to Buenos Aires. This experiment ended, like the earlier French effort, as a total fiasco.

The Paraguayan government learned from these failures, and in 1881 enacted comprehensive legislation to promote IMMIGRATION. This law authorized establishment of new agricultural colonies, with grants of land to each colonist, free passage from the point of embarkation, and maintenance for a maximum of one year. One provision of the law granted twelve square leagues to any company or private party who would introduce 140 families within a two-year period.

The new legislation brought an immediate response from German colonists, who came in considerable numbers to found a colony at San Bernardino, on the shores of picturesque Lake Ypacaraí. This colony enjoyed some impressive successes not only in agriculture but also in the production of high-quality soaps, jellies, and alcoholic beverages. San Bernardino prospered to such an extent that in 1901 it became a full-fledged municipality.

The success of San Bernardino attracted immigrants to other areas of Paraguay. New groups of Germans, as well as Italians, French, Swedes, and, in one case, a group of Australian utopian socialists, soon established colonies in various parts of eastern Paraguay. Few of these communities thrived, but few were outright failures.

By far the most successful colonists in Paraguay, how-

Mennonite immigrants building houses in Paraguay, 1930s. MENNONITE LIBRARY AND ARCHIVES, BETHEL COLLEGE.

ever, were German-speaking MENNONITES from Canada and Russia who began arriving in 1926. Attracted by government promises to grant them perpetual exemption from military service, the Mennonites founded three colonies—Menno, Fernheim, and Neuland—in some of the most inaccessible areas of the Chaco. These settlements had a combined initial population of 6,143 colonists. Despite the terrible odds against them, the Mennonites managed to tame the harsh environment and created a sizable agricultural and dairy complex in the Chaco. They soon founded new Mennonite colonies in eastern Paraguay. Today the various Mennonite communities are home to thousands of people who still proudly claim a lifestyle and language different from their Paraguayan neighbors.

In addition to the Mennonites, the twentieth century saw the arrival of colonists from many other countries, including Poland, Russia, Ukraine, Slovakia, and Japan, and, after World War II, a new influx of German refugees. It was estimated in 1958 that Paraguay contained 75,000 immigrants out of a total population of 1.8 million, and the number has grown decidedly since then, swollen not only by natural increases but also by the appearance of new immigrants who came individually from Taiwan, Brazil, South Korea, Vietnam, and, since 1990, from the former Soviet Union.

JOSEPH WINFIELD FRETZ, *Immigrant Group Settlements in Paraguay: A Study in the Sociology of Colonization* (1962); R. ANDREW NICKSON, "Brazilian Colonization of the Eastern Border Region of Paraguay," in *Journal of Latin American Studies* 13 (1981):111–131; HARRIS GAYLORD WARREN, *Rebirth of the Paraguayan Republic: The First Colorado Era, 1878–1904* (1985), pp. 243–271.

THOMAS L. WHIGHAM

IMPERIALISM. The various senses of *imperialism* require definition and an outline of their historical and theoretical components. According to *The Oxford Universal Dictionary* the word "imperial" comes from the Latin *imperium*, meaning "pertaining to an empire or emperor;" it defines imperialism as "the rule of an emperor, especially when despotic" or "the principle or spirit of empire." Other dictionaries define imperialism as "the policy of extending a nation's authority by territorial acquisition or by the establishment of economic and political hegemony over other nations," or "the policy of seeking to extend the power, dominion, or territories of a nation." The historian Tony Smith defines imperialism as "the effective domination by a relatively strong state over a weaker people whom it does not control as it does its home population, or the effort to secure such domination" (*The Pattern of Imperialism*, p. 6). He notes that the imperial power commonly permits the local population some areas of control. Any of these definitions allows for formal and informal imperialism.

The term *imperialism* has at heart subordination and the clash of sovereignty. In formal imperialism, the dominant power assumes sovereignty over the subject people in the form of annexation, colonialism, or an avowed protectorate. In informal imperialism, the dominant power asserts control over the sovereignty of subject peoples through various forms of domination (all of which carry the implied threat of force or other forms of harm). For example, the MONROE DOCTRINE was a policy that restricted the sovereignty of the Latin American nations because it denied them (without their consent) sovereignty over their territory (they could not alienate it) and over their political systems (they could not choose a form unacceptable to the United States). Imperialism was the product of the quest for glory, a higher purpose (God, the nation, civilization, or destiny), gold and wealth, and the strategic need for ports, outposts, and resources to achieve the first three objectives (or to protect early successes in achieving them).

RELATIONSHIPS OF STATES

World systems theory, associated with American sociologist Immanuel Wallerstein but based upon the work of the great French historian Fernand Braudel, defines the relationships of states within the world economy as metropole (core), semiperiphery, and periphery. A metropole power is defined, in part, by its urge to incorporate areas beyond its sovereignty into its political economy in order to enlarge the pool of land, labor, and capital from which its entrepreneurs accumulate profit. A metropole state not only controls the factors of do-

His Hat (Monroe Doctrine) Is in the Ring. Cartoon by Charles L. "Bart" Bartholomero. *Minneapolis Journal* (1912). REPRODUCED FROM JOHN J. JOHNSON, *LATIN AMERICA IN CARICATURE* (AUSTIN, 1980).

mestic production and distribution, but also acquires the political power and technology to control foreign factors of production and distribution in the periphery and semiperiphery. Metropoles are constantly in a state of competition with each other as they strain to obtain hegemony within the world economy. A semiperiphery state functions both as exploited and exploiter in the world economy. Metropoles and semiperiphery states exploit areas of the periphery (such as Central America), which lack some factors of production or are unable to control them. Metropole states preserve their political stability and improve the lifestyle and capital accumulation of their working and entrepreneurial classes in part by manipulating the periphery. Mexico, Brazil, and Argentina are three countries that acquired semi-peripheral status in the late nineteenth or twentieth centuries. They acquired considerable control over land and labor, and some capacity to distribute the imports and exports necessary for their economies. But they are still dependent upon foreign capital to a considerable extent and also rely upon foreign communications and transportation to an appreciable degree.

The explorers were the first foreign intruders into New World society. While the Viking raiding parties and the French and British fishermen were transitory, the adventurers and captains in the service of the Spanish, British, Portuguese, French, Dutch, Swedish, Danish crowns, and Italian states marked the New World

societies permanently with maps, ports, and settlements. The outward thrust of Europe was a response to its commercial expansion and its desire to reach the East more directly. Spanish experience with several centuries of reconquest of its peninsula from the Moors influenced its conquistadors; the mental and physical activity of many Spanish noble families had been directed toward conquest for generations. The Portuguese and the Dutch stressed trade more than settlement; the Spanish did a bit of both, while the British were heavily involved in both. Latin America was exploited for land, labor, and communication routes. The chief products of export under the Spanish and Portuguese were gold, silver, SUGAR, TOBACCO, chocolate, COTTON, hides, dyes and dyewoods, and fruit.

The European mercantilists of the fifteenth through the eighteenth centuries overran the whole New World. In addition to the Spanish Empire, which stretched from the Great Plains to Cape Horn, the Portuguese, Dutch, French, British, Russian, Danish, and Swedish nations established colonies in the New World. Centuries of competitive European expansion contributed to the formation of modern Latin America.

The European states used ship-building and navigational technology for exploration, and they employed military technology for domination and acquisition of territory. The elements of Western expansion in Latin America were the missionaries, settlers, and adventurers, the latter of which was reemphasized in new forms (filibusterers and economic adventurers) in the nineteenth century in the greed unleashed by the philosophy of liberalism and material progress. Western expansion (based on written records and maps and the transatlantic ties to settlers and colonists) attempted to alter empty or lightly settled regions, or regions occupied by peoples without advanced technology and sociopolitical organizations. Europe's technology, economic power, and advanced political and social organization developed from the geographical closeness of its states and the internecine and feudal wars fought to reestablish a centralized authority after the decline of the Roman Empire. The Renaissance enthusiasm for knowledge, new things, and new experiences of the mind also encouraged expansion. The European interaction with the indigenous peoples of Latin America in the sixteenth and seventeenth centuries was very one-sided: Europe borrowed some crops, but little else. Spanish, British, French, and Portuguese ideas, diseases, technology, and power carried the day.

Spanish and Portuguese institutions, the world economy, and the pre-Columbian societies shaped the agrarian structures in modern Latin America. The first two are part of the imperial order. The INCAS, AZTECS, and MAYAS had communal property (*capulli* for Aztecs and *ayllu* for Incas) but little private property. The Hispanics instituted private property and land grants to reward the soldiers and their leaders. The Spanish used *encomiendas* and the Portuguese *sesmarias* to distribute land and coerced labor for the production or extraction of wealth. In subsequent centuries, foreigners continued to assume a right to the land and labor needed to amass wealth. The church lands were also private, but held in *mano muerto* (dead hand or inalienable), hence outside the marketplace. Thus church property became a target of laissez-faire liberals and the ambitious nineteenth-century bourgeoisie.

Missionaries were important in the dissemination of European imperial rule because they penetrated the backlands and rain FORESTS that were without the gold or silver which attracted adventurers in the colonial period.

Except for the United States and Canada, the New World nations quickly became mixed racial and ethnic societies—mulattoes, MESTIZOS, and ZAMBOS. Anthropologist Marvin Harris has argued that the various racial and cultural components in Latin America were "in large measure the consequence of the attempt to harness the aboriginal population on behalf of European profit-making enterprises." Admittedly the REPARTIMIENTO was the cheapest form of labor in the New World because it required no capital investment as SLAVERY did. Still, if one adds land and resources to the harnessing of New World factors for European profit, the thought is more accurate.

ONE ECONOMIC SYSTEM
The age of exploration and discovery (fifteenth to eighteenth centuries) and of imperialism (nineteenth and twentieth centuries) completed the bonding of the world into one economic system. The "new imperialism" of the 1870–1931 period was more emotional and nationalistic and also tied closely to industry and cultural consciousness. Nationalism, liberalism, and the industrial revolution influenced and shaped European and U.S. imperialism in the late eighteenth and the nineteenth centuries. The imperialism and nationalism of the sixteenth through the early twentieth centuries left much of Africa, Latin America, Asia, and the Middle East with political boundaries and populations that suited the objectives of European imperial divisions of authority and economic power rather than local and indigenous factors of language, kinship, culture, or geography.

The imperial rivalry occurred within the world system which integrated all political units that controlled land, labor, capital, and distribution into a world economy. The Old World came to the New World quite consistently, although once the ties were made and the nature of the European and U.S. offerings became clear and evident, the indigenous peoples and the ethnically mixed authorities and businessmen of the New World states often solicited aid or programs. Desmond C. M. Platt argues that only after 1860 did U.S. and European economic ties with Latin America grow important and industrial markets more focused, drawing upon non-European labor and land (for raw materials and food) to foster material progress.

The shock waves of the world economic crisis of 1873–1898 persuaded political, business, and military leaders in metropole nations to expand through formal colonialism and informal imperialism in the years between 1870 and 1929. Around 1910, various European thinkers (Vladimir I. Lenin, John Hobson, and Joseph Schumpeter) advanced theories to explain the European expansion of the late nineteenth century. The time period strongly influenced these thoughtful and provocative explanations, which are linked to the question of power and to the economic, social, and strategic consequences of the liberal and Social Darwinian competition of industrial states. This focus upon the economic and strategic aspects of imperialism, however, overlooks an unusually enduring quality of imperialism: it restricted the sovereignty of the subject peoples. While European thinkers and politicians debated the merits of Marxist-Leninist and leftist critiques of European expansion, inhabitants of Latin America were more likely to debate the merits of pursuing European liberalism (most often in a positivist form) or condemning such a course through appeals to cultural nationalism (rooted in either Hispanic or indigenous cultures) or some variation of socialism.

U.S. efforts to plant and nurture the idea of a Western hemisphere became intense in the 1880s, but followed a vacillating course thereafter. U.S. officials cited a special relationship or shared Pan-Americanism, but they have continually encountered significant resistance among parts of all classes of Latin America. The special relationship was less cultural and emotional than fixed to a need for raw materials, markets for production, and investment opportunities. U.S. investment in Latin America rose dramatically from $308 million in 1897 to almost $5.5 billion in 1929. Trade rose almost as spectacularly from about $63 million in the late 1870s to $986 million in 1929. This era saw the rise of the *hispanismo* movement (Spanish efforts to rekindle cultural ties and then economic bonds with Latin America) and anti-Americanism, perhaps best evident in the APRA (Alianza Popular Revolucionaria Americana movement of Peru to redeem "Indo-America" and to resist "Yankee imperialism").

By the early twentieth century, much of the world had become colonies of metropole states or succumbed to the influence of multinational corporations. Metropole firms frequently controlled the production and distribution systems (often in enclaves) that drove the political economies in the periphery (those societies lacking most factors of production or unable to control them). Large transnational firms dominated the shipping, transoceanic telegraph cables, maritime services, and marketing operations that serviced Latin America. Other international organizations (dealing in labor, health, legal, cultural, and other matters) developed the capacity to interact with the gigantic firms at the level of the world economy. Through these large transnational institutions, metropole states dominated the political, judicial, social, cultural, labor, and professional organizations of the periphery.

SOCIAL IMPERIALISM

Social imperialism and dependency theory are useful tools for analyzing the international history of Latin America. Social imperialism (defined as metropole policies that ameliorated domestic problems such as labor dissatisfaction, social disorder, and unemployment by transferring them abroad to peripheral states) sheds light on the impulses operating within many metropoles, and dependency theory (which focuses on political sovereignty and economic and social autonomy) illuminates the consequences of metropole intrusions in the periphery.

The historians Bernard Semmel, Hans-Ulrich Wehler, and Thomas McCormick have described social imperialism as a policy through which the metropole hoped to ameliorate domestic social woes and preserve its wellbeing and security through exploitation of opportunities in the periphery. McCormick has described policies that aimed ''to export the social problem'' and ''to export the unemployment.'' Policy makers commonly discussed the impact of their foreign relations on their own domestic economy, but they rarely examined the consequences of their policies upon the host peripheral and semiperipheral states.

Social imperialism frequently brought dependent status to the societies on the periphery. Fernando H. Cardoso, Enzo Faletto, André Gunder Frank, and Samir Amin have described *dependencia* well. They have pointed out that metropole development in the competitive world economy required the underdevelopment of the periphery: if the periphery ever became developed, the option to exploit and extract accumulation would dissipate. Dependency theory focuses on the international structure as a means to restrict weaker participants rather than as a system to distribute bilateral justice in the metropole-periphery relationship.

The world economy, of course, is not a static structure, but a dynamic, changing system. Since ancient times, some producers and distributors have recognized that the exchange of commodities over large distances generates a large accumulation of value. The variety of products received from distant interchange by raising popular expectations, redefining the notion of wellbeing, and expanding the possibilities for accumulation became the motor for economic growth. As some European states applied technology to mass-produce goods and to develop new products, their need for raw materials and food expanded. Pressure grew to incorporate more areas into Europe's accumulation system—its production and distribution network. The European and North American statesmen, entrepreneurs, and military leaders contemplated the narrow land strip at the Central American isthmus as a key spot in a distribution system encompassing the whole world. This interest in world trade routes explains much of the urgency, intensity, and determination shown by metropole and Latin American geopoliticians, entrepreneurs, and intellectuals in the nineteenth and early twentieth centuries.

In the nineteenth century, informal means did not entirely replace formal imperial control in Latin America. Even after the formal Spanish (ca. 1820s) and Portuguese (1822) rule ended, the European states and the United States pursued political and economic authority in the New World, using formal colonialism or acquisition upon occasion. The British control of the FALKLAND ISLANDS (1833); the Spanish in Santo Domingo (1862) and the Chincha Islands (1864–1866); the British in the Bay Islands, Belize, and the Mosquito Coast (ca. 1860s); the French in Mexico (1861–1867); and the United States in Puerto Rico (1898), the Virgin Islands (1917), Guantánamo Bay (1898), and the Panama Canal zone (1903–1999) are some examples of formal imperial authority, in an age when power was more commonly exercised through informal means.

By the late nineteenth century, the leaders in the metropoles needed to implement policies of social imperialism and simultaneously to mediate the internal discord arising from the bitter domestic competition during the crisis of comparatively unrestricted laissez-faire industrial capitalism. The mediating order they created was organized (or corporate) capitalism, which developed into a varied body of economic, political, social, and cultural organizations (as well as ideas and common wisdom), many of which formed symbiotic relations to government regulatory agencies (often at the wish of the giant entrepreneurs and financiers). Organized capitalism sought to preserve the image and the rhetoric of a laissez-faire system in order to justify privatization of profit and at the same time institutionalize cartel, oligopolistic, monopolistic, or holding-company arrangements that initially joined government and leaders of the economic sectors, but soon attempted to incorporate leaders of labor and social and cultural movements into cooperative situations.

Abroad, the United States and other metropoles implemented social imperialism through a variety of forms, but the most common forms were multinational corporations, nonbusiness transnational organizations, governmental or quasi-governmental agencies, and private social and cultural bodies. The metropoles provided social overhead capital abroad in the form of diplomatic and consular services, military forces to maintain order, special commissions, experts, subsidies, and tariff and tax advantages, all of which were indirect aid to corporations. These actions could be obscured abroad, and the greatly reduced standards of living and lower expectations in the periphery allowed organized capitalism to pursue policies there with smaller sums of money. The corporations and cartels struggled and competed to acquire use of the factors of production in the periphery which would ameliorate their own domestic problems.

Imperialism flourished in an era of intense competition between metropole states. It meant that the Latin

American nations—which had limited resource bases, smaller and less educated populations, and less development of capital, communications, and technology— bore some of the burden of metropole unemployment and social disorder in addition to their own problems. Not surprisingly, some of the internal disorder in the Latin American societies derived from their ties to the metropole states. Social imperialism relied upon the power of the informal authority of metropole financial, business, political, and military groups in alliance with compradors—usually members of the bourgeoisie or military on the periphery. The metropole states and the multinational corporations established comprador relations with individuals and groups in Latin America. The compradors had two chief functions: they facilitated the entrance of foreign corporations and political influence, and they managed the domestic order to favor foreign business enterprises.

Compradors normally collaborated with metropole wishes for stability and order to stifle the discontent generated by the loss of sovereignty and the protest of exploited workers. But political repression generated violent and nonviolent resistance, and the ensuing spectacle alienated supporters of democratic and human rights in the metropoles. Metropole officials—under siege because of the outcry against inhumane and undemocratic conduct by the compradors—sought rescue in the quick restoration of order, at times through military intervention, because disorder in the periphery was perceived as a threat to the home country.

Metropole entrepreneurs engaged corrupted laissez-faire ideology—evident in free-trade rhetoric covering government-supported multinational business ventures—to support their competition for land, labor, markets, and communication routes. This competition was clothed in strategic, political, social, and cultural language to reinforce the home countries' determination to assure maximum access to the capacity of Latin America and isthmian transit to generate wealth and security by linking the Atlantic and Pacific half-worlds.

The evidence for Western world extraction of value from Latin America changed in character over time, but it is overwhelming. There was capital in flight from Latin America's elite, extracted as profit or controlled by European-U.S.-Japanese investors when left in Latin America; labor was exploited but scarcely educated or trained; land and resources were exhausted, used, or controlled; communications (both domestic and international) were dominated; technology and research were stifled or located abroad. These forms of economic exploitation continue after five hundred years of European and North American contact with Latin America. In addition, the sovereignty of these states is still subject to foreign interference, as has been evident in U.S. activity in Guatemala (1954), Cuba (since 1961), the Dominican Republic (1964), Chile (1973–1974), Grenada (1983), Nicaragua (1981–1990), Panama (1991), and Haiti (1992–1994).

MARVIN HARRIS, *Patterns of Race in the Americas* (1964); STANLEY J. STEIN and BARBARA H. STEIN, *The Colonial Heritage of Latin America: Essays on Economic Dependence in Perspective* (1970); FERNANDO HENRIQUE CARDOSO and ENZO FALETTO, *Dependency and Development in Latin America,* translated by Marjory Mattingly (1979); JAMES D. COCKCROFT, ANDRÉ GUNDER FRANK, and DALE L. JOHNSON, *Dependence and Underdevelopment: Latin America's Political Economy* (1972); ARIEL DORFMAN and ARMAND MATTELART, *Para leer al pato donald: comunicación de masa y colonialismo* (1972); DESMOND C. M. PLATT, *Latin America and British Trade, 1806–1914* (1972); IMMANUEL WALLERSTEIN, *The Modern World System* (3 vols; 1974–1988); CIRO F. S. CARDOSO and HÉCTOR PÉREZ BRIGNOLI, *Centro América y la economía occidental (1520–1930)* (1977); FERNAND BRAUDEL, *Civilisation matérielle, économie et capitalisme, xve–xviiie siècle* (3 vols.; 1979), translated as *The Structures of Everyday Life, The Wheels of Commerce,* and *The Perspective of the World* (1984); TONY SMITH, *The Pattern of Imperialism: The United States, Great Britain, and the Late-Industrializing World Since 1815* (1981); RONALD H. CHILCOTE and JOEL C. EDELSTEIN, eds., *Latin America: Capitalist and Socialist Perspectives of Development and Underdevelopment* (1986); PETER KLARÉN and THOMAS J. BOSSERT, eds., *Promise of Development: Theories of Change in Latin America* (1986); E. BRADFORD BURNS, *Latin America: A Concise Interpretive History,* 5th ed. (1990).

THOMAS SCHOONOVER

INCAS. When the Spanish conquistadores arrived in Peru in 1532, they found the major part of Andean South America under control of the empire of TAHUANTINSUYU. The ethnic group that ruled this empire was known as the Incas, and their emperor was the Sapa Inca. Between 1438 and 1532 the Incas expanded their domain throughout the Andean region of modern Ecuador, Peru, Bolivia, northern Chile, and northwestern Argentina. They transformed the terrain through massive public works of engineering and architecture, and restructured society through social engineering. In the process, the Incas accumulated great wealth that eventually filled the coffers of the Spanish Empire. Inca domination of the Andes was brought to an end by the Spanish conquest led by Francisco PIZARRO in 1532.

HISTORY

Inca history during the reigns of the emperors who preceded the Inca PACHACUTI is known largely from myths and legends. These accounts tell that around 1200 a small band of highlanders migrated into the valley of Cuzco in the southern Peruvian sierra. Over the next few centuries, the huge empire of the Inca was to spring from this small group. According to Inca legends, their place of origin was the town of Pacaritambo, a few miles southwest of Cuzco, where their ancestors had come forth into the world from three caves. This original group was led by the first Inca or ruler, MANCO CAPAC, and was comprised of his three brothers and four sisters. After many adventures, Manco led his small band into the valley of Cuzco, where they established themselves by force of arms and brought order and civilization. Other stories held the place of origin to be an island in Lake Titicaca, south of Cuzco, from which the Incas were led by Manco north to the valley of Cuzco. Yet other accounts combined these two legends into one, having the Incas migrating underground from Lake Titicaca to Pacaritambo, where they emerged from the caves of origin.

Following their arrival in Cuzco, the Incas slowly increased their influence through intermarriage and by military raids against their neighbors during the reigns of the second through seventh Incas (Sinchi Roca, Lloque Yupanqui, Mayta Capac, Capac Yupanqui, Inca Roca, and Yahuar Huacac). The city of Cuzco probably grew from a preexisting settlement, but through the reign of the eighth Inca, it was little more than an ordinary Andean highland town. The turning point in the history of the city and the Incas themselves was the great Chanca war near the end of the reign of Inca Viracocha (1438). By this time, the Incas had increased their domain to include the whole of the valley of Cuzco, including the Oropesa and Lucre basins, and a large part of the neighboring Yucay valley. A powerful warlike confederation known as the Chanca began to expand to the south, probably from the Ayacucho basin, the earlier HUARI imperial seat. Cuzco was threatened and the Inca forces very nearly defeated. The Inca Viracocha abandoned the city and fled to the neighboring valley, but at the last moment one of the royal sons, Inca Yupanqui, rallied the Inca armies and, in a heroic effort, defeated the Chanca forces. Following this victory he deposed his father, whose failure to defend Cuzco was viewed as a disgrace. Inca Yupanqui took the name Pachacuti and assumed the throne to become the first of the great Inca emperors and the first to be considered a true historical personage.

PACHACUTI INCA

The name Pachacuti (or Pachacutec, as it is sometimes given in the chronicles) means ''he who shakes the earth'' or ''cataclysm'' in QUECHUA, the language of the Incas. It was an appropriate name for a man who literally reorganized the Inca world. His first acts as emperor included subduing the neighboring peoples in the Cuzco region. Whereas they had previously been associated rather loosely with the Incas, mostly by persuasion and family ties, they were now firmly brought under control as vassals of the lords of Cuzco. Pachacuti then launched a series of conquests that rapidly transformed what had been the tiny Inca domain into an expanding empire. He conquered large areas of the sierra, moving north into the central Peruvian highlands and south to the shores of Lake Titicaca. He also turned his attention to reorganizing and rebuilding the city of Cuzco and designing the empire.

Pachacuti set himself the task of reconstructing Cuzco as a suitable capital for the empire he envisioned. The city was constructed in the form of a PUMA, incorporating the fortress–temple of Sacsayhuaman as its head.

The body was comprised of residential buildings and palaces laid out in a grid between the Tullumayo and Saphi rivers. Like so many New World peoples, the Incas held felines, especially the puma or mountain lion, to be sacred. The basic building unit of the city plan was an architectural form called the *cancha*, which was comprised of a series of small houses arranged within a rectangular enclosure. The *cancha* form and the grid plan of the city may have been derived from the old HUARI imperial administrative center of Pikillacta, located in the lower end of the valley of Cuzco. Other architectural features, such as the double-jamb doorway, are seen earlier in the imperial style of Tiahuanaco. However, the distinctive style of stone working for which Inca architecture is justly famous, was purely a creation of the Incas. So skilled were their masons that walls laid without mortar achieved a near perfect fit between stones.

The city of Cuzco was conceived as the center of the empire where the four quarters into which it was divided came symbolically and physically together. Four highways, one coming from each of the four quarters (*suyus*) converged in the great central plaza of the city. From this four-part division the empire took its name of TAHUANTINSUYU, meaning ''the land of four quarters.''

In addition to rebuilding Cuzco, Pachacuti initiated building projects in the environs of Cuzco and on his royal estates in the Urubamba valley. The most famous of these is the ''lost city'' of MACCHU PICCHU; he also built royal estates at Ollantaytambo, Patallacta, and many smaller sites in the valley.

Other building projects initiated by Pachacuti included the famous royal highway of the Inca. It provided for communication within the expanding empire and supplied a means of rapidly moving the army wherever it was needed. Following and expanding the routes of the old highways of the earlier Huari empire, standardized highways, often walled and paved, linked the various regions of the growing empire to Cuzco. Storehouses (*qolqa*) and rest stops (*tambos*) were built to provision and serve the army as it marched. A system of relay runners (*chasqui*) formed an effective postal system for the transmission of verbal messages and instructions. Towns and provincial administrative centers were built by Pachacuti and his successors in the various conquered territories as the empire expanded.

TOPA INCA

Pachacuti's son, Topa Inca, succeeded him as emperor in 1471 and continued to expand the empire. Topa Inca moved the imperial frontier north into what is now Ecuador and south into what is now Bolivia, northern Chile, and northwestern Argentina. By 1476 he had achieved the conquest of the Chimú, the last serious rivals for total control of the Andean area. The absorption of the Chimú had an important impact on Inca art, especially on goldwork. CHIMÚ artisans were brought to the capital at Cuzco to create golden vessels for the royalty. On the north coast, a hybrid Chimú-Inca art style developed with stylistic elements from both cultures. Topa Inca reigned until 1493 and was succeeded by his son Huayna Capac.

HUAYNA CAPAC

HUAYNA CAPAC continued to expand the boundaries of the empire to the north and east, incorporating much of what is modern Ecuador and the northeastern Peruvian Andes. Compared with his father, however, his conquests were modest. Huayna Capac spent so much time on his difficult northern campaign that severe strains began to grow in the social fabric of the empire. He was absent for many years at a time. Surrogates had to stand in for him at important festivals and ceremonies, and the people of Cuzco began to feel out of touch with their emperor. A new and potentially rival court grew up around him at his northern headquarters at Tomebamba in Ecuador. Administratively the empire had become difficult to govern. Decisions from the emperor took a long time to reach Cuzco and even longer to be disseminated to the rest of the empire. Controlling the far-flung outposts of empire became increasingly difficult.

A severe crisis finally came when Huayna Capac suddenly died of what may have been smallpox in 1527. The disease, introduced by Europeans, preceded the Spanish conquistadores as they journeyed across South America. Thousands died in a very short space of time, including Huayna Capac's appointed heir, who survived his father by only a few days. The confusion about the succession created even more strain on Inca society, and finally a civil war broke out between two brothers who were rival claimants for the throne.

HUASCAR AND ATAHUALPA

HUASCAR, one of the two rival brothers, had succeeded to the throne in Cuzco in 1527. He was challenged by ATAHUALPA, who had been with his father and the imperial army in Ecuador at the time of Huayna Capac's death. A large part of the army rallied behind Atahualpa, and a bloody war ensued. The forces of Atahualpa, which took the city of Cuzco in 1532, eventually prevailed. Huascar was captured and imprisoned.

As Atahualpa moved south to Cuzco with a large army, he was met by the Spanish forces led by Francisco Pizarro at the town of Cajamarca in the northern highlands. In a stunning surprise move, Pizarro and his small band of 168 men attacked and captured Atahualpa in the midst of his huge army (November 1532). Pizarro held the emperor captive for nearly eight months, waiting for the ransom that would secure Atahualpa's release. The emperor had offered to fill a room once with golden objects and twice with silver. This treasure chamber measured twenty-two feet by seventeen feet and was filled to a height of over eight feet. In all, almost eleven tons of treasure was collected throughout the empire and sent to Cajamarca. While he was in captivity, Atahualpa had secretly sent orders to

have the Inca Huascar killed. He eliminated his rival but to no avail, since he himself was killed by the Spaniards shortly thereafter, in July 1533. With the death of Atahualpa, the last of the independent Inca rulers had fallen. The Incas continued to resist the Spanish for many years thereafter, but the Inca Empire ceased to exist.

INCA SOCIETY

Most of what is known of Inca society is based on the Spanish chronicles, some of which were eyewitness accounts. Inca history viewed the great emperor Pachacuti as the founding genius of the Inca state. His reconstruction of the Inca capital coincided with a complete reorganization of Inca society. At the apex was the emperor himself, called the Sapa Inca, and the noble families of pure Inca blood. This lineage or extended family owned the empire. All of the important governmental posts, the governors of each of the four quarters of the empire, the army, and the religious institutions were held by pure-blooded Incas. There were never more than about 500 adult males, and perhaps 1,800 people in all who

The Way the Incas Travel. Reproduced from Fray Martín de Murua, *Historia general del Peru: Origen y descendencia de los Incas* (1611). PRIVATE COLLECTION.

carried pure Inca blood. Below them were the Incas by adoption, or Hahua Incas, comprised of neighboring peoples held in high enough esteem by the pure-blood Incas to be trusted with important positions when there were not enough royal Incas to fill these posts.

Below these were provincial nobility, who were local ethnic lords confirmed by the Inca administration. At the bottom of the social pyramid were the *hatun runa* (big men), the common heads of households (the family being the basic taxpaying unit). *Hatun runa* were organized in groups of 10, 50, 100, 500, 1,000, 5,000, and 10,000 families for administrative purposes. Each decimal division had an official responsible for its administration. This organization was the key to the success of the empire. Each family provided a set amount of labor or service to the state rather than wealth in the form of material goods. The state, in turn, used this labor to generate wealth through the production of goods, cultivation of lands, construction projects, or military conquest of new territory.

The social organization of the empire was based on a complex series of reciprocal obligations between the rulers and the ruled. Taxes were paid to the imperial government in labor service by the *hatun runa*. In return, the government provided social services to protect the population in times of want and natural disaster. Food and other goods were collected and stored to form a surplus for use during times of drought or famine. Some income from government lands was set aside for widows and orphans. Maize beer and food were provided for ritual feasting on holidays. The imperial government ensured that every citizen was fed and clothed.

INCA RELIGION

Pachacuti organized Inca religion into an imperial institution. The major gods of the various peoples incorporated into the empire were included in the Inca pantheon, and appropriate temples and shrines for them were built and maintained. In addition to the Inca patron, INTI the sun god, there were ILLAPA, the god of thunder; PACHAMAMA, the earth-mother goddess; MAMACOCHA, the sea goddess; and MAMAQUILLA, the moon goddess. Above all was VIRACOCHA, the great creator deity of the Andean peoples. In a separate category were deities called HUACAS, animistic spirits that inhabited everything in nature. Their specific manifestations occurred in mountain peaks, unusual natural phenomena, odd-shaped stone outcrops, mummies, and stone idols.

Inca religion emphasized ritual and organization rather than mysticism or spirituality. Religious rites focused chiefly on ensuring the food supply and curing disease. Divination was also of considerable importance. The Incas maintained an elaborate ritual calendar of public ceremonies and festivals, most associated with stages in the agricultural cycle such as plowing, planting, and harvesting. Others were related to solstice observations, puberty rites, and new year celebrations.

Inca society was highly stratified, and upward mobility was very limited. The only way in which a person could improve his position was through success as a warrior or by being attached as a servant to an important noble household or being selected as an *aclla* (chosen woman). The state controlled most aspects of the lives of its citizens, and a strict code of law applied more harshly to the nobility than to the commoners. Travel and dress were strictly regulated; no one could move about the empire or change from his native costume without the state's permission. The basic social unit beyond the immediate biological family was called the AYLLU. Land was held communally by the members of the *ayllu*, and decisions were often taken collectively.

Inca culture was the culmination of thousands of years of Andean civilization. From their predecessors they had inherited a body of statecraft and much of the physical infrastructure for the empire. This does not in any way diminish their achievement, however. It was the peculiar Inca genius for organization that allowed them to make profitable use of their cultural inheritance. They alone of the late Andean societies were able to weave together the disparate elements of the many Andean cultures through military prowess and extraordinary statecraft, and through drawing on thousands of years of cultural inheritance. In terms of geographical extension, military power, and political organization, the Inca created the greatest of the pre-Columbian empires.

The best single source for Inca culture and history is in the classic article by JOHN H. ROWE, "Inca Culture at the Time of the Spanish Conquest," in *Handbook of South American Indians*, vol. 2 (1946), pp. 183–330. Additional sources include BURR CARTWRIGHT BRUNDAGE, *The Empire of the Inca* (1963) and *The Lords of Cuzco: A History and Description of the Inca People in Their Final Days* (1967). The definitive study of the Inca economy is JOHN VICTOR MURRA, *The Economic Organization of the Inca State* (1980). On the Spanish conquest, see JOHN HEMMING, *The Conquest of the Incas* (1970). For a discussion of Inca origin myths, see GARY URTON, *The History of a Myth: Pacariqtambo and the Origin of the Incas* (1990). The two most important and accessible Spanish chronicles are *The Incas of Pedro de Cieza de León*, translated by Harriet de Onís (1959); BERNABÉ COBO, *History of the Inca Empire*, translated by Roland Hamilton (1979).

GORDON F. McEWAN

See also **Archaeology.**

INCHÁUSTEGUI CABRAL, HÉCTOR (*b.* 25 July 1912; *d.* 5 September 1979), Dominican poet. Born in Baní, Incháustegui Cabral wrote a sort of social poetry that ranges from raw identification with the disinherited to meditations on love, death, and mankind's relationship to God. He is best known for *Poemas de una sola angustia* (1940). His poetic texts appear in *Obra poética completa: 1940–1976* (1978), published by the Universidad Católica Madre y Maestra, where he taught literature for many years. The verse novel *Muerte en el Edén* (1951); the autobiography *El pozo muerto* (1960); two collections of essays on Dominican writers; three plays in verse based on ancient Athenian themes; and the novel *La sombra del tamarindo* (1984), which appeared posthumously, complete his vast production. A diplomat and public official during the dictatorship of his friend, Rafael TRUJILLO, Incháustegui Cabral held prestigious government positions throughout his life. Despite his association with the Trujillo regime, his literary legacy has been highly regarded by subsequent generations of Dominican writers.

JOSÉ ALCÁNTARA ALMÁNZAR, *Estudios de poesía dominicana* and *Imágenes de Héctor Incháustegui Cabral,* in Contemporáneos 2 (1980); ANGEL FLORES, "Héctor Incháustegui Cabral," in *Spanish American Authors: The Twentieth Century* (1992).

SILVIO TORRES-SAILLANT

INCOME DISTRIBUTION, a term normally used to describe the process that determines directly the division of income and, indirectly, provides an indication of the division of consumption, saving, and welfare. The two-way relationship between income distribution and development in Latin America has been complex and everchanging. The relative, factoral, sectoral, and other aspects of the distribution of income and the issue of poverty, which are examined in the sections that follow, reveal diverse dimensions of the absolute and relative welfare of Latin Americans and of the forces that have determined it. We are interested in the relative (personal or size) income distribution because income represents purchasing power over commodities (goods and services) and thus provides an indirect measure of relative consumption, saving, welfare and well-being of people in Latin America.

The factoral (class or functional) distribution of income is important because it focuses on the welfare of persons as determined by the prices of the labor, land, and capital services they offer in the market, these being known as wages, rent, and interest-profit. It is also important because it focuses on the relationship between the price of these factor services and their supply, especially skilled labor and capital, which ultimately determine total output and welfare. Until the 1960s, most research focused on the forces determining the distribution of income between the labor and capitalist classes and their respective wage and profit income shares. Since the 1970s, research has focused almost exclusively on the nature and determinants of the relative distribution of income and poverty. Furthermore, we are interested in the sectoral distribution of income because it focuses on the welfare of people as determined, in a derived way, by the output value of the sectors (agriculture, mining, industry, finance, education, trade, transport, government, and other services) in which their incomes are generated.

Have a few families received most of the income in Latin America or has there actually been little inequality? Has the distribution of income been more or less unequal in Latin America than in other regions? In or-

der to answer these questions, we turn our attention to the *relative* distribution of income.

The relative distribution of income (wealth or consumption)—the terms *size, personal,* and *household* distribution have also been widely used—deals with the distribution of a mass of income (wealth, consumption) among the members of a set of economic units (families, households, individuals) considering either the total income (wealth, consumption) of each economic unit or its disaggregation by source of income, such as wages and salaries, property income, self-employment income (or by type of consumption, such as private, semipublic, or collective, or wealth, such as land, home equity, financial assets).

The relative distribution of income typically presents percentage income shares of *deciles* (tenths) or *quintiles* (fifths) of the total population of households, families, or individuals. The relative distribution of per capita household income in Latin America and the Caribbean primarily in 1989 is presented in quintiles in table 1. The distribution of income can be considered as being highly unequal if the income share of the poorest 20 percent is less than 3.0 percent or if the income share of the lowest 40 percent is less than 12 percent. According to the first criterion, relative income distribution was highly unequal in Brazil, Guatemala, Honduras, and Panama. If the second criterion is used, the distribution of income was also highly unequal in Chile, Colombia, and Mexico. The lowest degree of inequality is found in Paraguay and Uruguay.

The relative distribution of income is, most frequently, visually illustrated by the so-called Lorenz curve and numerically measured by the related Gini coefficient of income concentration. The "Lorenz curve," named after Max Lorenz, the statistician who invented it, is an ingenious device most widely used to graphically demonstrate and analyze the relative distribution of income (wealth, consumption). The Lorenz curve is a graph of the cumulative percentage of income (wealth, consumption) received (owned) by the cumulative percentage of population (families, households, individuals) arranged from the poorest to the richest. The difference between this graph and the line of perfect equality (the diagonal between the two corners of the square in which the Lorenz curve is graphed) is a visual illustration of the degree of inequality of an income (wealth, consumption) distribution.

In their 1993 study, Psacharopoulos et al. present Lorenz curves of the income distribution in most Latin American and Caribbean (LAC) countries, primarily in 1989 but also in a few preceding years. In order to demonstrate the use of this statistical device, we present in figure 1 the Lorenz curve of the per capita household income distribution in Brazil during the fourth quarter of 1989, along with the underlying statistics. From these statistics we can see that the lowest 10 percent of the population received 0.7 percent of per capita household income, the lowest 20 percent received 2.1 percent, the

TABLE 1   Relative Distribution of Per Capita Household Income in Latin America and the Caribbean

Country	Year	Lowest 20 percent	Second quintile	Third quintile	Fourth quintile	Highest 20 percent	Highest 10 percent
Argentina	1989	4.1	8.6	13.3	21.3	52.6	35.9
Bolivia	1989	3.5	7.7	12.0	19.3	57.5	41.2
Brazil	1989	2.1	4.9	8.9	16.8	67.5	51.3
Chile	1989	3.7	6.8	10.3	16.2	62.9	48.9
Colombia	1989	3.4	7.3	11.7	19.2	58.3	41.8
Costa Rica	1989	4.0	9.1	14.3	21.9	40.8	34.1
Dominican Republic	1989	4.2	7.9	12.5	19.7	55.6	39.6
Ecuador	1987	5.4	9.4	13.7	21.0	50.5	34.6
El Salvador	1990	4.5	9.4	14.5	21.7	50.0	33.6
Guatemala	1989	2.2	6.0	10.7	18.7	62.4	45.9
Honduras	1989	2.7	6.0	10.2	17.4	63.5	47.9
Jamaica	1989	5.1	9.5	14.4	22.0	49.2	32.5
Mexico	1989	3.9	7.7	12.1	19.3	57.0	41.3
Panama	1989	2.0	6.3	11.6	20.3	59.8	42.2
Paraguay	1990	5.9	10.5	14.9	22.6	46.1	29.5
Peru	1990	5.6	9.8	14.0	20.2	50.4	35.1
Uruguay	1989	5.4	10.0	14.7	21.5	48.3	32.6
Venezuela	1989	4.8	9.5	14.4	21.9	49.5	33.2

SOURCE: Calculated from statistics in Annex 3 of GEORGE PSACHAROPOULOS et al., *Poverty and Income Distribution in Latin America: The Story of the 1980s* (Washington, D.C.: World Bank, Latin America, and the Caribbean, Technical Department, Regional Studies Program, Report No. 27, Revised June 1993).

lowest 40 percent received 7.0 percent, the lowest 60 percent received 15.9 percent, and so on, until the lowest 100 percent received 100 percent of income. These points are then plotted on figure 1 to show the Lorenz curve of income distribution.

The Psacharopoulos monograph also contains a comprehensive analysis and bibliography of the vast number of studies of the relative distribution of income and consumption in Latin America in recent decades. It also describes and uses other, less common, measures of the relative distribution of total as well as workers' income.

The straight line between O and A is called the line of perfect equality or the egalitarian line. If the Lorenz curve coincides with the egalitarian line, it means that each unit receives the same income (wealth, consumption), which is the case of perfect equality of incomes (wealth, consumption). In the case of perfect inequality of incomes (wealth, consumption), the Lorenz curve coincides with OA and AB, which implies that all income (wealth, consumption) is received (owned) by only one unit. Since the Lorenz curve displays the deviation of each individual income (wealth, consumption) from perfect equality, it graphically captures, in a sense, the essence of inequality. The closer the Lorenz curve is to the line of perfect equality, the more equal the distribu-

tion of income (wealth, consumption) will be. The further the Lorenz curve is from the line of perfect equality, the more unequal the distribution of income (wealth, consumption) will be.

The Lorenz curve presented in figure 1 is far below the diagonal OA line of perfect equality, thus revealing a highly unequal relative distribution of income in Brazil. The richest 20 percent of households received 67.5 percent of total income, while the poorest 60 percent of households received only 15.9 percent of total income.

The most commonly used summary measure of distributional inequality is the Gini coefficient, which is defined as the ratio of the area enclosed between the 45-degree line of perfect equality and the Lorenz curve to the area of the entire triangle enclosed by the 45-degree line. The closer the Lorenz curve is to the diagonal, the closer the ratio of this area to the area below the diagonal would be to zero. On the other hand, the farther the Lorenz curve dips away from the line of perfect equality, the greater the area between the two and the closer the ratio of this area and all the area enclosed by the 45-degree line will be to 1. Hence, a Gini coefficient closer to zero indicates greater equality in a distribution, while one closer to 1 represents greater inequality in a distribution.

According to many scholars and studies, Latin Amer-

FIGURE 1   Per Capita Household Income Distribution: Brazil 1989

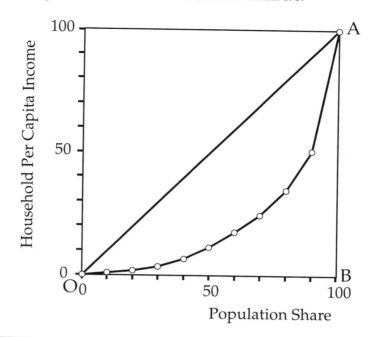

Income Decile	Income Decile Range (cruzados/month)	Mean Household per Capita Income* (cruzados/month)	Income Share (percent)
1	0–50	31	0.7
2	50–79	64	1.4
3	79–112	94	2.1
4	112–150	130	2.8
5	150–200	174	3.8
6	200–267	232	5.1
7	267–375	316	6.9
8	375–555	453	9.9
9	555–1001	742	16.2
10	1001 +	2,357	51.3
Sample mean:		459	100.0

Gini coefficient = 0.6331   Population represented by the sample = 141,407,443 individuals.

* Household per capita income from all sources including wages and salaries, and self-employed income.

SOURCE: GEORGE PSACHAROPOULOS et al., *Poverty and Income Distribution in Latin America: The Story of the 1980s* (Washington, D.C.: World Bank, Latin America, and the Caribbean, Technical Department, Regional Studies Program, Report No. 27, Revised June 1993), Annex 3, A3.8.

ica has historically exhibited a high degree of inequality in the relative distribution of income and consumption in comparison with the rest of the world. For example, according to a joint study by the World Bank and the International Labour Office (ILO) (cited by Psacharopoulos et al., p. 19), for years during the 1970s, and in some cases the 1960s, twenty non–Latin American and Caribbean countries had a mean Gini coefficient of 0.39 and a mean bottom 20 percent income share of 6.5 per-

cent of total income. In comparison, the three LAC countries in the World Bank/ILO study had a mean Gini coefficient of 0.52 and a mean bottom 20 percent income share of 3.1 percent of total income. Furthermore, the LAC countries in the Psacharopoulos study had a mean 1989 Gini coefficient of 0.50 and a mean bottom 20 percent income share of 4.0 percent of total income. Thus, although the World Bank/ILO study was based on data from the 1960s and the 1970s, the disparities that they find between LAC countries and non-LAC countries continued to hold true and may have even increased in the 1980s. During that decade, according to the Psacharopoulos study, and the statistics presented in table 2, the relative distribution of income, as measured by the Gini coefficient, became more unequal in Argentina (Buenos Aires), Bolivia (urban), Brazil, Guatemala, Honduras, Mexico, Panama, Peru (Lima), and Venezuela; it improved, however, in Colombia (urban), Costa Rica, Paraguay (Asunción), and Uruguay (urban). In 1989, the degree of inequality was highest in Brazil and lowest in Paraguay.

There does not exist, however, a consensus that the relative distribution of income in Latin America has been unusually high in the 1960s and 1970s. According to Miguel Urrutia (1993), Brazil, Colombia, Mexico, and Peru appear to have had high degrees of concentration

of relative distribution of income in the 1970s, but these rates were not too different from those found after the first phase of industrialization in England and Wales or Denmark. Since the explanations of the high inequality in relative income distribution are similar to those offered about poverty, they are discussed together at the end of this essay.

RELATIVE DISTRIBUTION OF LABOR INCOME
Few characteristics stand out in Latin America as much as the pervasive inequality in the relative (size, personal) distribution of labor income, that is, compensation of employees. Ever since Independence the high inequality in the relative distribution of total income has coincided with an equally pronounced high inequality in the relative distribution of labor income, that is, wages and salaries.

TABLE 2   Gini Coefficient and Bottom 20 Percent Share of Income at the Individual Level,*
Latin America and the Caribbean: 1980, 1989

Country	Year of Survey		Gini Coefficient		% Share of Income of Bottom 20% of Population	
			Circa 1980 (or earliest)	Circa 1989 (or latest)	Circa 1980 (or earliest)	Circa 1989 (or latest)
Argentina (Buenos Aires)	1980	1989	0.408	0.476	5.3	4.2
Bolivia (urban)	1986	1989	0.516	0.525	3.9	3.5
Brazil	1979	1989	0.594	0.633	2.6	2.1
Chile	—	1989	—	0.573	—	3.7
Colombia (urban)	1980	1989	0.585	0.532	2.5	3.4
Costa Rica	1981	1989	0.475	0.460	3.3	4.0
Dom. Republic	—	1989	—	0.503	—	4.2
Ecuador (urban)	—	1987	—	0.445	—	5.4
El Salvador (urban)	—	1990	—	0.448	—	4.5
Guatemala	1986–7	1989	0.579	0.587	2.7	2.2
Honduras[a]	1986	1989	0.549	0.591	3.2	2.8
Jamaica[b]	—	1989	—	0.435	—	5.1
Mexico	1984	1989	0.506	0.519	4.1	3.9
Panama	1979	1989	0.488	0.565	3.9	2.0
Paraguay (Asunción)	1983	1990	0.451	0.398	4.9	5.9
Peru (Lima)[b]	1985–6	1990	0.428	0.438	6.2	5.7
Uruguay (urban)	1981	1989	0.436	0.424	4.9	5.4
Venezuela	1981	1989	0.428	0.441	5.0	4.8

* Individual income has been calculated by dividing household income by the number of individuals in the household.
[a] Results are not strictly comparable due to differences in geographical coverage between the 1986 and 1989 surveys. The Gini coefficient based on urban households only for Honduras 1989 is 0.556 while the bottom 20 percent income share is 3.5 percent.
[b] Based on consumption data.
— Not available.

SOURCE: George Psacharopoulos et al., *Poverty and Income Distribution in Latin America: The Story of the 1980s* (Washington, D.C.: World Bank, Latin America, and the Caribbean, Technical Department, Regional Studies Program, Report No. 27, Revised June 1993), p. 18.

"Away with Special Privileges" banner carried by peasants demonstrating in Montevideo, Uruguay, 1930s. ORGANIZATION OF AMERICAN STATES.

There have been poor, middle, and rich workers, and the income differences among them have been vast. The average income of the richest workers (top decile) was 89 times the average income of the poorest workers (bottom decile) in Colombia in 1980 but only 29 times in 1989; it was 46 (1986) and 44 (1989) times in Guatemala; 46 (1979) and 68 times (1989) in Brazil; 12 (1980) and 22 times (1989) in Argentina; 30 (1981) and 20 (1989) times in Costa Rica; and 24 (1981) and 15 (1989) times in Uruguay (calculated from data presented in the Psacharopoulos study). High inequalities in the distribution of workers' income were also found in Chile between 1940 and 1973 (Mamalakis, 1975). Indeed, during much of the modern history of Latin America, the differences in income within the working class have been as great as, or even greater than, between the labor and capitalist classes. These differences have been so pronounced that they cast doubt about the existence of a homogeneous labor class, or proletariat, with common features, that is in conflict with a homogeneous capitalist class. To many, the Latin American problem of an unfair and unequal distribution of income has been primarily a problem of a highly unequal and unfair distribution of labor income, of income within the working class.

The high inequality in the relative distribution of workers' income has been evident as recently as the decade of the 1980s. According to the study by Psacharopoulos (chap. 3), the distribution of workers' income continued to be highly unequal in the 1980s in Argentina (Buenos Aires), Bolivia (urban), Brazil, Colombia (urban), Costa Rica, Guatemala, Honduras, Panama, Uruguay (urban), and Venezuela. The selection of the countries was determined solely on the basis of multiple data availability in 1980s.

The concentration of labor income in the hands of the richest 20 percent of workers was extremely high both in earlier years and in 1989. Presented here are only selected statistics for 1989, since these are the more recent ones.

The richest 20 percent of workers received 42.1 percent of total workers' income in Argentina, 46.9 percent in Bolivia, 67.2 percent in Brazil, 57.0 percent in Colombia, 47.1 percent in Costa Rica, 57.0 percent in Guatemala, 57.7 percent in Honduras, 49.6 percent in Panama, 47.7 percent in Uruguay, and 52.2 percent in Venezuela. In contrast, the poorest 20 percent of workers received only 1.6 percent of total workers' income in Argentina, 1.4 percent in Bolivia, 0.8 percent in Brazil, 1.1 percent in Colombia, 1.6 percent in Costa Rica, 0.9 percent in Guatemala, 1.1 percent in Honduras, 1.5 percent in Panama, 1.6 percent in Urugay, and 1.1 percent in Venezuela. Furthermore, even the poorest 40 percent of workers received extremely small fractions of total workers' income. This share was 14.2 percent in Argentina, 12.1 percent in Bolivia, only 7.8 percent in Brazil, 12.3 percent in Colombia, 16.0 percent in Costa Rica, 10.9 percent in Guatemala, 10.7 percent in Honduras, 14.1 percent in Panama, 15.5 percent in Uruguay, and 9.4 percent in Venezuela. The remaining, intermediate ("middle") 40 percent of workers (5th–8th deciles) received 33.7 percent of total workers' income in Argentina, 30.9 percent in Bolivia, 25.1 percent in Brazil, 30.7 percent in Colombia, 37.0 percent in Costa Rica, 32.2 percent in Guatemala, 31.0 percent in Honduras, 36.2 percent in Panama, 36.9 percent in Uruguay, and 38.4 percent in Venezuela.

The Gini coefficients for these countries (table 3) confirm the presence of high inequality in the distribution of workers' income. The highest degree of inequality in the distribution of income in 1989 was found in Brazil and Honduras; the lowest in Costa Rica and Uruguay.

Many factors have contributed to the differences in workers' incomes. Unequal endowments of human capital, for example, education, explains a significant part of these differences. Other factors include employment status (being an employee, self-employed, or an employer), age, gender, sector of employment, or belonging to indigenous populations.

The *class* or *factoral* distribution of income (the term *functional* distribution of income is also widely used) describes the levels of payments to the services provided by the trinity of land, labor, and capital factors of production—rents, wage rates, and rates of profits—and by extension the shares of these factors in the total income.

TABLE 3 Inequality in Workers' Income

Country	Gini Index	
	Early[a]	Late[a]
Argentina (Buenos Aires)	0.389	0.461
Bolivia (urban)	0.479	0.515
Brazil	0.574	0.625
Colombia (urban)	0.578	0.515
Costa Rica	0.451	0.410
Guatemala	0.532	0.528
Honduras[b]	0.528	0.533
Panama	0.376	0.446
Uruguay (urban)	0.452	0.420
Venezuela	0.512	0.498

[a] Most early Gini coefficients are for years around 1980. All later ones are for 1989.
[b] Early and late values are not strictly comparable due to differential survey coverage.

SOURCE: George Psacharopoulos et al., *Poverty and Income Distribution in Latin America: The Story of the 1980s* (Washington, D.C.: World Bank, Latin America, and the Caribbean, Technical Department, Regional Studies Program, Report No. 27, Revised June 1993), p. 36.

According to the classical school (Adam Smith, David Ricardo) and its followers, the class distribution critically affects income and welfare growth because landowners, the recipients of rents, and workers, the recipients of wages, largely consume their incomes, while capitalists, the recipients of profits, largely save them. Since the supply of capital in the long run is the supply of saving, a higher return (profit rate) on capital is expected to increase saving, investment, and income growth.

Since 1820 saving and investment have been low in most of Latin America, in spite of a favorable distribution of income, that is, a high profit share of capitalists. Saving and investment have been less than 20, or even 10, percent of GDP, while the share of profits (operating surplus) has fluctuated between 40 and 60 percent of GDP. During the so-called golden age of free trade and exports, which lasted from 1860 to 1930, vast operating surpluses and profit shares did not increase saving and investment enough to transform the underdeveloped Latin American countries into developed ones. Similarly, during the 1930–1980 era of protectionism, government intervention, and promotion of industry, saving and investment never reached the levels needed to transform Latin America into a developed region, in spite of high profit shares. Even during 1980–1995, high and rising profit shares did not give rise to the investment levels needed to achieve sustained development. Since 1820 the often fabulous resources of Latin America were used primarily for consumption rather than saving and investment.

The *sectoral distribution* of income examines the welfare of people in Latin America as determined by the creation and redistribution of sectoral incomes. By focusing on the sectoral aspect of the distribution of income, Mamalakis's *Theory of Sectoral Clashes and Coalitions* attempts to offer an explanation of both inequality and poverty. Before 1930, it is argued, the relative distribution of income was unequal because the fabulous riches created by agriculture and mining were appropriated primarily by the richest 40 percent of households. Even semipublic services funded by sectoral, export-generated, surpluses were provided largely to the privileged upper classes. These sectoral, or mesoeconomic, constitutions failed to generate either the demand for or the supply of skilled labor that could sustain rapid growth and eradicate poverty and extreme inequality. Use of sectoral surpluses primarily for consumption by the rich rather than for tangible and intangible human capital for all, but especially the poor, largely contributed to the failure of export "miracles" in Argentina, Brazil, Bolivia, Chile, Colombia, Cuba, Ecuador, Guatemala, Honduras, Mexico, Peru, Uruguay, Venezuela, and so forth.

Public policies shaping the sectoral distribution of income also slowed down growth and perpetuated inequality and poverty after 1930. Redistribution of sectoral income from agriculture and exports to industry led to agricultural and export, and ultimately, overall stagnation. Furthermore, systematic discrimination, that is, an unfair, artificially low share of income in financial services led to hyperinflation and chaos in much of the continent, but especially in Argentina, Chile (before 1973), Brazil, Nicaragua, and Peru. In Venezuela and Ecuador after 1973, it was once again the use of fabulous oil surpluses for consumption and entitlements by the privileged social groups that caused developmental "failure."

The policy implications are clear: unless all forms of discrimination in the sectoral distribution of income are eliminated, and sectoral surpluses are used for both tangible and intangible (human) capital, stagnation, inequality, and poverty will persist. Only nondiscriminatory sectoral (mesoeconomic) and microeconomic policies can guide resources to their most efficient uses—which is the function of income distribution—and accelerate growth. Such policies had been adopted in the 1990s in Chile, Argentina, and to a lesser extent, Mexico, Peru, Uruguay, and elsewhere.

ABSOLUTE POVERTY

Closely related to the various facets of income distribution is that of absolute poverty. While the former describes the distribution of income accruing to specific factors of production, income groups, sectors, regions, and so forth, the latter is a measure of those members of the population who have a welfare that is below some *absolute* standard. Latin America and the Caribbean have experienced high degrees of poverty throughout the 1820–1995 period. Absolute poverty has declined

TABLE 4 Percent of Individuals in Poverty and Extreme Poverty in Latin America and the Caribbean

Country	Survey	Year	Poverty Headcount Index[a] (% below $60 poverty line)		Extreme Poverty Headcount Index[b] (% below $30 poverty line)	
			($\approx$ 1980)[c]	($\approx$ 1989)[d]	($\approx$ 1980)[c]	($\approx$ 1989)[d]
Argentina (Buenos Aires)	1980	1989	3.0	6.4	0.2	1.6
Bolivia (urban)	1986	1989	51.1	54.0	22.5	23.2
Brazil	1979	1989	34.1	40.9	12.2	18.7
Chile	—	1989	—	10.0	—	1.5
Colombia (urban)	1980	1989	13.0	8.0	6.0	2.9
Costa Rica	1981	1989	13.4	3.4	5.4	1.1
Dominican Republic	—	1989	—	24.1	—	4.9
Ecuador (urban)	—	1987	—	24.2	—	4.0
El Salvador (urban)	—	1990	—	41.5	—	14.9
Guatemala	1986–7	1989	66.4	70.4	36.6	42.1
Honduras (urban)	1986	1989	48.7	54.4	21.6	22.7
Jamaica[e]	—	1989	—	12.1	—	1.1
Mexico	1984	1989	16.6	17.7	2.5	4.5
Panama	1979	1989	27.9	31.8	8.4	13.2
Paraguay (Asunción)	1983	1990	13.1	7.6	3.2	0.6
Peru (Lima)[e]	1985–6	1990	31.1	40.5[f]	3.3	10.1[f]
Uruguay (urban)	1981	1989	6.2	5.3	1.1	0.7
Venezuela	1981	1989	4.0	12.9	0.7	3.1

[a] "Poverty" is defined as having an income of $60 per person per month or less.

[b] "Extreme poverty" is defined as having an income of $30 per person per month or less.

[c] or earliest

[d] or latest

[e] Based on consumption data.

[f] Estimate based on extrapolation from 1985–1986 Peru poverty figure, adjusted for changes in poverty due to a fall in per capita income according to national accounts. This adjustment assumes an elasticity of poverty with respect to per capita income of -1.60, as determined by regression analysis.

SOURCE: GEORGE PSACHAROPOULOS et al., *Poverty and Income Distribution in Latin America: The Story of the 1980s* (Washington, D.C.: World Bank, Latin America, and the Caribbean, Technical Department, Regional Studies Program, Report No. 27, Revised June 1993), p. 62.

over time, even though it has increased during periods of severe crisis and unemployment. The most recent statistics of the percentage of individuals in poverty and extreme poverty are presented in table 4.

The ideal approach for making poverty assessments is to formulate a constant basket of commodities (goods and services) that satisfies a set of minimum basic needs with respect to nutrition, housing, clothing, education, and health, that is, a minimum level of composite consumption. The poor are then defined as those individuals whose consumption, or equivalent level of income, is less than the value of the poverty line. A uniform $60 income per person per month in 1985 purchasing power parity (PPP) dollars, that is, having the same purchas-

ing power in all countries, was chosen as the national poverty line for the entire Latin American and Caribbean region. In order to assess levels of extreme poverty, an additional extreme poverty line was chosen at $30 per month in 1985 PPP dollars. Psacharopoulos developed a regional absolute poverty standard that represents a uniform welfare level across all countries and presents the most comprehensive assessment of poverty in Latin America in the 1980s. Poverty was defined in terms of per capita household income because this is the single most identifiable factor for assessing welfare levels across the Latin American and Caribbean region through available household surveys.

The poverty lines for each Latin American country

were assessed as two times the cost of a basic food basket for metropolitan/urban areas, and 1.75 times the cost of a basic food basket in rural areas. The relative income distribution and poverty estimates of the Psacharopoulos study were based on thirty-one household surveys. These surveys covered eighteen countries for various years in the 1980s. Some countries counted only labor income, while less than half of the surveys included in-kind income or the value of owner-occupied housing. None of these surveys included estimates of the welfare benefits derived from the distribution of free educational, health, and other social services to households.

The simplest and most commonly used index of poverty is the headcount ratio, defined as the fraction of the population with income that is less than the poverty line. The headcount ratios for poverty and extreme poverty are presented in table 5. The highest degree of absolute poverty in 1989 was encountered in Guatemala, where the headcount index was 70.4 percent. High degrees of absolute poverty, as measured by a poverty headcount that was about 50 percent of the population, were also found in the urban regions of Bolivia and Honduras. The lowest poverty rates of 3.4 percent and 5.3 percent were observed in Costa Rica and Uruguay (urban), respectively.

A similar picture emerges when the headcount indices of extreme poverty are considered. Again, Bolivia (urban), Guatemala, and Honduras (urban) reveal headcounts of above 20 percent of the population living in extreme poverty. In contrast, the incidence of extreme poverty was the lowest in Argentina (Buenos Aires), Chile, Costa Rica, Jamaica, Paraguay (Asunción), and Uruguay (urban), with less than 2 percent of the population in each of these countries having an income below $30 per month in 1985 PPP dollars in the 1980s.

Estimates of the size and distribution of the total population in Latin America with income that was below the $60-per-month poverty reference in 1980 and 1989 are presented in table 5. In absolute terms, 131 million people in Latin America had a per capita income that was less than the $60-per-month poverty reference defined in the Psacharopoulos study. Poverty, which in 1989 was probably near its highest level for the entire decade, subsequently declined in countries experiencing rapid economic growth. A disproportionately large share (over 70 percent) of the poverty in the region, as compared to their population share (48 percent), was concentrated in Brazil, Peru, and the small, relatively impoverished, countries of Bolivia, El Salvador, Guatemala, Haiti, Honduras, and Nicaragua. More than 45 percent of the poor lived in Brazil, even though it had only one-third of the population in the region. Brazil's high degree of poverty reflected the extreme inequality that has historically characterized its income distribution. Over 9 percent of the poor were concentrated in Peru, and 19 percent in the aforementioned small countries.

The statistics of table 5 also reveal large, but changing, inequalities in regional and intraregional poverty and income distribution. In 1989 the percentage of people living in poverty was more than double in rural regions (53.4 percent), which were generally neglected by government, than in urban regions (22.0 percent). However, because Latin America has become increasingly urbanized, the absolute number of people living in 1989 in poverty in the cities (66.0 million) has exceeded those in the rural areas (64.8 million). Inadequate provision of social and public services by the state, that is, discriminatory mesoeconomics of government, has thus contributed not only to rural but also urban inequalities and poverty.

There exist numerous explanations of the high inequality in the distribution of income, and of persistent

TABLE 5 Changes in Rural and Urban Poverty, 1980–1989 (population in millions)

Year	LAC Region	Total Population	Population in Poverty	Headcount Index (% points)
1980	All	345.4	91.4	26.5
	Urban	227.4	38.2	16.8
	Rural	118.0	53.2	45.1
1989	All	421.4	130.9	31.0
	Urban	300.1	66.0	22.0
	Rural	121.3	64.8	53.4
Change 1980–1989	All	76.0	39.5	+17.0
	Urban	72.7	27.8	+31.0
	Rural	3.3	11.6	+18.4

SOURCE: GEORGE PSACHAROPOULOS et al., *Poverty and Income Distribution in Latin America: The Story of the 1980s* (Washington, D.C.: World Bank, Latin America, and the Caribbean, Technical Department, Regional Studies Program, Report No. 27, Revised June 1993), p. 71.

absolute poverty, in major parts of Latin America. Even though a complete consensus is absent, the following explanatory factors are emphasized by many.

Inequality has been more extreme and poverty more concentrated in Brazil, Peru, Guatemala, and Honduras because of vast differences in the quality of labor among socioeconomic groups. These differences in the quality of labor, which constitute a supply-side problem, have been attributed, in turn, to public policies that have failed to provide minimum levels of social services to the poor, often indigenous, populations. Inequality in labor skills contributed to inequality in income, welfare, and to absolute poverty. In turn, unequal incomes, and unequal consumption of the semipublic services of education, health, and welfare (that is, unequal and unequitable mesoeconomic constitutions) perpetuated inequalities in labor quality.

Inequality has persisted, and poverty has been aggravated also, however, by low, even declining income growth rates that barely have exceeded the growth of population. Low saving and investment levels, as a consequence of domestic policy failures and external factors, have been widely advanced as demand factors preventing the synchronous achievement of growth and equality.

Most of the statistical and related information of this essay was obtained from GEORGE PSACHAROPOULOS, SAMUEL MORLEY, ARIEL FISZBEIN, HAEDUCK LEE, and BILL WOOD, *Poverty and Income Distribution in Latin America, The Story of the 1980s* (Washington, D.C.: The World Bank, Regional Studies Program, Report No. 27, June 1993), which is the most comprehensive study of relative distribution and poverty in Latin America in the 1980s. This study, and consequently also the materials of this entry, has the same limitations as the household surveys on which it is based. The World Bank, the Inter-American Bank, and the Economic Commission for Latin America and the Caribbean have published numerous studies focusing on the relative distribution of income and the magnitude of absolute poverty in Latin America. A comprehensive review of major issues of distribution of income and poverty is found in WORLD BANK, *World Development Report 1990, Poverty, World Development Indicators* (1990), pp. xi, 1–260.

Useful background information is found in MIGUEL URRUTIA, ed., *Long-Term Trends in Latin American Economic Development* (1991), especially chapter 1 by Angus Maddison and chapter 2 by Miguel Urrutia. A detailed examination of relative income distribution in ten Latin American countries is presented in OSCAR ALTIMIR, "Income Distribution and Poverty Through Crisis and Adjustment," in *Latin America's Economic Future*, edited by Graham Bird and Ann Welwege (1994), pp. 265–302.

An introduction to the most recent methodological analysis of the distribution of income is found in COMMISSION OF THE EUROPEAN COMMUNITIES-EUROSTAT, INTERNATIONAL MONETARY FUND (IMF), ORGANISATION FOR ECONOMIC CO-OPERATION AND DEVELOPMENT (OECD), UNITED NATIONS (UN), WORLD BANK, *System of National Accounts, 1993* (Brussels/Luxembourg, New York, Paris, Washington, D.C.: Commission of the European Communities-Eurostat, etc., 1993).

A discussion of the factoral, international, sectoral, social class, and intralabor dimensions of the distribution of income in Chile from Independence to 1973 is found in MARKOS J.

MAMALAKIS, *The Growth and Structure of the Chilean Economy: From Independence to Allende* (1976), esp. chapters 3 and 10.

The role of the sectoral distribution of income is discussed in MARKOS J. MAMALAKIS, "The Theory of Sectoral Clashes," in *The Latin American Research Review* 4, no. 3 (1969): 3–46, and "The Theory of Sectoral Clashes and Coalitions Revisited," in *The Latin American Research Review* 6, no. 3 (1971): 89–126. The notion of mesoeconomics is defined and utilized in MARKOS J. MAMALAKIS, "Sectoral Clashes, Basic Economic Rights and Redemocratization in Chile: A Mesoeconomic Approach," in *Ibero-Americana, Nordic Journal of Latin American Studies* 22, no. 1 (1992), and in MARKOS J. MAMALAKIS, "Sectoral Conflicts in the U.S. and the Soviet Union: A Mesoeconomic Analysis," in *Eastern Economic Journal* 18, no. 4 (Fall 1992).

MARKOS J. MAMALAKIS

See also **Banking; Economic Development; Foreign Debt.**

INCONFIDÊNCIA DOS ALFAIATES (Conspiracy of the Tailors), an unsuccessful plot for independence in Salvador, Bahia, in 1798. The conspiracy was a two-stage response to changing economic and social conditions in Bahia as sugar growing experienced a resurgence within the context of increasing despair among Salvador's poor. Initially, Bahian elites, strongly influenced by French physiocratic thought and the ideas of the French Revolution disseminated by a newly formed Masonic society, the Knights of the Light, sought to lead a movement whose objectives were independence and free trade. As the plot developed, however, it became radicalized as a large number of working-class artisans (especially tailors), enlisted men, slaves, and ex-slaves became involved. The goals of this latter group constituted a radical agenda: an end to racism, equality of opportunity, equality before the law, abolition of slavery, and the establishment of an independent Catholic church. The political goals of the plotters included establishing a republic with leadership open to all, based on ability. Where the initial plot had been socially conservative, the second was a plan for social revolution.

The royal authorities discovered the plot because of the indiscreet actions of some of the participants and through informers. As with the INCONFIDÊNCIA MINEIRA, punishment fell disproportionately on the poorest of the plotters—four of whom were executed. The initial, elite plotters were punished either lightly or not at all. In some cases they were not even questioned.

The plot demonstrated the dichotomy between Brazilian elites, for whom independence did not imply social transformations, and the colony's poor, for whom independence was part of a process of radical social change.

LUIS HENRIQUE DIAS TAVARES, *História da sedição intentada na Bahia em 1798* ("A Conspiração dos Alfaiates") (1975); DONALD RAMOS, "Social Revolution Frustrated: The Conspiracy of the Tailors in Bahia, 1798," in *Luso-Brazilian Review* 13 (Summer 1976): 74–90.

DONALD RAMOS

INCONFIDÊNCIA MINEIRA, a plot for independence involving significant members of the elite of MINAS GERAIS, Brazil, in 1788–1789. Key plotters included Tomás Antônio GONZAGA, the royal judge of Vila Rica, poet, and satirist; Cláudio Manuel da COSTA, a local town councillor, poet, and the first historian of the mining zone; José Álvares Maciel, son of a local tax farmer and a recent graduate of Coimbra; Inácio José de Alvarenga Peixoto, a gold miner and poet; Francisco de Paula Freire de Andrade, the commander of dragoons; Father José da Silva de Oliveira Rolim, a priest, slave trader, and dealer in diamonds; and Joaquim José da SILVA XAVIER (Tiradentes), an ensign (*alferes*) in the dragoons. The plot was never implemented because the governor was informed and was able to arrest most of those involved.

Since the revolt was frustrated, the Inconfidência Mineira is less significant for its effects than for its symbolism and its implications for the end of Portuguese control over Brazil. It is important because key sectors of the elite of Minas Gerais, both lay and ecclesiastical, were involved in a plot to end Portuguese domination. The plot emerged from the alienation of a key segment of the Mineiro elite, which was bound by close familial ties. This alienation grew out of the economic impact of diminishing gold production. Several of the participants in the plot were heavily in debt.

Because of the failure to implement the plot, its objectives are known only through the investigation and questioning conducted by royal authorities. The objectives of the plotters included independence, although the extent of the plans for the new republic is not clear. The plotters sought to extend their efforts beyond Minas Gerais to include Rio de Janeiro and São Paulo. Recognizing the shift in the economic center of Minas Gerais, the plotters sought to move the capital from Vila Rica to São João del Rei and to create Brazil's first university in Vila Rica. The republic would be governed by a written constitution implemented by a parliament in the capital and smaller legislative bodies in each urban center. The plotters planned to establish industries—especially for gunpowder and iron, necessary for defense, and cheap agricultural and mining implements—thereby reviving the economy. There would also be free trade. On social issues the plotters were divided. Some supported the emancipation of slaves born in Brazil as a means of making them supporters of the new republic. Others favored maintaining slavery as an economic necessity. There was agreement on providing incentives for an increase in population. Finally, of great interest to many of the plotters, a pardon of debts owed to the treasury was proposed.

The Portuguese response to the plot reflects the nature of colonial rule. The activists and ideologues of the Inconfidência were brought to trial, but only Silva Xavier was executed. Key backers of the conspiracy were not tried, no doubt out of deference to their high social status. The plot demonstrated that there was sub-stantial dissatisfaction with the colonial status of Minas Gerais, the most powerful captaincy in Brazil. Although a failure, the Inconfidência Mineira demonstrated the existence of republican and nationalist values in a key part of colonial Brazil.

KENNETH R. MAXWELL, *Conflicts and Conspiracies: Brazil and Portugal, 1750–1808* (1973).

DONALD RAMOS

INDEPENDENCE. *See* **Wars of Independence.**

INDEPENDENT REPUBLICS (COLOMBIA), the regions of Sumapaz, Marquetalia, Río Chiquito, El Pato, Guayabero, and Viotá in central Colombia, which were "independent" of state control during the VIOLENCIA of the 1950s. These mountainous frontier zones were the sites of widespread land conflicts in the 1920s and 1930s, intensive mobilization efforts by GAITÁN Liberals and Communists in the 1930s and 1940s, and brutal Conservative repression in the late 1940s and early 1950s. After the ROJAS PINILLA amnesty of 1953, men such as Juan Cruz VARELA, Fermín Charry Rincón ("Charro Negro"), and Manuel Maralunda Vélez ("Tirofijo") helped organize peasant organizations to defend their agricultural and political autonomy. Although Cruz Varela entered the political mainstream in the 1960s, winning election to the House of Representatives, others faced military repression. Under the Plan Lazo, formulated with the assistance of the CENTRAL INTELLIGENCE AGENCY, the Colombian military brutally subdued the regions in the mid-1960s, prompting Tirofijo and others to form the Revolutionary Armed Forces of Colombia (FARC) in April 1966.

GERMÁN GUZMÁN CAMPOS, *La violencia en Colombia: Parte descriptiva* (1962); RICHARD GOTT, *Rural Guerrillas in Latin America*, rev. ed. (1973).

DAVID SOWELL

See also **Colombia: Revolutionary Movements.**

INDIAN POLICY, BRAZIL. The Indian Protection Service (Serviço de Proteção dos Indios—SPI) was founded in 1910 as a government institution specifically dedicated to the tutelage of Brazil's native peoples. In accordance with the positivist philosophy of its founder, Colonel Cândido Mariano da Silva RONDON, its mission was to bring Indians into contact with civilization by peaceful means, protect their lands and lives, and gradually, by education and example, assist their development as farmers and cattle raisers who, as Brazilians, would help to integrate the frontier regions with the rest of the country.

As a young army officer, Rondon had become acquainted with unacculturated Indians when he led expeditions to lay telegraph lines in remote regions of northwest Brazil. With a perspective common to many intellectuals of the time, he saw Indian societies as arrested at an early stage of cultural development, but capable of progressing when aided. At that time tribes were resisting the advance of German farmers who were opening up new lands for settlement in the south, and reports of these hostilities placed in jeopardy the government's plan to attract European immigrants. Many argued that any means necessary, including force, should be used to prevent Indians from standing in the way of this process. However, the legislation that established the SPI embodied Rondon's liberal ideas for acculturation and, while self-determination for tribal Indians was not a consideration, Brazil's Indian policy was perhaps the most enlightened of that of any nation in the early twentieth century.

Over the years, the SPI gained prestige for its success in attracting, pacifying, and eventually settling hostile Indian groups. Typically, a camp would be set up near the territory of the hostile group and "gifts" left along trails; these offerings consisted of knives, steel tools, aluminum pots, and other articles designated to impress the Indians with white technology. At the same time, the members of the expedition would attempt to assure the Indians of their friendly intentions. Even when their advances were met with arrows, the men of the Indian Protection Service were not to retaliate but to follow their motto, "Die if need be, but never kill." Eventually the Indians' curiosity would overcome their fears, and unarmed groups would venture out of the forest and accept face to face the gifts offered.

Once the Indians had become dependent on manufactured goods, they tended to settle near the government Indian post. Unfortunately, these new relations with the outside world were often fatal. Commonly 50 to 80 percent of the members of a newly contacted tribe succumbed within the first year to introduced infectious diseases. According to a 1970 text by Darcy Ribeiro, eighty-eight Indian tribes disappeared in the Brazilian Amazon between 1900 and 1957.

Although in principle one aim of the SPI was to preserve for the Indians the lands they occupied, in practice much of it was claimed by settlers once hostilities were no longer a threat. Government resources, which were freely expended for pacification, tended to dry up after the Indians were settled. As a result, the government agent assigned to an Indian post had little power to assist or protect the Indians.

As Rondon aged, the influence of his humanistic philosophy on the SPI grew weaker. The dedicated workers that Rondon had trained were replaced by military administrators for whom economic rather than humanitarian considerations were primary. The agency became increasingly corrupt and demoralized. In 1967 the Brazilian minister of the interior ordered an investigation of SPI practices, which resulted in a 20-volume report detailing crimes committed against Indians by SPI

personnel at all levels, and painting a shocking picture of corruption, greed, and sadism. When the results of the investigation were made public, they were widely reported in both the foreign and Brazilian press. After the scandal broke, the SPI was disbanded and replaced by the National Indian Foundation (FUNAI). However, the policy in defense of Indian rights initiated by the first governing board of FUNAI lasted only two years.

In 1970 the civilian president of FUNAI was succeeded by General Oscar Jerônimo Bandeira de Melo, a military man dedicated to carrying out the aggressive development policies of the authoritarian military regime headed by President Emílio Garrastazú Medici. The Indian policy instituted at this time was directed toward the rapid integration of native groups into the national economy and class structure of Brazil. The government saw FUNAI's mission as that of a buffer organization, providing limited assistance and protection to Indians, while at the same time making sure they did not impede the government's development plans.

The legal status of tribal Indians in Brazil is that of minors under tutelage. Indian reservations are not communal tribal property but federal lands held in trust for the Indians, with FUNAI acting as administrator. During the last twenty years, a network of roads has opened up the interior of Brazil to settlement and economic development, putting great pressure on Indian lands. The Indians have resisted these incursions, which has sometimes led to violent confrontations. The weak and ambiguous role of FUNAI made it distrusted by the Indians and probably led directly to increased Indian efforts, assisted by nongovernmental organizations, to organize in defense of their own interests.

By the early 1980s some Indian groups were growing in political sophistication as well as determination to preserve their distinct identity and traditions. As international concern about deforestation and environmental destruction in the Amazon increased, Indians found allies in organizations supporting conservation and the rights of tribal peoples. FUNAI came under pressure to expedite the official demarcation of Indian reservations, even as some powerful groups within the country, including the military, contended that granting large territories to Indians undermined Brazil's need to develop its resources, and constituted a threat to national security.

FUNAI has neither the resources nor prestige to arbitrate these positions. Essentially, the question is whether Brazil as a society is willing to accept the rights of its Indians, which make up less than 1 percent of the population, to maintain their cultural distinctiveness and to determine the course of their development.

DAVID STAUFFER, "The origin and establishment of Brazil's Indian Service: 1889–1910 (Ph.D. diss., University of Texas at Austin, 1955); DARCY RIBEIRO, A política indigenista brasileira (1962), and Os Índios e a civilização (1970); SHELTON H. DAVIS, Victims of the Miracle: Development and the Indians of Brazil (1977); ROBERTO CARDOZO DE OLIVEIRA, " 'Plural Society' and

Cultural Pluralism in Brazil," in *The Prospects for Plural Societies*, edited by David Maybury-Lewis (1982); DAVID PRICE, "Overtures to the Nambiquara," in *Natural History* 93 (October 1984), and *Before the Bulldozer: The Nambiquara Indians and the World Bank* (1989); DAVID MAYBURY-LEWIS, "Brazil's Significant Minority," in *The Wilson Quarterly* 14 (Summer 1990): 33–42; ANTÔNIO CARLOS DE SOUSA LIMA, "On Indigenism and Nationality in Brazil," and DAVID MAYBURY-LEWIS, "Becoming Indian in Lowland South America," in *Nation States and Indians in Latin America*, edited by Greg Urban and Joel Sherzer (1991).

NANCY M. FLOWERS

See also **Brazil: Organizations; Positivism.**

INDIAN SLAVERY AND FORCED LABOR. *See* **Slavery.**

INDIANISMO, a term used in studies of Brazilian literature to refer to the use of Indian characters and themes. In this type of literature, writers have combined aesthetic and ideological goals. In chronological order, the most significant examples are found in the mid-1800s with José de ALENCAR's romantic representation of an idealized inhabitant of the New World (e.g., *Iracema*, 1865); in the 1920s with the modernist Mário de ANDRADE's humorous fictional view of Brazilian national identity (e.g., *Macunaíma*, 1928; Eng. trans. 1976); and in the late twentieth century with Darcy RIBEIRO, whose novels incorporate an anthropological approach (e.g, *Maíra*, 1976).

An all-encompassing study is DAVID BROOKSHAW, *Paradise Betrayed: Brazilian Literature of the Indian* (1988).

PEDRO MALIGO

INDIANS

EARLY HUMAN SETTLEMENT

The term "Indian" applies to the indigenous peoples of North, Middle, and South America. The name was coined by COLUMBUS, who called the inhabitants of the West Indies "Indians" in the belief that he had reached the East Indies on his journey of exploration. In comparison with the rest of the Western Hemisphere, Latin America has always contained the largest number of Indians. At the time of first European contact, from 89 to 95 percent of the Indian population was in areas that later became Latin America. In spite of the devastation of Indian populations caused by European contact, the proportion of Indians in Latin American countries is still about the same. In 1978, 92 percent of the American Indian population was in Latin America. Today, the countries of Latin America contain about 26 million Indians. The following descriptions apply to these cultures at the time of first contact, unless otherwise noted.

Human beings came to the Americas rather late in their evolutionary history, at a time when modern humans, *Homo sapiens*, were fully developed. Controversy surrounds the effort to determine the time of their first arrival. When glaciers covered Canada and held enough water to lower the sea level, hunters occupied a large land area, called Beringia, that connected Siberia and Alaska. About 14,000 years ago the glaciers began to melt and the sea began to rise. Some of the hunters made the difficult trip southward, probably between the receding ice sheets. When they reached southern Canada, they found a rich environment filled with many large late-Pleistocene game animals such as the mammoth and giant sloth. The population of these post-Pleistocene hunters increased rapidly.

Tantalizing, sparse, and scattered evidence exists for even earlier human populations. Some scholars consider the evidence to be inconclusive; others are convinced that there were earlier populations. Radiocarbon techniques have produced dates for these earlier indications between 33,000 and 14,000 years before the present (B.P.), long before the arrival of the post-Pleistocene big-game hunters. The rarity of the earlier material, possible carbon contamination, indirect association with humans, and a lack of an understandable cultural pattern have allowed conservative scholars to reject a date earlier than 11,000 B.P. for the arrival of humans in the New World. Those who favor an earlier arrival point to the radiocarbon dates and to the implausibility of a very rapid growth and spread of populations after 10,000 B.P.

Migrations through the central ice-free corridor of Canada would have been difficult. Although a long coastal route was open at other times, the earliest cultures do not show a level of technology that could have exploited a coastal environment; however, culture could have regressed after arrival. As of the early 1990s, the exact route and time of the human entry into the New World were still unknown. Very possibly there were several migrations at different times and places. What is certain is that people came from northeastern Asia sometime, perhaps a long time, before 11,000 B.P.

The early hunting and gathering Indian cultures eventually evolved into a wide variety of different cultures. The sequence in which new cultures evolved was similar to that followed in the Old World. Intensive gathering and fishing was followed by incipient agriculture. Eventually agriculture reached the levels of productivity that permitted large, permanent, year-round settlements. In some areas, villages eventually amalgamated into chiefdoms and states, the legitimacy of which was maintained by religion. Conflict between villages, chiefdoms, and states raged during prehistoric times, and the more powerful native states conquered the weaker groups.

CULTURAL DEVELOPMENT

The major factor influencing the development of Indian cultures in Latin America was the natural ecology. Each ecosystem had different natural resources, different food-producing potentials, and different obstacles to

Latin American Indians

(Yaqui)

Gulf of Mexico

Yucatán

1

2

4

3

Caribbean Sea

Circum-Caribbean

Atlantic Ocean

Orinoco

5

Guiana Highlands

Casiquiare R.

Japurá

Negro

Amazon

Marajó Island

Coari

Tapajós

(Tupinambá)

Purus

A m a z o n

B a s i n

Brazilian Highlands

Coastal Brazil

Central Andean Highlands (Incas)

(Tupinambá)

(Payaguá)

Pacific Ocean

Gran Chaco

(Abipón)

(Guaraní)

6

Pampas

(Puelche)

7

Atlantic Ocean

Patagonia (Tehuelche)

750 miles
1205 kilometers

Tierra del Fuego (Ona)

Mesoamerica

1 Central Highlands
  (Nahua, Tarascans & Otomi)
2 (Zapotec & Mixtec)
3 (Highland Maya)
4 (Lowland Maya)
5 Orinoco Basin
6 Southern Andes
  (Araucanian & Mapuche)
7 Chilean Archipelago

communication. All of these factors led to the evolution of different Indian cultures in different parts of Latin America.

Some of the earliest traits that were later incorporated into Indian civilization, such as ceremonial architecture and towns, first appeared along the coasts of the Atlantic and Pacific oceans. Coastal Peru was host to very early village life. There, towns built around temples appeared after 4000 B.P. Permanent villages also appeared very early (7500 B.P.) along the lake shore in the Valley of Mexico. This has led to speculation that the extra food input from sea and lake resources permitted the earliest development of sedentary life and ceremonial activity. The OLMEC culture on the Gulf coast of Mexico produced temples and giant stone heads between 3000 and 2400 B.P. The earliest political systems without urban centers were probably governed by chiefs who may have been related to each other.

The most complex and advanced Indian civilizations eventually arose in the cool highlands of central Mexico and the central Andes. The hallmarks of civilization are intensive cultivation, class and economic stratification, cities, and the state. The two highland zones, central Mexico and the Andes, kept pace with each other, so that it is impossible to say that one or the other was the leader in the development of Indian civilizations.

One should not think of the cities of MESOAMERICA and the Andes as paralleling the great commercial metropolises of Europe. They were places from which elites governed an essentially rural population that lived in smaller towns and villages. A long growing season, good irrigation potentials, and few impediments to local transportation accelerated the evolution of these elaborate highland cultures. The high Andean mountain ranges made long-distance travel difficult. However, Robert Carneiro suggests that the confinements of the mountain ranges pushed the growing populations toward developing more complex and integrated social systems in order to maintain peace within a prosperous local area.

The civilized region that included all of Mexico south of the Mesa del Norte, Guatemala, and parts of Honduras is called Mesoamerica. Civilization was established there by A.D. 1. The area around Mexico City, where the TEOTIHUACÁN, TOLTEC, and AZTEC civilizations developed, was a catalyst to civilization elsewhere in Mesoamerica, which today is the home to millions of Indians. Classified by language in 1980, the largest groups of modern Indians in Mesoamerica are the Highland MAYAS, with 3.934 million speakers in Mexico and Guatemala; the Aztecs, today called NAHUA, with 1 million speakers; the Lowland Mayas, with around 555,000 speakers; the ZAPOTECS, with 283,000; the MIXTECS, with 233,000; and the OTOMÍ, with around 221,000. There are over fifty other Indian groups in Mesoamerica.

The development of civilization in the Andean area paralleled that in Mesoamerica. A religiopolitical system supported by sea resources got its start along the Peruvian coast around 4000 B.P. Sculpture and monumental architecture first appeared in CHAVÍN culture around 3000 B.P. Urbanization occurred after 2400 B.P. on the southern coast of Peru. Nazca and MOCHE cultures of the Peruvian coast produced fine textiles and pottery. Copper, gold, and silver were worked by a variety of techniques, including lost-wax casting, during the great florescence of the First Intermediate period (2250 to 1400 B.P.). The quality of the weaving in the Andean cultures was not surpassed elsewhere in the hemisphere. Conquest and violent war were probably the rule among the early Andean states as they were in Mesoamerica. The last Andean state, the Inca, was the largest, spreading northward into Ecuador and southward into Chile. Today, millions of Indian people speak the Quechua language that was spread by the INCA conquests. To the east, however, the forested *montaña* region stopped the spread of Andean civilization into the Amazonian basin, to which it was ill adapted. Modern Andean cultures, for example, AYMARA in Bolivia and Quechua in Peru, are numerous. Each has its unique qualities.

Along the western Sierra Madre of Mexico a number of farming and hunting cultures formed a bridge between central Mexico and the southwest United States. The Toltec expansion probably stimulated cultural advancement in this region during the Postclassic period. Today, the Tepehuan, HUICHOL, Tarahumara, YAQUI, and Mayo are examples of these cultures.

In the desert of Baja California and in the desert of the Mesa del Norte of Mexico, conditions were too dry to support agriculture, and so the Indian people there relied on hunting and gathering for subsistence. Living in small bands, these groups were derided as primitives by the civilized people to the south.

The hearth of Indian culture in the Caribbean area was the northern coast of South America. Large chiefdoms that integrated whole regions had formed by the time of the European arrival. The chiefdoms were varied and shared traits with Andean, Mesoamerican, and tropical forest areas. They can be separated into warlike conquering chiefdoms of the northern Andes and the religiously organized chiefdoms of the Greater Antilles and Venezuela. Large groups such as the Chibcha (also known as the MUISCA) disappeared under the weight of contact, and the Caribbean Indians today are composed of smaller ethnic units. Today, in northern South America, white cattle ranchers continue to take lands from Indians, such as the riverine hunting and gathering Cuiba of Colombia. The surviving Indians occupy ecological niches, such as those created by rivers, swamps, and forests, which are unattractive to commercial ranching.

CULTURAL TRANSITION

Indian culture spread into the Caribbean islands from Northern South America. Current theory based on the linguistic evidence postulates that Arawak-speaking groups first settled the islands. Following the South

American heritage, they formed large villages and organized under chiefs. Later, groups of more warlike CARIB speakers moved into the Lesser Antilles chain from the south and pressured the Arawaks. The TAINO Arawaks controlled the large Caribbean islands when Columbus arrived. Europeans overran the islands, and Indians fell to the main forces of the conquest: disease, warfare, and enslavement.

The agricultural potentials of the tropical forests of Latin America vary from region to region and within regions in small, significant microecological zones. The tropical forests of southern Mexico and Central America have high agricultural potentials. Within the forests of the southern Yucatán, Belize, and the Petén area of Guatemala, the Maya devised methods of intensive cultivation that allowed them to generate the surpluses needed to support an elite class. The agricultural potentials of the South American tropical forest are lower on the average, but vary widely. Complex urban civilizations such as the Maya never evolved there; however multivillage chiefdoms did arise in the agriculturally rich Amazonian flood-plain zone called the *várzea*. Chiefdoms flourished at Marajó Island and Santarém on the Amazon, where the people constructed large mounds and crafted fine ceramics before A.D. 1500.

The tropical forests of the Amazon and Orinoco basins of South America contain a variety of microecologies. The waterways of the two rivers connect via the Casiquiare River and Río Negro. Tributaries can be roughly divided into blackwater, clearwater, and whitewater rivers. The blackwater rivers are acidic, oxygen deprived, and sterile; they are notoriously low in agricultural potential. The clearwater rivers have more oxygen, and the whitewater rivers contain oxygen, suspended silt, and minerals that nourish the landscape. In blackwater regions, Indian populations such as the Makú are dispersed. The nutrient-poor acidic soils favor the cultivation of a form of MANIOC from which the Indians must remove poison before eating it. In the blackwater regions, Indians rely on hunting and fishing for much of their food.

In contrast, the whitewater rivers, such as the Amazon, nourish the *várzea* flood zone, which ranges from 10 to over 100 miles in width. The *várzea* was able to support Indian cultures with multivillage chiefs who raided the forest villages for slaves. Aboriginal occupation of the *várzea* was as early as that of coastal Peru and Ecuador, and the earliest pottery appears in the *várzea*. *Várzea* Indians, such as the Omagua, settled on the Amazon from the Japurá River to about halfway between the Coarí and the Purus rivers. They raised abundant quantities of manioc, MAIZE, beans, and peppers. The Omagua also kept large numbers of turtles in pens.

Another populous group, the Tapajós Indians, occupied the region around Santarém at the confluence of the Tapajós River, which now bears their name. Their principal crop was maize. Manioc and fruits were also cultivated. There was a large capital town that contained enough warriors to frighten the Portuguese. Because the waterways were the first routes of European incursion into Amazonia, the *várzea* culture pattern was destroyed within 150 years of the Conquest.

Most of the Amazonian Indians now live in the regions away from the largest rivers. Their survival depends on a wide variety of adaptations, including nomadic hunting and gathering, village agriculture, and fishing. Because tropical forest crops are low in protein, all groups rely on hunting or fishing to some extent. The forest Indians are generally warlike. Some, such as the SHUAR of Ecuador, successfully resisted white incursions into their territory, but most Amazonian natives suffered greatly after contact with Europeans. Their traditional warfare, often exacerbated by the pressures of white contact, pitted village against village. There was little pre-contact tribal solidarity. Since the 1940s, however, Amazonian native groups have successfully organized themselves to bring their problems and interests to the attention of South American countries and to the world.

To the north of the Amazon plain are the Guiana highlands. Smaller rivers have eroded the Guiana shield to produce a low, tropical forest environment. The Indians who live there were pushed back from the coast by white settlers. They now live in settlements of from forty to two hundred people. Their way of life differs little from that of the other Indian people of the tropical forests, except for a greater prevalence of matrilineal kinship systems.

A warlike group of Indians, collectively known as the TUPINAMBÁ, who lived along the coasts of Brazil, exploited the resources of the sea as well as those of the forest. In the past the Tupinambá were known for their constant warfare, revenge raids, and ritual CANNIBALISM. Villages were mutually hostile. Captives taken in raids were allowed to live, and even marry, in the captors' village until they were ritually sacrificed and eaten. Only after the Tupinambá had been embroiled in raids to capture slaves for the Europeans and had been enlisted as allies in the wars between the Portuguese and the French was their warlike nature known. Their patterns of violence, therefore, do not represent a pristine adaptation.

At the time of the Conquest, GUARANÍ Indians occupied the region from the Atlantic coast westward to the Paraguay River. They were related linguistically and culturally to the Tupinambá to the east. The Guaraní became involved with the Spanish colonists, who organized them in a defense against the warlike Guaycurú and PAYAGUÁ of the Chaco to the west. An intermingling of Guaraní and Spanish cultures occurred in the colonial ENCOMIENDAS (grant of Indians), from which a unique, rural Paraguayan culture emerged. Although Paraguayans are racially mixed with the original Guaraní and have retained their language, the present culture is not an aboriginal adaptation; yet, it derives a strong, independent national image from the historical involvement with the Guaraní.

Often not distinguished from the Amazon River basin, the Brazilian highlands are a geological shield similar to the Guiana shield. A region of dry, grassy upland areas interspersed with gallery forests, it is home to Indian cultures that differ somewhat from Amazonian groups; many are GÊ speakers. The Indians of the Brazilian highlands are essentially farmers who do not exploit river resources or use canoes. Some authorities believe they were originally hunters and gatherers who adapted tropical horticulture to the gallery forests. They have complex social organizations with a number of kinship divisions, moieties, age grades, and associations.

Within the forests of South America, between the more settled groups, lived other nomadic people who relied on hunting, gathering, and fishing for subsistence. Most of these people occupied regions inhospitable to agriculture. Much of their territory was swampy or was fed by blackwater rivers. The Macú hunt and gather in the blackwater regions of northern Brazil. Other groups, such as the Cuiba of Colombia and the Guató of Paraguay, move by canoe and exploit fish and other aquatic resources.

The Gran Chaco is climatically intermediate between the tropical forests to the north and the grassy pampas to the south. There, Indians hunted, gathered, fished, and practiced a limited seasonal agriculture. Society was organized primarily at the level of nomadic bands. The Chaco has a greater plant wealth than the tropical forest, and the bands of different groups, such as the Zamuco, Mataco, Tapieté, and Lengua, utilized different plants. The degree to which a certain resource was exploited was related to the migration pattern.

Raiding in the Chaco existed before the arrival of the Europeans. After acquiring horses from the Europeans, some Indians became particularly fierce nomadic raiders. They attacked other Indians and white settlers at long distances. Horse nomads like the ABIPÓN, MOCOBÍ, and MBAYÁ abandoned agriculture after the Conquest and obtained their plant food by looting other people's crops. The Chaco was dominated by these raiding Indians in the nineteenth century.

Numerous ARAUCANIAN populations occupied central Chile, where a Mediterranean climate favored agriculture. The Araucanians were village-oriented, but they lacked the state structure and urbanization of the Conquest states of the Andes to the north. They fed themselves with irrigated agriculture and animal husbandry. Food was obtained from guinea pigs and llamas. Llamas were used also for wool, bride price, and transportation. When threatened, villages could organize under a war chief to resist conquest, as they did under LAUTARO in the sixteenth century.

The Incas were unable to conquer the numerous Araucanian MAPUCHE and Huilliche. The Spanish fared no better, although they tried for three centuries. Since 1882, the Mapuche have been living at peace with the whites. Although the Mapuche and Huilliche now live on reservations, the Mapuche are still fiercely independent and they celebrate their five hundred years of resistance to foreign rule.

The cool grasslands of the pampas and Patagonia were unsuited to the aboriginal style of agriculture and, therefore, were sparsely populated. The nomadic Indians of the pampas, such as the TEHUELCHE, Puelche, QUERANDI, and Charrua, subsisted by hunting and gathering. After the arrival of the horse, Indians caught RHEA and GUANACO from horseback with *bolas* (a throwing weapon made of thongs with weights at their ends that entangles the legs of the animal) and killed them with spears. The horse increased predatory raiding, and Indians came together in larger nomadic bands. This process was similar to the cultural evolution of the Indians of the Great Plains of the United States.

Along the coast of southern Chile lies a long, windswept chain of islands known as the Chilean Archipelago. The islands and the fiord-cut mainland are covered by a dense forest that is unsuitable for agriculture except for a few areas in the north. Indians, such as the YAHGAN, subsisted mainly on sea resources. Women provided the majority of the food by diving for shellfish on the sea bottom; men hunted sea mammals and birds. The Indian bands were nomadic and moved by canoe along the rugged coast.

The lifeways of the ONA Indians of the Tierra del Fuego were similar to those of the people of Patagonia. They had a nomadic hunting and gathering life. Patrilineal bands claimed hunting rights in a well-defined territory. Young men and young women underwent separate initiation rites.

EUROPEAN COLONIZATION TO THE PRESENT
The European colonization of Latin America had a devastating impact on Indian populations. The primary effect was a dramatic loss of life due to European diseases to which the Indians had no immunity. Added to that were the military campaigns waged against Indians and various schemes to make them work for the colonists. All of this hardship reduced Indian populations drastically. Over 90 percent of the contact Indian population was lost. Indians survived best when they maintained independent communities removed from the areas of colonial exploitation. Catholic missionaries and the Spanish crown gave them some protection. Indian populations have only recently returned to pre-Conquest levels. Now, they have to contend with national politics controlled by large majorities of non-Indians.

The general situation of Indians today varies from country to country and from region to region within a country. Latin American nations are not as prosperous as their North American neighbors, and the attention they pay to Indian populations often depends on how much political influence the Indians are able to muster. Legal killing of Indians has disappeared, but some countries neglect Indian welfare. In Paraguay, Aché hunters and gatherers have been almost exterminated through neglect. Tropical forest dwellers have fared the worst, be-

Leaders of Brazil's indigenous peoples meet at Global Forum in Rio de Janeiro to treat with the government of Brazil, June 1992. AP / WIDE WORLD.

cause the lack of communication in these frontier zones makes it possible to commit even violent crimes without being punished. Because the settlers are usually better armed than the Indians, the Indians suffer. In Brazil and Venezuela, a standoff between liberal pro-Indianists and conservative proexpansionists has muted effective action to protect forest groups. Only in the 1980s have some Amazonian Indians, such as the Kayapó, organized to resist the colonization of their territory. There was a dramatic reversal of Indian policy in 1991 in Brazil, when forest reserves were set aside for the YANOMAMI in the northern blackwater region, the Kayapó in the Brazilian highlands, and seventy-one other groups. The needs of highland Indians in Mexico, Bolivia, and Ecuador have been incorporated more successfully into national political thinking because of their large numbers and their participation in land-reform movements. The Instituto Nacional Indigenista of the Secretaría de Educación Pública of Mexico is an Indian agency that is actively engaged in developing Indian areas. There are movements by Indian groups to organize themselves for adequate representation and political action. Among others, the following groups were in existence in 1991: União das Nações Indígenas (Brazil), Confederación de Nacionalidades Indígenas del Ecuador, Honduran Advisory Council for the Development of Autochthonous Ethnic People, Sejekto (La Voz del Indio, Costa Rica), Consejo de Todas las Tierras (Mapuche, Chile), Asociación Nacional Indígena de El Salvador (ANIS), Consejo de Organizaciones Mayas de Guatemala (COMG), and Frente Independiente de Pueblos Indios (FIPI, Mexico).

The many volumes of the following two handbooks are a major source of information: ROBERT WAUCHOPE, ed., *Handbook*

of Middle American Indians (1964–1976), and JULIAN H. STEWARD, ed., *Handbook of South American Indians* (1946–1950). A general survey is JULIAN H. STEWARD and LOUIS C. FARON, *Native Peoples of South America* (1979). Environmental influences are discussed in ROBERT L. CARNIERO, "Slash-and-burn Cultivation among the Kuikuru and Its Implications for Cultural Development in the Amazon Basin," in *The Evolution of Horticultural Systems in Native South America: Causes and Consequences; A Symposium*, edited by Johannes Wilbert (1961); BETTY MEGGERS, *Amazonia: Man and Culture in a Counterfeit Paradise* (1971), and RAYMOND B. HAMES and WILLIAM T. VICKERS, eds., *Adaptive Responses of Native Amazonians* (1983). A journal devoted entirely to studies of American Indian cultures is *América Indígena*. The history of the Brazilian Indians is given in JOHN HEMMING, *Red Gold: The Conquest of the Brazilian Indians* (1978), and *Amazon Frontier: The Defeat of the Brazilian Indians* (1987).

JAMES DOW

INDIGENISMO. Alone among the European colonizers in the New World, the Hispanic nations, beginning in the early years following the invasion of America, showed an interest in the cultures of the native peoples and tried to defend them against the tyranny of the majority of the oppressors. These advocates of the Indians were not always perceptive, accurate, or effective and, for much of the time since 1492, were a tiny minority of the dominant class, but their impact on our knowledge of Amerindians and on present-day attitudes has been far greater than their numbers.

Bishop Bartolomé de LAS CASAS (1474–1566) and Fray Bernardino de SAHAGÚN (ca. 1499–1590), the most famous of the early indigenists, were very different in character and purpose. Las Casas was an *encomendero*, cleric, and above all a polemicist who hoped to influence imperial policy toward the natives. He wrote historical propaganda that emphasized Spanish cruelty and the destruction of the native population. In a larger sense, far ahead of his time, he was an advocate of the self-determination of peoples. Sahagún, one of the fathers of modern anthropology, used native informants to compile inventories of Mexican Indian history and culture, with a view to recording them in the face of extinction, and in the hope of demonstrating their civilization and importance.

After the first generation much of the writing on Native American culture came from Europe itself. Reflections from afar on Native American customs, on their supposed barbarism, humanity, or nobility, were frequent from the time of Michel Montaigne (1533–1592) to François Chateaubriand (1768–1848), a founder of romanticism, whose *Atala* (1801) and *René* (1802) gave life to the image of the exotic "noble savage."

In the colonies themselves the crown continued to take its role seriously and treated its subject Indian population paternalistically. The RECOPILACIÓN DE LEYES DE INDIAS (1681) is a monument to these concerns. With the expulsion of Spanish government in the 1820s this protection was removed, and few nineteenth-century leaders of the new nations demonstrated great interest in their Indian peoples. Under various liberal regimes concentrated attacks on Indian landholdings in the name of laissez-faire free enterprise and individual ownership brought spirited resistance, but most sympathetic commentaries on the plight of native peoples came from foreign travelers. Some elite authors continued to write romantic tales of noble savages, leading to such paradoxical novels as *María* (1867) by Jorge Isaacs (1837–1895), a Colombian landowner.

It was from literature, however, that much of the first wave of protest came against the modern social conditions of the Indians of Spanish America. Clorinda MATTO DE TURNER (1852–1909), a Peruvian novelist, published *Aves sin nido* (1889; Birds Without a Nest), which, as the title suggests, laments the marginal, poverty-stricken lives of her Indian compatriots. Another pioneer was the Bolivian Alcides ARGUEDAS (1879–1946), whose volume of essays, *Pueblo enferno* (1909), while showing some racist and fatalistic overtones, deplored the treatment of his country's Indian majority. His later novel, *Raza de bronce* (1919; Race of Bronze), was more positive.

The egalitarian and revolutionary political movements of the early twentieth century were the true parents of the large intellectual forces that came to be called *indigenismo*; it was of particular importance in the nations with large indigenous populations, especially Peru, and, even more, Mexico. In Peru intellectual leaders such as José Carlos MARIÁTEGUI (1895–1930) sought to revive interest in the socialism that he perceived in Inca politics and statecraft. The American Popular Revolutionary Alliance (APRA), a Pan-American party, suggested that

the subcontinent be named *Indoamerica*. Becoming largely Peruvian, APRA gave further emphasis to the problem of how to integrate the Indian into the Peruvian mainstream. In literature the pro-Indian novel turned to realism. Its most famous author was, perhaps, Ciro ALEGRÍA (1909–1967), whose *El mundo es ancho y ajeno* (1941; Broad and Alien Is the World) achieved an international reputation. His Ecuadorian pioneering counterpart was Jorge ICAZA (1906–1978), given to even harsher realism in his depiction of injustice. His most famous novel was *Huasipungo* (1934; Peon's Smallholding).

In Mexico *indigenismo* was part of the MEXICAN REVOLUTION of 1910–1917, and it became part of government policy under President Lázaro CÁRDENAS (1934–1940). *Indigenistas* such as José VASCONCELOS (1882–1959) held government office, and his *Indología* (1927; Indology) presented ways in which Indians could be brought into national life via education, economic development, and legal change. Since the time of Cárdenas pro-Indian policies have been part of government programs and rhetoric in Mexico, although critics claim that this aspect of central government has been paternalistic, hypocritical, and ineffective.

Many scholars consider the cultural by-products of the political movement to be of at least equal importance. Archaeologists and anthropologists began to delve into the pre-Columbian past, and to reconstruct its monuments. A brilliant series of muralists and painters, such as Dr. ATL (1875–1964), Diego RIVERA (1886–1957), and José Clemente OROZCO (1883–1949), depicted Indian life both past and present; attacked clerical, military, upper-class, and North American exploiters of the Indian; and praised the Mexican Revolution. All were politically radical and achieved fame outside their homeland. Similar movements appeared in architecture, philosophy, and literature.

Mexican *indigenismo* spread to other countries with large Indian populations, although once again its cultural results were more impressive than the political ones. In Guatemala, where vast numbers of Indians were killed by the army and government in the 1980s–1990s, a series of brilliant folklorists and novelists made the world aware of their plight in an earlier age. Miguel Ángel ASTURIAS (1899–1974) won the Nobel Prize for literature, and among his novels *Hombres de maíz* (1949; Men of Maize) is perhaps the most Indianist. Similar movements arose in the 1940s and 1950s in Ecuador, Bolivia, and Paraguay.

By the 1960s *indigenismo* had suffered serious internal divisions and was under outside attack. Within the movement there was great debate over incorporation versus autonomy. Those who struggled to preserve "Indianness" accused those who sought to push economic development and incorporation of lack of empathy or even genocide, while the developmentally minded accused their opponents of romanticism and racism. The movement was also condemned for its paternalism and lack of results. Government programs and philosophical and fictional works were criticized for being from outside Indian society, about Indians rather than by Indians. Little success could be expected, these critics said, until Indians took charge of their own political, economic, and cultural futures.

Those criticisms appear to have had results. Novelists of importance such as José María ARGUEDAS (1911–1969) of Peru wrote in both Spanish and Quechua and tried to view Indian society, not only as an object of exploitation and a project for development, but also as an intrinsically interesting series of cultures. Today many Indian authors publish in their native languages. Nevertheless, the direction of the *indigenista* novel is diffused. Realism has given way to magical realism in some authors, and the Indian presence is hard to discern at times.

In politics changes have been more dramatic. Indian leaders now reject many of the ideas coming from government or outsiders and are forming pressure groups and cooperatives. Some claim that the non-Indian *indigenistas* from the past assigned the status of Indian to subordinate groups as one way of perpetuating their dependency and oppression. Others believe in electoral politics or popular revolution as the best methods for achieving just shares of national wealth and social and economic opportunities. *Indigenismo* as it was in the 1930s and 1940s has given way to other forces.

LEWIS HANKE, *The Spanish Struggle for Justice in the Conquest of America* (1949); ALFONSO CASO, *Indigenismo* (1958); HECTOR DÍAZ POLANCO, et al., *Indigenismo, modernización y marginalidad* (1979); EDGARDO J. PANTIGOSO, *La rebelión contra el indigenismo y la afirmación del pueblo en el mundo de José María Arguedas* (1981); GAILE MC GREGOR, *The Nobel Savage in the New World Garden: Toward a Syntactics of Place* (1988); ANTHONY PAGDEN, *The Fall of Natural Man: The American Indian and the Origins of Comparative Ethnology* (1982); STELIO CRO, *The Noble Savage: Allegory of Freedom* (1990); OMAR RODRÍGUEZ, *Contribución a la crítica del indigenismo* (1991); GREG URBAN and JOEL SCHERZER, eds., *Nation-States and Indians in Latin America* (1991).

MURDO J. MACLEOD

See also **Literature.**

INDIGO. The cultivation of indigo (*tinta añil*) in the New World dates to pre-Hispanic times. The Indians of northern Central America harvested wild indigo plants, called *xiquilite*, which they traded extensively and used as a rich blue dye for textiles.

During the late sixteenth century, the Spaniards domesticated the cultivation of indigo in Central America and established indigo plantations in Yucatán and along the fertile Pacific coasts of present-day El Salvador, Guatemala, and Nicaragua. Spaniards exported their first indigo in 1576, when a shipload was sent from Nicaragua to New Spain, where it was used in Mexico's nascent textile industry. By 1600, indigo had replaced cacao—until that time Central America's most profitable commodity—as the leading export. In the early seventeenth century, indigo also became the leading source of hard currency for the isthmus.

Indigo was highly valued in the Old World, where it supplanted more expensive blue dyes from the Far East and inferior dyes produced from woad in northern Europe. From 1580 to 1620 the Central American indigo industry thrived. *Añileros* (indigo planters) employed Indians for harvesting and processing the plant. Because the work was difficult and dangerous (extended contact with the toxins present in the indigo plant often proved fatal, as did constant exposure to the swamp waters used to extract dye from the plants), the industry was limited by the size of the indigenous labor supply. By the mid-seventeenth century, the indigo industry had stagnated. In the late seventeenth century, however, a resurgence in the size of the Indian population allowed the industry to expand again, at which time African slaves were imported to augment the labor force.

By 1635, San Vicente, El Salvador, had become the hub of the indigo trade, although other important centers were located in Guatemala and Nicaragua. The locus of the trade later shifted to Sonsonate, El Salvador, once the center of the colonial cacao trade, and to Guatemala. In addition to the European trade, Central American indigo also made its way to Mexico and Peru.

Indigo remained the most important export of the Kingdom of Guatemala throughout the colonial period. The industry reached its peak during the second half of the eighteenth century, when the expanding textile industry in northern Europe created a significant demand for the rich blue hue. The "free trade" economic policies of the Spanish Bourbons in the eighteenth century also enhanced the indigo trade, and in 1782 *añileros* formed an Indigo Growers Society based in Guatemala City. By the last years of the colonial period, indigo generated more than 2 million pesos worth of profits per year.

By the last decades of the eighteenth century, however, indigo exports from Central America began to decline, although the dye continued to bring heavy profits for planters in South Carolina, Venezuela, and the East Indies. In the mid-eighteenth century, Brazil's reformer, the Marquis de POMBAL, introduced indigo production to Rio de Janeiro and Maranhão, where the dye's high price helped compensate for the decline of sugar production in that country.

Indigo's importance as a commodity diminished worldwide during the nineteenth century, as cheaper synthetic dyes became available. El Salvador continued to export some indigo into the late nineteenth century.

RALPH LEE WOODWARD, JR., *Class Privilege and Economic Development: The Consulado de Comercio of Guatemala, 1793–1871* (1966); MURDO J. MAC LEOD, *Spanish Central America: A Socioeconomic History, 1520–1720* (1973); WILLIAM L. SHERMAN, *Forced Native Labor in Sixteenth Century Central America* (1979); WOODWARD, *Central America: A Nation Divided* (1985).

VIRGINIA GARRARD-BURNETT

See also **Free Trade Act; Slavery.**

INDUSTRIALIZATION, an increase in the proportion of total gross domestic product (GDP) resulting from the manufacture of goods in mechanized factories. This process began relatively late in Latin America and has, partly as a consequence, developed slowly and unevenly. Since the conquest and colonization of Latin America by European powers, the economies of the area have been oriented toward the production of agricultural commodities and mineral resources for export. While Latin America possesses the natural and mineral resources required for industrial growth, the international division of labor has not favored the creation of manufacturing enterprises. The export orientation of Latin America, fashioned during three hundred years of colonial rule, retarded the growth of a domestic market, limited the purchasing power of domestic consumers, and either obstructed or concentrated capital formation. Some development theorists explain the relative weakness of the industrial sector as a reflection of the natural comparative advantage enjoyed by Latin American countries in the production of tropical commodities such as coffee, sugarcane, and bananas. Others argue that agro-export specialization was forced on Latin America by imperial powers whose industrial growth required a steady supply of primary materials and captive markets for their manufactured products. Whatever the cause of industry's belated appearance, the fact remains that industrial production did not surpass agricultural output in any of the Latin American republics until the mid-twentieth century.

Industrialization resulted from deliberate government efforts to break out of an international division of labor in which Latin America specialized in agricultural exports. Government policies have been influenced by a bitter initial experience with free-trade policies in the early independence period. Spanish and Portuguese colonial policies permitted a degree of growth in small cottage industries. In colonial Mexico a primitive TEXTILE INDUSTRY developed in the eighteenth century. While English textile plants mechanized the production process, the Mexican plants (*obrajes*) mass-produced cotton textiles by using cheap manual labor working inefficient looms, yet satisfied a substantial portion of Mexican demand for cotton textiles. As less expensive and higher-quality English textiles flooded the market after the lifting of trade restrictions in the early independence period, these native industries were wiped out by the competition. Subsequent efforts to revive the textile manufacturers failed, but the political leadership in Mexico and elsewhere learned that weak native industries could not modernize and grow stronger without substantial government protection.

With the spread of liberalism in the nineteenth century, governments adopted policies that encouraged the development of mechanized factories. The first stage of industrial development occurred between 1850 and 1914, when a dramatic increase in export production, combined with indirect government incentives for industry, established the foundations for the region's first manufacturing plants. Railroad construction, designed primarily to facilitate agricultural exports, also stimulated industrial growth by reducing transportation costs and uniting the domestic market. New banking laws and the confiscation of communal and church lands fostered capital accumulation, while educational reforms and immigration incentives helped to produce a skilled labor force. Capital surpluses generated in the industrializing countries also made some capital available for investment in Latin America.

Yet the major impetus for industrialization came from the dramatic expansion of agricultural exports. In São Paulo, Brazilian entrepreneurs diverted some of the proceeds from the coffee boom (roughly 1830–1910) to the establishment of factories producing the bags in which

Industrialization. BENSON LATIN AMERICAN LIBRARY COLLECTION, UNIVERSITY OF TEXAS AT AUSTIN.

they exported a majority of the world's coffee. In and around Buenos Aires, a few meat-packing plants developed with the expansion of the cattle industry. While the early industries in Latin America were often tied to the export sector, the increase in agricultural productivity also expanded the domestic market for consumer goods. A few consumer-goods industries developed to supply domestic demand for processed foods, beer, cigarettes, shoes, and textiles.

Hence the first stage of industrialization is often referred to as an era of export-led industrial growth, characterized by the establishment of small, low-technology industries processing agricultural products or manufacturing light consumer goods for local consumers. The total contribution of industry to the GDP paled in comparison to the leading economic sector—exports of primary products—yet the foundations of Latin America's consumer-goods industry were laid in the late nineteenth century. The emergence of the manufacturing sector is reflected in the establishment of industrial organizations such as the Society of Manufacturing Development in Chile (1883), the Industrial Union of Argentina (1887), and the National Society of Industries of Peru (1897). Industry made its most significant advances in the largest countries, Argentina, Brazil, and Mexico, where natural and mineral resources, a relatively large domestic market, and a measure of capital accumulation favored the development of a manufacturing base. Mexico began producing steel in 1901, Argentina's industries employed 323,000 workers by 1915, and the Rio de Janeiro–São Paulo axis was a hub of industrial activity around the turn of the twentieth century. Even in the smaller countries of Central America a few consumer-goods industries had developed by 1900.

The onset of World War I disrupted international trading patterns and ushered in a second stage of industrial development, which lasted from 1914 to 1945. With war reducing demand for Latin American exports and cutting off imports, Latin Americans were faced with the choice of forgoing consumption of some manufactured goods or producing them in domestic plants. Governments chose to foster industrial development through import-substitution industrialization (ISI) strategies, a set of policies designed to promote the manufacture of products previously imported from foreign plants. While ISI is a development strategy associated with the post–World War II era, Latin American governments established the broad framework of ISI between 1914 and 1945. In their ad hoc responses to emergency situations, such as revenue shortages and scarcity, governments found that by increasing tariffs, a common practice for revenue-starved governments, and offering fiscal incentives, they could stimulate growth in the industrial sector. Protective tariffs and fiscal incentives made investment in industry more attractive to domestic entrepreneurs, who had always feared competition with British and American industries. Some foreign capitalists invested in South American industry,

but the stimulus for industrial expansion was generated locally. Governments gave greater incentives to industry because the new factories provided employment for a growing urban population, reduced the total cost of the country's imports, and improved the national balance of payments.

From 1914 to 1945, through two world wars and one Great Depression, import-substitution policies accelerated the rate of Latin American industrialization. Between 1915 and 1947, the number of industrial plants increased from 40,200 to 83,900 in Argentina and from 13,000 to 78,400 in Brazil. During the same period, industrial employment increased from 45,000 to 176,000 in Chile and from 323,000 to 1,921,000 in Argentina. Most of the industrial expansion occurred in the primary or consumer-goods sector, but a few intermediate and heavy industries were established. Chilean factories manufactured paper, glass, and cement; Brazil produced iron and steel; and Argentina manufactured farm machinery. By 1950, the industrial output of Latin America exceeded agricultural production. Import-substitution industrialization policies, while they were not popularly labeled as such at the time, had transformed the economic structure of Latin America.

Industrialization also contributed to significant changes in politics and society. With the emergence of industries came an industrial bourgeoisie, a proletariat, and a larger middle class, most of them resident in increasingly more populous urban centers. Urbanization reflected the growth of industry and also promoted it, for with a larger domestic market came greater incentive to increase manufacturing capacity. Moreover, the industrial bourgeoisie and the proletariat, occasionally united in populist political parties by a charismatic leader, penetrated the political structure and pushed forward development programs that accelerated industrial development. This was especially true during the populist regimes of Getúlio VARGAS in Brazil (1930–1945 and 1951–1954), Juan Domingo PERÓN in Argentina (1946–1955 and 1973–1974), and Lázaro CÁRDENAS in Mexico (1934–1940).

Populist politics of the post–1945 era ushered in the third stage of industrial development, an era one might label "dependent industrial growth" or "advanced import-substitution industrialization." Development issues took center stage in national politics, and reformists advocated more ambitious development projects to combat unemployment, raise the standard of living, and "catch up" with the more advanced industrial economies. Beginning in the late 1940s under the forceful leadership of Raúl PREBISCH, an Argentine economist, the United Nations ECONOMIC COMMISSION FOR LATIN AMERICA (ECLA) urged the republics to promote industrialization in order to escape increasingly unfavorable world-market conditions for raw-material exporters. In the minds of policymakers in Latin America and the United States, industrialization became a panacea for a whole range of economic, social, and political problems that plagued the region. By the end of the 1950s, virtually every nation of Latin America was committed to rapid industrial growth.

Political factors at the national level coincided with and were perhaps strengthened by conditions that favored the growth of multinational industries. Industries based in Europe and North America, looking for new markets and new outlets for their capital, began to invest more heavily in Latin American industry. Prior to 1945, foreign investment was concentrated in agriculture, transportation, and mining. In the postwar period, foreign capital flowed in ever larger amounts to the manufacturing sector. In 1949, the German multinational company Volkswagen set up a plant in Brazil, and it was followed by Ford, General Motors, and Mercedes Benz in the 1950s. In the third stage of industrial development, governments attempted to harness and coordinate the domestic and foreign factors that propelled industrial growth to its highest levels in the 1970s.

While a manufacturing base existed in 1945, plants were generally small, inefficient, and incapable of competing directly with foreign enterprises. Moreover, with some exceptions in the larger countries, few plants existed in the intermediate and capital-goods sectors, the industries that generate self-sustaining growth by producing tools, machines, and equipment that are subsequently utilized in other productive enterprises. Consequently, ISI in the post-1945 period has involved a higher degree of state intervention to expand manufacturing into the so-called heavy industries. States erected tariff barriers, subsidized and occasionally nationalized industries, funded industrial development banks, constructed hydroelectric plants and other power facilities, and loosened restrictions on foreign investment.

Government policies stimulated even higher levels of foreign investment, as multinational corporations were eager to get behind tariff barriers and take advantage of government incentives. Although foreign capital contributed less than 10 percent of total investment per year, it helped establish key industries like steel, petrochemicals, pharmaceuticals, automobiles, and other capital-goods industries. While ECLA economists and some political leaders would have preferred to industrialize with only national capital, others argued that foreign capital was a necessary ingredient in the total development program. Without it, few countries could have developed intermediate and heavy industries.

International political factors also contributed to an increase in industrial productivity. In an effort to correct the conditions that bred revolutionary movements in Latin America, the United States committed itself to finance the ALLIANCE FOR PROGRESS in 1961. Over the next ten years, the U.S. government made available billions of dollars in low-interest, long-term loans to finance economic diversification, infrastructural development, and other projects that governments could not have financed

TABLE 1   Average Annual Industrial Growth Rates, 1950–1978

	1950–1965	1965–1973	1973–1978
Argentina	4.8	5.9	−1.0
Brazil	7.3	12.0	6.3
Chile	5.5	3.4	−1.4
Colombia	6.2	7.7	5.4
Guatemala	5.4	7.7	6.2
Mexico	7.2	8.1	6.3
Latin America	6.3	8.2	4.5

SOURCE: Robert N. Gwynne, *Industrialization and Urbanization in Latin America* (1986), p. 36

otherwise on such flexible terms. A significant part of the development effort involved regional economic integration. Recognizing that the growth of industry required the expansion of markets, governments in Central and South America attempted to form common markets in which tariffs on manufactured goods would be gradually eliminated. While these integration measures failed to achieve all that had been intended, they helped to stimulate industrial exports and attract foreign investment.

A combination of domestic incentives, increased levels of foreign development assistance, direct foreign investment, and economic integration produced spectacular increases in industrial productivity. Between 1950 and 1978, Latin America's manufacturing sector grew at an average annual rate of 6.5 percent. The value of the industrial product increased more than five times, from $13 billion in 1950 to $77.2 billion in 1978. As shown in table 1, the growth in industrial productivity was greatest in Brazil, which recorded a remarkable 12 percent annual growth rate between 1965 and 1973, during the so-called Brazilian miracle.

As a result of these high growth rates, the industrial sector replaced agriculture as the leading economic sector. In 1950 the agricultural sector accounted for 25 percent of the GDP, while industrial output represented 19.6 percent of the GDP. By 1978 industry was the leading economic sector in Latin America, accounting for 26 percent of the GDP. Brazil led all Latin American countries in the value added by the manufacturing sector, producing a record $97.7 billion in 1987. Mexico's industrial sector, however, contributed a greater percentage of the country's gross domestic product, as shown in table 2.

High industrial growth rates were accompanied by significant changes within the manufacturing sector. The contribution of the consumer-goods sector to total GDP declined from almost 66 percent in 1950 to 40 percent in 1980. During the same period, the contribution of intermediate industries increased from 25 percent to 33 percent, and consumer durables increased from 11

TABLE 2   Level of Industrialization
(Manufacturing GDP as % of GDP)

	1950	1978	1990
Argentina	26	33	22
Brazil	22	30	27
Chile	23	24	21
Colombia	13	18	22
Guatemala	12	16	15
Mexico	19	26	28
Latin America	20	26	25

SOURCE: Robert N. Gwynne, *Industrialization and Urbanization in Latin America* (1986), pp. 37–38; Inter-American Development Bank, *Economic and Social Progress in Latin America: 1992 Report* (1992), pp. 286–291.

percent to 25 percent. The development of heavy industries was most successful in Argentina, Brazil, and Mexico, which even began to export industrial products in significant quantities during the third stage of industrial development.

The world recession of 1979–1984 slowed the rate of industrial growth throughout the region, and Latin American industry has still not recovered the high growth rates of the previous decades. Burdened by foreign debt and shortages of foreign exchange, the most industrialized countries were still registering negative growth rates in the mid-1980s. The recent decline in industrial productivity has forced policymakers to reconsider the strategies that had been so successful since World War II. Many countries have embarked on a neoliberal development strategy, eliminating tariff protection for industries, privatizing state corporations, and offering incentives to foreign manufacturers. The manufacturing sector showed signs of recovery in the 1990s, but the adoption of neoliberal policies will not likely reduce industry's dependence on foreign capital and the state. Some of the most productive Brazilian industries (automobiles, tires, cement, and pharmaceuticals) are controlled by multinational firms. As these firms are free to repatriate profits, critics are openly questioning the contribution of foreign enterprises to Brazilian development. Despite high growth rates in Brazil and elsewhere, industrialization has not been the panacea for the many social and economic problems faced by Latin America.

WERNER BAER, *Industrialization and Economic Development in Brazil* (1965); ALBERT O. HIRSCHMAN, "The Political Economy of Import-Substituting Industrialization in Latin America," in *Quarterly Journal of Economics* 82, no. 1 (1968): 1–32; WARREN DEAN, *The Industrialization of São Paulo, 1880–1945* (1969); CELSO FURTADO, *Economic Development of Latin America*, 2d ed. (1976); FERNANDO HENRIQUE CARDOSO and ENZO FALETTO, *Dependency and Development in Latin America* (1979); FREDERICK STIRTON WEAVER, *Class, State, and Industrial Structure: The Historical Process of South American Industrial Growth* (1980); ROBERT N. GWYNNE, *Industrialization and Urbanization in Latin America* (1986); STEPHEN H. HABER, *Industry and Underdevelopment: The Industrialization of Mexico, 1890–1940* (1989); FERNANDO FAJNZYLBER, *Industrialization in Latin America: From the "Black Box" to the "Empty Box"* (1990).

PAUL J. DOSAL

See also **Economic Development; Technology.**

INFANTE, JOSÉ MIGUEL (*b.* 1778; *d.* 9 April 1844), Chilean patriot and politician. Infante played a number of important roles in the Chilean struggle for independence and in its aftermath. As *procurador* (attorney) of the CABILDO (municipal government) of Santiago in 1810, he was active in putting forth the creole case for a national government. At the *cabildo abierto* (open town meeting) of 18 September 1810, he was given the task of making the keynote speech in favor of this change. He was a member of the first national congress (1811) and of the governing junta (1813–1814). He happened to be in Argentina at the time of the battle of RANCAGUA (1–2 October 1814), and remained there until 1817. Under Bernardo O'HIGGINS (1778–1842), Infante was briefly minister of finance (1818). He played one of the more important roles in the events of 28 January 1823, when O'Higgins relinquished power. As a senator in 1823 he was responsible for the law abolishing slavery in Chile.

Infante's moments of greatest influence came in the years 1824–1826, when his now strongly held "federalist" views dominated discussion in the Chilean congress. A federalist constitution, however, was never introduced, and Infante's influence quickly waned. Between 1827 and 1844 he published 206 issues of his own newspaper, *El Valdiviano Federal*, in which he continued to expound his increasingly dogmatic (and totally unfashionable) federalist views. He was widely respected as a man of great integrity. His death in 1844 made a deep impression on a new generation of Chilean liberals.

SIMON COLLIER, *Ideas and Politics of Chilean Independence, 1808–1833* (1967), chap. 8.

SIMON COLLIER

INFANTE, PEDRO (*b.* 18 November 1917; *d.* 15 April 1957), Mexican actor and singer. Born in Mazatlán, Sinaloa, Infante learned the trade of carpentry, then made a guitar and taught himself music. In 1939, while in Mexico City, he began his singing career on the radio. He was "discovered" by the director Ismael Rodríguez and cast in the film *La feria de las flores* (1942). One year later he became a major star in *¡Viva mi desgracia!* He starred in a total of forty-five films, including *Nosotros los pobres* (1947), *Ustedes los ricos* (1948), *Escuela de vagabundos* (1954), *Dicen que soy mujeriego* (1948), *Las Islas Marías* (1950), *Ahí viene Martín Corona* (1951), and *Dos tipos de cuidado* (1952). A versatile actor who performed comedy and drama with equal distinction, Infante has attained the status of a cultural icon in Mexico.

LUIS REYES DE LA MAZA, *El cine sonoro en México* (1973); E. BRADFORD BURNS, *Latin American Cinema: Film and History* (1975); CARL J. MORA, *Mexican Cinema: Reflections of a Society: 1896–1980* (1982); and JOHN KING, *Magical Reels: A History of Cinema in Latin America* (1990).

DAVID MACIEL

INFLATION. Latin America has customarily suffered more bouts of high inflation than many other parts of the world (see table 1). Although its inflationary experience spans centuries, the decades from 1950 to 1990 reflect different inflationary processes, distinct economic environments, and a plethora of government policies. There are, however, some Latin American countries (Colombia, Costa Rica, Mexico) that are not as prone to hyperinflation as others (Argentina, Brazil, and Chile). The period from 1950 to 1960 was marked by "easy import substitution" throughout Latin America. The following decade saw the exhaustion of that growth strategy and the beginning of an outward-looking (export-promoting) developmental model. From 1971 to 1981 the region pursued a "debt-led" development plan as nations continued to mix import-substitution and export-promotion strategies financed primarily by the accumulation of foreign debt. This policy resulted in a "debt crisis," initiated by the Mexican moratorium of August 1982 and the subsequent large negative resource transfers from Latin America to the industrialized world as it serviced this debt. During the last period, all Latin American countries experienced an upward trend in inflation rates, and even traditionally low-inflation countries such as Nicaragua and Peru joined the high-inflation leaders in undergoing hyperinflation (inflation above 50 percent per month). Unfortunately, Latin Americans have yet to find ways to eradicate inflation with minimal social cost and political strain.

The political effects of inflation are immense. It wreaks personal devastation on those with fixed incomes or frozen wages, whose lifetime savings can be wiped out literally overnight. The fears of the newly emerging middle class in such an environment cannot be overestimated and have been said to be responsible for the overthrow of civilian politicians in Brazil in 1964, Argentina in 1966 and 1975, Uruguay in 1971, and Chile in 1973. Thus, the issue of curbing inflation has ramifications for society that vastly exceed purely economic considerations. Several theories of inflation have evolved to explain its causes and cures, but none has yet proved fully adequate.

MONETARISM
According to the monetarist theory, growth in the money supply causes inflation, as do fiscal deficits. The typical Latin American country went through the import-substitution period without a central bank, leaving monetary issues directly in the hands of the treasury or of a central bank subservient to financing the needs of the treasury. Given that vigorous markets for government bonds also did not exist then, budget deficits became the primary source of monetary expansion and, therefore, of inflation. Monetarists believe that inflation interferes with economic growth for a number of reasons. It persuades those with means to put their savings into unproductive assets as a hedge: scarce financial resources will flow to projects based upon non-economic (nonprice) criteria and investors will avoid projects with long gestation periods in favor of those that promise lower re-

TABLE 1 Latin America: Average Annual Inflation Rates, 1950–1993

	1950–1959[b]	1960–1970[b]	1971–1981[b]	1982–1989[a]	1990–1993[a]	1950–1993[c]
Argentina	27.5	21.4	134.2	643.4	630.3	223.9
Bolivia	60.0	6.0	21.3	1746.3	14.8	345.8
Brazil	18.8	46.1	42.1	360.8	1549.3	237.7
Chile	36.1	33.0	164.6	19.9	15.9	63.3
Colombia	8.1	11.9	22.4	50.2	22.4	21.9
Costa Rica	1.8[a]	1.9[a]	16.2[a]	27.1	19.9	11.9
Mexico	7.1	3.5	19.2	80.4	18.7	24.0
Nicaragua	4.9	1.8	34.3	2587.1	2567.2	730.4
Peru	8.0	1.3	12.4	540.3	1787.2	272.0
Uruguay	17.0	44.0	61.2	59.4	78.4	48.8
Venezuela	2.0	1.0	9.2	23.1	26.9	9.8

[a] Measured by the consumer price index.
[b] Measured by the producer price index.
[c] Weighted average of the first five columns.

SOURCES: INTER-AMERICAN DEVELOPMENT BANK, *Economic and Social Progress Report*, various years; INTERNATIONAL MONETARY FUND, *International Financial Statistics*, various years; and WORLD BANK, *World Development Report*, various years.

turns in the shorter term; the real exchange rate will increase, hindering exports and enhancing imports, prompting governments to intervene in the foreign-exchange market and in trade flows as countries try to avoid the secondary inflationary effects of a devaluation; it lowers public utility rates or other public sector prices and thus reduces the financial health of these firms, leading to higher government deficits, while other price controls provoke shortages and underinvestment in those sectors.

Latin American countries signed policy packages with the International Monetary Fund (IMF) to receive balance-of-payments assistance and agreed to a set of commitments that included real depreciation of the currency, fiscal austerity coupled with increased prices for public transportation and basic commodities, monetary austerity, and wage freezes. The political and economic impacts of such prescriptions were enormous since they usually provoked long and deep recessions with a corresponding increase in unemployment. Many think the IMF inflation stabilizations fell too heavily on the working class, which responded with demonstrations and strikes.

STRUCTURALISTS
Raúl PREBISCH, Hans W. Singer, and their successors at the U.N. Economic Commission for Latin America and the Caribbean (ECLAC or CEPAL) postulated that inflation was caused by an inelastic food supply, chronic lack of foreign exchange, and structural government deficits arising from the necessary expansion of social overhead infrastructure. Structuralists believed that inflation (at reasonable levels) was not necessarily detrimental to economic growth since it poured savings into productive investment rather than into financial markets or fiscal schemes. They believed that industrial growth fueled rural-urban migration, resulting in higher food prices that forced workers to increase wage demands. But for various reasons, the food supply did not increase despite price hikes, and sparked inflationary pushes in the growth process. They also noted that since Latin American countries continued to demand increasing amounts of manufactured goods from industrialized nations while their primary exports could not keep pace with the chronic balance of payments deficits, the consequent lack of foreign exchange led to trade restrictions and currency devaluation, both of which are inflationary as was the growth of government during the expansion process. Although structuralists strongly criticized IMF stabilization policies as socially unacceptable, they presented no alternative to its imperatives.

RATIONAL EXPECTATIONS AND EXPECTATIONS MANAGEMENT APPROACHES
The "rational expectations" school agreed that inflation came from the money supply, but was rooted in present and future expected government deficits. In its view, governments could end inflation by undertaking cred-

ible reforms. In Latin America, this approach was generally associated with the CHICAGO BOYS in Argentina and Chile, who believed that a credible fiscal reform coupled with trade liberalization and slowing in the rate of devaluation of the currency would simultaneously stabilize the inflation rate at low levels and improve the balance of payments. Over time, the currency devaluation would fall to zero and the domestic inflation rate would come to equal that of the average for the country's trading partners. This framework propelled the so-called *tablita* and the corresponding liberalization policies imposed on Argentina, Chile, and Uruguay in the late 1970s.

Unfortunately the slowing of the depreciation rate led to extremely overvalued exchange rates and produced large trade deficits and corresponding increases in the foreign debt. Since domestic inflation did not converge to foreign inflation, the "credibility" of the exchange-rate policy declined, leading to devaluation expectations and a predictable run on the Central Bank's reserves followed by a large devaluation and a repudiation of the stabilization policy. A similar policy was undertaken in Mexico in 1988 at the end of the Miguel de la MADRID administration with its Economic Solidarity Pact and continued into the Carlos SALINAS DE GORTARI administration with the Pact for Economic Stability and Growth. In any event, Mexico's plan collapsed in late 1994 in a fashion similar to the collapses in the Southern Cone. But what distinguished Mexico's pacts is the incorporation of wage and price guidelines similar to those recommended by the New Structuralists.

NEW STRUCTURALISM
In order to provide an anti-inflation package in addition to a critique, the neostructuralists articulated the theory of "inertial" inflation. It concentrated on the role of formal and informal indexation of incomes, asserting that competing income sectors made claims on domestic product way in excess of its capacity. Inflation brought the claims into alignment with gross domestic products. Inertial inflation resulted from the fact that indexing reflected the last period's inflation as automatic inflation correction occurred on an economy-wide scale, making it difficult to shift. An incomes policy (wage and price freeze)–based inflation stabilization that removed the inertial aspects of inflation was supposed to reduce inflation at a lower cost to society. The "heterodox" stabilization measures of the Austral Plan (1985–1987) in Argentina and the Cruzado Plan (1986–1987) in Brazil presumably combined the policies of eradicating inertial inflation using incomes policies and monetary reform with the more orthodox policies of austere monetary and fiscal policy. Although these policies failed because of their reliance on wage, price, and exchange-rate pegging, the Plano de Ação Econômica do Governo (PAEG) in Brazil (1964–1972) and the recent stabilization attempt in Mexico (1988–1994) were more successful.

SUPER-MONETARIST-FISCALISM

The new monetarist-fiscalists no longer concentrate on the usual aspects of fiscal reform, but on the growth in the internal debt of the government. Needing to repay foreign loans, governments borrowed heavily internally, which accelerated the growth of the monetary base. Therefore, the Collor Plan in Brazil (March 1990) and a series of forced reschedulings in Argentina (December 1989 and January 1990) were based mainly on the effective repudiation of parts of the internal debt. The plans succeeded in "confiscating" a large portion of real liquidity of the economies and temporarily reducing inflation rates from hyperinflationary ones to high ones. But in early 1991 both plans collapsed and each country returned to its hyperinflationary environment.

The total loss in credibility in Argentina gave rise to the so-called Convertibility Plan. In March 1991, incoming Economy Minister Domingo Cavallo implemented a plan minimizing the discretion of the central bank to print money for any purpose. For the plan to work, the government would have to run a balanced budget or a surplus. The plan virtually turned the central bank into a so-called currency board; that is, the central bank can print money only when dollars come in. But it also has to destroy money when dollars go out. This puts large pressure on the banking system, and a banking panic could force a devaluation or a suspension of payments. The plan has worked brilliantly so far. Inflation fell from 1,700 percent in 1990 to 3.9 percent in 1994. But the Mexican devaluation in late 1994 led many Argentines to take their money out of Argentina, putting pressure on the Argentine banking system. Only time will tell if the Argentine convertibility plan will endure.

Since both structural and monetary forces are important in the inflation process in Latin America, policymakers need to resist the temptation to ignore orthodox adjustment during the initial success of incomes policies. One common denominator of successful inflation stabilization policies is the attainment of profound and lasting fiscal adjustment. The causes of government deficits and their subsequent monetization, however, cannot be separated from the specific socioeconomic context of each developing country. Hence, an integrated theory of Latin American inflation must contain a component that addresses the political economy of government budget deficits. Of related importance is the credibility of government inflation policies especially related to fiscal adjustments. Both structuralist and orthodox thinkers have generated some interesting work, but still fall short of a full-blown theory and set of policy recommendations. A large amount of literature explaining the link between politics and inflation was generated in the early 1990s. The new political economy is far too extensive to discuss in this essay, but Alesina (1994) contains a good review. Unfortunately, until a reliable remedy is found, the eradication of inflation in Latin America with minimal social cost and political strain is still a goal rather than a reality.

H. W. SINGER, "The Distribution of Gains Between Investing and Borrowing Countries," *American Economic Review* 40 (May 1950): 473–485; RAÚL PREBISCH, "Commercial Policy in the Underdeveloped Countries," *American Economic Review* 49 (May 1959): 251–273; GUILLERMO CALVO, "On the Time Consistency of Optimal Policy in a Monetary Economy," *Econometrics* 46 (November 1978): 1,411–1,428; LANCE TAYLOR, *Structuralist Macroeconomics* (1983); WERNER BAER and ISAAC KERSTENETZKY, eds., *Inflation and Growth in Latin America* (1984); ROQUE B. FERNÁNDEZ, "The Expectations Management Approach to Stabilization in Argentina During 1796–1982," *World Development* 13, no. 8 (1985): 871–892; THOMAS J. SARGENT, *Rational Expectations and Inflation* (1986); WERNER BAER and JOHN H. WELCH, eds., "The Resurgence of Inflation in Latin America," *World Development* 15, no. 8 (1987): 989–990; COLIN KIRKPATRICK and FREDERICK NIXSON, "Inflation and Stabilization Policy in LDCs," in Norman Gemmell, ed., *Surveys in Development Economics* (1987); MICHAEL BRUNO et al., *Inflation Stabilization* (1988); DAVID HEYMAN and FERNANDO NAVAJAS, "Conflicto distributivo y deficit fiscal: Notas sobre la experiencia argentina, 1970–1987" (Working Paper, Oficina de la CEPAL, Buenos Aires, 1989); ALBERTO ALESINA, "Political Models of Macroeconomic Policy and Fiscal Reforms," in Stephen Haggard and Steven Webb, eds., *Voting for Reform* (1994); JOHN H. WELCH, "Monetary Policy, Hyperinflation, and Internal Debt Repudiation in Argentina and Brazil," *Politica Internazionale*, forthcoming.

JOHN H. WELCH

INFORMAL ECONOMY, a somewhat vague concept, frequently defined as all economic activities that are performed outside the law and beyond regulation. Its origin, nature, magnitude, and implications have been heatedly debated, yet the notion has enjoyed a lasting appeal. The idea of the informal economy was introduced by Keith Hart in 1971 and was popularized by a 1973 International Labour Office study on employment in Kenya. Numerous studies of the informal economy in Latin America have been carried out under the auspices of the Regional Employment Program for Latin America and the Caribbean of the International Labour Office.

The informal economy and its evolution in Latin America are examined here in terms of their major production, income distribution, and capital formation components and characteristics. The framework used here aims to focus attention on the composite, complex, and heterogeneous origin, nature, and implications of the informal economy. It thereby hopes to provide a comprehensive understanding of the notion, its relation to the formal economy, and the changing structure and public policies of Latin America.

The informal economy was at Independence and still is today both large and highly heterogeneous. Its components and features have, however, changed significantly over time.

Although estimates of the size of the informal economy should generally be viewed with caution because of underlying conceptual and statistical problems, they nevertheless provide valuable insights. At Independence, the predominantly rural informal economy may have accounted for (these are highly speculative estimates) 80 to 90 percent of production and "employment" in some Latin American countries. By 1930 this may have fallen to 40 to 50 percent. By 1993 the combined rural and urban informal economy and employment accounted for approximately 35 to 40 percent, with the majority being urban.

Informal workers, defined as unpaid workers within the family, domestic servants, and the self-employed minus professionals and technicians, were, according to statistics presented by Manuel Castells and Alejandro Portes, 46.5 percent of the economically active population in Latin America in 1950 and 42.2 percent in 1980. If the estimated proportion of informal wage workers is added, the percentage in 1980 rises to 60.3.

Within nonagricultural employment in Latin America, the informal sector, which was concentrated in commerce and services, accounted for 26.1 percent in 1980 and 30.7 percent in 1985, according to Jacques Charmes. Family workers accounted for most of the urban informals, with the rest being employers and self-employed.

The first, and initially largest, autonomous component of the informal economy from Independence to 1930 encompassed those rural and urban activities from which the emerging, modern, market, and export-oriented economy drew resources. At first, informality implied small-scale, largely indigenous, preindustrial production of agricultural, mining, industrial, and service components of composite commodities with limited, if any, specialization, technological progress, capital goods, or support by governmental, education, and health services.

Although by no means a perfect term, "informality" better describes much of the production in regions of old indigenous and colonial settlement than do "agricultural," "rural," or "consumer." These activities coexisted with and complemented the formal economy. They persisted up to 1930 where (1) development was natural-resource based and nonindustrial and (2) formal meso-economic (i.e., sectoral, group-based and -oriented) policies in education, health, welfare, and other basic services favored the richest 40 percent of households. By 1930 this component included the activities and population that were unabsorbed by a rigid, formal economy within a production structure with increasingly plural (low, medium, and high productivity), segmented (minimally interacting) components.

The second component of the pre-1930 informal economy was made up of activities that absorbed workers who, having been part of the formal export-oriented or urban economy, returned to the informal hinterland, which acted as a sponge during seasonal, cyclical, or secular (long-term) downturns. This component first absorbed labor released by formal activities during recurrent cyclical downturns in 1860–1910, the golden age of exports. The component further expanded as the formal economy lost growth momentum during the 1910–1930 export slowdown. Its ranks swelled again during the export collapse and Great Depression of the 1930s, when the battered formal economy experienced a massive exodus of labor. The first and second component of the informal economy involved activities that do not fit easily into the traditional classification of employed, unemployed, and inactive population.

The third component of informal production, which emerged primarily after 1930, was induced by economic forces and policies. Its activities absorbed many of the illiterate and unskilled inhabitants of the sprawling slums, misery belts, and shantytowns of Latin America. Productivity, income, and expenditure in this group were, at best, marginal.

The fourth segment of the "informal economy" was defined in the famous Kenya report as activities characterized by ease of entry, reliance on indigenous resources, family ownership of enterprises, small-scale of operation, labor-intensive and adapted technology, skills acquired outside the formal school system, and unregulated and competitive markets. This informality is the antithesis of formal-sector activities that are characterized by difficult entry; frequent reliance on overseas resources; corporate ownership; large scale of operation; capital-intensive and often imported technology; formally acquired skills, often from foreign institutions; and markets protected through tariffs, quotas, and trade licenses.

The third and fourth components of the informal economy are largely the consequences of the post-1930 population explosion and structuralist developmental strategies. Unabsorbed surplus labor was forced to migrate into low-income, easy entry, unregulated informal activities as a consequence of capital-intensive, exclusive, nationalistic, populist, structuralist policies that favored import-substitution industrialization, penalized agriculture, and discriminated against financial, trade, transportation, and other services.

The fifth component of what is indeed an overlapping production continuum, encompasses activities originally belonging to the formal economy that were deliberately transferred to the informal economy either because they were crowded out by the state or in order to evade taxes, including social security, or to escape bureaucratic regulation and formidable transaction costs. The flight to informality served as an instrument of survival, escape, or enrichment for the middle and upper classes, who also operated within the formal, sometimes disintegrating economy. Animosity, inefficiency, corruption, and disintegration of the formal state have frequently accelerated this flight.

At the bottom of the informal totem pole are the truly destitute prostitutes, Brazil's black and mulatto *meninos a rua* (street kids), and self-employed adults engaged in petty trade, running drugs, begging, and stealing in order to survive. Inhabiting urban slums mired in poverty, violence, and despair, they amount to perhaps 100 million people, with 30 million in Brazil alone.

This informality of millions of Indians, blacks, mulattoes, mestizos, women, and children is a reflection of Latin America's imperfect social contracts. Masses of destitute informals subsist beyond the reach of educational, health, welfare, and other government services. Even though it is easy to enter the informal economy, mesoeconomic institutional barriers in the areas of education, health, and welfare inhibit efforts to exit from it. Thus, vast numbers are chained to absolute poverty for generations.

The intermediate (low- and middle-income) cohorts in Latin America's informal economy include an innovative, fiercely competitive, immensely dynamic archipelago of migrant, urban, self-employed minientrepreneurs. These informals perform, in the scenario of Hernando de Soto's celebrated *The Other Path* (1989), a critically productive role in Lima's retail trade (having built 83 percent of the city's markets), public transportation (delivering 95 percent), and housing (half of the population of Lima lives in houses built by black marketers).

The explosive growth of the informal economy in Peru and the rest of Latin America is caused by exorbitant costs of becoming and staying formal and legal. The exclusive nature of legal institutions, erected primarily by an executive branch controlled by monopolistic combines and their collaborative bureaucracies, bars the majority of the population from the antiquated formal economy. An onerous regulatory framework, inadequate legislation, excessive red tape, and inefficient bureaucracy turn free-market informality into the only viable, nonviolent "other path" for the poor. According to de Soto, only a complete overhaul of this archaic, "mercantilist" legal system can tear down the artificial barriers separating the parasitic, elitist formal economy from the dynamic informal segment, integrate the two, and restore growth. De Soto's approach, however narrow it may be, correctly focuses attention on the legal institutions that foster informality and on the power of special-interest groups that leads to their enactment.

At the apex of the informal distributional spectrum rises the rich, high-income component, which is often characterized, along with its formal complement, by high barriers to entry; oligopoly and monopoly power; human, physical, and financial capital intensity; access to formal education; variable scale of operation; and flexible ownership. Rich landowners, miners, merchants, industrialists, financiers, and professionals are forced or induced to transfer multifaceted formal activities into the informal economy. Far too often, privileged informals, including the Colombian, Peruvian, and Bolivian drug lords and contrabandists, enter marriages of convenience with corrupt segments of public administration and the military.

Capital formation and its investment, financial intermediation, and saving components, have played, through their heterogeneity and pluralism, a vital role in shaping the production and income-distribution structure of the informal economy.

The informal economy throughout the nineteenth and twentieth centuries included a large component forced to be self-employed because formal activities could not create the demand necessary to absorb all available labor. Before 1930 this component was important in those countries where naturally capital-intensive formal activities, especially in export mining and agriculture, limited their labor-absorbing capacity.

After 1930 declining savings, due to statization and export stagnation, and capital-intensive industrialization, further curtailed the formal economy's labor-absorbing capacity and strengthened the informal economy's role as an employer of last resort.

Disintegration of the financial system during structuralist phases and periods of hyperinflationary monetary and fiscal policies in Brazil, Argentina, Mexico, Peru, Chile, Bolivia, Nicaragua, and elsewhere contributed to capital flight into the informal economy. Furthermore, the induced disintegration of formal finance and capital flight into the informal economy, as well as overseas, have greatly curtailed formal capital formation, thus turning the informal economy into a last resort activity for millions of formally unabsorbed households.

This flight into informal finance and its pernicious side effects can be reversed when, as in Chile, Mexico, and Argentina, privatization, liberalization, deregulation, and orthodox fiscal and monetary policies are reintroduced. Squandering of vast export sector, private, and foreign savings on public and private consumption by privileged, formal, middle and upper classes has also contributed to the slow growth of the formal economy and the persistence of informality. Parts of the informal economy are major sources of saving, financial intermediation, and capital goods; incubators of vital entrepreneurship; and cradles of freedom, equality, and justice.

Traditionally, analysts like Aníbal Quijano, José Nun, and Fernando Cardoso characterized those participating in the low-income economy as "marginalized." They ascribed this phenomenon to insufficient job creation and have seen marginals as sources of antagonism and resentment. But according to Victor Tokman, the informal economy approach has superseded the concept of marginality in Latin America. The informal sector is seen as an employment response to the need to survive. The informal sector, which is subordinated to the modern one, is characterized by one segment that operates in residual markets found at the base of large-scale production. A second segment is located in competitive markets where economies of scale are not important and technological change is slow. An intermediate case is that of trade activities, in which market imperfections ensure the capacity of informal shops to compete efficiently with modern establishments.

According to the structuralist perspective, labor surplus and limited access to both markets and productive

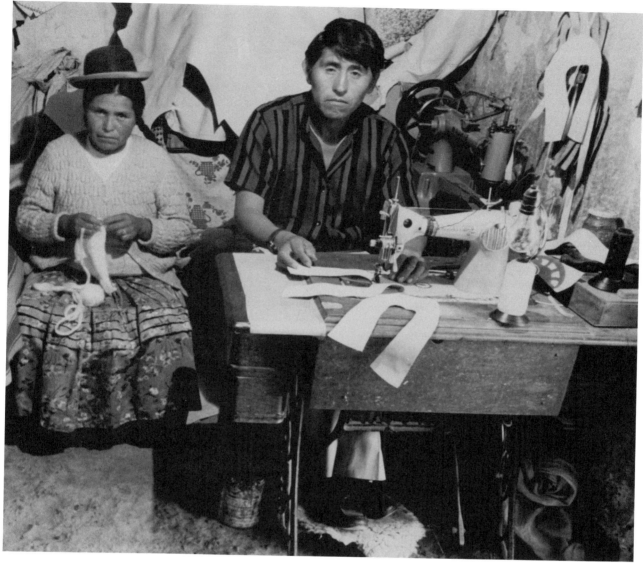

Workers in La Paz, Bolivia. ACCIÓN INTERNATIONAL; PHOTO BY GABRIELA ROMANOW.

resources, rather than institutional or legal factors, create the economic conditions for informal activities. Since informal production involves little capital and simple technology, wage employment is limited. They see the failure to observe the laws—that is, the inability and unwillingness to abide by complex and expensive regulations, including payment of social security taxes—as one of the results of operating informally, but not as its cause. Strong competition both in terms of product and labor results in incomes per person close to the minimum necessary for survival. According to a Marxist-oriented dependency perspective, prevailing institutions lead to the exploitation and impoverishment of informal labor. However, Castells and Portes postulate a functional exploitation perspective whereby in-

formality is a universal phenomenon attributable to the restructuring of the international system of production. The informal sector depresses the wages paid by modern firms (labor market impact) and produces low-cost goods (product market impact). The latter are used as either inputs for the modern firms or by workers of these firms for consumption (and so are referred to as wage goods), thereby increasing those firms' rate of profit.

According to the structuralist, neo-structuralist, and dependency schools, the expansion of the informal economy, as well as deindustrialization, unemployment, the debt crisis, income inequalities, and acute poverty have been caused in the late twentieth century by monetarist, neoconservative policies of liberalization

279

and privatization and the induced, excessive dependence on volatile external markets and foreign capital flows. Neoliberal economic restructuring in Chile, Argentina, Mexico, Peru, and elsewhere has led to a labor exodus out of the capital-intensive, often foreign-owned formal economy into the open entry, last resort informal one.

The informal economy in Latin America has been highly complex in terms of its origin, structure, and degree of interactions with the formal one. If the ultimate goal of integration with the formal one is to be achieved, new social contracts with enlightened production, income distribution, and capital formation pillars will probably be necessary.

The notions of informality and informal sector apparently were first introduced into the literature by KEITH HART in his influential article "Informal Income Opportunities and Urban Employment in Ghana," in *Journal of Modern African Studies* 11, no. 1 (1973): 61–89. According to Hart, the formal-informal dichotomy and analysis provide insights into the development process that the traditional urban-rural, employed-unemployed-inactive classifications and related migration theories are unable to generate.

The notion of informal-sector activities was, however, popularized by the pathbreaking study of the INTERNATIONAL LABOUR OFFICE (ILO), *Employment, Incomes, and Equality: A Strategy for Increasing Productive Employment in Kenya* (1972). The concept of the informal economy was widely disseminated in Latin America by the Regional Employment Program for Latin America and the Caribbean (PREALC) of the ILO, which has published numerous studies on this topic.

The literature on the informal economy in Latin America is vast. Probably the most complete bibliography is that prepared by PREALC, *Retrospectiva del sector informal urbano en América Latina: Una bibliografía anotada* (1991).

The relationship between informality and illegality is examined in *Beyond Regulation: The Informal Economy in Latin America*, edited by VÍCTOR E. TOKMAN (1992).

An extensive and generally favorable review of the idea and quantitative and qualitative evidence on the informal sector by scholars espousing the concept is found in *The Informal Sector Revisited*, edited by DAVID TURNHAM, BERNARD SALOMÉ, and ANTOINE SCHWARZ (1990). Detailed statistics on the size of the informal economy, some of which are presented in this entry, are found in chap. 1 by JACQUES CHARMES.

Also useful is *The Informal Economy: Studies in Advanced and Less Developed Countries*, edited by ALEJANDRO PORTES, MANUEL CASTELLS, and LAUREN A. BENTON (1989), which contains, in its first chapter, statistics cited in this entry.

A provocative libertarian analysis of the informal economy is in HERNANDO DE SOTO, *The Other Path: The Invisible Revolution in the Third World* (1989).

Explanation of informality as a response to an ossification of the formal economy caused by discriminatory governmental sectoral policies is found in MARKOS MAMALAKIS, "The Theory of Sectoral Clashes," in *Latin American Research Review* 4, no. 3 (1969): 9–46, and "The Theory of Sectoral Clashes and Coalitions Revisited," in *Latin American Research Review* 6, no. 3 (1971): 89–126.

As the notion of the informal sector gained popularity, its very meaning and usefulness have been questioned and criticized. A useful review of the evolution of the idea and its shortcomings is in LISA PEATTIE, "An Idea in Good Currency and How It Grew: The Informal Sector," in *World Development* 15, no. 7 (1987): 851–860.

MARKOS J. MAMALAKIS

See also **Economic Development.**

INGAPIRCA, "Inca wall" in Quechua, a name loosely applied to archaeological ruins throughout the former INCA Empire. In Ecuador, Ingapirca is the name given to the best preserved of Inca sites. Located in the Cañari region of the southern highlands, the site of Ingapirca contains both monumental architecture and high-quality stonework. The site is best known for a large oval structure of fine Cuzco masonry called the Castillo. The oval form is rare in Inca architecture. Other Inca constructions at the site include rectangular buildings, storage units, waterworks, and agricultural terraces.

Archaeological evidence indicates that many of the Inca structures at Ingapirca were erected over preexisting architectural features. Radiocarbon dates and associated Cashaloma pottery indicate that the site was occupied by the local Cañari population prior to the Inca invasion of the region. The sector of the site referred to as Pilaloma is believed to have been the original Cañari precinct. Excavations in this area revealed a walled enclosure containing a series of rectangular rooms organized around a central patio. A monolith in the center of the patio marked the location of a shallow sepulchre containing the remains of eleven individuals and a wealth of funerary offerings, including Cashaloma pottery vessels, copper objects, and *Spondylus* shell.

The Cañaris were conquered by Topa Inca Yupanqui the latter half of the fifteenth century. Ethnohistoric and archaeological data suggest that Ingapirca, known originally as Hatun Cañar, was the principal settlement and sacred origin place of the ancient Cañari nation. A well-known strategy of Inca imperial expansion was to symbolically subordinate local deities and sacred places to the state religion. The superimposition of Inca structures over the Cañari capital likely reflects a conscious effort on the part of the Inca lords to dominate and co-opt the sacred significance of this site.

On the archaeology of Ingapirca, see ANTONIO FRESCO, *La arqueología de Ingapirca (Ecuador): Costumbres funerarias, cerámica y otros materiales* (1984), or JOSÉ ALCINA FRANCH, "Ingapirca: Arquitectura y áreas de asentamiento," in *Revista Española de Antropología Americana* 8 (1978): 127–146. On the protohistoric Cañari ethnic group, see NIELS FOCK and EVA KRENER, "Los Cañaris del Ecuador y sus conceptos etnohistóricos sobre los Incas," in *Estudios Americanistas*, edited by R. Hartmann and U. Oberem, vol. 1 (1975), pp. 170–181. For a general discussion of the regional archaeology, see DONALD COLLIER and JOHN MURRA, "Survey and Excavations in Southern Ecuador," *Field Museum of Natural History, Anthropological Series no. 35* (1943).

TAMARA L. BRAY

INGENIEROS, JOSÉ (*b.* 24 April 1877; *d.* 31 October 1925), Argentine intellectual. Born in Buenos Aires, Ingenieros was one of early twentieth-century Argentina's most prolific and influential intellectual figures. A graduate of the medical school of the University of Buenos Aires, he was particularly interested in and wrote extensively on psychology, psychiatry, and criminology. Ingenieros was an early adherent of socialism, which he later abandoned, and was also active in the formation of the Unión Latino Americana, an organization of Latin American intellectuals and political leaders advocating continental solidarity against the growing influence of the United States in the region. In 1915, he took a teaching position in the school of philosophy and letters of the University of Buenos Aires and founded and edited two journals (the *Revista de Filosofía* and *La Cultura Argentina*), dedicated to literary and philosophical issues.

Ingenieros was the author of scores of articles and many books, his best-known publications being *El hombre mediocre* (1913), a discussion of the spiritually deadening effects of modern society, and *Evolución de las ideas argentinas* (1918–1920), a two-volume examination of Argentine history. Ingenieros was also a strong supporter of and inspiration for the university reform movement that began in 1918.

ANÍBAL PONCE, *José Ingenieros: Su vida y su obra* (1977); JANE VAN DER KARR, *José Ingenieros: The Story of a Scientist-Humanist* (1977).

RICHARD J. WALTER

INGENIOS (Port., *engenhos*), water-driven sugar mills established throughout Spanish and Portuguese America in the early sixteenth century. The *ingenios* became a major commercial enterprise for the colonies in Cuba and Brazil. SUGAR production in the New World was the most intensively organized agro-industry in the Indies. Mill ownership was often more important than land ownership as it meant the control of the actual production process. The *ingenios*, along with the animal-driven mills (*trapiches*) ground the sugar cane and processed sugar for export and local consumption. The *ingenio* was also a central social institution that fostered the development of permanent settlements. Modernization of the industry in the late nineteenth century led to their replacement with steam-drive mills, and the term "*ingenio*" fell out of common usage. In Cuba, for example, larger steam-powered "*centrales*" replaced the older *ingenios*.

LYLE MC ALISTER, *Spain and Portugal in the New World 1492–1700* (1984); JAMES LOCKHART and STUART B. SCHWARTZ, *Early Latin America: A History of Colonial Spanish America and Brazil* (1983).

HEATHER K. THIESSEN

INQUILINAJE, a rural labor system similar to peonage that is peculiar to Chile. In the colonial period, *inquilinos* were often ex-soldiers who resided on the fringes of large estates called *fundos* to protect them from incursion by squatters. When Chile's farms were converted from pastoral activities to cereal raising, landlords

Inquilinos in front of their huts. Central Chile, ca. 1910. LIBRARY OF CONGRESS.

moved the *inquilinos* closer to the main house to facilitate closer supervision of their labor. Housed in wretched hovels, paid in scrip, and deprived of their political rights through vote fraud and intimidation, the *inquilinos* seemed virtually defenseless, especially because the landlords often controlled the instruments of state power: the judiciary, the police, and the militia. As Chile's rural population grew, landlords increased the duties extracted from the *inquilinos,* who had to devote increasingly large amounts of their labor to maintaining the patron's fund.

Happily, the system began to collapse in the 1950s, and with the creation of the Corporation for Agrarian Reform (CORA), the state began to enforce labor laws in the countryside. The Christian Democratic agrarian reform program of the late 1960s eradicated the last vestiges of the *inquilino* system.

GEORGE M. MCBRIDE, *Chile: Land and Society* (1936); BRIAN LOVEMAN, *Struggle in the Countryside: Politics and Rural Labor in Chile, 1919–1973* (1976), p. 49.

WILLIAM F. SATER

See also **Chile: Organizations.**

INQUISITION, THE

Brazil

The Portuguese Inquisition was founded under King JOÃO III in 1536 and abolished in 1821, but no permanent tribunal of the Holy Office sat in Brazil. Inquisition business in the captaincies of Portuguese America was directly administered by the Lisbon Inquisition. The Inquisition was always most active in the states of Bahia, Rio de Janeiro, and Pernambuco, where there was the highest concentration of voluntary lay auxiliaries, the "familiars" (often Portuguese immigrant merchants not of New Christian descent). As a result of distance and its less effective system of repression, Brazil became a haven for New Christians, the descendants of converted Jews, who were particularly suspected of apostasy to Judaism. Denounced individuals were shipped to Lisbon if there seemed sufficient grounds for a trial. If found guilty, they could be punished by confiscation of their property, imprisonment, whippings, and even execution in Portugal. The number of individuals put to death after sentencing by the Inquisition for Judaizing in Brazil did not exceed 500. Arrests and confiscations at the behest of the Inquisition damaged the economic life of Portugal and its colonies by disrupting the system of personal credit drawn on rich New Christian merchants. Reforms carried out from 1768 to 1773 under the Marquês de POMBAL forbade the use of the term "New Christian" and ended Inquisitorial activity against them in Brazil for accusations of Jewish ritual practices.

Lisbon ordered a series of Inquisitorial visitations to Brazil in response to reports of moral and doctrinal laxity there. Father Heitor Furtado de Mendonça collected confessions and denunciations in Bahia from 1591 to 1593, then in Pernambuco from 1593 to 1595. Father Marcos Teixeira investigated in Bahia from 1618 through 1620. Father Giraldo de Abranches was active in Grão-Para from 1763 to 1769. The number of Inquisitorial investigations fluctuated from year to year in response to instructions sent from Lisbon and the zeal of the agents in Brazil. Much documentation of these visitations has been published during the twentieth century and has provided historians with information about colonial social conditions and religious beliefs. Outside of the visitation periods, denunciations were forwarded to Lisbon, which then instructed clerical commissaries resident in Brazil to investigate, and to arrest, if necessary, the accused, who were to stand trial in Portugal. Catholics were reminded annually by the Edict of the Faith of their duty to denounce a list of offenses, including the practice of Jewish rituals, bigamy, witchcraft, sodomy, clerical solicitation of penitents, and blasphemy. Those accused of these offenses in Brazil were usually white males. The proportion of white women, Native Americans, African-born slaves, and free blacks investigated was lower than their proportions of the total population. Article 9 of the 1810 Anglo-Portuguese Treaty of Alliance and Friendship signed in Rio specified that no tribunal would be set up in Portuguese America. In 1821 the Inquisition was abolished throughout Portuguese territories by the liberal CORTES that sat in Lisbon.

ARNOLD WIZNITZER, *Jews in Colonial Brazil* (1960); ANITA NOVINSKY, *Cristãos Novos na Bahia* (1972); SONIA A. SIQUEIRA, *A Inquisição portuguesa e a sociedade colonial* (1978); LAURA DE MELLO E SOUZA, *O diabo e a terra de Santa Cruz* (1986); RONALDO VAINFAS, *Trópico dos pecados: Moral, sexualidade e Inquisição no Brasil* (1989); ELIAS LIPINER, *Izaque de Castro: O mancebo que veio preso do Brasil* (1992); LUIZ MOTT, *Rosa Egipcíaca: Una santa africana no Brasil* (1993).

DAVID HIGGS

Spanish America

The Inquisition was a special tribunal for trying and punishing heresy. In its most basic form, it was one of several powers which the local bishop, as ordinary ecclesiastical justice, exercised.

Pope Sixtus IV approved the creation of the Spanish Inquisition in Seville in 1478. Four years later the pope allowed the Spanish kings to extend the Inquisition to all of their realms. The king governed the Holy Office in Spain and the colonies, in conjunction with the Supreme Council of the Inquisition, called the Suprema, one of several councils of state which functioned in the Spanish imperial system. The monarch appointed local inquisitors. The inquisitors did not necessarily have to be members of the clergy, although nearly all were. Secular authorities meted out the punishments decreed by the Inquisition in a public display, called an auto-da-fé.

Procession of religious judges (foreground) and of prisoners (center) entering the cathedral, where the sentences of the prisoners will be read. Reproduced from Duret, *Voyage de Marseille à Lima* (Paris, 1720). RARE BOOKS AND MANUSCRIPT DIVISION, THE NEW YORK PUBLIC LIBRARY, ASTOR, LENOX, AND TILDEN FOUNDATIONS.

In Spanish America, local bishops and prelates of religious orders, or their appointees, conducted inquisitions prior to 1569. In that year King PHILIP II created two jurisdictions of the Holy Office of the Inquisition in the New World: Mexico and Peru. With the creation of the Holy Office, direction of the Inquisition passed from the local ecclesiastical authorities to a bureaucracy developed under the king of Spain. In 1610 a third seat of the Holy Office was created in Cartagena with jurisdiction over New Granada.

Some of the most famous cases concerned Indians who had reverted to their traditional worship. In Mexico, in 1539, Don Carlos, the *cacique* of Texcoco, was exonerated from idolatry but found guilty of heretical dogmatizing and burned at the stake by Fray Juan de ZUMÁRRAGA, first bishop of Mexico, who had been given the authority of Apostolic Inquisitor by the Holy Office of Seville in 1535. Similarly in Yucatán, Fray Diego de LANDA, prelate of the Franciscan Order, conducted inquisitions against the local Indians on charges of idolatry. Eventually, the crown and Inquisition officials concluded that the Indians, as neophytes to the faith, could not be held to the same standard as Europeans. Under these circumstances, Indians were removed from the jurisdiction of the Holy Office, and local clergy undertook the extirpation of idolatry among the Indians.

The Inquisition customarily handled cases dealing with heresy and in general sought to maintain religious orthodoxy. Usually this involved cases against Protestants, Jews, and Muslims, as well as Catholics with a faulty comprehension of true doctrine. The Inquisition also raised suits against priests who broke their vows or who violated the sanctity of the sacraments. Common among these cases were priests who solicited sexual favors in the confessional. The Inquisition exercised censorship over books and maintained the Index of prohibited books. Simple issues among the faithful, such as fornication, homosexual acts, and the like, were not normally pursued by the Inquisition but rather by the office of the vicar-general and the diocesan courts. The bulk of the cases handled by the Inquisition then concerned heresy against religious orthodoxy; blasphemy, normally involving the swearing of oaths and other curses that got out of hand; sorcery, often involving local medical practitioners and diviners; and bigamy and other violations of the sanctity of the sacraments.

Each office of the Inquisition usually had four officials: two inquisitors; a *fiscal,* or prosecuting attorney; and a secretary or notary. These officials could then appoint others to assist them. Because the territories administered by the inquisitors were so large, initially there were Holy Offices only in Mexico and Lima, and the inquisitors appointed assistants in the major Spanish cities of the realm. These assistants, called *comisarios* (commissaries), normally came from among the ranks of the local clergy. Additionally, the Inquisition maintained a network of lay agents who were granted special status as familiars. In return for serving the Inquisition, these individuals enjoyed high social status and received the *fuero inquisitorial*. The inquisitorial FUERO was the privilege of having legal suits heard by the Inquisition rather than the royal courts.

Proceedings of the Inquisition were kept secret. The legal process could begin in any of several ways, but often a wrongdoer was denounced to an inquisitorial official. The Inquisition would then investigate the denunciation to weigh the merits of the case. If the Inquisitors felt that there was sufficient evidence to warrant a fuller investigation, they would take sworn testimony from witnesses, and eventually from the accused. During the investigation the accused was kept in the secret jail of the Inquisition and out of contact with family and friends.

Questioning of an accused followed a standard form. The accused was first asked to identify himself or herself. The Inquisitors asked if the accused or any relatives had ever been investigated or condemned by the Holy Office. Next the accused was asked to tell about his life. Only after these preliminary data had been collected did the Inquisitors ask the accused if he knew why he had been arrested. At this point the accused might confess the details of the case that interested the Inquisitors. It was also possible that the accused might incriminate himself on other charges, unknowingly. Often people had no idea why they had been arrested. If no testimony were forthcoming, the accused would be admonished to conduct a personal soul search for anything that might be against Christian doctrine in order to confess it at a later occasion. All witnesses, as noted, were sworn to secrecy. If the inquisitors were unable to secure a confession from the accused on the original grounds after several sessions of questioning, the accused could be subjected to judicial torture. This was an extremely serious step, and safeguards were included in the operating procedures of the Inquisition to avoid unnecessary torture. Furthermore, certain groups, such as clerics, could not be subjected to torture, except under very extreme circumstances.

Because the inquisitorial proceedings were so thorough, they could easily last several years. This meant that some defendants were imprisoned for long periods of time without any normal contact with family or friends. However, only a very small percentage of all cases initially considered by the Inquisition actually came to trial.

People found guilty by the Inquisition were subject to both penance and punishment. The penance was administered by the Inquisition, while punishment was meted out by secular authorities. Normal penance included wearing distinctive garb, such as the *sanbenito*, a small cape or scapulary worn around the shoulders; the saying of prayers and other devotions; and public humiliation in the auto-da-fé. Punishments ran the gamut from whipping and other corporal punishment to execution. Many of those convicted were exiled, either from their place of residence, the immediate territory, or from the Americas. In some situations, persons convicted by the Holy Office in the New World, once exiled, found themselves arrested by the Inquisition in Seville upon arrival there. The property of those convicted could also be confiscated by the Holy Office and sold, the proceeds used to pay court costs. The principle behind sentencing was the eventual reconciliation of the sinner with the body of the church. Consequently, punishments and penances were meant to provide not only a public ceremony where society could see the wages of sin but also occasions for private repentance. Executions were, therefore, to be used only against the most obdurate sinners who refused reconciliation or whose crimes had significantly destroyed the local social fabric.

Over the course of the 250-year history of the Inquisition in Spanish America, the main targets were foreigners, members of the clergy, and suspected Jews. Executions and large public autos-da-fé were far more frequent early in the history of the Holy Office than later on. The last formal execution in Mexico, prior to the upheavals of the Wars of Independence, occurred in 1781, and only fourteen people were executed in the 100 years prior to that. The Holy Office of the Inquisition was first suppressed by the CORTES OF CÁDIZ in 1813, only to be restored by Ferdinand VII in 1814, when he gained the throne. Consequently, the Inquisition was used against some of the leaders of the Independence movements in Spanish America. Eventually, with the triumph of liberal forces in Spain, the Holy Office came to its final end in 1820.

Although the Holy Office was staffed by clerics, and had the charge to maintain the purity of Christian doctrine, in effect it was a secular institution, under the control of the monarch. The high officials were appointed by the monarch, and policies established by the Suprema were subject to the monarch's approval. Making no distinction between religious and political philosophy because it assumed that the former determined the latter, the Inquisition sought to maintain the homogeneity of the body politic by assuring the existence of only one religious philosophy. On the other hand, because the Inquisition fell beyond the normal authority of local officials, either royal or ecclesiastical, it had a relatively high degree of independence from immediate oversight. By and large, however, the Spanish population of the Indies supported the actions of the Inquisition and did not themselves feel threatened by it.

HENRY C. LEA, *The Inquisition in the Spanish Dependencies: Sicily, Naples, Sardinia, Milan, the Canaries, Mexico, Peru, New Granada* (1908); JOSÉ T. MEDINA, *Historia del Tribunal del Santo Oficio de la Inquisición en México*, 2d ed. (1952), and *Historia del Tri-*

bunal de la Inquisición de Lima, 2d ed., 2 vols. (1956); RICHARD E. GREENLEAF, *Zumárraga and the Mexican Inquisition* (1961) and *The Mexican Inquisition of the Sixteenth Century* (1969).

JOHN F. SCHWALLER

INSTITUTE OF NUTRITION OF CENTRAL AMERICA AND PANAMA (INCAP),

a regional nutritional research and development agency located in Guatemala City. Representatives of the five Central American countries plus Panama met in 1946 under the auspices of the Pan-American Health Organization to consider regional health problems. They decided to create a cooperative organization to work on common nutritional problems. The government of Guatemala agreed to erect the building to house the institute, the W. K. Kellogg Foundation provided funds for staff-development scholarships and for initial equipment, and the Pan-American Health Organization gave administrative support. Money for continuing operating costs was provided by member countries and by supporting international agencies.

INCAP was inaugurated on 15 September 1949. Its program has included the study of nutritional problems in the region, the search for solutions to those problems, and assistance to the member countries in implementing those solutions. One of INCAP's major successes has been the introduction of iodized salt to counter a widespread incidence of goiter. A high-protein, child-feeding supplement called Incaparina was developed with private manufacturers. Other programs have focused on vitamin A deficiencies and on child survival techniques. INCAP has been a leader in studying the nutritional status of specific populations and the relationship between prenatal and postnatal malnutrition and the development of children, including learning and behavior.

NEVIN S. SCRIMSHAW and MOISÉS BEHAR, eds., *Symposium on Nutrition and Agricultural and Economic Development in the Tropics* (1976); INCAP, *Desarrollo del proceso de planificación multisectorial de la alimentación y nutrición en Centro America y Panama* (1979).

DAVID L. JICKLING

INSTITUTIONAL ACTS,

decrees issued by Brazil's military regime during the 1960s to provide legal justification for its assumption of greater power. Designed to restructure the political system, the seventeen Institutional Acts, of which the first and fifth are most significant, enabled the regime to establish an authoritarian government.

The first Institutional Act was announced on 9 April 1964, eight days after a military coup had left the office of the presidency vacant. Under this act, the chief executive could cancel electoral mandates, suppress individual political rights, and suspend constitutional liberties. The act limited the power of Congress by forbidding it to increase the amount of any expenditure measures submitted by the president and giving it only thirty days to consider executive-proposed amendments to the constitution. Another provision of the act established an electoral college that chose General Humberto CASTELO BRANCO to lead the new government.

The military regime hoped to maintain popular support while using the first Institutional Act to create a national security state capable of eliminating subversion. When the government's party fared poorly in the October 1965 elections, however, hard-liners convinced Castelo Branco to issue a second Institutional Act. This act's strictures, viewed as temporary measures needed to ensure the regime's control over government, abolished the existing political parties, provided for the indirect election of the president, restricted the amount of time Congress could consider legislation before it automatically became law, and stipulated that persons accused of crimes against national security were to be subject to military justice.

Brazil's next president, General Artur COSTA E SILVA, was aligned with the less moderate military faction. On 13 December 1968, in response to student protests, labor strikes, and congressional noncompliance, he issued his first Institutional Act, the fifth overall. This notorious act suspended constitutional and individual liberties and signaled an attempt by hard-liners to increase the military regime's control over Brazil. In the following year, the government issued twelve Institutional Acts of lesser significance but accompanied by Supplementary Acts and other decrees that canceled upcoming elections, suspended Congress indefinitely, and further expanded the powers of the executive.

MARIA HELENA MOREIRA ALVES, *State and Opposition in Military Brazil* (1985); THOMAS SKIDMORE, *The Politics of Military Rule in Brazil, 1964–85* (1988); ALFRED STEPAN, *Rethinking Military Politics* (1988).

MICHAEL POLL

INSTITUTO HISTÓRICO E GEOGRÁFICO BRASILEIRO

(IHGB), Brazilian research center characterized by its patriotic historiography and amateur scholarship. Its origins date to 1838 and are associated with the beginnings of Brazilian romantic nationalism, a milieu heavily indebted to contemporary French ideas and institutions. The institute was founded under the official protection of the emperor PEDRO II, who often presided over its meetings. Founders included celebrated literati, imperial statesmen, and associates of the French Institut Historique. Establishment backgrounds remained the rule through the monarchy and the Old Republic (1889–1930). The IHGB continues to include members of traditional elite families, including the former dynasty, and to enjoy an official link to the national government.

The mission of the institution was to strengthen the new empire by identifying it with, and defining, the national past. To that end, the IHGB has collected, organized, and published historical and geographical doc-

285

uments and has established relations with similar foreign organizations. It has also published the *Revista do Instituto Histórico e Geográfico Brasileiro*, which since 1839 has been fundamental to Brazilian studies. The IHGB library has more than 100,000 volumes; its archives hold 50,000 documents and 5,000 maps. Among its great strengths, perhaps foremost, is its material on the monarchy and its personal archives for statesmen of that era and the Old Republic.

ROLLIE E. POPPINO, "A Century of the *Revista do Instituto Histórico e Geográfico Brasileiro*," in *Hispanic American Historical Review* 33, no. 2 (1953): 307–23; MANOEL LUÍS SALGADO GUIMARÃES, "Nação e civilização nos trópicos," in *Estudos Históricos* 1 (1988): 5–27.

JEFFREY D. NEEDELL

See also **Varnhagen, Francisco Adolfo de.**

INTENDANCY SYSTEM, administrative and territorial subdivisions of viceroyalties, headed by an intendant or superintendent, and implemented in Latin America in the last half of the eighteenth century. The BOURBON dynasty assumed the Spanish throne in 1700 and began a series of reforms to centralize its power, reduce creole influence, increase its revenues, and eliminate corruption both on the Peninsula and throughout the empire. PHILIP V ordered intendancies created in Spain in 1718 but full implementation of the decree was delayed until 1749. A study of the economic conditions of the empire written by José del Campillo y Cossío in 1743 recommended that a series of investigations be conducted throughout the empire to identify the problems of each region and suggested utilization of the intendancy system to correct them. With the return of Havana to Spanish control in 1762, CHARLES III adopted Campillo's recommendations and sent José de GÁLVEZ to examine New Spain and Alejandro O'REILLY to study the Caribbean colonies. Cuba, changed by its exposure to international trade during the British occupation, received first attention, and in 1764 Charles created an intendancy for the island. José de Gálvez submitted the reports of his investigation in New Spain to the crown in 1768, recommending solutions to the problems of that colony and calling for implementation of the intendancy system throughout the empire. Resistance from New Spain's viceroy, Antonio María de BUCARELI, delayed application of this recommendation until 1782.

In that year, the king issued the Ordinance for Intendants, creating a position in Buenos Aires for a superintendent with nominal control over the remaining seven intendancies in the Viceroyalty of Río de la Plata, including Upper Peru. The following year, the plan was applied to Venezuela and in 1784 to Peru and the Philippines. By 1786, a revision of the initial ordinance appeared called the New Code for Intendants, issuing instructions to create twelve intendancies for New Spain, and its provisions were applied to the remainder

of the empire. In 1812 the intendancy of Cuba was divided into three jurisdictions, with a superintendent in Havana and separate intendancies in Santiago and Puerto Principe. In some cases, as in Spain, the governor of a region also served as intendant, although Gálvez recognized this as a source of corruption and inefficiency. The last intendancy filled in 1814 separated the positions on the island of Puerto Rico.

Older studies of the intendancies tended to suggest that all were alike, created for the same reasons, and existing under the same rules and regulations. There were, however, functional and territorial distinctions that made them different. The theoretical role of all intendants, nevertheless, was the same. Their instructions asked them to streamline the bureaucracy, promote efficiency, eliminate corruption and contraband, increase the tax yields, develop new raw materials for export to Spain, widen the colonial markets for Spanish goods, improve colonial facilities, promote education and technology, foster immigration to colonize agricultural areas, stimulate activities of the *cabildos*, and reorganize the militia. In order to achieve these ends, they took powers from all officials from the top down. In the vice-regal centers of New Spain and Peru, and in Central America, they replaced the *alcaldes mayores* and *corregidores* in Indian regions, jurisdictions long plagued by low salaries and massive corruption. For example, the twelve intendancies created in New Spain replaced 200 of these officials. However, the provinces created in that colony were so large that the intendancies were divided into districts (*partidos*) and the intendants appointed subdelegates in each to serve in their stead. Because of continuing low salaries and a lack of qualified individuals, many of the former officials became subdelegates and continued the corruption and exploitation of Indian populations.

In practice, all intendants had jurisdiction over taxation and financial aspects of the military. The Caribbean colonies, limited to these two areas, suffered constant jurisdictional disputes with the captains-general and other officials. Their situation was different from that on the mainland since the Caribbean colonies had no major Indian populations and had a disproportionate concern with trade and international interests because of their locations. Caribbean intendants had limited jurisdictions until the end of the system in 1853. The intendants on the mainland colonies enjoyed expanded powers that included administrative and judicial functions and stronger control over the military. They were given powers to examine and correct deficiencies in administration, and they became the first court of appeal in matters regarding trade and commerce, controlling function, composition, and movement of the military.

To further wrest colonial power and control from the creole elites, the crown generally appointed peninsular Spaniards to these positions. The intendants generally had good educations and approached their positions with the zeal evident in the late Bourbon period. They often received the appointment based on experience. For example, those named in Nicaragua and Honduras required prowess in martial skills to counter contraband and foreign colonization efforts. Those in Chiapas and El Salvador, regions with serious economic and legal problems, required men with fiscal and judicial expertise.

In general, the intendants increased revenues appreciably through commercial and agricultural diversification and a more efficient tax collection system, though they seem to have been more successful in peripheral areas than in the viceregal centers. Abuses of Indian populations did not cease because of the subdelegados, and in fact Indian tribute declined in New Spain because of the greater subdivision of territory. The bureaucracy created by the system increased the costs of administration, but the increased revenues, channeled into development of each region, did tend to benefit its residents. Immigration programs brought Spaniards into commercial centers and they, not the creole merchants, derived the benefits of the reforms. The appointment of peninsular Spaniards to most of the positions and the effects of their reforms further exacerbated creole frustration and animosity against Spain. In some areas, like Chile, the immigration program changed the face of the colony by whitening the population. The geographic divisions created regional autonomy and its creoles developed a regional loyalty rather than the hoped-for loyalty to Spain. During the wars for independence, the emerging states took on physical boundaries similar to those created under the system.

Differences in regions governed and in individual personalities determined the success or failure of a particular intendant. Early historians praised the system for achieving Bourbon goals. Some condemn the system altogether and say it caused more problems than it solved. Others believe some were successful while others were not. Studies of the careers of individual intendants are few, so an accurate conclusion on the effectiveness of the system is impossible. The available evidence shows that the force of the intendant and the cooperation of creoles in the Caribbean and Central America allowed progress, but that an entrenched system of creole elite power and uncooperative officials thwarted chances of success in Chile.

The basic study is LILLIAN FISHER, *The Intendant System in Spanish America* (1929). Various regions are discussed in JOHN R. FISHER, *Government and Society in Colonial Peru: The Intendant System 1784–1814* (1970); JOHN LYNCH, *Spanish Colonial Administration, 1782–1818: The Intendant System in the Viceroyalty of the Río de la Plata* (1958); ALTAGRACIA ORTIZ, *Eighteenth Century Reforms in the Caribbean* (1983); and HECTOR HUMBERTO SAMAYOA GUEVARA, *El régimen de intendencias en el Reino de Guatemala* (1978). Most individual studies are doctoral dissertations, but two are published, M. ISIDRO MÉNDEZ, *El Intendente Ramírez* (1944), and JACQUES BARBIER, *Reform and Politics in Bourbon Chile, 1755–1796* (1980).

JACQUELYN BRIGGS KENT

INTER-AMERICAN CONGRESS OF WOMEN, an international conference held in Guatemala City, Guatemala, 21–27 August 1947. Sponsored by the Committee of the Americas of the Women's International League for Peace and Freedom and hosted by the Guatemalan Union of Democratic Women, the meeting was comprised of representatives of women's groups from nineteen western hemisphere nations who convened to "denounce the hemispheric armament plan under discussion at the Rio Conference" and demand that "the cost of the arms program be used to support industry, agriculture, health, and education for our people."

The belief that "women of our continent" have a particular right to speak out on "inter-American political problems," as stated in the minutes of the congress, had a long precedent, as did the delegates' concern with international peace and issues of social and economic justice. The women sent cablegrams to the Rio Conference asking that the delegates respect the peaceful intent of the Charter of the United Nations and urging that "the expansion of communism will not be contained by force of arms." Their efforts were unrequited.

The Primero Congreso Interamericano de Mujeres (to give the official title) was not the "first" inter-American congress of women; rather, the title underscored the discontinuity of the historical record of women's activities at the international level. Convening the congress demonstrated the women's conviction that a separatist strategy continued to be necessary for women to make their voices heard on political issues in the post-World War II world. The legacy of the congress is clear in the 1949 mandate to the Inter-American Commission of Women in the charter of the Organization of American States.

The papers of the Primero Congreso Interamericano de Mujeres, 1947, are in the Collection of Alicia Moreau de Justo, Montevideo, Uruguay. See also FRANCESCA MILLER, "Latin American Feminism and the Transnational Arena," in *Women, Culture, and Politics in Latin America* (1990) and *Latin American Women and the Search for Social Justice* (1991).

FRANCESCA MILLER

See also **Feminism; Pan-American Conferences; Rio Treaty.**

INTER-AMERICAN DEVELOPMENT BANK (IDB), an international organization, headquartered in Washington, D.C., that was created by a 1959 agreement among Western Hemisphere governments; it began operations on 1 October 1960. Founded by nineteen Latin American countries and the United States, it has forty-five members (1992), including Caribbean islands, Canada, most European countries, Israel, and Japan. The extraregional countries began to join in 1976. The IDB's original capitalization was $1 billion, consisting of $850 million ordinary capital, of which a fraction was paid in and the remainder callable (guarantee capital), plus

$150 million in the Fund for Special Operations. By 1992, subscribed capital amounted to $54 billion. At the end of 1992, the IDB had approved 1,987 loans for a total of $56.8 billion and had made available $1.9 billion for technical cooperation. Over $41.7 billion had been disbursed. The total cost of projects financed exceeded $57 billion.

The IDB's charter stipulates that its purpose is to further the economic and social development of the regional members, individually and collectively. The United States, Canada, and the nonregional members do not borrow from the IDB. Loans are made to governments or government-guaranteed entities, although the charter does not prohibit lending to private enterprise; for this purpose the IDB sponsored the formation of the Inter-American Investment Corporation (1989), composed of most member countries. Most IDB loans have been for economic and social infrastructure, particularly agriculture, energy, industry, transportation, public health and the environment, education, science and technology, and urban development.

The IDB uses the callable portion of its capital to back its borrowings by means of bond issues in international capital markets; its bonds have a rating of AAA (investment grade), which enables it to lend at close to market rates. During 1992 the interest rate was about 7.5 percent. Loans from the Fund for Special Operations, available to the financially weaker member countries, are granted at between 1 and 4 percent.

Early efforts to establish an inter-American financial entity go back to the nineteenth century, although the original purposes were closely related to commercial banking activities. The First International American Conference (Washington, D.C., 1889–1890) encouraged governments to grant concessions for the development of inter-American banking operations and to establish an International American Bank. The Seventh International American Conference (Montevideo, 1933) unanimously recommended the establishment of an inter-American bank, primarily to function as a regional central bank. Despite support by U.S. President Franklin Roosevelt, the U.S. Congress did not ratify the proposal. In the aftermath of World War II, the creation of the World Bank seemed to make an inter-American financial organization less urgent than the reconstruction of war-torn Europe.

The decade of the 1950s underscored the need for external cooperation with Latin America, given declining terms of trade and reserves. Moreover, Latin American countries were unhappy with the World Bank's decision-making format, which, in their opinion, gave little consideration to the requirements of recipients and was said to be dominated by the stronger countries. A 1954 report by Raúl PREBISCH recommended the creation of an industrial and agricultural development fund; at the November 1954 Quitandinha (Brazil) meeting of the hemisphere's finance ministers, President Juscelino KUBITSCHEK of Brazil (later supported by President Alberto Lleras Camargo of Colombia) adopted the plan in substance, with the endorsement of the finance ministers, and called for Operación Panamericana, a series of measures in international public financing. In 1958 the United States indicated its readiness to support a regional development agency. A negotiating commission was established by the Eisenhower administration in 1959, and on 30 December of that year the requisite number of countries ratified the IDB charter.

The first president of the IDB was Felipe Herrera of Chile (1960–1970); he was succeeded by Antonio ORTIZ MENA of Mexico (1971–1987) and Enrique V. Iglesias of Uruguay (since 1988).

JULIO BROIDE, *Banco Interamericano de Desarrollo, sus antecedentes y creación* (1968); SIDNEY DELL, *The Inter-American Development Bank, a Study in Development Financing* (1972); JOSÉ D. EPSTEIN, "Interamerican Development Bank," in *International Banking Handbook,* edited by William H. Baughn and Donald K. Mandich (1983), pp. 503–521; G. POPE ATKINS, *Latin America in the International Political System* (1989), pp. 202–236. See also *IDB Annual Reports,* esp. the 1976 and 1991 reports, which mention issues related to IDB history, and the annual *IDB Economic and Social Progress in Latin America* (1985, 1991).

JOSÉ D. EPSTEIN

See also **Banking; Economic Development; Pan-American Conferences.**

INTER-AMERICAN FOUNDATION (IAF), an autonomous U.S. government corporation created in December 1969 as the Inter-American Social Development Institute. It arose from concern among key congressional members and executive branch officials in the development community that the efforts of the ALLIANCE FOR PROGRESS during the 1960s had failed to produce a noticeable effect on the social conditions of the poor in Latin America and the Caribbean, in spite of the advances shown by macroeconomic indicators. This lack of significant social progress was partly attributed to an undue emphasis on basic infrastructural projects as opposed to social policy and human resource development. However, it was also felt that the customary linkage of U.S. development assistance to short-term foreign policy interests related to host-country governments unnecessarily constrained what ought to be a long-term process of support related to host-country people.

Thus, under the congressional leadership of Representative Dante Fascell, the new agency was given considerable autonomy from the executive branch, particularly the State Department and the U.S. AGENCY FOR INTERNATIONAL DEVELOPMENT, and a mandate to take its development assistance directly to the beneficiaries, bypassing government institutions in the host countries. To emphasize this autonomy, the new agency was to be governed by a nine-member board of directors appointed by the White House; six of its members were to come from the private sector. Most unusual, perhaps, the legislation emphasized the experimental nature of the initiatives to be undertaken by the new agency, granting it the privilege to take risks—and thus sometimes to fail— and the responsibility to document the lessons learned. It was to be funded by direct congressional appropriations and—after subsequent negotiations—from the U.S.-funded Social Progress Trust Fund in the INTER-AMERICAN DEVELOPMENT BANK. After selection of board members and president, negotiations about its modus operandi, and debate about its location and even its name, the IAF opened for business in 1971.

Operationally, the IAF functions much like a private foundation. Its programs of direct grants, organized by country and region rather than by topic, are directed by appointed foundation representatives with administrative support. All its staff members are U.S. civil servants. Until 1994 the IAF has made a total of $425 million in grants in 26 countries to more than 4,500 organizations. Grants typically range in size from several thousand to several hundred thousand dollars, and durations range from several months to (rarely) more than three years, although continuation of projects for longer periods through amendments is common. For fiscal year 1994 the IAF had an authorized staff of 75 and a total budget of $31 million, 80 percent of which was devoted to programs. It accepts proposals on an ongoing basis and has no set format or schedule for these presentations.

By design, and to emphasize its autonomy from U.S. foreign policy interests, the IAF bases all of its staff in its U.S. headquarters in Arlington, Virginia. To compensate for the lack of a permanent country presence, it has relied on a very experienced staff, frequent visits, and an intensely hands-on style of relating to grantees and other country nationals. In the early 1980s the IAF began experimenting with a supplemental system of contracted in-country support services for administration, information clearinghouse, logistics, and evaluation of projects. By the 1990s the system had expanded to a network of support centers in all countries, some with a capacity to handle disbursements for small projects.

In line with its mandate to experiment and document, the IAF maintains an active learning and dissemination effort based on its quarterly journal, *Grassroots Development,* and frequent publication of books and occasional papers by staff and outside experts.

ROBERT W. MASHEK, *The Inter American Foundation in the Making* (1981).

RAMON E. DAUBON

INTER-AMERICAN ORGANIZATIONS, the constituent organizational, institutional, and legal-constitutional elements of the INTER-AMERICAN SYSTEM. From 1889 to the present there has been a gradual evolution of the Inter-American System, the successive creation of inter-American organizations, first through the Pan-American

Union and then through the Organization of American States (OAS).

ORGANIZATION OF AMERICAN STATES
The OAS is the central inter-American institution. The principal components of the OAS include the following:

General Secretariat The central, permanent institution of the Inter-American System that implements the programs and policies as directed by the General Assembly and the various decision-making councils. The General Secretariat is headquartered in Washington, D.C., with national offices and specialized institutes located in member countries.

General Assembly The supreme decision-making organ of the OAS. The Assembly, which meets at annual sessions in one of the member states or at OAS headquarters in Washington, D.C., sets the policy and budget for the OAS and its agencies.

Meetings of Consultation and Ministers of Foreign Relations Conferences may be convened (by the OAS Permanent Council at the request of a member state) "to consider problems of an urgent nature and of common interest" (OAS Charter) or in cases of attack or threats to peace and security.

Permanent Council Body that guides and monitors the daily business of the OAS. It is comprised of permanent representatives (holding ambassadorial rank) from each of the thirty-four active member states. The Council meets more than twice a month at OAS Headquarters in Washington, D.C.

Inter-American Council for Integral Development (CIDI) The "Protocol of Managua," approved at the June 1993 OAS General Assembly and now subject to ratification, merges the Inter-American Social and Economic Council (CIES) and Inter-American Council for Education, Science and Culture (CIECC) into a single Inter-American Council for Integral Development, which will provide greater coordination and efficiency of technical cooperation programs.

INTER-AMERICAN SPECIALIZED AGENCIES
The other inter-American organizations which, together with the councils of the OAS comprise the Inter-American System, include the INTER-AMERICAN DEVELOPMENT BANK, the Inter-American Defense Board, and the following specialized institutions and agencies:

Inter-American Institute for Cooperation on Agriculture (IICA) Founded in 1942 and based in Costa Rica, the Institute initiates projects to help member states plan and evaluate agriculture policies, develop and share technology, promote rural development, improve animal health, and generate trade.

Pan-American Health Organization (PAHO) Based in Washington, D.C., this agency cooperates closely with governments of the hemisphere to promote health care. Founded as the Pan-American Sanitary Bureau in 1902, it is both an OAS specialized organization and a regional arm of the World Health Organization.

Inter-American Commission of Human Rights (IACHR) Created in 1969, it is governed by the American Convention on Human Rights, which was signed in 1969 and put into force in 1978. The Commission, based in Washington, D.C., has seven members, who are proposed by member states and elected, in their own right, by the OAS General Assembly. The IACHR represents the thirty-five member states of the OAS.

Inter-American Court of Human Rights Created by the Pact of San José in 1969, the court is an autonomous judicial institution whose purpose is to apply and interpret the American Convention of Human Rights. It is composed of seven jurists from OAS member countries and is located in San José, Costa Rica.

Inter-American Drug Abuse Control Commission (CICAD) Established by the General Assembly of the OAS in 1986, it has a current membership of twenty-four states, which will increase to twenty-nine by 1995. CICAD's mandate is to promote and facilitate close cooperation among the member countries in the control of drug trafficking, production, and use in accordance with the Inter-American Program of Action of Rio de Janeiro (1986).

Inter-American Commission of Women (CIM) A specialized agency of the OAS, which was established in 1928 at the Sixth International Conference of American States in Havana, Cuba. It is the first official intergovernmental agency created expressly to ensure recognition of the civil and political rights of women in the Americas—the first not only in the region, but in the world.

Inter-American Children's Institute (IACI) Founded in 1927 and located in Montevideo, Uruguay, the IACI strives to achieve better health and living conditions for children and the family. The Institute serves as a center of social action, carrying out programs in the fields of health, education, social legislation, social service, and statistics.

Pan-American Institute of Geography and History (PAIGH) Founded in 1928 and located in Mexico City, the PAN-AMERICAN INSTITUTE OF GEOGRAPHY AND HISTORY seeks to encourage, coordinate, and publicize geographic, historical, cartographic, and geophysical studies in the Americas.

Inter-American Indian Institute (IAII) Created in 1940 and located in Mexico City, the IAII is concerned primarily with initiating, coordinating, and directing research for better understanding of Indian groups in the hemisphere and for the solution of their health, educational, economic, and social problems. It provides technical assistance in establishing programs of Indian community development.

CHARLES G. FENWICK, *The Organization of American States: The Inter-American Regional System* (1963); HENRY H. HAM, *Problems and Prospects of the Organization of American States* (1987); ORGANIZATION OF AMERICAN STATES, *The OAS and the Evolution of the Inter-American System* (1988); L. RONALD SCHEMAN, *The Inter-American Dilemma: The Search for Inter-American Cooperation at the Centennial of the Inter-American System* (1988); and G. POPE ATKINS, *Latin America in the International Political System*, 2d. rev. ed. (1989).

MICHAEL GOLD-BISS

See also **Pan-American Conferences.**

INTER-AMERICAN SYSTEM. The Inter-American System originated with the First International Conference of American States (Washington, D.C.; 1889), which established the International Union of American Republics and the Commercial Bureau of the American Republics in Washington, D.C. This effort built on the unsuccessful series of international "Americanismo" and Pan-Americanism–driven congresses, which tried to form a Spanish American union, beginning with the PANAMA CONGRESS OF 1826 and ending with the Second Lima Congress of 1865. Parallel endeavors for regional cooperation were the international law conferences held from 1887 to 1889. Such attempts were unsuccessful until, with encouragement of the United States, the American republics managed to place their hopes for political cooperation in a union governed by the rule of international law. The principal missions of the Inter-American System have included the maintenance and guarantee of peaceful relations and the nonviolent resolution of conflicts, security, and development. Its initial mandate was the establishment of the rule of international law to replace the rule of force in inter-American relations.

Representatives of American nations attended a series of conferences that created the treaties, conventions, and legal instruments upon which the multilateral cooperation between those nations is based. The conferences included eleven International Conferences of American States, thirteen Meetings of Consultation of Ministers of Foreign Affairs, eight Special Inter-American Conferences, and dozens of specialized conferences that focused on particular areas of concern from agriculture to public health.

The first International Conference of American States, held in Washington, D.C., from 1889 to 1890 bore fruit in 1910 in the form of the Pan-American Union, which served as the permanent secretariat for the Pan-American conferences and, after 1948, for the ORGANIZATION OF AMERICAN STATES (OAS). After 1890 the International Conferences of American States met every five years except during the two world wars. The Second International Conference of American States (Mexico City, 1901) adopted a protocol of adherence to the conventions framed by the First Hague Peace Conference in 1899. The Third International Conference (Rio de Janeiro, 1906) set conventions regarding copyright law, commercial arbitration, and international law, a process continued by the Fourth (Buenos Aires, 1910), which established conventions related to patents, artistic property, and commercial statistics, and set standards for the Pan-American railroad. The Fifth Conference (Santiago, 1923) adopted the GONDRA TREATY to avoid conflicts between American states and approved the formation of the PAN-AMERICAN HIGHWAY system. The Sixth Conference (Havana, 1928) approved conventions on political asylum, maritime neutrality, private international law (the Bustamante Code), extradition, and the duties of states in the event of civil strife.

The three conferences in the 1930s as well as the first three Meetings of Consultation of Ministers of Foreign Affairs (1939, 1940, 1942) responded to U.S. concerns about the increasing likelihood of war in Europe, the need to guarantee inter-American cooperation in that event, and U.S. and Latin American participation in the war effort. In 1933, the Seventh International Conference of American States (Montevideo) adopted the Convention of the Rights and Duties of States. Article VII of the Convention established that "no state has the right to intervene in the internal affairs of another." This Convention drew on the CALVO and DRAGO doctrines of non-intervention. The 1936 Special Conference for the Maintenance of Peace (also known as the Buenos Aires Conference) established procedures for the peaceful settlement of disputes in the event of an international war outside the hemisphere, and the Eighth International Conference (Lima, 1938) created the mechanism for meetings of consultation of ministers of foreign affairs.

The Special Inter-American Conference on the Problems of War and Peace (Mexico City, 1945) created the Inter-American Economic and Social Council and adopted the Act of CHAPULTEPEC, which declared that an act of aggression against any of the American states would be considered aggression against them all. The Special Inter-American Conference for the Maintenance of Continental Peace and Security (Rio de Janeiro, 1947) established principles for collective defense in the form of the Inter-American Treaty of Reciprocal Assistance, or RIO TREATY, that served as the basis for security arrangements in the Americas for the next forty years. The Ninth Conference (Bogotá, 1948) approved the Charter of the Organization of American States (OAS), the American Declaration of the Rights and Duties of Man, and conventions granting civil and political rights to women. The Tenth Inter-American Conference (Caracas, 1954) approved the creation of the economic, social, and cultural development programs of the OAS and adopted conventions on territorial and diplomatic ASYLUM. In 1959, the INTER-AMERICAN DEVELOPMENT BANK (IDB) was established to promote economic development, following suggestions offered by the United Nations ECONOMIC COMMISSION FOR LATIN AMERICA and its executive secretary, Raúl PREBISCH. At the Fifth Meeting of Consultation (Santiago, 1959) the Inter-American Commission on Human Rights was created. During the meeting of American Chiefs of State (Punta del Este, Uruguay, 1961), the Declaration to the Peoples of the Americas and the Charter of Punta del Este, creating the ALLIANCE FOR PROGRESS, were adopted.

Economic cooperation was soon overshadowed by the tension caused by the cold war, which climaxed with the 1962 expulsion of the government of Cuba from the OAS. Cuba's ouster was based on the understanding that "the adherence by any member of the Organization of American States to marxism-leninism is incompatible with the Inter-American System." Following the 1964 intervention by the United States in the Dominican Republic, the OAS created the Inter-American Peace Force, which helped end the fighting in that country and allowed elections in order to reestablish a constitutional government.

After 1970, in accordance with the 1967 revision of the OAS Charter, the International Conferences of American States were replaced by annual meetings of the General Assembly of the OAS. In the ensuing years, the OAS met to condemn and respond to various security-related incidents, including Cuban aggression against Venezuela, Bolivia, and other American states; the armed conflict between El Salvador and Honduras; the clash between Nicaragua and Costa Rica in 1978; the Nicaraguan crisis that ended with the triumph of the Sandinistas in 1979; the Peruvian-Ecuadorian clashes of 1981; and the FALKLANDS/MALVINAS WAR between Argentina and Great Britain in 1982. This last event threatened to undermine the Inter-American System because the United States supported the British venture to regain the islands, despite the Latin American perception that Great Britain was an extracontinental aggressor as defined by the Rio Treaty. The U.S. invasions of Grenada in 1983 and Panama in 1989 further weakened the cohesion of the Inter-American System, but the return to democratic rule in every American republic except Peru revived the OAS.

The future of the Inter-American System in the post–cold war era of economic integration and competition is contingent on the continued cooperation of all the hemisphere's nations. The integration efforts of the United States, Canada, Mexico, and Chile are being followed with great interest by the rest of the hemisphere, given the lack of success of such subregional efforts as the CENTRAL AMERICAN COMMON MARKET and the ANDEAN PACT. Cooperation continues on other matters, including health issues (for example, AIDS and cholera), resource development and management, energy security, environmental protection, narco-trafficking and violence, and nuclear proliferation.

The most important Pan-American conferences are treated in individual articles below. They are listed alphabetically under the name of the city in which they took place.

PAN AMERICAN UNION, *The Pan American Union and the Pan American Conferences* (1940); FRANCISCO CUEVAS CANCINO, *Del Congreso de Panamá a la Conference de Caracas, 1826–1954* (1955); JOHN D. MARTZ and LARS SCHOULTZ, eds., *Latin America, the United States, and the Inter-American System* (1980); L. RONALD

SCHEMAN, *The Inter-American Dilemma: The Search for Inter-American Cooperation at the Centennial of the Inter-American System* (1988); and, especially, G. POPE ATKINS, *Latin America in the International Political System*, 2d rev. ed. (1989).

MICHAEL GOLD-BISS
JAMES PATRICK KIERNAN

INTER-AMERICAN TREATY OF RECIPROCAL ASSISTANCE. *See* Rio Treaty (1947).

INTERNATIONAL COFFEE AGREEMENT,

the 1962 and 1983 accords reached by the coffee-producing and consuming nations of the world to stabilize the international coffee market and to alleviate the difficulties related to excessive fluctuations in the levels of world supplies, stocks, and prices of coffee. The agreements sought to establish a balance between supply and demand and to maintain prices at equitable levels. The principal mechanism of the agreements was the apportionment of export quotas, adjusted to world demand, among the producing nations.

The first international agreement to protect the COFFEE INDUSTRY was the 1940 Inter-American Coffee Marketing Agreement, which expired in 1948. Aimed at providing a market for fourteen Latin American coffee-producing countries who were affected by the closing of European markets during World War II, the agreement established U.S. import quotas at reasonable prices. Surplus production and falling prices in the late 1950s led Portugal and Latin American producers to create the International Coffee Organization to promote international consumption of coffee and to research ways of improving the quality of coffee and the reduction of production costs.

The short supply of coffee and changing production conditions after 1970 led to disagreement between producing and consuming nations that might have jeopardized the continuation of the 1962 treaty. In 1983, a new agreement endorsed the same principles outlined in the 1962 treaty and highlighted, in addition, the promotion and maintenance of employment and income in member countries to help bring about fair wages, higher living standards, and better working conditions.

HELEN DELPAR, ed., *Encyclopedia of Latin America* (1974); Department of State, *International Coffee Agreement, 1983, Between the United States of America and Other Governments* (1983).

NANCY PRISCILLA S. NARO

INTERNATIONAL PETROLEUM COMPANY (IPC),

foreign oil concern active in Peru. Breaking Latin American legal precedent, Simón BOLÍVAR granted to one of his followers outright ownership of the subsoil of the oil fields on the haciendas La Brea and Pariñas in the department of Piura in 1824. They were later developed by the London and Pacific Petroleum Company, which was sold to the Standard Oil Company—to become the International Petroleum Company (IPC) in 1913. While the legal ownership of the La Brea and Pariñas fields became a long-standing matter of dispute between the government of Peru and IPC, the company expanded its holdings and profits over the years. Because of the enclave nature of the industry, among other things, those profits amounted to around 70 percent of gross income from oil exports. The government consented to such high profit rates largely because of the company's repeated willingness to provide for its short-term financial support, particularly at times of severe deficit crises. Continued high-profit repatriation, charges of company intervention in Peru's internal and external affairs, as well as corruption and the legal dispute over ownership, all combined to intensify public resentment against IPC, which became a focal point in later years of nationalist sentiment. The government's complicity in the company's abuses became the pretext for the overthrow of the BELAÚNDE TERRY regime in 1968 by the armed forces and the subsequent nationalization of the company that year.

ROSEMARY THORP and GEOFFREY BERTRAM, *Peru 1890–1977: Growth and Policy in an Open Economy* (1978).

PETER F. KLARÉN

INTERNATIONAL RAILWAYS OF CENTRAL AMERICA (IRCA, FICA),

United States–based company that controlled key RAILROADS in Guatemala and El Salvador. In 1912 IRCA assumed ownership of nearly all Guatemalan railways, including Guatemala's only link with the Caribbean, and purchased a major Salvadoran Railroad. The company connected the Guatemalan and Salvadoran lines in 1929 to provide El Salvador with access to the Caribbean. The UNITED FRUIT COMPANY of Boston purchased controlling interest in IRCA in 1936. IRCA and its parent company became targets of economic nationalism and labor activists during the Guatemalan Revolution (1944–1954). Critics attacked IRCA's monopoly on freight transportation and its inequitable rate structures. United Fruit sold much of its IRCA holdings after the revolution. The government purchased IRCA in December 1968 and placed rail transportation under the auspices of a state-owned agency, Ferrocarriles de Guatemala (FEGUA).

CHARLES D. KEPNER and J. W. SOOTHILL, *The Banana Empire: A Case Study of Economic Imperialism* (1935; repr. 1967); STACY MAY and GALO PLAZA, *The United Fruit Company in Latin America* (1958; repr. 1976); RICHARD H. IMMERMAN, *The CIA in Guatemala: The Foreign Policy of Intervention* (1982); STEPHEN C. SCHLESINGER and STEPHEN KINZER, *Bitter Fruit: The Untold Story of the American Coup in Guatemala* (1983); RALPH LEE WOODWARD, JR., *Central America: A Nation Divided*, 2d ed. (1985), esp. pp. 179–182.

STEVEN S. GILLICK

INTI, special patron deity of the INCAS. The most important servant of the creator was the sun god Inti, who was believed to be the divine ancestor of the Inca dynasty. The Incas referred to themselves as Intip Churin, which means in QUECHUA "children of the sun." The sun was conceived of as male and was represented by an idol in the form of a golden disk with rays and a human face. The sun idol was kept in the temples of the sun throughout the empire along with the other members of the Inca pantheon. The sun was believed to protect and mature crops, a function of vital importance to a farming-based economy.

JOHN H. ROWE, "Inca Culture at the Time of the Spanish Conquest," in *Handbook of South American Indians,* vol. 2 (1946), pp. 183–330. Additional sources include BURR CARTWRIGHT BRUNDAGE, *The Empire of the Inca* (1963) and *The Lords of Cuzco: A History and Description of the Inca People in Their Final Days* (1967).

GORDON F. McEWAN

IQUITOS, the only major city in the Peruvian jungle and the capital of Loreto Department, Peru's largest in area. Its 1981 population of 178,100 was the eighth largest in the country. Founded in 1863, it is located on the west bank of the Amazon river about 2,000 miles from its mouth and some 500 miles downriver from Pucallpa, the only other sizable city in the jungle of Peru. Iquitos can be reached only by air or by water; there are no roads connecting it to the rest of the country. The city more than tripled in size between 1961 and 1981, largely as the result of commercial activity associated with oil exploration and production in the Peruvian Amazon region.

Iquitos grew from a fishing village to a major commercial base of operations during the rubber boom of 1890–1920. While the economic impact of the rubber bonanza was felt primarily in Iquitos and the lower Amazon Basin of eastern Peru, the oil boom affected the country's western coastal region much more, due to the construction in the mid-1970s of an oil pipeline over the Andes to the Pacific. Currently the major administrative center of the government and military in the northeastern region of Peru, Iquitos contains impressive architecture dating from its heyday in the nineteenth century.

ROSEMARY THORP and GEOFFREY BERTRAM, *Peru 1890–1977: Growth and Policy in an Open Economy* (1978); RICHARD F. NYROP, ed., *Peru: A Country Study,* 3d ed. (1981).

DAVID SCOTT PALMER

See also **Petroleum Industry; Rubber Industry.**

IRALA, DOMINGO MARTÍNEZ DE (Captain Vergara; *b.* 1509; *d.* 3 October 1556), Spanish explorer and conquistador. The youngest of six children, Irala was born in Vergara, Guipúzcoa, Spain, to a family of hidalgos.

His father, Martín Pérez de Irala, was a royal office holder.

In 1534, Irala went on an expedition to the RÍO DE LA PLATA, with the *adelantado* Pedro de MENDOZA. In 1535 he participated in the founding of Buenos Aires. The following year, he went on an expedition to the PARANÁ RIVER with his friend Juan de AYOLAS. On 2 February 1537, Ayolas founded the port of Candelaria on the PARAGUAY RIVER, and then continued north, leaving Irala in command.

In 1537 the *veedor* (colonial inspector) of the Río de la Plata, Alonso Cabrera, appointed Irala lieutenant governor. Soon after this appointment, Irala went to Asunción and founded several new settlements.

Irala participated in many other expeditions, such as an exploration of the Paraguay River and a region near Peru. In 1543 he participated in an Indian campaign under the second *adelantado* of the Río de la Plata, Alvar Núñez CABEZA DE VACA. He was also the main force behind the arrest of Cabeza de Vaca on 26 April 1544. When Irala sent him back to Spain one year later, he became the undisputed master of Paraguay.

In late 1547 and early 1548, Irala faced a rebellion in Asunción by some of Cabeza de Vaca's followers. He quelled the rebellion, and in order to ensure peace in the region, he gave his four daughters in marriage to four of the leaders. In 1555, the crown appointed him governor. He died the following year.

ENRIQUE DE GÁNDIA, *Historia de la conquista del Río de la Plata y del Paraguay; los gobiernos de don Pedro de Mendoza, Alvar Núñez y Domingo de Irala, 1535–1556* (1931); JORGE ROBERTO PAYRO, *El capitán Vergara (Domingo Martínez de Irala)* (1932); RICARDO DE LA FUENTE MACHAIN, *El gobernador Domingo Martínez de Irala* (1939).

JUAN MANUEL PÉREZ

IRIGOYEN, BERNARDO DE (*b.* 18 December 1822; *d.* 27 December 1906), cattle baron and politician in Buenos Aires province and Argentina. Born in Buenos Aires, Irigoyen received his law degree from the University of Buenos Aires in 1843. He obtained his first important political position in 1844, when Federalist dictator Juan Manuel de ROSAS appointed him intervenor in Mendoza Province.

As a member of the National Autonomist Party, he was elected to the Buenos Aires Province Chamber of Deputies in 1873 and advanced to the provincial Senate two years later.

In the 1880s, he returned to national politics. Under presidents Nicolás AVELLANEDA (1874–1880) and Julio ROCA (1880–1886) he held various cabinet-level positions. Although he broke from the National Autonomist Party, helping form the Civic Union Party and the Radical Civic Union Party, he remained influential. In the final decades of his life he served as governor and national senator of Buenos Aires Province.

OSCAR CORNBLIT ET AL., "La generación del ochenta y su proyecto—antecedentes y consecuencias," in *Argentina, sociedad de masas,* edited by Torcuato S. di Tella, et al. (1956), pp. 18–59; NATALIO R. BOTANA, *El orden conservador: La política argentina entre 1880 y 1916,* 2d ed. (1985).

DANIEL LEWIS

See also **Argentina: Political Parties.**

IRIGOYEN, HIPÓLITO. *See* **Yrigoyen, Hipólito.**

IRISARRI, ANTONIO JOSÉ DE (*b.* 7 February 1786; *d.* 10 June 1868), Spanish-American patriot, diplomat, historian, and journalist. Born in Guatemala, Irisarri settled in 1809 in Chile, where he played a prominent part in patriot politics during the PATRIA VIEJA, among other things as editor of *El Semanario Republicano* from 1813 to 1814. His pen rarely idle, he also wrote many political works. Obliged to leave Chile in August 1814 because of his opposition to José Miguel CARRERA, he went to England, where, together with Andres BELLO, he published the pro-independence *El Censor Americano.* Upon his return to Chile in 1818, he was appointed a diplomatic agent by Bernardo O'HIGGINS and sent back to Europe, where he contracted the £1 million Chilean loan of 1822. In 1826 he moved back to his native Guatemala, but in 1830 resettled in Chile. He was appointed Intendant of Colchagua in November 1835. He accompanied the first Chilean expedition to Peru in 1837, during the war against the PERU-BOLIVIA CONFEDERATION, and negotiated the Treaty of Paucarpata (17 November 1837) with Andrés de SANTA CRUZ. Seen as ignominious in Chile, the treaty was repudiated.

Finding it inadvisable to return to Chile, Irisarri spent the remainder of his life in Ecuador, Colombia, Venezuela, and the United States, finally settling in New York in November 1849. In 1855 he became ambassador of Guatemala and El Salvador to the United States, and was named as plenipotentiary for Nicaragua at the time of William WALKER's FILIBUSTERING incursions. Irisarri died in Brooklyn.

RICARDO DONOSO, *Antonio José de Irisarri,* 2d ed. (1966); JOHN D. BROWNING, *Vida e ideología de Antonio José de Irisarri* (1986).

SIMON COLLIER

Antonio José de Irisarri. Reproduced from Carlos García Bauer, *Antonio José de Irisarri: Diplomático de América* (Guatemala, 1970). COURTESY OF HARVARD COLLEGE LIBRARY.

IRISARRI Y LARRAÍN, JUAN BAUTISTA (*b.* ca. 15 February 1740; *d.* 4 May 1805), Guatemalan merchant, banker, and planter. Irisarri was born in Aranaz, Spain. After coming to Guatemala he was successful in finance, commerce, and INDIGO production. By 1805 he was regarded as the wealthiest man in the kingdom. An active member of the Sociedad Económica de Amigos del País de Guatemala, he especially promoted the development of a Pacific coast port in the late colonial period. His second marriage linked him to the prominent creole Arrivillaga family. He also had family ties in Chile, where his illustrious son, Antonio José (1786–1868), migrated after independence.

RALPH LEE WOODWARD, JR., *Class Privilege and Economic Development: The Consulado de Comercio of Guatemala, 1793–1871* (1966); EDGAR JUAN APARICIO Y APARICIO, "La familia de Irisarri," in *Revista de la Academia guatemalteca de estudios genealógicos, heráldicos e históricos* 1 (1967):17–25.

RALPH LEE WOODWARD, JR.

IRMANDADES. *See* **Brotherhoods.**

IRON AND STEEL INDUSTRY. Two of the principal factors that have driven Latin America's industrialization during the past three decades are iron and steel. In 1992 Latin America produced 27.5 million tons of steel, or roughly 6 percent of total world output. Only four countries in Latin America have the capacity to produce over 1 million metric tons of raw steel: in 1992 Brazil ranked first, producing 13.8 million tons or 57 percent of Latin America's steel; Mexico ranked second, with 4.8

million tons; Venezuela was third, with 2.1 million tons; and Argentina was fourth, with 1.5 million tons.

The iron and steel industries in Latin America have had a checkered history marked by foreign domination, nationalization, global competition, and the privatization of the sector. Until recently all of Brazil's steelworks were state-owned enterprises (SOEs), but in the early 1990s the Brazilian government began aggressively auctioning off its steelworks to private investors and for-profit SOEs. This process of mixing privatization with the establishment of for-profit SOEs in Brazil has been viewed as a model for other Latin American countries to follow. Although Venezuela has kept its steelworks in government hands, the other Big Three steelmakers are taking the state out of the steel-making business.

The major iron ore deposits in Latin America are found in Brazil, Venezuela, Chile, Peru, and Mexico. The quality of the ore mined by CVRD (Companhia Vale do Rio Doce) of Brazil, Hierro of Peru, and Ferrominera of Venezuela is equal to the best in the world. CVRD, the world's largest iron ore mining company, is still owned by the Brazilian state. It recently acquired shares in two steel companies, Usiminas (Usina de Minas Gerais) and CST (Companhia Siderurgica de Tubarão), and established upstream-downstream linkages, including a special distribution network in the country. CVRD with its Japanese partner, Kawasaki Steel, now manufactures steel in a California plant it bought and refurbished to sell in the U.S. market. Other Latin American countries have taken steps to adapt to the globalization of the steel industry. Peru sold its iron ore mining monopoly to Shougang of the People's Republic of China, which has plans to modernize and expand the mine operation. Mexico is allowing foreign mining companies to operate in the country by using a ''trust fee'' system of 100 percent access to minerals coupled with long-term leasing of land from Mexican banks—a system that circumvents the constitutional restrictions imposed on foreign investment in Mexico. Venezuela has been actively negotiating with foreign investors for iron ore projects.

Since iron and steel production is no longer considered the key sign of industrial prowess, Latin American governments are demonstrating more willingness to transfer steel SOEs to private hands, including foreign private hands. Moreover, since there are now many substitutes for iron and steel, such as aluminum, plastics, ceramics, polymer, and other man-made materials, Latin American governments no longer consider iron and steel production as essential for industrialization. For these reasons, Latin American steel production has been in decline for the past five years.

No country in Latin America possesses all the ingredients necessary for converting iron into raw and specialty steels. Steel-making technologies have gone through significant changes through the years. Latin America has no industrial-grade coking coal, so this vital element in steel production has always been imported, primarily from the United States. During the 1950s the push for industrialization to end Latin America's dependence on foreign imports led to the expulsion of foreign iron-mining behemoths and the nationalization of mining and iron- and steel-making plants. The desire for national security and fear of communism during the cold war era led the military and civilian industrialists to promote steel making as the key to economic progress and to self-sufficiency in arms production. During the 1960s state-owned power industries provided steelworks with subsidized low-cost energy that enabled them to expand. For the next two decades a boom in the construction and auto manufacturing industries increased demand for domestic steel and stimulated further growth of the iron and steel sectors.

Steel technology went through revolutionary changes as the old coking-coal method gave way to basic oxygenized furnaces, continuous casting and annealing, vacuum degassing, and computer-monitored quality control. These new technologies, including the use of new alloys, produced stronger and lighter steel. The oil price crises in the 1970s and early 1980s forced automobile industries around the world to use aluminum, plastics, and other substitutes for steel to make cars lighter and more fuel efficient. Energy costs became the critical factor in newer methods of steel making. Brazil, Argentina, Trinidad and Tobago, Venezuela, and other countries with cheap energy sources quickly abandoned the old methods in favor of the newer ones. Brazil boasted a dozen state-owned and private steel mills. Usiminas and Grupo Gerdau have adopted the most modern technology from Japan, the United States, and Europe. Trinidad and Tobago took advantage of its abundant cheap natural gas to provide the energy for its steel making. Argentina emerged as a major producer of seamless steel pipes for the oil industry. Chile has tapped its abundant reserve of molybdenum, an important raw material in steel making, to build its own competitive steel industry.

A number of factors, including mounting external debt, declining economic output, and political crises prompted by the military's retreat from national politics, have pushed country after country in Latin America to adopt fundamental macroeconomic reforms, such as the liberalization of foreign trade, thus allowing the importation of foreign-made steel and the privatization of bloated, inefficient, state-owned mining companies and steel mills. Argentina's Techint acquired the army-owned steel mill complex; Chile privatized Compañía Acera del Pacífico, its integrated steelwork; Mexico and Venezuela deregulated much of their mining codes to allow both private and foreign capital into mining; and Brazil has sold off its steel sector to banks and pension funds. Brazil is also amending its Constitution of 1988 to allow foreign companies to invest in mining. Such joint ventures between the public sector and private firms will continue in the iron and steel industries of Latin America.

WERNER BAER, *The Development of the Brazilian Steel Industry* (1969); JANET KELLY ESCOBAR, "Comparing State Enterprises Across International Boundaries: The Corporación Venezolana de Guayana and the Companhia Vale do Rio Doce," in *Public Enterprises in Less-Developed Countries,* edited by Leroy P. Jones (1982); UNITED STATES TRADE COMMISSION, *Certain Carbon Steel Products from Brazil* (1984); CATHY A. RAKOWSKI, *Women in Nontraditional Industry: The Case of Steel in Ciudad Guayana, Venezuela* (1985); SIDNEY WEINTRAUB, ed., *Industrial Strategy and Planning in Mexico and the United States* (1986); ISABEL MARSHALL LAGARRIGUE, *Restructuring and Protectionism in the U.S. Steel Industry: The Impact on Brazil* (1987); ORLANDO MARTINO, JEROME MACHAMER, and IVETTE TORRES, *The Mineral Economy of Mexico* (1992); UNITED STATES BUREAU OF MINES, *Mineral Commodity Summaries 1991* (1992).

EUL-SOO PANG

See also **Industrialization.**

IRRIGATION, the artificial watering of crops. Much of Latin America receives insufficient precipitation for farming. To expand and improve arable land, pre-Hispanic horticulturalists had developed water management systems by the first millennium B.C. in both MESOAMERICA and the Andes. The simplest method, pot irrigation, is familiar to all gardeners and leaves few, if any, archaeological traces. Water is carried by hand and applied to individual plants. Very effective use is made of limited amounts of water, but labor demands are high, so early farmers began to devise other methods of redirecting water's natural flow.

In central Mexico, rubble or earthen storage dams may have been built across natural channels to collect ephemeral surface runoff at the site of Teopantecuanitlán, in northern Guerrero State between 1200 and 1000 B.C., and in the TEHUACÁN Valley, between 750 and 600 B.C. However, the earliest undisputed remains of a Mex-

ican irrigation system are at Santa Clara Coatitlán, now within metropolitan Mexico City. Here unlined canals branched off a channelized gully and took water to fields from about 900 B.C. Near the present city of PUEBLA, canal networks carried water from ephemeral stream channels by the middle of the first millennium B.C. In Tlaxcala State, there is evidence that terraced fields were watered by a dam, reservoir, and canal system around the same time.

A canal fed from a dammed reservoir is found just below the archaeological site of MONTE ALBÁN, Oaxaca. Part of this canal is cut into bedrock, demonstrating that its builders had the theoretical knowledge to plan water flow without trial and error. The Monte Albán canal carried water from about 550 to 250 B.C. By A.D. 200, mortared masonry storage dams and aqueducts were functioning near Monte Albán.

By 1519, when Hernán Cortés arrived in the Valley of Mexico, hydraulic works had reached monumental proportions. TENOCHTITLÁN, the Mexica (AZTEC) capital, occupied an island in Lake Tetzcoco. The Mexica redirected rivers and constructed aqueducts, dams, dikes, and open canals. Mortared aqueducts carried sweet water from springs at Chapultepec (now a park in Mexico City) and Coyoacán across the lake to Tenochtitlán, where it was used for drinking, bathing, and watering gardens.

The Peruvian and north Chilean coasts receive little or no precipitation, so agriculture is dependent upon irrigation. Dozens of small rivers and streams, many seasonally dry, flow down the western slopes of the Andes, through the coastal deserts, and into the Pacific. Pre-Hispanic farmers drew water directly off these rivers; directed water in long-distance canals from higher, moister elevations; diverted spring flow; and dug wells and trenches down to the water table. The early prehistory of Andean irrigation is unclear, but simple canals

Raised fields with potatoes in the growing season. Huatta, Peru. PHOTO BY CLARK L. ERICKSON.

were probably built as early as the second millennium B.C. to extend floodwater farming of coastal valleys.

On Peru's north and central coasts, attempts were made in the mid-first millennium A.D. to build open canal irrigation networks supplied by two or more rivers. However, some of the long-distance linkages, including a 71-mile canal joining the Chicama and MOCHE drainages, may never have functioned. In the Chilca Valley, and elsewhere on Peru's central coast, ancient farmers dug a few meters to the water table, creating moist sunken fields called *mahames* or *hoyas*. This practice extended agriculture into areas without surface water.

The Andean Central Highlands receive unreliable precipitation during a wet season from November to April. To extend the growing time, or to produce two crops per year, agriculturalists made extensive use of open canals combined with terraces. These techniques were well established by the mid-first millennium A.D., the apogee of the Wari state. By 1500 the INCAS had brought basic irrigation to near perfection. Water was so important to the lords of CUZCO that they conceptualized their whole social structure in terms of its natural and artificial flow.

In parts of Latin America, waterlogged or flooded fields are a major problem for farmers. Both in lowland Mesoamerica and the Lake Titicaca basin, indigenous cultivators built extensive systems of ridges and furrows for planting and water containment. Some Maya cities and the early Andean state of TIWANAKU depended heavily upon such raised fields. However, construction of some Andean raised fields predated the rise of the Tiwanaku state by more than one thousand years. Remnants of CHINAMPAS, or "floating gardens," can still be observed in the Valley of Mexico. These are artificial planting platforms constructed and maintained in shallow lakes.

The aridity of Spain and Portugal stimulated the development of Iberian irrigation and made the conquistadores appreciative of the sophisticated indigenous hydraulic systems they encountered in the New World. Native waterworks and concomitant social structure were often retained. However, the requirements of sugarcane, water mills, and horses meant that Iberians needed more water than the pre-Conquest Indians. The most remote branches of canals were often abandoned to provide greater volume and flow elsewhere. This has preserved remnants of ancient systems, especially in the valleys of Peru's north coast. The Spanish introduced many Old World hydraulic devices, including the arched aqueducts that were a hallmark of ancient Roman technology. Examples can still be seen in Mexico near Zempoala and Hidalgo and at the city of Querétaro; in Peru at Cuzco; and in Brazil at Rio de Janeiro.

Another Iberian introduction may have been filtration galleries, also called *minas, qanats, foggaras,* or *puquois*. Such galleries are lines of vertical wells linked at their bottoms by slightly sloping tunnels with the main water outlet at the tunnel's mouth. The largest and best-studied Spanish water *mina* is in Madrid. It was begun in the early thirteenth century under Christian control. Spanish engineers built several filtration gallery systems in Mexico, including those at Tehuacán and Puebla. Dozens of others were constructed in the Andes during the viceregal period, but many scholars believe that the systems in the NASCA drainage were built in the first millennium A.D. by people of the indigenous Nasca culture.

Latin American agriculture remains dependent upon irrigation. Ambitious, high-tech projects have become almost impossible to finance in the wake of the 1980s debt crisis. However, in remote areas farmers continue to employ the agricultural technology of their pre-Columbian and Spanish ancestors.

For an excellent survey of ancient Mexican hydraulic technology see WILLIAM E. DOOLITTLE, *Canal Irrigation in Prehistoric Mexico* (1990). A study of the important prehistoric, colonial, and modern Tehuacán system can be found in KJELL I. ENGE and SCOTT WHITEFORD, *The Keepers of Water and Earth: Mexican Rural Social Organization and Irrigation* (1989). A good general work on the central Andes is MICHAEL E. MOSELEY, *The Incas and Their Ancestors: The Archaeology of Peru* (1992). A beautifully illustrated pioneering study of ancient Andean waterworks is PAUL KOSOK, *Life, Land, and Water in Ancient Peru* (1965). An influential article on the social organization governing canals is PATRICIA J. NETHERLY, "The Management of Late Andean Irrigation Systems on the North Coast of Peru," in *American Antiquity* 49, no. 2 (1984): 227–254. Sunken fields have been described in ANA MARÍA SOLDI, *Chacras excavadas en el desierto* (1979). A general discussion of raised fields can be found in CLARK L. ERICKSON, "Prehistoric Landscape Management in the Andean Highlands: Raised Field Agriculture and Its Environmental Impact," in *Population and Environment* 13, no. 4 (1992): 285–300. For a controversial study of Andean filtration galleries see MONICA BARNES and DAVID FLEMING, "Filtration-Gallery Irrigation in the Spanish New World," in *Latin American Antiquity* 2, no. 1 (1991) : 48–68; an opposing point of view is RONALD I. DORN et al., "New Approach to the Radiocarbon Dating of Rock Varnish, with Examples from Drylands," in *Annals of the Association of American Geographers* 82 (1992): 136–151. A solid book on highland irrigation, with emphasis on present practice, is WILLIAM P. MITCHELL and DAVID GUILLET, *Irrigation at High Altitudes: The Social Organization of Water Control Systems in the Andes* (1994).

MONICA BARNES

See also **Agriculture; Potato.**

ISAACS, JORGE (*b.* 1 April 1837; *d.* 17 April 1895), Colombian poet, politician, and ethnologist. Born in Cali, to an English father—a Christian convert from Judaism—and a Catholic Spanish mother, Isaacs was also Indian, Catalan, and Italian. He epitomized the Spanish American quest for personal and cultural identity in his life and his works. Educated in Cali and Bogotá, he soon showed his strong, varied, and captivating personality. At seventeen he enlisted in a revolutionary army; he later fought in several civil wars and summarized the history of one failed revolution in *La revolución radical en Antioquia* (1880). Although he entered politics as a Conservative, his rebellious nature pushed him to the Liberal Party, whereupon he declared "I have moved from shadow to light." Once involved in politics, he applied either democratic or authoritarian means to make good on his party's programs.

Isaacs traveled through La Guajira as secretary of a scientific commission for the study of natural resources. Lacking even experienced guides, the daring Isaacs began the exploration on his own and succeeded in finding coal mines and oil fields.

More than as a poet, explorer, politician, or ethnologist, Isaacs is known as a novelist for his only and unique novel. *María* (1867; *Maria,* 1890) won him a place in history and in the hearts of millions around the world. Published in every Spanish-speaking country and translated into many languages, *María* caused critics to proclaim it the "most exquisite sentimental novel" and "one of the most beautiful creations and . . . closest to perfection" for its "clear aesthetic conscience." America, in its postindependence search for identity, found itself in *María*'s landscape and humane romantic soul. After a life dedicated to his country and in the midst of economic hardships, Isaacs died of a disease contracted during his exploratory treks.

J. DAVID SUÁREZ-TORRES

ISABEL, PRINCESS OF BRAZIL (*b.* 29 July 1846; *d.* 14 November 1921), heiress to the Brazilian throne. Isabel was the daughter of PEDRO II and Empress Teresa Cristina Maria of Bourbon. Married to Gastão of Orléans, count d'Eu, on 15 October 1864, she assumed the regency in her father's absence in 1871, 1876, and 1887. Strong-willed, she displayed an uncommon ability to govern during her first regency. In Brazilian history her name is associated with emancipation and the abolition of SLAVERY. In 1871 she signed the Law of the Free Womb (FREE BIRTH LAW), which freed newborn slaves. Her major achievement was the *Lei Aurea* of 13 May 1888, which abolished slavery. Her experience in government, combined with her abolitionist views, led Princess Isabel to evaluate correctly the chaotic political climate created by the abolitionist movement in the first months of 1888 and to decide that the crown had to intervene directly to end slavery. She disregarded some of the unwritten rules followed by her father for decades when she forced the resignation of the Cotegipe cabinet, selected the head of the cabinet that was to abolish slavery, and did not seek the advice of the plenary Council of State, the emperor's advisory body.

Despite her achievements, Princess Isabel was plagued by a degree of unpopularity caused by several factors. Her marriage to a Frenchman led to suspicion of foreign influence and dominance, and her husband's unpopularity had a ripple effect of its own. Her Catholicism was equally unpopular, for fear of papal influence in the affairs of state. Above all, the fact that she was a woman made her in the view of many unsuitable to govern. The adulation that surrounded her after she abolished slavery was ephemeral. With the fall of the monarchy on 15 November 1889, she was exiled with her family and spent the last part of her life in France.

HERMES VIEIRA, *Princesa Isabel, uma vida de luzes e sombras* (1990).

LYDIA M. GARNER

ISABELLA I OF CASTILE (*b.* 22 April 1451; *d.* 26 November 1504), called "la Católica," Spanish queen of CASTILE and León (1474–1504). The daughter of John II of Castile, and his second wife, Isabella of Portugal, Isabella faced a rival claimant to the throne, Juana La Beltraneja, the daughter of her half-brother, Henry IV of Castile. Although Juana's paternity was in doubt, Henry IV and the powerful Mendoza family supported her claim. In 1468 Henry IV acknowledged Isabella's claim on the condition that she marry Alfonso V, king of Portugal. Isabella chose to ignore this arrangement and secured the approval of her noble supporters, led by the archbishop of Toledo, to marry FERDINAND II OF ARAGON in 1469. Her assertion of independence prompted Henry IV to disown her, and his death in 1474 initiated a civil war of succession between Isabella and Juana's noble supporters and Isabella's husband, Ferdinand, and Juana's suitor, Alfonso of Portugal. Isabella and Ferdinand's titles were secured by a peace treaty (1479) and Juana retired to a convent, although she asserted her claims until her death in 1530.

The primary task of Ferdinand and Isabella was to bring peace and order to their realms through the exercise of direct personal authority. Isabella traveled throughout Castile, covering as much as 1,200 miles in a single year. She also revived the medieval brotherhoods (*hermandades*) to restore law and order in the towns. Isabella governed with a Royal Council (*Consejo Real*) staffed by university-trained legists (LETRADOS) and dispensed justice (after 1489) through AUDIENCIAS established in major cities.

Isabella was determined to assert royal authority over the powerful Castilian nobility and recover territories and rights alienated by her ancestors. During her reign, the crown reclaimed the most recently alienated parcels and took three strategic cities—Cádiz, Gibraltar, and Cartagena—from their respective lords. She also brought the wealthy and powerful military orders under royal control when Ferdinand became their grand master.

Unchristian and heretical influences in Spain disturbed the devoutly Catholic queen and in 1480 she commissioned a newly established INQUISITION to root out heresy. In 1492 Isabella expelled the Jews who, because they were not baptized Christians, could not be classified as heretics. The monarchs also launched a crusade against the Moorish kingdom of Granada in 1482 and triumphantly claimed the capital city in 1492. Initial religious tolerance ended with the advent of the archbishop of Toledo and queen's confessor, Francisco Jiménez de Cisneros who, with Isabella's support, forced conversion through mass baptism (1499). Similarly, Isabella offered the choice of conversion or exile to the Moors elsewhere in Castile (1502) and thus limited Islamic and Jewish influence in her realm. Isabella's concern with Christian conversion extended to the native populations in the New World.

In addition to eliminating religious plurality in Spain, Isabella increased crown control over the Catholic church. During her reign, Pope ALEXANDER VI granted the crown patronage over all ecclesiastical appointments in Granada, the Canaries, and the New World. The monarchs also acquired greater control over the nomination of bishops in Castile.

When Christopher COLUMBUS was rebuffed by the king of Portugal, he sought backing from the Castilian monarch; after much bargaining, he received Isabella's support in 1492. However, she opposed his enslavement of Indians and encouraged the formation of ENCOMIENDAS and payment for wage labor. Her propitious decision to finance the first voyage was soon followed by the Treaty of TORDESILLAS (1494), which legitimated present and future Spanish claims in the New World.

WILLIAM H. PRESCOTT, *History of the Reign of Ferdinand and Isabella* (1838); TARSICIO DE AZCONA, *Isabel la Católica* (1964); L. SUÁREZ FERNÁNDEZ and M. FERNÁNDEZ, *La España de los reyes Católicos (1474–1516)* (1969); J. N. HILLGARTH, *The Spanish Kingdoms*, vol. 2, *1410–1516: Castilian Hegemony* (1978); PEGGY K. LISS, *Isabel the Queen* (1992).

SUZANNE HILES BURKHOLDER

ISAMITT ALARCÓN, CARLOS (*b.* 13 March 1887; *d.* 2 July 1974), Chilean composer and painter. Along with Carlos Lavín and Pedro Humberto Allende, Isamitt, who was born in Rengo, Chile, is noted for his extensive research on the native music of the ARAUCANIAN Indians. In 1932, he published a seminal classification of the Araucanian musical repertoire according to performance medium and function. In 1936, Isamitt became one of the founding members of the Asociación Nacional de Compositores de Chile. His early music could be described as nationalistic, expressed through the spirit and techniques of musical impressionism. Later, however, his work became more abstract through use of the twelve-tone technique, of which he was one of the first exponents in Chile. Isamitt is a major figure in the trend called "musical Indianism" in Chile, although he also explored creole folklore. For his use of indigenous folklore in his own compositions, he was awarded Chile's Premio Nacional de Arte in 1965. He held the posts of director of the Santiago School of Fine Arts and artistic director of the primary schools in Santiago. His large musical output includes music for orchestra, chamber groups, voice, piano, and ballet.

PAUL H. APEL, *Music of the Americas, North and South* (1958); RAQUEL BARROS and MANUEL DANNEMANN, "Carlos Isamitt: Folklore e indigenismo," in *Revista musical chilena* 20, no. 97 (1961): 37–42; MAGDALENA VICUÑA, "Carlos Isamitt," in *Revista musical chilena* 20, no. 97 (1961): 5–13; JOHN VINTON, ed., *Dictionary of Contemporary Music* (1971); SAMUEL CLARO VALDÉS and JORGE URRUTIA, *Historia de la música en Chile* (1973); GÉRARD BÉHAGUE, *Music in Latin America: An Introduction* (1979); SAMUEL CLAROS VALDÉS, *Oyendo a Chile* (1979); SAMUEL CLAROS VALDÉS et al., *Iconografía musical chilena*, vols. 1 and 2 (1989).

SERGIO BARROSO

ISLAM. Muslims were introduced in Latin America several centuries before immigrants from the Middle East arrived in the region, and mostly hailed from non-Arabic-speaking parts of the Islamic world. In fact, of the three historical strands of Muslim arrivals in Latin America, only the most recent one was part of the major migration from Lebanon, Syria, and Palestine.

The first strand was composed of large numbers of Islamized West Africans, especially from Ghana, Dahomey (now Benin), Mali, and Nigeria, who were among the millions of Africans enslaved and shipped to work in Brazilian and Caribbean plantations until the second half of the nineteenth century. Most became Christian, at least in name, while others were reported to have held secretly to their Islamic faith, which appears to have been the case in the Brazilian cities of Salvador and Rio de Janeiro. Although little survives of this first strand, some have traced elements of Afro-Brazilian religions such as UMBANDA, CANDOMBLÉ, and Xango to Islam.

The second strand is intimately linked to the abolition of slavery in the colonial possessions of Great Britain and the Netherlands in the Indian subcontinent and Southeast Asia. Indeed, while the British introduced indentured labor to India, the Dutch did the same in Indonesia. By 1917 the British had encouraged some 250,000 Indians to settle in Guyana, where legislation dating back to 1871 exempted their children from attending Christian schools. Nearly one-sixth of these East Indians were Muslim. By 1940, the Dutch had succeeded in settling 33,000 Javanese Muslims in today's Suriname. Some 34,000 Indians, less than a fifth of them Muslim, were also introduced in that country. Although their work contracts included the provision of return fares at the end of a five-year stint, few indentured laborers managed to accumulate the wealth they had originally envisaged; therefore, they settled for land in lieu of passage to their home countries. Against this backdrop, Panama is the only Latin American state where the Islamic presence is partly due to the more recent arrival of Indian Muslim businesspeople, attracted by the country's role as a regional trade entrepôt.

The MIDDLE EASTERN strand of Muslim arrivals in

Libyan community in a religious ceremony, 1974. Islamic Center, Buenos Aires. ARCHIVO GENERAL DE LA NACIÓN, BUENOS AIRES.

Latin America dates back to the end of the nineteenth century and, unlike the two previous influxes, was not a result of recruitment, but rather a move to improve their economic circumstances and to avoid conscription into the Ottoman army. Most Arab Muslims sought to go to the United States but, because of strict health screenings and tightened immigration quotas, landed instead in Argentina and Brazil, whence they moved to neighboring countries. Reliable figures are hard to come by, but various estimates suggest that most settled in Argentina and Brazil. The Institute of Muslim Minority Affairs estimated in 1980 that nearly 94 percent of the region's Muslims of all origins today live in Brazil (500,000), Argentina (370,000), Trinidad and Tobago (115,000), Suriname (104,500), and Guyana (74,500).

East Asian Muslims have long achieved recognition for openly practicing and furthering Islam among their offspring. Not surprisingly, the largest network of Muslim institutions in Latin America is in Britain's former colonies in the region. This includes more than two hundred mosques, as well as Koranic and other schools. In Guyana, the Muslim school system enjoys state subsidies, and Muslim religious festivals are recognized as national holidays. The same is the case in Suriname, where Muslims are said to make up 22 percent of the population. On the other hand, conflict between the African-descended majority and the Asian Muslim minorities has been more the rule than the exception in the Caribbean.

Muslims in the Catholic countries of Luso–Spanish America have not enjoyed the same degree of legitimacy as in Suriname and Guyana. Unpropitious circumstances at the receiving end—such as the erroneous assumption that all Muslims, including the penniless migrants, were polygamous, and intolerance of religious pluralism—pushed Muslim newcomers into a self-effacing posture. Some adopted Hispanic identities, and many more abandoned their faith while retaining their original names. Whereas Argentina's Syrian 'Alawite-descended president Carlos Saúl MENEM and Druze-descended military leader Muhammad Alí Seineldín are among the latter, Zulema Yoma was Latin America's first Muslim first lady before becoming estranged from Menem.

Those who held to their faith established social and mutual-help institutions, but generally refrained from building mosques, in a reluctance to call attention to themselves in these Catholic countries. Not surprisingly, therefore, most purpose-built prayer houses and Islamic centers in Brazil and the Spanish-speaking countries date back to the 1973 rise of the Gulf States, as well as to Iranian activism among the Muslims since the ouster of Shah Muhammad Reza Pahlavi in 1979. In Argentina and Mexico, for instance, mosques went up in the 1980s with Tehran's help, a fact suggesting that a proportion of the Muslim immigrants are Shiite. Saudi- and Iranian-backed proselytism is not unknown in Latin America, as intimated by the mid-1980s revelation by an Iranian diplomat that the number of conversions in Argentina was on the increase. It is possible that a sizable proportion of these are none other than the descendants of earlier Muslim immigrants now becoming more assertive of their identity.

R. GUEVARA BAZÁN, "Muslim Immigration to Spanish America," in *Muslim World* 56 (1966); "Les musulmans dans le monde," la documentation française (August 1952); ROLF RIECHERT, "Muslims in the Guyanas: A Socio-Economic Overview," in *Journal Institute of Muslim Minority Affairs* (Winter

1981): 120–126; S. A. H. AHSANI and OMAR KASULE, "Muslims in Latin America: A Survey," in *Journal Institute of Muslim Minority Affairs* (July 1984): 454–457; ESTELA BIONDI ASSALI, "L'insertion des groupes de langue arabe dans la société argentine," in *Revue Européenne des Migrations Internationales* 7, no. 2 (1991): 139–153; CLAYTON G. MACKENZIE, "Muslim Primary Schools in Trinidad and Tobago," in *The Islamic Quarterly* (First Quarter 1989): 5–16; IGNACIO KLICH, "Argentine-Ottoman Relations and Their Impact on Immigrants from the Middle East," in *The Americas* (October 1993).

IGNACIO KLICH

See also **Arab–Latin American Relations.**

ISRAELI–LATIN AMERICAN RELATIONS. During the first United Nations debates on Palestine in 1947, democratic and liberal Latin American regimes generally supported the creation of a Jewish state in parts of that territory, while conservative Catholic governments took a reserved attitude. Thus, Guatemala and Uruguay followed a marked pro-Zionist line in the United Nations Special Committee on Palestine (UNSCOP), which prepared the Partition of Palestine proposal. Eventually, thirteen out of twenty Latin American countries voted in favor of the Partition Plan in November 1947, and eighteen Latin American countries supported Israel's admission to the UN in May 1949.

Guatemala recognized Israel three days after its establishment in May 1948, and the other Latin American countries followed suit in 1948 and 1949. Peronist Argentina, which had abstained in the partition vote, was the first to open an embassy in Tel Aviv, then Israel's capital. It was followed by Brazil and Uruguay. In 1955 Guatemala set up the first Latin American representation in Jerusalem. Israel established its first diplomatic missions in Uruguay, Argentina, Brazil, and Mexico from 1949 to 1953.

In the 1960s relations between Israel and most Latin American states flourished, due partly to Israeli agricultural aid programs. There were by then fourteen Latin American embassies in Israel (of which ten were located in Jerusalem), while the number of Israeli embassies in Latin America had risen to sixteen. The closer relations manifested themselves within international organizations. In the UN General Assembly in 1967, after the Six Day War between Israel and Arab nations, the Soviet Union and nonaligned countries demanded Israel's unconditional withdrawal from the occupied territories. Twenty Latin American states then sponsored a resolution based on withdrawal, an end of belligerency, and "coexistence based on good neighborliness." The Latin American draft was defeated, but its presentation was a decisive factor in the rejection of the Soviet-nonaligned proposals and later in the formulation of Security Council Resolution 242.

In the 1970s Israeli–Latin American relations deteriorated in the wake of political changes in Latin America, such as left-wing military rule in Peru (1968–1980), the

Allende government in Chile (1970–1973), the reestablishment of a Peronist regime in Argentina (1973–1976), and the Sandinista regime in Nicaragua (1979–1990). These states adhered to the nonaligned movement, of which Fidel CASTRO's Cuba was already a member. They were gradually followed by other left-leaning Latin American countries. An additional factor was the emergence, between the 1960s and the 1980s, of fifteen new Caribbean states which felt, because of ethnic ties, close to Africa and to third-world ideologies. The result was significant Latin American participation in international political and economic alignments that pursued anti-Israeli policies.

The oil crises of 1973–1974 and 1979, which severely affected the Latin American economies, created a dependence on the cartel known as the Organization of Petroleum Exporting Countries (OPEC) and its Arab members. Brazil turned pro-Arab, while oil-producing Latin American states like Venezuela, Ecuador, and Mexico strengthened their relationships with Arab OPEC countries.

In several Latin American states there was also an awakening of political consciousness among the population of Arab origin (about 3 million persons, as against less than half a million Jews). All this led to the growth of diplomatic relations between Latin American and Arab states and the opening of Palestine Liberation Organization embassies and offices in Cuba, Nicaragua, Peru, Mexico, Brazil, and Bolivia. In the UN in 1975, five Latin American and Caribbean states (Brazil, Cuba, Guyana, Grenada, and Mexico) supported Resolution 3379, which equated Zionism with racism and questioned the moral ground for Israel's existence. Ten Latin American countries voted against the resolution and eleven abstained. By the 1980s some countries such as Mexico, and to a lesser extent Argentina, Brazil, and Peru, routinely supported anti-Israeli resolutions.

The change in the UN also affected bilateral relations. In 1980, after Israel had adopted a law declaring Jerusalem as its capital, the Security Council called on all states whose diplomatic missions were located in Jerusalem to "withdraw them from the Holy City." In consequence all twelve Latin American embassies in Jerusalem were transferred to Tel Aviv. (Costa Rica returned its embassy to Jerusalem in 1982 and El Salvador did the same in 1984.) Three Latin American states broke diplomatic relations with Israel: Cuba in 1973, Guyana in 1974, and Nicaragua in 1982. Nevertheless, the Israeli diplomatic network in Latin America continued to grow, and in the early 1990s Israel had eighteen embassies in Latin America and hosted seventeen Latin American missions. Significant developments included the visits of President Chaim Herzog to Argentina in 1990 and of President Carlos Menem to Israel in 1991. In 1990 Israel maintained technical assistance missions in several Central American and Caribbean countries and hosted about 600 trainees each year from Latin America.

Israeli–Latin American trade relations were always of

secondary importance. In 1990 Israeli exports to Latin America reached $98 million (not including classified military exports and oil supplies), and Israeli imports from there amounted to $43 million.

EDY KAUFMAN, YORAM SHAPIRA, and JOEL BARROMI, *Israel-Latin American Relations* (1979).

JOEL BARROMI

ITABORAÍ, VISCONDE DE (Joaquim José Rodrigues Tôrres; *b.* 1802; *d.* 1873). Born into a landowning family of Rio province, Itaboraí graduated from Coimbra University in 1825 and became an instructor at the Rio Military Academy. A doctrinaire Liberal, he served as a minister in 1831 and 1833. Converted to Conservative views, he was prominent in the Regresso movement (1835–1839) in favor of central authority and law and order. He was elected a deputy in 1834 and was named a senator in 1844. After PEDRO II's majority, Itaboraí served as minister in the Conservative cabinet of 1843–1844. On the Liberals' fall from office in 1848, he became minister of finance and, over the next five years, reorganized the fiscal system. He was prime minister from May 1852 to September 1853. Appointed president of the Bank of Brazil, he exerted considerable influence on monetary questions. In July 1868, Itaboraí formed a cabinet that, despite financial and political difficulties, brought the WAR OF THE TRIPLE ALLIANCE to a successful end. Himself a *fazendeiro* (plantation owner) and opposed to any meddling with slavery, Itaboraí voted but did not speak against the FREE BIRTH LAW of 1871. Very much the intellectual in politics, Itaboraí was perhaps the most capable and is certainly the most understudied leader of Pedro II's reign (1840–1889).

JOÃO LYRA FILHO, *Visconde de Itaboraí, a luneta do império* (Rio de Janeiro, 1986).

RODERICK J. BARMAN

ITAIPÚ HYDROELECTRIC PROJECT, power station and reservoir located on the PARANÁ RIVER on the border between Brazil and Paraguay. Itaipú has an installed capacity of 12,600 megawatts and an annual output of 77,000 gigawatt-hours, making it the largest and one of the most productive hydroelectric projects in the world. The dam complex is 4.6 miles long, reaches a maximum height of 216 yards, and houses eighteen 715-megawatt Francis turbines. Technologically distinctive features of the Itaipú project include the most powerful hydrogenerators and turbines, the highest direct-current transmission voltages and power ever used (±600 kilovolts and 6,300 megawatts), and some of the longest transmission lines in the world (about 600 miles of 765-kilovolts alternating current transmission). Both 50-hertz and 60-hertz generators were required in order to meet each country's national frequency standard.

The energy potential of the Paraná River has been known since at least the mid-1950s and has been previously exploited in a series of smaller dams within Brazil. The Acta Final (Acta de Iguaçú), signed in June 1966, ended a border dispute between Brazil and Paraguay and provided that the energy potential of the river between the site of the border dispute and the mouth of the Iguaçú River would be shared in condominium. Feasibility studies were undertaken and in April 1973, the Itaipú Treaty was signed, establishing a binational entity owned by the two state-owned electric utilities, the Administración Nacional de Electricidad (ANDE) in Paraguay and the Centrais Elétricas Brasileiras S.A. (Eletrobras) in Brazil. With an initial capital of $100 million, the binational entity secured financing from Brazilian agencies and international commercial banks (with the guarantee of the government of Brazil) to finance construction of the project. The Itaipú Dam created a 540-square-mile reservoir, which flooded the disputed area in October 1982. The first generator began commercial operation in 1984 and the project was completed in 1991 at an estimated total cost of $18 billion. Itaipú Binacional operates the facility, selling electric power to the two owners.

GERD KOHLHEPP, *Itaipú: Socio-economic and Ecological Consequences of the Itaipú Dam* (1987) provides a good overview of the Itaipú project, especially in the Brazilian context. The text of the Itaipú Treaty and definitive coverage of the debate surrounding it is found in E. E. GAMON, *Itaipú: Aguas que valen oro* (1975). RICARDO CANESE, *Itaipú y la cuestión energética en el Paraguay*, Biblioteca de Estudios Paraguayos, vol. 7 (1983), provides an excellent discussion of the project, the pricing of its electric power, and the potential uses of its energy in Paraguay. The impact of the Itaipú project on the Paraguayan economy may be found in WERNER BAER and MELISSA H. BIRCH, "Expansion of the Economic Frontier: Paraguayan Growth in the 1970s," in *World Development* 12, no. 8 (1984): 783–798. For technical information, see JULIVAL DE MORAES and VICTOR F. SALATKO, "Coming: 12,600 megawatts at Itaipú Island," in *IEEE Spectrum* (August 1983): 46–52.

MELISSA H. BIRCH

See also **Boundary Disputes (Brazil).**

ITU, CONVENTION OF (18 April 1873), a meeting of the newly formed Paulista Republican Party in the São Paulo town of Itu to discuss the future of republicanism in that province. The convention was attended by 133 individuals, 76 of whom were planters. The Paulista Republicans, having attracted more wealthy planters than had Republican parties elsewhere in Brazil, staunchly supported slavery and resented the relative exclusion of São Paulo planters from politics at the national level. The party thus favored a federalist republic but opposed the abolition of slavery. During the last years of the empire, Republicans gained their greatest strength in the province of São Paulo, where they came to control 25 percent of the electorate.

HEITOR LYRA, *História da queda do império*, 2 vols. (1964), esp. vol. 1, pp. 22–26; EMILIA VIOTTI DA COSTA, *The Brazilian Empire* (1985), esp. pp. 226–228.

JOAN MEZNAR

See also **Brazil: Political Parties.**

ITURBIDE, AGUSTÍN DE (*b.* 27 September 1783; *d.* 19 July 1824), military figure and emperor of Mexico. Born in Valladolid, Morelia, Iturbide entered the militia at age sixteen. Although vaguely involved with the VALLADOLID CONSPIRACY OF 1809, he refused to join the revolt of Miguel HIDALGO Y COSTILLA in 1810. Instead, he served the royal government, distinguishing himself as an able officer and an implacable foe of the insurgents. In 1816 Colonel Iturbide was relieved of command because of charges of corruption. He spent the next years in Madrid defending himself. There he came into contact with important members of the elite who favored autonomy within the Spanish Empire. While New Spain's elite had reached a consensus regarding autonomy, only Iturbide acted decisively.

Restored to command, Iturbide negotiated in 1821 with the leading royalist officers as well as with the principal insurgents, convincing them to accept autonomy under the Plan of IGUALA, which called for a constitutional monarchy with the Spanish king as sovereign, recognized the Constitution of 1812, and established equality among all groups. Independence was assured when Juan O'DONOJÚ, the newly appointed Spanish *Jefe Político Superior* (Superior Political Chief) ratified the plan by signing the Treaty of CÓRDOBA (24 August 1821). Thereafter, the autonomists, New Spain's elite who had sought home rule since 1808, rapidly came into conflict with Iturbide. While they believed that the legislature should be dominant, he insisted on exercising his personal power resulting from the immense popularity that he had gained when he proclaimed independence. When Spain refused to ratify Mexican autonomy, Iturbide crowned himself emperor on 19 May 1822 with the backing of the army and strong popular support.

The new nation faced immense problems, among them the near bankruptcy of the government. Although there was a widespread national desire to form a strong and unified nation, the empire failed primarily because Iturbide proved unwilling to accept the figurehead role that the new Spanish-Mexican parliamentary tradition required. As a result, he and Congress were continually at odds. On 26 August 1822 he ordered the arrest of sixty-six persons, including twenty congressmen, for conspiracy, and on 31 October he dissolved congress. Discontent emerged in the provinces, but the military finally undermined him. The Plan of CASA MATA, which provided the provinces the opportunity to gain home rule, ultimately forced him to abdicate on 19 March 1823. He and his family were exiled to Italy, but supporters convinced him to return in July 1824 in an effort to regain the throne. He was captured, court-martialed, and executed. Although he succeeded in emancipating his country, he failed, like his contemporaries throughout the region, to establish a stable regime and, thus, became an ambiguous figure in Mexican history.

WILLIAM S. ROBERTSON, *Iturbide of Mexico* (1952); JAIME E. RODRÍGUEZ O., "From Royal Subject to Republican Citizen: The Role of the Autonomists in the Independence of Mexico," CHRISTON I. ARCHER, " 'La Causa Buena': The Counterinsurgency Army of New Spain and the Ten Years' War," and BARBARA A. TENENBAUM, "Taxation and Tyranny: Public Finance During the Iturbide Regime, 1821–1823," in *The Independence of Mexico and the Creation of the New Nation*, edited by Jaime E. Rodríguez O. (1989); TIMOTHY E. ANNA, *The Mexican Empire of Iturbide* (1990); JAIME E. RODRÍGUEZ O., "The Struggle for the Nation: The First Centralist-Federalist Conflict in Mexico," in *The Americas* 49 (July 1992): 1–22.

JAIME E. RODRÍGUEZ O.

ITURBIDE, GRACIELA (*b.* 16 May 1942), Mexican photographer. A native of Mexico City, Iturbide uses the camera to interpret the daily lives and rituals of indigenous peoples. She studied at the Center for Cinematographic Studies of the National Autonomous University from 1969 to 1972. Her most extensive body of work, executed in the 1980s, centers on the matriarchal culture of the Zapotecs of Juchitán, a town near the Isthmus of Tehuantepec on Mexico's southern Pacific coast. Among other projects, she has documented the singular manner in which the Mexican people approach death, and, in East Los Angeles, the daily lives of *cholos*, young Mexican American street gang members. Following in the tradition of her mentor, the photographer Manuel ÁLVAREZ BRAVO, Iturbide works in black-and-white; although her images are photojournalistic, they are characterized by a level of intimacy and candor not necessarily associated with the documentary tradition. Exhibitions of her work have been mounted internationally, and her photographs are included in the permanent collections of many major museums.

GRACIELA ITURBIDE, *Sueños de papel* (1985); GRACIELA ITURBIDE and ELENA PONIATOWSKA, *Juchitán de las mujeres* (1989); GRACIELA ITURBIDE, "Mexican Street Gangs of Los Angeles and Tijuana," in *Desires and Disguises: Five Latin American Photographers*, edited and translated by Amanda Hopkinson (1992); ELIZABETH FERRER, "Manos Poderosas: The Photography of Graciela Iturbide," in *Review: Latin American Literature and Arts*, no. 47 (1993): 69–78.

ELIZABETH FERRER

See also **Photography.**

ITURRIGARAY, JOSÉ DE (*b.* 27 June 1742; *d.* 1815), fifty-sixth viceroy of New Spain (1803–1808). A military man, he obtained the post of viceroy as a protégé of Spanish Prime Minister Manuel GODOY (1767–1851). He won the sympathies of New Spaniards with programs such as smallpox vaccinations. He organized the defense of the viceroyalty and stationed troops to protect the road to Mexico City. He took every opportunity to amass wealth, as evidenced by his implemention of the Royal Law of Consolidation (26 December 1804), from which he received a percentage of the amount collected.

When news arrived that King CHARLES IV (1748–1819) had abdicated in favor of NAPOLEON I (1769–1821), the Ayuntamiento (city council) of Mexico City proposed the establishment of a junta of authorities while an assembly of cities was convened. The Audiencia of Mexico, fearful that such action might lead to independence, proposed, instead, the recognition of one of the juntas formed in Spain. Backing the Ayuntamiento, Iturrigaray held several meetings, to which the Audiencia responded by encouraging a coup d'état. On the night of 15 September 1808, Gabriel de YERMO (1757–1813), at the head of 300 Spaniards, imprisoned the viceroy and detained several members of the Ayuntamiento as well as Fray Melchor de TALAMANTES (1765–1809). Thereafter, the conflict between *criollos* and PENINSULARES became acute. Removed from command, Iturrigaray was sent to Spain, where he was prosecuted for disloyalty, but his case was stayed. He underwent a *juicio de residencia,* which posthumously found him guilty of peculation. He died in Madrid in 1815.

ENRIQUE LAFUENTE FERRARI, *El virrey Iturrigaray y los orígenes de la independencia de Méjico* (1941); JOSÉ M. DE SALAVERRÍA, "Relación o historia," in *Documentos históricos mexicanos,* edited by Genaro García, vol. 2 (1985), pp. 296–469.

VIRGINIA GUEDEA

ITUZAINGÓ, BATTLE OF, the most important contest in the war between the Brazilian Empire and the UNITED PROVINCES OF THE RÍO DE LA PLATA (1825–1828) over the territory referred to by some as the Provincia Oriental and by others as Cisplatine Province. Ituzaingó is located in present-day Argentina. The battle took place 20 February 1827 and ended in a decisive victory for the troops of Río de la Plata. The number of combatants is estimated at approximately 16,000. The Brazilian forces were slightly superior in numbers and more so in arms and supplies. General Carlos de ALVEAR commanded the troops of Río de la Plata, among whom figured 3,000 men from the Provincia Oriental, led by General Juan Antonio LAVALLEJA. The victory of the forces of Río de la Plata at Ituzaingó dealt a strong blow to Brazilian hopes of extending its territory to Río de la Plata. Brazil was further frustrated in this effort by the Preliminary Peace Pact of 1828, out of which was born the independent nation of Uruguay.

ALFREDO CASTELLANOS, *La Cisplatina: La independencia y la república caudillesca, 1820–1838* (1974); WASHINGTON REYES ABADIE and ANDRÉS VÁZQUEZ ROMERO, *Crónica general del Uruguay,* vol. 2 (1984).

JOSÉ DE TORRES WILSON

ITZCOATL (*b.* ca. 1380; *d.* 1440), Aztec ruler from 1426 to 1440. Itzcoatl ("Obsidian Serpent"), fourth Mexica ruler or TLATOANI ("speaker"), was the son of Acamapichtli, the first *tlatoani,* and a slave woman. Itzcoatl led the rebellion against the Tepanac polity centered at Azcapotzalco, to which the Mexica had been tributaries. Itzcoatl's nephew (half-brother in some sources) and predecessor, Chimalpopoca (r. 1415–1426), died under mysterious circumstances. The accession of Itzcoatl, a mature man with a low-ranking mother, may have been engineered by Mexica leaders desiring to fight the Tepanecs. A skilled warrior and strategist, Itzcoatl joined forces with the Acolhua under NEZAHUALCOYOTL and the dissident Tepanecs of Tlacopan (Tacuba), forging the "Triple Alliance" that defeated Azcapotzalco's ruler, Maxtla, in 1428. According to native tradition, Itzcoatl then destroyed the manuscript records of Mexica history, thus obscuring the humble origins of the now-triumphant Mexica. To the nascent Aztec Empire, Itzcoatl added Coyoacan, Xochimilco, and Cuitlahuac. He was succeeded by his nephew, MOTECUHZOMA I.

BURR CARTWRIGHT BRUNDAGE, *A Rain of Darts: The Mexica Aztecs* (1972); NIGEL DAVIES, *The Aztecs: A History* (1980); DIEGO DURÁN, *The Aztecs: The History of the Indies of New Spain,* translated by Doris Heyden and Fernando Horcasitas (1964).

LOUISE M. BURKHART

IVALDI, HUMBERTO (*b.* 1909; *d.* 1947), Panamanian painter. He trained initially under Roberto LEWIS and later at the San Fernando Academy in Madrid (1930–1935). In Panama, he became an art teacher and later director of the Escuela Nacional de Pintura, where he influenced a generation of Panamanian artists. A frustrated man, he left many unfinished works and his early death is presumed to have been a suicide.

Ivaldi's academic background stands out in his traditional still lifes and numerous portraits. However, his more "modern" genre paintings and landscapes, for example, *Viento en la Loma* (1945), are characterized by expressive brush strokes, dynamic compositions, and the rich atmospheric quality of his colors.

H. CALAMARI, "Breves apuntaciones sobre la obra de Humberto Ivaldi," in *El Panamá América, Suplemento Literario* (23 March 1947); RODRIGO MIRÓ, "Lewis, Amador, Ivaldi," in *Revista Lotería,* no. 219 (May 1974): 72–80.

MONICA E. KUPFER

IXIMCHÉ (Ee-sheem-cháy), capital city of the KAQCHIKEL (Cakchiquel) Maya from around 1470/1480 to 1524. In return for Kaqchikel support during the Conquest, the Spaniards made Iximché the first Spanish capital (Santiago) in the Kingdom of Guatemala. However, Spanish abuses soon led the Kaqchikel to revolt, and the Spaniards abandoned Iximché in 1526.

According to Kaqchikel history, Iximché was founded

by Huntoh and Vukubatz after the Kaqchikel broke with the neighboring ᴋ'ɪᴄʜᴇ'. This marked the end of K'iche' subjugation and the beginning of Kaqchikel expansion, during which they subjugated former K'iche' territory.

The site of Iximché is located near modern Tecpan, Guatemala, a town settled in the sixteenth century by former residents of Iximché. Iximché occupies a naturally defensible position, atop a plateau that is surrounded on three sides by deep ravines. The site is divided into a residential precinct and a civic precinct that consists of temples, palaces, ball courts, altars, and plazas. Some buildings in the civic zone were painted with murals. Archaeological investigations have been conducted periodically at Iximché since the early 1950s, and today portions of the civic precinct have been reconstructed.

GEORGE F. GUILLEMIN, ''Urbanism and Hierarchy at Iximché,'' in *Social Process in Maya Prehistory,* edited by Norman Hammond (1977); JOHN W. FOX, *Quiché Conquest* (1978), esp. pp. 176–187.

JANINE GASCO

IZABAL (Puerto Izabal, Puerto del Golfo), the main port for commerce entering Guatemala from the Caribbean after its establishment in 1804 until the completion of the railroad, Ferrocarril del Norte, in 1908. The port was located on the south shore of Lake Izabal, the largest lake in Guatemala, known during the nineteenth century as the Golfo Dulce. The Río Dulce connects the lake to the Caribbean. Goods and passengers traveled up the river and lake by steamship and then were carried from Izabal to Guatemala City overland by mule train, crossing the Sierra de las Minas and following the Motagua River valley to the city.

Spanish authorities established Izabal after publicly declaring the necessity of relocation because of unhealthy conditions at the old port of Bodegas, about 4 miles to the east. Archival records indicate, however, that the shift was made in order to control customs taxes then collected by the Dominican order of the Roman Catholic church, which had dominated Bodegas from its founding in 1567.

Great Britain became the main international trade partner of Guatemala after the country gained independence from Spain in 1821. Commerce came to Izabal by steamship via ʙᴇʟɪᴢᴇ, then a British colony. Nearly all imported goods entered Guatemala by this route until the early 1850s. At that time a railway across Panama made the Pacific port of Iztapa, nearer and more accessible to Guatemala City, the major port of entry for the country. After that time the route was used mainly by travelers to Guatemala on the Atlantic route, and Izabal was a transshipment point for coffee and bananas from the eastern part of the country.

With the arrival of the railroad at ᴘᴜᴇʀᴛᴏ ʙᴀʀʀɪᴏs on the Caribbean, Izabal was abandoned as a port. Today it

is a small fishing and farming village. Ruins of the church and army garrison remain as evidence of its earlier role.

For a nineteenth-century view of Izabal, see JOHN L. STEPHENS, *Incidents of Travel in Central America, Chiapas and the Yucatán,* 2 vols. edited by Richard L. Predmore (repr. 1969), esp. pp. 34–41. Great Britain's role in Guatemala's economic history is examined in ROBERT A. NAYLOR, *Influenica británica en el comercio centroamericano durante las primeras décadas de la independencia (1821–1851),* translated by J. C. Cambranes (1988).

REBECCA J. OROZCO

IZAPA, an archaeological site located on the Pacific coast of the Isthmus of Tehuantépec in the Soconusco district of the state of Chiapas, Mexico. It is a regional center famous for its hundreds of Late Formative Guillen (300–50 B.C.) sculptures. The Izapan style, temporally and stylistically intermediate between the Olmec and the Maya, is distributed along the Pacific coast and in the highlands of Guatemala.

Izapa is a large ceremonial center of 1.5 square miles. Boulder-faced platforms define eight large plazas. Structures are oriented to astronomical events and the Tacaná Volcano. Distributed throughout the plazas are stone monuments, including stelae, altars, and thrones, just over fifty of which are carved.

The Izapan sculptures are important for their unique style. Stelae are decorated with low-relief narratives. Unlike later Maya sculptures of deified humans, they show scenes of ritual confrontation involving human figures with feline, serpentine, or crocodilian characteristics or of communication with serpentine deities. The art depicts rituals of sacrifice and death, water and fertility, worldview and creation, and astronomy. Such scenes are usually framed top and bottom by stylized zoomorphic beings and terrestrial bands, respectively.

Izapa has been interpreted as having been a residence for religious rulers and a pilgrimage center. The ceremonial and symbolic stone art, evidence of incense burning, and large ritual deposits of valuable materials are evidence of its importance as a religious center.

V. GARTH NORMAN, *Izapa Sculpture,* 2 vols., New World Archaeological Foundation Paper 30 (1973–1976); JACINTO QUIRARTE, *Izapan-Style Art: A Study of Its Form and Meaning,* in *Studies in Pre-Columbian Art and Archaeology,* no. 10 (1973); GARETH LOWE, THOMAS A. LEE, JR., and EDUARDO MARTÍNEZ ESPINOSA, *Izapa: An Introduction to the Ruins and Monuments,* New World Archaeological Foundation Paper 31 (1982).

EUGENIA J. ROBINSON

See also **Mayas: Mesoamerica; Olmecs.**

IZQUIERDO, MARÍA (*b.* 1902; *d.* 2 December 1955), Mexican artist. María Izquierdo was largely self-taught. In the early 1930s she was the companion of Rufino ᴛᴀᴍᴀʏᴏ, with whom she shared stylistic affinities.

305

Izquierdo's works include self-portraits, in which her Indian features are proudly evident, still lifes, and landscapes. "My greatest strength," she said about her work, "is that my painting reflects the Mexico that I know and love. . . . In the world of art, a painting is an open window to the human imagination." Along with her populism, she celebrated her passion for color, texture, and careful composition while maintaining a delight in spontaneity. Her palette changed over time from more obscure tones to contrasting and rich ones close to those of textiles, ceramics, and lacquered folk ware. Despite her often brilliant use of color, there is a tragic or melancholy undertone to many works along with a wry humor.

MIGUEL CERVANTES, ed., *María Izquierdo* (1986): RAQUEL TIBOL, "María Izquierdo," in *Latin American Art* 1 (Spring 1989): 23–25.

SHIFRA M. GOLDMAN

JAAR, ALFREDO (*b.* 1956), Chilean artist. Born in Santiago, Jaar received degrees in filmmaking from the American Institute of Culture (1979) and in Architecture from the University of Chile in Santiago (1981). In 1982 he moved to New York, where he received fellowships from the Guggenheim Memorial Foundation (1985), the National Endowment for the Arts (1987), and the Deutscher Akademischer Austauschdienst Berliner Kunstlerprogram (1989). Employing over-life-size and close-up photographs, light boxes, mirrors, and digital signs in his installations, Jaar addresses themes related to environmental decay and the inequality of human groups and nations. The exportation of toxic industrial waste by developed countries to Nigeria was the subject of his *Geography = War* (1991), and the plight of the Vietnamese boat people was depicted in *(Un)Framed* (1987–1991). Jaar has traveled to and meticulously researched each site he selects as a theme. The simplicity of his installations has prompted comparisons with the minimalist artists Robert Morris and Donald Judd.

ASHTON DORE and PATRICIA C. PHILLIPS, *Alfredo Jaar: Gold in the Morning* (1986); W. AVON DRAKE et al., *Alfredo Jaar: Geography = War* (1991); ALFREDO JAAR, "Artists' Statements" in *Art Journal* 51 (1992):18–19.

MARTA GARSD

JACOBINISM, a term that refers to Brazil's urban radical nationalism, particularly in the early Old Republic (1889–1930). Associated with positivist-influenced militants in the Republican Party, especially those connected with the dictatorial presidential administration (1891–1894) of General Floriano PEIXOTO (hence, Florianistas), its adherents were generally middle-class civilians and army officers. Jacobinos defended Peixoto's regime during the Naval Revolt (1893–1894) and engaged in street riots and, more rarely, assassinations (including an attempt on President Prudente de MORAIS in 1897), targeting monarchists and Portuguese, especially, as threats to the imperiled Republic and as economic parasites.

Rooted in the abolitionist and Republican mobilization and in the economic difficulties of the 1880s and 1890s, and hostile to the political tradition of the monarchy's parliamentary and planter elites, the Jacobin leaders often supported a post-positivist authoritarianism, statist intervention and developmentalism in the economy, and paternalist labor policies. They also feared the restoration of the monarchy and the old agriculture-based oligarchies. Triumphant under Peixoto, Jacobins remained a threat to the emerging power of the state oligarchies and Paulista federal hegemony, at least until the Revolta Contra Vacina of 1904 (the coup and popular revolt associated with the government's forced vaccination against smallpox), and were seemingly influential in the *salvacionista* military coups against state oligarchies of the 1910s. Their thinking remained influential among the military officer corps, the radical-wing elders of the Republican Party, and the political elite of Rio Grande until the Revolution of 1930.

JUNE E. HAHNER, *Civilian-Military Relations in Brazil, 1889–1898* (1969); AFONSO ARINOS DE MELO FRANCO, *Rodrigues Alves*, vol. 1 (1973); JUNE E. HAHNER, "Jacobinos Versus Galegos," in *Journal of Inter-American Studies and World Affairs* 18, no. 2 (1976): 125–154; SUELY ROBLES REIS DE QUEIROZ, *Os radicais da república* (1986); JOSÉ MURILO DE CARVALHO, *Os bestializados* (1987); JEFFREY D. NEEDELL, "The *Revolta Contra Vacina* of 1904," in *Hispanic American Historical Review* 67 (May 1987): 233–269.

JEFFREY D. NEEDELL

See also **Brazil: Political Parties.**

JAGUAR (*Panthera onca*), the biggest, most powerful New World member of the cat family. A male jaguar can weigh between 200 and 250 pounds. Although jaguars rarely attack human beings, in folklore they are man-eaters. For many ancient and recent cultures in Latin America, this mighty hunter has symbolized political and military power. The jaguar is also associated with shamans or priests.

For its size and weight, the jaguar has the most powerful bite of any large cat. Its head is flexible, and it has wide-field binocular vision and eye cells that take in all possible light. Its eyes seem mirrorlike. Although it prefers moist, lowland, tropical forest, it can survive in many environments. It is a good swimmer, climbs trees, and may sleep in caves or crannies; thus, it fits human symbolic concepts of the levels of the world. Its tawny color makes it a sun symbol in some cultures, and because it hunts at night and seeks dark places, it is also linked to the underworld and the "other" world.

Jaguars are companions and avatars of pre-Columbian gods, whose pictures and statues often include jaguar attributes or wear jaguar skins, although jaguars are rarely gods as such. In the last millennium B.C., OLMEC art in Mexico and CHAVIN art in Peru featured jaguar depictions. Later, Classic MAYA kings sat on jaguar thrones, wore jaguar-skin garments, and took jaguar names. Jaguar remains have been found in royal Maya burials. On the north coast of Peru, MOCHE gods had feline fangs, and Moche rulers wore jaguar headdresses. At the time of the Spanish conquest, the major orders of warriors in AZTEC Mexico were named after the jaguar and the eagle. Jaguars were associated with human sacrifice in these cultures. In TOLTEC sculpture in Mexico, jaguars are shown eating human hearts. South American depictions of a jaguar with a man may be interpreted sometimes as a protector figure, a companion spirit, or alter ego; sometimes as the recipient or agent of human sacrifice; or sometimes as a shaman undergoing initiation.

The words for "jaguar" and "shaman" or "priest" are the same in many indigenous languages. In recent ethnographic literature, accounts of a shaman's transformation into a jaguar to protect his people are widespread. The shaman usually acquires the jaguar's power in ritual by using a psychoactive drug. Jaguar masks, sometimes with mirror eyes, are worn in some regions for special rites. Jaguar teeth or claws are used on shaman's belts or necklaces. Pre-Columbian rulers also had shamanic powers and supernatural aspects and used these to enhance personal power, presumably for the good of their people.

Archaeological objects and recent ethnographic literature suggest that some groups thought of themselves as People or Children of the Jaguar, with a jaguar ancestor, male or female, in the mythic past. Jaguars are often addressed as Father, Grandfather, Uncle, or Mother.

The jaguar is now classified as an endangered species.

PETER T. FURST, "The Olmec Were-Jaguar Motif in the Light of Ethnographic Reality," in *Dumbarton Oaks Conference on the Olmec*, edited by Elizabeth P. Benson (1968), pp. 143–178; ELIZABETH P. BENSON, ed., *The Cult of the Feline* (1972); ALAN RABINOWITZ, *Jaguar: Struggle and Triumph in the Belize Jungle* (1986); NICHOLAS J. SAUNDERS, *People of the Jaguar: The Living Spirit of Ancient America* (1989).

ELIZABETH P. BENSON

JAGUARIBE GOMES DE MATOS, HÉLIO (*b.* 1923), Brazilian political scientist. During the second half of the twentieth century, Jaguaribe distinguished himself as one of Brazil's foremost social scientists whose research interests and publications consistently presented innovative approaches to issues of political and social development in modern Brazil and Latin America. Best known for his studies on the role of political nationalism and social organization in Brazilian modernization, Jaguaribe's works are widely read among Latin Americanists in the Americas and Europe. Some of his most provocative early writings include the controversial *O nacionalismo na atualidade brasileira* (1958), *The Brazilian Structural Crisis* (1966), and *Economic and Political Development: A Theoretical Approach and a Brazilian Case Study* (1968), as well as collaborations with the journal *Cadernos de nosso tempo*. His later works, including *Crise na república* (1993) and *Brasil: Reforma ou caos* (1989), concentrate on the institutional, social, economic, and political problems involved in the transition from authoritarian to democratic rule, particularly in Brazil.

A native of Rio de Janeiro, Jaguaribe received a law degree from the Pontífica Universidade Católica of Rio de Janeiro (1946) and a doctorate from Mainz University in Germany (1983). After receiving his law degree, Jaguaribe worked as a lawyer, entrepreneur, and industrialist in the states of Rio de Janeiro and Espírito Santo. After entering academics in the mid-1950s, Jaguaribe taught extensively in Brazil, serving as a faculty member of the Instituto Superior de Estudos Brasileiros (1956–1959) and the Universidade de São Paulo, and abroad, as visiting professor at Harvard (1964–1966), Stanford (1966–1967), and the Massachusetts Institute of Technology (1968–1969). In the early 1990s, Jaguaribe served as dean of the Instituto de Estudos Políticos e Sociais do Rio de Janeiro.

DARYLE WILLIAMS

JAGUNÇO, a bodyguard, hired gun, or assassin. Originating in northeastern Brazil in the early nineteenth century, *jagunços* were an integral part of rural life throughout the country well into the twentieth century. They formed the heavily armed military forces of *coronéis* (local political bosses) during regional power struggles and were also employed as enforcers of property rights against sharecroppers and squatters. Some *jagunços* became CANGACEIROS (bandits), while many fought alongside Antônio CONSELHEIRO during the millenarian CANUDOS conflict in Bahia (1896–1897). As Brazil modernized, they declined, but competition for land in the Amazon Basin has led to their resurgence under the name of *capanga*.

EUCLIDES DE CUNHA, *Rebellion in the Backlands (Os Sertões),* translated by Samuel Putnam (1944); JORGE AMADO, *Jubiabá,* translated by Margaret A. Neves (1984); AFONSO ARINOS, *Os jagunços: Novela,* 3d ed. (1985).

ROBERT WILCOX

See also **Coronel.**

JALISCO, state in west central Mexico that is sixth largest in the area (30,941 square miles), and fourth largest in population (5,278,987 in 1990). The indigenous population that settled the area beginning about 15,000 years ago was less dense and more linguistically and culturally diverse than that of central Mexico. By the early sixteenth century, the area included well-developed sedentary chiefdoms and numerous nomadic peoples. Nuño Beltrán de GUZMÁN's campaign of conquest (1529–1536) was bloody even by standards of the time. Further conflicts reduced the area's indigenous population by some 90 percent by 1560. Today Indian elements are notably scarce in Jalisco's culture, and with the exception of some 65,000 Indians, mostly *huicholes,* the state is predominantly *criollo* and mestizo. GUADALAJARA, the chief city, has been the seat of a bishopric since 1548. It was the capital of Nueva Galicia and seat of New Spain's only independent *audiencia* since 1560.

Under Spanish rule in the seventeenth century, the area developed haciendas (great landed estates) as well as an occasionally spurious local nobility. Peninsular Spanish immigrants, who often succeeded as merchants because Guadalajara was such an important entrepôt in New Spain's trade network with the northern provinces, then intermarried with landed families to integrate an oligopoly based on agriculture, commerce, and mining. Discovery of silver at Bolaños initiated a period of growth in 1747 that was boosted by a relaxation of trading restrictions in 1773. This development broadened the economic base, created a more mobile and wage-oriented labor force, and thus laid the groundwork for future industrial development.

The Wars of Independence from Spain, beginning in 1810, devastated the local economy. The insurgents' temporary seizure of Guadalajara in late 1810 foreshadowed a period of several decades when the capital was to be the political and military football first of royalists and insurgents, later of centralists and federalists, then of monarchists and constitutionalists. Real recovery did not begin until the peace imposed by dictator Porfirio DÍAZ between 1876 and 1910.

By the time the revolution against Díaz broke out in 1910, Jalisco was losing influence relative to Sonora, Nuevo León, and other rival states. As a bastion of conservative Spanish Catholicism, Jalisco in this period is perhaps best remembered as the focal point of the proclerical CRISTERO REBELLION (1916–1929), a bitter reaction to the anticlerical policies of the revolutionary leaders Alvaro Obregón and Plutarco Elías Calles. Even today, the ruling party (Institutional Revolutionary Party—PRI) is often sharply challenged by opposition parties and prochurch elements with power bases in Jalisco.

Guadalajara was a somewhat distant second to Mexico City in size and influence until the nineteenth century. As early as 1840, the city had begun to develop an industrial base dominated by paper and printing, clothing, and food products. Today, Guadalajara is a major industrial and commercial center, with photographic and electrical goods, textiles, tequila, and steel leading the list of local products. Other important municipalities in the state include Puerto Vallarta (home of the state's second international airport), Lagos de Moreno, Tepatitlán, Ciudad Guzmán, and Ocotlán.

Jalisco is still the country's top maize producer and the second-largest cattle producer, and trade accounts for approximately 20 percent of the state's domestic product. The state is popularly identified with such *criollo* cultural monuments as tequila, *charros* (elaborately costumed cowboys), and MARIACHI music, and with the international beach resort of Puerto Vallarta. Outsiders encounter the state's culture through the works of such prominent twentieth-century natives as writers Agustín YÁÑEZ and Juan RULFO and the muralist José Clemente OROZCO, as well as through *huichol* yarn paintings, pottery from Tonalá, and hand-blown glass from Tlaquepaque.

References in English consist mainly of topical monographs and dissertations that can be located through the Library of Congress, *Handbook of Latin American Studies,* and University Microfilms, *Dissertation Abstracts.* The new standard source in Spanish is JOSÉ MARÍA MURIÁ, *Historia de Jalisco,* 4 vols. (1980–

1982); a much shorter version, *sans* bibliography, is his *Breve historia de Jalisco* (1988). Relatively recent Spanish-language sources can be found in JAIME OLVEDA and MARINA MANTILLA TROLLE, *Jalisco en libros* (1985). A more general bibliography is RAMIRO VILLASEÑOR Y VILLASEÑOR, *Bibliografía general de Jalisco*, 2 vols. (1958, 1983).

RICHARD LINDLEY

JAMA-COAQUE, the name originally given to the prehistoric culture occupying northern Manabí Province, Ecuador, during the Regional-Developmental period, (500 B.C.–A.D. 500). More recent research has established that the Jama-Coaque tradition represents four phases of occupation beginning around 550 B.C. and continuing until the Spanish conquest in 1531. Although its territory may have fluctuated over time, it minimally extended along the northern Manabí coast from Bahía de Cojimíes in the north to Bahía de Caráquez in the south. To the east, limited archaeological evidence suggests that Jama-Coaque influence extended to the Andean foothills.

Jama-Coaque was originally defined by the Ecuadoran archaeologist Emilio Estrada in the late 1950s, on the basis of limited test excavations at the littoral type sites of Coaque and Jama. The culture is best known for its tradition of elaborate ceramic figurines and modeled vessels depicting a wide range of anthropomorphic and zoomorphic imagery. It shares many characteristics with the BAHÍA culture to the south, such as ceramic house models and neck rests, suggesting shared Asiatic influences. Also common to both cultures are several vessel forms and decorative techniques, such as negative painting, postfire multicolored painting, and nicked or cutout flattened rims on shallow polypod bowls, but enough differences exist to differentiate the two styles clearly. Jama-Coaque figurines are commonly mold-made, and even the larger, hollow, modeled figurines depicting elite personages or dragonlike animals typically exhibit detailed ornamentation assembled from standardized mold-made pieces. Other typical pottery artifacts include both flat and cylindrical stamps or seals, incised spindle whorls, zoomorphic whistles and flutes, and anthropomorphic masks that may have functioned as pendants. A number of these ceramic objects, as well as specific costumes and ornamentation depicted on figurines, have stylistic parallels in Mesoamerica, suggesting maritime contacts with western Mexico.

Both the costumes depicted on figurines and the evidence of numerous fabric impressions in clay suggest a well-developed textile industry. Feather-working is also depicted on some figurine costumes. Lithic industries included a sophisticated lapidary technology of carved and polished greenstone and jadeite. Obsidian was imported from highland sources near the Quito Basin, and a well-developed prismatic blade industry is present at several sites. Artifacts of cut and polished *Spondylus* shell were crafted into sumptuary ornaments and may have been traded to highlanders for obsidian. The abundance and standardization exhibited by many of these artifact categories suggest a well-developed craft specialization.

Archaeological research in the Jama Valley, at moister higher elevations inland from the coast, have shed new light on the nature of Jama-Coaque settlement dynamics and subsistence production. High population densities and multitiered settlement hierarchies are present throughout the sequence, along with intensified agricultural production based on maize and root crops. The Jama-Coaque polities were stratified chiefdoms that minimally controlled a large river valley. It is also possible that a single paramount from a large ceremonial civic center ruled over all of northern Manabí at various times in the prehistoric past. One such regional center is the site of San Isidro, in the middle Jama Valley some 15 miles inland from the coast. It has over 125 acres of thick habitation refuse and is dominated by a large central platform mound measuring 110 yards in width at the base and some 19 yards in height. Smaller platform mounds have been documented at secondary centers throughout the valley.

By the time of Pizarro's march through Coaque and Pasao in 1531, the Jama-Coaque peoples may have been coming under the progressive domination of the MANTEÑO polity to the south. Although not conclusive, the presence of Manteño burnished black pottery in several Late Integration sites suggests the establishment of enclave communities that perhaps administered tribute payments from the local Jama-Coaque populations.

EMILIO ESTRADA, *Prehistoria de Manabí* (1957); CLIFFORD EVANS and BETTY MEGGERS, "Mesoamerica and Ecuador," in *Handbook of Middle American Indians*, edited by Robert Wauchope, vol. 4 (1966); BETTY MEGGERS, *Ecuador* (1966); ROBERT A. FELDMAN and MICHAEL E. MOSELEY, "The Northern Andes," in *Ancient South Americans*, edited by Jesse D. Jennings (1983); JAMES A. ZEIDLER and DEBORAH M. PEARSALL, eds., *Regional Archaeology in Northern Manabí, Ecuador*, vol. 1, *Environment, Cultural Chronology, and Prehistoric Subsistence in the Jama River Valley* (1994).

JAMES A. ZEIDLER

See also **Atacames; Guangala.**

JAMAICA, an island in the West Indian archipelago that encircles the Caribbean Sea. Its land area encompasses 4,471 square miles, an area slightly smaller than the state of Connecticut. The climate is mostly tropical, with a temperate interior. The terrain is predominantly mountainous, reaching a height of 7,400 feet in the Blue Mountain range. The nation's population in 1990 was approximately 2.4 million, 49 percent of which lived in urban areas. The ethnic divisions are as follows: 76.3 percent African; 15.1 percent Afro-European; 3.4 percent East Indian and Afro–East Indian; 3.2 percent European; 2 percent other. Ethnic diversity plays a major role in Jamaican history.

Although recorded Jamaican history began with European arrival in the New World, Jamaica has a rich pre-Columbian history. Its earliest inhabitants were the peaceful Arawak Indians who sought refuge from the more aggressive CARIBS. Unfortunately, little remains of their culture. Archaeologists have been able to reconstruct some patterns from kitchen middens, burial caves, and other artifacts. Although Jamaica provided the necessary refuge from the Caribs, no such haven could protect the Arawaks from the Europeans.

Christopher Columbus, on his second transatlantic voyage, arrived in Jamaica on 5 May 1494, going ashore at what is today called Discovery Bay. He received a less than hospitable welcome from native inhabitants. On further excursions, he found the natives living on the western part of the island more amiable. As Jamaica was not a source of gold, Spain used it mainly as a supply base. While the first Spanish community, Sevilla la Nueva, was unsuccessful, other settlements and townships, most notably St. Jago de la Vega (Spanish Town), became well established. Settlers introduced the banana and most citrus fruits.

English interest in the island dated from at least 1569, but not until 1643 did the British attach much importance to it. During this time, Spanish-English relations became more tenuous. In 1655, under Cromwell's "Western Design," Admiral William Penn and General Oliver Robert Venables attacked Jamaica after being routed by the Spaniards at Santo Domingo, having relatively little trouble taking the island. The Spaniards, intent on making British occupation temporary, freed their black slaves, who escaped to the mountains and aggravated the British through guerrilla warfare. These guerrillas would later become known as MAROONS.

In 1656, some 1,600 colonists came to the island, settling around Port Morant. While the soil was healthy, the surrounding area was swampy, and within three months 1,200 colonists had died. The Spaniards tried at various times to recapture the island but failed. Jamaica was legally ceded to the English by the Treaty of Madrid (1670), but the island received only nominal English attention. It was not until large SUGAR plantations displaced the small independent settler that the island increased in political importance.

Beginning with the seventeenth century, sugar and SLAVERY were central factors in Jamaica's development. By 1673, sugar had become Jamaica's staple crop, the "gold" sought by the Spaniards. For the most part, absentee ownership was the preferred form of plantation management. Slaves and intensive labor were needed to tend sugarcane. During the eighteenth century, approximately five thousand slaves a year were brought to Jamaica. The slaves brought their customs and religions, which were often an important force in slave rebellions.

The maroons, the freed Spanish slaves who had escaped to the dense forest interior, also carried out rebellions. They molested the English from the very beginning, swooping down from the hills, raiding farms and towns, and burning fields. Escaped slaves flocked

to the maroons, swelling their numbers and strengthening their position. Conflict with the maroons lasted until 1796 and cost the British approximately £250,000.

Resolving the maroon conflict, however, did little to rectify social inequalities for the Jamaican slave. Men and women continued to suffer under the prevailing system. Foreign events promoted the continued use of slavery on Jamaica. First, wars with both the United States and France were costly, and Jamaica's sugar and COFFEE were important commodities in financing the wars. Second, as ideas from the French Revolution filtered to the Caribbean and especially Haiti, slaves of that nation clamored for freedom. After a failed attempt to take Haiti, but having witnessed its slave rebellions, the British returned to Jamaica determined to prevent similar uprisings.

In 1838, humanitarian efforts in England coupled with resistance to slavery led to emancipation. As in many nations, however, the abolition of slavery brought new social struggles. In Jamaica, two distinct societies continued to exist. At times social diversity led to increased tensions, as with the Morant Bay Rebellion of 1865, in which the peasantry revolted against the planter class.

Social tensions exacerbated a declining economy. Jamaica's agricultural industry remained highly susceptible to fluctuating world markets and economic conditions, and continued to decline until the pre–

Road from Gordon Town to Guarva Ridge, Jamaica, 1975. ORGANIZATION OF AMERICAN STATES.

World War II era, when England reinstituted isolationist policies and subsidies for its colonies. This refuge was temporary.

When Jamaica received its independence in 1962, social tensions continued to permeate Jamaican life. The black shoulder continued to bear Jamaica's poverty. Out of these conditions grew the influential Rastafarian religious movement. Founded in the 1930s, the Rastafarians advocated black nationalism and recognized the ties of the people to Africa. Black nationalism was strengthened by the civil rights movement in the United States. In 1963, Jamaicans took to the streets of Kingston, inspired by Martin Luther King, Jr. The Kingston protests were strongly anti-imperialist and pro-socialist; the calls for an end to social injustices, however, fell on deaf ears at the official level.

This intransigence was made all too clear when popular Guyanese lecturer Walter Rodney, an advocate of black power, was denied entrance into Jamaica by Prime Minister Hugh Shearer on 15 October 1968. The following day, black Jamaicans once again took to the streets in protest. The demonstration resulted in substantial property damage and the loss of two lives. Shearer labeled Rodney a subversive and a Communist. Although calls for reform sounded from many parts of the country, legislators were slow to respond.

In the 1970s, the failure to respond to social injustice allowed a socialist government under the leadership of Michael Manley and the People's National Party to come to power. Poor economic world trends, however, produced many hardships for Jamaica, and while Manley's government did make gains in social justice, real economic changes were hindered. The socialist experiment failed in 1980, after which Jamaica was ruled by the more conservative Labour Party. Under Prime Minister Edward Seaga, Jamaica reestablished ties with the International Monetary Fund, yet continued to struggle with its debt. Economic and social conditions were exacerbated when, in 1988, Michael Manley once again returned to power. Enacting austerity measures and continuing a free-market approach, the People's National Party was positive about Jamaica's future. Manley was able to convince major world powers to forgive a substantial portion of Jamaica's debt.

PETER ABRAHAMS, *Jamaica: An Island Mosaic* (1957); CLINTON V. BLACK, *The Story of Jamaica from Prehistory to the Present* (1965); MICHAEL MANLEY, *Jamaica: Struggle in the Periphery* (1982); G. BECKFORD and MICHAEL WITTER, *Small Garden, Bitter Weed: The Political Economy of Struggle and Change in Jamaica* (1982); K. E. INGRAM, *Jamaica* (1984); ROBERT E. LOONEY, *The Jamaican Economy in the 1960s* (1986); REX NETTLEFORD, *Jamaica in Independence* (1989); FRANKLIN W. KNIGHT and COLIN A. PALMER, eds., *The Modern Caribbean* (1989); FRANKLIN W. KNIGHT, *The Caribbean: Genesis of a Fragmented Nationalism* (1990).

ALLAN S. R. SUMNALL

See also **British–Latin American Relations; Buccaneers.**

JAMES, CYRIL LIONEL ROBERT (*b.* 4 January 1901; *d.* 31 May 1989), historian, philosopher, literary critic. C. L. R. James is well known outside his island home of Trinidad and Tobago as one of the twentieth century's leading intellectuals. His illustrious career as a writer spans several disciplines. His contributions to cultural studies, political philosophy, and West Indian creative and historical literature both predict and inform the late twentieth century's preoccupation with postcolonial studies and have earned him a place of high respect as an interpreter of both Marx's and Lenin's philosophies.

Throughout his life James was recognized as a brilliant student and teacher. When he emigrated to England in 1932, he established himself as a keen cricket commentator, writing for the *Manchester Guardian*. Later in his career he combined the history of cricket with autobiography to create a stunning cultural critique of the West Indies in *Beyond a Boundary* (1963). His novel *Minty Alley*, written in 1927, is a foundational text in the Caribbean literary tradition. His historical work, *The Black Jacobins: Toussaint L'Ouverture and the San Domingo Revolution* (1938), remains a universally acclaimed account of the Haitian war for independence in relationship to the French Revolution.

James was a major figure in the Pan-African movement in the 1930s. The continual development of his political ideologies can be traced through his numerous and diverse essays, collected in several volumes. Both his essays and full-length works reflect a keen interest in and healthy skepticism for Marxism, Trotskyism, socialism, and notions of American democracy. In association with Trotsky's organization, with which he later broke, James spent fifteen years in the United States (1938–1953) lecturing and organizing black workers. A casualty of the McCarthy era, he was asked to leave the country because his activities were considered too radical. While awaiting deportation, James wrote *Mariners, Renegades, and Castaways: The Story of Herman Melville and the World We Live In* (1953), a literary critique of Herman Melville's novel *Moby Dick*, but also a political commentary on totalitarianism and American democracy. James periodically revisited the Caribbean and also traveled through Europe and Africa. In 1968, he was allowed to reenter the United States, where he taught at Federal City College for ten years. During the last decades of his life he continued to write and lecture widely, and received awards and accolades from around the world. He died in London, England, his adopted home.

PAUL BUHLE, ed., *C. L. R. James: His Life and Work* (1986), and *C. L. R. James: The Artist As Revolutionary* (1988); ANNA GRIMSHAW, *The C. L. R. James Archive: A Reader's Guide* (1991); PAGET HENRY and PAUL BUHLE, eds., *C. L. R. James's Caribbean* (1992); ANNA GRIMSHAW, ed., *The C. L. R. James Reader* (1992).

NICOLE R. KING

JANGADA, a raft made of lightweight logs secured with wooden pegs or lianas, used for fishing by various indigenous groups in precolonial Brazil. Pero Vaz da Caminha recorded the first description of a *jangada*, mis-identifying it as a pirogue. Tupi names for these vessels were many: *itapaba, igapeba, candandu, piperi,* and *cata-marã.* The Portuguese adopted and modified the original raft, eventually labeling it *jangada,* from the Hindustani *janga* with the augmentative *ada,* meaning "larger."

The raft was first made of three logs, had no sail, and was guided by a fisherman who sat with legs extended. It was later expanded to five or six logs with a rudder (also used for a paddle). A stone on a woven rope was, and still is, used to anchor the *jangada.* A mast for a triangular sail was developed by the seventeenth century. There are small (about 10 feet by 2½ feet), medium (about 15 feet by 5 feet), and "classic," or large, *jangadas,* which measure about 26 to 30 feet by 6½ feet and require six to seven logs. The larger rafts may carry a crew of up to four men, each having a special title and function and receiving a certain portion of the catch according to his station, as recorded by noted authority Luís da Câmara Cascudo.

Jangadas are found primarily along Brazil's Northeastern coast from Bahia to Pernambuco to Ceará, and in each state a distinctive vocabulary exists to label the logs, vessel size, auxiliary equipment, and crew. Used today only by the poorest fishermen, the *jangada* has become a symbol of the Northeast, immortalized in prose, poetry, and song.

LUÍS DA CÂMARA CASCUDO, *Dicionário do folclore brasileiro,* 3d ed. (1972); NEARCO BARROSO GUEDES ARAÚJO, *Jangadas,* 2d ed. (1990).

GAYLE WAGGONER LOPES

JANITZIO, island in Lake PÁTZCUARO (Michoacán, Mexico). Janitzio is home to one of the many distinctive TARASCAN communities that settled on and around Lake Pátzcuaro. During the Mexican wars for independence from Spain the insurgents built a fort on the island that was attacked in 1816 by royalist forces. The heroic defense mounted by the insurgents is commemorated by an enormous 132-foot statue of José María MORELOS Y PAVÓN (1765–1815). The statue, in its strikingly beautiful setting, along with the picturesque butterfly fishing nets made and used by the island people (today mainly viewed in postcards, in light of the decline of the lake), have made Janitzio the subject of popular songs and a place of tourism.

PABLO G. MACÍAS, *Pátzcuaro* (Morelia, 1978).

MARGARET CHOWNING

JAPANESE–LATIN AMERICAN RELATIONS. The history of Japanese relations with Latin America dates from the early seventeenth century. By means of the MANILA GALLEON, Japanese and other Asian merchants devel-

oped a thriving trade with New Spain. Throughout most of the Tokugawa shogunate (1639–1857), however, Japan remained isolated from most foreign contact. The impetus for modernization, begun during the Meiji Restoration of the late nineteenth century, led Japan to cultivate commercial and diplomatic relations with the Pacific nations of Latin America. Seeking a precedent for the establishment of co-equal treaties with the major world powers, Japan signed a commercial treaty with Mexico in 1888. These initial trade ventures with Mexico, and later Peru and Chile, were soon overshadowed by Japanese government-sponsored IMMIGRATION to Latin America. Designed to alleviate increasing economic distress among Japan's agricultural population, these first immigrants (*nikkei*) were recruited mainly from southern Japan and particularly the island of Honshu. Later, these *nikkei* would be joined by immigrants from Okinawa.

While some of the first *nikkei* learned Spanish and converted to Roman Catholicism, most remained determined to promote the Japanese language and culture within their Latin American immigrant communities. Cultural organizations such as Peru's Nihonjin Doshi-kai (Japanese Brotherhood Association) and Mexico's Confederación de las Asociaciones Japonesas en la República Mexicana, enhanced Japanese cultural awareness and solidarity. Second-generation Japanese (*nisei*) in Latin America were generally educated in Japanese language schools, and the children of prosperous *issei* (first generation) were frequently sent to Japan to complete their education. Ironically, the very success of Latin American *issei* and *nisei* in building prosperous and culturally cohesive communities was at once their greatest strength and most significant vulnerability.

The first Japanese *nikkei* faced the same opposition earlier Chinese immigrants to the Western Hemisphere had encountered. After the Gentlemen's Agreement of 1907, Japanese immigration in the hemisphere was redirected from the United States and Mexico to the South American nations, where the *issei* made their livelihoods in commercial agriculture and later in urban commerce, with Brazil becoming the destination for the vast majority of Japanese. On the eve of World War II, approximately 190,000 of Latin America's 250,000 Japanese resided in Brazil, largely in agricultural cooperatives in São Paulo State.

Japanese militarism in the 1930s and the early financial success of many Latin American *nikkei* exacerbated the existing ill will and suspicion displayed by many Latin Americans toward the highly insular Japanese communities. After Pearl Harbor, nearly 2,000 Latin American Japanese, mostly from Peru, Central America, and Mexico, were deported from their adopted countries and interned in camps in the western United States. The Mexican government adopted a domestic internment policy similar to that of the United States, while Brazil, Bolivia, and Paraguay allowed their *nikkei* populations to remain in relatively isolated agricultural colonies where minimal security measures were taken. Tokyo made only limited attempts to establish espionage networks in Latin America during the war. These efforts were largely confined to the Japanese diplomatic communities in Argentina and Chile before both nations broke relations with the Axis. Japanese nationals in Latin America were generally instructed to maintain a low profile, and the vast majority did so, with the exception of the fanatically nationalistic Shindō Remmei patriotic league in Brazil.

By the early 1950s, Japanese immigration to Latin America resumed with the governments of Paraguay and Bolivia actively seeking these new colonists. As Japan emerged to become an economically powerful nation in the 1960s, many Latin American nations began to perceive themselves as Pacific Rim states and sought active trade relations with Tokyo to counterbalance the dominance of the United States in the hemisphere. By the 1980s, Japanese economic power made that country the second largest trading partner with Peru and Chile, and the third largest investor in Mexico. Japanese immigration to Latin America effectively ceased by the late 1960s as the Japanese agricultural sector attained unprecedented levels of prosperity.

There have been major changes among the Japanese in Latin America in the 1990s. Thousands of Latin American Japanese, mostly Brazilian *nisei* and *sansei* (third generation), are immigrating to Japan now that foreign-born Japanese can more easily obtain work permits. In Peru the election of *nisei* Alberto FUJIMORI to the presidency in 1990 has elevated public awareness of the Japanese presence in Latin America. But given the questionable economic future of many Latin American nations, it now seems clear that the historic pattern of Japanese immigration and settlement is not likely to be renewed. In the future, Japan's influence is likely to grow, but more through trade and culture than through settlement of new groups of pioneering *nikkei*.

JAMES L. TIGNER, *The Okinawans in Latin America* (1954); NORMAN STEWART, *Japanese Colonization in Eastern Paraguay* (1967); PHILIP STANIFORD, *Pioneers in the Tropics: The Political Organization of the Japanese in an Immigrant Community in Brazil* (1973); NOBUYA TSUCHIDA, "The Japanese in Brazil, 1908–1941" (Ph.D. diss., UCLA, 1978); AMELIA MORIMOTO, *Fuerza de trabajo immigrante japonesa y desarrollo en el Perú* (1979); C. HARVEY GARDINER, *Pawns in a Triangle of Hate: The Peruvian Japanese and the United States* (1981); MARIA ELENA OTA MISHIMA, *Siete migraciones japonesas en Mexico, 1890–1978* (1982); SUSAN KAUFMAN PURCELL and ROBERT M. IMMERMAN, eds., *Japan and Latin America in the New Global Order* (1992).

DANIEL M. MASTERSON
JOHN F. BRATZEL

JARA, VÍCTOR (*b.* 28 September 1934; *d.* 14/15 September 1973), Chilean singer, songwriter, and theater director. One of the leading figures of the New Chilean Song movement of the later 1960s and early 1970s, Jara was born into a peasant family in Lonquén, near Talagante,

in central Chile. After his military service (1952–1953), he studied acting at the University of Chile drama school, later acquiring a reputation as a theater director. Given his innate musical skill and his work with folk groups such as Cuncumén, with whom he toured Latin America and Europe, he soon found a place among the musicians gathering at the Peña de los Parra, an informal club founded in 1965 by Ángel and Isabel Parra, which was the focal point of New Chilean Song as it took shape. Several of Jara's songs (many pointed, some controversial) were to become true classics of the period, while his singing gained popularity.

A loyal but undogmatic Communist, Jara was a devoted supporter of President Salvador ALLENDE and became an immediate victim when the military seized power in September 1973. He was arrested, brutally beaten, and shot in one of the most tragic events of a tragic time.

JOAN JARA, *An Unfinished Song: The Life of Víctor Jara* (1983).

SIMON COLLIER

JARAMILLO LEVI, ENRIQUE (*b.* 11 December 1944), Panamanian writer, dramatist, and editor. Born in Colón, Jaramillo Levi attended La Salle High School and in 1967 received a degree in English from the University of Panama. He earned master's degrees in creative writing (1969) and in Latin American literature (1970) from the University of Iowa. In 1973, on a scholarship from the Center of Mexican Writers, he traveled to Mexico, where during the next twelve years he taught at Universidad Autónoma Metropolitana, founded *Editorial Signos*, and published several books, articles, and anthologies. From 1987 to 1990 he was a Fulbright scholar in the United States and also published the anthology *When New Flowers Bloomed: Short Stories by Women Writers from Costa Rica and Panama* (1991). His works include *Duplicaciones* (1973; *Duplications and Other Stories*, 1994), *El búho que dejó de latir* (1974; The Owl Who Stopped Throbbing), *Renuncia al tiempo* (1975; Renounce to Time), *Fugas y engranajes* (1982; Flights and Gears), *Ahora que soy él* (1985; Now That I Am He), *Extravíos: Poesía* (1989), and *El fabricante de máscaras* (1992; The Masks Maker).

Aside from enriching the innovative literary tradition started by Rogelio SINÁN, Jaramillo Levi's writings have opened new avenues of expression with emphasis on universality and aesthetic experimentation. He has received many literary prizes. He is founder and editor of *Maga* and director of Editorial Universitaria.

RODRIGO MIRÓ, *La literatura panameña* (1972); KAY GARCÍA, "El agua: Un signo polisémico en la obra literaria de Enrique Jaramillo Levi," in *Confluencia* 5, no. 2 (1990): 149–153; RICARDO SEGURA T., et al, *Puertas y ventanas: Acercamiento a la obra literaria de Enrique Jaramillo Levi,* (1900); DAVID FOSTER, *Handbook of Latin American Literature,* 2d ed. (1992), p. 466; ELBA D. BIRMINGHAM-POKORNY, "Las realidades de Enrique Jaramillo-Levi: Una entrevista," in *Confluencia* 8 and 9, nos. 1 and 2 (1993): 185–198.

ELBA D. BIRMINGHAM-POKORNY

JÁUREGUI, AGUSTÍN DE (*d.* 27 April 1784), viceroy of Peru (1780–1784). Although the date and place of Jáuregui's birth are uncertain, it is known that he was of noble Navarrese descent and served as equerry to PHILIP V before a period of military service in Cartagena, Cuba, and Honduras in the 1740s.

Following his return to Spain, he began a new period of service in America in 1773, with his appointment as captain-general of Chile, a post from which he was promoted to Lima in 1780 in succession to the disgraced Manuel de GUIRIOR. His period of office was complicated by widespread internal insurgency (notably the rebellion of TÚPAC AMARU I), the fear of British attack and the high costs of coastal defense occasioned by this fear, and the administrative reorganization that culminated in the introduction of the intendant system in 1784. Replaced as viceroy by Teodoro de CROIX on 3 April 1784, Jáuregui died later that month.

SEBASTIÁN LORENTE, ed., *Relaciones de los virreyes que han gobernado el Perú*, vol. 3 (1872); RUBÉN VARGAS UGARTE, *Historia del Perú: Virreinato (Siglo XVIII) 1700–1790* (1956), esp. pp. 393–433.

JOHN R. FISHER

JAURETCHE, ARTURO M. (*b.* 13 November 1901; *d.* 25 May 1974), Argentine nationalist intellectual, born in Lincoln, in Buenos Aires Province. Along with Luis DELLEPIANE and Raúl SCALABRINI ORTIZ, Jauretche founded the Radical Orientation Force of Argentine Youth (FORJA) in 1935. The FORJA criticized the country's liberal order and especially its quasi-colonial relationship with Great Britain as part of a deep historical revisionism with political goals. Its members embraced a vitriolic anti-imperialism replete with epithets (e.g. *vendepatria*) that would become an integral part of Argentine political discourse over the next several decades. In its scorn for the oligarchy's cosmopolitan, antinational culture, its denunciations of the ROCA-RUNCIMAN PACT, and criticisms of what it saw as U.S. pretensions to hegemony in Latin America, the FORJA helped contribute to the popular nationalism that would crystallize under Juan Domingo PERÓN. Jauretche was the most effective disseminator of the FORJA's ideas in books such as *Libros y alpargatas: civilizados o bárbaros* (1983) and *El medio pelo en la sociedad argentina* (1966).

The FORJA remained primarily an intellectual movement; expelled from the Radical Party, it never constituted an independent political force in its own right.

NORBERTO GALASSO, *Jauretche y su época* (1985); DAVID ROCK, *Authoritarian Argentina: The Nationalist Movement, Its History and Its Impact* (1993).

JAMES P. BRENNAN

JÊ. *See* **Gê.**

JECKER BONDS, promissory notes that provided a pretext for the FRENCH INTERVENTION in Mexico (1862–1867). Jecker, Torre, and Company was one of three French banking houses in Mexico City. Late in 1859 the Conservative MIRAMÓN regime entered into a bond-conversion arrangement with Jecker. In return for ready cash not even totalling 1 million pesos, Miramón issued bonds whose value came to 15 million pesos. Jecker agreed to pay 3 percent interest on these bonds over a five-year period in return for 15 percent of the face value of each new bond at the moment of conversion of an old bond for a new one. The Duc de Morny, half-brother of NAPOLEON III, had been Jecker's partner at the time of the issue. His close collaborator, Count Pierre Dubois de Saligny, French minister in Mexico (1860–1863), pressed the Jecker claims. The JUÁREZ government, however, refused to recognize the Jecker debt. But afterwards, the Mexican Empire paid Morny's claim in regular installments until his death in 1865, as provided by the Treaty of Miramar (March 1864).

NANCY N. BARKER, ''The Duke of Morny and the Affair of the Jecker Bonds,'' in *French Historical Studies* 6 (1970): 555–561, and *The French Experience in Mexico, 1821–1861* (1979).

BRIAN HAMNETT

JEFE POLÍTICO, a term designating the chief political officer (civil governor) at the provincial or departmental level, especially in nineteenth-century Latin America and Spain. The term was recognized in the Spanish CONSTITUTION OF 1812 and was incorporated into many subsequent Latin American constitutions. The office of *jefe* (or *gefe*) *político* replaced that of CORREGIDOR and was especially popular with liberal governments that sought to replace Spanish colonial terminology with new terms. Usually appointed by the president, the *jefe político* often exercised great power at the local level. In Argentina, the term is used to designate the chief of police.

Constitución política de la monarquía española promulgada en Cádiz a 19 de marzo de 1812, título VI (1820); MARIO RODRÍGUEZ, *The Cádiz Experiment in Central America, 1808 to 1826* (1978).

RALPH LEE WOODWARD, JR.

JEREZ, FRANCISCO DE (Xerez, Francisco de; *b.* 1497), Francisco PIZARRO's secretary at CAJAMARCA during the capture of ATAHUALPA in 1532 and author of one of the earliest and most widely read chronicles of the Conquest. Born in Seville, Jerez came to the New World in 1514 in the fleet of Pedro Arias de ÁVILA. He accompanied Pizarro on his three trips to Peru in 1524, 1526, and 1531, serving as the conqueror's secretary on all three. He witnessed the encounter with Atahualpa, as well as the Inca's subsequent kidnapping and execution at Cajamarca. While at Cajamarca, Jerez broke his leg, and used his convalescence to write his chronicle. He returned to

Spain in 1533, a much wealthier man, and his chronicle was published a year later in Seville. Titled *True Relation of the Conquest of Peru,* and written in part to refute the chronicle of Cristóbal de Mena, it soon became the standard account of the Conquest. Written in dry and unembellished soldier style, it describes in detail Pizarro's march from TUMBES to Cajamarca, the Inca's entourage, his capture, the story of the ransom, and so on. Jerez used his new wealth to establish himself as an important merchant in Seville, but his business failed to prosper. He later petitioned the court to allow him to return to America. Whether he actually returned to the New World is not known, nor is the date of his death.

RAÚL PORRAS BARRENECHEA, *Cronistas del Perú, 1528–1650* (1962); JAMES LOCKHART, *The Men of Cajamarca* (1972).

JEFFREY KLAIBER

JEREZ, MÁXIMO (*b.* 8 June 1818; *d.* 11 August 1881), Nicaraguan general and diplomatic figure. Jerez was born in León, the center of Nicaraguan liberalism. Political conditions forced his family to relocate to Costa Rica until 1825, when they returned to Nicaragua. Although his father had hoped he would join the family business as a painter, Jerez instead studied civil and canon law at León's university. He received his degree in 1837 and intended to become a priest; however, his scientific orientation led him to a second degree in philosophy the following year. In 1844 he worked for the noted jurist Francisco Calderón as a member of a diplomatic legation to European parliaments. Despite his youth, Jerez earned a reputation as a hard-working, honest, dedicated, and affable individual. His capabilities prompted President José León SÁNDOVAL to name Jerez to his cabinet in 1845. However, Jerez's liberal sympathies were becoming more pronounced, and he declined this position in a government led by a Conservative from Granada; instead, the ministry went to Fruto CHAMORRO.

Jerez joined the Liberal militia opposed to Sándoval and Chamorro and quickly distinguished himself in action. On 17 August 1845, Jerez was wounded in the battle of Chinandega; he was named colonel and major-general of the army. He recovered and took up the struggle with renewed vigor. In 1847 he was elected representative to the Central American Diet in Nacaome, where he formed an alliance with other Liberals and the pro-unionists José Sacasa and José Francisco BARRUNDIA and embarked on a lifelong friendship with the Honduran general Trinidad CABAÑAS. In 1848–1849 Jerez served as secretary of the legation to Great Britain, where he was very much affected by Lord Aberdeen's criticism of Nicaragua's inability to meet its treaty obligations. In 1853, Jerez was a Liberal delegate from León to the Constituent Assembly called by Fruto Chamorro to amend the 1838 Constitution. A crisis ensued when Chamorro overruled the Liberal opposition and exiled Jerez, Francisco Castellón, and José Guerrero on charges of conspiracy.

When William WALKER invaded Nicaragua in 1855, Jerez viewed him as the last hope of Central American liberalism and joined Walker's puppet government as cabinet minister for a short while until he grasped the true nature of Walker's designs. Jerez then defected to the opposition and led the Nicaraguan western army into Managua on 24 September 1856. Other Central American and legitimist troops followed. Jerez served as co-president in a provisional coalition with the Conservative Tomás MARTÍNEZ until November 1857, when Martínez alone was elected to continue. Jerez served in various diplomatic positions until his death in Washington.

WILLIAM WALKER, *The War in Nicaragua* (1860; repr. 1985); JOSÉ DOLORES GAMEZ, *Apuntamientos para la biografía de Máximo Jerez* (1910); PEDRO JOAQUÍN CHAMORRO, *Máximo Jerez y sus contemporáneos* (1948); SOFONÍAS SALVATIERRA, *Máximo Jerez Comentario polémico inmortal:* (1950); ALBERT Z. CARR, *The World and William Walker* (1963).

KAREN RACINE

JESUITS. The Society of Jesus, popularly known as the Jesuits, is a Roman Catholic religious order of men founded by the Spaniard Ignatius Loyola in the sixteenth century. In 1534 Ignatius and six companions studying in Paris vowed themselves to poverty, chastity, and work in the Holy Land. In 1540 the Roman Catholic church approved the establishment of the group as a religious order.

PURPOSE

The purpose of the group was the salvation of their own souls and that of their neighbors. Members include ordained priests, who take the vows of poverty, chastity, and obedience, plus an additional vow of special obedience to the pope, or spiritual coadjutors, priests who take the three vows but not that of obedience to the pope, and lay brothers, who perform tasks for which the priesthood is not needed. Candidates for the priesthood, called scholastics, are also members of the Jesuits.

ORGANIZATION

The Jesuits are highly centralized. A superior general in Rome is the head of the order. Geographic units headed by provincials report to the central office in Rome, and each house or residence, headed by a rector or superior, reports to the provincial. Required written correspondence between a local superior and provincial, and between provincial and the superior general assure a tightly knit bond and a continual flow of information and directives in both directions. Many of these documents dating from the sixteenth century are preserved in the central Jesuit archives in Rome.

The Society of Jesus grew rapidly in the sixteenth and seventeenth centuries. In 1556, at the death of Ignatius Loyola, there were 936 members. In 1626 there were 15,544. In Counter-Reformation Europe, Jesuits founded colleges, wrote theological and philosophical treatises, preached itinerant missions, and were influential at the Council of Trent (1545), thus gaining reputations for superior intellect, theological knowledge, and moral probity.

From the early days of the Jesuits, foreign missions were given high priority. The sixteenth century witnessed the expansion of Europe, and the church saw the opportunity to convert vast numbers of souls to Christianity. Jesuits were sent to the Portuguese colonies of West Africa, Francis Xavier began the evangelization of India (1541), and in 1549 Manuel da NÓBREGA began mission work in Brazil. The first Jesuits arrived in French Canada in 1611.

MISSIONS IN LATIN AMERICA

Jesuit mission work in Latin America had a relatively late start. The Spanish king, PHILIP II (1527–1598), hesitated to send the Jesuits to his domains in the New World. The Dominicans (Hispaniola) and Franciscans (Mexico) had preceded the Jesuits, and the danger of rivalry and jurisdictional disputes made the king uneasy. In addition, the Jesuits, based in Rome, had a certain independence that did not sit well with the king. Nevertheless, because they were well trained and well organized, they were permitted to establish missions in America.

Florida was the first American mission field of the Jesuits. Between 1565 and 1571 the Jesuits worked with the Indians on the shores of eastern and western Florida. Few converts were made, but the Jesuits acquired valuable lessons about the importance of learning the Indian languages and customs, establishing a solid economic base apart from the promises of king and CONQUISTADORES, and formulating clear goals for a mission area. These were lessons they carried with them to future mission experiences in America.

The Jesuits left Florida in 1571 and joined a group of Jesuits sent to Mexico in 1572. In Mexico the Jesuits established residences in Mexico City, Oaxaca, and Guadalajara, and later founded colleges in other major towns. Indian and Spanish parishioners were served, and the northern and western frontiers witnessed major Jesuit mission activity. In 1582 Jesuits arrived in Guatemala. In 1568, three decades after PIZARRO conquered the INCAS, and when there were already 2,500 Spanish settlers in Peru, five Jesuits arrived in Lima. The pattern of establishing a college, residences, and missions for the Indians was followed. In 1585 the Jesuits entered Tucumán, in present-day Argentina, and the following year they traveled north from Lima to Quito. By 1593 a

Jesuit house was established in Chile. In the Jesuit expansion north and south, the major focus of their labor was the urban college or university.

COLLEGES AND UNIVERSITIES

The models for the Jesuit colleges founded in Latin America were those of Europe. The college was the spearhead of Jesuit strategy during the Counter-Reformation in Germany, France, and Poland. Indoctrinating young Catholic minds to be wary of the pitfalls of PROTESTANTISM was a primary goal. Solid classical learning was another. In Latin America as well, the college was viewed as an instrument for Catholic and secular education. It was also seen as an ideal vehicle for proselytizing. The college always had a church attached to it, and the pulpit served as a powerful means of instruction and persuasion. Itinerant missions that swept through the countryside, exhorting the old faithful and encouraging the new, were initiated in the college. Social works of mercy that encompassed the surrounding neighborhood were also based in the college. So the college was not solely an educational institution; it was supposed to be a storehouse of energy that radiated outward, incorporating numerous ministries and housing Jesuits engaged in a variety of activities.

Large Latin American cities such as Lima, Mexico City, and Córdoba, in Argentina, had colleges with thirty or forty Jesuits. Smaller ones, such as those in Cuenca or Latacunga, in Ecuador, had only four or five. Colleges charged their students no tuition. Financial support came from a complex of farms and estates that each college had to possess as an endowment before being allowed to open. The larger the college, the greater the number of students and Jesuits to be provided for, and the more extensive the estates and farms required. Large SUGAR plantations and vineyards on the coast of Peru supported the college in Lima. Sheep farms and associated TEXTILE mills were the financial mainstay of the college of Quito, and cattle ranches and farms supplied the Jesuit college in Mexico City with most of its income. Many documents dealing with Jesuit landholdings and agrarian operations are extant, and shed a great deal of light on colonial Latin American rural society and development.

The Jesuits ran eight universities in colonial Latin America. The most famous were Córdoba in Argentina, San Pablo in Lima, and that of Mexico City. A university was a prestigious institution that could confer doctoral degrees. The universities and colleges were a focus of cultural life as well. Philosophical disputations, theater, panegyrics, processions, and degree conferrals added colorful pageantry to colonial life. In 1767 the Jesuits staffed more than thirty-five colleges throughout Latin America.

Brazil had no Jesuit universities but by 1578 the college in Bahia was conferring master's degrees, and mission work focused on trying to settle surrounding

Ruins of Jesuit mission in Misiones, Argentina. INSTRUCTIONAL RESOURCES CORP.

Indians in fixed towns called ALDEIAS. Financial support was provided by sugar plantations.

EVANGELIZATION

The frontier of the Latin American world beckoned the Jesuit missionary. In 1594 Jesuits began evangelizing Sinaloa, in northwestern Mexico. The mission to the Mainas Indians along the Marañón River in Peru was begun in 1639 by three Jesuits, and the Moxos Indians were evangelized in 1668. The Indians of Pimería Alta, in northwestern Mexico (Arizona), were evangelized by Eusebio KINO, who also showed that California was not an island (as hitherto had been believed). The Jesuit missions of Baja California operated from 1697 to 1767. During this time fifty-nine Jesuits established a chain of mission farms, villages, and ranches from Cabo San Lucas to the present international border. Jesuits stationed in the Andean regions of Cuzco and La Paz (Bolivia) evangelized the Altiplano.

Jesuits in Brazil traveled up the Amazon and thrust their way into the interior by the end of the sixteenth century. The order founded almost 400 missions in their 200-year history in Brazil. António VIEIRA became the Indians' most eloquent spokesman, charging Portuguese colonists with killing over two million Indians in their quest for workers and slaves. By the seventeenth century over 258 Jesuits had been sent to Portuguese Brazil. Labor in the mission village was organized for the benefit of either the religious order, the crown, or the colonists. In 1757 a royal decree freed Indian villages from missionary control.

THE REDUCTIONS OF PARAGUAY

The most famous of the Jesuit MISSIONS in Latin America were the reductions in northern Argentina and Paraguay. The term "reduction" comes from the Spanish noun *reducción,* the closest English meaning of which is "reservation." The first reductions were begun by the Franciscans, but the prototype of the Jesuit reductions was probably the Jesuit mission of Juli, on the shores of Lake Titicaca. The reductions were self-sufficient GUARANI Indian settlements. No Spaniards other than missionaries were permitted to enter a reduction. The "corrupting influence" of merchants or settlers was to be kept far from the neophytes. Isolation and indoctrination were the hallmarks of the reductions. A major project of the reductions was YERBA MATE, a tea that when boiled provided a tasty and popular beverage. Indians who sold reduction tea in Buenos Aires received low prices from Buenos Aires middlemen, so the Jesuits took over the sale and eventually the distribution of the tea, which became known as Jesuit tea. As a result, the order was criticized for operating an extensive commercial enterprise.

The reductions protected the Indians from the slave-raiding BANDEIRANTES, who periodically attacked the missions from São Paulo, Brazil. These villages allowed the missionaries to indoctrinate the Indians on a regular basis. Reduction town planning included elaborately constructed churches, the ruins of which still survive as tourist attractions.

In 1750 Spain and Portugal signed the Treaty of Limits that transferred some of the missions to Brazilian territory. The Jesuits and Indians protested with armed resistance, but to no avail.

When the Jesuits were expelled from the Spanish domains in 1767, government officials immediately repossessed the reductions, expecting to find mines of precious metals and hoards of SILVER and GOLD. Nothing was found. Eventually the mission Indians drifted into the mainstream of colonial agrarian society. The charge that the Jesuits had made the Indians thoroughly docile and helplessly dependent was untrue; many Guaraní took up trades in urban centers.

CRITICISM

Animosity and resentment had built up against the Jesuits during the two hundred years that they worked in Latin America. The network of colleges, estates, and slaves working on the estates created a political and economic force unrivaled by colonial economic groups. The Jesuits' economically integrated institutions were able to withstand the wild fluctuations of the colonial economic climate. Those of laypersons could not. Large estates and ostentatious construction fueled rumors of wealth and power. The European Bourbon monarchs, who resented the Jesuits for their own reasons, were confirmed in their wildest suspicions.

A propaganda campaign waged by the prime minister of Portugal, José de Carvalho, Marqués of POMBAL, convinced the king that the Jesuits were subverting royal authority and using the missions as economic benefices. In 1759, six hundred Jesuits were expelled from their colleges and missions in Brazil and from the other Portuguese domains. Eventually this was followed by their expulsion from the Spanish domains in 1767, and the order was suppressed in 1773.

EXPULSION

Over 2,000 college, mission, and parish personnel gathered in port cities (the sick and infirm remained) and were exiled to Italy. Jesuit estates, houses, movable property, and real estate were auctioned off by a committee of *temporalidades* (tangible possessions), and the income went to the crown. Schools and colleges were staffed by other religious orders. However, the academic quality of the universities and colleges suffered enormously, Indian missions collapsed, and the cultural and economic life of the region declined. Indian protests and revolts occurred in Mexico and Brazil.

RESTORED SOCIETY

In 1814 the Society of Jesus was restored by the papacy, but Jesuits did not return to Latin America until the middle of the nineteenth century. By then the independence movement and political upheavals had changed the educational and economic structures so the Jesuits never regained the influence that they had enjoyed in education, economics, and politics.

After the Second Vatican Council (1962–1965), the Jesuits in Latin America began to choose what was called the "option for the poor," associating themselves with many of the rural land-reform movements and the creation of Christian base communities (*comunidades de base*). These movements were often locally opposed, and Jesuits were accused of being Communist sympathizers. LIBERATION THEOLOGY was another movement that individual Jesuits supported. Jesuit theologians and writers such as Juan Luis Segundo and Gustavo GUTIÉRREZ proposed the Bible as a vehicle for political and individual liberation from oppression. Many Jesuits today in Latin America are in the forefront of economic and theological reforms.

PETER MASTEN DUNNE, *Pioneer Black Robes on the West Coast* (1940); MAGNUS MÖRNER, *The Economic and Political Activities of the Jesuits in the La Plata Region: The Hapsburg Era* (1953); GUILLERMO FURLONG CARDIFF, *Misiones y sus pueblos de Guaraníes* (1962); C. R. BOXER, *The Golden Age of Brazil, 1695–1750* (1965); MAGNUS MÖRNER, *The Expulsion of the Jesuits from Latin America* (1965). LUIS MARTÍN, *The Intellectual Conquest of Peru: The Jesuit College of San Pablo, 1568–1767* (1968); JUAN LUIS SEGUNDO, *The Liberation of Theology*, translated by John Drury (1976); HERMAN KONRAD, *A Jesuit Hacienda in Colonial Mexico: Santa Lucía, 1576–1767* (1980); NICHOLAS P. CUSHNER, *Lords of the Land: Sugar, Wine, and Jesuit Estates of Coastal Peru, 1600–1767* (1980); *Farm and Factory: The Jesuits and the Development of Agrarian Capitalism in Colonial Quito, 1600–1767* (1982); *Jesuit Ranches and the Agrarian Development of Colonial Argentina, 1650–1767* (1983); DAURIL ALDEN, "Sugar Planters by Necessity, Not Choice: The Role of the Jesuits in the Sugar Cane Industry of Colonial Brazil," in *The Church and Society in Latin America*, edited by Jeffrey A. Cole (1984), pp. 139–170.

NICHOLAS P. CUSHNER

JESUS, CAROLINA MARIA DE (*b.* 1914; *d.* 1977), Brazilian writer. A fiercely proud black woman, Jesus spent most of her life in obscurity, raising her three children in São Paulo's Canindé FAVELA, and supporting herself and them by scavenging paper. Her diary, published in

1960 through the help of journalist Audálio Dantas, who discovered her accidentally, made her an overnight sensation. It described the misery of *favela* life and expressed her thirst to escape it and provide a better life for her children. Within a year, it had become Brazil's all-time best-selling book, and it ultimately was translated into thirteen languages and sold in forty countries. But her fame and fortune did not last. She moved out of the *favela* into a house in a middle-class neighborhood, where she was rejected by her new neighbors; she spent much of the money she received unwisely, giving large sums away to needy people she hardly knew; and because she was unwilling to control her outspokenness, she alienated the members of the elite for whom she had been fashionably chic. Even at the height of her fame, most Brazilians never took Jesus seriously. The Left rejected her because she did not speak out against the exploitation of the poor. The literary establishment rejected her writing as childlike; indeed, she enjoyed a much more positive reputation outside of Brazil, where her book was called "one of the most astonishing documents of the lower-class depths ever printed."

All of Jesus's subsequent books lost money, so that within a few years of her exceptional success, she was forced to move out of her house with her children. She became a recluse in a distant semirural district. Times were so hard for her that she had to walk back to the city to scavenge for refuse, and her family again suffered hunger. She died at the age of sixty-three, so poor that her children had to ask for charity to bury her. Her diary, translated into English as *Child of the Dark*, was still in print in many foreign countries, although it had been largely forgotten in Brazil.

CAROLINA MARIA DE JESUS, *Child of the Dark*, translated by David St. Clair (1962); ROBERT M. LEVINE and JOSÉ CARLOS BOM MEIHY, *The Life and Death of Carolina Maria de Jesus* (1995).

ROBERT M. LEVINE

JEWS. Varying patterns of immigration, as well as differing degrees of acculturation, adaptation, and assimilation, have characterized the diverse Jewish population in Latin America and the Caribbean. Ashkenazim (Jews of Central and Eastern European ancestry) currently constitute the majority of the approximately half a million Jews in the region, but the first Jews to land in the New World came from Spain and Portugal. Early arrivals have been traced back to the initial voyages of exploration undertaken by Columbus and others sailing on behalf of Spain. These voyages represented Spain's outward expansion and were a direct result of Spanish unification and of the end of the war against the Moors. They were undertaken at the height of the power of the Spanish Catholic church, during the INQUISITION.

The impact of the Inquisition cut a path across the Atlantic, for only those who could document their Catholic ancestry were sanctioned to enter these new lands. Nevertheless, *conversos* and suspect "New Christians"

(Jewish converts to Christianity), along with a handful of Jews who managed to elude state edicts, in fact became the earliest Jewish settlers of the Americas. A tolerant environment and distance from the Inquisition's reach were major factors in the initial establishment of Jewish communities in both Spanish- and Portuguese-controlled territories and, shortly thereafter, in the Dutch-ruled possessions of Pernambuco and Bahia on the mainland and Curaçao and Suriname in the Caribbean. The experience of the descendants of Spanish and Portuguese *marranos* (converts to Christianity who secretly maintained their Judaism), who saw themselves as "La Nación," constitutes a unique chapter in the history of Jewish settlements in the Caribbean, which began to flourish in the seventeenth century.

It is both ironic and tragic that the best sources for Jewish life in the early colonial period are dossiers that document persecution and autos-da-fé, such as the destruction of Luis de CARVAJAL and his family in Mexico and the trial of Francisco Maldonado de Silva in Tucumán, then under the aegis of the Viceroyalty of Peru; detailed records of the Inquisition also portray the daily life of New Christians in Brazil. Many of the New Christians were eventually assimilated into the region's mainstream population, and only occasional traces (names and isolated but telling customs) link descendants to their Jewish origins. The modified Jewish traditions still being observed by the inhabitants of Venta Prieta (Mexico), and by some inhabitants of Loja (Ecuador), attest to non-Christian roots.

While a relatively small number of Jews had already settled in Latin America and on several Caribbean islands as the independence movements unfolded (Jews were, for instance, among the supporters of Simón BOLÍVAR), today's Jewish population must be seen in the context of nineteenth-century migration waves, and linked to World War I and World War II. This holds true for both Ashkenazi and for Sephardic Jews from Northern Africa and the Middle East. Official immigration plans played a role in attracting Europeans, Jews among them, to the nascent republics. Beyond these plans, however, the dominant factor in the migration of Jews to Latin America and the Caribbean, whether in the sixteenth or in the twentieth century, has been the possibility of finding a haven from persecution (oftentimes, since the 1800s, as a second choice to the United States) and access to opportunities that had been foreclosed in European towns and villages.

A notable example of a prompt and coordinated response to persecution—especially pogroms—under czarist Russia was framed by Baron Maurice de Hirsch and, under his guidance, by the Jewish Colonization Association (JCA) by resettling Jews in an agricultural setting in Argentina. The experiment, lauded by Alberto Gerchunoff as an unmitigated success that delivered a new Zion for the Jews, began to falter as the descendants of the colonists opted for urban life. Contrary to patterns elsewhere, a significant segment of the Jewish immigrants to several Latin American nations became an integral part of the urban labor force. Socialist and anarchist tenets among the urban proletariat contributed to anti-Semitic outbursts and pogroms during labor struggles. In 1919, the SEMANA TRÁGICA (Tragic Week) served as a powerful reminder of Argentina's painful readjustment to the changing economic order and to the reweaving of its social fabric; it was also a reminder that anti-Jewish feeling had taken root on this side of the Atlantic. Today, most of Argentina's approximately quarter million Jews—the largest Jewish community in Latin America—live in Buenos Aires, where over a third of the country's population resides, and are engaged in occupations that range from retail merchandising (one of the earliest Jewish trademarks in the city) and industry to careers in the liberal professions and scientific fields.

In addition to various official plans aimed at attracting European immigrants—plans that varied greatly among the countries that possessed them—conditions that propitiated the establishment of Jewish institutions and allowed for the development of a Jewish way of life were a significant inducement for this minority culture. Following traditional ethnic patterns of immigration, local aid societies were established along trade lines, and by city or area of origin. Religious tolerance and economic incentives, particularly in the form of industrial growth and of an accommodating climate, determined the initial inflow as well as the sustained growth of Jewish communities. In wartime, the availability of visas (or of quasi-legal permits) sufficed to direct passage into one or another country. In this regard, Bolivia and the Dominican Republic (where an agricultural experiment by German-Jewish colonists took place in Sosua), constitute paradigmatic responses to World War II refugees. Other countries soon opened their doors, albeit under quotas, to fleeing Jews.

With few exceptions, the largest Jewish centers in Latin America are in the region's major cities. Buenos Aires, São Paulo, Rio de Janeiro, Montevideo, Santiago, Mexico City, and Caracas are hubs of Jewish life, possessing established communal, religious, and educational networks that reflect the ideological and religious plurality of the community. From strictly Orthodox to secular Zionist to "lay Yiddishist" and, in recent years, to Conservative and Reform trends that replicate those of the United States, Jews have been provided in most Latin American nations with a suitable environment for all aspects of Jewish life.

Jews demonstrating for peace and the defense of their values, Buenos Aires, 6 August 1922. Reproduced from *La Nación*. ARCHIVO GENERAL DE LA NACIÓN, BUENOS AIRES.

As elsewhere, Ashkenazic and Sephardic communities have developed independently of each other, with the added splintering that corresponds to points of origin. In some cases, however, they have come together under representative umbrella organizations, such as Asociación Mutual Israelita Argentina (AMIA) and other mutual aid societies. Even before the establishment of the State of Israel in 1948, Zionism had been a mainstay of educational and communal associations. This tends to explain the rapid integration into Israeli life of first- and second-generation Latin American Jews. It is important to note, however, that economic fluctuations, political repression, and anti-Semitic outbursts and sentiments also enter into the equation that motivates emigration to Israel and, particularly since the 1970s, to other countries. Besides Tragic Week, anti-Semitism has included the "Golden Shirts" pro-Nazi elements in Mexico, the July 1994 bombing of the AMIA Building in Buenos Aires, and the ongoing circulation of anti-Semitic publications. It is also important to note that since 1948, relations between Israel and its Arab neighbors have had a direct impact on the Jewish communities (which disagreed on Middle Eastern politics) in Latin America. The 1970s United Nations statement equating Zionism with racism, for instance, generated lost tourist revenue in Mexico and its Jewish community, due to a Jewish-American boycott.

Early life in the major Latin American centers had a distinctly Yiddish flavor: newspapers and magazines—such as *Die Yiddishe Zeitung* and *Die Presse* in Argentina and *Havaner Lebn* in Cuba—and theater and radio programs echoed the dominant presence of Ashkenazi Jews. The growth of a vibrant Spanish- and Portuguese-language journalism in these communities indicate the degree of integration that has occurred in the countries that are home to Latin American Jews. This sentiment is manifested in first-rate literary and cultural expressions that continue to earn critical acclaim. In the political arena, integration is also evident—except for periods of heightened anti-Semitism or of official and unofficial proscription—in the number of Jews who have joined their respective governments, as well as in the relatively high proportion of Jewish youth who in the 1970s and early 1980s actively opposed the dictatorial regimes of the Southern Cone, notably in Argentina. Radical political transformations have also produced a different mass reaction, as witnessed by the emigration of most Cuban Jews at the beginning of the revolution and a similar move by the Nicaraguan Jews at the triumph of the Sandinista revolution. These demographic shifts in turn affected several Caribbean locations as well as South Florida.

Today, most Latin American Jews belong to the middle sectors of the socioeconomic spectrum. Beyond their measurable financial security, however, and contrary to widespread popular notions, a significant number of urban Jewish families remain indigent and require communal support for their sustenance. Entry into the Latin American mainstream can also be gauged by the high rate of intermarriage and assimilation, and constitutes a reason for communal concern over the lasting presence of Jewish life in a number of smaller centers. Other indicators are equally significant to an understanding of the current status of Jews in Latin America. These include ongoing Christian-Jewish dialogues that build on the conclusions of the Second Vatican Council (1962–1965), a shift in ethnic politics, the growing participation of Jews in longtime and reestablished democracies, the high profile of Jewish scientists and artists, the open recognition of minority contributions to the mosaic of national cultures, the expansion of moderate religious and cultural practices among younger segments of the population, and the unintended solidarity among persecuted minorities created in response to anti-Jewish terrorism and anti-Semitic acts.

BOLESLAO LEWIN, *Los judíos bajo la inquisición en Hispanoamérica* (1960); ANITA NOVINSKY, *Cristãos novos na Bahia* (1972); SEYMOUR B. LIEBMAN, *The Inquisitors and the Jews in the New World: Summaries of 'Procesos,' 1500–1810, and Bibliographic Guide* (1975); COMITÉ JUDÍO AMERICANO, INSTITUTO DE RELACIONES HUMANAS, *Comunidades judías de Latinoamérica, 1973; 1974; 1975* (1977) [similar reports exist for other years]; HENRIQUE RATTNER, *Tradicão e mudanca: a comunidade judaica em São Paulo* (1977); MARTIN H. SABLE, *Latin American Jewry: A Research Guide* (1978); JACOBO SCHIFTER SIKORA, LOWELL GUDMUNDSON, and MARIO SOLERA CASTRO, *El judío en Costa Rica* (1979); ROBERT WEISBROT, *The Jews of Argentina: From the Inquisition to Perón* (1979); JUDITH LAIKIN ELKIN, *Jews of the Latin American Republics* (1980); SEYMOUR B. LIEBMAN, *New World Jewry, 1493–1825: Requiem for the Forgotten* (1982); JUDITH LAIKIN ELKIN and GILBERT W. MERKX, eds., *The Jewish Presence in Latin America* (1987); LEONARDO SENKMAN, comp., *El antisemitismo en Argentina*, 2d ed. (1989); HAIM AVNI, *Argentina and the Jews: A History of Jewish Immigration*, translated by Gila Brand (1991); GUNTER BOHM, *Los sefardíes en los dominios holandeses de América del Sur y del Caribe, 1630–1750* (1992); JUDIT BOKSER DE LIWERANT, *Imágenes de un encuentro: la prescencia judía en México durante la primera mitad del siglo XX* (1992); ROBERT DI ANTONIO and NORA GLICKMAN, eds., *Tradition and Innovation: Reflections on Latin American Jewish Writing* (1993); ROBERT M. LEVINE, *Tropical Diaspora: The Jewish Experience in Cuba* (1993).

SAÚL SOSNOWSKI

See also **Arab–Latin American Relations; Israeli–Latin American Relations.**

JÍBARO, a term describing the rural subsistence population of the inland regions of Puerto Rico. During the 1890s and early twentieth century, the *jíbaro* was characterized as an untrustworthy and uncultured peasant. In the 1960s, under the nationalist program of the Popular Democratic Party and its leader, Luis MUÑOZ MARÍN, the *jíbaro* reemerged as a symbol of Puerto Rican identity. While perhaps poor in material wealth, the *jíbaro* was considered to be rich in cultural traits: hospitable, honorable, and hardworking. The virtues of *jíbaro* culture became identified with an idealized political image of Puero Rican nationality. This depiction was adopted by both pro-independence and pro-statehood political groups. Despite the effects of modernization and urbanization, which produced migration from rural to urban areas in the 1940s, the rural image of the *jíbaro* remains a powerful symbol of *puertorriqueñidad*. "Estado Jíbaro" was the term coined by Governor Luis A. Ferré to describe a state in which Puerto Rican culture would exist within a multicultural society.

JOSÉ C. ROSARIO, *The Development of the Puerto Rican Jíbaro and His Present Attitude Towards Society* (1935); KENNETH R. CARR, *A Historical Dictionary of Puerto Rico and the Virgin Islands* (1973); and RAYMOND CARR, *Puerto Rico: A Colonial Experiment* (1984).

HEATHER K. THIESSEN

JIMÉNEZ, ENRIQUE A. (*b.* 1888; *d.* 1970), president of Panama (June 1945–October 1948). Nicknamed "el submarino" for his apparent ability to fire on political opponents and to surface at the most opportune moment, Jiménez was supposed to be an interim president. He was supported by the Partido Renovador and Don Pancho Arias Paredes, who expected to succeed Jiménez but met an untimely death before elections were scheduled. With his support gone, Jiménez faced stiff opposition from Arnulfo ARIAS MADRID, who unsuccessfully attempted a coup d'état in December 1945, and was imprisoned for most of 1946. Although Jiménez negotiated an agreement with the United States regarding U.S. bases in Panama, anti-Yankee demonstrations led to its rejection by the National Assembly. Jiménez responded to the growing domestic agitation caused by students and labor with the iron fist of the National Police, which was under the leadership of José Antonio RÉMON CANTERA. Jiménez's political fortunes ended when his chosen successor, Domingo DÍAZ AROSEMENA, died of a heart attack (1946) and Remón installed Arias as president.

WALTER LA FEBER, *The Panama Canal* (1979), 2d ed., pp. 100–101; LESLIE BETHELL, ed., *The Cambridge History of Latin America*, vol. 7 (1990), pp. 624–626.

MICHAEL A. POLUSHIN

JIMÉNEZ DE QUESADA, GONZALO (*b.* 1509; *d.* 16 February 1579), Spanish CONQUISTADOR. Jiménez was born into a Jewish converso family in Córdoba, which had moved to Granada by 1522. Both he and his father were lawyers who practiced before the Audiencia in Granada. His family's subsequent financial ruin, the result of a lawsuit, made emigration inviting. In 1535, Jiménez joined a New World–bound expedition led by Pedro Fernández de Lugo, the experienced governor of the Canaries and at that time governor of the troubled colony at SANTA MARTA in what is now Colombia. As lieutenant to Governor Fernández, Jiménez was to oversee judicial and administrative procedures, not to command as conquistador.

The situation in Santa Marta was chaotic and grim: too many Spaniards and hostile Indians, and not enough food or gold. An expedition to the interior was an obvious solution, but Governor Fernández's son abandoned the project and returned to Spain. Suddenly, at the age of twenty-seven, unseasoned and inexperienced, Jiménez was given command as captain-general. Leaving Santa Marta on 5 April 1536, his force of 670 Spaniards made the difficult journey up the Magdalena and Opón rivers before reaching the Eastern Cordillera near Vélez in March 1537. The trek had taken its toll; fewer than 200 had survived.

But then their luck changed. They had reached the Chibchas (MUISCA), the largest group of Indians in Colombia. Jiménez and his group seized more than 200,000 pesos in gold and 1,815 large emeralds, distributed the Indians in *encomienda*, founded Santa Fé de Bogotá, and named the rich kingdom New Granada. The sudden appearance of Nicolás FÉDERMAN's and Sebastián de BELALCÁZAR's expeditions endangered this success, but Jiménez negotiated astutely. Leaving his brother Hernán in command, Jiménez traveled to Spain with Féderman and Belalcázar. There, however, he faced a hostile and pro-Indian Council of the Indies that ordered his imprisonment. He fled to France, Portugal, and Italy before returning to Spain in 1545. In the interval, the civil war in Peru and chaos in New Granada led the council to reconsider his merits.

Although he was not allowed to govern, Jiménez did return to New Granada in 1551 as *adelantado* (governor), marshal, senior *regidor* (alderman) in the Bogotá cabildo, and chief spokesman for the fast-disappearing conquistadores. He wrote at least four or five works, one running to more than 500 folios, of which only *El epítome* (1547) and *Antijovio* (1567) survive. The latter is an ambitious and complex work whose importance is still being debated.

In 1560 Jiménez exchanged his 2,000-ducat annual salary for *encomiendas* of equal value and joined the *encomendero* class. However, great wealth escaped him. In 1569, at the age of sixty—some say seventy—hounded by debt and lawsuits, still mesmerized by the El Dorado legend, he organized and commanded a disastrous expedition into the llanos. Of 300 Spanish and 1,500 Indians, only 50 Spaniards and 30 Indians returned alive in 1572. Yet, at the request of the Bogotá *audiencia*, he was pacifying hostile Indians in the Central Cordillera near Mariquita in 1574. He died there in 1579, suffering from what was described as leprosy.

An authoritative biography with accompanying documents is JUAN FRIEDE, *El Adelantado Don Gonzalo Jiménez de Quesada*, 2 vols. (1979). On whether Jiménez wrote *El Epítome*, see DEMETRIO RAMOS PÉREZ, *Ximénez de Quesada en su relación con los cronistas y el "Epítome de la conquista del Nuevo Reino de Granada"* (1972). For Jiménez's own work, see *Antijovio* (1952). On the importance of *Antijovio*, see VICTOR FRANKL, *"El Antijovio" de Gonzalo Jiménez de Quesada, y las concepciones de realidad y verdad en la época de la contrarreforma y del manierismo* (1963).

In English a lively read is JOHN HEMMING, *The Search for El Dorado* (1978). A very dated translation is GERMÁN ARCINIEGAS, *The Knight of El Dorado: The Tale of Don Gonzalo Jiménez de Quesada*, trans. Mildred Adams (1942; repr. 1968).

MAURICE P. BRUNGARDT

JIMÉNEZ OREAMUNO, RICARDO (*b.* 6 February 1859; *d.* 4 January 1945), president of Costa Rica (1910–1914; 1924–1928; 1932–1936). Born in Cartago, Costa Rica, Ricardo Jiménez earned his law degree from the University of Santo Tomás in San José in 1884. The following year he was named president of the municipality of San José and sent on a diplomatic mission to Mexico, where he successfully gained Mexican support for Costa Rica's battle against Justo Rufino BARRIOS, the Guatemalan general who was attempting to create forcibly one Central American republic. Upon completion of his mission, Jiménez left for Washington, D.C., where in January 1886 he published his most notable essay, ''Colegio de Cartago,'' in which he condemned JESUIT control of schools and argued for complete separation of church and state. The essay not only established Jiménez as one of the leading liberal theorists of the Costa Rican Generation of '89, but served as that group's credo.

In the years that followed, Jiménez held several government posts. In November 1886 he was appointed secretary of state in the Office of the Interior, Police, and Public Works. In September 1889 he assumed the post of secretary of state in the Office of Foreign Relations, only to quit after eight days on the job. In November he was named secretary of the interior, foreign relations, and finance, and the following year he was named president of the Supreme Court. In 1892 he resigned his post in objection to the dictatorship of José Joaquín Rodríguez. In 1906 he was elected to the Costa Rican Congress and made a name for himself as the country's chief critic of the UNITED FRUIT COMPANY's preferred economic status.

Jiménez was elected and served his first term as president from 1910 to 1914. After a brief retreat from politics he was elected representative of the provinces of San José and Cartago in 1921. He went on to serve as president of Costa Rica twice more (1924–1928 and 1932–1936). Jiménez was a highly accomplished leader best known for his foreign relations successes in protecting the sovereignty and neutrality of Costa Rica amidst Central American political strife. In 1939, at the age of eighty, Jiménez ran for a fourth term of office; however, he withdrew from the race due to a shortage of campaign funds. He remained an active voice in politics during his latter years and was honored as *Benemérito de la Patria* by a unanimous vote of Congress in 1942.

EUGENIO RODRÍGUEZ VEGA, *Los días de don Ricardo Jiménez* (1971); JOAQUÍN VARGAS COTO, *Crónicas de la época y vida de don Ricardo* (1986).

DOUGLAS R. KEBERLEIN

JIMENO Y PLANES, RAFAEL (also Ximeno; *b.* ca. 1760; *d.* 1825), painter. Born into a family of artists, Jimeno was trained at the ACADEMIA DE SAN CARLOS in Valencia and also spent time in Madrid and in Rome absorbing the neoclassical style. In 1794 he arrived in New Spain to teach painting at the Academia de San Carlos; four years later he became its general director and continued to teach there for the rest of his life. His portraits of fellow academicians Jerónimo GIL and Manuel TOLSÁ are considered his best work, but just as significant were his paintings in the dome of the cathedral of Mexico City (1809–1810) and in the Capilla del Señor in the Church of Santa Teresa (1813), both lost. Important paintings in the chapel of Tolsá's Palacio de Minería (1812–1813) survive. Jimeno also did drawings for engravings, notably for illustrations of *Don Quixote* in Spain and of the Plaza Mayor of Mexico City after the installation of Tolsá's equestrian statue of CHARLES IV.

MANUEL TOUSSAINT, *Colonial Art in Mexico* (1967); XAVIER MOYSSÉN ECHEVERRÍA, *El pintor Rafael Ximeno y Planes, su libreta de dibujos* (1985).

CLARA BARGELLINI

JÍVAROS. *See* **Shuar.**

JOÃO I OF PORTUGAL (*b.* 11 April 1357; *d.* 14 August 1433), king of Portugal (1385–1433) and founder of the house of Aviz (or Avis). The illegitimate son of PEDRO I, he ascended to power first as regent in 1383 and then as king despite opposition from the aristocracy and upper clergy. Through the Portuguese defeat of Castilian forces in the Battle of Aljubarrota (1385), the establishment of close alliances with England and Burgundy, and the creation of a new aristocracy with middle-class roots, João centralized power in the hands of the monarchy.

The marriage of João to Philippa of Lancaster, daughter of John of Gaunt, reinforced Portuguese-English relations and produced several children who contributed to the future of independent Portugal. Isabel was wed to Philip the Good, duke of Burgundy, thereby solidifying relations with Flanders. Henrique, or HENRY THE NAVIGATOR, devoted his energies to increasing the economic power of Portugal by attempting to establish a direct trade route to the Far East. Duarte (*b.* 1391) succeeded his father but died in 1438, leaving his brother Pedro as regent. Pedro's regency assured the house of Aviz's position as the ruling dynasty of Portugal until 1580, when Castilian forces seized the throne for PHILIP II OF SPAIN. The house of Aviz promoted intensive overseas exploration and expansion not only to perpetuate the Aviz name but also to placate their initial supporters, the Portuguese mercantile community.

H. V. LIVERMORE, ed., *Portugal and Brazil* (1963), pp. 58–62, 84, 89; *The Cambridge History of Latin America*, ed. Leslie Bethell, vol. 1 (1984), p. 154.

LESLEY R. LUSTER

JOÃO II OF PORTUGAL (*b.* 3 March 1466; *d.* 25 October 1495), the great-grandson of JOÃO I and fourth Portuguese king (1481–1495) of the Aviz (Avis) dynasty. Also known as John the Perfect, he succeeded to the throne after the death of his father, Afonso V, in 1481. João is credited with reasserting the power of the crown over the nobility, reestablishing the Portuguese priority of overseas exploration as a means of economic expansion, and smoothing relations with Ferdinand and Isabella of Castile by successfully negotiating the TREATY OF TORDESILLAS in 1494. The policy of economic growth through exploration led to the establishment of the fortress of São Jorge da Mina (Elmína, in present-day Ghana) in 1482 as a protective measure to encourage Portuguese trade with Guinea, Diogo Cão's discovery of the mouth of the Congo, the successful and lucrative colonization of the Atlantic Islands of MADEIRA and the AZORES, and, more important, Bartolomeu Dias's successful rounding of the Cape of Good Hope in 1488.

H. V. LIVERMORE, ed., *Portugal and Brazil* (1963), pp. 61–62, 89; E. BRADFORD BURNS, *A History of Brazil* (1980), p. 24; LYLE N. MC ALISTER, *Spain and Portugal in the New World, 1492–1700* (1984).

LESLEY R. LUSTER

JOÃO III OF PORTUGAL (*b.* 6 June 1502; *d.* 11 June 1557), king of Portugal (1521–1557). Also known as John the Pious, he was the great-nephew of JOÃO II, son of MANUEL I, and the sixth ruler of the Aviz dynasty.

Under João the Portuguese development of Brazil began in earnest. He divided the Brazilian coastline into captaincies that he awarded to hereditary proprietors (*donatarios*). He sent Tomé de SOUSA to Bahia to establish a government there in order to end the threat of French invasion and Indian revolts. Jesuit priests were sent to pacify, convert, and acculturate the Indians. At home, João established the INQUISITION and permitted the entry into Portugal of the JESUITS, whose influence on education became marked during his reign.

Despite the fact that Portugal was at the height of its powers at João's ascension, during his reign the country began its decline. The French and English challenges to the Portuguese monopoly of trade, the falling prices of Asian goods, the tremendous expense of maintaining the fleets and overseas posts, and the burden of crown debt caused by wasteful spending all contributed to the waning of the PORTUGUESE EMPIRE that was to culminate under his successors.

H. V. LIVERMORE, ed., *Portugal and Brazil* (1963), pp. 62, 92–93, 114, 168, 205–209, 350; E. BRADFORD BURNS, *A History of Brazil* (1980), pp. 29–36, 47, 99; JAMES LOCKHART and STUART B. SCHWARTZ, *Early Latin America: A History of Colonial Spanish America and Brazil* (1983); LESLIE BETHELL, ed., *The Cambridge History of Latin America*, vol. 1 (1984), pp. 156, 261–262, 267–268, 350; LYLE N. MC ALISTER, *Spain and Portugal in the New World, 1492–1700* (1984).

LESLEY R. LUSTER

JOÃO IV OF PORTUGAL (*b.* 19 March 1604; *d.* 1656), son of the seventh duke of Bragança, Dom Teodósio, and his wife, Dona Ana de Velasco. Born in the ancestral palace in Vila Viçosa, he married Dona Luísa Francesca de Guzmán of the Spanish house of Medina Sidonia (12 January 1633). Following the success of the December Revolution (1640) against Portugal's Spanish rulers, he was acclaimed king (15 December) and became the founder of the BRAGANÇA dynasty, thereby fulfilling 60 years of dreams of his family and his nation. He inherited a government devoid of funds, an effective army, or a competitive navy, but despite these weaknesses his rule survived a serious pro-Spanish conspiracy (1641). He came to rely upon the Jesuits for advice and diplomatic service and the members of his councils, including the Overseas Council, which he created for the management of the empire. Although he was unable to save Portugal's eastern empire, beset by heavy pressure from the Dutch, or to resume the once lucrative silk trade between Macao and Japan, he supported popular Brazilian uprisings against occupying Dutch forces in northeastern Brazil and lived to learn of their definitive surrender (1654). João IV was a conscientious, prudent monarch whose interests were hunting and music and the welfare of his subjects.

JOEL SERRÃO, ed., *Dicionário de história de Portugal* (1971), vol. 2, pp. 620–623; JOAQUIM VERÍSSIMO SERRÃO, *História de Portugal*, vol. 5 (1980).

DAURIL ALDEN

JOÃO V (*b.* 22 October 1689; *d.* 31 July 1750), king of Portugal (1706–1750). The grandson of JOÃO IV, João V was "neither feared nor owed," thanks to gold and diamond discoveries in Brazil. At the time largely untapped, this great wealth enabled him to build massive royal works [the palatial monastery at Mafra (1717–1735); the Lisbon Aqueduct of Free Waters (1732–1748)], support cultural establishments like the Royal Academy of History (1720), and indulge in extended patronage of the church. It also afforded him freedom from the CORTES, without whose intervention he ruled with increasing absolutism. João experienced recurring bouts of illness (possibly epilepsy) that worsened after 1742, and the queen, Maria Ana of Austria, assumed the regency until his death. He was succeeded by his son JOSÉ I.

MANUEL LOPES DE ALMEIDA, "Portugal na época de D. João V: Esboço de interpretação político-cultural da primeira metade do século XVIII," in *International Colloquium on Luso-Brazilian Studies* (1953); CHARLES R. BOXER, *The Golden Age of Brazil, 1695–1750: Growing Pains of a Colonial Society* (1962); H. V. LIVERMORE, *A New History of Portugal* (1966), pp. 205–212; ALAN DAVID FRANCIS, *Portugal, 1715–1808* (1985).

CATHERINE LUGAR

JOÃO VI OF PORTUGAL (*b.* 13 May 1767; *d.* 10 March 1826), regent (1799–1816) and king (1816–1826). João

325

was the second son of Queen MARIA I and Pedro III of Portugal who became heir to the crown when his elder brother José died in 1788. In 1785 he married CARLOTA JOAQUINA, the daughter of the Spanish king Carlos V. When Queen Maria became mentally ill, João took the government in his hands in 1792 and was officially declared regent in 1799. With the invasion of Portugal by NAPOLEON Bonaparte's troops in 1807, he embarked with the royal family and his court for Brazil. After a short stay in Bahia, he chose Rio de Janeiro as the seat of his government.

Among his first reforms was the opening of Brazilian ports to international trade, which changed the colony considerably. The capital became crowded with civil servants, aristocrats, and foreigners, a demographic and cultural change for which the police intendant general, Paulo Fernandes Viana, sought to prepare the urban space. The regent and the royal family were housed in a *chácara* (farm) in São Cristóvão that had belonged to a rich merchant. The Portuguese elite took refuge in the beautiful neighborhoods, where they built the noble houses to which they were accustomed in Portugal. The downtown shops and warehouses occupied by Portuguese and foreign merchants began to display European goods and fashions. Court life contributed to the development of a luxury trade, and the life-style changed in many aspects: housing, furniture, transportation, fashions.

Dom João soon adjusted to the Brazilian environment and enjoyed the musical events in church and in the palace. Every day he received his subjects in a ceremony called *beija-mão*, and on special occasions he favored them with a promotion in military rank, an honor in the Order of Christ, or a public office in some part of the Brazilian territory. When Bonaparte was defeated in Europe (1815), Dom João and the royal family were supposed to return immediately to Portugal, but the regent preferred to stay in Brazil. On 9 March 1816, after Queen Maria's death, he became King João VI.

The PERNAMBUCAN REVOLUTION OF 1817 was the result of the struggle between absolutism and liberalism that began after the fall of Napoleon. The conspiracy was put down, but, in Portugal, the king's continued absence was a major grievance. In 1820 the commander in chief of the Portuguese army, the English officer William Carr BERESFORD (1768–1854), left for Brazil in order to warn the king of the imminence of revolution in Portugal and the urgent need for his return. João VI was not a man of quick decisions. He always listened to his ministers, and since they held differing views about monarchy, the constitution, and the cortes, the king delayed his return.

After many ministerial discussions, the opinion prevailed that the king should return to Portugal, leaving his elder son PEDRO in Brazil. João VI and the court finally sailed 26 April 1821, after the city of Rio de Janeiro had been the stage of a violent coup attempt and

the persecution of those who defended the immediate adoption of the Spanish Constitution of 1812—unpleasant events for which the king was not directly responsible. Rather, they were the result of Pedro's personal interference and of his fear of a more democratic form of constitutional government. The years before João VI's death in 1826 in Portugal were troubled by the absolutist movement conducted by his younger son Miguel (1802–1866) in 1823 and 1824.

PEDRO CALMON, *O rei do Brasil: Vida de D. João VI*, 2d ed. (1943); MANUEL DE OLIVEIRA LIMA, *D. João VI no Brasil, 1808–1821*, 2d ed. (1945); ANGELO PEREIRA, *D. João VI príncipe e rei* (1953–1956); MARIA BEATRIZ NIZZA DA SILVA, *Cultura e sociedade no Rio de Janeiro, 1808–1821*, 2d ed. (1978); MARIA CÂNDIDA PROENÇA, *A Independência do Brasil: Relações externas portuguesas, 1808–1825* (1987); RODERICK J. BARMAN, *The Forging of a Nation* (1988).

MARIA BEATRIZ NIZZA DA SILVA

JOÃO PESSOA, capital of the Brazilian state of Paraíba. Known as Parahyba until 1930, when it was renamed in honor of the assassinated governor João PESSOA, the city was founded as Filipéia in 1585. Located six miles from the sea, on several hills overlooking the Paraíba River at its confluence with the Sanhauá, the city included the colonial port of Varadouro, which received ocean vessels until the late nineteenth century. Politically incorporated into adjacent Pernambuco (as part of the province of Paraíba) several times during the colonial period and economically subordinate to the regional entrepôt of Recife, Parahyba exported dyewood, SUGAR, hides, skins, vegetable waxes, and COFFEE. COTTON, which gained ascendancy in the nineteenth century, eventually led to Varadouro's decline, since river navigation depended on favorable tides. The Atlantic port of Cabedêlo, eleven miles away and constructed during the cotton boom of the 1920s, enabled Parahyba's exporters to remain competitive.

Famous for its beautiful beaches, the exquisitely restored colonial church of São Francisco, and its museum of regional popular art, and having direct access to the sugar plantation zone, João Pessoa is today an important tourist and convention center.

LINDA LEWIN, *Politics and Parentela in Paraíba: A Case Study of Family-Based Oligarchy in Brazil* (1987).

LINDA LEWIN

JOAQUIM, LEANDRO (*b.* ca. 1738; *d.* ca. 1798), Brazilian painter and architect. Born in Rio de Janeiro, Joaquim studied with the painter João de Sousa and was a colleague of Manuel da Cunha. He collaborated with the sculptor Valentim da FONSECA E SILVA (Mestre Valentim) on the Passeio Público and designed sets for the Teatro de Manuel Luis. Although his oeuvre consists primarily of religious paintings and portraits of governmental dignitaries, his few secular compositions have received particular acclaim. They include *Incendio do Recolhimento do Parto* and *Reconstrução do Recolhimento do Parto* and six oval panels commissioned for a pavilion in the Passeio Público. The latter are aesthetically among his best works but are also iconographically significant because they document social life and urban transformation in late-eighteenth-century Rio.

Arte no Brasil, vol. 1 (1979), esp. pp. 264–267.

CAREN A. MEGHREBLIAN

JOASEIRO DO NORTE. *See* **Juazeiro do Norte.**

JOBIM, ANTÔNIO CARLOS "TOM" (*b.* 25 January 1927; *d.* 8 December 1994), Brazilian composer. The most famous Brazilian songwriter, inside and outside of Brazil, Jobim was born in Rio de Janeiro. He studied with Lúcia Branco and Tomas Teran and was profoundly inspired by the works of Brazilian composer VILLA-LOBOS. As a young man, Jobim worked for a time as an architect but soon gave that up to pursue music as a full-time career. He began playing in nightclubs as a pianist around 1950, then got a job with the Continental record label in 1952 transcribing music, followed by a post with Odeon as artistic director, and then worked for various artists as an arranger. During the mid- to late-1950s, he would compose songs (alone and in collaboration with Newton Mendonça, Luiz Bonfá, and poet Vinícius de Moraes) that prefigured and then defined the BOSSA-NOVA style. Jobim wrote the music for such enduring songs as "Garota de Ipanema" (The Girl from Ipanema), "Samba de uma nota só" (One Note Samba), "Desafinado" (Off-Key), "Aguas de março" (Waters of March), "Dindi," "Corcovado" (English title: "Quiet Nights of Quiet Stars"), "Insensatez" (English title: "Foolishness"), and other standards often recorded by musicians in many countries. While singer-guitarist João GILBERTO provided the bossa-nova style with its beat, Jobim contributed its most important melodic and harmonic elements.

Jobim's compositions are warm and intimate and incorporate difficult harmonies even as the composer strove for a subtle simplicity. He sometimes wrote his own lyrics, but usually collaborated with songwriters such as Vinícius de Moraes, with whom he wrote the ground-breaking bossa standard "Chega de saudade" (No More Blues [1956]), songs for Moraes's play *Orfeu da conceição* (1956), tunes such as "A Felicidade" for the 1959 film *Orfeu Negro* (Black Orpheus), and later classics like "Garota de Ipanema" (1962). Jobim arranged João Gilberto's "Chega de saudade" (1959), considered the first bossa-nova album, and supplied several of its songs.

Jobim achieved international fame as a songwriter in the 1960s and recorded numerous albums over the next three decades as a singer-pianist. Some of Jobim's albums were strictly in the bossa vein, while others, such as *Urubu* (1976), which incorporated Brazilian regional music and evoked impressionistic classical music, ventured into other styles. Jobim (like João Gilberto) had a strong influence on succeeding generations of Brazilian musicians as well as on American jazz musicians in the 1960s and 1970s.

JOSÉ EDUARDO HOMEM DE MELLO, *Música popular brasileira* (1976); AUGUSTO DE CAMPOS, *Balanço da bossa e outras bossas* (1978); RUY CASTRO, *Chega de saudade* (1991); CHRIS MC GOWAN and RICARDO PESSANHA, *The Brazilian Sound: Samba, Bossa Nova, and the Popular Music of Brazil* (1991).

CHRIS McGOWAN

JOCKEY CLUB, upper-class institution serving as a center for socialization, communication, and recruitment among Latin American elites, with exorbitant membership dues guaranteeing exclusivity. The Jockey Club was established in Buenos Aires by Argentine President Carlos PELLEGRINI in 1882. Besides breeding fine horses (with government subsidies), the club sported excellent wine cellars and a collection of European art. After an inflammatory speech by Juan Domingo PERÓN in April 1953, an angry crowd of *descamisados* (shirtless ones), deeming it the heart of the oligarchy and its foreign collaborators, sacked and gutted the building housing the prestigious club, located on La Florida, while the fire department lagged in its response. The club was later rebuilt and serves, together with the Palermo racetrack, as one of the finest sporting venues in South America.

JOSEPH A. PAGE, *Perón: A Biography* (1983), esp. pp. 270–273 and 311; JORGE NEWTON and LILY DE NEWTON, *Historia del Jockey Club de Buenos Aires* (1966); DOUGLAS W. RICHMOND, *Carlos Pellegrini and the Crisis of the Argentine Elites, 1880–1916* (1989), pp. 24 and 80.

CHRISTEL K. CONVERSE

JONGO, a Brazilian dance-song indigenous to southern-central Brazil. The jongo is an African slave dance-style performed for social and recreational purposes. Many scholars believe the jongo to be of Angolan origin, while others have identified a form of the same title in northern Ghana. Accompanied by a highly syncopated ⅔ drum pattern, the male and female participants of the jongo dance in a circle, moving in a counterclockwise direction. Performing with a rattle in his hand, the singer jumps to the center of the circle and sings a verse. After the singer is answered by the chorus, he stamps his feet and then, near the end of the chorus, rejoins the dancers. The dance resumes when one of the spectators moves to the center of the circle.

Songs of the jongo dance, known as *pontos*, are usually sung in improvised one- and two-line verses, or *voltas*, which parallel the percussion accompaniment. In

São Paulo the lead singer and a harmonized second voice are answered by the dancers in an improvised call-and-response pattern. The jongo continues to survive in a few areas within the former southern-central slave regions.

NICHOLAS SLONIMSKY, *Music of Latin America* (1972).

JOHN COHASSEY

JOSÉ I OF PORTUGAL (*b.* 6 June 1714; *d.* 24 February 1777), king of Portugal (1750–1777). Called the ''idle king,'' in contrast to his energetic chief minister, Sebastião José de Carvalho e Melo, Count of Oeiras (known as the Marquês de POMBAL), José was eclipsed as Pombal pushed absolutist tendencies to despotic heights following the cataclysmic Lisbon earthquake of 1755. The king never challenged Pombal's attacks on the aristocracy, his suppression of the JESUITS, or his extensive administrative, economic, and fiscal reforms that worked toward a more bourgeois and secular state. José's marriage to the Spanish Bourbon princess Mariana Victoria (1729) produced four daughters. The oldest, the future MARÍA I, inherited the throne at his death.

JOÃO LÚCIO DE AZEVEDO, *O Marquês de Pombal e a sua época* (1922); H. V. LIVERMORE, *A New History of Portugal* (1976), pp. 212–238; ALAN DAVID FRANCIS, *Portugal, 1715–1808* (1985).

CATHERINE LUGAR

JOURNALISM. Latin American journalism has pulled itself up by its own bootstraps. The United Nations estimates that almost 40 percent of the region's people are functionally illiterate and 70 percent never see a daily newspaper. Radio and television have reached more *incomunicados* (those beyond communication), but the print medium has had greater long-range historical impact by influencing the opinion makers. This oligarchical press, which represents the social and economic interests of its owners, has been challenged by voices of protest.

The first printing press was set up in New Spain (Mexico) in 1535, soon after the Conquest and a century before the establishment of the first printing press in the British North American colonies. This first press, at the Royal and Pontifical University of New Spain, was used primarily to produce religious material to support the Roman Catholic church. The Viceroyalty of Peru acquired a printing press in 1568, and one first appeared in Argentina in 1705.

Under close government control, however, the early presses did not print newspapers until the eighteenth century. The first newspaper in Spanish America was *La Gazeta de México y Noticias de Nueva España*, founded in Mexico City in 1722; the first daily paper did not appear until 1805. This early press, largely religious and literary, was followed by a vituperative political phase.

The movements for independence from Spain be-tween 1809 and 1825 saw the birth of patriot propaganda organs, such as *El Despertador Americano* (The American Alarm Clock) in Mexico and *Aurora* (Dawn) in Chile. As the nineteenth century progressed, however, newspapers began to lose their political coloration and became a source of information for the masses.

In Chile, for example, *El Ferrocarril* (The Railroad, 1855–1911) was the first newspaper supported mainly by advertising, thus allowing a national and antisectarian orientation. Likewise, in Mexico the founding by Rafael Reyes Spíndola of *El Imparcial* (1896), which sold for one centavo (other papers charged six centavos), removed the press from dependence on political support by widening circulation and thus increasing advertising revenues. Newspapers were an important medium for fledgling parties, such as *La Vanguardia* for the Argentine Socialist Party. Short-lived organs were published by anarchists, syndicalists, and fascists.

As the twentieth century opened, some newspapers fought to preserve entrenched privilege. During the MEXICAN REVOLUTION, which began in 1910, some conservative Mexico City newspapers deliberately undermined the fragile democratic government of Francisco I. Madero (1911–1913). This made Madero appear vulnerable and led to the counterrevolution of General Victoriano Huerta, plunging Mexico into six more years of bloodshed.

In Bolivia, scene of the next social and economic revolution, the distance between the press and the people was even greater. The Big Three tin-mine owners controlled the three leading newspapers until the advent of *La Calle* (The Street, 1936–1946). Politicized by the disastrous CHACO WAR with Paraguay (1932–1935), the *La Calle* journalists drummed up support for the Movimiento Nacionalista Revolucionario (Nationalist Revolutionary Movement), which began the modernization of Bolivia after 1952.

In Cuba, the corrupt and venal press under Fulgencio BATISTA (1934–1959) accepted $450,000 a month in bribes to support the dictator. After Fidel CASTRO gained power in 1959, he instituted state control of the press. *Granma* became the unchallenged voice of the Cuban Communist Party, and therefore of the state, and Prensa Latina started operations as the Third World's first international news agency.

Other newspapers strove to be independent. In Uruguay, *El Día* championed the progressive programs of President José Batlle y Ordóñez. *La Prensa* of Buenos Aires, founded by Ezequiel Paz in 1869 and the best known Latin American newspaper before its closure by Juan PERÓN in 1951, refused to accept subscriptions from government employees and vowed not to discuss the private lives of public figures. Its stout opposition to Perón's demagoguery led to harassment, curtailment of newsprint supplies, and ultimate expropriation until 1955. Bartolomé MITRE founded Argentina's influential paper *La Nación*.

The liberal *Excélsior* of Mexico also felt the wrath of

the government. Founded in 1917, and one of the few successful newspaper cooperatives in the world, *Excélsior* was edited by Julio García Scherer until the government of Luis Echeverría engineered his ouster in 1976. Neither *Excélsior* nor *La Prensa* of Argentina has recovered its international prestige.

In Brazil, during the early Portuguese colonial period, there was no printing press or periodicals of any kind, since prohibitions against the press were rigorously enforced. The Dutch (1630–1654) installed a press from Amsterdam, but it was later destroyed by the Portuguese authorities. The first Brazilian newspaper was the weekly *La Gazeta do Río de Janeiro*, established in 1808.

The nineteenth century saw the emergence of such distinguished journalists as Joaquim María Machado de ASSÍS (1839–1908), who along with Rui BARBOSA (1849–1923) combined journalism with literature, not uncommon in Latin America, to illuminate a class, if not a caste, society.

In modern times, giants of the Brazilian press such as *O Estado de São Paulo* and *Jornal do Brasil* opposed the reformist president João GOULART (1961–1964), contributing to his overthrow and ushering in twenty-one years of military rule. But once censorship was lifted in 1978, Brazilian newspapers were instrumental in opposing continued military domination and fostering a return to democracy in 1985.

Perhaps the single most influential voice decrying the many dislocations in Brazilian life came not from a professional journalist but from a woman of the *favela* (shantytown), Carolina María de Jesús (1914–1977). Her diary, scribbled on scraps of paper and discovered by a Brazilian reporter, was first serialized in the influential magazine, *O Cruzeiro*, and later became a world classic under the title, *Child of the Dark*.

But nowhere was the dispute between government and press more sharply etched than in Chile during the freely elected presidency of Marxist Salvador ALLENDE (1970–1973). While Allende granted complete freedom of the press, the opposition press, confusing freedom with license, undermined his government and made possible, if not inevitable, the military coup of 11 September 1973. EL MERCURIO, the longest continuously published newspaper in the Spanish language (founded 1827), accepted $1,650,000 from the Central Intelligence Agency to wage verbal warfare against Allende. His successor, General Augusto PINOCHET, clamped sixteen years of dictatorial rule on Chile and did not permit freedom of expression.

There were other approaches toward the relationship between government and the press in Latin America. In Peru a group of technocratic military officers who gained power in 1968 nationalized the eight leading newspapers in 1974. They promised to turn these dailies over to various sectors of the people, such as the campesinos and labor, but this was never accomplished. An elected civilian government returned the papers to their owners in 1980.

In recent years, Latin Americans have challenged their dependency on the industrial world. They are inundated by entertainment and information—even about themselves—from the North. The United States has insisted on a "free flow of information," while UNESCO and Latin Americans have demanded a "balanced flow" in a New World Information and Communication Order.

At times, intervention by U.S. journalists has proved decisive in Latin America. James CREELMAN's interview with the aging Mexican dictator Porfirio DÍAZ (1876–1911), published in *Pearson's Magazine* in March 1908, contained Díaz's assertion that he would not run for an eighth term in 1910. Intended only for foreign consumption, the interview was translated and circulated by the underground press in Mexico, which set the political pot bubbling and led to revolution.

Likewise, Herbert L. Matthews of the *New York Times* made a historic trek into the Sierra Maestra in 1957 to prove that Fidel Castro was still alive. Critics charged that Matthews glorified Castro and was instrumental in his coming to power, but Matthews replied that this was like blaming the weatherman for the weather.

Journalism is a prestigious profession in Latin America, although underpaid reporters often hold two or more jobs, unaware of possible conflicts of interest. They are also susceptible to bribes. To restrict the labor market and improve standards, thirteen Latin American countries now have the *colegio* or guild system, under which only graduates of journalism schools or those with substantial experience can work in the field. Proponents say this is no different from licensing physicians or lawyers, so long as the government does not do the licensing.

Government harassment of the press can be fierce. Some 98 newsmen were killed in Argentina during the "Dirty War" (1976–1983), and some 400 fled the country. Journalists also have been on the front lines, sometimes paying with their lives, in the drug wars of Colombia and the Sendero Luminoso (Shining Path) Maoist guerrilla campaign in Peru.

Direct censorship, such as that wielded by the Sandinistas of Nicaragua against the opposition LA PRENSA in the 1980s, is increasingly rare because of adverse international publicity. More insidious, however, is *auto-censura* (self-censorship) by which governments indirectly intimidate journalists, who are still largely unaware of their adversarial relationship to those who rule.

The first journalism school in Latin America was created by the Círculo de Periodistas (Circle of Journalists) in La Plata, Argentina, in 1934, but widespread instruction in the field did not exist until after World War II. The Centro Internacional de Estudios Superiores de Periodismo para la América Latina (International Center of Advanced Studies in Communication for Latin America) began operation in Quito, Ecuador, in 1960. It is a center for research as well as for training teachers of journalism.

Good historical overviews are GUSTAVO ADOLFO OTERO, *El periodismo en América* (1946); and MICHAEL BRIAN SALWEN and BRUCE GARRISON, *Latin American Journalism* (1991). Significant treatments of the Latin American press in the twentieth century are ROBERT N. PIERCE, *Keeping the Flame: Media and Government in Latin America* (1979); and MARVIN ALISKY, *Latin American Media: Guidance and Censorship* (1981). ELIZABETH FOX, ed., *Media and Politics in Latin America: The Struggle for Democracy* (1988), gives more attention to radio and television. For critical national studies, see JERRY KNUDSON, ''The Press and the Mexican Revolution of 1910,'' *Journalism Quarterly* 46 (Winter 1969): 760–766; *Bolivia: Press and Revolution, 1932–1964* (1986); *The Chilean Press During the Allende Years, 1970–73* (1986); *Herbert L. Matthews and the Cuban Story* (1978); ''The Nicaraguan Press and the Sandinista Revolution,'' *Gazette* (The Hague) 27 (1981): 163–179; and NELSON WERNECK SODRÉ, *A História da Imprensa no Brasil* (1966).

JERRY W. KNUDSON

JOVELLANOS, SALVADOR (*b.* 1833), Paraguayan president (1871–1874).

The decade after the disastrous WAR OF THE TRIPLE ALLIANCE was a difficult period for Paraguay, with political factions shifting constantly and foreign armies in control of the streets of Asunción. Under such circumstances, obscure men sometimes achieved high political office. Salvador Jovellanos was one example. He had been chosen by President Francisco Solano LÓPEZ to study in Europe. After López was killed, Jovellanos was chosen as Cirilo Antonio RIVAROLA's vice president solely, it seems, on the basis of his charming manner. He in turn succeeded to the presidency when opponents forced out Rivarola in 1871. His charm notwithstanding, Jovellanos never gained the trust of any major faction. His administration was marred by four revolts and by two notorious loans negotiated in London in an effort to restore the country's wrecked economy.

CHARLES J. KOLINSKI, *Historical Dictionary of Paraguay* (1975); HARRIS GAYLORD WARREN, *Paraguay and the Triple Alliance: The Postwar Decade, 1869–1878* (1978), pp. 177–193.

THOMAS L. WHIGHAM

JUAN DIEGO (*b.* 1474?; *d.* 1548?), according to tradition, a neophyte Christian Indian who saw the Virgin Mary 9–12 December 1531.

Details of his native town, time of marriage, and age at the time of the apparitions exist in various traditions. None of the information about him antedates the first published account in 1648. He inspired no cult, except for some hints in the 1660–1661 archdiocesan inquiry, and the place of his burial—today unknown—never became a place of devotion. He is inextricably linked with the apparition account, but there is no such evidence of this account prior to 1648. Because of the legendary nature of the tradition of the Virgin of GUADALUPE, the existence of Juan Diego is dubious at best, and in all probability he was no more than a fictional creation. He was beatified by Pope John Paul II in 1989.

LAURO LÓPEZ BELTRÁN, *La historicidad de Juan Diego* (1977, 1981), and *La primera historia guadalupana de México impresa* (1981); FRANCISCO DE LA MAZA, *El guadalupanismo mexicano* (1981); EDMUNDO O'GORMAN, *Destierro de sombras* (1986); STAFFORD POOLE, C.M., *Our Lady of Guadalupe: The Origins and Sources of a Mexican National Symbol, 1531–1797* (1994).

STAFFORD POOLE, C.M.

JUAN FERNÁNDEZ ISLANDS, three volcanic islands

belonging to Chile that lie about four hundred miles west of Valparaiso. Although possibly sighted by MAGELLAN, they were discovered in 1574 by the Spanish navigator Juan FERNÁNDEZ. He named them after saints, but those names were soon supplanted by Más a Tierra (Nearer Land) and Más Afuera (Farther Out) for the two principal islands and Santa Clara, or Goat Island, for the small island just off the tip of Más a Tierra. They became important aids to navigation along the Pacific coast of South America and served as bases for Spain's rivals during the seventeenth and eighteenth centuries.

In October 1704 a British privateer marooned Scottish seaman Alexander Selkirk on Más a Tierra, where he remained until rescued by Captain Woodes Rogers in February 1709. Selkirk's story provided the factual basis for Daniel Defoe's *Robinson Crusoe* (1719).

Colonization efforts failed until 1750, when the Spanish established San Juan Bautista at Cumberland Bay, Más a Tierra, to defend the island against rival nations. As a penal colony, it held a number of prominent Chilean creoles during the wars for independence. The Chileans abandoned the island in 1837, following a Peruvian raid. Chileans returned later to San Juan Bautista (today called Robinson Crusoe), used it as a penal colony again, and eventually developed a small fishing and agricultural community. In the twentieth century it became primarily a lobster fishing center.

During World War I, Cumberland Bay was the site of a naval encounter in which British forces sank the German light cruiser *Dresden* in March 1915. Since then the island has attracted some tourist activity. In January 1966 the Chilean government renamed Más a Tierra for Robinson Crusoe and Más Afuera for Alexander Selkirk.

BENJAMÍN VICUÑA MACKENNA, *Juan Fernández, historia verdadera de la isla de Robinson Crusoe* (1883); RALPH LEE WOODWARD, JR., *Robinson Crusoe's Island: A History of the Juan Fernández Islands* (1969).

RALPH LEE WOODWARD, JR.

JUAN SANTOS. *See* Atahualpa (Juan Santos).

JUAN Y SANTACILIA, JORGE (*b.* 5 January 1713; *d.* 5 July 1773), Spanish scientist.

Born in Novelda, near Alicante, Juan was orphaned at three but nevertheless received a first-rate education, first in Malta, then at the prestigious new Spanish naval academy (Guardia Marina) in Cádiz, and finally with the Spanish fleet plying the Mediterranean (1730–1734). In 1734 PHILIP V chose him and Antonio de ULLOA, another brilliant young naval officer, to join the French scientists Louis Godin and Charles Marie la Condamine on an expedition to the Indies to measure the exact length of a degree on the equator.

Finally reaching Quito in May 1736, the group immediately began their measurements, with Juan assigned to the ostensible leader of the expedition, Louis Godin, with whom he made observations at thirty-two sites. Juan's stay in Ecuador was not without controversy, however. Both he and Ulloa became embroiled with the president of the Audiencia of Quito and also with the French in a protocol dispute over whose names and royal coat of arms were to be placed on the pillars erected on the equator.

Called to Lima early in the WAR OF JENKINS'S EAR, the two officers advised the viceroy on military and naval matters before returning to Quito in January 1744 to make their own scientific observations. Late in October they left for Spain, where they began writing a four-volume descriptive work on their travels, *Relación histórica del viage a la América meridional* (Historical Report on the Voyage to America), published in 1748. In 1749 they completed a secret report for crown officials on conditions in the Indies.

Juan never returned to the Indies. After that last assignment, he became a royal troubleshooter in his native country, where he improved ventilation in the mercury mines at Almadén, strengthened the sea walls at Cartagena, built a new arsenal at El Ferrol, and served as ambassador to Morocco, among other duties. Spending his last days in Madrid as head of the Royal Seminary of Nobles, Juan was noted for his deep-seated attachment to ENLIGHTENMENT ideas, confirmed by the posthumous publication of his book on astronomy in 1774.

JOHN J. TEPASKE and BESSE CLEMENT, eds. and trans., *Discourse and Political Reflections on the Kingdoms of Peru . . .* (1978).

JOHN JAY TEPASKE

JUANA INÉS DE LA CRUZ, SOR (*b.* 12 November 1651 or 1648; *d.* 17 April 1695), the major poet of the Spanish colonies. Born in San Miguel de Nepantla, near the capital city of Mexico, Juana Inés de Asuaje y Ramírez was the illegitimate daughter of Isabel Ramírez de Santillana and Pedro Manuel de Asuaje y Vargas Machuca; her illegitimacy may explain the uncertainty about the year of her birth. Taken to the Spanish viceroy's court as a child prodigy, she became a nun in 1667, first with the CARMELITES for a short time and then definitively, in 1669, in the Jeronymite Convent of San Jerónimo, where, with the religious name of Sor Juana Inés de la Cruz, she had her own collection of books and some free time for study and writing. Toward the end of her life she was

Sor Juana Inés de la Cruz. PHOTO BY BOB SCHALKWIJK.

more strictly ascetic. She died taking care of her sister nuns during a plague.

Almost all of Sor Juana's works were initially published in Spain in three different volumes (1689, 1692, and 1700). Her works include many different genres of poetry, dramatic works in verse, and prose works of a more doctrinal or autobiographical sort.

Personal Lyrics Her secular lyric poetry is among her best-known work. We have, for example, such highly original works as her verse portrait of her beloved Marquise of Paredes (a viceroy's wife); her sonnet on a painted portrait of herself as a vain attempt to save her body from annihilation; several "carpe diem" sonnets centered on the image of the rose; and various poems on hope and the vanity of human illusions, on feminine fidelity, on absence and the sufferings of love, and on the imagination within which we can imprison the beloved.

Religious Writings and "Villancicos" Among Sor Juana's devotional writings are the interesting prose *Ejercicios de la Encarnación* (Exercises on the Incarnation), in which she presents the Virgin Mary as a model of feminine power and wisdom, almost on the same level as God. Her *villancicos*, or carol sequences, written for festive performance in cathedrals, allow us a glimpse of her religious and social sensibility. This popular genre, with many different voices, permitted the poet to speak for marginal social groups such as black slaves, Indians, and women, and to make fun of masculine clerical types such as the student. These songs present women as intellectual as well as devout, as for example in the figure of Saint Catharine of Alexandria. Her black voices speak a special dialect of Spanish, and her Indians speak NAHUATL, to address God directly and to complain about how they are treated by Spanish representatives of the Church or State.

The "Sueño" Sor Juana's lengthy *Sueño* (Dream) occupies a unique place among her works. In her highly significant autobiographical *Respuesta* (Reply), she refers to the *Sueño* as the only poem that she had written for her own pleasure. It is a compendium of contemporary scholastic and scientific knowledge, ranging from the ancient philosophers and church fathers to Florentine hermetic wisdom and the contemporary ideas of Athanasius Kircher and perhaps even of René Descartes. Literarily, the poem draws on Renaissance poetic commonplaces, recast in Spanish baroque forms. Its narrative structure is based on the arrival and departure of night, framing the dream itself, which is an adventure of the intellectual Soul in search of a complete understanding of the universe, a journey that represents the author's own crisis as a religious woman interested in the physical sciences. She seems to identify with Phaëthon, the illegitimate son of Apollo struck down by his father and thus made famous, and with other mythological figures, mostly feminine, such as Night. The Soul, who is the protagonist of the poem, comes back to earth in the final lines of the poem and is identified with the poet herself, who wakes up and, for the first time, asserts her feminine presence grammatically in the very last word of the poem.

The "Respuesta" In 1690 the bishop of Puebla published Sor Juana's critique of a Portuguese JESUIT's sermon, along with a public letter of his own addressed to her over the pseudonymous signature of a nun. In her critique (*Carta atenagórica* or *Crisis sobre un sermón*), Sor Juana had refuted in a highly sophisticated and learned way the argument of Father Antonio de VIEIRA, in which he rejected interpretations by the fathers of the church and proposed his own. The bishop's letter, although somewhat ambiguous, reveals how much he admires her intellectually as he urges her to use her intelligence in the study of divine rather than secular matters. The bishop's critique provided Sor Juana with an excuse for a full-scale apologia in her *Respuesta a sor Filotea de la Cruz.* This eloquent and warmly human document fully explains the nun's intellectual vocation by recalling her childhood eagerness to learn to read and write and her adolescent rejection of marriage and choice of the convent as a place to study. She cites many famous women from the Bible and from classical antiquity in her defense of equal feminine access to study and to writing. She implies that women as scientists have empirical advantages when she asserts, "If Aristotle had done some cooking, he would have written even more." Such a feminist apologia is unique in the seventeenth-century Hispanic world. (In a letter, "Carta de Monterrey," discovered a few years ago, which Sor Juana wrote to her confessor long before her *Respuesta,* we find her defending her rights in even stronger terms.)

Neptuno alegórico (Allegorical Neptune) is, for the modern reader, a difficult work; it is an official *relación* or explanation of the triumphal arch erected in November of 1680 for the reception of the new viceroy, the Marqués of La Laguna, and his wife. The nun presents as an allegorical model for the viceroy the mythological figure of Neptune, in her poetic description of the arch. This is a highly learned text in which she displays her most arcane erudition and ingenuity.

Theater Sor Juana's theatrical works consist of several *loas* (short dramatic prologues) that are largely mythical and allegorical; three *autos sacramentales,* or allegorical dramatizations of sacramental theology in the tradition of Calderón, written, with their *loas,* for the feast of Corpus Christi; and two full-length "cape and sword" plays in the tradition of Lope de Vega. The *loas* that precede her *autos* are especially interesting for their presentation of AZTEC feminine characters, who defend pre-Christian religious practices. Of the *autos, El cetro de José* (Joseph's Scepter) is based on a story from the Bible; *El mártir del Sacramento, San Hermenegildo* (The Martyr of the Sacrament . . .) is hagiographic; and *El Divino Narciso* (Divine Narcissus), the best of the three, is an ingenious allegorization of the pagan mythological Narcissus as the redeeming Christ. Narcissus (Christ), having rejected the advances of Echo (the Devil), who is the rival of Human Nature, sees the latter reflected in the Fountain of Grace, which unites God to Human Nature at the moment of the Incarnation; then Narcissus, in love with himself as reflected in Human Nature, falls into the fountain and drowns, allegorically crucified. One of the secular plays, *Amor es más laberinto,* was written in collaboration with Juan de Guevara; the other, *Los empeños de una casa,* has strong leading female roles, especially that of Leonor, which is a sort of autobiographical figure. The comic character Castaño, a mulatto servant from the New World, speaks satirically of the machismo of white Spaniards in a metatheatrical scene parodying the "cape and sword" comedy as a literary genre.

From the baroque intellectual world of her convent cell Sor Juana sends messages that intimate her deep concerns as a woman and a *criolla.* She is a key figure for understanding colonial Mexico.

Editions include *Obras completas,* 4 vols. edited by Alfonso Méndez Plancarte and Alberto G. Salceda (Mexico, 1951–1957); *Obras selectas,* edited by Georgina Sabat de Rivers and Elias L. Rivers (Barcelona, 1976); *Inundación castálida,* edited by Georgina Sabat de Rivers (Madrid, 1982); and ALAN TRUEBLOOD, *A Sor Juana Anthology* (Cambridge, Mass., 1988).

Secondary works by GEORGINA SABAT-RIVERS include *El "Sueño" de Sor Juana Inés de la Cruz: Tradiciones literarias y originalidad* (1976); "Sor Juana Inés de la Cruz," in *Latin American Writers,* edited by Carlos A. Solé and Maria Isabel Abreu, pp. 85–105; *"Esta de nuestra América pupila": Hacia Sor Juana Inés* de la Cruz: Poetas barrocos de la Colonia (1991); and ''A Feminist Rereading of Sor Juana's 'Dream,' '' in *Feminist Perspectives on Sor Juana Inés de la Cruz* (1991), pp. 142–161.

Other studies include ELECTA ARENAL, ''Sor Juana Inés de la Cruz: Speaking the Mother Tongue,'' *University of Dayton Review* 16 (1982): 93–105; MARIE-CÉCILE BÉNASSY-BERLING, *Humanismo y religión en Sor Juana Inés de la Cruz* (1983); JEAN FRANCO, *Plotting Women* (1989); ASUNCIÓN LAVRIN, ''Unlike Sor Juana? The Model Nun in the Religious Literature of Colonial Mexico,'' in *Feminist Perspectives on Sor Juana Inés de la Cruz* (1991), pp. 61–85; JOSEFINA LUDMER, ''Tricks of the Weak,'' in *Feminist Perspectives on Sor Juana Inés de la Cruz* (1991), pp. 86–93; OCTAVIO PAZ, *Sor Juana; or, The Traps of Faith* (1988); and NINA SCOTT, '' 'If you are not pleased to favor me, put me out of your mind . . .': Gender and Authority in Sor Juana Inés de la Cruz,'' (Plus the translation of the ''Carta de Monterrey''), *Women's Studies International Forum* 2 no. 5 (1988): 429–438.

GEORGINA SABAT-RIVERS

JUÁREZ, BENITO (*b.* 21 March 1806; *d.* 18 July 1872), president of Mexico (1858–1872). Juárez led the liberals and Republicans during the War of the REFORM (1858–1861) and the FRENCH INTERVENTION (1862–1867). For many Mexicans, and in the official pantheon of national heroes, Juárez is a preeminent symbol of Mexican nationalism and resistance to foreign intervention. His critics, however, continue to charge that Juárez resorted to dictatorial methods to prolong his presidency, undermined the property rights of rural villages, and sacrificed Mexican sovereignty to the United States.

Juárez was born in the village of San Pablo Guelatao, Oaxaca. His parents were Zapotec Indian peasants who died before he reached the age of four. Juárez was raised by relatives and worked in the fields until the age of twelve, when, in hopes of getting an education, he left his village and walked the forty miles to the city of Oaxaca to live with his sister. There, he was taken in by Antonio Salanueva, a bookbinder and Franciscan monk, who immediately took Juárez to be confirmed and encouraged him to attend the seminary for his education. Still lacking a primary education and with no more than the rudiments of Spanish grammar, Juárez began studying Latin. After two years, Juárez convinced his patron to allow him to study the arts since he was still too young to be ordained a priest. Juárez completed his secondary education in 1827. Lacking the financial resources and the inclination to receive holy orders, he rejected an ecclesiastical career in order to study law at the newly established Institute of Sciences and Arts, where he received his degree in 1834.

Even before Juárez received his law degree, his political career had begun with election to the City Council of Oaxaca in 1831. Two years later he was elected to the state legislature. He made a living as a lawyer, and in 1841 he was appointed a civil judge. In 1843, he married Margarita Maza. The following year, he was appointed secretary of government by the state governor, Antonio

León, and then to the post of prosecutor with the state supreme court. In 1845, Juárez was elected to the state legislature, but that body was soon dissolved in a conservative rebellion led by General Mariano PAREDES. Juárez was then named by liberal forces to the executive committee for the state. Elected to the national congress the following year, Juárez supported President Valentín GÓMEZ FARÍAS in his attempt to use church property to pay for the war with the United States. Organized opposition to these efforts, the Rebellion of the Polkos (1847), brought Antonio López de SANTA ANNA back to the presidency, ended the liberal government, and forced Juárez to return to Oaxaca.

In Oaxaca, liberals regained control of the state and elected Juárez governor in 1847. At the end of his term in 1852, he accepted the post of director of the Institute of Sciences and Arts. When Santa Anna returned to the presidency in 1853, he exiled Juárez and other leading liberals. Juárez eventually ended up in New Orleans, where he met Ponciano ARRIAGA, Melchor OCAMPO, and other opponents of Santa Anna, and where he earned his living making cigars.

With Juárez and his allies providing the political platform for the liberal Revolution of Ayutla in 1854, Juárez

Portrait of Benito Juárez by Diego Rivera, 1948. ARCHIVO CENIDIAP.

traveled to Acapulco to serve as a political aide. When Juan ÁLVAREZ forced Santa Anna into exile the following year, liberal exiles were able to return to Mexico. President Álvarez named Juárez his minister of justice and ecclesiastical affairs. Juárez wrote the LEY JUÁREZ (eliminating the right of ecclesiastical and military courts to hear civil cases), which President Álvarez signed in November 1855. Juárez resigned the following month, returning to Oaxaca, where he took office as governor in January 1856 and served for nearly two years. Juárez supported and swore to uphold the Constitution of 1857, but he took no direct role in drafting that document. President Ignacio COMONFORT designated Juárez minister of government in November 1857. Elected president of the Supreme Court (and first in line of succession to the presidency), Juárez took the oath of that office on 1 December 1857. Ten days later President Comonfort ordered Congress closed and Juárez arrested. Juárez was freed in January 1858 and escaped from the capital, just before conservative militarists overthrew Comonfort and declared Félix ZULOAGA president. The coup notwithstanding, in accordance with the Constitution of 1857, Juárez succeeded Comonfort in the presidency, taking the oath of office on 19 January 1858 in Guanajuato, thereby leaving Mexico with two presidents and civil war.

During the War of the REFORM, or Three Years' War (1858–1860), Juárez fled to Guadalajara, where he was captured and nearly executed by conservative forces. Later he made his way to Colima, then Manzanillo, and by way of Panama, Havana, and New Orleans to Veracruz, where the liberal governor, Manuel Gutiérrez Zamora, allowed Juárez to establish his government. With the support of the radical liberals (known as PUROS) like Miguel LERDO DE TEJADA and Melchor Ocampo, Juárez issued the reform laws separating the church and state, establishing civil marriage and civil registration of births and deaths, secularizing the cemeteries, and expropriating the property of the church. The conservative forces held most of central Mexico but were unable to dislodge the Juárez government from Veracruz. Perennially short of funds to pay and provision the improvised forces that fought the conservatives, the liberal government expropriated and sold church property and negotiated with the United States.

During the war, Juárez authorized arrangements with the United States that have been the source of enduring controversies about his patriotism. The MC LANE–OCAMPO TREATY, which Juárez's secretary of foreign relations Melchor Ocampo negotiated with the U.S. diplomat Robert M. McLane in 1859, permitted United States protection of transit over routes across Mexican territory in exchange for several million dollars. The treaty was rejected by the U.S. Senate. In what is known as the Antón Lizardo incident, President Juárez authorized U.S. ships to attack conservative vessels flying the Mexican flag at anchor in the port of Antón Lizardo, Veracruz, in 1860. Juárez's critics charge that he con-

doned foreign intervention and sold out to the United States.

Further concessions were not necessary before liberal forces under Jesús González Ortega defeated the conservative army and recaptured Mexico City in December 1860. At the end of Comonfort's term in 1861, there were new elections, which Juárez won. His government's suspension of payments on the foreign debt led to the intervention of Spain, France, and Great Britain. Spanish and British forces soon withdrew, but French forces, supporting the creation of a Mexican empire, advanced toward Mexico City in early 1862, and in 1864 the Austrian archduke MAXIMILIAN von Habsburg took the throne as Maximilian I.

The French Intervention (1862–1867) provides conflicting images of Juárez. A heroic Juárez led the Republican forces that tenaciously defended Mexico and its Republican constitution during desperate years of struggle against foreign and imperial armies. But Juárez's critics charge that he illegally extended his presidency when his constitutional term ended in 1865 and that he arbitrarily ordered the arrest and imprisonment of Jesús González Ortega, who ought to have succeeded to the presidency. The defeat of the imperial armies and the execution of Maximilian in 1867 provided a moment of unity for Mexican liberals, but Juárez's attempt to alter the constitution and strengthen the presidency by referendum again prompted critics to charge him with dictatorial methods. Many liberals opposed his reelection, but Juárez retained enough support to win the presidential elections of December 1867.

The liberals divided into three major factions backing Sebastián Lerdo de Tejada, Porfirio DÍAZ, and Juárez. The president repeatedly resorted to grants of extraordinary power to combat revolts and to maintain order. His critics maintained that Juárez was corrupted by power and increasingly dictatorial. By the time of the 1871 elections, Juárez could no longer count on a majority of votes, and the election passed to Congress, which elected him to another term. Porfirio Díaz resorted to rebellion, but Juárez was able to defeat him, again with an extension of extraordinary powers.

Not long afterward, on the evening of 18 July 1872, Juárez died. Controversial during his lifetime, he became a premier symbol of Mexican nationalism after his death. Ironically, Porfirio Díaz, as president, played a major role in creating the Juárez myth. As a national hero, Juárez has been most commonly invoked by presidents seeking to create an image of continuity with the past during times when stability and economic growth rather than reform have been the major concerns of government.

The major biographies of Juárez in English are RALPH ROEDER, *Juárez and His Mexico: A Biographical History*, 2 vols. (1947); CHARLES ALLEN SMART, *Viva Juárez: A Biography* (1963); and IVIE E. CADENHEAD, JR., *Benito Juárez* (1973). On Juárez's role in Mexican politics, see WALTER V. SCHOLES, *Mexican Politics During the Juárez Regime, 1855–1872* (1957); DANIEL COSÍO

VILLEGAS, *Historia moderna de México*, vol. 1, *La república restorada, vida política* (1959); LAURENS BALLARD PERRY, *Juárez and Díaz: Machine Politics in Mexico* (1978); RICHARD N. SINKIN, *The Mexican Reform, 1855–1876: A Study in Liberal Nation-Building* (1979); and DONATHON C. OLLIFF, *Reform Mexico and the United States: A Search for Alternatives to Annexation, 1854–1861* (1981). On the creation and use of the Juárez myth, see CHARLES A. WEEKS, *The Juárez Myth in Mexico* (1987).

D. F. STEVENS

See also **Anticlericalism.**

JUÁREZ, JOSÉ (*b.* 1617; *d.* 1661), painter. The son of Luis Juárez, José was surely introduced to painting in his father's workshop. He has been considered by some to be the best painter of colonial Mexico. These claims are often accompanied by assertions that he must have received training in Spain. Others consider that the presence of Sebastián López de Arteaga and of original works by Francisco de Zurbarán in New Spain would have been sufficient for someone of his talent to develop as he did. Juárez's works show the influence not only of Zurbarán but also of compositions by Peter Paul Rubens, known in New Spain through prints. Probably his best-known painting is a complex composition depicting martyrdom and glorification, *Saints Justus and Pastor*.

ROGELIO RUÍZ GOMAR, *Historia del arte mexicano*, vol. 2 (1982), pp. 38–40.

CLARA BARGELLINI

JUÁREZ, LUIS (*b.* ca. 1585; *d.* ca. 1635), Mexican painter. Juárez was the founder of an important dynasty of colonial Mexican painters. Although the place of his birth is unknown, his mannerist style can clearly be identified as Mexican—influenced, of course, by the Spanish masters who preceded him, particularly the Sevillian Alonso Vázquez, who came to New Spain in 1603 and died there in 1608. The works of Juárez are remarkably uniform in style and feeling, usually showing religious figures in an elegant yet subdued and direct manner. Scattered throughout Mexico are nearly one hundred paintings that can be attributed to Juárez, evidence that he was well and widely known.

ROGELIO RUÍZ GOMAR, *El pintor Luis Juárez* (1987).

CLARA BARGELLINI

JUÁREZ CELMAN, MIGUEL (*b.* 29 September 1844; *d.* 14 April 1909), president of Argentina (1886–1890). Juárez Celman, born in Córdoba, took a strong anticlerical position in promoting secular education. After serving as a legal adviser, legislator, and provincial minister, he became an unconditional supporter of Julio Argentino ROCA. He married Roca's sister, and Roca married Juárez Celman's sister. In 1882, Roca decided that his brother-in-law should govern Córdoba. Impressed with Juárez Celman's political machine, Roca then imposed him as president of the republic.

As chief executive, Juárez Celman was self-serving and corrupt. His regime promoted European immigration, foreign investment, public works, and economic growth. Unfortunately, wild speculation, galloping inflation, and a tripling of the public debt occurred. A particularly irresponsible issue of paper currency resulted in the loss of political legitimacy. When Juárez Celman belatedly took measures to head off the financial crisis, his supporters refused to back him in Congress.

Angry investors and those who suffered a decline in their standard of living joined with Catholic activists and the Unión Cívica (Civic Union) in demanding honest government. Three days of rebellion, known as the 1890 Revolution, resulted in Juárez Celman's resignation on 6 August, 1890. Once worth over $30 million, he died in obscure poverty at Capitán Sarmiento Arrecites.

Discussions relating to Juárez Celman are THOMAS MC GANN, *Argentina, the United States and the Inter-American System, 1880–1914* (1957); and A. G. FORD, *The Gold Standard, 1880–1914* (1962). A concise statement is GUSTAVO FERRARI, "La presidencia Juárez Celman," in *La Argentina del ochenta al centenario*, edited by GUSTAVO FERRARI and EZEQUIEL GALLO (1980). For the early background of Juárez Celman, see JUAN CARLOS AGULLA, *Eclipse of an Aristocracy: An Investigation of the Ruling Elites of Córdoba*, translated by BETTY CROUSE (1976).

DOUGLAS W. RICHMOND

JUAZEIRO DO NORTE (until 1944 Joaseiro or Joazeiro), one of the principal cities of the state of CEARÁ in Brazil. Located in the Carirí Valley in the uplands of Ceará's interior, the city has a population of 173,300 (1990) and serves as a commercial and manufacturing center, depending primarily on the processing of SUGAR and COTTON.

Drawn by rumors of a miracle, pilgrims flocked from the Brazilian backlands to the town during the 1890s. In 1889 and again in 1891, the host reputedly turned to blood during mass celebrated by local priest Padre Cícero Romão Batista (1844–1934). Although the Catholic church refused to accept the alleged miracle and threatened Padre Cícero with excommunication if he persisted in insisting on its validity, thousands of peasants regarded the priest as a saint, and Joaseiro's population reached thirty thousand by 1914. Such growth helped to make the city an industrial and commercial center of the SERTÃO.

Padre Cícero's spiritual power quickly translated into political influence. His actions in state and national politics were closely tied to maneuvers of José Gomes Pinheiro Machado but were also influenced by shifts in Ceará's economy, by the complex interplay of church-state relations, and by the instability of his own relations with the church hierarchy. Maintaining his base in

Joaseiro, Padre Cícero held sway over much of the state and was instrumental in toppling the state government of Marcos Franco Rabelo in March 1914.

Despite excommunication in 1916, Padre Cícero retained his spiritual and political influence until his death in 1934. Juazeiro do Norte remains a pilgrimage center as well as an important political bailiwick.

AMÁLIA XAVIER DE OLIVEIRA, *O Padre Cícero qui eu conheci: Verdadeira história de Juazeiro do Norte* (1969); RALPH DELLA CAVA, *Miracle at Joaseiro* (1970); LUITGARDE O. C. BARROS, *A Terra da Mãe de Deus: Um estudo do movimento religioso de Juazeiro do Norte* (1988).

CARA SHELLY

See also **Messianic Movements: Brazil.**

JUDICIAL SYSTEMS

Brazil

During the empire, Brazil had a unitary judicial system. Like France, however, administrative or public law disputes were decided by the Council of State, an executive body outside the judiciary. Pursuant to the 1891 Constitution, which was modeled on the U.S. Constitution, Brazil instituted a dual judicial system of federal and state courts. The state courts have general jurisdiction, while the federal courts have limited jurisdiction. The jurisdiction of the federal courts is generally limited to cases in which federal questions are presented, in which the federal government (or its public enterprises or autarchies) has an interest, in which a crime involves federal property or services, or in which an international concern is present. Since 1891, the Brazilian courts have been given jurisdiction over cases involving both public and private law. Brazil also has three specialized court systems within the judiciary: labor, electoral, and military courts.

Brazil has a career judiciary, although there is lateral entry into the higher courts. A Brazilian national between the ages of twenty-three and forty-five, who has practiced law for two years, can begin a judicial career by passing written and oral tests. Those who pass start their careers in entry-level judicial districts (*comarcas de entrância*) and eventually are promoted to the higher courts, either on merit or seniority. Those completing a two-year probationary period are guaranteed tenure until retirement age. Their salaries may not be reduced, nor may they be involuntarily transferred.

THE FEDERAL JUDICIARY

Supreme Federal Tribunal Brazil's highest court is the Supreme Federal Tribunal (STF), which consists of eleven justices (*ministros*), usually sitting in panels of five. They are appointed by the president, with the approval of an absolute majority of the Senate. The present constitution has redefined the STF's jurisdiction to make it primarily a constitutional court. Direct actions challenging the constitutionality of any federal or state law

or normative act can now be brought directly before the STF, whose decision is binding. The right to bring a direct action of unconstitutionality, however, is limited to the president; the procurator general; the executive committees of the Senate, Chamber of Deputies, or state legislatures; state governors; the Federal Council of the Bar Association; any political party represented in Congress; and any syndical confederation or national class (management or labor) entity. The STF has original jurisdiction to decide all requests for issuance of a mandate of injunction, another form of direct constitutional action used to try to make Congress or some other federal agency issue a law or rule necessary to implement a constitutional right.

The STF has ordinary appellate jurisdiction in matters involving habeas corpus, writs of security, habeas data and mandates of injunction decided originally by the Superior Tribunals if they have denied such requests, and in political crimes. The STF also has jurisdiction to hear extraordinary appeals if the appealed decision is contrary to a provision of the Constitution, declares a treaty or federal law unconstitutional, or upholds the constitutionality of a local law or act.

Superior Tribunal of Justice Directly below the STF in the hierarchy is the Superior Tribunal of Justice (STJ). Created by the 1988 Constitution, the STJ is the court of last resort for much of the appellate caseload formerly decided by the STF. The STJ has thirty-three judges appointed by the president from lists of candidates nominated by courts, the Bar Association, and the Public Ministry. The STJ sits in chambers with five judges each.

The original jurisdiction of the STJ is quite limited, for it functions predominantly as an appellate court. Its ordinary appellate jurisdiction includes cases involving denials of habeas corpus or writs of security by other tribunals below it, and cases in which the parties are a foreign state or an international organization taking legal action against a county or a person resident or domiciled in Brazil. It has jurisdiction to decide on special appeal cases decided by the lower tribunals if the appealed decision is contrary to a treaty or federal law, or denies the effectiveness of a treaty or federal law; upholds a law or act of local government challenged as contrary to federal law; or interprets federal law differently from another tribunal.

Federal Regional Tribunals Below the STJ are five Federal Regional Tribunals (FRT), located in Rio de Janeiro, Brasília, São Paulo, Pôrto Alegre, and Recife. These courts, each of which has at least seven judges, were created by the 1988 Constitution to replace the former intermediate federal appeals court, the Federal Tribunal of Recourses. The FRTs also have very limited original jurisdiction. Their primary function is to hear appeals from cases decided by federal judges and by state judges exercising federal jurisdiction within their particular region.

Federal Judges The federal judges are essentially courts of first instance for cases in which the federal government has an interest. Federal judges are career judges, chosen by competitive examinations. If there is no federal judge in a particular judicial district, a state judge may be permitted to decide federal cases. In such event, an appeal may be taken to the FRT.

Labor Courts The Labor Courts are regular members of the Brazilian federal judiciary. Nevertheless, they differ from the regular judiciary in that their jurisdiction is limited to labor matters and they operate collegially at all levels. Moreover, they are mixed tribunals, composed of both professional judges and lay representatives of labor and management. All Labor Courts have the power to decide any matter connected with labor law. The Labor Court system is exclusively federal; state courts may not decide labor law questions. The Labor Courts have jurisdiction to conciliate and adjudicate individual and collective labor disputes. If collective bargaining negotiations fail to produce an agreement, the parties may appoint arbitrators. If any party refuses to negotiate or to arbitrate, the respective management or labor syndicate may litigate a collective bargaining dispute, and the Labor Courts will establish the rules and conditions for the contractual provisions and the protection of labor.

At the head of the Labor Court system is the Superior Labor Tribunal (SLT), which has twenty-seven judges appointed by the president after approval by the Senate.

Below the SLT are the Regional Labor Tribunals. Every state has at least one Regional Labor Tribunal, as does the federal district. The baseline courts of the Labor Court system are the Boards of Conciliation, which have at least one labor judge and two temporary representatives, one from labor and the other from management.

Electoral Courts The Electoral Justice system consists of the Superior Electoral Tribunal (SET), the Regional Electoral Tribunals, electoral judges, and the electoral boards. The Electoral Courts are responsible for supervising the integrity of the electoral process. Unlike other Brazilian courts, they are staffed by members of other courts who serve two to four years. Decisions of the SET are not appealable except on constitutional grounds or if they deny writ of habeas corpus or writ of security.

The Regional Electoral Tribunals are misnamed. Each state capital and the federal district has a Regional Electoral Tribunal, whose jurisdiction is statewide rather than regional. The Regional Electoral Tribunals have seven judges, who serve for at least two years, but never more than two consecutive terms.

The baseline courts for the Electoral Justice system are the electoral judges, who sit alone. Usually, the state judge in the electoral district performs the functions of the electoral judge; if there are several judges in the district, the Regional Tribunal selects a judge to serve as electoral judge for a two-year term.

Election returns are supervised by election boards. These boards consist of a law judge and two to four citizens of outstanding reputations nominated by the presiding judge with the approval of the Regional Tribunal.

Federal Military Courts The Military Courts have jurisdiction to try military personnel (and those equated with such personnel) for military crimes, as defined by law. This court system consists of the Superior Military Tribunal, the Councils of Justice, and professional military judges. The Superior Military Tribunal has fifteen judges with life tenure, appointed by the president with the approval of the Senate.

The judges of first instance are called auditors. They are lawyers and career judges, chosen through competitive examinations. They perform many of the functions of an investigative magistrate or prosecutor. Trials are held before Councils of Justice, made up of one auditor and several military officers.

THE STATE JUDICIARIES

Tribunals of Justice The highest court in every state is called the Tribunal of Justice. The number of judges, called *desembargadores*, on the Tribunal of Justice varies from state to state. In the more populous states, where the Tribunals of Justice typically have about one hundred judges, they sit in panels (*câmaras*) or groups of panels. In more sparsely populated states, the Tribunals of Justice hear appeals directly from courts of first instance.

Intermediate Appeals Courts More populous states have an intermediate court of appeals, the *Tribunal de Alçada*. (The busiest court system, São Paulo, has three: two civil and one criminal.) The intermediate court divides jurisdiction with the Tribunal of Justice, hearing appeals relating to leases, labor accidents, fiscal matters, most summary proceedings, and less serious criminal offenses.

State Military Courts States also have their own systems of military justice. The court of first instance, called the Council of Military Justice, tries military police and firemen for military crimes. In some states appeals from these Councils are heard directly by the state Tribunals of Justice; other states have created their own Tribunals of Military Justice to hear such appeals. These courts usually consist of seven judges, four chosen from colonels in active service in the military police and three civilians.

Courts of First Instance Each state is divided into judicial districts, and each district has at least one titular law judge (*juiz de direito*). The state courts of the first instance generally sit as a single judge and have jurisdiction over all matters not specifically allocated to the exclusive jurisdiction of other courts by the Constitution or statute.

Jury Tribunals Intentional crimes against human life are usually tried by a Jury Tribunal, which consists of one professional judge who presides and seven lay jury members chosen by lot from an array of twenty-one persons. The jury decides whether a crime was committed, the nature of the crime, its gravity, and who committed it.

Verdicts of the Jury Tribunal may be appealed, but

the appellate tribunal can only modify the decision with respect to the decisions of the presiding judge and only to correct an error or injustice in his application of the penalty. The appellate tribunal may only make the judgment correspond to what the law establishes and what the jury found. If the appellate court determines that the jury's decision was manifestly contrary to the evidence on the record, it will vacate the jury verdict and remand for retrial by the same Jury Tribunal. A second appeal may not be taken after a retrial.

Small Claims Courts Since authorizing legislation was passed in 1984, many states have created Small Claims Courts, which decide less complex civil cases and minor criminal infractions. Disputes can be resolved inexpensively through conciliation, arbitration, or trial before a law school graduate. Appeals from these Small Claims Courts are decided by groups of judges of the first instance.

Justices of the Peace At the very bottom of the state judicial system are justices of the peace, who do not enjoy the constitutional guarantees of the regular judiciary. They are nominated by state governors from a list of three prepared by the president of the Tribunal of Justice. They perform marriages and attempt conciliations, but they have no real jurisdictional functions.

CONCLUSIONS

Brazil has a sophisticated and complex judicial system that looks better on paper than it is in practice. Most courts have huge backlogs, and cases frequently creep through the system at a snail's pace. More resources need to be allocated to the judiciary, and more judges need to be appointed, particularly in urban areas. Excessive formalism needs to be pruned from the procedural codes. The entire judicial system badly needs major streamlining in order to function efficiently. Justice delayed is justice denied, and unfortunately much justice in Brazil is delayed.

The jurisdiction and manner of selection of the Brazilian courts is set out in Articles 92 to 126 of the Constitution of 1988. For detailed commentary on these provisions, see JOSÉ CRETELLA JÚNIOR, *Comentários à Constituição Brasileira de 1988* 2d ed., vol. 6 (1993), pp. 2995–3287. Useful diagrams of the various judicial systems appear in LAERTE ROMUALDO DE SOUZA, *III breviário de organização judiciária*, 2d ed. (1990). Helpful overviews are ATHOS GUSMÃO CARNEIRO, "Política judicial no Brasil: Estrutura do poder judiciário brasileiro conforme a Constituição de 1988," *Ajuris* 20 (November 1993): 236–252; and PAULO ROBERTO DE GOUVÊA MEDINA, "O poder judiciário na Constituição de 1988," *Revista Forense*, 305 (January–March 1989): 351–371. The law regulating the organization of the judiciary is the Organic Law of the National Judiciary (*Lei orgânica da magistratura nacional*), Complementary Law 35 (14 March 1979). An overview of Brazilian civil procedure appears in KEITH S. ROSENN, "Civil Procedure in Brazil," *American Journal of Comparative Law* 34 (1986): 487–525.

KEITH S. ROSENN

See also **Brazil: Constitutions.**

Spanish America

Spanish America's colonial civil-law legacy remains the core of its modern judicial systems. That legacy is most clearly evident in judicial method and approach. The organizational architecture of the modern judicial institutions derives from the nineteenth-century adaptation of the doctrine of the division of powers and the simplified first-, second-, and third-instance hearing process to promote prompt and efficient administration of justice.

After the papacy sanctioned Spain's formal right to rule New World lands in the Treaty of TORDESILLAS (1494), the Spanish crown introduced and modified Iberian judicial institutions and the civil law inherited from the Roman Empire. At the heart of the Spanish judicial system was the AUDIENCIA. In Spain an *audiencia* was an ordinary-jurisdiction, local and regional appellate court. In the Americas the crown expanded *audiencia* duties to include oversight of civil administration and consultation with various colonial fiscal and administrative offices. First introduced in Santo Domingo in 1511, the *audiencia* became the main pillar of Spanish governance in the Americas. At the local level in major Spanish population centers, municipal judges adjudicated most first-instance, ordinary-jurisdiction civil and criminal cases. In towns and villages, ALCALDES MAYORES, royal officials with local administrative, fiscal, and judicial responsibilities, adjudicated most of those cases.

During the colonial era the Spanish government created an array of special-jurisdiction courts, ranging from Indian courts and probate courts for intestate peninsulars to tax fraud and mining courts. The regional *audiencia* ministers adjudicated most appellate cases from the special first-instance courts. In addition, the Catholic church and the military maintained privileged-jurisdiction (FUERO) courts for civil and criminal cases in addition to canon-law and military-law cases.

The introduction of the doctrine of the separation of powers and the simplified hearing process accompanied the initiation of a constitutional tradition in Spain in 1812. Following the emergence of new republics, political leaders throughout Spanish America built on those innovations and augmented their political systems with constitutional-jurisdiction courts (supreme courts). Political leaders also sought to restrict ecclesiastical-jurisdiction courts to canon-law cases and military courts to military-law cases; restricting those two jurisdictions emerged as among the most volatile issues, as political leadership sought to transform colonial corporatist polities into republican polities. Most Spanish American republics introduced universal civil- and criminal-law courts and developed universal legal codes within three generations of independence. Today all of the constitutional republics have universal ordinary-jurisdiction courts and constitutional-jurisdiction supreme courts.

The jurisprudential common denominator throughout Spanish America is that all judicial systems are rooted in the colonial civil-law legacy. That legacy includes investigatory or inquisitorial procedures, rather than the accusatory procedures of common-law heritage states, and judicial decision making based on written legal codes and texts, rather than judicial opinions and precedent. Lawmakers in many Spanish American republics have augmented their colonial civil-law legacy with innovative laws to protect individual constitutional rights (AMPARO) and to strengthen international laws concerning the scope and significance of sovereignty (the principle of nonintervention).

The most comprehensive bibliographic guide in English is AMERICAN ASSOCIATION OF LAW LIBRARIES, *Workshop on Latin American Law and Law-Related Reference Sources* (1988), a compilation of workshop papers and annotated jurisdictional bibliographies that survey all fields of law. The principal study in English is ALBERT S. GOLBERT and YENNY NUN, *Latin American Laws and Institutions* (1982). For a succinct discussion of the differences between common-law and civil-law heritage systems, see FERNANDO ORRANTIA, "Conceptual Differences Between the Civil Law System and the Common Law System," in *Southwestern University Law Review* 19, no. 4 (1990): 1161–1170. The most recent study in English that reflects the depth and scope of that literature on the colonial system is PATRICIA SEED, *To Love, Honor, and Obey in Colonial Mexico: Conflicts over Marriage Choice, 1574–1821* (1988). The most recent work in Spanish on the colonial legal environment is VICTOR TAU ANZOÁTEGUI, *La ley en América Hispana: Del descubrimiento a la emancipación* (Buenos Aires, 1992). See also FRANK GRIFFITH DAWSON, "Contributions of Lesser Developed Nations to International Law: The Latin American Experience," in *Case Western Reserve Journal of International Law* 13 (Winter 1981): 37–81; and MARCOS KAPLAN, comp., *Estado, derecho y sociedad* (Mexico City, 1981).

LINDA ARNOLD

See also **Constitutions** (under individual countries).

JUJUY, province in northwestern Argentina with an area of 20,548 square miles and a population of 502,694 (1989) that stretches from the Andes into their foothills. A great number of the population are descended from the AYMARA Indians of the Bolivian Puna and Altiplano. The landscape is similar, in many respects, to the southern Bolivian highlands, with extensive salt flats, barren high mountains, and fertile river oases in the piedmont. The region was part of the Inca Empire upon the arrival of the Spaniards and became a dependency of Tucumán in 1593, intended to protect trade caravans to Alto Peru (Bolivia) from the attacks of Humahuaca and Calchaquí Indians. To pacify and evangelize the Indians, Franciscan and Jesuit MISSIONS were established in the areas most populated by Indians. In the Jesuit missions the cultivation of sugarcane and cotton was introduced, while in the settlements dominated by Spaniards, cattle ranching and the cultivation of tobacco, corn, oranges, and rice prevailed. In colonial times these activities lent significance to this northwesternmost corner of the RÍO DE LA PLATA viceroyalty.

The decline of Jujuy started with the expulsion of the Jesuits in 1767, followed by the WAR OF INDEPENDENCE and several decades of internecine wars. It was not until 1853 that Jujuy exited its most turbulent period, but in the meantime the fragile agricultural bases of its economy had been severely damaged.

Irrigation works and the completion of a railroad in 1990 connecting Jujuy with Buenos Aires and another linking it with La Paz (Bolivia) eased that city's isolation while at the same time opening the way for an exodus of natives to Buenos Aires and for an influx of impoverished Bolivians that continues today. Mineral exploitation is an important pillar of the province's economy. Antimony and tin are mined in Rinconada, and Sierra del Aguilar and Nevado del Chañi have the richest deposits of lead, zinc, silver, and iron of Argentina. Iron from the Zapala mine is processed in the iron mill of Palpalá. Sugar refineries and wood-processing plants are elements of the industrial development of the province.

EUGENIO TELLO, *Descripción de la provincia de Jujuy* (San Salvador, 1989).

CÉSAR N. CAVIEDES

JULIÃO, CARLOS (*b.* 1740; *d.* 18 November 1811), officer in the Portuguese army and artist. Born in Italy, Julião began a military career in Portugal in 1763 and by 1800 had been promoted to colonel. During his thirty-seven years in military service, he traveled to India, China, and South America. He recorded his travels in a pictorial travel account that was published posthumously in 1960 by the Brazilian National Library. One section of the account consists of forty-three watercolors without text. Entitled *Ditos de figurinhos de brancos, negros dos usos do Rio e Serro do Frio,* the watercolors depict diverse social and cultural aspects of the Portuguese colony of Rio de Janeiro during the late eighteenth century. They show members of the white elite at work and in their domestic life; slaves working in the mines, at festivals, and in the cities; and Indians. These watercolors are iconographically and sociologically significant because they document daily life in colonial Rio de Janeiro through the eyes of a Portuguese official.

CARLOS JULIÃO, *Riscos illuminada de figurinhos de brancos e negros dos usos do Rio de Janeiro e Serro do Frio* (1960).

CAREN A. MEGHREBLIAN

JULIÃO ARRUDA DE PAULA, FRANCISCO (*b.* 16 February 1915), honorary president, Peasant Leagues of Brazil. Born to a once-prominent landowning family in Pernambuco State, Julião became a lawyer and politician who defended peasants and advocated land reform. He was twice elected state legislator in 1954 and 1958 and entered Congress in 1962. In 1964 the military imprisoned him, and in 1965 Mexico granted him asylum. Exiled, Julião returned to Brazil once in 1979 and again in 1986, when he ran unsuccessfully for Congress. Rejected by voters, he returned to Mexico.

Julião was a controversial figure in the rural labor movement. He believed that feudalism reigned in Brazil and only a bourgeois revolution could bring progress. He pushed for radical agrarian reform—the quick redistribution of large landholdings without compensating owners in cash—and the complete enfranchisement of the rural poor. Fiercely independent, he devised his own spiritually rich discourse of revolt and resisted the directives of organizations, even his own.

Key supporters of the rural movement, such as the Brazilian Communist Party, distanced themselves from Julião. Within the Peasant Leagues, his independence spawned factionalism, with some members forcefully seizing land and others supporting legal methods of change. All the same, Julião did more to popularize the cause of the rural poor in Brazil and abroad than any other individual.

FRANCISCO JULIÃO, *Cambão—The Yoke, The Hidden Face of Brazil,* translated by John Butt (1972); JOSEPH A. PAGE, *The Revolution That Never Was: Northern Brazil, 1955–1964* (1972).

CLIFF WELCH

JUNÍN, BATTLE OF, the decisive engagement of the Peruvian struggle for independence. A patriot army led by General Simón BOLÍVAR defeated the Spanish royalist forces under General José Canterac at the battle of Junín on 6 August 1824. The battle was fought on the 9,000-foot-high Plains of Junín, near the central highland city of Jauja. Bolívar's 9,000-man force was outnumbered by almost 7,000, but in a short, decisive cavalry engagement, the patriots carried the day. Even though casualties were low on both sides, Bolívar gained the critical initiative. Shortly thereafter, after returning in triumph to Lima, Bolívar was recalled to Colombia. However, his lieutenant, General Antonio José de SUCRE, went on to defeat the royalist army at the battle of AYACUCHO on 9 December 1824, effectively ending three hundred years of Spanish rule in America.

TIMOTHY E. ANNA, *The Fall of Royal Government in Peru* (1979).

PETER F. KLARÉN

JUNTA

Brazil

The juntas of Brazil were extralegal governmental boards of prominent men of the local elites that functioned as parallel forms of local government. Displaying an independent spirit, they often challenged the Portuguese governor and ruled at the local level through the municipal *senados da câmara*. Juntas became more common in the early nineteenth century than they had been

in the colonial period, although the crown did introduce judicial juntas in the mining regions to inflict capital punishment on the nonwhite population without any appeals. When news of the Portuguese revolution of 1820 reached Brazil, new governments (*juntas administrativas*) were formed in each capital city. José Bonifácio de ANDRADA E SILVA was chosen to be a member of the *junta governativa*. Delegates were sent from Brazil's juntas to the Portuguese CORTES. The delegates were willing to remain within the Portuguese empire provided they were allowed representation in the Cortes. Juntas in the nineteenth century came to represent local interests and elites against the Portuguese ruling class, especially during the independence struggle.

LESLIE BETHELL, ed., *The Cambridge History of Latin America,* vol. 2 (1984); EMILIA VIOTTI DA COSTA, *The Brazilian Empire, Myths and Histories* (1985).

PATRICIA MULVEY

Spanish America

Junta is the Spanish word for any board or council. During the political crisis of the early 1800s when NAPOLEON invaded Spain, numerous juntas developed out of the municipal councils of important cities in the New World. When the Central Junta fled from Seville to Cádiz in 1810, the Spanish American juntas took over in the New World. They either declared their support for the exiled Spanish king or declared their right to independence from the Central Junta in Spain.

In the twentieth century, juntas in Spanish America have become associated with groups of military officers who collectively exercise the powers of government. A military junta is usually established following a coup d'état. Juntas are often headed by ranking officers of the army, navy, and air force. The exclusion of all civilians from the executive and the ban on all political parties indicate the military's complete rejection of the previous system and its belief in its ability to define and protect the country's national interest.

HEATHER K. THIESSEN

JUNTA DO COMÉRCIO (Portuguese Board of Trade), established in 1755 to replace the *mesa do bem commun,* whose members had vigorously opposed the crown's formation of monopoly companies. The marquês de POMBAL established the Junta do Comércio as a principal part of his strategy to reinvigorate Portugal's economy by creating a central agency that would coordinate the empire's commercial activity. The Junta's statutes, confirmed in 1756, called for a *provedor* (superintendent), secretary, *procurador* (advocate), six deputies (four from Lisbon and two from Porto) together with a judge conservator, and a solicitor of the exchequer. Only well-established businessmen who were Portuguese-born or naturalized could be appointed deputies. The

Junta's commission authorized it to supervise "all affairs connected with the commerce and navigation of these kingdoms and dominions." It administrated the Brazil fleets and customhouses, set freight prices, issued passports, oversaw the loading and unloading of cargoes to prevent contraband, and managed the proceedings surrounding bankruptcies. In 1759 it helped establish the Aula de Comércio (Commercial School) to train aspiring merchants. Eventually, it licensed the operation of Lisbon's shops and oversaw apprentice training.

The Junta's charge soon went beyond administrating commerce to directly influencing economic policy. After 1700 it became the basic administrative organ for stimulating Pombal's industrial program by channeling funds and giving special privileges to public and private enterprises. Industries such as cotton and glass manufacturing and the production of luxury goods like silk, china, and jewelry were encouraged toward the goal of making Portugal independent of foreign manufactures. After Pombal's fall, the Junta do Comércio went into eclipse as his successors reversed his centralized administrative structure. In 1788 it became a royal tribunal with the title Real Junta do Comércio, Agricultura, Fabricas, e Navegação, but with considerably less real power, and was finally dissolved in 1834.

KENNETH MAXWELL, *Conflicts and Conspiracies: Brazil and Portugal, 1750–1808* (1973); JOEL SERRÃO, ed., *Dicionário de história de Portugal,* vol. 2. (1979).

WILLIAM DONOVAN

JUNTA SUPREMA DE CARACAS, the highest junta of the Venezuelan government, established by the *cabildo* of Caracas as a result of the *cabildo*'s defiance of the captain-general of Venezuela, Vicente EMPARÁN, and its effective declaration of independence on 19 April 1810. When the *cabildo* of Caracas demanded the resignation of Emparán, the Supreme Governing Junta was created to defend the privileges of Ferdinand VII. This junta assumed control of the government of the province of Caracas and sent delegates to the other provinces to obtain support for the decision not to recognize the regency of Spain.

Once its governing authority was established, the junta sent representatives out of the country to win support for the independence movement, abolished the SLAVE TRADE, eliminated export duties, and called for elections to establish a constituent congress. The junta dissolved once the Constituent Congress was installed in March 1811.

INSTITUTO PANAMERICANO DE GEOGRAFÍA E HISTORIA, *El 19 de Abril de 1810,* no. 11 (Caracas, 1957); ANDRÉS PONTE, *La revolución de Caracas y sus próceres* (1960); and P. MICHAEL MC KINLEY, *Pre-Revolutionary Caracas: Politics, Economy, and Society, 1777–1811* (1985).

INÉS QUINTERO

JUNTAS PORTUGUESAS, the administrative organs governing Portugal from the revolution of 24 August 1820 until the return of the king from Brazil in 1821. Marking the beginning of Portuguese liberal practice, the leaders of the constitutional movement promised to convoke the General Cortes to draw up a constitution, and they formed a Provisional Junta of the Supreme Government of the Realm, composed of military leaders and representatives of the clergy, the magistracy, and the commercial bourgeoisie of Pôrto. With the adherence of Lisbon to the revolution on 15 September 1820, it became necessary to avoid weakening the revolution by the division of authority. To this end, the governments of Pôrto and Lisbon organized into two distinct bodies, with the Pôrto Junta concerning itself with public administration, and the Provisional Preparatory Junta of the Cortes taking responsibility for all activities necessary for the implementation of the *cortes.* The two juntas gathered the principal leaders of the 1820 movement, including the brigadier Antônio da Silveira Pinto da Fonseca, the judge of the Court of Appeals Manuel Fernandes Tomás, and the Count of Sampaio. Although they attempted to control the workings of the state, the juntas did not cease to proclaim their loyalty to the church and the monarchy, in the person of JOÃO VI.

JOEL SERRÃO, "Vintismo," *Dicionário de história de Portugal,* vol. 4 (1971), pp. 321–329; JOAQUIM VERÍSSIMO SERRÃO, *História de Portugal,* vol. 7 (1984), pp. 354–360.

LÚCIA M. BASTOS P. NEVES

JUSTO, JOSÉ AGUSTÍN PEDRO (*b.* 26 February 1876; *d.* 11 January 1943), general and president of Argentina (1932–1938); leader of the CONCORDANCIA. Born in Concepción del Uruguay, Entre Ríos Province, Justo gained national prominence as a member of the Argentine army. After graduating from the Military College of San Martín in 1892, he rose rapidly through the ranks. He gained influence over a generation of military officers as the director of his alma mater between 1915 and 1922.

Having achieved the rank of brigadier general, he entered national politics in 1922, when President Marcelo T. de ALVEAR (1922–1928) appointed him minister of war. Along with other members of the Alvear administration, Justo joined the Anti-Personalist wing of the Radical Civic Union. In opposition to the second administration of President Hipólito YRIGOYEN (reelected 1928), he joined with the planners of the Revolution of 1930. When the military, led by General José Félix URIBURU, seized power, he participated in the provisional government as commander-in-chief of the army.

Justo became the leading spokesman for conservative politicians who hoped to impose limits on democracy and to use the government to protect their interests. When support for Uriburu faded in 1931, the provisional government sponsored elections engineered to favor the conservatives, and Justo, with the support of the National Democratic Party and the Anti-Personalist

José Agustín Pedro Justo. ORGANIZATION OF AMERICAN STATES.

head of a local clinic and as a professor at the school from which he had recently graduated. In these positions, he introduced modern sanitary and scientific techniques into Argentina's operating rooms.

In the 1890s, Justo's interests began to shift from medicine to politics. His concern with the many environmentally induced illnesses he was called on to treat made him determined to attack the social conditions producing them. In 1893 he began to meet with like-minded professionals and skilled workers to found a socialist newspaper. The result was the appearance in 1894 of *La Vanguardia,* destined to be the most influential socialist publication in Argentina. Soon thereafter, Justo helped found the Socialist Party of Argentina, which in 1896 began to participate in local and national elections on a regular basis.

As the Socialist Party evolved and expanded, Justo emerged as its principal leader and guiding force. A man of great intellectual ability, he molded the party in his own image and directed it along the path—mostly a moderate one—he believed best suited to Argentine conditions. One of the few Argentine Socialists well versed

Radicals, was elected president. Serving from 1932 to 1938, he directed the consolidation of the Concordancia, a coalition of conservative political forces that controlled Argentine politics until 1943.

Justo's administration maneuvered Argentina through the Great Depression. The fiscal innovations initiated under Justo, including the ROCA–RUNCIMAN PACT (1933), the Pinedo Plan, the establishment of a national income tax, and the creation of Argentina's Central Bank, were overshadowed by the growing reliance on electoral fraud, censorship, and repression that maintained the Concordancia in power.

ROBERT A. POTASH, *The Army and Politics in Argentina, 1928–1945: From Yrigoyen to Perón* (1969); DAVID ROCK, *Argentina, 1516–1987: From Spanish Colonization to Alfonsín,* rev. ed. (1987), pp. 216–231.

DANIEL LEWIS

JUSTO, JUAN B. (*b.* 28 June 1865; *d.* 8 January 1928), Argentine Socialist congressman, senator, and party founder. Born in the city of Buenos Aires, Justo graduated from the medical school of the local university in 1888. After travel to Europe, he returned to Argentina in the early 1890s to serve as a surgical specialist at the

Juan B. Justo. ARCHIVO GENERAL DE LA NACIÓN, BUENOS AIRES, ARGENTINA.

in Marxist theory (he produced the first Spanish translation of *Das Kapital*), he closely followed various European models of socialist theory, organization, and practice, adjusting them whenever necessary to local circumstances and conditions. Among his several publications, *Teoría y práctica de la historia* (1909) best describes and explains Justo's particular brand of socialism.

Under Justo's direction, the Socialist Party of Argentina grew in size, strength, and support. Justo himself was elected three times to the national Chamber of Deputies (1912–1916, 1916–1920, and 1920–1924) and once to the national Senate (1924–1928) from the federal capital. As a legislator, Justo was a forceful advocate for his party's programmatic agenda and an acerbic critic of the governments in power. His speeches were characterized by careful and often compelling reasoning, extensive documentation, frequent references to foreign examples, and sardonic wit. The acknowledged leader of his party, he also served as the head of its congressional delegation.

Justo's brilliance and leadership attracted many like-minded and able young men to the party. He developed a coterie of protegés, notably Nicolás Repetto and Enrique DICKMANN, who were closely tied to him not only by philosophy but also by marriage. Throughout the first three decades of the twentieth century, Justo and his allies dominated the editorial board of *La Vanguardia* as well as the main directive positions and candidate lists of the Socialist Party.

Although the party flourished under Justo's direction, there were many who chafed and occasionally rebelled against his tight discipline and the control he exercised from the top. Dissident reaction against the "family elite," a constant and repeated complaint, resulted in several serious schisms within the party in these years. Rarely, however, was open criticism directed against Justo himself, who remained the most widely respected, and by some revered, socialist in Argentina. The impact of Justo's ideas continued to have a substantial influence on the direction of Argentina's Socialist Party well after his death in 1928.

DARDO CÚNEO, *Juan B. Justo y las luchas sociales en la Argentina* (1956).

RICHARD J. WALTER

JUZGADO GENERAL DE INDIOS, a court of appeal for Indians. From the earliest days of conquest and settlement, the Spanish crown was concerned about the well-being of the native population. This concern included providing the Indians with access to judicial recourse in civil and criminal matters. In Peru an elaborate but inefficient protective system was developed that involved provincial judges and a staff in Lima, all supported by Indian taxation. In Mexico the crown in 1592 established a special tribunal in Mexico City, the General Indian Court, to hear Indian cases without charge to the individual and supported by a special tax. The Mexican court, which existed until 1820, had jurisdiction in suits of Indians against Indians and Spaniards against Indians, although other courts could hear such cases as well. It also heard numerous complaints by Indians against Spanish officials and clergy. Its existence helped to rein in the excesses of provincial governors, and Indians found it preferable to other judicial alternatives and used it extensively.

WOODROW BORAH, *Justice by Insurance: The General Indian Court of Colonial Mexico and the Legal Aides of the Half-Real* (1983).

MARK A. BURKHOLDER

See also **Criminal Justice; Judicial Systems.**

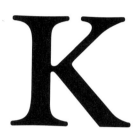

KAGEL, MAURICIO RAÚL (*b.* 24 December 1931), Argentine composer who became a naturalized German citizen. He was born in Buenos Aires. At the University of Buenos Aires he studied literature and philosophy until 1955. He trained with private instructors, most notably with Juan Carlos PAZ. For a few years he worked as a pianist and conductor for opera preparation at the Teatro Colón in Buenos Aires. In 1957 he moved to Germany where he studied with Werner Meyer-Eppler at the Institute for Research in Phonetics and Communications in Bonn. His career developed rapidly as a composer, conductor, writer, and lecturer. He founded the Cologne Ensemble for New Music in 1961.

Since 1965, Kagel has written for what is now called "musical theater," and he has written and directed his own films. His early compositions, written while he was still living in his native country, were very pitch conscious and precisely structured. The String Sextet (1953, revised 1957) uses polymetric rhythms and microtonal writing. His more experimental *Musique de tour* for tape with light projections (1953), required a light system projected from a steel tower and sound broadcast from twenty-four loudspeakers. Other influential compositions by Kagel include *Anagrama* for spoken choir, four soloists, and chamber orchestra (1957–1958), based on a palindrome by Dante; *Transición* no. 1 for electronic mu-

sic (1958–1960); and *Transición* no. 2 for piano and tape recorder (1958–1959). Theatrical components became very important in his works *Sur scène* for instrumental theater (1959–1960); *Pandorasbox* for bandoneon, a type of accordion (1960–1962); *Ludwig van* (1970), a homage to Beethoven that appeared in several versions, including a German television film and a recorded version with Kagel's ensemble playing distorted music of Beethoven; and *Staatstheater* (1970), the prototype of a veritable anti-opera.

Other significant works by Kagel include *Match* for two cellos and percussion (1964); *Tremens,* instrumental theater for two actors and electronically amplified instruments (1963–1965); *Pas de cinq,* variable scenes for five actors (1965); *Music for Renaissance Instruments* (1965–1967); *Halleluja* for voices (1967–1968); *Atem* for one wind instrument, tape recorder, and two loudspeakers (1970); *Con voce* for three silent players (1972); *Zwei Mann Orchester* for two performers (1971–1973); *1898* for children's choir (1972); *Mare nostrum* for contralto, baritone, and chamber ensemble (1973); *Exotica* for non-European instruments (1972); *Die Mutation* for children's voices and piano obbligato (1971); *Siegfriedp* for cello (1971); *Bestiarium* sound fable for three actors, bird calls and other objects, and tape (1974); *Die Umkehrung Amerikas* (1975–1976), a radio play; *Unguis in-*

345

carnatus est for piano (1972); *Morceau de concours* for solo trumpet and tape (1971), a competition piece; *Variationen ohne Fuge* for orchestra and two actors, Brahms and Handel (1971–1972); *Tango alemán* for bandoneon (1978); *Vox humana?* cantata for narrator, choir, and orchestra (1979); *Rrrrrr . . . .* a radio fantasy for different instrumental combinations (1982); *Pan* for piccolo flute and string quartet (1985); *Ein Brief* for mezzo-soprano and orchestra (1986); *Zwei Akte* for saxophone and harp (1988–1989); *Les idées fixes,* rondo for orchestra (1989); and *Der Windrose* for salon orchestra (1988).

Films written and directed by Kagel include *Antithèse* (1965); *Match* (1966); *Solo* (1966–1967); *Duo* (1968); *Halleluja* (1967–1968); *Sous tension* (1975); *Blue's Blue* (1981); and *Dressage* (1985). He also wrote the music for the film *MM51* (1977).

RODOLFO ARIZAGA, *Enciclopedia de la música argentina* (1971), pp. 187–188; "Dossier Kagel," in *Musique en jeu,* no. 7 (1972): 98–100, 113, 117–123; JOHN VINTON, ed., *Dictionary of Contemporary Music* (1974). pp. 386–387; GÉRARD BÉHAGUE, *Music in Latin America: An Introduction* (1979), pp. 337–338; ALCIDES LANZA, "Music Theatre: A Mixed Media Realization of Kagel's 'Ludwig van,'" in *Interface 8* (1979): 237–248; *New Grove Dictionary of Music and Musicians* (1980).

ALCIDES LANZA

KAHLO, FRIDA (*b.* 6 July 1907; *d.* 13 July 1954), Mexican artist. Kahlo was born in Coyoacán, the daughter of the Hungarian Jewish immigrant photographer Guillermo Kahlo and Matilde Calderón. She studied at the Escuela Nacional Preparatoria, one of thirty-five girls in a student body of two thousand. In 1925, she suffered a fractured spine and pelvis in a traffic accident that left her in constant pain. During her convalescence, she began to paint.

In 1929 Kahlo married the famed muralist Diego Rivera. Together they became international celebrities, honored by the art world and the political left. Among their friends, they counted Leon Trotsky, Max Ernst, Tina Modotti, Henry Ford, John D. and Nelson Rockefeller, Pablo Neruda, André Breton, and Isamu Noguchi. To complement Diego Rivera's extravagant character, Frida Kahlo created her own flamboyance. Drawing upon the Mexican cultural nationalist movement, she elevated Tehuana dress to haute couture and coiffed her hair in indigenous styles embellished with ribbons, bows, combs, and flowers. Necklaces, earrings, and rings completed her costume along with a prominent cigarette. A vivacious, engaging, and playful presence, Frida Kahlo was a living work of art, self-constructed to fight her constant physical agony and her sorrow at being unable to conceive a child and having to endure her husband's infidelities.

Most of Kahlo's paintings are small, intricately crafted self-portraits combining the real and the fantastic. They capture her spiritual and physical suffering in anatomical, surgical detail cast in traditional Mexican art forms like the *retablo,* using Catholic and pre-Colombian symbolism and imagery. Her subject matter is distinctly female: motherhood, fertility, the womb, childbirth, childhood, children, and family. Her art is precociously feminist in her concern with domestic violence, adultery, and her drive to control her own body. Often interpreted as surrealist, her depiction of flowing blood and wounded bodies in fact derives from Mexican popular culture. In her fantastic depiction of monkeys, prickly pears, and rainforest, she achieves a degree of sensual expression unequalled in Mexican art. André Breton wrote: "There is no art more exclusively feminine, in the sense that, in order to be as seductive as possible, it is only too willing to play alternately at being absolutely pure and absolutely pernicious. The art of Frida Kahlo is a ribbon about a bomb" (Herrera, p. 214).

Kahlo died in July 1954 at the age of forty-seven. By the 1980s, her art had received the international recognition that had eluded her in her lifetime.

DIEGO RIVERA, with GLADYS MARCH, *My Art, My Life: An Autobiography* (1960); BERTRAM D. WOLFE, *The Fabulous Life of Diego Rivera* (1963); MAC KINLEY HELM, *Modern Mexican Painters* (1968); RAQUEL TIBOL, *Frida Kahlo, crónica, testimonios y aproxi-*

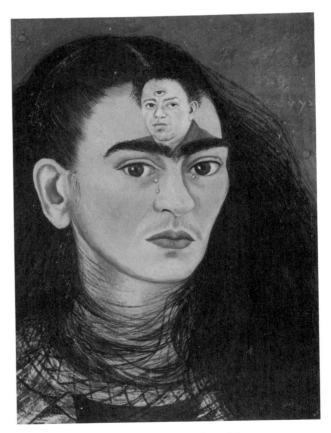

Diego y yo. Oil on masonite by Frida Kahlo, 1949. MARY-ANNE MARTIN / FINE ART.

maciones (1977); HAYDEN HERRERA, *A Biography of Frida Kahlo* (1983).

MARY KAY VAUGHAN

KAMINALJUYÚ, a Formative and Classic Period MAYA site in (and mostly destroyed by) the suburbs of modern Guatemala City. The source of its importance was the El Chayal obsidian deposits 12 miles northeast. Through exploitation of this resource, it became sufficiently strong to resist OLMEC inroads into the southern highlands. Its location provides trade access to the west and north across the Isthmus of TEHUANTEPEC to the Gulf, northward into the Petén and the southern Maya lowlands, and southward to the Pacific Coast and Central America. Though independent of the Olmecs, Kaminaljuyú must have served as a major conduit of cultural influences reaching the MAYAS from the Olmec region via IZAPA, to which Kaminaljuyú is stylistically linked.

As TEOTIHUACÁN rose to power about A.D. 150, Kaminaljuyú became a major trading partner or a colony. The distinctive Teotihuacán *talud-tablero* (sloping-table) style of terrace facings on platforms and pyramids appears on several structures in one area of the site tied to this era. Teotihuacán dress on sculptured monuments and funerary furnishings in elaborate tombs further document the Teotihuacán links. (Alfred V. Kidder and E. M. Shook excavated two tombs in Structure E-III-3 and reported finding sacrificial victims, jadeite beads, a mask, headdress, obsidian blades, stingray spines, stuccoed gourds, and quartz crystals.) Some scholars believe that Kaminaljuyú was initially conquered by Teotihuacán warriors, integrated into the Teotihuacán trade networks, and sustained by the rule of the descendants of local marriages. Kaminaljuyú was both a commercial and dynastic link between TIKAL and Teotihuacán; and perhaps Curl Nose (ruler of Tikal, late fourth century A.D.) married into the Tikal ruling lineage from Kaminaljuyú.

ALFRED V. KIDDER, J. D. JENNINGS, and E. M. SHOOK, *Excavations at Kaminaljuyú, Guatemala* (Carnegie Institution of Washington, publication 561, 1946); E. M. SHOOK and A. V. KIDDER, *Mound E-III-3, Kaminaljuyú, Guatemala* (Carnegie Institution of Washington, publication 596, 1952); WILLIAM T. SANDERS and J. W. MICHELS, *Teotihuacán and Kaminaljuyú: A Study in Prehistoric Cultural Contact* (1977).

WALTER R. T. WITSCHEY

KAQCHIKEL, MAYAN Indians of south-central Guatemala (1992 pop. 750,000). The Kaqchikel (formerly known as Cakchiquel) came to highland Guatemala between 1200 and 1250 as warriors accompanying the K'ICHE' (Quiché) and the TZ'UTUJIL (Zutuhil). By 1470 an independent Kaqchikel nation ruled forty towns from the capital, IXIMCHE'. Although by 1520 the population had been decimated by European plagues, continued strife with the K'iche' and Tz'utujil forced the Kaqchikel to enlist Spanish military aid. Pedro de ALVARADO (known as Tonatiw) marched into Iximche' as an ally in 1524. But after further joint campaigns against the PIPILES and the Tz'utujil, planned at and launched from Iximche', Alvarado broke with the Kaqchikel, demanding tribute. The Kaqchikel leaders abandoned Iximche' to lead guerrilla resistance that lasted over a decade.

Between 1519 and 1550 the Maya population of Guatemala dropped by 80 percent, and between 1550 and 1800 by another 60 percent.

The centrally located Kaqchikel supplied labor and provender for the Spanish settlements while reestablishing pre-Columbian trade networks through exchange of their minimal excess produce. Many adopted Catholic religious practices, though the sacred 260-day calendar round was maintained. Holy places, particularly the dawn altars, the caves, and the obsidian emblematic stelae brought from Tula, endured as often clandestine centers of worship.

The Indian policies of the Spanish and Guatemalan governments alternated between assimilationism and integrationism. The politically knowledgeable Kaqchikel have consistently used the courts to oppose discrimination and to petition for equal rights. While maintaining their own ethnicity, they have incorporated multiethnic Indian resettlements into Kaqchikel communities. At the time of the downfall of the Liberal regimes of Jorge UBICO and Federico Ponce (1944), they tried to secure their traditional lands. Under Juan José ARÉVALO, they formed farm labor unions. Successive governments tried to assure access to Indian labor by cultivating dependence through economic and educational subordination.

Through unions, cooperatives, education, and commerce, the Kaqchikel are freeing themselves from debt peonage and manual labor constraints. Although ties to the land are still important, many families are no longer primarily farmers. Robert M. Brown found that most Kaqchikel families have four sources of income in addition to farming. Between the 1964 and the 1981 censuses, both the absolute and the relative population figures for Kaqchikel increased, despite the toll of the 1976 earthquake.

Although the violence of 1979–1985 slowed Kaqchikel population growth, the average educational level, involvement in macropolitical and macroeconomic spheres, and commitment to revitalizing Kaqchikel culture are building steadily. The 1986 Guatemalan constitution recognizes the indigenes' rights to maintain their languages and cultures.

In 1987 the government established official alphabets for Mayan languages. Kaqchikel, as one of the four major indigenous languages, is now served by the national bilingual/bicultural education program. Mayan scholars are again turning to the classic sources of the 1500s, such as the ANNALS OF THE KAQCHIKELS and the POPOL VUH, as inspiration for novels, histories, textbooks, poetry, and for constructing a new worldview, a modern Mayan reality. In 1990 a Kaqchikel poet, Kab'raqän, wrote: "So we too emerge from the heavy shadows, the dark night. Because all of their shadowy voices, the voices of our grandmothers, our grandfathers are crying in our hearts."

FRANCISCO HERNÁNDEZ ARANA XAJILA and FRANCISCO DÍAZ GEBUTA QUEJ, *Memorial de Tecpán-Atitlán: Anales de los Cakchiqueles,* translated by José Antonio Villacorta C. (1934); ADRIÁN RECINOS, *Crónicas indígenas de Guatemala* (1957); SOL TAX, *Penny Capitalism* (1963); MANNING NASH, "Guatemalan Highlands," in *Handbook of Middle American Indians,* vol. 7, *Ethnology,* pt. 1 (1969); SOL TAX and ROBERT HINSHAW, "The Maya of the Midwestern Highlands," in *Handbook of Middle American Indians,* vol. 7, *Ethnology,* pt. 1 (1969); DOUGLAS E. BRINTNALL, *Revolt Against the Dead: The Modernization of a Mayan Community in the Highlands of Guatemala* (1979); SHELDON ANNIS, *God and Production in a Guatemalan Town* (1987); ROBERT MC KENNA BROWN, *Language Maintenance and Shift Among the Kaqchikel Maya* (1991).

JUDITH M. MAXWELL IxQ'ANIL

See also **Closed Corporate Peasant Community.**

KEARNY, STEPHEN W. (*b.* 30 August 1794; *d.* 31 October 1848), a soldier who gained fame during the MEXICAN WAR (1846–1848). Kearny, of Dutch and Irish parentage, was raised in New Jersey and New York City. He served with distinction during the War of 1812 and as an officer commanding various posts on the western frontier. When the Mexican War broke out, he was given the command of the Army of the West. He marched 1,600 troops into Santa Fe, New Mexico, and served as military governor from August to September 1846.

From Santa Fe Kearny led an army of about one hundred to California to assist in the American conquest of the far West. On 6 December 1846, at San Pasqual, near San Diego, in a brief but bloody skirmish, he encountered a Californio force led by Andrés Pico that blocked his advance for several days. Later Kearny assisted in the recapture of Los Angeles. For many months he quarreled with John C. Frémont over who was the chief commander of California. Eventually Kearny was vindicated and Frémont was court-martialed.

In 1847 Kearny was sent to Mexico and served as the civil governor of Vera Cruz and later of Mexico City. He died the following year in St. Louis, of a tropical disease contracted in Vera Cruz.

HUBERT HOWE BANCROFT, *History of California,* 7 vols. (1884–1890); JUSTIN HARVEY SMITH, *The War with Mexico,* 2 vols. (1919); ALLAN NEVINS, *Frémont* (1922; repr. 1963); DWIGHT CLARKE, *Stephen Watts Kearny: Soldier of the West* (1961).

RICHARD GRISWOLD DEL CASTILLO

KEITH, MINOR COOPER (*b.* 19 January 1848; *d.* 14 June 1929), Costa Rican railroad builder and founder of

UNITED FRUIT COMPANY. Born in Brooklyn, New York, Keith received only a grade-school education before beginning to work in the cattle business out west. In 1871 his uncle, Henry MEIGGS, obtained and transferred the contract to build the Costa Rican railroad to Minor's elder brother, Henry Meiggs Keith. Henry Keith soon had Minor in Costa Rica working on the railroad, which quickly became Minor C. Keith's project. He completed the Costa Rican Railway on 7 December 1890.

Minor Keith encouraged banana production along the railroad line in order to have a return freight during the period before the railroad reached the Mesa Central. He used the Tropical Trading and Transport Company to control all the banana land in the early decades. Later he organized the Colombian Land Company, Limited, and the Snyder Banana Company as his fruit business expanded. He joined with Andrew W. Preston of Boston Fruit Company to form the UNITED FRUIT COMPANY, incorporated in New Jersey on 30 March 1899. Preston became president and Keith first vice president, but Keith ceased any active role in the company by 1912. He had received $4 million in United Fruit shares for his various fruit operations when United Fruit organized.

On 31 October 1883, Keith married Cristina Castro Fernández, the daughter of José María CASTRO, who served twice as president and once as chief justice of Costa Rica, and Pacífica Fernández de Castro, who designed Costa Rica's flag and coat of arms. Minor and Cristina had no children.

Later in life, Keith pursued other interests. He collected and turned over to the Costa Rican National Museum (founded in 1887) many Costa Rican antiquities. About 1905, he acquired fruit lands in Guatemala for United Fruit and built the International Railroads of Central America by purchasing existing railroads and acquiring concessions for additional lines in Guatemala and El Salvador. He had interests in Brazilian railroads and Cuban sugar mills among his many and varied Latin American business holdings.

J. FRED RIPPY, "Relations of the United States and Costa Rica During the Guardia Era," *Bulletin of the Pan American Union* 77, no. 2 (1943): 61–68; WATT STEWART, *Keith and Costa Rica* (1964); JOHN E. FINDLING, *Dictionary of American Diplomatic History,* 2d ed. (1989), p. 279.

THOMAS SCHOONOVER

KEMMERER, EDWIN WALTER (*b.* 19 June 1875; *d.* 16 December 1945), U.S. financial adviser in Latin America. Born in Scranton, Pennsylvania, Kemmerer attended Wesleyan University (B.A., 1899) and Cornell (Ph.D., 1903). One of the most famous U.S. economists in the opening decades of the twentieth century, Kemmerer was a professor at Cornell (1906–1912) and Princeton (1912–1943). He helped design the Federal Reserve System in 1911, edited the *American Economic Bulletin* and the *American Economic Review,* and became president of the American Economic Association in

1926. He was renowned as an expert on money and banking. His greatest achievement, however, was his success as an adviser to foreign governments. A product of the Progressive Era, Kemmerer saw himself as a professional technician bringing universal, scientific advances to underdeveloped countries and their poorer citizens. He became known as the "money doctor."

Throughout the world, Kemmerer spread the gospel of the gold standard and central banks. His teams of experts stabilized exchange, modernized financial and fiscal institutions, and thus made countries more attractive to foreign investors, particularly during the lending boom of the 1920s. He played many of the roles later assigned to international financial institutions, principally the International Monetary Fund.

Kemmerer's overseas economic reforms began with the United States–Philippine Commission in 1903–1906. From 1917 to 1934 he conducted similar crusades against inflation in Mexico, Guatemala, Colombia, Germany, Chile, South Africa, Poland, Ecuador, Bolivia, China, Peru, and Turkey. In most cases, Kemmerer and his colleagues were invited independently by foreign governments, although the U.S. State Department heartily approved of his missions.

After the Great Depression, Kemmerer's influence faded, as he continued to espouse monetary stability based on the gold standard. Although his ideas lost sway, his institutions—such as the central bank, the superintendency of BANKING, and the national comptroller—continued as major instruments of economic policy-making in Latin America. Moreover, the pattern he set for the role of foreign advisers in Latin America's financial development forecast the operations of international institutions, academics, and technocrats in subsequent decades.

EDWIN W. KEMMERER, "Economic Advisory Work for Governments," in *American Economic Review* 17, no. 1 (March 1927): 1–12; ROBERT N. SEIDEL, "American Reformers Abroad: The Kemmerer Missions in South America, 1923–1931," in *Journal of Economic History* 32, no. 2 (June 1972): 520–545; PAUL W. DRAKE, *The Money Doctor in the Andes: The Kemmerer Missions, 1923–1933* (1989).

PAUL W. DRAKE

KENNECOTT COPPER COMPANY. See **Gran Minería**.

K'ICHE' (Quiché) Indians are Guatemala's most numerous MAYA ethnolinguistic group, with an estimated total population of between 1.5 and 2 million concentrated in the western departments of Guatemala, the great majority in the highlands and the remainder in the Pacific and northern lowlands. Caught in the middle of a harsh and bloody civil war, since the late 1970s the K'iche' have suffered widespread internal dislocation, involving many deaths and the destruction of numerous communities. Thousands have emigrated to Mexico, the United States, and Canada. Some joined the guerrillas in the 1970s and early 1980s, and many more have been conscripted into the army, whose counterinsurgency campaign of torture and death has claimed thousands of Maya victims.

The Spanish conquest was characterized by K'iche' and other Maya bravely opposing forces favored by superior technology. Beginning in 1524, the Spanish conquerors enslaved and forcibly resettled (*congregación*) the K'iche'. They destroyed K'iche' cultural-religious symbols and required the people to practice the Catholic religion. The K'iche' were compelled to give labor and tribute to their new lords (*encomenderos*). While late-twentieth-century violence has been horrific for the K'iche', in the 1524–1675 period they lost 80–90 percent of their population, primarily to Old World diseases. The K'iche' population numbered some 925,000 about 1520 and declined to probably fewer than 100,000 in the seventeenth century. Recovery over the next three centuries to more than 1.5 million is ample testimony to the K'iche' ability to survive despite unfavorable odds.

The key to K'iche' resistance to a multitude of destructive forces, including the more subtle Spanish and Guatemalan efforts to integrate the Maya into a colonial or national polity, lies in the strength of K'iche' cultural traditions and the ability to maintain ancestral towns and lands. Both of these factors have deep roots in the pre-Conquest period, when the early K'iche' (ca. thirteenth century) and their predecessors formed villages, then more complex patrilineal clans and chiefdoms, and finally a state structure.

For at least several centuries prior to the Spaniards' arrival, the K'iche' were the dominant highland group, directly ruling both their own regions and those peoples who later broke away to form the independent TZ'UTUJIL and KAQCHIKEL polities. Other Maya, like the MAM, were subordinate tributaries under indirect K'iche' authority. Lacking a rich resource base near their capital, Gumaarcaj (UTATLÁN), the K'iche' expanded into lower-lying areas rich in agricultural commodities like cacao and cotton.

Preconquest K'iche' writings include the POPOL VUH, elaborate calendars, and clan histories (*títulos*) by priests and chroniclers. All were lost or destroyed, but Maya versions in the Roman alphabet took their place. Despite Spanish efforts to extirpate the pagan past—notably by destroying temples and killing religious leaders—much survived, often in modified form. Woven textiles for both daily wear and ceremonial occasions are an obvious example.

Such political and cultural achievements bestowed strength, a measure of continuity, and a distinct identity on the K'iche' inhabitants of numerous hamlets and towns. In recent decades, new levels of cultural identity based on these antecedents have emerged, giving the K'iche' both a new pan-Maya identity and a growing sense of belonging to a particular group.

Still, the struggle for K'iche' and Maya survival in

Guatemala is likely to remain difficult. Institutional violence persists, racism is deeply entrenched, and poverty has increased as population expansion and environmental destruction have put new strains on the carrying capacity of the land.

Fundamental works are ROBERT M. CARMACK, *Quichean Civilization: The Ethnohistoric, Ethnographic, and Archaeological Sources* (1973), and *The Quiché Mayas and Utatlán: The Evolution of a Highland Guatemalan Kingdom* (1981). An intriguing comparison of past and present events is W. GEORGE LOVELL, "Surviving Conquest: The Maya of Guatemala in Historical Perspective," in *Latin American Research Review*, 23, no. 2 (1988): 25–57.

A number of authors focus on K'iche' towns as a mechanism for analyzing a period stretching from the pre-Hispanic era to the present. Noteworthy are ROBERT M. CARMACK, *Historia social de los Quiché* (1979); ROBERT M. HILL II and JOHN MONAGHAN, *Continuities in Highland Maya Social Organization: Ethnohistory in Sacapulas, Guatemala* (1987); and JEAN PIEL, *Sajcabajá: Muerte y resurección de un pueblo de Guatemala, 1500–1970* (1989).

Important analyses of postcolonial Guatemalan Maya society are ROBERT M. CARMACK, "Spanish-Indian Relations in Highland Guatemala, 1800–1944," in *Spaniards and Indians in Southeastern Mesoamerica: Essays on the History of Ethnic Relations*, edited by Murdo J. MacLeod and Robert Wasserstrom (1983); CAROL A. SMITH, ed., *Guatemalan Indians and the State, 1540–1988* (1990).

Essential for understanding the impact of revolution and institutionalized repression on the K'iche' and other Maya peoples is ROBERT M. CARMACK, ed., *Harvest of Violence: The Maya Indians and the Guatemalan Crisis* (1988).

CHRISTOPHER H. LUTZ

KINNEY, HENRY L. (*b.* 3 June 1814; *d.* July 1861[?]), U.S. FILIBUSTER and borderlands entrepreneur. A Pennsylvanian by birth, Kinney farmed and speculated in land in Illinois in the 1830s. Ruined in the Panic of 1837, he migrated to the Republic of TEXAS. In 1840, at the mouth of the Nueces River, within territory disputed by Texas and Mexico, he established a trading post/smuggler's nest that became known as Kinney's Rancho. Kinney, who became bilingual, survived border strife by providing information and supplies to Texan and Mexican forces alike, sometimes serving as intermediary between them. His ranch became the nucleus of a boomtown, Corpus Christi, after General Zachary Taylor stationed his army in its vicinity prior to the MEXICAN–AMERICAN WAR. During that conflict, Kinney apparently was division quartermaster on the general staff of the Texas Volunteers and then agent of the U.S. Quartermaster Department, serving as supplier, scout, interpreter, and dispatch carrier.

Kinney served in the Republic of Texas's Ninth and Tenth congresses, as well as the Texas Constitutional Convention of 1845 (where he championed the interests of Spanish-speaking inhabitants). Although elected to the Senate of the first four Texas legislatures, he never took his seat in the second legislature and abandoned

his seat in the fourth. After the Mexican–American War, he became involved in the publication of the *Corpus Christi Star* (later the *Nueces Valley*), Texas Ranger affairs, and promotion of Texas's first state fair (1852), held both to boost Corpus Christi and to raise aid for José María Carvajal's Republic of the Sierra Madre.

From 1854 to 1858 Kinney devoted himself to the Central American Land and Mining Company, designed to colonize—really filibuster—Central America's MOSQUITO COAST, on the basis of an invalid land grant. Kinney ruled GREYTOWN (San Juan del Norte) as "civil and military governor" for part of this period. In 1859, Kinney served as Texas governor Sam Houston's agent to investigate Juan Cortina's raid on Brownsville. Elected a representative in Texas's eighth legislature, Kinney opposed secession and, in March 1861, was forced to give up his seat. Several undocumented accounts assert that he died at Matamoros, Mexico.

WILLIAM O. SCROGGS, *Filibusters and Financiers: The Story of William Walker and His Associates* (1916), esp. pp. 93–132; JOSEPH MILTON NANCE, *After San Jacinto: The Texas–Mexican Frontier, 1836–1841* (1963); JAMES T. WALL, *Manifest Destiny Denied: America's First Intervention in Nicaragua* (1981), esp. pp. 29–70.

ROBERT E. MAY

KINO, EUSEBIO FRANCISCO (*b.* 10 August 1645; *d.* 15 March 1711), JESUIT missionary and explorer of northwestern New Spain. A native of Segno, near Trent, in the Italian Tyrol, educated in Austria and Germany, Kino was among the foreign-born Jesuit missionaries permitted by the Spanish crown under quota to serve in the Spanish Indies. He excelled in mathematics, astronomy, and cartography, and could have had a university chair in Europe. Instead, he put these skills to good use during a thirty-year career in New Spain, first as royal cosmographer of Admiral Isidro de Atondo's failed effort to occupy BAJA CALIFORNIA in the mid-1680s and then as the pioneer missionary of PIMERÍA ALTA (present-day northern Sonora and southern Arizona), capstone of the Jesuits' northwest missionary empire.

An irrepressible expansionist, Kino's restless nature better suited him for exploration and first contact with the Pimas and Pápagos (Tohono O'odam) than for everyday administrative routine at mission Dolores, which he established as his headquarters in 1687. On numerous expeditions, traveling the valleys of the San Pedro, Santa Cruz, Gila, and Colorado rivers, he introduced cattle, created demand for European goods, and mapped the country. His crowning cartographic achievement, which he drew the year before his death, showed California not as an island, a misconception of the seventeenth century, but as a peninsula.

In 1966, Kino's grave was discovered in Magdalena, Sonora, since renamed Magdalena de Kino. The JESUITS are promoting his cause for canonization. A mineral, a hospital, a table wine, and much else bear his name, and statues abound.

Eusebio Francisco Kino. Reproduced from Herbert Eugene Bolton, *The Padre on Horseback*. BENSON LATIN AMERICAN COLLECTION, UNIVERSITY OF TEXAS AT AUSTIN.

The standard treatment is HERBERT E. BOLTON, *Rim of Christendom: A Biography of Eusebio Francisco Kino, Pacific Coast Pioneer* (1936; repr. 1984), supplemented by the works of ERNEST J. BURRUS, e.g., *Kino and the Cartography of Northwestern New Spain* (1965) and *Kino and Manje, Explorers of Sonora and Arizona, Their Vision of the Future* (1971). See also CHARLES W. POLZER, *Kino Guide II*, rev. ed. (1987).

JOHN L. KESSELL

KISSINGER COMMISSION. The Reagan administration convened the U.S. National Bipartisan Commission on Central America in 1984 in hopes of reversing flagging congressional support for its Central American policy, particularly with respect to aid to the Nicaraguan CONTRAS and military assistance for the government of El Salvador. Former Secretary of State Henry Kissinger chaired the conservative, twelve-member commission, whose mandate was to study contemporary conflicts in Central America and make policy recommendations.

The report of the Kissinger Commission was released in January 1984. It contained an overview of Central American development and addressed what the commission believed to be the immediate causes of the military conflicts afflicting the region in the early 1980s. Members of the commission concurred with other observers that peace in Central America was dependent upon improvements in economic and social conditions and that those developments were not likely to occur until the civil wars came to an end.

Regarding the region's economic problems, the report recommended that the United States mount a large aid program for Central America; it envisioned much more external assistance than was actually forthcoming in the 1980s. The sections dealing with security issues, however, created the most public controversy, and only partially succeeded in gaining congressional support. Especially contentious aspects of the report were its insistence that Central American revolutionary movements relied heavily on support from Cuba and the Soviet Union, the commission's refusal to fully acknowledge United States' backing of the contras, and arguments in favor of increasing U.S. military assistance to El Salvador.

Report of the National Bipartisan Commission on Central America (1984); RICHARD E. FEINBERG, "The Kissinger Commission Report: A Critique," in *World Development* 12, no. 8 (1984): 867–876; WILLIAM M. LEO GRANDE, "Through the Looking Glass: The Kissinger Commission Report on Central America," *World Policy Journal* 1, no. 2 (1984): 251–284.

MARY A. CLARK

KNOX–CASTRILLO TREATY (1911), a loan convention signed in Washington, D.C., on 6 June 1911 between U.S. Secretary of State Philander C. Knox and Nicaraguan minister Salvador Castrillo. Reflecting the U.S. government's desire to provide financial, and by extension political, stability for Nicaragua, the convention called for the Nicaraguan authorities to negotiate a loan for the purpose of re-funding the nation's internal and external debts. The bonds floated for the loan would be secured by Nicaraguan customs duties, and the customs would be supervised by a collector general approved by the U.S. government. Although ratified almost immediately by Nicaragua, the treaty languished for nearly a year in the U.S. Senate Foreign Relations Committee. In May 1912, when the committee finally voted, the treaty failed to secure the necessary support for a favorable report to the Senate. The Nicaraguan government then decided to negotiate directly with U.S. bankers for a short-term loan, a financial arrangement that did not carry the official sanction and guarantees that treaty status would have provided.

Papers relating to the Foreign Relations of the United States, 1912 (1919), esp. pp. 1,071–1,104; DANA G. MUNRO, *Intervention and Dollar Diplomacy in the Caribbean, 1900–1921* (1964), esp. pp. 186–204.

RICHARD V. SALISBURY

See also **Dollar Diplomacy.**

KOELLREUTTER, HANS JOACHIM (*b.* 2 September 1915), German-born teacher and composer, who has lived in Brazil since 1937.

Koellreutter's effect on young Brazilian composers has been enormous. In 1939 he formed the group Música Viva Brasil and in 1940 began publishing a magazine of the same name. Through his group and his periodical, Koellreutter set out to introduce new music to Brazilian audiences. He championed the theories and music of Arnold Schoenberg, and encouraged his music students to employ the twelve-tone technique when writing music. Koellreutter's modernist agenda prompted Brazil's principal nationalist composer, Camargo GUARNIERI, to write the famous ''Carta aberta aos músicos e críticos do Brasil'' (Open letter to musicians and critics of Brazil), in which he attacked the idea that serial technique could be a suitable means of expression for nationalist music. Composers such as César Guerra PEIXE, Claudio SANTORO, and others who studied with Koellreutter went on to develop their own individual styles, but the ideas and teaching of Koellreutter made a major contribution to twentieth-century Brazilian music.

GÉRARD BÉHAGUE, *Music in Latin America: An Introduction* (1979); DAVID P. APPLEBY, *The Music of Brazil* (1983).

DAVID P. APPLEBY

KORN, ALEJANDRO (*b.* 3 May 1860; *d.* 9 October 1936), Argentine philosopher. Together with José VASCONCELOS and Antonio CASO in Mexico, Carlos VAZ FERREIRA in Uruguay, and Alejandro DEUSTUA in Peru, Korn belonged to a group of Latin American philosophers who were prominent at the end of the nineteenth and beginning of the twentieth centuries and who represented the beginning of a more professional approach to philosophy.

Korn was born in San Vicente, Buenos Aires Province, and educated in medicine at the University of Buenos Aires. He began his career as professor of philosophy at the University of Buenos Aires in 1906, while still engaged in his main profession as a psychiatrist. In the beginning, he was influenced by POSITIVISM, but he soon abandoned this position because of its naturalist determinism, which he felt made moral responsibility impossible. His Kantian-based philosophy was later influenced by the work of Europeans such as Wilhelm Dilthey and Henri Bergson.

Korn conceived of philosophy as a knowledge of the subjective, or the human, world, as opposed to science, which was the exact knowledge of the natural world. Philosophy was to him axiology, or the analysis of values and valuations as sources of all human action. Although it is not openly revealed in his philosophical writings, the base of his worldview is an intensely religious, but not dogmatic, feeling. His ethic is voluntarist and considers action as the way out of perplexities of theoretical antinomies. Although he considered Marxism an antiquated philosophy of the nineteenth century, he adhered to ''ethical socialism,'' a form of socialism based on the moral reasoning of social justice.

Korn was the author of a classic work on the interpretation of the history of ideas in Argentina, *Influencias filosóficas en la evolución nacional* (1936). His philosophical writings have been collected in *Obras*, 3 vols. (1938–1940) and *Obras completas* (1949).

SOLOMON LIPP, *Three Argentine Thinkers* (1969); DANIEL E. ZALAZAR, *Libertad y creación en los ensayos de Alejandro Korn* (1972); JUAN CARLOS TORCHIA ESTRADA, *Alejandro Korn: Profesión y vocación* (1986).

JUAN CARLOS TORCHIA ESTRADA

KÖRNER, EMIL (*b.* 10 October 1846; *d.* 25 March 1920), German army officer and founder of the modern Chilean army. Emil Körner Henze, as he was called in Chile, was born in Wegwitz, Saxony. He entered the army in 1866. He was a student and later taught at the Artillery and Engineer's School (Charlottenburg) and was decorated after Sedan. He graduated from the Kriegsakademie (staff school) in 1876 and served in Italy, Spain, and Africa. After nearly twenty years of service in the kaiser's army, Captain Körner had established a good record but, as a Saxon and a commoner, had a limited future as an officer of the imperial army. His military career took a sharp turn in 1885 because of the Chilean government's decision to professionalize its army. Impressed with what he had read of Chile's recent victory over Peru (WAR OF THE PACIFIC, 1879–1884), Körner accepted an offer to teach artillery, infantry, cartography, military history, and tactics; to serve as subdirector of the Escuela Militar; and to oversee establishment of a Chilean staff school. In Chile he ultimately rose to the rank of inspector general.

A year after his arrival he helped inaugurate the Academia de Guerra, and the Chilean army began a new life. Under Körner's direction the new staff school provided advanced training and the army adopted the general staff system in order to be prepared for war at any time. By 1889, the popular Körner was advocating wide-reaching reforms in military training. Two years later he helped the forces of the National Congress with the support of the Navy and some Army leaders to win a civil war against President José Manuel BALMACEDA. Subsequently Körner was given great latitude in the continual modernization of the army. He attracted several German missions to Chile in the last decade of the century, and by 1910, when he retired, Chile's army was superficially a creole copy of the kaiser's. Körner died in Berlin, but his remains were brought to Santiago in 1924.

CARLOS SÁEZ MORALES, *Recuerdos de un soldado*, vol. 1, *El ejército y la política* (1933); FREDERICK M. NUNN, ''Emil Körner and the Prussianization of the Chilean Army: Origins, Process, and Consequences, 1885–1920,'' in *Hispanic American Historical Review* 50 (May 1970): 300–322; FREDERICK M. NUNN, *Yesterday's Soldiers: European Military Professionalism in South America, 1890–1940* (1983).

FREDERICK M. NUNN

KOSICE, GYULA (*b.* 26 April 1924), Argentine painter and sculptor, born in Hungary. Kosice came to Argentina at age three. He studied at free academies from 1937 to 1942 and later at the School of Philosophy and Letters of the University of Buenos Aires and at the National School of Fine Arts. He founded the GRUPO MADÍ art movement as well as the Asociación de Arte Concreto-Invención, a nonfigurative group. ("Madí," like Dada, is an arbitrary word.) Kosice designed the Hydrospatial City. He is the creator of hydrokinetic art and neon luminal sculpture. A member of the Argentine Writers' Society (SADE), Kosice wrote eight books, among them *Herbert Read* (1955), *Poème hydranlique* (1960), *Arte Hidro-cinético* (1968), *Arte y arquitectura de agua* (1974), and *Arte Madí* (1980, 1982). His works are highly personal and imaginative, effecting a sense of tranquillity.

VICENTE GESUALDO, ALDO BIGLIONE, and RODOLFO SANTOS, *Diccionario de artistas plásticos argentinos* (1988).

AMALIA CORTINA ARAVENA

KOSMOS LINE, a Hamburg shipping line organized in early 1872 primarily to enter the competition for the Pacific coast freight service. Known as the Deutsche Dampfschiffahrts-Gesellschaft Kosmos (German Steamship Service Company Kosmos), it originally served only South America's Pacific coast, but by the early 1880s, it was running ships up to Central America during the six-month coffee season. Later, Kosmos extended its service northward to San Francisco. About 1880, Bremen shippers responded with the formation of the Roland Line to compete with Kosmos for the trade of the Pacific coast. Later Kosmos also developed trade with the Caribbean area, and it received a British mail subsidy to establish the first regular steamer service to Las Malvinas (FALKLAND ISLANDS). In 1901, the HAMBURG-AMERIKA LINIE (HAPAG) obtained a large interest in Kosmos through an agreement by which they shared access to the Pacific coast. Kosmos suspended service to Latin America from 1914 until mid-1921. In 1926, HAPAG absorbed Kosmos, but re-formed a shipping company for Latin American service under this name in 1976.

EDWIN J. CLAPP, *The Port of Hamburg* (1911); OTTO MATHIES, *Hamburgs Reederei 1814–1914* (1924); LUDWIG WENDEMUTH and W. BÖTTCHER, *The Port of Hamburg* (1932); RAYMOND A. RYDELL, *Cape Horn to the Pacific: The Rise and Demise of an Ocean Highway* (1952).

THOMAS SCHOONOVER

KOTOSH, an archaeological site in the Huallaga drainage of highland Peru. Known for its monumental architecture, Kotosh was built during the third millennium B.C., centuries before the introduction of ceramics. It is located in a rain shadow along the eastern slopes of the Andes at 6,600 feet above sea level. It is dominated by two mounds, the larger of which reached a height of 45 feet. Excavations showed that the featureless mounds were eroded terraced pyramid-platforms and that their impressive scale was the end product of centuries of intentional filling and renovation, a process sometimes called "ritual entombment." The core of the mounds contains a sequence of similar public structures superimposed one on top of the other.

The most important of these buildings are small stone chambers with a square ground plan and a central subfloor firepit attached to subterranean flues. The structures often feature a distinctive two-level floor in which a recessed zone surrounds the central stone-lined hearth. The exterior and interior walls of these chambers were plastered with light clay, and in some cases the entryway was painted red. These buildings are generally interpreted as chambers designed for rituals involving burnt offerings.

The best known of the Kotosh buildings, the Temple of the Crossed Hands, has two clay friezes flanking the main axis of the building: the eastern one depicts a small set of hands with the left arm overlapping the right, while the western one shows a similar but slightly larger set with the right arm on top of the left. These images constitute one of the oldest known examples of public art in the Americas, and they may symbolize dual opposition, a principle fundamental to later Andean ideology.

Preceramic structures similar to those at Kotosh have been found at other sites, including Shillacoto in Huánuco, Huaricoto in the Callejón de Huaylas, and La Galgada in the Tablachaca drainage. These structures probably housed comparable ceremonies, and the groups responsible for them are thought to have shared a similar belief system, sometimes referred to as the Kotosh Religious Tradition.

Following the Preceramic occupation (known as the Mito phase), Kotosh continued to be occupied during the second millennium B.C. by farmers who supplemented their diet with hunted game, especially deer. These groups produced elaborate ceramic assemblages known as the Kotosh Waira-jirca and Kotosh Kotosh styles; the form and decoration of this pottery display link to styles of the tropical forest, highlands, and coast. This pottery and occasional exotic imports from the eastern lowlands constitute evidence of the role that Amazonian cultures played in the development of early Andean civilization. During the first millennium B.C. Kotosh developed strong ties to CHAVÍN DE HUÁNTAR, and the local population participated in the Chavín sphere of interaction.

A synthesis of Kotosh and the Kotosh religious tradition is presented in RICHARD L. BURGER, *Chavín and the Origins of Andean Civilization* (1992). The University of Tokyo excavations at the site were published in SEIICHI IZUMI and T. SONO, *Andes 2: Excavations at Kotosh, Peru, 1960* (1963), and S. IZUMI and KAZUO TERADA, *Andes 4: Excavations at Kotosh, Peru, 1963 and 1966* (1972). SEIICHI IZUMI discussed the implications of Kotosh investigations in "The Development of the Formative Culture in the Ceja de Montaña" in *Dumbarton Oaks Conference on Chavin*, edited by Elizabeth Benson (1971).

RICHARD L. BURGER

KRAUSISMO is the Spanish version of the teachings of Karl Christian Friedrich Krause (1781–1832). Reminiscent of the mysticism of earlier centuries and of Erasmus's impact in sixteenth-century Spain, Krausismo appealed to the Iberian fondness for idealism and spiritualism, and offered alternatives of conservatism and POSITIVISM. Its "harmonious rationalism" provided a needed force for moral renewal. Introduced by Julián Sanz del Río and propagated through the works of Heinrich Ahrens, Karl David August Roeder, and Guillaume Tiberghien, Krausismo was a dominant influence from 1854 to 1874, with centers in Madrid, Oviedo, and Seville/Granada. Both the coup of 1868 and the First Republic of 1873–1874 were *krausista* phenomena.

Spain produced several *krausista* generations, and Krausismo also reached all of Latin America, especially Argentina and Uruguay (Hipólito YRIGOYEN and the *Radicales*; José BATLLE Y ORDÓÑEZ and the *Colorados*), as well as Guatemala (Juan José ARÉVALO's "spiritual socialism"). Krausismo is still a force in both Spain and Latin America (Raúl ALFONSÍN, for example).

ARTURO ARDAO, *Espiritualismo y positivismo en el Uruguay: Filosofías universitarias de la segunda mitad del siglo XIX* (1950); JUAN LÓPEZ MORILLAS, *El krausismo español: Perfil de una aventura intelectual* (1956); JUAN JOSÉ GIL CREMADES, *El reformismo español: Krausismo, escuela histórica, neotomismo* (1969); ARTURO ANDRÉS ROIG, *Los krausistas argentinos* (1969); FUNDACIÓN FRIEDRICH EBERT, INSTITUTO FE Y SECULARIDAD, *El krausismo y su influencia en América Latina* (1989).

O. CARLOS STOETZER

KRAUZE, ENRIQUE (*b.* September 1947), Mexican historian and intellectual. Best known for his popular series of illustrated presidential biographies produced and marketed for the general public, Krauze has authored important historical works, most notably *Caudillos culturales en la revolución mexicana* (1976). His political essays in *Vuelta* often provoke critical discussion.

Born in the Federal District, Krauze graduated from the National University with an engineering degree and earned a Ph.D. from the Colegio de México. Awarded a Guggenheim fellowship for 1979–1980, he has collaborated closely with Nobel Prize winner Octavio PAZ as managing editor and subdirector of *Vuelta* since 1976. Krauze is the intellectual disciple of Daniel COSÍO VILLEGAS and Paz.

RODERIC AI CAMP, *Who's Who in Mexico Today* (1988).

RODERIC AI CAMP

KRIEGER, EDINO (*b.* 17 March 1928), Brazilian composer. Born in the state of Santa Catarina, Brazil, Krieger was the son of Aldo and Gertrudes Krieger. His father was a well-known violinist, conductor, and composer who undertook the musical instruction of his son when the boy was only seven. During the next seven years, Edino Krieger gave several recitals as a violinist, and at the age of fourteen received a scholarship to study violin at the Conservatório Brasileiro de Música in Rio de Janeiro. In 1944 he wrote an improvisation for solo flute and in 1945 became associated with a group of composers, Música Viva, under the leadership of Hans Joachim KOELLREUTTER, a pupil of Paul Hindemith. Three years later he won first prize in a competition sponsored by the Berkshire Music Center in Massachusetts. He later enrolled in the Juilliard School of Music in New York City, where he studied with Aaron Copland, Peter Mennin, and Darius Milhaud.

Krieger has combined a career as a composer of works of stylistic originality and powerful dramatic qualities with significant achievements as director of the music section of Brazil's National Foundation of the Arts. During his administration, the foundation contributed to a vitalization of musical performance throughout the nation and published scores of historical works by Brazilian composers, providing a heightened sense of the nation's cultural achievements. Important compositions by Krieger include his *Ludus symphonicus*, commissioned by the Instituto de Cultura e Bellas Artes de Venezuela, and his oratorio *Rio de Janeiro*, a dramatic narration of the birth of Brazil from its period of Portuguese colonization. Both these works were performed in Rio de Janeiro in 1988 at a special concert celebrating the composer's sixtieth birthday.

DAVID P. APPLEBY, *The Music of Brazil* (1983).

DAVID P. APPLEBY

KRIEGER VASENA, ADALBERTO (*b.* 1920), a prominent Argentine economist. Educated at the University of Buenos Aires and in the United States, he received his doctorate in 1944 with a dissertation on "An Estimate of National Income." He has served on the faculties of the universities of Córdoba and La Plata and has held numerous posts. He served in the Ministry of the Treasury (1957–1958) and the Ministry of Economy and Labor (1967–1969). He is a member of the Economic Advisory Committee of the Stock Exchange of Buenos Aires and a member of the board of the Latin American Research Foundation and the board of the International Center for Economic Growth. He was chief of the Argentine delegation to the sixth meeting of the General Agreement on Tariffs and Trade (GATT) and has been an executive officer of numerous private companies. Dr. Krieger has written numerous articles and the book *Latin America: A Broader World Role*.

ROBERT SCHEINA

KUBITSCHEK, MÁRCIA (*b.* 23 October 1943), Brazilian cultural and political figure. The only natural daughter of President Juscelino KUBITSCHEK (another, Maria Estela, was adopted; he had no sons), she was born in Belo Horizonte, capital of Minas Gerais, while her father was its mayor. With the end of her first marriage, to a Brazilian investment banker, she married the renowned Cuban American ballet dancer, Fernando Bujones, in New York City in 1980. Kubitschek has administered various cultural activities, including the Ballet of Rio de Janeiro, the Ballet of Brazil Foundation, the Brazilian Tourist Authority in New York City, and the Brasília 2000 Olympics Association. A political centrist, she was elected a member of the Brazilian Constituent Assembly of 1987–1988. The assembly reconstituted the country along civilian lines after the military dictatorship of 1964–1985, which had barred her father from campaigning for a second term as president. In the first direct gubernatorial elections held in the Federal District (Brasília), in 1991, she became lieutenant governor of the national capital built just over a generation before by her father. She lost a senatorial bid in 1994 although a record number of five women won seats that year to the Brazilian Senate.

See *Travel Weekly,* 26 August 1985, for her work at the Brazilian Tourist Authority, and *Veja,* 19 October 1994, for her 1994 senatorial candidacy.

EDWARD A. RIEDINGER

KUBITSCHEK DE OLIVEIRA, JUSCELINO (*b.* 12 September 1902; *d.* 22 August 1976), president of Brazil (1956–1961), founder of Brasília (1960). Born in Diamantina, Minas Gerais, an impoverished colonial diamond-mining town, Kubitschek and his older sister were raised on the spare resources of their resolute and independent schoolteacher mother. Their father died when they were very young. A great-uncle had been prominent in early republican (late nineteenth century) state politics, favoring transfer of the capital from the baroque Ouro Prêto to a new, planned city, Belo Horizonte. Studying grade school with his mother and completing secondary education at a local seminary, Kubitschek entered the medical school of Belo Horizonte in 1922. Supporting himself as a telegraph operator, he became a doctor in 1927.

Income from his first years of medical practice allowed him to pursue specialized study in Europe during most of 1930. He established his own practice in Belo Horizonte the following year. That year he married Sarah Gomes de Lemos, member of a socially and politically prominent family. During an uprising in 1932 by the neighboring state of São Paulo against the federal government, Kubitschek was called to the borderline front as a medical officer. It was at this time that he met and impressed Benedito Valadares, a local politician serving as head of the military police in the region, who became Kubitschek's political mentor.

In 1933 President Getúlio VARGAS appointed Valadares interventor, or chief executive, of Minas Gerais. Valadares made Kubitschek his chief of staff. Actively extending the political network of his boss, and building a base for himself in Diamantina, Kubitschek was elected a federal deputy the following year, occupying

this position until the Vargas coup of 1937 closed Congress and established the authoritarian ESTADO NÔVO.

Uneasy about such a regime, he returned to his medical practice and profitably revived it. However, he entered public life again in 1940 when Valadares appointed him mayor of Belo Horizonte. His mayoralty gave singular impetus to the urban infrastructure of the still-developing city, augmenting streets, parks, water, and sewage systems; enhancing real estate; and encouraging commercial and industrial development. The model neighborhood of Pampulha became a signature of his administration with its dramatically modern church, designed by Oscar NIEMEYER and bearing murals by Cândido PORTINARI.

As the strength of the Estado Nôvo withered by 1945 under the victory of democratic forces in World War II, Vargas and his state interventors sought to maintain their political control in the emerging era of political liberty. They organized the Social Democratic Party (PSD) as a powerful opponent to the anti-Vargas forces, which had coalesced in the National Democratic Union (UDN).

Kubitschek became the organizing secretary of the PSD in Minas Gerais, the largest section of the party in the country, extending throughout the state his network of contacts. Removed from the mayoralty of Belo Horizonte with the ouster of Vargas near the end of 1945, Kubitschek was voted in by a substantial margin as a federal deputy that year and began his term in the Constituent Assembly in 1946.

Maneuvering himself within the factions of the PSD of Minas Gerais, Kubitschek ran successfully for the governorship of the state in the election of 1950. He obtained the tacit support of Getúlio Vargas, who won the presidential election the same year through another party he had founded, the trade-union-based Brazilian Labor Party (PTB).

With a campaign slogan of ''energy and transportation,'' Kubitschek began in 1951 an intensive gubernatorial administration dedicated to activating the state's economy through industrialization. He expanded or inaugurated numerous hydroelectric plants; brought the West German steel company, Mannesmann, to the state; enlarged the road network by many hundreds of miles; and built many clinics, schools, and bridges. These projects were financed through federal funds, foreign capital, and mixed public and private enterprises, a pattern he would also apply at the federal level.

Using the success of his administration in Minas Gerais, Kubitschek prepared himself for the presidential succession of 1955. He launched his campaign in the shadow of the August 1954 suicide of Vargas, who had been charged with massive corruption by the military and the UDN. Attempting to acquire the power base of the fallen president, Kubitschek renewed the alliance of the PSD and PTB by selecting as his vice presidential running mate the political heir of Vargas, João GOULART. He thereby also acquired the ire of the anti-Vargas forces. Kubitschek campaigned with an extensive plan for national development, pledging himself to fulfill a series of economic targets that would culminate in the building of a new national capital, Brasília, on the central plateau of the country. He won the October election, however, with only one-third of the votes, the lowest in Brazilian history, since he was relatively unknown in national politics and bore the burden of anti-Vargas sentiment. Only a protective coup the following month allowed Kubitschek and Goulart to take office for their five-year term in January 1956.

Because Kubitschek entered the presidency under such bitter and delicate circumstances, diligent execution of his campaign promise of "fifty years of progress in five" became paramount for solidifying his national support. Campaign targets were achieved as the production of concrete, steel, energy, and other components of industrial expansion dramatically increased. The automobile industry was created, soon making the country almost self-sufficient in such production. The latter years of the Kubitschek government witnessed economic growth at annual rates averaging over 7 percent. In April 1960 he inaugurated the futuristic and controversial new capital, Brasília, with buildings by Niemeyer and an urban design of Lúcio COSTA, a bravura feat strikingly affirming national accomplishment.

The cost of such progress, however, was inflation. Kubitschek encouraged extensive foreign investment, and the vast market potential of a growing Brazil attracted it. However, declining income from Brazilian exports created a shortage of capital, pressuring inflation. Kubitschek was cooperative in international relations, suggesting Operation Pan American, a hemisphere-wide approach to Latin American problems, to U.S. president Dwight D. Eisenhower. But in 1959 Kubitschek rejected the International Monetary Fund's (IMF) efforts to make him reduce inflation by cutting his economic expansion program. As a result, inflation accelerated. This and charges of graft and favoritism, along with the fact that Kubitschek was constitutionally barred from succeeding himself, enabled the candidate of the opposition, Jânio QUADROS, to win the 1960 presidential election.

Still popular personally, Kubitschek was elected a senator from Goiás the same year. However, with the establishment in 1964 of a military regime, the political rights of Kubitschek were canceled for ten years, thereby ending his plans to return to the presidency in the election of 1965. He went into intermittent exile in Europe or the United States, supporting an unsuccessful Frente Ampla, a broad front of civilian leaders allied across the political spectrum. After 1967 he remained in Brazil, becoming an investment banking executive. He died in 1976 in an automobile accident on a highway between São Paulo and Rio de Janeiro. His funeral procession in Brasília produced one of the greatest popular outpourings of grief in the history of the city, and the military government was forced to decree three days of official mourning.

Although Kubitschek dominated the Brazilian national scene for a relatively brief period, his memory has proved lasting due to a concentration of exceptional personal, economic, political, and cultural factors. Possessed of great ambition and energy, he was able as an administrator to take advantage of economic opportunities resulting from increased Brazilian exports during World War II and then from the resurgence of international capital in the recovery from that war. He represented a generation of Brazilian elites that legitimized itself through modernization based on industrialization and accommodated itself to trade unionism growing from that development. During his presidency there occurred a rare combination of intensive economic production within a fully functioning democratic government. His administration bore, moreover, a cultural style, expressed in architecture, landscape design, sculpture, and even the rhythms of BOSSA NOVA, which

Juscelino Kubitschek de Oliveira. ICONOGRAPHIA.

projected itself as the embodiment of international modernism, giving Brazilians a sense of confidence and promise.

FRANCISCO MEDAGLIA, *Juscelino Kubitschek, President of Brazil: The Life of a Self-Made Man* (1959); FRANCISCO DE ASSIS BARBOSA, *Juscelino Kubitschek: Uma Revisão na Política Brasileira* (1960); JUSCELINO KUBITSCHEK, *Meu Caminho para Brasília,* 3 vols. (1974–1978), and *Por Que Construí Brasília* (1975); MARIA VICTÓRIA BENEVIDES, *O Governo Kubitschek: Desenvolvimento Econômico e Estabilidade Política, 1956–1961* (1976); OSVALDO ORICO, *Confissões do Exílio: JK* (1977); ABELARDO JUREMA, *Juscelino & Jango: PSD & PTB* (1979); CARLOS HEITOR CONY, *JK, Memorial do Exílio* (1982); SÍLVIA PANTOJA and DORA FLAKSMAN, "Kubitschek, Juscelino," in *Dicionário Histórico-Biográfico Brasileiro, 1930–1983,* vol. 2 (1984), pp. 1,698–1,717; EDWARD ANTHONY RIEDINGER, *Como Se Faz um Presidente: A Campanha de J.K.* (1988); ROBERT J. ALEXANDER, *Juscelino Kubitschek and the Development of Brazil* (1991).

EDWARD A. RIEDINGER

See also **Brazil: Political Parties.**

KUMATE RODRÍGUEZ, JESÚS (*b.* 12 November 1924), Mexican health official and medical researcher. A native of Mazatlán, Sinaloa, Kumate graduated from Mexico's Military Medical School (1946), later obtaining a Ph.D. in biomedical sciences in 1963. Kumate taught at both the Military Medical School and the National University, and served as research coordinator of the Children's Hospital, Mexico City, an institution he later directed (1979–1980). In 1974 he was invited to become a member of the National College, and in 1983 the secretary of health appointed him coordinator of the National Institutes of Health for the entire country. He became assistant secretary of health in 1985, and in 1988 President Carlos SALINAS selected Kumate as his secretary of health.

COLEGIO NACIONAL, *Memoria,* vol. 8 (1974), pp. 265–274.

RODERIC AI CAMP

KUNA (CUNA), the spoken language and common name applied to the Tule Indians of Panama and Colombia. There are four principal groups of the Kuna. The most well-known are those who inhabit the San Blas archipelago off the Caribbean shore of Panama. Other groups include the Kuna Brava, in the center of the Darién jungle; the Bayano Kuna, of the Bayano River region of Panama; and those who live in Colombian villages near the Panamanian border.

The Kuna are descendants of Carib peoples. They are physically short, only slightly taller than pygmies. They have bronze skin and black hair, but also have the highest rate of albinism in the world.

The Spanish conquistador Vasco Núñez de BALBOA came into contact with the Kuna in the early sixteenth century, but Spanish cruelty under the subsequent rule of Governor Pedrarias Dávila became a highly signifi-

Kuna Indians in Panama, ca. 1930s. ORGANIZATION OF AMERICAN STATES.

cant part of Kuna mythology. By the seventeenth century the Kuna, as well as other natives along the eastern coast of Central America, were favoring the English and helping them in their struggles against Spain in this region.

In the nineteenth century the Kuna moved from their mainland villages to the coral islands along Panama's east coast. Of the more than 365 islands of the San Blas archipelago, only about fifty are inhabited, with about a hundred more used for coconut and food production.

Property in Kuna society has traditionally been owned and passed on through the female line. Women are also the ones to choose their mates. The principal wealth in Kuna society is based on coconuts, a business that the women normally own and manage. The Kuna did not intermarry with other peoples and have maintained their own strict standards of morals and conduct. During the building of the Panama Canal, the men were contracted in teams for specific periods of labor, but most returned to their home islands when their contract was up.

After a 1925 skirmish with Panamanian police, the comarca (territory) of San Blas became an autonomous region within Panama. Elected Kuna chiefs called saylas preside over council meetings. The Kunas own the land, but the Panamanian government has established an office on the island of El Porvenir, where a government official supervises the village chiefs, pays their salaries, and is the connecting link between the San Blas Kuna and the government in Panama City.

In the twentieth century the Kuna have become notable for their art forms, whose motifs are very similar to those found on gold and ceramics from the Conte

archaeological site in Coclé Province, which date from approximately A.D. 500 to 1100. The Kuna have long worn golden ornaments, but according to legend the atrocities of the Spanish conquistadores caused gold working to become taboo and goldsmiths were prohibited from even landing on the islands. Thereafter, the Kuna purchased gold jewelry from merchants who came to the islands in boats.

The practice of colorful body painting has long been a Kuna trait. In 1680, the buccaneer surgeon Lionel Wafer noted the colors of their body painting as being mostly red, yellow, and blue, depicting "figures of birds, beasts, men and trees or the like." Twentieth-century Kuna are known for their interpretive needlework, used originally on their molas, or blouses. The use of reverse appliqué of Kuna native symbolism, cartoon art, and religious scenes on fine European cottons in solid colors has created an art form sought by major museums and individual collectors. The molas developed from the late nineteenth century forward in imitation of traditional body painting, but the styles and techniques of mola artisans gradually changed. After World War II the colorful molas suddenly burst upon the art scene with unique cartoon images derived from everything from foreign graphic art to domestic political statements, more recently including Christian religious art.

CLYDE E. KEELER, Cuna Indian Art: The Culture and the Craft of Panama's San Blas Islanders (1969); ANN PARKER and AVON NEAL, Molas: Folk Art of the Cuna Indians (1977); MARY W. HELMS, Ancient Panama: Chiefs in Search of Power (1979); JAMES HOWE, The Kuna Gathering: Contemporary Village Politics in Panama (1986).

SUE DAWN McGRADY

LA BREA Y PARIÑAS, since colonial times a tar-producing estate in the province of Talara in northern Peru, which was later developed into the Negritos oil-field, a source of dispute between several Peruvian governments and foreign oil companies until its expropriation by the military government in 1968. Through dubious legal means, Genaro Helguero bought the Hacienda La Brea y Pariñas and then obtained tax exemptions and property rights over surface and sub-soil. In 1888 he sold the property to Herbert Tweddle, who organized the London and Pacific Petroleum Company under British law. In 1913, Standard Oil of New Jersey bought control of the British firm and under Canadian law merged it into the INTERNATIONAL PETRO-LEUM COMPANY. This company exported Peruvian oil at huge profits made possible by advantageous tax deals with the Peruvian government (paying only 6 percent tax on its profits since 1916). The other local and foreign companies that controlled two other important oilfields in northern Peru, Lobitos and Zorritos, paid a higher tax rate. The legal dispute over Negritos was one of the main reasons for President Fernando BELAÚNDE's ouster by a military coup in 1968. According to studies, Peru's economy would have been better off without the presence of the International Petroleum Company.

ADALBERTO PINELO, *The Multinational Corporation as a Force in Latin American Politics: A Case Study of the International Petroleum Company in Peru* (1973); ROSEMARY THORP and GEOFFREY BERTRAM, *Peru, 1890–1977: Growth and Policy in an Open Economy* (1978).

ALFONSO W. QUIROZ

LA CENTINELA, the capital of the CHINCHA kingdom. The archaeological site of La Centinela lies near the modern town of Chincha Baja and near the mouth of the Chincha valley. It consists of a group of impressive adobe compounds that were built during the period of the Chincha kingdom but continued to function during the following period of INCA domination. In the midst of these local architectural compounds the Inca built a compound of their own. While the earlier Chincha construction was of the coursed adobe known as *tapia*, the Inca compound was constructed of adobe bricks. It also contained a rectangular plaza and had the trapezoidal niches and doorways typical of Inca architecture. But alongside the buildings that appear to have served as an Inca palace stood a pyramidal platform more reminiscent of earlier Chincha architecture even though it was constructed of adobe bricks and constituted a formal part of the compound of the dominant Inca. Several of the compounds built of *tapia* had been modified with adobe bricks, in one case extensively, indicating Inca alteration of existing structures. Scholars suspect that these local compounds were related to Chincha social units and were the settings for important ceremonies and rituals, probably including initiation, marriage, and other rites of passage. Archaeological evidence of extensive manufacturing or other purely economic activities has not been found.

Differences in Inca architectural modification to the Chincha compounds may have been related to differences in the ways the Inca supported and controlled various groups. Though they exerted control indirectly, the Inca were obviously not content to leave the mechanisms by which they carried it out entirely in local hands. Elements of Inca identity were made evident at many points in the social and political ceremonies that held together the upper levels of local society.

La Centinela was probably part of a broader network of population centers and other kinds of sites in the Chincha valley. These were linked by a system of roads, one of which was part of the Inca road system during the times of the Inca Empire. The nearby sites of Tambo de Mora and La Cumbe were perhaps visualized as part of the same large complex during pre-Columbian times. La Cumbe served mainly as a cemetery.

MAX UHLE, ''Explorations at Chincha,'' in *University of California Publications in American Archaeology and Ethnology* 21, no. 2 (1924): 55–94.

CRAIG MORRIS

See also **Archaeology; Indians.**

LA CIUDADELA, a fortress in the center of Mexico City. It was the scene of many military rebellions. Antonio González Velázquez built it in 1793 as the Royal Cigar and Cigarette Works. It obtained its military features from Miguel Costansó and Ignacio Castera when in 1808 they finished transforming it into a gunpowder storage facility for the Spanish army. The rebel leader José María MORELOS was imprisoned in La Ciudadela in 1815. In the period of SANTA ANNA (late 1820s–mid-1850s) it served as the bastion for the generals in revolt, and its importance continued during The REFORM (1857–1860) and the French intervention. In 1871, Sóstenes Rocha seized it in order to crush a rebellion against Benito JUÁREZ. In 1913, Manuel Mondragón and Félix DÍAZ rebelled against Francisco MADERO and for ten days (DECENA TRÁGICA) bombarded the center city and principal neighborhoods from La Ciudadela. The treaty that the rebels signed there with their adversary, General Victoriano HUERTA, was backed by U.S. Ambassador Henry Lane WILSON and resulted in the assassination of Madero and the dictatorship of Huerta from 1913 to 1914.

After the Revolution, La Ciudadela was declared a historic monument and became a center of fine culture.

In its surroundings began the student movement of 1968. Between 1987 and 1991 it was refurbished under the direction of Abraham Zabludovsky and today houses the Mexican Library.

La Ciudadela: Biblioteca México (1991); ANTONIO SABORIT et al., *La Ciudadela de fuego: A ochenta años de la decena trájica* (1993).

J. E. PACHECO

LA DEMOCRACIA, a town in the Pacific coastal department of Escuintla, Guatemala, notable for its central park, which is adorned with sculptures from the site of Monte Alto and contains an archaeological museum.

The site of Monte Alto, on the Pacific coast of Guatemala, has about fifty earthern mounds and is notable for its colossal stone heads, full-figure boulder sculptures, and full-round potbelly sculptures, which most likely date between 500 and 200 B.C. The boulder heads, which are bald, have closed eyes and closed mouths, indicating that they represent deceased individuals. These heads appear to depict severed trophy heads of elites. Full-figure boulders have expansive bodies, their limbs are wrapped around them, and their faces are similar to the boulder heads. The full-round potbelly sculptures are smaller and squatter than the boulder sculptures, but otherwise have similar stylistic features.

Excavations at Monte Alto revealed that sculptures had specific placements. One sculpture was located on the central north-south axis of the site. Colossal stone heads and human-effigy boulder sculptures were found in irregular rows on the east and west sides of the mound group; these may not have been their original placements.

Stylistic affinities of these sculptures with those of the OLMECS, combined with their comparative crudity, suggest that they might predate the Olmec (1200–500 B.C.). They were considered evidence that the beginning of Mesoamerican civilization was in the Pacific lowlands of Guatemala. Secure dating of potbellied figures in El Salvador shows that they postdate the Olmec, thus suggesting that they are a regional development outside of the Olmec heartland.

JEFFREY PARSONS, ''Excavation at Monte Alto, Escuintla, Guatemala,'' in *National Geographic Society Research Reports* (1976), pp. 325–332, and ''Post-Olmec Stone Sculpture: The Olmec-Izapan Transition on the Southern Pacific Coast and Highlands,'' in *The Olmec and Their Neighbors: Essays in Memory of Matthew W. Stirling,* edited by Elizabeth P. Benson (1979), pp. 257–288; Arthur Demarest, *The Archaeology of Santa Leticia and the Rise of Maya Civilization,* Middle American Research Institute (Tulane University) Publication 52 (1986).

EUGENIA J. ROBINSON

See also **Mesoamerica.**

LA ESCALERA, CONSPIRACY OF. In December 1843 Esteban Santa Cruz de Oviedo, a planter with major holdings in the western province of Matanzas, Cuba, claimed to have uncovered a conspiracy to promote revolt by the slaves of Cuba's sugar plantation heartland. The authorities tortured suspects, then executed the "confessed" ringleaders. Captain-General Leopoldo O'Donnell, Cuba's new chief executive, doubting that all the guilty had been found, widened the circle of investigation. Persecution and torture spread throughout much of western Cuba in the first months of 1844. Officials eventually concluded that a vast revolutionary conspiracy involving slaves, free people of color, Cuban-born whites, and foreigners existed. They implicated Domingo DEL MONTE and José de la LUZ Y CABALLERO, two of Cuba's preeminent dissident intellectuals; they convicted in absentia David Turnbull, an abolitionist and former British consul in Havana, of being the '"prime mover" behind the conspiracy; and they executed the prominent free mulatto poet PLÁCIDO for being the leader of a revolutionary faction of people of color. By the end of 1844, thousands of people of color, free and slave, had been banished, imprisoned, tortured, or executed; many others had simply disappeared. The alleged conspiracy acquired the name La Escalera—the Ladder—from the principal instrument to which suspects were bound before interrogation accompanied by the lash. The year 1844 has gone down in Cuban history as el Año del Cuero, the Year of the Lash.

Generations of Cuban scholars have debated the reality of the conspiracy. Although it was clearly exaggerated by unscrupulous officials who wanted to silence dissidence, by venal whites who wanted to despoil rising members of Cuba's free colored class, and by panic-stricken slaveholders who feared a replay of the Haitian Revolution, La Escalera probably existed as a conjunction of several different conspiracies. Each drew energy from British abolitionism; each had distinct cores involving whites, slaves, and free people of color; each overlapped, if only in some cases, at the margin; and each expanded or contracted at different points between 1841 and 1844.

La Escalera decimated the leadership of Cuba's free colored class and encouraged many Cuban whites to look more favorably upon Cuba's annexation by the United States. It was the last major act of collective resistance by Cuba's people of color before their participation in the TEN YEARS' WAR.

DAVID R. MURRAY, *Odious Commerce* (1980), chaps. 8 and 9; ENILDO A. GARCÍA, *Cuba: Plácido, poeta mulato de la emancipación, 1809–1844* (1986); ROBERT L. PAQUETTE, *Sugar Is Made with Blood* (1988).

ROBERT L. PAQUETTE

LA GALGADA, Peruvian site of ruins dating from the Late Preceramic period (3000–2000 B.C.). Andean South America is one of the regions where civilization arose independently before 3000 B.C. The ruins of La Galgada (Rockslide) have provided some of the richest evidence in Peru of early cultural development. Located 72 miles from the coast on the banks of the Tablachaca, a tributary of the Santa River, the largest river on Peru's Pacific coast, the town was a center on routes connecting the coastal desert, the highlands, and the Amazon Basin. Isolation and aridity account for the well-preserved buildings, irrigation canals and field patterns, and burial tombs containing offerings of gourd vessels, baskets, cotton and bast cloth, stonework, shell and turquoise jewelry, and even feathers. The similarity of the material from La Galgada to that from such contemporary sites as KOTOSH, Huaricoto, and Huaca Prieta reveals a widespread shared culture before the introduction of pottery about 2000 B.C.

The earliest excavated structures, about 2800 B.C., are small circular or rectangular temples with plastered stone walls painted white and flat roofs. The rituals seem to have included putting food offerings in the small central fire pit. The temple chambers were converted into tombs by building a stone roof supported by a massive stone column. The tomb was buried under earth fill, leaving a shaft to the surface, and a new temple was built on top. Four levels of such temple–tombs are known, spanning the period 2600–2000 B.C.

Cotton, the principal crop, was used to make cloth by pre-loom techniques, much of it evidently for trade. Several dye colors are among the oldest specimens known. With the introduction of the heddle loom along with pottery about 2000 B.C., there were style changes in cloth, jewelry, and architecture, heralding the CHAVÍN style, which dominated northern Peru for the next two millennia.

TERENCE GRIEDER and ALBERTO BUENO MENDOZA, "Ceremonial Architecture at La Galgada," in *Early Ceremonial Architecture in the Andes,* edited by Christopher B. Donnan (1985), pp. 93–109; TERENCE GRIEDER, "Preceramic and Initial Period Textiles from La Galgada, Peru," in *The Junius B. Bird Conference on Andean Textiles,* edited by Ann Pollard Rowe (1986), pp. 19–29; TERENCE GRIEDER, ALBERTO BUENO MENDOZA, C. EARLE SMITH, JR., and ROBERT M. MALINA, *La Galgada, Peru* (1988).

TERENCE GRIEDER

LA LIBERTADORA REVOLUTION (1901–1903), the last in a series of civil conflicts that plagued Venezuela during the nineteenth century. When CIPRIANO took power in 1899, he began a process of military and political transformation that tended to centralize power and eliminate the political factionalism that was typical of the nineteenth century. The urgent need for financial resources and the chaotic budgetary situation of the country pitted Castro against the most notable bankers, creating a climate of tension which led to the revolution.

The uprising was financed and organized by Manuel Antonio Matos, an important Caracas banker, backed by the New York and Bermúdez Company, whose interests in the asphalt business were being affected by Castro's rule, as well as by important caudillos in the country. The revolution broke out in 1901 and rapidly spread throughout the entire country. The last battle took place in 1903. The government's triumph consolidated the politics of centralism and ended the politics of *caudillismo*, which had characterized late nineteenth-century politics in Venezuela.

ELEAZAR LÓPEZ CONTRERAS, *Páginas para la historia militar de Venezuela* (1945); ORRAY THURBER, *Orígenes del capital norteamericano en Venezuela* (1983); and Inés Quintero, *El ocaso de una estirpe: la centralización restauradora y el fin de los caudillos históricos* (1989).

INÉS QUINTERO

LA OROYA, town and mineral smelting center in the central highlands of Peru (1990 population 33,594). At 12,200 feet, La Oroya stands at the crossroads of the central RAILWAY and HIGHWAY systems connecting the MINING center of Cerro de Pasco and the commercial city of Huancayo with the country's capital, Lima. The railway reached La Oroya in 1893 and a year later the CERRO DE PASCO CORPORATION, formed with U.S. investment capital (Guggenheim interests), began to establish a smelting complex to treat minerals from Cerro de Pasco, Morococha, and other nearby mining areas. This gave the Cerro de Pasco Corporation the technological advantage to displace foreign and domestic competition. The smelter was upgraded by 1922. Pollution from the smelter modified the agrarian landscape and made possible the purchase of rich pasture lands formerly owned by the native Cattlemen's Society of Junín. With the nationalization of mining interests between 1968 and 1975, La Oroya smelter was managed by a state company.

FLORENCIA MALLON, *The Defense of Community in Peru's Central Highlands: Peasant Struggle and Capitalist Transition, 1860–1940* (1983); ELIZABETH DORE, *The Peruvian Mining Industry: Growth, Stagnation, and Crisis* (1988).

ALFONSO W. QUIROZ

LA PAZ, city and region of Bolivia, located in the western part of the nation; the city is situated some 50 miles southeast of Lake Titicaca. Covering an area of 51,732 square miles, the department of La Paz contains four distinct ecological zones: altiplano (12,000 feet or higher), high valley (12,000–8,000 feet), *yungas* or steep valleys (8,000–4,000 feet), and the Amazon basin (4,000–1,000 feet). Each is characterized by distinct agricultural production. Potatoes and barley are grown on the altiplano, corn in the valleys, and tropical fruits at lower elevations. The city of La Paz is located in a high valley zone and in 1976 contained a population of 635,000 out of a total departmental population of 1,465,000.

When Alonso de Mendoza founded the city of La Paz on 20 October 1548, he chose a site amid densely populated AYMARA villages. The tribute lists of the first *encomiendas* (1560) showed why La Paz attracted Spanish settlers. Items delivered to the *encomenderos* included wool in the form of manufactured garments, llamas, sheep, pigs, corn, salt, fish, eggs, potatoes, coca, and cotton. *Encomiendas* also regularly supplied labor for the Spanish farms near the city and for the alluvial goldfields in the province of Larecaja.

After the demise of the *encomienda*, Aymaras continued to be important components of the Spanish economic system. The large number of surviving villagers on the altiplano paid tribute in coin derived from their labor at the Potosí mine and the marketing of their agricultural surplus in urban centers. Other villagers migrated to the Spanish-owned haciendas either on the altiplano or in the valley zones, where they became resident COLONOS fulfilling obligations of labor and personal service to the owners. By the 1830s, out of a total Indian population of 500,000 in the department of La Paz, 70 percent resided in Indian villages and 30 percent on haciendas.

For the Spaniards, the city of La Paz served not only as a repository of goods from the immediate area but also as a trade center on the route from Potosí to Lima and an administrative center for Spanish authorities. Because of those functions, the city grew from a population of almost 6,000 in 1586 to 30,000 by independence in 1825.

During the colonial period only two uprisings occurred: an artisan tax revolt of 1661 led by Antonio Gallardo and an Indian uprising of 1781 led by Julián Apaza TÚPAC CATARI. After the Indian siege had been lifted by Spanish troops in 1781, and rebel leaders had been executed, the memory of the rebellion reminded Indians and creoles alike of the deep divisions in colonial society.

During the early independence period, 1825–1880, regional caudillos, many of whom received their military training in the republican armies, dipped their hands generously into the treasury of La Paz, which was the largest in Bolivia because of Indian tribute payments. Thus, although Sucre was the official capital, La Paz became the de facto center of government. Once in power, however, caudillos altered colonial social relations very little.

In 1880 silver barons from southern Bolivia seized political control and stressed export-led development. They not only opened trade, built railroads, and established banks but also removed government protection for Indian communities and sponsored hacienda expansion. In the department of La Paz between 1880 and 1916, approximately 30 percent of Indian communal householders sold their land to elite residents of the city of La Paz. Meanwhile, La Paz became the official "second" capital of Bolivia, confirmed in the Federalist War of 1899. After the railroad reached the city in 1905, La Paz became the terminus of the import trade and the business headquarters for banks and exporters involved in the rubber and tin trade. By 1942 the city of La Paz had about 287,000 inhabitants and included a large, politically active middle class.

La Paz with Mount Illimani in the background. PHOTO BY PETER MC FARREN.

During the 1940s, the National Revolutionary Movement (MNR) galvanized the latent political strength of the urban middle class when the party branded the government a tool of the tin mine owners. The 1952 revolution took place in the streets of La Paz and ushered in a reform government. But while MNR leaders expropriated the largest tin mines, implemented an agrarian reform that returned land to the tillers, and opened the electorate to all adults, other demographic and political forces proved stronger than the reform program. Despite having legal access to land, Indians increasingly moved into the city because population growth exceeded available land resources. Simultaneously, the government enlarged the bureaucracy and expanded state-run enterprises, and private, small-scale capitalists developed a manufacturing sector, particularly in textiles and food processing. Under these conditions, the city population increased to 655,000 by 1976. Thus, alongside modern office buildings and cosmopolitan hotels, Indians have their own markets and form the majority of inhabitants in certain sectors of the city.

CHOLOS (mestizos) comprise the largest portion of the city's population. They are defined by their cultural characteristics. *Cholos* speak both Spanish and Aymara, dress in a Western style, and participate in the national economy and political system. Their jobs and incomes vary greatly. They are waiters, truck drivers, merchants, mechanics, store owners, factory employees, white-collar workers, construction workers, and artisans of all sorts. *Cholos* comprise the rank and file of urban political parties and staff the government's bureaucracy and

army. They are proud of their Indian heritage but do not consider themselves Indian. They value education highly, but they are not unified politically.

La Paz is a multi-ethnic city in which Indian and Western cultures collide daily. The outcome of these cultural collisions is not so much the blending of cultures as it is the creation of distinctions and the establishment of boundaries among social groups.

ALBERTO CRESPO R., *El corregimiento de La Paz 1548–1560* (1972); WOLFGANG SCHOOP, *Ciudades bolivianas* (1981), 47–89; HERBERT S. KLEIN, *Bolivia: The Evolution of a Multi-Ethnic Society* (1982).

ERWIN P. GRIESHABER

See also **Bolivia: Political Parties.**

LA PLATA, an island approximately 5.5 square miles in size, lying just south of the equator, 14 miles off the central coast of Ecuador. Archaeological evidence indicates that the island was an important offertory and religious center during the pre-Columbian era. Findings of Valdivia, Machalilla, Chorrera, Bahía, Jama-Coaque, Manteño, and Inca pottery at various sites around the island indicate that it was utilized from the Early Formative Period (around 2450 B.C.) through the Inca conquest.

Large quantities of broken clay figurines, engraved stones, and processed *Spondylus* (thorny oyster) shell have been found at archaeological sites on La Plata. The figurines exhibit a wide range of styles and are generally of crude manufacture. The nature of the deposits suggest that they were ritually smashed and left as offerings. The engraved stones are found in similar offertory contexts. *Spondylus* shell was highly valued by Andean cultures throughout the pre-Columbian era. The amount of *Spondylus* shell found on La Plata suggests that it may have been an important source of this material, which in turn may have contributed to the ritual significance of the island.

In 1892 George A. Dorsey was the first to undertake archaeological investigations on La Plata. His discovery of an Inca burial on the island marks the northernmost limits of Inca expansion along the Pacific coast. The grave was found to contain a wealth of materials including gold, silver, and copper figurines, a gold bowl, *tupus* (metal pins), and Inca polychrome pottery. The type of figurines found in this burial is known from only a limited number of sites around the empire, most of which were of extreme ritual importance to the Inca. It has been suggested that the burial on La Plata may have been associated with the state rite of *capac hucha*, which involved the ceremonial sacrifice of children and served to define the sacred and political boundaries of the Inca Empire.

GEORGE A. DORSEY, *Archaeological Investigations on the Island of La Plata, Ecuador* (1901), Field Columbian Museum, Anthropological Series, Publication 56, vol. 2 (1901), and JORGE MARCOS and PRESLEY NORTON, "Interpretación sobre la arqueología de la Isla de La Plata," in *Miscelánea antropológica ecuatoriana* 1 (1981): 136–154.

TAMARA L. BRAY

LA QUEMADA, one of the principal settlements of Mesoamerica's northern periphery, located in central Zacatecas, Mexico, on the grasslands bordering the eastern slope of the Sierra Madre Occidental. The main occupation of La Quemada apparently dates to the Epiclassic period (A.D. 600–900), although earlier and later dates have been recovered. The site was established atop the dominant peak in the valley, a readily defensible location. By construction of numerous terraces, many of which are interconnected by stairways and causeways, the peak was transformed into an imposing architectural space. It contains perhaps fifty patio complexes, one central ball court that is among the longest in MESOAMERICA, at least two smaller ones, thirteen or more pyramids, a large colonnaded hall, and a massive wall that encloses the central parts of the site that are not protected by natural cliffs. In the valley below are numerous present-day villages, many of which are linked by a system of ancient roads that centered on La Quemada. Archaeologists assume that La Quemada was the elite administrative and religious center of this group of settlements.

In virtually all parts of the site excavated to date, extensive human skeletal deposits have been found, including piles of disarticulated, cut, and burned bone,

suspended skulls and long bones, and subfloor burials. Some of the bones are probably those of revered ancestors, and others belonged to enemies. All apparently were displayed to symbolize a social order rooted in violence.

Archaeologists have varying opinions about the causes of growth and decline of La Quemada, as well as whether it should be included in the Chalchihuites culture. Some perceive colonization by more sophisticated societies to the south as an important force, whereas others see the developments as indigenous. The new chronological evidence that places La Quemada's occupation within the Epiclassic Period does not support the previously popular notion that La Quemada was built to serve as an outpost for TOLTEC (A.D. 900–1150) trade in turquoise with the American Southwest. By the time the Toltecs were in their ascendancy, La Quemada was apparently abandoned or much reduced in size. The late dates obtained from the nucleus of the site may represent its occasional, postoccupational use as a camp or shrine.

J. CHARLES KELLEY, "Settlement Patterns in North-Central Mexico," in *Prehistoric Settlement Patterns in the New World*, edited by Gordon R. Willey (1956), pp. 128–139; PHIL C. WEIGAND, "The Prehistory of the State of Zacatecas: An Interpretation," in *Anthropology* 2, no. 1 (1978): 67–87, and no. 2 (1978): 103–117; MARIE-ARETI HERS, *Los toltecas en tierras chichimecas* (1989); PETER JIMÉNEZ BETTS, "Perspectivas sobre la arqueología de Zacatecas," in *Arqueología* 5 (1989): 7–50; CHARLES D. TROMBOLD, "A Reconsideration of the Chronology for the La Quemada Portion of the Northern Mesoamerican Frontier," in *American Antiquity* 55, no. 2 (1990): 308–323; BEN A. NELSON, J. ANDREW DARLING, and DAVID A. KICE, "Mortuary Practices and the Social Order at La Quemada, Zacatecas, Mexico," in *Latin American Antiquity* 3, no. 4 (1992): 298–315.

BEN A. NELSON

LA SALLE, RENÉ-ROBERT CAVELIER, SIEUR DE (*b.* 22 November 1643; *d.* 19 March 1687), French explorer. A native of Rouen, France, La Salle was educated by the Jesuits but left the order and went to Canada in 1666 to enter the fur trade. In 1679 he built and launched the first sailing vessel to ply the Great Lakes. By canoe, he descended the Mississippi River to its mouth in 1682, claiming for France all the lands of its drainage.

La Salle envisioned a warm-water port on the Gulf of Mexico to serve his commercial aims and French designs of empire. Returning to France, he won royal support for a voyage to the Mississippi through the Gulf to establish a colony on the lower river. He sailed from La Rochelle on 24 July 1684. Because of geographical uncertainty, he missed the mouth of the Mississippi and landed his 280 colonists at Texas's Matagorda Bay on 20 February 1685. Realizing his error, he sought his post on the Illinois River by land, but was slain by a disenchanted follower near the Trinity River in eastern Texas.

La Salle was responsible for opening the Mississippi Valley for development. His Gulf of Mexico expedition sparked a renewal of Spanish exploration in the Gulf that led to Spanish occupation of eastern Texas and Pensacola Bay. Because of La Salle, the United States asserted a claim to Texas as part of the Louisiana Purchase, giving rise to a boundary dispute with Spain that lasted until 1819.

FRANCIS PARKMAN, *La Salle and the Discovery of the Great West* (repr. 1963); PATRICIA K. GALLOWAY, ed., *La Salle and His Legacy: Frenchmen and Indians in the Lower Mississippi Valley* (1982); ROBERT S. WEDDLE, ed., *La Salle, the Mississippi, and the Gulf: Three Primary Documents* (1987); ROBERT S. WEDDLE, *The French Thorn: Rival Explorers in the Spanish Sea, 1682–1762* (1991), esp. pp. 3–84.

ROBERT S. WEDDLE

See also **Explorers and Exploration.**

LA SERENA, city of 106,617 inhabitants (1987), on the mouth of the Elqui River and on the Pan-American Highway some 265 miles north of Santiago, Chile, and capital of the Coquimbo region (1990 population 486,493). The city was founded in 1544 by Juan Bohón, one of Pedro de Valdivia's lieutenants, to secure the land route toward southern Peru. It became a center of the mining activities conducted in the southern part of the NORTE CHICO and of the fruit and brandy industry of the Elqui Valley. The well-protected port of Coquimbo, 10 miles to the south, has served as its outlet to the sea. Overwhelmed by the political hegemony of Santiago and the commercial prowess of Valparaíso, La Serena has become a placid provincial city without major ambitions, beautified by the public works with which past president Gabriel GONZÁLEZ VIDELA commemorated his city of birth.

GUIDO VELIZ CANTUARIAS, "Conurbación La Serena–Coquimbo," in *Revista Geográfica* (Mexico) 111 (1990): 219–258.

CÉSAR N. CAVIEDES

LA SERNA, JOSÉ DE (*b.* 1770; *d.* 6 July 1832), last viceroy of Peru and commander of the Spanish forces at the BATTLE OF AYACUCHO (1824). A native of Jerez de la Frontera, Spain, he was a professional soldier who fought in the defense of Ceuta in 1790, and later against England and France. He was sent to Peru in 1816 as one of the generals under Viceroy Joaquín de la Pezuela. He criticized the latter's decision to hold on to LIMA at all costs, and in 1821, following Pezuela's overthrow, he was acclaimed viceroy by his fellow commanders. He negotiated briefly with General José de SAN MARTÍN, especially over the idea of placing Peru under a crowned head. The negotiations came to naught, and in July 1821, he abandoned Lima and took his army to the highlands, where he established his seat of command in HUANCAYO and later in CUZCO. On 9 December 1824, on a plain near Ayacucho, he led the last royal army in South America against General Antonio José de SUCRE,

Simón Bolívar's chief lieutenant. La Serna was defeated, and with that loss Spain's empire in the New World, save its Caribbean possessions, disappeared. La Serna was taken prisoner and returned to Spain, where he received the title Count of the Andes. He subsequently held the post of captain-general of GRANADA (1831). He died in Seville.

RUBÉN VARGAS UGARTE, *Historia general del Perú*, vol. 6, *Emancipación (1816–1825)* (1966); TIMOTHY E. ANNA, *The Fall of the Royal Government in Peru* (1979).

JEFFREY KLAIBER

LA VENTA, an important center of the archaeological OLMEC culture located on a swamp island 30 miles west of Villahermosa, Tabasco, Mexico. Excavations conducted at La Venta in the 1940s and 1950s have played a pivotal role in shaping current interpretations of Olmec culture. Dating to as early as 1150 B.C., La Venta appears to have reached its apogee between 800 and 400 B.C. Originally interpreted as an empty ceremonial center, the site is now known to have supported a considerable population of fishermen and agriculturalists who made their homes on the banks of the many creeks and rivers that surrounded the site center. The ceremonial precinct

Colossal head from La Venta. Olmec, 1000–600 B.C. PHOTO BY LEE BOLTIN.

of La Venta was dominated by a court enclosed by a fence constructed of basalt columns and a 33-foot-high great Pyramid resembling a fluted cone. Scattered throughout La Venta were a large number of stone monuments, including four colossal heads. The majority of these monuments are currently displayed at La Venta park in Villahermosa. During the 1950s the site of La Venta was in danger of destruction due to both the construction of a nearby petroleum refinery and the encroachment of the modern town of La Venta. The site is now protected as an archaeological park.

PHILIP DRUCKER, ROBERT F. HEIZER, and ROBERT J. SQUIER, *Excavations at La Venta, Tabasco* (1959); MICHAEL D. COE, *America's First Civilization* (1968); REBECCA GONZÁLEZ LAUCK, "Proyecto arqueológico La Venta," in *Arqueología* 4 (1988): 121–165; WILLIAM F. RUST and ROBERT J. SHARER, "Olmec Settlement Data from La Venta, Tabasco, Mexico," in *Science* 242 (1988): 102–104.

F. KENT REILLY III

LABARCA HUBERTSON, AMANDA (*b.* 5 December 1886; *d.* 1975), Chilean educator and feminist. Born in Santiago to Onofre and Sabina Pinto, Labarca studied at the Pedagogic Institute of the University of Chile in Santiago, at Columbia University in New York, and at the Sorbonne in Paris. She married educator and politician Guillermo Labarca Hubertson, a Radical Party activist who was minister of justice and education during the first presidency of Arturo Alessandri. Amanda Labarca taught most of her life and was active in the Radical Party. Her books on women's issues include *A dónde va la mujer?* (Whither Women?, 1934) and *Feminismo contemporáneo* (Contemporary Feminism, 1947). Labarca worked in the women's suffrage movement and was president of Mujeres de Chile (Chilean Women). A devoted secondary school teacher, she also served as director of a high school and later taught courses on education at the University of Chile. She wrote important books about education, including *Realidades y problemas de nuestra enseñanza* (Realities and Problems in Chilean Education, 1953), *La escuela secundaria en los Estados Unidos* (Secondary Schools in the United States, 1919), and *Historia de la enseñanza en Chile* (History of Chilean Education, 1939). Labarca also wrote essays and fiction during her early years, including *La lámpara maravillosa* (1921) and *Impresiones de juventud* (1909). With a handful of Latin American women, Labarca played a prominent role in focusing attention on women's issues and was an active participant in international feminist congresses during the first half of the twentieth century.

BIBLIOTECA DEL CONGRESO, CHILE, *Amanda Labarca: bibliografía selectiva* (1983); ROBERTO MUNIZAGA AGUIRRE, *Educatores chilenos de ayer y de hoy*, vol. 5 (1983–1992); JORDI FUENTES et al., *Diccionario histórico de Chile*, 10th ed. (1989).

GEORGETTE MAGASSY DORN

See also **Feminism.**

LABASTIDA Y DÁVALOS, PELAGIO ANTONIO DE (*b.* 1816; *d.* 1891), bishop of Puebla, archbishop of Mexico, opponent of the Reform. Born in Zamora, Michoacán, Labastida was ordained in 1839. He became rector of the seminary in Morelia and governor of the diocese in the early 1850s, and was bishop of Puebla from 1855 to 1863. Labastida protested against President Ignacio COMONFORT's 31 March 1856 decree punishing the Puebla clergy for the rebellion of Zacapoaxtla, which he had not supported, and the loss of the city to the Conservatives. Banished from Mexico, he went to Rome and became a strong opponent of liberalism and the Reform movement. Labastida returned with the FRENCH INTERVENTION, and on 21 June 1863 General Élie-Frédéric Forey appointed him to the three-man executive power. On 17 November Marshal François BAZAINE removed him as an obstacle to French efforts to find a compromise with moderate Liberals. Labastida opposed Maximilian's ecclesiastical policy, which sought to conciliate Liberal opinion by upholding the disamortization (the transfer of corporate properties to private ownership) policies of the period 1856–1863. Exiled in 1867 by JUÁREZ, he attended the First Vatican Council (1869–1870) in Rome. He was allowed to return to Mexico in 1871 and died in Oacalco, Morelos.

JAN BAZANT, *Alienation of Church Wealth in Mexico: Social and Economic Aspects of the Liberal Revolution, 1856–1875*, translated and edited by Michael P. Costeloe (1971); MICHAEL P. COSTELOE, *Church and State in Independent Mexico: A Study of the Patronage Debate, 1821–1857* (1978).

BRIAN HAMNETT

LABOR MOVEMENTS. The history of organized labor in Latin America is rich and varied. From the mid-nineteenth century to the present, workers have sought to further their collective interest by forming unions, by taking direct action, by supporting friendly candidates, and by forming their own political groupings. These efforts have met with uneven success, although at times workers have wrested concessions, willingly or not, from their employers and played an important role in shaping national history. Overall, labor's trajectory can be divided into roughly three somewhat overlapping periods. During the first period, spanning roughly 1850–1870 to the 1930s, workers' organizations emerged. Workers organized their first significant collective actions and, for the most part, took a marked oppositional and apolitical stance toward the state and toward both the dominant agrarian and the emerging industrial elites. During the second period, covering the 1920s through the decades after World War II, labor became increasingly incorporated into the political and economic equation, and political parties formed that catered to organized labor and workers but often sought to control both, although not always successfully. Finally, the 1960s to the present make up a third period, when the traditional labor movement lost much of its power owing to military takeovers and the imposition of neoliberal economic policies.

THE EMERGENCE OF WORKERS' ORGANIZATIONS
Sometime after 1850, urban workers emerged as a group demanding notice in most Latin American societies, although the population remained predominantly rural. This phenomenon coincided with Latin America's entrance into the world economy as an exporter of primary products and importer of manufactured goods, which resulted in a growth of local industry and of urban areas. Rail, port, and mine workers were among the first to organize, although artisans preceded them in many cases. Transport, dock, and mine workers could strike serious blows at local economies by blocking exports and/or imports. Although such action in the export sector drew immediate hostile attention from the state, workers sometimes managed considerable gains through concerted action.

In the rapidly growing cities, there was a large body of artisans who, under pressures from the increasing subordination of labor to the modern large factory, often banded together. With some exceptions, such as the Brazilian textile industries, most enterprises remained small (less than five people), as did the percentage of factory workers within the total numbers of salaried individuals. A modern industrial proletariat really formed only after 1930. Textile factories usually represented the largest enterprises, but flour mills and meatpacking plants in Argentina also employed several hundred people, as did mining companies in Mexico and Chile. Construction, which was at best part-time or seasonal work, also provided considerable employment.

Obstacles Many factors, however, hindered organizing. In most countries, a substantial jobless pool existed. In Buenos Aires, 10,000 men might appear for the morning shape-up at the docks. São Paulo imported immigrants for the coffee plantations, and the Argentine government recruited in Europe. Competition kept wages close to survival level and jobs at a premium, but skilled workers fared much better. Many immigrants, particularly in the period 1880–1910 in the more dynamic Southern Cone economies, for example, thought that they could advance from worker to owner to entrepreneur. Just enough did so to keep the hope alive, although opportunities closed off as industry demanded more capital and technology after 1900. Local bourgeoisies proved intransigent toward workers' demands and organization. These attitudes stemmed from the competitiveness of relatively small industrial establishments and from the fact that owing to lack of mechanization, the wage bill represented a hefty percentage of costs. Ideological and institutional coercion had not yet fully developed, and so repression often proved to be the standard response of owners and the state to workers' movements. Agrarian elites, not always directly concerned with urban affairs, agreed that repression was the best answer to agitation.

Foreign ownership of most major export industries (railroads in Argentina, mines in Chile and Mexico, as well as important textile plants in Mexico and Peru, for example) served as a rallying point for workers, particularly native ones. While workers in foreign enterprises occasionally won a sympathetic hearing from local governments, in most cases the state defended foreign capital as fiercely as local capital. In Brazil, where planters became involved in industrial and commercial activities after the 1890s, a state policy of repression emerged, although its ferocity varied from area to area. Elsewhere, when workers did not directly threaten the export sector, they sometimes could avoid immediate state action. Nevertheless, many instances of heavy repression mark the period up to 1930, including massacres after strikes in Veracruz at the Orizaba (1906) and Río Blanco (1907) textile mills and the mining areas around Iquique, Chile (1907). Numerous workers and their families lost their lives in these encounters, perhaps more than a thousand in the latter incident.

Other factors pressured workers and their organizations. Governments protected strikebreakers, banned and forcefully dispersed meetings, closed union halls, shut down working-class newspapers, and used agents provocateurs. On the pretext that foreigners lay behind growing labor unrest, Argentina, Brazil, Chile, Cuba, and Uruguay all passed laws allowing for expulsion of foreign-born persons, who formed a significant part of working-class leadership, for disturbing the social peace. The first labor laws appeared before 1920, many designed to control rather than protect workers, but also arising from Catholic social action, which advocated Sunday rest and protection for women and children. Exceptionally, in Uruguay, President José BATLLE Y ORDÓÑEZ (1903–1907, 1911–1915) passed comprehensive social legislation, including social services and protective measures, as part of his larger program, which courted popular support to counter the viselike grip of the old agrarian oligarchy.

In countries with the most advanced economies, immigrants, mostly Italians and Spaniards (Portuguese in Brazil), formed the bulk of the urban working class. In Argentina, Uruguay, and southern Brazil, for example, this foreign influence had numerous consequences. Some immigrants brought previous labor movement experience, although most newcomers possessed little political consciousness. Many immigrants wanted only to make money and return home and so steered clear of potentially troublesome activities. A refusal by many to become citizens hurt strategies that depended upon working-class votes. Ethnic diversity led to rivalries between foreigners and between foreigners and nationals. Those born abroad became subject to nationalistic campaigns and right-wing jingoism personified in such paramilitary right-wing organizations as the Argentine Liga Patriótica, which emerged after 1910.

Accomplishments Workers achieved much before 1930. Living and working conditions helped mobilize

367

people. Workers lived in abysmal circumstances even compared with salaried or middle-sector employees. Lack of social services and extensive slums were prevalent and led to alarming public health problems. But large numbers of workers crowded together helped build a certain sense of solidarity at home as well as at work. Working-class districts, such as La Boca in Buenos Aires or Brás in São Paulo, grew into militant centers of activity. Workers in mining camps, mill towns, and plantations developed a similar affinity, often leading to organization. Everywhere job conditions remained difficult. Owners imposed draconian work rules and applied them arbitrarily. Work hours totaled as much as twelve to sixteen hours a day, six days a week. Few safety measures existed, and occupational diseases represented a serious threat in many industries. Employers fired workers almost at will, particularly if they resisted industrial discipline. Most workers experienced unstable work histories. The average worker had little or no control over his or her own fate in the labor market, but gravitated both geographically and sectorally to where jobs existed or were rumored to exist. Many workers set up their own small enterprises, often failing and returning to the status of employee. A fortunate few, however, succeeded, giving rise to the proverbial immigrant success story.

ANARCHOSYNDICALISM

Anarchists or utopian socialists controlled the first attempts at organization. Gradually, however, anarchosyndicalism emerged as the dominant tendency among activists. All shades of anarchists believed in confronting the state and not participating in traditional politics. Later, there emerged a syndicalist current that assigned primacy to unions but concentrated upon immediate economic gains. Strongest in Argentina and Brazil, syndicalists negotiated with governments when necessary. A reformist socialism, akin to that of Europe, also attracted some workers, particularly in the Southern Cone. Since it was dedicated to electoral politics, however, the fact that immigrants could not vote weakened its appeal. Catholic-leaning organizations and independent unions that took no set positions also arose. Most workers, even those who were unionized, probably held no set ideological positions, but acted on the basic desire to improve their living and working conditions however possible. Workers often bargained collectively and sometimes won partial or full victories. Strikes, however, proved to be the most common and effective form of direct action. Mostly these occurred in one or more shops, but sometimes affected a whole industry and occasionally turned into generalized movements. Some of the latter briefly closed major cities, such as Buenos Aires and Montevideo in the early 1900s and São Paulo in the following decade. Workers also used slowdowns, boycotts, and other tactics to gain their ends.

GROWTH OF THE MOVEMENT

Until 1920, the strongest labor movements had emerged in Argentina, Chile, Brazil, and Mexico. Unions, however, existed in almost every country except for primarily agrarian nations, where only a few artisans organized. In the first three countries, significant federations formed, grouping important numbers of unions and workers. The largest of them, the Argentine syndicalist Federación Obrera Regional Argentina (FORA), claimed 20–25 percent of Buenos Aires's working force by 1918. Despite divisions, particularly between anarchists and syndicalists, the Argentine movement remained numerically the strongest. In Chile miners led the way, along with workers in the larger cities. The militant Partido Obrero Socialista (POS) arose in 1912 and elected its leader, Luis Emilio RECABARREN, to Congress, although the elites refused to seat him. In Brazil a national confederation, the Confederação Operária Brasileira (COB), emerged in 1908, hewing to an anarchosyndicalist line, and several general strikes shook both Rio de Janeiro and São Paulo in the following years. In Mexico at least 250 strikes took place during the regime of Porfirio DÍAZ (1876–1911). Widespread state repression doomed most of them, although they put social issues squarely on the agenda and undermined Díaz.

Labor and the State The MEXICAN REVOLUTION (1910) ushered in a new relationship between labor and the state. Segments of the labor movement, located predominantly in Mexico City, signed a pact (1915) with the upper-middle-class faction led by Venustiano CARRANZA and Álvaro OBREGÓN under which, in return for support, they could organize freely. But tensions soon arose and a general strike in Mexico City against unfavorable government policies led to repression that weakened the radical wing of the labor movement and strengthened more collaborationist elements. The Constitution of 1917 incorporated a whole section of labor clauses. These progressive measures, however, remained largely a dead letter until the 1930s or later owing to a lack of government enforcement. But the document presaged a time when social and labor questions would increasingly become a part of the state's purview throughout Latin America.

After 1917, a close relationship developed between the ruling cliques and labor leaders, such as Luis MORONES, who controlled the Confederación Regional Obrera Mexicana (CROM), Mexico's leading labor confederation, which existed with government approval. CROM organized workers and kept more radical elements within the labor movement under check, often aided by state violence. CROM's greatest influence was evident during the 1920s, when its connections allowed it to offer members material benefits. The government often pressured CROM's rivals. This pattern of state-labor collaboration, where power lies with the state, has marked Mexican labor relations ever since. Even today, the relationship between the ruling Institutional Revolutionary Party (PRI) and the largest labor confederation, the Mexican Confederation of Workers (CTM), continues. The government and the CTM, which represents labor, now sign annual social pacts that limit wage increases. Although these matched or even outran the pace of inflation during the expansionary 1950s and 1960s, from about 1985 to 1995 workers steadily lost ground. By some estimates, real salaries plummeted as much as 60 percent in that time.

WORLD WAR I

World War I brought substantial economic dislocations, which resulted in mass layoffs and rapid inflation throughout Latin America. This situation was reflected in a burst of labor unrest from 1917 to 1920, which included major general strikes and increased organization, often in trades previously nonunionized. Working-class actions in such countries as Colombia, Cuba, Peru, and Uruguay reached new heights. Labor gained a stronger bargaining position owing to the cutoff of imports and to more demand for skilled labor, which helped some workers attain their goals. Most workers generally achieved limited gains, and many experienced defeats. The outburst, however, led politicians and employers to rethink the question of labor relations.

THE 1920S: NEW TRENDS

In the 1920s there were several new trends. A postwar depression halted the upsurge in activity. The state and ruling groups strengthened the repressive apparatus and rethought strategies to dampen workers' rebellion and protest. Although comprehensive legal controls emerged only after 1930, their roots lie in this period. Governments now sought to co-opt labor or at least to neutralize it. Mexico and Uruguay led the way, but the same phenomenon appeared in Argentina and Chile, not coincidentally countries where the labor movement proved to be strongest. Some governments promulgated labor codes that regulated work relations and the ways in which workers could organize. States tried to see that these codes effectively governed relations between labor and capital, although they did not always succeed. Increased social legislation represented an attempt to domesticate labor; with better conditions and wages there would be more contented workers, higher productivity, and thus more profits.

Three other developments shaped the 1920s. First, the failure of confrontational strategies brought an eclipse of ANARCHISM and anarchosyndicalism. Second, workers more and more sought to bargain with the state and/or employers and to resort to direct action only in extreme instances. Third, newly formed Communist parties tried to organize a labor movement with long-term revolutionary objectives, at the same time also pursuing electoral ends. The appearance of Communist parties that won solid working-class constituencies created new cleavages within the labor movement. The rise

of such parties also frightened both agrarian and industrial elites. Communism represented yet another divisive ideological tendency, although Communists at times collaborated with others to oppose foreign capital and the capitalist system. Communism provided another reason for official repression of any workers' protest on the ground that foreign agitators manipulated a well-intentioned local labor force. But the rise of communism also opened the way for a more systematic analysis of imperialism, which appealed to workers exploited by foreign capital and even sometimes to local industrialists.

Rural labor remained generally unorganized before the 1930s. The Mexican Revolution, however, stirred up considerable peasant agitation and the beginnings of organization. Agrarian tenants' movements also arose. In Argentina, for example, they sometimes connected with urban labor. Strictly rural unions remained scarce, but peons often protested forcefully against working conditions. Nonurban workers, other than those outside agrobusiness, seldom joined organizations, let alone led collective action. Still, the massive peasant uprising in El Salvador in 1932 and its brutal repression, in which perhaps 30,000 persons perished, and strikes on banana plantations in Central America and Colombia in the late 1920s and early 1930s, as well as the massive uprisings by estate workers across the Caribbean (1931–1938), show that rural workers did not remain totally passive.

Industrialization The Great Depression and World War II accelerated industrialization. The working class expanded markedly and, as immigration slowed, the class became more national. Political parties and politicians courted labor support more seriously after 1930 and particularly after 1945, both in response to labor's new strength and in hopes of gaining an ally against their enemies. Mechanisms of control over labor also expanded in terms of labor relations systems and corporatist controls. Global depression after 1930 generated more worker agitation against deteriorating conditions. Some organizations became more collaborationist and others more militant, with mixed results in terms of permanent gains for workers. Repression, however, remained a major response to workers' unrest. The years 1930–1950, nonetheless, ushered in an era during which organized labor slowly emerged as a new force in society.

The Emerging Movement The democratic movements that grew across Latin America in the immediate postwar years often included a labor component. After years of pent-up frustration due to depression and war, workers sought to recover lost ground, with varied results. The war had been fought in the name of democracy, and workers demanded the fruits of the system. Politicians or political movements often co-opted these efforts, giving limited economic benefits or more room to organize in return for state support of labor and workers' votes at election time. Peronism is a classic case. In

Argentina, General Juan D. PERÓN emerged as leader of a military junta (1943–1946), and labor rallied to his support, attracted by incentives he had granted as Secretary of Labor and Social Welfare. Workers formed the backbone of Perón's electoral bids, and their votes carried him to victory in 1946 and 1952. The Peronist-dominated labor Confederación General de Trabajo (CGT), however, remained largely under the control of a bureaucracy pledged to Perón. Workers (even rural ones), at least until 1950, received real gains in terms of social and labor legislation and income. Perhaps most important, they gained a sense of dignity and of their collective power. After 1950, when the economy turned down, workers took the brunt of cuts that eroded support for the increasingly dictatorial Perón. Despite this loss, however, the Peronist Party still received the support of a substantial majority of Argentine workers even after Perón's ouster in 1955; labor did not forget the gains won under him.

In Mexico strikes by white-collar unions as well as electrical and rail workers in the 1950s and early 1960s led to repression and more state control over the CTM and other labor organizations. Significant postwar activity occurred in Brazil. A labor upsurge from 1945 to 1947, sparked by the Partido Trabalhista Brasileiro (PTB), founded by longtime ruler Getúlio VARGAS, and the Partido Comunista Brasileiro (PCB), brought a violent reaction on the part of upper- and middle-class politicians, which included the outlawing of the PCB and prohibition of its elected candidates from office. But in 1950, Vargas, running as a populist with an appeal to labor, won. Labor autonomy, however, remained limited, and docile leaders headed most major unions, although independent elements continued to operate. Vargas's overthrow in 1954 failed to sever labor's links to populist politicians, although it resulted immediately in regimes markedly less favorable toward workers and unions. Like Perón in Argentina, Vargas, despite his control over the state, could not simply manipulate labor at will. Even with imbalances in power, a degree of negotiation always existed between the two sides.

In Bolivia, the revolution in 1952 depended heavily upon the support of militant miners' unions hewing to leftist doctrines. The Confederación Obrera Boliviana (COB) demanded and received co-government of the mines, and the minister of mines came from labor's ranks. Although the ruling party, Movimiento Nacional Revolucionario (MNR), moved steadily rightward and miners lost their power owing to both economic and political factors, their unions continued to exercise influence at the national level until the TIN INDUSTRY's collapse in the 1980s. In fact, COB became the main vehicle for labor and leftist politics both in opposition and when allied with the government, as in the brief regime of Juan José TORRES (1970–1971), when the Asamblea Popular (Popular Assembly) functioned in place of traditional parliamentary bodies.

Institutionalization The decades after 1950 brought accelerated industrial growth and urbanization. The working class rapidly increased in numbers and became a more important actor at the political level. This situation, in turn, reflected a process of institutionalization, one designed to contain industrial conflict as well as to mobilize support for elite-led political parties and governments. Organized workers often received or won economic benefits plus favorable social legislation in return for support. Real wages for workers in more dynamic industrial sectors probably tended upward, although patterns varied country by country. In Mexico, for example, the ruling PRI tightly controlled organized labor. It accomplished this end through a policy of divide and rule (more than a thousand unions existed by the 1960s), keeping white-collar and peasant unions separate from blue-collar ones; a forceful imposition of corrupt leadership; repression of independent actions; and granting real wage gains. Labor also became a battleground between contending political parties and/or competing ideologies. Occasionally, one party captured the bulk of labor support as in the cases of Peronism in Argentina or Acción Democrática (AD) in Venezuela. But in Colombia, Catholics and Communists vied for workers' allegiance. In Peru, the Peruvian Aprista Party (PAP/APRA) and the Communists did the same. In Chile, socialists, Communists, Radicals, and Christian Democrats all controlled labor blocs in the 1960s.

In Cuba, labor divided between the centrist Auténticos, aided by government intervention from 1944 to 1952, and the Communists, hurt by repression during that same period. After 1952, the TWENTY-SIXTH OF JULY labor movement and Communist-influenced unions, both of which played a role in the struggle against Fulgencio BATISTA, formed the unified Confederación de Trabajadores de Cuba (CTC). Unions continued to represent workers' interests, but within the bounds of the Revolution and with often mixed results.

In Chile, organized labor had an important opportunity to see many of its goals realized. Workers solidly backed the Popular Unity ticket, which elected a socialist, Salvador ALLENDE, to the presidency in 1970. His policies benefited the working class in material and organizational terms. But when his nationalization measures slowed, militant workers forced his hand by seizing factories. Eventually they formed worker-run zones (*cordones industriales*). The 1973 reactionary military coup, however, found labor almost totally unprepared to defend the regime in any significant manner.

During the 1960s and 1970s there was also marked growth of rural unions in several countries. Agricultural workers' and peasants' unions, for example, became an important segment of the labor movement in Brazil, Bolivia, Chile, Peru, and Central America. Sometimes national federations emerged, as in Chile, Brazil, and Peru. In Mexico an official confederation existed. Despite this phenomenon, however, the vast majority of Latin American rural workers remained unorganized.

LABOR AND THE MILITARY

By the 1960s, before the military takeovers that swept across Latin America, the ranks of organized workers had risen markedly in almost every country, from some 4.5 million in 1945 to 6–7 million in 1960–1970. The greatest militancy in the labor movement had shifted from transport or dock workers to those in the modernized sectors, such as the metal trades, but not excluding mining and oil. Public sector unions also grew as government bureaucracy expanded. Labor in most countries had become firmly allied with or tied to specific political parties such as AD in Venezuela, APRA in Peru, Peronism in Argentina, or the PRI in Mexico. These ties created tensions between political platforms and workers' demands. The question became to what degree workers should bow to the agenda set by non-working-class politicians and abandon labor autonomy. Labor had become a significant actor not only because it influenced or controlled votes, but also because it could threaten to disturb political stability, which could bring down governments.

The military takeovers from 1964 through the early 1980s brought reactionary forces to power. The military deemed labor organizations subversive and acted to curb their power, usually by force, as in the cases of Argentina, Chile, and Brazil. In the latter country, during 1967 not a single major strike took place. But in Argentina, the military governments after 1966 failed to crush the Peronist resistance in the unions, leading to Perón's ill-fated return in 1974. A second round of military dictatorship ending in 1983 fared no better. Everywhere, however, military rule weakened labor by arresting, torturing, and exiling leaders and middle-level organizers.

NEW PATTERNS

The 1970s and 1980s brought other new patterns. First, neoliberal economic policies in conjunction with built-in structural imbalances resulted in a marked shrinkage of the industrial sector. Privatization also reduced the number of blue- and white-collar jobs in the state sector. This situation weakened once strong industrial and public sector unions and labor's traditional bargaining power. The International Monetary Fund mandated austerity programs in a dozen countries, drastically lowering working-class living standards. Despite general strikes against such programs in Argentina, Brazil, Bolivia, Colombia, the Dominican Republic, Ecuador, Peru, and elsewhere, almost nowhere did labor and its allies ultimately succeed in changing economic policies, if occasionally it did postpone or ameliorate them. Second, explosive informal sector growth changed the composition of the working class. Informal sectors proved notoriously difficult to organize because they had no

General strike in Buenos Aires, ca. 1990. OWEN FRANKEN / STOCK, BOSTON.

locus of work. Many people opposed collective action, considering themselves to be individual entrepreneurs. Even in cases where unions emerged within the sector, such as that of street vendors in La Paz, they have proved fragile and transient. Third, in countries where the military ruled over a long period, years of clandestine or severely limited activity for labor, and also for progressive political parties, served to weaken the traditional links between the two. As a result, labor emerged into the period of redemocratization perhaps less powerful but more independent, opening the possibility that it could forge a more truly independent path.

A TURNING POINT

At the start of the 1990s, labor appeared to be at a crossroads. Traditionally strong sectors had weakened numerically. In Peru, for example, where a once vibrant labor movement had played a major role in forcing the military out of power in 1980, by 1991 it looked powerless against the strong antilabor policies of the government of Alberto FUJIMORI. In Argentina a "Peronist" president pursued antilabor measures, and in Mexico the long-term collaboration between the PRI and the CTM seemed to be on the verge of collapse, with labor receiving fewer benefits. But in Brazil, as a result of the massive strikes led by metallurgical workers in the state of São Paulo in the 1970s, a new labor party formed. Hewing to a social-democratic position, the Partido dos Trabalhadores (PT) soon turned to national politics. Its candidate, the charismatic Luís Inácio da SILVA (Lula), ran a strong second in the presidential elections of 1990 and 1994, and the PT even captured the city of São Paulo in the first campaign. Whether the party could retain its momentum remained a question.

By the mid-1990s, the immediate prospects for Latin American labor seemed far from rosy. Widespread and continuing neoliberal programs undercut unions, and often class solidarity, through massive layoffs and drastic cuts in the PUBLIC SECTOR. Increased competition in newly formed free trade areas (such as NAFTA and MERCOSUR) led companies to downsize and, at least in the latter area, resulted in massive flows of labor from low- to high-wage areas. This trend eroded pay scales in high-wage jobs. Finally, politicians discovered that controlling rampant INFLATION, which includes holding down wages and benefits, wins more votes than prolabor platforms. As in the case of the Peronist Party in Argentina or the ruling center-left coalition in Chile, even traditionally labor-friendly parties have distanced themselves from unions. Almost everywhere labor finds itself on the defensive. Only in Brazil, where the PT remains a significant force, or in Uruguay, where many unions allied with the Frente Amplio (a progressive electoral coalition that won over 30 percent of the vote in the 1994 elections), do things look more hopeful.

Clearly workers must formulate new strategies to meet the challenges of the 1990s and beyond. As prime victims of the restructuring of local and global capital, they must broaden the appeal of their movements to include new groups, such as those in the INFORMAL SECTOR, WOMEN, and even the unemployed. Furthermore, as capital internationalizes, labor organizations must do the same. Indeed, some dialogue between workers inside the free trade areas has already taken place with the idea of increasing cooperation between national movements.

HOBART A. SPALDING, *Organized Labor in Latin America: Historical Case Studies of Workers in Dependent Societies* (1977); CHARLES BERGQUIST, *Labor in Latin America: Comparative Essays on Chile, Argentina, Venezuela, and Colombia* (1986); MICHAEL HALL and HOBART SPALDING, "The Urban Working Class and Early Latin American Labour Movements, 1880–1930," in *The Cambridge History of Latin America*, vol. 4, edited by Leslie Bethell (1986); JOHN FRENCH, ed., *Latin American Labor Studies Bibliography*, vols. 1–4 (1989–1993); PABLO GONZÁLEZ CASANOVA, ed., *Historia del movimiento oberero en América Latina*, 4 vols. (Mexico City, 1984–1985); IAN ROXBOROUGH, "Labor Since 1930," in *The Cambridge History of Latin America*, vol. 13 (forthcoming).

HOBART A. SPALDING

See also **Organizations** (under individual countries).

LABRADOR RUÍZ, ENRIQUE (*b.* 11 May 1902; *d.* 1991), Cuban novelist, journalist, and short-story writer. Labrador Ruíz was born in Sagua la Grande in the province of Las Villas. Self-taught, he started out as a journalist for the newspaper *El Sol* in the city of Cien-

fuegos and eventually became one of its editors. When the paper moved to Havana, he, too, moved and once there, began to write for other newspapers and magazines. In 1946 he received the National Short Story Prize for "El conejito Ulán." In 1950 he was awarded the National Prize for his novel *La sangre hambrienta*, and in 1951 he received the Juan Gualberto Gómez prize for journalism. His work appeared in publications all over the Americas, including *Orígenes* (Cuba), *The American News* (United States), and *Babel* (Chile).

After the Cuban Revolution of 1959, Labrador Ruíz became editor of the National Publishing House. Although he was initially supportive of the Cuban government, he eventually broke with it and emigrated to Miami, where he died in 1991. His work is considered to be a precursor of the modern Latin American novel.

Among Labrador Ruíz's most important works are the novels *El laberinto de sí mismo* (1933, repr. 1983), *Cresival* (1936), *Carne de quimera: Novelines neblinosos* (1947, repr. 1983), and *La sangre hambrienta* (1950), and the short stories *El gallo en el espejo* (1953) and *Cuentos* (1970).

RITA MOLINERO, *La narrativa de Enrique Labrador Ruíz* (1977) and *Homenaje a Enrique Labrador Ruíz* (1981).

ROBERTO VALERO

LACALLE HERRERA, LUIS ALBERTO (*b.* 13 July 1941), president of Uruguay, elected in 1989 and took office 1 March 1990. He was the first Blanco (National Party) president of Uruguay elected in the twentieth century. The grandson of the great Blanco leader Luis Alberto de HERRERA, Lacalle graduated from law school and gravitated toward a political career. He was elected a deputy to Congress in 1971 but lost his position in 1973 when Congress was closed in the coup that brought the military to power for the next twelve years.

In 1981 Lacalle founded a political group within the Blancos known as the National Herrerist Council, and by 1982 he was on the Blanco board of directors. In the national elections permitted by the military in November 1984, Lacalle was elected to the Senate. In 1987 he served as vice president to the Senate. In July 1988, Lacalle declared himself a presidential candidate. With the 1988 death of the last political caudillo, Blanco Senator Wilson FERREIRA ALDUNATE, Lacalle emerged as the leader of the party. On 26 November 1989, aided by infighting in the ruling Colorado Party and a stagnant economy, Lacalle was elected president, with his party receiving 39 percent of the vote.

Lacalle is an articulate, center-right politician who is attempting to steer Uruguay away from its welfare-state orientation. His major goals are to privatize, or at least to bring mixed ownership to, such state-owned operations as the airline and telephone company. He is also attempting to reform the social-security system, which is a heavy drain on government resources. On 26 March 1991 he signed an agreement with the presidents of Brazil, Argentina, and Paraguay for the creation by 1995 of a common market (MERCOSUR) among these nations. Lacalle has written on political and economic matters, and he authored a book about his grandfather, *Herrera, Un nacionalismo oriental* (1978).

MARTIN WEINSTEIN, "Consolidating Democracy in Uruguay: The Sea Change of the 1989 Elections" (Bildner Center for Western Hemisphere Studies of the Graduate Center of the City University of New York, Working Paper Series, 1990); CHARLES G. GILLESPIE, *Negotiating Democracy: Politicians and Generals in Uruguay* (1991).

MARTIN WEINSTEIN

LACANDON FOREST, the largest surviving tropical wilderness area in modern Mexico and a major segment of the once vast rain forest belt of Middle America. Located in the Usumacinta River basin in the states of Chiapas and Tabasco, it harbors a considerable, if largely unstudied, diversity of flora and fauna. This humid, lowland region was once a part of the heavily populated heartland of Classic MAYA civilization that flourished between A.D. 300 and 900. The forest is named for the later Lacandon Indians, who fled to the region from the direction of the Yucatán Peninsula in the centuries following the abandonment of the ancient cities.

This great forest, which covered at least 520,000 square miles in 1875, was, in spite of much manual lumbering of hardwoods, largely intact and isolated until 1950. Yet by 1990 it had suffered extreme alteration and at least a 70 percent reduction, to approximately 156,000 square miles, as a result of mechanized lumbering, road construction, excessive settlements, extensive cattle ranching, massive uncontrolled burning, and large-scale energy projects for oil exploitation and planned hydroelectric dams. During the last decade of the twentieth century, efforts were undertaken to regulate the forest area and to formalize the Montes Azules Biosphere Reserve to preserve a significant remaining upland portion.

The classic description of the forest before radical alteration is FRANS BLOM and GERTRUDE DUBY, *La Selva Lacandona* (1955). Visual data from that period are also presented in GERTRUDE DUBY BLOM, *Bearing Witness* (1984). The current state of the forest is examined in S. JEFFREY K. WILKERSON, "The Usumacinta River: Troubles on a Wild Frontier," in *National Geographic Magazine* 168 (October 1985):514–543; "The Last Forest: Exploring Mexico's Lacandon Wilderness," in *America's Hidden Wilderness: Lands of Seclusion,* edited by Donald J. Crump (1988), pp. 36–61; and "Damming the Usumacinta: The Archaeological Impact," in *Sixth Palenque Round Table* 8 (1991):118–134.

S. JEFFREY K. WILKERSON

LACANDONES, MAYA Indians of the tropical rain forest of eastern Chiapas, Mexico, who speak a dialect of Yucatec Mayan. Numbering fewer than four hundred in-

dividuals, they are divided into two branches, the Southern and Northern Lacandones, who live in three major settlements, Najá and Metzabok in the north and Lacanjá in the south. The groups differ in language, traditions and religion, and residence patterns.

Disagreement among scholars as to the descent of present-day Lacandones is characterized by discussion of whether the Lacandones are directly descendant of the Classic Maya. Some divide the Lacandones into Historical Lacandones, who disappeared before 1700, and the ancestors of the Lacandones of today, who began migrations from Yucatán or Petén beginning in 1850.

The Spanish were never successful in dominating the Lacandones, who died or fled into the jungle when the Spanish attempted to confine them in settlements. The Lacandones were protected in the isolation of the rain forest until the 1870s, when the prosperous mahogany business brought timber-cutters into contact with them during the following fifty years. Beginning in the 1940s and 1950s, Tzeltal, Chol, and Tzotzil Indians migrated to the jungle in search of land. They, followed by crocodile hunters and chicle gatherers, seriously damaged the Lacandon environment. In 1971 the Lacandones were granted 1,535,800 acres as national park by the Mexican government. While the lumber industry continues to cut trees, the Lacandones receive percentage payments for lumber rights.

In the past the Lacandones were scattered in the jungle and lacked political leadership. By the second half of the twentieth century, Lacandones lived in settlements of single households or compounds of two of more households. Furthermore, Lacandones had religious leaders and political deputies to represent them at the state and federal levels of government.

The northern group of Najá continue to practice native Maya religion. Many of their ceremonies are closely

Young Lacandon in a boat, 1957. PHOTO BY GERTRUDE DUBY BLOM / NA-BOLOM (FOTOTECA).

related to those of the classic Maya. The Metzabok Lacandones, however, were converted by Seventh Day Adventists, and the southern group at Lacanjá converted to Protestantism beginning in the 1950s.

As in the past, the present-day Lacandones continue to cultivate maize, black beans, squash, tomatoes, chile peppers, cassava, sweet potatoes, and a large variety of fruits. Tobacco is grown for both local consumption and as a cash crop. The land is planted after clearing trees and burning small growth, then used for two years and abandoned for seven years until replanted. Immigrant groups contribute to the environmental destructiveness of slash-and-burn agriculture by increasing stress on limited land. The Lacandones supplement agriculture by exploiting rain-forest products such as fish, game, wild honey, cotton, vanilla, and cacao.

House construction consists of pole and thatch, although houses of cement block with zinc roofs are becoming more common. Canoes are made of dugout mahogany trees. Bows and arrows are handmade, while hunting tools consist chiefly of guns, knives, and fishhooks. Cloth is hand woven on a backstrap loom. Dress for men and women consists of a long white tunic, although western clothing is also worn. Craft items of wood and pottery are sold to tourists.

FRANS F. BLOM and GERTRUDE DUBY, *La Selva Lacandona* (1955); DIDIER BOREMANSE, "Final Link with Maya Indians," in *Geographical Magazine* (January 1981): 250–256; VICTOR PERERA and ROBERT D. BRUCE, *The Last Lords of Palenque: The Lacandon Mayas of the Mexican Rain Forest* (1982); ANDRÉS AUBRY E INAREMAC, "Nueva luz sobre los Lacandones," in *Boletín del Archivo Histórico Diocesano* 2, no. 5–6 (Chiapas, 1985); LAURA L. WOODWARD and RALPH LEE WOODWARD, JR., "Trudi Blom and the Lacandon Rain Forest," in *Environmental Review* 9 (1985): 226–236.

LAURA L. WOODWARD

LACERDA, CARLOS FREDERICO WERNECK DE (*b.* 30 April 1914; *d.* 21 May 1977), famous for combative oratory and journalism that contributed to the fall of Brazilian presidents. According to historian José Honório Rodrigues, "No single person exerted as much influence on the Brazilian historical process" from 1945 to 1968.

Lacerda, born in the city of Rio de Janeiro, was a rebellious, intense youth who preferred to educate himself by reading instead of taking formal courses. In 1935 he dropped out of the Faculdade Nacional de Direito (Rio Law School) without obtaining a degree. His ardent oratorical and journalistic work for communism ended in 1940 with his "expulsion" from the Communist Party, which he had in fact never joined. Continuing to condemn the dictatorship of Getúlio VARGAS, he contributed to the achievement of democracy in 1945. His articles, such as those after 1949 in his own *Tribuna da Imprensa*, gained him admirers as an anticommunist and a courageous crusader against corruption. After his

revelation of scandals in the final Vargas administration (1951–1954), supporters of the president killed a military officer while trying to assassinate Lacerda. Following Vargas's suicide (24 August 1954), mobs shouted "death to Lacerda." The latter, however, became the congressman who received the greatest number of votes.

Calling for a reform of the political system, Lacerda demanded in 1955 that President-elect Juscelino KUBITSCHEK be prevented from taking office. Kubitschek, inaugurated with the help of a military coup, in turn would not allow Lacerda, Brazil's most sensational orator, to broadcast, and tried unsuccessfully to have him removed from Congress. As congressional opposition leader, Lacerda secured passage of legislation to reform education and was active in advancing the campaign that brought Jânio QUADROS to the presidency early in 1961.

When Quadros, attacked by Lacerda for harboring dictatorial plans, unexpectedly resigned in August 1961, the presidency went to Vice President João GOULART, despite Lacerda's wishes. Lacerda, who had been elected governor of Guanabara state, gave his state a brilliantly constructive administration while denouncing Goulart and the president's Communist allies in labor unions. During the military coup that overthrew Goulart in 1964, Lacerda dramatically prepared the governor's palace against a possible assault by Goulart's forces.

As a presidential candidate, Lacerda denounced the new military regime and its unpopular anti-inflation measures. After an institutional act ended direct presidential elections, he found allies in Kubitschek and Goulart for organizing an antidictatorial front. The increasingly repressive military regime jailed him for a week in 1968 and deprived him of his political rights for ten years. Lacerda then concentrated on business affairs, writing, and book publishing, activities to which he had turned in 1965 following a political setback. He died of a heart attack.

JOSÉ HONÓRIO RODRIGUES, Introduction to *Carlos Lacerda, Discursos parlamentares* (1982); JOHN W. F. DULLES, *Carlos Lacerda, Brazilian Crusader* (1991).

JOHN W. F. DULLES

See also **Lacerda, Maurício Paiva de.**

LACERDA, MAURÍCIO PAIVA DE (*b.* 1 June 1888; *d.* 23 November 1959), popular politician and journalist who contributed to the collapse of Brazil's Old Republic in 1930 through his passionate oratory. Always attacking those in power, Lacerda stirred the masses in the streets and encouraged workers to strike. He named his son Carlos Frederico, after Marx and Engels.

Maurício de Lacerda was born in Vassouras, Rio de Janeiro State. He was the oldest son of Sebastião de Lacerda, a prominent politician of the state who became a cabinet minister and supreme court justice. Before the willful Maurício obtained his degree at the Rio Law

School, he was a student leader, director of a newspaper in Vassouras, and participant in an ineffective antigovernment conspiracy. As a congressman (1912–1920) from his home state of Rio de Janeiro, Lacerda introduced labor legislation. The antigovernment revolts of 1922 and 1924 were insufficiently labor-oriented to attract him, but he was nevertheless arrested on both occasions. Following his imprisonment (1924–1926) he allied himself with the "Cavalier of Hope," Luís Carlos PRESTES, leader of the revolutionary Long March (1925–1927), but in 1929–1930 he angered Prestes by supporting the Liberal Alliance and its uprising, which brought Getúlio VARGAS to the presidency.

Lacerda denounced the economic policies and what he saw as the fascist viewpoints of the new Vargas regime, and in 1935 he joined the Aliança Nacional Libertadora, whose honorary president, Prestes, was by then a Communist in hiding. Following the unsuccessful uprising of Prestes and his followers that year, Lacerda was jailed, again without cause, for a year. During most of the Vargas dictatorship (1937–1945), he did legal work for the Rio de Janeiro municipality. He ran unsuccessfully for Congress when the dictatorship fell.

JOHN W. F. DULLES, *Anarchists and Communists in Brazil, 1900–1935* (1973); MICHAEL L. CONNIFF, *Urban Politics in Brazil: The Rise of Populism, 1925–1945* (1981); JOHN W. F. DULLES, *Carlos Lacerda, Brazilian Crusader*, vol. 1 (1991).

JOHN W. F. DULLES

See also **Lacerda, Carlos Frederico Werneck de.**

LACERDA, OSVALDO (*b.* 23 March 1927), Brazilian composer and teacher. Lacerda's formal music training started at age nine, when he began piano study in the city of São Paulo, where he was born. From 1945 to 1947 he studied harmony, and in 1952 he became a composition student of Camargo GUARNIERI. In 1963 he became the first Brazilian to win a Simon Guggenheim grant for study in the United States. He studied with Vittorio Giannini in New York City, and with Aaron Copland at Tanglewood. In 1965 he participated in the Inter-American Seminar of Composers at Indiana University and in the Third Inter-American Composers Seminar, held in Washington, D.C. In an era in which most Brazilian composers reject obvious national elements in their works, Osvaldo Lacerda remains an important spokesman for neonationalism with compositions such as nine *Brasiliana* suites for piano based on Brazilian themes and dances. He also excels in writing songs and choral works, such as *Poema da necessidade*, for four-part chorus, based on a poem by Carlos Drummond de ANDRADE.

MARCOS ANTÔNIO MARCONDES, ed., *Enciclopédia da música brasileira: Erudita, folclórica e popular* (1977); GÉRARD BÉHAGUE, *Music in Latin America: An Introduction* (1979); DAVID P. APPLEBY, *The Music of Brazil* (1983).

DAVID P. APPLEBY

LADINO, a Spanish word derived from the Latin *latinus,* meaning a person who spoke the Latin language, in contrast to speakers of Arabic. In medieval Spain, the word was used to describe Moors who had learned the Spanish language with such care and precision that they were scarcely distinguishable from Spaniards. From there, the word's meaning (documented as early as 1596, and also described as such in Covarrubias's 1611 *Tesoro de la lengua castellana*) was broadened to designate a crafty person, one who is cunning or astute, especially in learning foreign languages. In Spain, it was applied to the Moors and Spanish Jews (the Sephardic Jews of the Spanish diaspora are still known as ladinos), or any "foreigner" who learned the Spanish language, and implied a certain adaptation to Spanish customs. In the New World, usage expanded to incorporate New World Indians, African slaves, and the offspring of Spanish and Indians (mestizos), who were proficient Spanish-speakers and reasonably well-adapted to Spanish customs. Generally, the term described a person of non-Hispanic ethnic or racial background who successfully learned the Spanish language and customs of the Spaniards. In Guatemala, although originally applied to mestizos, it now connotes any person who is culturally not Indian. This purely cultural significance means that it describes both individuals of European descent and those of purely indigenous descent whose cultural identity and language align them with European rather than Indian culture.

SEBASTIÁN DE COVARRUBIAS, *Tesoro de la lengua castellana o española* (1611); JOAN COROMINAS and JOSÉ A. PASCUAL, *Diccionario crítico etimológico castellano e hispánico* (1980); THOMAS M. STEPHENS, *Dictionary of Latin American Racial and Ethnic Terminology* (1989).

J. DAVID DRESSING

LADRÓN DE GUEVARA, DIEGO (*b.* 1641; *d.* 9 November 1718), bishop and viceroy of Peru (1710–1716). Born in Cifuentes, Ladrón studied in Alcalá and Sigüenza before entering the church, serving as a canon in both Sigüenza and Málaga. He was sent to America in 1689 as bishop of Panamá and was subsequently promoted to Huamanga (Peru) in 1699, and Quito in 1703.

Following the death in office in 1710 of the viceroy of Peru, marqués de Castelldosríus, Ladrón, as the AUDIENCIA's third choice as interim successor, took office when the other two nominees died. Although recalled to Spain in 1713, he remained in office until 1716 and stayed in Lima for two further years to defend himself (unsuccessfully) against charges of corruption, permitting contraband, and incompetence in defending shipping in the Pacific against English intruders. He left Peru for Acapulco in March 1718 and died in Mexico City later that year.

RUBÉN VARGAS UGARTE, *Historia del Perú: Virreinato (Siglo XVIII) 1700–1790* (1956), esp. pp. 67–96; GEOFFREY J. WALKER,

Spanish Politics and Imperial Trade, 1700–1789 (1979), esp. pp. 61–62, 80–83.

JOHN R. FISHER

LAGÔA SANTA, Brazilian archaeological site. A complex of calcareous caves situated in the Rio das Velhas valley in the state of Minas Gerais, it was discovered by the Danish scientist Peter Wilhelm Lund (1801–1880). The exploration of the Lagôa Santa site began in 1833; Lund, working by candlelight, studied hundreds of caves, the main ones being Lapa Nova de Maquiné, Lapa da Cêrca Grande, Lapa do Saco Comprido, and Lapa do Mosquito. The total of 115 identifiable mammal specimens proved that giant toothed animals—*Megatherium, Mylodon, Glyptodon, Pachyterium, Chlamydotherium*—dominated in Brazil. In 1843 the first human bones were found.

A fossil discovered in 1935 in the Lapa dos Confins initiated a scientific debate about the contemporaneity of Pleistocene animals and prehistoric humans. In 1956 Brazilian and foreign specialists had yet to find a satisfactory answer to that question after systematically exploring eight different sites at Lagôa Santa. The early archaeological finds have been preserved in Copenhagen since 1859, in the Universitets Zoologiske Museum. Lund, considered the father of Brazilian paleontology, is buried at Lagôa Santa.

ANIBAL MATTOS, *Peter Wilhelm Lund no Brasil* (1939); PETER WILHELM LUND, *Memórias sôbre a paleontologia brasileira* (1950); CARLOS DE PAULD COUTO, ed., *Resumo de memórias de Lund sôbre as cavernas de Lagôa Santa e seu conteúdo animal,* translated by H. C. Orsted (1956); H. V. WALTER, *Archaeology of the Lagôa Santa Region (Arqueologia da região de Lagôa Santa)* (1958).

ELIANA MARIA REA GOLDSCHMIDT

See also **Archaeology.**

LAGOS, RICARDO (*b.* 2 May 1938), a leader of Chile's moderately socialist Partido por la Democracia (PPD) and minister of education (1990–) in the government of President Patricio AYLWIN AZCÓCAR. A lawyer who was once active in the Radical Party, Lagos staunchly supported the Popular Unity government of Salvador ALLENDE and taught in the United States following its overthrow in 1973. During the mid- and late-1980s, he was affiliated with the Socialist Party's Nuñez wing and helped to build the broad movement that opposed and ultimately forced from power the government of General Augusto PINOCHET. In a television appearance early in 1987, he issued a direct challenge to General Pinochet that helped to launch the eventually successful plebiscite campaign. Although he far outpolled all senatorial candidates in the 1989 general election except the Christian Democrat who was his ticketmate, Lagos was denied the second seat from Santiago because their combined totals fell just short of the requisite two-thirds of the votes cast.

Partido por la Democracia (Chile) (1989), and *Qué es el PPD: Documentos oficiales* (1989); A. CAVALLO et al., *La historia oculta del regimen militar* (Santiago, 1989); P. CONSTABLE and A. VALENZUELA, *A Nation of Enemies* (1991).

MICHAEL FLEET

LAGUERRE, ENRIQUE ARTURO (*b.* 3 May 1906), Puerto Rican novelist. Born in Moca, a rural community in the western part of the island, Laguerre is Puerto Rico's foremost novelist. Educated at the University of Puerto Rico, in 1924 Laguerre embarked upon a lifelong teaching career spanning from elementary to postgraduate education.

Laguerre's twelve novels form a saga of Puerto Rico's land, people, and history in the late nineteenth and twentieth centuries. Two of them, *El laberinto* (1959; The labyrinth, 1960) and *Los amos benévolos* (1976; Benevolent masters, 1976); are available in English. *La llamarada* (The blaze), a classic since its publication in 1935, deals with the exploitation of the sugarcane worker. *Solar Montoya* (Montoya Plantation, 1941) takes place in the coffee fields, and *Los dedos de la mano* (The fingers of the hand, 1951) in tobacco country. Other novels deal with the Puerto Rican in San Juan, New York, and abroad; university life, feminism, and the religious practices of SANTERÍA. Puerto Rican identity and values are central themes in *Cauce sin río* (Riverbed without a river, 1962), *El fuego y su aire* (Fire and its air, 1970), and *Infiernos privados* (Private infernos, 1986). Associated with the 1930s generation, Laguerre creates a historical consciousness by enriching the past with legends, folklore, and myths, especially in *La resaca* (The undertow, 1949) and *Los gemelos* (The twins, 1992). Laguerre's novels treat the plight of oppressed women, children, and workers; the effects of affluence and power on the individual; and conflicts of conscience. In his writing he has embraced both traditional and innovative forms.

LUIS O. ZAYAS MICHELI, *Lo universal en Enrique A. Laguerre: Estudio conjunto de su obra* (1974); ESTELLE IRIZARRY, *Enrique A. Laguerre* (1982), ''*La llamarada,*'' *clásico puertorriqueño: Realidad y ficción* (1985) and *La novelística de Enrique A. Laguerre: Trayectoria histórica y literaria* (1987).

ESTELLE IRIZARRY

LAGUNA, SANTA CATARINA, a seaport in southern Brazil, founded in 1684 by Domingos de Brito Peixoto. In an effort to drive out the encroaching Spanish Jesuits, the Portuguese crown encouraged settlement at Laguna. Between 1682 and 1706 the Spanish Jesuits founded the missions of the Seven Peoples, the Sete Povos, which flourished in what is now Rio Grande do Sul. The presence of the Sete Povos threatened Portuguese territorial ambitions in the region. Moving with geopolitical and economic motivations, Portugal staked her claim to the region. Settled by PAULISTAS and Azorean couples sent by the crown, Laguna quickly became part of Portuguese Brazil. By 1694 settlers had transformed the region from a farming-fishing community to one dependent on grazing. Laguna later developed into an out-migration area as Lagunistas themselves migrated south to the plains of Rio Grande do Sul. In the eighteenth century a newly opened road for the livestock trade linked Laguna to São Paulo and the mines of Minas Gerais.

Leslie Bethell, ed., *The Cambridge History of Latin America,* vol. 2 (1984), p. 472; ROLLIE E. POPPINO, *Brazil: The Land and People,* 2d ed. (1973), p. 83

ORLANDO R. ARAGONA

LALEAU, LÉON (*b.* 3 August 1892; *d.* 1979), Haitian writer, journalist, and diplomat. Léopold Sédar Senghor cited Laleau as "one of the best representatives among Haitian poets using the vein of blackness." Laleau made many contacts with European and Latin American writers during his diplomatic assignments in Rome, Paris, London, Lima, and Santiago de Chile. Influenced by French symbolism at first, he later became acutely conscious of the catastrophic effects of the U.S. occupation of Haiti (1915–1934). He began to move toward the writers of *La revue indigène* and to use Haitian themes in the volume of verse, *Musique nègre* (1931), and in his novel about the occupation, *Le choc* (1932). Laleau also managed *Haïti journal, Le nouvelliste,* and *Le matin* at different periods. He wrote for the *Mercure de France, Le divan, Le Figaro littéraire,* and *Paris soir,* among other French journals. A collective volume of Laleau's *Oeuvre poétique* ("À voix basse," 1919; "La flèche au coeur," 1926; "Le rayon des jupes," 1928; "Abréviations," 1929; "Musique nègre," 1931; "De bronze et d'ivoire," 1978) won the literary prize of Éditions Henri Deschamps for 1978.

Other works include *Amitiés impossibles* (theater, with Georges Léger, 1916); *Une cause sans effet* (theater, 1916); *L'étau* (theater, 1917); *La pluie et le beau temps* (theater, 1919); *La danse des vagues* (novel, 1919); *Le tremplin* (theater, 1921); *Maurice Rostand intime* (biography, 1926); and *Apothéoses* (essays, 1952).

Conjonction, nos. 87–88 (1963), special issue dedicated to Laleau; NAOMI M. GARRET, *The Renaissance of Haitian Poetry* (1963), pp. 48–50; 139–144; F. RAPHAËL BERROU and PRADEL POMPILUS, *Histoire de la littérature haïtienne illustrée par les textes,* vol. 2 (1975), pp. 480–514, 666–691, 737–750.

CARROL F. COATES

LAM Y CASTILLA, WIFREDO (*b.* 9 December 1902; *d.* 11 September 1982), Cuban painter. Born in Sagua la Grande of a Chinese father and mulatto mother, Lam received a scholarship from the town council in 1921 to

Lisamona. Oil on canvas by Wifredo Lam y Castilla, 1950. STEVEN M. GREENBAUM.

study in Havana. From 1923 to 1937 he studied in Madrid, and from 1937 to 1939 he worked in Paris with Pablo Picasso and rediscovered his African ancestry. The events of World War II forced Lam to Marseilles in 1939 and out of France in 1941 with a group of three hundred intellectuals who chose exile from the Vichy government. Seven months after leaving France, he returned to Cuba. In 1942–1943, he painted *The Jungle,* his best-known work. He lived in Paris, New York, and Havana from 1946 to 1964, finally settling in the Italian town of Albissola Marina. In 1966, he returned to Cuba and painted *The Third World* for display in the Presidential Palace. His works run the gamut from postimpressionist to surrealist to postcubist styles, yet he never lost his devotion to the African influence. His paintings are unique in depicting African Cuban VODUN spirits in a style based on Picasso and West Indian devices. Internationally acclaimed, he stands as Cuba's foremost modern painter.

Few works are available in English. See MAX-POL FOUCHET, *Wilfredo Lam* (1976), with reproductions of many works. In Spanish, see ANTONIO NÚÑEZ JIMÉNEZ, *Wilfredo Lam* (1982); *Exposición antológica "Homenaje a Wilfredo Lam" 1902–1982,* issued by the Museo Nacional de Arte Contemporaneo, Madrid (1982).

JACQUELYN BRIGGS KENT

LAMADRID, GREGORIO ARÁOZ DE (*b.* 28 November 1795; *d.* 5 January 1857), Argentine military and political leader in the Río de la Plata during the independence and early national periods. Born in Tucumán, Lamadrid entered the local militia in 1811. His revolutionary duties included fighting under Manuel BELGRANO, José RONDEAU, and José de SAN MARTÍN in 1812–1820. Lamadrid sided with the Unitarists of Buenos Aires against the Federalists of the interior and, accordingly, fought against Juan Facundo QUIROGA of La Rioja after assuming the governorship of Tucumán in 1825. He later fought against the dictatorship of Juan Manuel de ROSAS. In addition to his personal service in the struggles for Argentine independence and nation building, Lamadrid wrote two basic sources concerning these events: his autobiography and a work on José María PAZ that he completed shortly before his death in Buenos Aires.

JACINTO R. YABEN, *Biografías argentinas y sudamericanas,* vol. 1, (1938–1940), pp. 278–285; ERNESTO QUESADA, *Lamadrid y la Coalición del Norte* (1965); LILY SOSA DE NEWTON, *Lamadrid* (1971).

FIDEL IGLESIAS

See also **Wars of Independence.**

LAMAR, MIRABEAU BUONAPARTE (*b.* 16 August 1798; *d.* 19 December 1859), president of the republic of Texas (1838–1841). Born near Louisville, Georgia, Lamar founded (1828) and published the Columbus *Enquirer,* and served as secretary to Georgia governor George M. Troup and as state senator before moving to the Mexican province of Texas in 1835. Lamar was soon caught up in Texas's revolt against Mexico. His distinguished military service led to a succession of elected and appointed offices, including secretary of war, commander in chief of the army, vice president, and president of the Republic of Texas.

Lamar's presidency was characterized by many innovative, and often radical, programs. Texas became the first nation in the world to ensure that a person's home and livelihood could not be taken away because of debts. He also established a system of public education endowed entirely from the public domain. But improvident adventures, such as the Santa Fe Expedition, which tried to wrest that trade center from Mexico in 1841, and the republic's continued financial troubles overshadowed the positive aspects of Lamar's administration. Following his retirement from the presidency, Lamar spent much of his time writing poetry and history. He also served in the MEXICAN-AMERICAN WAR (1846–1848) and as minister to Nicaragua and Costa Rica (1858–1859). He died in Richmond, Texas, two months after returning from Central America.

ASA K. CHRISTIAN, *Mirabeau Buonaparte Lamar* (1922); PHILIP GRAHAM, *The Life and Poems of Mirabeau B. Lamar* (1938); CHARLES A. GULICK, ed., *The Papers of Mirabeau Buonaparte Lamar,* 6 vols. (1968); STANLEY SIEGEL, *The Poet President of Texas: The Life of Mirabeau B. Lamar, President of the Republic of Texas* (1977).

MICHAEL R. GREEN

See also **Texas Revolution.**

LAMARQUE PONS, JAURÉS (*b.* 6 May 1917; *d.* 11 June 1982), Uruguayan composer and pianist. Lamarque Pons was born in Salto, where he began his music studies with María Victoria Varela (piano). Later he moved to Montevideo and took advanced piano lessons with Wilhelm Kolischer. He took courses in harmony, counterpoint, and instrumentation with Tomás Mujica and Guido Santórsola. In 1949 he enrolled in the composition classes of the Spanish composer Enrique Casal-Chapí. His *Aires de milonga* premiered in 1943. Lamarque's earlier music was universalist in character and included piano pieces, chamber music, and vocal works. He later composed in the nationalist style, using popular urban melodies, such as old tangos and *milongas* and the rhythms of the Afro-Uruguayan *tamboril.* From that period came his opera *Marta Gruni* (1965), with a libretto from the Uruguayan playwright Florencio SÁNCHEZ. After its 26 February 1967 premiere at the TEATRO SOLÍS under his baton, it became one of the most frequently performed Uruguayan operas. Other important works of Lamarque Pons include the ballet *Suite según Figari* (1952), *Suite Rioplatense* (1954), and the ballet-pantomime *El encargado* (1956). He also composed music for stage and films. Lamarque Pons died in Montevideo.

Composers of the Americas, vol. 16 (1970), pp. 102–107; SUSANA SALGADO, *Breve historia de la música culta en el Uruguay,* 2d ed. (1980).

SUSANA SALGADO

LAMBADA, musical style and dance from northern Brazil. *Lambada* became nationally popular at the end of the 1980s and flourished briefly as an international dance craze. Lambada originated in the mid-1970s in the state of Pará, where musicians such as Joachim de Lima Vieira were fusing Afro-Brazilian *carimbó* with merengue and elements of other Caribbean styles. The sensual *lambada* dance, in which the partners' thighs press close together, was a hybrid of the *maxixe, forró,* and merengue. *Lambada* gained popularity in Bahia and from there was exported to Europe. In 1989, the song "Lambada" (based on Gonzalo and Ulises Hermosa's "Llorando se fue") by the band Kaoma, was the number-one hit in fifteen countries.

CHRIS MC GOWAN and RICARDO PESSANHA, *The Brazilian Sound: Samba, Bossa Nova, and the Popular Music of Brazil* (1991).

CHRIS McGOWAN

LAMBAYEQUE, the name of a modern Peruvian town, district, province, and department. The department, which was created by law 10 December 1874, is bounded by the department of Piura on the north, the department of La Libertad on the south, the department of Cajamarca on the east, and the Pacific Ocean on the west. Its territory encompasses the desert coast; fertile, irrigated river valleys; and the western slopes of the Andes Mountains.

The town of Lambayeque became increasingly important during the colonial period. Encompassing a large community of Indians, at the time of the Spanish Conquest, Lambayeque became a very valuable *encomienda* entrusted by Francisco Pizarro in 1536 to Juan de Barbarán, his loyal supporter and confidant. By the earliest years of the seventeenth century, the town had become an important stopover on the overland route to Lima. Twice thereafter, the town became a refuge for the provincial elite: first, on 14 February 1619, following an earthquake that damaged Trujillo, and second, after the flood of 1720, which destroyed the provincial capital of Saña. As a consequence of the flood, Saña's citizens made Lambayeque the de facto administrative center of the area, a function it performed into the nineteenth century.

During the early nineteenth century, Lambayeque was the third department, after Ica and Tarma, to choose independence. In the late twentieth century, the department is known for its sugar production. The town of Lambayeque has been eclipsed by the departmental capital and bustling commercial emporium of Chiclayo.

RICARDO A. MIRANDA, *Monografía general del Departmento de Lambayeque* (1927); DAVID P. WERLICH, *Peru: A Short History* (1978); and HANS HEINRICH BRÜNING, *Estudios monográficos del Departmento de Lambayeque* (1989).

SUSAN E. RAMÍREZ

LAMBITYECO was one of the principal ZAPOTEC settlements in the Valley of Oaxaca occupied during the MONTE ALBÁN IV period (750–1000). During this period Monte Albán, which had served as the regional capital for over 1,200 years, was gradually abandoned. As its political and economic power waned, other centers in the valley such as Lambityeco, Macuilxochitl, and Jalieza increased in power and influence. This decentralization was accompanied by a low degree of formal political integration and a secularization of authority, trends that characterized the Postclassic throughout Mesoamerica.

Located in the eastern arm of the Valley of Oaxaca, a little over a mile west of the modern town of Tlacolula, Lambityeco is the Period IV sector of a larger site known as Yegüih, which has more than 200 mounds over an area of about 188 acres. Lambityeco, in the northwest sector of the site, consists of about seventy mounds.

Excavations in two of the larger mounds (Mounds 190 and 195) revealed that they were elite residences. In their earliest versions, they were simple houses with a single patio. Mound 190 was reconstructed at least five times, and Mound 195 was rebuilt at least once before being converted into a pyramid. Both structures had family tombs. The tomb in Mound 195 had lifelike stucco representations of a man and a woman above the door and two stucco friezes each depicting a man and a woman in possible marriage scenes. The tomb in Mound 190 contained a large number of ceramic vessels characteristic of Period IV, carved bones, bone tools, and unfired clay vessels.

The unfired clay vessels and millions of pottery sherds on the surface suggest local ceramic production at Lambityeco, and a clay source has been identified at the site. A standardized bowl form apparently was produced on a massive, commercial scale. Another important local industry was SALT production. It also seems likely that the site served an important function as a central marketplace.

JOHN PADDOCK, "Lambityeco," in *The Cloud People: The Divergent Evolution of the Zapotec and Mixtec Civilizations,* edited by Kent V. Flannery and Joyce Marcus (1983), pp. 197–204; RICHARD E. BLANTON, STEPHEN A. KOWALEWSKI, GARY FEINMAN, and JILL APPEL, *Ancient Mesoamerica: A Comparison of Change in Three Regions,* 2d ed. (1993).

WILLIAM R. FOWLER

LAME, MANUEL QUINTÍN (*b.* 31 October 1883; *d.* 7 October 1967), Colombian indigenous leader and author. The son of Páez sharecroppers, Lame organized the Indians of the departments of Cauca and Tolima. His efforts, which met with severe repression by Colombia authorities, revolved around the following demands: (1) defense of the RESGUARDO, a communal landholding corporation of indigenous people; (2) consolidation of the CABILDO (*resguardo* council) as a center of political authority; (3) reclaiming of lands usurped from the *resguardo*; (4) refusal by sharecroppers to pay rent; and (5) reaffirmation of indigenous cultural values.

Although Lame's program was obstructed in Cauca, where his 1910–1921 campaign provoked military occupation, police violence, and the eventual imprisonment of Lame and his associates, his efforts in Tolima were more successful. The pressure exerted by the growth of the coffee economy upon indigenous landholdings in Tolima resulted in the division of *resguardos*. Lame's campaign, which lasted from 1922 to 1939, restored the *resguardo* status of Ortega and Chaparral, thus reversing over a century of land loss under capitalist expansion.

Lame is best known for a 118-page manuscript, "Los pensamientos del indio que se educó dentro de las selvas colombianas" (The Thoughts of the Indian Who Was Educated in the Colombian Forests). Although it was completed in 1939, *Los pensamientos* was published only posthumously in 1971 as *En defensa de mi raza* (In Defense of My Race). This autobiographical treatise outlines Lame's political philosophy, offers an idiosyncratic vision of indigenous history, and denounces specific crimes against Colombian Indians. *Los pensamientos* is a philosophical attack on capitalism, called "civilization" by its author, and is strongly messianic in character.

DIEGO CASTRILLÓN ARBOLEDA, *El indio Quintín Lame* (1973); GONZALO CASTILLO-CÁRDENAS, *Liberation Theology from Below: The Life and Thought of Manuel Quintín Lame* (1987); JOANNE RAPPAPORT, *The Politics of Memory: Native Historical Interpretation in the Colombian Andes* (1990)

JOANNE RAPPAPORT

LAMPIÃO (Virgulino Ferreira da Silva: *b.* 7 July 1897; *d.* 28 July 1938), Brazilian bandit. Brazil's best-known bandit of all time, Lampião was a world-class bandit as well. Son of a modest rancher and hauler in the backlands of Pernambuco, he went astray when he and his brothers began to feud with neighbors. As violence increased on both sides, the Ferreiras, of lower social status than their adversaries, were branded, not unjustly, as outlaws. After 1922, Lampião became the preeminent figure in the *cangaço*, the name given to the organized brigandage that flourished in the region from the 1870s to the 1930s. He seemingly verged on legality in 1926, when Father Cícero Romão Batista of Juàzeiro had him commissioned a captain in forces hastily raised to oppose Luís Carlos PRESTES's wandering revolutionaries. But the patent proved to be worthless, and he reverted to outlawry. For sixteen years, roaming over seven states; living from extortion, robbery, and abductions; and enjoying protection from sometimes reluctant ranchers, political bosses, and even for a time a state governor, he and his band so vanquished police and army forces sent against them that they virtually dominated portions of the backlands. Conscious of his image and ever catering to the press, he became one of the nation's most newsworthy figures, and the story of his exploits reached abroad. Partly the result of strengthened efforts, but largely by luck, the police killed him, his companion, Maria Bonita, and several others of his band in a surprise attack in Sergipe in 1938. Thus the *cangaço* ended. Lampião, whose preserved head long lay in a museum in Salvador, survives in folkore and history.

RANULPHO PRATA, *Lampeão* (1934); OPTATO GUEIROS, *"Lampião": Memórias de um oficial excommandante de forças volantes* (1952); BILLY JAYNES CHANDLER, *The Bandit King: Lampião of Brazil* (1978).

BILLY JAYNES CHANDLER

See also **Bandits** (with illustration); **Cangaceiro.**

LAND LAW OF 1850 (BRAZIL). The Lei de Terra made purchase the only means of acquiring public lands by abolishing the right to acquire legal title through simple occupancy. Containing 108 articles, the law was subject to long debate. Passed on 18 September 1850, it was not published and put into effect until 30 June 1854. The law created a service called the General Bureau of Public Lands (*Repartição Geral das Terras Públicas*) to control access and promote colonization.

The Land Law represented a reformulation of land policy in Brazil. During the colonial period land was acquired through effective occupation, purchase, inheritance, or donation. Donations (SESMARIAS) were crown grants of public lands awarded to petitioners in recognition of their service to the crown, or for the purpose of settlement. At independence, donations of *sesmarias* were abolished and effective occupation, purchase, and inheritance of land became the prevailing forms of acquisition until 1850.

The Land Law vested the ownership of all free land in the state. It confirmed the pre-1850 claims of existing occupants and provided for the official registration and surveying of those claims, upon presentation of proof concerning effective occupation and cultivation. The Land Law limited the size of claims to the dimensions of the largest *sesmaria* in each district. It required a vast bureaucracy at the local level, since it delegated to police officers and judges the responsibility for informing the government of the existence and location of public lands. It also empowered parish priests to register lands after local civil servants located and measured the claim. Funds from land sales and the registration of private claims were to be dedicated to measuring public lands and defraying the costs of settling European colonists.

According to some interpretations, the intent of the Land Law was to stimulate the occupation and colonization of public lands, while others link the abolition of the transatlantic SLAVE TRADE and the passage of the Land Law to a reevaluation of public policy regarding land and labor. In conjunction with a general refocusing of the national economy, from the sugar production of the Northeast to the coffee farming of the Center South, the public regulation of land and labor restricted access to land in favor of the increasing demands of the external capitalist market. The clause that linked the official recognition of claims to a deed of purchase permitted the establishment of a complex bureaucracy to control access to public lands, thus favoring commercial use of land. As a result, the Land Law of 1850 transformed land into a marketable product and legitimized the alienation of unclaimed lands by monied and propertied interests, thereby reinforcing the tendency toward land concentration begun by the *sesmarias*.

Lack of human resources to implement the registration and measurement of lands, a weak bureaucracy at the local level, and resistance by local landowners contributed to the minor impact the law had on the agrarian structure of the country.

EMÍLIA VIOTTI DA COSTA, *The Brazilian Empire: Myths and Histories* (1985).

NANCY PRISCILLA SMITH NARO

See also **Fazendas.**

LAND TENURE

Brazil

There are two principal types of land tenure in Brazil. The first dates back to the legal ownership of land by deed, officially granted by SESMARIAS (crown grants) in the sixteenth century. The other form of land tenure, which paralleled that of legal claim, was related to title through occupation or squatting and through cultivation of the land. After Brazilian independence in 1822, the granting of *sesmarias* was discontinued. Until the LAND LAW OF 1850, claim to land was recognized by its effective occupation and cultivation.

Land usage varied throughout Brazil. A *chácara*, or country establishment on the outskirts of a town or city, was typically a small or medium-sized farm where the proprietor owned both the land and its produce, often foodstuffs. Other small holdings for subsistence cultivation and some livestock breeding usually contained a small cabin or two and might also have included primitive processing facilities for manioc, beans, and corn. These units existed on unclaimed plots of land and also within FAZENDAS (large rural properties). Among many things, they were referred to as *rocas*, *sítios*, and *situações*. Their occupants were squatters or leaseholders (*posseiros*), renters (*arrendatários*), tenants (*foreiros*), or sharecroppers (*parceiros*), many of whom paid an annual rent in cash and labor services to the landowner and owned small numbers of slaves. During the nineteenth century, small farms within the confines of large ones or within plantations could be freely exchanged or sold by their occupants without the prior knowledge of or consultation with the landowner. This arrangement began to change when landowners, faced with increasing production costs and diminishing prices for slave labor in the 1880s, began to control land use and labor through contracts and other formal agreements.

NANCY PRISCILLA SMITH NARO, "Customary Rightholders and Legal Claimants to Land in Rio de Janeiro, Brazil, 1850–1890," in *The Americas* (April 1992).

NANCY PRISCILLA SMITH NARO

LAND TENURE: SPANISH AMERICA. *See* Hacienda.

LANDA, DIEGO DE (*b.* 1524; *d.* 1579), Castilian Franciscan missionary. Born in Cifuentes, Landa entered the monastery of San Juan de los Reyes in Toledo when he was sixteen. In 1549 he journeyed to Yucatán, where he learned the Maya language and ministered to the Maya people. Landa, one of the earliest Franciscans in Yucatán, helped convert the Maya to Christianity, only to discover that they refused to abandon their traditional religion. Suspecting them of carrying out human sacrifice using Catholic ritual, he organized an inquisition (1562) that eventually led to the imprisonment and torture of 4,400 Indians. After extracting confessions, and after more than 170 people had died under torture or by committing suicide, Landa held an auto-da-fé (day of judgment, punishment, and penance) on 12 July 1562 and pardoned the survivors. He was later charged with misconduct in the affair but defended himself successfully and in 1564 returned to Spain, where he wrote his book about Maya history and culture (*Relación de las cosas de Yucatán*). He returned to Yucatán in 1573 as bishop and died there seven years later without further controversy.

JUAN FRANCISCO MOLINA SOLÍS, *Historia de Yucatán durante la dominación española*, vol. 1 (1904); INGA CLENDINNEN, *Ambivalent Conquests: Maya and Spaniard in Yucatán, 1517–1570* (1987).

ROBERT W. PATCH

LANDALUZE, VÍCTOR PATRICIO DE (*b.* 1828; *d.* 8 June 1889), Cuban painter and cartoonist who is considered the precursor of graphic political satire in Cuba. Born in Bilbao, Spain, Landaluze emigrated in the 1850s to Havana, where he founded the newspaper *Don Junípero* (1862). Between 1868 and 1878, he was the political cartoonist for *La Charanga*, *El Moro Muza* (under the pseudonym of Bayaceto), *Don Circunstancias*, and *Juan Palomo*, weekly journals through which he satirized the Cuban struggle for independence. He was both professor at and director of the Academy of San Alejandro in Havana.

In oil and watercolor paintings, he depicted popular Cuban stereotypes such as the *guajiro* (a rustic type), the landowner, the slave, and the *ñañigo* (a member of a secret black society), and illustrated the books *Tipos y costumbres* (Types and Customs) and *Cuba pintoresca* (Picturesque Cuba), both published in 1881.

His ironic attitude toward the Cuban independence movement earned him the antipathy of art critics. Ironically, his painting of the backward *campesino* Liborio became a Cuban national symbol. With the exception of an oil painting of a fugitive slave cornered by dogs and soldiers (*El cimarrón* [The Runaway Slave]), Landaluze's work is often considered biased in his presentation of blacks as lazy and lascivious. Much of his production, however, recorded with exactitude the costumes and rituals of the different nations of Cuban blacks. He died in Guanabacoa.

ADELAIDA DE JUAN, *Pintura cubana: Temas y variaciones* (1980), pp. 25–26, 33–36, 46; DAWN ADES, *Art in Latin America: The Modern Era, 1820–1980* (1989), p. 85.

MARTA GARSD

LANDÁZURI RICKETTS, JUAN (*b.* 19 December 1913), archbishop of Lima and primate of Peru (1955–1988), cardinal (1962–). Landázuri led the Peruvian Catholic church through a period of transformation in that institution's understanding of its mission in society. A Franciscan, and considered a church moderate, Landázuri championed the church's commitment to the reform of social and economic structures. Enjoying great prestige among fellow bishops, he copresided over the Second CONFERENCE OF LATIN AMERICAN BISHOPS (CELAM) at Medellín, Colombia, in 1968 and served as the vice president of the Latin American Bishops' Council at the time of its third general conference in Puebla, Mexico (1979). Under his leadership, the Peruvian church distanced itself from the state and traditional elites, democratized church decision-making procedures, and turned its attention to organizing the poor. Though famous for his mediation skills, Landázuri's defense of the LIBERATION THEOLOGY of Gustavo GUTIÉRREZ, a Peruvian priest, culminated in the 1980s in clashes with the Vatican and division among an increasingly conservative Peruvian hierarchy.

CATALINO ROMERO, *Iglesia en el Perú: Compromiso y renovación (1958–1984)* (1987); PENNY LERNOUX, *People of God* (1989), esp. pp. 98–102, 114–115.

MATTHEW J. O'MEAGHER

LANDÍVAR, RAFAEL (*b.* 27 October 1731; *d.* 1793), Guatemalan Jesuit priest and writer, born in Santiago de los Caballeros de Guatemala, today known as Old Guatemala City. He graduated from San Borja School and earned his Ph.D. in philosophy from the Pontifical University of San Carlos at the age of sixteen. Later he traveled to Mexico (1749) and in 1750 joined the Jesuit order. Five years later he was ordained a priest. In 1761 he returned to Guatemala, where he assumed the position of rector at the College of San Francisco de Borja.

When CHARLES III expelled the Jesuits from the American continent six years later, Landívar and his colleagues roamed the ports of Europe for a year, an odyssey which finally ended when the Jesuits were allowed to settle in Italy. Though Charles III prohibited the members of the Jesuit order from performing priestly duties and writing books, this didn't prevent Landívar from writing in Bologna. His works include *Oración fúnebre a la muerte del arzobispo de Guatemala, Francisco Figueredo y Victoria*, two odes in Latin and one in Castilian, and the collection of poems entitled *Salva cara parens*. His most outstanding work, however, is *Rusticatio mexicana*, a mournful song of his native land in which he describes its natural attributes, its customs, and its disasters such as volcanic eruptions and earthquakes. The first edition was published in Modena in 1781 and the second in Bologna in 1782. It is the first ode to the Guatemalan homeland by a political exile and is considered the best verse about Latin America ever written in Latin.

ANTONIO BATRES JÁUREGUI, *Landívar e Irisarri: literatos guatemaltecos*, 2d ed. (1957); JOSÉ MATA GAVIDIA, ed., *Landívar, el poeta de Guatemala* (1979); CATALINA BARRIOS Y BARRIOS, *Rafael Landívar: Vida y obra* (1982).

FERNANDO GONZÁLEZ DAVISON

LANUSSE, ALEJANDRO AUGUSTO (*b.* 28 August 1918), president of Argentina (1971–1973). Born in the city of Buenos Aires, Lanusse became an officer in the cavalry. In 1956 he was special envoy to the Vatican and was the Argentine military attaché in Mexico from 1958 to 1960.

When Lanusse assumed the presidency on 26 March 1971, following a nonviolent coup, there were no fewer than five separate guerrilla armies; wildcat strikes were wrecking the economy; and there was student unrest. Although staunchly anti-PERÓN, Lanusse allowed the former dictator to return from exile, hoping to be bailed out of his predicament. Perón, in the meantime, allowed his subordinate, Héctor José CÁMPORA, to precede him in the presidency. The remainder of Lanusse's career was tarnished by his alleged involvement in the David Graiver affair and the murder of his daughter-in-law by left-wing guerrillas.

FÉLIX LUNA, *Argentina de Perón a Lanusse, 1943–1973* (1974); LUIS BERTONE DES BALBES, *Cronología militar argentina, 1806–1980* (1983).

ROGER GRAVIL

LANZA, ALCIDES (*b.* 2 June 1929), Argentine composer. Born in Rosario, Argentina, Lanza studied composition with Julián Batista and Alberto GINASTERA. He continued his studies with Maderna, Copland, Messiaen, Loriod, and Malipiero at the Instituto Di Tella in Buenos Aires (1963–1964). From 1959 to 1965 he was a member of the artistic staff of the Teatro Colón in Buenos Aires, where he became one of the founding members of Agrupación Música Viva. Awarded a Guggenheim Fellowship in 1965, he studied with Ussachevsky and Mimaroglu at the Columbia-Princeton Electronic Music Centre in New York. Since 1971, he has been professor of composition and electronic music at McGill University in Montreal. From 1972 to 1973, he was composer in residence in Berlin. Director of the Electronic Music Studio at McGill since 1974, Lanza has also been artistic director and conductor of GEMS (Group of the Electronic Music Studio) at McGill and a member of the CEC (Canadian Electroacoustic Community) since its inception in 1987.

Showing the influence of his earlier architectural studies, his scores are based on ideograms, graphisms, and drawings, all intended to give a direct representation of his musical ideas. A substantial amount of Lanza's production includes electroacoustics either on tape, live processing, or both. Except for some mostly earlier solo tape pieces and a recent work for keyboard-controlled synthesizers with tape, this output consists of mixed compositions wherein an important role is assigned to some acoustic element. Notable are several pieces written for his life and artistic partner the actress-singer Meg Sheppard, with whom he has performed extensively in Canada and elsewhere promoting his music and that of many Latin American and Canadian avant-garde composers. Lanza's scores and recordings are published by Editions Shelan Publications in Montreal.

JOHN VINTON, ed., *Dictionary of Contemporary Music* (1971); GÉRARD BÉHAGUE, *Music in Latin America: An Introduction* (1979); ANDRÉE LAURIER, "Le compositeur à l'ère de l'électronique et des nouvelles facilités de la composition," in *Le compositeur canadien* (mars 1984): 15–19.

SERGIO BARROSO

LAPLANTE, EDUARDO (*b.* 1818; *d.* ?), Cuban lithographer and painter. Born in France, Laplante was among the first to portray Cuban rural life as it existed in reality. He devoted particular care to details in his art, making his work useful for historians and students of mid-nineteenth-century Cuban planter society. Laplante is most famous for his collection of twenty-eight lithographs, *Los ingenios de Cuba* (1857), which provides detailed views of both external appearances and internal social conditions in Cuba's major SUGAR plants. With these lithographs Laplante achieved a realistic portrait of Cuban race and class relations as well as the operation of the rural sugar economy.

ADELAIDA DE JUAN, *Pintura Cubana: Temas y variaciones* (1978) and *Two Centuries of Cuban Art, 1759–1959* (1980).

KAREN RACINE

LAPRIDA, FRANCISCO NARCISO DE (*b.* 28 October 1786; *d.* 28 September 1829), Argentine patriot. Born in San Juan and educated in Buenos Aires and Santiago de Chile, Laprida returned to his native city in 1811 to practice law and participate in local politics. He was president of the Congress of TUCUMÁN when, on 9 July 1816, it adopted the Argentine declaration of independence.

Laprida served briefly as acting governor of San Juan in 1818. As a liberal professional and eager to promote progressive innovations, he collaborated from 1822 to 1824 with the radical reformist government of Salvador María del Carril in his home province and then with the abortive national government of Bernardino RIVADAVIA and his Unitarist party. He was vice president of the Constituent Congress that issued the centralist 1826 Constitution. In the civil strife that followed adoption of the Constitution, he was a committed Unitarist. Laprida was killed by victorious Federalists in the immediate aftermath of the battle of Pilar, in Mendoza province.

EMILIO MAURÍN NAVARRO, "Dr. Francisco Narciso de Laprida," in his *Precursores cuyanos de la independencia de América y patriotas sanjuaninos de la hora inicial* (1968); and JOSÉ F. SIVORI, *Francisco Narciso de Laprida* (1971).

DAVID BUSHNELL

LARA, AGUSTÍN (*b.* 30 October 1900; *d.* 6 November 1970), renowned Mexican composer of popular songs.

Lara was born in Tlacotalpan, Veracruz. He began composing in the mid-1920s, when the regional music of Mexico had not yet become popular, and joined Radio XEW with his own program, "Hora Azul" (Blue Hour), on which he showcased his own compositions, often playing them on the piano. He wrote almost 600 songs, mostly in the International Latin style, including "Farolito," "Enamorada," "Mujer," "Cada noche un amor," and "Solamente una vez" ("You Belong to My Heart"), which achieved global fame. His choice to use an international rather than native Mexican styles brought extensive criticism from many Mexican musicians, scholars, and critics, who regarded his work as not truly Mexican. The song "Granada" became so popular in Europe and the Americas that he received honorary Spanish citizenship.

See *New Grove Dictionary of Music* (1980); CLAES AF GEIJERSTAM, *Popular Music in Mexico* (1976).

GUY BENSUSAN

LAREDO BRU, FEDERICO (*b.* 23 April 1875; *d.* 8 July 1946), president of Cuba 1936–1940. A veteran of the war of independence, Bru served as governor of Las Villas Province and as secretary of the interior under President José Miguel GÓMEZ. In 1923 he led an uprising of disgruntled veterans against President Alfredo ZAYAS. Bru was elected vice president of Cuba in January 1936, and when President Miguel Mariano GÓMEZ was impeached by a Senate subservient to army chief Fulgencio BATISTA, he was installed as the new figurehead president. He nevertheless discharged the duties of his office with great aplomb and dignity, counterbalancing military interference as much as possible. A law completely restructuring the SUGAR INDUSTRY, one of the most important pieces of legislation of the period, was passed during his term in office. It was also under Laredo Bru that the 1940 constitution was framed by a freely elected constituent assembly.

Very little has been written about Bru, but some information may be found in HERMINIO PORTELL-VILÁ, *Nueva historia de la República de Cuba* (1986), pp. 474–510.

JOSÉ M. HERNÁNDEZ

See also **Cuba: War of Independence.**

LARKIN, THOMAS (*b.* 16 September 1802; *d.* 27 October 1858), California merchant and U.S. consul in Monterey, California. A Bostonian, Thomas Larkin came to CALIFORNIA in 1832 to work for his half-brother, Captain Juan Bautista Rogers Cooper, in Monterey. Larkin soon began his own successful career trading in flour and hides, provisioning vessels, and collecting debts for eastern U.S. merchants. His wide network of merchant contacts in Mazatlán, Mexico, Honolulu, Hawaii, and the U.S. made natural his appointment as U.S. consul in

1843. His diligence and his wide circle of acquaintances among the leading citizens of Mexican California led to his appointment as confidential agent by President James K. POLK in 1846. Larkin was successful in warding off European influence in California, in persuading leading *Californios* to favor acquisition by the U.S., and in mediating between them and Americans intent on acquiring California by force. He later became a major land speculator in the San Francisco area.

GEORGE P. HAMMOND, ed., *The Larkin Papers: Personal, Business, and Official Correspondence of Thomas Oliver Larkin, Merchant and United States Consul in California,* 10 vols. (1951–1968); JOHN A. HAWGOOD, ed., *First and Last Consul: Thomas Oliver Larkin and the Americanization of California,* 2d ed. (1970); HARLAN HAGUE and DAVID J. LANGUM, *Thomas O. Larkin, A Life of Patriotism and Profit in Old California* (1990).

E. JEFFREY STANN

LARRAZÁBAL UGUETO, WOLFGANG (*b.* 5 March 1911), Venezuelan naval officer and politician. Born in Carúpano, Larrazábal studied at the Escuela Naval (1928–1932). He became commander of the naval base at Puerto Cabello and held successively higher posts, finally rising to commander of the navy in 1957. As the senior navy officer, he joined forces with other military and civilian leaders to overthrow Marcos PÉREZ JIMÉNEZ in January 1958. When the dictator fled, Larrazábal headed the interim governing junta (23 January–13 November 1958) as provisional president. Prior to elections in December, he resigned from the military to run as a presidential candidate of the Democratic Republican Union and the Communist Party. His enormous personal popularity in Caracas and other cities enabled him to capture 34 percent of the popular vote. He lost to Rómulo BETANCOURT of Democratic Action, however, who received 50 percent. Larrazábal is noted for his support of democracy at a time when many military leaders preferred to rule. He backed the electoral process and encouraged the military to support the transition to civilian rule during his transition government. Larrazábal ran for president again in 1963 as the Popular Democratic Force candidate but won only 9.4 percent of the vote. He remained a political figure in the 1980s but broke with the Force to form a splinter group.

JOSÉ UMANA BERNAL, *Testimonio de la revolución en Venezuela* (1958); JOHN D. MARTZ, *Acción Democratica: Evolution of a Modern Political Party,* (1966); AGUSTIN BLANCO MUÑOZ, *El 23 de enero: Habla la conspiración,* (1981); JUDITH EWELL, *Venezuela. A Century of Change,* (1984).

KATHY WALDRON

See also **Venezuela: Political Parties.**

LARREA, JUAN (*b.* 1782; *d.* 1847), Spanish-born merchant and member of the first Argentine patriot junta. Larrea arrived in Buenos Aires prior to 1806. He fought British invaders as a captain in the battalion of Volunteers of Catalonia. An early champion of independence, he was initially associated with the Spanish-dominated Partido Republicano, which controlled the *cabildo,* or town council. In 1810 Larrea joined Mariano MORENO and other creoles participating in the CABILDO ABIERTO on 22 May, and became a member of the first patriot junta. During the ensuing controversy between federalists and centralists, Larrea continued to support Moreno and was exiled to San Juan after Moreno's resignation and the revolt of May 1811. In January 1813 Larrea represented Buenos Aires at the constitutional assembly. Named minister of the treasury under Supreme Director Gervasio Antonio de POSADAS, Larrea and Carlos María de Alvear were charged to acquire a naval squadron. Larrea accomplished this with the aid of the North American merchants Guillermo Pío White and William BROWN. The unraveling of the "united" provinces in 1815 forced Larrea, once again, into exile and obscurity. Reestablished as a merchant, he was appointed Argentine consul general in France several years later. Larrea eventually returned to Buenos Aires, where he died.

IONE S. WRIGHT and LISA M. NEKHOM, *Historical Dictionary of Argentina* (1978), pp. 476–477; CARLOS ALBERTO FLORIA and CÉSAR A. GARCÍA BELSUNCE, *Historia de los Argentinos,* vol. 1 (1971), pp. 244 and 322–337; DIEGO ABAD DE SANTILLÁN, *Historia Argentino,* vol. 1 (1965), pp. 516–528.

CHRISTEL K. CONVERSE

LARRETA, ENRIQUE RODRÍGUEZ (*b.* 4 March 1873; *d.* 7 July 1961), Argentine dramatist. Enrique Rodríguez Larreta was born in Buenos Aires of Uruguayan parents and belonged to the cattle-baron oligarchy; he earned a doctorate in law from the University of Buenos Aires. Larreta exemplifies the phenomenon of the gentleman literatus made possible by the enormous economic prosperity and international ties that characterized Argentine life in the federal capital of Buenos Aires and the province of Buenos Aires between 1880 and 1930. True to his class, Larreta specialized in a literature (basically narrative and lyrical dramas) that focused on questions of national identity from the perspective of the ruling creoles. This meant an emphasis on a chthonic definition of Hispanic roots, with or without the dimension of their forceful domination of indigenous elements. Larreta's most famous work, *La gloria de don Ramiro; una vida en tiempos de Felipe II* (1908), in the context of a decadent prose with important French parallels, explores contradictions of the Hispanic substratum of Latin American society and is most notable for its rereading of the Spanish racialistic obsession with the "purity of the blood." Larreta correlates Don Ramiro's nonpurity with his failure in the New World, a plot configuration that has strident ideological implications for early-twentieth-century political beliefs in an Argentina that opposed immigration (especially its Jewish components) and non-Hispanic liberalism, while at the same time calling for a reaffirmation of an authentic Hispanic heritage. Larreta, thanks in great part to the strains of literary decadence to which he was exposed, may not have been as facile in these matters as Leopoldo LUGONES (1874–1938) or the harsh-minded nationalists, but there is no question that his writing strikes a counterpoint to the dominant cultural liberalism of the modernists. One cannot help but be struck by the juxtaposition in Larreta of significant manifestations of an aesthetist posture and the mythmaking force of an austere Spanish traditionalism, a feature of his writing also evident in *Zogoibi* (1926), set in the legendary Argentine pampas.

AMADO ALONSO, *Ensayo sobre la novela histórica: El modernismo en* La gloria de don Ramiro (1942); JUAN CARLOS GHIANO, *Análisis de* La gloria de don Ramiro (1968); GABRIELLA IBIETA, *Tradition and Renewal in "La gloria de don Ramiro"* (1986).

DAVID WILLIAM FOSTER

LARS, CLAUDIA. *See* **Brannon de Samayoa Chinchilla, Carmen.**

LAS CASAS, BARTOLOMÉ DE (*b.* ca. August 1474; *d.* ca. 17 July 1566), Spanish bishop, defender of human rights, author. Bartolomé de Las Casas remains one of the most controversial figures in Latin America's conquest period. His exposé of Spanish mistreatment of Amerindians produced public outrage that was directed at both the conquistadores who were committing the atrocities and at the writer who had made them public. Las Casas's vast output of political, historical, and theological writing forms one of the basic sources for contemporary understanding of the conquest period and of some of the most important individuals involved in the initial colonization of the Spanish Indies.

The early years of Las Casas's life seemed destined to propel him toward the newly discovered Indies and its inhabitants. He was the son of a Seville merchant, Pedro de Las Casas. In 1493 the young Bartolomé saw Christopher COLUMBUS's triumphant return to Spain and the small group of Taino Indians Columbus brought with him. Las Casas remained at home in school while his father and other members of his family accompanied Columbus as colonists on the second voyage to the Indies. Five years later Pedro de Las Casas returned to Spain for a short period, bringing with him a Taino boy named Juanico. While his father was at home, Bartolomé declared his desire to become a priest and went to Salamanca to learn canon law. He also began to learn about the Indies from Juanico, with whom Las Casas struck up a lifelong friendship. In 1502 Las Casas quit school and sailed to the West Indies. His first years in Hispaniola were spent helping his father and aiding in the provisioning of Spanish military expeditions. At the same time, young Las Casas began learning several na-

tive languages and befriending local Indians; he had already begun deploring the violence he witnessed. He returned to Europe, first to Spain and then to Rome where, in 1507, he was ordained a priest.

In 1510 Las Casas returned to Hispaniola. These years were to be crucial both for Las Casas and for the nature of Spanish-Indian relations. His return coincided with the arrival of the DOMINICANS. In 1511 the Dominican priest Antonio de Montesino represented his order in a highly public condemnation of the ENCOMIENDA system that outraged the island's entire Spanish community. The message was not lost on Las Casas, who then held Indians as an *encomendero* (land grantee). Las Casas was ordained priest in 1512 or 1513, and in 1513 he joined Diego de VELÁZQUEZ and Pánfilo de NARVÁEZ in the conquest of Cuba. Las Casas preached to and converted the natives in preparation for the Spanish conquistadores, and those efforts largely succeeded. In reward for his services, Las Casas received land together with a grant of Indians and by all appearances had established himself as a typical *encomendero*.

The decimation of Cuba's native population by Spanish *encomenderos* through overwork, starvation, and murder made Las Casas realize that the real solution for Indian mistreatment lay not with challenging the conduct of individual *encomenderos* but by calling into ques-

Fray Bartolomé de Las Casas. Reproduced from J. A. Llorente, *Oeuvres de Don Barthélemi de Las Casas, évêque de Chiapa . . .* (Brussels, 1822). ORGANIZATION OF AMERICAN STATES.

tion the entire system and its relationship to Christian morality. In 1514 he astonished his parishioners by condemning the *encomienda* in its entirety, freeing his Indians, and then vigorously interceding with local authorities on the natives' behalf. Failing to convert even a single *encomendero* to his position, he went to Europe in 1515 to plead his case with the king of Spain. Las Casas spent the next six years arguing that the period for military conquest of the Indians had passed. The time had arrived, he claimed, for peaceful conversion of natives and the promotion of agricultural colonization. He did not stand alone in condemning Spanish cruelties against Indians. Other voices had begun to sound in the Americas, and a small but influential group of royal ministers and Spanish churchmen supported the goal of protecting Indians. After heated debate, Emperor Charles V (CHARLES I OF SPAIN) sided with Las Casas in 1519, ruling that the Indies could be governed without the force of arms. The ruling, however, had little practical effect in the distant Western Hemisphere.

During the next quarter century, Las Casas repeatedly suffered defeats in his efforts to defend the Americas' native populations. In 1520 he left Spain to establish a settlement in Venezuela, hoping to peacefully convert local Indians and create an economically self-sufficient community. But opposition from *encomenderos* and colonial officials helped to incite an Indian rebellion that wrecked the project. Despondent over its failure, he entered the Dominican order as a monk in 1523. The years that followed were ones of intellectual growth and personal frustration for Las Casas. He outlined his program for peaceful conversion, in opposition to military conquest, in *Del único modo de atraer a todos los pueblos a la verdadera religión* (1537; *The Only Way*). While in the monastery, he began his monumental *Apologética historia* (*In Defense of the Indians*) and the *History of the Indies* and continued a lifelong passion of collecting documents. One of Las Casas's critics charged that he once arrived in Tlaxcala, Mexico, "with twenty-seven or thirty-seven [Indian] carriers—and the greatest part of what they were carrying was accusations against the Spaniards, and other rubbish."

Although colonial Spaniards scorned any attempt to ameliorate the Indians' plight, moral encouragement arrived from Europe in the form of Pope Paul III's bull *Sublimis Deus* (1537), which proclaimed that American Indians were rational beings with souls, whose lives and property should be protected. During the same year Charles V supported an effort by Las Casas and the Dominicans to establish missions in Guatemala based on the precepts laid out in *Del único modo*. The high point of the crown's efforts came in 1542 with the so-called New Laws, which forbade Indian SLAVERY and sought to end the *encomienda* system within a generation by outlawing their transference through family inheritance. Las Casas, who was in Spain at the time, directly influenced the direction of the NEW LAWS in part by reading the first version of *The Devastation of the*

Indies (a much longer text than the one he published in 1552) to a horrified royal court.

In 1544 he sailed to the Indies for a brief and tempestuous tenure as the bishop of Chiapas. Although he had been offered the Cuzco bishopric, the richest in the Americas, Las Casas instead accepted one of the poorest. When he tried to implement the New Laws in his see, local clergy who had ties to *encomenderos* defied him. After Las Casas denied final absolution to any Spaniard who refused to free his Indians or pay restitution, he received threats against his life. Proclamation of the New Laws brought outright revolt in parts of Spanish America and fierce antagonism everywhere. Even the Viceroyalty of New Spain and its high court openly refused to enforce them. In 1545 colonial opposition persuaded Charles V to revoke key inheritance statutes in the New Laws. Las Casas went to an ecclesiastical assembly in Mexico City and persuaded his fellow bishops to support a strongly worded resolution defending Indian rights. At the same time he publicly humiliated the viceroy, Antonio de MENDOZA, for attempting to silence him. But he left his most defiant act for last.

Just after arriving, Las Casas issued a confessor manual for the priests in his diocese that essentially reinstituted the inheritance statutes of the New Laws. His *Confesionario* produced public outrage by reiterating that all Spaniards seeking last rites must free their Indians and make restitution, even if the Indians were part of a deeded estate. Las Casas justified his decision by arguing that all wealth acquired through *encomiendas* was ill-gotten, declaring, "There is no Spaniard in the Indies who has shown good faith in connection with the wars of Conquest." This last statement put at issue the very basis of Spain's presence in the Americas. Las Casas contended that the Spanish had acquired all their wealth by unjustly exploiting Indians; if all of their activities since Columbus's landing were unjust, so too, logically, was the crown's American presence. Not surprisingly, the Council of the Indies recalled Las Casas to Spain in 1547 and ordered all copies of the *Confesionario* confiscated.

Colonial and Spanish opposition to Las Casas coalesced around Juan Ginés de SEPÚLVEDA, one of Spain's leading humanists. Sepúlveda used Aristotle's doctrine of just war to defend Spanish conduct in the Americas. The vigor of Las Casas's counterattack led the Council of the Indies to call for a court of jurists and theologians to ascertain "how conquests may be conducted justly and with security of conscience." Charles V then ordered the two men to debate their positions before the court.

Much popular misconception has surrounded the 1550 "great debate" between Las Casas and Sepúlveda in the Spanish city of Valladolid. The two men never debated face to face but stated their cases individually before the court. Sepúlveda's three-hour defense of just wars against Indians rested on four points. First, the Indians had committed grave sins by their idolatry and sins against nature. Second, their "natural rudeness and inferiority" corresponded with Aristotle's view that some men were born natural slaves. Third, military conquest was the most efficacious method of converting Indians to Christianity. Finally, conquering Indians made it possible to protect the weak amongst them. In rebuttal, Las Casas took five days to read his *Apologética historia sumaria*. In the end, the majority of judges sided with Las Casas but, perhaps fearing controversy, refused to render a public decision. Legislation by the crown continued to move slowly toward the abolition of Indian slavery and some of the egregious features of the *encomienda* system.

Las Casas left Chiapas in 1547 and, in August 1550, resigned the Chiapas bishopric. He assumed residency in the Dominican San Gregorio monastery, where in 1552 he produced his most important work, *The Devastation of the Indies: A Brief Account. A Brief Account* was immediately translated into several languages and ignited a firestorm of controversy that continues today. Next came his two largest works. The first, *Apologética historia sumaria*, argued for the rationality of American Indians by comparing them favorably to the Greeks and Romans. After research in Hernando Columbus's library; he rewrote his three-volume *History of the Indies*, which remains a standard source on Columbus and Spain's first decades in the Americas.

Las Casas continued to champion Indian rights in the final phase of his life. His last great success occurred in 1555, when Peruvian conquistadores offered 8 million ducats to PHILIP II in exchange for perpetual *encomiendas*. Las Casas adroitly had the decision postponed while he gained the power of attorney, enabling him to act officially on the Indians' behalf. With their backing, he made a counteroffer that surpassed the conquistadores' bribe and led to its summary withdrawal. Despite that triumph, Las Casas's final years were characterized by urgent pleas about the Indians' circumstances and the belief that God might destroy Spain for its sins against them. On the day he died, Las Casas voiced regret for not having done more. He was buried in the convent chapel of Our Lady of Atocha in Madrid.

Today Las Casas is largely remembered for *A Brief Account* and his role in the controversy surrounding the BLACK LEGEND of Spanish conquest. Whether or not Las Casas exaggerated Spanish atrocities, as his critics claim, does not alter the fact that *A Brief Account* remains one of the most important documents ever written on human rights. The issues Las Casas raised in 1552 remain pertinent today. Modern scholarship has supported Las Casas's staggering toll of native deaths but assigns the principal responsibility to Afro-European diseases rather than Spanish cruelty. Recent work has also refuted the claim that Las Casas promoted the African SLAVE TRADE as a substitute for Indian slavery, pointing out that his *History of the Indies* explicitly condemns African slavery. Although Las Casas never claimed to be

an impartial historian, his historical texts continue to provide information on the conquest period. Ultimately, however, it is Las Casas as a crusader and symbol of the struggle for human rights that keeps him in our historical memory. Perhaps no one else in history has been more insistent or clear in articulating Western culture's moral responsibility to the oppressed.

LEWIS HANKE, *Aristotle and the American Indians* (1959); HENRY R. WAGNER, *The Life and Writings of Bartolomé de las Casas* (1967); CHARLES GIBSON, ed., *The Black Legend: Anti-Spanish Attitudes in the Old World and the New* (1971); GUSTAVO GUTIÉRREZ, *Las Casas: In Search of the Poor of Jesus Christ* (1994); HELEN RAND, *Las Casas: The Untold Story* (forthcoming).

WILLIAM DONOVAN

LAS HERAS, JUAN GREGORIO DE (*b.* 11 June 1780; *d.* 6 February 1866), Argentine general and hero of the wars of independence. Born in Buenos Aires and seemingly destined for a commerical career, he enrolled in the militia and fought against the British during the "English invasions" of 1806–1807. In 1813 he went to Chile with a force of Argentine auxiliaries and distinguished himself in the early campaigns of Chile's wars of independence. Following the collapse of patriot Chile (October 1814), he joined José de SAN MARTÍN's Army of the Andes, in which he commanded a division. He fought in many other actions, including the battles of CHACABUCO (12 February 1817) and MAIPÚ (5 April 1818), and later served as San Martín's chief of staff on the expedition to liberate Peru (1820–1821).

When San Martín withdrew from Peru, Las Heras returned to his native land. He became governor of Buenos Aires Province in 1824 and chief executive of Argentina in 1825. During his brief period in office, war was declared on Brazil. With Bernardino RIVADAVIA's assumption of the Argentine presidency (1826), Las Heras returned to Chile and resumed his military career. He was cashiered in 1830 for refusing to recognize the new Chilean Conservative regime. He was reinstated in 1842, after which he immediately retired. He spent the rest of his life in Chile. His remains were repatriated to Buenos Aires in 1906.

SIMON COLLIER

LAS VEGAS, the culture characteristic of the people of southwestern Ecuador in the preceramic period between 10,000 and 6,600 years ago (based on 22-radiocarbon dates). The Las Vegas culture may be a local variant of the preceramic culture distributed in the coastal zones of northern Peru, Colombia, and Panama in the same period. In Ecuador, it is the only preceramic-stage culture reconstructed in detail. Las Vegas lithic technology lacked stone projectile points and bifacial flaking techniques, both of which were characteristic of the preceramic tool kits found in the highlands of Ecuador.

The way of life of the Las Vegas people has been reconstructed from abundant remains excavated at Site 80, a large camp or village on the seasonal Las Vegas River, and from limited excavations and surface reconnaissance of thirty-one sites on the semiarid and recently deforested SANTA ELENA Peninsula. Lithic, shell, and bone artifacts; 192 human skeletons; faunal remains; charcoal; pollen; phytoliths; minerals; and settlement data have been analyzed. The human skeletons recovered from the site show that the people, who lived there 6,600 to 8,250 years ago, were biologically like other early Native Americans, and that they were relatively healthy and did not suffer from the deleterious effects of intensive agriculture (such as anemia and tooth decay). The sample included 122 adults and 70 subadults who were buried in various ways, reflecting a complex set of burial customs probably associated with ancestor worship. This is evidence that there was an intensification in the social activities of the local group in the period after 8,000 years ago.

The Las Vegas people were unspecialized gatherers, hunters, and fishermen living in a tropical, littoral zone with high biotic potential. The people exploited comprehensively an environment which included a seasonally dry tropical forest, more heavily wooded river bottoms, limited mangrove swamps, estuaries, beaches, and a very productive marine ecosystem. The animal bones recovered from the midden at Site 80 suggest that the ancient environment was similar to the present one (semiarid), although it had not yet suffered the desertification caused by deforestation: the ancient environment was not very moist, because tropical forest animals were not identified from bones in the Las Vegas sites.

Counting the animal bones recovered from Site 80 suggests that the people consumed calories from animal sources in the following proportions: terrestrial fauna (like deer) accounted for about 54 percent of the calories, while fish contributed about 35 percent and shellfish about 11 percent. It is likely that plant food contributed most to the people's diet, but ancient plant remains are only rarely preserved in these sites. Evidence of squash, bottle gourd, and primitive maize found in Site 80 indicates that the people added plant cultivation to their subsistence system before 8,000 years ago. At that time they occupied Site 80 on a semipermanent basis, moving irregularly to subsidiary camps. A trench suitable for supporting the wall poles of a shelter is evidence that the earliest Las Vegans built circular huts about 6 feet in diameter.

Preceramic people like those of Las Vegas probably inhabited both the lowlands of the Guayas River basin and the littoral zones of the coast of Ecuador, where they exploited a wide variety of tropical resources from permanent villages, but regrettably preceramic sites have been identified only on the Santa Elena Peninsula, and there is a gap of over 1,000 years at the end of the preceramic period. Still, the proto-agricultural way of life of the Las Vegas preceramic people on the coast and in the Guayas basin may have been the foundation for the development of the ceramic-stage VALDIVIA culture around 5,000 years ago.

Three interpretive works by KAREN E. STOTHERT describe the Las Vegas data: "Review of the Early Preceramic Complexes of the Santa Elena Peninsula, Ecuador," in American Antiquity 48, no. 1 (1983):122–127; "The Preceramic Las Vegas Culture of Coastal Ecuador," in American Antiquity 50, no. 3 (1985):613–637; and La prehistoria temprana de la península de Santa Elena: Cultura Las Vegas (1988).

KAREN E. STOTHERT

See also **Puná Island.**

LASO, FRANCISCO (b. 8 May 1823; d. 14 May 1869), Peruvian artist and writer. A painter influenced by the French romantic tradition who focused on Peruvian subjects, Laso was born in Tacna and studied at the Academy of Painting and Drawing in Lima, where he was assistant to Ignacio Merino, director of the academy. He went to Paris in 1842 to study with the painter Hippolyte Delaroche. On visits to Rome and Venice he was influenced by Titian and Veronese. In 1847 he returned to Peru and traveled throughout the countryside, sketching Indians. During a second trip to Europe he studied with the genre painter Marc Gabriel Charles Gleyre in Paris. In Gleyre's atelier, Laso finished his famous El indio Alfarero (The Indian Potter, also known as Dweller in the Cordillera, 1855), a painting of a young Indian holding a Mochica ceramic piece, which is considered a forerunner of Peruvian indigenist art in the twentieth century. Upon his return to Peru in 1856, he was commissioned to paint The Four Evangelists for the Cathedral of Lima and the Saint Rose of Lima (1866) in the municipal palace. Laso worked as a Red Cross volunteer during the yellow fever epidemic of 1868 in Peru and fell victim to it. He died at the height of his career.

JUAN E. RÍOS, La pintura contemporánea en el Perú (1946); DAWN ADES, Art in Latin America: The Modern Era, 1820–1980 (1989), p. 39; ORIANA BADDELEY and VALERIE FRASER, Drawing the Line: Art and Cultural Identity in Contemporary Latin America (1989), p. 17.

MARTA GARSD

LASTARRIA, JOSÉ VICTORINO (b. 22 March 1817; d. 14 June 1888), intellectual and politician, the most active and brilliant mid-nineteenth-century Chilean Liberal. Lastarria had more than a touch of vanity. "Tengo talento y lo luzco" (I have talent, and it shows), he once told the Chilean congress. He did have talent. As a politician, his finest moments were in 1849–1850, when he was congressional leader of the resurgent Liberal opposition to the Conservative regime, a role for which he was arrested in November 1850 and briefly exiled to Peru. In 1851 he was expelled from congress. Later he held the office of minister of finance (1862) and minister of the interior (1876–1877). He was elected six times to the Chamber of Deputies (1849, 1855, 1858, 1864, 1867, 1870) and was a senator from 1876 to 1882. His many public services included diplomatic missions to Peru (1863), Argentina (1864), and Brazil (1879), and membership on the supreme court (1882–1887).

Lastarria's talent for active politics and diplomacy was limited. His true interests were intellectual and literary. He contributed to numerous newspapers and journals, serving as editor of *El Siglo* (1844–1845) and helping to found *La Revista de Santiago* (1848). An indefatigable "cultural entrepreneur," he was instrumental in founding the Sociedad Literaria (Literary Society) of 1842, an event regarded as the first real stirring of cultural life in postcolonial Chile. In a notable opening address to this society, Lastarria pleaded for an authentic national literature within the canons of modern romanticism. His own fiction, for example, *Don Guillermo* (1860), does not read well today, but his promotion of literature was tireless, and the several circles and academies he sponsored are vividly described in his *Recuerdos literarios* (1878), a remarkable intellectual autobiography. At his death, he left unfinished a prologue he had promised Rubén DARÍO (1867–1916) for his path-breaking *Azul* (1888).

Lastarria urged a "philosophical" approach to historical writing and engaged in a famous polemic on the subject with Andrés BELLO (1781–1865), whose ideas proved more enduring. Of greater positive influence was Lastarria's political-constitutional thought. Consistently liberal and democratic, it is best represented in his books *Elementos de derecho constitucional* (Elements of Constitutional Law, 1846), *Bosquejo histórico de la Constitución chilena* (Historical Outline of the Chilean Constitution, 1847), *Historia constitucional de medio siglo* (Constitutional History of Half a Century, 1853), and *Lecciones de política positiva* (Lessons in Positive Philosophy, 1874), the last of which reflects POSITIVIST influence, Lastarria having assimilated the thought of Auguste Comte (though not uncritically) in the 1860s.

JOSÉ VICTORINO LASTARRIA, *Obras completas*, 14 vols. (1906–1934); BERNARDO SUBERCASEAUX, *Cultura y sociedad liberal en el siglo XIX: Lastarria, ideología y literatura* (1981); ALLEN WOLL, *A Functional Past: The Uses of History in Nineteenth-Century Chile* (1982), chaps. 1–2.

SIMON COLLIER

LASUÉN, FERMÍN FRANCISCO DE (*b.* 7 June 1736; *d.* 26 June 1803), Franciscan missionary in California. Born in Victoria, Spain, Lasuén arrived in New Spain in 1759, posted first in Baja California and later in Alta California. While stationed at San Francisco de Borja mission in Baja California between 1768 and 1773, he directed the construction of a large adobe church and other buildings, the ruins of which still exist behind a later Dominican-constructed stone facade.

Between 1773 and 1803 Lasuén was stationed at the

José Victorino Lastarria, ca. 1865. PHOTOGRAPHIC ARCHIVE, UNIVERSIDAD DE CHILE.

San Gabriel, San Diego, and San Carlos missions in Alta California. In 1785 he became the superior of the Alta California missions, directing the development of the MISSIONS until his death at San Carlos. During his tenure as superior, nine missions were established, including four in the summer of 1797 alone. As part of the maturation of the mission system, mission herds expanded and the Franciscans planted larger crops. The danger of food shortages passed, and the missionaries recruited larger numbers of Indians. To accommodate growing populations of converts, the Franciscans directed ambitious building projects, including the construction of larger churches. The stone structure that Lasuén began constructing at San Carlos in 1793 became the church that stands today.

ZEPHYRIN ENGELHARDT, O.F.M., *Missions and Missionaries of California*, 4 vols. (1929–1930); MAYNARD J. GEIGER, O.F.M., *Franciscan Missionaries in Hispanic California, 1769–1848: A Biographical Dictionary* (1969).

ROBERT H. JACKSON

LATIFUNDIA, a system of land tenure dominated by large rural estates (latifundios). Concentration of landownership began during the Conquest, with sizable royal grants establishing a system of land concentration that persists in much of Latin America today. Figures from Milton Esman indicate that in 1978, 60 percent of rural Mexican households were landless or near landless; the figure was 66 percent in Colombia and 70 percent in Brazil. Latifundia has been especially persistent in cattle-ranching regions.

Chile is among the extreme cases of a latifundia-dominated society. From colonial times onward, a rural elite controlled the best lands in the central valley around Santiago. In 1924 fewer than 3 percent of farms in the fertile central valley controlled 80 percent of the arable lands. The rural poor (*huasos; inquilinos,* or sharecroppers; migrant workers; and squatters) remained subservient to a powerful patron. The Christian Democratic government of Eduardo FREI (1964–1970) passed but did not enforce land-reform legislation. The socialist regime of Salvador ALLENDE (1970–1973) attempted unsuccessfully to reform the latifundia system.

Mexico's landowners established the first association in the Western Hemisphere to promote rural interests. In 1529 town councilmen in Mexico City organized the MESTA, patterned on a powerful organization of sheep ranchers in Spain. While not as powerful as its Spanish predecessor, the Mexican Mesta appointed many important rural officials and shaped rural legislation. As a public official recorded in 1594, ranching and agriculture were "in the hands of the rich and of those possessing Indians under the ENCOMIENDA system." While latifundia was not universal in Mexico, on the northern grazing lands the large HACIENDAS ably described by François Chevalier dominated into the twentieth century. Even the great upheaval of the MEXICAN REVOLUTION only replaced one set of latifundistas with another.

Similar circumstances prevailed in Uruguay and Argentina. Spanish colonial policy promoted land concentration and the marginalization of the GAUCHOS and others of the rural lower classes. Rich, landed Uruguayan families—the Viana, de la Quadra, and others—dominated the countryside and, after Independence, the country. Argentina, with vast lands and a small population, also experienced latifundia, especially on the PAMPAS. Colonial and national policies granted control of the vast plains to the few.

Great estates (*hatos*) also developed on the Venezuelan and Colombian LLANOS during the early eighteenth century. In mid-eighteenth-century Venezuela, about thirty families owned forty ranches covering 219 square leagues on which about 300,000 cattle grazed.

Independence speeded land concentration in much of Latin America. Land granted to war veterans quickly passed to the hands of caudillos and wily speculators. Venezuelan caudillo José Gregorio MONAGAS distributed land to followers in 1848, but more than half the total went to ten concessions. Owing to the income and prestige of landownership, latifundistas have retained strong political clout. Through rural societies and associations, they continue to promote their interests at the regional and national levels.

FRANÇOIS CHEVALIER, *Land and Society in Colonial Mexico,* translated by Alvin Eustis, edited by Lesley Byrd Simpson (1963); CHARLES H. HARRIS III, *A Mexican Family Empire: The Latifundio of the Sánchez Navarros, 1765–1867* (1975); BRIAN LOVEMEN, *Struggle in the Countryside: Politics and Rural Labor in Chile, 1919–1973* (1976); MILTON J. ESMAN, *Landlessness and Near-Landlessness in Developing Countries* (1978); RICHARD W. SLATTA, *Cowboys of the Americas* (1990).

RICHARD W. SLATTA

See also **Estancia; Fundo.**

LATIN AMERICA, term commonly used to describe South America, Central America, Mexico, and the islands of the Caribbean. As such, it incorporates numerous Spanish-speaking countries, Portuguese-speaking Brazil, French-speaking Haiti and the French West Indies, and usually implies countries such as Suriname and Guyana, where Romance languages are not spoken. The term *Latin America* originated in France during the reign of Napoleon III in the 1860s, when the country was second only to England in terms of industrial and financial strength. The French political economist Michel Chevalier, in an effort to solidify the intellectual underpinnings of French overseas ambitions, first proposed a "Pan-Latin" foreign policy in the hopes of promoting solidarity between nations whose languages were of Latin origin and that shared the common cultural tradition of Roman Catholicism. Led by France, the Latin peoples could reassert their influence throughout the world in the face of threats from both the Slavic peoples of eastern Europe (led by Russia) and the Anglo-Saxon peoples of northern Europe (led by England). In the Western Hemisphere, Pan-Latinists distinguished between the Anglo north and the Latin south, which they gradually began to refer to as *América latina*. From the French *l'Amérique latine,* the term came into general use in other languages.

JOHN L. PHELAN, "Panlatinismo, la intervención francesa en México y el origen de la idea de latinoamerica," in *Latino América aunuario/estudios latinoamericanos* 2 (1969): 119–141.

J. DAVID DRESSING

LATIN AMERICAN FREE TRADE ASSOCIATION (LAFTA), an organization comprised of eleven nations dedicated to furthering economic integration in Latin America. Established by a treaty signed in Montevideo, Uruguay, on 18 February 1960, the Latin American Free Trade Association (LAFTA) served as a forum for the creation of greater economic ties among Latin American nations. The Montevideo agreement was initially signed by representatives of Argentina, Brazil,

Chile, Colombia, Ecuador, Mexico, Peru, and Uruguay. Bolivia, Paraguay, and Venezuela became members shortly thereafter.

The treaty signed at Montevideo proposed the gradual easing of trade barriers between the member nations, culminating with completely free trade by 1973. A permanent body was created to facilitate periodic tariff reductions and regular negotiations between the members. LAFTA met with some early success, as these nations had traded very little in the years preceding the agreement. However, progress toward integration moved slowly throughout the 1960s as the disparities of the member nations became more apparent.

Frustrated by the slow process of integration, the LAFTA nations signed the Caracas Protocol in 1969, thereby extending the deadline for free trade to 1980. The divisiveness and imbalance that had threatened LAFTA throughout the 1960s only increased during the 1970s. Many members, whose level of industrialization at this time might be described as intermediate, felt ill equipped to compete with the large industrialized nations—Argentina, Brazil, and Mexico. The perceived inequity inherent in LAFTA led to the 1969 ratification of the ANDEAN PACT by Bolivia, Chile, Colombia, Ecuador, Peru, and, later, Venezuela, which pursued their own agendas for integration independent of LAFTA, an action which further inhibited LAFTA's original goal of free trade throughout the hemisphere. In 1980, the year in which free trade in Latin America was to have occurred, the members of LAFTA formed the Latin-American Integration Association (LAIA), initiating a renewed effort toward integration.

EDWARD S. MILENKY, *The Politics of Regional Organization in Latin America: The Latin American Free Trade Association* (1973).

JOHN DUDLEY

LATORRE, LORENZO (*b.* 28 July 1840; *d.* 18 January 1916), military leader and president of Uruguay (1876–1880). Latorre was the country's strongman after the uprising of 1875. His dictatorship from March 1876 until his resignation in March 1880 initiated the militarist period. The son of an immigrant warehouse-keeper, he began his military career as a soldier in Venancio FLORES's Colorado revolution and, later, as a professional soldier fought in the WAR OF THE TRIPLE ALLIANCE (1865–1870) against Paraguay. The Blanco caudillo Timoteo Aparicio's civil war between 1870 and 1872 created a power vacuum. The government that ruled until 1875 was one of cultured professionals, but lacked support from the military and the dominant economic groups—factors that provided the conditions for the establishment of militarism.

Latorre's program responded to the interests of the rural upper classes and to those of the financial and commercial classes who supported the gold standard and resisted the introduction of paper currency. His administration saw the escalation of fencing on the ranges that had begun in 1872, the reform of the Rural Codes, which tended to guarantee landownership and order in rural areas, and the extension of the authority of the army and the police. It sought balance in fiscal matters and guaranteed the continuation of the gold standard. Latorre was granted constitutional legitimacy in 1878.

Upon his resignation in 1880, Latorre was replaced by Francisco A. Vidal, president of the Senate. In 1882 another military leader, General Máximo Santos, assumed control of the government. Latorre, who settled in Buenos Aires after his resignation, was taken by surprise by a decree of permanent exile issued by the new dictator. Another military leader, Máximo TAJES, succeeded Santos and began the slow transition to civilian government.

ALBERTO ZUM FELDE, *Proceso histórico del Uruguay*, 5th ed. (1967); ENRIQUE MÉNDEZ VIVES, *El Uruguay de la modernización* (1977).

FERNANDO FILGUEIRA

LAUGERUD GARCÍA, EUGENIO KJELL (*b.* 25 January 1930), president of Guatemala 1974–1978. Brigadier General Kjell Laugerud García succeeded Carlos ARANA OSORIO as president of Guatemala in 1974. It is widely believed that the 1974 elections were fraudulent and that Efraín RÍOS MONTT was the actual winner.

Laugerud initially tried to implement a program of slight social and political reform. During his first years in office, membership in labor unions nearly tripled. Laugerud also inaugurated colonization programs for landless peasants in the Petén and along the Mexican border.

Laugerud's reform programs were cut short when a massive earthquake on 4 February 1976 caused enormous destruction and catalyzed social unrest. The last years of Laugerud's presidency were overshadowed by growing political violence. In May 1978, the army massacred one hundred civilians thought to be subversives in the village of Panzós, Alta Verapaz. One month later, Fernando Romeo LUCAS GARCÍA succeeded Laugerud as president of the republic.

JIM HANDY, *Gift of the Devil: A History of Guatemala* (1984); RICHARD F. NYROP, ed., *Guatemala: A Country Study*, 2d ed. (1984).

VIRGINIA GARRARD-BURNETT

LAUTARO (*b.* 1535?; *d.* 29 April 1557), ARAUCANIAN warrior and leader. Captured at an early stage of the warfare between the Araucanians and the Spaniards under Pedro de VALDIVIA (1500–1553), Lautaro spent some time as a groom in the conquistador's entourage, where he learned much about Spanish military capacity. Escaping back to Araucanian territory, he emerged as a great military leader of his own people. Toward the end of 1553 his forces successfully attacked and destroyed the Spanish fort at Tucapel: a desperate counterattack by Valdivia himself led to the conquistador's death (December 1553). From this resounding victory, Lautaro went on to defeat the Spaniards at Marigueñu (February 1554) and to force the evacuation of Concepción. Re-founded by the Spaniards, the settlement was attacked and destroyed a second time by Lautaro in December 1555. The following year the brilliant Araucanian launched an offensive to the north of the river Maule. But the Araucanians were never as effective away from their own territory as they were on home ground. Repulsed by Pedro de Villagra (1508?–1577) near the river Mataquito in November 1556, Lautaro fell back on a safe position near the mouth of the Itata. On 29 April 1557 a second attack to the north of the Maule was countered by Francisco de VILLAGRA (1511–1563) at the battle of Peteroa (sometimes called the second battle of Mataquito), in which Lautaro received a fatal wound either from an arrow or a sword.

Lautaro's deeds were frequently evoked as an inspiring precedent by creole patriots at the time of independence. His name (like those of other Araucanian heroes of the period) has often been used as a given name for Chilean boys even in the twentieth century.

FERNANDO ALEGRÍA, *Lautaro, joven libertador de Arauco* (1981).

SIMON COLLIER

LAUTARO, LOGIA DE, a lodge founded in Buenos Aires in 1812 by José de SAN MARTÍN, Carlos María de ALVEAR, and José Matías Zapiola, following the models of the lodges of Spain and England. Its most important goal was to spread the idea of independence, and many of the sympathizers of independence belonged to it. A highly disciplined political pressure group, the Lautaro Lodge helped revitalize the Sociedad Patriótica of Buenos Aires. In October 1812, the Lautarianos played a key role in the overthrow of the first triumvirate (then the executive body of Argentina), of which Juan Martín de PUEYRREDÓN was a member. However, dissension soon appeared, and the lodge had to be reorganized in 1815. The lodge was instrumental in the mobilization of resources for San Martín when he was preparing the expedition to liberate Chile. After San Martín left, and without his influence, dissension arose once again, and the lodge became more and more involved in the intricate web of the Argentine politics of the period. By 1820 it had lost practically all of its influence.

ANTONIO R. ZÚÑIGA, *La Logia "Lautaro" y la independencia de América* (1922); RICARDO ROJAS, *San Martín: Knight of the Andes,* translated by Herschel Brickell and Carlos Videla (1945); RICARDO PICCIRILLI, *San Martín y la Logia Lautaro: Conferencia pronunciada el 13 de agosto de 1958* (1958); JAIME EYZAGUIRRE, *La Logia Lautariana y otros estudios sobre la independencia* (1972).

JUAN MANUEL PÉREZ

LAVALLE, JUAN GALO (*b.* 17 October 1797; *d.* 9 October 1841), Argentine general. Born in Buenos Aires, Lavalle entered the military soon after the outbreak of revolution against Spain. He earned a reputation for valor tinged with rashness, distinguishing himself both in José de SAN MARTÍN's crossing of the Andes and in later service with Argentine expeditionary forces in Peru and Ecuador. He returned to Buenos Aires in 1824 and won further distinction in the war of 1825–1828 against Brazil.

Like most of the professional military, Lavalle was a supporter of the Unitarist faction against the Federalists. He thus opposed the Federalist governor of Buenos Aires, Manuel DORREGO, whom he accused of inflicting a disorderly and arbitrary rule upon the province and of ending the Brazilian war on unfavorable terms. On 1 December 1828, Lavalle seized power in Buenos Aires by a coup. Twelve days later he had the former governor shot, thereby setting off a backlash of anger that in the end doomed Lavalle's government. Faced with counterrevolutionary uprisings throughout Buenos Aires Province, he held power less than a year.

For roughly ten years Lavalle lived as an exile in Uruguay, until in 1839 he launched a major invasion of Argentine territory, aiming to overthrow the Federalist dictatorship established by Juan Manuel de ROSAS. He penetrated deeply into Buenos Aires Province, but Rosas was able to assemble superior forces. In the meantime, Lavalle's alliance with the French forces intervening in the Río de la Plata made him vulnerable to charges of betraying national interests. He withdrew to the Argentine interior, where he suffered eventual defeat at the hands of Rosas's allies in 1841. Fleeing toward Bolivia, he was assassinated in Jujuy. Lavalle would remain a dashing hero in the middle of some; but the execution of Dorrego dogged his historical image just as it did his entire subsequent career.

PEDRO LACASA, *Vida militar y política del general argentino don Juan Lavalle* (1973) is an account by one of Lavalle's closest collaborators. LILY SOSA DE NEWTON, *Lavalle* (1967) is a modern popular biography. See also the references in JOHN LYNCH, *Argentine Dictator: Juan Manuel de Rosas 1829–1852* (1981).

DAVID BUSHNELL

LAVALLE URBINA, MARÍA (*b.* 24 May 1908), lawyer, public official, and early Mexican feminist. A native of Campeche, she grew up in an important political family. She graduated in law from the state university in 1945, and immediately entered public life. She became the first woman to serve as a state superior court justice (1947), after which she joined the federal bureaucracy. The first female senator to be elected from her home state (1964), she later served as undersecretary of education in 1976. She has written many articles on delinquency, human rights, and women; served on United Nations and national commissions in these areas; and presided over the Mexican Alliance of Women in the

1960s. She directed the Textbook Commission from 1982–1984.

Hispano Americano (3 February 1975): 8–9.

RODERIC AI CAMP

LAVALLEJA, JUAN ANTONIO (*b.* 20 June 1784; *d.* 22 October 1853), Uruguayan military leader and a hero in the struggle for Uruguayan independence. Born in Santa Lucía to a family of cattle ranchers, he began his military career in 1811 in José ARTIGAS's revolutionary movement for independence from the Spanish dominion. From 1816 to 1818 he fought against the invaders from the Luso-Brazilian Empire, and in 1818 he was taken prisoner and confined for three years in Río de Janeiro. Once freed, he returned to his homeland, now called the CISPLATINE PROVINCE, and joined the revolutionary movement for independence. Discovered, he was forced into exile in Buenos Aires, where he prepared the "liberation crusade." The final epic of national independence, Artigas's offensive was brought to a close in 1828 with a preliminary peace agreement and finally ended in 1830 with the establishment of a constitutional government.

Lavalleja's adherence to federalist ideals caused him on more than one occasion to favor forms of political unity with Argentina, but he finally renounced these to pursue an independent nation. The liberation crusade was the zenith of his career as well as the beginning of his rivalry with the other national caudillo, President Fructuoso RIVERA, against whom Lavalleja rose up in arms in 1832 and 1834. Defeated, he went into exile in Brazil. He returned in 1836 to fight against Rivera again, this time along with the constitutionalist forces of then President Manuel ORIBE. He defeated Rivera at the battle of CARPINTERÍA, where for the first time the colors symbolizing the traditional parties of Uruguay, red (*colorado*) for Rivera and white (*blanco*) for Oribe, were used. The war ended in 1851, and in 1853, Lavalleja joined the governing triumvirate—a short-lived one, since he died that same year.

ALFREDO CASTELLANOS, *La Cisplatina, la independencia y la república caudillesca* (1974); ANIBAL BARRIOS PINTOS, *Lavalleja: La patria independiente* (1976).

MAGDALENA GUTIÉRREZ

See also **Cisplatine War.**

LAVISTA, MARIO (*b.* 3 April 1943), Mexican composer, editor, and administrator. Lavista was among the talented group of young musicians who in the 1960s matriculated at the Carlos Chávez composition workshop in the National Conservatory of Mexico. Others were Eduardo MATA and Hector QUINTINAR, the latter also one of Lavista's teachers. Study with leaders of Europe's avant garde—Karlheinz Stockhausen, György Ligeti,

and Iannis Xenakis—and his own pioneering creative impulses led Lavista to discoveries of new sonorities coaxed from traditional instruments; however, he has not eschewed electronic sound synthesis, which he studied in Japan. Lavista has taught theory and composition at the National Conservatory, edited the music journal *Pauta,* and headed the music section of the National Council for Culture and the Arts.

JOSÉ ANTONIO ALCARAZ et al., "Período contemporáneo," in *La música de México,* edited by Julio Estrada, vol. 1, pt. 5 (1984).

ROBERT L. PARKER

LAVRADIO, MARQUÊS DO (Dom Luís de Almeida Portugal Soares Alarção Eça Melo Pereira Aguilar Fiel de Lugo Mascarenhas Silva Mendonça e Lencastre; *b.* 27 June 1729; *d.* 2 May 1790), governor of Bahia and viceroy of Rio de Janeiro. Born in Lisbon, the son of an army officer who served as captain-general of Angola and briefly as the last viceroy of Brazil at Bahia de Todos os Santos, Lavradio became the forty-fifth governor and captain-general of Bahia (1768–1769) before being promoted to Rio de Janeiro, where he became the third viceroy to reside there (1769–1779). As had his predecessors, Lavradio found his authority far more circumscribed than his exalted title would suggest. His regime coincided with the climax of a century-long dispute between Spain and Portugal over the temperate lands between present-day São Paulo and the Río de la Plata. In spite of his best efforts, he was unable to prevent vastly superior Spanish forces from gaining control over the southern portions of that disputed territory. Acutely aware of the fact that Brazil's first gold boom was already over, Lavradio tried to stimulate new sources of royal income by encouraging the production of tobacco, cereals, fibers, whale products, and dyestuffs and to curtail illicit foreign trade with Brazilian ports. Toward the end of his viceregency he drafted an illuminating, markedly modest account of his administration, one of the few such terminal reports ever prepared by senior administrators of colonial Brazil. Subsequently, he became a member of the Council of War and president of the senior judicial tribunal of the kingdom, the DESEMBARGO DO PAÇO, but left no trace of his role in either body.

DAURIL ALDEN, *Royal Government in Colonial Brazil* (1968); JOHN ARMITAGE, *The History of Brazil . . . 1808 to . . . 1831,* 2 vols. (London, 1836), 2: 161–242.

DAURIL ALDEN

LAVRADOR DE CANA, in Brazil a farmer who planted and harvested sugarcane, which was then sent to a mill for processing into sugar. In colonial Bahia, cane farmers were associated with the dominant sugar export economy, slavery, and the political interests of the sugar sector. Most *lavradores* were white and were socially an adjunct of the mill-owner elite, although many were themselves people of humble background and resources.

Land determined one's social position and the relationship of cane farmers to the mill. Those who owned land outright, who were the most privileged, generally divided the pressed cane on a fifty–fifty basis with the mill owners. Among the less fortunate were those who owned land that was under obligation, and sharecroppers and tenants, who leased or rented ENGENHO lands with restrictions both on land use and on the disposal of the cane produced. *Lavradores de cana* owned varying numbers of slaves and in some cases also had capital sufficient to purchase or negotiate access to the oxen, lumber, and firewood necessary for sugar production.

STUART B. SCHWARTZ, *Sugar Plantations in the Formation of Brazilian Society: Bahia, 1550–1835* (1985).

NANCY PRISCILLA SMITH NARO

See also **Plantations; Slavery; Sugar Industry.**

LAW OF THE SEA. The Latin American and Caribbean states were very active in the Third United Nations Conference on the Law of the Sea (UNCLOS III), 1973–1982. In fact, three Latin American states (Chile, Ecuador, and Peru) precipitated a controversy in the 1950s when they claimed a 200-mile zone to protect tuna, a claim that had to be resolved at the conference. Their claim was on the basis of the Declaration of Santiago on the Maritime Zone (1952), which the United States particularly opposed on the ground that it violated the traditional area of the high seas considered to be open to all—most states accepted that this was the area beyond the three-mile territorial sea. (Other states in the region soon followed suit with similar claims.) The enforcement of these states' claimed right to regulate tuna fishing resulted in the Tuna War when Ecuador and Peru seized and fined United States private fishing boats in the 1950s and 1960s.

In preparation for the conference, the Caribbean states met in the Dominican Republic in 1972 and approved the Declaration of Santo Domingo, which set the territorial sea and fishing limits for these states. The first session of UNCLOS III was held in New York in 1973, the second in Caracas, Venezuela, in 1974 (the other sessions were held mainly in New York and Geneva). This long conference differed from the earlier ones—UNCLOS I (1958) and UNCLOS II (1960)—in that it had some 150 participants versus some 80 for them. While the earlier ones had been on an East (Soviet bloc)–West (led by the United States) political axis, this conference was on a North (developed and industrialized)–South (developing) economic and political axis. The latter group of states, a majority, used the conference to challenge the North and to bring about the New International Economic Order (NIEO). This would help transform the traditional system so that it would better serve the interests and needs of the South, especially

economically. The Group of 77 (G-77), formed in the 1960s and including Latin America, developed a unified bloc in the United Nations in general and in UNCTAD (UN Conference on Trade and Development) in particular to advance the movement toward the NIEO. The UN General Assembly passed a declaration on the establishment of an NIEO in 1974 and later the same year approved the Charter of Economic Rights and Duties of States.

During UNCLOS III the South used bloc caucusing and bargaining to deal with the North. The G-77 was one bloc along with both an African group and a Latin American group (it had twenty-eight members), all trying to have a common position on major issues. Several Latin American and Caribbean states were especially influential at UNCLOS III: the Bahamas, Brazil, Chile, Jamaica, Mexico, Peru, Trinidad and Tobago, and Venezuela. Two compromises between the North and the South that favored the latter were a territorial sea of 12 miles and an Exclusive Economic Zone of 188 miles (200 miles total). In the final vote on the 1982 Law of the Sea Convention, only four states voted against it (including the United States and Venezuela); seventeen abstained (among the North); the South, including Latin America and the Caribbean, voted for it. The required sixty ratifications were obtained in late 1993; they included twelve COMMONWEALTH CARIBBEAN and seven Latin American states. The Convention went into effect in November 1994. The United States signed in August 1994; Senate approval was still needed.

ROBERT L. FRIEDHEIM and WILLIAM J. DURCH, ''The International Seabed Resources Agency Negotiations and the New International Economic Order,'' in *International Organization* 31, no. 2 (Spring 1977): 349–352, 378–382; EDWARD MILES, ''The Structure and Effects of the Decision Process on the Seabed Committee and the Third United Nations Conference on the Law of the Sea,'' in *International Organization* 31, no. 2 (Spring 1977): 161–166, 177–179, 185–192; DOUGLAS M. JOHNSTON, ed., *Regionalization of the Law of the Sea: Proceedings* (1978); BERNARD H. OXMAN, DAVID D. CARON, and CHARLES L. O. BUDERI, eds., *Law of the Sea: U.S. Policy Dilemma* (1983), chaps. 2 and 4; FRANCISCO ORREGO VICUÑA, *Exclusive Economic Zone: A Latin American Perspective* (1984).

LARMAN C. WILSON

LE BRETÓN, TOMÁS ALBERTO (*b.* 1868; *d.* 1959), Argentine politician and statesman. Born in Buenos Aires, Le Bretón trained as a lawyer at the university there and received his degree in 1891. He became a specialist in patent law and used this expertise to represent Argentina at the 1904 Berlin Industrial Property Congress as well as at a subsequent congress in Stockholm. Although Le Bretón is now remembered mostly for his dominant role in Radical Party politics after his election to the Chamber of Deputies in March 1914, he was also instrumental in promoting land colonization in the CHACO REGION as part of a process of government support for the nascent cotton industry there. He probably became interested in the matter as a member of the Administrative Commission of Land and Colonies in 1920, but he did not become officially active in this regard until 1923, following a term in the United States (1919–1922) as Argentine ambassador. As minister of agriculture from 1922 to 1925 he thoroughly reorganized the ministry, paying particular attention to the prospects of cotton cultivation. Le Bretón contracted with U.S. agronomist Dr. Ernest Tutt to provide the most modern agricultural and marketing information. These resources, along with the opening of government lands to settlers and provision by the government of free cotton seed to farmers, together served to promote the rapid development of this industrial fiber.

Le Bretón's links to the Antipersonalist Radical Civic Union led to his reentry into politics. In later years the conservative governments of General José Augustín P. JUSTO and Roberto M. ORTIZ appointed him to several important diplomatic posts. In 1936 Le Bretón was called upon to represent Argentina in commercial negotiations with Great Britain. He also served as Argentine ambassador to Great Britain from 1938 to 1941.

DONNA J. GUY

LEAGUE OF NATIONS. Hoping to counterbalance the growing political and economic power of the United States and the economic dominance of Britain in Latin America, nine Latin American countries (Bolivia, Brazil, Cuba, Guatemala, Haiti, Honduras, Nicaragua, Panama, and Peru) became charter members of the League of Nations in 1919, followed by several others that joined during the 1920s.

After World War I, Latin America continued to fear the possibility of direct foreign intervention in hemispheric affairs, not having forgotten European attempts, both direct and indirect, to do so during the 1800s and the U.S. buildup in the Caribbean in Theodore Roosevelt's day. The "big stick," the ROOSEVELT COROLLARY to the Monroe Doctrine, and DOLLAR DIPLOMACY had left their mark. In spite of Woodrow Wilson's declaration on 27 October 1913 that the United States would never again seek territory through conquest, and of some goodwill he gained by accepting Latin American leadership in the mediation of the MEXICAN REVOLUTION, Latin American political leaders sought clarification of the Monroe Doctrine in the international arena. Just as Baron RIO BRANCO had closely aligned Brazil with unpopular U.S. policies in order to use the prestige of the U.S.-Brazilian alliance to escape British domination while establishing a favorable western boundary, Latin American leaders aligned themselves with the League of Nations.

Unfortunately, the League usually ignored Latin America and proved to be the wrong forum for negotiation, since the U.S. Senate failed to ratify the League's Covenant and the United States thus did not become a member. During the 1920s and 1930s, U.S. manufac-

tured goods flooded Latin American markets while U.S. investments, particularly in Brazil, dominated Latin American economic development.

The League did get involved, however, in two incidents of open fighting in Latin America. In July 1932, the League began to investigate sporadic fighting between Bolivia and Paraguay over an area called the Gran Chaco. Paraguay formally declared war on 10 May 1933. More than 100,000 lives were lost while the League's fact-finding commission, headed by Álvarez del Vayo of Spain, investigated and made its way back to Geneva in December of that year. The League proposed a peace treaty, which both sides rejected, and then an arms embargo. The CHACO WAR dragged on mainly because, despite U.S. imposition of a separate arms embargo, existing arms contracts to Bolivia for the defense of the oilfield owned by Standard Oil of New Jersey were not affected. The war ended 14 June 1935 when Paraguay ran out of matériel.

The League was even less effective in settling open fighting between Peru and Colombia over Leticia, a small town with a strategic location on the upper Amazon. Both sides ignored League mediation efforts, but the conflict came to an end when Peru's president, Luis Sánchez Cerro, was assassinated in 1933. League commissioners administered the area around Leticia for a year and then returned it to Colombia.

By 1938, Chile, Brazil, Paraguay, Nicaragua, Guatemala, Costa Rica, and Honduras had dropped out of the League, which they viewed as powerless, and turned to direct negotiations with the United States.

E. BRADFORD BURNS, *The Unwritten Alliance: Rio-Branco and Brazilian-American Relations* (1966); JOSEPH S. TULCHIN, *The Aftermath of War: World War I and U.S. Policy Toward Latin America* (1971); ELMER BENDINER, *A Time for Angels: The Tragi-comic History of the League of Nations* (1975); ROBERT F. SMITH, ed., *The United States and the Latin American Sphere of Influence* (1981); F. S. NORTHEDGE, *The League of Nations: Its Life and Times, 1920–1946* (1986).

LESLEY R. LUSTER

LEAL, FERNANDO (*b.* 1896; *d.* 1964), Mexican painter. Born in Mexico City, Leal studied briefly at the San Carlos Academy of Fine Arts and at the Open Air Painting School in Coyoacán under Alfredo Ramos Martínez. He was a teacher of drawing and printmaking at the Open Air School for seven years. In 1921, together with Jean Charlot, he devoted himself to woodcuts, reviving the once popular medium with images of contemporary life. Leal was among the first Mexican painters to use subjects from the Mexican Revolution in his canvases, including *Zapatista Camp* (1922). Later that year, he was invited by Education Minister José Vasconcelos to paint on the walls of the National Preparatory School. The result was the large encaustic mural *The Feast of Our Lord of Chalma*, which depicted the Indian dances dedicated to the Black Christ of the village of Chalma. In

1927 Leal decorated, in fresco, the entrance to the laboratories of the Department of Public Health. In 1931, again using encaustic, he painted the vestibule of Bolívar Hall, incorporating various events from the Wars of Independence in South America.

Unlike many of his contemporaries, who were leftists and anticlerical, Leal was a devout Catholic, and in the late 1940s he was involved in mural decorations for the Church of Our Lady of Guadalupe in Mexico City. He also served as art critic for the newspaper *El Nacional Revolucionario* in 1934–1935. Although he ceased mural painting in the last decade of his life, he continued to produce many easel paintings of landscapes, figures, and still lifes, as well as woodcuts, until his death.

JEAN CHARLOT, *The Mexican Mural Renaissance* (1962); ANTONIO RODRÍGUEZ, *A History of Mexican Mural Painting* (1969).

ALEJANDRO ANDREUS

LEANTE, CÉSAR (b. 1 July 1928), Cuban novelist and essayist. Leante was born in Matanzas and spent part of his childhood in Mexico. From 1944 to 1950 he was a member of the Socialist Youth Movement and later the Popular Socialist Party. In 1954 he began writing radio scripts and continued until 1959, the year he joined the staff of the newspaper *Revolución*. In 1961 he became an editor for the news agency Prensa Latina. He also taught theater at the National School for Instructors in the Arts until 1963, when he was named cultural attaché at the Cuban embassy in Paris. Leante went on to represent his country officially in international activities and to occupy prestigious posts at the Ministry of Foreign Relations and at the Cuban Union of Writers and Artists (UNEAC), which recognized his novel *Padres e hijos* with an honorable mention in 1965. He translated into Spanish the works of Simone de Beauvoir and Antoine de Saint-Exupéry.

Leante served as literary adviser to the National Council on Culture and enjoyed favorable treatment from the Cuban regime until opting not to return to Cuba while on an official trip to Europe. Since then he has published in Spain, his adopted home, and elsewhere in the Americas. One of his best-known works is the 1973 novel *Muelle de caballería*. Among his other works are *Tres historias* (1977), *Calembour* (1988), and *Fidel Castro* (1991). His novels have been translated into several languages.

ROBERTO VALERO

LECHÍN OQUENDO, JUAN (b. 19 May 1914), Bolivian labor leader. Born in the small mining town of Corocoro to an Arab father and a mestizo mother, Lechín studied at the American Institute in La Paz. He was a founding member of Bolivia's Federation of Miners (Federación Sindical de Trabajadores Mineros de Bolivia—FSTMB)

and for over forty years (1944–1986) served as its permanent secretary. In 1952, Lechín joined the revolution of the Nationalist Revolutionary Movement (MNR) that nationalized the MINING INDUSTRY, declared universal suffrage, and carried out an extensive land reform program, playing a key role in the formation of the new regime. As minister of labor, Lechín was instrumental in the establishment of the Bolivian Workers Central (COB), an umbrella organization in which he presided as secretary general until the mid-1980s. He was also instrumental in securing worker cogovernment and comanagement in COMIBOL (the Mining Corporation of Bolivia).

In 1960, Lechín was elected vice president of Bolivia on the MNR ticket headed by Víctor PAZ ESTENSSORO. This relationship, however, was short-lived as Lechín resigned from the MNR to form his own Revolutionary Party of the Nationalist Left (Partido Revolucionario de Izquierda Nacionalista—PRIN) and then conspired with the military to topple Paz Estenssoro in 1964.

Lechín's support for the military coup did not prevent his joining the MNR leadership in exile while the new military government cracked down on labor. Ironically, between 1982 and 1985 Lechín was largely responsible for the erosion of labor's power. In an attempt to replay the 1950s, he demanded and obtained worker comanagement in Comibol; significantly, he rejected worker cogovernment. At the same time, however, Lechín launched numerous general strikes that crippled the government's attempts to stabilize the economy.

A year after the launching by the MNR of Bolivia's New Economic Policy in 1985, Lechín suffered a humiliating defeat when the miners he had served since 1944 refused to reelect him permanent secretary of the FSTMB. Earlier he had lost his position as secretary general of the COB. Since 1986, Lechín has become a marginal player in labor and in Bolivian politics.

LUPE CAJÍAS, *Historia de una leyenda: Vida y palabra de Juan Lechín Oquendo* (1988); JAMES M. MALLOY and EDUARDO GAMARRA, *Revolution and Reaction: Bolivia, 1964–1985* (1988).

EDUARDO A. GAMARRA

See also **Bolivia: Organizations.**

LECLERC, CHARLES VICTOR EMMANUEL (b. 17 March 1772; d. 2 November 1802), commander of the French military expedition to Saint-Domingue in 1802. In December 1802 a French funeral ship docked at Marseilles. On board were the body of Leclerc and his grieving widow, Pauline. Napoleon officially declared his court in mourning and announced a state funeral for his brother-in-law.

Leclerc, a native of Pontoise, first served under Napoleon at the siege of Toulon (1793) and attained the rank of general in 1797 for his service in Italy. Leclerc married Pauline Bonaparte in 1797 and played an important role in Napoleon's coup against the Directory in 1799.

In 1801, Napoleon selected Leclerc to lead a French expedition against Toussaint L'OUVERTURE and the black rebels of Saint-Domingue. Leclerc encountered unexpected resistance from the rebels, attempted to restore slavery in the former colony, and arrested Toussaint L'Ouverture. He then contracted yellow fever and died at Cap Français. At the time of his death, Jean-Jacques DESSALINES had organized the island's blacks for victory and independence from France.

CYRIL L. R. JAMES, *The Black Jacobins* (1938); JAMES LEYBURN, *The Haitian People* (1941); GEORGES LEFEBVRE, *Napoleon*, 2 vols., translated by Henry F. Stockhold (1969); THOMAS OTT, *The Haitian Revolution, 1789–1804* (1973).

THOMAS O. OTT

LECONTE, MICHEL CINCINNATUS (*d.* 8 August 1912), president of Haiti (1911–1912). Leconte was one of six Haitian presidents who ruled for very brief periods between 1911 and 1915, an era of chronic political instability that encouraged the U.S. military to intervene in Haitian affairs in 1915. Leconte staged a successful coup against President Antoine SIMONE. Lasting only from 14 August 1911 to 8 August 1912, Leconte's presidency was subject to the pressures produced by U.S. and German banking and commercial interests that were competing for control over Haitian economic life. With the support of the German merchants in Haiti, Leconte sought to appease native elite elements unhappy about the corruption that had occurred in Simone's dealings with U.S. bankers and railroad businessmen. U.S. diplomatic pressure, as epitomized by the visit of U.S. Secretary of State Philander Knox, encouraged him to impose order upon the country. Leconte reorganized the army and began developing a system of public education before he was killed in a mysterious explosion at the presidential palace in Port-au-Prince.

RAYFORD W. LOGAN, *Haiti and the Dominican Republic* (1968); DAVID NICHOLLS, *From Dessalines to Duvalier* (1979).

PAMELA MURRAY

LECUONA Y CASADO, ERNESTO (*b.* 6 August 1895; *d.* 29 November, 1963), Cuban pianist and composer. Lecuona, born in Guanabacoa, began to play the piano when he was barely four years old—he had to climb on a box to reach the keyboard. As the great Ignacy Jan Paderewski once noted, he gave the impression that "he had nothing to learn. Nature had made him a prodigious pianist." Thus pianists sometimes have difficulty

playing many of his works because they were composed by an extraordinary master of the keyboard. He had the same natural gift for composing. Many times his works went straight to the publisher without Lecuona's having played them even once.

In this somewhat undisciplined fashion Lecuona's creative genius produced three groups of works. The first encompasses the bulk of his early BOLEROS, *guarachas,* and *criollas*—Cuban music with European roots. The second is made up of Afro-Cuban compositions, which he began to write around 1920, the best known of which is probably the elegant and sensuous dance "La Comparsa." The third, less numerous group is his Spanish-style works, among which the seven pieces that form his suite *Andalucía* stand out. It is said that the celebrated French musician Maurice Ravel believed that the semiclassic "Malagueña," one of these Spanish-style works, was more melodic and beautiful than his own "Bolero." Lecuona also wrote a number of works for the theater, from frivolous revues to tragic zarzuelas (Spanish operettas). Many of his best-known songs come from his stage work, among them "Siboney," one of his most popular pieces outside Cuba.

Plácido Domingo, the world-acclaimed tenor, won the 1985 Grammy Award for Latin American songs for his performance of "Always in My Heart," the theme song that Lecuona wrote for the film of the same title, released in the early 1940s. Lecuona died in Santa Cruz de Tenerife, Spain.

For a short biography of Lecuona, see JOSÉ I. LASAGA, *Cuban Lives: Pages from Cuban History* (1988), vol. 2, pp. 411–424. Further details may be found in GLORIA CASTIEL JACOBSON, "The Life and Music of Ernesto Lecuona" (Ph.D. diss., University of Florida, 1982).

JOSÉ M. HERNÁNDEZ

LEDUC, PAUL (*b.* 11 March 1942), Mexican film director. Leduc was born in Mexico City, where he attended the National Autonomous University of Mexico (UNAM) before receiving a scholarship to study film direction at the Institute of Graduate Film Studies in Paris. Upon his return to Mexico, he organized numerous film clubs and began his career as an assistant director and producer of various important documentaries. He debuted as a director of feature films with the acclaimed *Reed: México insurgente* (1970). A series of noted and controversial films followed. One of the most creative and original directors of current Latin American cinema, Leduc is equally adept at narrative film and documentary. He has consistently preferred to work as an independent film director. Leduc's other films are *Historias prohibidas de Pulgarcito* (1981), *La cabeza de la hidra* (1983), *Frida, naturaleza viva* (1985), *Como vas* (1989), *Barroco* (1990), and *Latino Bar* (1991).

LUIS REYES DE LA MAZA, *El cine sonoro en México* (1973); E. BRADFORD BURNS, *Latin American Cinema: Film and History*

(1975); CARL J. MORA, *Mexican Cinema: Reflections of a Society: 1896–1980* (1982); and JOHN KING, *Magical Reels: A History of Cinema in Latin America* (1990).

DAVID MACIEL

See also **Cinema.**

LEEWARD ISLANDS. The British Lesser ANTILLES are divided into the WINDWARDS (south) and the Leewards (north). The Leewards comprise ANTIGUA, BARBUDA, Redonda, MONTSERRAT, SAINT CHRISTOPHER (Saint Kitts)-Nevis, ANGUILLA, DOMINICA, and the British VIRGIN ISLANDS. Except for Dominica, they are a geographical and historical unit having a common legislature from about 1650 until 1798 that was revived in 1871.

In 1493 Christopher COLUMBUS discovered the Leewards. The Spanish ignored the islands, although they were strategically located. Consequently they became a haven for such privateers as Sir Francis DRAKE and Richard Hawkins. In the seventeenth century they were the first English and French Caribbean sugar colonies.

In 1623, Saint Christopher (Saint Kitts) became the first permanent colony. In 1625 Charles I of England granted Saint Kitts, Nevis, Antigua, Montserrat, and BARBADOS to Charles Howard, first earl of Carlisle. In the same year, the French and English allied against the CARIBS, and formally divided Saint Kitts in 1627. Initial amity turned to struggle, and the two nations alternated in controlling Saint Kitts until the 1713 Peace of Utrecht gave the island to England.

The English governor, Thomas Warner, sent non-Anglicans to settle other islands, and in 1628 they crossed a two-mile channel to Nevis. After they were temporarily expelled from Saint Kitts in 1666, the English made Nevis the Leeward capital.

The Leewards separated from Barbados in 1671, and in 1687 the capital was moved to Antigua, the most windward, and therefore most secure, island from French raids. The corruption of the colonial administration led to the mobbing of Governor Daniel Parke in 1709.

Dominica is the southernmost and largest of the Leewards. Twice declared a neutral Carib sanctuary, it was nevertheless colonized by the French because it is strategically located between the French islands of GUADELOUPE and MARTINIQUE. England dominated the Caribbean when it gained the island after it won the naval battle of the SAINTES (12 April 1782).

Saint Kitts, Nevis, and Antigua were the pioneers of the colonial TOBACCO and SUGAR economies, but sugar declined after England declared the emancipation of SLAVES in 1833. The smaller Leeward Islands traditionally relied on "wrecking" (pillaging stranded ships), fishing, agriculture, and herding. The economy remains undiversified: TOURISM and off-island migration have taken the place of sugar; in the 1960s 50 percent of tiny Montserrat's labor force worked off the island.

The Leewards' political development lagged behind the larger islands after the 1962 collapse of the WEST INDIES FEDERATION delayed their independence. Now the Leewards are ministates belonging to the CARIBBEAN COMMON MARKET and the Organization of Eastern Caribbean States.

ALGERNON ASPINALL, *The Handbook of the British West Indies, British Guiana, and British Honduras* (1926); SIR ALAN BURNS, *History of the British West Indies*, rev. 2d ed. (1965); GORDON K. LEWIS, "The Incubus of Crown Colony: The Leeward Islands," in *The Growth of the Modern West Indies* (1968); ROBERT L. BREEDAN, ed., *Isles of the Caribbean* (1980); FRANKLIN W. KNIGHT, *The Caribbean: The Genesis of Fragmented Nationalism* (1990).

PAT KONRAD

LEGUÍA, AUGUSTO BERNARDINO (*b.* 19 February 1863; *d.* 7 February 1932), Peruvian politician, businessman, and landowner, and twice president of Peru (1908–1912, 1919–1930) at a time of distressing economic modernization and social upheaval. Initially an important representative of the Civilista political elite, and an example of the rise of the more business-oriented sector of the Peruvian agro-export elite, Leguía broke with the Civilista Party over issues of executive initiative and state interventionism. In his second presidential term, Leguía used both popular and elite support to enhance the role of the state aided by foreign loans which became excessive after 1925.

Leguía was born in Lambayeque and studied accounting in a British school in Valparaíso. After the WAR OF THE PACIFIC he was tied through marriage to agro-exporting landed interests. He also developed financial ties with foreign and local banks and insurance companies. He established the British Sugar Company in 1896 and the South America Insurance Company in 1900. He rose meteorically in politics, first serving as finance minister under Presidents Manuel CANDAMO and José PARDO. As a presidential candidate with the official Civilista Party blessing, Leguía was elected president in 1908. His first term of office was traumatic. In an attempted coup in 1909, Leguía almost lost his life but also demonstrated considerable courage. His attempts at modernizing the state lost him favor among the Civilistas. From 1908 to 1910 Leguía also had to face international crises with neighboring Ecuador, Colombia, and Chile. In his second term Leguía was able to settle most of these old boundary disputes.

After 1913 Leguía lived abroad, mainly in London. In 1918 he returned to Peru with strong popular support. Leguía won the presidential elections of 1919, but fearing congressional opposition by his political enemies, he rallied military support for a coup to reinforce his presidential powers. Subsequently, his efforts to establish a New Fatherland (*Patria Nueva*) resulted in rigged reelections in 1924 and 1929. He exiled or imprisoned many of his political adversaries. His public works in Lima and the provinces (road construction, urbanization), state modernization, and encouragement of local capitalist interests seriously floundered during the financial crisis that led to the depression of the 1930s. He was ousted by a military coup led by Colonel Luis SÁNCHEZ CERRO and died in prison in Callao.

MANUEL CAPUÑAY, *Leguía, vida y obra del constructor del gran Perú* (1952); ALFONSO QUIROZ, *Domestic and Foreign Finance in Modern Peru, 1850–1950: Financing Visions of Development* (1993).

ALFONSO W. QUIROZ

See also **Peru: Political Parties.**

LEIGHTON GUZMÁN, BERNARDO (*b.* 16 August 1909), Chilean politician. Bernardo Leighton Guzmán served as minister of the interior during the first half of Christian Democrat Eduardo FREI's presidency in the mid-1960s. Along with Frei, Radomiro TOMIC, and Rafael Agustín Gumucio, he was among the many young, middle-class Chilean Catholics attracted to the liberal currents of Catholic social thought that emerged during the 1920s and 1930s. After several years of burrowing from within the country's traditional Conservative Party, this group left the party in 1938 to establish the Falange Nacional, which in 1957 became the Christian Democratic Party (PDC).

Known affectionately as Hermano Bernardo (Brother Bernard), Leighton was one of the most congenial and widely respected of the Christian Democrats. He served in the cabinets of Liberal (Arturo ALESSANDRI) and Radical (Gabriel GONZÁLEZ VIDELA) governments, and throughout his career maintained cordial relationships with virtually all political forces, particularly those of the Left. Although one of the most trusted confidants of the strongly anticommunist Frei, he was among the minority of Christian Democrats who condemned the 1973 military coup and publicly criticized those who encouraged and supported it. He and his wife were attacked and left for dead by unknown assailants in Rome in 1978. He eventually recovered, but remains partially paralyzed.

MICHAEL FLEET, *The Rise and Fall of Chilean Christian Democracy* (1985).

MICHAEL FLEET

LELOIR, LUIS F. (*b.* 6 September 1906; *d.* 2 December 1987), Argentine scientist and winner of the Nobel Prize in chemistry in 1970. Born in Paris to a wealthy Argentine landowning family, Leloir was brought to Argentina when he was two years old. He received an M.D. from the University of Buenos Aires in 1932, after which he briefly practiced medicine. In 1934 he joined the research team at the Institute of Physiology under the leadership of Dr. Bernardo A. Houssay, the pioneering Argentine scientist and 1947 Nobel Prize winner in physiology and medicine. From 1936 to 1937, Leloir pursued his interest in the young field of biochemistry at Cambridge University, England, with Sir Frederick

Gowland Hopkins, another Nobel Prize winner (1929). He returned to Buenos Aires and rejoined the Institute of Physiology (1937–1943), where he studied the oxidation of ethanol and fatty acids, and later worked on the mechanism of renal hypertension.

In 1944, disagreements with the Juan PERÓN government led Leloir (and many other scientists) to pursue research abroad. Initially, he worked on the formation of citric acid as a research associate at Washington University in Saint Louis, and later joined the Enzyme Research Laboratory at the College of Physicians and Surgeons in New York City. In 1947, he returned to Argentina and became the first director of the Biochemical Research Institute in Buenos Aires, a research group formed and led by Leloir and financed by businessman Jaime Campomar. On Campomar's death in 1957, the U.S. National Institutes of Health provided a grant that allowed the institute to continue its research.

Leloir was awarded the 1970 Nobel Prize for the work he and his staff did at the institute in the late 1940s and early 1950s that led to the discovery of sugar nucleotides and their role in the biosynthesis of carbohydrates. His more than seventy scientific articles have been published in international scientific journals. Leloir's dedication and many scientific successes, despite an often astonishing lack of financial support for even basic equipment and laboratory space, attest to his genius and contradict the image of Latin American disinterest in science.

LUIS LELOIR, *Opera selecta* (1973) and "Far Away and Long Ago," in *The Excitement and Fascination of Science,* edited by Joshua Lederberg, vol. 3, pt. 1 (1990), pp. 367–381.

J. DAVID DRESSING

LEMÁCHEZ, QUIRINO. *See* **Henríquez, Camilo.**

LEMUS, JOSÉ MARÍA (*b.* 22 July 1911), president of El Salvador (1956–1960). Born in La Unión of humble origins, Lemus attended the National Military Academy. He served as El Salvador's undersecretary of defense (1948–1949), and as President Oscar OSORIO's (1950–1956) minister of the interior (1950–1955); in the latter post he antagonized his colleagues by fighting corruption. Lemus was Osorio's choice to succeed him, and in 1956 he won a disputed election.

A man of democratic impulses, he brought a number of distinguished civilians into government. He repealed Osorio's antisedition law and permitted political exiles to return to El Salvador, thereby antagonizing the military. He also offended the press by requiring newspapers to print replies to news stories and editorials.

The use of production controls to combat the 1958 drop in coffee prices infuriated the growers, while rising prices and unemployment alienated the workers. A disputed congressional election in 1960 exacerbated tensions. Lemus responded by announcing reforms in health, education, and minimum wages. With the support of the Roman Catholic church, he organized a mass rally in support of the government. This was followed by student demonstrations praising the Cuban revolution. The subsequent roundup of students and other dissidents led to Lemus's arrest and exile on 26 October 1960.

FRANKLIN D. PARKER, *The Central American Republics* (1964); STEPHEN WEBRE, *José Napoleón Duarte and the Christian Democratic Party in Salvadoran Politics, 1960–1972* (1979); JAMES DUNKERLY, *The Long War: Dictatorship and Revolution in El Salvador* (1982).

ROLAND H. EBEL

LENCA, a group of Indian peoples who inhabited central, south, and western Honduras and southeast El Salvador at the time of the Spanish conquest. Origins of the Lenca are still unclear. Ancestors may have been Late Preclassic populations of central Honduras. The Salvadoran Lencas built the Classic-Period QUELEPA on the Pacific coastal trade route. The term *Lenca* encompasses the Potón, Guaquí, Care, Chato, Dule, Paraca, and Yara Indians. The Lencan language family includes extinct Honduran Lenca and Salvadoran Lenca, of which there are few surviving speakers.

The Lenca gathered foods and cultivated maize, beans, curcubits (squash and pumpkins), chiles, tobacco, cacao, and plantains. Their stratified political organization was headed by caciques (high chieftains) and lesser chiefs, followed by priests, soldiers, and commoners. Chiefdoms made up at least four provinces: Care, Cerquín, Potón, and Taulabe.

War was important to the Lenca way of life; their main weapon was the poison-tipped lance. They also built mounds and hilltop fortresses called *penoles*. The Lenca made peace agreements and formed alliances against the Spanish, who enslaved them for work in mines and the REPARTIMIENTO system of labor partitioned by the Spanish for their own use.

Disagreement among scholars on whether to include the Lenca in the Mesoamerican cultural category is due to their mix of northern and southern cultural traits. Mesoamerican traits include agricultural and religious practices, the use of wooden swords with obsidian and cotton armor for war, and a calendar of eighteen months of twenty days each. Poisonous weapons and the panpipe, however, are characteristic of South American cultures.

DORIS STONE, *The Archaeology of Central and Southern Honduras* (1957); ANNE CHAPMAN, "Los Lencas de Honduras en el siglo XVI," *Estudios Antropológicos e Históricos*, no. 2 (1978); JOHN M. WEEKS, NANCY BLACK, and J. STUART SPEAKER, "From Prehistory to History in Western Honduras: The Care Lenca in the Colonial Province of Tencoa," in *Interaction on the Southeast Mesoamerican Frontier*, edited by Eugenia J. Robinson (1987), vol. 1, pp. 65–94.

LAURA L. WOODWARD

See also **Mesoamerica.**

LENCINAS, CARLOS WÁSHINGTON (*b.* 13 November 1889; *d.* 10 November 1929), Argentine caudillo. Born in Rivadavia in the province of Mendoza, Argentina, Lencinas studied law at the University of Córdoba. Upon returning to Mendoza, he followed in the political footsteps of his father, José Néstor Lencinas, who in 1918 became the first governor from the Radical Civic Union (UCR) to rule the province. When his father died in office in 1920, Lencinas, who that year had been elected a representative to Congress, took the reins of the party and eventually formed a new one, the Lencinista UCR. In 1922 he was elected governor of Mendoza and ruled in a populist fashion. He was popularly called "el gauchito Lencinas." In 1924 his government was "intervened," an Argentine constitutional device that under specific conditions allows Congress or the central government to assume administrative control of a province; thus ended Lencinas's short-lived governorship. Two years later Lencinas was elected national senator by Mendoza's legislature, but his credentials were rejected by Congress. On 10 November 1929, Lencinas was assassinated while addressing a crowd in Mendoza. As his assailant was also shot and killed, the motivation for the crime was never clearly determined. A popular and charismatic leader, Lencinas established pioneer social reforms such as the minimum-wage salary, the eight-hour workday, and an employee pension system. These provincial measures were the harbinger of national social reforms instituted a generation later by Juan Domingo Perón.

DARDO OLGUÍN, " . . . Y en el medio de mi pecho Carlos Wáshington Lencinas . . . !" in *Todo es historia*, no. 24 (1969): 8–35; CELSO RODRÍGUEZ, *Lencinas y Cantoni, el populismo cuyano en tiempos de Yrigoyen* (1979); PABLO LACOSTE, "Carlos Wáshington Lencinas: Su vigencia póstuma," in *Todo es historia* 23, no. 270 (1989): 82–97.

CELSO RODRÍGUEZ

LEÑERO, VICENTE (*b.* 9 June 1933), Mexican writer and journalist. Leñero was born in Guadalajara, Jalisco. He earned a degree in engineering, which he practiced very briefly. During the early 1960s Leñero was a full-time journalist, and subsequently he continued working in that profession. He has produced short stories, novels, dramas, and cultural reports, and he has made decisive contributions to some of the most important journalistic and cultural enterprises in recent Mexican history. Since 1976 he has been assistant director of the magazine *Proceso*.

Inspired by the exemplary works of Juan RULFO and Juan José ARREOLA, Leñero published his first book, *La polvareda y otros cuentos*, in 1959. Published two years later was his first novel, *La voz adolorida*, a revised version of which later appeared under the definitive title *A fuerza de palabras*. This work began a novelistic career unique in Mexican literature. Perhaps because of his engineering background, Leñero is very conscious of the structure of his novels and in each of them displays a will to master a radically different and complex structure. This formal preoccupation has produced at least one masterpiece, *Los albañiles* (1964), winner of the Biblioteca Breve prize for a novel in 1963, at that time the most prestigious recognition that existed in the Spanish language.

Although some critics consider the spontaneity of Leñero's works excessive and even detracting, his approach has led him to explore the most diverse novelistic subgenres while reflecting with clarity and honesty on some of the most critical moral problems of our time.

DANNY J. ANDERSON, *Vicente Leñero: The Novelist as Critic* (1989).

JORGE AGUILAR MORA

LENG, ALFONSO (*b.* 11 February 1894; *d.* 11 November 1974), Chilean composer. Born in Santiago, Leng was largely a self-taught composer, he attended the conservatory in Santiago for less than a year (1905). Leng was a member of the *Grupo de los diez* (Group of the Ten), which had been formed by fellow composers Próspero Bisquertt, García-Guerrero, Acario COTAPOS, and Carlos Lavín, whose works introduced the concept of modernism into the Chilean cultural aesthetic. By about 1906 Leng had acquired his definitive style, as shown in such compositions as *Preludio no. 2* (1906) and his five *Doloras* for piano (1901–1914). In 1921 he composed *La muerte de Alsino,* a symphonic poem. Leng's style was strongly connected with German late romanticism. He wrote a considerable number of works for voice and piano as well as choral works. He was awarded the National Art Prize in Music in 1957. A noted dentist, he wrote several major papers on odontology. He died in Santiago.

Revista Musical Chilena (Leng issue), 98 (1966); *Composers of the Americas,* vol. 15 (1969), pp. 156–160; JOHN VINTON, ed., *Dictionary of Contemporary Music* (1974); *New Grove Dictionary of Music and Musicians,* vol. 10 (1980).

SUSANA SALGADO

LEO XIII, POPE (*b.* 2 March 1810; *d.* 20 July 1903), considered the first modern pope (1878–1903). Although he retained many of the attitudes of his predecessor, Pius IX, toward the modern world, especially his reservations regarding liberalism and the application of scientific method to religion, Pope Leo opened the doors for Catholics notably in the realm of social thought. After a short diplomatic career he served as bishop of Perugia, Italy, for thirty-two years. Elected pope in 1878, he attempted to give a more positive response to many of the great intellectual and social questions of the day: industrialism, capitalism, democracy, and nationalism. He is most famous for his encyclical *Rerum Novarum* (1891), the first major papal statement on the rights of workers and social justice. In that and other writings, Leo XIII

criticized socialism and economic liberalism, but he also called for a just and democratic social order. His ideas inspired the creation of the Christian Democratic parties of Europe and Latin America. At his invitation, the bishops of the CATHOLIC CHURCH in Latin America held a plenary council in Rome in 1899.

EDWARD T. GARGAN, ed., *Leo XIII and the Modern World* (1961); LILLIAN PARKER WALLACE, *Leo XIII and the Rise of Socialism* (1966).

JEFFREY KLAIBER, S.J.

LEÓN, the second city of Nicaragua and the traditional center of liberal political groups. León was first established on the western shores of Lake Managua in 1524. It was moved a few miles to the west to its present site in 1610 as the result of an eruption of nearby Momotombo volcano. During the colonial period, it shared leadership of the country with the rival city of Granada but was the provincial capital within the captaincy general of Guatemala. León's cathedral is the largest in Central America. The present structure, designed by the prominent colonial architect Diego de PORRES, was completed in 1780. Built of cut stone, it withstood repeated earthquakes. On occasion it has served as a fortress. Rubén DARÍO (1867–1916), Nicaragua's most beloved poet, spent much of his early life in León and is buried within the cathedral under a statue of a lion. The city has grown in recent years, but not as rapidly as Managua. León is estimated to have a population of 130,000 (1990).

ALFONSO ARGUELLO, *Historia de León Viejo* (1969).

DAVID L. JICKLING

LEÓN, ALONSO DE (*b.* 1637; *d.* ca. 25 March 1691), first governor of COAHUILA (1687–1691) and leader of early colonization efforts in Texas. The son and namesake of an important chronicler of Nuevo León, León was born in León, Spain. He grew up on Mexico's northern frontier, earned a reputation as an explorer and soldier, and rose to the rank of general in 1687. That same year, León became the first governor of the newly created province of Coahuila, which was intended to serve as a bulwark against the threatening French presence in the Gulf of Mexico. At first, he concentrated on internal affairs, distributing land grants and mining licenses, reorganizing the presidio system, and attempting to pacify the indigenous population. But imperial matters soon took precedence. In 1689 and 1690, León led expeditions to Texas. The first came across the remains of a French fort built by Sieur de La Salle, already destroyed by Indians. On the second, León's party founded the first Texas mission, San Francisco de los Tejas. However, such missionary activity—underfinanced, poorly supplied, and insufficiently defended—could not be sustained in the face of a hostile Indian response and was abandoned within a few years. Spain would not establish a permanent base in Texas until 1716. León died in Santiago de Monclova, which he had founded in 1689.

VITO ALESSIO ROBLES, *Coahuila y Texas en la época colonial* (1938); DAVID J. WEBER, *The Spanish Frontier in North America* (1992).

R. DOUGLAS COPE

LEÓN DE LA BARRA, FRANCISCO (*b.* 16 June 1863; *d.* 22 September 1939), president of Mexico (26 May 1911–6 November 1911). The son of a Chilean immigrant who fought for the Liberals in the War of the Reform, León de la Barra was a native of Querétaro. He graduated in 1886 from the School of Jurisprudence that was later absorbed into the National University. An outstanding international lawyer and career diplomat, León de la Barra was Mexico's ambassador to the United States when the Revolution of 1910 began. After being elevated constitutionally to the presidency by the Treaty of Ciudad Juárez, he presided over the most democratic elections held until that time.

Nicknamed the "White President" because of his apolitical behavior, León de la Barra walked with some success the slippery tightrope between demands for peace and order and the quest for social change. Although some interpretations have made his presidency the scapegoat for Francisco MADERO's inadequacies, more recent studies have been more favorable, pointing out that he allowed a free press and initiated labor and agrarian reforms. León de la Barra served Victoriano HUERTA briefly as secretary of foreign relations (1913), was ambassador to France in 1913–1914, and then retired to Europe, where he played a role in the post–World War I settlement. He died in Biarritz, France.

See STANLEY R. ROSS, *Francisco I. Madero: Apostle of Mexican Democracy* (1955), for the traditional interpretation; for a fresher evaluation, see PRESIDENCIA DE LA REPÚBLICA, *Los presidentes de México: Discursos políticos, 1910–1988* (1988), vol. 1, esp. pp. 17–21.

PETER V. N. HENDERSON

LEÓN-PORTILLA, MIGUEL (*b.* 22 February 1926), leading Mexican scholar of ancient Mexican literatures, philosophy, and culture. Born in Mexico City, Léon-Portilla received B.A. degrees at the Instituto de Ciencias in Guadalajara (1944) and Loyola University in Los Angeles (1948). In 1951 he graduated with an M.A. from Loyola and received a Ph.D. from the National University of Mexico in 1956. León-Portilla has held several positions since then, including professor in the Faculty of Philosophy and Letters at the National University of Mexico; director of the Inter-American Indigenist Institute (1960–1963); director of the Institute of Historical Research of the National University of Mexico (1963–

1975); and delegate of Mexico to UNESCO. His honors include Mexico's 1981 National Prize in the Social Sciences, History, and Philosophy. León-Portilla's revised Ph.D. dissertation, *La filosofía Nahuatl estudiada en sus fuentes*, first published in 1959, set the stage for his life-long scholarly endeavors. His more than 40 monographs, over 200 professional articles, instrumental involvement in the publication of numerous primary sources, and his editorships of *Estudios de cultura Nahuatl* and *Tlalocan* demonstrate his pivotal role in developing and furthering Aztec studies.

Among León-Portilla's major contributions has been his willingness to grapple with questions of Aztec worldview and philosophy, based on documentary sources that are incomplete and subject to interpretation. His translations of primary Aztec documentation have made a large and complicated corpus accessible to intensive study; his interpretations and analyses have stimulated scholarly research and debate; and his numerous syntheses of Aztec literature and culture have extended an understanding of ancient Mexico to a worldwide audience.

Among León-Portilla's many influential works are *Visión de los vencidos* (1950); *Aztec Thought and Culture* (1963); *Trece poetas del mundo azteca* (1967); and *Pre-Columbian Literatures of Mexico* (1969). For background, see the preface by JORGE KLOR DE ALVA, "Nahua Studies, the Allure of the 'Aztecs,' and Miguel León-Portilla," in LEÓN-PORTILLA's *The Aztec Image of Self and Society* (1992), vii–xxiii.

FRANCES F. BERDAN

LEONI, RAÚL (*b.* 26 April 1906; *d.* 5 July 1972), Venezuelan president (1964–1968). Raúl Leoni was one of the founding fathers of Venezuela's most important twentieth-century political party, Acción Democrática (AD). He began his political career when, as president of the Venezuelan Students Federation, he organized a Students' Week in February 1928 to protest the repressive regime of Juan Vicente GÓMEZ. Although the protest sparked a more general outcry against the regime, including an aborted rebellion led by young army officers, it also forced Leoni and his colleagues into exile for eight years. While in Barranquilla, Colombia, Leoni and other exiles plotted their return and drew up the *Plan de Barranquilla*, a nationalist reform document that foreshadowed the program of the AD. The plan stressed the need for political democracy and social justice in Venezuela and sought to curb the virtually unbridled power of the country's foreign-owned petroleum companies. Leoni returned to Venezuela after the death of Gómez, and in 1936 he was elected to the Venezuelan Chamber of Deputies as a member of the Partido Democrático Nacional (PDN), precursor of AD. However, Leoni was deported by President Eleazar LÓPEZ CONTRERAS in 1937 and was unable to take his seat.

After earning a law degree at the Universidad Nacional de Colombia in Bogotá, Leoni returned to Venezuela, where he became one of the main organizers of AD, which was legally recognized in September 1941. Leoni and Rómulo BETANCOURT led the party into power for the first time by cooperating with dissident army officers who, in 1945, overthrew dictator General Isaías MEDINA. As minister of labor during the heady years that followed, Leoni oversaw the unionization of Venezuelan workers and supervised the first collective bargaining agreement between the oil companies and their workers in 1946. When AD fell victim to its own mistakes and a military coup against President Rómulo GALLEGOS in November 1948, Leoni left the country again, this time to work for the International Labor Organization of the United Nations and with fellow AD exiles who formed part of a larger community of exiled Caribbean democratic-left leaders.

With the fall of the dictatorial General Marcos PÉREZ JIMÉNEZ in January 1958, Leoni returned to Venezuela to help his party regain power. After becoming president of AD the following year, he succeeded his old ally Rómulo Betancourt as president of Venezuela between 1964 and 1968. Relying initially on support from the AD-affiliated labor groups, Leoni largely continued the nationalist, reformist policies inaugurated by Betancourt. These included promotion of industrialization, agrarian reform, and expansion of public education. Leoni also proved to be an innovator by seeking conciliation with the radical Left which had launched a guerrilla war several years earlier, and by legalizing the Communist Party in 1968. Finally, by proposing a law to levy an excess profits tax on the oil companies, he goaded the latter into accepting a compromise arrangement that increased the industry's benefit to the national government. This step paved the way for future efforts to increase the government's share of Venezuelan oil wealth.

JOHN MARTZ, *Acción Democrática: The Evolution of a Modern Political Party in Venezuela* (1966); CHARLES D. AMERINGER, *The Democratic Left in Exile: The Antidictatorial Struggle in the Caribbean, 1945–1959* (1974); ROBERT J. ALEXANDER, ed., *Biographical Dictionary of Latin American and Caribbean Political Leaders* (1988).

PAMELA MURRAY

See also **Venezuela: Political Parties.**

LEOPOLDINA, EMPRESS (Maria Leopoldina de Hapsburg; *b.* 22 January 1797; *d.* 11 December 1826), empress consort of Brazil (1822–1826). Daughter of Emperor Francis I of Austria, Archduchess Leopoldina married Pedro, prince of Brazil and heir to the Portuguese throne, in ceremonies in Vienna and Rio de Janeiro in 1817. The marriage became a factor in the acceptance of Brazil's independence from Portugal—declared by Pedro with Leopoldina's strong support in 1822—by Austria and the "Holy Alliance" of conservative European monarchies. Pedro and Leopoldina were proclaimed emperor and empress of Brazil on 12 October 1822.

Intelligent and well educated, especially in the natural sciences, Leopoldina came under the intellectual influence of her husband's chief minister, José Bonifácio de ANDRADA E SILVA, though she retained her innate political conservatism. Pedro's banishment of José Bonifácio in 1823 distressed her, and subsequent revelations of her husband's infidelities added to her unhappiness. While the emperor's political enemies publicly sympathized with his long-suffering wife, Leopoldina remained devoted to the unfaithful Pedro. She bore him four daughters, including the future Queen MARIA II of Portugal, and two sons, one who died in infancy and one who became Emperor PEDRO II of Brazil. Barely a year after the birth of her second son, Leopoldina died of complications following a miscarriage.

AMILCAR SALGADO DOS SANTOS, *Imperatriz D. Leopoldina* (1927); CARLOS H. OBERACKER, JR., *A imperatriz Leopoldina: Sua vida e sua época* (1973).

NEILL MACAULAY

LEPE, DIEGO DE (*d.* before 1513), Andalusian explorer, possible discoverer of the Orinoco River in present-day Venezuela. A native of Palos, in southwest Spain, Lepe was one of several leaders of a series of minor expeditions from Spain's southern Atlantic ports that led to important advances in geographic knowledge of New World coasts. Leading a small fleet of two boats, Lepe left Seville in mid-November 1499, pursuing the course set two weeks earlier by Vicente Yáñez PINZÓN, who commanded four ships. Lepe followed the route of Pinzón, passing the Cape Verde Islands, then sailed to Cape San Agustín (Pinzón reached it on 26 January 1500) on the Brazilian coast. Pinzón seems to have been the first European to discover the Amazon estuary and enter the great river; he sailed upstream for a time and made contact with peoples along its banks. Diego de Lepe and his men followed within days.

At this point the account becomes confused. Some say Lepe sailed southward along Brazil's coast as far as the Río de la Plata; others argue he went northwestwardly, encountering several important rivers, including the Orinoco, of which he took possession in the name of the Spanish monarchs, calling it the Marañón. In skirmishes he lost eleven men but captured thirty-six Native Americans, whom he later presented as slaves to Bishop Juan de Fonseca in Seville. Given that Lepe's fleet and that of Pinzón came together in the Gulf of Paria, the second version of Lepe's voyage seems most likely.

From the north coast of South America, Lepe's boats headed to the Isla de San Juan (Puerto Rico) in May 1500, while the Pinzón group sailed to Hispaniola's north coast in June of the same year. From Puerto Rico, Lepe sailed directly to Spain, reaching Seville several weeks earlier than Pinzón. He had an audience with the monarchs in Granada on 15 November 1500, and later secured an agreement for a new voyage on 14 September 1501. It is unclear if this expedition ever took place. Lepe died in Portugal sometime before 1513.

Both Pinzón and Diego de Lepe came upon Brazil several months prior to the official Portuguese discovery of Pedro Alvares CABRAL on 22 April 1500. Their logs, maps, and reports were used by cartographer Juan de la Cosa for his famous world map of 1500.

JUAN MANZANO MANZANO, *Los Pinzones y el descubrimiento de América* (1988); FRANCISCO MORALES PADRÓN, *Andalucía y América* (1988).

NOBLE DAVID COOK

See also **Explorers.**

LÉPERO, a pejorative term used primarily in the nineteenth century to refer to Mexico City's underclass. During the long period of economic stagnation and political instability after Independence in 1821, Mexico City's elite grew obsessed with the suspected volatility, moral turpitude, and criminal activities of the vast majority of the urban population, who led lives of poverty and uncertainty. The term *lépero* or *populacho* indiscriminately lumped together underemployed artisans and manual laborers with beggars and criminals. Successive governments implemented various legal measures, such as a special vagrancy court, to fight the perceived infestation of idlers and thieves, but such legislation did little to eliminate the city's problems, which were primarily a result of the country's chronic political and economic crises and not the criminal proclivities of its residents.

A *lépero* (left) and a public scribe in Mexico City. Reproduced from M. Alcide D'Orbigny, *Voyage pittoresque dans les deux Amériques* (Paris, 1836).
HARVARD COLLEGE LIBRARY.

The term *lépero* is of obscure origin and was also used as a pejorative in parts of Central America and Ecuador. In Cuba, however, it was equivalent to LADINO.

TORCUATO S. DI TELLA, "The Dangerous Classes in Early Nineteenth Century Mexico," in *Journal of Latin American Studies* 5, no. 1 (1973): 79–105; FREDERICK J. SHAW, JR., "Poverty and Politics in Mexico City, 1824–1854," (Ph.D. diss., University of Florida, 1975); SILVIA M. ARROM, "Popular Politics in Mexico City: The Parián Riot, 1828," in *Hispanic American Historical Review* 68 (May 1988): 245–268; ERIC VAN YOUNG, "Islands in the Storm: Quiet Cities and Violent Countrysides in the Mexican Independence Era," in *Past & Present* 118 (1988): 130–155.

RICHARD WARREN

See also **Acordada, Revolt of; Parián.**

LERDO DE TEJADA, MIGUEL (*b.* 1812; *d.* 22 March 1861), Mexican politician, author of the LEY LERDO, and brother of Sebastián Lerdo de Tejada. A native of the city of Veracruz, Lerdo was elected to the Mexico City *ayuntamiento* (city council) in 1849 and became its president in 1852. Lerdo was a close associate of many of the *agiotistas* (moneylenders) of Mexico City and Veracruz and a consistent advocate of infrastructure development. Lerdo was deputy minister and later minister of development during the last presidency of Antonio López de SANTA ANNA (1853–1855). As finance minister for Ignacio Comonfort, Lerdo issued the Law Disamortizing Urban and Rural Property, commonly called the Ley Lerdo, on 25 June 1856. Lerdo served Benito JUÁREZ as finance minister (1858–1859, 1859–1860) and as minister of development (1859, 1860). On 12 July 1859, after Lerdo had threatened to resign, the liberal government issued a decree nationalizing all property of the regular and secular clergy, suppressing religious orders, and separating the church and the state. Lerdo hoped to use church property as collateral for a loan from the United States to adequately fund the liberal government and its war against the conservatives. He traveled to New Orleans, New York, and Washington, D.C., in 1859, but was unsuccessful in acquiring funds. Lerdo resigned in June 1860, when Juárez rejected his proposal to suspend payment on the foreign debt, but the real difference between the two men was Lerdo's position in favor of either negotiating peace with the conservatives or inviting U.S. intervention, neither of which Juárez would accept. After the liberal victory, Lerdo became a candidate for the presidency of the republic. During the campaign he died of typhus in Mexico City.

CARMEN BLÁZQUEZ, *Miguel Lerdo de Tejada: Un liberal veracruzano en la política nacional* (1978); RICHARD N. SINKIN, *The Mexican Reform, 1855–1876: A Study in Liberal Nation-Building* (1979); BARBARA A. TENENBAUM, *The Politics of Penury: Debt and Taxes in Mexico, 1821–1856* (1986), pp. 133, 156–163.

D. F. STEVENS

See also **Anticlericalism.**

LERDO DE TEJADA, SEBASTIÁN (*b.* 1823; *d.* 1889), president of Mexico (1872–1876). The younger brother of Mexican politician Miguel Lerdo de Tejada, Sebastián Lerdo was born in Jalapa, Veracruz. After renouncing an ecclesiastical career, he moved to Mexico City in 1841. Lerdo took a teaching post at the Colegio de San Ildefonso in 1849 and became rector in 1852. President Ignacio COMONFORT appointed him minister of foreign relations in 1857, but Lerdo remained in Mexico City as the rector of San Ildefonso and took no part in the War of the REFORM. In 1861, he was elected to the national legislature, where he served as president of the Congress on three occasions. During the FRENCH INTERVENTION, Lerdo accompanied President Benito JUÁREZ as a representative of the Congress. Juárez appointed Lerdo to head the ministries of government and foreign relations.

Along with Juárez and José María IGLESIAS, Lerdo was among the most prominent politicians in the Republican government. He wrote decrees (8 November 1865) explaining the extension of Juárez's presidential term until the end of the war and eliminating the possibility of succession for Jesús GONZÁLEZ ORTEGA. According to some sources, Lerdo convinced Juárez not to pardon MAXIMILIAN. Lerdo wrote the *convocatoria* of 1867, which sought to increase presidential power through an unconstitutional plebiscite.

Despite increasing opposition to him, Lerdo was elected vice president. He inherited the presidency on the death of Juárez in July 1872 and later that year was elected to a constitutional term. His presidency was marked by the completion of the Mexico City–Veracruz railroad (1873), the elimination of several regional caciques, and anticlerical reforms. As minister of foreign relations, Lerdo had consistently resisted U.S. encroachments on Mexican territory. As president, he delayed railroad construction in the north, saying "Between strength and weakness, the desert," but finally granted a concession to a U.S. firm. After announcing his intention to seek reelection in 1876, Lerdo faced two opposition movements, one led by José María IGLESIAS, the other by Porfirio DÍAZ. Although Lerdo was reelected, he was not able to defeat his armed opponents. He resigned the presidency on 20 November 1876 and fled into exile on 25 January 1877. He died in New York City.

FRANK A. KNAPP, *Sebastián Lerdo de Tejada, 1823–1889: A Study of Influence and Obscurity* (1951; repr. 1968); DANIEL COSÍO VILLEGAS, *Historia moderna de México, Vol. 1: La república restorada, La vida política* (1959); LAURENS BALLARD PERRY, *Juárez and Díaz: Machine Politics in Mexico* (1978); RICHARD N. SINKIN, *The Mexican Reform, 1855–1876: A Study in Liberal Nation-Building* (1979); *Diccionario Porrúa de historia, biografía y geografía de México*, 5th ed. (1986), vol. 2, pp. 1654–1655.

D. F. STEVENS

LERMA RIVER, a waterway in west-central Mexico. Beginning in the Toluca basin, in the state of Mexico, the river drops sharply into the basin of Guanajuato, winds through the fertile agricultural basin known as the BAJÍO, and empties into Lake CHAPALA in Jalisco, 350 miles away. From Chapala, the river continues as the Río Grande de Santiago, which flows through the agricultural lands of Jalisco before plunging over the western edge of the central plateau toward the Pacific. Collectively, the Lerma-Chapala-Santiago system forms the largest river basin located wholly within the borders of the Republic of Mexico.

Since the Lerma is one of the largest perennial waterways serving the densely populated southern portion of the central plateau, it is used extensively for drinking water, irrigation, and hydroelectric power. Water diversion from the Lerma began during the colonial period, to irrigate the important wheat- and cornfields of the Bajío, the breadbasket of Mexico. Much of the river is also diverted by aqueduct to meet the growing water needs of Mexico City.

Throughout the twentieth century, human and natural stresses on the Lerma have deteriorated its water quality and flow. Such problems are exemplified by the receding shores of Lake Chapala.

DAVID BARKIN and TIMOTHY KING, *Regional Economic Development: The River Basin Approach in Mexico* (1970), pp. 68–69, 113–115; JORGE L. TAMAYO, *Geografía moderna de México*, 9th ed. (1980), pp. 239–275; MICHAEL E. MURPHY, *Irrigation in the Bajío Region of Colonial Mexico* (1986), esp. pp. 1–8.

MARIE D. PRICE

LÉRY, JEAN DE (*b.* 1534; *d.* 1611), Huguenot pastor who traveled to Brazil in 1556 as part of a colony established by French adventurer Durand de VILLEGAGNON near present-day Rio de Janeiro. In 1578 Léry published *Histoire d'un voyage fait en la terre du Brésil*, in which he recalled his voyage to the New World, his flight from the French colony, and the two months he spent living among the TUPINAMBÁ Indians. Léry's remarkably comprehensive and largely sympathetic discussion of Indian life included descriptions of physical appearance, housing, cuisine, ceremonial rituals (including cannibalism), warfare, marriage customs, and child rearing.

OLIVIER REVERDIN, *Quatorze Calvinistes chez les Topinambous: Histoire d'une mission genevoise au Brésil* (*1556–1558*) (1957); JANET WHATELY, "Une révérence réciproque: Huguenot Writing on the New World," in *University of Toronto Quarterly* 57, no. 2 (Winter 1987/1988): 270–289.

KATHLEEN JOAN HIGGINS

LESCOT, ÉLIE (*b.* 1883; *d.* 1974), Haitian dictator (1941–1946). Lescot, a native of Saint-Louis-du-Nord, was educated in Cap Haitien and received his doctorate from Laval University in Québec. Subsequently he was secretary of public education, justice, and the interior; envoy to the Dominican Republic; and a diplomat in the United States. His regime was known for its tyranny and corruption as well as for its close cooperation with U.S. government and business interests. Lescot established his dictatorship, in part, by taking advantage of circumstances produced by U.S. national and hemispheric security concerns after the outbreak of World War II. In the name of protecting Haiti from the Axis powers, he not only confiscated the property of Germans and Italians within the country, but also suspended the Haitian constitution. The regime also benefited from an influx of U.S. military and economic aid during the war period. U.S.-sponsored development projects went to enrich Lescot's family and friends. These included a project to grow sisal financed by the U.S.-controlled Société Haïtienne-Américaine du Développement Agricole (SHADA), to which Lescot made huge land concessions and which, in turn, led to the displacement of thousands of peasants.

Lescot's policies favored members of the country's mulatto elite and, generally, denied the aspirations and interests of blacks. Lescot excluded blacks from important positions in his government. He also attacked black folk culture by supporting the Roman Catholic church's campaign against the vodun religion. Although this attack proved short-lived, it helped provoke widespread nationalist opposition to the regime. Lescot altered the constitution in order to extend his term of office and postponed elections, ostensibly because of World War II. By the end of 1945, students, workers, and intellectuals openly demanded an end to the dictatorship. Following the Revolution of 1946, Lescot was forced to resign on 11 January 1946. He was exiled to Canada.

DAVID NICHOLLS, "Haiti Since 1930," in *The Cambridge History of Latin America*, vol. 7, edited by Leslie Bethell (1990), pp. 545–577; MICHEL ROLPH-TROUILLOT, *Haiti: State Against Nation* (1990).

PAMELA MURRAY

LESSEPS, FERDINAND MARIE, VICOMTE DE (*b.* 19 November 1805; *d.* 7 December 1894), French statesman who organized construction of the Suez Canal in the 1860s and attempted to build a canal in Panama in the 1880s.

Born into a distinguished diplomatic family with connections in the Middle East, de Lesseps entered the foreign service in the 1820s and received a number of postings, including a seven-year tour in Egypt. While there he became acquainted with a group of development-minded engineers from France committed to material progress, Saint-Simonians, who tried to build a canal linking the Red Sea and the Mediterranean.

After his removal from the foreign service following the 1848 revolution, de Lesseps temporarily retired from public life. However, two of the connections he had made were to lead to eventual triumph: his cousin married the Emperor Napoleon III, providing access to the

court, and a prince he had known became Viceroy of Egypt. De Lesseps soon parlayed these advantages into a project to build a canal at Suez modeled on the Saint Simonians' plans. For fifteen years he mesmerized Europe with his tremendous vigor and promotional talents, and he received world acclaim upon opening the canal in 1869.

Within a few years de Lesseps determined to repeat his triumph in Central America, and he devoted his energies to organizing a new company for the project. He sponsored a series of meetings to make geographical and engineering plans, but he steered that planning toward a decision he had already made: to build a sea-level canal in Panama. In 1879, ready to raise capital, he formed the Compagnie Universelle du Canal Interoceanique de Panama and acquired a concession from the Colombian government. The following year he managed to raise a vast sum of money through public subscription, a tribute to his reputation as *le Grand Français*. Work began in February 1881.

For eight years the French company labored heroically in Panama but accomplished only a fraction of the necessary excavation. It went bankrupt in 1889, a victim of many ills. First, de Lesseps's insistence on a sea-level canal was mistaken, given the technology and resources available. Second, from the beginning he had spread around graft and spent with such extravagance that his capital soon ran out. Third, yellow fever, malaria, smallpox, tuberculosis, and other DISEASES devastated the French and West Indian work forces. By now old and infirm, de Lesseps was shielded from the tremendous scandal that accompanied the crash of the Compagnie Universelle.

The French debacle eventually led to the U.S. canal project of the 1900s. The year de Lesseps died, stockholders and receivers created a new company to manage the assets and preserve the Colombian concession. The French excavations, maps, buildings, and equipment helped convince the U.S. government to build there rather than in Nicaragua.

GERSTLE MACK, *The Land Divided* (1944); MARON J. SIMON, *The Panama Affair* (1971); DAVID MC CULLOUGH, *The Path Between the Seas* (1977); JAMES M. SKINNER, *France and Panama* (1989).

MICHAEL L. CONNIFF

LETELIER DEL SOLAR, ORLANDO (*b.* 13 April 1932; *d.* 21 September 1976), Chilean ambassador to the United States and cabinet minister under President Salvador ALLENDE. Born in Temuco to an upper-class family, Letelier graduated from the University of Chile with degrees in law and economics. After several years in the government's Department of Copper, he worked for Felipe Herrera at the INTER-AMERICAN DEVELOPMENT BANK in Washington, D.C., from 1960 to 1971. A long-time Allende supporter, he was appointed Allende's ambassador to the United States, a post in which he faced a hostile Nixon administration committed to subverting the Chilean government. During Allende's hectic final four months in office, Letelier served in his cabinet as minister of foreign relations, interior, and defense, successively. He was arrested in the 11 September 1973 coup and, with other ranking officials and supporters of the fallen government, he was sent to the prison camp on DAWSON ISLAND in the frigid Strait of Magellan. Exiled a year after the coup, Letelier went to Venezuela before accepting a position as associate fellow at the Institute for Policy Studies in Washington, D.C., where he was prominent among Chileans attempting to rally opposition to the Augusto PINOCHET regime. Agents of the Dirección Nacional de Inteligencia (DINA) blew up his automobile on 21 September 1976, killing him and his assistant Ronni Moffitt. U.S. courts tried and sentenced five DINA agents: Michael Townley (a U.S. citizen) and four Cuban exiles. Chile rejected extradition requests for three of its citizens indicted for the crime, straining relations with the Carter and Reagan administrations. In November 1993, a Chilean court sentenced former DINA head Manuel Contreras Sepúlveda and his assistant, Pedro Espinoza Bravo, to seven to ten years of prison; an appeal was pending in 1994.

JOHN DINGES and SAUL LANDAU, *Assassination on Embassy Row* (1980); DONALD FREED with FRED SIMON LANDIS, *Death in Washington: The Murder of Orlando Letelier* (1980).

THOMAS C. WRIGHT

LETELIER MADARIAGA, VALENTÍN (b. 16 December 1852; d. 20 June 1919). Chilean thinker and political figure, often considered the chief Chilean disciple of POSITIVISM. Born in Linares City, he qualified as a lawyer in 1875 and later held a number of official jobs, including the secretaryship of Chile's legation in Germany (1880–1885). He was a deputy in the Congress of 1888–1891 and, as a leader of the Radical Party, was one of the signers of the act deposing President José Manuel BALMACEDA in January 1891 (for which he was later imprisoned and exiled by Balmaceda). In 1906 Letelier became rector of the University of Chile, where he instituted important reforms. At the third Radical Party convention in 1906, Letelier successfully advocated ''socialist'' (i.e., social reform) principles that were the direct opposite of the ''individualism'' espoused by his chief adversary, the brilliant speaker Enrique MAC IVER RODRÍGUEZ. Letelier's pen was rarely idle; his numerous works, which incline to the ponderous, cover history, law, sociology, and philosophy.

LUIS GALDÁMES, *Valentín Letelier y su obra* (1937); SOLOMON LIPP, *Three Chilean Thinkers* (1975).

SIMON COLLIER

LETELIER VALDÉS, MIGUEL FRANCISCO (b. 29 September 1939), Chilean organist and composer. Born in Santiago, Letelier Valdés is the son of composer Alfonso Letelier Llona. He received his early musical education at the National Conservatory of the University of Chile. Later studies included work in France with Max Deutsch, André Jolivet, and Jean-Jacques Grünenwald. In Argentina, where he eventually took up residence, he studied with Alberto GINASTERA. Letelier Valdés, who has given recitals throughout South America and Germany, has composed for orchestra, piano, chamber groups, and voice. The originality of his work makes it difficult to identify him with a particular style or tendency, but his later music shows an affinity with the work of György Ligeti and Luciano Berio.

JOHN VINTON, ed., *Dictionary of Contemporary Music* (1971); SAMUEL CLARO VALDÉS and JORGE URRUTIA, *Historia de la música en Chile* (1973).

SERGIO BARROSO

LETICIA DISPUTE, a conflict in the 1930s between Colombia and Peru over control of the town of Leticia and surrounding territory (about 4,000 square miles) near the Amazon River. The Leticia quadrilateral or corridor was awarded to Colombia in the SALOMÓN–LOZANO TREATY (1922), which ceded to Peru Colombian territory south of the Putumayo River. Acquisition of Leticia, founded by Peruvians in 1867, was deemed desirable by Colombia because of its location on the northern bank of the Amazon. The treaty was meant to settle a longstanding boundary dispute but was unpopular in Peru.

On 1 September 1932 an armed force of about 200 Peruvian civilians and soldiers seized Leticia and expelled the Colombian residents. On 21 October 1932, Peruvians captured Tarapacá, another town on the Putumayo. President Luis SÁNCHEZ CERRO of Peru probably did not authorize the action at Leticia but was pressured by public opinion to use the incident to secure revision of the 1922 treaty. Colombia's president, Enrique OLAYA HERRERA, was also determined to regain Leticia and dispatched an expedition of 1,000 men and five ships, which was able to reach the disputed area only by sailing to Pará, Brazil, and thence up the Amazon. Early in 1933 the Colombians recaptured Tarapacá and took the Peruvian fort at Güepí, also on the Putumayo. Further hostilities were averted by the assassination of Sánchez Cerro in April and the accession of Oscar BENAVIDES, who was more amenable to the return of Leticia to Colombia. This finally was accomplished by mid-1934 through the efforts of the League of Nations and the mediation of Afrânio de MELO FRANCO, foreign minister of Brazil.

BRYCE WOOD, *The United States and Latin American Wars, 1932–1942* (1966), esp. pp. 167–251; JORGE BASADRE, *Historia de la República del Perú*, 6th ed., vol. 14, (1968), esp. pp. 347–402; EDWARD P. LEAHY, ''Man and Environment in the Leticia Corridor,'' in *Southeastern Latin Americanist* 25 (March 1982):1–12.

HELEN DELPAR

LETRADOS, university graduates (literally "men of letters") and synonymous with lawyers and judges. *Letrados* comprised a special group, equal to knights and noblemen (*fidalgos*), who occupied most of the judicial and many of the administrative positions of government. Members of this group usually were educated at the University of Coimbra in Portugal and were schooled in canon law or civil law before entering royal service. *Letrados* were closely associated with the crown and often were appointed to one of the king's councils, to knighthoods and to military orders. As members of the bureaucracy, *letrados* established and ran the administration of the Portuguese Empire, including colonial Brazil.

STUART B. SCHWARTZ, *Sovereignty and Society of Colonial Brazil* (1973).

ROSS WILKINSON

LEVINGSTON, ROBERTO MARCELO (*b.* 10 January 1920), president of Argentina (18 June 1970–March 1971). With the fall of Juan Carlos ONGANÍA, Alejandro LANUSSE stayed in the background while the military junta recalled Levingston from the post of military attaché in Washington, D. C., to assume the presidency. The first item on his agenda after taking office was to salvage Onganía's stabilization plan. When that attempt failed, Levingston brought in Aldo Ferrer as economic minister. By October 1970 he and Ferrer had expanded credit, initiated a 6 percent pay hike, and promoted exports through a "buy Argentine" campaign.

Levingston's reform program notwithstanding, unrest burgeoned among labor, guerrillas, and political parties, with the latter forming a broad coalition, including Peronists, called the "Hour of the People." When Córdoba's governor, José Luis Camilo, dubbed some political agitators "vipers," he sparked the *viborazo*, a guerrilla insurrection. Alarmed, the military deposed Levingston and installed Lanusse as president, marking the end of the "Argentine Revolution."

ANDREW GRAHAM-YOOLL, *De Perón a Videla* (1989).

ROGER GRAVIL

LEVINSON, LUISA MERCEDES (*b.* 5 January 1914; *d.* 4 March 1988), Argentine writer. Born in Buenos Aires, Levinson was part of the *La Nación* dynasty, the oligarchic Buenos Aires daily whose literary supplement continues to be a powerful voice in Argentine letters. Perhaps best known as the mother of writer Luisa VALENZUELA, Levinson exemplifies one literary alternative in Argentina during the turbulent 1950s and 1960s: the projection of an internationalist commitment to contemporary themes such as the individual against the "massification" and cultural commodification of society, the problematics for a woman of sustaining an intrinsic dignity and integrity in the wasteland of modern life, and the psychological depth of solitary lives. *La pálida rosa de Soho* (1959) deals in a highly poetic fashion with the experiences of a London prostitute, while the stories of *La hermana de Eloísa* (1955) were written in collaboration with Jorge Luis BORGES, with whom she was long associated. *El último zelofonte* (1984) is especially notable for its psychopathic eroticism and the possibilities it presents as a political allegory of contemporary Argentina.

PERLA GIORNO, *Soledad y búsqueda: Dos novelas latinoamericanas* (1976); CELIA CORREAS DE ZAPATA, "Elementos fantásticos y mágicos-realistas en la obra de Luisa Mercedes Levinson," in her *Ensayos hispanoamericanos* (1978), pp. 245–277; SOLOMÓN LIPP, "Los mundos de Luisa Mercedes Levinson," in *Revista Iberoamericana* 45, nos. 108–109 (1979): 583–593; BERNARDO A. CHIESI, *La manifestación del animus en "A la sombra del búho"* (1981); DELFÍN LEOCADIO GARASA, "Prólogo," in Luisa Mercedes Levinson, *Obra completa*, vol. 1 (1986), pp. 7–14.

DAVID WILLIAM FOSTER

LEVY, ALEXANDRE (*b.* 10 November 1864; *d.* 17 January 1892), Brazilian composer, pianist, conductor, and critic. A composer of French and Swiss descent, he enjoyed the musical advantages of being a member of one of São Paulo's most renowned musical families. His father was a clarinetist and owner of Casa Levy, a music store as well as a recital hall in which concerts of local and visiting artists took place. Alexandre Levy performed in public for the first time at the age of eight in a concert in which he and his brother played the piano, and his father the clarinet. Since his father owned a publishing business, several of the compositions he wrote as a teenager were published.

The last two decades of the nineteenth century in Brazil were marked by rising republican sentiment which culminated in the end of the empire and the establishment of the republic in 1889. The importance of Levy's work as a composer consisted of the fact that a respected Brazilian musician with excellent European training began to employ systematically the use of Brazilian folk and popular music in his compositions at a time when Brazilian musicians were attempting to break the bonds of European artistic domination. Levy also introduced Brazilian audiences to a significant number of European works unknown to them in his programming of works for the Haydn Club, of which he was program director and frequent conductor. Two of Levy's best-known works are *Variations on a Brazilian Theme* (Vem cá, Bitú [1887]), and *Suite brésilienne* (1890). On 17 January at a dinner on the country estate of his family, he complained of feeling unwell and died before the family was able to summon a physician. He was only thirty-one years old.

DAVID P. APPLEBY, *The Music of Brazil* (1983); GÉRARD BÉHAGUE, *Popular Musical Currents in the Art of Music of the Early Nationalistic Period in Brazil* (Ph.D. diss., Tulane Univ., 1966).

DAVID P. APPLEBY

LEWIS, ROBERTO (*b.* 1874; *d.* 1949), Panamanian painter. In the 1890s, Lewis studied under Albert Dubois and Leon Bonnat in Paris, where he was later named Panamanian consul (1904–1912). Upon returning to Panama, he became director of the Academia Nacional de Pintura from its founding until the late 1930s.

Lewis is well known for the official neoclassical paintings with which he decorated the interiors of public buildings such as the Teatro Nacional, the Palacio de Gobierno, and the Presidencia. He also painted many portraits, including all of the national presidents from 1904 to 1948. Unlike the academic portraits, Lewis's landscapes, including the famous *Tamarindos de Taboga* (1936), are characterized by the luminous colors and lively brushwork which reflect the influence of post-impressionism on his style.

RODRIGO MIRÓ, "Lewis, Amador, Ivaldi," in *Revista Lotería*, no. 219 (May 1974): 72–80; P. PRADOS, *Exposición Maestros-Maestros* (1987).

MONICA E. KUPFER

LEY DE LEMAS. *See* **Uruguay: Electoral System.**

LEY IGLESIAS, a Mexican law regulating the cost of church sacraments, named for José María IGLESIAS, its principal author. The law was promulgated 11 April 1857, while its author was minister of justice under President Ignacio COMONFORT. The law stipulated that the poor were not to be charged for baptisms, marriage banns, weddings, or burials. All who earned no more by their honest toil than would provide for their daily subsistence were to be considered poor. All others could be charged reasonable fees. The Comonfort administration had earlier taken from the church the responsibility for registering births, marriages, adoptions, and deaths. Registration of these events and the administration of cemeteries were turned over to civil officials, but these changes were not technically part of the Ley Iglesias. These Reform Laws were later adopted as part of the Constitution of 1857.

WALTER V. SCHOLES, *Mexican Politics During the Juárez Regime, 1855–1872* (1957); THOMAS GENE POWELL, *El liberalismo y el campesinado en el centro de México, 1850–1877* (1974); THOMAS GENE POWELL, "Priests and Peasants in Central Mexico: Social Conflict During 'La Reforma,'" in *Hispanic American Historical Review* 57, no. 2 (1977):296–313.

D. F. STEVENS

See also **Anticlericalism.**

LEY JUÁREZ, a Mexican law abolishing military and ecclesiastical FUEROS (privileges) named for Benito JUÁ-REZ, its principal author. The law, dated 11 November 1855, was promulgated by President Juan ÁLVAREZ, while Juárez was his minister of justice. The law contained seventy-seven main articles that had the effect of abolishing all special tribunals except the military and ecclesiastical courts. Although the Ley Juárez did not abolish these courts, it did end the military and ecclesiastical *fueros* in civil cases. Priests and military officers could no longer change the venue of trials for civil offenses to the ecclesiastical or military courts. Sinkin argues that the law accepted the basic corporate structure of society and did not abolish the entire *fuero* system since the church courts retained the right to hear criminal cases. As the first of the Reform Laws, the Ley Juárez was approved as part of the Constitution of 1857.

RICHARD N. SINKIN, *The Mexican Reform, 1855–1876: A Study in Liberal Nation-Building* (1979), pp. 98–99, 123–124.

D. F. STEVENS

See also **Anticlericalism.**

LEY LERDO, a Mexican law disamortizing church property, named for Miguel LERDO DE TEJADA, its principal author. The law was promulgated 25 June 1856, while Lerdo served as finance minister for President Ignacio COMONFORT. It declared that civil and ecclesiastical corporations, such as the Catholic church and local and state governments, would be prohibited from owning real property not directly used in everyday operations. The church could retain its sanctuaries, monasteries, convents, and seminaries, and local and state governments their offices, jails, and schools, but both had to sell all other urban and rural real estate. Tenants were given preference during the first three months the law would be in effect, and the annual rent was considered as 6 percent of the value of the property for sale. The government would collect a 5 percent tax on these sales. The law prohibited civil and ecclesiastical corporations from acquiring property in the future, but it did not confiscate their wealth. Intended to raise revenue and promote the development of markets, its actual effects on property ownership are disputed, but it seems to have raised litle revenue for the government. The Ley Lerdo was adopted as part of the Constitution of 1857. It was later superseded by decrees confiscating church property.

JAN BAZANT, *Alienation of Church Wealth in Mexico: Social and Economic Aspects of the Liberal Revolution, 1856–1875* (1971); THOMAS GENE POWELL, *El liberalismo y el campesinado en el centro de México, 1850–1876* (1974); ROBERT J. KNOWLTON, *Church Property and the Mexican Reform, 1856–1910* (1976); CHARLES R. BERRY, *The Reform in Oaxaca, 1856–76: A Microhistory of the Liberal Revolution* (1981).

D. F. STEVENS

See also **Anticlericalism.**

LEY, SALVADOR (*b.* 2 January 1907; *d.* 21 March 1985), Guatemalan composer and pianist. Ley was born of German parents who had settled in Guatemala City. At the age of fifteen Ley won a scholarship to study music in Berlin. He remained in Germany from 1922 until 1934, when he returned to Guatemala to teach and serve as the director of the National Conservatory of Music. In 1937, Ley moved to New York City, where he made his North American debut in January 1938. His subsequent tour of the United States included a performance at the White House. Ley returned to Guatemala and resumed the directorship of the National Conservatory from 1944 to 1953. In the latter year he returned to the United States and taught at the Westchester Conservatory of Music in White Plains, New York. Ley has composed orchestral works, including *Copla triste* and *Danza exótica*, the opera *Lera*, and works for piano and voice.

OTTO MAYER-SERRA, *Música y músicos en Latinoamérica*, vol. 2 (1947), pp. 556–557; J. VICTOR SOTO DE ÁVILA, *Quién es quién en Centroamérica y Panamá* (1954), p. 111; Enrique Anleu Díaz, *Esbozo histórico-social de la música en Guatemala* (1978), p. 97.

STEVEN S. GILLICK

LEYVA SOLANO, GABRIEL (*b.* 1871; *d.* 13 June 1910), precursor of the Revolution in Sinaloa. From northern Sinaloa, educated at the state *colegio* (preparatory school) in Culiacán, Leyva became a schoolteacher on a large rural estate. There, and in neighboring villages, he observed the misery and the atrocities of local political authorities which the country folk suffered. This, combined with reading of Porfirian abuses in the nation, led him to cultivate opposition sentiment among peasants. In time, as a lawyer's assistant, Leyva began representing the dispossessed in legal proceedings. An avid follower of Francisco MADERO, after the latter's tour of the state in 1909, Leyva espoused the Maderista cause among peasants and workers in northern Sinaloa. Harassed by authorities, he gathered a revolutionary band around him in May 1910. But within a month he was betrayed, captured, and executed without trial, an early martyr of the Revolution.

ERNESTO HIGUERA, *Gabriel Leyva Solano: Ensayo biográfico* (1954); AMADO GONZÁLEZ DÁVILA, *Diccionario geográfico, histórico y estadístico del Estado de Sinaloa* (1959); HECTOR R. OLEA, *Breve historia de la Revolución en Sinaloa* (1964).

STUART F. VOSS

LEZAMA LIMA, JOSÉ (*b.* 19 December 1910; *d.* 9 August 1976), Cuban poet and novelist. Possibly the greatest Cuban novelist and one of the greatest Cuban poets of all time, Lezama Lima was born in Havana. He graduated from the law school of the University of Havana in 1929 and worked as a lawyer until 1941, when he received a post at the cultural office of the Ministry of Education. Aside from his own arduous literary creations, he promoted literature in Cuba by founding and directing four literary publications that were pivotal to the development of Cuban literature: *Verbum*, while he was a law student; *Espuela de Plata*, with Guy Pérez Cisneros and Mariano Rodríguez (1939–1941); *Nadie Parecía*, with Ángel Gaztelu (1942–1944); and *Orígenes*, with José Rodríguez Feo (1944–1956). This last publication became the center of Cuban literary and artistic life. It published only previously unpublished material and provided a forum for the work of Cuban writers of merit, both known and unknown, including Alejo CARPENTIER, Virgilio PIÑERA, Lydia CABRERA, Eliseo DIEGO, and Eugenio FLORIT. It also published the graphic work of great Cuban artists, among them Wilfredo LAM and Amelia PELÁEZ, as well as a section of reviews. Aside from attracting the best talent in Cuba, *Orígenes* also published the work of varied figures of international renown, such as Albert Camus, Gabriela MISTRAL, Juan Ramón Jiménez, Octavio PAZ, Paul Valéry, giving Cuban cultural activity an unprecedented entry into the international scene.

Lezama Lima's official standing after the Cuban Revolution of 1959 was initially good. He was almost enthusiastic about the new regime, and he occupied several key posts in the Cuban cultural establishment: he was one of the vice presidents of the National Union of Cuban Writers and Artists (UNEAC), director of the Department of Literature and Publications of the National Council of Culture, and researcher and consultant at the Institute of Literature and Linguistics at the National Academy of Sciences. Although he never publicly dissented from the government, in his later years he was harassed and marginalized because he failed to be actively supportive of official aims and policy.

Lezama Lima's best-known work, the novel *Paradiso*, was published in Cuba in 1966 to immediate acclaim there and abroad. Yet its distribution in Cuba was extremely limited, and shortly after its publication it mysteriously disappeared from bookstores and became very difficult to obtain. He became an internationally known and revered author, receiving many invitations to cultural events abroad, but the Cuban government repeatedly denied him permission to travel. He lived in Cuba until his death.

Lezama Lima is one of the most complex, baroque authors in the history of the Spanish language. An unabashed proponent of "art for art's sake" in a milieu that favored art as an instrument for social change, he spurned references to reality and sought to create a hermetic and self-referent world through language. His best-known works include *Oppiano Licario* (1977), the sequel to *Paradiso*; the essay *Las eras imaginarias* (1971); and a volume of his poetic work, *Poesía completa*, published in 1975. His novels and poetry have been translated into many languages.

RAYMOND SOUZA, *The Poetic Fiction of José Lezama Lima* (1983); GUSTAVO PELLÓN, *José Lezama Lima's Joyful Vision: A Study of "Paradiso" and Other Prose Works* (1989); EMILIO BEJEL, *José Lezama Lima: Poet of the Image* (1990).

ROBERTO VALERO

LIAUTAUD, GEORGES (*b.* 1899; *d.* after 1988), Haitian artist and sculptor. Liautaud, who has been described as Haiti's most consistently original artist, did not begin his career until middle age. He received an above-average education but also expressed an early interest in mechanics. He spent several years in the Dominican Republic working as a repairman for the railroads before returning to Haiti as a blacksmith and manufacturer of hardware. In 1953 DeWitt Peters, the director of the Centre d'Art in Port-au-Prince, discovered Liautaud's metal crosses and began to commission more such works of pure art. After this Liautaud shifted to one dimensional figures, especially representations of a half-woman, half-fish spirit known as Maîtresse La Sirène. Today his unique pieces can be found in galleries in Paris, New York, and Rotterdam.

SELDEN RODMAN, *The Miracle of Haitian Art* (1974); ELEANOR INGALLS CHRISTENSEN, *The Art of Haiti* (1975); UTE STEBICH, *Haitian Art* (1978).

KAREN RACINE

LIBERAL PARTY (CENTRAL AMERICA). Central American LIBERALISM arose during the movement toward independence—achieved in 1821—in the heart of the Captaincy General of the Realm of Guatemala. Those who opposed the continuance of the system of privileges authorized by the crown and defended by the conservatives, who were considered crooked and reactionary, founded a group to advance the ideas of the French Enlightenment. They referred to the conservatives as "fevers" or "cowards." They were self-declared defenders of the ideology of the French Revolution and placed hope in the Spanish liberalism of the period.

In the beginning, both liberals and conservatives were criollos. The former desired federalism as a system of government for the United Provinces of CENTRAL AMERICA, while the latter sought centralism. The tension between these two factions would cause hate and bloodshed lasting into the twentieth century. After Central American independence, the liberals held power for several decades. In the 1830s Francisco MORAZÁN headed a government that confronted the disinterest of the provinces, which failed to provide enough funds for its very existence. The conservatives capitalized on this situation, and the United Provinces were divided into the several states currently found on the isthmus. The conservatives dominated the political scene through the first half of the nineteenth century, the only exception

being Costa Rica, where a patriarchal democracy predominated until 1948.

In Guatemala, the 1871 triumph of the so-called Liberal Revolution had a determining influence on the diffusion of liberalism in the other countries, especially in Honduras and El Salvador. Two decades earlier, the President of El Salvador, Gerardo BARRIOS, promoted both liberal principles and coffee production. In so doing, he followed the lead of Costa Rica's COFFEE INDUSTRY under that country's liberal President Braulio Carrillo. In Guatemala, Justo Rufino Barrios increased coffee production and put an end to the conflicts between liberals and conservatives by imposing liberal absolutism. This was more forceful in Guatemala, El Salvador, and Honduras than in Nicaragua. A good number of new, land-owning mestizos were incorporated into the ranks of the liberals.

Liberal ideology spread by intellectuals such as Guatemala's Lorenzo MONTÚFAR adopted the principles of French POSITIVISM and became rooted in the liberal, anticlerical, Latin American world of the time. Those who called themselves liberals defended freedom of expression, secular education, abolition of the death penalty, and limited terms of office for those in power. But they were far from actually realizing these ideals. In essence—excepting Costa Rica once again—the expanding coffee industry revitalized the feudal system. Democratic principles such as freedom of work and movement were impossible with the state finding it necessary to use its power to forcibly recruit laborers. Also, in an attempt to avoid the disorder caused by conflicts with the conservatives, freedom of thought and expression were also restricted. And although the liberals considered themselves anticlerical due to the relationship that existed between the church and the conservatives, liberal governments permitted the functioning of the church, and their members attended Mass, even, as in Guatemala, at churches whose possessions had been confiscated. All the Central American countries except Costa Rica distanced themselves from predominant liberal ideologies in the decades surrounding 1900.

The contradiction between what was preached and what was practiced was evident. The Liberal Party produced such memorable dictators as Justo Rufino BARRIOS, Manuel Estrada Cabrera, and Jorge UBICO in Guatemala, Terencio Sierra in Honduras, and José Santos ZELAYA and Anastasio SOMOZA in Nicaragua. In their time, just as the conservatives did, the liberals resorted to foreign intervention for partisan rather than national reasons, inhibiting the march of progress. A mark in favor of liberal governments is that they established infrastructural bases that would aid free trade and production in archaic societies: the railroad, the telegraph, and electricity. This brought about the rise of a small, urban middle class. Nevertheless, social development was scarce. The economic growth that did occur was at the expense of peasants, who only grew poorer.

411

At the beginning of the twentieth century, the Central American isthmus became a colony for ever-increasing foreign interests: bananas for North America, coffee for Germany, and sugar for Great Britain. These interests surpassed the power of the State and brought about liberal dictatorships. Rather than being driving forces behind democracy, these foreign interests maintained the liberal status quo. The conservatives of course took every advantage to criticize the liberals, whose governments began to fall. In turn-of-the-century El Salvador, differences with conservatives dissolved when the oligarchy agreed to a power-sharing arrangement. Guatemala saw the fall of the dictator Jorge Ubico in 1944 and Nicaragua that of the Somoza dynasty in 1979. The survival of liberalism in Honduras is due to its articulating relatively democratic principles, as was the case in Costa Rica with its Revolution of 1948. Despite the fact that liberalism was no longer an important ideological tendency in the mid-1990s, the Liberal International had various Central American political parties as members.

MARIO RODRÍGUEZ, *The Cádiz Experiment in Central America, 1808 to 1826* (1978); R. L. WOODWARD, JR., "The Rise and Decline of Liberalism in Central America: Historical Perspectives on the Contemporary Crises," in *Journal of Inter-American Studies and World Affairs*, 26 (1984): 291–312, and *Central America: A Nation Divided* (1985).

FERNANDO GONZÁLEZ DAVISON

LIBERALISM was at first a European and later a worldwide intellectual and political movement whose aim was to promote greater freedom and liberty for the individual. It had its roots in the struggle for power between church and state during the Middle Ages. Liberals tended to see both institutions as inimical to the interests of the individual and therefore wanted to limit their power. The political agenda of nineteenth-century liberalism was to liquidate the remaining power of the medieval church, already broken in northern Europe as a result of the Protestant Reformation, and to promote individual economic and political power, under the doctrine of laissez-faire, against the political power of the state. Liberals hoped that the economic growth from such reforms would expand the size of the middle class, increase the number of citizens admitted to political power, and thereby bolster the ranks of liberalism.

Latin American liberalism was part of this wider movement. Since the Iberian world had been untouched by the Protestant Reformation, its liberals faced a far more powerful church antagonist than the liberals of northern Europe, a reality that explains the primacy of ANTICLERICALISM in the liberal movement in Spain, Portugal, and Latin America. Moreover, Europe's experience with economic development, civil war, and revolution was such that the state's power to impose corporate and economic restraints on the individual was much weaker there by the nineteenth century than in the Iberian/Latin American world.

The battle against the power of the church was pan-European and began in the Enlightenment, whose secular and optimistic vision of the future greatly molded liberal thinking. In Iberia, the opening round was the expulsion of the JESUITS from the Portuguese and Spanish empires in 1759 and 1767, respectively. Their properties were confiscated, for a brief time administered by the state, and eventually auctioned off. The second round took place during the Napoleonic Wars, when the state's economic problems produced similar results. In 1798 the Spanish Bourbons ordered the forced sale of all church property in Spain that sustained chantries and pious foundations. In 1804 the measure was extended to Spanish America. Already in the air, therefore, were some of the components that would mark future liberal thinking.

The seeds of other liberal issues of the Iberian world—greater economic and political freedom—also go back to the eighteenth century. While the goal of many was greater absolutism, the particulars of the agenda could just as easily be pushed forward in the name of individual freedom. Free trade, for example, advanced on various fronts by fits and starts, so that by the end of the century mercantilism was in decline. On the political front, the introduction of the INTENDANCY SYSTEM and local militias gave the central government a real presence at the provincial level, but it also created the regional organizational structures that enabled regions to resist central authority and set the stage for the federalist–centralist struggles of the nineteenth century.

Much of liberal ideology was crystallized in the Spanish CONSTITUTION OF 1812. The constitutional crisis brought on by the 1808 French invasion of Spain prompted an immediate "modernization" of the political system. The constitution severely limited monarchical government, ended the Inquisition, restricted the military and ecclesiastical FUEROS, created provincial deputations and militias as a counterweight to centralized authority, and provided for universal manhood suffrage. The constitution also went into effect in Mexico and Central America, where elections were soon held. The constitution was annulled in 1814 by FERDINAND VII, but was forced on him again in 1820. Mexican and Central American leaders broke definitively with Spain in 1820 in order to avoid a return of its version of liberalism. The 1812 Constitution socialized a generation of Mexican and Central American liberals and accounts for some of the virulence of the federalist–centralist struggles there.

Liberals identified with federalism and the separation of powers because they provided a check on the absolute power of the centralized state and tended to enhance the autonomy and freedom of the individual. The problem of what the proper balance between central and provincial authority should be occupied liberals from early on. They were not always consistent in their answer. They frequently acted illiberally and imposed their own views on others. Liberals were often selective in what principles they chose to support; their decisions usually depended on the political, economic, and social context of their own region and what was in their personal interest and/or what was politically possible. Pragmatic considerations such as survival, self-defense, access to power, and domination often won out over ideological consistency in the liberal agenda, especially in the area of the federalist–centralist debate. This debate was especially intense in Mexico, Central America, Colombia, Brazil, and Argentina.

Regarding the economic order, liberals wanted to liquidate much of the colonial legacy of state control, state taxation, and church, corporate, and state interference in economic matters. In general, liberals supported the movement toward free trade and a lowering of the tariff. They believed that these changes would produce more trade and commerce, which in turn would prompt the economic growth that would transform the whole economy. An end to state subsidies and monopoly rents like tobacco and *aguardiente* were logical parts of the liberal program. But where falling government revenues endangered the ability of the central government to pay its soldiers and bureaucrats, or where the reaction from sugar, tobacco, and cotton growers or artisan producers was too great, liberals usually moderated their principles.

A basic premise of liberalism was the right of the individual to be treated equally before the law. Thus it was logical that Indian tribute and communal lands, special categories like ecclesiastical and military *fueros*, entailed estates, and slavery and other forced labor institutions would come under attack. Freedom of the press and many civil liberties taken for granted elsewhere were not always espoused by, let alone supported by, Latin American liberals. Liberals in multiracial and unequal societies frequently compromised and even betrayed their principles. Such was the case in Mexico, Guatemala, Ecuador, Peru, and Bolivia, where liberals excluded Indians from their push to increase individual liberties, and in Brazil, Venezuela, and Cuba, where liberals closed their eyes to the plight of the enslaved.

Since the church had been such a close partner of the state in the colonial period, it had held onto functions and powers that the churches of post–Reformation Europe and North America had long since relinquished. The church's role as the recorder of vital statistics, such as births, marriages, and deaths, was a frequent battleground between the Latin American church and its liberal opponents. Religious toleration and church control of education were other areas of conflict. State control of church appointments and tithes, the colonial *patronato*, was claimed by the liberals, and used to mold and "modernize" the church hierarchy. What to do with the religious orders was a thorny problem. For many liberals, they were a vestige of the Middle Ages. Their suppression had several advantages from the liberal point of view. A sell-off of their wealth would raise money for the state, put property back into circulation that had been in "dead" hands, and eliminate some of the financial support for, and hence the attractiveness of joining, the clerical estate. The church–state conflict was especially bitter in Mexico, Guatemala, and Colombia.

The liberal advance in Latin America was anything but uniform. Country-by-country differences are a testimony to Latin America's fabled diversity. The bewildering possibilities for just one country are captured in Gabriel GARCÍA MÁRQUEZ's portrayal of the liberal struggle in Colombia in his novel *One Hundred Years of Solitude*. But each region is a case study that frequently disproves the general rule. In Central America, liberals from the outlying provinces had won a seemingly definitive victory in their struggle with conservative centralists in Guatemala City in the late 1820s, and thought they would have the power to force Guatemala to share its income and resources with the rest of Central America. Beginning in 1830, the liberal federation president, Francisco MORAZÁN of Honduras, pursued a centralist policy and carried out the most radical liberal program in Latin America up to that time, with the abolition of tribute, the ecclesiastical *fuero*, regular orders, and compulsory tithes. These measures, as well as a head-tax, making divorce legal, and allowing civil marriage, led to an inevitable reaction.

In Guatemala it coalesced around the proclerical CAUDILLO Rafael CARRERA, who led the conservatives to victory over Morazán in 1840. Guatemalan conservatives, fearing a resurgence of liberal power throughout the isthmus, flip-flopped and adopted a federalist stance. Liberal aid in Nicaragua to the interventionist effort of the American filibuster William WALKER confirmed conservative fears and discredited liberals throughout Central America. Walker's intervention plus Carrera's reign until 1865 delayed a return to liberal rule in Central America. When Liberals did recover power in Guatemala under Justo Rufino BARRIOS in 1871, their disestablishment of the church was even more total than that in Mexico later. With the social control provided by the church gone, liberals ruled Guatemala's Indians in a repressive and exploitative fashion.

' In Mexico the colonial church, establishment, and legacy, especially in Mexico City, were much stronger. Liberals were not immediately victorious as in Central America, and had to proceed in a more piecemeal fashion. They had to ensure that the institutional framework protected their liberal base in the provinces, especially against special interest groups in Mexico City like the Army. The liberal agenda in the 1820s and 1830s was pushed forward on the federal structure outlined in the 1824 constitution by regional politicians like Valentín GÓMEZ FARÍAS of Zacatecas, José María Luis MORA of Guanajuato, and Lorenzo de ZAVALA of Yucatán. The individual states had considerable powers, including their own state legislatures, state militias, and state-elected governors.

Liberals finally achieved national power when Antonio López de SANTA ANNA overthrew the centralist government of Anastasio BUSTAMANTE in 1832 and installed Gómez Farías as acting president in 1833. Liberal laws closed down the clerically run national university, secularized Franciscan missions, disentailed church property, and ended compulsory tithes. But other liberal measures, such as ending tariff protection, abolishing the tobacco monopoly, decreasing the size of the army, and ending the military *fuero*, threatened too many vested interests. Santa Anna sided with the centralists in 1834 and defeated a coalition of state militias headed by Zacatecas. But Texas escaped and became an independent republic in 1836 with Zavala as its vice president. The debacle continued and soured many liberals on federalism.

A divided house was obviously a conquered one, and the loss of much of northern Mexico in the MEXICAN–AMERICAN WAR (1846–1848) confirmed the suspicion that federalism put liberals at a competitive disadvantage both nationally and internationally. When liberals drew up the Constitution of 1857, they made sure it was much more centralist than the Constitution of 1824. It also enshrined the LEY JUÁREZ and LEY LERDO that abolished the ecclesiastical and military *fueros* and provided for the sale of corporately owned church and Indian real estate. The church's belligerent reaction and support for the conservatives in the War of the Reform (1858–1861) and French intervention (1862–1867) made the liberals determined to establish the church completely. While the disestablishment was reconfirmed in the Constitution of 1917, the church continued to endure in Mexico.

In Argentina liberals faced a weaker colonial establishment, traded directly with Europe, and resided in the capital of Buenos Aires rather than in the provinces (as in Mexico). Under the leadership of Bernardino RIVADAVIA and other PORTEÑO leaders, they imposed a UNITARIO or centralist order, first on the province of Buenos Aires in 1820 and then on the rest of the country with their rigorously centralist constitution of 1826. The liberals' program of modernization was truly impressive. They took the *fuero* from the army and church, reduced the size of the former, and took over assets and property, and many of the educational and welfare functions, of the latter. In their economic program liberals pushed infrastructure development, greater foreign trade, increased immigration, and new investment. But religious freedom, tax modernization, and the war with Brazil over Uruguay were too radical for the interior provinces, and the liberal experiment ended in 1827 in civil war, Rivadavia's departure, and Juan Manuel de ROSAS's rise to power. With the defeat of Rosas in 1852, the Unitario liberals regained power in Buenos Aires, and within ten years they had forced themselves on the rest of Argentina. While the Constitution of 1853 was federalist and the capital was eventually federalized, the constitutional right of the president to intervene in the provinces, and

the income and growth of Buenos Aires, ensured a centralization in favor of *porteño* liberals that would have gladdened the hearts of the Unitarios.

In Brazil the chief force for liberalism was the monarch Dom PEDRO I, more liberal than his subjects. Favoring a constitutional monarchy, religious toleration, civil liberties, and an end to slavery, he pushed the Constitution of 1824 on his reluctant subjects. But it was not long before the parliamentary system he created evolved to the point where the majority resisted his liberalism and centralization. As a result he abdicated in 1831 in favor of his five-year-old son, Dom PEDRO II. By 1842 a system had developed by which the emperor would dissolve parliament, and the elections would be fixed to favor the opposition party; conservative or liberal made no difference. This sham continued until the monarchy was overthrown in 1889.

In Colombia, Venezuela, and Ecuador, independence colleagues Francisco de Paula SANTANDER, José Antonio PÁEZ, Juan José FLORES, and Vicente ROCAFUERTE provided strong leadership and carried out some liberal reforms without them being recognized as such, and a formal liberal–conservative division was postponed until the 1840s. When Colombia's liberal reform came in earnest in the 1850s and 1860s, it surpassed Mexico's in its laissez-faire and individual and states' rights. With the backing of the relentless Tomás Cipriano MOSQUERA, it imitated the Mexican example in suppressing religious orders and seizing all church property.

In Chile, too, federalism produced disorder and chaos in the 1820s. While the problems with ultrafederalism were not admitted by liberals until the second half of the nineteenth century, ultrafederalism was out of step with the need for a state to be strong enough to face the world, maintain order, and get infrastructure projects like transportation and port systems developed so commerce and trade could evolve effectively. This was Chile's response under the guidance of Diego PORTALES and the Constitution of 1833, and the nation's unparalleled success by the end of the nineteenth century was an important lesson for the rest of Latin America. In Colombia, where a shortage of national revenues led to a shedding of national government functions and a turn to extreme federalism from 1863 to 1885, the results were such that the liberal Rafael NÚÑEZ MOLEDO drew the same conclusions Portales had, and orchestrated a rapprochement with the conservatives and the church; together they produced the highly centralized Constitution of 1886.

Toward the end of the century, reaction had set in among other liberals as well. In Mexico under Porfirio DÍAZ, in Venezuela under Antonio GUZMÁN BLANCO, and in Central America under other liberal dictators, the "order and progress" doctrines of the POSITIVISTS brought more authoritarian and centralized rule. Although liberal in economic and religious matters, these dictators and their supporters sacrificed other liberal principles, such as an independent judiciary, a free press, and political democracy, for the economic progress order was supposed to bring. On the other hand, in Chile liberals chipped away at presidential power and moved toward parliamentarism, while Brazil moved toward decentralization. And in Argentina, liberal reform brought the middle class to power for the first time in 1916, when the radicals won as a result of the 1912 SÁENZ PEÑA election law.

As the twentieth century opened, the worldwide economic development brought by the industrial revolution had created powerful new forces like corporate businesses that threatened the individual. As a consequence, the political agenda of liberalism changed and increasingly had a social program that looked once again, as it had in its struggle against the church, to the state to protect the individual from the awesome economic power of private capitalism. This change in liberalism was evident in the rule of José BATLLE Y ORDÓÑEZ in Uruguay, Hipólito YRIGOYEN in Argentina, Arturo ALESSANDRI PALMA in Chile, and Alfonso López PUMAREJO in Colombia.

In many places the demands of the middle classes and the masses were not met by liberalism, and the old order was swept away, as was the case in the MEXICAN REVOLUTION of 1910. At the same time, economic difficulties and the worldwide Great Depression of the 1930s saw the rise of mass-based authoritarian political movements. FASCISM and COMMUNISM spread throughout Latin America while the APRA (Alianza Popular Revolucionaria Americana) appeared in Peru, the PRI (Partido Revolucionario Institucional) in Mexico, and the Peronist Party in Argentina. Many saw these groups as national and international threats; where liberals held power, they invoked the countervailing power of the state for protection. For some this worldwide struggle culminated in World War II. With the victory of the Allies, the global threat of fascism was virtually eliminated, but the postwar settlement left the world divided between East and West. As the twentieth century came to a close, the perceived threat from international communism was much reduced by the collapse and breakup of the Soviet Union, and many mass-based formerly authoritarian political movements like APRA, PRI, and Peronism tried to gain respectability by transforming themselves into something akin to liberal parties.

Liberals were now more openly divided over the role of the state. Those who focused on economic concerns like the threat of inflation, budgetary deficits, trade problems, and the inability of the state to solve a wide array of social ills were known as "Neoliberals." They called for a reduced role for the state, a sell-off of state-run enterprises, and a return to the laissez-faire principles of nineteenth-century liberalism. Others looked at the same economic problems, the rise of the third world, nuclear proliferation, and environmental pollution as the main causes of an unstable world order and as the chief threats

to individual liberties, and they argued for a continued strong role for the state. Whatever the case, all liberalism—whether old or new, right or left—was about restraining power for the benefit of the individual.

For a clearly written and cogently argued survey of liberalism in general, see HARRY K. GIRVETZ, From Wealth to Welfare: The Evolution of Liberalism, rev. ed. (1966). On Latin America, the best survey by far is DAVID BUSHNELL and NEILL MACAULAY, The Emergence of Latin America in the Nineteenth Century, 2d ed. (1994). For church–state relations, see JOHN L. MECHAM, Church and State in Latin America: A History of Politico-Ecclesiastical Relations, rev. ed. (1966), which, though overly legalistic, is still serviceable. Individual country surveys in which the role of liberalism is particularly well explained include DAVID BUSHNELL, The Making of Modern Colombia: A Nation in Spite of Itself (1993); RALPH L. WOODWARD, JR., Central America: A Nation Divided, 2d ed. (1985), and HUGH THOMAS, Cuba: The Pursuit of Freedom (1971). For the role of the Constitution of 1812, see NETTIE LEE BENSON, The Provincial Deputation in Mexico: Harbinger of Provincial Autonomy, Independence, and Federalism (1992) and NETTIE LEE BENSON, ed., Mexico and the Spanish Cortes, 1810–1822 (1966). An excellent in-depth political history of liberalism and federalism in early independent Chile is SIMON COLLIER, Ideas and Politics of Chilean Independence, 1808–1833 (1967). The study of liberalism as intellectual history in a single country has no equal to CHARLES A. HALE, Mexican Liberalism in the Age of Mora, 1821–1853 (1968) and The Transformation of Liberalism in Late Nineteenth-Century Mexico (1989). The crucial Mexican Reform period is superbly handled by RICHARD N. SINKIN, The Mexican Reform, 1855–1876: A Study in Liberal Nation-Building (1979). The impact of the expropriation of church wealth is analyzed in JAN BAZANT, Alienation of Church Wealth in Mexico: Social and Economic Aspects of the Liberal Revolution, 1856–1875 (1971). Although liberalism in the twentieth century has not been adequately studied, the economic issues are outlined in JOSEPH L. LOVE and NILS JACOBSEN, eds., Guiding the Invisible Hand: Economic Liberalism and the State in Latin American History (1988).

MAURICE P. BRUNGARDT

See also **Constitutions** (under individual nations).

LIBERATION THEOLOGY represents a major change in the way Christianity approaches the social problems of Latin America. The changes began in the 1960s with the Second Vatican Council and the growth of CHRISTIAN BASE COMMUNITIES. The first major publication was the Spanish edition of Gustavo GUTIÉRREZ's A Theology of Liberation (1971). Gutiérrez is still a key figure.

Liberation theology has eight basic themes: (1) praxis (our action in the world) is the starting point of theology; (2) history is the locus of theology (God acts in historical time); (3) the world should be viewed as a whole, favoring the Hebraic holistic view over Greek dualism; (4) sin is social and systemic, not just individual; (5) God is on the side of the oppressed; (6) the present world order must be transformed; (7) the purpose of theology is primarily to act and to change the world, not just to understand it; (8) the kingdom of God (the reign of God) has begun in this life, and the purpose of humanity is to increase the kingdom by human actions in the world.

In the colonial period and until about 1960, the church generally promoted the fatalistic view that the poor would receive their reward in the afterlife, implying that they should not strive for social change in this life. Liberation theology uses biblical themes like the Exodus to teach the poor that God is on the side of the oppressed and favors their liberation. Thus the post-Vatican II church has a "preferential option for the poor." The focus is to work for justice and social change in solidarity with the poor.

Liberation theology is closely connected to Christian base communities (*comunidades eclesiales de base*), small communities that began about 1960 to empower the poor to work for social change. There are thousands of base communities all over Latin America. The movement is strongest in Brazil, Nicaragua, and El Salvador, and weakest in Bolivia and Colombia.

There is much controversy over liberation theology and the base communities. They are a challenge to the current power structures in both civil society and the Catholic church. Because they have empowered the poor in many countries, the Vatican fears a laity that sees power as coming from the grass roots and not just from the hierarchy. Liberation theology has redefined the church. Thus, Leonardo BOFF's *Ecclesiogenesis: The Base Communities Reinvent the Church* (1986) defines the church as the people, and deemphasizes the institutional church. Governments are threatened by the poor masses who are organizing as a result of this movement and who have rising expectations of more control over their lives. These organized groups work for social change, sometimes in a revolutionary mode, as happened in Nicaragua in the 1980s.

Liberation theology is often linked with Marxism, but most liberation theologians do not accept all of Marxism, and certainly not its atheistic materialism. Rather they use Marxism as a source for their questions, not their answers. Liberation theologians use Marxist economic analysis to ask probing questions about the economic injustice endured by the poor in Latin America.

Liberation theology defines theology as reflection on praxis (experience); that is, theology is the work of the corporate community of Christians reflecting on the happenings in their lives in light of the Scriptures. Thus the poor who are members of base communities reflect on their economic and political oppression and see that God liberated his people in the Exodus and elsewhere. Their faith in the Scriptures gives them hope, and the organization of their Christian communities gives them the means. The power of religion is no longer a magic formula reserved for priests; it is also held by the people, according to liberation theology. Power is to be used for good, so politics is a proper field for Christian action.

Liberation theology has been criticized for being too

Soup kitchen for the unemployed in Villa Francia, Santiago, Chile, 1978. HELEN HUGHES.

naive about Marxist economics and DEPENDENCY THEORY. In its early years biblical scholars criticized its weakness in exegesis (interpretation). Its greatest competition from within Christianity comes from the Pentecostal and Evangelical groups, which concentrate on individual conversion and avoid community politics and social issues. These groups do not require literacy and commitment to social action, as the base communities usually do. In some areas of Brazil, for instance, the base communities are in direct competition with Pentecostals for the population in poor barrios or *favelas* (slums).

Major Latin American liberation theologians include Gustavo Gutiérrez, a priest who lives in a poor section of Lima; Leonardo Boff, a former Franciscan seminary professor from Brazil who resigned his priesthood in 1992, after many battles with the Vatican; Juan Luis Segundo, an Uruguayan Jesuit; Jon Sobrino, a Spanish Jesuit who has lived in El Salvador for many years; Hugo Assmann, a Brazilian priest who founded the Departamento Ecuménico de Investigaciones (DEI) in Costa Rica, a Christian institute that publishes books on liberation theology; José Míguez Bonino, an Argentine Methodist pastor; Segundo Galilea, a Chilean priest who was director of the Latin American Pastoral Institute for many years and writes on Christian spirituality; and Pablo Richard, a Chilean priest who has worked at DEI in Costa Rica for many years. All but Gutiérrez and Galilea have spent most of their careers as university professors. A major publisher of liberation theology books is Orbis Books, in MARYKNOLL, New York.

In the history of ideas, liberation theology may be the first intellectual movement from Latin America that has been adopted as part of a global culture. The dominant European and U.S. cultures have sought, translated, and integrated a Latin American idea system into their own.

GUSTAVO GUTIÉRREZ, *A Theology of Liberation: History, Politics, and Salvation,* translated and edited by Sister Caridad Inda and John Eagleson (1973); JOSÉ MÍGUEZ BONINO, *Doing Theology in a Revolutionary Situation* (1975); JON SOBRINO, *The True Church and the Poor,* translated by Matthew J. O'Connell (1984); PHILLIP BERRYMAN, *Liberation Theology: The Essential Facts About the Revolutionary Movement in Latin America and Beyond* (1987); LEONARDO BOFF and CLODOVIS BOFF, *Introducing Liberation Theology,* translated by Paul Burns (1987); JUAN LUIS SEGUNDO, *The Liberation of Theology* (1988); ARTHUR F. MC GOVERN, *Liberation Theology and Its Critics* (1989); ALFRED HENNELLY, ed., *Liberation Theology: A Documentary History* (1990); WARREN EDWARD HEWITT, *Base Christian Communities and Social Change in Brazil* (1991); RONALD G. MUSTO, *Liberation Theologies: A Research Guide* (1991).

THOMAS NIEHAUS

LIDA, RAIMUNDO (*b.* 15 November 1908; *d.* 20 June 1979), Argentine literary scholar. Born in Lemberg, Austria (Lvov, Poland), Lida arrived with his family in Argentina at the age of two and was educated at the University of Buenos Aires, as a student of Amado ALONSO and Pedro HENRÍQUEZ UREÑA. His literary scholarship represented the best of the philological tradition, while displaying a strong interest in aesthetics, philosophy of language, and newer critical methodologies. Lida became secretary of the Institute of Philology at the University of Buenos Aires under the directorship of Alonso. In 1948 Alfonso Reyes appointed him director of the Center of Linguistic and Literary Studies of the Colegio de México, where he also became the founding managing editor of the *Nueva Revista de Filología Hispánica (NRFH)*. Lida's distinguished career as professor at Harvard University began in 1953; in 1968 he became Smith Professor of Romance Languages. His *Letras hispánicas: Estudios, esquemas* (1958) is a collection of essays on philosophy, Latin American literature (Rubén DARÍO, Gabriela MISTRAL, and Jorge Luis BORGES, among others), and the prose works of Francisco de Quevedo, to which he dedicated much of his scholarly career. Nine of his later articles on Quevedo were collected posthumously as *Prosas de Quevedo* (1981). *NRFH* published a special issue titled *Homenaje a Raimundo Lida* (vol. 24, no. 1) in 1975. Known for his scholarly precision in addressing historical contexts and stylistic questions, and for the economy and subtle wit of his own critical style, Lida placed great emphasis on his role as mentor to several generations of Hispanists who shaped U.S. scholarship on the literature of medieval and early modern Spain and present-day Latin America.

ANA MARÍA BARRENECHEA, "Bibliografía de Raimundo Lida," in *Nueva Revista de Filología Hispánica* 24, no 1 (1975): v–x; "En Memoria de Raimundo Lida," in *Revista Iberoamericana* 46, no. 112–113 (July–December 1980): 517–521; JORGE GUILLÉN, "Raimundo Lida," in *Insula: Revista Bibliográfica de Ciencias y Letras* 36, no. 421 (December 1981): 1, 3; IRIS M. ZAVALA, "Las letras hispánicas de Raimundo Lida (1908–1979)," in *Insula: Revista Bibliográfica de Ciencias y Letras* 36, no. 421 (December 1981): 4–5.

EMILIE BERGMANN

LIENDO Y GOICOECHEA, JOSÉ ANTONIO (*b.* 3 May 1735; *d.* 2 July 1814), Central American educator and scientist, founding member of the Economic Society of Guatemala. Born to a creole family in present-day Cartago, Costa Rica, Goicoechea was instrumental in introducing the Enlightenment to late colonial Central America. He entered the Franciscan order in his native Costa Rica, and it was during his studies to enter the order that he was first exposed to scientific training. In 1767 he earned a bachelor's degree from the University of San Carlos. He moved to Guatemala sometime during the late 1760s, and in 1769 he published a paper on experimental physics. In the 1780s Goicoechea visited Spain, where he was exposed to the "new learning" so popular at the time. He examined the libraries, botanical gardens, and natural history exhibits of Spain, an experience that provided him with the basis for his later work in Guatemala. He returned to Guatemala in 1788.

Along with other "enlightened" figures, on 20 November 1794 Goicoechea signed a petition to the crown calling for the establishment of an economic society modeled on those existing in Europe. He and his associates hoped that the society could help to enliven Guatemala's moribund economy, so backward in comparison with what Goicoechea had seen in Spain. But economic revival threatened many entrenched interests, and the crown ordered the suppression of the society in 1800, ostensibly because Goicoechea and another member, Antonio Muró, argued that Indians should be allowed to wear European-style clothing.

Goicoechea taught a generation of Guatemalans destined to lead the former Spanish colony as an independent nation. In addition to his article on Indian clothing, he wrote articles on indigo cultivation, the Indians of Comayagua, and poverty in the capital city. He died in Santiago de Guatemala.

JOHN TATE LANNING, *The Eighteenth-Century Enlightenment in the University of San Carlos de Guatemala* (1956); ROBERT JONES SHAFER, *The Economic Societies in the Spanish World, 1763–1821* (1958); ELISA LUQUE-ALCALDE, *La Sociedad Económica de Amigos del País de Guatemala* (1962); RALPH LEE WOODWARD, JR., *Class, Privilege, and Economic Development: The Consulado de Comercio of Guatemala, 1793–1871* (1966).

MICHAEL POWELSON

See also **Guatemala: Organizations.**

LIHN, ENRIQUE (*b.* 3 September 1929; *d.* 10 July 1988), Chilean poet. Lihn was the prominent Chilean poet of his generation and one of the most original voices of contemporary Latin American poetry. *La pieza oscura* (1963) (*The Dark Room and Other Poems* [1978]) marks the initial maturity of his poetry of biographical experience and the manifestation of the strange and ominous. *Poesía de paso* (1966) develops a poetry of circumstance, which emanates from visits to art museums and famous cities and travel to foreign countries. It parodies art criticism and the language of travelogues. *Escrito en Cuba* (1969) and *La musiquilla de las pobres esferas* (1969) present an ironic vision of life and poetry, which marks a new stage of Lihn's work.

During the military dictatorship Lihn produced a series of books, which included *Por fuerza mayor* (1974), *París, situación irregular* (1977), *A partir de Manhattan* (1979), *Estación de los desamparados* (1982), *El paseo Ahumada* (1983), *Pena de extrañamiento* (1986), *Al bello aparecer de este lucero* (1983), *La aparición de la Virgen* (1988), and *Album de toda especie de poemes* (1989), published posthumously. These books played with all kinds of allusions to social, cultural, and political circumstances. Lihn also wrote three novels of parody, a collection of short stories, *Agua de arroz* (1964), plays, and numerous

essays, and he did a number of original drawings. *Diario de muerte* (1989) is a collection of poems written when the author was suffering from cancer.

PEDRO LASTRA, *Conversaciones con Enrique Lihn* (1980); RODRIGO CÁNOVAS, *Lihn, Zurita, Ictus, Radrigán* (1986); DAVE OLIPHANT, "On translating the poetry of Enrique Lihn," *Dactylus* 6 (1986): 61–63; CEDOMIL GOIC, *Historia y crítica de la literatura hispanoamericana* (1990), vol. 3, pp. 241–243.

CEDOMIL GOIC

See also **Literature.**

LIMA, ALCEU AMOROSO (*b.* 11 December 1893; *d.* 14 August 1983), Brazilian writer, publicist, and Catholic leader, whose career started in 1919 as a literary critic for the recently founded Rio de Janeiro newspaper *O Jornal*. Cautious that his activities as a writer could detract from the respectability of his position as an industrialist, he chose the pen name Tristão de Athayde, which was destined to make him famous. As an intellectual and a writer, he embraced many different roles simultaneously. These included social activist on Catholic issues, political doctrinaire, essayist at large, professor of literature and, of course, literary critic, which was his main persona throughout his life, with only sporadic interruptions.

His life was marked and divided by the year 1928, when, hitherto religiously indifferent, he converted not only to Catholicism but to militant Catholic causes. For a long time he was an intellectual of the rightist, conservative, ideology, but, after the military political coup of 1964 in Brazil, he identified himself progressively with left-of-center positions. As a matter of fact, he eventually belonged to the so-called Catholic Left, not going so far, however, as to join the Theology of Liberation.

Lima's influence was enormous, although it abated somewhat after his death. In any case, he personified the traditional Catholic thinker par excellence. Although he wrote hundreds of books and essays, the five volumes of his *Estudos* (1927–1933) may be taken as a largely representative introduction to the whole of his work.

CARLOS DANTE DE MORAES, *Tristão de Athayde e outros ensaios* (1937); M. A. M. ANCILLA O'NEILL, *Tristão de Athayde and the Catholic Social Movement in Brazil* (1939); ANTÔNIO CARLOS VILLAÇA, *O pensamento católico no Brasil* (1975) and *O desafio da liberdade* (*A vida de Alceu Amoroso Lima*) (1983); VERA REGINA TEIXEIRA, "Alceu Amoroso Lima," in *Latin American Writers,* edited by Carlos A. Solé and Maria Isabel Abreu, vol. 2 (1989), pp. 781–790.

WILSON MARTINS

LIMA, JORGE DE (*b.* 23 April 1895; *d.* 16 Nov. 1953), Brazilian poet, physician, politician. Lima was born in the northeastern state of Alagoas, where he completed secondary school. While drawn to the priesthood, he chose medicine as a career and went to Salvador to study. Having specialized in public health, he returned in 1915 to practice in Alagoas. In 1926, he became involved in public affairs, winning election to the state chamber of deputies as a candidate of the Republican Party. In 1930 he moved to Rio, where he was active in political causes while continuing his medical career. In 1946, he served on the governing council of the Federal District, and in 1949 he began to teach at the University of Brazil and the Catholic University.

Like many well-known intellectuals of the period, he participated in the Catholic movement of renovation. While the first poetry he published followed Parnassian models, Lima achieved recognition only in the second phase of modernism as a member of a spiritually oriented group in Rio. His poetry, inspired by his Christian faith, gave way to surreal verse of self-searching abstraction. In literary circles, Lima's most admired single work is *Invenção de Orfeu* (Invention of Orpheus, 1952), a dense ten-canto lyrical epic.

In terms of cultural nationalism, Lima's cult of northeastern regionalism, especially of the black cultural presence, is noteworthy. He was born into a family that had been active in the abolition movement, and a concern for the black experience marks his writing from the 1920s on. One of his most noteworthy works is *Poemas Negros* (1947), which invokes African deities. In addition to eighteen books of verse, Lima wrote five works of long fiction, but they are not of the same distinction as his verse. He also produced children's literature, biography, and art criticism.

MARIE F. SOVEREIGN, "The Double Itinerary of Jorge de Lima's Poetry," in *Luso-Brazilian Review* 11, no. 1 (1974): 105–113; RICHARD A. PRETO-RODAS, "The Black Presence and Two Brazilian Modernists: Jorge de Lima and José Lins do Rego," in *Tradition and Renewal: Essays on Twentieth-Century Latin American Literature and Culture*, edited by Merlin Forster (1975); LUCIANA STEGAGNA PICCHIO, "Jorge de Lima: Universal Poet," in *Portuguese Studies* 1 (1985): 151–167.

CHARLES A. PERRONE

LIMA, PEDRO DE ARAÚJO (Marquis of Olinda; *b.* 22 December 1793; *d.* 7 June 1870), Brazilian politician. He received a degree in canon law from Coimbra University in Portugal. His career covered the last part of the colonial period, independence, the First Empire, Regency, and most of the Second Empire. In 1821 he was a member of Pernambuco's delegation to the Portuguese constitutional convention in Lisbon, and in 1823 he was Pernambuco's delegate to the Brazilian constitutional convention. Lima was minister of empire during the First Empire; president of the Chamber of Deputies, and last regent of the empire (1837–1840) during the minority of PEDRO II; senator for Pernambuco; four times president of the Council of Ministers in the Second Empire; and councillor of state.

Lima's political views and actions were influenced by the excesses of the theoretic parliamentarism he witnessed in the Portuguese and Brazilian constitutional conventions; by the solid English parliamentarism of Lord Liverpool, George Canning, and Robert Peel; and by the unconstitutional actions of Charles X of France. They were also profoundly marked by the chaos and disorder that engulfed Brazil during the Regency (1831–1840). He developed a marked distaste for parliamentary demagoguery and theories, advocated strict adherence to the constitution, called for a strong central government as an antidote to disorder and chaos, developed a willingness to share power with the opposition, and acquired an ingrained fear of political and territorial fragmentation of the state.

Lima's regency signaled the end of Liberal experiments in political and administrative decentralization, promoted the prestige of the monarchy, and strove to regain the prerogatives lost by the executive power during the period of decentralization. In 1841, he was among the first to be appointed to the Council of State, the emperor's advisory body. As councillor of state for twenty-eight years, he strongly defended political and administrative centralization and governmental control over the church. He served mostly in the Section of Empire, where he advised the ministers of empire and of agriculture. He specialized in the incorporation of Brazilian joint-stock companies, whose bylaws he scrutinized with the utmost care, and thus molded the commercial legislation affecting companies. As president of the Council of Ministers he was gifted in his ability to select as his ministers men of recognized talents and prestige, regardless of their political affiliation. As a result, important pieces of legislation were approved during his stewardships.

One of the Conservative national political leaders and the undisputed Conservative leader in the province of Pernambuco, he later became one of the founders of the Progressive Party, a league of moderate Conservatives and Liberals. In 1854 he was granted the title of marquis of Olinda. His position as former regent, as well as his political, institutional, and administrative knowledge of the life of the empire made him one of the most powerful and influential politicians of the Second Empire.

LUIS DA CAMARA CASCUDO, *O marques de Olinda e seu tempo (1793–1870)* (1938).

LYDIA M. GARNER

LIMA BARRETO, AFONSO HENRIQUES DE (*b.* 13 May 1881; *d.* 1 November 1922), Brazilian author. A fin-de-siècle realist writer, memorialist, and journalist from Rio de Janeiro, he produced novels, stories, and essays containing scathing critiques of the Brazilian plutocracy, the bureaucratic state, racism, and social injustice. The grandson of African slaves on both sides, he was for decades compared—almost always unfavorably—with Joachim Maria MACHADO DE ASSIS. Although both wrote urban fiction set in Rio, Machado's style was generally considered more sophisticated in form, whereas Lima Barreto's fiction was seen as a poorly articulated paraphase of his own life.

His fictional works, including his four major novels—*Recordações do escrivão Isaías Caminha* (1909; Memoirs of the Clerk Isaías Caminha), *O triste fim de Policarpo Quaresma* (1915; *The Patriot*, 1978), *Vida e morte de M. J. Gonzaga de Sá* (1919; *The Life and Death of M. J. Gonzaga de Sá*, 1979), *Clara dos Anjos* (1923; *Clara dos Anjos*, 1979)—were based on an aesthetic in which literature is seen as "liberating from all forms of prejudice." Initially devalued as romans à clef or autobiographical recollections, these works have more recently received favorable critical reappraisals for their antiliterary attitude and direct prose style.

A fierce opponent of the highly rhetorical, French-inspired "literature of the salons" promoted by his contemporary Henrique COELHO NETO, Lima Barreto was also a self-proclaimed anarchist who espoused virulent anti-Americanism. His best-known novel, *O triste fim de Policarpo Quaresma*, is a utopian novel and an overt attack on the Republican government of Floriano PEIXOTO. The hero, a fanatic nationalist obsessed with Brazil's redemption, dies a madman. In his diaries, Lima Barreto, who died at age forty-one, describes his own life as a tragic one, marked by alcoholism, discrimination, and economic hardship.

ROBERT HERRON, "*Isaías Caminha* as a Psychological Novel," in *Luso-Brazilian Review* 8 (December 1971): 26–38; FRANCISCO DE ASSIS BARBOSA, *A vida de Lima Barreto* (1975); MARIA LUISA NUNES, ed. and comp., *Lima Barreto: Bibliography and Translations* (1979); FRANCISCO DE ASSIS BARBOSA, "A. H. de Lima Barreto," in *Latin American Writers,* edited by Carlos. A. Solé and Maria Isabel Abreu, vol. 2 (1989), pp. 565–573.

MIRIAM AYRES

LIMA E SILVA, LUÍS ALVES DE (duque de Caxias; *b.* 25 August 1803; *d.* 7 June 1880), patron of the Brazilian army and Brazil's most famous soldier. Caxias began his military career at age five as a cadet. His father, Francisco de Lima e Silva, was prominent in national politics and served as a member of the Regency from 1831 to 1835. Caxias saw action in the struggle for independence. During the Regency period (1830–1841), in which three political parties were grappling for power following the abdication of Dom PEDRO I, he served the goals of the moderate Chimango Party by dissolving the unruly army created by the former ruler. Then, with a corps of four hundred loyal officers (the Sacred Battalion) heading up units of the newly created National Guard, Caxias suppressed various regional uprisings. In 1840 he was appointed president of Maranhão Province, which was in rebellion. The seizure of the town of Caxias was crucial in bringing that area under control, and he was given the title of baron (later viscount,

Cartoon on the War of the Triple Alliance published in *A Vida Fluminense* magazine. Below, Caxias; above, Solano López. ICONOGRAPHIA.

count, marquis, and duke) of Caxias. Subsequently, he was able to suppress revolts in the provinces of São Paulo, Minas Gerais, and Rio Grande do Sul.

Caxias is remembered as the providential figure in establishing and maintaining political stability for the empire and as a very active member of the Conservative Party, serving as minister of war, deputy, senator, and, on two occasions, as prime minister. He characterized himself as being "more of a soldier than a politician." Others described him as "the most civilian soldier." Although he demonstrated his military abilities in the campaign to topple the Argentine dictator Juan Manuel de ROSAS in 1852, it was as commander of Allied forces during the Paraguayan War (1865–1870) that Caxias met his greatest test both militarily and politically. Certain Liberal Party leaders in power at that moment subjected Caxias to a constant barrage of criticism in Parliament and the press, to which Caxias responded with a threat to resign. Dom PEDRO II removed the Liberal regime and, although the episode was complicated by other factors, Liberal leaders blamed the whole affair on "militarism."

Caxias, his health broken, and bitter over the way civilian leaders had allowed partisan considerations to affect their obligation to support him and the army in the war, returned home to further evidences of ingratitude. No hero's welcome was arranged, he continued to be criticized in Parliament, and the size of the army was cut drastically against his wishes. Although he subsequently served in various governmental positions, Caxias died disillusioned with the treatment accorded him and the army by civilian political leaders of the empire.

In the view of Brazilian military leaders, Caxias stands as the example of how the army, under the leadership of patriotic officers, could serve as the principal institution for maintaining the national unity needed for governing an essentially undisciplined society whose civilian leaders purportedly have lacked an adequate sense of patriotism. Thus, the term *Caxiasism* becomes synonymous with the term *civics*.

AFFONSO DE CARVALHO, *Caxias*, 2d ed. (1940); OLYNTHO PILLAR, *Os patronos das forças armadas* (1966), pp. 15–56; PAULO MATOS PEIXOTO, *Caxias: Nume tutelar da nacionalidade*, 2 vols. (1973); E. BRADFORD BURNS, *A History of Brazil*, 2d ed. (1980), pp. 177–178, 282.

ROBERT A. HAYES

See also **War of the Triple Alliance.**

LIMA, capital city of Peru, a large metropolitan area with a population of 6,980,000 (1990); also a province and department of the same name. Like other Latin American megalopolises, Lima's size continues to increase as people move from the interior provinces seeking better economic opportunities. Lima is by far the most important industrial, commercial, banking, and political center of the country. It is situated in the central coastal region and connected with the rest of the country by a network of highways, including the longitudinal coastal Pan-American Highway and the Central Highway, which reaches the central highlands. On the Pacific Ocean coast, the port of Callao, once separated from Lima by a few miles but now part of a continuous urban sprawl, and the nearby international airport handle approximately 80 percent of the country's imports and 50 percent of its exports.

Lima extends from and beyond the Rímac River valley, a narrow fringe of dwindling agricultural land similar to other valleys (Huara, Chancay, Chillón, Mala, Cañete) in the department that sporadically interrupt the vast coastal desert. These valleys were among the most productive SUGAR and COTTON areas up to the 1920s, when the decline of export prices and growing real estate developments helped drastically reduce the arable land. Although situated in a tropical region, Lima has a humid and mildly cold climate during the months of April to November because of cloud cover from the effects of the cold Humboldt current off the coast. Dur-

ing the summer months of December to March, the weather is sunny and hot.

Before the arrival of the Spaniards, the valley of Lima was under the influence of the important religious center of Pachacámac. This god was accepted by Inca rulers and worshipped as the one responsible for the periodic earthquakes. For defensive reasons Francisco PIZARRO abandoned his initial plan to make the central highland town of Jauja the political center of the conquered Incan territory. He decided instead to establish the future administrative center of the Viceroyalty of Peru in the valley of Lima. Thus Ciudad de los Reyes (City of the Kings), as Lima was known in early colonial times, was founded on 18 January 1535.

Under Spanish colonial rule, Lima consisted of well-protected squared blocks of dwellings at the center of which was the Plaza de Armas, the square bordered by the government and municipal palaces and Lima's cathedral, as well as the most notable families' houses. This core, characterized by one- and two-story houses of distinct colonial architecture, Moorish balconies, and ornate baroque and rococo churches, is today known as the downtown area of Old Lima. In one of the city's old sections, Pachacamilla, the syncretic and popular religious cult of the Señor de los Milagros (Lord of Miracles), invoked for protection against earthquakes (the most destructive of which occurred in 1630, 1687, 1746, 1941, and 1970), began initially among the urban SLAVES of the owner of the Pachacamac estate just south of Lima.

Lima's old boundaries were modified by the mid-nineteenth century, when Henry MEIGGS was contracted to demolish the remnants of the old colonial wall surrounding Lima. At the time, Lima, Callao, and the port of Pisco south of Lima were the main beneficiaries of the income produced by the booming export of GUANO, a fertilizer deposited on islands off the central coast by seabirds. Beyond the post-Independence political struggle that made Lima the target of conspiracies and coups by military chieftains, a rising civilian economic and social elite built new houses and summer ranches in Lima, Miraflores, and Chorrillos. However, by the end of the WAR OF THE PACIFIC and the Chilean occupation of the city (1881–1883), Lima's urban development was in decline.

Starting in the first two decades of the twentieth century, and especially in the 1920s, Lima's real estate boom began in earnest. New avenues and streets raised the price of land in and around Lima. New neighborhoods funded by profitable financial institutions extended considerably the urban area. A process of gradual industrialization, a growing urban market, and a rise in commercial and other services since the 1890s provided jobs and entrepreneurial opportunities. By the 1950s, however, the first slums appeared on Lima's outskirts, the result of a housing shortage as the massive immigration from the interior provinces steadily increased. By the 1970s, Lima was surrounded by an impressive

Cathedral in the Plaza de Armas, Lima, Peru. LIBRARY OF CONGRESS.

and populous ring of slums, which by the 1990s contained almost a third of the city's population. In these vast and precarious concentrations, such as Comas and Villa El Salvador, the inhabitants seek better urban services.

As a political and cultural center, Lima is the head of the government and the judicial system and is home to several universities, among them the oldest in the Americas, San Marcos University. It is a city that has inspired the witty anecdotes of Ricardo PALMA, the tragicomic short stories of writer Julio Ramón Riveiro, and the skeptical novels by Mario VARGAS LLOSA. The main financial center of Peru, Lima possesses disproportionate financial and economic resources as a result of the unequal distribution of wealth and income in Peru. During periods when the democratic system is in place, Lima's voting population is decisive. Despite the extended poverty and obvious corruption in the Peruvian capital, people in Lima can enjoy a wide variety and richness of food, representing a blend of ethnic origins.

JOSÉ BARBAGELATA and JUAN BROMLEY, *Evolución urbana de Lima* (1945); DAVID COLLIER, *Squatters and Oligarchs: Authoritarian Rule and Policy Change in Peru* (1976); ALBERTO FLORES GALINDO, *Aristocracía y plebe: Lima, 1760–1830,* (1984); MARÍA ROSTOWOROWSKI, *Pachacámac y el Señor de los Milagros* (1992); ALFONSO QUIROZ, *Domestic and Foreign Finance in Modern Peru, 1850–1950: Financing Visions of Development* (1993).

ALFONSO W. QUIROZ

LIMA CONFERENCE (1847–1848), a meeting of representatives of the republics of Bolivia, Chile, Ecuador, New Granada, and Peru at Lima. Initiated by Peruvian President Ramón CASTILLA, it was an attempt to revive the Bolivarian ideal of Latin American solidarity, and an early antecedent of the Pan-American Union, which sought to confront the dangers of European intervention through a defensive confederation. (In 1846 conservative Ecuadorian politician and former dictator Juan José FLORES had conspired in Spain and France to establish a European monarchy in Ecuador.) The conference also considered the consequences and dangers for Latin America of the outcome of the MEXICAN-AMERICAN WAR and the French and British intervention in Argentina. The Lima Conference was followed by a similar meeting in Santiago in 1856.

JORGE BASADRE, *Historia de la República del Perú,* vol. 2 (1963).

ALFONSO W. QUIROZ

See also **Pan-Americanism.**

LIMA CONFERENCE (1938). *See* **Pan-American Conferences.**

LIMA, TREATY OF (1929), a diplomatic agreement between Chile and Peru, signed on 16 April 1929, that finally resolved the TACNA-ARICA DISPUTE. Under the Treaty of ANCÓN, signed in 1883, Chile retained temporary possession of the two provinces Arica and Tacna. It refused, however, to carry out the remaining terms of the treaty, which called for a plebiscite to determine the ownership of this territory. After years of haggling, Peru and Chile signed the Treaty of Lima. According to this arrangement, Chile retained Arica but Tacna was awarded to Peru along with 6 million pesos. While it settled the long-simmering boundary dispute between Chile and Peru, the Treaty of Lima unfortunately did not deal with Bolivia's loss of its seacoast, an issue (dating from the WAR OF THE PACIFIC) which continues to complicate the relationship between Santiago and La Paz to this day.

FREDRICK B. PIKE, *Chile and the United States, 1880–1962* (1963), pp. 229–230; WILLIAM F. SATER, *Chile and the United States: Empires in Conflict* (1990), pp. 100–101.

WILLIAM F. SATER

LIMANTOUR, JOSÉ YVES (*b.* 26 June 1854; *d.* 26 August 1935), Mexican secretary of the treasury (1892–1911), a leader of the CIENTÍFICOS. In 1892 Limantour became secretary of the treasury in the government of Porfirio DÍAZ after serving for a year as *oficial mayor* of the ministry under Matías ROMERO. Faced with a severe economic crisis, he initially was forced to secure a series of foreign loans at disadvantageous terms, to maintain Mexico's solvency, but eventually he reformed government finances to the extent that he produced a surplus in 1895 and for years thereafter. In 1899 he renegotiated the nation's foreign loans at significantly better rates.

His most pressing dilemma, however, was the decline in the value of silver during the 1890s. He determined that the best solution was to convert Mexican currency to the gold standard, and he did so in 1904.

Limantour presided over the period of Mexico's most dynamic economic development until after 1940. His policy was based on the encouragement of foreign investment. After 1900, however, Limantour, like Díaz, became increasingly concerned about the vast economic presence of U.S. investors in the country. In 1902, worried by the likelihood that the two largest U.S.-owned railroad companies, the Mexican Central and the Mexican National, would swallow up other lines, Limantour initiated the government purchase of two railroad companies, the Interoceanic and the National. When this jeopardized the delicate financial situation of the Mexican Central, Limantour engineered its takeover by the government in 1906. Two years later, he merged all these lines together to form the Ferrocarriles Nacionales de Mexico. In 1908 Limantour sponsored a new banking law that reined in the unfettered growth of banks and attempted to curb abuses and corruption that marked the banking system.

Despite his reforms, the Mexican economy experienced a severe downturn in 1907 due to the decline in mineral prices on the world market. Foreign investment temporarily dried up and the country plunged into a depression, which, when coupled with a series of disconcerting political developments, badly destabilized the Díaz regime.

Between 1900 and 1910 Limantour led the *científicos*, one of two major factions within the Díaz dictatorship. Technocrats who sought to modernize the nation through positivist principles, they believed fervently in rational decision making. The opposing faction was a group of Porfirian generals, the most notable of whom was Bernardo REYES OGAZÓN, the political boss of Nuevo León. Their politics centered around personal relations with those who depended on their goodwill.

The rivalry between Limantour and Reyes took in more importance in 1904, when the aged dictator agreed to run for president for another term with a vice president for the first time. Two years earlier the finance minister had won a cabinet struggle that resulted in Reyes's ouster as minister of war and he triumphed again when Díaz chose *científico* stalwart Ramón CORRAL VERDUGO as his vice president. During this period, the *científicos* obtained the governorships of several key states. The division in *Porfirista* elite ranks badly weakened the government when it confronted the challenge of rebellion in 1910.

On 25 May 1911 Limantour resigned his post as finance minister and went into exile in France, where he lived for the next twenty-four years.

See DANIEL COSIO VILLEGAS, ed., *Historia moderna de México*, 9 vols. (1955–1970). JOSÉ Y. LIMANTOUR, *Apuntes sobre mi vida pública* (1965), is a defense of his career. See also WALTER F. MC CALEB, *Present and Past Banking in Mexico* (1920); ANTONIO MANERO, *La revolución bancaria en México* (1957); and CHARLES HALE, *The Transformation of Liberalism in Late Nineteenth Century Mexico* (1989).

MARK WASSERMAN

LINARES, JOSÉ MARÍA (*b.* 10 July 1808; *d.* 6 October 1861), president of Bolivia (1857–1861). Linares was born in Tilcala into an important Spanish family from colonial Potosí. Heir to one of the largest fortunes in Bolivia, he became the first civilian president in Bolivia's history. After the death of General José BALLIVIÁN in exile, Linares became the undisputed champion of the enemies of Manuel Isidoro BELZÚ (president, 1848–1855), who had mobilized Bolivia's lower classes to remain in power. A widely read and charismatic man, Linares, with his supporters, known as the "Rojo," conspired ceaselessly to overthrow the government. When they finally did so, he quickly established a dictatorship because he felt that this was the only way to reform Bolivian society. In particular, Linares attempted to rid the government of the corruption inherent in previous military regimes. Although a devout Catholic and pro-

clerical, on other issues Linares was a precursor to later liberal administrations, fostering the MINING industry and free trade and trying to inculcate European culture into Bolivian society. He tried to do this through dictatorial means, however, and ultimately failed. He was overthrown by members of his own administration in 1861.

Linares engendered a large political historiography soon after his death, but there are fewer recent works. Some newer efforts include MANUEL FRONTAURA ARGANDOÑA, *El dictador Linares* (1970). See also ALCIDES ARGUEDAS, *Historia de Bolivia: La dictadura y la anarquía* (1926). A short description of the Linares regime is contained in HERBERT S. KLEIN, *Bolivia: The Evolution of a Multi-Ethnic Society* (1982), pp. 130–134.

ERICK D. LANGER

LINARES, PEDRO (*b.* 29 June 1906; *d.* 26 January 1992), a Mexican papier-mâché artist (*cartonero*) who developed an expressive, one-of-a-kind style from folk art forms and traditional, ephemeral fiesta accoutrements. He is best known for two genres—the *alebrije* (fantastic animal) and the *calavera* (animated skeleton)—based on Holy Week Judas and Day of the Dead *calavera* miniatures.

Trained as a child by his father, Linares passed the family métier on to his three sons—Enrique, Felipe, and Miguel—who extended the imaginative possibilities of the medium. Grandsons Leonardo, Ricardo, and David have also taken up the work.

Alebrijes, a term coined by Linares, combine the body parts of serpents, scorpions, lions, reptiles, and butterflies and accentuate a playful outlook on reality. Intricate surface patterning in an array of bright colors and detailed tactile textures (spikes, bumps, curves) add dimension. Linares's *calaveras* touch on a pre-Hispanic rooted belief that death is an extension of life. Thus, *calaveras* engage in a wide variety of activities, such as guitar-playing, picture-taking, and skateboarding. Many of Linares's *calavera* scenes are inspired by the prints of José Guadalupe POSADA, most notably La Catrina, El Panteón, Don Quixote, and revolutionary figures.

CARLOS ESPEJEL, *Las artesanías tradicionalis en México* (1972); JUDITH BRONOWSKY, *Artesanos Mexicanos* (1978); RODOLFO BECERRIL STRAFFON and ADALBERTO RÍOS SZALAY, *Los artesanos nos dijeron . . .* (1981); VICTOR INZÚA CANALIS, *Artesanía en papel y cartón* (1982) and *El imaginativo mundo de los Linares* (1987); SUSAN N. MASUOKA, *En Calavera: The Papier-Mâché Art of the Linares Family* (1994).

SUSAN N. MASUOKA

LINARES ALCÁNTARA, FRANCISCO (*b.* 13 April 1825; *d.* 30 November 1878), president of Venezuela (1877–1878). Linares Alcántara began his political and military career before the FEDERAL WAR (1859–1863). He participated in that as a proponent of liberalism and remained a prominent figure in the Liberal Party. In

1873 President Antonio GUZMÁN BLANCO named him first appointee of the republic, and as such he took on the duties of the first magistracy on various occasions.

With Guzmán's support Linares Alcántara was elected president in 1877. He brought together a cabinet composed mostly of civilians, promoted the politics of reconciliation by declaring a general amnesty, and supported freedom of the press and an administrative decentralization of funds destined for construction of public works. During his administration, a reaction against Guzmán, which Linares Alcántara tacitly encouraged, gained strength, and there were calls for a return to the Constitution of 1864. After Linares Alcántara's sudden death, his followers continued to participate in the reaction against Guzmán. The reinstatement of the Constitution of 1864 and the nullification of General Guzmán Blanco's statutes resulted in the Revolución Revindicadora (Revindicating Revolution) of December 1878, by which power was returned to Guzmán.

FRANCISCO GONZÁLEZ GUINÁN, *Historia contemporánea de Venezuela,* vols. 10 and 11 (1954).

INÉS QUINTERO

LINATI, CLAUDIO (*b.* 1790; *d.* 1832), Italian printer. Linati was born in Parma, Italy. At seventeen he belonged to the Engraving Society in Parma. In 1809 he went to Paris, where he attended the atelier of Jacques-Louis David. In Belgium, Linati met the Mexican diplomat Manuel E. Gorostiza, who awarded him a loan and a contract from the Mexican government to bring the first lithographic press to Mexico. In 1825, Linati arrived in Veracruz with Gaspar Franchini, whom he knew through his political activities in Parma with the Carbonaris. In Mexico he founded *El Iris,* and in 1826 he joined Florencio Galli and the Cuban writer José María HEREDIA. Later joined by Onazio de Attellis, marques de Santangelo, an Italian, they used their printing skills in polemics. A liberal and revolutionary opposed to all forms of tyranny, Linati was exiled. The press, however, remained at the Academy of San Carlos, where a course in lithography was offered for one year; however, use of the press to illustrate publications was tightly restricted.

Back in Europe, Linati completed and published in Brussels a series of lithographs entitled *Les costumes civils, militaires, et religieux du Méxique* (1826?), which portrayed various Mexican costumes and customs. It is an important book in that it provides a glimpse of the way in which Europeans imagined the social life of a country that so attracted them. Linati died in Tampico, Tamaulipas, Mexico.

MANUEL TOUSSAINT, *La litografía en México en el siglo XIX* (1934); EDMUNDO O'GORMAN, *Documentos para la historia de la litografía en México* (1955).

ESTHER ACEVEDO

LINDLEY LÓPEZ, NICOLÁS, one of the important Peruvian army leaders of the institutional military coup of 18 July 1962. The coup was officially justified by the allegation that the contested elections of that year had been fraudulent. None of the three main contenders in the elections, Víctor Raúl HAYA DE LA TORRE, Fernando BELAÚNDE, and Manuel ODRÍA, had been able to obtain the number of votes necessary to become president. The formation of a coalition between the Aprista Party and Odría's party and the congressional designation of Haya as president prompted the anti-Aprista forces in the military to stage the coup.

Together with generals Ricardo PÉREZ GODOY (army) and Pedro Vargas Prada (air force) and Vice Admiral Juan Francisco Torres Matos, Lindley López formed the executive of an interim government that held new elections in 1963, which were won by Belaúnde. After the forced retirement of Pérez Godoy, Lindley López became the de facto president. The military government restored constitutional guarantees, attempted a localized agrarian reform, and confronted strikes and armed insurrections led by Hugo BLANCO and Javier Heraud. The new technocratic attitude among the military was the basis for the far more consequential coup of 1968.

ARNOLD PAYNE, *The Peruvian Coup d'État of 1962: The Overthrow of Manuel Prado* (1968); DANIEL MASTERSON, *Militarism and Politics in Latin America: Peru from Sánchez Cerro to "Sendero Luminoso"* (1991).

ALFONSO W. QUIROZ

LINDO ZELAYA, JUAN (*b.* 1790; *d.* 24 April 1857), president of Honduras (1847–1852) and El Salvador (1841–1842). Lindo was born in Comayagua, Honduras, the son of Joaquín Fernández Lindo and Barbara Zelaya. He studied in Mexico as a youth and later was appointed interim colonial governor of Honduras by Governor José Gregorio Tinoco de Contreras (ruled 1819–1821). The Constituent Assembly of Honduras, then reappointed him to the post, at which he served from 21 November 1821 to 11 February 1824. While president of El Salvador, he established in 1841 the Colegio de la Asunción, which was later elevated in status, becoming the University of El Salvador in 1847. He also raised the Honduran Academía Literaria in status and renamed it the University of Honduras (1847). Its curriculum, under his direction, included law, philosophy, and Latin.

On 12 February 1847, Lindo became president of Honduras with the support of Honduran Conservatives and the approval of neighboring Guatemala. Technically, his term expired on 16 July 1848, when the 4 February 1848 constitution took effect, and his second term began on the same date and lasted until 1 January 1852. Domestic unrest due to disputes with Great Britain over loan agreements marred his term of office, as did Liberal revolts in Tegucigalpa on 4 February 1849 and 12 February 1850, which forced him to flee. Liberal forces under General Santos GUARDIOLA, his successor, were eventually suppressed with the aid of Guatemala and El Salvador. Lindo's refusal to run for reelection and his belief in the 1848 constitution led him to allow a Liberal to take office unopposed.

RÓMULO E. DURÓN Y GAMERO, *Biografía de don Juan Nepomuceno Fernández Lindo* (1932); LUIS MARIÑAS OTERO, *Honduras*, 2d ed. (1983).

JEFFREY D. SAMUELS

LINE OF DEMARCATION (1493), papal donation of temporal authority in the Indies to the Spanish crown. Following the successful completion of Christopher COLUMBUS's first voyage to the New World, Pope ALEXANDER VI (a Spaniard) extended to the crown of Castile by a series of bulls (May–September 1493) dominion over all those lands and peoples to the west of a meridian that were not already under the control of another Christian prince. The line ran roughly 100 leagues west of the AZORE or CAPE VERDE Islands. Other western European seafaring nations, especially England and France, questioned the claims: Francis I purportedly asked to be shown the clause in Adam's will excluding the French from a share in the newly discovered lands; the English outright rejected papal authority in the matter; and the Portuguese demanded bilateral discussions with the Spanish to redraw the boundary, which resulted in the TREATY OF TORDESILLAS.

C. H. HARING, *The Spanish Empire in America* (1963); LYLE N. MC ALISTER, *Spain and Portugal in the New World: 1492–1700* (1984).

NOBLE DAVID COOK

LINHA DURA (hard line), the term used to characterize the authoritarian views of a faction of young officers (called *duristas,* or hard-liners) in the Brazilian military following the 1964 coup d'état. Aimed first at armed revolutionaries and left-wing political activists, the hard-line was expanded to include union leaders, social workers, journalists, students, and teachers, under the alleged effort to fight communism. The ascendancy of the hard-liners (1968–1974) was heralded on 13 December 1968 by the declaration of Institutional Act 5, which abrogated civil liberties, suspended habeas corpus, adjourned Congress indefinitely, and gave the government discretionary power to purge the bureaucracy, military, universities, and trade unions. The incapacitation by a stroke in 1969 of President Artur da COSTA E SILVA, who had argued for a quick return to constitutional government, further facilitated the in-house coup known as "the revolution within the revolution." General Emílio Garrastazú de MÉDICI was named president (1969–1974) by the military high command and presided over the most violent and repressive period of the regime. While the economy boomed, arrests, torture, and illegal detention aroused vociferous opposition domestically and internationally. The 1974 inauguration of Ernesto GEISEL, who with his colleague General Golbery Couto y Silva represented moderate factions within the military government, marked the beginning of a politics of *abertura,* or "opening." The strategy of gradual liberalization was repeatedly challenged by hard-liners, but prevailed through a precarious alliance with civil groups, including women's movement organizations, labor organizers, the Brazilian Bar Association, and leaders of the Brazilian Catholic church. Geisel's dismissal of hard-liner Army Minister Sylvio Frota in 1977 and the amnesties extended to political exiles and prisoners in 1978 and 1979 signalled the ascension of *abertura* politics and the decline of the hard-line.

PETER FLYNN, *Brazil: A Political Analysis* (1978); MARIA HELENA MOREIRA ALVES, *State and Opposition in Military Brazil* (1986); ALFRED STEPAN, ed., *Democratizing Brazil* (1989).

FRANCESCA MILLER

See also **Institutional Acts.**

LINIERS Y BREMOND, SANTIAGO DE (*b.* 25 July 1753; *d.* 26 August 1810), viceroy of Río de la Plata (1807–1809). Born in Niort, France, Liniers was the son of a French naval officer from the Poitou region. At age twelve, he joined the Order of Malta as page to the grand master. He entered the service of the Spanish king in 1774 as an army officer in the Moroccan campaigns. Liniers first arrived in the Río de la Plata with the CEVALLOS expedition (1776) and returned in 1788. Married to María Martina de Sarratea, daughter of Martín de Sarratea, a prominent Spanish-born merchant, Liniers served as the head of the naval squadron charged with the protection of Montevideo, and then as interim governor of Misiones.

Present at the time of the second British invasion (1806–1807), Liniers was instrumental in reorganizing the militia that defeated the British invaders. Awaiting the arrival of a new viceroy to replace the discredited SOBREMONTE, who had fled during the invasions, Liniers was named interim viceroy and given the title of count of Buenos Aires. He was instrumental in putting down the ÁLZAGA rebellion of January 1809 and ruled until replaced by the newly arrived Viceroy CISNEROS in August 1809. He then retired to Alta Gracia, Córdoba.

Upon hearing of the dramatic action of the *cabildo abierto* (open town council meeting) of Buenos Aires, Liniers helped organize the royalist opposition to the Buenos Aires revolutionary troops. He was captured and executed as a traitor to the revolutionary cause.

PAUL GROUSSAC, *Santiago de Liniers* (1943); ENRIQUE UDAONDO, *Diccionario biográfico colonial argentino* (1945), pp. 502–505.

SUSAN M. SOCOLOW

LINS, OSMAN DA COSTA (*b.* 5 July 1924; *d.* 8 July 1978), Brazilian writer. A prolific author whose body of work includes short stories, drama, essays, and teleplays, Lins is best known for several novels exemplifying an important existentialist trend in Brazilian literature between the 1950s and the early 1980s. Lins's themes concerned the moral and ethical issues that must be confronted in everyday life, while the formal aspect of his fiction steadily evolved from simplicity to complex experimentation in language. His efforts to create innovative narrative techniques stand out in one of his best novels, *Avalovara* (1973; Eng. trans. 1980).

ANATOL ROSENFELD, "The Creative Narrative Processes of Osman Lins," in *Studies in Short Fiction* 8, no. 1 (1971): 230–244.

PEDRO MALIGO

LINS DO REGO, JOSÉ (*b.* 3 June 1901; *d.* 12 September 1957), Brazilian writer. Author of numerous volumes of speeches, personal and travel memoirs, and children's literature, Lins do Rego is known principally as a novelist, most notably for the six volumes of the Sugarcane Cycle. Critics have traditionally included him in a group referred to as the Northeastern Generation of 1930, a half dozen novelists whose fiction came to dominate the Brazilian literary scene during the 1930s and 1940s. Indeed, he and another member of the group, Jorge AMADO, took turns writing many of the best-sellers at the time, and both had a sufficiently high profile to merit the attentions, generally unfavorable, of the government of Getúlio VARGAS. He was also affiliated with the Region-Tradition movement founded in 1926 by Brazilian sociologist Gilberto FREYRE, at least in the sense that his novels seemed to be the most faithful to the tenets of the regionalist movement.

Lins do Rego was born into the rural aristocracy and thus had a unique insider's perspective on the society he depicted in his works. He was born on his grandfather's plantation in Paraíba, was raised by his maiden aunts after his mother's death when he was only eight months old, and attended both a boarding school and law school in Recife. Each of these episodes is the theme of one of the novels of the cycle. A common criticism of his work as a novelist, in fact, is that he was more of a memorialist than a creator, but this perceived shortcoming is an advantage from the perspective of social history, for his novels provide perhaps the most complete, and certainly the most readable, portrait of the rural Brazilian society of the period. Lins do Rego is regarded as one of the masters of the "sociological novel," a rather vague category referring to his portrayal of characters who are at once affecting and convincing.

Freyre's notion of regionalism, detailed in his *Manifesto regionalista de 1926*, grew out of his opposition to the modernists of Rio de Janeiro and São Paulo, whom he considered too citified, too cosmopolitan, and too European to qualify as spokesmen for a still essentially rural Brazil. Today the manifesto sounds almost quirky, with its praise for regional cuisine and such things as palm thatch roofing, but it was at the time as much at the center of intellectual debate as the political question of left versus right, a matter rendered nearly moot by the Vargas coup of 1930 and utterly so by the declaration of the Estado Novo in 1937.

The modernists became urbane vanguardists, and the regionalists of the Generation of 1930 defined themselves as chroniclers of that "other," more real Brazil with its mansions and shanties, a Brazil in which the heritage of a colonial past lay just beneath the surface. Regionalism versus MODERNISM was at the center of intellectual ferment of the period, although in hindsight it is clear that both groups were attempting, by quite different avenues, to accomplish the same end—to create a literature that could be clearly identified as truly Brazilian. The unstated agenda, and the factor that made Lins do Rego such an important writer of the time, was that the regionalists were consciously writing social documents, a posture that whether intentional or not, made the creation of art a secondary part of the exercise. There is no doubt that the public preferred such artlessness, but it is a factor that inhibits such documents from translating well into subsequent decades. From a historical perspective, however, this unadorned memorialism has its positive value, because the appeal of these works at the time of their publication was based in large degree on the fact that the Brazilian reading public *recognized* the characters and scenes and stories, which meant that their fidelity to the realities of Brazilian society was the key to their success.

It is not clear why the Vargas government regarded such writing as a threat to its well-being, but perhaps the very accuracy of the social portrayals made the government edgy. There is also some suspicion that Lins do Rego's works were targeted simply as a matter of guilt by association, because he was associated in the minds of many with other members of the generation who were in fact also members of the illegal Communist Party and whose works often made these sympathies more than evident. But the clearest sentiment evident in his works themselves is probably nostalgia, hardly a subversive quality.

The Sugarcane Cycle is largely a chronological account of the life of Carlos de Melo, who, like Lins do Rego, is the scion of a wealthy planter family. The first novel, *Menino de Engenho* (1932), deals with the early years of the timid and lonely young man, and the second, *Doidinho* (1933), continues with his trials at boarding school. *Bangüê* (1934) chronicles the years spent in Recife in law school, and *O Molegue Ricardo* (1935) tells the similar story of the black childhood companion of Carlos, who moves to the city and becomes involved in a union movement. *Usina* (1936) recounts the death of Ricardo and the transformation of the Santa Rosa plantation from the old labor-intensive plantation system into a modern, mechanized (and dehumanized) factory.

The final novel, not originally included in the cycle by

José Lins do Rego. ICONOGRAPHIA.

its author, is also universally regarded as his best—*Fogo Morto* (1943). This volume, a tripartite narrative centering on three very different people, contains not only the best-drawn characters but also the fullest insights into a society on the verge of decadent collapse. The first central character is a saddle maker who lives on the plantation of Seu Lula, the second character, a member of the hereditary aristocracy who is the central character of the second part of the novel. The final segment features the third character, a local eccentric and his manic and misdirected exploits. Although each character is from a different social stratum and each has his own foibles and strengths, the narrative is in essence the story of a social system in which the fabric seems to be unraveling, where all assumptions about outcomes are thwarted. Lins do Rego also wrote fiction about other uniquely Brazilian and mostly rural issues, such as messianic movements and banditry, but his best works remain those most closely drawn from his own experiences. It is certainly this latter body of work that assures his place as one of the most important Brazilian writers of the century.

A short section of *Fogo Morto* has been translated by Susan Hertelendy and appears in *Borzoi Anthology of Latin American Literature*, vol. 1 (1977), pp. 446–458. The first three novels of the cycle are collected in a single volume entitled *Plantation Boy*, translated by Emmi Baum (1966). Another novel, *Pureza*, exists in a British edition entitled *Pureza: A Brazilian Novel*, translated by Lucie Marion (1948). Commentary and criticism can be found in ÁLVARO LINS, OTTO MARIA CARPEAUX, and FRANKLIN THOMPSON, *José Lins do Rego* (1952); FRED P. ELLISON, *Brazil's New Novel: Four Northeastern Masters* (1954), pp. 45–79; JOÃO PACHECO, *O mundo que José Lins do Rego Fingiu* (1958); JOSÉ ADERALDO CASTELO, *José Lins do Rego: Modernismo e regionalismo* (1961); CLAUDE L. HULET, *Brazilian Literature*, vol. 3 (1975), pp. 271–272; WILSON MARTINS, *The Modernist Idea* (1975), pp. 285–288; BOBBY J. CHAMBERLAIN, "José Lins do Rego," in *Latin American Writers*, vol. 2, edited by Carlos Solé and Maria Isabel Abreu (1989), pp. 909–913; and EDUARDO F. COUTINHO and ÂNGELA BEZERRA DE CASTRO, *José Lins do Rego* (1990).

JON S. VINCENT

LINSEED. The flax plant has been cultivated in Europe, North Africa, and the Middle East—especially Egypt, the Caucasus, and the Black Sea—since antiquity. In Latin America it has been cultivated in Mexico, Chile, and Brazil. In Argentina, however, it became an especially important crop that provided the necessary infrastructure for several industries. Agronomist Martín José de Altolaguirre first introduced it to Argentina as an experiment in 1784. He grew the plant at his farm near the convent of La Recoleta in Buenos Aires and then extracted oil from the seed (linseed). In Argentina the plant was more greatly appreciated for that seed than for its use in the production of linen. After 1850 European immigrants began to cultivate the plant in Buenos Aires, Santa Fe, Córdoba, and Entre Ríos provinces. From 1899 until the 1940s, the acreage devoted to its cultivation steadily increased.

At the beginning of the twentieth century, the Bemberg Company began growing linseed in Baradero and Rojas in the province of Buenos Aires. A key ingredient in the production of paints and printer's ink, linseed was exported as raw material for European manufacturers until the 1950s. By 1913 Argentina was exporting more than a million tons of linseed each year and was devoting more acreage to this crop than any other country. The value of Argentine linseed exports was exceeded only by that of wheat, corn, and oats.

During World War I, Argentine exporters began to ship crushed, rather than whole, seed in order to reduce cargo space. The Depression and the development of modernized seed processing stimulated import substitution so that companies previously involved in exporting seed began to invest in domestic processing plants to extract oil and other by-products. World War II accelerated the growth of domestic seed oil production, and exports of Argentine linseed oil grew dramatically until the industry began a gradual decline after the 1960s.

CARLOS DE ALBERTI GIROLA, *El cultivo del trigo para la producción de la semilla en la Argentina* (1915); RAÚL RAMELLA, *El lino oleaginoso* (1944); EMILIO A. GRUGET, *Aprovechamiento industrial de los rastrojos del lino oleaginoso* (1949); CARLOS REMUSSI, *El lino textil* (1951).

DONNA J. GUY

LIRCAY, BATTLE OF (17 April 1830), a seminal military encounter which brought the Conservative Party to power in Chile. Tired of political unrest, a combination of Conservative and regional interests selected General Joaquín Prieto Vial to lead a coup. Progovernment forces under General Ramón FREIRE SERRANO advanced from Santiago, only to be defeated at the Lircay River. The Conservative triumph, while perhaps issuing in what became known as the "weight of the night" ended the political anarchy that had plagued Chile since the fall of Bernardo O'HIGGINS in 1823. After Lircay, Chile would enjoy stability, albeit at some substantial damage to political rights, that would bring economic recovery and national progress.

LUIS GALDAMES, *A History of Chile* (1941), p. 236; SIMON COLLIER, *Ideas and Politics of Chilean Independence, 1808–1833* (1967), pp. 327–328, 348.

WILLIAM F. SATER

See also **Chile: Political Parties.**

LISBOA, ANTÔNIA FRANCISCO. *See* **Aleijadinho.**

LISBOA, JOAQUIM MARQUES (Almirante Tamandaré; *b.* 13 December 1807; *d.* 20 March 1897), patron of the Brazilian navy. Tamandaré graduated from the Naval Academy in 1826. He was appointed to noble status (baron, viscount, count, and marquis Tamandaré) by Dom PEDRO II for suppressing various rebellions, including the CONFEDERATION OF THE EQUATOR (1824), the BALAIADA REBELLION (1838–1841), and the PRAIEIRA REVOLT (1848–1849). As commander of Brazilian naval forces in the Rio de La Plata in 1864, Tamandaré was involved in bringing pressure on the Uruguayan regime of Atanásio Cruz Aguirre by leading the attacks against Salto and Paissandú. He supported the mission of Counselor José Antônio SARAIVA, who was seeking satisfaction of Brazilian claims against the Uruguayan government. Tamandaré's testy, impulsive nature created problems for himself and the Brazilian government. He incurred the displeasure of the diplomatic corps when he tried to impose a blockade on Montevideo during a time of peace. He quarreled bitterly with other leaders of the high command of the forces of the Triple Alliance, and, despite numerous minor victories, he was strongly criticized for hesitating to attack the Paraguayan stronghold of HUMAITÁ. He was finally relieved of his command in December 1866 and returned to Brazil, where, because of his long service, he was maintained on the active list until shortly after the creation of the Republic (1889). Tamandaré carried out an endless campaign to exonerate his name, a goal that was finally achieved via the Supreme Military Tribunal a few days before his death. His birthday is celebrated as Sailors' Day.

OLYNTHO PILLAR, *Os patronos das forças armadas*, vol. 1 (1961), pp. 148–153; PEDRO CALMON, *História do Brasil*, vol. 7 (1963), pp. 1788, 1791–1792, 1824, 1871, 1890; CHARLES J. KOLINSKI, *Independence or Death! The Story of the Paraguayan War* (1965), pp. 13, 58, 106, 128, 139; PELHAM HORTON BOX, *The Origins of the Paraguayan War* (1967), pp. 124, 130, 220–224, 233, 237–239.

ROBERT A. HAYES

See also **War of the Triple Alliance.**

LISBON EARTHQUAKE, a devastating disaster that occurred on the morning of 1 November 1755, the feast of All Saints. It struck with extraordinary intensity in a series of violent shocks that left Lisbon's central commercial district and major public buildings, churches, and palaces in ruins. But the major cause of damage derived from the ensuing fire, which in the following six days razed most of the city's other neighborhoods. Although casualty figures vary enormously, at least 15,000—and perhaps as many as 30,000—people died from the quake and fire. Hundreds of thousands were left homeless, and extensive damage remained conspicuous into the nineteenth century.

The earthquake had an enormous effect on Portugal's economy and politics. It ruined many Lisbon merchants, and the enormous cost of rebuilding the city and its infrastructure consumed much of the country's and empire's revenues for years to come. The earthquake precipitated the political rise to power of Sebastião de Carvalho, the future marquês de POMBAL, who used the emergency to assume vital dictatorial power, which he held until 1777. The rebuilt city owed much to Pombal's energy and vision. From the ashes of medieval Lisbon arose a symmetrical city whose wide streets, open squares, and central grid reflected Enlightenment ideas of harmonious architecture and rational city planning.

T. D. KENDRICK, *The Lisbon Earthquake* (1956); MARIA LEONOR MACHADO DE SOUSA, *O Terromoto de 1755: Testemunhos britânicos—The Lisbon Earthquake of 1755: British Accounts* (1990).

WILLIAM DONOVAN

LISCANO VELUTINI, JUAN (*b.* 7 July 1915), Venezuelan poet, folklorist, literary critic, essayist, and editor. Following early studies in Europe, Liscano returned to Venezuela, where he has been a central figure in national literary and intellectual life and founder and director of several journals, most notably the literary supplement of *El Nacional* (1943–1950) and *Zona Franca* (1964–1984), and of the publishing houses Monte Avila (1979–1983) and Mandorla. He participated in resistance activities during the dictatorship of Marcos PÉREZ JIMÉNEZ and spent the years 1953–1958 exiled in Europe. An independent thinker of greater erudition, he has written extensively, often polemically, on literature and art and on cultural, social, philosophical, and political issues. He is one of the most important literary critics of Venezuela. Although he won the Premio Nacional de Poesía in 1952, his best work is found in the more than a dozen books of poetry published since that date. In his early poetry, which culminates in the neoepic *Nuevo Mundo Orinoco* (1959), the themes of American nature, history, and experience predominate. His later work explores individual perception, metaphysics, and universal myth. More modern essays reflect his interest in the erotic, psychology, esoterica, and historical cultural patterns.

Tiempo desandado (1964) and *Fuegos sagrados* (1990) contain good selections of Liscano's rich and varied essayistic production. His *Panorama de la literatura venezolana actual* (1973) and *Lecturas de poetas y poesía* (1985) are basic contributions, as are his several books on Rómulo Gallegos. *Nombrar contra el tiempo* (1968) is a useful anthology of his early poetry. *Nuevo Mundo Orinoco* (1959; 2nd ed. 1976; 3rd ed. 1992), *Rayo que al alcanzarme* (1978), *Fundaciones* (1981), *Myesis* (1982), *Vencimientos* (1986), and *Domicilios* (1986) contain his mature poetry. AR-LETTE MACHADO, *El apocalipsis según Juan Liscano* (1987) is a largely autobiographical document in interview form. OSCAR RODRÍGUEZ ORTIZ has edited a volume containing the major criticism on Liscano's work, *Juan Liscano ante la crítica* (1990).

MICHAEL J. DOUDOROFF

LISPECTOR, CLARICE (*b.* 10 December 1925; *d.* 9 December 1977), Brazilian writer. After nine novels, six collections of stories, four children's books, translations, interviews, and a wealth of *crônicas* (newspaper columns), Lispector's literary reputation rests on three features, all of which, from the early years of her career, were a positive influence on Latin American narrative: a lyrical and metaphoric style conveying her philosophical subject matter; a structure based chiefly on interior monologue and stream of consciousness; and themes concerning anxiety, isolation, and the need for self-realization. A writer of greatly refined poetic prose, but one with a strong social conscience, Lispector is one of Latin America's most original and powerful authors of the post–World War II era.

The youngest of three daughters of Ukrainian immigrants, she read avidly, doing little else in her spare time, whether as a student or journalist. In general, her life seems to have paralleled the content, themes, and style of her works. Existential and mystical in nature, they reveal her innermost self acting upon more than reacting to exterior reality. Never very methodical, she finally learned at least to jot down her ideas and feelings as they came to her and before they were lost forever. Later she could piece them together as she understood them, and, except for *A maçã no escuro*, all her works were composed in this rather unstructured manner.

Never a popular author in the sense that great numbers of people read her works, she was from the beginning of her career in 1942 an important author, one whose achievements had already attracted a discerning international audience as well as a national one. Lispector was less interested in events than in the repercussions these events produced in the minds of her characters—an approach to fiction writing that put her

largely at odds with what was then current in the Brazilian novel and short story. Not surprisingly, then, very little happens in a typical Lispector tale: plot, if defined in terms of the traditional realistic novel, is virtually nonexistent. The conflict of the work is based, almost invariably, in the mind of the character most centrally involved, the character whose hermetic and at times even claustrophobic point of view dominates both the telling and the structuring of the story. More than anything else, Lispector's narratives, her novels and her shorter pieces, are philosophical and poetic exercises that probe the complex and shifting inner realities of modern men and women. Her work has been praised for its brilliant use of language, its structural inventiveness, and its depiction of the alienated and frustrated modern human condition.

As a Brazilian writer, Lispector is best remembered for having opened new roads for Brazilian narrative, for having helped to lead it away from the productive but ultimately limiting kind of regionalism that had dominated the literary scene in Brazil for several decades. Lispector's first novel, *Perto do coração selvagem* (1942), broke radically with this deeply rooted tradition and established a new set of criteria that would help internationalize Brazilian literature and end its cultural and linguistic isolation.

The storm center of *Perto do coração selvagem*, and a character who, in her inner verisimilitude and complexity, can be taken as the prototype for later protagonists of Lispector, is a young woman, the first of a series of

Clarice Lispector. ICONOGRAPHIA.

striking female characters the author would create. Ranging from timid Ermelinda (*A maçã no escuro*), to the middle-class housewife Ana ("Amor"), to the hopelessly crippled refugee Macabéa (*A hora da Estrela*), to the existential voice of *Um sopro de vida*, Lispector's characters, whether female or male, all relate in one way or another to the issues of feminism, fulfillment, courage, freedom, and love.

Although many critics find her stories superior to her novels, because of the striking dramatic intensity that characterizes them, there can be no doubt that Lispector was a major precursor of the "new novel" in Latin America.

BENEDITO NUNES, *O mundo de Clarice Lispector* (1966), and *Leitura de Clarice Lispector* (1973); OLGA DE SÁ, *A escritura de Clarice Lispector* (1978); EARL FITZ, *Clarice Lispector* (1985).

RICHARD A. MAZZARA

See also **Literature: Brazil.**

LITERACY, in its most basic definition, the ability to read and write simple messages. An issue of concern affecting the general populace, it has been widely addressed in Latin America, primarily in the last half of the twentieth century. Before 1950, the formal education systems of the region were largely designed to serve the interests of the ruling elite. After 1960, informal, community-based, or "popular education," programs were mounted on a large scale. According to Miguel Roca, as late as 1950, 40 percent of the population of Latin America fifteen years of age or older was illiterate, and the mean level of education for this group was less than one year. By 1985, however, illiteracy had dropped to approximately 17 percent in the same age group. While the overall percentage of illiterates declined, however, the absolute numbers of illiterates remained relatively stable. This marked improvement in the literacy rate can be explained in large part by the expansion of the formal education system and by the provision of informal, or popular, education programs for adults who either never entered or dropped out of the formal system.

The expansion of educational opportunities was dramatic after 1950 for reasons that were economic, political, and social. Moreover, the commitment of such international groups as UNESCO, UNICEF, the ORGANIZATION OF AMERICAN STATES, and the ECONOMIC COMMISSION FOR LATIN AMERICA AND THE CARIBBEAN to educational development in the region was significant. Finally, several regional meetings of Latin American ministers of planning and education held during this period served to establish a region-wide educational agenda. These efforts notwithstanding, marginal populations disproportionately represented by women, indigenous groups, and rural populations continued to lack access to schools, attended infrequently, repeated grades, and/or dropped out at a high rate during the first years of primary schooling.

By the 1960s, national-level literacy campaigns were a visible manifestation of the effort to reach marginalized groups. The two campaigns that stand out—those in Cuba in 1960 and in Nicaragua in 1980—were both associated with revolutionary governments. They were both acclaimed internationally as having achieved unparalleled success. Cuba, for example, was credited with practically eliminating illiteracy within a single year. Similarly, in Nicaragua, literacy brigades in the department with the highest rate of illiteracy (Río San Juan) reduced illiteracy from 96 percent in 1979 to 3.7 percent in 1987. Not all literacy campaigns have been associated with revolutionary governments, however. Once illiteracy was seen as an obstacle to economic development, numerous campaigns were begun in the 1960s and 1970s, including those in Argentina, Bolivia, Brazil, Colombia, Chile, Ecuador, El Salvador, Honduras, Jamaica, Mexico, Peru, the Dominican Republic, and Venezuela.

Literacy education in Latin America received additional impetus at the Regional Conference of Ministers of Education (1979). From this conference came the Major Project of Education, an ambitious twenty-year plan organized and administered by UNESCO to overcome the region's educational problems. This region-wide project pledged by 1999 to ensure universal access to schooling, eliminate illiteracy, expand educational opportunities for adults, and improve the quality of education at all levels. Unfortunately, the economic recession of the 1980s adversely affected progress toward these goals, and illiteracy remained a serious problem into the 1990s, especially among the traditionally underserved groups. On the eve of the United Nations National Literacy Year (1990), there were still an estimated 44 million illiterates in Latin America (virtually unchanged from 1970, at 44.4 million, and 1980, at 44.3 million).

Most of the literacy campaigns mentioned appear to have concentrated on imparting an ability to read and write a simple message. This definition, while helping boost claims of success, does not consider the uses to which literacy is put. Those who argue for *functional literacy* define it as a person's capacity to make decisions concerning his or her economic, civic, political, and day-to-day life. In fact, enabling people to enjoy meaningful and active participation in all areas of national life constitutes the greatest challenge to literacy campaigns in Latin America—the challenge of ensuring that people will retain and use their newly acquired literacy skills.

Literacy recidivism—the relapse to illiteracy—is widespread and serious in Latin America and threatens to undermine the success of both literacy campaigns and government efforts to universalize primary education. This phenomenon leaves its victims worse off than ever, more destitute and less motivated. Bernard Dumont proffers several recommendations for postliteracy programs that serve to maintain and expand literacy skills, including production of appropriate educational materials (easy-to-read, practical general education books;

rural newspapers and supplements in urban newspapers containing current and practical information and written specifically for the newly literate; entertaining comic books and picture stories; and radio, film, and TV programs), creation of "literary environments" (through, for example, road signs and newspapers), and access to positions of higher responsibility. It is clear that to be successful, future programs must focus on the postliteracy needs of the newly literate.

PAULO FREIRE, *Pedagogy of the Oppressed,* translated by Myra Bergman Ramos (1972); VALERIE MILLER, *Between Struggle and Hope: The Nicaraguan Literacy Crusade* (1985); IRENE CAMPOS CARR, "The Politics of Literacy in Latin America," in *Convergence* 23, no. 2 (1989): 58–68; JOSÉ RIVERO, "Learning for Autonomy," in *International Review of Education* 35, no. 4 (1989): 445–461; W. ROSS WINTEROWD, *The Culture and Politics of Literacy* (1989); JUAN B. ARRIEN, *Nicaragua: Mobilizing the Local Community for Literacy and Post-Literacy* (ERIC Document: ED321043, 1990); BERNARD DUMONT, *Post-Literacy: A Pre-Requisite for Literacy* (ERIC Document: ED321058, 1990); MIGUEL SOLER ROCA, *Literacy in Latin America: Progress, Problems, and Perspectives* (ERIC Document: ED321054, 1990).

EVERETT EGGINTON

See also **Education.**

LITERATURE

Brazil

Along with that of the rest of the New World, Brazilian literature from the Discovery to Independence and beyond was subject to the influences of Portugal and thereby of Europe. To be sure, those of the new environment were very powerful also. The mixture produced new forms of behavior and ways of thinking that became constants in Brazilian spiritual life, with the native elements serving to put new life into the forms brought from Europe.

The medieval period, far more important for Brazil than the Renaissance, provided the metrics of poetry, the popular and courtly lyrics derived from the troubadours, the collections of romances, and the traditional dramatic genres developed by Gil Vicente and the JESUITS and perpetuated in Brazil by Father José de ANCHIETA and others.

Successive waves of enchantment with the New World gave rise to the chauvinistic lyricism of local things and landscapes that has been a constant of Brazilian literature from Indianism to regionalism. If Renaissance metric and poetic forms were unsuccessful in the Brazilian imitators (such as Nuno Marques Pereira) of CAMÕES and Sá de Miranda through the eighteenth century, and the Brazilian sonnet did not reach the heights of those of the Renaissance until the seventeenth century with Gregório de Matos, there were numerous other reflections of the Renaissance in the baroque that almost directly replaced the medieval in Brazil in the seventeenth and eighteenth centuries. As important as Greco-Roman culture was in the work of the Jesuits (notably Anchieta and Father Manuel da NÓBREGA, especially in *autos* staged for the instruction of their catechumens) were local languages and motifs. Many of these elements are to be found also in letters and reports sent home for the edification of the court, as well as in the sermons of Father Antônio VIEIRA.

The expression "colonial literature" defines a certain phase of Brazilian literary history in keeping with the political history of the country. Politically homogeneous, this phase corresponds to the period during which Brazil had colonial status; in literature, however, such was not the case. According to stylistic criteria, applicable to Brazil as well as Europe, "colonial literature" is divided into baroque, rococo, and classical. These styles include all Brazilian poets of that period, regardless of geography or genre. To the baroque belong Gregório de MATOS and Manuel Botelho de OLIVEIRA, and to the rococo, Antônio José da SILVA (the "Jew") and Father Domingos Caldas BARBOSA. As for classicism, it may be divided into "ilustrado," that of the encyclopedia, such as Cláudio Manuel da COSTA, and the sentimental "pre-romantic," such as Father José de Santa Rita DURÃO. Barbosa, a mulatto priest and author of MODINHAS, is a figure typical of colonial Brazil. Although he lived most of his life in Lisbon, his type of lyricism clearly makes him Brazilian. Less classical in some respects were the poets of Minas Gerais, in whose works are found the political, sentimental, and exotic (Brazilian) elements of European pre-romanticism. In the case of Tomás Antônio GONZAGA, the many editions of his *Marília de Dirceu* make clear that, after Camões, Gonzaga is the most read lyric poet in Portuguese. After 1860, however, Brazilians found greater intensity of sentiment in the romantics. The most "Arcadian" of the poets in Minas is Manuel Inácio da Silva Alvarenga, who freely displays his personal feelings despite the stylistic conventions in his work.

Despite the excesses and a certain sterility brought about by the almost exclusive emphasis on imported classical culture, its beneficial discipline and stimulation cannot be denied. In Brazil, a classicist, or neoclassicist, was a disciple of Alfieri, Chénier, and Goethe who combined the style of antiquity and liberal patriotism—a type best represented by José Bonifácio ANDRADA E SILVA.

There are three distinct phases in Brazilian romanticism: the pre-romantic of the eighteenth century; the conservative and religious; and the liberal and revolutionary. In the eighteenth century, colonial Brazil, subject to the classical traditions of Portugal, did not experience more than pale reflections of the exoticism and sentimentalism of pre-romanticism in the poets of the INCONFIDÊNCIA. Pre-romantic authors like Gonçalves de MAGALHÃES returned to classical models. As conservative romanticism declined in Europe, the movement split and became either revolutionary or popular, with the latter using various bourgeois moral and sentimental elements, especially those of French romantic literature, designed to please the public. Although not a romantic, the comedic dramatist Luís Carlos Martins PENA took advantage of the decline of classical theater to put many realistic popular types on the stage.

In Brazil there were two generations of romantic poets. Gonçalves de Magalhães and Antônio Gonçalves DIAS are the principal poets of the first; the second includes Junqueira Freire and Antônio de CASTRO ALVES. Despite chronology, certain writers, notably the great MACHADO DE ASSIS, are far more important for contributions other than their romantic poems. Although Castro Alves is more widely read and admired than Gonçalves Dias, many consider the latter the greatest Brazilian romantic and perhaps the greatest poet of Brazil. He is known for his strength and humanistic culture, and some of his works, Indianist or personal in theme, are perennial favorites. Both poets are more nationalistic than individualistic and, therefore, more popular than the other romantics mentioned here. As for prose writers, some of whom initiated the regionalism later in great vogue, José Martiniano de ALENCAR is the foremost exponent, and his works, *O Guarani, Iracema,* and others, have had great lasting success. These national historical novels assure their creator the same place in the development of Brazilian prose that Gonçalves Dias occupies in poetry and make him as popular as Castro Alves. Although also very romantic in their lyricism and idealism, Alencar's novels of manners point the way to the works of the great Machado de Assis. The foremost liberal political writer who has remained an idol in Brazil is Joaquim NABUCO, an aristocrat and Christian who possessed both human and literary virtues.

Realism developed in the nineteenth century out of romanticism, and, in some instances, blended with another aesthetic style, for example, impressionism (Euclides da CUNHA). The most important development of realism in Brazil was the emergence of regionalism, already found in the romantic Franklin Távora. As usual, foreign influences acted upon local materials to produce something unique.

Despite his obvious imitation of Zolá, Aluísio AZEVEDO remains the leading naturalist novelist; his works rival those of Alencar and Machado de Assis. Corresponding to naturalist prose was Parnassian poetry, among whose chief practitioners in the late nineteenth and early twentieth centuries were Olavo BILAC and Vicente de Carvalho. Those Parnassians who wrote prose, such as Henrique COELHO NETO and Rui BARBOSA, were much more preoccupied with style than were the naturalists. A statesman, jurist, journalist, grammarian, and orator, above all, Barbosa influenced literature more through his cultivated speech than his publications.

Popular elements have played an extraordinary part in Brazilian literature. The common fund of traditions may become the raw materials of literature: religious rituals, archetypical heroes, myths, and symbols. Brazilian lyricism has its roots deep in the oral tradition of the earliest troubadours of the towns and backlands when slaves tried to express their feelings in a new, sometimes hostile environment that stimulated their imaginations. Moreover, Indian and African traditions gave rise to an entire mythology that became incorporated in the popular psychology, symbolizing attitudes and behavior. Particularly significant are the constant preoccupation with the SERTÃO and the myth of the backlander of the Northeast, including the CANGACEIRO (bandit), such as LAMPIÃO, in the setting of the periodic drought. In the South the figure of the GAÚCHO has similar prominence.

Usually heralded as the beginnings of MODERNISM, the MODERN ART WEEK of 1922 in São Paulo was the culmination of a long period of incubation. Author of *Canaan,* a sociological novel of Recife, Graça ARANHA was at first hailed as the leader of modernism. His style, however, is not modernistic, and he, too, like MONTEIRO LOBATO and LIMA BARRETO, must be considered only one of many precursors. Although European in origin, modernism served as a catalyst to the spirit of renewal that had existed in part in reaction to symbolism and Parnassianism from before the turn of the century in Spain, Portugal, and Brazil, as well as other parts of Latin America. In contrast to the "ancients," the "moderns," whether in prose or poetry, share certain characteristics: images and constructions increasingly modeled on daily speech rather than on bombastic oratory, sequences of images based on association rather than logic or cause and effect, emphasis on the usual as opposed to the cosmic, interest in the subconscious, interest in ordinary human beings, and interest in the social order instead of heaven and nature.

Its most productive phase was 1924 to 1930, during which modernists such as Oswaldo de ANDRADE, Cecília Mireiles, and Mário de ANDRADE (not related to Oswaldo) emphasized aesthetic research and creative freedom in poetry and prepared the way for the second phase, more philosophical and religious in its concerns, of Vinícius de MORAIS, Jorge de LIMA, Augusto Frederico Schmidt, and Carlos Drummond de ANDRADE. More glorious than its poetry was the prose of the second phase, featuring Gilberto FREYRE and novelists José LINS DO REGO, Graciliano RAMOS, Jorge AMADO, Rachuel de QUEIRÓS, and Érico VERÍSSIMO. Since 1945, there has been an effort in poetry for greater formal, emotional, and linguistic discipline, and in prose, for new psychological, technical, and linguistic expression such as that in the works of João Guimarães ROSA and Clarice LISPECTOR.

Post–World War II writers, in the third phase of modernism, called attention to the frustration and despair of people attempting to live lives based on materialism. In their relationships with others, pathetic characters reveal the shallowness and inauthenticity of their lives.

433

Readers understand them well, sensing their own terrible burden of inauthenticity. Like the modernists of the second phase, especially the two Andrades in their novels or Cassiano Ricardo and Raul Bopp in poetry, Clarice Lispector's lyrical prose seeks always what is most universally true and human in each individual, Brazilian or otherwise. Although in the late 1950s Western literature began to be influenced by the *roman nouveau*, which stressed the connection between language and objective reality, there seems no direct French influence on Lispector or other Brazilians, for they are less concerned with "objective" descriptions of the material world than with the many possible human responses to concrete reality, sharing an affinity with Nathalie Sarraute, Virginia Woolf, and Albert Camus in the lyrical exploration and discovery of the self. Representative of modernist Brazilian literature of the third phase, the work of Lispector, Rosa, and others fits into a line that is technically innovative yet socially aware. The general belief in literary reform emphasized that language, even more than characters, themes, or social relevance, was the author's main preoccupation.

Despite many links with earlier Brazilian modernism, the literature of the third phase established that Brazilian works could exist on a par with European literary art. Often it did little to re-create "authentic" aspects of national culture or identity, and therefore for a time found scant public acceptance. Nor did many critics feel comfortable praising it. In theme and especially in language it embodied the highest aesthetic purpose of early Brazilian modernism, but the resultant extreme originality made its practitioners "difficult" authors for the average reader until recently.

Much that has been said of Brazilian prose and poetry is true also of Brazilian THEATER, which has come into its own, particularly in this century. Like their colleagues elsewhere, Brazilian dramatists such as Arano Vilar SUASSUNA, Jorge ANDRADE, and Alfredo DIAS GOMES have made use of history and civilization in their writing in various yet similar ways to accomplish their objectives.

SÁBATO MAGALDI, *Panorama do teatro brasileiro* (1962); OTTO MARIA CARPEAUX, *Pequena bibliografia crítica da literatura brasileira* (1964); EMIR RODRÍGUEZ MONEGAL, *Fiction in Several Languages* (1968); AFRÂNIO COUTINHO, *An Introduction to Literature in Brazil*, translated by Gregory Rabassa (1969); NELSON WERNECK SODRÉ, *História da literatura brasileira*, 5th ed. (1969); CLAUDE HULET, *Brazilian Literature*, vols. 1–3 (1974–1975); MALCOLM SILVERMAN, *Moderna ficção brasileira* (1978).

RICHARD A. MAZZARA

See also **Indianismo (Brazil).**

Spanish America

Spanish American literature shares many European literary and cultural patterns and at the same time gives voice to a distinct and different American reality. For the most part, period styles in Spanish American literature correspond to those in Europe (for example, Renaissance, baroque, neoclassicism, romanticism, realism). Vigorous national literatures are in evidence in a number of Spanish American countries (the most notable examples being Mexico, Cuba, Colombia, Peru, Chile, and Argentina), and many first-rank individual writers have achieved international distinction.

TERMINOLOGY AND PERIODIZATION

Well-defined national literatures, it could be argued, make ineffective the use of the more general Spanish American construct that is here being applied. There is a large degree of commonality among the nationals, stemming in large part from the relative constancy of the Spanish language and the numerous similarities in literary movements and period styles. In spite of some legitimate concerns about its usefulness, the Spanish American construct offers a valid framework for literary study and commentary in this diverse area of the world.

An even more complex question is the particular approach to be used in considering the development of a multifaceted literary expression in Spanish America. One could focus, for example, on the various literary genres (i.e., Spanish American poetry, for example, or the Spanish American novel), on various aesthetic or thematic patterns that transcend national boundaries (i.e., the literary conceptualization of Spanish America, the regionalist "novel of the land," or social and political themes in literature), or on a series of major figures who exemplify the peculiar mix of European and local elements in Spanish America. The most productive design for a general discussion, however, is a combination of several of those approaches, in which political period, epoch style, and genre development find expression in a complex literary interweaving that has been in process for nearly five centuries. The principal periods can be divided into pre-Hispanic literature; the colonial period (extending from 1520 to 1820 and including accounts of exploration, conquest, and consolidation during the sixteenth century; baroque literature during the seventeenth century; and neoclassicism during the eighteenth and early nineteenth centuries); independence and the development of national literatures from 1820 until 1915 (including romanticism, realism-naturalism, and modernism); and the development of modern literature after 1915.

PRE-HISPANIC LITERATURE

Any consideration of Spanish American literature should take as a point of departure the cultural richness of the well-developed pre-Columbian civilizations in the Western Hemisphere, a richness that is expressed in languages other than Spanish. The principal indigenous cultures encountered in the European conquest were those of the NAHUATL-speaking AZTECS in central Mexico, the MAYAS of southern Mexico and Guatemala, and the Quechua speakers of the Andean Incan empire.

434

Other cultures were those of the OTOMÍ, the ZAPOTECS, the MIXTECS, and the TARASCANS in Mexico; the Cunas in Central America; Arawaks and CARIBS in the Caribbean; and the Chibchas, AYMARAS, GUARANI, and ARAUCANIANS in South America. At the time of the Conquest all those cultures enjoyed a more or less developed literary expression, most often in orally transmitted form, although in some areas written transcription was in use.

In the Nahuatl-speaking area of Mexico a very elaborate historical and artistic expression was recorded and transmitted in both oral form and by means of pictographic codices inscribed on such materials as *amate* paper or leather. A few of these documents survived the Conquest, but most of our present-day information comes from the efforts of certain Spanish clerics, in particular Fray Bernardino de SAHAGÚN, whose informants transcribed Nahuatl materials using the Latin alphabet. Poetry (religious, war-making, epic, lyric, dramatic) is the most significant literary genre, showing a notable richness of imagery and awareness of form. Several individual poets can be identified, foremost among them NEZAHUALCÓYOTL (king of Tetzcoco, 1402–1472).

The Maya culture in Yucatán and Central America showed a much greater variation in linguistic patterns than the Nahuatl but had a similar combination of oral and written traditions. An ideographic/phonetic system was developed in the lowlands, and various kinds of historical and literary materials were recorded on paper codices and engraved on stone. As in central Mexico, however, the most important collections of literary materials are those transcribed after the Conquest using the Latin alphabet. The most famous of these texts, for example, is the POPOL VUH, or the *Libro del Consejo*, a narrative and mythological text transcribed from Guatemalan K'ICHE'-Maya and translated into Spanish in the eighteenth century by Fray Francisco XIMÉNEZ. The various mytho-historical texts known as the CHILAM BALAM books were transcribed from Yucatecan Maya; the best known, the *Chilam Balam de Chumayel*, was found and published in the mid-nineteenth century. In those same years the K'iche' tragedy *Rabinal Achí* was also transcribed from an ancient theatrical tradition.

The Quechua-speaking cultural area in the Andes (the Inca Empire) also had a well-developed literary tradition, but in contrast to the high cultures to the north it lacked a formalized writing system. The cords, knots, and colors of the mnemonic *quipu* apparently aided in the transmission of statistical, historical, mythical, and even literary information, but the system was essentially different from the pictographs or the ideographs used in the other centers. Once again, the principal sources of cultural and literary information in this area are the post-Conquest chronicles, in particular Cristóbal de Molina's *Relación de las fábulas y ritos de los Inkas* (1575), Juan Santacruz Pachacuti's *Relación de antigüedades de este Reyno del Perú* (1598), and El Inca GARCILASO DE LA VEGA's *Comentarios reales* (1609). As in the Nahuatl area, poetry was the preferred literary genre, and anonymous creators used a number of traditional forms to express their ideas (i.e., the sacred or heroic *jailli*, the sentimental *arawi*, the musical *wayñu*, or the funereal *wanka*). The Quechua-language *Ollantay*, an anonymous dramatic text discovered in the early years of the nineteenth century, is generally considered to be of pre-Hispanic origin.

EXPLORATION, CONQUEST, AND CONSOLIDATION (1520–1620)
An essentially Hispanic culture was established and refined in the New World, a culture built around the linguistic, social, and religious values imposed by a European power structure that attempted to repress all vestiges of indigenous cultures. That very process of colonization and *mestizaje* (racial mixing), which brought together in differing proportions the European settlers, the aboriginal Indian populations, and imported African slaves, is the hallmark of what has come to be seen as a distinctive Spanish American society. Literature was an essential component of that developing Hispanic society. The New World attracted the attention and, on occasion, the presence of distinguished Spanish writers, among them Gutierre de Cetina, Tirso de Molina, and Mateo Alemán. Such figures, together with the clerics and other educated persons who were a part of the early colonization efforts, were very much influenced by the humanistic Renaissance style then current in Europe, a relationship that ensured that most of the early literature in Spanish America followed that same Renaissance model.

The most important literary genres from this early period are the *crónica* (the expository prose texts of exploration and conquest, including letters, accounts, histories, etc.) and epic poetry. The earliest of the chroniclers are Christopher COLUMBUS (1451–1506), whose diary and letters (perhaps the best known of which is a letter dated 1493 to Luis de Santangel, a secretary to FERDINAND and ISABELLA) describe and justify his discoveries in the New World, and Hernán CORTÉS (1485–1547), who recounted his exploits in the conquest of Mexico to King CHARLES I in his *Cartas de relación* (1519–1536). More compelling as a chronicle of conquest is the account of one of Cortés's foot soldiers, Bernal DÍAZ DEL CASTILLO (ca. 1495–1584), whose *Historia verdadera de la conquista de la Nueva España* (finished in 1568 but not published until 1632) presents the most vivid and readable account of the conquest of Mexico. The most famous chronicler of the period is probably Fray Bartolomé de LAS CASAS (1474–1566), whose polemical treatise *Brevísima relación de la destrucción de las Indias* (1552) was translated rapidly into a number of other languages and contributed to the so-called BLACK LEGEND of the Spanish conquest. Most of Las Casas's other voluminous writings were not published until well after his death.

The first major chronicler born in the New World was El Inca GARCILASO DE LA VEGA (1539–1616), the MESTIZO son of an INCA princess and a Spanish captain. Following his early years in Cuzco, the Inca Garcilaso completed his education and spent the remainder of his life in Spain. His most important works, *La Florida del Inca* (1605) and the *Comentarios reales* (1609, 1617), reflect a unique dual culture. On the one hand, El Inca is clearly a Hispanic writer, and, on the other, his command of Quechua and his access to primary sources through personal family experience give unusual authority to his historical commentary.

The most important epic poet was Alonso de ERCILLA Y ZÚÑIGA (1533–1594), who as a young Spanish officer took part in the wars of conquest against the Araucanians in Chile. His personal experiences were the basis for *La araucana* (published in three parts in 1569, 1578, and 1589), a long narrative poem that in many ways can be seen as a rhymed chronicle of the Spanish conquest of Chile. At the same time Ercilla's poem is probably the best example of the Renaissance epic (on the model of Ariosto and others) in Spanish literature. *Arauco domado* (1596), by Pedro de OÑA (1570–ca. 1643), follows in the epic tradition set by Ercilla. Bernardo de BALBUENA (ca. 1562–1627) wrote *Grandeza mexicana* (1604), a descriptive epic in terza rima on Mexico City, as well as the heroic epic *El Bernardo, o Victoria de Roncesvalles* (1624). *La Cristíada* (1611) was a religious epic on the Passion of Christ written by Diego de Hojeda (ca. 1571–1615).

BAROQUE (1620–1750)
By the mid-seventeenth century a solid Hispanic social structure had been consolidated in the Spanish American colonies, with the viceregal capitals of Mexico City and Lima as the two political and cultural centers. The relative turbulence of the Conquest had long since passed, and colonial life was carried forward with a sense of stability and coherence, most especially in the upper levels of society. Affluence and conspicuous luxury were much in evidence, and the often exaggerated forms of the European baroque were used as models in colonial art, architecture, music, and literature.

The first major literary figure in this period was Juan RUIZ DE ALARCÓN Y MENDOZA (1580–1639), a poet and playwright whom Alfonso Reyes has called the "first universal Mexican." Alarcón spent most of his life in Spain, where he wrote and saw produced a number of first-rank dramas, among them *La verdad sospechosa* and *Las paredes oyen* (both published with other plays in 1628 and 1634). The central figure of the baroque period, however, was Sor JUANA INÉS DE LA CRUZ (ca. 1648–1695), an extraordinary Mexican writer and intellectual whose works place her in the first rank of Spanish American authors from all periods. Her literary work is varied and extensive, including a number of dramas of different types, several significant prose texts, and a large body of poetry. Her best-known plays are *Los empeños de una casa* (1683) and *El Divino Narciso* (1690); her prose works include *Carta athenagórica* (1690), a learned commentary on a sermon by Antonio VIEIRA, and *Respuesta a Sor Filotea de la Cruz* (1691), an unusual autobiographical justification of her intellectual life. The best of her poetry is to be found, perhaps, in a series of masterly love sonnets and in *Primero sueño* (1692).

The acerbic verses of the satirical Peruvian poet Juan del Valle y CAVIEDES (ca. 1652–ca. 1697) circulated widely in manuscript outside his local area (for example, Sor Juana wrote from her convent in Mexico requesting copies of his texts), but his *Diente del Parnaso* was not published definitively until 1873. Carlos de SIGÜENZA Y GÓNGORA (1645–1700), a leading Mexican intellectual and scientist, produced a number of literary works, among them a gongorine poem entitled *Primeravera indiana* (1668) and *Los infortunios de Alonso Ramírez* (1690), a first-person narrative chronicle. Another leading figure is the Peruvian intellectual Pedro de Peralta BARNUEVO Y ROCHA (1663–1743), whose accomplishments as a scientist, historian, and creative writer place him in the transition between the seventeenth-century baroque and the enlightenment of the eighteenth century. His best-known work is a long epic poem on Pizarro entitled *Lima fundada* (1732).

ENLIGHTENMENT AND NEOCLASSICISM (1750–1820)
The eighteenth century in the Spanish colonies was a period of further cultural and political development in which the liberal ideas of the French ENLIGHTENMENT provided a kind of ideological framework. By the middle of the century, the extremes of the baroque style in art and literature had largely been replaced by the more playful lightness of the rococo, which in turn soon gave way to more controlled neoclassical patterns. In politics the impact of the American and French revolutions was widely felt; by the end of the century the now rather frail colonial institutions seemed ripe for change, which swept through the colonies in the early decades of the nineteenth century.

The most notable representative of Enlightenment ideas in Spanish America was Andrés BELLO (1781–1865), who had a distinguished career as a public figure, educator, scholar, and writer in both Venezuela and Chile. Among his best-known works are the neoclassical *silvas* "Alocución a la poesía" (1823) and "La agricultura de la zona tórrida" (1826). The Ecuadorian José Joaquín de OLMEDO expressed in heroic style several of the battles in the struggle for independence. The most striking is *La victoria de Junín, canto a Bolívar* (1825), a long *silva* that celebrates Bolívar's 1824 victory with grandiose images. José María HEREDIA Y HEREDIA (1803–1839) is a transitional figure between the waning of neoclassicism and a developing romanticism. Born in Cuba, he spent most of his life in exile, a tension visible in many of his poetic works. His two best-known texts are neoclassical odes. "En el Teocalli de Cholula" (1820) uses the Mexican pyramid for a reflection on tyranny and the passage of time; "Niágara" (1824) describes the famous cataract in precise terms but at the same time is an impassioned comment on exile.

Two major prose writers of this period should be mentioned. Under the pseudonym "Concolorcorvo," Alonso Carrió de la Vandera (ca. 1715–1783) wrote *El lazarillo de ciegos caminantes* (1773), a first-person picaresque description of a journey from Buenos Aires and Montevideo to Lima. José Joaquín FERNÁNDEZ DE LIZARDI (1776–1827), known also by his pseudonym "El Pensador Mexicano," was strongly influenced by Enlightenment ideas and by a desire for social reform. His most famous work is *El Periquillo Sarniento* (1816), a four-volume picaresque novel sharply critical of social conditions in prerevolutionary Mexico and often considered to be the first Spanish American novel. The best dramatist of this period was Manuel Eduardo de GOROSTIZA (1789–1851), whose work was identified both with Mexico and Spain. He wrote a number of plays and adaptations, the best known of which is *Contigo pan y cebolla* (1833).

ROMANTICISM (1820–1880)

The coming of independence in Spanish America initiated an extended period of national definition. In the postconflict decades many of the developing national entities were either anarchical or dominated by dictatorial strongmen, and it was not until well into the latter part of the nineteenth century that the now independent Spanish American nations were able even to glimpse the stability and democracy envisioned by the liberators.

Literary expression during these decades was centrally influenced by romanticism, which placed itself in opposition to the rational streams of neoclassicism and proposed to give a dominant place to strong human emotions. In keeping with a culture in the process of consolidation, the Spanish American romantics differed in many ways from the Europeans. They described a distinct landscape, for example, with regional languages and customs and with the Indian and the GAUCHO as romantic heroes. They expressed as well the ongoing Spanish American conflict between rural and urban values or, as Domingo Faustino SARMIENTO (1811–1886) expressed it, between "civilization" and "barbarism."

After extended residence in Paris the Argentine Esteban ECHEVERRÍA (1805–1851) became one of the principal standard-bearers for romanticism in Spanish America. He found himself in conflict with the despotic Juan Manuel de ROSAS, and his literary associations and publications are colored by that tension. His best-known poem is "La cautiva" (1837), a work that applies European aesthetic ideas to an Argentine reality. He is most remembered, however, for his vivid short story "El matadero," a brutal denunciation of Rosas probably written in 1839 but not published until 1871.

Several romantic poets should be mentioned here. The most memorable works of the Cuban mulatto poet "Plácido" (Gabriel de la Concepción VALDÉS, 1809–1844) are the ballad "Jicoténcal" and the ode "Plegaria a Dios." Gertrudis GÓMEZ DE AVELLANEDA (1814–1873)

was born in Cuba but spent much of her life in Spain, and in many ways was the prototypical anguished romantic. She wrote poetry (including such emotional texts as "Al partir" and "Al destino"), theatrical works, legends, and novels. Perhaps her most remembered work is the antislavery novel *Sab* (1841). Gaucho poetry in the River Plate region developed as a significant late romantic expression. Among the foremost poets are two Argentines: Estanislao del CAMPO (1834–1880), whose comic poem *Fausto* (1866) makes a unique contribution to this subgenre, and José HERNÁNDEZ (1834–1886), whose two-volume mock epic *Martín Fierro* (*El gaucho Martín Fierro*, 1872; *La vuelta de Martín Fierro*, 1879) has become Argentina's national work. In Hernández's poem the gaucho is no longer comic or folkloric, but in the person of Fierro is rather a tragic figure who must deal with the contradictory demands of modern society. The Uruguayan poet Juan ZORRILLA DE SAN MARTÍN (1855–1931) wrote an extensive lyrical epic entitled *Tabaré* (1888), whose indigenous theme and musical language represent a point of transition between romanticism and modernism.

The prose writing of the period was varied and included both narrative and expository forms. Sarmiento, a central Argentine figure of romanticism, wrote the classic prose work *Civilización i barbarie: La vida de Juan Facundo Quiroga* (1845), generally known simply as *Facundo*, which is neither novel nor history; rather, it is a dialectical attempt to capture the essence of an area under development. The novel as such was carried forward by such writers as the Argentine José MÁRMOL (1817–1871), whose *Amalia* (1851) was the best political novel of the period; by the Colombian Jorge ISAACS (1837–1895), whose *María* (1867) was the prototypical sentimental romantic novel; and by the Chilean Alberto BLEST GANA (1830–1920), whose *Martín Rivas* (1862) used realistic detail to depict the society of its time. The Peruvian Ricardo PALMA (1833–1919) occupies a unique place among late romantic prose writers. His *Tradiciones peruanas*, published in several series beginning in 1872, are short narrative pieces that allow Palma to make effective use of an encyclopedic knowledge of the colonial period and an unusual verbal inventiveness. The major essayist of the period was Juan MONTALVO (1832–1889) of Ecuador, whose masterwork *Siete tratados* (1882) placed him among the best prose writers in the Spanish language. Also important is *Moral social* (1888), by the Puerto Rican Eugenio María de HOSTOS Y BONILLA (1839–1903).

REALISM-NATURALISM (1880–1915)

By 1880 the majority of the Spanish American nations had enjoyed some fifty years of political independence, and from that point through the turn of the century they began to enjoy a modicum of stability and economic prosperity. Reflecting a concern for renovation, the literary expression of these decades can best be seen in two distinct and parallel dimensions: first, the development of prose fiction and other associated genres influenced by realism and naturalism and, second, the studied cultivation of poetic discourse in what came to be designated as MODERNISM.

The beginnings of realism in Spanish America can be traced to Blest Gana and other writers of the preceding period. During the decades around the turn of the century, however, there are several very significant novelists and short-story writers who bring this focus to fuller development. First among them might be the Peruvian Clorinda MATTO DE TURNER (1852–1909), whose *Aves sin nido* (1889) is considered to be the first true *indigenista* novel in Spanish America. Tomás CARRASQUILLA (1858–1940) of Colombia developed an engaging regionalist view of his own native area, in which popular language and situations are used effectively. His best works are *Frutos de mi tierra* (1896) and *En la diestra de Dios Padre* (1903). Roberto J. Payró (1867–1928) presented a picaresque view of Argentine life in *El casamiento de Laucha* (1906) and *Pago Chico* (1908).

Naturalism, especially the work of Émile Zola, was a determining influence for several Spanish American writers. Carlos Reyles (1868–1938) of Uruguay, for example, wrote naturalistic novels, among them *Beba* (1894) and *La raza de Caín* (1900). Another Uruguayan, Javier de Viana (1868–1926), used the gaucho setting for a number of collections of naturalistic short stories, such as *Campo* (1896), *Leña seca* (1911), and *Yuyos* (1912). The Chilean coal mines, factories, and farms provided settings for the short stories of Baldomero Lillo (1867–1923), who was clearly influenced by Zola. *Sub terra* (1904), a very successful collection protesting mine conditions, contains such well-known texts as "El chiflón del diablo" and "La compuerta número 12." *Sob sole* (1907), a second collection dealing with the problems of peasants and other workers, is not of the same quality.

It is appropriate to consider under realism the works of the Uruguayan playwright Florencio SÁNCHEZ (1875–1910), who is the first major figure of the modern Spanish American theater. His principal works—*M'hijo el dotor* (1903), *La gringa* (1904), and *Barranca abajo* (1905)—represent in realistic terms the tension between rural and urban values.

MODERNISM (1880–1915)

The period of relative political stability after 1880 favored the parallel development of what is now known as modernism, which extended over some three or four decades, well into the new century, and gave rise to major literary centers (Mexico City and Buenos Aires, among others) and to significant literary journals (such as *Revista Azul* and *Revista Moderna*). Modernist writers, central among them such figures as José MARTÍ, Rubén DARÍO, and Leopoldo LUGONES, were motivated by the desire to revitalize what they saw as antiquated literary discourse in Spanish, and, using the French Parnassian and symbolist poets as models, they strove for musical-

ity and perfection of form in their works. Figurative language was rich and sensorial, with preference given to chromatic imagery and elegant symbolism (i.e., the color blue or the graceful figure of the swan). Themes were exotic or introspective, and a profound disenchantment with mediocre surroundings led many modernists to take refuge in invented "ivory tower" worlds.

The multifaceted literary work of the Cuban patriot José Martí (1853–1895) is at the center of a first group of modernist writers. Martí's political activities forced him to spend much of his life in exile, and his sizable literary production is closely related to his life-long profession as a journalist. His prose writings (essays, *crónicas*, short stories, and *Amistad funesta*, a novel published in 1885) represent an important contribution to the renovation of prose style during the modernist years. His books of poetry are, however, his most significant literary contribution: *Ismaelillo* (1882), short poems written to his absent son, and *Versos sencillos* (1891), a collection of musical eight-syllable poems containing some of Martí's best-known lines. Two other collections, *Versos libres* (written around 1882 but not published until 1913) and *Flores del destierro* (written between 1882 and 1891 but not published until 1933), appeared after Martí's death. Other early modernists were the Mexican Manuel GUTIÉRREZ NÁJERA (1859–1895), the Cuban Julián DEL CASAL (1863–1893), and the Colombian José Asunción SILVA (1865–1896). Nájera, a recognized journalist, founded the well-known modernist journal *Revista Azul*. His musical and strikingly chromatic verses appeared largely in literary journals and were collected after his death as *Poesías* (1896). Casal's sensorial poetry, particularly that published in *Nieve* (1892) and *Bustos y rimas* (1893), expressed in a most poignant way modernism's pessimistic dimension. Silva's poems also appeared first in literary journals, and only after he committed suicide were they finally collected and published as *Poesías* (1908). Silva's "Nocturno" is his best-known single work; its sensuality and novel use of a four-syllable rhythmic foot earned the poet a considerable international reputation.

Rubén Darío (pseudonym of Nicaraguan writer Félix Rubén García Sarmiento, 1867–1916) is the central figure of a second grouping, and indeed can be seen as *the* quintessential modernist presence. He left his native Central America as a young man and with varied diplomatic and journalistic assignments spent many years in South America and Europe. His extensive literary production, which includes short stories, essays, and travel commentaries, as well as a number of volumes of poetry, reflects a varied international life. Darío's *Azul . . .* (1888; 2d ed., 1890) combines prose and poetry and is often cited as a key early modernist work. More innovative than his poems, are Darío's lyrical short stories (e.g., "El pájaro azul"), especially in the 1888 edition. The *Prosas profanas y otros poemas* (1896; 2d ed., 1901) is the high point in Darío's luxuriant and aristocratic modernist art. The third work is *Cantos de vida y esperanza. Los cisnes y otros poemas* (1905), perhaps Darío's best single poetry collection and one that represents at the same time a period of maturity in modernist development. Darío's later collections, *El canto errante* (1907) and *Poema del otoño y otros poemas* (1910), continue this same introspection but do not reach the level attained in *Cantos de vida y esperanza.*

Other poets who with Rubén Darío contributed to the second modernist group include the Bolivian Ricardo Jaimes Freyre (1868–1933), the Mexican Amado NERVO (1870–1919), the Colombian Guillermo VALENCIA (1873–1943), the Peruvian José Santos CHOCANO (1875–1934), and the Uruguayan Julio HERRERA Y REISSIG (1875–1910). In his unusual work *Castalia bárbara* (1899), Jaimes Freyre made novel use of Nordic myths and imagery and also experimented with metrical form. Nervo's voluminous work revolves around religious and existential concerns, in particular the anguish resulting from the loss of a loved person. In form, his poetry moved from the modernist patterns of *Perlas negras* and *Místicas*, both published in 1898, toward the spare presentations of *Serenidad* (1914) and *Elevación* (1917). Valencia's *Ritos* (1899) shows modernist elegance and precision in its attention to metrical form and chromatic imagery. Chocano's principal work, and the one most closely aligned with modernism, is the torrential *Alma América; poemas indo-españoles* (1906). One of the most fascinating and difficult figures of the entire movement, Herrera y Reissig represented in many ways the epitome of a bohemian and extravagant modernist life-style, and his published poetic work, collected the year of his death in a volume entitled *Los peregrinos de piedra* (1909), has at its center a most demanding metaphorical structuring.

The central figure in a third modernist group is the Argentine Leopoldo LUGONES (1874–1938), whose some thirty-five published volumes include poetry, prose fiction, political commentary, historical treatises, and literary and cultural studies. His very sizable contributions to prose fiction came with such titles as *La guerra gaucha* (1905) and *Las fuerzas extrañas* (1906); similar contributions to history, culture, and literary studies are in *Historia de Sarmiento* (1911) and *El payador* (1916). His major poetic works are *Las montañas del oro* (1897), a collection of rather audacious texts using an innovative prose-like form; *Los crepúsculos del jardín* (1905), a volume of carefully worked texts in modernist style; *Lunario sentimental* (1909), a curious mix of poetry, fiction, and dramatic pieces using the lunar theme; and *Las horas doradas* (1922), simple contemplations on the beauties of the natural world.

Other poets to be considered in this third group are the Mexicans Enrique GONZÁLEZ MARTÍNEZ (1871–1952) and José Juan TABLADA (1871–1945), and the Peruvian José María EGUREN (1874–1942). The early works of González Martínez are very much within the modernist poetic, but his sonnet "Tuércele el cuello al cisne" (in

Los senderos ocultos, 1911) appeared to call for a violent end to Darío's modernism. Tablada published a collection of modernist verses under the title of *El florilegio* (1899), and then, in books like *Li-Pó y otros poemas (poemas ideográficos)* (1920), turned to experimentations with miniature Oriental forms and visual poetry. Eguren's delicately chromatic verses, generally in short lines and also with figures in miniature, were collected in *Simbólicas* (1911) and *La canción de las figuras* (1916).

Three other modernist prose writers deserve mention. The most important novel by Venezuelan Manuel Díaz Rodríguez (1871–1927) is *Sangre patricia* (1902), a poetic work that uses a shifting point of view to examine the internal dimensions of its central character. The best modernist narrative work, however, is *La gloria de don Ramiro* (1908), a historical novel written by the Argentine Enrique LARRETA (1873–1961) in which sixteenth-century Ávila, Spain, is brought to life in a veritable symphony of places, persons, and sensorial impressions. The principal essayist of modernism is the Uruguayan academic José Enrique RODÓ (1872–1917), whose most famous work is *Ariel* (1900), a philosophical essay in six chapters that uses Shakespeare's character to speak in support of morality and beauty and to inveigh against materialism, especially that of the United States. *Motivos de Proteo* (1909) is a fragmented gathering of parables, exhortations, confessions, and allegories that together illustrate Rodó's working out of a kind of spiritual autobiography.

Connecting the final stages of modernism and the beginning experimentation of the vanguardists is a transitional grouping, to which the Mexican Ramón López Velarde (1888–1921) clearly belongs. His first two poetry collections, *La sangre devota* (1916) and *Zozobra* (1919), are largely in the modernist tradition; his later work, published posthumously as *El son del corazón* (1932), anticipates a number of the stylistic complexities of the vanguardists. Another major figure is Chilean Gabriela MISTRAL (pseudonym of Lucila Godoy Alcayaga, 1889–1957), who in 1945 was the first Spanish American to be awarded the Nobel Prize for literature. Her principal collections—*Desolación* (1922), *Tala* (1938), and *Lagar* (1954)—reveal a poetic discourse that evolved away from the decorative aspects of modernism toward an impassioned and anguished simplicity. Also a part of this group are the Uruguayan Juana de IBARBOUROU (1895–1979), whose sensual verses appeared in *Las lenguas de diamante* (1919) and *Raíz salvaje* (1922); the Uruguayan Delmira AGUSTINI (1886–1914), whose best-known work is *Los cálices vacíos* (1913); and the Argentine Alfonsina STORNI (1892–1938), whose acid feminist verses are best represented in *Ocre* (1925).

Several essayists belong to this transitional group. The Mexican Alfonso REYES (1889–1959), a talented poet as well as a novelist and an essayist, produced in *Visión de Anáhuac* (1917) a major contribution to the consolidation of a Spanish American cultural unity. A fellow Mexican, José VASCONCELOS (1882–1959), commented on the cultural role of the mestizo and the Indian in *La raza cósmica* (1925), and the Peruvian José Carlos Mariátegui (1894–1930) dealt with similar concerns in his *Siete ensayos de interpretación sobre de la realidad peruana* (1928). The writings of Pedro HENRÍQUEZ UREÑA (1884–1946) of the Dominican Republic displayed wide interest in language, culture, and literature; one of his best works is *Seis ensayos en busca de nuestra expresión* (1928).

VANGUARDISM (1915–1945)

Three major political events during the second decade of the twentieth century introduced a period of rejection of established values: the Mexican Revolution (1910–1917), World War I (1914–1918), and the Russian Revolution (1917). As was the case in the preceding period, Spanish American literary expression in the two or three decades following 1920 once again developed essentially in two distinct but parallel dimensions: the intense and multiform experimentations in poetic discourse now generally designated as vanguardism and the equally significant exploration of Latin American problems and values in regional *criollista* prose fiction.

Vanguardism was strongly influenced by such experimental European movements as cubism, futurism, and surrealism, but in its Latin American setting vanguardism was primarily a rejection of the modernist aesthetic. Truth and beauty were no longer to be found in musicality, order, and careful delineation; the destruction of such "antiquated" concepts was necessary in order to fashion altered poetic worlds envisioned by the "new" poet or those to be found in the disordered flow of the subconscious. Free verse took the place of metered form; nonregular structures, hermetic imagery, and visual typographic experimentations became hallmarks of vanguardist poetic discourse.

The most important vanguardist figure is without doubt the Chilean Vicente HUIDOBRO (1893–1948), who spent significant periods of his life in France and Spain and whose work includes both the elaboration of a theory he called "creationism" and a very substantial poetic praxis. At the center of Huidobro's theory are the concepts that the "new" poet has divine powers in his small realm (Huidobro averred in one of his most famous lines that the poet is a minor god) and that imitative conventionalities should not interfere with those powers. Huidobro's poetry was published in both Spanish and French, with such titles as *El espejo de agua* (1916), *Horizon carré* (1917), and *Poemas árticos* (1918). His masterwork is *Altazor, o el viaje en paracaídas* (1931), whose descending imagery is at once the culmination and the destruction of the poet's theoretical ideas.

A second major figure, though one not so centrally identified with the theoretical issues of vanguardism, is the Peruvian César VALLEJO (1892–1938). Vallejo also spent significant portions of his life in Europe, principally in France and Spain, and in his essays and prose fiction took a committed political stance. His best works, however, are still his three volumes of poetry. In *Los heraldos negros* (1918), *Trilce* (1922), and *Poemas humanos* (1939), Vallejo experiments with structure and figurative language but at the same time communicates a profound and tragic vision of human existence. Other important figures in a first vanguardist group are the Argentines Oliverio Girondo (1891–1967) and Jorge Luis BORGES (1899–1986), and the Cuban Mariano BRULL (1891–1956). Girondo and Borges made major contributions to the development of ultraism in Argentina, the first with his collections *Veinte poemas para ser leídos en el tranvía* (1922) and *Calcomanías* (1925), and the second with *Fervor de Buenos Aires* (1923), *Luna de enfrente* (1925), and *Cuaderno de San Martín* (1929). Brull's playful sonorities are best represented in *Poemas en menguante* (1928).

A second vanguardist group followed the central figure of the Chilean Pablo NERUDA (pseudonym of Neftalí Ricardo Reyes Basoalto, 1904–1973), whose voluminous poetic production extended over almost five decades and earned him the Nobel Prize for literature in 1971. In contrast to Huidobro, Neruda paid little attention to theoretical concerns, preferring to express in poetry the ever-changing vision of the world around him. His first major work, *Veinte poemas de amor y una canción desesperada* (1924), over the years became Neruda's most popular single book. His most vanguardist verses are *Tentativa del hombre infinito* (1926) and *Residencia en la tierra* (1933, 1935), the second reflecting Neruda's often anguished consular service in the Orient. Beginning with *España en el corazón* (1937), an incandescent protest volume on the Spanish Civil War, a political and openly Marxist commitment became increasingly evident in Neruda's poetry: *Tercera residencia* (1947); *Canto general* (1950), which includes the well-known "Alturas de Macchu Picchu" (the Incan fortress city); *Canción de gesta* (1960), a celebration of the Cuban Revolution; and *Incitación al Nixonicidio* (1973), a scathing denunciation of the United States. Neruda also developed a spare, columnar poetic form to represent the small details of his surrounding world. These novel texts appeared first in *Odas elementales* (1954) and were continued in several additional collections during the 1950s.

Other important figures in the second vanguardist group are the Puerto Rican Luis PALÉS MATOS (1898–1959), the Cuban Nicolás GUILLÉN (1902), and the Mexicans José GOROSTIZA (1901–1973) and Xavier VILLAURRUTIA (1903–1950). Palés Matos and Guillén are the most important representatives of the vanguardist experimentation in Afro-Antillian forms and rhythms, Palés with *Tuntún de pasa y grifería* (1937) and Guillén with *Motivos de son* (1930), *Sóngoro consongo* (1931), and *West Indies, Ltd.* (1934). Gorostiza and Villaurrutia combined complexities of language and death imagery with carefully worked poetic form; Gorostiza's *Muerte sin fin* (1939) is one of the great twentieth-century poems in the

Spanish language, and Villaurrutia's major collection is *Nostalgia de la muerte* (1938).

THE REGIONAL NOVEL AND SHORT STORY (1915–1945)
Prose fiction during these decades showed a pattern of development parallel to but distinct from that of the experimental poetic forms of vanguardism. The jungles, the plains, the cities, and the conflicts of modernization became the settings for a number of compelling works, as first-rank writers established an international readership and set the stage for the Boom period in the latter half of the century.

The Mexican Revolution of 1910 provided the motivation for one of the most significant examples of a regionally specific prose fiction. The central figure is Mariano AZUELA (1873–1952), a novelist and medical doctor who himself fought in the Revolution. His most famous novel, and the prototypical novel of the Revolution, is *Los de abajo* (1915), in which Azuela depicts with graphic detail and a cyclic structure the disorderly development of the conflict. Other significant novels by Azuela are *La Malhora* (1923) and *La luciérnaga* (1932). The most famous work of Martín Luis GUZMÁN (1887–1976) is *El águila y la serpiente* (1928), not really a novel but rather a representation of important personalities and events during the revolutionary years. Once again, the author was himself a participant, and his personal view of such figures as Carranza and Villa make his account an especially compelling one. José Rubén ROMERO (1890–1952) wrote several novels on the Revolution, among them *Mi caballo, mi perro y mi rifle* (1936), but he is probably best known for his salacious depiction of Mexican life contained in the picaresque *La vida inútil de Pito Pérez* (1938).

Both the Venezuelan Rómulo GALLEGOS (1884–1969) and the Colombian José Eustasio RIVERA (1888–1928) situate their novels in northern South America. Gallegos's masterwork, *Doña Bárbara* (1929), is set on the Venezuelan *llano*, and depicts through a strong female central character the struggle between the same antagonistic forces of civilization and barbarity that Sarmiento had earlier studied. Rivera chose the rubber-growing region of the Colombian jungle as the setting for *La vorágine* (1924). His protagonist is ultimately swallowed up by the "green hell" of the jungle, and Rivera's vivid first-person descriptions remain the most significant dimension of the novel.

Social protest is a central concern of the indigenist novel, particularly that set in the Andean region. In his *Raza de bronce* (1919) the Bolivian Alcides ARGUEDAS (1879–1946) represented the unresolved conflict between Indians and landowners, though more in a spirit of submission than protest. The protest is intensified in the works of the Ecuadorian Jorge ICAZA (1906–1978), whose *Huasipungo* (1934) is probably the most representative indigenist novel. The Indians mount a disorganized and unsuccessful rebellion against the despotic landholders who want to remove them from their small parcels of land (*huasipungos*). The most famous work of the Peruvian Ciro Alegría (1909–1967) is *El mundo es ancho y ajeno* (1941), a novel that once again deals with the dispossession of Indian community lands by a rapacious landowner.

Many of the short stories of the Uruguayan Horacio QUIROGA (1878–1937), most especially those from *Cuentos de amor, de locura y de muerte* (1917), reveal a sharp awareness of both the remote Argentine-Uruguayan setting of Misiones and the unusual narrative techniques of Edgar Allan Poe. The Argentine Ricardo GÜIRALDES (1886–1927) wrote poetry and short stories but is best known for his splendid gaucho novel *Don Segundo Sombra* (1926). The "master" Don Segundo is seen through the eyes of his young admirer Fabio, and becomes the shadowy embodiment of the entire gaucho tradition.

The Chileans Eduardo BARRIOS (1884–1963) and Pedro PRADO (1886–1952) should be considered here, through their best novels are not necessarily regional in setting. Barrios is best known for *El hermano asno* (1922), a psychological study of the closed world of a monastery; Prado's masterwork is *Alsino* (1920), a fanciful poetic novel about a young boy who grows wings.

POETRY, DRAMA, AND THE ESSAY SINCE 1945
The last half of the century has been a period of considerable tension, brought on by the cold war, the Cuban Revolution, widespread guerrilla movements, and the growing drug trade. Against that backdrop, however, literary expression has shown extraordinary development in all genres. In poetry the major figure is the Mexican Octavio PAZ (1914), whose imposing work won him the Nobel Prize in 1990. *Libertad bajo palabra* (1949, expanded in 1960) is a compilation of his earlier poetry; *Blanco* (1967), *Pasado en claro* (1975), and *Árbol adentro* (1987) represent his later work. Paz is also a brilliant cultural and literary essayist; *El laberinto de la soledad* (1950), a commentary on modern Mexican culture, and *Los hijos del limo* (1974), on the interconnections between romanticism and the avant garde, are only two of many influential works. Other important poets who are roughly contemporaneous with Paz are the Cuban José LEZAMA LIMA (1910–1976), the Nicaraguan Pablo Antonio CUADRA (b. 1912), and the Chileans Nicanor PARRA (b. 1914) and Gonzalo Rojas (b. 1917). Lezama's anguished and self-reflective poetry found its fullest expression in *La fijeza* (1949) and *Dador* (1960); both his essays and his novel *Paradiso* (1966) reveal similar complexities. Cuadra's poetry develops a central view of his native country; *Cantos de Cifar* (1971), set in the central lake region of Nicaragua, and *Siete árboles contra el atardecer* (1980), a totemic vision of a multiple Nicaraguan reality, are examples of that view. Parra is best known for *Poemas y antipoemas* (1954), which set in motion a denunciatory poetic style. Rojas is passionate, irreverent, and at the same time brilliantly sensorial in his poetic language.

Materia de testamento (1988) is an excellent collection of his recent work.

A number of writers born in the 1920s or later have made significant contributions to the development of contemporary poetry, but there is space here only for the most schematic of representations. Important poets born in the 1920s, for example, would include Álvaro MUTIS (Colombia, 1923), Ernesto CARDENAL (Nicaragua, 1925), Rosario CASTELLANOS (Mexico, 1925–1974), Jaime Sabines (Mexico, 1925), Roberto Juárroz (Argentina, 1925), Carlos Germán Belli (Peru, 1927), and Enrique LIHN (Chile, 1929–1988). Significant poets born in the 1930s include Juan Gelman (Argentina, 1930), Roque DALTON (El Salvador, 1935–1975), Alejandra PIZARNIK (Argentina, 1936–1972), Óscar Hahn (Chile, 1938), and José Emilio PACHECO (Mexico, 1939). Among those poets born in the 1940s or later who should be mentioned are José Kozer (Cuba, 1940), Antonio Cisneros (Peru, 1942), Rosario Ferré (Puerto Rico, 1942), Arturo Carrera (Argentina, 1948), Néstor Perlongher (Argentina, 1948), David Huerta (Mexico, 1949), and Coral Bracho (Mexico, 1951).

The drama has enjoyed spectacular development over the past several decades, a transformation that critics have referred to as the "new" Spanish American theater. Significant initial contributions to that development were made by the Mexicans Xavier VILLAURRUTIA (1903–1950) and Rodolfo USIGLI (1905–1979). Villaurrutia's best full-length play is a reworking of the Hamlet theme entitled *Invitación a la muerte* (1943; staged in 1947); Usigli is best known for his use of Mexican culture and history, particularly in *El gesticulator* (1943; staged in 1947) and *Corona de sombra* (1943; staged in 1947). René MARQUÉS (Puerto Rico, 1919–1979), Carlos GOROSTIZA (Argentina, 1920), and Carlos Solórzano (Guatemala, 1922) made substantial contributions in the 1950s. Marqués's best plays are the ever-popular *La carreta* (1952), which depicts the disintegration of Puerto Rican rural life, and *Los soles truncos* (1959), in which the pressures of the modern world produce the suicide of three aging sisters. In *El juicio* (1954) and *El pan de la locura* (1958), Gorostiza uses realistic staging for pointed social commentary. *Las manos de Dios* (1956), Solórzano's best play, also carries a strong social message but one that is expressed in the more symbolic terms of traditional religious drama.

In the 1960s, a group of brilliant younger dramatists began to make their presence known and have continued to express themselves up to the present. Emilio CARBALLIDO (Mexico, 1925) is a major figure, whose extensive work includes such successes as *Yo también hablo de la rosa* (1970), a commentary on multiple reality, *Tiempo de ladrones* (1983), a long melodramatic presentation based on the bandit-hero Chucho el Roto, and *Rosa de dos aromas* (1986), a double-sided spoof on traditional machismo. The plays of Egon WOLFF (Chile, 1926), especially *Los invasores* (1964) and *Flores de papel* (1970), depict the invasion and destruction of middle-class values. Loss of freedom and movement is the dominant theme in the plays of Griselda GAMBARO (Argentina, 1928), as seen sharply in *Los siameses* (1967) and *El campo* (1967, staged in 1968). Fellow Argentine Osvaldo DRAGÚN (1929) is best known for his *Historias para ser contadas* (1982), a series of whimsical but often sharply critical one-act plays. *El cepillo de dientes* (1967), depicting bizarre everyday rituals by El and Ella, is an obvious incursion into theater of the absurd by Jorge DÍAZ (Chile, 1930). Equally absurdist but considerably more violent is *La noche de los asesinos* (1965, staged in 1966) by José TRIANA (Cuba, 1933): the three characters act out over and over the murder of their parents. The plays of Eduardo Pavlovsky (Argentina, 1933) deal with the violence of recent Argentine history: *El señor Galíndez* (1973), for example, is set in a well-equipped torture chamber that becomes increasingly visible as the play progresses. Vicente LEÑERO (Mexico, 1933) makes adroit use of everyday Mexican language in his *Jesucristo Gómez* (1986; staged in 1987), a present-day reworking of the Gospel of Luke in which Christ becomes an ordinary bricklayer, and in his *Nadie sabe nada* (1988), a searing denunciation of Mexican journalism and public life.

PROSE FICTION SINCE 1945

The novel and the short story have also enjoyed extraordinary development over the past several decades, and critics have used the stock-market term "boom" in discussing what has been seen as the new narrative in recent Spanish American literature. This development really began before 1945, with the publication of *La última niebla* (1934) and *La amortajada* (1938) by the Chilean María Luisa BOMBAL (1910–1980). These two novels represent a sensitive probing of the feminine psyche but at the same time make effective use of a poetic style and experimentation in point of view. In the 1940s the movement toward a new narrative can be seen clearly in the works of Jorge Luis Borges (Argentina, 1899–1986), whose brilliant short fiction was collected first in *Ficciones* (1944) and then in *El aleph* (1956). The labyrinthine circularities of Borges's best tales, among them "La biblioteca de Babel," "El jardín de senderos que se bifurcan," "La muerte y la brújula," and "Las ruinas circulares," call into question the very processes of writing and reading. *El informe de Brodie* (1970) contains some of Borges's best later work. Miguel Ángel ASTURIAS (Guatemala, 1899–1974) is best known for *El señor presidente* (1946) and *Hombres de maíz* (1949), two novels that combine sophisticated narrative technique, social message, and indigenous myths. Asturias was awarded the Nobel Prize for literature in 1967. Eduardo MALLEA (Argentina, 1903–1982) was a prolific and expansive novelist; his best works are *La bahía de silencio* (1940) and his masterpiece, *Todo verdor perecerá* (1941), both intense psychological studies presented in a complex narrative style. The unusual historical and musical background of Alejo CARPENTIER (Cuba, 1904–1980) found brilliant expression in his novels and short sto-

From left: Juan Rulfo, Mario Vargas Llosa, Octavio Paz, Gabriel García Márquez, Julio Cortázar, Carlos Fuentes, and Jorge Luis Borges. Painting by Abel Quezada for *New York Times Magazine* cover (13 March 1983). PHOTO COURTESY OF JOLANDA QUEZADA.

ries, especially in *El reino de este mundo* (1949), a novel based on the Haitian revolution, and the shorter historical pieces of *Guerra del tiempo* (1958). Agustín YÁÑEZ (Mexico, 1904–1980) is best remembered for *Al filo del agua* (1947), a novel that uses sophisticated narrative techniques to present the tensions of a small Jalisco village at the beginning of the Mexican Revolution. Juan Carlos ONETTI (Uruguay, 1909) is a prolific novelist and short-story writer, whose masterworks are *La vida breve* (1950), a complex interplay between fiction and reality, and *El astillero* (1961), in which the pointless rebuilding of a ruined shipyard becomes an allegorical reference to Uruguayan reality.

In the 1950s other younger writers began to contribute to the developing new narrative. José María ARGUEDAS (Peru, 1911–1969) published *Los ríos profundos* (1958), an unusual novel that uses both Spanish and Quechua in the communication of a multicultural Andean reality. Augusto ROA BASTOS (Paraguay, 1917) has received international attention for *Hijo de hombre* (1960) and *Yo, el*

supremo (1974), the second a contribution to the so-called dictator novel. Juan RULFO (Mexico, 1918–1986) produced two masterworks. The first is *El llano en llamas* (1953), a collection of short stories set in rural Jalisco, and the second is the extraordinarily complex *Pedro Páramo* (1955), a novel in whose pages the living hell of the created town of Comala and its inhabitants can be experienced. Juan José ARREOLA (Mexico, 1918) is best known for his brilliant and highly intellectual short fiction, collected first in *Confabulario* (1952) and then in *Confabulario total* (1962). In *Balún Canán* (1957) and *Oficio de tinieblas* (1962), Rosario CASTELLANOS (Mexico, 1925–1974) uses the Indian setting of her native state of Chiapas in making a memorable contribution.

The 1960s and 1970s saw the publication of an unusually large number of first-rank narrative works, and the consequent coining and wide use of the Boom terminology to characterize the production of those decades. The oldest of the principal figures is Julio CORTÁZAR (Argentina, 1914–1984), whose novel *Rayuela*

443

(1963) was one of the opening salvos in this war of innovation. The most celebrated feature of the novel is an open-ended "Table of Instructions," which invites readers to follow an idiosyncratic and rather whimsical pattern established by the author or to invent their own approaches to the reading of the novel. The first novel by Carlos FUENTES (Mexico, 1928) was *La región más transparente* (1958), a mythical-realistic incursion into the roiling world of Mexico City; in *La muerte de Artemio Cruz* (1962) Fuentes uses an unusual triadic structure to delve into a contradictory personality that is representative of post-Revolutionary Mexico. *La ciudad y los perros* (1963), a complex narration set in a real Lima military academy, was the prize-winning first novel by Mario VARGAS LLOSA (Peru, 1936); even more involved was his second novel, *La casa verde* (1966). Guillermo CABRERA INFANTE (Cuba, 1929) published the highly inventive and very Cuban *Tres tristes tigres* in 1967. The best-known work of Gabriel GARCÍA MÁRQUEZ (Colombia, 1928), who received the Nobel Prize in 1982, is *Cien años de soledad* (1967), the paradigmatic Boom novel. Set in the banana-growing region of Colombia, the work develops the history, often in magical terms, of the fictional town of Macondo and its leading family. García Márquez's successful later novels include *Crónica de una muerte anunciada* (1981) and *El amor en los tiempos de cólera* (1985). The principal contributions of Manuel PUIG (Argentina, 1932–1990) came with *La traición de Rita Hayworth* (1968) and *Boquitas pintadas* (1969), novels that demonstrated connections to the cinema and other popular art forms. José DONOSO (Chile, 1924) contributed to the wave of new fiction with *El obsceno pájaro de la noche* (1970), a dark representation of Chilean society, and then with *Casa de campo* (1978), an allegory of the 1973 military coup.

There are a number of post-Boom prose fiction writers who deserve attention, among them are Severo SARDUY (Cuba, 1936–1992), Luisa VALENZUELA (Argentina, 1938), José Emilio PACHECO (Mexico, 1939), Alfredo BRYCE-ECHENIQUE (Peru, 1939), Gustavo SAINZ (Mexico, 1940), Antonio SKÁRMETA (Chile, 1940), Eduardo GALEANO (Uruguay, 1940), Cristina PERI ROSSI (Uruguay, 1941), Isabel ALLENDE (Chile, 1942), Rosario Ferré (Puerto Rico, 1942), and Reinaldo ARENAS (Cuba, 1943–1990).

An excellent general approach to the area is provided by *Latin America and the Caribbean: A Critical Guide to Research Sources* (1992), edited by Paula H. Covington. In this guide see especially the essay and bibliography on Spanish American literature by ENRIQUE PUPO-WALKER, ROBERTO GONZÁLEZ-ECHEVERRÍA, and HENSLEY C. WOODBRIDGE (pp. 443–493), together with the essay and bibliography on Latin American drama by LESLIE DAMASCENO and LIONEL LOROÑA (pp. 589–604). WALTER RELA, *A Bibliographical Guide to Spanish American Literature: Twentieth-century Sources* (1988), is a reliable source for data on materials from this century. For information and up-to-date bibliography on individual authors see the excellent three-volume *Latin American Writers* (1989), edited by Carlos A. Solé and Maria Isabel Abreu. Of particular interest are the in-

troductory essays and chronological table by the editors (vol. 1, xiii–lxxxvi). A similar multivolume work in Spanish, now nearing publication in Caracas, is the *Diccionario enciclopédico de las letras de América Latina*, edited by José Ramón Medina and Nelson Osorio T.

ENRIQUE ANDERSON IMBERT's two-volume *Spanish American Literature: A History*, 2d ed. (1969) is an indispensable source of information, although now dated in its coverage of recent developments. The same can be said of the excellent one-volume histories by JEAN FRANCO, *An Introduction to Spanish-American Literature* (1969) and LUIS LEAL, *Breve historia de la literatura hispanoamericana* (1971). A more recent multivolume work that provides a historical context, up-to-date bibliography, and selected critical essays is *Historia y crítica de la literatura hispanoamericana* (1988), with CEDOMIL GOIC as general editor. DAVID WILLIAM FOSTER, *Handbook of Latin American Literature*, 2d ed. (1992), takes the form of detailed surveys of literary development on a country-by-country basis, with each essay done by a recognized expert. For information on prose fiction consult: FERNANDO ALEGRÍA, *Nueva historia de la novela hispanoamericana* (1986); JOHN S. BRUSHWOOD, *The Spanish American Novel: A Twentieth-Century Survey* (1975) and *Genteel Barbarism: New Readings of Nineteenth-Century Spanish-American Novels* (1981); MARGARET SAYERS PEDEN, *The Latin American Short Story: A Critical Survey* (1983). On poetry, see GORDON BROTHERSTON, *Latin American Poetry: Origins and Presence* (1975); MERLIN H. FORSTER, *Historia de la poesía hispanoamericana* (1981); ÓSCAR RIVERA RODAS, *La poesía hispanoamericana del siglo XIX* (1988); JACOBO SEFAMÍ, *Contemporary Spanish American Poets* (1992). On the drama, consult SEVERINO JOÃO ALBUQUERQUE, *Violent Acts: A Study of Contemporary Latin American Theatre* (1991); LEON F. LYDAY and GEORGE W. WOODYARD, *Dramatists in Revolt: The New Latin American Theater* (1976); DIANA TAYLOR, *Theatre of Crisis: Drama and Politics in Latin America* (1991). MARTIN S. STABB, *In Quest of Identity: Patterns in the Spanish American Essay of Ideas, 1890–1960* (1967) provides excellent commentaries on major Spanish American essayists.

MERLIN H. FORSTER

See also **Gauchesca Literature.**

LIVESTOCK

Origins People in southeastern Europe domesticated wild cattle (*B. primigenius*) at least 8,500 years ago. Herders in southern Asia domesticated *Bos indicus* (zebu or Brahman cattle) about the same time. Since then, humankind has taken advantage of the wide range of useful products that cattle provide: meat, leather, milk, power, and tallow.

The zebu comes from India. These animals tolerate heat and resist disease and insect attacks better than most breeds. Their distinctive hump of cartilage and fat above the neck and withers give the large zebu a somewhat menacing look. Colors range from various shades of gray to red. Unlike most breeds, zebus can tolerate hot, humid climates. Ranchers from Texas to Venezuela and Brazil have raised the breed. A relative newcomer to western-hemisphere ranching is the Charolais, a native to France. Beef producers initially thought very little of this large, muscular, all-white breed. However, the Charolais's fast growth and heavier weight at a younger age soon attracted adherents.

Specialized markets have opened new opportunities to livestock raisers. The venerable Corriente breed, for example, is much in demand for team roping competitions. The Corriente developed in colonial Mexico from cattle imported from Spain. Like its cousin, the Longhorn, the hardy Corriente is a tough survivor.

Animal husbandry—raising and domesticating animals for food, transportation, power, clothing fiber, or building materials—is an ancient activity. South Americans of the pre-Columbian era domesticated many animals, including the alpaca and the LLAMA. After the arrival of the Spanish, cattle, sheep, mules, and goats joined the ranks of indigenous livestock.

Llamas, alpacas, vicuñas, and guanacos—members of the family Camelidae—were native to the Andean highlands. Guanacos, never domesticated, were hunted for their MEAT. Llamas, alpacas, and vicuñas may have been domesticated by about 2000 B.C. They stand about 4 feet high at the shoulders, may reach more than 4 feet in length, and weigh up to 300 pounds. Indians wove their wool into yarn and used their flesh as food. Llamas also were used as pack animals.

The Colonial Era Thanks to Spanish explorers and rich grasslands, herds of wild cattle proliferated quickly in the Río de la Plata during the early colonial period. Indians learned to herd horses and cattle, and developed a livestock trade across the Andes to Chile. GAUCHOS (most often Indian or mestizo) hunted the wild cattle for their HIDES.

By the mid-eighteenth century, ranchers established ESTANCIAS and began domesticating wild cattle and claiming control of land and water. They raised the tough, rangy creole cattle for their hides and increasingly for the salted meat trade to Brazil and Cuba. Oxen, the most important draft animals, pulled high-wheeled carts across the pampas and up to Alta Peru.

During the latter decades of the nineteenth century, ranchers began improving their creole stock with imported breeds, in order to compete in the growing refrigerated beef export market. Thanks to their control of the pampas, Argentina's wealthy livestock producers remained politically powerful into the twentieth century.

Longhorns Longhorn cattle are descended from the creole cattle brought to Mexico and South America during the sixteenth century. During the eighteenth century, Spanish priests brought the breed to missions that they established in Texas, New Mexico, and California. Longhorns likewise provided the basis for the beef industries of Brazil and Argentina. Their hardiness made the Longhorn well-suited to less hospitable ranges, such as the semi-desert regions of northern Mexico and the south Texas brush country.

Growing up wild on open range or in the dense thickets of the Texas brush country, Longhorns did not take kindly to being herded. Longhorns come in an amazing variety of colors and patterns. With horn spreads sometimes exceeding ten feet, they posed dangers to horses and riders. Fiercely protective, they used their horns against wolves and other enemies.

Despite their virtues, Longhorns had deficiencies that ultimately doomed them as the mainstay of the beef cattle industry. They take longer to mature: ten years versus six years for so-called "American breeds," such as Herefords, Angus, Devon, and Shorthorn. Longhorns are a lean breed, and the beef-eater's pallet came to demand fatty, marbled beef. Finally, the unwieldy horns created havoc in close quarters, such as the confines of

Cattle auction, Argentina. ARCHIVO GENERAL DE LA NACIÓN, BUENOS AIRES.

feedlots. During the late nineteenth century, other breeds pushed aside the venerable Longhorn.

In 1927 the U.S. Forest Service acted on a congressional mandate to establish a national herd of Longhorns. Rangers could locate only three bulls, twenty cows, and four calves. They removed those animals to the Wichita Mountains Wildlife Refuge at Cache, Oklahoma. During the following decades, government and private efforts established the "Seven Families" of different gene pools to rebuild the breed. Today breeders raise tens of thousands of Longhorns.

Brazil Like livestock producers everywhere, those in the Brazilian Northeast faced many problems. Rustlers, runaway slaves, and bandits posed threats to cowboys and herds. DROUGHTS still strike the region periodically. Despite the problems, by the early eighteenth century Bahia held an estimated 500,000 cattle and Pernambuco 800,000. This marked the high point of VAQUEIRO life.

During the eighteenth century, the economy, population, and political power in Brazil shifted south toward Rio de Janeiro. This demographic shift left the Northeast politically and economically marginalized and contributed to a decline in the northern livestock industry toward the end of the eighteenth century. Minas Gerais, also a mining center, became Brazil's new livestock center. Still further to the south gaúchos herded cattle in Rio Grande do Sul. JESUIT missionaries moved some livestock into southern Brazil in the 1620s. Ranchers and priests brought many more animals during the following decade. The Brazilian southern plains, called Campo Gerais during the colonial era, had an abundance of well-watered pasture land.

In 1793 the captaincy of Rio Grande exported 13,000 arrobas of dried meat. About a decade later the figure had jumped to 600,000 arrobas as *charqueadas* (beef-drying plants) multiplied. (An arroba is 11.5 kg or about 25 pounds.) Slaves in Cuba provided a ready market throughout the nineteenth century.

Not until the mid-nineteenth century did ranchers in southern Brazil begin to furnish cattle with salt. Some ranchers added wire fencing after the 1880s, but borderlands cattle production, work techniques, and social relations changed very little. Ranchers in Rio Grande and nothern Uruguay continued to raise cattle for the traditional hides and jerky markets for decades after ranchers elsewhere diversified into the more lucrative chilled beef trade.

Mules and Sheep The Spanish and Brazilians also bred mules, the sterile offspring of a donkey and a mare. In mountainous regions, such as Salta, mules served as mounts. In many areas, including mining centers, like Potosí, they were used as work and pack animals. Muleteers (*arrieros*) drove long trains of more than eighty mules from Potosí and Chile to cities in the Río de la Plata. During the colonial period, the pampas around Córdoba became an important mule-breeding center.

Sheep have long been raised, especially for their WOOL and MEAT. Beginning in the 1820s, British ranchers began importing sheep and grazing them in cooler areas of the Argentine pampas. Despite resistance from traditional cattle ranchers, the sheep population grew gradually. Initially, ranchers raised merino sheep and exported wool to French and British textile mills. Both men and women earned relatively high wages during the busy shearing season. During the 1860s, thicker fleeced Rambouillet sheep replaced the merinos. With the development of the technology to ship refrigerated meat, ranchers imported Lincoln and Romney Marsh sheep, breeds that provided good mutton and wool. By 1895, Argentina's sheep population numbered nearly 75 million head. Today Argentina remains among the world's top ten sheep and cattle producers.

J. FRANK DOBIE, *The Longhorns* (1941); JOHN E. ROUSE, *World Cattle* (1970); RICHARD W. SLATTA, *Gauchos and the Vanishing Frontier* (1983) and *The Cowboy Encyclopedia* (1994); DAVID ROCK, *Argentina, 1516–1987* (1987).

RICHARD W. SLATTA

See also **Saladero; Vaquería.**

LIVINGSTON CODES, a set of civil penal reform codes written by U.S. lawyer and statesman Edward Livingston in the 1820s and later adopted by Guatemala. Written for Louisiana, that state rejected his *System of Penal Law* in 1826. When Livingston became Andrew Jackson's secretary of state in 1831, he offered the codes to Guatemala's liberal governor, José Francisco BARRUNDIA, who viewed it as a needed replacement for his country's Hispanic criminal code. With the help of Barrundia's active advocacy in the legislature, the codes were adopted by Guatemala in December 1835 during the administration of Governor Mariano Gálvez. They went into effect on 1 January 1836.

The Livingston Codes provided trial by jury, habeas corpus, and jails with separate cells; they also vested the appointment of all judges in the governors of the various states within Guatemala. Despite their progressive nature, they proved to be impractical for Guatemala and quickly resulted in the alienation of a number of sectors of Guatemalan society, in particular attorneys and rural peasants who were conscripted into forced labor gangs to construct new jails. Trial by jury proved impractical, especially in rural areas, and the change in the appointment system of judges alienated powerful landed interests. The association of the Livingston Codes with centralization efforts of the Liberals in Guatemala City also aroused opposition to them. Rafael CARRERA demanded the abolition of the Livingston Codes during his 1837 rebellion, and after he gained power the codes were repealed in 1839.

MARIO RODRÍGUEZ, "The Livingston Codes in the Guatemalan Crisis of 1837–1838," in *Applied Enlightenment: Nineteenth*

Century Liberalism, Middle American Research Institute, Tulane University, Publication 23, no. 1 (1972), pp. 1–32, is the best source for this topic. On the origins of the codes, see GRANT LYONS, "Louisana and the Livingston Criminal Codes," in *Louisiana History* 15 (1974): 243–272, and IRA FLORY, JR., "Edward Livingston's Place in Louisana Law," in *Louisiana Historical Quarterly* 19 (1936): 328–389. For the resistance to the codes, see RALPH LEE WOODWARD, JR., *Rafael Carrera and the Emergence of the Republic of Guatemala, 1821–1871* (1993), pp. 53–83.

HEATHER K. THIESSEN

LLAMA. The llama, alpaca, guanaco, and vicuña are four species of camelid native to the high-altitude zones of the central and southern Andes in Peru. Raised by Andean peoples on the grasslands of the high plateau, the domesticated camelids, llamas and alpacas, are valued primarily for their wool, hides, and meat. Although not as large as the Old World camel, llamas are prized as pack animals for transporting food products to and from lower altitudes. The wild vicuña, the smallest of the species, is used mainly for its soft fine wool. The undomesticated and increasingly rare guanaco is hunted for meat and especially for pelts. Ranchers consider guanacos a threat to pastureland needed for livestock.

Llamas and alpacas have been central to the livelihood of Andean peoples since their domestication between 4000 and 3000 B.C. In the INCA state (ca. 1430–1532) Andean communities developed large herds of llamas and alpacas in order to maintain a steady supply of wool, meat, and animals for ritual sacrifice. As a hedge against famine the Inca state promoted the storage of dried llama meat (*charqui*). Indian pastoralists under Spanish colonial rule produced alpaca wool for export. For most of the nineteenth and early twentieth centuries the economy of southern Great Peru revolved around the export of high-grade alpaca wool to Britain. The collapse of the wool export boom in the 1920s, coupled with the expansion of cattle raising, has led to a sharp reduction in camelid herds. Nevertheless, the Peruvian government has begun to assist Indian communities in building up alpaca herds.

BENJAMIN S. ORLOVE, *Alpacas, Sheep, and Men: The Wool Export Economy and Regional Society in Southern Peru* (1977); WILLIAM L. FRANKLIN, "Biology, Ecology, and the Relationship

Llama. PHOTO BY MARTÍN CHAMBI. COURTESY OF JULIA CHAMBI.

Alpacas. PHOTO BY JESUS NAZARENO.

A vicuña. LATIN AMERICAN LIBRARY, TULANE UNIVERSITY.

to Man of the South American Camelids," in *Mammalian Biology of South America,* edited by M. A. Mares and H. H. Genoways (1982); SHOZO MASUDA, IZUMI SHIMADA, and CRAIG MORRIS, eds., *Andean Ecology and Civilization* (1985).

STEVEN J. HIRSCH

See also **Wool Industry.**

LLANOS (COLOMBIA). The eastern tropical plains of Colombia cover approximately 98,000 square miles, or one-fifth of the national territory. Stretching eastward from the Eastern Cordillera to the Venezuelan border, the llanos are bounded on the north by the Arauca River and on the south by the Guaviare River. Included within the sparsely populated region are the departments of Arauca, Casanare, Meta, and Vichada, which had a combined population of about 592,000 in 1985. Villavicencio, the capital of Meta and the largest city in the llanos, had a population of 177,000 in 1985.

Cut off from the heart of Colombia by the Eastern Cordillera, the llanos have played a marginal role in the country's history. Although Europeans seeking EL DORADO began to explore the region in the 1530s, few Spaniards settled there. In 1778 the llanos were home to only 1,535 whites, who were devoted mainly to cattle raising. In the mid-seventeenth century missionaries moved into the area to proselytize the Indians, who were gathered into mission towns, which numbered thirty-one by 1760.

The llanos became a battleground during the WARS OF INDEPENDENCE as well as a place of refuge for patriots during the Spanish reconquest (1816–1819). The region suffered population loss and economic disruption because of the conflict and experienced little growth during the nineteenth century. One significant nineteenth-century change was the decline of the northern llanos and the shift of population south to Meta. Villavicencio, founded in 1850, had a population of nearly 5,000 by 1918.

After 1930 the national government regularized regional administration and created an infrastructure to encourage settlement and development. Cattle raising remained a major economic activity, supplemented by petroleum production and the cultivation of rice and other commercial crops. The llanos were a center of Liberal guerrilla activity during La VIOLENCIA, especially during the period 1949–1953, and the scene of agrarian conflict during the 1970s and 1980s.

By 1994 Casanare had become Colombia's leading oil-producing department because of the exploitation of large reserves (about two billion barrels) found there by British Petroleum in association with Ecopetrol, the state petroleum agency, and other foreign firms.

JANE RAUSCH, *A Tropical Plains Frontier: The Llanos of Colombia, 1531–1831* (1984), and *The Llanos Frontier of Colombia, 1830–1930* (1993).

HELEN DELPAR

LLANOS (VENEZUELA). The low-lying plains of the Orinoco Basin, occupying almost one-third of Venezuela's national territory, run from the Andes to the Atlantic. Approximately 600 miles long and 200 miles wide, they are bounded on the north by coastal mountains and on the south by the Guiana Highlands. Treeless, they are covered largely by a mixture of savanna and scrub woodland. The climate of the llanos is divided into a rainy season from roughly April to November and a dry season from November to April. The rainy season causes extensive flooding: the lowlands along the streams are inundated and livestock are driven to safer ground to the north. The dry season is characterized by severe drought. As the waters recede and the grasses are scorched by the sun, livestock must retreat toward the Orinoco River to seek food and water.

The human population of the llanos is sparse, owing to drought and flooding, extreme heat, abundance of insects, and disease. Most of the population is clustered in river towns, the largest and more important of which is Ciudad Bolívar, which lies 200 miles up the Orinoco. Traditionally cattle raising has been the principal economic activity despite weather extremes, transportation problems, poor-quality forage, and disease. The local cowboys, or *llaneros,* are legendary for their independence and for their fighting skills, which they demonstrated in the independence wars and the civil wars of the nineteenth century.

In the later twentieth century there has been significant agricultural development in the northern llanos, facilitated by land settlement, irrigation projects, and the construction of a major dam on the Guárico River. Large oil and gas deposits lie beneath the eastern portion of the llanos, including the giant Orinoco heavy oil belt, which, if world oil prices warrant, is scheduled to be on-stream by the end of the twentieth century.

AMERICAN UNIVERSITY, *Foreign Area Studies Division, Area Handbook for Venezuela* (1964); RAYMOND E. CRIST and EDWARD P. LEAHY, *Venezuela: Search for a Middle Ground* (1969); JOHN V. LOMBARDI, *Venezuela: The Search for Order, the Dream of Progress* (1982); PRESTON E. JAMES and C. W. MINKEL, *Latin America,* 5th ed. (1986).

WINFIELD J. BURGGRAAFF

LLANQUIHUE, province of southern Chile. With 221,561 inhabitants (1982), it is the core of the Lake Region. The green landscape dotted with lakes and mountain peaks—most of them snowcapped volcanoes—attracted Chilean and European colonists during the second half of the nineteenth century. Dairy and grain-growing farms, interspersed with large cattle ranches, prospered. Labor for many of these enterprises was supplied by migrant workers from CHILOÉ. Today, nearly 40 percent of the population is of European ancestry, and the rest are natives from Llanquihue and Chiloé. The largest city is Puerto Montt (1987 population 113,488), which connects with the island of Chiloé via ferry, with the province of Aisén in northern Patagonia via an all-weather road, and with Bariloche (Argentina) via the Pérez Rosales Pass and Puerto Blest.

JEAN-PIERRE BLANCPAIN, *Les allemands au Chili (1816–1945)* (Cologne, 1974); and INSTITUTO GEOGRÁFICO MILITAR, "La región de Los Lagos," in *Geografía de Chile,* vol. 32 (1986).

CÉSAR N. CAVIEDES

LLERAS, LORENZO MARÍA (*b.* 7 September 1811; *d.* 3 June 1868), Colombian politician. As an educator, publicist, and politician, Lleras's moderate liberalism characterized an important current in early national Colombian politics. Born in Bogotá, Lleras received his education in his native city. His activity as a lawyer facilitated his political activity with General Francisco de Paula SANTANDER and Florentino GONZÁLEZ in the 1830s, especially as editor of *La Bandera Nacional.* Lleras was rector of the Colegio Mayor de Nuestra Señora de Rosario (1842–1846) before establishing the Colegio Mayor de Espíritu Santo, where he trained numerous influential Liberals. His *El Neo-Granadino* promulgated Draconiano Liberalism in the 1850s, an ideology he championed in the congress and in the cabinet of President José María OBANDO.

Lleras's association with members of the Democratic Society of Artisans led to his brief incarceration after the 1854 coup of José María MELO. He backed anti-Conservative forces in the 1859–1862 civil war and was a delegate to the RIONEGRO CONVENTION (1863). Lleras and Clotilde Triana, his second wife, parented fifteen children, establishing a lineage that included Liberal presidents Carlos LLERAS RESTREPO (1966–1970) and Alberto LLERAS CAMARGO (1958–1962).

ANDRES SORIANO LLERAS, *Lorenzo María Lleras* (1958); ROBERT H. DAVIS, "Acosta, Caro, and Lleras: Three Essayists and Their Views on New Granada's National Problems," (Ph.D. diss., Vanderbilt University, 1969).

DAVID SOWELL

See also **Colombia: Political Parties.**

LLERAS CAMARGO, ALBERTO (*b.* 3 July 1906; *d.* 4 January 1990), president of Colombia (1945–1946 and 1958–1962). Born into a middle-class Bogotá family, Lleras Camargo briefly attended university but was quickly drawn into Liberal journalism and politics. Elected to Congress in 1930, he became the youngest interior minister in Colombian history during the first term of Alfonso LÓPEZ PUMAREJO (1934–1938). In López's troubled second term (1942–1945), Lleras was ambassador to the United States; he completed López's term upon the latter's resignation in July 1945, a period of severe political and labor unrest. He served as secretary general of the Organization of American States (1948–1954) and rector of the University of the Andes in

Bogotá (1954). In 1956–1957 he negotiated with exiled Conservative leader Laureano GÓMEZ the agreements that formed the basis for the bipartisan National Front; in May 1958 he was elected president under that agreement. Lleras's regime faced serious problems of pacification and rehabilitation after more than a decade of violence; the western department of Caldas, plagued by murderous *bandoleros*, proved especially intractable. Reform projects inspired by the ALLIANCE FOR PROGRESS, such as a 1961 Agrarian Reform Law, produced indifferent results. After leaving office, Lleras edited the magazine *Visión*; in 1978 he retired from public life, though not before expressing dissatisfaction with the Liberal leadership of the late 1970s.

JOHN MARTZ, *Colombia: A Contemporary Political Survey* (1962); ROBERT H. DIX, *Colombia: The Political Dimensions of Change* (1967); IGNACIO ARIZMENDI POSADA, *Presidentes de Colombia, 1810–1990* (1990), pp. 245–248.

RICHARD J. STOLLER

See also **Colombia: Political Parties.**

LLERAS RESTREPO, CARLOS (*b.* 14 April 1908; *d.* 27 September 1994), president of Colombia (1966–1970). The son of a prominent but poor Bogotá scientist, Lleras Restrepo was already a rising Liberal politician when he received his law degree in 1930. He served as comptroller and finance minister during the regimes of Alfonso LÓPEZ PUMAREJO and Eduardo SANTOS (1934–1942). A leader of the Liberals' "civil resistance" during the Conservative regime of Mariano OSPINA PÉREZ (1946–1950), he was forced into exile in 1952, during the presidency of Laureano GÓMEZ. A leading backer of the bipartisan National Front, he reached the presidency in 1966 promising an analogous "national transformation" on the social and economic fronts. A technocrat by temperament, Lleras Restrepo organized "decentralized institutes" in fields as diverse as sports and scientific research. In 1968 he forced through a constitutional reform increasing the executive's budgetary and planning powers. In the late 1970s, through his influential magazine *Nueva Frontera*, Lleras Restrepo was a vocal opponent of the Liberal regime of Julio César TURBAY. Lleras Restrepo's writings include the multivolume autobiography, *Historia de mi propia vida* (1983–).

IGNACIO ARIZMENDI POSADA, *Presidentes de Colombia, 1810–1990* (1990), pp. 275–280.

RICHARD J. STOLLER

See also **Colombia: Political Parties.**

LLORENS TORRES, LUIS (*b.* 14 May 1876; *d.* 16 June 1944), Puerto Rican poet. Born into a comfortable family in Juana Díaz, in southern Puerto Rico, Llorens began writing verse at the age of twelve. He studied law in Barcelona and Granada, Spain, where he also wrote articles on Puerto Rican and Caribbean history for several periodicals. Llorens practiced law in Puerto Rico, while at the same time engaging actively in journalistic writing. In 1913 he founded and directed the journal *Revista de las Antillas*, which established new directions for the poetry of Puerto Rico, and two years later established the satirical weekly *Juan Bobo* (with Nemesio R. CANALES). He published articles under the pseudonym Luis de Puerto Rico and in 1914 wrote a historical drama, *El grito de Lares* (The cry of Lares, 1927). Llorens defined his philosophy of art as "everything is beauty" and "everything is poetry." Llorens wrote poems of intense patriotic sentiment about Spanish American history and the Caribbean; about Puerto Rico's towns, women, customs, heroes, history, folklore, natives, and landscape, and verse both admiring and protesting the United States. He was also a member of Puerto Rico's House of Representatives from 1908 to 1910, and was a supporter of self-determination for Puerto Rico. When Llorens became gravely ill in New York in 1944, President Franklin D. Roosevelt arranged to have him flown to Puerto Rico, so that he could die in his homeland.

His major works are *América* (1898), *Al pie de la Alhambra* (At the foot of the Alhambra, 1899), *Sonetos sinfónicos* (Symphonic sonnets, 1914), "*La canción de las Antillas*" *y otros poemas* ("Song of the Antilles" and other poems, 1929), *Voces de la campana mayor* (Voices of the great bell, 1935), and *Alturas de América* (Heights of America, 1940).

CARMEN MARRERO, *Luis Llorens Torres: Vida y obra (1876–1944)* (1953); THERESA ORTIZ DE HADJOPOULOS, *Luis Llorens Torres: A Study of His Poetry* (1977); NILDA S. ORTIZ GARCÍA, *Vida y obra de Luis Llorens Torres* (1977); DAISY CARABALLO-ABREU, *La prosa de Luis Llorens Torres: Estudio y antología* (1986).

ESTELLE IRIZARRY

LLORENTE Y LAFUENTE, ANSELMO (*b.* 1800; *d.* 1871), bishop of Costa Rica (1851–1871). In 1850 Pope Piux IX created the diocese of Costa Rica, separating it from the diocese of León, Nicaragua. On 7 November 1851 Llorente, a native of Cartago, was consecrated its first bishop. Aside from failing to convince the legislature to provide funds for a seminary, Llorente's relationship with the government was harmonious until 1858, when the legislature, supported by President Juan Rafael Mora, passed a hospital tax. Since clergymen were not exempt from the tax, Llorente publicly opposed it, ordering his priests not to pay it. Consequently, he was expelled from the country. He went to Nicaragua but was able to return in August 1859, when Mora was overthrown, largely due to outrage at the bishop's banishment. From then until his death, Llorente maintained a cordial relationship with civil authorities.

VICTOR SANABRIA MARTÍNEZ, *Anselmo Llorente y Lafuente, primer obispo de Costa Rica: Apuntamientos históricos* (1933);

PHILIP J. WILLIAMS, *The Catholic Church and Politics in Nicaragua and Costa Rica* (1989), pp. 99–100.

EDWARD T. BRETT

See also **Anticlericalism.**

L'OLONNAIS, FRANCIS (*b.* 1630; *d.* 1670), notorious French buccaneer who preyed upon Spanish shipping in the Caribbean and terrorized settlements along the Spanish Main and the coast of Central America. He was born Jean David Nau but known as L'Olonnais after his birthplace, Sables d'Olonne in Brittany. L'Olonnais came to the West Indies as an indentured servant but on gaining his freedom, he quickly earned respect as a successful and unusually murderous buccaneer. With the support of the governor of Tortuga, L'Olonnais used that island as his base of operations, equipping his expeditions there and drawing his crew from its unsavory population. His greatest achievement was the capture and plunder of treasure from the relatively well-defended towns of Maracaibo and San Antonio de Gibraltar in the Gulf of Venezuela. L'Olonnais died at Islas Barú, Darién, Panama at the hands of a group of Indians allied to the Spanish. The natives tore his body apart and threw it, limb by limb, into a fire.

JENIFER MARX, *Pirates and Privateers of the Caribbean* (1992); ALEXANDER O. EXQUEMELIN, *The Buccaneers of America* (1993).

J. DAVID DRESSING

See also **Buccaneers and Freebooters.**

LOMBARDO TOLEDANO, VICENTE (*b.* 16 July 1894; *d.* 16 November 1968), Mexican labor leader, intellectual, and opposition party leader. Along with Manuel GÓMEZ MORÍN and Alberto Vázquez del Mercado, Lombardo was a member of the important intellectual generation known as the "Seven Wisemen," which founded the Society of Conferences and Concerts. His intellectual orientation began with Christian Democracy and early in his adult life moved toward socialism. He was a labor activist best remembered as an organizer and secretary general of the Mexican Federation of Labor (CTM), Mexico's most powerful union. He lost control over this union to a group that included Fidel Velásquez, who dominated it from the mid-1940s to the 1990s. In 1948, disenchanted with the government, Lombardo Toledano founded his own opposition Partido Popular, which predated the Popular Socialist Party (1960), later an ally in Cuauhtémoc CÁRDENAS's 1988 electoral front.

Born in Teziutlán, Puebla, he was a childhood friend of Manuel ÁVILA CAMACHO. His grandparents were Italian immigrant peasants, and his father, who married into an old Spanish family, served as mayor of his hometown. Two of his sisters married leading intellectual contemporaries, Alfonso CASO and Pedro HENRÍQUEZ UREÑA. Lombardo Toledano completed his preparatory studies at the National Preparatory School and went on to obtain a law degree and an M.A. from the National University in 1919 and 1920, respectively. A professor for many years, he founded and directed the night-school program at the National Preparatory School (1923) and the Workers University of Mexico (1936–1968). A student leader in college, he worked for the Federal District, and at the age of twenty-nine, became interim governor of his home state, Puebla. He served in the Chamber of Deputies from 1924 to 1928 and again from 1964 to 1966, and held major union posts as secretary general of the National Federation of Teachers and secretary general of the Federation of Workers of the Federal District. When he lost his influence as the government co-opted labor unions after 1940, he founded and presided over the Federation of Latin American Workers from 1938 to 1963. He also organized and served as secretary general of the Socialist League (1944). He contributed many essays to popular magazines and newspapers.

ROBERT P. MILLON, *Vicente Lombardo Toledano, Mexican Marxist* (1966): VICENTE LOMBARDO TOLEDANO, *A un joven socialista mexicano* (1967); ENRIQUE KRAUZE, *Caudillos culturales en la revolución mexicana* (1976).

RODERIC AI CAMP

See also **Mexico: Political Parties.**

LONARDI, EDUARDO (*d.* 22 March 1956), president of Argentina (September–November 1955). General Lonardi ruled for only fifty days and would have been forgotten but for the fact that he managed to oust Juan D. PERÓN when all others had failed. Lonardi had previously promoted an abortive revolt, which resulted in his own forced retirement in 1951. Terminally ill with cancer, Lonardi planned the coup while a patient at the Buenos Aires Military Hospital.

Though his presidency was brief, there were nevertheless distinguishing features. Once Perón was exiled (September 1955), Lonardi was magnanimous toward the Peronists, launching the slogan "neither victors nor vanquished." On the economic front, he appointed Raúl PREBISCH to prepare a "what is to be done?" report.

Though ailing, Lonardi did not die in the presidency. Pedro Eugenio ARAMBURU ousted him on 13 November 1955 only to be confronted with a "Bring Back Lonardi" movement, but Lonardi died four months later.

MARTA LONARDI, *Mi padre y la revolución del '55* (1980).

ROGER GRAVIL

LONDON, TREATY OF (1604), agreement between Spain and England ending a protracted conflict highlighted by the famous defeat of the Spanish Armada in

1588. Issues raised in negotiations during the summer of 1604 included English demands for trade with Spanish colonies, but the demands were denied and there is no mention of them in the final treaty signed 19 August 1604. The treaty was restricted to arrangements in Europe and included an end to English aid to the Dutch and protection of Spanish ships in the English Channel. Outside Europe ("beyond the line"), war between the colonial powers and England's policy of "effective occupation" continued unabated. The treaty, however, ended a war that was disastrous for Spain and marked the end of the age of Queen Elizabeth and Sir Francis DRAKE and the beginning of Anglo-Spanish cooperation (aided by the accession [1603] in England of James I).

CHARLES HOWARD CARTER, *The Secret Diplomacy of the Habsburgs, 1598–1625* (1964).

SUZANNE HILES BURKHOLDER

LONGINOS MARTÍNEZ, JOSÉ (*b.* ca. 1755; *d.* 1803), naturalist in New Spain (1787–1803). A native of Calahorra, Spain, Longinos studied botany at the Royal Botanical Garden in Madrid before traveling to Mexico in 1787. Longinos preferred the study of animals and spent his time in Mexico studying birds, butterflies, fish, and mammals. He traveled through Lower and Upper California in 1791 and 1792, and kept a detailed journal on Indian life and customs, geography, and fauna and flora. Following his assignment in California, Longinos went to Guatemala, where he opened a small museum and gave lessons in botany. He died of tuberculosis on a trip to Campeche in Yucatán.

LESLEY BYRD SIMPSON, ed. and trans, *Journal of José Longinos Martínez: Notes and Observations of the Naturalist of the Botanical Expedition in Old and New California and the South Coast, 1791–1792* (1961); IRIS H. W. ENGSTRAND, *Spanish Scientists in the New World: The Eighteenth-Century Expeditions* (1981).

IRIS H. W. ENGSTRAND

LÓPEZ, AMBROSIO (*b.* 1809; *d.* 19 June 1881), Colombian artisan and political activist. Ambrosio López illustrates the potential social mobility afforded by nineteenth-century patron-client relations. Born in Bogotá to the tailor Jerónimo López and the *chichera* (brewer) Rosa Pinzón, López used political associations with, first, General Francisco de Paula SANTANDER, and then Tomás Cipriano de MOSQUERA to secure various appointments. López helped found the Democratic Society of Artisans in 1847, only later (1851) to quit the organization because he thought that Liberal anti-Catholicism had corrupted it. Ambrosio supported Mosquera in opposing the 1854 revolt of José María MELO, for which he was rewarded with the post of director of waters for Bogotá during the 1860s. He participated in several Catholic mutual aid organizations, favored a more traditional political economy, and op-

posed Liberalism on most points. In the 1870s, Ambrosio ran the distillery Los Tres Puentes, owned by the SAMPER brothers. His association with the Sampers later enabled his son, Pedro, to become an important banker; his grandson, Alfonso LÓPEZ PUMAREJO, served as president of the country in the 1930s.

AMBROSIO LÓPEZ, *El desengaño o confidencias de Ambrosio López, primer director de la Sociedad de Artesanos de Bogotá, denominada hoi "Sociedad Democrática" escrito para conocimiento de sus consocios* (1851); ALFONSO LÓPEZ, *Mi novela: Apuntes autobiográficos de Alfonso López,* edited by Hugo LaTorre Cabal (1961).

DAVID SOWELL

LÓPEZ, CARLOS ANTONIO (*b.* 4 November 1792; *d.* 10 September 1862), president of Paraguay (1844–1862). López was the second of the three major nineteenth-century, post-Independence rulers of Paraguay, after José Gaspar Rodríguez de FRANCIA. Elite contemporaries and traditional historians have viewed him as a benevolent despot who discouraged opposition but was less ruthless, more self-interested, and more receptive to foreigners and the elite than was Francia. Revisionist historians see López's administration as having modernized Paraguay and developed commerce and foreign ties.

Born and educated in Asunción, López graduated from the Real Colegio y Seminario de San Carlos. He won a competition in 1814 for the chair of arts and another in 1817 for the chair of theology. A lucrative law practice served to introduce him to influential clients and friends. When Francia gained control of the elite, López retired to his family home in Recoleta. In 1826 he married Juana Pabla Carillo, who had an ESTANCIA in Olivares, southeast of Asunción. They had five children.

In February 1841, when Colonel Mariano Roque ALONSO, an uneducated soldier, won the power struggle that ensued at the death of Francia, López became his secretary. On March 12 a national congress appointed Alonso and López to a three-year joint consulate and elected López president in 1844, 1854, and 1857.

During his first term, López continued many of Francia's foreign and domestic policies. Paraguay, continuing its isolation from the countries along the Río de la Plata, regulated foreign commerce and migration. In his second and third terms, López sought to modernize Paraguay. The bureaucracy grew and taxes increased, but the budget was balanced. The government strengthened its army, developed a river navy, and improved internal transportation and communication. In 1852 the López government established steamship service between Asunción, Paraná, Rosario, Buenos Aires, and Montevideo. In 1853, López signed commercial treaties with Great Britain, France, and the United States that brought Paraguay international recognition. Although government regulation of major exports—YERBA MATÉ, lumber, and hides—continued, commercial treaties signed with Brazil in 1850 and with Argentina in 1856 defined borders, permitted free navigation of the Paraguay and Paraná rivers, and increased trade. In 1861, López inaugurated a railroad from Asunción to Santísima Trinidad, which was extended almost to Areguá before his death.

Pursuing his program of modernization further, López expanded rural primary schools, reopened the seminary that Francia had closed, and encouraged European immigration. He also contracted with European and North American technicians, engineers, educators, and advisers who, among other things, carried out a national geological survey; established medical services; developed industries such as a gun factory, iron foundry, and shipyard; and encouraged education and artistic endeavors. Although López limited free expression, he supported publication of Paraguay's first newspapers: *El Paraguayo Independiente* (1845–1852) and *El Semanario de Aviso y Conocimientos Útiles* (1853–1868). Under López agricultural production expanded and the government helped improve the quality of Paraguay's export cotton and tobacco. López ended the African slave trade, recognized Indian villagers as Paraguayan citizens, and used the army to end indigenous border raids.

Although López's vision for Paraguay was more self-serving than Francia's, his administration ensured that the GUARANI peasantry remained the basis of Paraguayan society. López bequeathed a unified, prosperous nation without foreign debt to his eldest son, Francisco Solano LÓPEZ.

JOHN HOYT WILLIAMS, *The Rise and Fall of the Paraguayan Republic, 1800–1870* (1979), the best available nineteenth-century history, has an extensive description and analysis of López and his administration. THOMAS J. PAGE, *La Plata, the Argentine Confederation, and Paraguay* (1859), by a contemporary, provides a useful description of López's policies. The U.S. minister to Asunción from 1862 to 1868, CHARLES A. WASHBURN, in *The History of Paraguay, with Notes of Personal Observations and Reminiscences of Diplomacy Under Difficulty*, 2 vols. (1871), provides biased criticism of both José Gaspar Francia and C. A. López but nevertheless remains an important source. JUAN F. PÉREZ ACOSTA, *Carlos Antonio López, obrero máximo, labor administrativa y constructiva* (1948), based on extensive archival research, describes the economic accomplishments and administration of C. A. López. JULIO CÉSAR CHAVES, *El Presidente López*, 2d ed. (1968), uses multi-archival research to analyze the political and diplomatic developments of the C. A. López administration. PETER A. SCHMITT, *Paraguay y Europa 1811–1870* (1990), translated from the German by Frank M. Samson, provides diplomatic information. A work from the FUNDACIÓN CULTURAL REPUBLICANA, *Mensajes de Carlos Antonio López* (1987), is a useful collection of López's speeches.

VERA BLINN REBER

LÓPEZ, ENRIQUE SOLANO (*b.* 2 October 1859; *d.* 19 November 1917), Paraguayan journalist, teacher, and politician who left a large library and archives. Son of Francisco Solano López and Elisa LYNCH, he worked ceaselessly to revive his late father's reputation, which had been shattered due to his haste in bringing Paraguay into the bloody and disastrous WAR OF THE TRIPLE ALLIANCE in 1864. López traveled throughout Europe, and directed the conservative Colorado Party newspaper *La Patria*. He served as the national superintendent of primary schools (1897–1899) and was a Colorado Party senator (1912–1917) and mayor of Asunción in 1912. He ended his illustrious political and writing career as a professor at the National University.

CHARLES KOLINSKY, *Historical Dictionary of Paraguay* (1973); OSVALDO KALLSEN, *Asunción y sus calles* (1974).

MIGUEL A. GATTI

See also **Paraguay: Political Parties.**

LÓPEZ, ESTANISLAO (*b.* 22 November 1786; *d.* 15 June 1838), governor of the province of Santa Fe (1818–1838). Born in the city of Santa Fe, Argentina, López studied in the local convent school. At the age of fifteen he joined the BLANDENGUES who patrolled the northern frontier, where he learned the hit-and-run tactics that his *montonero* soldiers would later use. He participated in the reconquest of Buenos Aires (1806) and in the struggles for independence in the littoral. SAN MARTÍN early won him over to his ideas. On 23 July 1818, López separated the province of Santa Fe from Buenos Aires by proclaiming himself its interim governor; the following year, he was elected governor, and remained so until his death. In 1819 he gave the province its first constitutional statute. He joined José Gervasio ARTIGAS and Francisco RAMÍREZ in their war against Buenos Aires. He and Ramírez defeated Buenos Aires at Cepeda (1 February 1820) and compelled its CABILDO to dissolve the national congress and to sign the Treaty of PILAR (23 February). Peace was reestablished between Buenos Aires and Santa Fe with the Treaty of Benegas (24 November). With the death of Ramírez in 1821, López became the dominant leader in the littoral. On 22 January 1822 he signed the Quadrilateral Treaty, and on the eve of the Brazilian invasion of Uruguay he approved an alliance with Montevideo (13 March 1823).

In 1828, López presided over the national convention in Santa Fe that approved the peace treaty with Brazil and appointed him commander of the national army to fight the unitarian José María PAZ. At his initiative, the FEDERALIST PACT was negotiated and signed in Santa Fe (4 January 1831). As governor, he encouraged trade and economic development, pushed the provincial borders farther into the CHACO, improved the administration of justice, and established elementary schools, including one in an Abipón village, and a secondary school. His influence diminished as that of Juan Manuel de ROSAS increased.

YSABEL F. RENNIE, *The Argentine Republic* (1945); H. S. FERNS, *Britain and Argentina in the Nineteenth Century* (1960); JOSÉ LUIS ROMERO, *A History of Argentine Political Thought*, translated by

Thomas F. McGann (1963); TULIO HALPERÍN-DONGHI, *Politics, Economics, and Society in Argentina in the Revolutionary Period*, translated by Richard Southern (1975); JOHN LYNCH, *Argentine Dictator: Juan Manuel de Rosas, 1829–1852* (1981); LESLIE BETHELL, ed., *Spanish America After Independence, 1820–1870* (1987); JOSEPH T. CRISCENTI, ed., *Sarmiento and His Argentina* (1993).

JOSEPH T. CRISCENTI

LÓPEZ, FRANCISCO SOLANO (*b*. 24 July 1826; *d*. 1 March 1870), president of Paraguay (1862–1870) and the third of its three major nineteenth-century post-Independence administrators. Paraguayans traditionally have viewed López as a national hero, whereas revisionists have judged him to be an ambitious nationalist who overestimated the economic significance and military strength of Paraguay and involved it in the disastrous WAR OF THE TRIPLE ALLIANCE.

Born in Asunción as the eldest son of Carlos Antonio LÓPEZ, raised on the family *estancia* in Olivares, and privately educated by tutors, López became his father's principal adviser, confidant, and heir apparent. When Carlos Antonio López declared war on Juan Manuel de ROSAS of Argentina in 1845, he made eighteen-year-old Francisco Solano a brigadier general. From 1853 to 1854, the younger López negotiated contracts for technicians and arms in Europe, where he met Elisa Alicia Lynch, who became his mistress and bore him five sons. As commander of the army and vice president, he dominated the triumvirate that ruled at his father's death. On 16 October 1862 a congress elected him president of Paraguay for a ten-year term.

General López continued the political system and economic policies of his father. He sought to make Asunción similar to European capitals—socially vibrant and culturally stimulating, with regular theater performances and fashionable events. He encouraged trade and provided government loans for commercial enterprises, railroad expansion, and telegraph construction. His administration increased the number of doctors, engineers, teachers, and skilled workers and also centralized education and the economy. Although López accumulated his own land and wealth, he was well accepted by both the peasantry and the elite.

When López sought to increase Paraguay's international role in the Río de la Plata area, he clashed with Argentina and Brazil. After leading the armed forces in the War of the Triple Alliance (1864–1870) for more than five years, he was killed at the battle of CERRO CORÁ.

JOHN HOYT WILLIAMS, *The Rise and Fall of the Paraguayan Republic, 1800–1870* (1979), provides the most recent material in English. JUAN EMILIANO O'LEARY, *El Mariscal Solano López*, 3d ed. (1970), describes the political and military accomplishments of Paraguay's national hero. R. B. CUNNINGHAME GRAHAM, *Portrait of a Dictator* (1933), provides the standard foreign condemnation and thus should be considered carefully.

VERA BLINN REBER

LÓPEZ, JOSÉ HILARIO (*b*. 18 February 1798; *d*. 27 November 1869), president of Colombia (1849–1853). Born in Popayán, López joined the patriots in 1814 and was imprisoned by the royalists from 1816 to 1819. Freed, he fought in Venezuela and in southern Colombia, becoming a colonel in 1826. He rejected Simon BOLÍVAR's dictatorship, and at the Ocaña Convention in 1828 he remained antidictator. Later that year, López and Colonel José María OBANDO defeated Bolívar's surrogate, Colonel Tomás Cipriano de MOSQUERA, and won control of Cauca. In 1830 López was promoted to general, and with Obando he raised an army that ousted General Rafael URDANETA in May 1831. López served in key gubernatorial posts from 1833 to 1837 and was the Colombian chargé d'affaires to the Vatican (1839–1840).

López did not join Obando in the WAR OF THE SUPREMES (1839–1842). Having married into the Neiva elite, he devoted himself to managing his estates until he was elected president. As chief executive, he carried out a liberal agenda. Education was made more secular, the clergy put on salary, the Jesuits expelled, tithe collection secularized, the ecclesiastical *fuero* abolished, clerical posts made elective, and Archbishop Manuel José MOSQUERA exiled. Also, slavery was abolished and legislation aimed at improving the status of women was

Francisco Solano López. ORGANIZATION OF AMERICAN STATES.

enacted. López fought against the Melo Revolt (1854). He joined the Liberal Revolution (1860–1862) late, but contributed to its victory. He participated in the Rionegro Convention (1863).

ABEL CRUZ SANTOS, *General José Hilario López, 1869–noviembre 27–1969* (1969) and *José Hilario López, o el soldado civil* (1970); JUAN PABLO LLINAS, *José Hilario López* (1983). See also LÓPEZ's *Memorias del general José Hilario López* (1857), which covers 1814 to 1839.

J. LEÓN HELGUERA

LÓPEZ, NARCISO (*b.* 19 October 1797; *d.* 1 September 1851), Cuban revolutionist. A native of Caracas, Venezuela, López joined the Spanish army in his mid-teens, participated in campaigns against Simón Bolívar's independence movement, and achieved the rank of colonel. When Spanish forces withdrew to Cuba in 1823, López accompanied the army to the island. There he married the sister of a creole planter, and acquired landholdings and mines. In 1827 López went to Spain, where, during the Carlist wars, he served as aide-de-camp to General Gerónimo Valdés in support of the queen-regent, María Cristina, and her daughter, Isabella, against the claims to the succession of Don Carlos, brother of the late Ferdinand VII. While in Spain, López rose to the rank of brigadier general. López returned to Cuba when Valdés became captain-general of the colony in 1841. During Valdés's tenure, López served as president of the Executive and Permanent Military Commission and governor of Trinidad Province—posts which he lost when General Leopoldo O'Donnell replaced Valdés in 1843. This loss of patronage, as well as financial setbacks, may have contributed to López's conversion to anticolonialism in the mid-1840s.

López's overt revolutionary activities commenced in 1848 with a plot named after his mines—Conspiracy of the Cuban Rose Mine. Set to erupt in late June, the uprising was postponed until mid-July in deference to the wishes of the Havana Club, which favored annexation of Cuba to the United States. Alerted by the U.S. government to the pending revolt, Spanish authorities took preemptive action. Having escaped arrest in the resultant crackdown, López reached the United States, where he organized a private military—or "FILIBUSTERING"—expedition to liberate Cuba. In 1849 the Zachary Taylor administration thwarted this effort, which, like all filibustering expeditions, violated U.S. neutrality statutes, by blockading López's troops assembled at Round Island, off the Gulf coast, and by seizing his ships and supplies in New York City.

Undaunted, López and associated exiles announced a junta based in New York City but with a Washington, D.C., address. On 19 May 1850, López and some 520 followers captured Cárdenas, on Cuba's northern coast. His forces outnumbered by Spanish reinforcements, López fled to Key West, Florida. He was indicted in June 1850 for violating American neutrality laws but never stood trial (charges were dismissed after three juries failed to convict a coconspirator).

Federal authorities upset his next invasion scheme when, in April 1851, they seized the vessel *Cleopatra* in New York and arrested several filibuster leaders. However, that August, López eluded federal authorities and invaded Cuba with some 453 men. His force debarked the coasting packet *Pampero* near Bahía Honda, west of Havana. López mismanaged the ensuing military campaign, which was doomed to failure because Spanish authorities repressed developing resistance prior to the landing. Many of López's followers died in battle. The rest, except for a couple of officers who had returned to the United States for reinforcements, were captured. Spanish authorities released a few, but executed fifty invaders on 16 August and later sent some 160 captives to imprisonment in Spain. López was garroted in Havana on 1 September, in a public display. News of the 16 August executions sparked riots in New Orleans, Mobile, and Key West that did thousands of dollars' worth of damage to Spanish property. Disputes arising from the López invasions complicated for years diplomatic relations between the United States, Spain, and Great Britain and France—the latter two seeking to dominate the Gulf-Caribbean region economically—and left a legacy of fear of American intentions among Spanish officials ruling Cuba.

Some authorities, noting the disproportionate number of Americans in López's filibuster armies, his flag modeled upon the banner of the Republic of Texas, and his contacts with both Americans and Cubans favoring the annexation of Cuba to the United States as a new slave state, portray López as a conservative who intended to integrate Cuba into the United States. A few scholars, however, view López as a liberal nationalist—an early martyr to the cause of Cuban independence.

ROBERT G. CALDWELL, *The López Expeditions to Cuba, 1848–1851* (1915); HERMINIO PORTELL VILÁ, *Narciso López y su época*, 3 vols. (1930–1958); BASIL RAUCH, *American Interest in Cuba, 1848–1855* (1948); PHILIP S. FONER, *A History of Cuba and Its Relations with the United States*, vol. 2 (1963), esp. pp. 41–65; CHARLES HENRY BROWN, *Agents of Manifest Destiny: The Lives and Times of the Filibusters* (1980), esp. pp. 21–108.

ROBERT E. MAY

LÓPEZ, VICENTE FIDEL (*b.* 24 April 1815; *d.* 30 August 1903), Argentine historian and political figure. Born in Buenos Aires and the son of Vicente López y Planes, who wrote Argentina's national anthem, López as a young intellectual became involved during the 1830s in Esteban ECHEVERRÍA's Asociación de Mayo. Fearing possible persecution by the Juan Manuel de ROSAS dictatorship, López fled to Chile, where he worked as an educator and liberal publicist. Returning to Buenos Aires after the fall of Rosas in 1852, he served briefly in the provincial government, then emigrated to Uruguay until national unity was finally effected.

Once permanently reestablished in Buenos Aires, López served as university rector, finance minister, and in other capacities, as well as practicing journalism. However, he is best known for his work as a historian. That career began in Chile with the publication of historical novels and essays, and it culminated when he both published historical documents and authored a series of major works of Argentine history, notably his ten-volume *Historia de la República Argentina* (1883–1893). His writing was highly partisan and made use of a lively imagination rather than depending on rigorous documentation, a trait that drew him into a bitter polemic over historical method with Bartolomé MITRE. He was, however, a skilled writer and enjoyed a wide following in his time.

RÓMULO D. CARBÍA, *Historia crítica de la historiografía argentina* (1939), pp. 121–148; RICARDO PICCIRILLI, *Los López: Una dinastía intelectual* (1972).

DAVID BUSHNELL

LÓPEZ, WILEBALDO (*b.* 3 July 1944), Mexican playwright. Born in Queréndaro, he studied acting, received a Writers' Guild Fellowship, and was the first dramatist of his generation to achieve recognition. Two of his early plays were widely staged in Mexico: *Los arrieros con sus burros por la hermosa capital* (1967) and *Cosas de muchachos* (1968). His others include *Yo soy Juárez* (1972) and *Malinche Show* (1977), adaptations of Mexican history in modern terms. His recent works have not enjoyed the same popularity as the earlier ones with audiences and critics.

MALKAH RABELL, *Decenio de teatro 1975–1985* (1986); GUILLERMO SCHMIDHUBER DE LA MORA, "*Los viejos* y la dramaturgia mexicana," *Cahiers du C.R.I.A.R.,* no. 7 (1987): 127–133; RONALD D. BURGESS, *The New Dramatists of Mexico* (1991).

GUILLERMO SCHMIDHUBER

LÓPEZ ARELLANO, OSWALDO (*b.* 30 June 1921), the dominant military officer in Honduras from 1957 until 1975. Born in Danlí, López Arellano joined the armed services in 1939 and was schooled in military aviation in the United States. As commander of the armed forces beginning in 1956, he was installed as provisional president after the coup of 3 October 1963. This coup, carried out ten days before scheduled elections, reflected the Conservatives' and the military's displeasure with the prospect for a victory by the Liberal candidate, Modesto Rodas Alvarado. López continued as provisional president until a new constitution confirmed him as president in 1965. During his presidency the poor performance of the military in the war with El Salvador (1969) brought discredit on the armed services. López maintained a mild military dictatorship during his term,

which continued until 1971. The National Party became his personal political vehicle.

In 1971 Ramón Ernesto CRUZ was elected president, but López, as chief of the armed forces, remained in control. In 1972, López again seized power and acted as president until he was toppled by his fellow officers in 1975. At that time, he was charged with corruption in accepting a bribe from United Brands (formerly UNITED FRUIT) to obtain lower banana export taxes. López subsequently became the president of the national airline, Servicio Aereo de Honduras, S.A. (SAHSA).

RAÚL ALBERTO DOMÍNGUEZ, ed., *Ascenso al poder y descenso del General Oswaldo López Arellano* (1975); JAMES A. MORRIS, *Honduras: Caudillo Politics and Military Rulers* (1984).

DAVID L. JICKLING

See also **Honduras: Political Parties.**

LÓPEZ BUCHARDO, CARLOS (*b.* 12 October 1881; *d.* 21 April 1948), Argentine composer and teacher. Born in Buenos Aires, López Buchardo began his musical studies with Héctor Belucci and studied piano with Alfonso Thibaud. He studied harmony with Luis Forino and Constantino GAITO. Later he moved to Paris to attend the composition classes of Albert Roussel. Returning to Buenos Aires, López Buchardo founded the eponymous Conservatorio López Buchardo (1924) and directed it until his death.

López Buchardo began to compose as a young man, starting with pieces for the stage, some musicals, and an early opera, *Il sogno di Alma,* which premiered in Buenos Aires on 4 August 1914. He was an excellent melodist with an extraordinary gift for vocal works, and his numerous song cycles, which are based on Argentine folk tunes and themes, were popular worldwide. Among his symphonic works is the *Escenas argentinas* (1920), in which he utilized two popular dances, the *milonga* and *gato;* it premiered under Felix Weingartner with the Vienna Philharmonic Orchestra in Buenos Aires in 1922. The following year López Buchardo received the Municipal Prize in Music. He was founder and director of the school of fine arts at the University of La Plata, where he was professor of harmony. He was also president of the Wagnerian Association, twice member of the board of TEATRO COLÓN, and director of music and art for the stage for the Ministry of Public Instruction. He died in Buenos Aires.

Composers of the Americas, vol. 12 (1966); ABRAHAM JURAFSKY, *Carlos López Buchardo* (1966); *New Grove Dictionary of Music and Musicians,* vol. 11 (1980).

SUSANA SALGADO

LÓPEZ CAPILLAS, FRANCISCO (*b.* ca. 1615; *d.* ca. 18 January 1673), Mexican composer and organist. López Capillas may have been born in Andalusia and was probably a pupil of Juan de Riscos, the *maestro de capilla* of Jaén. Ordained a priest, he was named organist and bassoonist for the Puebla cathedral in December 1641. In 1645 he became first organist and singer. In May 1648 he went to Mexico City, where he was hired by the cathedral organist Fabián Ximeno, who had heard López Capillas on a visit to the Puebla cathedral and been impressed with his talent. He presented a volume of his choir compositions to the Mexico cathedral in April 1654, and on 21 May he was appointed *maestro de capilla* and organist of the cathedral. He was supervisor of the musical services and presented the cathedral with several excellently illuminated choirbooks. López's compositions are considered among the best written in New Spain; his eight Masses, eight Magnificats, and numerous other religious works are composed with extraordinary artfulness. His use of the polyphony, canon, and difficult mensural practices were remarkably competent. The arrival in Madrid of some of his choirbooks generated a court decree (1672) to bestow him a full prebend, but he died in Mexico City before the order became effective.

ROBERT STEVENSON, "Francisco López Capillas," in *Heterofonía* 6 (1973), and *Renaissance and Baroque Musical Sources in the Americas* (1970); *New Grove Dictionary of Music and Musicians*, vol. 11 (1980).

SUSANA SALGADO

LÓPEZ CONTRERAS, ELEÁZAR (*b.* 5 May 1883; *d.* 2 January 1973), president of Venezuela (1936–1941). Having completed high school in 1898, López Contreras joined the army of Cipriano CASTRO in 1899. In 1908, he left the army with the rank of colonel, but in 1913 he returned as commander of the barracks of Ciudad Bolívar, and in 1914 assumed command of an infantry regiment at Caracas. In 1919 he became minister of war and marine, and undertook the acquisition of war matériel from Europe and the United States. As a loyal supporter of Juan Vicente GÓMEZ, he used military force against students, workers, dissident army officers, and other opposition groups. For his reward, he rose through the ranks during the 1920s, taking over as commander in chief in 1930. From 1931 until December 1935, he again served as minister of war and marine.

Following Gómez's death López became president of the republic. He quickly ended popular demonstrations by students and workers. In so doing, he became the first Venezuelan president to speak to the nation by radio. In February 1936, he introduced a broad reform program aimed at appealing to everyone. On the one hand, he checked the power of the army. On the other, he followed Arturo USLAR PIETRI's call to "sow the petroleum" by using oil revenues to finance educational and institutional reforms. The government established a new teacher training institution, the Instituto Pedagógico (1936), and gave further assistance to child care

by creating the Consejo Venezolano del Niño (1939), the Instituto Preorientación para Menores (1939), and the Casa de Maternidad Concepción Palacios (1938). New cabinet departments included the Ministry of Agriculture and Livestock and the Ministry of Labor and Communications.

López's administration guided Venezuela toward a more democratic government. He tolerated opposition movements, although he exiled Communists and radicals. Like Gómez, he followed an anticommunist policy and limited the activities of labor organizations. The government also imposed more control over the economy by creating the Industrial Bank and the National Exchange Office, as well as the Central Bank of Venezuela.

In 1938, the López government enacted petroleum legislation aimed at giving the nation more control over the industry and a larger share in the revenue, but for various reasons, including corruption, little was done to enforce the laws. In 1941, López stepped down from power, the presidential term having been reduced from seven to five years, and turned the government over to his chosen successor, Isaías MEDINA ANGARITA. Following the overthrow of the latter, López Contreras went into exile and effectively dropped out of politics.

HENRY J. ALLEN, *Venezuela: A Democracy* (1941); ELEÁZAR LÓPEZ CONTRERAS, *Proceso político social, 1928–1936* (1965); WINFIELD J. BURGGRAAFF, *The Venezuelan Armed Forces in Politics, 1935–1959* (1972); ALFRED TARRE MURZI, *López Contreras: De la tiranía a la libertad*, 2d ed. (1982); *López Contreras, el último general* (1983); JUDITH EWELL, *Venezuela: A Century of Change* (1984); EMILIO PACHECO, *De Castro a López Contreras* (1984).

WINTHROP R. WRIGHT

LÓPEZ DE ARTEAGA, SEBASTIÁN (*b.* 15 March 1610; *d.* 1652), painter. Born in Seville, López de Arteaga was examined as a painter in 1630. In 1638 he was in Cádiz; around 1640 he embarked for New Spain, where in 1642 he erected and decorated an arch with mythological subjects to celebrate the arrival of Viceroy García SARMIENTO DE SOTOMAYOR y Luna. López de Arteaga is credited with introducing into New Spain the tenebrist style of Francisco de Zurbarán, who some scholars claim had been his teacher. He sought, and with some success won, the patronage of the Inquisition. Although documents attest to López de Arteaga's considerable activity, only eight paintings can be ascribed to him with certainty, and even some of those are problematic. One of the most famous is the *Incredulity of Saint Thomas* (1643). More difficult is the *Marriage of the Virgin*, quite dissimilar and the subject of much discussion over what constitutes this master's style.

MANUEL TOUSSAINT, *Colonial Art in Mexico* (1967); XAVIER MOYSSEN, "Sebastián de Arteaga, 1610–1652," in *Anales del Instituto de investigaciones estéticas* 59 (1988): 17–34.

CLARA BARGELLINI

LÓPEZ DE CERRATO, ALONSO (also Cerrato, Alonso López; *b.* ca. 1490; *d.* 5 May 1555), president of the Audiencia of Santo Domingo (1543–1547); president of the AUDIENCIA DE LOS CONFINES, later Guatemala (1548–1555). Of obscure origins but educated and enjoying royal favor, Cerrato was appointed to serve in Santo Domingo and then Guatemala to enforce the NEW LAWS OF 1542 and other proindigenous legislation. Stern and uncompromising, he freed Indian slaves in both jurisdictions, lowered tributes, and corrected abuses in Central America. Supported by Bartolomé de LAS CASAS (1474–1566) and other reformers and indifferent to local public opinion, he earned the enmity of Spanish settlers, who accused him of nepotism. He died while serving his *residencia*.

MURDO J. MacLEOD

LÓPEZ DE COGOLLUDO, DIEGO (*b.* ca. 1612; *d.* ca. 1665), Franciscan historian and missionary. Born in Alcalá de Henares, Spain, Friar López de Cogolludo arrived as a missionary in Yucatán in 1634, and after years of work among the MAYA he rose to be the chief (provincial) of the Franciscan province. In the 1650s he wrote *Historia de Yucathan*, a major source not only for the history of Yucatán but also for the study of Maya culture. The book was published posthumously in Madrid in 1688; later editions appeared in 1842 (Campeche), and 1846 and 1867–1868 (Mérida). Reprints and new editions also appeared in the twentieth century.

GABRIEL FERRER DE MENDIOLEA, "Historia de la historiografía," *Enciclopedia yucatanense*, vol. 5 (1944), pp. 815–846; J. IGNACIO RUBIO MAÑÉ, "Preface," in DIEGO LÓPEZ DE COGOLLUDO, *Historia de Yucathan*, 3 vols. (1954–1957).

ROBERT W. PATCH

LÓPEZ DE LEGAZPI Y GURRUCHÁTEGUI, MIGUEL (*b.* 1510; *d.* 1572), *escribano mayor* (senior clerk of the Mexico City *cabildo* (municipal council) from January 1542 to 3 June 1557. López perhaps epitomizes the career of a sixteenth-century bureaucrat who, arriving late in a conquest area, had to work to achieve upward mobility. An *hidalgo* (nobleman) from Zumárraga, Guipúzcoa, in the Basque country, López departed for New Spain in 1528. On 19 January 1530 he became the *escribano de cabildo* of Mexico City, serving in that capacity until the end of 1541. For a period after 1535 he was secretary in the government of Viceroy Antonio de MENDOZA. After serving as *escribano mayor* of the *cabildo*, he transferred his rights to his son, Melchor de Legazpi.

López's offices, while not providing the opportunity to acquire an *encomienda* (grant of tribute from an indigenous polity) in New Spain, did permit the development of contracts, status (his wife, Isabel Garcés, was the sister of Julián Garcés, first bishop of Tlaxcala), and other assets that he parlayed into a license to settle the Philippine Islands. On 21 November 1564 his armada of 5 ships, 150 sailors, 200 salaried employees, some 25 settlers, and 4 Augustinian friars left Mexico. The navigator for the expedition was the Augustinian friar Andrés de URDANETA. López was governor of the Philippines when he died in Manila.

IGNACIO BEJARANO, *Actas de cabildo de la Ciudad de Mexico*, vols. 2, 4, and 6 (1889); JOSÉ ROGELIO ÁLVAREZ, ed., *Enciclopedia de México*, vol. 8 (1975), p. 4785; and PETER BOYD-BOWMAN, *Índice geobiográfico de cuarenta mil pobladores españoles de América en el siglo XVI*, vol. 2 (1968).

ROBERT HIMMERICH Y VALENCIA

LÓPEZ DE QUIROGA, ANTONIO (*b.* ca. 1620; *d.* late January 1699), silver mine owner in Potosí. López de Quiroga was born near Triacastela in the province of Lugo, in northwestern Spain. He was the leading silver producer of Potosí (and possibly of all Spanish America) in the seventeenth century, owning mines and refineries at Potosí itself as well as at other sites widely scattered over its district. Between 1661 and 1699, these operations provided about 14 million ounces of silver, a seventh or an eighth of the Potosí district's total output in that period.

About 1648 López came to Potosí, where he used his prior commercial experience to set himself up as an importing merchant. He quickly married Doña Felipa Bóveda y Savavia, daughter of a prosperous local family from Galicia, close to his own birthplace in Spain. He benefited from an investigation of coinage adulteration at the Potosí mint, which led to the removal of most of the existing *mercaderes de plata* (silver traders and coinage supervisors) thereby paving the way for his eventual entrance to that profession in the 1650s. From this position, he moved into silver production about 1660, and in that decade rapidly expanded his holdings of mines and refineries in Potosí. In the 1670s and 1680s he extended his activities to Porco, Ocurí, San Antonio del Nuevo Mundo, and other sites in the district, often reviving old mines through the excavation of deep drainage galleries. To expedite this process, about 1670 he introduced the technique of blasting with gunpowder, probably for the first time in Spanish-American silver mining.

López placed many relatives in governmental positions in the Potosí district during the 1670s and 1680s, thus safeguarding his own interests. He became a large landowner and used his estates to supply goods useful in mining. Though he was unsuccessful in acquiring a title of nobility, he ended his days an already quasimythical figure in Potosí.

BARTOLOMÉ ARZÁNS DE ORSÚA Y VELA, *Historia de la Villa Imperial de Potosí*, edited by Lewis Hanke and Gunnar Mendoza I. 3 vols. (1965), vol. 2; PETER BAKEWELL, *Silver and Entre-*

preneurship in Seventeenth-Century Potosí: The Life and Times of Antonio López de Quiroga (1988).

PETER BAKEWELL

See also **Coinage; Mining.**

LÓPEZ DE ROMAÑA, EDUARDO (b. 1847; d. 1912), president of Peru from 1899 to 1903. When President Nicolas de PIÉROLA created the post of minister of development, he chose López de Romaña to fill it. López de Romaña successfully undertook an ambitious public works program and pledged to continue Piérola's progressive plans if the president in turn agreed to support him as the next president. On the basis of that agreement and with an alliance formed between Democrats and Civilistas, López de Romaña became president in 1899. In 1901 he began to reorganize the nation's schools to give more emphasis to technical skills in higher education. But his political naïveté made him susceptible to Civilista manipulation, and other progressive programs had less success. By the 1903 election the coalition of parties had split, some members joining the new Liberal Party and others returning to the Civilista Party. Even Piérola had abandoned him in favor of an old friend, Manuel CANDAMO, the Civilista candidate who won the election. The elite political machinations of the post-Piérola years thus kept power in the hands of the national oligarchy.

STEVE STEIN, *Populism in Peru: The Emergence of the Masses and the Politics of Social Control* (1980); ALFONSO W. QUIROZ, *Domestic and Foreign Finance in Modern Peru, 1850–1950: Financing Visions of Development* (1993).

VINCENT PELOSO

See also **Peru: Political Parties.**

LÓPEZ DEL ROSARIO, ANDRÉS. See **Andresote.**

LÓPEZ JORDÁN, RICARDO (b. 30 August 1822; d. 22 June 1889), military leader and staunch defender of provincial autonomy. Born in Paysandú, Uruguay, López Jordán was a nephew of Francisco RAMÍREZ and Justo José de URQUIZA. He attended the Colegio de San Ignacio in Buenos Aires, and began his military career at the age of nineteen as a soldier in the escort of Urquiza. He served in the forces of Urquiza and the Uruguayans Manuel ORIBE, Eugenio Garzón, Lucas Moreno, and César Díaz. Twice military commandant of Concepción del Uruguay, he became extremely popular when he stopped an invasion of his jurisdiction by General Juan Madariaga. He later taught military science at the Colegio del Uruguay, where among his students was Julio A. ROCA (who later defeated him in battle and became president of Argentina). He represented Paraná in the national congress (1858) and accompanied Urquiza to

Asunción to settle an international dispute (1859). López Jordán served as minister of government in the provincial government of Urquiza (1860) and as president of the provincial legislature (1863–1864), but was unsuccessful in his candidacy for governor because of Urquiza's opposition (1864).

During the WAR OF THE TRIPLE ALLIANCE, López Jordán's troops were the only ones not to disband at Basualdo, and he escorted Urquiza home. The day after Urquiza was assassinated, an act for which he assumed responsibility, he was elected governor (12 April 1870). When President SARMIENTO refused to recognize the election and ordered the intervention of the province, the legislature authorized López Jordán to defend provincial autonomy. Sarmiento then besieged the province. Warships patrolled the Uruguay and Paraná rivers, and federal troops, eventually armed with imported Remington rifles, advanced into the province from Gualeguaychú and Corrientes.

López Jordán was supported by the people, many young intellectuals, and the partisans of Adolfo ALSINA. His secretary at the time was José HERNÁNDEZ, author of the epic poem *Martín Fierro*. Defeated at Naembé (26 January 1871), he fled to Brazil. Following an unsuccessful invasion in 1873, he returned to Brazil. His secretary now was Francisco F. Fernández. In 1876, in his last attempt at revolution, which received weak support, López Jordán was captured in Corrientes, but he was able to escape to Montevideo. In 1888, President JUÁREZ CELMAN granted him a pardon. He returned to Buenos Aires, where he was assassinated. Some view him as the last defender of provincial autonomy.

YSABEL F. RENNIE, *The Argentine Republic* (1945), pp. 117–118; MARÍA AMALIA DUARTE, *Urquiza y López Jordán* (1974) and *Tiempos de rebelión, 1870–1873* (1988); JOSEPH T. CRISCENTI, ed., *Sarmiento and His Argentina* (1993), p. 83.

JOSEPH T. CRISCENTI

LÓPEZ MATEOS, ADOLFO (b. 26 May 1910; d. 22 September 1969), president of Mexico (1958–1964). The accession of López Mateos to the presidency in 1958 represented the control of a postrevolutionary generation of politicians who, for the most part, were born in the first two decades of the twentieth century. López Mateos also represented politicians who had opposed the Mexican establishment in the 1929 presidential campaign, in which he and a prominent group of students joined forces with José VASCONCELOS in a bitter and unsuccessful campaign. During the transitional period of his presidency, from 1958 to 1959, López Mateos faced a most difficult labor strike, that of the railroad workers' union, led by Valentín Campa. This strike revealed the union leadership's failure to represent the rank and file and demonstrated the willingness of the new, untried president, who had achieved the office largely on the basis of his skill as labor secretary in avoiding such confrontations, to apply force when necessary. As a result of his use of army intervention, government-dominated union leadership strengthened its hold over this and other unions. In 1960 López Mateos briefly risked his early political successes by refusing to join the United States and most of the rest of Latin America in breaking relations with Castro's Cuba. In fact, he only succeeded in reinforcing Mexico's independent course in foreign affairs—a strategy followed by most of his successors.

On the economic front, López Mateos inherited a devalued peso, but in spite of pressures to devalue once again, he pursued a moderate economic philosophy, promoting the stabilization of the peso and the gradual, steady expansion of the economy. He appointed as treasury secretary Antonio ORTIZ MENA, who became the financial architect of an unprecedented twelve years of growth and continued at the helm of the treasury in the next administration. The López Mateos administration's repressive control of the urban working classes extended to the countryside, as exemplified by the notorious execution of peasant leader Rubén Jaramillo while in the hands of government troops. The forced sacrifices of the Mexican working class were what made possible the economic growth of the 1958–1964 period. This expansion in turn produced a growing middle class and the beginnings of an important industrial infrastructure. There is probably no president in recent times who inherited a better economic and political situation than López Mateos's successor, Gustavo DÍAZ ORDAZ.

López Mateos was born in Atizapán de Zaragoza, México. His father, a dentist, died when he was quite young, leaving his mother to support five children. He attended the Colegio Francés in Mexico City on a scholarship, and completed his secondary and preparatory studies in Toluca, México. A student activist at a young age, he joined the Anti-reelections movement in 1929, working as a librarian to support himself. He attended law school at the National University (1929–1934). Disenchanted with Vasconcelos's failure to win the presidency, he attached himself to the president of the ruling National Revolutionary party (1931–1933). In 1934, he began working for the government printing office, becoming a labor representative of the National Workers Development Bank in 1938 and later serving in the secretariat of public education. President Miguel ALEMÁN VALDÉS, whom López Mateos represented on numerous assignments abroad, selected him as one of the PRI's candidates for senator from his home state in 1946. In 1951, while still a senator, he became secretary general of the party, organizing the campaign committee for Adolfo RUIZ CORTINES's presidential bid (1951–1952). Ruiz Cortines rewarded him for his efforts by appointing him secretary of labor, a position he served in successfully until his own candidacy for the presidency in 1957. He became the only person in the history of the party to win the presidential office from the labor post. After he left the presidency in 1964, president Díaz Ordaz asked him to organize the 1968 Olympic Games in

Mexico City. Severe illness prevented him from fulfilling this assignment, and he died after a stroke.

TOMÁS CONTRERAS ESTRADA, México y Adolfo López Mateos (1959); ROBERT E. SCOTT, Mexican Government in Transition, rev. ed. (1964); FRANK BRANDENBURG, The Making of Modern Mexico (1964); L. VINCENT PADGETT, The Mexican Political System (1966); OLGA PELLICER DE BRODY and JOSÉ LUIS REYNA, Historia de la Revolución Mexicana, 1952–1960, vol. 22 (1978); OLGA PELLICER DE BRODY and ESTEBAN L. MANCILLA, Historia de la Revolución Mexicana, 1952–1960, vol. 23 (1978).

RODERIC AI CAMP

See also **Mexico: Political Parties.**

LÓPEZ MICHELSEN, ALFONSO (*b.* 30 June 1913), president of Colombia (1974–1978). The son of Alfonso LÓPEZ PUMAREJO (president 1934–1938 and 1942–1945), López Michelsen was educated in Bogotá, the United States, and Europe, and received his law degree in 1936. In 1958 he organized the leftist Liberal Revolutionary Movement (MRL) in opposition to the bipartisan National Front. A decade later López rejoined the official Liberal fold, becoming governor of Cesar Department in 1967, and later foreign minister. In 1974 he won the first post-Front presidential election; his program included a series of fiscal reforms and an opening to the nonviolent left. Growing popular discontent fueled by rising inflation turned violent in the general strike of September 1977. The resurgence of guerrilla activity led López, once a critic of emergency powers, to impose a state of siege in June 1975. Running again in 1982 López was defeated by the Conservative Belisario BETANCUR CUARTAS. López's writings include *Cuestiones colombianas* (1955) and the novel *Los elegidos* (1953).

HERNANDO GÓMEZ BUENDÍA, Alfonso López Michelsen (1978); IGNACIO ARIZMENDI POSADA, Presidentes de Colombia, 1810–1990 (1990).

RICHARD J. STOLLER

See also **Colombia: Political Parties.**

LÓPEZ PORTILLO, JOSÉ (*b.* 16 June 1920), president of Mexico (1976–1982). López Portillo took office at a time when Mexico first began undergoing a series of political and economic crises, beginning a long cycle of problems extending to the 1990s. When his predecessor, Luis ECHEVERRÍA, left office, he also left a legacy of devaluation, an unstable peso and inflation (for the first time in recent history), the distrust of the private sector, and a populist political heritage. Those disenchanted with the Echeverría administration were hopeful when López Portillo was inaugurated. The new president, with some intellectual credentials, and without a long career in the federal government, seemed to offer something new to expectant Mexicans. To mend fences with the alienated business leadership, the president made it clear that he would need its assistance to reverse the economic deficits created by his predecessor and that the government wanted to reestablish a cooperative relationship with the business community. With the participation of many of Mexico's leading capitalists, he succeeded in creating the Alliance for Production. Initially, this association enjoyed considerable success, and until the last year of his administration, the economy appeared to be growing steadily. But by 1982, after another devaluation, and the near bankruptcy of Mexico's leading industrial enterprise, Grupo Industrial AIFA, confidence in the government declined precipitously and capital flight rose to new highs. Mexico's foreign debt reached an estimated $83 billion. In desperation, the president took the extraordinary measure in his 1 September 1982 State of the Union address of nationalizing the domestically owned banking industry, blaming the bankers and, indirectly, the private sector for Mexico's economic woes. The president's decision to nationalize the banks not only failed to restore public confidence in the economy but also raised doubts about his ability to govern. His political decisions brought Mexico to the point of its lowest political legitimacy in modern times, leaving his successor, Miguel de la MADRID, with nearly insurmountable political and economic problems.

Politically, López Portillo, under the direction of Jesús Reyes Heroles, briefly flirted with serious party and electoral reforms, but failed in his attempts. The president, perhaps fearful of internal instability as well as problems caused by the presence of Central American refugees in Mexico, increased the size and budget of the Mexican military, beginning a pattern of increasing modernization. On the intellectual front, he further alienated support when, in the last year of his administration, he censored his most vociferous critic, the leftist weekly *Proceso,* publicly announcing in April that he would require all government agencies to withdraw advertising from the magazine. His actions produced a pall over the media, underlining their dependency on government goodwill. The level of popular dissatisfaction with his political and economic legacy was reflected in the vote tallies for Miguel de la Madrid in the 1982 elections, in which he obtained 71 percent, leaving López Portillo with the lowest figure up to that date for a government party candidate.

López Portillo is the son of engineer José López Portillo y Weber, a military officer, and Margarita Weber y Narvárez, and the grandson of a prominent political figure in the administration of Victoriano Huerta (1913–1914). He was born in Mexico City, where he completed all of his schooling. He and his predecessor, Luis ECHEVERRÍA, were high school classmates. After graduating from the National University in 1946, he became a professor of general theory of the state there and founded the course in political science and government policy in Mexico. He obtained a doctorate in law from the University of Santiago, in Chile. During these years he also practiced law.

López Portillo did not hold his first public office until 1960, when he became director general of the federal board of material and moral improvement of the secretariat of national properties. In 1965, he served as director of legal advisers to the secretariat of the presidency, and three years later, became the assistant secretary of the presidency. In 1970, in the administration of Luis Echeverría, he became assistant secretary of national properties. During a mid-term cabinet shuffle, the president appointed him secretary of the treasury 29 May 1973, and he served in this capacity until his 22 September 1975 nomination as the official party presidential candidate. With at least half a dozen potential candidates, López Portillo was considered a dark horse. Since leaving the presidency he has lived abroad, largely because of his unpopularity in Mexico.

SUSAN K. PURCELL, ed., *Mexico-United States Relations* (1981); MIGUEL BASÁÑEZ, *La lucha por la hegemonía en México* (1982); JUDITH A. HELLMAN, *Mexico in Crisis,* 2d ed. (1983); ROBERTO G. NEWELL and LUIS F. RUBIO, *Mexico's Dilemma: The Political Origins of Economic Crisis* (1984); PETER WARD, *Welfare Politics in Mexico: Papering Over the Cracks* (1986); DANIEL LEVY and GABRIEL SZEKELEY, *Mexico: Paradoxes of Stability and Change,* 2d ed. (1987); JUDITH A. TEICHMAN, *Policymaking in Mexico: From Boom to Crisis* (1988); JOSÉ LÓPEZ PORTILLO, *Mis tiempos: Biografía y testimonio político,* 2 vols. (1988).

RODERIC AI CAMP

LÓPEZ PUMAREJO, ALFONSO (*b.* 31 January 1886; *d.* ca. 20 November 1959), president of Colombia (1934–1938, 1942–1945). One of the most influential presidents in the history of Colombia, López's impact can be measured by the fact that almost all legislation that "modernized" Colombia was passed during his first term in office.

Born in Honda (Tolima), López studied at the College of San Luis Gonzaga and then at the Liceo Mercantil (Mercantile Lyceum) in Bogotá, specializing in business. Afterward, he took courses at Bright College in England and worked in New York before returning to Colombia.

The 1929 world depression exposed the weakness of the Conservative Party—in power since 1886—which had no program to cope with economic collapse and social unrest. López became president in 1934 and, accompanied by an energetic group of young Liberal reformers, began pushing a "New Deal" type of economic, social, labor, and educational legislation to which the patriarchal society was unaccustomed. The most controversial of López's reforms, the Land Law 200 of 1936, has been misnamed the Agrarian Reform Law. In essence, what this law tried to accomplish was the legalization of titles to land and the affirmation of the "social function" of property, particularly landed property.

Reelected for a second term (1942–1946), López was forced to resign in 1945 because of the opposition of both the Conservatives and a sizable fraction of his own party, which together effectively blocked most of his initiatives.

EDUARDO ZULETA ANGEL, *El Presidente López* (1966); GERARDO MOLINA, *Las ideas liberales en Colombia, 1915–1934* (1978); THOMAS C. TIRADO, *Alfonso López Pumarejo, el Conciliador* (1986); ALVARO TIRADO MEJÍA, "López Pumarejo: La Revolución en marcha," in *La nueva historia de Colombia, I: Historia política, 1886–1906,* edited by Dario Jaramillo Agudelo (1976), pp. 305–348; ROBERT J. ALEXANDER, ed., *Biographical Dictionary of Latin American and Caribbean Political Leaders* (1988), pp. 265–266.

JOSÉ ESCORCIA

LÓPEZ REGA, JOSÉ (*b.* 17 October 1916; *d.* 9 June 1989), retired police corporal, onetime singer, spiritist, and disciple of the occult. López Rega rose from humble beginnings in Buenos Aires to become Isabel PERÓN's private secretary in the 1960s in Madrid and eventually to be the most powerful, and sinister, figure in Argentina during the 1973–1976 Peronist governments. He personally organized and, out of the Social Welfare Ministry, oversaw the activities of the infamous right-wing death squad, the so-called Triple A (Alianza Anticomunista Argentina), which committed political assassination and created a climate of terror in the country. After Perón's death in July 1974, he emerged as the power behind the throne and convinced Isabel to abandon the "Pacto Social" and to adopt a hard line toward organized labor. Protests by the latter and demands for his removal led to his resignation in July 1975.

JOSEPH A. PAGE, *Perón: a Biography* (1983); TOMÁS ELOY MARTÍNEZ, *La novela de Perón* (1985).

JAMES P. BRENNAN

LÓPEZ TRUJILLO, ALFONSO (*b.* 8 November 1935), Colombian churchman who as president of the COUNCIL OF LATIN AMERICAN BISHOPS (CELAM) led a conservative movement against LIBERATION THEOLOGY and other progressive tendencies in the Latin American Catholic church. Born in Villahermosa, department of Tolima, he entered the seminary in Bogotá and was ordained a priest in 1960. He received a doctorate in philosophy at the University of Saint Thomas Aquinas, Colombia. In 1971 he was appointed auxiliary bishop of Bogotá. He became archbishop of Medellín in 1978 and was raised to the rank of cardinal in 1983. From 1987 to 1990 he was president of the Colombian episcopal conference. He was elected secretary-general of CELAM in 1972 and served as its president from 1979 to 1983. As secretary of CELAM he was in charge of the third meeting of the Latin American bishops, held in Puebla, Mexico, in 1979. In 1990 he was named president of the Pontifical Commission on the Family, in Rome.

ALFONSO LÓPEZ TRUJILLO, *Liberación marxista y liberación cristiana* (1974); PENNY LERNOUX, *People of God: The Struggle for World Catholicism* (1989).

JEFFREY KLAIBER

LÓPEZ VALLECILLOS, ITALO (*b.* 15 November 1932; *d.* 9 February 1986), Salvadoran journalist, historian, playwright, poet. As leader of the Generación Comprometida (Committed Generation) that emerged about 1950, López called for revision of Salvadoran literary values. His early poetry, most notably *Imágenes sobre el otoño* (1962), expressed the Committed Generation's sensitivity to the need for social change and relevance in literature. López raised Salvadoran historiography to a higher level of professionalism with his *Biografía de un hombre triste* (1954); *El periodismo en El Salvador* (1964), articles on the independence of El Salvador; *Gerardo Barrios y su tiempo* (1967); and many articles on twentieth-century El Salvador. As director of the press of the Universidad Centroamericana and as a frequent contributor to *ECA—Estudios Centro Americanos*, he was an important intellectual leader of the country in the difficult period after 1972. The versatile López also wrote plays, notably *Las manos vencidas* (1964), *Burudi Sur* (1969), and *Celda noventa y seis* (1975).

LUIS GALLEGOS VALDÉS, *Panorama de la literatura salvadoreña del período precolombino a 1980,* 3d ed. (1989), esp. pp. 140, 150–153, 168, 415–445.

RALPH LEE WOODWARD, JR.

LÓPEZ VELARDE, RAMÓN (*b.* 15 June 1888; *d.* 19 June 1921), Mexican poet. López Velarde was born in Jerez, Zacatecas, and died in Mexico City. He was educated in the Seminarios Consiliares of Zacatecas and Aguascalientes and the Instituto Científico y Literario de Aguascalientes and received a degree from the Law School in San Luis Potosí. A lawyer, literary historian, and militant in the National Catholic Party, he occupied posts in revolutionary governments. As a poet, he abandoned Latin American modernism and in some respects moved toward the avant garde. *La sangre devota* (1916) expresses the conflict of provincial people, forced from their towns by the Revolution of 1910–1917, and the drama of a young Catholic who confronts his sexuality and a world that has rejected traditional beliefs. The great poetry of López Velarde springs from his relationships with two women with whom he never became intimate: Fuensanta (Josefa de los Rios), who represents childhood and the idyllic, and Margarita Quijano, symbol of the city and a woman of high culture who introduced him to French poetry. *Zozobra* (1919) carries rhyme and free verse beyond the point at which Leopoldo LUGONES had left them and speaks of death and passion in a way that is both diaphanous and mysterious. His celebrated poem "La sauve patria," written in 1921 during the period of nationalist renewal associated with José VASCONCELOS, was included posthumously in *El son del corazón* (1932). His prose poems and chronicles are collected in *El minutero* (1923), *El don de febrero* (1952), and *Prosa política* (1953). The best critical edition of his *Obras* is that of José Luis Martínez (2d ed., 1990). Several of his poems appear in *Mexican Poetry* (1985), translated by Samuel Beckett. López Velarde died in Mexico City.

OCTAVIO PAZ, "El camino de la pasión," in *Cuadrivio* (1965); ALLAN W. PHILLIPS, "Ramón López Velarde," in *Latin American Writers,* edited by Carlos A. Solé and Maria Isabel Abreu, vol. 2 (1989); GUILLERMO SHERIDAN, *Un corazón adicto* (1989).

J. E. PACHECO

See also **Literature: Spanish America.**

LÓPEZ Y FUENTES, GREGORIO (*b.* 1892; *d.* 1966), Mexican novelist and journalist. As a young man, López fought in the Mexican Revolution. In the post-Revolution period, he began a distinguished career as a journalist at *El Universal,* becoming general editor of the newspaper in 1948 and serving in that capacity until the 1960s. Considered one of the major exponents of the "novel of the Revolution," López addressed in his works the principal social issues of his time. His novels include *Acomodaticio; Arrieros; Campamento; Cuentos campesinos de México; El Indio; Entresuelo, Huasteca; Los peregrinos inmoviles; ¡Mi general!; En Milpa, potrero y monte;* and *Tierra.* He also wrote a series of short stories for children entitled *Cartas de niños* and *El campo y la ciudad.* His fiction is distinguished by the anonymous nature of the characters; representation of types takes precedence over the individual.

DAVID MACIEL

LORENZANA Y BUITRÓN, FRANCISCO ANTONIO DE (*b.* 22 September 1722; *d.* 17 April 1804), Spanish intellectual, archbishop of Mexico (1766–1772), and cardinal-archbishop of Toledo, Spain (1772–1804). Born in León, Spain, Lorenzana studied under the JESUITS in that city. He served as bishop of Plasencia (1765–1766), then as archbishop of Mexico, where he founded the Home for Abandoned Children in 1767. Among his accomplishments was the Fourth Mexican Provincial Council, held in 1771. Known as a promoter of culture and charity, Lorenzana was elected a cardinal in 1789 and was named envoy extraordinary to the Holy See by CHARLES IV of Spain in 1797. He organized the conclave at Venice that in 1800 elected the successor to Pope Pius VI. He then accompanied the new pope, Pius VII, to Rome, where he resigned his archbishopric. Lorenzana died in Rome.

Lorenzana's writings include *Concilios provinciales primero, y segundo* (1769); *Cartas pastorales y edictos* (1770); *Concilium mexicanum provinciale III* (1770); *Historia de Nueva España escrita por su esclarecido conquistador Hernán Cortés* (1770); *Missa gothica seu mozarabica* (1770); and *SS. PP. Toletanorum,* 3 vols. (1782–1783).

FRANCISCO SOSA, *El episcopado mexicano,* edited by Alberto María Carreño (1962); LUIS SIERRA NAVA-LASA, *El cardenal Lorenzana y la ilustración* (1975).

W. MICHAEL MATHES

LORENZO TROYA, VICTORIANO (*b.* 1864; *d.* 15 May 1903), native leader in the Panamanian province of Coclé during the WAR OF THE THOUSAND DAYS (1900–1903). In 1891, Lorenzo was accused of murder and the following year was sentenced to nine years in prison. He remained in jail until 1898. When the war broke out, he joined the liberal side and fought with Belisario PORRAS in Panama (then a department of Colombia) hoping that a liberal victory would end the abuses against the Indians. Lorenzo and his Indian followers made a formidable fighting force, practically unbeatable in the mountains. Their exploits became widely known during the war. After the failure of the liberals to take Panama City with their defeat at the Calidonia bridge (24 July 1900), Lorenza went back to Coclé, where he organized a guerilla group and rejoined Porras. In 1902 he was betrayed by the liberal general Benjamín HERRERA, who handed him over to the government. Despite the fact that he should have been protected under the terms of the peace of 21 November 1902, which ended the civil war between liberals and conservatives, the government executed him by a firing squad.

He execution was considered by many a great miscarriage of justice and there are many theories as to why he was executed. First, General Herrera, a Colombian liberal always looked with disdain to the Panamanian liberal leaders and wanted to impose his own authority on them. The fact that Lorenzo was only loyal to Porras—who at the time of his execution was in El Salvador—may have contributed to his arrest by Herrera. Second, the conservative government feared him a great deal and he was seen by them as an obstacle to a permanent peace. During the war, the conservatives had sent an expeditionary force to Coclé to capture him, but failed. Many Panamanian historians speculate that during the peace negotiations between liberals and conservatives, a secret agreement was reached by which the liberals would hand Lorenzo to the conservatives. In 1966, the Panamanian National Assembly, as a tribute to this popular leader, invalidated the proceedings in Lorenzo's trial, indicating that it was a violation of the peace treaty.

ERNESTO DE JESÚS CASTILLERO REYES, *Historia de Panamá,* 7th ed. (1962); JORGE CONTE PORRAS, *Panameños ilustres* (1978) and *Diccionario biográfico ilustrado de Panamá,* 2d ed. (1986).

JUAN MANUEL PÉREZ

LORETO, the largest department of Peru (135,000 square miles) and one of the least populated (1981 population 445,368), encompassing most of the Peruvian Amazonian rain forest. Loreto has only one major highway, which links its western boundary with Tarapoto and Yurimaguas. The department's capital, Iquitos, is the easternmost port in Peru, a major tourist attraction, and the region's most active commercial center, with 40 percent of Loreto's population. Located between two affluents of the Amazon, Iquitos has no highway connection with other Peruvian provinces but has an international airport. Iquitos has traditionally traded mostly with Peru's neighbor, Brazil, especially since its impressive growth due to the RUBBER BOOM of the early years of the twentieth century. Loreto's production includes timber, rubber, agricultural products (yuca, rice, corn), and oil from the area of Trompeteros, which is linked to the coast through a system of oil pipes.

RICHARD COLLIER, *The River That God Forgot: The Story of the Amazon Rubber Boom* (1968); EDMUNDO MORALES, *Cocaine: White Gold Rush in Peru* (1989).

ALFONSO W. QUIROZ

LOS ALTOS, a region in western Guatemala, bounded on the north and west by Mexico and on the south by the Pacific Ocean. The Sierra Madre crosses the region from northwest to southeast, producing a great deal of geographic and climatic diversity. The surface elevations of its area of 9,200 square miles range from near sea level to more than 12,000 feet in the northern uplands of the Cuchumatanes; its fertile mountain valleys, at altitudes of about 8,000 feet, have been home since pre-Columbian days to a dense Indian population of Maya descent. Its population, estimated to be about 3.5 million in 1990, is about 40 percent of the national total.

When the Spaniards arrived in 1524, Los Altos was dominated by four distinct and warring ethnic states: the MAM, the K'ICHE', the KAQCHIKELS, and the TZ'UTU-JILS. After a bloody and protracted war, Pedro de ALVARADO finally imposed Spanish rule in 1528. Following his death, the region functioned as the *alcaldía mayor* of Zapotitlán, a subdivision of the Audiencia of Guatemala. Crown officials and missionaries were charged with consolidating Spanish political-military and spiritual control over the area and, more important, with collecting the royal tribute from the conquered communities.

Devoid of mineral and agricultural wealth, Los Altos attracted relatively few Spanish colonists. Thus, left relatively unmolested, its Indian communities were able to recover successfully from the demographic disaster that accompanied the Conquest. Most continued to engage in subsistence agriculture and textile weaving on their communal lands.

The BOURBON REFORMS of the eighteenth century substantially altered this traditional pattern. The indigo boom of the latter half of the century integrated the region into the expanding Central American economic network. Attracted by the growing commercial opportunities in cloth and food staples, new Spanish as well as mestizo colonists established themselves in the area, often at the expense of Indian land and labor. As a result, urban centers such as Quetzaltenango and Totonicapán became dynamic centers of economic and, later, political activity.

By the early nineteenth century, these new colonists had consolidated their hold on the region. Quetzal-tenango, the most prosperous village, became the focus of a vigorous regionalist movement whose chief goal was to secure for Los Altos greater political and economic autonomy vis-à-vis the financial and administrative control of the capital. Led by the Quetzalteco patricians, the efforts of Los Altos finally crystallized in 1838, when the region became the sixth state of the Central American Federation. The Federation collapsed, however, and the area was forcibly reintegrated into Guatemala by the Conservative dictator Rafael CARRERA in 1840. Following Carrera's temporary ouster in 1848, the region again seceded, but the movement was easily suppressed by an army under the orders of the Liberal government in Guatemala City. In 1871 Los Altos General Justo Rufino BARRIOS led the revolution that restored the Liberals to power in Guatemala for the next seventy years. Barrios became Guatemalan dictator in 1873 and proceeded to develop the economic infrastructure of Los Altos as well as to encourage the cultivation of coffee, the new cash crop destined to become the mainstay of the nation's economy. The piedmont area of Los Altos remains an important coffee-producing region.

Juan José ARÉVALO's revolution of 1944 tried to relieve the plight of the Indians, but despite numerous decrees, the Liberal land tenure system remained intact. Under Jacobo ARBENZ GUZMÁN (1951–1954), thousands of acres were distributed among peasants, vagrancy laws were abolished, and a national syndicate of peasants was organized.

In 1954, however, those gains were lost to a military coup which restored to power the Liberal land-owning elite, who were this time allied with the military. While paying lip service to reform, the new regimes continued to dispossess peasants and encourage the growth of large agro-export enterprises. Organized peasant and Indian resistance has been met with brutal repression by the army.

HAZEL INGERSOLL, "The War of the Mountain" (Ph.D. diss., George Washington University, 1972); CAROL SMITH, *The Domestic Marketing System in Western Guatemala* (1972); JORGE H. GONZÁLEZ, "Una historia de Los Altos, el sexto estado de la federación centroamericana" (M.A. thesis, Tulane University, 1989); GEORGE LOVELL, *Conquest and Survival in Colonial Guatemala: A Historical Geography of the Cuchumatán Highlands, 1500–1821* (1992).

JORGE H. GONZÁLEZ

LOSADA, DIEGO DE (*b.* 1511; *d.* 1569), Spanish conquistador and founder of Caracas, Venezuela. Losada traveled to America as part of the conquistador armies. He passed through Puerto Rico and later, in 1533, joined Antonio Sendeño's expedition on the Meta River. When Sendeño was assassinated, Losada moved on to the city of Coro. From there he was sent eastward with Juan de VILLEGAS in 1543 to search for provisions and men.

Losada later traveled to Santo Domingo and returned

to Venezuela in 1546 in the company of Juan PÉREZ DE TOLOSA, governor and captain-general of the province. He took part in the founding of Nueva Segovia de Barquisimeto, received various Indian *encomiendas,* and performed diverse duties within the colonial administration.

In 1565 Losada was assigned the mission of subduing the Caraca Indians, a task at which others had failed. After heavy fighting, he occupied the valley of El Guaire, where he founded the city of Santiago de León de Caracas on 25 July 1567. Losada attempted to win the post of governor and captain-general of the province of Venezuela. To this end he traveled to Santo Domingo to send his petition to the king, but his attempt was unsuccessful.

FELIPE FELIPE FERRERO, *Don Diego de Losada, o el fundador de Caracas* (1968); HERMANO NECTARIO MARÍA, *Diego de Losada, fundador de Caracas* (Caracas, 1967); and JOSÉ MARÍA CRUXENT, *La ruta de Losada* (1971).

INÉS QUINTERO

LOTT, HENRIQUE BATISTA DUFFLES TEIXEIRA

(*b.* 16 November 1894; *d.* 19 May 1984), Brazilian minister of war (1954–1960), politician, and presidential candidate (1959). A native of Sítio, in Minas Gerais, Lott attended the military school of Realengo in Rio de Janeiro. Upon graduation he enlisted in the army in 1911 and was commissioned five years later.

A dedicated professional, Lott remained loyal to the government during the military upheavals of the 1920s and on through the Revolution of 1930, the São Paulo constitutional revolt of 1932, the Communist uprising of 1935, and the 1938 Fascist putsch.

Lott studied abroad at the Superior War College in Paris and at the U.S. Army Command and General Staff College in Fort Leavenworth, Kansas. These courses further enhanced his well-deserved reputation as an instructor at the general staff school and other Brazilian military academies, where he became known for strong opinions and stern discipline. Posted to Italy with the BRAZILIAN EXPEDITIONARY FORCE (FEB) during World War II, he was denied command, thus widening the split with the so-called SORBONNE GROUP of military reformers. Promoted to general at the age of fifty, he commanded the Second Military Region in São Paulo.

The suicide of President Getúlio VARGAS in 1954 brought Lott into politics with his appointment by acting president João CAFÉ FILHO, who named him minister of war because of his reputation for being apolitical. Café Filho's resignation in November 1955, ostensibly for health reasons, brought in Carlos Luz, president of the chamber of deputies, as chief executive. Allied with the Sorbonne Group, he soon resigned when Lott pronounced in favor of Nereu Ramos, the senate's president.

This institutional crisis coincided with the disputed presidential election of Brazilian Labor Party candidate Juscelino KUBITSCHEK. Lott favored Kubitschek's inauguration as the legitimate candidate, thus easing unrest and ensuring his own reappointment as war minister. He held this post until February 1960, although he retired, with the rank of marshal, in 1959 to run for president on the Labor Party ticket. Defeated by reformist Jânio QUADROS, Lott nevertheless remained a powerful figure, opposing both the military interventions against Vice President João GOULART in 1961 and his ousting as acting president in April 1964. Lott's 1965 attempt to present himself as a candidate for the governorship of the state of Guanabara was vetoed by the revolutionary military regime.

IRVING L. HOROWITZ, *Revolution in Brazil* (1964); JOHN W. F. DULLES, *Unrest in Brazil: Political-Military Crises, 1955–1964* (1970); ALFRED C. STEPAN, *The Military in Politics: Changing Patterns in Brazil* (1971); E. BRADFORD BURNS, *A History of Brazil* (1980); ROBERT AMES HAYES, *The Armed Nation: The Brazilian Corporate Mystique* (1989).

LEWIS A. TAMBS

LOUISIANA, a Spanish colonial province that included the Louisiana Purchase territory and, at certain periods, lands in the area from the junction of the Ohio and Mississippi rivers to Pensacola, Florida.

Spain's interest in the northern coast of the Gulf of Mexico was dictated by desires to protect the mines of northern Mexico and shipping transiting the northern Gulf of Mexico on the way to Havana. This interest dictated its initial (1699–1723) efforts to dislodge the French colony of Louisiana and its acceptance in 1763 of Louis XVI's gift of the part of Louisiana that lay west of the Mississippi River and the line defined by Bayou Manchac, the Amite River, and Lakes Maurepas and Pontchartrain.

This interest dictated that Spain take advantage of Great Britain's involvement in the U.S. Revolutionary War to seize in 1779–1781 the areas north and east of that border that had been given to Great Britain in 1763. Once in control of the Mississippi Valley below the Ohio River, Spain attempted to prevent American settlement west of the Appalachian Mountains by denying those settlements use of the Mississippi for trade (1784–1788) and then, when that policy failed, to extend its influence over those settlements by conspiring with James Wilkinson and others, leaders in Kentucky and Tennessee, to foment rebellion in the West. This expansive policy began to collapse with Kentucky's statehood in 1792 and the opening of New Orleans to friendly and allied shipping in 1793, and came to an end with the implementation of Pinckney's Treaty (1795) in 1798. Weakened by defeats at the hands of the French (1793–1795) and the British, Spain could do no more than make the best trade possible with France: Louisiana for the Kingdom of Etruria, for Charles IV's brother-in-law, Prince Louis of Parma. When Napoleon I decided to sell Louisiana (as defined in 1763) to the United States, Spain protested in vain. The United States took possession on 20 December 1803.

Spain's trade and Indian policies in Louisiana differed sharply from those elsewhere in its empire. Although the long-term goal remained the integration of Louisiana into the system of imperial *comercio libre* (free trade), officials on the spot had to tolerate British smuggling that accounted for as much as 85 percent of the colony's ship traffic from 1763 to 1777, and then a French and French West Indian commerce that accounted for about 60 percent of the colony's shipping from 1777 to 1793. After 1793, U.S. ships carried 45 percent to 60 percent of the colony's trade (depending on year). Spanish shipping never amounted to more than 35 percent of the colony's total, and generally was under 25 percent. By their very nature, Louisiana's exports of indigo, tobacco, skins and furs, and lumber and imports of flour, alcoholic beverages, and manufactures did not fit well with the imperial economic system, even as modified during the 1760s and 1770s. Well before 1803, Louisiana had become part of the U.S. economy.

Spain's Indian policies involved forging alliances with, and arming, the Creek, Choctaw, and Chickasaw rather than attempting to subjugate them in a mission system. The goal was to use these Indians and their lands as a barrier to check advancing American settlement. The Nogales Treaty of 1793 culminated this policy, which was abandoned with the implementation of Pinckney's Treaty. Another unusual feature of Spain's Indian policy was that it relied on the Scots firm of PANTON, LESLIE, AND COMPANY to supply the trade goods and presents needed for the alliance system, since Spanish firms did not produce products of the right types and qualities.

Demographically, Louisiana grew from a total of 13,000 persons to 50,000 persons, largely because of immigration. More than half of the population were African slaves. Acadians, Canary Islanders, and Germans were notable minorities.

ARTHUR P. WHITAKER, *The Spanish-American Frontier, 1783–1795* (1927), and *The Mississippi Question, 1795–1803* (1934); LAWRENCE C. FORD, *The Triangular Struggle for Spanish Pensacola, 1689–1739* (1939); JOHN F. BANNON, *The Spanish Borderlands Frontier, 1513–1821* (1974); JUAN JOSÉ ANDREU OCARIZ, *Luisiana Española* (1975); ANTONIO ACOSTA RODRÍGUEZ, *La población de Luisiana Española (1763–1803)* (1979); WILLIAM S. COKER and THOMAS WATSON, *Indian Traders of the Southeastern Spanish Borderlands: Panton, Leslie, & Company and John Forbes & Company, 1783–1847* (1989); PAUL E. HOFFMAN, *Luisiana* (1992), in Spanish.

PAUL E. HOFFMAN

LOUISIANA REVOLT OF 1768, rebellion against Spanish rule by French colonists of Louisiana. The revolt was the result of a conspiracy by the leading merchants and planters of New Orleans against the colony's first Spanish governor, Antonio de ULLOA. Without any bloodshed, they succeeded in driving him out of the colony with the help of colonists who had been both tricked and bullied into supporting the rebel cause.

Confusion had surrounded Ulloa's arrival in 1766, well after the 1762 Treaty of Fontainebleau, which transferred Louisiana from French to Spanish rule. Ulloa kept his distance, both socially and politically, from the local elite, which had been accustomed to a prominent role in all decision making. More than this reticence, what most upset the leading colonists, however, were Ulloa's trade reforms eliminating contraband and regulating the fur trade. Yet even with the support of the former French governor, Charles Philippe Aubry, Ulloa lacked the military force to impose his will. On 28–29 October 1768, the Spanish regime was overthrown and Ulloa and other officials fled to Spain.

Many colonists withdrew their initial support for the rebels after Ulloa's removal. A chaotic period followed until General Alejandro O'REILLY arrived in August 1769 with 2,000 troops to put down the revolt. The five ringleaders (Nicolas Chauvin de La Frenière, Pierre Marquis, Pierre Caresse, Jean Baptiste Noyan, and Joseph Milhet) were executed. A sixth, Joseph Villeré, died before the execution, and six others received lesser sentences. O'Reilly calmed fears with a general pardon, reestablished order, and became the second Spanish governor.

CHARLES GAYARRÉ, *History of Louisiana*, vol. 2, *The French Domination* (1885), pp. 158–361; VICENTE RODRÍGUEZ CASADO, *Primeros años de dominación española en la Luisiana* (1942), pp. 99–350; JOHN PRESTON MOORE, *Revolt in Louisiana: The Spanish Occupation, 1766–1770* (1976).

PHILIPPE L. SEILER

L'OUVERTURE, TOUSSAINT (*b.* ca. 20 May 1743; *d.* 7 April 1803), leader of the slave rebellion in Saint-Domingue (Haiti) (1794–1802). As the sounds of martial music intermingled with the gentle tropical breezes that floated across the Palace d'Armes, the central square of Le Cap François, a small, ornately clad black man led a military procession of 2,000 smartly dressed troops into the city under an arch of triumph. He was Toussaint L'Ouverture, and this day, 22 November 1800, marked his greatest moment. He had defeated both his foreign and domestic enemies. More important, he had governed Saint-Domingue well, rebuilt its economy, and sought a program of racial harmony. The swell of pride must have been his when, at the end of his triumphant military procession, a beautiful woman from one of the colony's most prestigious white families greeted him. The mixed crowd of whites, mulattoes, and blacks burst forth with the "Marseillaise." In just over two years from this moment, this victorious "Black Spartacus" would be coughing and dying of pneumonia in a French prison.

François Dominique Toussaint was the first of his parents' eight children. His grandfather had been an Arada chief. Pierre Baptiste Simon may have been his father or his godfather. For the next forty-seven years Toussaint lived on the Bréda plantation and went through two name changes—Toussaint Bréda and finally Toussaint L'Ouverture. The significance of this last name change is unclear but may refer to his ability to move quickly to openings on the battlefield.

Toussaint lived about as well as any slave ever did in Saint-Domingue. He had a lifelong friendship with one of the plantation managers (Bayou de Libertad), had read books from the big house, married Suzanne Simon-Baptiste when he was forty, and settled down to the life of a coachman. He knew smatterings of ancient history, Stoic philosophy, and a few Latin phrases taught to him by his father.

Just what Toussaint's role was in the great slave rebellion that exploded in Saint-Domingue on 22 August 1791 is unclear, despite biographer Ralph Korngold's contention that he actively participated in igniting the conflict. It is clear, however, that once under way, the conflagration, as Saint-Domingue sugar planters liked to call it, swept up the Black Spartacus and set him ablaze with revolutionary fervor. He saw to the safety of his old friend Bayou de Libertad and joined the armies of generals Jean-François and Georges Biassou already fighting for the Spanish. Third in command,

Portrait of Toussaint L'Ouverture. Watercolor, 1802. BIBLIOTHÈQUE NATIONALE.

Toussaint had the rank of "Doctor of the King's Armies" because of his knowledge of medicinal herbs.

After three years of service with Biassou and François, Toussaint defected to France and on 25 June 1794 joined forces with the embattled General Etienne Laveaux. The abolition of slavery by the French National Convention undoubtedly prompted his action, as did his own greed for power. Both C. L. R. James and Thomas O. Ott have recognized the complexity of these motives in their histories of the Haitian Revolution. Dedication to his people's freedom, though, was Toussaint's main consideration.

Over the next eight years, Toussaint enjoyed a mercurial rise from lieutenant governor to dictator of Saint-Domingue. And over that period he gave special emphasis to the domestic problems of a devastated land. He attempted to maintain the large plantations, invited former planters to return as "managers," and parceled out vast amounts of land to favorite generals to hold their loyalty. At one time, Jean Jacques DESSALINES owned thirty plantations. On these estates, Toussaint and his generals enforced *fermage* (a system of forced labor not unlike sharecropping). The laborer could not leave his plantation assignment without permission and was subject to severe corporal punishment for lazy habits. By 1800, Saint-Domingue had regained two-thirds of its economic prosperity of 1791. Most historians have joined Ralph Korngold to acclaim this a triumph, but biographer Pierre Pluchon labeled the Black Spartacus's program a failure.

Toussaint also gave attention to his people's religious training. He suppressed voodoo, made Catholicism the religion of state, and appointed Father Mainville the Catholic bishop for Saint-Domingue. Never reticent about interfering in their personal lives, he demanded the participation of "colonials" in compulsory religious parades and made divorce illegal. Though he kept many mistresses, Toussaint demanded monogamy and marital fidelity in his subjects.

Failure to incorporate the mulattoes into his revolutionary state constituted Toussaint's greatest domestic failure. Emotionally, he hated them, and sometimes he let this attitude break through his rational attempts to include them in his state. Finally he squared off against the mulattoes, led by André RIGAUD, in the War of the Knives (1799–1800). When he won, Toussaint encouraged Dessalines to bathe himself in their blood in South Province.

On the foreign front, Toussaint scored notable victories by defeating the British invasion (1793–1798) and by maintaining good relations with the United States. But France proved too delicate an operation for him. While swearing loyalty to the First Republic, Toussaint ever so gently removed the agents of France and sent them home. But he committed a major blunder when he proclaimed the Constitution of 1801 and himself governor-general for life with the right to appoint his successor. He had, moreover, proclaimed the constitution without the First Consul's approval. Napoleon was not fooled; he knew that Toussaint intended to make Saint-Domingue independent.

Historian Shelby McCloy believed Toussaint's high-handed acts alone prompted Napoleon to send the expedition of General Charles LECLERC to Saint-Domingue. But Napoleon's imperial ambitions for a Western empire and planter influence were probably more persuasive factors in his decision, according to historians J. Christopher Herold and Thomas O. Ott.

After holding his own against Leclerc for a few months, Toussaint suddenly surrendered to France on 6 May 1802. Korngold argued that Toussaint capitulated as a trick. Once yellow fever did its deadly work, Toussaint would come out of retirement and lead Saint-Domingue to independence. Ott, however, saw the surrender as the best deal Toussaint could make to ensure the freedom of his people. A month later, 7 June, Leclerc arrested the Black Spartacus and deported him to France to die. Leclerc believed that Toussaint was his main obstacle to the restoration of slavery in Saint-Domingue. Dessalines and the Haitians proved him wrong.

THOMAS MADIOU, *Histoire d'Haiti*, 4 vols. (1847–1904); C. L. R. JAMES, *The Black Jacobins* (1938); RALPH KORNGOLD, *Citizen Toussaint* (1944); STÉPHEN ALEXIS, *Black Liberator: The Life of Toussaint Louverture* (1949); J. CHRISTOPHER HEROLD, *The Age of Napoleon* (1963); SHELBY T. MC CLOY, *The Negro in the French West Indies* (1966); HUBERT COLE, *Christophe: King of Haiti* (1967); GEORGES LEFEBVRE, *Napoleon*, 2 vols. (1969); THOMAS O. OTT, *The Haitian Revolution, 1789–1804* (1973); WENDA PARKINSON, *This Gilded African: Toussaint L'Ouverture* (1978); PIERRE PLUCHON, *Toussaint L'Ouverture* (1979).

THOMAS O. OTT

LOZADA, MANUEL (*b.* 1828; *d.* 19 July 1873), Mexican cacique and rebel leader. Considered by some to be a precursor of later agrarian reformers, Lozada was a mestizo bandit whose extreme violence and invincibility earned him the attribute "El Tigre de Alica." Although still a controversial figure, he led one of the most serious uprisings of the nineteenth century.

Cacique of the Cora and Huichol Indians of western Jalisco, Lozada worked as a peon on the Hacienda de Mojarras. After a dispute with the administrator, he fled to the sierra. In his absence, the administrator was said to have maltreated Lozada's mother, misconduct for which Lozada returned to kill him. A self-designated general, he assumed leadership of the ongoing Indian resistance to European penetration of the Nayarit zone.

Armed conflict broke out in 1847 and reached a climax after the disamortization law of 1856. In his defense of community lands against privatization and hacienda penetration, he received the private support of the San Blas-based Barron and Forbes Company, which was heavily involved in contraband. His tacit support of the Conservative cause during LA REFORMA (the Civil War

Manuel Lozada. Lithograph by Rodrigo Guadal. BENSON LATIN AMERICAN COLLECTION, UNIVERSITY OF TEXAS AT AUSTIN.

of the Reform, 1858–1861), together with his control of western Jalisco, threatened the Liberal position in Jalisco and Sinaloa. In March 1864, however, Lozada rallied to the empire, received a cash subsidy, and was decorated with the Legion of Honor. He abandoned the imperial cause in December 1866 and was thereafter virtually protected from his enemies by JUÁREZ.

Lozada's circular of 12 April 1869 had a distinctly agrarian character and provided for direct action by villages for the recovery of land. His power was broken at Mojonera, near Guadalajara, by General Ramón CORONA, after an ill-considered invasion of central Jalisco. Betrayed, he was executed on 19 July 1873.

SILVANO BARBA GONZALEZ, *La lucha por la tierra: Manuel Lozada* (1956); JEAN MEYER, "El ocaso de Manuel Lozada," in *Historia Mexicana* 18, no. 4 (1969): 535–568; JOSÉ MARÍA MURIÁ ET AL., *Historia de Jalisco*, vol. 3 (1981), pp. 348–357.

BRIAN HAMNETT

LOZANO, PEDRO (*b.* 16 September 1697; *d.* 1752), JESUIT historian. Lozano was born in Madrid, and a year after entering the Society of Jesus (at fourteen years of age), he was sent to the Province of Paraguay. It was fairly common at the time to send young Jesuits to America for their novitiate training. In theory, they adapted more readily to the customs of the place and learned the local languages more easily. Lozano was assigned for most of his life to the College of Córdoba, where he taught philosophy and theology. He traveled extensively throughout the province, visiting missions and consulting Jesuit records in Santa Fe, Esteco, and Buenos Aires.

In 1730 Lozano began writing the first of the histories for which he became known, *Descripción corográfica del Gran Chaco Gualamba* (1733). He also wrote *Historia de la Compañía de Jesús en la Provincia del Paraguay* (2 vols., 1754–1755), and five volumes of the *Historia civil del Río de la Plata*, as well as two volumes titled *Historia de las revoluciones de la Provincia del Paraguay (1721–1735)*. His most famous history, now a classic, is *Historia de la conquista de la Provincia del Paraguay, Río de la Plata y Tucumán* (1905). In 1750 he was given the task of preparing a report on why the Treaty of Limits (1750) would be harmful to the Indians. Lozano died in Humahuaca.

NICHOLAS P. CUSHNER

LOZANO DÍAZ, JULIO, president of Honduras (November 1954–October 1956). Vice president under Juan Manuel GÁLVEZ, Lozano Díaz seized the presidency at a time of political ferment and trade-union agitation in Honduras. In 1954 a strike against the UNITED FRUIT and STANDARD FRUIT and Steamship companies coincided with a three-way contest for the presidency between the Liberal Party candidate Ramón VILLEDA MORALES, Abraham Williams of the Movimiento Nacional Reformista, and Tiburcio CARÍAS ANDINO of the Partido Nacional. Although Villeda Morales had garnered nearly 50 percent of the vote, the Carías-controlled Congress refused to sanction a Liberal presidency and Lozano Díaz settled the issue by declaring himself interim president in November 1954. He successfully warded off an attempted coup on 1 August 1956 and orchestrated the victory of his party, the Partido Union Nacional, in the 7 October congressional election. The three opposition parties declared the election fraudulent, and on 21 October members of the Honduran military, led by General Roque J. Rodríguez, brought down the Lozano Díaz dictatorship and established a military junta.

RALPH LEE WOODWARD, JR., *Central America: A Nation Divided* (1976), pp. 255 and 301; JAMES A. MORRIS, *Honduras: Caudillo Politics and Military Rulers* (1984), esp. pp. 11–12; LESLIE BETHELL, ed., *The Cambridge History of Latin America*, vol. 7 (1990), pp. 298–299.

MICHAEL A. POLUSHIN

LOZZA, RAÚL (*b.* 27 October 1911), Argentine painter, craftsman, and illustrator. Lozza was born in Alberti, Buenos Aires Province, and was self-taught. He was a founding member of the Asociación de Arte Concreto-Invención, a nonfigurative group, as well as the creator of *perceptismo,* a theory of color and open structure in painting that he called ''cualimetría de la forma plana.'' Lozza's two- and three-dimensional works reveal an almost scientific concern for the intelligent use of technology, and the tonal values in his paintings are intensified or reduced with mathematical precision. Lozza has had numerous exhibitions, including a retrospective in 1985 at the Fundación San Telmo in Buenos Aires. He is the recipient of several awards, including the Palanza Prize (1991) and the Konex Award (1992).

Raúl Lozza. Cuarenta años en el arte concreto (sesenta con la pintura), Catalog of the Fundación San Telmo Exhibition, 22 July–18 August 1985; VICENTE GESUALDO, ALDO BIGLIONE, and RODOLFO SANTOS, *Diccionario de artistas plásticos en la Argentina* (1988); *Raúl Lozza. Pintura y arte concreto, 1945–1955*. Catalog of the Fundación Banco Patricios Exhibition, 8 September–1 October 1993.

AMALIA CORTINA ARAVENA

LUCAS GARCÍA, FERNANDO ROMEO (*b.* 24 July 1924), president of Guatemala (1978–1982). Brigadier General Lucas García succeeded Kjell LAUGERUD as president in June 1978. It is widely believed that the 1978 election was fraudulent, and that Enrique PERALTA AZURDIA was the real winner.

Romeo Lucas García presided over an administration that was generally perceived to be riddled with corruption, cronyism, and violence. During Lucas's tenure the Guerrilla Army of the Poor (EGP) gained significant support and territory from the mainly indigenous inhabitants of the western highlands. Political violence from the Far Right increased, particularly in urban areas, where students, union members, and professionals were regularly ''disappeared'' by DEATH SQUADS. During this period, the U.S. government under Jimmy Carter refused military aid to Guatemala because of human rights violations.

By 1980, Guatemala's once-vital economy had begun to weaken, due to world recession and a decline in tourism. Dissatisfaction with Lucas García within the military became acute, and on 23 March 1982 he was overthrown in a coup. Lucas was succeeded by a three-man junta consisting of General Efrain RÍOS MONTT, General Horacio Maldonado Schad, and Colonel Francisco Gordillo.

JIM HANDY, *Gift of the Devil: A History of Guatemala* (1984); RICHARD F. NYROP, ed., *Guatemala: A Country Study,* 2d ed. (1984); JEAN-MARIE SIMON, *Guatemala: Eternal Spring, Eternal Tyranny* (1987).

VIRGINIA GARRARD-BURNETT

LUDWIG, DANIEL KEITH (*b.* 24 June 1897; *d.* 27 August 1992), American billionaire. In 1967, Ludwig purchased property on both sides of the Jari River in western Pará and Amapá for $3 million and named it Jari. He bought this Brazilian property, the size of Connecticut, so he could grow and manufacture pulpwood. President Humberto CASTELLO BRANCO granted Ludwig such concessions as ten-year tax exemptions and a guarantee that he could run his operation as he pleased without interference from the Brazilian government. Jari included housing for workers at Monte Dourado, the town Ludwig had built; 2,500 miles of dirt roads; and 50 miles of railroad tracks.

Although Ludwig planned to plant most of the area in *Gmelina arborea* seedlings, a fast-growing East India tree, the huge machines used to level the forest packed down the nutritionless soil, and most of the *Gmelinas* died. He finally covered one-third of Jari in the hardier Caribbean pine, which survived but takes sixteen years to mature. Ludwig did profit from rice he had planted around the Jari River; kaolin, used in the manufacture of porcelain; and bauxite deposits. These earnings however, did not offset his losses because the remaining *Gmelina* seedlings failed to mature on schedule.

Despite this setback, in 1976 Ludwig spent $269 million on a pulpwood processing factory with a wood-burning power plant that was built in Japan and floated 15,500 miles across the ocean up the Amazon River to Jari. Ludwig had neither enough pulpwood to operate the factory at full capacity nor enough wood to keep his power plant fueled. He realized he would never recover his $1 billion investment. He sold Jari in 1982 for $300 million to a consortium of twenty-three companies backed by the Brazilian government. Jari continues to operate and has made profits from kaolin.

GWEN KINKEAD, "Trouble in D. K. Ludwig's Jungle," in *Fortune*, 20 April 1981; ROGER D. STONE, *Dreams of Amazonia* (1985); JERRY SHIELDS, *The Invisible Billionaire, Daniel Ludwig* (1986); SUSANNA HECHT and ALEXANDER COCKBURN, *The Fate of the Forest: Developers, Destroyers, and Defenders of the Amazon* (1990).

CAROLYN JOSTOCK

LUGONES, LEOPOLDO (*b.* 13 June 1874; *d.* 18 February 1938), Argentine poet and social historian.

Lugones occupies a central position in the history of Hispanic-American modernism for his perfection of form and rich, original imagery in works such as *Los crepúsculos del jardín* (Garden Twilights, 1905). Lugones used his prodigious intellect and formidable learning to make his ideas known in literature, education, politics, government, and public affairs. He began his career as a journalist at the age of sixteen, writing articles for a newspaper in his native Córdoba. He came to Buenos Aires in 1896 and there published his first book of poems, *Las montañas de oro* (The Golden Mountains, 1897). In 1897, he cofounded *La Montaña* as a forum for his socialist—and at times anarchist—ideas. In 1899, he became director of the General Archives of the postal services and in 1904 general inspector of the secondary schools.

Lugones strongly opposed the ultraliberal revolutionary activities of 1904 and in 1907 launched a virulent attack on President Figueroa Alcorta from the columns of *El Diario*. When the Argentine Congress passed an electoral reform bill in 1912, Lugones protested strenuously. His views, which were frequently self-contradictory, suffered radical changes throughout his life. After World War I, he extolled the Versailles Treaty and was critical of German military leadership. Yet he also attacked democracy and was convinced that the use of force was necessary to secure social order and progress. Lugones supported the Argentine university reform laws enacted in 1918, but he opposed universal suffrage and populist solutions to national problems. With the reelection of Hipólito YRIGOYEN as president in 1928, Lugones's militarism became more extreme, and he participated actively in the September 1930 revolution that overthrew that regime. In his later years he began using a religious approach in his writing. He took his own life on 18 February 1938.

Best known as a poet and prose writer, Lugones is also the author of numerous books revealing his ardent nationalism, his profound insights into Argentine history, and his identification with the people and traditions of Argentina's provincial regions. Such works as *El imperio jesuítico* (1904), *Historia de Sarmiento* (1911), and *El estado equitativo* (1932) have had a strong impact on the way Argentines view themselves and have contributed to Lugones's stature as one of the foremost intellectual figures of his time.

JUAN CARLOS GHIANO, *Poesía Argentina del siglo XX* (1957), pp. 29–40; JULIO IRAZUSTA, *Genio y figura de Leopoldo Lugones* (1968); ALFREDO CANEDO, *Aspectos del pensamiento político de Leopoldo Lugones* (1974); DANIEL C. SCROGGINS, "Leopoldo Lugones' Defense of the Monroe Doctrine in the *Revue Sud-américaine*," in *Rivista Interamericana de Bibliografía* 28, no. 2 (1978): 169–175; CARLOS A. SOLÉ and MARIA ISABEL ABREU, *Latin American Writers*, vol. 2 (1989), pp. 493–502.

MYRON I. LICHTBLAU

See also **Literature.**

LUÍS PEREIRA DE SOUSA, WASHINGTON (*b.* 26 October 1870; *d.* 4 August 1957), president of Brazil (1926–1930). Although known as the consummate defender of the political and economic interests of the state of São Paulo, Luís was born and schooled in the state of Rio de Janeiro. After moving to São Paulo in 1888, Luís steadily rose within São Paulo's political circles, serving as state deputy (1904–1906, 1912–1913), state secretary of justice (1906–1914), mayor of the city of São Paulo (1914–1919), governor of the state of São Paulo (1920–1924), and senator (1924–1926). In 1926 Luís was elected president of Brazil. He remained president until October 1930, when he was forced from office and into exile during the one-month civil war later known as the Revolution of 1930.

Luís was one of the most prominent members of the

Partido Republicano Paulista (PRP), and his political career was representative of the oligarchic-led politics of Brazil's First Republic (1889–1930). He was a fiscal conservative who promoted state autonomy (particularly for the state of São Paulo) and economic policies favorable to COFFEE cultivation, nascent industrialization, and infrastructural improvements (especially in rail and roads). An advocate of stricter policing and opponent of organized labor, Luís coined the republican elite's dictum that the social question was a police question. However, his close association with the oligarchic interests of the First Republic also proved to be his downfall, as Luís failed to convince the reformist interests from Minas Gerais and Rio Grande do Sul supporting Getúlio VARGAS's 1930 presidential candidacy that Luís's hand-picked successor, *paulista* Júlio PRESTES, could best manage Brazil's extremely precarious position amidst the onset of the Great Depression. During the Revolution of 1930, Luís and President-elect Prestes were stripped of their political powers and Vargas became chief of the provisional government. Exiled, Luís lived in Europe and the United States. Upon returning to Brazil in 1947, Luís remained far from politics, concentrating his energies on his personal life and his interest in *paulista* history and culture.

THOMAS E. SKIDMORE, *Politics in Brazil, 1930–1964: An Experiment in Democracy* (1967), pp. 1–8; JOSEPH L. LOVE, *São Paulo in the Brazilian Federation, 1889–1937* (1980); "Luís, Washington," in *Dicionário histórico-biográfico brasileiro, 1930–1983*, vol. 3 (1984), pp. 1,952–1,955.

DARYLE WILLIAMS

See also **Brazil: Revolution of 1930.**

LUISI, LUISA (*b.* 1888; *d.* 1940), Uruguayan poet, critic, and educator; her work is grouped with the generation of Uruguayan "realist poets" between 1885 and 1935. Luisi's books of poetry include *Sentir* (1916), *Inquietud* (1921), *Poemas de la inmovilidad y canciones al sol* (1926), and *Polvo de días* (1935). Her early poetry was conceptual and based on philosophical ideas, but an illness that left her without the use of her legs brought forth in her later poetry an anguish over her immobile state. Her tone became melancholic and reflected a spiritual restlessness and dismay that she was unable to realize her full potential. Luisi's critical prose include *A través de libros y autores* (1925).

Luisi was educated in Montevideo in both private schools and at the Normal Institute for Girls, qualifying to teach in the first, second, and third grades. She later became a school principal, taught reading and declamation in the Normal Institute for Girls, and remained active in Uruguayan education her entire life, despite retiring from teaching in 1929. Luisi, along with her two remarkable sisters, Clotilde and Paulina, broke down many barriers in Uruguayan society for female intellectual activity and for the advancement of WOMEN in other areas. Clotilde Luisi distinguished herself as the first woman lawyer in Uruguay and as professor of moral philosophy and religion at the Normal Institute for Girls. Paulina LUISI, one of the few and among the earliest Uruguayan women to become a doctor, held teaching posts and headed the gynecological clinic at the Faculty of Medicine.

WILLIAM BELMONT PARKER, *Uruguayans of Today* (1921), pp. 307–308; MERCEDES PINTO, "Las poéticas," in Carlos Reyles, ed., *Historia sintética de la literatura uruguaya*, vol. 2 (1931); SARAH BOLLO, *Literatura uruguaya, 1807–1975* (1976).

J. DAVID DRESSING

LUISI, PAULINA (*b.* 22 September 1875; *d.* 17 July 1950), physician, educator, feminist, diplomat, social reformer. Luisi was the first Uruguayan woman to receive a medical degree. Her lifelong work on behalf of children (president of the Uruguayan delegation to the First American Congress of the Child, Buenos Aires, 1916) and women's health (Uruguayan delegate to the International Congress on Social Hygiene and Education, Paris, 1923; member of the League of Nations consultative committee on the Treaty to End Traffic in Women and Children, 1922, 1923, 1924, 1925) was paralleled by her commitment to woman suffrage and female education. She founded the Uruguayan branch of the National Women's Council in 1916 and represented Uruguay at the International Congresses of Women in Geneva and Cristiana, Norway, in 1920 and Rome in 1925. She was the first woman in the Western Hemisphere to represent her government as an officially appointed delegate to an intergovernmental conference (Fifth International Conference of American States, Santiago, 1923). Luisi also served as head of the Uruguayan delegation to the League of Nations. With her colleague, Argentine feminist and socialist Alicia MOREAU DE JUSTO, Luisi believed that female education and equal political rights were crucial to improving working conditions and health care for women and children.

INTER-AMERICAN COMMISSION OF WOMEN, *Libro de Oro* (1980), and MARIFRAN CARLSON, *¡Feminismo! The Woman's Movement in Argentina from Its Beginnings to Eva Perón* (1988).

FRANCESCA MILLER

See also **Feminism and Feminist Organizations.**

LUJÁN, city of 39,000 inhabitants (1980) located 35 miles west of Greater Buenos Aires. Its origin dates to a shrine to the Virgin Mary, erected in 1630, which has become the major Argentine center of religious pilgrimage. In the central nave, the gothic-style basilica commemorates the adherence to Catholicism of the Argentine provinces and in the two lateral aisles, the loyalty of Uruguayans and Paraguayans. The city is also known for its *cabildo* (local council house), built in 1750, and the colonial museum of Buenos Aires. Greater Buenos Aires's western gateway to the PAMPA, Luján is an important hub of the General San Martín railway and the starting point of the highway leading to the region of CUYO and Chile.

JOSÉ R. TORRE, *La casa cabildo de la villa de Luján* (Buenos Aires, 1942); and FELISA C. ECHEVERRÍA, *Romancero de la villa de Luján* (Luján, 1975).

CÉSAR N. CAVIEDES

LUJÁN, VIRGIN OF, the most popular figure of devotion and most venerated shrine in Argentina. Around 1630 a Portuguese ranch owner had two images of the Virgin Mary brought from Brazil for his chapel. When one of the images, borne by oxen, "refused" to move beyond a certain point, a site thirty-six miles west of Buenos Aires, local inhabitants took it as a sign that the Virgin wished to stay there. A popular devotion grew around the image, and the *villa* of Luján itself grew up around the chapel housing the virgin. It soon became the center of Argentine Catholic religiosity. Generals Manuel BELGRANO and José de SAN MARTÍN paid their respects to the Virgin of Luján. A major basilica to house the image, under the care of the Vincentian fathers, was begun in 1887 and opened in 1910. Declared the patroness of Argentina, the Virgin of Luján attracts many pilgrims each year, especially in the months of November and December.

JORGE MARÍA SALVAIRE, *Historia de Nuestra Señora de Luján* (1885); RUBÉN VARGAS UGARTE, *Historia del culto de María en Iberoamérica,* 3d ed., vol. 1 (1956).

JEFFREY KLAIBER

LULA. *See* **Silva, Luís Inácio Lulu da.**

LUMBER INDUSTRY. Much of Latin America is denuded of commercial timber, but select areas have supplied specialized markets. Europeans were early attracted to the variety of subtropical trees, both dyewoods and construction wood, formerly available only from the Orient. Craftsmen and builders prized Caribbean mahogany; textile manufacturers coveted BRAZIL-WOOD, Nicaragua wood, and logwood. The best wood commanded high prices in European markets, but the quality was inconsistent and the risks of obtaining it were considerable. Valuable trees such as mahogany were widely scattered. Finding and removing them was a major undertaking. Costs were proportional to overland haulage; the greater the distance, the higher the cost. The competition for accessible trees that consequently arose often provoked international controversy. The dyewood trade suffered from inroads by such other natural dyes as Mexican and Guatemalan COCHINEAL and was destroyed by synthetic dyes after 1856.

Brazilwood, which yielded a brilliant red dye, was the premier wood. It grew along the coast from the state of Pernambuco (Recife) to that of Rio de Janeiro, and provided the economic base for the first Portuguese settlements in the early sixteenth century. Overcoming a French challenge, the Portuguese crown monopolized the brazilwood trade for 300 years. The trade peaked before 1600 and was followed by a sharp drop attributed to the decimation of the coastal forests and Indian laborers. Exports in the seventeenth century averaged only 100 tons annually, even less in the eighteenth century, and ceased altogether in 1875.

Nicaragua wood, a brazilwood substitute that furnished a less intense and less durable red coloring, grew on the Pacific coast of Central America, particularly near Lake Nicaragua. The trade enjoyed a brief boom in the 1830s, when ships rounded Cape Horn to trade along the Pacific.

Logwood yielded a bluish-red dye that was the basic fixing dye for almost every other color used in the textile industry. The major source was the Yucatán, where the Spanish monopoly was threatened in the seventeenth century by English interlopers from Belize. Failing to expel them, Spain finally conceded woodcutting privileges in 1786. By then most of the logwood had been shipped overseas. Moreover, technical changes adopted by the dyemakers, plus the availability of better natural dyes, reduced the demand for logwood. Consequently, loggers shifted to the mahogany resources of the region.

The market for mahogany expanded in the nineteenth century to include building construction, shipbuilding, and railway carriages. Although mahogany grew elsewhere in the Caribbean, the Bay of Honduras was by far the major supplier for the boom that lasted into the 1850s, when exports from the region averaged 25,000 tons annually. As accessible mahogany within the Belize borders became exhausted, aggressive cutters expanded into Mexico, Guatemala, and Honduras, thereby precipitating controversies that questioned the status of both Belize and the resurrected Mosquito Kingdom. As the market declined, the tensions that had accompanied the expansive phase subsided.

ARTHUR M. WILSON, "The Logwood Trade in the Seventeenth and Eighteenth Centuries," in *Essays in the History of Modern Europe,* edited by Donald Cope McKay (1936, repr. 1968), 1–15; ALEXANDER N. MARCHANT, *From Barter to Slavery: The Economic Relations of Portuguese and Indians in the Settlement of Brazil, 1500–1580* (1942, repr. 1966); WILLIAM J. GRIFFITH, *Empires in the Wilderness: Foreign Colonization and Development in Guatemala, 1834–1844* (1965); SUSAN FAIRLIE, "Dyestuffs in the Eighteenth Century," in *Economic History Review* 2d ser., 17 (April 1965): 488–510; ROBERT A. NAYLOR, "The Mahogany Trade as a Factor in the British Return to the Mosquito Shore in the Second Quarter of the 19th Century," in *Jamaica Historical Review* 7 (1967): 40–67; *Influencia británica en el comercio centroamericano 1821–1851* (1988); and *Penny Ante Imperialism: The Mosquito Shore and the Bay of Honduras, 1600–1914* (1989).

ROBERT A. NAYLOR

See also **Forests.**

LUNA PIZARRO, FRANCISCO JAVIER DE (*b.* 1780; *d.* 9 February 1855), Peruvian Roman Catholic priest. Born in Arequipa, in his youth he admired liberal ideas and found politics as practiced in the United States to be worthy of emulation. After the protectorate of José de SAN MARTÍN ended in 1822, Luna Pizarro organized the liberal leadership in the national congress that formulated the constitutions of Peru from 1823 through 1834. This leadership favored free trade, administrative decentralization, a carefully restricted electorate, establishment of Roman Catholicism as the religion protected by the state, and the prohibition of all other views. Churchmen and the military retained the special privileges awarded them in the colonial era. Luna Pizarro later abandoned his support of the government's right to protect the church and appoint its priests. Regaining the favor of Rome, he then became a conservative archbishop of Lima (1845–1855).

JEFFREY L. KLAIBER, *Religion and Revolution in Peru, 1824–1976* (1977) and *The Catholic Church in Peru, 1821–1985: A Social History* (1992), esp. pp. 38–58.

VINCENT PELOSO

See also **Peru: Constitutions.**

LUNA Y ARELLANO, TRISTÁN DE (*b.* ca. 1500/10; *d.* 16 September 1573), soldier and governor of La Florida (1559–1561). Born in Aragón, Luna came to New Spain with Hernán CORTÉS around 1530, returned to Spain, and came back to New Spain in 1535. In 1558 Luna, a veteran of the CORONADO expedition to the American Southwest as well as of military exploits in Oaxaca, received a charter to establish a colony on the Gulf coast. Planned and outfitted in Mexico, the expedition of eleven vessels, five hundred soldiers, and a thousand colonists and servants (including Mexican natives) sailed from San Juan de Ulúa on the Gulf coast of Mexico on 11 June 1559 for the port of Ochuse (Pensacola Bay).

A hurricane sank most of the ships with their supplies before they could be offloaded. The colony quickly fell into disarray, a process hastened by Luna's illness, which at times incapacitated him. Colonists and scouting parties sent into the interior to seek food and shelter from native peoples were largely unsuccessful. In March 1561, Luna was relieved of the governorship and ordered to Spain; the colony was withdrawn.

HERBERT I. PRIESTLEY, ed. and trans., *The Luna Papers: Documents Relating to the Expedition of Don Tristán de Luna y Arellano for the Conquest of La Florida in 1559–1561*, 2 vols. (1928; repr. 1971); ROBERT S. WEDDLE, *Spanish Sea: The Gulf of Mexico in North American Discovery, 1500–1685* (1985), esp. pp. 251–284; CHARLES HUDSON, MARVIN T. SMITH, CHESTER B. DE PRATTER, and EMILIA KELLEY, "The Tristán de Luna Expedition, 1559–1561," in *First Encounters: Spanish Explorations in the Caribbean and the United States, 1492–1570*, edited by Jerald T. Milanich and Susan Milbrath (1989).

JERALD T. MILANICH

LUNDU, a Brazilian dance and song form. Of African, most probably Angolan, origin, *lundu* was popular in the eighteenth century. Like BATUQUE and SAMBA, the dance form consisted of a couple performing within a *roda* (spectators' circle) by tapping their feet, accentuatedly swaying their hips, and engaging in the characteristic *umbigada* (smacking of stomachs). Often compared with the Spanish fandango and the Portuguese *fofa* in its dance form, *lundu* was popularized as a song form with humorous lyrics by the Brazilian poet Domingos Caldas BARBOSA at the Portuguese court in the eighteenth century. In its song form, *lundu* is played in 2/4 time, with the first beat syncopated. According to Mário de Andrade, it was the first black musical form to be widely accepted into Brazilian "high" society, and left its formal imprint on Brazilian music through its "systematization of syncopation" and the "reduced seventh."

ONEYDA ALVARENGA, *Música popular brasileira* (1982); MÁRIO DE ANDRADE, *Dicionário musical brasileiro,* coordinated by Oneyda Alvarenga and Flávia Camargo Toni (1982–1989); CHARLES A. PERRONE, *Masters of Contemporary Brazilian Song* (1989).

ROBERT MYERS

See also **Maxixe; Música Popular Brasileira.**

LUNFARDO, a local vocabulary incorporated into the colloquial Spanish of BUENOS AIRES. The word itself probably comes from the Italian (Roman dialect) word *lombardo,* or thief (cf. the Sicilian *lummardo,* or "dirty man"). The large-scale Italian migrations to the Río de la Plata from 1880 to 1930 left permanent traces on the local variant of Spanish. The richest such trace, *lunfardo,* was initially a thieves' cant, many of whose expressions passed into the language (especially the slang) of Buenos Aires. The Italian derivations are usually clear, for example, *pibe* (boy) from the Genoese *pivetto; morfar* (to eat) from the Italian slang *morfa* (mouth); *mufa* (bad temper) from the Venetian *star muffo* (to feel blue); and the like. Closely associated with *lunfardo* is *vesre,* a form of back slang with the words rearranged as in *choma* (from *macho*), *dorima* (from *marido*), *gotán* (from *tango*), and so on. Valuable studies of *lunfardo* and other facets of Buenos Aires's popular culture have been fostered by the Academia Porteña del Lunfardo, founded in Buenos Aires in 1962.

JOSÉ GOBELLO, *Nuevo diccionario lunfardo* (1990).

SIMON COLLIER

LUPERÓN, GREGORIO (*b.* 8 September 1839; *d.* 21 May 1897), president of the Dominican Republic (6 October 1879–1 September 1880). A black, born in Puerto Plata in the north, Luperón won great distinction as a general during the War of Restoration (1863–1865) and the defeat of Spain. He became a leading soldier-statesman and patriot dedicated to ending turmoil and uniting the country. For many years, he was a strong supporter of Ulises ESPAILLAT, who urged Luperón to become president in 1876. He regularly resisted assuming the office but finally agreed to serve as a provisional president in 1879. As president he reorganized the army and local administration, paid government workers their back pay of three years, and adjusted all foreign claims. In the early 1880s, he served as a diplomat in Paris, representing the democratically elected government of his successor, Father Fernando Arturo de Meriño.

EMILIO RODRÍGUEZ DEMORIZI, *Luperón y Hostos* (1939), pp. 14–15, 20–21, 26, 31–32; SUMNER WELLES, *Naboth's Vineyard: The Dominican Republic, 1844–1924*, vol. 1 (1966), chap. 6; HUGO TOLENTINO DIPP, *Gregorio Luperón (Biografía Política)* (1977), chap. 2; FRANK MOYA PONS, *Manual de historia dominicana* (1977), pp. 367–368, 371–374, 384–402, 407–416.

LARMAN C. WILSON

LUQUE, HERNANDO DE (*d.* 1534), an early-sixteenth-century Spanish cleric who accompanied Pedro Arias de ÁVILA (Pedrarias) in 1514 on an expedition to colonize Panama. When Pedrarias took command at Darién, de Luque's friendship with the governor allowed him to establish a number of influential contacts. In Panama, de Luque joined in a business partnership with the conquistadores, Francisco PIZARRO and Diego de ALMARGO. In the early 1520s, the three men embarked on a plan to explore the regions south of Panama and to undertake the conquest of Peru. De Luque was instrumental in raising the necessary funds for the 1524 and 1526 expeditions into the Andean region. Acting as an agent for wealthy investors, including the judge Gaspar de Espinosa, who condemned BALBOA, de Luque raised two hundred pounds of gold bars. He was nicknamed ''Fernando de Loco,'' the mad priest, for undertaking the venture. Later scholars have suggested it was de Luque who planned and organized the expeditions as well as arranged for the necessary financial backing. He did not accompany Pizarro and Almargo on the expeditions, remaining instead in Panama to manage their business affairs. De Luque died before the conquest was completed.

FREDERICK A. KIRKPATRICK, *The Spanish Conquistadors* (1934); C. HEDRICK BASIL, and ANN K. HEDRICK, *A Historical Dictionary of Panama* (1970); JAMES LOCKHART and STUART B. SCHWARTZ, *Early Latin America: A History of Colonial Spanish America and Brazil* (1983); LESLIE BETHELL, ed., *Colonial Spanish America* (1987); MARK A. BURKHOLDER and LYMAN L. JOHNSON, *Colonial Latin America* (1990).

HEATHER K. THIESSEN

LUSINCHI, JAIME (*b.* 1924), Venezuelan president (1984–1989). While studying medicine at the Central University of Venezuela and the University of the East, Lusinchi became active in Venezuela's Democratic Ac-

tion (Acción Democrática—AD). From 1952 to 1958 he was exiled by the military dictatorship. After his return, the young pediatrician became a member of the national executive committee of AD. He also served in the Chamber of Deputies and the Senate. From 1980 to 1983 he was the party's secretary-general. In the 1983 presidential election he defeated Rafael Caldera, the candidate of the Social Christian COPEI (Comité de Organización Política Electoral Independiente) Party. As president, Lusinchi presided over a period of low oil prices and rising discontent; scandals also plagued his administration.

OLMEDO LUGO, *Políticos de Venezuela* (1969); JAIME LUSINCHI, *Frente al futuro* (1983); JUDITH EWELL, ''Venezuela Since 1930,'' in *The Cambridge History of Latin America,* edited by Leslie Bethel, vol. 8 (1991), pp. 785–789.

WINFIELD J. BURGGRAAFF

LUSO-BRAZILIAN, term that is used to describe a person or to refer to the mixture of Brazilian and Portuguese culture. *Luso* refers to Portugal and more specifically to Lusitania, the name of Portugal during the Roman Empire. Luso-Brazilian culture evolved from the mixture of Portuguese, African, and coastal Indian influences. Portuguese colonists imposed some Western-oriented cultural traditions on the indigenous society, such as the Roman Catholic church, but the farther away they were from coastal towns, the more likely were colonists and their descendants to adopt TUPI Indian language and customs. Importation of African slaves, which began in the sixteenth century, introduced a new cultural element. Brazil retained many features of Portuguese life, but was distinct from Portugal because of the preponderance of people of color. The society that evolved in Brazil was marked by racial and ethnic diversity, but also by a social hierarchy based on plantations, SLAVERY, and polygamous patriarchal paternalism. Another reflection of the mix of cultures is in language. During colonial times, many words from the Tupi Indian languages came into use alongside Portuguese. Africans, from diverse linguistic groups, added to the vocabulary. Portuguese spoken in Brazil, therefore, includes African as well as Tupi terms.

GILBERTO FREYRE, *The Masters and the Slaves* (1946); JOAQUIM MATTOSO CÂMARA, JR., *The Portuguese Language* (1972); BAILEY W. DIFFIE and GEORGE D. WINIUS, *Foundations of the Portuguese Empire, 1415–1850* (1978); STUART B. SCHWARTZ, *Sugar Plantations in the Formation of Brazilian Society: Bahia, 1550–1835* (1985).

ROSS WILKINSON

LUTZ, BERTHA MARIA JULIA (*b.* 2 August 1894; *d.* 16 September, 1976), the principal leader of the Brazilian woman's suffrage movement. Bertha Lutz was born in São Paulo to a Swiss-Brazilian father, Adolfo Lutz, a pioneer in the practice of tropical medicine in Brazil, and an English mother, Amy Fowler, a former volunteer nurse who cared for lepers in Hawaii. Lutz was educated first in Brazil and then in Europe, receiving her licencié ès sciences from the Sorbonne in 1918. Later, in 1933, she earned a degree from the Faculty of Law in Rio de Janeiro.

Following seven years of study in Europe, Lutz returned to Brazil and helped to initiate a formal woman suffrage movement. Unlike many of her contemporaries, she felt that this was the time to organize, rather than just inform and educate, women. In 1920 she founded her own woman's rights organization. Two years later, immediately after Lutz's return from the United States, where she had served as Brazil's official delegate to the first Pan American Conference of Women, this small local group was transformed into the Brazilian Federation for Feminine Progress (Federação Brasileira pelo Progresso Feminino—FBPF), affiliated with the International Woman's Suffrage Alliance. Lutz served as its president from 1922 to 1942. The main suffrage organization in Brazil, the FBPF led the campaign for the vote, because no other suffrage association attained a similar size, geographic range, or network of personal contacts. In 1932, it achieved its major goal when a new civil code enfranchised women under the same conditions as men (illiterates of both sexes were still denied the vote).

More than other leaders of the FBPF, Lutz linked women's economic emancipation with their political and social emancipation. She repeatedly warned women that the franchise was not an end in itself, and she understood that without access to education and jobs, political rights would remain mere abstractions. In print and in public, she spoke out against the exploitation of the working class, and particularly of its lower-class women. But even though the professional women leading the FBPF tackled problems of concern to the working class, such as salaries, shorter working hours, working conditions, and maternity leaves, interclass linkages were not very strong.

Following the promulgation of the 1932 civil code that enfranchised women, Bertha Lutz served on the committee that drafted a new constitution for Brazil. The Constitution of 1934 confirmed the women's 1932 victory by specifically guaranteeing women the vote and equal political rights with men. Lutz ran twice for Congress; elected as an alternate deputy, she entered the Chamber of Deputies late in 1936 to fill the vacancy created by the death of the incumbent. During her year in Congress, she helped create the Commission on the Code for Women, which she headed. Through the commission, she pushed vigorously for enactment of a statute on women, a comprehensive law concerning women's legal status and social rights. But the establishment of the dictatorial ESTADO NOVO in 1937 ended electoral politics and women's participation in them until 1945.

Although Lutz, like the FBPF, never regained a preeminent position as a voice for Brazilian women, she continued to work for woman's rights in Brazil while also pursuing her own scientific work in botany and

Bertha Lutz campaigning for women's suffrage, early 1930s. ICONOGRAPHIA.

herpetology. In 1973 she published a major work on Brazilian species of hyla. She also participated in international woman's rights activities, attending numerous women's conferences abroad, including the International Women's Year conference held in Mexico City in 1975, a year before her death at the age of eighty-two.

JUNE E. HAHNER, *Emancipating the Female Sex: The Struggle for Women's Rights in Brazil, 1850–1940* (1990).

JUNE E. HAHNER

See also **Feminism; Women.**

LUTZENBERGER, JOSÉ ANTÔNIO (*b.* 17 December 1928), Brazilian ecologist. Lutzenberger served as Brazil's first secretary of the environment (1990–1992), a cabinet-level post created by President Fernando Collor de MELLO in part to address growing international criticism of Brazil's Amazon policy as articulated during predecessor José SARNEY's presidency. Lutzenberger, an agronomist with a special interest in the AMAZON REGION and a native of Rio Grande do Sul, had long been a critic of government development policies. He accepted the cabinet post only after Collor de Mello guaranteed that his administration would halt expansion of the controversial BR-364 highway across the southern Amazon, respect the rights of the indigenous peoples of the Amazon, and end all economic incentives to environmentally destructive development projects. Lutzenberger also supported debt-for-nature swaps, unlike the Sarney administration.

Lutzenberger was known for making bombastic gloom-and-doom pronouncements and was often criticized for his adherence to the scientifically unproven "Gaia" theory, which held that the Earth is a closed physiological system capable of altering the planet's climate at will. In late 1991, the Brazilian Chamber of Deputies, along with conservative politicians and the military, complained that Lutzenberger was "internationalizing" the Amazon to the point of compromising Brazilian national sovereignty and hence called for his resignation. Color de Mello replaced him in March 1992.

Lutzenberger enjoyed an international reputation, initially based on his active opposition to the use of pesticides. In 1971 he was a founder of the Association for the Protection of the Natural Environment of Rio Grande do Sul (Associação Gaúcha de Proteção Ambiente Natural—AGAPAN), the first ecological entity organized in Brazil. He was the 1988 recipient of the Swedish government's Right Livelihood Award, the environmental equivalent of the Nobel Prize.

"Um verde do outro lado," in *Veja* 23 (7 March 1990): 35; "New President Appoints Ecologist to Head Environmental Secretariat," in *International Environment Reporter: Current Report* 13 (11 April 1990): 152–153; and NIRA BRONER WORCMAN, "Brazil's Thriving Environmental Movement," in *Technology Review* 93 (October 1990): 42–51.

LAURA JARNAGIN

See also **Environmental Movements.**

LUZ Y CABALLERO, JOSÉ DE LA (*b.* 11 July 1800; *d.* 22 June 1862), Cuban philosopher and educator. Luz y Cabellero was one of the three most influential Cuban thinkers of the nineteenth century, the other two being Father Félix VARELA Y MORALES and José Antonio SACO. A native of Havana, he initially studied for the priesthood but ended up a lawyer, although he never practiced law. Instead, he traveled extensively in Europe and the United States, becoming acquainted with most of the important writers of his time. He was influenced by the work of Francis Bacon, Étienne Bonnot de Condillac, and René Descartes, and came to embrace John Locke's nominalism, the denial that abstract entities or universal principles have real existence.

In Cuba, Luz y Caballero was a respected and popular teacher at the San Carlos Seminary (Cuba's most prominent institution of higher learning at the time) and later at the Colegio El Salvador, which he founded. His ideas and his teaching methods involved him in ardent polemics that provoked the hostility of the Spanish authorities, especially when he was accused of participating in the Conspiracy of la Escalera (1844), an attempted slave revolt. Luz y Caballero opposed violence, however, and held that Cuba was not prepared for self-government. His approach to the problem of slavery was cautious; he believed it should end gradually, by means of the suppression of the slave trade. Despite his timidity, however, he represented a progressive tendency in Cuban society; through his lectures and writings he helped to develop strong nationalistic feelings in a whole generation of Cubans. Luz y Caballero died in Havana.

The available sources in English on Luz y Caballero are too scanty. Perhaps the best discussion of his ideas is still that of his disciple MANUEL SANGUILY Y GARRITE, *José de la Luz y Caballero* (1926). See also MEDARDO VITIER, *Las ideas en Cuba* (1969), vol. 2.

JOSÉ M. HERNÁNDEZ

LYNCH, BENITO (*b.* 25 July 1880; *d.* 23 December 1951), Argentine journalist and writer. Lynch came from an old, distinguished family of *estancieros* (ranchers) and spent his childhood on an ESTANCIA in Buenos Aires Province. In 1890 he settled in La Plata, where he later worked for the conservative newspaper *El Día*. From 1904 to 1941 he devoted himself to writing fiction. His novels *Los caranchos de la Florida* (1916; *The Vultures of La Florida*) and *El inglés de los güesos* (1924; *The English Boneman*), both later adapted for stage and film, made him one of the most prominent Hispanic novelists. However, to preserve his privacy, Lynch shunned the trappings of success, refusing royalties and academic honors. A member of the generation presided over by Leopoldo LUGONES and Ricardo ROJAS, Lynch maintained his reclusiveness, his keen loyalty to his social class, his conservatism, and his divorce from contemporary political and literary life even when confronted with the innovative MARTÍN FIERRO group. His narratives almost exclusively concern life on the *estancias* of Buenos Aires Province around the beginning of the twentieth century, contrasting city life with the sedentary, stable life of the peasantry. An admirer of Zola, his naturalism contrasts with a sentimental vision of love and friendship, despite his basic distrust of the human race. Lynch's novels are considered models of linguistic frugality and well-adjusted plots.

GERALD L. HEAD, "Characterization in the Works of Benito Lynch" (Ph.D. diss., University of California, Los Angeles, 1964), "La muerte del paisano de Benito Lynch," in *Romance Notes* 12 (1970): 68–73, and "El extranjero en las abras de Benito Lynch," in *Hispania* 54 (1971): 91–97; ELBA TORRES DE PERALTA, "Actitud frente a la vida de los personajes en *El inglés de los güesos* de Benito Lynch," in *Explicación de textos literarios* 5 (1976): 13–22; DAVID WILLIAM FOSTER, "Benito Lynch," in *Latin American Writers,* edited by Carlos A. Solé and Maria Isabel Abreu, vol. 2 (1989), pp. 559–563.

ANGELA B. DELLEPIANE

LYNCH, ELISA ALICIA (*b.* June 1835; *d.* 27 July 1886), Irish mistress of Paraguayan dictator Francisco Solano LÓPEZ.

Born into impoverished circumstances, Lynch left Ireland at age fifteen when she married Xavier Quatrefages, a French military surgeon. Theirs was evidently a loveless marriage, and within a few years Lynch was on her own in Paris. In 1853, after having lived with several lovers, she met Solano López, son of the Paraguayan president Carlos Antonio López, who was then on an official tour of Europe.

Unable to marry López because of her then undocumented marital status, Lynch nonetheless accompanied him back to Paraguay. She was less than well received by the Paraguayan elites, who regarded her in a scandalous light. López installed her in a sumptuous residence in Asunción, however, and there she attempted to re-create in Paraguay a salon that included musicians, literary figures, and interesting foreign visitors. She introduced the piano in Paraguay, and popularized Parisian fashions. She had five children with López. Upon his accession to the presidency in 1862, Lynch became de facto first lady.

The outbreak of the WAR OF THE TRIPLE ALLIANCE in 1864 found Lynch at the front, together with her consort. Detractors later claimed that she was responsible for many of López's excesses, particularly the mass executions at San Fernando in 1868. Two years later, after a long and sanguinary retreat, López was killed in the northeastern region of CERRO CORÁ. Lynch witnessed his death, as she did that of their firstborn son, an army colonel.

At the end of the war, the Brazilian authorities deported Lynch, but after a few years she returned to Asunción to try to lay claim to lands that had been transferred to her name during the fighting. These legal efforts failed and she returned to Paris, where she died penniless in 1886. In the 1960s, the Stroessner government repatriated her remains.

WILLIAM E. BARRETT, *Woman on Horseback: The Biography of Francisco López and Eliza Lynch* (1938); GILBERT PHELPS, *Tragedy of Paraguay* (1975) *passim;* ELISA A. LYNCH, *Exposición y protesta* (1987); FERNANDO BAPTISTA, *Madame Lynch: Mujer de mundo y de guerra* (1987).

MARTA FERNÁNDEZ WHIGHAM

LYNCH, MARTA (*b.* 8 March 1925; *d.* 8 October 1985), Argentine writer. Born in Buenos Aires, Lynch was the daughter of an important political figure and the wife of a powerful corporate director. She is notable for making use of the circumstances of her socioeconomic privilege to portray a complex network of cultural oppressions in Argentina, with special reference to the victimization of middle-class women whose lives project a facade of passive comfort. *La señora Ordóñez* (1967) may be the first Argentine treatment of a woman's explicit sexual discontent, while *Al vencedor* (1965) centers on class conflict and its humiliations in Argentina during the so-called Argentine Revolution that followed the Peronist period. But Lynch's best writing focuses on the devastating social and personal price paid by Argentines for the DIRTY WAR of the late 1970s, especially in the short stories of *Los dedos de la mano* (1976), *La penúltima versión de la Colorada Villanueva* (1978), and *Informe bajo llave* (1983). With her death, Lynch joined a line of notable Argentine women authors who have committed suicide.

MARTHA PALEY DE FRANCESCATO, "Marta Lynch," in *Hispamérica* 4, no. 10 (1975): 33–44; DIANE S. BIRKEMOE, "The Virile Voice of Marta Lynch," in *Revista de Estudios Hispánicos* 16, no. 2 (1982): 191–211; ELIANA MOYA RAGGIO, "Conversación con Marta Lynch," in *Letras Femeninas* 14, no. 1–2 (1988): 104–111; NAOMI LINDSTROM, *Women's Voice in Latin American Literature* (1989), pp. 73–95; BIRGITTA VANCE, "Marta Lynch," in *Spanish American Women Writers: A Bio-Bibliographical Source Book* (1990), pp. 292–302; DAVID WILLIAM FOSTER, "Raping Argentina: Marta Lynch's *Informe bajo llave,*" in *Centennial Review* 3, no. 3 (1991): 663–680.

DAVID WILLIAM FOSTER

M

MACCIÓ, RÓMULO (*b.* 24 March 1931), Argentine artist. Born in Buenos Aires, Macció was trained as a graphic designer and worked as an illustrator in advertising agencies. He took up painting in 1956, joining the New Figuration group in 1961. His early work consisted of paintings of anthropomorphic fragments, halfway between abstraction and figuration. After 1964 he began to paint distorted figures in expressionistic and surrealistic styles. He consciously sought to generate visual and thematic contradictions, such as the overlapping of planar and volumetric structures and the coexistence of two different subjects in the same painting. In 1967 he won the International Di Tella Prize. A rational and orderly composition characterized his paintings of the mid-1970s, although surreal traits remained present in melancholic portraits of lonely figures, often self-portraits (*Self-Portrait with Easel*, 1976; *At Seven O'Clock in Highbury Place*, 1976). In the late 1970s, he painted human figures as stylized silhouettes with spiritual and mystical connotations (*Amalfi*, 1980; *Adriatic*, 1979). Macció's tendency to expressionism became more evident in the 1980s (*Castel Sant' Angelo*, 1980). His most recent paintings are views from his atelier and subjects with some classical mythological overtones. He participated in the Venice Biennale in 1988 and exhibited in Paris, Milan, and Rome in 1991.

GILBERT CHASE, *Contemporary Art in Latin America* (1970), pp. 152–153; RÓMULO MACCIÓ, *Rómulo Macció: Selected Paintings, 1963–1980,* translated by Kenneth Parkin (1980); FÉLIX ANGEL, "The Latin American Presence," in *The Latin American Spirit: Art and Artists in the United States, 1920–1970,* by Luis R. Cancel et al. (1988), p. 259; MIGUEL BRIANTE ET AL., *Nueva Figuración: 1961–1991* (1991); p. 59.

MARTA GARSD

MACEDO, JOAQUIM MANUEL DE (*b.* 24 June 1820; *d.* 11 April 1882), Brazilian novelist. Joaquim Manuel de Macedo was not the first Brazilian to publish novels, but he was the great popularizer of the genre in the nation's literature. His two earliest novels, *A moreninha* (1844) and *O moco loiro* (1845), achieved enormous popularity; indeed, *A moreninha* is still widely read and enjoyed in Brazil, particularly by adolescent readers. Macedo's sentimental tales of adventure and romance never challenged established social norms; after a good many implausible plot devices, his aristocratic young heros and heroines always manage to find precisely the mates society and family would have chosen for them. The primary value of his texts today is their detailed documentation of upper-class mores in Imperial Rio de Janeiro. (Macedo was tutor to the children of Princess ISABEL.)

Macedo continued to publish fiction after *O moco loiro*, but his skills as a novelist did not develop and his reputation as a writer was increasingly overshadowed by that of José de ALENCAR. The most interesting of Macedo's later works, none of which attracted the audience his earliest novels had enjoyed, is *As vítimas-algozes* (1869), a collection of three antislavery novellas.

ANTÔNIO CÂNDIDO, "O honrado e facundo Joaquim Manuel de Macedo," in *Formação da Literatura Brasileira*, 5th ed. (1975), vol. 2, pp. 136–145; JOSÉ ANTÔNIO PEREIRA RIBEIRO, *O universo romântico de Joaquim Manoel de Macedo* (1987).

DAVID T. HABERLY

MACEHUALLI (pl. *macehualtin*), a Nahua social category taken into Spanish as *macehual* (pl. *macehuales*), that usually refers to an indigenous commoner. It also had the occasional meaning of "vassal," reflecting the political dimension of a commoner's life, and, when pluralized, "the people." Forming the majority of the population of central Mexico in pre-Hispanic and colonial times, *macehualtin* farmed, fished, and produced utilitarian goods. As members of *calpulli* and *altepetl* (neighborhoods, towns, and regional states), they had usufruct rights to land. With those rights came the responsibilities of tribute and labor drafts owed to local authorities. Over time, the concepts of *macehualli* and *indio* merged, reflecting changes in colonial society.

JACQUES SOUSTELLE, *Daily Life of the Aztecs on the Eve of the Spanish Conquest* (1961); FRANCES F. BERDAN, *The Aztecs of Central Mexico* (1982); JAMES LOCKHART, *The Nahuas After the Conquest* (1992), pp. 95–96, 114–115.

STEPHANIE WOOD

MACEIÓ (formerly Macayo), capital of the state of ALAGOAS, Brazil, with a population of about 527,220 (1989 est.). Founded in 1815 when a small settlement received official recognition, Maceió became the state capital in 1839. On the Atlantic coast approximately 120 miles south of Recife, the city's port deals mainly in sugar, cotton, and rum. The primarily industrial economy of Maceió encompasses sugar refineries, textile mills, distilleries, chemical factories, and steel, iron, and zinc foundries. The city is famous for a lighthouse built on an eminence in a residential area about a half mile from the ocean, and local beaches are considered among the best in Brazil.

CARA SHELLY

MAC ENTYRE, EDUARDO (b. 20 February 1929), Argentine artist. A self-taught painter, Mac Entyre was born in Buenos Aires, where he still lives.

In 1959 Mac Entyre, with Ignacio Pirovano and Miguel Angel Vidal, founded a movement called Generative Art, which they defined as "engendering a series of op-

tical sequences which are produced by the evolving of a given form." Mac Entyre uses geometrically precise sequences of exquisitely colored lines that give the canvas a magical effect of depth and appear to generate their own movement as they glide or whirl through space. In liberating his paintings from a static state, he achieved an important goal of twentieth-century avant-garde artists.

A pillar of geometric art in Argentina, Mac Entyre still adheres to the same principles while creating a tremendous variety of forms of his poetic geometry. In 1986 the Organization of American States and the Museum of Modern Art of Latin America honored Mac Entyre for his contribution to the development of the modern art of the Americas.

SAMUEL PAZ, "Los diez últimos años de pintura y escultura argentina, 1950–1960," in *150 años de arte argentino* (Buenos Aires, 1961); RAFAEL F. SQUIRRU, *Eduardo Mac Entyre* (1981); *Selections from the Permanent Collection of the Museum of Modern Art of Latin America* (Washington, D.C., 1985); *Mac Entyre* (Buenos Aires, 1993).

IDA ELY RUBIN

MACEO, ANTONIO (b. 14 June 1845; d. 7 December 1896), second in command of Cuba's independence army. Maceo was one of the greatest guerrilla fighters of the nineteenth century and certainly the most daring soldier ever born on Cuban soil. Cubans familiarly refer to him as the Titan of Bronze, as he was dubbed by an admiring speaker at a patriotic rally in New York City in 1895.

Maceo was the son of a Venezuelan mulatto émigré and a free Cuban black, Mariana Grajales, the mother of thirteen children, all of whom swore at her behest to free their country from Spanish domination or die in the attempt. When Cuba's TEN YEARS' WAR began in 1868, Maceo enlisted in the rebel army as a private; five years later he achieved the rank of general. From the outset he showed a superior ability to outsmart and outmaneuver the Spanish commanders and occasionally inflicted heavy losses on them. He also displayed extraordinary leadership and determination. Throughout his military career, which spanned the Ten Years' War and the 1895–1898 war, it is estimated that he fought in more than 900 actions. Since he never sought the safety of the rear guard, he sustained twenty-six wounds. Perhaps his greatest military feat was to lead an invasion of western Cuba in 1895–1896, a brilliant operation during which he covered more than a thousand miles in 92 days while engaging the Spanish army in 27 battles or skirmishes and capturing more than 2,000 rifles and 80,000 rounds of ammunition. When Maceo was killed, in a scuffle of little consequence, he had risen to the rank of second in command of the Cuban liberating army.

Maceo's place in Cuban history is as a symbol of tenacity and unwavering patriotism. On 11 February 1878 most of the generals of the Cuban liberating army realized that it would be impossible to defeat the Spanish

Antonio Maceo Grajales, ca. 1890s. ORGANIZATION OF AMERICAN STATES.

For this reason, he wrote, "I enjoin my own people not to ask for anything on the basis of the color of their skin."

This confidence in the ability of Cubans was probably the key to Maceo's attitude toward the United States. He favored the recognition of Cuban belligerency by the powerful republic to the north, but he did not think that American intervention was needed to defeat Spain. He believed that Cubans should depend on their own efforts, adding that it was better to rise or fall without help than to contract debts of gratitude with a neighbor as powerful as the United States. He wrote to the *New York World:* "I should not want our neighbor to shed their blood for our cause. We can do that for ourselves if, under the common law, we can get the necessary elements to overthrow the corrupted power of Spain in Cuba." And on another occasion he said: "Do you really want to cut the war down? Bring Cuba 25,000 to 35,000 rifles and a million bullets. . . . We Cubans do not need any other help."

There are numerous biographies in Spanish, notably JOSÉ LUCIANO FRANCO, *Maceo, apuntes para una historia de su vida,* 3 vols. (1975). The best narrative of his military exploits is JOSÉ MIRÓ ARGENTER, *Crónicas de la guerra, las campañas de invasión y de occidente, 1895–1896,* 3 vols. (1945). In English, see PHILIP S. FONER, *Antonio Maceo: The "Bronze Titan" of Cuba's Struggle for Independence* (1977).

JOSÉ M. HERNÁNDEZ

See also **Cuba: War of Independence.**

forces and thus accepted the Pact of ZANJÓN to end the Ten Years' War. At this juncture Maceo refused to capitulate. He held a historic meeting, known as the Protest of Baraguá, with Spanish marshal Arsenio Martínez Campos, at which he demanded independence for Cuba and the total abolition of slavery. When Martínez Campos rejected these conditions, Maceo resumed fighting. Since the situation of the liberators was truly hopeless, Maceo eventually had to desist and ultimately leave Cuba. But his gesture remained a source of inspiration for future combatants and earned him the acclaim of Cubans and foreigners alike. The American and Foreign Anti-Slavery Society was among the groups praising him warmly for his stand on slavery.

Maceo identified closely with the predicament of the men and women of his race. Although he himself suffered the attacks of racists within the Cuban liberating army, who accused him of attempting to create a black republic in Cuba, his defense of the rights of blacks was based on the theoretical notion of the rights of men rather than any ethnic affinity. "The revolution has no color" was his indignant rejoinder to his accusers. He trusted that "Now, tomorrow, and always there shall exist in Cuba men who will do justice to the people of my race."

MACGREGOR, GREGOR (*b.* 1786; *d.* 4 December 1845), British soldier of fortune and speculator in colonization. MacGregor was often regarded as either a visionary idealist or an unscrupulous promoter. A young man of twenty-five with some experience in the British army, this flamboyant Scottish army captain arrived in Venezuela in 1811 to support the cause of independence. MacGregor fought with distinction under Francisco de MIRANDA and Simón BOLÍVAR and was decorated. During his years with the insurgents he cruised the Caribbean from Florida to Venezuela. At some point he saw his fortune interwoven with the lush tropical environment he had adopted.

Sailing for New Granada in 1819, MacGregor occupied the island of San Andrés off the Nicaragua coast and later landed on the desolate MOSQUITO COAST, where an assortment of European adventurers had long maintained close ties with the Indians. The imaginative MacGregor concocted a visionary scheme to establish an overseas Acadia on the Mosquito Coast as a haven for surplus population in his native Scotland and as a staging point for introducing the Presbyterian faith to the natives. On 29 April 1820 he received from the compliant Mosquito king, George Frederick, title to the Black River (Río Tinto) district of Honduras, abandoned by the British in 1787.

Styling himself "His Excellency General Sir Gregor

MacGregor, Prince of POYAIS,'' he returned home in 1821 to launch his grandiose project on an unsuspecting public, looking to Scotland for settlers and to London for funds. Although preoccupied with financing, MacGregor sent four ships with more than 300 settlers to Black River, where Governor Hector Hall had elaborate instructions on how to proceed. Totally unprepared for frontier survival, two-thirds of the settlers died of malaria, yellow fever, or dysentery. Belize Superintendent Edward Codd authorized Marshall BENNETT and George Weston to evacuate the survivors in 1823. About forty-five eventually reached England, where their revelations blackened the name of MacGregor.

Still seeking support, MacGregor returned to England, paid a fine, and then was arrested in France in 1825 but acquitted. Attempts by Poyais bondholders to revive the project in 1837, under various names, failed. MacGregor gave up, leaving England in 1839 for Venezuela, where he was reinstated in his former military rank and granted a pension.

An unsympathetic account is ALFRED HASBROUCK, ''Gregor MacGregor and the Colonization of Poyais Between 1820 and 1824,'' in *Hispanic American Historical Review* 7 (1927): 438–459. A popular account is VICTOR ALLEN, ''The Prince of Poyais,'' in *History Today* 2 (1952): 53–58. On attempted revivals, see WILLIAM J. GRIFFITH, *Empires in the Wilderness: Foreign Colonization and Development in Guatemala, 1834–1844* (1965); and ROBERT A. NAYLOR, *Penny Ante Imperialism: The Mosquito Shore and the Bay of Honduras, 1600–1914* (1989).

ROBERT A. NAYLOR

MACHADO, GUSTAVO (*b.* 1898), leader of Venezuelan Communist Party. Born into a wealthy Caracas family, Machado, while still in high school, became a revolutionary in opposition to the dictatorship of Juan Vicente Gómez (1908–1935). Over the course of his political career, he spent many years in exile and in prison for his revolutionary and Communist activities. During the Democratic Action *trienio* (1945–1948), the Communist Party now legalized, he was a vocal member of the Constituent Assembly and later of the Chamber of Deputies. In 1947 Machado ran for president on the Communist ticket, finishing third and last. After the military dictatorship (1948–1958) Machado returned from exile and was again elected to the Chamber of Deputies (1958), where he served as head of the Communist delegation. He was subsequently imprisoned (1963–1968), however, for allegedly fomenting guerrilla insurgency. After his release he resumed command of the Communist Party, but he renounced armed violence and instead stressed the peaceful road to socialism.

ROBERT J. ALEXANDER, *The Communist Party of Venezuela* (1969); JUAN BAUTISTA FUENMAYOR, *Historia de la Venezuela política contemporánea, 1899–1960*, 10 vols. (1978–); ROBERT J. ALEXANDER, ed., *Biographical Dictionary of Latin American and Caribbean Political Leaders* (1988).

WINFIELD J. BURGGRAAFF

MACHADO DE ASSIS, JOAQUIM MARIA (*b.* 21 June 1839; *d.* 29 September 1908), the greatest figure in Brazilian letters. Machado was a novelist, short-story writer, poet, essayist, playwright, and literary critic; fiction, however, gave him eminence in Brazilian literature. A contemporary of the romantics, who to some extent influenced him in his formative years, Machado developed a highly personal style.

Machado was born in a slum of Rio de Janeiro, the son of a black house painter and a Portuguese woman from the Azores Islands. At an early age, he became an orphan and began to earn his own living. He did not receive much formal education. He worked as a typesetter, proofreader, editor, and staff writer. In 1869 he married Carolina, the sister of his friend the Portuguese poet Faustino Xavier de Novais. At thirty-five he joined government service.

When still very young, Machado entered the field of letters, writing poetry, plays, opera librettos, short stories, newspaper articles, and translations. Active in artistic and intellectual circles, he was, however, a man of restrained habits who spent thirty-five years as a civil servant. Some of his biographers believe that the bureaucratic routine permitted Machado to devote himself completely to letters. Others view his hardships as having benefited his literature. Machado's anxieties regarding his race and social origin, the epilepsy that tortured him, and his stuttering all had powerful influences on his art. Literature was his relief.

Machado's first volume of poems, *Crisálidas* (Chrysalis), was published in 1864. Other publications followed: *Falenas* (Moth, 1870), *Contos fluminenses* (Tales of Rio de Janeiro, 1870), his first novel, *Ressurreição* (Resurrection, 1871), *Histórias da meia-noite* (Midnight Tales, 1873), *A mão e a luva* (The Hand and the Glove, 1874), *Americanas* (American Poems, 1875), *Helena* (1876), and *Iaiá Garcia* (1878).

In spite of this substantial accomplishment, Machado had not yet defined his identity, still searching for his own creative principles. At thirty-nine, sick and exhausted, he was granted a leave of absence, which he spent in the resort city of Nova Friburgo, near Rio. This period marks a turning point in his work. After his return to Rio he began one of the masterpieces that characterize the second part of his writing career, *Memórias póstumas de Brás Cubas* (1881; *Epitaph of a Small Winner*, 1952).

This rise to greatness has been explained in different ways. Most modern critics, however, interpret his achievement as the consequence of a long desire for perfection and as the result of the struggle between romantic ideals and Machado's creative intuition with which they conflicted. There was not a sudden change between the two phases; the first phase prepared the second. It was a maturation process. After 1875 the technique of his short stories improved. As a result, the collections published after 1880 include several true masterpieces, such as ''Missa do galo'' (Midnight Mass),

Joaquím Maria Machado de Assis, 1864. ORGANIZATION OF
AMERICAN STATES.

"Noite de almirante" (An Admiral's Evening), "A causa
secreta" (The Secret Cause), "Uns braços" (A Pair of
Arms), "O alienista" (The Alienist), "O enfermeiro"
(The Male Nurse), "A cartomante" (The Fortune Teller),
and "O espelho" (The Mirror).

Machado's first novel of the second phase, *Memórias
póstumas de Brás Cubas,* is a fictional autobiography written by the dead hero. Starting with his death and funeral, the novel represents a complete break with the
literary conventions of the time and Brazilian literature,
which allowed an exploration of themes not utilized
before. With psychological acuity, the author observes
people in trivial, cynical, and egocentric conditions. He
also portrays Brazilian society at the end of the empire.

The next novel is *Quincas Borba* (1891; *Quincas Borba:
Philosopher or Dog?,* 1954). Rubião, a teacher from Minas
Gerais, inherits from Quincas Borba a huge amount of
money and a crazy philosophy. As he leaves for Rio,
Rubião meets a pair of crooks, Christiano Palha and his
beautiful wife, Sofia, with whom he falls in love. The
couple, who become Rubião's close friends, slowly steal
everything from him. Many other people belonging to a
marginal and mobile society are involved. Rubião ends
up poor and insane. The conclusion proclaims universal
indifference in the face of human suffering and the
abandonment of man by supernatural forces.

Machado reached the highest expression of his art in
Dom Casmurro (1890; *Dom Casmurro,* 1971). This masterpiece is artistically superior to his other works; novelistic
elements such as narrative structure, composition of
characters, and psychological analysis are employed
with incomparable genius. Bento Santiago wanted to join
the two ends of life and restore youth in old age. For this
purpose he had a replica of his childhood home constructed. Because the plan did not work, he decided to
write about his past. Bento and Capitu are in love, but he
must become a priest to comply with his mother's vow.
Capitu's plotting convinces Bento's mother to allow him
to leave the seminary. Bento receives his law degree, and
finally the couple are united in a blissful marriage. They
have only one child. Escobar, Bento's best friend, has
married Capitu's best friend, and the two couples live in
perfect friendship. As Escobar dies, Bento becomes convinced that his friend and Capitu have committed adultery. Bento tells his own story, which seems smooth on
the surface. Implicitly, however, this is a tragic tale of
evil, hatred, betrayal, and jealousy. This content, along
with the outstanding artistic qualities of the book, makes
Dom Casmurro Machado's most powerful work.

In *Esaú e Jacó* (1904; *Esau and Jacob,* 1965), Machado
adds a new dimension to his treatment of symbolic and
mythical elements. The novel contains more political
allegories than do any of his other works. Two identical
twins, Pedro and Paulo, differ from each other in every
respect but their love for the same girl, Flora. The political atmosphere of the newly proclaimed Brazilian Republic is incorporated into the narrative.

Also in 1904, Machado was overwhelmed by the
death of his wife. He wrote a very touching poem, "À
Carolina," which appeared as an introduction to a new
collection of short stories, *Relíquias da casa velha* (Relics
of an Old House, 1906). *Memorial de Aires* (1908; *Counselor Ayres' Memoirs,* 1972), his last novel, is a love story
and reminiscence of his life with Carolina. Very ill and
frail, Machado died the same year.

Machado de Assis was a powerful writer who im-
presses us intellectually and emotionally. His writing is
predominantly psychological, but the best of his fiction
combines the social, philosophical, and historical dimensions with the psychological to make a whole. His extraordinary ability to evoke the past is one of the secrets
of his success. His stylistic traits include a simple, exact,
and clear syntax and short, discontinuous sentences
without rhetorical effects. Metaphor and simile are evident in his writing, but conciseness marks his style and
is responsible for its greatness. The underlining philosophy is a pessimistic one that envisions man as solitary,
depraved, and lost. Compatible with his tragic view of
life, his themes embrace death, insanity, cruelty, ingratitude, disillusion, and hate. Machado found refuge for
his nihilism in beauty. His heaven is the aesthetic ideal.

Additional collections of short stories included *Papéis
avulsos* (1882), *Histórias sem data* (1884), *Várias histórias*
(1896), *Páginas recolhidas* (1899), and *Outras relíquias*

(1910). Many of these stories have been published in English. A three-volume collection of his complete works is *Obra completa* (1959).

HELEN CALDWELL, *The Brazilian Othello of Machado de Assis: A Study of "Dom Casmurro"* (1960); AFRÂNIO COUTINHO, *Machado de Assis na literatura brasileira* (1960); HELEN CALDWELL, *Machado de Assis* (1970); CLAUDE HULET, "Machado de Assis," in *Brazilian Literature,* edited by Claude Hulet, vol. 2 (1974), pp. 95–118; MARTA PEIXOTO, "Aires as Narrator and Aires as Character in *Esaú e Jacó,*" in *Luso-Brazilian Review* (Summer 1980): 79–92; MARIA LUÍSA NUNES, *The Craft of an Absolute Winner: Characterization and Narratology in the Novels of Machado de Assis* (1983); JOHN GLEDSON, *The Deceptive Realism of Machado de Assis: A Dissenting Interpretation of "Dom Casmurro"* (1984); AFRÂNIO COUTINHO, "Machado de Assis," in *Latin American Writers,* edited by Carlos A. Solé and Maria Isabel Abreu, vol. 1 (1989), pp. 253–268.

MARIA ISABEL ABREU

MACHADO Y MORALES, GERARDO (*b.* 28 September 1871; *d.* 29 March 1939), president and dictator of Cuba (1925–1933). A man of humble origins, Machado joined the rebels during Cuba's second war of independence (1895–1898), rising to the rank of brigadier general. After peace returned, he became a prominent politician and businessman. In association with American capitalists, he invested in public utilities. He had become wealthy by the early 1920s, when he managed to win control of the Liberal Party and, with a platform of national "regeneration," was elected president in 1924 in a relatively fair election.

Although Machado is usually condemned by historians for eventually turning into a dictator, in his first presidential term not only did he appear to be genuinely concerned with "regenerating" the nation, but he also embarked on an impressive public works program that included the completion of a much-needed central highway and the construction of a national capitol building. In addition, he made a serious attempt to regulate sugar production and became the first president to promote Cuban sovereignty vis-à-vis the United States. His most important step in this direction was a tariff reform bill he sponsored in 1927 that provided protection to emerging Cuban industries.

Betraying his electoral promises, however, Machado did contract several loans with U.S. banks to finance his public works program. He also showed a disposition to resort to force in order to solve problems, so that striking workers, restless students, and other dissidents at times suffered from his actions. On the whole, however, in 1928–1929 he was still popular and had a grip on the political situation.

Ironically, this control proved to be Machado's undoing, for through bribes and threats he brought all the opposition parties under his influence and subordinated the Congress and the judiciary to his will. He was consequently able to push forward a change in the constitution that allowed reelecting himself virtually

Gerardo Machado y Morales, February 1931. LIBRARY OF CONGRESS.

unopposed for a new six-year term. At the time of his second inauguration, 20 May 1929, he was still being hailed as the savior of the fatherland. But after that the number of people forced into active opposition increased considerably, and when shortly afterward the shock waves of the worldwide depression reached Cuba, the anti-Machado movement assumed the characteristics of a revolutionary upheaval.

In 1930 there were several antigovernment demonstrations, the most serious of which culminated in the closing of all the schools in the country. The following year, the leaders surviving from the wars of independence staged a full-scale military uprising in the countryside. Machado succeeded in crushing these revolts because he could count on the army, which he had transformed into the overseer of the civil government. But not even the full resources of the army could prevent the revolutionary struggle from degenerating into a vicious fight (as it did from 1932 onward) between the government's brutally repressive forces and clandestine opposition groups such as the so-called ABC movement and the Student Directorate, which were bent upon overthrowing the regime through sabotage and terrorism.

When Franklin D. ROOSEVELT became president of the United States in 1933, political stability was seen as essential for the successful development of New Deal

Cuban policy. Thus, Sumner WELLES was sent as ambassador to Havana for the purpose of finding a peaceful solution to the Cuban imbroglio. At first he tried to mediate between the Machado government and its opposition, but as the negotiations went on, he began to push Machado toward making concessions to his enemies. Playing for time, Machado accepted some of the conditions, but he soon drew the line and refused to yield to further pressure, paradoxically assuming the same nationalistic stand as radical opposition groups such as the Student Directorate, which had earlier rejected Welles's good offices. Thus the attempted mediation ended in a deadlock that was resolved only when a general strike paralyzed the nation. Machado then offered favorably disposed Communist labor leaders legal recognition and official support if they would use their influence to end the strike. This maneuver failed, however, and on 12 August 1933 Cuba's armed forces, fearing U.S. armed intervention, moved against the president.

Thus the defiant Machado, who even at the last minute sought to arouse the populace to defend Cuba against a U.S. landing, was finally forced to take a plane to Nassau in the Bahamas. He eventually settled in the United States, where he died, six years later, in Miami Beach. Cuban governments since have refused to authorize the transfer of his remains to his native soil.

The best account of Machado's presidency available in English is in LUIS E. AGUILAR, *Cuba 1933: Prologue to Revolution* (1972).

JOSÉ M. HERNÁNDEZ

See also **Cuba: Revolution of 1933.**

MAC-IVER RODRÍGUEZ, ENRIQUE (*b.* 15 July 1845; *d.* 21 August 1922), a prominent Chilean lawyer, political figure, intellectual, and journalist. As a deputy to Congress, Mac-Iver supported the rebellion against President José Manuel BALMACEDA FERNÁNDEZ in 1890–1891. He also served as a senator (1900–1922) and as a government minister, and was a grand master of the Masonic Order. An astute social critic, he lamented the decline in Chile's political morality, the nation's international reputation, and the quality of its leaders. In a 1906 convention of the Radical Party, Mac-Iver unsuccessfully argued against Valentín LETELIER MADARIAGA that the state should not become involved in developing the economy and backing social reforms. At the same time, he questioned the capacity of the lower classes to participate in political life.

FREDRICK B. PIKE, *Chile and the United States, 1880–1962* (1963); KAREN L. REMMER, *Party Competition in Argentina and Chile* (1984).

WILLIAM F. SATER

MACHU PICCHU, the most famous Inca settlement. A royal estate of the emperor Inca PACHACUTI, Machu Picchu lies about fifty-four miles northwest of the city of Cuzco at approximately 9,000 feet above sea level, in the cloud forest of the rugged *montaña* region on the eastern watershed of the Peruvian Andes. Machu Picchu is believed to have been abandoned at the time of the Spanish conquest and was never found by the conquistadores. It lay in obscurity until Hiram BINGHAM's 1911 expedition in search of the last Inca capital, VILCA-

Machu Picchu. PHOTO BY MARTÍN CHAMBI, COURTESY JULIA CHAMBI.

BAMBA. His explorations were publicized by the National Geographic Society, and Machu Picchu became famous as the "Lost City of the INCAS."

In fact Machu Picchu was neither lost nor a city. Bingham found local farmers living there when he arrived, and the site was known to the local people. Bingham was the first, however, to clear the site extensively and to recognize it as a major Inca monument. The function of Machu Picchu has long been debated. Bingham believed it to be the last capital of Vilcabamba, the Inca rump state established after the Conquest. Recent research, however, indicates that the site was not a city but an estate of the emperor Pachacuti. Machu Picchu's importance, aside from its beauty and aesthetic qualities, lies in the fact that the Spanish never discovered it. It is therefore one of only a very few examples of an imperial Inca installation that was not altered or affected by the European invasion.

Sources on Machu Picchu include HIRAM BINGHAM, *Machu Picchu, a Citadel of the Incas* (1930) and *Lost City of the Incas* (1948); PAUL FEJOS, *Archaeological Explorations in the Cordillera Vilcabamba, Southeastern Peru* (1944); JOHN HEMMING, *Machu Picchu* (1981); and JOHAN REINHARD, *Machu Picchu the Sacred Center* (1991).

GORDON F. McEWAN

See also **Archaeology.**

MACULELÊ, an African Brazilian warrior dance, possibly of southern Angolan, Congolese, Mozambican, and Portuguese origin, traditionally found in Salvador, Bahia, on the feast of Our Lady of the Immaculate Conception. The dance is performed by ten or twenty men dressed in white cotton shirts, holding wooden sticks in each hand. The dancers, in animated synchronicity, perform a mock battle, rhythmically cross-striking their wooden bastinadoes. Similar stick dances date to at least the nineteenth century in Brazil. Exhibitions of *maculelê* may be seen in Salvador and Rio de Janeiro during Carnival. They are often danced by the same men who perform CAPOEIRA.

LUIS DA CAMARA CASUDO, *Dicionário do folclore brasileiro*, 5th ed. (1984); MARY C. KARASCH, *Slave Life in Rio de Janeiro* (1987).

BERNADETTE DICKERSON

MADEIRA ISLANDS, Atlantic island group 400 miles west of Morocco. Madeira was unoccupied before its discovery by the Portuguese in 1420. João Gonçalves Zarco and Tristão Vaz, lieutenants of HENRY THE NAVIGATOR, were the first to land on Madeira. Shortly after, colonies were established with financial support from the revenues of the MILITARY ORDER of Christ. The capital was called Funchal, the Portuguese word for "fennel," which grew abundantly on the island. The island was ruled by DONATÁRIOS until 1497, when the captain-cies were abolished and the Portuguese crown took direct control of Madeira.

The Portuguese first established sugar plantations on Madeira, an experiment that introduced the islands to the African SLAVE TRADE. During the late fifteenth century, Madeira was at the height of its prosperity as the world's largest producer of sugar. This condition changed, however, when the Madeira model for sugar production was introduced to Brazil. By 1620 the SUGAR INDUSTRY on the island was in decline as the competition from Brazil proved overpowering. There was a brief respite while the island was under Spanish domination (1580–1640) during the Eighty Years' War, but when the Dutch were forced out of Brazil in 1654, Madeira's sugar industry gradually declined, in spite of strong protectionist legislation meant to save it.

Twice during the nineteenth century the island was occupied by the British, who developed a taste for the local wine. It was believed that the wine was improved by a visit to the tropics, so it was shipped first to Brazil before it was returned to Europe and sold in England.

ELIZABETH NICHOLAS, *Madeira and the Canaries* (1953); C. R. BOXER, *Four Centuries of Portuguese Expansion, 1415–1825* (1969); ALFRED W. CROSBY, *Ecological Imperialism: The Biological Expansion of Europe, 900–1900* (1986).

SHEILA L. HOOKER

MADEIRA–MAMORÉ RAILROAD, a transportation company linking Bolivia and Brazil. Ever since the first Europeans descended the treacherous falls and rapids between the Mamoré and MADEIRA rivers in the eighteenth century, developers dreamed of opening a more direct connection between them. Upriver were great quantities of RUBBER, quinine, sarsaparilla, hardwoods, and other forest products.

A railroad was first proposed by U.S. entrepreneur George E. Church. Between 1869 and 1872 he obtained Bolivian and Brazilian concessions to build a 220-mile line around a dozen major falls. He raised money in London and began work, but within a year the project collapsed. In 1878 he launched another attempt, this time financed in Philadelphia. It, too, failed; and in 1881 the Brazilian government shut it down with only 11 miles of track laid.

The U.S. magnate Percival FARQUHAR completed construction of the line early in the twentieth century. Having been successful in his ventures in southern Brazil, he won contracts to modernize the port of BELÉM. At the same time he acquired the Amazon Navigation Company, which earned great profits by transporting rubber from the headwaters.

The railroad was inaugurated in 1912, just as the rubber boom was being undermined by cheap rubber exports from Asia. Farquhar lost the railroad, as well as his holdings in the port of Pará and the steamships. The railroad ceased operation in 1972.

FRANK W. KRAVIGNY, *The Jungle Route* (1940); CHARLES A. GAULD, *The Last Titan: Percival Farquhar* (1964).

MICHAEL L. CONNIFF

MADEIRA RIVER, an Amazonian tributary that competes with the Amazon for the volume of water that flows through it. Four major rivers merge to form the Madeira before it begins its 2,000-mile journey to join the Amazon 90 miles east of Manaus: the Madre de Dios, the Beni, the Mamoré, and the Guaporé, which forms the border between Rondônia and Bolivia. JESU-ITS and SLAVE raiders began pushing up the river in 1639. Along their way, the Jesuits converted and captured Indians until after 1719, when the Portuguese settlers eliminated the Torá Indians, who lived near the Madeira's mouth. The Mura, who were brilliant at guerrilla warfare, reclaimed the Torá's territory and prevented settlement along the upper Madeira for most of the eighteenth century.

During the RUBBER boom of the late nineteenth century, the Madeira and its tributaries were used to transport rubber to waiting markets. Steamships began operating on the river in 1873 and could navigate for 800 miles before encountering the Alto Madeira Falls. After that point, rapids and turbulent waters extend for 260 miles and make passage impossible. When the rubber boom ended, Brazilians fished the Madeira mainly for local consumption.

No other major product was extracted from the river until the GOLD RUSH of the 1980s. Indians found gold in the river's bottom where the Madeira passes through Rondônia. An estimated half million prospectors battle with malarial mosquitos and other prospectors as they work in rapids and waters up to 60 feet deep to bring up gold from the deep. The mercury used to extract gold from the sand has polluted the Madeira and has poisoned the fish.

R. KAY GRESSWELL and ANTHONY HUXLEY, eds., *Standard Encyclopedia of the World's Rivers and Lakes* (1965); ALEX SHOUMATOFF, *The Rivers Amazon* (1986); DAVID CLEARY, *Anatomy of the Amazon Gold Rush* (1990); SUSANNA HECHT and ALEXANDER COCKBURN, *The Fate of the Forest: Developers, Destroyers, and Defenders of the Amazon* (1990).

CAROLYN JOSTOCK

MADERO, FRANCISCO INDALECIO (b. 30 October 1873; d. 22 February 1913), revolutionary leader and president of Mexico (1911–1913). Madero is best known for his key role in the overthrow of the dictator Porfirio DÍAZ in 1911 and his forced resignation and assassination in February 1913 by antirevolutionary elements headed by Victoriano HUERTA.

Madero was born on the Hacienda de El Rosario, Parras de la Fuente, Coahuila, to one of the wealthiest industrial and landowning families in Mexico, headed by his grandfather, Evaristo Madero, and his father,

Francisco Madero Hernández. He studied in Parras, Coahuila, and at the Jesuit Colegio de San Juan, Saltillo, Coahuila, before taking business courses at Mount Saint Mary's College near Baltimore, Maryland (1886–1888). In France he attended the Liceo de Versailles and the Higher Business School in Paris (1887–1892). Subsequently he took classes in agriculture at the University of California at Berkeley (1893). Upon his return to Mexico, Madero founded a business school in San Pedro de las Colonias, Coahuila, where he also administered a family business and practiced homeopathic medicine, spiritism, and vegetarianism.

While working in rural Mexico, Madero came into direct contact with many of its problems, which he attributed to the lack of a liberal, democratic political system. When Porfirio Díaz claimed in the CREELMAN INTERVIEW that he would be willing to step down and allow free and open elections, Madero published *La sucesión presidencial en 1910* (The Presidential Succession of 1910 [1908]), which called for freedom of suffrage, nonreelection of high public officials, and rotations in office. The book's appeal (the initial run of 3,000 copies sold out in three months) and its author's dogged determination and persuasive powers led to the formation in May 1909 of the Anti-Reelectionist Center of Mexico.

Within a few months, Madero's anti-reelectionist movement, and then party, had attracted a large enough following to pose a serious threat to the dictatorship. Madero traveled constantly throughout the country, dedicating himself to propagandizing, recruiting, and helping establish political clubs for the cause. The party's national convention, held in Mexico City in April 1910, attracted nearly 200 delegates from all the states and territories but four.

In early June 1910 authorities arrested Madero in Monterrey, Nuevo León, and then transferred him to the city of San Luis Potosí. He was incarcerated in order to remove him from the political scene until after the 26 June 1910 election, which Díaz and his vice-presidential running mate, Ramón CORRAL VERDUGO (1854–1912), using fraudulent means, won handily. During that summer in San Luis Potosí, Madero made the decision to escape and challenge the Díaz regime with arms. In early October he fled north to San Antonio, Texas, where he and others drew up the PLAN OF SAN LUIS POTOSÍ, which called for revolution on 20 November 1910.

The arrests of Madero agents resulted in the confiscation of documents outlining the revolutionary plans for all of central Mexico, thus forcing the conspirators' hands. As a result, Aquiles Serdán (1877–1910) prematurely and futilely raised his revolt on 18 November in the state of Puebla, thus ending any chance of catching the government by surprise. The rebellion sputtered and nearly died, and Madero fled back to Texas for safety.

Only in the state of Chihuahua did any significant rebel activity continue, principally under the leadership of Pascual OROZCO. His successes, along with others in the northwest part of the country, convinced Madero to

Francisco Indalecio Madero standing up in car waving his hat, 1911. LA FOTOTECA DEL INAH.

return to Mexico in mid-February 1911. Within weeks the insurgency spread to many areas of the nation and involved thousands of fighters, including followers of Emiliano ZAPATA (1879–1919) in Morelos. On 10 May 1911, the important border city of Ciudad Juárez, Chihuahua, fell. On 21 May Díaz signed the Treaty of Ciudad Juárez, thereby relinquishing power to an interim government headed by his ambassador to Washington, Francisco LEÓN DE LA BARRA. Madero's revolutionaries took control of the country.

Following elections, Madero assumed the constitutional presidency on 6 November 1911, but much of the popular support he had enjoyed the previous May had already disappeared. Once in office Madero proved incapable of stemming the disintegration of his movement.

Madero's difficulties arose from several complex and interrelated factors. First, Madero's social and political outlook had little in common with that of the majority of his followers. He came from a moderately conservative upper-class family that believed in elite rule and a paternalistic relationship with the lower classes. Madero felt comfortable with the upper classes and barely related to the peasants and workers in his movement, most of whom had rural, traditional backgrounds.

Madero's social values in turn shaped his political ideas. He believed that the establishment of a liberal, constitutional, democratic political system would ensure the free election of good men who then would deal with such problem areas as labor, land, education, and taxes. He therefore rejected many of his lower-class and rural supporters' calls for rapid and far-reaching socioeconomic reforms and advocated the more conservative positions of middle- and upper-class elements, many of whom were former supporters of the Díaz regime.

Second, the heterogeneous and disorganized nature of Madero's movement contributed greatly to its demise. The revolution between November 1910 and May 1911 mobilized several thousands of mainly radical, rural, and lower-class fighters throughout the country. The vast majority took advantage of Madero's call to arms to seek redress of local and sometimes personal grievances; they were unaware of or indifferent to Madero's pronouncements. This large, dispersed, and varied movement wanted immediate satisfaction of its demands. Incapable of satisfying his more radical supporters, Madero lost control in the rural areas where they were mainly based.

Third, Madero made a series of political decisions in the weeks following Díaz's surrender that quickly alienated his more radical adherents (and some moderates) and gave his conservative opponents a chance to regroup. Although professing a policy of nonintervention in state and local affairs (he left the Porfirian-era state legislatures intact), Madero intervened in the selection of many other state and local officials. For example, he named governors who generally were middle-aged, educated, and urban-oriented rather than the revolutionary leaders who fought to put him into power.

Madero also alienated many of his followers when he created a new political party, the Constitutionalist Progressive Party (PCP) to replace the Anti-Reelectionist Party. They felt that Madero was discarding an important symbol of the revolution and betraying a loyal supporter, Francisco Vázquez Gómez (1860–1934), whom Madero replaced as his vice presidential running mate. At the same time, Madero compounded the ill feeling toward him by agreeing to the ouster from his cabinet of Emilio Vázquez Gómez (1858–1926), Francisco's brother and one of the staunchest defenders of the left wing of the movement.

Maderista officers and troops also chafed over Madero's decision to demobilize them and maintain the Porfirian army as the only official force in Mexico. When they resisted and clashed with federal units (most notably in Puebla City in mid-July 1911), Madero resorted to the hated draft to build up the regular army and converted newly demobilized insurgents into *rurales* (rural police during Díaz's regime) to fight their former colleagues.

Finally, Madero proved slow to implement the reform program he had promised. The federal government could and did undertake some measures, such as the creation of a labor department and the construction of schools. However, the lack of resources, Madero's belated assumption of the presidency, his selective reluctance to interfere in nonfederal governmental affairs, and the fact that most reforms directly involved state and local levels of administration meant that Madero mostly had only an indirect say in what reforms were implemented.

Beginning in the summer of 1911, the disillusionment of much of his left wing and the continued adamant opposition of the conservatives, supported in part by backsliding moderate Maderistas who feared the increasingly violent masses, led to a series of rebellions, two of which most seriously threatened the regime.

After Díaz's fall, the Zapatistas waited for Madero's government to fulfill its promises, especially those regarding the restitution and protection of communal lands. They became especially angered when federal authorities demanded their demobilization. Zapata tried to reason with Madero, but President León de la Barra, who considered the Zapatistas rural bandits, sent General Victoriano HUERTA to subdue them. Thus provoked into rebellion in August 1911, the Zapatistas were soon operating over a wide area of south-central Mexico. In November 1911, they issued the PLAN OF AYALA, their formal declaration of rebellion, which called for agrarian reform and the overthrow of Madero. Although never able to topple the national government during the Madero period, the Zapatistas made life miserable for provincial authorities and elites, sapped the government's resources, and undermined its military and political credibility.

The second major rebellion occurred in Chihuahua, where Pascual Orozco, financed by the conservative Terrazas-Creel clan, rebelled in early March 1912. His defeat of the federal army at Rellano, Chihuahua, on 23 March forced Madero to turn to Huerta to save the regime. Huerta defeated Orozco's forces at Rellano on 23 May 1911. The Orozquistas fled to the mountains from where they, too, carried on guerrilla warfare, thus also sapping the limited resources of the regime and forcing Madero to focus on a military solution to his problems.

In early 1913, with his movement in tatters, his credibility gone, and his government bankrupt and besieged, Madero faced a rebellion (whose events are referred to as the DECENA TRÁGICA, or tragic ten days

[9–19 February 1913]) within the federal army, which was led by Félix DÍAZ, Manuel Mondragón, and Bernardo Reyes. The seriousness of the revolt forced Madero once again to turn to Huerta to save his government. During the ensuring battle, Huerta, with the aid of U.S. Ambassador Henry Lane WILSON (1857–1932), plotted with the rebels against Madero. On 19 February, Huerta forced Madero to resign and assumed the interim presidency. On 22 February, government agents executed Madero and his vice president, José María PINO SUÁREZ (1869–1913), probably upon Huerta's orders.

Madero became a martyr, and his name entered the pantheon of revolutionary heroes as the father of the MEXICAN REVOLUTION of 1910. He has been portrayed as a well-meaning, progressive democrat who was betrayed by the dark forces of dictatorship and foreign intervention. A more recent assessment, however, depicts him as the person who catalyzed the heterogeneous and dispersed revolutionary movement that managed to overthrow the Díaz regime, yet who did not have the ability or vision to institutionalize that movement and carry out the fundamental socioeconomic reforms necessary to meet the demands of the vast majority of his followers who put him into power. In fact, he oftentimes used autocratic methods to keep those very followers in check to the benefit of Mexico's more conservative and economically privileged groups.

CHARLES C. CUMBERLAND, *Mexican Revolution: Genesis Under Madero* (1952); STANLEY R. ROSS, *Francisco I. Madero: Apostle of Mexican Democracy* (1955); ALFONSO TARACENA, *Francisco I. Madero: Biografía* (1969); WILLIAM H. BEEZLEY, *Insurgent Governor: Abraham González and the Mexican Revolution in Chihuahua* (1973); HÉCTOR ÁGUILAR CAMÍN, *La frontera nómada: Sonora y la revolución mexicana* (1977); WILLIAM H. BEEZLEY, ''Madero: The 'Unknown' President and His Political Failure to Organize Rural Mexico,'' in *Essays on the Mexican Revolution: Revisionist Views of the Leaders,* edited by George Wolfskill and Douglas W. Richmond (1979), pp. 1–24; RAMÓN EDUARDO RUÍZ, *The Great Rebellion: Mexico, 1905–1924* (1980), esp. pp. 139–152; FRANÇOIS-XAVIER GUERRA, *Le Mexique de l'ancien régime à la révolution,* 2 vols. (1985); ALAN KNIGHT, *The Mexican Revolution,* 2 vols. (1986); JOHN M. HART, *Revolutionary Mexico: The Coming and Process of the Mexican Revolution* (1987), esp. pp. 237–262; DAVID G. LA FRANCE, *The Mexican Revolution in Puebla, 1908–1913: The Maderista Movement and the Failure of Liberal Reform* (1989) and ''Many Causes, Movements, Failures, 1910–1913,'' in *Provinces of the Revolution: Essays on Regional Mexican History, 1910–1929,* edited by Thomas Benjamin and Mark Wasserman (1990), pp. 17–40.

DAVID LaFRANCE

MADRAZO, CARLOS A. (*b.* 1915; *d.* 4 June 1969), Mexican political leader. Born in Villahermosa, Tabasco, Madrazo pursued his early education there before attending preparatory and law school at the Universidad Nacional Autónoma de México in Mexico City. Associated with Left, progressive groups, he was a spellbinding orator and leader in the Bloc of Revolutionary Youth of the Red Shirts (1933–1935) under Tabasco's radical governor Tomás GARRIDO CANABAL. He served as private secretary to Luis I. Rodríguez during the latter's tenure as governor of Guanajuato and later as president of the Party of Mexico Revolution (PRM), forerunner to the Institutional Revolutionary Party (PRI). His friendship with Gustavo DÍAZ ORDAZ, later president of Mexico (1964–1970), dated from the time when both served in the national Chamber of Deputies. Madrazo served as governor of Tabasco during 1959–1964.

A controversial figure, Madrazo's significance for modern Mexican political life stems from his failure as president of the PRI in 1964–1965 to make the party more democratic and independent of the presidency. Defeated by an alliance of state governors and cabinet ministers, Madrazo remains a symbol for the still-unrealized renovation of the party.

THOMAS J. BOSSERT, "Carlos A. Madrazo: The Study of a Democratic Experiment in Mexico" (Senior thesis, Princeton University, 1968); JOHN BAILEY, *Governing Mexico: The Statecraft of Crisis Management* (1988), chap. 5.

JOHN BAILEY

MADRID, TREATY OF (1670), agreement between England and Spain that recognized England's possessions in the New World. It was one of a series of treaties between Spain and other European powers recognizing "effective occupation" in return for promises not to trade with Spanish colonies. By 1680 European colonial powers were collaborating in an attempt to restrain the activities of buccaneers. The Treaty of Madrid superceded the Treaty of TORDESILLAS (1494) which had proved unworkable and had been repeatedly violated. The new basis for determining colonial boundaries was effective possessions (at the time of the Treaty of Madrid) rather than prior discovery or an imaginary line.

J. H. PARRY, *The Spanish Seaborne Empire* (1966), esp. pp. 251–271.

SUZANNE HILES BURKHOLDER

MADRID, TREATY OF (1750), agreement between Spain and Portugal that affected Brazil and the Río de la Plata. In the Treaty of Madrid, Portugal ceded to Spain Colônia, an important center of contraband trade, lands adjoining the Río de la Plata, and its free navigation of the river in exchange for two areas along the border of Brazil and an agreement to move seven Jesuit MISSIONS (along with thirty thousand GUARANÍ INDIANS) located in one of the territories. Signed on 3 January 1750, the treaty's terms faced vehement opposition in both countries. Among its detractors were the powerful Portuguese minister POMBAL (Sebastião José de Carvalho e Melo), the future CHARLES III (1716–1788) of Spain, and the JESUITS, who protested but obeyed. The Portuguese

did the most to subvert the treaty, but the Jesuits in Spain (and government supporters of the order) suffered the most from its political repercussions when the attempt to evacuate the missions was met with bloody resistance in 1754 and 1756. The Treaty of Madrid was annulled by the Treaty of El Pardo (12 February 1761) which restored the Jesuits to their missions but renewed territorial disputes.

GUILLERMO KRATZ, *El tratado hispano-portugués de límites de 1750 y sus consecuencias* (1954); DAURIL ALDEN, *Royal Government in Colonial Brazil* (1968), esp. pp. 86–96.

SUZANNE HILES BURKHOLDER

See also **Jesuits.**

MADRID HURTADO, MIGUEL DE LA (*b.* 12 December 1934), president of Mexico (1982–1988). Miguel de la Madrid took office at the Mexican presidency's lowest level of legitimacy in modern times. Confronted with a major economic crisis consisting of rapidly increasing inflation, a downturn in growth, high rates of unemployment, extraordinary capital flight, and massive external debt, the president pursued an orthodox strategy of economic austerity. Having achieved only moderate economic success, de la Madrid is likely to be remembered more for having provided the groundwork for his successor's liberalization and privatization programs. However, de la Madrid's administration did bring inflation under relative control, renegotiate the debt, and begin the process of selling off state-owned enterprises.

Politically, de la Madrid restored the shattered relationship between the private and public sectors, a step necessary for the success of his economic strategy. While he initially attempted moderate electoral reforms, the government's mishandling of earthquake rescue efforts in 1985 provoked the development of numerous popular opposition movements. Worse still was the electoral fraud in Chihuahua in 1986, which brought, for the first time in four decades, formal denunciations from the church hierarchy and encouraged a more activist church posture in politics. In 1986, de la Madrid introduced a new electoral code mandating an increase in the number of proportional seats in the Chamber of Deputies from 100 to 200 (raising the total number of seats from 400 to 500), and thus setting the stage for the extraordinary representation of the opposition in the 1988 chamber.

Internally, de la Madrid reinforced the growing tendency of the two preceding administrations toward the dominance of political technocrats: younger, bureaucratically experienced, highly educated (often abroad), urban decision makers with few ties to the PRI or the electoral scene. The control of these leaders continued to exacerbate internal disputes between the more traditional leadership and reform-minded younger technocrats. Finally, de la Madrid's designation of Carlos SALINAS as his party's candidate and the unbending treatment of party dissidents Cuauhtémoc CÁRDENAS and Porfirio MUÑOZ LEDO, who formed their own party, led to the most disputed presidential election in the party's history, in which it captured only a bare majority of the votes cast.

Miguel de la Madrid was born in Colima, Colima, the son of Miguel de la Madrid Castro, a lawyer and government employee murdered by wealthy landowners after he defended peasant rights. His mother, Alicia Hurtado, took Miguel and his sister to Mexico City, where he attended the Colegio Cristóbal Colón and the National Law School, from which he graduated with an honorary mention 8 August 1957. An outstanding student, de la Madrid had the second-highest grades of his 732 law school classmates. In 1965, on a fellowship from the Bank of Mexico, de la Madrid obtained an M.A. degree in public administration from Harvard University, the first Mexican president with a graduate degree as well as the first with a degree from abroad. He also taught constitutional law at the National University from 1958 to 1967. As a student, he worked in the National Foreign Trade Bank under Ricardo J. Zevada, his professor, to support himself at school. After graduation, he obtained his first government post at the Bank of Mexico as an adviser to Mario Ramón Beteta through his professor, Daniel J. Bello. Beteta became the president's early mentor, and when he moved to the secretariat of the treasury, he took de la Madrid along as his subdirector general of credit (1965–1970). In 1970, de la Madrid became assistant director of finances for the government oil company, Pemex, but moved back to his mentor's agency as director general of credit (1972–1975). When Beteta became treasury secretary in 1975, he appointed de la Madrid as assistant secretary of credit, a post he continued to hold in the next administration. On 17 May 1979 President José LÓPEZ PORTILLO appointed him secretary of programming and planning. Although considered a dark horse candidate for the presidential nomination, he became the party's candidate on 25 September 1981. His ties to José López Portillo, who chose him as his successor, extended back to law school, where he studied under his predecessor. After de la Madrid left the presidency in 1988, his successor, Carlos Salinas, appointed him director of the government-funded publishing firm Fondo de Cultura Económica.

WAYNE A. CORNELIUS, "The Political Economy of Mexico under de la Madrid: Austerity, Routinized Crisis, and Nascent Recovery," in *Mexican Studies* 1, no. 1 (1985): 83–124; RODERIC A. CAMP, ed., *Mexico's Political Stability: The Next Five Years* (1986); JUDITH GENTLEMAN, ed., *Mexican Politics in Transition* (1987); JOHN BAILEY, *Governing Mexico: The Statecraft of Crisis Management* (1988); SUSAN K. PURCELL, ed., *Mexico in Transition, Implications for U.S. Policy: Essays from Both Sides of the Border* (1988); RIORDAN ROETT, ed., *Mexico and the United States: Managing the Relationship* (1988); RODERIC A. CAMP, *Entrepreneurs and Politics in Twentieth-Century Mexico* (1989); MIGUEL BASÁÑEZ, *El pulso de los sexenios: 20 años de crisis en México* (1990).

RODERIC AI CAMP

MADUREIRA, ANTÔNIO DE SENA (*b.* 1841; *d.* 1889), Brazilian military leader. Sena Madureira graduated from the military academy with a degree in science and mathematics. He was training in Europe when the WAR OF THE TRIPLE ALLIANCE (1864–1870) broke out, and served in the war with distinction. An abolitionist and a republican, Madureira's historical significance stems from his launching, in 1884, of the famous "military question," concerning the civil rights of the military. This occurred when his command gave a hero's welcome to the celebrated abolitionist Francisco de Nascimento. The minister of war labeled the episode a breach of discipline and censured Madureira. A related incident followed when a liberal colonel cited some irregularities in a command headed by a captain of conservative leanings. The captain felt aggrieved and turned to a conservative deputy, who verbally attacked the colonel in the Chamber of Deputies. The colonel responded in the press and was censured by the minister of war. Madureira joined in the debate by writing provocative articles in a republican newspaper. The minister of war sought to administer discipline but found that Madureira was under the direct command of General Deodoro da FONSECA, the most prestigious military officer in the army. Fonseca refused to censure his subordinate, since the matter involved Madureira's criticism of civilian authority, and not a breach of military hierarchy. The affair centered on the rights of the military to express their political views publicly. The Supreme Military Tribunal ruled in favor of the officers, and Madureira's punishments were revoked. The split between military and monarchist leaders remained, however, and the monarchy was overthrown by a military coup in 1889.

JOÃO PANDIÁ CALÓGERAS, *A History of Brazil*, edited and translated by Percy Alvin Martin (1939); NELSON WERNECK SODRÉ, *História Militar do Brasil* (1965), esp. pp. 143–153; *Dicionário de História do Brasil* (1976); ROBERT A. HAYES, *The Armed Nation: The Brazilian Corporate Mystique* (1989).

ROBERT A. HAYES

See also **Military Question of the 1880s.**

MÃE MENININHA. *See* **Menininha de Gantois, Mãe.**

MAGALHÃES, BENJAMIN CONSTANT BOTELHO DE. *See* **Constant Botelho de Magalhães, Benjamin.**

MAGALHÃES, DOMINGOS JOSÉ GONÇALVES DE (*b.* 1811; *d.* 1882), considered the "father" of Brazilian romanticism. Magalhães was a doctor, a poet, and an influential diplomat of the empire who enjoyed the favor of Emperor Dom Pedro II. While living in Paris he fell under the influence of the European romantics. In 1836, along with the romantic painter and poet Manuel de Araújo PORTO ALEGRE (1806–1879) and Alberto Torres Homem, he cofounded a literary review, *Niterói: Revista Brasiliense*. While his early poetical works reflected the conservatism of the neoclassical literary canon, they also contained slight echoes of nascent liberalism.

His first collection of poems, *Suspiros poéticos e saudades* (1836), offered a pantheistic view of life: nature is omnipresent in, and consequently the major influence on, the poetic art. That same year, influenced by the romantic concept of nationalism, he published the first "history" of Brazilian literature, "Discurso sobre a história da literatura do Brasil." Romantic nationalism is also evident in his most notable drama, *António José; ou, O poeta e a inquisição* (1839), about the eighteenth-century Luso-Brazilian writer condemned by the Inquisition. Although he continued to write throughout his lifetime, his last major work (and the one for which he remains best known today) is the epic poem *A confederação dos Tamojos* (1856), in which he legitimizes the total destruction of an Indian tribe in the pursuit of independence and the establishment of the empire.

DAVID MILLER DRIVER, *The Indian in Brazilian Literature* (1942); RAYMOND SAYERS, *The Negro in Brazilian Literature* (1956).

IRWIN STERN

MAGALLANES, name given to the territories around the Strait of MAGELLAN and the southernmost province of Chile (1992 population 143,058). PUNTA ARENAS (1990 population 120,030) is the capital city. Most of the territory consists of fjords, channels, glaciated mountains, and impenetrable rain forests or peat moss. The cold steppes of Chilean Patagonia, east of the Andes, hold some potential for raising sheep, the major centers of which are in Puerto Natales and Porvenir. Oil discovered in 1940 near Cerro Sobrero (Tierra del Fuego) met the nation's needs until the mid-1960s. Since the early 1990s there has been a resurge in petroleum exploitation in the eastern segment of the Strait of Magellan. Wool and mouton exports also contribute to the region's economy.

ALBERTO M. DE AGOSTINI, *Magallanes y canales fueguinos* (Punta Arenas, 1960); and *Instituto Geográfico Millitar*, "La región de Magallanes y la Antártica chilena," in *Geografía de Chile*, vol. 34 (Santiago, 1987).

CÉSAR N. CAVIEDES

MAGAÑA, SERGIO (*b*. 24 September 1924; *d*. 23 August 1990), Mexican dramatist and novelist. Magaña contributed to the formation of a new generation of playwrights with his first play, *La noche transfigurada* (1947), and mainly with his popular play *Los signos del zodíaco* (1951), which depicts the lower class in Mexico City through the simultaneous staging of various scenes. With the collaboration of Emilio CARBALLIDO, he founded a literary group called Atenea, which later became the School of Philosophy and Letters theater group, and exerted a great deal of influence on the avant-garde scene. Both *Los argonautas* (1953) and *Moctezuma II* (1954) concern the Spanish Conquest, while *Santísima* (1980), a stylized musical about a prostitute's life, uses characters from Federico GAMBOA's novel *Santa*. He has also written novels, such as *El molino del aire* (1953).

WILLIS KNAPP JONES, *Behind Spanish American Footlights* (1966); CARLOS SOLÓRZANO, *Testimonios teatrales de México* (1973).

GUILLERMO SCHMIDHUBER

MAGDALENA RIVER, a waterway in Colombia, important for centuries as the principal artery linking the interior of the country with the Caribbean Sea. Navigable for most of its length of 956 miles, the Magdalena flows northward between the Central and Eastern Cordilleras and empties into the Caribbean near BARRANQUILLA. Its major tributary is the CAUCA RIVER.

The mouth of the river was first sighted by Rodrigo

View of the Magdalena River. Engraving based on drawings by Riou, 1877. Reproduced from *Geografía pintoresca de Colombia* (Bogotá, 1971).

de BASTIDAS and Juan de la Cosa in 1501. With the establishment of SANTA MARTA nearby in 1526, Spaniards became interested in exploring the river in order to move south and possibly reach Peru. In 1536 the ships of the expedition led by Gonzalo JIMÉNEZ DE QUESADA reached a point on the river near modern BARRANCA-BERMEJA before Jiménez abandoned the river to strike inland to the east. From the founding of Bogotá in 1539 until well into the twentieth century, the Magdalena offered the only practical means of transporting cargo and passengers between the interior and the Caribbean coast. Indian canoes and keelboats were initially used to navigate the river; steam-powered vessels began to flourish in the mid-1840s. By the late twentieth century, the construction of roads and railways and the development of aviation had lessened the economic importance of the river, but it remained a vital part of Colombia's transportation system.

ROBERT LOUIS GILMORE and JOHN P. HARRISON, "Juan Bernardo Elbers and the Introduction of Steam Navigation on the Magdalena River," in *Hispanic American Historical Review* 28 (1948): 335–359.

HELEN DELPAR

MAGDALENA VALLEY. The Magdalena is the principal river of Colombia, and a diverse and long archaeological sequence has been recognized in its valley. The early evidence of human occupation begins with hunters and gatherers. Projectile points and choppers were found in the region of Carare in the middle Magdalena Valley (8500–8000 B.C.). More archaeological information is found for ceramic times in the lower Magdalena Valley and includes the sites of Bucarelia and El Bongal (4000–3000 B.C.). Both belong to the PUERTO HORMIGA tradition. Other pottery complexes such as Monsú, Guájaro, and Malambo (2600–1000 B.C.) are also present and yield evidence of populations that subsisted on riverine resources as well as on collection of food plants. Sites such as Malambo have been considered by some authors to be part of the Barrancoid pottery tradition. This tradition has been reported to occur from the Magdalena Valley to the lower Orinoco and Amazon rivers, and appears to be related to the peopling of the Lesser Antilles. In relation to the development of agriculture and settled life in the valley, nothing is known. In more recent times (300 B.C.–A.D. 700), complex adaptations to the flooded region of the Mompos Depression occurred. The Mompos Depression has more than 250,000 acres of modified landscape in the form of raised fields that work as agricultural drainage systems for the area during the rainy season. Settlements were dispersed along the artificial channels. High-ranking individuals were buried in earth mounds with pottery and GOLDWORK. Goldwork manufacture illustrating faunal iconography was present.

Another archaeological expression of the Magdalena Valley is what has been called the burial urn horizon. This horizon is characterized by the urns depicting a regional diversity of style that were always used for secondary burials (bones reburied in a pottery container made specifically for them). Examples include the anthropomorphic urns of Tamalameque, Puerto Serviez, Puerto Nare, Honda, Girardot, and El Espinal. The burial urn horizon seems to be a late development (900–1600). Some authors link this horizon to a migration of Carib speakers to the area. The horizon also is considered to be related to ethnic groups that the Spanish encountered, such as the Pantágoras, Pijao, Panche, and Carare. Information related to these settlements is scarce (Mayaca site). However, settlements seem to have included a common long house similar to the MALOCA known in the Amazon River region. No hard evidence has been found concerning the subsistence base, but it very likely centered on maize, manioc, and fishing. The archaeological information for the upper Magdalena Valley is more complete and centered on the town of SAN AGUSTÍN, which gave its name to the culture.

On the middle Magdalena Valley, see CARLOS EDUARDO LÓPEZ, *Investigaciones arqueológicas en el Magdalena Medio* (1991). For the lower Magdalena Valley, see GERARDO REICHEL-DOLMATOFF, *Arqueología de Colombia* (1986).

AUGUSTO OYUELA-CAYCEDO

MAGDALENO, MAURICIO (*b.* 13 May 1906; *d.* 30 June 1986), Mexican writer. Born in Villa del Refugio, Magdaleno wrote drama, novels, and movie scripts, most of which address the achievements, failures, and contradictions of the Mexican Revolution. In the 1930s Magdaleno founded the theater group Teatro de Ahora in partnership with Juan Bustillo Oro; he also published his most important novel, *El resplandor* (Sunburst, 1937). In the 1940s Magdaleno wrote many successful screenplays for the growing Mexican film industry. Named to the Mexican Academy of Language in 1957, Magdaleno later held a variety of bureaucratic and political offices, including a period as senator for the state of Zacatecas (1958–1964).

JOHN S. BRUSHWOOD, *Mexico in Its Novel: A Nation's Search for Identity* (1966), pp. 19–21, 217–218, 226; JOSEPH SOMMERS, *After the Storm: Landmarks of the Modern Mexican Novel* (1968), pp. 23–36; GUILLERMO SCHMIDHUBER, "Díptico sobre el teatro mexicano de los treinta: Bustillo y Magdaleno, Usigli y Villaurrutía," in *Revista Iberoamericana* 55, no. 148–149 (1989): 1221–1237.

DANNY J. ANDERSON

MAGELLAN, FERDINAND (*Port.* Fernão de Magalhães e Sousa; *Span.* Fernando de Magallanes; *b.* 1480 [?]; *d.* 27 April 1521), Portuguese navigator who, under the service of the king of Spain, discovered the westward route to the Orient and initiated the first voyage to circumnavigate the globe.

Ferdinand Magellan was born near Oporto, Portugal, and in 1504 entered service to the Portuguese throne under Francisco de Almeida, viceroy of the Portuguese

East Indies. Magellan served in Mozambique under Nuño Vaz Pereira before fighting in battles with the Muslims in India and later taking part in successful attacks on Goa and Malacca in 1511.

After service in Morocco, Magellan returned to Lisbon, where he was denied a promotion in the Portuguese military. Dissatisfied with his status in Portugal, Magellan sought support from King Charles I of Spain in 1517, the same year in which he married Beatríz Barbosa, daughter of an important official in Seville. Magellan persuaded the king to send him in search of a westward route to the Indies, whose islands Spain claimed as its rightful territory. On 20 September 1519, Magellan set sail with five ships from Sanlúcar de Barrameda in search of the western passage.

The vessels stopped briefly in Madeira and, after reaching the shores of Brazil, headed south along the coast of South America. In January 1520, Magellan entered the Río de la Plata and explored the region, finding the site that would later become Montevideo and discovering the Uruguay River. In March, Magellan entered the Bay of San Julián, where he chose to stay for the winter. During this time, a mutiny among some of his captains threatened Magellan's command, but it was successfully suppressed.

Portrait of Ferdinand Magellan from an old German print. Reproduced from Ernst and Johanna Lehner, *How They Saw the New World* (New York, 1966). TUDOR PUBLISHING COMPANY.

On 21 October 1520, the voyage entered the straits between the mainland and Tierra del Fuego that were to bear Magellan's name and, after a difficult passage, emerged on 28 November in the Pacific. Heading northwest, Magellan landed at Guam on 6 March 1521, after spending months on the open sea without encountering inhabited islands.

Soon after, the ships reached the Philippines, where Magellan made the mistake of taking part in a territorial dispute with local chieftains and was killed in a battle on the island of Mactan on April 27. The voyage continued, with only one ship, under the command of Juan Sebastian de ELCANO, returning to Spain on 8 September 1522, thus achieving the first circumnavigation of the globe.

EDOUARD RODITI, *Magellan of the Pacific* (1972); DONALD G. PAYNE, *Magellan and the First Circumnavigation of the World* (1973); MAURICIO OBREGON, *La primera vuelto al mundo: Magellanes, Elcano y el libro perdido de la nao Victoria* (1984).

JOHN DUDLEY

MAGELLAN, STRAIT OF, a narrow body of water, about 330 miles long and 2.5 to 15 miles wide, separating mainland South America from TIERRA DEL FUEGO and the numerous other islands to the south. Named after its discoverer, Ferdinand MAGELLAN, a Portuguese navigator in the service of King CHARLES I of Spain, the strait, except for the eastern mouth, which is Argentine, lies entirely within Chile. It provides a protected inland waterway between the Atlantic and Pacific oceans, but is difficult to navigate because of its winding course and the fog and wind that prevail.

Embarked on a voyage of global circumnavigation, Magellan wanted to establish that the Spice Islands (the Moluccas) lay in the Spanish sphere of influence under the 1494 Treaty of TORDESILLAS. His voyage took him to Brazil, the Rio de la Plata, Patagonia, and, on 21 October 1520, to the strait which bears his name. The passage through the strait was difficult, taking him thirty-eight days. Magellan was killed in the Philippines a few months later, but one of his captains, Juan Sebastian de Elcano, completed the voyage.

In the nineteenth century the Chilean city of PUNTA ARENAS on the strait was an important coaling station, but its value diminished markedly with the opening of the PANAMA CANAL in 1914. In recent years the region has grown in importance as Chile's principal oil and gas production area, as well as the staging base for Antarctic tourism and logistical support. Punta Arenas, along with Ushuaia in Argentina, are the southernmost cities in the world, and were the first to feel the impact of the depletion of the ozone layer over Antarctica.

ANTONIO PIGAFETTA, *Magellan's Voyage Around the World* (1906); HUBERT C. HERRING, *A History of Latin America* (1963).

JACK CHILD

See also **Beagle Channel Dispute.**

MAGLOIRE, PAUL EUGÈNE (*b.* 1907), president of Haiti (1950–1956). Born in Cap Haitien into a family of the country's black elite, Magloire received an education at the Lycée Philippe Guerrier, at the military academy, and at the National University, where he earned a law degree. As commander of the Palace Guard, he and two mulatto officers organized the coup that toppled the dictatorship of Élie LESCOT in January 1946. After serving as minister of the interior under President Dumarsais ESTIMÉ, Magloire again conspired against his superior: when Estimé sought to prolong his rule in violation of Haiti's constitution, Magloire joined in the coup to overthrow him.

Supported by the Roman Catholic church, the Haitian military, and the U.S. government, Magloire's presidency, from December 1950 to December 1956, represented a return to power of Haiti's mulatto elite in cooperation with blacks like Magloire himself. Instead of continuing the social reforms started by his predecessor, Magloire focused on economic modernization with the help of private, foreign (mainly U.S.) investments, U.S.-government aid programs, and U.S.-backed international agencies like UNESCO. While lavishing money on showy development projects such as the Point Four–sponsored irrigation project in the Artibonite Valley, the regime did little for the bulk of the country's population. It not only suppressed civil liberties and independent unions, but also aggravated conditions for the peasantry by allowing the country's best land to be taken over by foreign-owned agro-export industries. By increasing Haiti's dependence on agro-exports, Magloire contributed to the ecological and human disaster

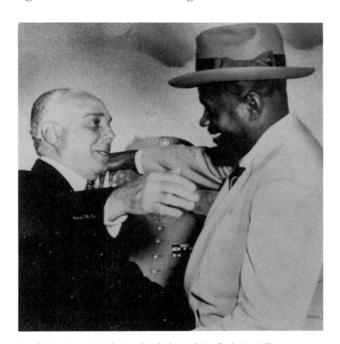

Paul Eugène Magloire (right) and Rafael Trujillo.
ORGANIZATION OF AMERICAN STATES.

that explains the poverty of most Haitians today as well as the heavy migratory overflow that has characterized the country since his time.

DAVID NICHOLLS, *From Dessalines to Duvalier: Race, Colour, and National Independence in Haiti* (1979); MICHEL-ROLPH TROUILLOT, *Haiti: State Against Nation* (1990).

PAMELA MURRAY

MAGOON, CHARLES EDWARD (*b.* 5 December 1861; *d.* 14 January 1920), joined the U.S. War Department in 1899, served as governor-general of the PANAMA CANAL Zone in 1905–1906, and was named by President Theodore ROOSEVELT as provisional governor of Cuba during the U.S. occupation of 1906–1909. His role in Cuba is very controversial. Cuban historians blame Magoon for wasting the monies amassed by the first Cuban president, Tomás ESTRADA PALMA, through granting sinecures and promoting questionable public works, thus establishing the pattern of venality that plagued successive Cuban governments. In actuality, he was not corrupt but inclined to reward a generation of former revolutionary Liberals with posts, which prevented effective enforcement of the civil service law. He was also accused of letting public works contracts to favored U.S. firms. His secretary of justice, General Enoch CROWDER, presided over the writing of Cuba's electoral law.

ALLAN R. MILLETT, *The Politics of Intervention: The Military Occupation of Cuba, 1906–1909* (1968); DAVID LOCKMILLER, *Magoon in Cuba: A History of the Second Intervention, 1906–1909* (1969).

LESTER D. LANGLEY

See also **United States–Latin American Relations.**

MAHOGANY. *See* **Lumber Industry.**

MAINE, U.S.S. The battleship *Maine* was sent to Havana in January 1898, at the height of Cuba's second war of independence, for the purpose of protecting American lives and property should the turmoil prevailing in that country make it necessary. At 9:40 P.M. on February 15 the ship blew up in Havana harbor, where it was anchored. Out of a complement of 355 officers and men, a total of 260 were killed. It is likely that the explosion was caused by the detonation of the *Maine*'s own gunpowder, but official inquiries conducted at the time were inconclusive. Inflamed by the yellow press and certain U.S. government officials, public opinion in the United States quickly placed the responsibility for the tragedy on the Spaniards. Two weeks later, Congress appropriated $50 million for war preparations, and on April 11 President William McKinley sent to Congress a war resolution. For this reason, the destruction of the *Maine* traditionally has been regarded as the chief causal explanation of the SPANISH–AMERICAN WAR. More re-

Destruction of the U.S. battleship *Maine*. Havana Harbor, 15 February 1898. LIBRARY OF CONGRESS.

cently, however, historians have emphasized the need to reconceptualize the origins of the war in the context of U.S. policy toward Cuba in the nineteenth century. For even if the explosion of the *Maine* had faded into the background of the Cuban War of Independence, the fact remains that the United States and Spain were on a collision course because of Cuba and neither showed any willingness to turn aside.

LOUIS A. PÉREZ, JR., "The Meaning of the *Maine*: Causation and the Historiography of the Spanish–American War," in *Pacific Historical Review* 58, no. 3 (Aug. 1989): 293–322; GUILLERMO G. CALLEIA LEAL, "La voladura del Maine," in *Revista de Historia Militar* 34, no. 59 (Spain, 1990): 163–196. The latter is especially interesting in that it reflects the Spanish perspective on the episode.

JOSÉ M. HERNÁNDEZ

MAIPO RIVER, a 150-mile-long waterway located at the southern edge of the basin of SANTIAGO, 12 miles from the city's center. It springs from the foothills of the Volcán Maipo and is fed by winter rains and spring snowmelt. The soils on both sides of the Maipo River are rich in mineral nutrients from the volcanic and fluvial deposits carried from the ANDES. Here the best vineyards of the country thrive, and the choicest wines of Chile bear the Maipo Valley provenance labels.

CÉSAR N. CAVIEDES

MAIPÚ, BATTLE OF, a conflict that took place near Santiago, Chile, on 5 April 1818. A revolutionary army com-

posed of Argentines and Chileans and commanded by General José de SAN MARTÍN defeated a royalist army composed primarily of American loyalists and commanded by General Mariano Osorio. This decisive victory eliminated Spanish influence in Chile. The battle raged for six hours and the entire royalist army was destroyed. Two thousand royalists were killed and 2,432 captured. Only a handful, including General Osorio, escaped. The insurgents sustained about 1,000 casualties. The victory at Maipú was an important milestone in San Martín's grand strategy to cross the Andes, defeat the royalists in Chile, and then attack Peru by amphibious assault. Revolutionary forces had previously tried to attack Peru via the land route through Bolivia but were repeatedly defeated.

MARTIN SUÁREZ, *Atlas histórico-militar argentino* (1974); CHRISTIÁN GARCÍA-GODOY, ed., *The San Martín Papers* (1988).

ROBERT SCHEINA

MAÍZ, FIDEL (*b.* 1828; *d.* 1920), Paraguayan cleric and figure in the WAR OF THE TRIPLE ALLIANCE. Born in the tiny hamlet of Arroyos y Esteros, Maíz was little more than an obscure country priest until the late 1850s, when he gained the attention of the all-powerful López family. One story has it that Maíz was the only Paraguayan priest willing to baptize the offspring of Francisco Solano LÓPEZ (the future president) and his Irish mistress Eliza Lynch. In any case, Maíz went on to officiate at the September 1862 funeral of President Carlos Antonio LÓPEZ, and to participate in the subsequent congressional meetings called to choose a new government. Some ill-chosen words at the latter assembly put Maíz in prison for several years, but in 1866, he was reprieved by Solano López and named army chaplain.

Two years later, Maíz played an infamous role in one of the ugliest episodes of the war: he acted as government prosecutor at a series of conspiracy trials, often referred to as the *tribunales de sangre*. Convened at San Fernando, the trials were characterized by their expediency and, more particularly, by the use of torture to obtain confessions. In this fashion, Maíz elicited confessions from scores of men said to be plotting against López. Many were condemned and bayoneted to death on the same day. In fact, however, historians today question whether any conspiracy ever existed.

After the war, Maíz was imprisoned for a time by the Brazilians and then censured by the Roman Catholic church. He traveled to Rome to appeal his case to the pope, was absolved, and returned to Arroyos y Esteros, where he spent the remainder of his life composing polemical tracts, memoirs, and textbooks for the little church school he ran.

FIDEL MAÍZ, *Etapas de mi vida* (1919); CARLOS ZUBIZARRETA, *Cien vidas paraguayas*, 2d ed. (1985), pp. 172–176.

THOMAS L. WHIGHAM

MAIZE (*Zea mays mays*), a coarse annual plant of the grass family (*Gramineae*). The staple crop of most Latin American countries, it is the most important native crop in the Western Hemisphere and is second only to wheat in commercial value. Maize is also the most photosynthetically efficient of the domesticated grains.

On 5 November 1492 two sailors returned from a reconnaissance mission into the interior of Cuba and reported to COLUMBUS a grain called "maiz . . . a grain which was well tasted, bak'd, dry'd and made into flour." At that time maize was grown from southern Canada to southern Chile, from sea level to 10,000 feet. In the English-speaking world maize became known as Indian corn, "corn" being a common European term for cereal grain. In Latin America it continued to be called *maíz*.

There are six major types of maize, all developed by Native Americans in response to various environmental and cultural factors: (1) flint corn, with its hard kernels, is resistant to fungus and stores well in cooler and damper climates; (2) flour corn, with its soft, easily ground kernels, is best suited to warmer and drier climates; (3) dent corn, the most common "field corn," combines the hard features of flint with a flour "dent" over its soft center; (4) sweet corn, which accounts for only 3 percent of overall production because it cannot

Aztec depiction of maize cultivation, from the Codex Florentino. LIBRARY OF CONGRESS.

be dried and stored as easily as the preceding types; (5) popcorn, characterized by small and extremely hard kernels that must be parched or exploded before they can be further processed or eaten; and (6) pod corn, which is raised as a curiosity and represents a "primitive" race in that each kernel is surrounded by its own chaff (husk). Maize is unusual among the domesticated grains because it cannot effectively seed itself. Its seeds (kernels) are enclosed in a modified leaf (husk) and are so tightly attached to the spike (cob) that they cannot be easily dispersed.

ORIGIN

Considerable controversy has surrounded the origin of domesticated maize. Unlike other major cereals, wild races of maize have not been discovered. Two competing theories have been proposed to explain the origin of domesticated maize. Paul Mangelsdorf, Richard Mac-Neish, and others have argued that maize was domesticated from a wild form that subsequently became extinct. They base their arguments on excavated material from the Valley of TEHUACÁN, Puebla, Mexico, which they dated as early as 5000 B.C.E. (now redated to 3600 B.C.E.), and on maize pollen from Valley of Mexico lake sediments originally dated as early as 80,000 B.C.E. (now redated to as recent as the beginning of the common era). George Beadle, Hugh Iltis, and others have argued that maize was domesticated from one of the subspecies of teosinte (*Zea mays mexicana, Zea mays parviglumis*), a closely related wild grass. Current research on plant genetics utilizing molecular analysis supports the teosinte theory, and points to the BALSAS RIVER drainage of southwestern Mexico as the most probable region for first domestication.

Once domesticated, the cultivation of maize spread rapidly, first as a supplement to the diet of hunting and gathering populations. It may have reached the highlands of Peru as early as 4000 B.C.E., and southern South America soon after. As new races of maize were developed in South America they hybridized with the more ancient races from Mexico, which led to the rapid evolution of hundreds of varieties of domesticated maize.

Maize also spread north. By 2000 B.C.E. it was present at Bat Cave in west-central New Mexico. Within 600 years these first primitive ears found north of Mexico were followed by more productive varieties. Similar varieties, *chapalote* and *naltel*, are still grown in Mexico.

Unraveling the origin of maize has important consequences for the future of Latin American farmers. Current research on the recently discovered perennial teosinte species *Zea diploperennis* holds the promise of providing genetic material that can be used to increase the disease resistance of *Zea mays*. The incorporation of genetic material from ancient races of Mexican maize into modern hybrids can increase resistance to environmental stresses.

HISTORY

From its humble beginnings as a dietary supplement, maize was rapidly transformed into the essential crop that supported the growth of the first civilizations of the Americas. It was prepared with lime water or wood ash to release chemically bonded nutrients. When maize was combined with beans, squash, chiles, and small amounts of animal protein, it provided a diet far superior to any known in sixteenth-century Europe.

Throughout temperate Latin America maize was the staff of life. In the tropical lowlands of Mexico and Central America it became the dominant crop, and in Amazonia it became an important supplement to MANIOC-based diets. Maize was grown to its environmental limits in the Andes, but in the higher altitudes it was often replaced as a staple by POTATOES and quinoa. It is not surprising that maize was incorporated into the religious life of all pre-Columbian civilizations.

When maize was first introduced to Europe, prominent herbalists referred to it as Turkish corn or wheat. Maize then had a brief vogue in the Mediterranean countries, but it was not prepared properly, nor nutritionally balanced with other crops. As a result, the dietary-deficiency disease pellagra became common in areas where maize was farmed, and it was abandoned as a food crop.

Since maize was associated with the conquered people of the Western Hemisphere, it remained unpopular among Europeans, and was thought by some to be, in the words of English herbalist John Gerard, "a more convenient food for swine than for man" (Charles B. Heiser, Jr., *Seeds to Civilization*, new ed., 1990, p. 92). This colonial attitude did not develop in sub-Saharan Africa, however, where maize was soon incorporated into indigenous subsistence systems and cuisines. Maize also became a staple crop in areas of India and China.

In Latin America maize remains the basis of most traditional meals and is prepared in over 300 ways; even the pollen and fungus (smut) is eaten; in Mexico, the latter, known as *huitlacoche*, is considered a delicacy. Maize also is fermented to produce the traditional maize beer (*chicha*) of the Andes.

TODAY

Almost 350 million acres of maize were planted worldwide in 1985–1986. In North America it is primarily grown for animal feed and industrial products, while in Latin America it is primarily grown for food. Latin America accounts for approximately 42 million acres of the world's maize production. Four countries, China, Brazil, India, and Mexico, account for more than 50 percent of the total area planted to maize in the Third World.

Today, most processed foods contain starch, oil, or sugar from maize. Biodegradable products from diapers to "paper" bags are being produced from processed corn starch, and ethanol, an alcohol distilled from corn starch, is being mixed with gasoline for fuel. A quality-protein maize nearly twice as nutritious as normal maize is currently under development.

PAUL WEATHERWAX, *Indian Corn in Old America* (1954); ALEXANDER GROBMAN, *Races of Maize in Peru* (1961); PAUL C. MANGELSDORF, RICHARD S. MAC NEISH, and W. C. GALINAT, "Domestication of Corn," in *Science* 143 (1964): 538–545; HOWARD WALDEN, *Native Inheritance: The Story of Corn in America* (1966); GEORGE W. BEADLE, "The Ancestry of Corn," in *Scientific American* 242 (1980): 112–119; HUGH H. ILTIS, "From Teosinte to Corn: The Catastrophic Sexual Transmutation," in *Science* 222 (1983): 886–894; STEPHEN J. GOULD, "The Short Way to Corn," in *Natural History* 93 (1984): 12–20; PAUL C. MANGELSDORF, *Corn: Its Origin, Evolution, and Improvement* (1984); RANULFO CAVERO CARRASCO, *Maíz, chicha y religiosidad andina* (1986); BRUCE F. BENZ, "Racial Systematics and the Evolution of Mexican Maize," in *Studies in the Neolithic and Urban Revolutions,* edited by Linda Manzanilla (1987); INTERNATIONAL MAIZE AND WHEAT IMPROVEMENT CENTER, *The 1986 CIMMYT World Maize Facts and Trends: The Economics of Commercial Maize Seed Production in Developing Countries* (1987); MUSEO NACIONAL DE CULTURAS POPULARES, *El maíz, fundamento de la cultura popular mexicana,* 3d ed. (1987); NATIONAL RESEARCH COUNCIL, *Quality-Protein Maize* (1988); PROCEEDINGS OF THE GLOBAL MAIZE GERMPLASM WORKSHOP, *Recent Advances in the Conservation and Utilization of Genetic Resources* (1988); FLAVIO ROJAS LIMA, *La cultura del maíz en Guatemala* (1988); *Maydica* 35 (1990), special issue devoted to *Zea diploperennis;* CHARLES B. HEISER, JR., *Seeds to Civilization: The Story of Food,* new ed. (1990); SIMPOSIUM NACIONAL DEL MAÍZ, *El maíz en la década de los 90* (1990); ROBERT E. RHOADES, "The Golden Grain," in *National Geographic* 183 (1993): 92–117.

DAVID E. MCVICKER

MAJANO, ADOLFO ARNOLDO (*b.* 1938), Salvadoran army officer and member of the provisional junta (1979–1980). Majano was briefly the most visible representative of reformist forces within El Salvador's officer corps. A participant in the coup d'état that overthrew the regime of Carlos Humberto ROMERO on 15 October 1979, Majano later served as one of two military members on the junta that replaced him. Considered honest and progressive, Majano supported the junta's reforms and urged greater respect for human rights and an opening to the Left. But he was not an effective leader, and rightist forces within the military eventually outmaneuvered him. Ousted from the junta in December 1980, Majano went into exile the following year.

TOMMIE SUE MONTGOMERY, *Revolution in El Salvador: Origins and Evolution* (1982); SHIRLEY CHRISTIAN, "El Salvador's Divided Military," in *Atlantic Monthly* (June 1983): 50–60.

STEPHEN WEBRE

MALARIA. *See* Diseases.

MALASPINA, ALEJANDRO (*b.* 5 November 1754; *d.* 9 April 1810), Spanish naval officer and explorer. Alejan-

dro Malaspina, a Spanish subject born in Mulazzo, in the Duchy of Parma, Italy, entered Spain's navy in 1774 as a midshipman and rose quickly through the ranks. After serving in Gibraltar, he circumnavigated the earth from 1786 to 1788 as commander of *La Astrea.* As a captain, Malaspina was given command of a five-year around-the-world scientific exploratory mission departing from Cádiz on 30 July 1789. The expedition sailed around the tip of South America and surveyed various Spanish ports. From Acapulco, Malaspina explored northward to the sixtieth parallel, visiting Alaska, Nootka Sound (Vancouver Island), and Monterey, California. His men gathered scientific data and charted the coastline before returning to Mexico. The ships sailed for the Philippines and Australia before recrossing the Pacific to South America and Spain. Prior to publishing his materials, Malaspina fell victim to court intrigue in 1795; he was imprisoned and stripped of his rank. After about eight years in jail, Malaspina was exiled to Parma, where he died.

Not until 1885 did a one-volume account of his expedition appear in print. Today, however, Malaspina's work has added valuable scientific and visual data to existing knowledge about the natural history of New World areas during the late eighteenth century.

PEDRO NOVO Y COLSON, ed., *Viaje político-científico alrededor del mundo por las corbetas Descubierta y Atrevida* (1885, 1984); DONALD C. CUTTER, *Malaspina in California* (1960); IRIS H. W. ENGSTRAND, *Spanish Scientists in the New World: The Eighteenth-Century Expeditions* (1981); CARMEN SOTOS SERRANO, *Los Pintores de la Expedición de Alejandro Malaspina* (1982).

IRIS H. W. ENGSTRAND

MALDONADO, department in the southeastern corner of Uruguay (1985 population 94,500), on the Atlantic Ocean. The major town is Maldonado (1985 population 33,498), 80 miles from Montevideo and famous for its several monuments dating to colonial times. The town has been overshadowed by the dramatic development of the neighboring sea resort PUNTA DEL ESTE, which, with a population of only 6,608 (1985), is capable of lodging 80,000 in the summer months. The major economic activity along the coast is TOURISM. Sheep graze in the rugged hills of the interior, and on the flatter terrain, vegetables, sugar beets, and wheat are grown. A cement factory as well as granite and marble quarries add extractive industries to the economic profile of Maldonado.

ELZEAR GIUFFRA, *La república del Uruguay* (Montevideo, 1935).

CÉSAR N. CAVIEDES

MALDONADO, FRANCISCO SEVERO (*b.* 1775; *d.* 1832), Mexican politician and reformer. Born in Tepic, Nayarit, Maldonado studied in Guadalajara and became a priest and a scholar. Joining HIDALGO's movement when the insurgent army arrived in Guadalajara in 1810, he published the revolutionary *El despertador americano* and began drafting a constitution. After the battle of Calderón, Maldonado was put on trial. He renounced his earlier views and began to write for a royalist periodical, *El telégrafo de Guadalaxara* (1811). He supported both the Constitution of 1812 and the PLAN OF IGUALA, and served in the early congresses. His social and political ideas, expressed in various editions of a work he called *Nuevo pacto social* and *Contrato de asociación* (1823), may have influenced Mariano OTERO. Maldonado's plans are, in the words of Charles Hale, "an odd blend of liberal individualism, utopian socialism, and traditional corporate theory." His views on land reform and corporate society have been seen by some as presaging the Constitution of 1917.

CHARLES A. HALE, *Mexican Liberalism in the Age of Mora, 1821–1853* (1968), pp. 74–75; *Diccionario Porrúa de historia, biografía y geografía de México*, 5th ed. (1986).

D. F. STEVENS

MALDONADO, RODRIGO DE ARIAS

MALDONADO, RODRIGO DE ARIAS (*b*. 25 December 1637; *d*. 23 September 1716), the moving force behind the organization in Guatemala of the religious order of BETHLEHEMITES to serve the poor. Born into the Spanish nobility, Maldonado went with his parents as a child to Costa Rica, where his father served as governor. He took over the governorship when his father died in 1662. As governor of Costa Rica he subdued the Talamanca Indians, and he was expected to go on to higher posts. He moved to Santiago de Guatemala, opened a great house, and lived ostentatiously. He then came under the influence of Hermano Pedro de BETHANCOURT, who had established a hospital and was extending services to the poor. The king appointed Maldonado marquis de Talamanca, but he refused the honor and turned to a life of service. When Hermano Pedro died, leadership of the group known as the Bethlehemites passed to Maldonado, called Rodrigo de la Cruz within the church. Maldonado went to Rome in 1674 and again in 1685 to gain authorization to establish the order of the Bethlehemites. He then traveled to Mexico and Peru, founding hospitals and churches in the name of the new order. Upon his death he was buried in one of the churches that he had established in Mexico City.

JOSEPH GARCÍA DE LA CONCEPCIÓN, *Historia Belemitica*, 2d ed. (1956).

DAVID L. JICKLING

MALESPÍN, FRANCISCO

MALESPÍN, FRANCISCO (*b*. 1790; *d*. 25 November 1846), president of El Salvador (1844–1845). Following Rafael CARRERA's defeat of Francisco MORAZÁN, Carrera imposed Malespín as commander of El Salvador's army in March 1840. Regarded as Carrera's puppet, Malespín

effectively resisted Morazán's attempt to return to El Salvador in 1842. Collaborating with Bishop Jorge VITERI Y UNGO, Malespín broke with Salvadoran President Juan José Guzmán in December 1843 and took over the presidency on 1 February 1844. He stopped ex-President Manuel José ARCE's attempt to return to El Salvador to regain office, but his involvement in the liberal-conservative intrigues of the period led him into war with Nicaragua in October 1844. He captured LEÓN on 24 January 1845, but Gerardo BARRIOS and Trinidad CABAÑAS meanwhile pressured Acting President Joaquín Guzmán to depose Malespín on 2 February 1845. When Malespín ordered a priest executed later that year, Bishop Viteri y Ungo excommunicated him. Malespín's efforts to regain power led to war between Honduras and El Salvador in mid-1845. Malespín launched a new invasion of El Salvador in November 1846, but was murdered in a personal dispute at San Fernando, Chalatenango.

PHILIP FLEMION, *Historical Dictionary of El Salvador* (1972), pp. 83–84; CARLOS C. HAEUSSLER YELA, *Diccionario general de Guatemala*, vol. 2 (1983), pp. 950–951; RALPH LEE WOODWARD, JR., *Rafael Carrera and the Emergence of the Republic of Guatemala, 1821–1871* (1992).

RALPH LEE WOODWARD, JR.

MALFATTI, ANITA CATARINA

MALFATTI, ANITA CATARINA (*b*. 2 December 1889; *d*. 6 November 1964), Paulista artist who helped ignite the Brazilian modernist movement. Her oils, drawings, engravings, pastels, and watercolors were exhibited for fifty years in museums in Brazil, France, the United States, Argentina, and Chile.

Malfatti's Italian-born father died before she was thirteen. Her mother, a North American of German descent, was her first art teacher. Born with an atrophied right arm and hand, Malfatti received extensive training to use her left hand. After attending the Escola Americana, Malfatti graduated from Mackenzie College, and later taught at both institutions. Her uncle, Jorge Krug, sent her to Berlin (where she studied with Fritz Burger, Lovis Corinth, and Bischoff-Culm from 1910 to 1914). From 1914 to 1916 she took classes in New York at the Art Students League and at the Independent School of Art with Homer Boss. In 1915 her illustrations appeared in *Vogue* and *Vanity Fair* and she also painted some of the oils (*O japones, O homen amarelo, A boba, A mulher de cabelos verdes*) that led to the "Anita Malfatti Affair."

After returning to São Paulo in 1916, Malfatti painted two other controversial oils, *Tropical* and *O saci*, which were shown at her "Exposicão de pintura moderna" in São Paulo from December 1917 through January 1918. At first the exhibit was a success. But then an influential newspaper critic's hostile remarks led to demands for refunds and a flood of articles pro and con. Following this "Anita Malfatti Affair," a small group of young writers, other artists, and musicians began planning an

A Estudante Russa. Oil on canvas by Anita Malfatti.
PHOTO BY LUIZ HOSSAKA / COLLECTION MUSEU DE ARTE DE SÃO PAULO ASSIS CHATEAUBRIAND.

event, the MODERN ART WEEK, held in São Paulo in 1922, to vindicate her "martyrdom" and to modernize the Brazilian arts. The event did not change public opinion, however. With other members of the "Grupo dos Cinco" (Mario de ANDRADE, Tarsila do AMARAL, Oswaldo de ANDRADE and Menotti del Picchia) and other Brazilians, including Lucilia Guimarães Villa-Lobos, Heitor VILLA-LOBOS, Victor Brecheret, and Emiliano DI CALVALCANTI, Malfatti traveled to Europe, where she stayed until 1928.

Malfatti had many exhibitions in Brazil, including major shows at the Salão Paulista de Arte Moderna (1932), the Salão de Arte de Feira Nacional de Indústrias (1941), the Salão Bahiano de Belas Artes (1949), and the Bienales do Museu de Arte Moderna (1951, and retrospective 1963). She was president and director of the Sindicatos dos Artistas Plásticos from 1941 to 1946.

MARTA ROSSETTI BATISTA, *Brasil.* Vol. 1, *Tempo Modernista—1917/29: Documentacão* (1972), and *Anita Malfatti (1889–1964)* (1977); MARY [LUCIANA] LOMBARDI, "Women in the Modern Art Movement in Brazil: Salon Leaders, Artists, and Musicians, 1917–1930" (Ph.D. diss., University of California at Los Angeles, 1977).

MARY LUCIANA LOMBARDI

See also **Art: Twentieth Century; Modernism: Brazil.**

MALINALCO, site of an Aztec ceremonial center on a hilltop and cliffs overlooking the modern town of Malinalco, Morelos, Mexico. Subjugated by the Aztecs in 1476, Malinalco became the site of an important Aztec temple complex begun in 1501, during the reign of the Aztec ruler Ahuizotl and completed in the reign of his successor, MOTECUHZOMA II. Ethnohistoric documents allude to the use of forced labor in the construction of the complex.

The impressive temple complex consists of several structures that were carved out of bedrock on the cliff face. The principal structure is round, with an entrance in the form of the jaws of a serpent, symbolizing the entrance to a cave. Inside is a semicircular bench with four sculpted jaguar and eagle seats that presumably were occupied by high-ranking military officers. A small hole cut into the floor of the chamber suggests that the temple was the site of coronation rituals in which an incoming ruler dropped his own blood into the "heart of the earth" to symbolize his bond with the land. Similar ceremonies were performed in ritual caves elsewhere in the Aztec realm.

The Aztecs may have chosen Malinalco as the site for this important temple or shrine because of the historical significance of the place. According to Aztec (or Mexica) myth, during the long migration from Aztlan to the Valley of Mexico, a faction of the group was abandoned. This faction was led by Malinalxochitl, sister of HUITZILOPOCHTLI, the Mexica leader. Malinalxochitl and her group were thought eventually to have founded the town of Malinalco.

Excavations were carried out in the temple complex in the 1930s. More recently research has been conducted on the hilltop, the location of the original settlement.

RICHARD F. TOWNSEND, *The Aztecs* (1992); MURIEL PORTER WEAVER, *The Aztecs, Maya, and Their Predecessors*, 3d ed. (1993).

JANINE GASCO

MALINCHE (Marina; Malintzin; *b.* ca. 1504; *d.* 1527), Indian interpreter for Hernán CORTÉS. According to the Indian historian Domingo Chimalpahin Cuauhtlehuanitzin and Francisco Javier Clavijero, Malinche's complete indigenous name was Malinali Tenepal. She was baptized Marina and given the nickname Malinche, perhaps a distortion of Malintzin. (The termination *tzin* denotes nobility.) Several places of birth are given. Some historians, following Francisco López de Gómara, say she was born in the present-day state of Jalisco, while the more accepted version, based on Bernal DÍAZ DEL CASTILLO, locates her birthplace in the vicinity of Coatzacoalcos, in southern Mexico, probably in Painala but possibly in Oluta or Jaltipán. These historians also provide different accounts of her life before the arrival of the Spaniards. According to Gómara, she was stolen by some merchants during a war and then sold as a slave. Díaz's account lends her the semblance of a Greek tragic figure or the heroine of an Old Testament story.

According to Díaz, Malinali's parents were caciques of the town of Painala. After her father died, her mother married another cacique, with whom she had a son. To keep Malinali from succeeding them as cacique, one night they sold her to some merchants from Xicalanco and proclaimed her dead. At that time the child of one of their slave women had died, and they passed the dead girl off as Malinali. The merchants from Xicalango sold Malinali to other Indians in Tabasco, who in turn gave her to Cortés along with nineteen other women sometime in the spring of 1519.

After the twenty women were baptized, Cortés distributed them among his officers. He gave doña Marina, who was barely fifteen at the time, to Alonso Hernández Portocarrero. After Portocarrero returned to Spain on 26 June 1519, she became Cortés's interpreter and lover. The language skills of Marina, who spoke Nahuatl and Maya, complemented those of Jerónimo de AGUILAR, who had learned Maya during his captivity in the Yucatán. One can hardly exaggerate the importance of her role in the conquest of Mexico. In addition to her function as a translator, Marina possessed information about the Aztecs as well as the political structures of central Mexico. This knowledge was indispensable to Cortés's alliances with traditional enemies of Tenochtitlán. Her presence in numerous indigenous portraits of Cortés testifies to this fact.

In 1522, Marina gave birth to a son, whom Cortés named Martín Cortés and eventually recognized as legitimate. From November 1524 to June 1526 Marina served as Cortés's interpreter in the expedition to the Hibueras (present-day Honduras). During the expedition, Cortés married her to Juan Jaramillo. It was also during this expedition that, according to Díaz, she encountered her mother and half brother. They feared she would punish them for having sold her, but she consoled them and gave them gifts. She also told them that she was fortunate to be a Christian, to have a son by her master, Cortés, and to be married to a gentleman like Juan Jaramillo.

Marina had a daughter named María with Juan Jaramillo. As dowry, Cortés gave Marina and Jaramillo the *encomiendas* of Olutla, and Jilotepec, near Coatzacoalcos. She died, still very young, most likely from smallpox, probably in Mexico City. Today in Mexico, as in most of its history, Malinche is identified as a prostitute or a traitor, as someone who sold out to the invaders. Thus, the term *malinchismo* names the tendency to prefer what is foreign. More recently, however, Mexican and Chicana (Mexican American) women writers and artists have sought to rescue Malintzin from the misogynist perceptions that have prevailed in the past.

BERNAL DÍAZ DEL CASTILLO, *The Discovery and Conquest of Mexico, 1517–1521*, translated and edited by A. P. Maudslay (ca. 1568; 1970, esp. chaps. 35, 36; FEDERICO GÓMEZ DE OROZCO, *Doña Marina, la dama de la conquista* (1942); MARIANO G. SOMONTE, *Doña Marina, "La Malinche"* (1969); MARGARET SHEDD, *Malinche and Cortés* (1971); JOSÉ LUIS MÁRTINEZ, *Hernán Cortés* (1990), esp. pp. 160–173; and SANDRA MESSINGER CYPESS, *La Malinche in Mexican Literature from History to Myth* (1991).

JOSÉ RABASA

MALLARINO–BIDLACK TREATY. *See* **Bidlack Treaty (Treaty of New Granada, 1846).**

MALLEA, EDUARDO (*b*. 14 August 1903; *d*. 12 November 1982), Argentine novelist and essayist. Of a distinguished colonial family, Eduardo Mallea was born in Bahía Blanca, a wind-swept seaport 300 miles south of Buenos Aires. His father, an eminent physician whose integrity and patriotism were beyond question, strongly influenced the young Mallea during his intellectual and artistic development. The Mallea family moved to Buenos Aires in 1916, and in 1920 Eduardo entered law school at the university, but never completed his studies. Instead, he devoted himself completely to literature, publishing his first book in 1926, a collection of short stories entitled *Cuentos para una inglesa desesperada* (Stories for a Desperate Englishwoman).

Mallea was Argentina's intellectual novelist; in him Argentina found the spokesman for its most authentic values and beliefs. Influenced by Jean-Paul Sartre and Martin Heidegger, Mallea was Hispanic America's most important existential fiction writer. In novels such as *La bahía de silencio* (The Bay of Silence, 1940) and *Todo verdor perecerá* (All Green Shall Perish, 1941), Mallea portrayed the emotional crisis of contemporary man seeking to find reason in an irrational and chaotic world. If Mallea's predecessors, the *criollista* novelists, portrayed the spirit of America as a physical presence, Mallea captured the spirit of man as an individual, in his fundamental essence, of man not necessarily in conflict with nature or his environment, but in a more basic conflict with himself and his emotions.

Mallea's life was his writing. In 1914 he began a long-time association with *Sur*, one of the most influential literary magazines in the Americas. He also contributed regularly to other journals and newspapers and in 1923 founded the magazine *Rivista de América*. Mallea also had close ties to *La Nación* as editor of that newspaper's literary supplement from 1934 to 1955.

In 1937, Mallea published *Historia de una pasión Argentina* (History of an Argentine Passion), a book-length essay that is both his spiritual autobiography and Argentina's most influential biography of the 1930s. In this work Mallea's stance is that of the liberal intellectual who saw this period as dominated by a repressive oligarchy subverting the truth and moral order on which the country had been built. Revealing Mallea's anguish over the destruction of Argentina's basic values and the bankruptcy of its ideals, *History of an Argentine Passion* contains many themes that appear later in his novels, notably the concept of a visible Argentina—the materialistic, ostentatious false veneer that the country (especially Buenos Aires) lives with from day to day—versus an invisible one—the genuine soul of the country, its true being, which lies submerged beneath the crass surface.

In 1940, Mallea became president of the Argentine Association of Writers. In 1955, he served as Argentina's delegate to UNESCO in Paris, and in 1956 he traveled to New Delhi to represent his country at a UNESCO conference. His fiction writing never abated. In 1957, he published *Simbad*; in 1967, *La barca de hielo* (The Ice Ship); in 1971, *Triste piel del universo* (Sad Skin of the Universe); and in 1982, *La mancha en el marmol* (The Stain on the Marble).

JOHN H. R. POLT, *The Writings of Eduardo Mallea* (1959); MYRON I. LICHTBLAU, *El arte estilístico de Eduardo Mallea* (1967); MARTIN S. STABB, *In Quest of Identity: Patterns in the Spanish American Essay of Ideas, 1890–1960* (1967), pp. 161–169; VICTORIA OCAMPO, *Diálogo con Mallea* (1969); EMIR RODRÍGUEZ MONEGAL, *Narradores de esta América*, vol. 1 (1969), pp. 249–269; H. ERNEST LEWALD, *Eduardo Mallea* (1977).

MYRON I. LICHTBLAU

See also **Literature.**

MALOCA, a Portuguese word of Araucan origin, *malocan* was transformed by the Spanish into *maloca*. It was used originally to mean hostile or aggressive actions. The conquest of the pampas added a new meaning to the word, which also came to designate "Indian village." Today, the term refers to "Indian home," "shel-

ter," or "hiding place," giving rise to the Brazilian Portuguese verb *malocar* (to hide or fool). The indigenous *maloca* is a large building of strong beams with large diameters, which support smaller, flexible pieces of wood, over which is woven a roof of straw made from palm or banana leaves or grass. Brazilian Indian cultures produced many forms of *malocas* to shelter extended families.

HAMILTON BOTELHO MALHANO

MALONES (also called *malocas*), a term from the Mapuche *malocan*, meaning "hostilities toward or among enemies involving raiding of goods and property." In Chile, the term *malocas* was used by Spanish colonists in the sixteenth century to describe Mapuche hostilities, but when the MAPUCHES expanded into the Argentine pampas at the turn of the nineteenth century, the Argentines called the raids *malones*.

In the course of four centuries of resistance, first to INCA and then to Spanish conquest, the Mapuche *malon* functioned as a formidable defense. In classical historiography, the Indian *malones* usually have been viewed as obstacles to progress or modernization but have not always been analyzed in cultural context. More recent analytical literature, which has begun to document the quantity and extent of Mapuche *malones* against CREOLE property, indicates dramatic changes within Mapuche society as a result of the integration of European goods and resources obtained through *malones* within Mapuche systems of exchange and redistribution.

Kapayo Malocas, village of Aukre, Brazil. © 1988 ALEXANDER DE MOURA KING.

As an institution, intra-Mapuche *malones* functioned to regularize the distribution of material resources, status, and wife-exchange. Allegations of malevolence and witchcraft affecting the health of individuals in a community or band prompted *malones* against other bands and also motivated Mapuche *malones* against creole frontier settlements in Chile and Argentina.

Over the centuries, the organization of the *malones* changed. By the eighteenth century, *malones* were organized, interband military operations, in some cases mirroring Spanish military forms. By the nineteenth century, the intertribal *malones* against Argentine *estancias* were clearly motivated by market objectives as well as by anger at treaty violations. In the course of these developments, however, Mapuche participation in the *malones* continued to be at the discretion of each individual kin leader, rather than dictated through a hierarchy. Even so, by the late nineteenth century confederations involving over 200 individual bands organized major *malones* against ranching interests in Argentina. It was not until boundary issues between Chile and Argentina were resolved that those national governments were able to effectively combat the Mapuche *malon*.

MADALINE W. NICHOLS, "The Spanish Horse of the Pampas," in *American Anthropologist* 41 (January 1939):119–129; ALFRED TAPSON, "Indian Warfare on the Pampa During the Colonial Period," in *Hispanic American Historical Review* 42 (February 1962):1–28; JUDITH EWELL and WILLIAM BEEZELEY, eds., *The Human Tradition in Latin America: The Nineteenth Century* (1989), pp. 175–186; LEONARDO LEON SOLIS, *Maloqueros y conchavadores en Araucanía y las Pampas, 1700–1800* (1990).

KRISTINE L. JONES

See also **Araucanians; Calfucurá; Namuncurá, Manuel; Pehuenches; Ranqueles.**

MALUF, PAULO SALIM (*b.* 3 September 1931), Brazilian politician. Maluf was born in São Paulo, the son of Salim Farah Maluf and Maria Estefano Maluf. He married Silvia Luftalla, with whom he had four children. Although trained as an engineer, Maluf has been a long-time political figure both locally and nationally. Owner of Eucatex and other enterprises, Maluf started his political career in 1967, when President Costa e Silva appointed him president of the Caixa Econômica Federal (Federal Savings Bank) of São Paulo, a post he held for two years. In 1969, he was appointed *prefeito* (mayor) of his hometown and served until 1971, when he was appointed secretary of transportation for the state of São Paulo. In 1979, Maluf was indirectly elected under the ARENA Party banner as state governor. In spite of corruption charges, the politician was elected federal deputy in 1982, having received more than 600,000 votes.

Maluf ran for the presidency in 1984, but in spite of military backing, was defeated in the electoral college by Tancredo de Almeida Neves. Later, he suffered additional defeats in his campaigns for governor of São

Paulo state in 1986 and mayor of São Paulo in 1988, and in his candidacy for the presidency in 1989. The former governor attempted to regain the São Paulo governorship in 1990, but without success. He has remained politically active.

IÊDA SIQUEIRA WIARDA

MALVINAS, LAS. *See* **Falklands Islands.**

MAM, one of twenty-nine extant Mayan languages spoken in Guatemala, Mexico, Belize, and Honduras. With approximately 600,000 speakers it is among the four largest languages and is spoken in fifty-six townships in the departments of Huehuetenango, Quetzaltenango, and San Marcos in Guatemala, as well as in the hills surrounding the border towns in Mexico such as Mazapa, Amatenango, Motozintla, and Tuzantán. Mam belongs to the Mamean branch of the Eastern Division of Mayan languages, along with Tektiteko (Teco/Tectiteco), Awakateko (Aguacateco), and Ixil. It is bordered by Q'anjob'alan (Kanjobalan) languages to the north and K'ichean (Quichean) languages to the east. It is the most internally divergent Mayan language, with three major dialect zones each consisting of a number of separate dialects. Mam diverged from other Mamean languages between 1,500 and 2,600 years ago. It is spoken today in a territory similar to that occupied in 1524, though somewhat reduced, through K'iche' (Quiché) incursion, from its maximum area. Although Mamean languages are historically most closely related to the K'ichean, Mam shows a number of innovative similarities to Q'anjob'alan (Western Division) languages that are due to long-term contact in the Huehuetenango region. Mam is suffering extensive loss in the western area, some loss in the south, and very little loss in the north.

See NORA C. ENGLAND, *A Grammar of Mam, a Mayan language* (1983), for a reference grammar, and "El Mam: Semejanzas y diferencias regionales" in *Lecturas sobre la lingüística maya*, edited by Nora C. England and Stephen R. Elliott (1990), for dialect differences.

NORA C. ENGLAND

MAMACOCHA. The INCAS revered the Pacific Ocean as the goddess Mamacocha, which translates from the QUECHUA as "Lady Sea" or "Mother Sea." Streams and springs, considered to be daughters of the sea, were venerated and given offerings of shells.

JOHN H. ROWE, "Inca Culture at the Time of the Spanish Conquest," in *Handbook of South American Indians*, vol. 2 (1946), pp. 183–330. See also BURR CARTWRIGHT BRUNDAGE, *The Empire of the Inca* (1963).

GORDON F. McEWAN

MAMAQUILLA, the Inca name for the moon. Mamaquilla was believed to be a goddess and wife of the sun.

She was important to the INCAS for calculating time and regulating the ritual calendar. Represented by a large silver disk, her idol was kept in the temples of the sun, along with the other members of the Inca pantheon.

JOHN H. ROWE, "Inca Culture at the Time of the Spanish Conquest," in *Handbook of South American Indians*, vol. 2 (1946), pp. 183–330. Additional sources include BURR CARTWRIGHT BRUNDAGE, *The Empire of the Inca* (1963) and *The Lords of Cuzco: A History and Description of the Inca People in Their Final Days* (1967).

GORDON F. MCEWAN

MAMELUCO, a person of mixed blood, that is, of Portuguese and Indian parents. While the term is not used in modern Brazil, *mameluco* appears frequently in the historical documents of the sixteenth and seventeenth centuries. *Mameluco* men participated in many ENTRADAS into the interior, for their facility with Indian language, customs, and terrain made them valuable middlemen between the coastal townsfolk and the inhabitants of the wilderness. *Mameluca* women assimilated easily into Portuguese society by marrying Portuguese men. *Mamelucos* profoundly influenced frontier societies such as São Vicente and Maranhão, which were characterized by extensive interactions with the interior and the late introduction of significant numbers of African slaves.

JOHN HEMMING, *Red Gold: The Conquest of the Brazilian Indians* (1978); ALIDA C. METCALF, *Family and Frontier in Colonial Brazil* (1992).

ALIDA C. METCALF

MAÑACH Y ROBATO, JORGE (*b.* 14 February 1898; *d.* 25 June 1961), Cuban writer, born in Sagua la Grande. Mañach was learned in Cuban history and culture and participated in Cuban political life as senator of the Cuban republic (1940–1944) and as minister of state (1944). After studying in Cuba and going to Spain in 1907, where he attended Escuelas Pías in Getafé from 1908 to 1913, he was educated at Harvard, from which he graduated in 1920. In France he studied law at the Sorbonne and experienced the rich cultural and artistic life of Paris during the 1920s. Back in Cuba, Mañach took up a career in journalism (1922) on the famous journal *Diario de la Marina*. His first book, *Glosario* (1924), is a collection of the chronicles of his European and Cuban travels. This work comprises three genres: travel chronicles, *cuadros costumbristas* (works of local color), and essays of literary and art criticism. His essay *Indagación del choteo* (1928), which brought him recognition, deals with the humorous peculiarities and irreverent spirit of the Cuban personality. In *Martí: El apóstol* (1933), a biography in novel form, praise for the Cuban patriot José Martí is based on historical facts rather than on the subjective view of Martí given by the first republican generation. Exalting Martí as a hero, Mañach sought to restore political health to Cuba, which was then under

the dictatorship of Gerardo MACHADO (1925–1933). Mañach rejected autocratic systems and considered the individual's inalienable right to freedom to be the foundation necessary for a social and political regime. And though his writings in the magazine *Bohemia* supported Fidel CASTRO, Mañach ultimately rejected the tenets of both Castro and Fulgencio BATISTA. Other important works by Mañach are *Examen del quijotismo* (1950), a phenomenological study of *Don Quijote*, and *Teoría de la frontera* (1970), which synthesizes the values of North American and Latin American culture, and suggests the potential for a good relationship between the two.

ROSALYN K. O'CHERONY, "The Critical Essays of Jorge Mañach" (Ph.D. diss., Northwestern University, 1970); JORGE LUIS MARTÍ, *El periodismo literario de Jorge Mañach* (1977); NICOLÁS EMILIO ÁLVAREZ, *La obra literaria de Jorge Mañach* (1979).

JUAN CARLOS GALEANO

MANAGUA, the capital of Nicaragua. Located on the southern shores of Lake Managua, the city's site had been an ancient Indian settlement of the Chorotega called Manahuec. Before 1855, however, it was an obscure village. At that time it was chosen as a compromise capital to avoid conflict between the competing centers of LEÓN and GRANADA. The city grew rapidly after the completion of the railroad to coffee-producing areas in 1898 and to the Pacific port of Corinto in 1903. Although it was a late starter among Central American capitals, Managua is now the commercial and political center of Nicaragua. U.S. Marines came to Managua in 1912 to back a Conservative Party revolt. They returned in 1927 to enforce a political settlement between the Conservatives and Liberals. Remaining until 1932, they also supervised elections and trained the National Guard.

A severe earthquake destroyed a large part of the city in 1931, and a major fire caused widespread destruction in 1936. Another earthquake in December 1972 leveled the center of the city. Over 10,000 people were killed, and 300,000 were left homeless. A pattern of decentralization was decided upon in rebuilding, because the fault lines clearly concentrated in the city center. The principal commercial ventures moved to the southern part of the city.

In 1978–1979 the city led the general strikes held to oppose the government of Anastasio SOMOZA DEBAYLE. Heavy fighting with the Sandinista opposition took place in the city's slum areas in 1979. By the year 2000 it is expected that Managua's population will exceed 1 million and will represent over one-third of the total population of Nicaragua. It is nearly ten times the size of León, the second-largest city of the country. Managua is governed as a national district under the control of the central government, rather than as a typical municipality. It shares with León the main campuses of the National Autonomous University. The Central American University (UCA), a Jesuit institution, was founded in Managua in 1962. The Central American Institute of Business Administration (INCAE) has its original campus to the south of the city.

GRATUS HALFTERMEYER, *Historia de Managua* (1971).

DAVID L. JICKLING

MANAUS, capital of the Brazilian state of Amazonas. Founded in 1669, Manaus is located on the RIO NEGRO, about 1,000 miles upriver from the mouth of the AMAZON, and is the main port in the Amazonian interior.

Manaus was a small settlement in 1867, when the Brazilian government opened the Amazon River to international trade. The forests surrounding Manaus were rich in RUBBER trees, and from the 1870s on, Brazilian and foreign merchants flocked to the inland capital to profit from the booming rubber trade.

The city entered its heyday in the 1890s, when Manaus became the major center for Amazonian exports; by 1910 the urban population had grown to nearly 100,000 inhabitants. A classic boomtown, Manaus boasted the first electric street lighting in Brazil, piped water and gas, a system of floating docks, an ornate customshouse, and an elaborate opera house, crafted almost entirely from imported materials.

As an entrepôt that relied almost entirely on the rubber trade, Manaus was hit hard by the collapse of the wild rubber market in 1911. Population declined, trade plummeted, and the abandoned, decaying opera house stood as a monument to the excesses of the boom years. However, as the sole significant urban center in the western Amazon, Manaus survived the boom–bust cycle. In an effort to revive the Amazonian economy, in 1967 the Brazilian government declared Manaus a free port, thus generating a sharp increase in commercial activity and industrial development. Along with factories processing local products, Manaus is now home to several large, foreign-owned manufacturing plants producing consumer durables for the Brazilian market. As of 1985, Manaus had a population of 835,000.

E. BRADFORD BURNS, "Manaus, 1910: Portrait of a Boom Town," in *Journal of Inter-American Studies* 7, no. 3 (1965): 400–421; RICHARD COLLIER, *The River that God Forgot* (1968); BARBARA WEINSTEIN, *The Amazon Rubber Boom, 1850–1920* (1983).

BARBARA WEINSTEIN

MANCO CAPAC, founder of the Inca dynasty (the dates of his reign are unknown). In Inca myth Manco Capac emerged, together with his three brothers and four sisters, from three caves at Pacariqtambo, the Inca place of origin in the Peruvian highlands, a few miles southwest of the valley of Cuzco. Manco married his sister Mama Ocllo, founding the Inca bloodline, and led his siblings into the valley of Cuzco, establishing the city of Cuzco and the Inca dynasty around 1200. According to the legend, at the end of his life, Manco Capac turned into a stone that became one of the most sacred HUACAS of the INCAS.

Sources on Manco Capac and the founding of the Inca dynasty include JOHN H. ROWE, "Inca Culture at the Time of the Spanish Conquest," in *Handbook of South American Indians*, vol. 2 (1946), pp. 183–330; BURR CARTWRIGHT BRUNDAGE, *The Empire of the Inca* (1963); GARY URTON, *The History of a Myth: Pacariqtambo and the Origin of the Incas* (1990).

GORDON F. McEWAN

MANCO INCA (*b.* ca. 1516; *d.* 1545), Inca emperor during the early colonial period (reigned 1533–1545). Manco Inca was one of the sons of the emperor HUAYNA CAPAC. After the deaths of his brothers Atahualpa, HUASCAR, and the first Spanish puppet Inca, another brother named Topa Huallpa, Manco Inca was chosen by the Spanish conquistadores to rule as Inca emperor under their control. Crowned in 1533, he was treated badly by the Spanish, who abused him and his family and publicly insulted them. As a result, in 1536 he rebelled and fled with a large group of followers into the *montaña* region of eastern Peru, where he formed the rump state VILCABAMBA. Leading a vigorous resistance to the Conquest, he was killed by the Spanish.

JOHN HEMMING, *The Conquest of the Incas* (1970); BURR CARTWRIGHT BRUNDAGE, *The Lords of Cuzco: A History and Description of the Inca People in Their Final Days* (1967).

GORDON F. McEWAN

See also **Incas.**

MANDAMIENTO. In the political and economic chaos of Guatemala immediately after-independence, there was little need for the forced wage labor (*repartimientos*) that had characterized the late colonial period. The onset of large-scale COFFEE production after 1860, however, prompted the state and expectant planters to revive and expand coerced labor, now universally labeled *mandamientos* (from *mandar*, "to order"). The labor law of 1877, for example, gave Guatemala's Indian population the choice of accepting contracts for seasonal work on the coffee plantations or of finding themselves subjected to repeated forced drafts for the same purposes. Under the *mandamiento* system a planter in need of labor might request workers from one of the regional governors, paying the necessary wages and travel expenses in advance; the governor designated a community to supply the workers and required local Indian officials to mobilize and deliver them. Coercion kept wages low, but because *mandamiento* Indians were a reluctant and resentful work force, planters turned to them only in emergencies or to staff properties notorious for egregious abuse or particularly unhealthful conditions. The more important function of *mandamientos* was to force Indians into DEBT PEONAGE. Officially abolished in the 1890s, *mandamientos* in fact persisted until the overthrow of President Manuel ESTRADA CABRERA in 1920.

CHESTER LLOYD JONES, *Guatemala: Past and Present* (1940), chap. 12; DAVID MC CREERY, " 'An Odious Feudalism': *Mandamiento* Labor and Commercial Agriculture in Guatemala, 1858–1920," in *Latin American Perspectives* 13, no. 1 (Winter 1986): 99–117.

DAVID MCCREERY

MANDU LADINO (*d.* 1719), leader of one of the largest Indian rebellions in the Brazilian colonial period. Mandu Ladino was a "civilized" (ladino means "latinized" or "civilized") Indian, who had been educated by the JESUITS. The revolt began in 1712 because of TAPUIA resentment of forced labor in support of a Portuguese garrison. The Tapuia also wanted to avenge Indian killings committed by the Portuguese commander, Antônio da Cunha Souto-Maior, and his men, whose brutality including decapitating Indians for sport.

Mandu's 400 men sacked military garrisons, burned ranches, and killed Portuguese soldiers and settlers in Ceará, Piauí and Maranhão, but they spared missionaries. When Portuguese troops attacked a group of TUPI Indians, they too joined the rebellion and killed 88 people. Rebels destroyed at least 100 ranches, causing substantial losses.

Several Portuguese military expeditions against Mandu failed. The governor of Maranhão led one expedition in 1716 and surrounded Mandu's village, but a premature shot alerted the Indians and allowed them to escape. A rival group of the Tapuia, the Tobajara, defeated Mandu Ladino in a series of engagements, reducing his force to about 50 men. They killed him as he attempted to escape across a river.

JOHN HEMMING, *Red Gold* (1979).

ROSS WILKINSON

See also **Slavery: Indian.**

MANILA GALLEON. From 1571 to 1814, the richly laden Manila galleons sailed across the Pacific Ocean between Mexico and Manila in the Philippines. This trade route linked America with Asia, and more particularly, the Viceroyalty of New Spain with its farthest province, the Philippine Islands. The galleon trade was noted for the length and duration of its voyages—over 6,000 miles and six to nine months' sail from Manila to Acapulco. It was also notable for the enormous size of many of the galleons (up to 2,000 tons, comparable only to the largest of the Portuguese East Indiamen) and the mystique of the Asian luxuries it made available.

In 1571, after gaining control of the Malay trading center of Manila for Spain, Miguel LÓPEZ DE LEGAZPI

sent two ships back to Mexico laden with Chinese silks and porcelains, to be exchanged for needed provisions. In this way the Manila galleon trade was established. Spain was uniquely well prepared to conduct this commerce because of the convenient geographical location of Manila and America's large supply of silver. Chinese merchants, eager for silver, carried to Manila fine silks, damasks and other fabrics, gemstones, finely worked gold jewelry, and porcelain. Other products shipped aboard the galleons were brought from India (cottons and other fabrics); Japan (lacquerware and screens); the islands of the Indonesian archipelago (aromatic substances, pepper, cloves, nutmegs, mace); Indochina (gemstones and hard woods); and the Philippine Islands themselves (cinnamon, coconut products, beeswax, and fabrics).

Merchants in Spain found that inexpensive, high-quality merchandise from Asia competed too successfully with Spanish exports to America, and argued for severe restrictions on the volume of the trade—over the loud complaints of Mexican and Philippines advocates. This purposeful limitation after 1593 led to the proliferation of contraband trading.

Precise estimates of the extent of illegal trade are elusive for obvious reasons, but scattered information gleaned from official records, secondhand commentary, testimony from English captors of galleons, and accounts of infrequent inspections suggest that as much as ten times the permitted amount of cargo was being shipped. Contraband trading was fairly common throughout the Spanish Empire, but that on the Pacific galleons was notorious.

The westbound galleons rode the trade winds, and typically reached Manila without incident in three months. Eastbound galleons faced the harder challenge. Oversized, with decks piled high and provisions frequently foregone in order to carry additional merchandise, the unwieldy galleons sailed from Cavite, in Manila Bay. It took a month for the galleons to clear the Philippine archipelago and sail out into the open water of the Pacific. This leg of the journey needed to be completed before the onset of the typhoon season, which required that the galleons depart Manila by the end of June. This feat was rarely achieved, however, and many ended their journeys wrecked in fierce typhoons—as many as forty-four are known to have been lost—or by making the return (*arribada*) to Manila.

Even a successful voyage from Manila to Acapulco could be trying, lasting from six to nine months. This made the problems of provisions and health daunting. It was not unusual for more than 100 persons to die en route.

When first news arrived of the approach of the galleons to Acapulco—usually in January or February—plans were made for a festive trade fair. The ships were met by officials who came from Mexico City for the occasion. The sick were disembarked, ships' manifest and cargo cursorily examined, and merchandise unloaded to be sold at the fair. Residents of the Spanish colonies, both Spaniards and Amerindians, festooned themselves and their homes with Oriental goods.

The Manila Galleon trade made significant contributions to colonial Spanish culture. It helped to fashion the very society of the Philippines, which relied upon its income, its merchandise, and the services of Chinese, Malay, and other participants. In Mexico, the infusion of Chinese goods and art forms into Hispanic and Native American material culture remains visible today.

The economy of the whole empire was affected by the trade. From the Spanish (and official Mexican) point of view, the Philippine colony and its commerce were liabilities, even though much sought-after Chinese products were acquired. Manila and the galleons cost enormous sums to maintain and succeeded in directing vast quantities of American silver away from the imperial treasury. Many individual merchants risked and lost their lives, but sizable fortunes were accrued. Upon arrival at Acapulco in 1634, the traveler Fray Sebastián Manrique noted, "this profit made all hardships and dangers appear as nothing."

WILLIAM LYTLE SCHURZ, *The Manila Galleon* (1939); PIERRE CHAUNU, *Les Philippines et le Pacifique des Ibériques* (1960); GIOVANNI FRANCESCO GEMELLI CARERI, *A Voyage to the Philippines, 1696–1697* (1963); NICHOLAS CUSHNER, *Spain in the Philippines* (1971); ROBERT R. REED, *Colonial Manila: The Context of Hispanic Urbanism and Process of Morphogenesis* (1978); O.H.K. SPATE, *The Spanish Lake* (1979); CARMEN YUSTE LÓPEZ, *El comercio de la Nueva España con Filipinas, 1590–1785* (1984); LOUISA SCHELL HOBERMAN, *Mexico's Merchant Elite, 1590–1660* (1991), esp. pp. 183–222.

WILLIAM McCARTHY

MANIOC, a tropical root crop, also known as mandioca, cassava, aipim, or yuca. The manioc plant (*Manihot esculenta*) grows from 5 to 12 feet in height, with edible leaves of five to seven lobes. What most people use for food, however, are the roots, which are 2 to 6 inches in diameter and 1 to 2 feet in length. Each plant may yield up to 17 pounds of roots. When fresh, the roots are a source of carbohydrates, whereas the leaf has protein and vitamin A. Fresh roots may also contain calcium, vitamin C, thiamine, riboflavin, and niacin.

Of the two principal varieties of manioc, the sweet ones can be harvested in six to nine months, peeled, and eaten as a vegetable. The bitter varieties, however, require twelve to eighteen months to mature and have high levels of prussic acid, which must be removed by grating and soaking in water to avoid poisoning.

The indigenous populations of Latin America mastered the technology to render bitter manioc harmless and useful. Amerindian women wash, peel, and grate the roots to convert them into a snowy white mass, which they put into a cylindrical basket press, the *tipiti*. One end of the *tipiti* is tied to a tree, the other to the ground in order to squeeze out excess liquid. The pulpy

mass is removed, put through a sieve, and then toasted on a flat ceramic griddle or metal basin. The starchy pulp may also be boiled in a mush, baked into a bread, and even eaten as a pudding (tapioca). Manioc meal (farinha) can be preserved and stored in a tropical climate.

Manioc was domesticated in the Americas; possible areas of origin include Central America, the Amazon region, and the northeast of Brazil. Although the oldest archaeological evidence comes from the Amazon region, actual remains of manioc date from 1785 B.C. in and near the Casma Valley of Peru. In Mexico manioc leaves and manioc starch found in human coprolites are 2,100 to 2,800 years old. Manioc was also a staple of the MAYAS in MESOAMERICA. Evidence of ancient manioc cultivation also exists for the Caribbean, where the Arawaks and CARIBS utilized manioc griddles and named the plant *kasabi* (Arawak) and *yuca* (Carib).

The first European description of what the Spanish came to call *yuca* is that of Peter MARTYR (1494), who reported on "venomous roots" used in preparing breads. The Portuguese soon thereafter discovered manioc on the coast of Brazil. Two early descriptions are by Hans Staden (1557) and Jean de Léry (1578). Coastal settlers and their slaves rapidly adopted manioc as a principal food staple in South America. The Iberian conquerors also doled out manioc bread to their troops in the frontier wars, and it has been a military ration since the sixteenth century.

By the end of the colonial period, manioc was widely

"Manioc preparation." Reproduced from *Il gazzettiere americano* (Livorno, 1763). COURTESY OF THE JOHN CARTER BROWN LIBRARY AT BROWN UNIVERSITY.

cultivated by small farmers, the enslaved, and the impoverished of tropical Latin America, either for their own families or for sale to sugar planters, towns, and cities. Its cultivation, transport, and commerce contributed significantly to the internal economy of the tropics, but manioc did not become a cash crop for export, possibly because the Portuguese introduced it to the rest of the world in the sixteenth century. It was, however, widely used in the SLAVE TRADE between Brazil and Africa from at least the 1590s to 1850. In the twentieth century, most manioc production occurs outside of Latin America—Asia and Africa accounted for three-fourths of global production in contrast to Latin America's one-fourth in the 1980s.

HANS STADEN, *Duas viagens ao Brasil,* translated by Guiomar de Carvalho Franco ([1557], 1974); JEAN DE LÉRY, *History of a Voyage to the Land of Brazil, Otherwise Called America,* translated by Janet Whatley ([1578], 1990); LEON PYNAERT, *Le manioc,* 2d ed. (1951); WILLIAM O. JONES, *Manioc in Africa* (1959); MILTON DE ALBUQUERQUE, *A mandioca na Amazônia* (1969); DONALD W. LATHRAP, *The Upper Amazon* (1970); ANNA CURTENIUS ROOSEVELT, *Parmana: Prehistoric Maize and Manioc Subsistence Along the Amazon and Orinoco* (1980); PINTO DE AQUIAR, *Mandioca—Pão do Brasil* (1982); JAMES H. COCK, *Cassava: New Potential for a Neglected Crop* (1985); ROBERT LANGDON, "Manioc, A Long Concealed Key to the Enigma of Easter Island," *Geographical Journal* 154, no. 3 (1988): 324–336; TIMOTHY JOHNS, *With Bitter Herbs They Shall Eat It: Chemical Ecology and the Origins of Human Diet and Medicine* (1990); MAGUELONNE TOUSSAINT-SAMAT, *History of Food,* translated by Anthea Bell (1992).

MARY KARASCH

MANN, THOMAS CLIFTON (*b.* 11 November 1912), career diplomat. Mann, born near the border town of Laredo, Texas, became bilingual at an early age. After working in the family law firm, he joined the State Department in 1942, specializing in Latin American affairs. He became a foreign service officer in 1947 and served as ambassador to El Salvador and as one of President Lyndon B. Johnson's principal advisers on Latin American policy. Mann advocated private, rather than public, investment and feared that Communists manipulated local nationalist movements in the Western Hemisphere. Therefore, he supported the Central Intelligence Agency's planned overthrow of Guatemala's Jacobo ARBENZ GUZMÁN in 1954. Mann served as Assistant Secretary of State for Economic Affairs in the Eisenhower administration (1957–1960) when it shaped many of the policies subsequently found in the ALLIANCE FOR PROGRESS. After a stint as Ambassador to Mexico, Mann became Under Secretary of State for Economic Affairs in 1965. His advocacy of unilateral action by the United States in the Dominican Republic crisis of 1965 caused widespread criticism and contributed to his resignation in 1966.

ABRAHAM F. LOWENTHAL, *The Dominican Intervention* (1972); STEPHEN G. RABE, *Eisenhower and Latin America: The Foreign Policy of Anticommunism* (1988); FEDERICO GIL, "The Kennedy-Johnson Years," in *United States Policy in Latin America: A Quarter Century of Crisis and Challenge, 1961–1986,* edited by John D. Martz (1988).

THOMAS M. LEONARD

See also **Dominican Revolt.**

MANNING, THOMAS COURTLAND (*b.* 14 September 1825; *d.* 11 October 1887), Louisiana lawyer, public official, and U.S. minister to Mexico. Manning was educated at the University of North Carolina before reading law. On 18 January 1848, he married Mary Blair. Before moving to Louisiana in 1855, he taught school and practiced law in North Carolina. During the Civil War he was a brigadier general in the Confederate army. He served as an associate justice of Louisiana's Supreme Court in 1864–1865 and 1882–1886, and as chief justice from 1877 to 1880.

He was envoy extraordinary and minister plenipotentiary to Mexico from 30 August 1886 until 21 September 1887. In December 1886, he filed a claim against Mexico for the killing of Captain Emmet Crawford, a U.S. citizen, by Mexican rural volunteers. During his short service he intervened on behalf of various U.S. entrepreneurs, especially in mining, railroads, and real estate.

National Cyclopedia of American Biography, vol. 4 (1892), p. 344; *Biographical and Historical Memoirs of Louisiana,* vol. 1 (1892), pp. 93, 97, 112; JAMES MORTON CALLAHAN, *American Foreign Policy in Mexican Relations* (1932); *Dictionary of American Biography,* vol. 6 (1961), p. 253; LUIS G. ZORRILLA, *Historia de las relaciones entre México y los Estados Unidos de América, 1800–1958,* 2 vols. (1965–1966).

THOMAS SCHOONOVER

MANRIQUE DE ZÚÑIGA, ALVARO (marqués de Villamanrique; *d.* ca. 1593), seventh VICEROY of New Spain. Villamanrique is thought by some to have been the low point of viceregal government in Mexico in the sixteenth century. Governing from 1585 to 1590, Villamanrique is credited with having begun the process whereby the northern frontier was pacified. He sought to increase royal control over the distribution and sale of mercury, WINE, and meat. In keeping with royal legislation of 1574, Villamanrique helped strengthen royal control over the CATHOLIC CHURCH. Because of these and other policies many residents of New Spain opposed the viceroy. In 1588 a jurisdictional dispute with the neighboring Audiencia of New Galicia was portrayed in Madrid as approaching a civil war, a prospect that prompted the crown to remove Villamanrique and to subject him to a judicial review. In 1589 he was arrested by the bishop of Puebla, don Diego Romano, and returned to Spain, suffering the sequester of his personal possessions.

RICHARD GREENLEAF, "The Little War of Guadalajara, 1587–1590," in *New Mexico Historical Review* 43 (1968): 119–135.

JOHN F. SCHWALLER

MANSILLA, LUCIO VICTORIO (*b.* 23 December 1831; *d.* 8 October 1913), Argentine soldier, explorer, diplomat, and author. The second of four children, Mansilla was an undisciplined student and, as a consequence, his father pulled him from school and sent him as his representative on business trips to India, Egypt, and Europe. Mansilla's lasting influence lay in Argentina, however. Properly speaking, Mansilla was more of a tutor to than a member of the Argentine Generation of 1880, the group that secured the liberal hegemony responsible for the modernization of the country following the tyranny of José Manuel de ROSAS, which ended in 1852. (Mansilla's mother was Rosas's sister.) Nevertheless, Mansilla is in many respects an emblematic figure of 1880. Published in 1888, his *Entre-nos, causeries del jueves* (note the Francophile title) first appeared in the newspaper *Sud América*, important as an ideological platform during the period. Mansilla's underscoring of the urbane dilettantism, the drawing room and café society, and the emphasis on public, oral performance characteristic of the period makes these sketches undoubtedly a principal sociocultural document.

Nevertheless, Mansilla is most known for his *Una excursión a los indios ranqueles* (1870), for many generations of Argentines (typically, Argentine boys) one of the first works of national literature to be read. Mansilla recounts with attention to detail—backed up by extensive European learning that made him a symbol of Argentine cultural sophistication—the expedition he led in mid-1870 to indigenous settlements in an attempt to establish boundaries that would put an end to Indian raids against the creole settlers encroaching on those settlements. Based on the belief that an understanding of Indian society and culture would enhance pacification, *Una excursión* is of undeniable value as a sort of protoanthropolitical document and a predecessor of Claude Lévi-Strauss's *Tristes tropiques*. This protoanthropolitical quality is relevant to what Mansilla's text cannot relate: how the 1879–1880 CONQUEST OF THE DESERT imposed a violent military solution to indigenous opposition to white settlement of the pampas.

ENRIQUE POPOLIZIO, *Vida de Lucio V. Mansilla* (1954); JOSÉ LUIS LANUZA, *Genio y figura de Lucio V. Mansilla* (1965); DAVID WILLIAM FOSTER, *The Argentina Generation of 1880: Ideology and Cultural Texts* (1990), pp. 14–31.

DAVID WILLIAM FOSTER

MANSO DE MALDONADO, ANTONIO (*b.* ca. 1670; *d.* 5 November 1755?), military figure and president of the Audiencia of Santa Fe de Bogotá (1724–1731). Drawn from the officer corps of the Barcelona garrison, Manso went to America as *audiencia* president and governor and captain-general of the New Kingdom of Granada in order to conduct the RESIDENCIA (end-of-tenure review) of the first viceroy of New Granada, Jorge de VILLALONGA (1719–1724), under whose leadership viceregal rule had failed to meet royal expectations, and to oversee the reestablishment of political order in the colony. Manso arrived in New Granada in February 1724 and immediately began to gather testimony on Villalonga. Although faced with voluminous contradictory reports, he largely absolved the former viceroy of wrongdoing. The difficulties of rule, the opposition to his authority, and his scandalous private life left the president bitter and anxious to return to a military post in Spain. Manso's administration is generally considered to have been ineffective or even inept. Returning to Spain in 1731, he served as governor of Cueta and then as inspector of Spanish and foreign infantry.

An important and straightforward examination of Manso's role in the experiment with viceregal rule in New Granada is MARÍA TERESA GARRIDO CONDE, *La primera creación del virreinato de Nueva Granada (1717–1723)* (1985). See also the discussion in SERGIO ELÍAS ORTIZ, *Nuevo Reino de Granada: El virreynato, 1719–1753,* in *Historia extensa de Colombia,* vol. 4 (1970), pp. 61–95; and Manso's own report of his administration in GERMÁN COLMENARES, ed., *Relaciones e informes de los gobernantes de la Nueva Granada,* vol. 1 (1989).

LANCE R. GRAHN

MANSO DE VELASCO, JOSÉ ANTONIO (*b.* 1688; *d.* 5 January 1767), count of Superunda and viceroy of Peru, 1745–1761. Born in Logroño, Spain, Manso followed a military career from an early age, rising to lieutenant general. From 1737 to 1745 he governed Chile with vigor and ability, founding a number of settlements.

On 24 December 1744, King PHILIP V named Manso viceroy of Peru, the first of the military officers who governed the viceroyalty in place of the traditional noblemen and diplomats. After the earthquake and tidal wave that devastated Lima and Callao in 1746, Manso rebuilt the city and port. He put down an Indian rebellion in Huarochirí but had less success with that of Juan Santos. For his services, King FERDINAND VI named him count of Superunda in 1748. Manso established the royal tobacco monopoly (*estanco de tabaco*) in 1752 and reformed the mints in Lima and Potosí. His sixteen-year tenure, until 12 October 1761, was the longest of any Peruvian viceroy.

Returning to Spain, he was in Havana when the British captured the port in 1762. As the senior official present, although in transit, Manso was blamed for the debacle. Sentenced to exile in Granada, he died there in 1767, a sad end to a distinguished career.

DIEGO OCHAGAVÍA FERNÁNDEZ, ''El I Conde de Superunda,'' in *Berceo* 58–63 (1961–1962); JOSÉ A. MANSO DE VELASCO, *Relación y documentos de gobierno del virrey del Perú, José A. Manso de Velasco, Conde de Superunda (1745–1761),* edited by Alfredo Moreno Cebrián (1983).

KENDALL W. BROWN

MANTEÑO, the name given to the prehistoric culture occupying much of the Ecuadorian coast during the Integration period (A.D. 500–1531). Manteño's territorial boundaries extended from the Bahía de Caráquez in the north to the Gulf of Guayaquil in the south, where it is sometimes referred to as the Huancavilca culture. It is widely considered the preeminent society of coastal Ecuador prior to the Spanish conquest due to its monopoly on balsa raft navigation and a far-flung network of maritime trade, which included a wide variety of sumptuary goods such as artifacts of gold, silver, and copper; elaborate textiles of cotton and wool; richly decorated ceramic vessels and figurines; turquoise, greenstone, and lapis lazuli; and the highly prized *chaquira* (small beads of red and white marine shell).

With the PUNÁ Islanders, the Manteños formed a League of Merchants, although it is unclear to what extent this exchange was strictly commercial or an extraction of religious tribute from dominated coastal peoples. The Manteños themselves were probably subject to Inca influence in a peripheral zone of that expanding empire. Although no permanent Incaic presence has been documented in coastal Ecuador, LA PLATA Island, off the coast of southern Manabí, has yielded clear evidence of a royal Incaic burial ritual commonly employed as a territorial marker throughout Tawantinsuyu.

The largest regional centers of Manteño culture were divided in quadripartite fashion, with one of the four local communities playing a paramount sociopolitical role. The two most important of these centers, or *señoríos*, were Salangome in southern Manabí (at modern Agua Blanca) and Jocay in central Manabí (at modern Manta). Others existed in inland riverine settings, such as Picuazá (near modern Portoviejo), but have received less archaeological attention. Many of these sites are true urban centers having well-ordered platform mounds and numerous buildings with stone wall foundations. Jocay is reported to have had an important religious shrine to which regular pilgrimages were made on ritual occasions. There was also a substantial Manteño settlement of the hill country of central and southern Manabí in areas such as Cerro de Hojas, Cerro Jaboncillo, and Cerro de Paco. Sites here are usually smaller than those on the coast and represent habitation sites often associated with agricultural terracing on hillsides.

One of the chief hallmarks of Manteño culture is the use of stone carving for the manufacture of large ceremonial objects. These include heavy U-shaped seats placed over three-dimensional feline or anthropomorphic imagery and large rectangular stelae with heraldic female figures carved in bas-relief. The seats are widely considered to be associated with high-status civic/ceremonial functions and may symbolize authoritative powers of the chiefly elite.

A second hallmark of Manteño culture is its distinctive pottery, characterized by burnished black designs on grayware bowls, pedestaled *compoteras* with zoomorphic modeled figures, grayware ollas with fine-line in-

cision, and anthropomorphic figurine-vessels with flaring rim on the head and a pedestal base. Solid mold-made figurines, as well as larger, hollow, modeled figurines are common. The latter often depict elite personages with elaborate tattooed designs, especially on the shoulders and neck.

A complex social division of labor is indicated by occupational specialization in economic pursuits as well as in craft manufacture; certain settlements were dedicated exclusively to a narrow range of subsistence and craft pursuits. Uncovered at Los Frailes in the *señorío* of Salangome was an extensive shell artifact workshop that was dedicated to the manufacture of plaques, sequins, beads, and other ornaments from the pearl oysters *Pteria sterna* and *Pinctada mazatlantica*, as well as beads and pendants of the thorny oyster *Spondylus*. Because of their very strong symbolic connotations, these were highly sought-after luxury items throughout the Andean area.

The existence of a complex social hierarchy in these *señoríos* is also suggested by the diversity of human burial patterns found throughout Manteño territory. These include primary interments in simple pits, primary burials in platform mounds, secondary urn burials, and deep shaft-and-chamber tombs in hilltop ceremonial centers such as Loma de los Cangrejitos in the southern Manteño area.

FRANCISCO DE XEREZ [1528], "La relación Sámano-Xerez," in *Colección de documentos inéditos para la historia de España*, vol. 5 (1844), pp. 193–201; EMILIO ESTRADA, *Los Huancavilcas: Últimas civilizaciones pre-historicas de la costa del Guayas* (1957); BETTY J. MEGGERS, *Ecuador* (1966); ROBERT A. FELDMAN and MICHAEL E. MOSELEY, "The Northern Andes," in *Ancient South Americans*, edited by Jesse D. Jennings (1983); ANNE M. MESTER, "Un taller manteño de madre de perla del sitio Los Frailes, Manabí, Ecuador," in *Miscelánea antropológica ecuatoriana* 6 (1986); 131–143; COLIN MC EWAN and MARÍA SILVA "¿Que fueron a hacer los Incas en la costa central del Ecuador?" In International Congress of Americanists, *Relaciones interculturales en el área ecuatorial del Pacífico durante la época precolombiana*, edited by Jean François Bouchard and Mercedes Guinea Bueno, BAR International Series 503 (1989), pp. 163–185.

JAMES A. ZEIDLER

See also **Atacames; Jama-Coaque.**

MANUEL I (*b.* 31 May 1469; *d.* 13 December 1521), king of PORTUGAL (1495–1521). Born in Alcochete, Manuel was the youngest child of Prince Fernando, second duke of Viseu and first duke of Beja, master of the Orders of Christ and Santiago, and Dona Beatriz, daughter of Prince João. Both parents of Manuel were grandchildren of King JOÃO I (reigned 1385–1433), and Prince Fernando was the younger brother of King Afonso V (reigned 1438–1481). One of Manuel's sisters, Leonor, was married to King JOÃO II (reigned 1481–1495). Another sister, Isabel, was married to Dom Fernando, third duke of Bragança, who was executed for treason in 1483.

An older brother of Manuel was Dom Diogo, fourth duke of Viseu and third of Beja, master of the Order of Christ, who was stabbed to death in 1484 by King João II for conspiring against the monarch. Manuel, who was only fifteen years old at the time of Diogo's death, had earlier been adopted by King João II, his cousin and brother-in-law, and was allowed to succeed his deceased brother as duke of Viseu and Beja and master of the Order of Christ. In July 1491, João II's only legitimate child, Crown Prince Afonso, who had married Princess ISABEL, daughter of the Catholic monarchs FERDINAND of Aragon and ISABELLA I of Castile, was fatally injured in a horseback-riding accident. Although João II had an illegitimate son, Dom Jorge, who by 1492 had become master of the Orders of Santiago and Avis, the monarch was pressured to name Manuel as heir to the throne and did so in his last will and testament.

When João II died in 1495, Manuel was acclaimed king of Portugal on 25 October. In 1496, King Manuel recalled the Braganças to Portugal from exile in Castile and restored that family's properties and titles, which earlier had been confiscated by the crown. In 1498, Manuel named his nephew, Dom Jaime, fourth duke of Bragança, heir presumptive to the Portuguese throne. The previous year, in hopes of unifying the Iberian Peninsula under Portuguese rule, Manuel married Isabel, the widow of Prince Afonso. Isabel, who had become crown princess of Aragon and Castile because of the death of her brother Juan, died in childbirth in 1498. Manuel and Isabel's son, Miguel, heir to the thrones of Portugal, Castile, and Aragon, died in 1500. King Manuel then married Isabel's younger sister, Maria. Among their many children were future King JOÃO III (reigned 1521–1557); Princess Isabel (who married Emperor Charles V in 1526); Cardinal-King Henrique (reigned 1578–1580), who was also Grand Inquisitor of Portugal; Prince Luis (father of the illegitimate Dom Antônio, prior of Crato, pretender to the Portuguese throne in 1580); and Prince Duarte (father of Dona Catarina, sixth duchess of Bragança and grandmother of King João IV, the first of Portugal's Bragança monarchs). In 1518, following Queen Maria's death the previous year, King Manuel married Leonor, oldest sister of Charles V and Catherine of Austria (future wife of Manuel's son, King João III).

The most controversial action of Manuel's reign was the forced conversion to Christianity of all Jews living in Portugal. At the prodding of Princess Isabel and her parents, Manuel issued an edict in December 1496, giving all Jews in Portugal from January to October of 1497 to convert to Christianity or to leave Portugal. Contrary to what is frequently written, relatively few Jews were expelled or allowed to depart from Portugal since Manuel did all in his power to prevent them from leaving the country. With few exceptions, Jews in Portugal either voluntarily accepted Christianity or were forcibly baptized. Among the crown's incentives to conversion was the taking of all children under fourteen years of age from Jewish parents who would not convert and giving them to Christians throughout Portugal to raise. By the end of 1497, the process of forced conversion was completed. In 1498, Manuel issued an edict allowing twenty years' grace regarding the sincerity of the conversions. An additional sixteen years was later granted. The result of this forced conversion was a new group in Portuguese society called "New Christians," who later were hounded by the INQUISITION and subjected to "purity of blood" statutes until 1773, when King JOSÉ I (reigned 1750–1777), at the urging of the marques de POMBAL, abolished these distinctions.

During his reign, Manuel I presided over numerous financial, legislative, and administrative reforms, including an updated codification of Portuguese law. The monarch replaced the Ordenações Afonsinos of his uncle with the Ordenações Manuelinas, which began to be printed in 1512. A new corrected edition was published in 1521, the year of Manuel's death. Manuel's reign is probably most famous for the great overseas discoveries he sponsored. On 8 July 1497, he sent Vasco da GAMA and four ships to find a sea route to India. This aim was achieved with da Gama's arrival in Calicut on 20 May 1498. By the end of August of 1499, two of da Gama's ships had arrived back in Portugal. On 9 March 1500, a follow-up expedition of thirteen ships, headed by Pedro Álvares CABRAL, left Lisbon. On 22 April, Monte Pascoal in Brazil was sighted, and on 2 May, Cabral continued to India, but not before sending his supply ship back to Portugal with news of his discovery. In 1501, Manuel sent three ships under the command of Gonçalo Coelho to explore the eastern coast of Brazil. Upon Coelho's return the following year, Manuel leased out Brazil for three years to a consortium headed by Fernão de Loronha. However, Manuel was more interested in North Africa, East Africa, and Asia than in America, and concentrated his energies on those regions.

The best biography is ELAINE SANCEAU, *The Reign of the Fortunate King, 1495–1521* (1969), which focuses chiefly on Portuguese expansion. There is no definitive study of Manuel's reign in any language. Historians have been content to rely on DAMIÃO DE GÓIS, *Crónica do Felicíssimo Rei D. Manuel*, first published in 1566–1567. The best modern edition was published in four volumes, 1949–1955.

FRANCIS A. DUTRA

See also **Portuguese in Latin America.**

MANUMISSION, the voluntary freeing of slaves. Throughout Latin America and the Caribbean, the freeing of captives (who, from the mid-sixteenth century onward, were largely Africans or of African descent) implied that enslavement constituted a legal status that was not necessarily permanent. This transformation from SLAVERY to freedom, requiring the relinquishing of control over "property" or "human capital," was of considerable significance to all individuals directly in-

Manumitted slaves in Brazil. Reproduced from Jean-Baptiste Debret, *Voyage pittoresque et historique au Brésil*, vol 2. (Paris, 1839). BY PERMISSION OF THE HOUGHTON LIBRARY, HARVARD UNIVERSITY.

volved in the change, as well as to governing officials and family relations of both masters and slaves. The actual act of freeing an individual slave was, therefore, regularly recorded, most commonly in a notarized letter of liberty (in Spanish a *carta de libertad;* in Portuguese a *carta de alforria*).

The historical significance of manumission rests on an evaluation of such factors as its frequency or availability within a given slave society, the motivations of masters in releasing individual slaves from their control, and the impact that manumission had on freed slaves, their descendants, and the larger slave societies in which both groups lived. Studies of such factors indicate that the significance and impact of freeing a slave or of becoming a freed slave depended on where one lived in Latin America. *When* one lived in a particular slave society was also quite crucial, as the quality of liberty for an ex-slave and the impact of the newly freed slave on the larger society varied according to the climate for manumission at a particular historical moment. An understanding of slave manumission in Latin America is, therefore, tied to the differing contexts in which it occurred.

Slaves were freed primarily through the individual action of a slaveholder. (The exceptions were the cases of colonial, revolutionary, or national governments who emancipated slave soldiers fighting on their behalf.) Whether these masters freed their captives as an act of charity or in exchange for market value, or in order to relieve themselves of a financial burden, their view of

the deed was fundamentally limited to one involving themselves and their human property. The impact upon the slaveholder's community was not as significant a concern as the personal gain to be derived from the act. Even when it benefited the freed slave, manumission was, at bottom, not a social act but a selfish one.

It was the job of government officials, not slaveholders, to concern themselves with the long- and short-term consequences of manumission: independent wage workers who could decide when and for whom to work; sick or elderly freed captives too weak to care for themselves and dying on the streets; healthy and reproductive slaves who competed, or threatened to compete, with free whites for economic standing, social status, and in some cases the numerical majority within the free population as a whole. Throughout Latin America, colonial and later national governments bemoaned what the emancipating slaveholders had wrought—a nonslave population of color struggling for security amid difficult material conditions and unwelcoming free whites.

In both the colonial and national periods, there were laws that formally discriminated against freed slaves and their freeborn descendants. In addition, the Catholic church barred ex-slaves from the priesthood, and some churches segregated nonwhites from whites in their services, brotherhoods, and burial grounds. Whites also petitioned their governments to bar free blacks and mulattoes from training in crafts and entrance into artisan guilds. Despite the clear and persistent evidence that manumission did not protect a freed individual from legal and illegal acts of discrimination, slaves throughout Latin America continued to seek grants of manumission from their owners, preferring a restricted state of freedom to none at all.

The distribution of grants of manumission among slaves in Latin America was neither random nor entirely consistent. Certain subgroups of the slave population, such as male and female children and adult women, were overrepresented among the manumitted, but several studies have shown that the proportions of these subgroups within manumitted populations differed according to regions and, within a region, could change over time. In addition, grants of manumission contained a wide variety of terms, which ranged from dismissal without further obligation to payment and/or further years of service by the slave. Grants sometimes required that a slave wait until the owner's death before his or her release, and sometimes stipulated that a period of service be rendered to the owner's heirs. The specific terms of manumission have been linked to such mutable factors as the economic conditions within a given slave society, the relationship of the slave to the manumittor, and the emergence in some places of large numbers of female slaveholders.

To date, every empirical study of manumission in Latin America and the Caribbean has indicated that less than 2 percent of slaves were freed annually. Nonetheless, manumissions contributed to the freed and free people of color ultimately representing a significant percentage of the total populations of many slave regimes—in some areas of Brazil as much as 40 percent. A mechanism that allowed individual masters considerable flexibility in manipulating the labor and lives of their human property, manumission could have the unintended and unwelcome impact of threatening the numerical majority of whites in the free population. Thus, the practice was cautiously tolerated, but not wholeheartedly embraced, as a method of social control within Latin American slave societies.

DAVID W. COHEN and JACK P. GREENE, eds., *Neither Slave Nor Free: The Freedman of African Descent in the Slave Societies of the New World* (1972); KATIA M. QUEIRÓS MATTOSO, "A próposito de cartas de alforria na Bahia, 1779–1850," in *Anais de História* 4 (1972): 23; STUART B. SCHWARTZ, "The Manumission of Slaves in Colonial Brazil: Bahia, 1684–1745," in *The Hispanic American Historical Review* 54 (November 1974): 603–635; FREDERICK P. BOWSER, "The Free Persons of Color in Lima and Mexico City: Manumission and Opportunity, 1580–1650," in *Race and Slavery in the Western Hemisphere: Quantitative Studies,* edited by Stanley L. Engermen and Eugene D. Genovese (1975); JAMES PATRICK KIERNAN, "The Manumission of Slaves in Paraty, Brazil, 1789–1822" (Ph.D. diss., New York University, 1976); LYMAN L. JOHNSON, "Manumission in Colonial Buenos Aires, 1776–1810, in *The Hispanic American Historical Review* 59 (May 1979): 258–279; JEROME S. HANDLER and JOHN T. POHLMAN, "Slave Manumissions and Freemen in Seventeenth-Century Barbados," in *William and Mary Quarterly* 3, 41 (July 1984); ROSEMARY BRANA-SHUTE, "The Manumission of Slaves in Suriname, 1760–1828" (Ph.D. diss., University of Florida, 1985); KATHLEEN J. HIGGINS, "Manumissions in Colonial Sabará," chap. 4 in "The Slave Society in Eighteenth-Century Sabará, A Community Study in Colonial Brazil" (Ph.D. diss., Yale University, 1987); MARY C. KARASCH, "The Letter of Liberty," in her *Slave Life in Rio de Janeiro, 1808–1850* (1987); "Special Issue: Perspectives on Manumission," in *Slavery and Abolition* 10, no. 3 (December 1989).

KATHLEEN JOAN HIGGINS

MANZANO, JUAN FRANCISCO (*b.* 1797; *d.* 19 July 1853), Cuban poet, narrator, and playwright. The only slave in Spanish American history to become an accomplished writer, Manzano is one of the founders of Cuba's national literature. Born to Toribio Manzano and María Pilar Infazón and slave to Doña Beatriz de Justiz, Marquesa de Justiz de Santa Ana, Manzano published his first collections of poems, *Poesías líricas*, in 1821, and *Flores pasageras* [*sic*] in 1830.

In 1835, at the request of the literary critic and opponent of SLAVERY Domingo DEL MONTE, Manzano wrote his autobiography. In it, Manzano tells of his good and bad moments under slavery: he was treated as a privileged slave by his first mistress and was punished as a common one by the marquesa de Prado Ameno. Manzano concludes with his escape from his last mistress in 1817. Manzano learned to read and write on his own and his autobiography contains numerous grammatical errors. To make it more presentable, it was corrected but also altered by Anselmo Suárez y Romero, who made the slave's antislavery stance even stronger than Manzano intended. This version was translated into English by Richard Madden as "Life of the Negro Poet," and published in London in 1840. The original was lost until 1937.

After writing his autobiography and reading his autobiographical poem "Thirty Years" in the Del Monte literary circle in 1836, Del Monte and other Cuban intellectuals purchased Manzano's freedom for 800 pesos. Manzano continued to write poetry, publishing much of it in periodicals of the period, and he wrote a continuation of his autobiography, which was lost by Ramón de Palma. In addition, Manzano published his only play, *Zafira*, in 1842. In 1844 Manzano and Del Monte were falsely accused by the mulatto poet Gabriel de la Concepción VALDÉS (Plácido) of participating in the antislavery Ladder Conspiracy. Manzano was imprisoned for one year. Once released, and fearful that his writing might implicate him in other liberal activities, he never wrote again.

JOSÉ LUCIANO FRANCO, "Juan Francisco Manzano, el poeta esclavo y su tiempo," in his *Autobiografía, cartas y versos de Juan Francisco Manzano* (1937); ROBERTO FRIOL, *Suite para Juan Francisco Manzano* (1977); WILLIAM LUIS, "Autobiografía del esclavo Juan Francisco Manzano: Versión de Suárez y Romero," in *La historia en la literatura iberoamericana* (1989), pp. 259–268; *Literary Bondage: Slavery in Cuban Narrative* (1990), pp. 82–100;

ANSELMO SUÁREZ Y ROMERO, *Autobiografía de Juan Francisco Manzano y otros escritos*, edited by William Luis (forthcoming).

WILLIAM LUIS

MAPOCHO RIVER, stream arising in the ANDES of SANTIAGO and draining the northern portion of the Santiago basin in Chile. After a short but precipitous course (62 miles), it joins the MAIPO RIVER at El Monte. Santiago was chosen by Pedro de VALDIVIA as the capital of his governancy because the river offered the water needed by the settlement. Cerro Santa Lucía on the southern bank served as a defense post against Indian attacks, and both riverbanks were densely populated by natives engaged in successful agricultural production in the fertile soils along the Mapocho. In the early 1990s the waters had become badly contaminated by city sewage and industrial waste.

BENJAMÍN VICUÑA-MACKENNA, *Historia de Santiago* (Santiago, 1938); and JEAN BORDE, *Les Andes de Santiago et leur avant-pays* (Bordeaux, 1966).

CÉSAR N. CAVIEDES

MAPUCHES (also called ARAUCANIANS), the largest indigenous population in the Southern Cone. Composed of several ethnic subgroups, the Mapuches live primarily in communities in Chile south of the Bío-bío River (Mapuche) and in reserves in Argentina in the southern cordillera north and south of Lake Nahuel Huapi (Araucanian). The term *Mapuche* is commonly used in Chile and in Argentina to refer to all of the Araucanian (the Spanish term) ethnic subgroups. The Mapuches (*mapu*, meaning "land," and *che*, "people") most commonly identified themselves according to territoriality, for example, Huilliche (people of the south), Picunche (people of the north), Lafkenche (people of the coast), Lelfunche (people of the plains), PEHUENCHE (people of the pines—an ethnic subgroup of the cordillera region incorporated within Araucania), and so on.

Archeological studies indicate three prehistoric phases in the ethnogenesis of the Mapuche culture, beginning in the second half of the first millennium A.D. Following the unsuccessful attempts of the INCA Empire in the mid-fifteenth–early sixteenth century to incorporate the Mapuches and the even less successful attempts of the Spaniards to conquer them in the sixteenth century, the Mapuches (excepting the Picunches) maintained relative cultural and political autonomy throughout the seventeenth and eighteenth centuries, during which time they incorporated many technological and even cultural features of the Spanish. Mapuche sovereignty was threatened by the breakdown of treaty protections following the independence of Chile and the subsequent territorial expansion resulting from the expansion of Chilean capitalism in the second half of the nineteenth century.

Following the military subjugation that was part of the pacification policies of the Chilean government in the late nineteenth century, the Mapuches were reduced to living on communally held reservation lands. In the first half of the twentieth century, Mapuche poverty and dependence increased, and the reservation system lost land to expanding Chilean latifundios. Agrarian reform measures in the 1960s and 1970s temporarily halted the disintegration of Mapuche territory, but the gains were reversed under the military dictatorship when the system of communally held territory was legally challenged. In 1991 a new law was proposed to protect further disintegration of communally held lands in Chile.

JULIAN H. STEWARD, ed., *Handbook of South American Indians*, vol. 2 (1946), pp. 687–760; BERNARDO BERDICHEWSKY, "Araucanian," in *Encyclopedia of Indians of the Americas*, vol. 2 (1975); JOSÉ BENGOA, *Historia del pueblo Mapuche* (1985); ROLF FOERSTER and SONIA MONTECINO, *Organizaciones, líderes y contiendas Mapuches (1900–1970)* (1988).

KRISTINE L. JONES

See also **Calfucurá; Malones; Namuncurá; Ranqueles.**

MAQUILADORAS, Mexican assembly plants, sometimes referred to as "in-bond" plants or "twin" plants, that are part of the phenomenon of production-sharing manufacturing characteristic of globalization of the world economy. Owing to advances in communications and transportation, under production sharing, manufacturing processes can be divided into those that are capital- and technology-intensive and those that are labor-intensive. Under the Mexican variant of production sharing, components are imported from the United States or another industrialized country, principally Japan and Southeast Asian countries, then assembled in Mexico and exported to the United States. Under Mexican law, machinery, components, and supplies are imported duty-free, or "in bond," as long as the assembled product is exported. Under U.S. Tariff Codes, raw materials and components originating in the United States are not assessed when reentering the country as a part of a finished product; tariffs are paid only on the value added in Mexico—mainly labor. Initially, all assembled goods had to be exported, but by 1994 *maquiladoras* were permitted to sell up to 50 percent of their production in the Mexican market.

The maquiladora option was established in Mexico in 1965, partly in response to the termination of the BRACERO program, which employed thousands of Mexican temporary workers in the United States. Confined to Mexico's northern border until 1972, the industry grew slowly until the economic collapse of Mexico in the early 1980s, when the devaluation of the Mexican peso significantly reduced the cost of Mexican labor in dollar terms to the point that it was competitive with labor in other parts of the developing world. By 1993, the maquiladora

515

Douglas Furniture Company *maquiladora* in Tijuana.
© DON BARTLETTI / LOS ANGELES TIMES.

industry included more than 2,000 plants and nearly one-half million employees. Assembly plants produce electronics and consumer electronics, apparel, wood products, and auto parts, and carry out other labor-intensive operations such as sorting supermarket coupons and shelling walnuts.

The maquiladora industry is controversial. Critics claim that maquiladoras result in the export of large numbers of jobs from the United States, that they cause severe pollution problems in Mexican and U.S. border cities, that they exploit the largely female work force, and that they are not integrated with the Mexican economy. Furthermore, critics say they have caused infrastructure shortages in border cities, they cease operation and leave the country at the first sign of labor difficulties, and they have not produced significant transfers of technology. Proponents of the option point to the stability of many firms in the industry, job creation in the stagnant Mexican economy, the increasingly capital-intensive nature of maquiladoras, increased training and transfers of technology (including managerial skills), high levels of worker satisfaction, and the generation of foreign exchange as benefits of the industry. Opponents of the NORTH AMERICAN FREE TRADE AGREEMENT (NAFTA), mainly U.S. organized labor and its supporters, in 1992 and 1993 focused on the maquiladora industry in their attacks on the treaty.

Implementation of NAFTA began 1 January 1994, and over an eight-year period many of the special privileges enjoyed by maquiladoras will be extended to other manufacturing operations in Mexico. Maquiladoras will gain full access to the Mexican market and will, in essence, become integrated into the Mexican manufacturing sector. Inflows of capital and technology into the maquila-dora industry, as well as lower tariffs under the NAFTA framework, location of the industry adjacent to the U.S. market, and competitive wage rates in Mexico will assure continued importance of the maquiladoras.

JOSEPH GRUNWALD and KENNETH FLAMM, eds., *The Global Factory: Foreign Assembly in International Trade* (1985); NORRIS C. CLEMENT et al., *Exploring the Mexican In-Bond/Maquiladora Option in Baja California, Mexico* (1989); LESLIE SKLAIR, *Assembling for Development: The Maquiladora Industry in Mexico and the United States* (1993). For current information, see the trade magazine *Twin Plant News*.

PAUL GANSTER

See also **Economic Development.**

MAR, JOSÉ DE LA (*b.* 1778; *d.* 1830), one of the first military presidents of Peru (1827–1829). Born in Cuenca, Ecuador, he was trained as a royalist officer in Spain. He was appointed governor of the Callao fortress in 1816. After initially fighting against the naval attacks led by Lord Thomas COCHRANE, La Mar capitulated to General José de SAN MARTÍN's independence forces in 1821. In 1822, La Mar received the title of grand marshal and, when San Martín left Peru, he was put in charge of the government until his dismissal because of his lack of success against the loyalist resistance. However, Simón BOLÍVAR later recruited La Mar to fight in the definitive battles of JUNÍN and AYACUCHO against the remaining Spanish forces. In 1827, La Mar was elected president but, while in a campaign against Colombian forces, a coup in 1829 forced him out of office and into exile. He died in San José, Costa Rica.

JORGE BASADRE, *Historia de la República del Perú*, vol. 1 (1963); CELIA WU, *Generals and Diplomats: Great Britain and Peru 1820–40* (1992).

ALFONSO W. QUIROZ

MAR DEL PLATA, coastal city of Argentina in the province of Buenos Aires, 250 miles from the capital. The bustling city (1981 population of 414,700) has developed into the favorite sea resort of the inhabitants of the capital. The nearby spa of Huincó, where the mineral water has a moderate calcium carbonate content, attracts many patients with lung problems. Mar del Plata is also an important fish-processing center, with packing plants, paper mills, grain mills, and apparel manufactories. Two universities, the University of the Province of Buenos Aires and the Catholic University Stella Maris, as well as an institute of marine biology, enhance the cultural life of the city. The navy station at Mar del Plata ensures the presence of the Argentine armed forces in the Atlantic.

ROBERTO CAVA, *Síntesis histórica de Mar del Plata* (Mar del Plata, 1968).

CÉSAR N. CAVIEDES

MARACAIBO, second largest city in Venezuela, a major seaport situated on the western bank of the channel between Lake Maracaibo and the Gulf of Venezuela. Maracaibo is the capital of the state of Zulia. Its population grew from less than 50,000 in 1915 to over 750,000 by 1980. Settled first by Ambrosio Alfinger, it was officially founded in 1571 under the leadership of Alonso Pacheco Maldonado. The city has long served as a major port for western Venezuela and eastern Colombia, especially for the export of mountain-grown coffee. In 1667 the Dutch attacked Maracaibo, and in 1669 Henry Morgan captured it. During the twentieth century the city has flourished due to the discovery of oil in the region. Throughout its history, Maracaibo has served as the center of numerous separatist movements. Its population includes descendants of German immigrants, who comprise a significant part of the city's merchants.

JOHN V. LOMBARDI, *People and Places in Colonial Venezuela* (1976) and *Venezuela: The Search for Order, the Dream of Progress* (1982); JUDITH EWELL, *Venezuela: A Century of Change* (1984).

WINTHROP R. WRIGHT

MARACATU, an Afro-Brazilian dance procession performed during CARNIVAL in Recife, Pernambuco. The *maracatu* originated in the seventeenth and eighteenth centuries, when plantation owners allowed slaves to elect kings and queens and parade during holidays—singing, dancing, and drumming—while dressed in the costumes of European royal courts. These groups, which were then known as CONGADAS and were linked to black religious brotherhoods, mixed Catholicism with African religious practices. After the abolition of slavery (1888) this tradition was incorporated into the Carnival celebrations of Recife and given the name *maracatu*. These groups now parade during carnival dressed in elaborate Louis XV costumes of various stock characters: king, queen, princes, princesses, ambassadors, Roman soldiers, *baianas* (Bahian women), and slaves. A central figure is the *dama do paço* (court lady), who carries a small doll representing an ancestor of the group.

Accompanying the royal court is a large percussion orchestra of double-headed drums, metal shakers, and large iron bells. The rhythms are elaborate, interlocking, and highly syncopated, with large *bombos* (bass drums) taking the lead role. *Toadas* (songs) are sung by a lead singer and chorus in a call-and-response form that typically combines Portuguese and Yoruba words. In the 1940s, the *maracatu rural*, a new type of group combining Afro-Brazilian and mestizo traditional patterns developed in the sugarcane area around Recife.

CÉSAR GUERRA-PEIXE, *Maracatus do Recife*, 2d ed. (1980); KATARINA REAL, *O folclore no carnaval do Recife*, 2d ed. (1990), esp. pp. 55–82.

LARRY N. CROOK

See also **Music: Popular Music and Dance.**

MARAJÓ ISLAND, an island located at the mouth of the AMAZON River on the Atlantic coast of Brazil. Approximately 45,000 square miles in area, Marajó is the world's largest river island. The climate of the island is tropical savanna, and rain falls seasonally from January to July (80–100 inches per year). During the rainy season most (70 percent) of the island floods. Evidence of human habitation on Marajó dates back to the early Holocene period (3,000 to 8,000 B.P.). The island was home to the Pre-Colombian MARAJOARA culture, which, according to evidence, developed elsewhere and then moved to the island. At the time of European arrival, the population of Marajó may have stood at 36,000.

The people on Marajó Island resisted European encroachment for over 150 years, until Padre Vieira persuaded the Nheengaiba and other tribes to accept Portuguese rule in 1659. After the Portuguese took control, the island was entrusted to the Jesuits, who began raising cattle with Indian cowboys to manage the herds. Around 1900, Indian water buffalo were introduced into the Marajó ecology. According to local tradition water buffalo that were originally intended for British Guiana arrived via a shipwreck. Today, cattle and water buffalo are raised commercially for meat and transportation needs.

BETTY J. MEGGERS, *Amazonia: Man and Culture in a Counterfeit Paradise* (1971); JOHN HEMMING, *Red Gold: The Conquest of the Brazilian Indians, 1500–1760* (1978); ANNA C. ROOSEVELT, *Moundbuilders of the Amazon: Geophysical Archeology on Marajó Island, Brazil* (1991).

MICHAEL J. BROYLES

MARAJOARA. Known since the nineteenth century for its elaborate polychrome funerary pottery and numerous monumental earthern mounds, the Marajoara culture at the mouth of the Amazon in Brazil was attributed by early professional archaeologists to an invasion from the Andes, because the tropical forest was considered to be too poor to support large human populations and complex cultures. However, the habitat of the Marajoara is not *terra firme* (upland) tropical forest lowland but floodplain, so the influence of the habitat need not have been as limiting as assumed earlier. The culture has now been dated with twenty-four radiocarbon dates, and these reveal that the culture is earlier than related Andean cultures, and the physical anthropology of the people affiliates them with Amazonian populations, rather than Andeans. Thus, Marajoara now must be presumed a local development of the tropical lowlands. The Marajoara mounds had been characterized by earlier archaeologists as purely ceremonial, but recent geophysical surveys and excavations show them to be large platforms for entire villages of earth, pole, and thatch longhouses with adjacent cemeteries and garbage dumps. The fishbones, seeds, and tools of exotic rocks in the mounds indicate a mixed economy of FISHING, gathering, trade, and horticulture, and several carbon-

Marajoara funeral urn (left) and idol (right). COURTESY
AMERICAN MUSEUM OF NATURAL HISTORY; PHOTO BY CHARLES H. COLES.

ized MAIZE specimens were recovered in the excavations. Despite the achievements of this culture, the settlement pattern that has emerged from research does not suggest a centralized and hierarchical political organization. Whether the society was socially ranked or stratified has not yet been determined.

HELEN CONSTANCE PALMATARY, *The Pottery of Marajó Island, Brazil* (1950); BETTY J. MEGGERS and CLIFFORD EVANS, *Archaeological Investigations at the Mouth of the Amazon* (1957); ANNA CURTENIUS ROOSEVELT, *Moundbuilders of the Amazon: Geophysical Archaeology on Marajó Island, Brazil* (1991).

ANNA CURTENIUS ROOSEVELT

MARANHÃO (MODERN), state in northeastern Brazil bounded by the Atlantic Ocean to the north, Piauí to the east/southeast, Pará to the west, and the Tocantins River to the south/southeast. Maranhão is relatively flat: more than 90 percent of its total area (about 131,000 square miles) is less than 990 feet above sea level. The climate is hot (average year-round temperature of 75°F) and rainy (approximately 81 inches per year) owing to its location near the equator. Northeastern Maranhão is pre-Amazon rain forest, while the babassu (*Orbignya martiana*) palm forest dominates the southwest, along with significant concentrations of buriti and carnauba palms. South America's largest coral reef lies off the coast. Mangrove swamps, which help sustain rich coastal marine life, are rapidly disappearing.

Maranhão's population of 5,404,827 (1990), 43 percent of which is urban, has an average density of nine in-habitants per mile. The largest cities are the capital of SÃO LUÍS (781,374), Imperatriz (262,757), Caxias (157,884), and Codó (130,426). Historically, most Maranhenses have inhabited the low coastal and river basins in the Northeast, where agriculture predominates. Armed land conflicts between wealthy property owners and poor squatters have intensified in recent years.

Agricultural production remains the base of the state's economy, with significant exports of rice, corn, beans, soybeans, and manioc. Because of drought and pest infestations, the state's harvest fell almost 60 percent in 1990. Babassu and carnauba, along with hardwoods, are exported, as are substantial quantities of fish and seafood. Since 1984 exports of pig iron, iron ore, manganese, aluminum, and alumina have grown steadily. An annual trade of more than 36 million tons established the Maranhão port system as the second in total tonnage nationwide for 1990.

The state has only 1,797 miles of paved roads, including the two federal highways that link the capital to neighboring Belém in Pará (480 miles) and Teresina in Piauí (295 miles), the latter also connected by railway. In 1984, the Companhia Vale do Rio Doce (CVRD) inaugurated a railway for mineral exports linking Carajás in Pará with São Luís (534 miles). CVRD also built a deepwater port in the capital. The Norte-Sul Railway joining Goiânia in Goiás and Açailândia in Maranhão (900 miles) is partially completed. The Alcântara Satellite Base, begun in 1985, is now in operation.

Since 1984, with the opening of the CVRD railway and port, the Alumar (Alcoa/Billiton-Shell) aluminum factory, and the satellite base, the state has regained national importance. Maranhão is also the birthplace of former president José SARNEY, whose term (1985–1990) encompassed this period of expansion and development.

PAULO LYRA for Alcoa Alumínio S/A, *Maranhão* (1981).

GAYLE WAGGONER LOPES

MARANHÃO, ESTADO DO, colonial Brazil's administrative center. Because prevailing winds made northern Brazil more accessible by sea from Lisbon than from Salvador, the state of Maranhão was formed as a separate government in 1621. It initially included the captaincies of Ceará (later made dependent upon Pernambuco), Maranhão, and Grão Pará, which included the Amazon Valley. During the seventeenth century the capital moved between the towns of São Luís do Maranhão and Belém do Pará, but when CACAO, harvested from the Amazonian rainforest, became the leading export in the eighteenth century, Belém, the leading port, also became the permanent capital. Until their removal in 1759–1760, the JESUITS were the dominant missionaries, but they were joined by CARMELITES, FRANCISCANS, and MERCEDARIANS. The expulsion of the Jesuits coincided with the legal end of Indian SLAVERY in Maranhão and the introduction of substantial numbers of African slaves. The arrival of the blacks led to the development of plantation-produced staple exports, mainly COTTON and rice. As part of the administrative reorganization of Brazil during the 1760s and 1770s, the state was abolished as a separate entity in 1774.

CÉZAR AUGUSTO MARQUES, *Diccionário histórico-geográphico do Maranhão* (Maranhão, 1870); RODOLFO GARCIA, *Ensaio sôbre a história política e administrativa do Brasil (1500–1810)* (Rio de Janeiro, 1956), chap. 11.

DAURIL ALDEN

MARAÑÓN RIVER, an important waterway that joins the Ucayali River to form the Amazon River in the rain forest or Montaña region of Peru. Originating in the Peruvian central Andes, the Marañón flows northward until its confluence with the Santiago River and then eastward in the low Montaña region, where it is joined by the Huallaga River and later the Ucayali. It is a navigable river used commercially since the introduction of STEAMSHIPS in 1866, its banks supporting both industry and agriculture, including the mining of GOLD and limestone and the production of COFFEE, cacao, wheat, and fruits. In 1542, Francisco de ORELLANA, the Spanish explorer, was able to navigate through it and across the Amazonian jungle to reach Spain.

JAVIER PULGAR-VIDAL, *Análisis geográfico sobre las ocho regiones naturales del Perú* (1967).

ALFONSO W. QUIROZ

MARBLEHEAD PACT (1906). On 20 July 1906 official representatives of Guatemala, El Salvador, and Honduras met aboard the U.S.S. *Marblehead*, anchored off the Guatemalan port of San José. Honorary representatives of Costa Rica and Nicaragua were also present. The United States and Mexico, sponsors of the conference, had brought the isthmian nations together in an effort to resolve the conflict that had erupted between El Salvador and Honduras, on the one hand, and Guatemala on the other. The Marblehead Pact, signed by the three belligerents, called for the ending of hostilities, the release of political prisoners, expanded efforts to control the activities of political émigrés, and a commitment to negotiate, within two months, a general treaty of "peace, amity, and navigation." The conferees designated San José, Costa Rica, as the site for the forthcoming isthmian conference and agreed that in the interim any difficulties involving the signatory powers would be submitted to the arbitration of the presidents of Mexico and the United States.

Papers Relating to the Foreign Relations of the United States, 1906 (1909), esp. pp. 835–852; DANA G. MUNRO, *Intervention and Dollar Diplomacy in the Caribbean, 1900–1921* (1964), esp. pp. 144–146.

RICHARD V. SALISBURY

See also **San José Conference; Washington Treaties.**

MARCELIN BROTHERS (Philippe Thoby-Marcelin [*b.* 11 December 1904; *d.* 13 August 1975]; Pierre Marcelin [*b.* 20 August 1908]), Haitian writers.

Philippe Thoby-Marcelin added to his own name that of an uncle who adopted him. He published early verse in *La nouvelle ronde* and in *La revue indigène*. Studying in Paris, Philippe met Valéry Larbaud, who published some of his poems in *La revue européenne* (1928). He worked along the lines of the Indigenist movement to cast off French influence and write in a Haitian vein. From the forties onward, Thoby-Marcelin continued to make contact with a number of major writers—Nicolás GUILLÉN, Alejo CARPENTIER, Aimé CÉSAIRE, André Breton, Malcolm Lowry (who dedicated the French translation of *Under the Volcano* to him), Langston Hughes, and others. He was cofounder of the Haitian Popular Socialist Party in 1946. He later served as an employee of the Haitian Department of Public Works and the Pan American Union.

Pierre Marcelin received his early schooling at Saint-Louis de Gonzague in Port-au-Prince. He lived in Cuba with his diplomat father for several years and published fiction in collaboration with his brother. Their *Canapé-Vert* (1942) was awarded first prize for the Latin American novel in 1943. The fiction of both Marcelins has been accused of offering a superficially touristic view of Haiti, but it has achieved greater readership than that of many Haitian writers.

PHILIPPE THOBY-MARCELIN: *La négresse adolescente* (poetry, 1932); *Dialogue avec la femme endormie* (poetry, 1941); *Lago-Lago* (poetry, 1943); *À fonds perdu* (poetry, 1953); *Panorama de l'art haïtien* (1956); and *Art in Latin America Today: Haiti* (1959).
PHILIPPE THOBY-MARCELIN and PIERRE MARCELIN: *La bête de Musseau* (novel, 1946), translated as *The Beast of the Haitian Hills* (1951); *Le crayon de Dieu* (novel, 1946), translated as *The Pencil of God* (1951); *Contes et légendes d'Haïti* (1967), translated as *The Singing Turtle and Other Tales* (1971); and *Tous les hommes sont fous* (novel, 1980), translated as *All Men Are Mad* (1970).
See also EDMUND WILSON, "The Marcelins—Novelists of Haiti," *The Nation* (14 October 1950): 341–344; NAOMI M. GARRET, *The Renaissance of Haitian Poetry* (1963), pp. 93–106; "In Memoriam, Philippe Thoby-Marcelin (1904–1975)," *Présence Haïtienne* 2 (September 1975): 11–15; F. RAPHAEL BERROU and PRADEL POMPILUS, *Histoire de la littérature haïtienne illustrée par les textes*, vol. 3 (1977), pp. 143–150.

CARROL F. COATES

MARCH OF THE EMPTY POTS (also known as the *Ollas vacías* or *Marcha de cacerolas*), a demonstration against the regime of Chilean President Salvador ALLENDE mounted by upper- and middle-class women in Santiago on 1 December 1972 to complain about high prices and food shortages. The president's supporters, many of whom apparently belonged to the Movement of the Revolutionary Left (MIR), attacked the women, prompting the government to declare a state of emergency and impose a curfew. The demonstration, which occurred during a visit of Cuba's Fidel Castro to Chile, clearly embarrassed Allende. It also alienated various people, who denounced the government for ordering the police to use tear gas on the women. Similar demonstrations took place in May and September 1983, when upper- and middle-class women again banged their empty pots to protest the economic policies of President PINOCHET.

PAUL E. SIGMUND, *The Overthrow of Allende and the Politics of Chile, 1964–1976* (1977), pp. 162–164; JULIO B. FAÚNDEZ, *Marxism and Democracy in Chile* (1988), p. 218.

WILLIAM F. SATER

MARCHA, a political, intellectual, and cultural weekly review, founded in Montevideo in 1939 by Carlos QUIJANO. By November 1974, when it was finally closed by Uruguay's military dictatorship, *Marcha* had published 1,676 issues, with a circulation reaching 30,000, and had established an international reputation for its vigorously independent and principled views. Reflecting the growing strength of anti-imperialist sentiment and disaffection with the traditional political parties in Uruguay during the 1960s, its editorials became increasingly confrontational, which assured its closure after the coup in 1973.

Throughout its history *Marcha* was central to the cultural and intellectual life of Uruguay, but in spite of the prestigious names who wrote for it, *Marcha* always remained closely identified with its founder. Quijano had been a member of the Independent Nationalist faction of the Blanco Party in the 1930s, in opposition to the Herrarists who had backed Gabriel TERRA's coup in 1933. After 1938, Quijano took little part in party politics, abstaining until 1946 and abandoning his Blanco affiliation in 1958. His social-democratic convictions eventually led him to support the left-wing FRENTE AMPLIO coalition, formed to contest the 1971 elections. Quijano died in exile in 1984, as Uruguay negotiated its return to democracy.

HUGO R. ALFARO, *Navegar es necesario: Quijano y el semanario "Marcha"* (1984); GERARDO CAETANO and JOSÉ PEDRO RILLA, *El joven Quijano, 1900–1933* (1986).

HENRY FINCH

MARECHAL, LEOPOLDO (*b.* 11 June 1900; *d.* 26 June 1970), Argentine novelist, poet, playwright, and essayist. Born in Buenos Aires, Leopoldo Marechal re-creates in his works his life experiences: his childhood in Buenos Aires, the countryside of Maipú, years spent as a teacher, and trips to Europe are revealed through the written word. His first book, *Los aguiluchos* (1922), is a poetic vision of enjoyment found in the beauty of nature. *Días como flechas* (1926), a second book of poetry, alludes to the biblical story of creation and shows greater structure and harmony in the platonic world constructed by the poet. Marechal collaborated on

MARTÍN FIERRO (1924), a seminal literary review that reflected experimental and stylistic changes in literature as they occurred in Europe, and he also contributed to *Proa,* an avant-garde literary journal.

In his longest, most complex, and highly influential novel, *Adán Buenosayres* (1948), Marechal explores themes that remained constant throughout his works. As an effort to reinterpret biblical themes symbolically through a protagonist simultaneously representing Adam and a contemporary resident of Buenos Aires, the novel oscillates between the symbolic and the realistic, examining the transformations of Argentine society brought about by massive immigration and industrialization. In spite of a favorable review by Julio CORTÁZAR, then a critic and aspiring writer aligned with Victoria OCAMPO's SUR, the novel was coolly received and left unattended for more than twenty years. This has been attributed, in part, to Marechal's identification with the Peronist Party. More recent writers consider the novel as one of their primary influences and as a precursor to the technical and thematic literary experimentation of the 1960s.

El banquete de Severo Arcángelo (1965), considered to be Marechal's most important experimental novel, reflects the interplay of illusion and reality also found in plays such as *Antígona Vélez* (1951) and *Las tres caras de Venus* (1966), as well as in his essays, including *Cuaderno de navegación* (1966). Marechal is best known for his use of religious and mystical motifs, for the poetic qualities interwoven throughout his narrative and essays, and the epic narrative style of his poetry. He died in Buenos Aires.

RAFAEL F. SQUIRRU, *Leopoldo Marechal* (1961); LEOPOLDO MARECHAL et al., *Interpretaciones y claves de Adán Buenosayres* (1966); ALFREDO ANDRÉS, *Palabras con Leopoldo Marechal, Reportaje y antología: Alfredo Andrés* (1968); DANIEL BARROS, *Leopoldo Marechal, poeta argentino* (1971); ELBIA ROSBACO DE MARECHAL, *Mi vida con Leopoldo Marechal* (1973); GRACIELA COULSON, *Marechal: La pasión metafísica* (1974); *Poesía: 1924–1950 por Leopoldo Marechal* (1984); VALENTÍN CRICCO et al., *Marechal, el otro: Escritura testada de Adán Buenosayres* (1985).

DANUSIA L. MESON

MARGARITA, an island about 12 miles off the eastern coast of Venezuela, which, with TORTUGA, Cubagua, and Coche, comprises part of the state of Nueva Esparta. It was discovered in 1498 by Christopher Columbus. The Spanish set up pearl fisheries at Cubagua in 1515. In 1524, Emperor Charles V gave Margarita to Marceto Villalobos. In 1561, Lope de AGUIRRE plundered Asunción before going on to raid the mainland. Besides pearls, the island's population depended upon fishing and saltmaking for their livelihoods.

Margarita played a crucial role in the return of Simón BOLÍVAR from exile in Haiti. In 1816, he landed on Margarita and in early 1817 defeated royalist troops before he moved his headquarters to the Orinoco region. In return for its loyalty, Bolívar made Margarita part of a new state and promised to create a free trade zone there. This finally occurred in the final quarter of the twentieth century, and as a result the island has become a major tourist attraction.

JOHN V. LOMBARDI, *People and Places in Colonial Venezuela* (1976) and *Venezuela: The Search for Order, the Dream of Progress* (1982); JUDITH EWELL, *Venezuela: A Century of Change* (1984).

WINTHROP R. WRIGHT

MARGIL DE JESÚS, ANTONIO (*b.* 18 August 1657; *d.* 6 August 1726), missionary and founder of missionary colleges in Guatemala and New Spain. A native of Valencia, Spain, Antonio Margil was ordained a FRANCISCAN priest in 1682 and the following year volunteered for service in New Spain. Shortly after his arrival in the New World, he was sent to Central America, where he served in Yucatán, Guatemala, Costa Rica, and Nicaragua from 1684 to 1697. In 1701, during a second tour in Guatemala, he founded the Colegio de Cristo Crucificado, a missionary college.

Following his appointment as guardian of the new missionary college of Nuestra Señora de Guadalupe de Zacatecas in 1706, Margil spent the remainder of his life working in northern New Spain. From his base at the college, he conducted missionary activity among both Spanish and Indian populations of Nayarit, Nueva Galicia, Zacatecas, Nuevo León, and Coahuila. He participated in the permanent occupation of TEXAS, founding three missions in the eastern part of the province in 1716–1717 and another in San Antonio in 1720.

PETER P. FORRESTAL, "The Venerable Padre Fray Antonio Margil de Jesús," in *Preliminary Studies of the Texas Catholic Historical Society* 2, no. 2 (1932); EDUARDO E. RÍOS, *Fr. Margil de Jesús, apóstol de América* (1955).

JESÚS F. DE LA TEJA

See also **Catholic Church.**

MARGINAL, MARGINALIDADE. A *marginal* is an individual peripheral to or excluded from mainstream Brazilian society. In the colonial period this term referred to the landless, colored poor occupying a stratum between masters and slaves. As neither slaves nor salaried workers in an export-based, slave economy, they were denied steady employment. The Portuguese state tried to repress them and subject them to the most menial and dangerous forms of occasional employment, including manning frontier forts and capturing Indians, runaway slaves, and criminals.

In the late nineteenth century, *marginalidade* became associated with vagabondage. It was linked to modernization, urbanization, social dislocation, racial discrimination, and the breakdown of traditional social controls such as personal honor and rural patronage. The crim-

inalization of socially deviant forms of behavior such as drunkenness, unemployment, and banditry, and of the Afro-Brazilian form of self-defense known as CAPOEIRA, provided a source of free labor that eased the transition from slavery. Persons guilty of these forms of social deviance were arrested and forced to labor on public works projects, for private landowners, or as army recruits as part of their social redemption. Marginality offered a structural challenge to political stability and public order, two values that the Brazilian Empire and First Republic held dear. Today "marginality" is still used to describe the criminal behavior of those on the fringes: the poor, the homeless, the racially mixed, and the unemployed.

PATRICIA ANN AUFDERHEIDE, *Order and Violence: Social Deviance and Social Control in Brazil, 1780–1840* (1976); LAURA DE MELLO E SOUSA, *Desclassificados do ouro. A pobreza mineira no século XVIII* (1982); BORIS FAUSTO, *Crime e cotidiano: A criminalidade em São Paulo* (1984); MARTHA KNISELY HUGGINS, *From Slavery to Vagrancy in Brazil* (1985).

JUDY BIEBER FREITAS

See also **Coronel, Coronelismo.**

MARIA I (*b.* 17 December 1734; *d.* 20 March 1816), queen of Portugal (1777–1816). Born in Lisbon, Maria I was the oldest of four children (all girls) born to the future King JOSÉ I of Portugal (reigned 1750–1777) and his Spanish queen, Mariana Vitória. As heir presumptive to the throne, Maria was given the title of princess of Beira at her birth. When her father became king, she inherited the title of princess of Brazil. On 6 June 1760, Princess Maria married her father's younger brother, Prince Pedro, and they established their residence at Queluz palace. For the most part, Maria was removed from affairs of state during her father's reign. The marquês de POMBAL had hopes that Maria would abdicate her right to the throne and Prince José, oldest son of Maria and Prince Pedro, would succeed his grandfather as king. However, this plan fell through. In February 1777, just days before José I died and Maria succeeded him as ruler of Portugal, Prince José, then fifteen years of age, married his mother's younger sister, thirty-year-old Princess Maria Francisca Benedita. Prince José died of smallpox a little more than a decade later in 1788, leaving his younger brother Prince João to inherit the throne as JOÃO VI.

Maria I's reign is frequently described as the *viradeira* (turnabout) because of the reversal of many of the policies promulgated by the marquês de Pombal, her father's chief minister. However, the extent of the changes has sometimes been exaggerated. Maria's husband, who was given the honor and title of King Pedro III, died in 1786. It is not known exactly when Maria began showing signs of mental illness, due possibly to the loss of her father, husband, and son within a short period. However, by late January or early February of 1792, it was clear that she was unable to rule. By a decree of 10 February of that year, her surviving son, Prince João, took over the government of Portugal but was not officially given the title of regent until 1799. In November of 1807, the insane queen accompanied the Portuguese court when it fled to Brazil during the French invasion of Portugal. She died in Rio de Janeiro.

CAETANO BEIRÃO's *D. Maria I, 1777–1792,* first published in 1934, has gone through a number of editions.

FRANCIS A. DUTRA

MARIA II (*b.* 4 April 1819; *d.* 15 November 1853), queen of Portugal (1834–1853). Maria da Glória was born in the Palace of São Cristóvão in Rio de Janeiro, the oldest child of Crown Prince Pedro and his wife, Archduchess Leopoldina, daughter of the emperor of Austria, Francis I. When Maria was three years old, her father became PEDRO I, emperor of Brazil. When Pedro's father, King JOÃO VI, died in Portugal on 10 March 1826, Pedro I of Brazil was acclaimed PEDRO IV of Portugal. Shortly after receiving this news, Pedro, while still in Brazil, drew up a constitutional charter for Portugal and promised to abdicate the Portuguese throne in favor of Maria da Glória, who was then seven years old, on the conditions that Maria marry her father's younger brother, Prince Miguel, an exile in Vienna, and that Miguel accept the new constitution. In the meantime, Pedro's younger sister, Isabel Maria, would continue to serve as regent of Portugal. Miguel pledged to marry his niece and observe the new constitution. On 29 October 1826, the betrothal took place in Vienna by proxy.

On 5 July 1828, Maria departed from Rio de Janeiro for Vienna in the charge of Brazilian-born Felisberto Caldeira Brant Pontes, first marquis of Barbacena, to complete her education under the watchful eye of her maternal grandfather. However, after arriving at Gibraltar on 2 September 1828, Maria discovered that her husband-to-be Prince Miguel, had returned to Portugal from exile and had been acclaimed king of Portugal by an absolutist-controlled traditional Portuguese *côrtes* of the three estates. Sailing on to England and later to France, Maria met resistance to her claim to the throne by governments of George IV of England and Charles X of France, who were wary of the constitutional liberalism inherent in Pedro's charter of 1826. Therefore, Maria da Glória, along with the marquis of Barbacena and her father's wife-to-be, AMÉLIA, returned to Brazil, arriving in Rio de Janeiro on 16 October 1829.

On 7 April 1831, Pedro I abdicated the Brazilian throne in favor of Maria's brother, his five-year-old son Pedro, and, along with the Empress Amélia, sailed for Europe in the English corvette *Volage* while Maria traveled on the French brig *La Seine.* On 18 September 1834, after years of bitter civil war, fifteen-year-old Maria da Glória was acclaimed Maria II, queen of Portugal, by the newly elected Portuguese *côrtes.* On 28 January 1835, she married Prince Auguste Beauharnais, duke of Leuchtenberg (brother of her father's second wife, Empress Amélia), who died two months later. On 9 April 1836, Queen Maria II married Prince Ferdinand of Saxe-Coburg-Gotha, who in 1837 assumed the title of King Ferdinand II of Portugal. Two of their sons were also kings of Portugal: Pedro V (reigned 1853–1861) and Luis I (reigned 1861–1889). After a troubled reign, Maria II died in Lisbon while giving birth to her eleventh child.

There is no biography of Maria II in English. However, there are numerous references to her early life in NEILL MACAULAY, *Dom Pedro: The Struggle for Liberty in Brazil and Portugal, 1798–1834* (1986). A convenient short biography in Portuguese is found in AFONSO EDUARD MARTINS ZUQUETE, ed., *Nobreza de Portugal e do Brasil,* vol. 2 (1960), pp. 51–78. Two lengthier biographies are JULIO DE SOUSA E COSTA, *D. Maria II* (1947), and ESTER DE LEMOS, *D. Maria II (A Rainha e a Mulher)* (1954).

FRANCIS A. DUTRA

MARIACHI, an ensemble usually consisting of three violins, a six-string guitar, a bass (*guitarrón*), and two trumpets; also a member of such a group. Although the exact origins of mariachis are disputed and are variously traced to the Coca Indians, the French Intervention serenaders, or to colonial string bands, they have come to be regarded as typically Mexican. Local bands flourished in the west-central state of Jalisco in the late 1800s. They began to travel during the 1910 revolution and later became popular over Radio XEW. Sometime between 1860 and 1930 Gaspar Vargas began the Mariachi Vargas (de Tecalitlán), which was continued and expanded by his son Sylvestre. Early band members played by ear, but later musicians read music, especially after Rubén Fuentes became the arranger.

In the 1940s village mariachis and popular mariachis diverged in style, although both remained wandering troubadours who played for tips. In the 1950s bands began to experiment with new instruments (marimba, harp, clarinet, accordion, and organ), diversify their repertory, and arrange their music for concert halls. The best-known tunes are "La Negra" and "Guadalajara."

See *New Grove Dictionary of Music* (1980); CLAES AF GEIJER-STAM, *Popular Music in Mexico* (1976).

GUY BENSUSAN

See also **Music: Popular Music and Dance.**

MARIÁTEGUI, JOSÉ CARLOS (*b.* 14 June 1894; *d.* 16 April 1930), Peruvian essayist and political thinker. Born in Moquegua to a poor family, he was able to obtain only a primary education. In 1909, Mariátegui began as copy boy at the Lima daily *La Prensa;* four years later he was promoted to reporter. He worked as a columnist at several newspapers until his departure for Europe in 1919. There, he broadened his education and married an Italian girl. Won over by Marxism, Mariátegui returned to Peru in 1923, where he became an

José Carlos Mariátegui. © A. C. CRITON / SYGMA.

Just as Mariátegui's perception of Marxism exerted influence on his religious ideas, so his religiosity in turn modified his political outlook; he added a mystical dimension to his interpretation of socialism. Religion acquired a new meaning: it became a belief in the supreme good, translated into revolutionary action. At the same time his eclectic-Marxist approach to literature led him beyond a strict analysis of a work. Mariátegui felt the need for a global perspective that would blend previously utilized points of view with the Marxist position on art. He was a Marxist when he viewed art as an economic superstructure, conditioned by class struggle and subject to the changes in the market of intellectual work. He was an eclectic when, compelled by his basic precepts, he adopted heterodox ideas to check dogmatism, arbitrary authority, and the presumed infallibility of the high priests of intelligence, art, and politics. Mariátegui's open-ended ideology and his eclectic methodology of analysis presaged for him the ushering in of a new art, consonant with the socialist society he envisioned.

JOSÉ CARLOS MARIÁTEGUI, *Seven Interpretive Essays on Peruvian Reality,* translated by Marjory Urguidi (1971); EUGENIO CHANG-RODRÍGUEZ, *Poética e ideología en José Carlos Mariátegui* (1983); ANTONIO MELIS, ed., *José Carlos Mariátegui: Correspondencia* (1984); HARRY E. VANDEN, *National Marxism in Latin America: José Carlos Mariátegui's Thought and Politics* (1986); EUGENIO CHANG-RODRÍGUEZ, "José Carlos Mariátegui," in *Latin American Writers* (1989), vol. 2, pp. 791–796.

EUGENIO CHANG-RODRÍGUEZ

outstanding leftist personality while earning his livelihood as a free-lance writer. His house became a meeting place for avant-garde intellectuals and artists, university students, and labor leaders before and after both his legs were amputated because of an illness dating from his childhood. In 1925 he and his brother established a publishing house that printed two of his books. Mariátegui's prestige rests primarily on his *Siete ensayos de interpretación de la realidad peruana* (1928), translated into several languages; his editorship of the journal *Amauta* (1926–1930), the organization of the Peruvian General Federation of Workers (1929), and the founding of the Socialist Party of Peru (1928).

Traditionally, more emphasis has been placed on Mariátegui's contributions to politics than on his literary writings of his early youth (1914–1919) and mature publications (1920–1930). Lately, however, his articles on cultural events, short stories, poems, and plays, all written before 1920, have been reappraised because certain constant elements of this period remained in his later works: profound religiosity, romantic antipositivism, antagonism toward academia, exaltation of heroism, and heterodoxy. During the last seven years of his life Mariátegui molded European ideological and aesthetic currents in order to conform them to his own preferences and originality.

MARIEL BOATLIFT, the massive exodus from April to September 1980 of over 125,000 Cubans to the United States and other countries. Beginning in Havana as a dispute between Cuba and other Latin American countries, especially Peru, over the granting of political asylum, a crisis developed when thousands of Cubans seeking asylum took refuge on the grounds of the Peruvian embassy in Havana. U.S. president Jimmy Carter denounced the Cuban government's refusal to allow asylum seekers to leave the country and pointed to the crowd on the grounds of the Peruvian embassy as an illustration of the unpopularity and bankruptcy of the Cuban regime.

Cuban president Fidel CASTRO responded by allowing all who wished to leave Cuba to do so via the port of Mariel on the northern coast of the island. To this end Castro allowed small boats from Florida to enter the Cuban port to carry asylum seekers back to the United States. This move clearly caught the Carter administration off guard and at first it declared that all Cubans illegally entering U.S. waters would either be returned to Cuba or jailed in the United States. The Cuban government seized on this policy and charged the Carter administration with hypocrisy. Caught by what many believed was a brilliant move by Castro, President Carter was forced to change policy and announce that the U.S. would accept all Cuban refugees.

Commercial fishing boat overloaded with Cuban refugees heading for Key West. Mariel boatlift, 4 June 1980. UPI / BETTMANN.

The Carter administration's reversal, however, only exacerbated the problem since it encouraged even greater numbers of Cubans to make the difficult crossing to Florida. In addition, Cuba further embarrassed the U.S. by allegedly releasing thousands of prison inmates and mentally handicapped Cubans from jails and hospitals and allowing them, too, to emigrate to the United States. This created an atmosphere of panic in those areas of the United States that received Mariel refugees. Coupled with outbreaks of violence in refugee camps in the United States, U.S. response to the Mariel boatlift was a major foreign policy blunder for the Carter administration and a clear victory for Castro and the Cuban government. Since so many of the refugees were young, Castro was able to convey to the youth at home the pitfalls of leaving Cuba, which included not only a dangerous sea crossing, but also hostility and imprisonment once they entered the United States. Because of the size of the Mariel exodus, it was the Carter administration, not the Cuban government, that was finally forced to halt the influx of Cuban refugees to the U.S.

KENNETH N. SKOUG, *The U.S.-Cuba Migration Agreement: Resolving Mariel* (1988); U.S. HOUSE OF REPRESENTATIVES, COMMITTEE ON THE JUDICIARY, SUBCOMMITTEE ON IMMIGRATION, REFUGEES, AND INTERNATIONAL LAW, *Mariel Cuban Detainees* (1988).

MICHAEL POWELSON

See also **Asylum and Refugees.**

MARIGHELA, CARLOS (Marighella; *b.* ca. 1904; *d.* 4 November 1969), Brazilian architect of Latin American urban guerrilla warfare. Marighela was born in Salvador, the son of an Italian immigrant and, on his mother's side, the descendant of African slaves. He studied engineering at the Salvador Polytechnic but dropped out. He joined the Brazilian Communist Party (PCB) in 1927 and was imprisoned after the party's attempted armed revolt of 1935. Released in 1937, Marighela moved to São Paulo.

Disenchanted with the party's conservatism, he urged violent revolution and a guerrilla struggle. He was elected a deputy from the state of São Paulo to the new Congress in 1946, but was forced underground following the ban on the PCB in 1947. His 1960 acceptance of an invitation to Havana extended to the PCB leadership, which they refused, initiated a break with the party that was complete by 1964. Having rejected the revolutionary theory made popular by Ernesto (Che) GUEVERA as too spontaneous, and therefore doomed to failure, Marighela founded the Action for National Liberation (ALN) in 1968. His "Mini-manual of the Urban Guerrilla," written in 1969 as a training manual for the ALN and other guerrilla groups, is a mechanistic theory of urban guerrilla warfare and the most famous document to emerge from the urban struggle in Brazil. Marighela was killed in a police ambush in São Paulo.

ROBERT MOSS, "Marighella: Letter from South America," in *Encounter* 39, no. 1 (1972): 40–43.

MICHAEL L. JAMES

MARIJUANA. *See* **Drugs and Drug Trade.**

MARIMBA, a percussion instrument consisting of parallel, graduated, tuned wooden bars that are struck with a mallet. Known as the national instrument of Guatemala, the marimba is also found in southern Mexico, Central America, Cuba, Colombia, Ecuador, Brazil, and Peru. In the controversy over the marimba's origin, the Central Americans are nationalistic, but the earliest documentation dates only to the 1680s. Scholarly opinion favors the theory of African descent because of the similarity with the African xylophone, the linguistic parallel between the Peruvian and the Bantu word for the instrument, and the lack of early archaeological evidence in America.

Marimbas evolved in America, using local woods and gourds for buzzing and resonation. A nineteenth-century variation substituted wooden boxes for gourds, and another variation used a shoulder strap instead of supporting legs. In the 1890s the early diatonic tuning was modified into the fully chromatic scale played on the *marimba doble* by the Hurtado brothers (The Royal Marimba Band). The *grande* has eighty bars and is played by four musicians, while the *cuache* has fifty bars and is played by three. Village marimbas still use the older diatonic scale, while acculturated Indians prefer the chromatic scale and the popular and international repertory. Beginning in the late 1970s a revival of folk groups in Chile and Peru, which spread to Ecuador, Bolivia, Colombia, Venezuela, Mexico, the United States, and Europe, featured players such as Zeferino Nandayapa, who adapted Bach, Mozart, and Handel for use in concert halls as well as for television and commercial recordings.

See listings in *New Grove Dictionary of Music* (1980); F. MACCALUM, *The Book of the Marimba* (1968).

GUY BENSUSAN

MARINELLO, JUAN (*b.* 2 November 1898; *d.* 27 March 1977), Cuban poet and essayist. Marinello was born in Jicotea in Las Villas Province and received degrees in public and civil law from the University of Havana, where he was an outstanding student, receiving a scholarship for a year at Madrid's Central University (1921–1922). He was politically active from his student days, organizing and taking part in student protests and groups. He was among the founders of the Hispano-Cuban Culture Institution (1926) and the publication *Revista de avance* (1927). He was imprisoned repeatedly for his political activities, especially during the regimes of Cuban presidents Gerardo MACHADO and Fulgencio BATISTA. A life-long dedicated Communist and political activist, he embraced the Cuban Revolution of 1959 and in turn was wholeheartedly supported and promoted by the CASTRO regime until his death. Marinello became president of the University of Havana in 1962 and Cuban ambassador to UNESCO in 1963; he was elected by the Central Committee of the Cuban Communist Party to help draft the constitution of the Cuban socialist state. He also received such international honors as the Lenin Medal (1970) and was a part of the executive council of UNESCO in 1974. Although Marinello cultivated poetry in his youth, he is mostly known today for his essays and literary criticism. He compiled several anthologies on Cuban literary giant José MARTÍ, whose prose deeply influenced him. His best-known works are the essays *Españolidad literaria de José Martí* (1942), *Creación y revolución* (1973), and *Escritos sociales* (1980).

MARÍA LUISA ANTUÑA, *Bibliografía de Juan Marinello* (1975); "Cuba, les étapes d'une liberation: hommage a Juan Marinello et Noël Saloman," Actes du Colloque International des 22, 23 et 24 Novembre 1978 (Toulouse, 1979).

ROBERTO VALERO

MARINHO, ROBERTO (*b.* 1905), owner of the Globo Group. With a net worth of $1 billion, he is the third richest man in Brazil. This fortune is derived primarily from the TV Globo Network, other media, computer and telecommunications firms, as well as real estate and insurance companies (100 companies total in the group). He founded *O Globo*, one of the four main newspapers in Brazil, and Radio Globo, one of the most popular radio stations in Rio de Janeiro. In 1962, Marinho established TV Globo in joint venture with Time-Life. In 1968, after considerable controversy, that arrangement was found to violate the Brazilian Constitution and Time-Life was bought out by Marinho, who now owns 100 percent of TV Globo. By 1968, TV Globo had the first true network with simulcast programs in Brazil and began a dominance of audience ratings that has continued until today, although competition has grown. TV Globo was favored with military government advertising and infrastucture, such as satellite and microwave links.

The Brazilian managers Marinho hired took advantage of the growing Brazilian advertising market and built up a television production system that has been compared with the old Hollywood studios. TV Globo often produces twelve or more hours of programming a day for itself, including *telenovelas* (prime-time serials), music, news, comedy, public affairs, and talk shows. The Globo Group has expanded into records (Som Livre), magazines (*Globo Rural*, comic books), video and film distribution (Globo Video), and direct satellite broadcasting (GloboSat).

Marinho has moved into telecommunications and information technologies through joint ventures with NEC of Japan in areas including cellular telephony and a bid for the second generation of Brazilian telecommunications satellites. His charitable foundation, Fundação Roberto Marinho, produces television programs for education and funds historical preservation.

JOSEPH STRAUBHAAR, "Brazilian Television: The Decline of American Influence," in *Communication Research* 11 (April 1984): 221–240.

JOSEPH STRAUBHAAR

MARIÑO, SANTIAGO (*b.* 25 July 1788; *d.* 4 September 1854), Venezuelan Independence leader. From 1811 to 1821 the aristocratic General Mariño led patriot forces against Spanish rule, especially in his native eastern Venezuela, where he was the most powerful caudillo. Although he several times sought to assert his independence from Simón BOLÍVAR, Mariño served under him for many years and was Bolívar's chief of staff at the battle of CARABOBO (1821), which assured Venezuela's

independence from Spain. Later he was elected vice president of the ill-fated Gran Colombia confederation. After he lost the 1834 election for president of Venezuela, he rebelled unsuccessfully against the government of José María VARGAS (1835–1836). Defeated for the presidency again in 1850, Mariño closed his career as a caudillo by participating in the Revolution of May (1853) that sought to overthrow José Gregorio MONAGAS.

JULIO CÁRDENAS RAMÍREZ and CARLOS SAENZ DE LA CALZADA, eds., *Diccionario biográfico de Venezuela* (1953); CARACCIOLO PARRA PÉREZ, *Mariño y la independencia de Venezuela*, 5 vols. (Madrid, 1954–1957); GUILLERMO MORÓN, *A History of Venezuela* (1964); JESÚS MANUEL SUBERO, *En defensa del General Santiago Mariño* (1975).

WINFIELD J. BURGGRAAFF
INÉS QUINTERO

MARISOL (Marisol Escobar; *b.* 1930), Venezuelan pop art sculptor. Born in Paris to Venezuelan parents, Marisol traveled with them in Europe until 1935; the family subsequently commuted between the United States and Venezuela. She moved to Los Angeles in 1946 and then to New York City, where she studied with Yasao Kuniyoshi and Hans Hofmann. In 1954 she turned from painting to terra-cotta sculpture inspired by pre-Columbian art. Since 1960 she has been best known for her portrayals of modern life and famous people in multifigure ensembles that blend media images, found objects, and blocky materials. Her statues use painted

Self-Portrait by Marisol in wood, plaster, marker, paint, graphite, human teeth, gold, and plastic. 1961–1962. COLLECTION MUSEUM OF CONTEMPORARY ART, CHICAGO.

wood figures with other items, such as doorknobs, locks, or plaster. All of her works combine fantasy with reality, the grotesque with the humorous.

WORCESTER, MASSACHUSETTS, ART MUSEUM, *Marisol* (1971), an exhibition catalog; *Marisol* (1974), catalog of an exhibition at Ohio University and the Columbus Gallery of Fine Arts; ROBERT CREELEY, *Presences* (1976); NANCY GROVE, *Magical Mixtures: Marisol Portrait Sculpture* (1991), an exhibition catalog.

WINTHROP R. WRIGHT

MARKHAM, CLEMENTS ROBERT (*b.* 20 July 1830; *d.* 30 January 1916), British writer, translator, geographer, and historian. Born in Stillingfleet, Yorkshire, Markham was the son of the Reverend David F. and Catherine Markham. He studied at Westminster School and then, in 1844, he entered the navy.

Markham traveled and studied widely in Latin America and Asia. He spent a year in Peru (1852–1853), where he examined Inca ruins, learned the Quechua and Spanish languages, and translated some materials into English. He served as secretary (1858–1886) and later president (1889–1909) of the Hakluyt Society and translated and edited twenty-two books for that organization. He was also elected secretary (1863–1888) and president (1893–1905) of the Royal Geographical Society. In 1892, Markham wrote his *History of Peru*. Meanwhile, he sought to use some of what he learned in Peru to assist British development in India. In addition, he studied the irrigation systems of southeastern Spain. Critics claimed that while he had a remarkable career and eventually was knighted by the British government, his interests were too diverse and his work sometimes weakened by spreading himself too thin over too wide an academic area.

ALBERT H. MARKHAM, *The Life of Sir Clements R. Markham* (1917); BAILEY W. DIFFIE, ''A Markham Contribution to the Leyenda Negra,'' in *Hispanic American Historical Review* 16 (1936): 96–103; HARRY BERNSTEIN and BAILEY W. DIFFIE, *Sir Clements R. Markham as a Translator* (1937).

JACK RAY THOMAS

MÁRMOL, JOSÉ PEDRO CRISÓLOGO (*b.* 2 December 1817; *d.* 9 August 1871), Argentine poet, novelist, and journalist. Born in Buenos Aires, Mármol became one of the main literary figures of his time in the fight against the tyranny of General Juan Manuel de ROSAS. His works include *El poeta: Drama en cinco actos en verso* (1842), *A Rosas el 25 de mayo* (1843), *Amalia* (in two parts, 1844, 1850), and *Cantos del peregrino* (1846–1847). Most of his works were published in Uruguay. His complete works, including *Armonías* and *El cruzado, drama en cinco actos,* were published posthumously. His novel *Amalia* is considered one of the classics of Spanish American literature. It portrays life in Buenos Aires during the dictatorial regime of Juan Manuel de Rosas from the viewpoint of the opposition (the Unitarios).

Mármol suffered financial hardship during his childhood (the years he lived in Montevideo, his mother's city of origin) and after his mother's death in Brazil. His father distanced himself from his son, who returned to Buenos Aires and began his studies at the University of Buenos Aires.

In 1839, Mármol was jailed by the Rosas regime. In 1840 he was back in Montevideo, where he joined Esteban Echeverría's group of patriots in their fight against the Rosas government in Buenos Aires. His literary mentor was Juan Cruz VARELA, who also became his friend and supporter. Works from this period deal with the political battles against the tyranny of Rosas as well as with disagreements among the three political groups fighting Rosas: the Unitarios, the older political theoreticians among the Federales, and Echeverría's group, the Young Argentine Generation. In Rio de Janeiro, Mármol met Juan Bautista ALBERDI, who was returning from a trip to Europe. Alberdi convinced Mármol to go to Chile, where he could be more effective in the fight against Rosas, but Marmol's ship was not able to reach Chile. This experience is the source of his *Cantos del peregrino* (Songs of the Pilgrim).

After his abortive trip to Chile, Mármol returned to Brazil, where he remained until 1846. His exile, as well as that of his peers, ended in 1852, when Rosas was defeated by General Justo José de Urquiza's army in the battle of Caseros. During the years that followed, he wrote many articles on political issues, but he never completed the unfinished cantos of the *Cantos del peregrino*. Appointed director of the Public Library of Buenos Aires in 1858 (a post he held until his death), Mármol was much admired as the heir to the political ideas of Esteban ECHEVERRÍA. He is an important writer of the generation of the Romantics, whose life and work centered on beliefs in liberty and democracy for Argentina and South America.

STUART CUTHBERTSON, *The Poetry of José Mármol* (1935); DELFÍN LEOCADIO GARASA, ''José Mármol,'' in *Latin American Writers*, edited by Carlos A. Solé and Maria Isabel Abreu, vol. 1 (1989).

MAGDALENA GARCÍA PINTO

MAROONS (CIMARRÓNES), African fugitive slaves. *Marronage*—the flight of enslaved men and women from the harsh discipline, overwork, and malnutrition associated primarily with plantations—was a common occurrence in the Americas and Caribbean from the sixteenth through the nineteenth centuries. Originally believed to be of Spanish origin (*cimarrón*; French *marron*), the term ''maroon'' is now thought to derive from a Hispaniola TAINO root meaning ''fugitive,'' which converged with the Spanish *cimá* (mountaintop). The term was originally applied to livestock in the Hispaniola hills and to fugitive Amerindian slaves.

Grand marronage (desertion leading to the establishment of permanent, autonomous settlements on the fringes of plantations or in remote forest, swamp, or mountain areas) must be distinguished from *petit marronage* (individual absenteeism or permanent flight from country to town or sea, from one colonial society to another, where the fugitive could pass for free). This discussion concentrates on *grand marronage,* since neither absentees nor urban and maritime fugitives separated themselves permanently from the slaveowner's society.

Known variously as QUILOMBOS (Jaga *ki-lombo,* "war camp"), *mocambos* (Mbundu *mu-kambo,* "hideout"), and *palenques* (palisades or stockades), Maroon settlements developed from the southern United States to South America. Maroon communities were more numerous and longer-lived in territories where enslaved Africans vastly outnumbered Europeans.

Maroons developed a variety of military, social, and political relations with Amerindians as allies, domestic slaves, spouses, and advisers of chiefs. In northern Ecuador, for instance, the republic of ESMERALDAS emerged in the sixteenth century from the wreckage of a slave ship whose slave passengers escaped and settled among Amerindians. Their ZAMBO, or Afro-Amerindian offspring, dominated the new state. In sixteenth-century Venezuela, fugitive slave miners lived peacefully with the Jirajara on the San Pedro River in the first of numerous Maroon settlements uniting Africans and Amerindians. African Maroons and their Afro-Carib offspring came to dominate the Carib on the island of St. Vincent. In other instances, such as the Amerindian Miskito of Nicaragua and Honduras and Florida's Seminoles, Amerindians enslaved African fugitives. In the Seminole case, Maroons retained a separate identity and acted as political advisers. In other cases, however, Amerindians assisted Europeans in capturing or killing Maroons and destroying their communities.

Founded by west, central, and east Africans, Maroon societies blended many African, Amerindian, and European cultural traditions in ways based on the contemporary colonial situation, one aspect of which was the disproportion between women and men resulting from the slave trade, as well as from the low fertility of women in monocultural plantation environments. As long as Maroons remained at war with Europeans, the hardships of warfare and bush life tended to suppress fertility. Maroon men tried to solve the shortage of women by kidnapping women for wives, a major reason for raids on plantations and Amerindian settlements. Peaceful Maroon relations with Amerindians provided alternative access to wives, and one of the benefits of peace between Maroon communities and colonial states was a rise in the Maroon birthrate and a corresponding increase in the female Maroon population.

Their initial scarcity enhanced the value of Maroon women. As farmers and processors of food, women were responsible for the Maroon food supply. Women presided over Maroon villages; they assumed responsibility for children and the elderly while young men engaged in hunting, surveillance, war, and later in migrant wage labor that took them from the villages.

Females exercised authority through their role as spirit mediums. In the 1730s, an eastern Jamaican Maroon woman, Nanny, founded Nanny Town, later Moore Town, in the Blue Mountains, as a women's and children's refuge from English attacks. Maroons consider Nanny the greatest female Maroon sorcerer, crediting her with repulsing the English by supernatural means and averting Maroon starvation with pumpkin seeds obtained from the spirit world. In Suriname, 80 percent of the mediums of the three main Djuka Maroon spirit cults were women.

Like spirit mediums, twentieth-century female composers also enunciated women's grievances. Indeed, a career as a renowned singer preceded Ma Fiida's rise to leadership in the male-dominated Gaan Gadu cult. With lyrics expressing love and happiness tempered by sadness, rejection, jealousy, and despair, songs provided outlets for female grievances and aggression and brought fame and status to female composer-singers.

In spite of occasional male-female conflicts, Maroons maintained sufficient unity for the task of self-defense. They established stockaded, booby-trapped settlements of various sizes, strategically located in inaccessible swamps and forests or on hills or mountains. Networks of slave and Amerindian allies provided intelligence to Maroons and acted as middlemen in the exchange of Maroon produce and goods for arms and tools. Slaveowners and state officials feared Maroon raids, desertion of laborers, and the undermining of slave discipline.

Europeans counterattacked by passing fugitive slave acts, offering bounties for captured fugitives, and by dispatching armed units, including specially commissioned slave, free black, and Amerindian soldiers. Captured Maroons incurred severe punishment including imprisonment and execution, hamstringing, wearing of spiked metal collars, and deportation. Marronage could not be eradicated, however. Some settlements were destroyed, but others emerged and many have survived until the present time. Many Maroon groups forced colonial authorities to negotiate peace treaties that recognized Maroon semiautonomy and ceded land to Maroons in return for their cooperation in suppressing slave rebellions and hunting slave fugitives.

The extent of Maroon cooperation with European authorities varied, and peace treaties were broken repeatedly by both sides. Suriname's Maroons continued to welcome new fugitive slaves, for instance, and the Brazilian government and the seventeenth-century Maroon state of PALMARES frequently broke peace treaties until the final conquest of Palmares in 1697.

Mature Maroon communities developed complex economies. They grew a wide variety of fruits and vegetables, including rice, and often harvested surpluses. They also produced forest products like timber, salt, and palm wine, as well as building materials and utensils, hammocks, ropes, and beeswax candles. What they did not make they acquired by trade, developing widespread commercial networks with slaves, free people of color, and European settlers.

From the late nineteenth century, colonial economic development began to encroach on many Maroon communities, drawing them into the economic life of colonies and republics and, in some cases, depriving them of their lands. Colombia's San Basilio remained isolated until the early twentieth century, when men began to work in the expanding sugar industry and on the Panama Canal. Cuba's eastern Maroons played an important role in the island's first and second wars of independence in 1868 and 1899, only to lose their farms to North American land speculators and sugar companies and to be ousted from the labor market by Spanish and West Indian immigrants. They rebelled unsuccessfully in 1912. Post–World War II bauxite mining and dam construction proletarianized and displaced Suriname Maroons, alienating them from the urban ruling class. Between 1986 and 1991, Maroons formed the insurrectionary Jungle Commando, which gained control of most of southern and eastern Suriname. Their fate remains uncertain since their leader, Ronnie Brunswijk, negotiated a secret peace with the Suriname government in 1991.

JOSÉ LUCIANO FRANCO, *Los palenques de los negros cimarrones* (1973); ANGELINA POLLAK-ELTZ, "Slave Revolts in Venezuela," in *Comparative Perspectives on Slavery in New World Plantation Societies*, edited by Vera Rubin and Arthur Tuden (1977), pp. 439–445; RICHARD PRICE, ed., *Maroon Societies: Rebel Slave Communities in the Americas* (1979); KENNETH M. BILBY and FILOMENA CHIOMA STEADY, "Black Women and Survival: A Maroon Case," in *The Black Woman Cross-Culturally*, edited by Filomena Chioma Steady (1981), pp. 451–467; RICHARD PRICE, *First Time: The Historical Vision of an Afro-American People* (1983); SALLY PRICE, *Co-wives and Calabashes* (1984); GAD HEUMAN, ed., *Out of the House of Bondage: Runaways, Resistance, and Marronage in Africa and the New World* (1986); JUAN JOSÉ ARROM and MANUEL A. GARCIA ARÉVALO, *Cimarron* (1986); MAVIS CAMPBELL, *The Maroons of Jamaica, 1655–1796* (1988); H.U.E. THODEN VAN VELZEN and W. VAN WETERING, *The Great Father and the Danger: Religious Cults, Material Forces, and Collective Fantasies in the World of the Surinamese Maroons* (1988).

MONICA SCHULER

See also **Slave Revolts.**

MARQUÉS, RENÉ (b. 4 October 1919; d. 22 March 1979), Puerto Rican author. René Marqués showed an early interest in theater and cinema as a child in his native Arecibo. While studying drama at Columbia University, he wrote *Palm Sunday* (1956) in English; the book deals with a tragic episode in Puerto Rico's history. After returning to his homeland, Marqués began a seventeen-year association with the Department of Education's community education program in 1950 as a writer and head of the publishing section. In 1958 the Puerto Rico Athenaeum awarded him first prize in four genres: short story, novel, essay, and drama. Marqués taught courses and theater workshops at the University of Puerto Rico, in Río Piedras.

Marqués's first staged work was *El sol y los MacDonald* (The sun and the MacDonald Family, 1950), a tragedy set in the southern United States. His most celebrated work is *La carreta* (The oxcart, 1952), about the trials of a family displaced from rural Puerto Rico to the island's capital and then to New York. Another masterwork of intense national and poetic symbolism is *Los soles truncos* (The truncated suns), staged in the First Puerto Rican Theater Festival in 1958. Historical events are featured in *La muerte no entrará en palacio* (Death shall not enter the palace, 1958) and *Mariana o el alba* (Mariana or the dawn, 1965); biblical events in *Sacrificio en el Monte Moriah* (Sacrifice on Mount Moriah, 1969) and *David y Jonatán. Tito y Berenice* (1970); and futuristic events in *El apartamento* (The apartment, 1965).

Marqués's writings, which include essays and criticism, theater, movie scripts, short stories, poetry, and a novel, show deep concern with the destiny of Puerto Rico and its dependence on the United States. The problem of national identity and cultural conflict is likewise central to his innovative books of short stories, *Otro día nuestro* (Another day, 1955), *En una ciudad llamada San Juan* (In a city called San Juan, 1960 and 1970), and *Inmersos en el silencio* (Immersed in silence, 1976).

CHARLES PILDITCH, *René Marqués: A Study of His Fiction* (1977); ELEANOR J. MARTIN, *René Marqués* (1979); BONNIE HILDEBRAND REYNOLDS, *Space, Time, and Crisis: The Theatre of René Marqués* (1988).

ESTELLE IRIZARRY

MARQUESADO DEL VALLE DE OAXACA, the vast estate encompassing 23,000 indigenous vassals granted by the crown to Hernán CORTÉS in 1529. By the end of the sixteenth century, the marquesses enjoyed the rights to tribute, justice, and administration in seven major jurisdictions: Charo, Coyoacán, Cuatro Villas de Oaxaca, Cuernavaca, Jalapa, Toluca, and Tuxtla. The marquessate's administrative structure was very similar to the royal government's, and until 1771 its indigenous citizens had recourse to either bureaucracy. The *estado*, as the marquessate was also known, was frequently embroiled in litigation concerning the exact scope of the grant, and it was sequestered by the crown on several occasions. In 1629 the marquessate passed to the fourth marquess's niece, wife of the duke of Terranova, and by the end of the century, by a similar process, into the hands of the Neapolitan Pignatellis, the dukes of Monteleone. Thereafter, the marquesses, and the dukes of Terranova and Monteleone, resided in Spain and Italy, leaving the direction of the state to its chief administrator in Mexico.

The marquessate weathered the wars of independence and early national period with difficulty, and in 1825 the duke of Monteleone and Terranova asked his friend, Lucas ALAMÁN, to oversee the liquidation of the estate, which was completed by the end of 1849.

An excellent source for the administrative history of the marquessate is WOODROW BORAH, *Justice by Insurance: The General Indian Court of Colonial Mexico and the Legal Aides of the Half-Real* (1983). There have been studies of several of the *estado*'s jurisdictions and enterprises, including WARD BARRETT, *The Sugar Hacienda of the Marqueses del Valle* (1970); G. MICHEAL RILEY, *Fernando Cortés and the Marquesado in Morelos, 1522–1547* (1973); CHERYL ENGLISH MARTIN, *Rural Society in Colonial Morelos* (1985); and ROBERT HASKETT, *Indigenous Rulers: An Ethnohistory of Town Government in Colonial Cuernavaca* (1991). The basic study of the estate remains BERNARDO GARCÍA MARTÍNEZ, *El marquesado del Valle: Tres siglos de régimen señorial en Nueva España* (1969).

ROBERT HASKETT

MÁRQUEZ, JOSÉ IGNACIO DE (*b.* 7 September 1793; *d.* 21 March 1880), president of New Granada (1837–1840). Born in Boyacá, Márquez received a law degree from the Colegio de San Bartolomé in Bogotá at age twenty. In 1821 he served in the Congress of Cúcuta and was elected presiding officer. In 1830–1831, Márquez served as finance secretary, and his 1831 *Memoria de hacienda* stands as the classic statement of protectionist thought in nineteenth-century Colombia. From March to October 1832, Márquez served as acting president pending the return to New Granada of Francisco de Paula SANTANDER, whereupon he assumed the vice presidency. In 1837 he was elected president by the Congress after a bitterly divisive three-way contest against José María OBANDO and Vicente Azuero. Although Márquez was a sound administrator with some mildly progressive ideas, his presidency was poisoned by the rivalry between his ministerial grouping and the defeated *progresistas* gathered around Santander. Márquez's purge of *progresista* officials further exacerbated political tensions. In 1839 a rebellion erupted in the southwestern Pasto region, initially directed against a Márquez decree on the suppression of small convents, but which soon came under the leadership of Obando. Throughout 1840 other regional rebellions, known collectively as the WAR OF THE SUPREMES and led by quasi-retired military men and disgruntled local elites, snowballed into a major crisis for the Márquez regime, especially after Santander's death in May 1840 removed a major brake on *progresista* intrigues. On 7 October 1840, after receiving news of a government defeat at Polonia (near Socorro in the northeast), Márquez temporarily stepped down from the presidency—ostensibly for health reasons—but resurfaced in Popayán two weeks later, rallying government forces. Márquez never returned to office, but by early 1842 the rebellions were defeated. He later served as representative for Tunja (1842–1845), interior secretary (1845–1846), and senator for Bogotá (1847–1850).

CARLOS CUERVO MÁRQUEZ, *Vida del doctor José Ignacio de Márquez*, 2 vols. (1917).

RICHARD STOLLER

MÁRQUEZ, LEONARDO (*b.* 1820; *d.* 1913), Mexican general. His military career began in the 1830s in the Texas campaign. During the War of the Reform (1858–1860), he fought on the side of the Conservatives and later to support the monarchy of MAXIMILIAN during the period of the FRENCH INTERVENTION (1862–1867). He is best known for three episodes: his order to execute captured Liberal officers and some doctors and medical students after the battle of Tacubaya (11 April 1859), an act that earned him the nickname of "Tiger of Tacubaya"; his 1861 orders to execute Melchor OCAMPO, leading Liberal statesman, and General Leandro Valle; and his role in the mid-1867 siege of Querétaro, where he left Maximilian to find reinforcements and never returned, thus leaving the emperor to his fate. After the fall of the Empire, Márquez went into exile in Cuba. He returned to Mexico in the 1890s, but upon the ouster of Porfirio DÍAZ, he went back to Havana, where he died three years later.

LEONARDO MÁRQUEZ, *Manifiestos (el imperio y los imperiales)* (1904); JESÚS DE LEÓN TORAL, *Historia militar: la intervención francesa en México* (1962).

CHARLES R. BERRY

MARRIAGE AND DIVORCE. Throughout the colonial period, the nurturance and preservation of marriage and the family in Latin America was a primary concern of the state and the Catholic church. While the state provided a legal basis for the family and for intrafamily relations, the church watched over the morality of gender relations and of women. In the case of women, their "predestination" to marriage and the domestic sphere was sanctioned by the church. Ecclesiastical courts dealt meticulously and at length with cases of marital abandonment, adultery, concubinage, bigamy, incest, and dispensation of consanguinity for marriage.

Marriage rites in Latin America were both complicated and expensive during the colonial period and most of the nineteenth century. Many persons avoided or delayed marriage, forming consensual unions instead. Although a woman's honor was said to be "lost" if she entered a premarital sexual relationship, the frequency of such relationships was high. Often women entered into premarital involvements because of the promise of marriage, which was legally binding. After deflowering a woman, a man who wished (or was forced) to marry her would request dispensation from the impediment of previous sexual relationships from ecclesiastical authorities. The argument often used to support his petition was that the woman would otherwise be dishonored.

Contract or ceremony of marriage in seventeenth-century Peru. Note Jesuits presiding and indigenous leaders observing. HARTH-TERRÉ COLLECTION, LATIN AMERICAN LIBRARY, TULANE UNIVERSITY.

The "morality argument" was also helpful in circumventing the consanguinity limits for spouses. Canon law did not allow marriages within four degrees of kinship or between ritual kin. However, endogamous marriages within elite Latin American families represented a common strategy to consolidate property and for political mobilization. These marriages between cousins or between uncles and nieces, were not "unequal" marriages. Although the church objected to them on moral grounds, in most cases ecclesiastical authorities were less concerned about consanguineous marriages than they were about irregular sexual relationships and illegitimate births. This order of concern is obvious from the dispensation records. For example, in nineteenth-century Chile, three-fourths of couples seeking the dispensation of consanguineous impediments cited sexual involvement as a justification, and half of these had conceived at least one child. After presumably "debasing" the woman, the man would use stereotyped arguments of a potentially worse fate for the woman and assume the role of her savior through marriage.

During the nineteenth century marriage continued to be practiced mainly by an elite minority in Latin America. For example, studies of several nineteenth-century cities find that from 20 to 60 percent of births were illegitimate. These patterns existed because of insufficient clergy available to conduct marriages, the high costs of marriage, parent-child conflicts over marriage choices and inheritance, and power inequities related to gender and race. An example of the latter from nineteenth-century Cuba is that of poor, colored women who often preferred a consensual union with a higher-class male to marriage with a man of their own class, because the former could support them. While changes occurred at different rates among specific countries, more socially conscious governments in the twentieth century spurred an expansion in legal marriages through increased social rewards for married citizens such as social security, family allowances, and health care. Other changes, often associated with the expansion of education, were a higher age of marriage (or coupling), and a decline in fertility and illegitimacy.

The history of interracial marriages has provoked sharp debate among scholars. Most believe that race had declined as a criterion of social status in the eighteenth century, a view consistent with the increased occurrence of interracial marriage for all races. However, several studies suggest that race continued to be a significant constraint on marital choice and that endogamous unions continued to be favored. These studies emphasize the continuation of substantial endogamy among Spaniards and among Indians at the end of the eighteenth century.

Changes in mating and reproductive practices in Latin America during modernization are consonant with the directions of change elsewhere in the modern world. In spite of these changes, the most common sexual relationship in Latin America continues to be the "visiting" relationship, in which a woman usually has her own house (though occasionally she lives with her parents) at the same time that she receives some financial or "in kind" support from her male companion; children are very

531

common in these relationships. The second most common sexual relationship in Latin America is the consensual union which is like marriage, except that it is not formalized. Nevertheless, the proportion who legally marry at some age is growing. Illegitimacy is also declining, though undoubtedly the data understate its incidence. In many countries the increase in legal civil marriage is associated with advantages related to taxes, subsidies, and inheritance. Moreover, women with university educations are marrying later and having fewer children, whereas men are generally marrying somewhat earlier.

Research on Colombia, Peru, Panama, Jamaica, and Trinidad indicates both that visiting and consensual unions have some stability and financial and social cooperation built into them, and that marriage is by far the most stable form of relationship. First relationships, particularly those of rural teenage females, are especially volatile, no matter what form they take. In Jamaica the visiting relationship is practiced by all classes, often as a prelude to marriage.

Many women express a preference for the visiting relationship over common-law marriage because common-law unions "demand" too much, and men fail to take responsibility for their children. They support marriage because of the "respectability" it confers and the legal benefits it gives children. However, women express fear of being victims of their partners' violent behavior and abuse even in marriage. A common view supporting the visiting relationship is that women under thirty are considered old enough to have children but not old enough for a committed relationship. Frequently the woman continues living with her parents, who are heavily involved in the socialization and care of the grandchild or grandchildren.

Family values in the lower classes, but also in the middle and upper classes, include different priorities of relationships for men and women. Scholars assert that lower-class children in Venezuela and Chile are bound more to their mothers than to their fathers, and stay with their mothers if the marriage dissolves. Men may desert their families; instances of maternal desertion are rare and subject to severe criticism. Children of single mothers are frequently reared by their maternal grandmothers while their mothers work outside the home as domestics.

Some authors assert that a son is expected to care for his parents in their old age, whereas a young woman's first obligation is to her husband. Men have greater obligations to their mothers and sisters than to their fathers, wives, or their own children. Female-headed households are more likely to be extended or complex households (including nonrelated members) than are couple-headed households, which implies the frequent presence of aged parents within female-headed households, often partly to assist with child care.

It is not obvious from the literature that elderly parents would receive more assistance from sons than from single, divorced, or widowed daughters. What is probably true is that sons are more likely to give financial support to their parents in times of need, while daughters will offer a place to live or companionship and care. Daughters also are more likely to be able to profit from the child care offered by parents while they work.

During the colonial period, divorce was not allowed by the Catholic crowns of Spain and Portugal. Unhappy marriages might be dissolved either through annulment (usually available only if a marriage had not been consummated) or through a separation of board and bed. There were numerous suits in Brazil and in Spanish America of the latter type, predominantly instituted by women because of desertion, physical violence, or lack of support. The return of the dowry was a major issue in many cases, since the dowry was supposed to provide security for the woman. Civil codes allowing divorce and remarriage have been enacted in most countries of Latin America in the twentieth century, some very recently. However, divorce has not been easy or common, and women and men have often been treated differently by the law. For example, although adultery was considered a cause of divorce by the Mexican Constitution of 1917, a wife's adultery always constituted a cause of divorce, a husband's only in certain cases. This difference in treatment was not corrected until the Civil Code of 1985.

VERENA MARTÍNEZ-ALIER, *Marriage, Class, and Colour in Nineteenth-Century Cuba: A Study of Racial Attitudes and Sexual Values in a Slave Society* (1974); SILVIA ARROM, *La mujer mexicana ante el divorcio eclesiastico (1800–1857)* (1976); *Journal of Family History*, special issues on Latin America: 3, no. 4 (1978), 10, no. 3 (1985), and 16, no. 3 (1991); ASUNCIÓN LAVRIN, "In Search of the Colonial Woman in Mexico: The Seventeenth and Eighteenth Centuries," in *Latin American Women: Historical Perspectives*, edited by Asunción Lavrin (1978), pp. 4–23; ROBERT MC CAA, *Marriage and Fertility in Chile: Demographic Turning Points in the Petorca Valley, 1840–1976* (1983); ELIZABETH KUZNESOF, "Household and Family Studies," in K. Lynn Stoner, ed., *Latinas of the Americas: A Source Book* (1989), pp. 305–388; ASUNCIÓN LAVRIN, ed., *Sexuality and Marriage in Colonial Latin America* (1989); RAMÓN A. GUTIÉRREZ, *When Jesus Came, the Corn Mothers Went Away: Marriage, Sexuality and Power in New Mexico, 1500–1846* (1991).

ELIZABETH KUZNESOF

See also **Family.**

MARROQUÍN, FRANCISCO (*b.* ca. 1499; *d.* 9 April 1563), first bishop of Guatemala (1537–1563). Probably a native of Santander, Spain, Marroquín was a diocesan priest and a protégé of Francisco García de Loaysa, bishop of Osma and president of the COUNCIL OF THE INDIES. In 1528, when Juan de ZUMÁRRAGA was named bishop of Mexico, Marroquín accompanied him to the New World. At the invitation of Pedro de ALVARADO, he settled in Guatemala in 1530 and served as a parish priest there. In 1532, Marroquín was appointed bishop

Portrait of Francisco Marroquín from the Palacio Arzobispal, Guatemala City. PHOTO COURTESY OF CHRISTOPHER LUTZ / CIRMA.

3 November 1898), president of Colombia (31 July 1900– 7 August 1904). Marroquín, a member of the upper class, is better remembered for his literary achievements than for his political performance. As a writer, he was concerned with form as well as substance, and published works on Spanish poetics and rhetoric. His poetry has been hailed as charming and assured. He was a charter member of the Mosaico group of *costumbristas* ("sketch of manners" writers) and probably was the best of them, employing gentle satire to prod and instruct his readers. He was also a novelist; his best-loved work in that genre, *El Moro* (1897), is a sentimental tale about a horse. As president and nominal head of a disintegrating faction of the Conservatives, Marroquín had the ill fortune to preside ineffectually over a Colombia being torn apart by the WAR OF THE THOUSAND DAYS (1899–1903) and dismembered by the U.S.-sponsored secession of PANAMA (1903).

JOSÉ MANUEL MARROQUÍN OSORIO, *Don José Manuel Marroquín íntimo* (1915); FRANK M. DUFFEY, *The Early Cuadro de Costumbres in Colombia* (1956), pp. 59–67; CHARLES W. BERGQUIST, *Coffee and Conflict in Colombia, 1886–1910* (1978), pp. 51–80, 196–219.

J. LEÓN HELGUERA

MARSHALS OF AYACUCHO. Several future Peruvian presidents served under General Antonio José de SUCRE at the battle of AYACUCHO, which ended Spanish rule in South America in 1824. They included Agustín GAMARRA of Cuzco (b. 1785), Miguel San Román of Puno (b. 1802), Manuel Ignacio VIVANCO (b. 1806), Felipe Santiago SALAVERRY (b. 1805), and Juan Crisostomo Torrico (b. 1808), all of Lima. The military and political skills of these generals, together with the public renown they received by serving at Ayacucho, helped them to reach the pinnacle of political power, however briefly, during the turbulent post-Independence period known as the "age of the caudillos."

TIMOTHY E. ANNA, *The Fall of Royal Government in Peru* (1979).

PETER F. KLARÉN

MARTÍ, AGUSTÍN FARABUNDO (*b.* 1893; *d.* 1 February 1932), Salvadoran Communist leader and labor organizer. Martí's father, a moderate landholder in Teotepeque, reputedly adopted his surname in honor of the Cuban patriot José MARTÍ. Young Farabundo grew up surrounded by poor campesinos, with whom he identified later in life. His biographers describe him as a precocious, sensitive child who could not understand the differences between men. When his father decided against dividing the family land among his sons, Martí enrolled in the Faculty of Jurisprudence and Social Sciences at the National University. From the beginning, however, he felt frustrated by the lack of open discus-

of the new diocese of Guatemala, and following papal approval, he was consecrated at Mexico City in 1537. Marroquín spent the rest of his life in Guatemala. During his long episcopacy, he showed great interest in the conversion of the Indians, in the settlement and development of the colony, and in education, especially for the Spanish population. He served briefly as cogovernor of Guatemala (1541–1542) and thereafter collaborated closely with the presidents of the Audiencia of Los Confines, which was established in 1542. From his earliest days in Central America, Marroquín had a long and stormy relationship with Bartolomé de LAS CASAS, with whom he disagreed regarding the best method of dealing with the native population.

LÁZARO LAMADRID, "Bishop Marroquín: Zumárraga's Gift to Central America," in *The Americas* 5, no. 3 (1949): 331–341; CARMELO SÁENZ DE SANTA MARÍA, *El licenciado don Francisco Marroquín, primer obispo de Guatemala (1499–1563): Su vida, sus escritos* (1964).

STEPHEN WEBRE

See also **Catholic Church; Guatemala, Audiencia of.**

MARROQUÍN, JOSÉ MANUEL (*b.* 6 August 1827; *d.* 19 September 1908), acting president (7 August 1898–

sion in his college and began independently reading anarchist and communist texts in the library. He became involved in the nascent labor movement and participated in the first strikes held in El Salvador (1920). At this same time, he provoked a duel with his professor, Victoriano López Ayala, over the nature of cognition. For this, Martí and his friend José Luís Barrientos were exiled to Guatemala in 1920.

There are only fragmentary records of Martí's movements for the period from 1920 to 1925, but it is generally believed that he spent this time living among the Quiché Maya and making contacts among the rural salaried workers of Guatemala. He traveled frequently, working as a baker and bricklayer and doing other odd jobs in Guatemala and Honduras; he also served with the Red Battalions in Mexico, becoming a sergeant. Martí apparently took a pessimistic view of the latter country's still-young revolution, for he once remarked, ''Disgracefully, the workers of Mexico have been captured by the bourgeoisie.'' In 1925, Martí and a few other dissident intellectuals founded the Central American Socialist Party in Guatemala City, which pledged to work for the unity of the isthmus. They had some brief success in persuading the legislatures of Guatemala, El Salvador, and Honduras to sponsor a tripartite republic but lacked support in Costa Rica and Nicaragua, and the party disintegrated.

Martí then found his way back to El Salvador, where he tried to raise the class consciousness of the rural

Agustín Farabundo Martí arriving for detention in Los Angeles, 1931. BETTMANN ARCHIVE.

workers. In 1928, President Alfonso QUIÑONES MOLINA exiled Martí to Nicaragua. This move allowed Martí to link up with Augusto César SANDINO and serve as personal secretary to the Nicaraguan patriot. Martí failed to convert Sandino to Marxism-Leninism and returned to El Salvador in 1929, but Martí retained the highest personal regard for Sandino. Shortly before his execution in 1932, Martí declared that there was no greater patriot in all of Central America than General Sandino. For his own part, Martí was a hardened internationalist and a devout admirer of Leon TROTSKY; throughout the 1920s he wore a lapel pin that featured an image of Trotsky within a red star.

Martí spent the closing years of the 1920s in and out of Salvadoran jails, with intermittent periods of exile. He spent some time in California, where he met several sympathetic members of the International Labor Defense and secured a position as Salvadoran representative of the Socorro Rojo (Red Aid), a socialist labor organization. He made his way back to El Salvador in time for the December 1930 election campaign. That year, Martí and a few close associates, including Miguel Mármol, founded the Communist Party of El Salvador. Contrary to the established Moscow-directed approach, the Salvadoran Communists refused to participate in elections and instead concentrated their efforts on organizing the dispossessed rural peasantry. The Communists initially lost ground to the reformist experiment of President Arturo ARAUJO, but gained strength after a coup in December 1931 brought the military to power. A mass uprising was planned for 22 January 1932, but the government uncovered the plot and executed Martí, along with two student accomplices, on 1 February. The period of repression that followed is known as the MATANZA, or massacre. In 1980 several guerrilla groups joined forces and christened their umbrella organization the Farabundo Martí Liberation Front (FMLN) in honor of their model.

THOMAS P. ANDERSON, *Matanza: El Salvador's Communist Revolt of 1932* (1971); JORGE ARIAS GÓMEZ, *Farabundo Martí: Esbozo biográfico* (1972); JAMES DUNKERLEY, *The Long War: Dictatorship and Revolution in El Salvador* (1982); FMLN, *Farabundo Martí* (1982).

KAREN RACINE

See also **El Salvador: Revolutionary Movements.**

MARTÍ Y PÉREZ, JOSÉ JULIÁN (*b.* 28 January 1853; *d.* 19 May 1895), father of Cuba's independence. Even if he had done nothing for his native land, Martí would have gone down in history as a great literary figure. But besides being a poet, journalist, and orator of genius, Martí was a revolutionary and a politician, the architect and organizer of Cuba's 1895–1898 war against Spanish colonialism. For this reason he is best known as the apostle of Cuba's independence. Cubans today revere his memory and regard his teachings as the living gospel of the fatherland.

EARLY CAREER

Born in Havana of poor Spanish immigrants, Martí was able to go to high school owing to the support of Rafael María Mendive, an enlightened schoolmaster whose influence outweighed all others on his early youth. Martí was still in school when the first Cuban war of independence, the TEN YEARS' WAR, broke out in 1868. Like many of his classmates, he embraced the cause of freedom. In January 1869, aged sixteen, he founded his first newspaper, which he appropriately named *La Patria Libre* (Free Fatherland). Shortly afterward he was arrested and sentenced to six years of hard labor in a rock quarry, merely because he wrote a letter denouncing a pro-Spanish fellow student as an "apostate." After serving only a few months, however, Martí's sentence was commuted to banishment to Spain, where he arrived early in 1871. That same year he published his celebrated essay *El presidio político en Cuba,* a passionate indictment of conditions in Cuba's prisons.

After this, his first exile (during which he completed his schooling at the universities of Madrid and Saragossa), Martí revisited Cuba only twice before 1895: in 1877 for less than two months, and again from 31 August 1878 to 25 September 1879. Altogether Martí spent twenty-three years away from the land of his birth, during which period he worked as a journalist in Mexico, the United States, and Venezuela, and as a professor in Guatemala. Nevertheless, for the most part he made his home in New York, which was the center of his activities from 1881 until just before his death in 1895.

LITERARY WORK

It was during this period that Martí gained recognition throughout the hemisphere, partly as a chronicler of life in the United States. He was a keen observer of the grandeur and miseries of the nation during the Gilded Age, and he reported what he saw in his columns for the *Opinión Nacional* of Caracas, *La Nación* of Buenos Aires, and more than twenty other Spanish American newspapers. In 1884 Martí was famous enough to be appointed vice-consul of Uruguay in New York. By this time he had become one of the forerunners of literary modernism in Spanish with the publication of *Ismaelillo* (1882), a collection of poems for his only son. In 1889 Martí delighted Spanish-speaking youngsters with his *Edad de Oro,* a magazine for children written entirely by him, and in 1891 he published his *Versos sencillos,* which in many ways marks the culmination of his poetic career. Martí's literary output at this point of his life was enormous and included several translations from English, a not very successful novel, and a romantic play. Nowhere is his genius revealed, though, as in the highly personal style of his articles and essays, his mesmeriz-

José Julián Martí y Pérez. BROWN BROTHERS.

ing speeches, his political documents, and even his private correspondence. His prose is among the best in the Spanish language.

CUBAN INDEPENDENCE

Martí spent many of his years in exile plotting the independence of Cuba, a Herculean task. Not only did he have to hold in check those who favored the autonomy of the island under Spain or who endorsed its annexation to the United States, but he also had to cope with the threat of American expansionism and the authoritarian proclivities of the veteran generals of the Ten Years' War. Martí maintained that in order to avoid these pitfalls, Cuba's struggle for independence would have to be brief (so as to minimize the chances for U.S. intervention) and conducted with "republican method and spirit" (in order to prevent the island from falling prey to a military dictatorship after independence). Somewhere around 1887 he concluded that he would have to assume political leadership if these ends were to be attained. For this purpose, in 1892 Martí formed the Cuban Revolutionary Party, an essentially U.S.-centered organization through which he subsequently channeled his efforts to overthrow Spanish domination in Cuba. For more than three years, he worked untiringly until, by early 1895, he was ready to launch a new and more formidable rebellion on the island. The veteran generals would still be in command of the expeditions to sail from Fernandina, Florida, but they were now under the authority of the party and its leader.

At the last minute, however, U.S. authorities seized the boats and the war materials that Martí had clandestinely procured, and he could only join the fighting that had already started in Cuba on the sufferance of the military leaders. His leadership role declined as a result of the Fernandina fiasco. Once in Cuba, the generals challenged the principle of civil supremacy so dear to him, and he began to think of returning to the United States in order to cope with the threat of military authoritarianism that he had long feared. Thus, he was in a somber mood when he was killed in a skirmish of little consequence. The struggle continued, but his political doctrine had very little influence on subsequent developments. After the war ended, there were very few who thought that his statue should be erected in Havana's Central Park.

INTELLECTUAL AND POLITICAL LEGACY
Gradually, however, Martí became better known in Cuba. When the island was swept by a shock wave of nationalism in the late 1920s and early 1930s, he was vindicated, emerging as the political, moral, and spiritual mentor of a new generation of Cubans. It was at this time that the cultlike Cuban attitude toward Martí and his preachings took on its present form and substance.

Martí was so prolific that it is nearly impossible to offer an adequate insight into his thought. Often what may be considered as representative ideas are offset by completely different or even contradictory ones. For this reason he appears to be ambivalent on many subjects, while in other cases it seems that he simply refused to record an opinion. We look in vain, for example, for a passage stating his political program, the political system he preferred, or his constitutional doctrine.

It is not surprising, therefore, that leftist scholars and politicians should have found a Marxist slant in his writings. But Martí rejected the notion of the class struggle as well as the high level of violence employed by some of the labor leaders of his time. Furthermore, he condemned the idea of entrusting to the state the satisfaction of man's material needs. Therefore, while Martí may have sympathized with Marx's concern for the worker, he certainly was no Marxist.

Martí was not anti-American, nor did he ever intend to make an enemy of the United States, despite his well-known anti-imperialist stance. If anything, his view of the country, which he chose as his haven in exile, was critical, in the strictest sense of the word. He was aware of the sordid facets of life within its boundaries—and denounced them. But Martí also proclaimed his admiration for the dynamism and industry of Americans as well as his esteem for American thinkers and writers and "the wonderful men who framed the constitution of the United States of America." As Martí himself once said, he loved the land of Lincoln as much as he feared the land of Francis Cutting (a nineteenth-century adventurer who once tried to annex northern Mexico to the United States).

Although Martí was a pugnacious nationalist, when he worried about Cutting-like predators he was thinking not only about Cuba, but about Spanish America as well. He envisioned Spanish America as forming, from the Rio Grande to Patagonia, one single, colossal nation, which he called "our America," and which in his view would have a great future, "not as a conquering Rome but as a hospitable nation." Like Simón BOLÍVAR, therefore, he thought in hemispheric terms, and that is no doubt the reason why Rubén DARÍO, the great Nicaraguan poet, said that he belonged not to Cuba alone, but to "an entire race, an entire continent."

Martí's definitive biography remains to be written. Of the studies available in English, two of the most recent are PETER TURTON, *José Martí: Architect of Cuba's Freedom* (1986), and CHRISTOPHER ABEL and NISSA TORRENTS, eds., *José Martí: Revolutionary Democrat* (1986).

JOSÉ M. HERNÁNDEZ

MARTÍN FIERRO, the classic poem of Argentine GAUCHESCA LITERATURE, published in two parts (1872 and 1879). The poem contains a strong ethical, social, and political message, which its author, José HERNÁNDEZ, also delivered in his journalism and political life. Hernández sought to depict the destitute existence of a specific social class, re-creating its world view and particular language. He embodied that class in a fictional GAUCHO, Martín Fierro, who narrates his life before and after he was compulsorily sent to the frontier to fight the Indians—robbed of his family, home, and all his belongings. He escapes from virtual slavery at the fort, lives as a *gaucho matrero* (cunning outlaw), together with his friend Sargeant Cruz, and finds refuge among the Indians. Upon returning to his "pago" (the region in which he used to live), Martín Fierro finds two of his sons and the one of Cruz. After hearing the father's wise advice the four agree, for reasons not explained in the poem, to lead separate lives.

A vivid depiction of life in the fort and of Indian MALONES (surprise attacks), of Fierro's humiliating experiences as an unsalaried soldier, as well as of the abuses of his orphaned children, the poem is a denunciation of the profound injustices inflicted on the gauchos. An epic and lyrical piece of 7,210 verses, the poem not only achieved Hernández's sociopolitical purposes, but also won popular acclaim. Martín Fierro has ever since been the archetypical gaucho, symbolizing the "barbaric" inhabitants of the PAMPAS who were decimated in the name of "civilization."

NETTIE L. BENSON, "*Martín Fierro* at the University of Texas," in *Library Chronicle of the University of Texas* 8, no. 4 (1968): 13–27; TED LYON, "*Martín Fierro:* Narrative Fluctuation (as Key to Interpretation)," in *Chasqui* 1, no. 3 (1972): 26–35; NETTIE L. BENSON, "*Martín Fierro,* Best Seller," in *Américas* 25, no. 2 (1973): 8–12; FRANK G. CARRINO et al., trans., *The Gaucho Martín Fierro* (1974); FERMÍN CHAVEZ, "*Martín Fierro:* Sus contenidos ideológicos y políticos," in *Cuadernos Hispanoamericanos* 357 (March 1980): 525–540; MICHAEL J. CASEY, "El cantor y el mudo: Speech and Silence in *Martín Fierro,*" in *Chasqui* 11, no. 1 (1981): 53–57; NANCY VOGELEY, "The Figure of the Black *Payador* in *Martín Fierro,*" in *CLA Journal* 26, no. 1 (1982): 34–48; RODOLFO A. BORELLO, "La originalidad del *Martín Fierro,*" in *Cuadernos Hispanoamericanos* 437 (November 1986): 65–84, and "El *Martín Fierro* y la poesía gauchesca," in *Boletín de la Academia Argentina de Letras* 54, nos. 211–212 (1989): 97–129.

ANGELA B. DELLEPIANE

MARTÍNEZ, ANTONIO J. (*b.* 1793; *d.* 1867), Roman Catholic priest, publisher, and political leader of NEW MEXICO under Spanish, Mexican, and U.S. rule. Born in Abiquiu, New Mexico, Martínez was widowed after only one year of marriage. He subsequently studied for the priesthood in Durango, Mexico. As a pastor in Taos, Padre Martínez founded schools and published books and a newspaper called *El Crepúsculo de la Libertad* (The Twilight of Liberty). His was the first printing press west of the Mississippi River. Martínez's labors were characterized by a deep conviction about the importance of education for his people. He is best known for the often bitter controversies between himself and the first archbishop of Santa Fe, Jean-Baptiste Lamy, which exemplified the cultural conflicts between New Mexico (Hispano) Catholics and the European, especially French, priests sent to work in New Mexico after the territory passed to the United States in 1848. The clash revolved around the efforts of the Europeans, who viewed their ministry as being both religious and social, to Americanize the New Mexico Hispanics. They urged the New Mexicans to abandon their "old-fashioned" Catholicism for a more "modern" Jansenist Catholicism appropriate for Catholics in a Protestant nation. The Europeans, who were trained for the ministry in the austere seminaries of France, knew little about the deep cultural roots of New Mexican Catholicism. Padre Antonio J. Martínez has come to be viewed as a hero of New Mexico history and a forerunner of the Hispanic or Latino civil rights movement of the 1960s.

LUCIANO HENDREN synthesizes the life and work of Padre Martínez in *Fronteras: A History of the Latin American Church in the USA Since 1513* (1983), esp. pp. 195–207. CAREY MC WILLIAMS places Martínez's life within the larger framework of the history of the Spanish-speaking people of the United States in *North from Mexico* (1968), esp. pp. 118–119.

ALLAN FIGUEROA DECK, S.J.

MARTÍNEZ, ESTEBAN JOSÉ (*b.* 9 December 1742; *d.* 28 October 1798), Spanish naval officer, explorer of the Pacific Northwest. Born in Seville, Martínez studied at the Real Colegio de San Telmo. He was second pilot in the Department of San Blas in 1773 and sailed as provisional ensign with Juan Pérez to southern Alaska the following year. From 1775 to 1785 he commanded supply ships that sailed to Loreto, San Diego, Monterey, and San Francisco. Martínez was promoted to first pilot in 1781; commanded the *Princesa* and the *Favorita,* and met the expedition of Jean François de La Pérouse at Monterey in 1786; and became an ensign in 1787. With González López de Haro he searched the Northwest Coast for foreign encroachment as far as Unalaska and Kodiak islands. Martínez was commandant of Nootka in 1789 and, after fortifying it, returned to San Blas in December of that year. Subsequently, the British captain James Colnett was arrested for encroachment upon assumed Spanish territory, an event that led to conflict and to the convention of 1790. Martínez was posted to La Coruña in 1792 and returned to San Blas, as a lieutenant, in 1795. He died in Loreto. Among the proposals he had made to the crown were the occupation of the Sandwich Islands (modern Hawaii) and the establishment of a sea otter trade in the Californias.

ROBERTO BARREIRO-MEIRO, *Esteban José Martínez (1742–1798), Colección de diarios y relaciones para la historia de los viajes y descubrimientos,* vol. 6 (1964); and WARREN L. COOK, *Flood Tide of Empire: Spain in the Pacific Northwest, 1543–1819* (1973).

W. MICHAEL MATHES

See also **Explorers and Exploration.**

MARTÍNEZ, JUAN JOSÉ (*b.* ca. 3 January 1782; *d.* ca. 25 July 1863), a hero of Mexican independence whose existence has been widely questioned. When Miguel HIDALGO besieged Guanajuato in September 1810, the Spaniards fortified themselves in the ALHÓNDIGA de Granaditas granary. According to the legend, Martínez, a miner nicknamed Pípila (Turkey), joined the insurgents in their attack on the Alhóndiga. In the heart of battle he reached the great door of the granary by crawling under the protection of slab and set fire to the building, thus allowing the insurgents to enter. Lucas ALAMÁN, the greatest historian of the epoch, doubted that Martínez had existed, but his critic, José María de Liceaga, insisted on the veracity of the tale. In recent years, the Guanajuato historian Fulgencio Vargas has published articles claiming to possess documents that prove the existence of the hero.

LUCAS ALAMÁN, *Historia de Méjico desde los primeros movimientos que prepararon su independencia en el año 1808 hasta la época presente,* vol. 1 (1849), p. 430; JOSÉ MARÍA DE LICEAGA, *Adiciones y rectificaciones a la historia de México que escribió D. Lucas Alamán* (1868), pp. 113–114; JOSÉ MARÍA MIQUEL I VERGÉS, *Diccionario de insurgentes,* 2d ed. (1980), p. 364.

JAIME E. RODRÍGUEZ O.

MARTÍNEZ, TOMÁS (*b.* 21 December 1820; *d.* 12 March 1873), president of Nicaragua (1859–1867). In his early life Martínez was involved in commerce and agriculture, only later turning to the military. He became president in 1859, after the ouster of U.S. filibuster William WALKER during the NATIONAL WAR (in which Martínez emerged as a central figure). His administration developed a program that included the reorganization of agriculture, increased coffee cultivation, state support for secular schools, industrial growth, limitations on government monopolies, separation of church and state, abolition of the death penalty, establishment of trial by jury, and a plan for direct elections.

Ironically, although his administration ushered in thirty years of Conservative Party rule, his plan for direct elections ultimately caused the Conservative Party to split into four factions, creating a tumultuous situation that led to the installation of Liberal José Santos ZELAYA as president in 1893.

SARA LUISA BARQUERO, *Gobernantes de Nicaragua, 1825–1947* (1945), esp. pp. 117–124; BENJAMIN I. TEPLITZ, "The Political and Economic Foundations of Modernization in Nicaragua: The Administration of José Santos Zelaya, 1893–1909" (Ph. D. diss., Howard University, 1973), esp. p. 7; FRANCISCO ORTEGA ARANCIBIA, *Cuarenta años (1838–1878) de historia de Nicaragua* (1975).

SHANNON BELLAMY

MARTÍNEZ DE HOZ, JOSÉ ALFREDO (*b.* 10 July 1895), Argentine business magnate and former finance minister. Born in Buenos Aires to one of the wealthiest and most traditional families in Argentina, Martínez de Hoz occupied important economic posts during the governments of Arturo FRONDIZI and José María GUIDO. Former president of the National Grain Board and head of the country's largest steel company, Acindar, he was an important member of a giant conglomerate, the Roberts Group. He is infamous as the architect of the last military regime's (1976–1983) economic plan. As its finance minister from April 1976 to March 1981, Martínez de Hoz dismantled the protection for domestic industry, deregulated the financial sector, and curbed the power of Peronist trade unions. Convinced that state controls were the primary obstacles to economic growth, he deindustrialized the country, increased unemployment rates to unprecedented levels, and soon overvalued the currency, provoking massive balance-of-trade deficits and capital flight. The combination left Argentina with a $40 billion external debt. Martínez de Hoz was subsequently charged and convicted under the government of Raúl ALFONSÍN (1983–1989) for corruption and fraud.

JORGE SCHVARZER, *La política económica de Martínez de Hoz* (1987); WILLIAM L. SMITH, *Authoritarianism and the Crisis of the Argentine Political Economy* (1989); PAUL H. LEWIS, *The Crisis of Argentine Capitalism* (1990).

JEREMY ADELMAN

MARTÍNEZ ESTRADA, EZEQUIEL (*b.* 14 September 1895; *d.* 5 November 1964), Argentine writer. Born of Spanish parents in San José de la Esquina, province of Santa Fe, Martínez Estrada was one of the most important Argentine writers of the twentieth century. Some consider him as influential as Domingo Faustino SARMIENTO had been for the nineteenth century. His reputation is even more remarkable considering that he had little formal schooling and no university education.

With Martínez Estrada an intellectual movement began in Argentina, the major preoccupation of which was the reassessment of the country's character following the political decadence that began after the military coup of 1930. His book *Radiografía de la pampa* (1933; The X-Ray of the Pampa) is a condemnation of the elite for trying to impose European modes on the Argentine reality, rejecting what Martínez Estrada considered native traits. In this book he dissected Argentine society and searched for its true nature, as it struggled between urban and rural models. When he raised these questions, he brought everything into the open; he criticized those who emphasized only fragments of Argentine life. Basically, his works represented a search for the essence of Argentina's soul, and, therefore, he called on the Argentines not merely to evaluate their past but also to change the way in which they assessed it.

His literary work is characterized by a great sense of pessimism about the country's future as a result of the political decadence that had come about since 1930. His pessimism grew with the military revolts of the 1940s and with Juan Domingo PERÓN's anti-intellectual attitude. Martínez Estrada went into self-imposed exile from Buenos Aires to Bahía Blanca and from there to Mexico and Cuba. He wrote two other important books, *The Head of Goliath* (1940) and *Sarmiento* (1946), which also deal with social and political thoughts about Argentine society.

PETER G. EARLE, *Prophet of the Wilderness: The Works of Ezequiel Martínez Estrada* (1971); PEDRO G. ORGAMBIDE, *Genio y figura de Ezequiel Martínez Estrada* (1985); JUAN JOSÉ SEBRELI, *Martínez Estrada: Una rebelión inútil* (1986).

JUAN MANUEL PÉREZ

See also **Literature.**

MARTINIQUE AND GUADELOUPE, Départements d'Outre-Mer (DOMs) of France since 1946. Each elects three representatives to the French National Assembly and two to the Senate. The northernmost of French territories in the eastern Caribbean, the DOM of Guadeloupe consists of the large islands of Basse-Terre and Grande Terre and five dependencies: Marie-Galante, Désirade, Îles des Saintes, SAINT BARTHÉLÉMY, and half of Saint Martin. Most of the population of 342,000 (1990) is concentrated on the two large islands, primarily in Point-à-Pitre, the commercial center and major port, and secondarily in the political capital of Basse-Terre. Martinique has about a third of its 340,000 population in Fort-de-France, its capital and economic center, which has one of the best harbors in the Caribbean.

There are active volcanoes: Soufrière on Guadeloupe and Pelée on Martinique. The latter created a modern Pompeii in 1902 when it devastated Saint Pierre, then the largest city on Martinique, killing over 30,000 inhabitants in moments.

The first French settlers appeared on Martinique and Guadeloupe in 1635. Carib opposition and weak merchant support slowed the establishment of profitable plantations. In 1664 the French finance minister Jean-Baptiste Colbert, instituted policies that greatly stimulated SUGAR production with African slave labor and brought the colonies under firm crown control. The *exclusif* ended local attempts at economic diversification and competition with French industry. Local councils were only advisory, and officials were French. Governors answered to the governor-general in Martinique.

By the eighteenth century, French planters in Martinique, Guadeloupe, and Saint Domingue (later Haiti) were producing more sugar than the English, and selling it cheaper, even expanding their trade in British North America, which was legally a closed British market.

The end of plantation SLAVERY began with a massive slave rebellion in Saint Domingue (HAITI) in 1793. In 1794, the French Revolutionary government declared the end of slavery in all French colonies (the British occupation of Martinique made the declaration void there). In 1802 Napoleon decreed a reimposition of slavery in the remaining French possessions. The French agreed to end the African SLAVE TRADE to their colonies in 1815. Abolition came with a new Revolutionary government in 1848. After emancipation the planters were compensated for their lost slaves, and France offered support in locating indentured labor, primarily from India. From 1850 to 1914, about 25,000 Indians arrived in Martinique and 37,000 in Guadeloupe. Many died or migrated after their contracts were over.

The major political initiatives have come from the working class: a riot on Martinique (1870) and strikes on both Martinique and Guadeloupe in the 1890s and at the beginning of the twentieth century. Sugar and its derivatives continue to dominate the economy, as well as labor and social relations.

The contemporary social structure of Martinique reflects the legacies of a plantation society. The social and landed elite is made up of whites, the Békés, many of whom claim descent from the original colonizers. They maintain marriage with inheritance strictly within their group. The Békés reflect the values of the plantocracy. "Metropolitans" (whites who immigrated to Martinique, mostly from France) form part of the middle class. The larger part of the middle class is composed largely of *mulâtres,* most of whom are of mixed racial ancestry as a result of sexual liaisons between whites and blacks during slavery (particularly through the con-

cubinage commonly practiced by white males); of marriages among "free coloreds" during slavery; and, more recently, of marriages between "metropolitans" and descendants of Asian indentured laborers and blacks. This middle class which began its ascent after 1848, now dominates commerce, the professions, and political and bureaucratic offices.

The majority of the population and the lowest economic group is the *noirs* (blacks), although some members of this group are of mixed ancestry. The *noirs* tend to be more rural and to work in agriculture, many as wage laborers on plantations. Some ply trades, often in addition to agriculture; others reside on plantations for lack of their own land and employment alternatives; some are fishermen. The upper level of this class overlaps with the *mulâtres* as shopkeepers, bureaucrats, lawyers, and teachers in rural areas.

The Guadeloupan social structure closely resembles that of Martinique, except that the white elite is not as large, powerful, or racially exclusive. The comparative weakness of the white group is due in good part to the decimation it suffered at the hands of Victor Hugues, the French Jacobin who instituted the Terror in Guadeloupe, executing over 800 whites. Many of the remaining whites fled the island.

Both Martinique and Guadeloupe are intimately tied to the distant French metropole from which they derive their standard of living (very high, compared with their Caribbean neighbors); their defense, education, and health and welfare funding; their official language; and their Roman Catholicism. Independence is not a likely popular choice, largely because of the fear of economic decline without massive French subsidies. However, a growing awareness of cultural similarities to their Caribbean neighbors continues to fuel the search for greater local autonomy within the French nation.

LAFCADIO HEARN, *Two Years in the French West Indies* (1890); NELLIS MAYNARD CROUSE, *The French Struggle for the West Indies, 1665–1713* (1966); WALTER ADOLPHE ROBERTS, *The French in the West Indies* (1971); LÉO ELISABETH, "The French Antilles," in *Neither Slave nor Free: The Freedman of African Descent in the Slave Societies of the New World,* edited by David W. Cohen and Jack P. Greene (1972); BRIDGET BRERETON, "Society and Culture in the Caribbean: The British and French West Indies, 1870–1980," in *The Modern Caribbean,* edited by Franklin W. Knight and Colin A. Palmer (1989); DALE TOMICH, *Slavery in the Circuit of Sugar: Martinique and the World Economy, 1830–1848* (1990).

ROSEMARY BRANA-SHUTE

See also **Slave Revolts; Slavery.**

MARTORELL, ANTONIO (*b.* 18 April 1939), Puerto Rican artist. Martorell received his early training with Julio Martín Caro in Madrid (1961–1962). He studied printmaking with Lorenzo HOMAR from 1962 to 1965 at the Institute of Puerto Rican Culture's graphics workshop in New York City. In 1968 he founded the Taller Alacrán (Scorpion's Workshop). Martorell has also worked as a set designer, book illustrator, caricaturist, textile and graphic designer, art critic, and writer. Since 1985, he has worked collaboratively with Rosa Luisa Márquez as performer and set designer for graphic-theatrical performance pieces. He has taught at the National School of Fine Arts in Mexico City, the Institute of Puerto Rican Culture, and the Universidad Interamericana in San Germán, Puerto Rico. His posters, paintings, and installations have been exhibited internationally, and he has won numerous awards.

INSTITUTO DE CULTURA PUERTORRIQUEÑA, *Antonio Martorell, Obra gráfica 1963–1986. Exposición homenaje* (1986); ANTONIO MARTORELL, *La piel de la memoria* (1992); MUSEO DEL BARRIO (New York City), *Antonio Martorell and Friends: La Casa de Todos Nosotros/A House for Us All* (1992).

MIRIAM BASILIO

MARTYR, PETER (also Pietro Martire d'Anghiera; *b.* 1457 or 1459; *d.* 1526), early historian of the discovery and exploration of the New World. Born in Arona, Italy, Martyr moved to Rome in 1477 and became a noted academic. In 1487 he went to Spain, where he became a cleric and adviser to the Spanish monarchs Isabella I and Ferdinand V, and became a friend of Christopher Columbus. In 1520 he became court historian and secretary to the Council of the Indies. His close relationship to the Spanish court and with the early conquistadors during the time of the Conquest of America provided him with much data, from which he wrote *De orbe novo* (The New World). The first history of the Spanish Conquest, this work was published in eight parts, beginning in 1511. Although it contains many errors as a result of Martyr's heavy use of the reports of the conquistadors, who often embellished their accounts or relied on memory rather than documentary sources, it remains one of the most important of the early chronicles and reflects the Renaissance spirit of the explorations.

Early complete editions of *De orbe novo* were published in 1530 and 1587. A 1612 London edition, translated into English by Richard Eden, was *De nouo orbe, or The historie of the West Indies.* A more modern English edition, translated from the original Latin by Francis Augustus MacNutt, is *De orbe novo: The Eight Decades of Peter Martyr d'Anghera* (1912).

SUE DAWN McGRADY

MARYKNOLL ORDER. In 1911 the Catholic Foreign Mission Society of America, popularly known as Maryknoll, was founded in Ossining, New York. In 1920 the Maryknoll Sisters officially became a separate congregation. Prior to U.S. entrance into World War II, Maryknoll MISSION activities were limited to the Far East. Since the war forced Maryknoll to cut back on that com-

mitment, it decided to expand to Latin America, where it established missions in Bolivia in 1942 and opened its Instituto de Idiomas in Cochabamba, the largest of the order's language schools. It offers instruction in Spanish, Quechua, and Aymara, and trains missionaries for Maryknoll and thirty other Catholic religious orders, as well as for several Protestant groups. So successful has its program been that between 1965 and 1982 alone it taught about 3,500 missioners.

In 1942 Maryknoll also opened missions in Peru and Chile, and by the end of 1943, it had opened additional missions in Mexico, Guatemala, and Ecuador. Later Maryknoll expanded into El Salvador (1961), Venezuela (1966), Nicaragua (1971), Brazil (1976), and Honduras (1981). Its Ecuadoran operations, however, were terminated in 1948. Since a primary goal was to increase indigenous priestly vocations, Maryknoll opened a minor seminary in Puno, Peru, in 1944. Although more than 800 boys studied there, only 12 became priests. The seminary was closed in 1969.

When Maryknoll first entered Latin America, its superior general, James E. Walsh, noted that its missioners were "not going as exponents of any so-called North American civilization." Nevertheless, until the late 1960s the order's work was undeniably colored in part by a sense of U.S. superiority and an anticommunist mentality. Parishes were based on the U.S. Catholic model and when possible included a parochial school. The extensive North American presence in the area was seen as a positive force, and missioners often relied on local North American businessmen for moral and monetary support. Numerous development projects were started under the auspices of the ALLIANCE FOR PROGRESS, but many eventually failed because of local injustice and an overreliance on outside financial help.

As a result of the Second Vatican Council's emphasis on social awareness, Maryknoll began to rethink its role. In its 1966 general chapter, a new mission rationale was produced, placing more stress on the needs of the poor. Encouraged by the Second General Conference of Latin American bishops at Medellín, Colombia, in 1968, the society increased its efforts in training Catholic lay leaders. *Cursillos* (three-day retreats for lay people, followed by weekly meetings) were held. Catechetical training centers were opened, and CHRISTIAN BASE COMMUNITIES were organized. At its 1973 general chapter, Maryknoll emphasized its responsibility to make U.S. citizens aware of Third World poverty and injustice, and of the role the First World plays in their perpetuation. Already in 1970 it had created Orbis Books, in an attempt to offer the best of Third World theology to North American readers. After two decades, Orbis has become well known for its English translations of LIBERATION THEOLOGY, publishing works by such notables as Gustavo GUTIÉRREZ, Leonardo BOFF, Jon Sobrino, and Juan Luis Segundo. Its School of Theology at Maryknoll, New York, soon created programs in Hispanic ministry and in justice and peace studies, opening its doors to lay people as well as clergy and to non-Catholics and Catholics alike. In 1975 it began an innovative lay missionary program, which has become a model for other religious orders. Over the years Maryknoll has produced eight Latin American bishops. Four of its members were murdered while carrying out their duties. In 1990 it had 282 religious and lay missionaries stationed in ten Latin American countries, and the order was reputed to be one of the most aggressive in its commitment to the poor.

There is no study that offers a general overview of Maryknoll in Latin America. For the early years see ALBERT J. NEVINS, *The Meaning of Maryknoll* (1954), pp. 201–251. For Maryknoll sisters, see PENNY LERNOUX, *Hearts on Fire: The Story of the Maryknoll Sisters* (1993). Although not specifically treating Maryknoll, GERALD M. COSTELLO, *Mission to Latin America: The Successes and Failures of a Twentieth Century Crusade* (1979), contains some important information. The periodicals *Mission Forum* and *Maryknoll* are especially valuable.

EDWARD T. BRETT

MASCATES. *See* **War of the Mascates.**

MASFERRER, ALBERTO (*b.* 24 July 1868; *d.* 4 September 1932), Salvadoran journalist and political figure, most famous for his *mínimum vital,* a nine-point program designed to provide a minimum standard of living to his countrymen. As a youth Masferrer displayed exceptional sensitivity to the social problems he encountered throughout Central America. He objected to the outmoded, restrictive system of education and the appalling conditions in which many Salvadorans, particularly those in rural areas, lived. His basic ideas, present in their most rudimentary form in his first work, *Niñerías* (1892), were refined over the next four decades.

In 1895, President Rafael Gutiérrez appointed Masferrer consul to Costa Rica. Here he also began to dabble in journalism and forge links with the nascent labor movement, two interests that were to continue throughout his life. He was reassigned to Chile in 1901 and Belgium in 1911 but left the diplomatic corps in 1914 to pursue a career in journalism. Masferrer returned to El Salvador in 1916 and quickly espoused the cause of the working classes. In 1918 he organized the First Workers' Congress, which featured the future president Arturo ARAUJO, a landlord, as its keynote speaker. Throughout the 1920s, Masferrer continued to campaign for an improved standard of living and to achieve official respect for the working classes. He served as the editor of several short-lived journals before founding *La Patria* in 1928. In his opening editorial, Masferrer pledged that his newspaper would describe the life of Salvadorans as it actually was and committed himself to working for "the health, welfare, prosperity, culture, liberty, peace

and contentment of all." He wrote a series of articles known collectively as "El mínimum vital" (1928–1929) which called for adequate food, housing, clothing, education, work, recreation, and justice for all Salvadorans. In the 1930 campaign for the presidency Masferrer endorsed Arturo Araujo, who borrowed Masferrer's concept of *vitalismo* as his platform. Araujo easily won office after General Maximiliano HERNÁNDEZ MARTÍNEZ withdrew from the race, but his term lasted less than a year. Masferrer quickly realized that the Araujo administration was corrupt and powerless to effect real reforms, and left for self-exile in Guatemala. Upon hearing of the 1932 MATANZA, wherein thousands of Salvadorans were killed by government troops, Masferrer became despondent and sank into deep depression. He died of a cerebral hemorrhage later that year.

Masferrer is an important figure in the intellectual history of Central America. His thought is part of a broad anti-POSITIVIST movement that flourished in Latin America in the early decades of the twentieth century. Though his writings shied away from addressing directly the need for political reform, Masferrer's ideas included a clear social and economic agenda which implied that such changes were needed for a more

Alberto Masferrer. San Salvador, 4 October 1905. LATIN AMERICAN LIBRARY, TULANE UNIVERSITY.

smoothly functioning society. In his mind any truly national culture had an obligation to provide for its people their minimum spiritual and material well-being. His ideas reveal a strong affinity with the Roman Catholic church after *Rerum Novarum*, the 1891 papal encyclical that rejected both capitalism and socialism as paths for human development. His notion of an organic, harmonious nation that was hierarchical in organization and functioned along the lines of Christian charity and the dignity of all work is clearly typical of the intellectual flirtation with FASCISM that characterized so many thinkers of his generation. Masferrer was a reformer who did not seek to tear down the whole social order; he merely wanted to rid it of its worst abuses. Thus his ideas led directly into the Salvadoran Christian Democratic movement that flourished in the 1960s and similarly sought to improve general conditions through cooperation and conciliation rather than revolution. Masferrer remains a popular figure in El Salvador today.

MATILDE ELENA LÓPEZ, *Masferrer: Alto pensador de Centroamérica* (1954); MANUEL MASFERRER C., *Biografía del escritor Alberto Masferrer* (1957); RAFAEL ANTONIO TERCERO, *Masferrer: Un ala contra el huracán* (1958); ALBERTO MASFERRER, *Obras Escogidas* (1971); MARÍA LUISA ZELAYA DE GUIROLA, *Masferrer: Un grito en la noche de Centroamérica* (1975); MATILDE ELENA LÓPEZ, *Pensamiento social de Masferrer* (1984).

KAREN RACINE

MASONIC ORDERS. Freemasonry claims traditions that go back to ancient times, but its modern form and meaning reside in such principles as religious tolerance, social equality, philanthropy, and the belief in a powerful Grand Architect of the universe. In the Iberian colonies in the eighteenth century, records of the INQUISITION show that several individuals charged with practicing Freemasonry were tried and punished, but Masonic lodges with a primarily CREOLE composition and purpose did not make a formal appearance until the early nineteenth century.

Masonic societies are secret, primarily in terms of rites of initiation, ceremonies, and forms of identification and salutation. Since the nineteenth century, those in Latin America have been the most public of secret societies. They have been involved in many of the central issues affecting the region; their leaders have been publicly known as Freemasons; and they have made their views known through numerous publications. Probably the major significance of Latin American Freemasonry is the role the lodges played during Independence and their position with respect to church-state relations.

The origins of masonic orders having a specific Latin American orientation remain unclear, but Francisco de MIRANDA is widely believed to have played a role in their creation during his stay in Europe in the 1790s and the early years of the nineteenth century. The most significant lodge for the process of independence, the Lautaro lodge, first established in Cádiz, was carried to

Buenos Aires in 1812 and then to Mendoza and Santiago. Such prominent creoles as Simón BOLÍVAR, Andrés BELLO, Vicente ROCAFUERTE, José de SAN MARTÍN, Mariano MORENO, and Bernardo O'HIGGINS were initiated into this network of lodges. Although some may have been genuine believers in some Masonic rites, Independence leaders utilized the lodges primarily as vehicles for the struggle against Spain. Fifty-three such lodges were created between 1809 and 1828 in the Andean countries alone. In Brazil, Masons were a decisive force in the achievement of independence in 1822. Dom PEDRO himself was initiated in the Comércio e Artes lodge and became grand master of the Brazilian Grand Orient. Throughout the region, the composition of the lodges reveals a membership of merchants, lawyers, army officers, some artisans, and even members of the clergy.

Independence resulted in the decline of Freemasonry, but only temporarily. The major issue that allowed Freemasonry to flourish was the increasingly acrimonious struggle between church and state. Although Freemasonry welcomed Catholics, the lodges opposed the papacy at a time when the Latin American church sought to strengthen its ties with the Vatican. The very participation of Catholics in Masonic lodges—and the participation of Freemasons in Catholic associations—became a matter of contention. In Brazil, a serious crisis developed in the early 1870s, when the government imprisoned the bishops who upheld papal bulls anathematizing Freemasonry. At issue was the authority of the government to exercise patronage over the church. Freemasonry became the focus of attention in a struggle that eventually led to the separation of church and state in 1890.

Probably under the influence of the increasingly anti-Catholic stands of Freemasons influenced by the so-called Scottish rite, Latin American Freemasonry developed into a liberal, anticlerical force that fought for modernization and secularization, and paid preferential attention to education. In Argentina, such prominent Freemasons as Domingo Faustino SARMIENTO and Bartolomé MITRE worked first for the unification of the country and then concentrated on secularization of society and the advancement of lay education. In Mexico, Porfirio DÍAZ, himself a high-ranking Freemason, utilized the lodges as a vehicle to obtain the backing of business groups and the middle class for the advancement of his modernizing schemes. Mexican Freemasonry had been sharply divided in the 1820s, when the two main branches of Freemasonry, the YORQUINOS and the ESCOCESES, engaged in a bitter struggle over federalism and the expulsion of the Spaniards. By the late nineteenth century, consensus over Díaz's policy of industrialization and foreign investment had muted somewhat the tensions between the rites, but they exploded again during the revolution, when Freemasons became divided over the refusal of President Woodrow Wilson of the United States to recognize Victoriano HUERTA.

During the twentieth century, such prominent leaders as Arturo ALESSANDRI PALMA, Lázaro CÁRDENAS, and Hipólito YRIGOYEN were Freemasons. The institutionalization of political parties, however, during the century overshadowed the political influence of Freemasonry. Separation of church and state in most Latin American countries deprived Freemasons of a major issue, although echoes of the struggle continued to be heard in Argentina in the 1950s. The lodges continued to serve as vehicles for the transmission of Masonic traditions, but played a diminished social and political role.

SISTER MARY CRESCENTIA THORNTON, *The Church and Freemasonry in Brazil, 1872–1875: A Study in Regalism* (1948); AMÉRICO CARNICELLI, *La masonería en la independencia de América*, 2 vols. (1970); JOSÉ FERRER BENIMELI, *Masonería e Inquisición en Latinoamérica durante el siglo XVII* (1973); THOMAS B. DAVIS, *Aspects of Freemasonry in Modern Mexico: An Example of Social Cleavage* (1976); ROBERT MACOY, *A Dictionary of Freemasonry* (1989).

IVÁN JAKSIĆ

See also **Anticlericalism.**

MASSERA, JOSÉ PEDRO (*b.* 1866; *d.* 1942), Uruguayan philosopher, professor, and politician. From 1887 to 1927 Massera taught philosophy at the University of the Republic in Montevideo. His only published work during his lifetime was *Reflexiones sobre Rodó* (1920), but various of his essays were published posthumously, on subjects such as the works of Carlos Vaz Ferreira and Ribot, moral values, and moral philosophy. In 1937 he gave up teaching to pursue a political career in the national Senate.

WILLIAM H. KATRA

MASTROGIOVANNI, ANTONIO (*b.* 26 July 1936), Uruguayan composer. Born in Montevideo, Mastrogiovanni began musical studies with Nieves Varacchi and Héctor TOSAR. He studied composition under Carlos ESTRADA at the National Conservatory of Music (1963–1968), and was technical director of the music-publishing project at the conservatory. His *Monotemáticas* for violin and piano was well received at its premiere during the Second Latin American Festival of Montevideo (1966). He was awarded several prizes by the SODRE, the Association of Music Students, and the National Conservatory, and was honored by the Uruguayan Ministry of Culture (1960, 1961, 1963). *Sinfonía de Cámara* for orchestra (1965) and the piano concerto (1967) belong to that period. With *Contrarritmos* (1967), for two string orchestras and percussion, Mastrogiovanni shifted toward new composition techniques, in recognition of which he received a scholarship at the Latin American Center of Advanced Music Studies of the Di Tella Institute in Buenos Aires, where from 1969 to 1970 he studied under Gerardo GANDINI (analysis), Francisco Kröpfl

(composition), and von Reichenbach (electronic music). He received grants from the Organization of American States that enabled him to travel to Rome and Mexico to explore new composition techniques. His *Reflejos* and *Secuencial I* both won the Dutch Gaudeamus Foundation Prize (1970; 1971) and were premiered by the Utrech Symphony Orchestra. Other works of his include *Secuencial II* for tape (1970) and *Maderas* for ensemble (1974).

Since 1971, Mastrogiovanni's works have premiered throughout South America and Europe and have earned the composer awards both at home and abroad. He has taught at several prestigious institutions, including the Conservatorio Nacional de Música in Montevideo (1972–1973), the Conservatorio Nacional Juan José Landaeta in Caracas (1979–1988), and Montevideo's Escuela Universitaria de Música (1986–1993), where he also has served as director since 1988. In addition to composing commissioned works and conducting vocal and instrumental ensembles in Venezuela and Uruguay, he founded and organized an annual competition for advanced music students in Montevideo.

JOHN VINTON, ed., *Dictionary of Contemporary Music* (1974); *New Grove Dictionary of Music and Musicians* (1980); SUSANA SALGADO, *Breve historia de la música culta en el Uruguay*, 2d ed. (1980).

SUSANA SALGADO

MATA, EDUARDO (*b.* 5 September 1942; *d.* 4 January 1995), Mexican-born composer and conductor. His studies at the National Conservatory of Mexico focused on percussion and composition (with Carlos CHÁVEZ and Julian Orbón). He studied conducting with Max Rudolf and Eric Leinsdorf at the Berkshire Music Center in 1964. Mata has concentrated less on composition since his meteoric rise as a conductor, beginning in 1965 with orchestras at Guadalajara and the Free University of Mexico, and followed with Phoenix (1971–1977) and Dallas (1977–1991). He was appointed Fine Arts Opera director in Mexico City (1983) and was a guest conductor of the London Symphony Orchestra.

JOSÉ ANTONIO ALCARAZ et al., *Período contemporáneo*, in *La música de México*, edited by Julio Estrada, vol. 1, pt. 5 (1984).

ROBERT L. PARKER

MATACAPÁN, Middle Classic period (A.D. 400–700) urban center on Mexico's Gulf Coast in the Tuxtlas Mountains of southern Veracruz. The Tuxtlas lay within a region of remnant rain forests, numerous volcanoes, and a long rainy season that today supplies water to extensive areas cleared for agriculture and cattle production. Recent research at the site has uncovered the Formative and Olmec origins of settlement in the region, which now appear to stretch back into the second millennium B.C. Throughout the succeeding millennia the area was periodically devastated by volcanic eruptions that blasted nearby hillsides with enormous basaltic "bombs" and covered the surrounding countryside with a thick mantle of rich ash. Human occupation and population growth in the area, fueled by its agricultural potential, comprised a set of episodes punctuated by volcanic disasters. The longest period of growth culminated in the relatively dispersed urban sprawl at Matacapán with a resident population of perhaps 20,000 people distributed across an area perhaps as large as 5 square miles.

At its height Matacapán was the center of a diversified regional economy that specialized in industrial-level ceramic production, as evidenced by innumerable and well-preserved pottery kilns that have been uncovered throughout the ancient city. Matacapán also maintained far-flung economic and political links to the giant urban metropolis of TEOTIHUACÁN in the central Mexican highlands as well as to the more numerous MAYA population centers of the eastern lowlands. More than one hundred enormous earthen mounds comprising the monumental core of the Middle Classic city were mapped by archaeologists during the 1980s. Most of these monuments, however, have been leveled and destroyed by wealthy export tobacco farmers who control the region.

ROBERT S. SANTLEY, PONCIANO ORTÍZ CEBALLOS, and CHRISTOPHER A. POOL, "Recent Archaeological Research at Matacapán, Veracruz: A Summary of the 1982 to 1986 Field Seasons," in *Mexicon* 9 (1987): 41–48; THOMAS W. KILLION, "Residential Ethnoarchaeology and Ancient Site Structure: Contemporary Farming and Prehistoric Settlement Agriculture at Matacapán, Veracruz, Mexico," and ROBERT S. SANTLEY, "A Consideration of the Olmec Phenomenon in the Tuxtlas: Early Formative Settlement Pattern, Land Use, and Refuse Disposal at Matacapán, Veracruz, Mexico," in *Gardens of Prehistory: The Archaeology of Settlement Agriculture in Greater Mesoamerica*, edited by Thomas W. Killion (1992), pp. 119–149, 150–183.

THOMAS W. KILLION

See also **Mesoamerica.**

MATAMOROS Y GURIDI, MARIANO (*b.* 14 August 1770; *d.* 3 February 1814), MEXICAN INDEPENDENCE leader and corevolutionary of Father Miguel HIDALGO. Born in Mexico City, Matamoros studied theology at the Colegio de Santa Cruz de Tlatelolco. In 1811, he was interim curate of Jantetelco. He offered his services to the insurgent chief José María MORELOS, who named him a colonel and commissioned him to raise military forces. Matamoros accompanied Morelos to Taxco and was at Cuautla during the siege by the royalist army of Félix CALLEJA. Ordered to obtain provisions, on 21 April 1812, Matamoros and 100 dragoons broke through the royalist lines. When Morelos fled Cuautla, he dispatched Matamoros to reorganize the insurgent forces at Izúcar. A gifted military commander, Matamoros was a close adviser of Morelos during the Oaxaca campaign and was promoted to field marshal and later to lieutenant general. He was with Morelos at the abortive attack on Valladolid, Morelia, in 1814. Later, at Puruarán, Matamoros was captured by the royalists and executed.

LUCAS ALAMÁN, *Historia de México desde los primeros movimientos que prepararon su independencia en el año de 1808 hasta la época presente*, 5 vols. (1849–1852; repr. 1942); JOSÉ MARÍA LUIS MORA, *México y sus revoluciones*, 3 vols. (1961); WILBERT H. TIMMONS, *Morelos: Priest Soldier Statesman of Mexico* (1963).

CHRISTON ARCHER

MATANZA, the name given in El Salvador to the massacre perpetrated by the government after the abortive Communist-led revolt of January 1932. the revolt grew out of the anger of coffee workers and peasants over depressed living conditions and the agitation of Communist Party leaders, especially Secretary-General Augustín Farabundo MARTÍ. The revolt followed a coup d'état on 2 December 1931 that had overthrown the elected government of President Arturo ARAÚJO and replaced it with a military dictatorship headed by General Maximiliano HERNÁNDEZ MARTÍNEZ.

The Communists' revolt began in a confused manner on the night of 22 January, after Martí and other key leaders had been arrested four days earlier. It took place largely to the west of the capital in the departments of Ahuachapán, Santa Ana, and Sonsonate and just east of San Salvador, around Lake Ilopango. The rebels, armed mostly with machetes, failed to take any major garrisons and killed only a small number of civilians, along with some soldiers and police. By 25 January, military forces had largely regained control of the areas in revolt.

Although unsuccessful in seizing power, the rebellion created a great fear among the upper classes, and General Hernández Martínez decided on a policy of frightful repression in the department where the revolt took place. He instituted the Matanza (slaughter or massacre). Utilizing the regular army, police units such as the Policía Nacional and the Guardia Nacional, and the volunteer Guardia Cívica, drawn from among the upper classes, the government rounded up not only those known as Communists or as rebels, but also large numbers of peasants, often of PIPIL Indian origin, and proceeded to execute them by firing squad. The bodies were then buried in mass graves.

Estimates of the number of persons killed in the Matanza vary widely, running from 3,000 to 30,000. A reasonable guess is about 10,000 killed. Since Indians were especially targeted, the Pipil culture of western El Salvador was largely destroyed. Martí and his lieutenants, Alfonso Luna and Mario Zapata, were given the formality of a trial before being executed in the capital. One leader, Miguel Mármol, survived his firing squad and fled into exile. The effect of the massacre was to create a climate of fear among the masses that inhibited agitation for social change for some forty years.

JOAQUÍN MÉNDEZ H., *Los sucesos comunistas en El Salvador* (1932); JORGE SCHLESINGER, *Revolución comunista* (1946);

Mass grave of Salvadoran civilians killed by the military during La Matanza, 1932. ARCHIVE OF EDDIE BECKER.

THOMAS P. ANDERSON, *Matanza: El Salvador's Communist Revolt of 1932* (1971); ROQUE DALTON, *Miguel Mármol*, English ed. (1987).

THOMAS P. ANDERSON

MATÉ. *See* **Yerba Maté.**

MATIENZO, BENJAMÍN (*b.* 9 April 1891; *d.* May 1919), pioneer Argentine aviator. Born in San Miguel de Tucumán, son of a Bolivian-born jurist of the same name, Matienzo followed a military career. He became an aviation enthusiast at an early age and attended the Escuela de Aviación Militar in Palomar. In May 1919 he and two companions set out to fly over the Andes to Chile. Bad weather caused his companions to return to Mendoza; Matienzo, however, pushed ahead. His plane was forced down near Las Cuevas. While attempting to walk into the town, he froze to death. A monument commemorates his determination and sacrifice.

RONALD C. NEWTON

MATIENZO, JOSÉ NICOLÁS (*b.* 4 October 1860; *d.* 3 January 1936), Argentine jurist and statesman. Matienzo, a native of San Miguel de Tucumán, specialized in constitutional law. He was a professor at the universities of Buenos Aires and La Plata, wrote extensively on constitutional matters (see his *Cuestiones de derecho público argentino*, 1924, and *Lecciones de derecho constitucional*, 1926), and served as a member of the Supreme Court of the province of Buenos Aires (1910–1913) and as attorney general (*procurador general*) (1917–1922). He also drafted a project for a criminal code, in collaboration with Norberto Piñero and Rodolfo RIVAROLA. A liberal of reformist inclinations, he was the first president of the National Department of Labor (1907–1909). In 1910 Matienzo published *El gobierno representativo federal en la República Argentina*, a detailed study of the workings of the country's political system,

which he described as oligarchical. He shared with other members of his generation, particularly his friend Rivarola, editor of the *Revista Argentina de Ciencias Políticas*, a passionate interest in the reform of the country's political system. In 1922 he was appointed minister of the interior by President Marcelo ALVEAR, and in 1931 he was a candidate for the vice presidency on the ticket headed by Augustín Pedro JUSTO. He was elected to the National Senate in 1932, where he remained until his death in 1936.

For biographical works see FRANCISCO LUIS MENEGAZZI, *Biobibliografía de José Nicolás Matienzo* (1940); on the origins of the 1912 electoral reform, see NATALIO BOTANA, *El orden conservador: La política argentina entre 1880 y 1916* (1979); and for the general background, see EZEQUIEL GALLO, "Argentina: Society and Politics, 1880–1916," in *The Cambridge History of Latin America*, edited by Leslie Bethell, vol. 5 (1986).

EDUARDO A. ZIMMERMANN

MATO GROSSO, state in central-west Brazil, bordered on the southwest by Bolivia, on the south by the PARAGUAY RIVER, on the east by the ARAGUAIA RIVER, and on the north by various Amazon tributaries. The Chapada dos Parecis mountain range lies on the western border of the state. Mato Grosso also contains the Pantanal National Park in the southwest, and Xingu National Park in the Northeast.

The first Europeans to establish permanent settlements within Mato Grosso's interior were missionaries during the early seventeenth century, but until midcentury such settlements were frequently decimated by BANDEIRANTES, the frontiersmen and entrepreneurs of São Paulo in search of Indian slaves. In the first quarter of the eighteenth century the discovery of gold in Mato Grosso launched the first significant ranching settlements, and established the boom town of CUIABÁ.

Transportation and distance have historically impeded the economic development of Mato Grosso. In 1914 the railroad reached southern Mato Grosso, making Campo Grande the economic hub of the region; prior to this time most transportation depended upon

Mato Grosso's waterways. Partially to protect the water route from Rio de Janeiro to this western frontier, by way of Asunción and Buenos Aires, Brazil entered the WAR OF THE TRIPLE ALLIANCE in 1864. After World War II railroads were also instrumental in bringing coffee production to Mato Grosso.

On 1 January 1979 Mato Grosso was formally divided into two states, Mato Grosso and Mato Grosso do Sul. As of 1991 the population of Mato Grosso was about 1,486,111, and the total area was 352,400 square miles. The capital of Mato Grosso is Cuiabá (1991 population 220,000). Roughly half of the state remains forested, rural, agriculture-based and dependent upon coffee, cotton, timber, and rubber harvesting.

D. G. FABRE, *Beyond the River of the Dead*, translated by Eric L. Randall (1963); ROLLIE E. POPPINO, *Brazil: The Land and People* (1968).

CAROLYN E. VIEIRA

MATO GROSSO DO SUL, the state created from the southern portion of MATO GROSSO State on 1 January 1979. It lies in central-west Brazil and is bounded by Bolivia and Paraguay on the west, Paraguay on the south, and the PARANÁ RIVER on the east. In 1991 the population of Mato Grosso do Sul was 1,592,489; its area was 140,219 square miles. The capital is CAMPO GRANDE. The economy is dependent upon agriculture, cattle raising, and mineral exploration.

CAROLYN E. VIEIRA

MATOS, GREGÓRIO DE (*b.* 20 December 1636; *d.* 1696), Brazilian poet and satirist. Born in Salvador, Bahia, the son of a rich Portuguese immigrant and a lady of the local aristocracy, Matos was educated in Jesuit schools and then sent to law school in Coimbra, Portugal, in 1652. He graduated in 1661 and, after a period in Brazil, took up practice in Portugal as a guardian of orphans and as a criminal judge. He remained in the metropolis until his return to his native city in 1681. After taking minor religious orders, he was appointed by the archbishop to positions in the bishop's office and the treasury department.

His calling notwithstanding, Matos led a notorious bohemian life and earned a reputation locally as a poet and social observer. His verse was of three fundamental types: devotional, amorous, and satirical. He was especially sensitive to moral decay, corruption, exploitation, and injustice. Many of his poems are quasi-journalistic in nature, commenting on local events and personages. His biting verse earned him the nickname "Boca do Inferno" (Mouth of Hell) and the disfavor of powerful citizens. His unrelenting critical writing led to his exile in Angola (1686–1695). He died in Recife, Brazil, one year after his return from banishment.

Matos is generally considered the most important poet of the baroque period in Brazil. His work is an excellent example of the literary practice of his time, a style of conceit and formal play involving liberal borrowing and imitation. He did not publish a book in his lifetime; his poems circulated in manuscript form or were recited. It was not until the late nineteenth century that his work became widely known. The Brazilian Academy of Letters published his works in six volumes (1923–1933); a later commercial edition (1969) has seven volumes. The attribution of many texts, however, remains in dispute.

EARL E. FITZ, "Gregório de Matos and Juan del Valle y Caviedes: Two Baroque Poets in Colonial Portuguese and Spanish America," in *Inti* 5–6 (1977): 134–150; NORA K. AIEX, "Racial Attitudes in the Satire of Gregório de Matos," in *Studies in Afro-Hispanic Literature*, vol. 1 (1977), pp. 89–97.

CHARLES A. PERRONE

MATTA ECHAURREN, ROBERTO SEBASTIÁN ANTONIO (*b.* 1912), Chilean painter and printmaker. Known simply as "Matta," he was born in Santiago, Chile, and received his early education from French Jesuits. He went on to earn an architectural degree in 1933 from the Catholic University in Santiago, Chile. He took drawing classes in Santiago at the Academia de Bellas Artes. Matta left Chile in 1935 for Paris, where he worked for the architect Le Corbusier until 1937, by which time he had become a member of the surrealist group. He lived and worked in New York from 1939 to 1948. Shunned by the artistic community upon his return to Paris, he went to Rome. In the late 1950s he slowly regained acceptance in Paris, where, having become a French citizen, he spends part of each year. Matta resists being labeled a Latin American artist; rather, he sees himself in a universal context, as one who has integrated into his art elements of the many cultures with which he has come into contact.

VALERIE FLETCHER, *Crosscurrents of Modernism: Four Latin American Pioneers* (1992), pp. 228–287.

KATHERINE CLARK HUDGENS

MATTO DE TURNER, CLORINDA (Grimanesa Martina Matto Usandivaras; *b.* 11 November 1852; *d.* 25 October 1909), Peruvian novelist and journalist. She was born and raised in the ancient city of Cuzco. The family lived in the city as well as in the Hacienda Paullu Chico. Her mother died when she was ten years old, and she was sent to a Catholic school to be educated. At age eighteen she left school to look after her younger brothers. She learned English to prepare herself for study in the United States, but failed to travel to that country. She married Joseph Turner, an Englishman, in 1871. The couple first settled in the small town of Tinta, in the province of Canchis, which later served as the model for the imaginary Killac, the city of her most widely read work, *Aves sin nido* (Birds Without Nest). While living in Tinta she developed two of her major intellectual preoccupations: defending the rights of women and protesting the cruel exploitation of the Indians.

In 1876 Matto returned to Cuzco, where she directed the literary magazine *El Recreo del Cuzco* (Cuzco's Entertainment). As an active journalist during these years, she became a well-known celebrity in Peru. She traveled to Lima in 1877 and was warmly received by the intellectual elite. She attended the *salón literario* organized by Juana Manuela GORRITI and was hailed as an important literary voice of Peruvian letters.

When Matto's husband died in 1881, leaving her in dire economic straits, she returned to Tinta to manage her hacienda personally. During this time Chile and Peru were engaged in the WAR OF THE PACIFIC, which left the defeated Peru devastated. Matto aided her compatriots by raising funds for military equipment and donating her farmhouse for medical assistance to the troops. In 1883 she lost her hacienda and she went to

Arequipa, where she again worked as a journalist. In 1884 she published *Tradiciones cusqueñas: leyendas, biografías y hojas sueltas* (Cuzco's Traditions: Legends, Biographies, and Other Writings), a volume of articles published in newspapers and literary magazines between 1870 and 1882, with a preface by Peruvian writer Ricardo PALMA. In 1886 she published a second volume, *Tradiciones cusqueñas: crónicas, hojas sueltas,* with a preface by José Antonio Laval. These short stories (*tradiciones*) follow the model of the genre created by Palma.

In 1887, Matto returned to Lima and organized a *salón literario* that became an important meeting place for Peruvian intellectuals. She joined the Ateneo de Lima and Círculo Literario literary groups. Connected to these groups was the literary publication *El Peru Ilustrado,* of which Matto was appointed director in 1889. She insisted that the magazine reflect Peruvian concerns above all others. Together with writer Manuel GONZÁLEZ PRADA, she became known as a defender of the Indians. In 1889 she also published her best-known novel, *Aves sin nido.* It was the first indigenous novel that portrayed the life and social condition of the Indian population of Peru and the first favorable literary representation of the Indian cause, including a partial history of the abuse of the Indian by whites, mestizos, and the clergy in Spanish America. In 1892, Matto published her only play, *Hima sumac.* In 1893 she published *Leyendas y recortes.* Her other novels, *Indole* (1891) and *Herencia* (Inheritance, 1895), continue the Indian theme. *Boreales, miniaturas y porcelanas,* published in Buenos Aires in 1902, documents the difficult years of political turmoil in Peru and how they affected Matto. In 1895 she left Lima for Buenos Aires, where she wrote for *La Nación* and *La Prensa.* She founded the magazine *El Búcaro Americano* in 1897 and traveled to Europe in 1908. Her memoirs are collected in *Viaje de recreo* (Vacation Trips, 1910). She died in Buenos Aires of pneumonia, and her remains were returned to Peru in 1924.

ALBERTO TAURO, *Clorinda Matto de Turner y la novela indigenista* (1976); ANTONIO CORNEJO-POLAR, *La novela peruana* (1980; 2d ed. 1989); EFRAÍN KRISTAL, "Clorinda Matto de Turner" in *Latin American Writers,* edited by Carlos A. Solé and Maria Isabel Abreu, vol. 1 (1989).

MAGDALENA GARCÍA PINTO

Clorinda Matto de Turner, Lima, 1890. PHOTO BY EUGÈNE COURRET / ARCHIVO CARETAS.

MAUÁ, VISCONDE DE (Irineu Evangelista de Souza; *b.* 28 December 1813; *d.* 21 October 1889), Brazilian merchant, banker, industrialist, railroad magnate, rancher, and national politician who rose from obscure beginnings to become a major protagonist in imperial Brazil's banking, transportation, and industrial infrastructure. Born in Rio Grande do Sul, Mauá initiated his business-entrepreneurial career in Rio de Janeiro at age eleven as a cashier in a cloth store and was later employed in a British firm, where he learned British business methods and successively held the positions of partner and sole

Visconde de Mauá. Cover of a magazine published in his memory at the time of his death, 1889. ICONOGRAPHIA.

manager by the 1830s, when the firm's founder returned to England.

Mauá invested in a variety of modernizing endeavors, most of which initially were aimed at improving Brazil's transportation and industrial infrastructure. From the establishment of an iron foundry that supplied pipes for a new water system in Rio de Janeiro, Mauá acquired concessions for a tramway line, the first gas-lamp system built in the country, and the first steamship company to operate on the Amazon River. An investor in the Second Bank of Brazil, he founded the Bank of Mauá in 1854, the same year he constructed Brazil's first railroad line from the port of Mauá on Guanabara Bay in Rio de Janeiro to the interior highlands, where COFFEE production for the foreign market was the mainstay of the Brazilian economy. That year he also received the title of baron.

Mauá represented his native province of Rio Grande do Sul in the Chamber of Deputies from 1856 to 1873, and he received the title of viscount in 1874 after laying the first submarine cable between Brazil and Europe.

Mauá's widespread banking network extended to London, and his business ventures expanded to Argentina and Uruguay, where he held control over Uruguayan railroads, shipyards, gasworks, livestock farms, and meat-processing plants. His economic liberalism was not popular among conservative economic sectors in Brazil and Uruguay, and his creditors were not sympathetic to the losses he suffered in the Río de la Plata region during the WAR OF THE TRIPLE ALLIANCE (1864–1870). His finances declined in the 1870s, and in 1878 he was forced into bankruptcy. His "Exposition to the Creditors of Mauá and Company and to the Public," written in that year, attributed the reversal of his fortunes to his placing the well-being of the country before personal concerns, rather than to mismanagement or misdeeds. Mauá spent the remainder of his life managing a modest investment business.

ANYDA MARCHANT, *Viscount Mauá and the Empire of Brazil: A Biography of Irineu Evangelista de Sousa, 1813–1889* (1965); LIDIA BESOUCHET, *Mauá e seu tempo* (1978); RODERICK J. BARMAN, "Business and Government in Imperial Brazil: The Experience of Viscount Mauá," *Journal of Latin American Studies* 13, no. 2 (1981): 239–264.

NANCY PRISCILLA SMITH NARO

MAULE, historical region (1982 population 730,587) and name of a province in Central Chile dominated by the 140-mile-long Maule River and its affluents. The most important center is Talca (164,492 inhabitants in 1990), located in the Central Valley. During colonial and early republican times, the fertile lands of the region provided most of Chile's wine, dry meat, and wheat, which were shipped to Peru on wooden ships and barges built in Constitución on the Pacific shore. At the turn of the century, this important agricultural region deteriorated owing to intense soil erosion and the ensuing siltation of the river. Today most agricultural products (grapes, vegetables, and fruit) are grown in the Central Valley.

CÉSAR N. CAVIEDES

MAURITS, JOHAN (John Maurice, Count of Nassau-Siegen; *b.* 17 June 1604; *d.* 20 December 1679), governor-general of Dutch Brazil (1637–1644). Born in Dillenburg in what is now Germany, Maurits was the eldest son of Johann VII, count of Nassau-Siegen (1561–1623), and his second wife, Margaretha, princess of Holstein-Sonderburg. Johan's paternal grandfather was Johann VI (1536–1606), younger brother of William the Silent of Orange. Maurits served with distinction in a number of campaigns in the Thirty Years' War with the army of the Dutch States-General. In August 1636, Maurits formally accepted an offer from the DUTCH WEST INDIA COMPANY to be governor-general of Netherlands Brazil. Soon after his arrival in RECIFE on 23 January 1637, he successfully ousted the Portuguese military forces from the region north of the Rio São Francisco and forced them to retreat across the river to the captaincy of Sergipe del Rey. The entire captaincy of PERNAMBUCO fell into DUTCH hands.

Maurits then returned to Recife to restore order and

Johan Maurits. ICONOGRAPHIA.

encourage the Portuguese inhabitants to settle down and continue sugar production. As incentive, he allowed both Catholics and JEWS to worship publicly and promised them good treatment. At the same time, he improved fortifications, formed alliances with the neighboring Indians, and tried to encourage more northern European immigration. Later that year, he sent an expedition under Colonel Hans Coen to capture São Jorge da Mina (Elmina) on Africa's Gold Coast. Another expedition, under Admiral Jan Corneliszoon Lichthart, sailed along the coast of Brazil to intercept Portuguese shipping and raided the captaincy of Ilheus, south of Bahia. In November of 1637, Colonel Sigismund von Schoppe attacked the captaincy of Sergipe del Rey. By the end of Maurits's first year in Brazil, the northern captaincy of Ceará was also in Dutch hands.

On 17–18 May 1638, Maurits attempted to capture the Brazilian capital of Bahia, but failed even though he had a force of 3,600 Europeans and 1,000 Indians. In 1640, he successfully defended Dutch Brazil from the count of Torre's large Spanish-Portuguese armada. In reprisal for the damage done by Portuguese troops to plantations in Dutch Brazil, Maurits sent another expedition under Lichthart to attack Portuguese sugar mills in the region

around Bahia, and twenty-seven of them were destroyed. Other raids were made along the Brazilian coast, but not all were successful. After the Portuguese overthrow of Spanish rule (December 1640) and while a treaty between Portugal and the Netherlands was being negotiated, Maurits sent 3,000 men, including 240 Indians, to capture Luanda and Benguela in Angola, the islands of São Tomé and Ano Bom, and the fortress of Axim on the coast of Guinea, a task successfully completed during the second half of 1641 and early 1642. In November of 1641, São Luis do Maranhão was captured, giving the Dutch control over more than a thousand miles of Brazilian coastline. At this point, the Dutch West India Company reached its greatest territorial extension in the Atlantic world.

During his seven-year stay in Brazil, Maurits rebuilt Recife and founded a new town (Mauritsstad) on the neighboring island of Antônio Vaz. He also built two country houses (Vrijburg and Boa Vista) on the island. On his properties he collected a wide variety of Brazilian flora and fauna. Maurits brought with him to America a large entourage of scholars, artists, and craftsmen. The most important were Georg Marcgraf (1610–1644), the German naturalist and astronomer; Willem Piso (1611–1678), the governor-general's personal physician, who published on tropical medicine and diseases; the landscape painter Frans POST (1612–1680); and Albert ECKHOUT (ca. 1610–1665), whose paintings depicted Brazilians and the country's animals and plants. Also of interest are the paintings by the amateur Zacharias Wagener, a German soldier in the service of the Dutch West India Company.

After more than seven years of rule, Maurits, greatly beloved by the populace of Dutch Brazil, was recalled by the directors of the Dutch West India Company. He left for Europe in May of 1644. He became stadholder of Cleves (1647–1679) and was made a prince of the Holy Roman Empire in 1652. He served in various Dutch military posts, distinguishing himself in battle as late as 1674.

The best biography is PIETER J. BOUMAN, *Johan Maurits van Nassau, de Braziliaan* (1947). CHARLES R. BOXER, *The Dutch in Brazil, 1624–1654* (1957) has two fine chapters on Johan Maurits and his accomplishments (pp. 67–158) and a sketch of his activities in Europe after returning from Brazil (pp. 261–264). Two other useful accounts of the role of Maurits in Brazil are JOSÉ ANTÔNIO GONSALVES DE MELLO, *Tempo dos flamengos: Influência da ocupaçao Holandesa na vida e na cultura do norte do Brasil* (1947), and HERMANN WÄTJEN, *Das Hollandische Kolonialreich in Brasilien* (1921), which is available in a Portuguese translation (1938). Also of interest are the essays in E. VAN DEN BOOGAART, ed., *Johan Maurits van Nassau-Siegen, 1604–1679: A Humanist Prince in Europe and Brazil* (1979). Valuable plates are found in PETER J. P. WHITEHEAD and MARINUS BOESEMAN, *A Portrait of Dutch 17th Century Brazil: Animals, Plants, and People by the Artists of Johan Maurits of Nassau* (1989).

FRANCIS A. DUTRA

See also **Dutch in Colonial Brazil.**

MAXIMILIAN (*b.* 6 July 1832; *d.* 19 June 1867), emperor of Mexico (1864–1867). Born in the Schönbrunn Palace in Vienna, Maximilian was the younger brother of Emperor Francis Joseph. He served as Austrian governor of Lombardy and Venetia from February 1857 until April 1859, when his liberal policies caused a breach with the Vienna authorities. In July 1857, he married Charlotte (known in Mexico as CARLOTA), daughter of Leopold I of the Belgians, who had earlier declined the Greek throne and the offer of a Mexican crown on the grounds that financial support had been lacking. Carlota, however, fervently believed in the Mexican imperial idea.

Rather than a politician, Maximilian was a romantic who wanted to do something for humanity. Before NAPOLEON III's suggestion of the Mexican crown, he had traveled the Mediterranean, and by the end of 1859, had also visited Madeira and Brazil. Francis Joseph, reluctant to be drawn into the Mexican scheme, left the matter of the crown to Maximilian, who verbally accepted the offer on 3 October 1863. Following Maximilian's acceptance, Napoleon, in the secret convention of Miramar, agreed to maintain an army of 20,000 men in Mexico until 1867 and the Foreign Legion until 1873, while in exchange, Mexico would cover the entire cost as well as pay back its past debts. In September-October 1863, he was apparently studying Lucas Alamán's *Historia de México,* a pro-monarchy tract. On 10 April 1864, Maximilian formally accepted the crown offered to him by a delegation of Mexican monarchists. Four days later he and Carlota set sail, by way of Rome, where they received the blessing of Pope Pius IX, reaching Mexico City on 12 June, after a *Te Deum* celebrated at the shrine of Our Lady of Guadalupe by Archbishop LABASTIDA. Maximilian had no intention of restoring the position of the church to that held before the Reform Laws, an attitude that led to intense conflict with the bishops and the papal nuncio. He ignored the pope's request to suspend Liberal measures, which he himself had ratified, and issued imperial decrees confirming purchases of ecclesiastical properties (28 December 1864) and continuing sales—though providing for division of rural properties (26 February 1865).

Maximilian also was determined to free himself of the French and disliked Marshal François BAZAINE, the French commander in chief in Mexico, who had abandoned the attempt to create a Mexican army late in 1864. The French army encountered fierce guerrilla resistance across Mexico. At the same time, Maximilian made the serious mistake of sending Miguel MIRAMÓN and Leonardo MÁRQUEZ, the best Conservative generals, on missions in Europe.

Maximilian's Council of State and cabinet consisted in the main of moderates, since there existed little basis of support for the empire among Conservatives and the clergy. The emperor's competition for the middle ground was undermined further by Napoleon III's determination from late 1866 to evacuate all French forces. After Miramón's return to France in November, Maxi-

Portrait of Maximilian by Alberto Graefle. NATIONAL MUSEUM OF HISTORY, MUNICH; PHOTO BY BOB SCHALKWIJK.

milian for the first time became dependent on the Conservatives for his survival. He had in the meantime withdrawn to Orizaba for one month to ponder the question of abdication and indulge his passion for catching butterflies. Meanwhile, Carlota went to France to appeal to Napoleon III to save the empire by committing more funds. She reached Paris in August 1866, but to no avail.

Maximilian's decision to remain on the throne was made public on 30 November 1866. A junta of notables voted on 14 January 1867 in Mexico City to uphold the empire by one vote, in spite of Bazaine's reservations concerning the empire's military position. Maximilian refused to abandon Mexico City with the last French troops and departed for the interior to take personal command of his army. He was captured by forces loyal to President Benito JUÁREZ and was summarily tried and executed at Querétaro on 19 June 1867. The case against him rested on JUÁREZ's decree of 25 January 1862 for the execution of all collaborators, and the death sentence, which Juárez refused to commute, was determined by the imperial decree of 3 October 1865, which had established the death penalty for all members of rebel bands or bandit groups. Juárez refused all appeals for clemency and delayed sending the corpse to Europe.

Maximilian had attempted to alleviate agrarian problems in his imperial decrees of 26 June 1865, which vested communal ownership in village inhabitants in reversal of Liberal policy, and in those of 1 November 1865, which granted laborers the right to leave employment at will. He did not consider himself to be the dupe of Napoleon III or the pawn of the French army. His decision to remain in Mexico after February 1867 reflected his determination to uphold his honor as a Hapsburg. He had sought to identify with Mexico and believed that the country could attain peace under his rule. Anxious to rally moderate opinion to the throne, he alienated Mexican Conservatives and the Catholic hierarchy. Moreover, Maximilian was hampered by his own lack of political skill.

ÉMILE DE KÉRATRY, *L'elévation et la chute de l'Émpereur Maximilian* (1867); EGON CAESAR CORTI, *Maximilian and Charlotte of Mexico*, 2 vols., translated by Catherine A. Phillips (1928).

BRIAN HAMNETT

MAXIMÓN, a MAYA cult existing in the western highlands of Guatemala, practiced principally by Maya Indians in Santiago Atitlán, San Jorge La Laguna, Nahualá, and Zunil. The cult of San Simón of San Andrés Itzapa is closely related to that of Maximón and has more Ladino followers. The Maximón is a wooden image that is kept in a chapel or at home and dressed as a wealthy Indian or in a suit or military uniform. In exchange for prayers and offerings of money, cigars, liquor, tortillas, candles, and incense, Maximón performs miracles. While Maximón is considered a guardian of moral behavior, he is also associated with vices and sexual disorder.

Maximón is important as a representation of the mixing of Maya and Catholic religions characterized by both the destruction of the native religion and the lack of acceptance of Catholicism. Though unknown, his origins are related to beliefs about San Miguel (Saint Michael), Pedro de Alvarado, San Andrés, San Pedro, Judas Iscariote, and the Maya god MAM. He appeared at the end of the eighteenth century or the beginning of the nineteenth century. The Catholic church has been unsuccessful in efforts to crush the cult, and in Santiago Atitlán, Maximón parades with the Catholic saints during Holy Week.

E. MICHAEL MENDELSON, "Maximón: An Iconographical Introduction," in *Man* 59, no. 87 (1959): 57–60; MARIO RICARDO PELLECER BADILLO, *Un Encuentro con San Simón en San Andrés Itzapa* (1973); DIEGO F. MOLINA, *Las confesiones de Maximón* (1983).

LAURA L. WOODWARD

See also **Syncretism.**

MAXIXE, Brazilian song and dance form. Performed in syncopated 2/4 time, the maxixe was created from a fusion of elements of the European polka, the habanera, the LUNDU, and the Brazilian TANGO. The maxixe was popular from its first appearance in Rio de Janeiro around 1870 until approximately 1920. It has been variously described as the "first . . . truly national genre" by Charles Perrone, and "the first urban dance created in Brazil" by Oneyda Alvarenga. Its historical importance derives from its being the immediate and often indistinguishable precursor of the *samba carioca* (Rio de Janeiro SAMBA). The best-known maxixe composers are Ernesto NAZARETH and Marcelo TUPINAMBA, although both referred to their compositions as tangos.

ONEYDA ALVARENGA, *Música popular brasileira* (1982); GÉRARD BÉHAGUE, "Popular Music," in *Handbook of Latin American Popular Culture*, edited by Charles Tatum and Harold Hinds (1986); MÁRIO DE ANDRADE, *Dicionário musical brasileiro*, coordinated by Oneyda Alvarenga and Flávia Camargo Toni (1982–1989); CHARLES A. PERRONE, *Masters of Contemporary Brazilian Song* (1989).

ROBERT MYERS

See also **Música Popular Brasileira.**

MAY PACTS (1902). The Pactos de Mayo were a series of four diplomatic treaties between Chile and Argentina negotiated in 1902. Since the mid-nineteenth century, Buenos Aires and Santiago had disputed the location of their common border. The arguments became so hostile that both nations began modernizing their armies as well as engaging in a costly naval arms race in preparation for war. Great Britain convinced the two countries to negotiate a settlement, which resulted in the Pactos de Mayo.

The treaties achieved several goals: they established a mechanism for the peaceful settlement of the outstanding boundary issues and ended the naval competition by setting a rough parity between the two nations' fleets. More significantly, each country recognized the other's hegemony on its own coasts: Argentina promised not to intervene in the Pacific basin, and Chile respected Argentina's domination of the Atlantic. Thus, the treaties not only provided a mechanism for resolving their long-festering border dispute, they also recognized the rights of the signatories in their respective spheres of influence, thereby avoiding future possible irritants to international peace.

LUIS GALDAMES, *A History of Chile* (1941), pp. 406–407; ROBERT N. BURR, *By Reason or Force: Chile and the Balancing of Power in South America, 1830–1905* (1965), pp. 252–256.

WILLIAM F. SATER

MAYA, THE, one of the largest indigenous groups of the Americas, with a modern population estimated at more than six million. The largest concentration of modern Maya peoples is in Guatemala, where they make up over 40 percent of the population. In Mexico, Yucatecan Mayan speakers are the second largest indigenous group in the country. The Mayan language family, which includes twenty-four to thirty related but mutually unintelligible languages, is the most populous and diversified language family in Mesoamerica. With the exception of Huastec in the Mexican states of Veracruz and Tamaulipas, Mayan speakers are found today in northern Yucatán, Belize, Chiapas, and highland Guatemala. Linguists have estimated that the Mayan languages began diverging around 4,100 years ago. Before about 2200 B.C., ancestral Mayan speakers presumably spoke a single parent language, known as proto-Mayan, with their homeland possibly in the northwestern highlands of Guatemala.

The territory of the ancient Maya included the entire Yucatán Peninsula, Belize, most of Guatemala, western Honduras, and western El Salvador. This area is extremely varied topographically and physiographically, and differences in elevation, temperature, rainfall, soils, availability of water, natural plants and animals, and the distribution of natural resources such as salt and obsidian have resulted in great environmental diversity. The northern lowlands of Yucatán are low and flat, hot, relatively dry (rainfall averages less than seventy-eight inches annually), and characterized by poor soils and low forest and bush vegetation. The central lowlands, or the Petén region of Guatemala, are moister, with annual rainfall averaging more than seventy-eight inches, and are distinguished by many lakes, seasonal swamps, deep soils in some places, and good availability of natural resources such as chert, limestone, and hardwoods. The tropical forest in the central lowlands is lush, and animal life is rich and diverse. South of the Petén, the southern lowlands provide a transitional zone to the highlands. This region is characterized by abundant rainfall (78 to 117 inches annually), rich soils, and thick tropical rain forest. The Motagua Valley, which links the southern lowlands with the northern highlands, was an important source of precious greenstone.

The northern highlands are composed of the rugged mountains of the Sierra Madre of Central America, spanning Chiapas and Guatemala. This region is the natural habitat of the QUETZAL, whose feathers were coveted by Maya lords for resplendent headdresses. The southern highlands are made up of the great chain of volcanoes paralleling the Pacific coastal plain, some of which are still active. The most important mineral resource of the southern highlands is obsidian, or volcanic glass, used for making cutting and scraping implements. Both highland regions feature fertile valleys and basins with rainfall averaging 78 to 117 inches annually. Vegetation in the cool northern highlands consists of rich highland rain forest on higher slopes, and semitropical pine and oak forest on lower slopes. The original vegetation of the southern highlands, which are lower and warmer, probably consisted of mixed evergreen and deciduous forest; the region is so densely inhabited—and this has been true for thousands of

years—that the natural environment has been completely altered by human activity. Finally, the Pacific coastal plain and piedmont are hot and wet, with annual rainfall averaging more than 117 inches. Soils here are rich, the tropical vegetation luxurious, and animal life abundant and varied. One of the most important products of the piedmont was cacao—from which chocolate is produced—one of the most important commercial crops of ancient Mesoamerica.

The earliest secure evidence of human presence in the Maya area has been found in the northern highlands of Guatemala, where fluted projectile points similar to those known as the Clovis type, used by early hunters and gatherers in Northern and Middle America and dated to about 10,600 to 11,300 years ago, have been found at the sites of San Rafael and Los Tapiales. A Clovis-type point is also known from Ladyville, Belize. Belize also has a number of Archaic-period sites tentatively dated to about 7500–2000 B.C., but these sites may be much younger. A recent revision dates the Belize Archaic no earlier than about 2500 B.C. On the Pacific coastal plain of Chiapas, Late Archaic-period sites have been found dating to around 3000–2000 B.C. One of these, Tlacuachero, has produced evidence that shrimp processing was an important activity. During the Archaic period, semisedentary hunters and gatherers living in isolated villages depended primarily on natural plant and animal resources for their livelihood. Coastal dwellers probably traded salt, dried fish and shrimp, and shellfish for highland products such as obsidian and domesticated plant foods such as MAIZE.

Proto-Mayan vocabulary reconstructed by means of comparisons of modern Mayan languages provides a glimpse of the habitat, plants, and animals of the ancestral Mayas of the Archaic period. In addition to a number of terms for highland plants and animals, names for some lowland species also occur. The inference is that proto-Mayan speakers inhabited a highland zone bordering on the lowlands. Names for lowland plants and animals include crocodile, coyol palm, and ceiba tree. Other names for trees refer to the willow, oak, cypress, and pine. Referents for cultivated plants include avocado, chile, yellow squash, maize, sweet potato, bean, cotton, and tobacco. Domestic animals include the dog and turkey. Other animals are JAGUAR, cougar, deer, fox, squirrel, mouse, gopher, weasel, coyote, agouti, skunk, armadillo, crow, buzzard, hummingbird, owl, bat, hawk, toad, turtle, and fish. Names for insects include bee (which also means honey), fly, gnat, ant, spider, louse, tick, butterfly, and scorpion. Other important items of proto-Mayan vocabulary include words for food preparation (*metate* [grinding stone], to grind, to roast), containers (gourd, trough), construction and tools (bench, cord, mat, house, bed, axe), ritual (drum, rattle, to jump-dance-sing, paper, writing). There is no proto-Mayan word for ceramics, which did not appear in the Maya area until about 1800 B.C. Nor are there terms for *comal* (ceramic griddle) or tortilla, which were absent in the Maya area until probably the Postclassic period.

Early Preclassic villages on the coast of Chiapas, Guatemala, and western El Salvador, dated to 1800–1500 B.C., are characterized by elaborate and well-made ceramics. The presence of highland obsidian and foreign ceramics indicates long-distance trade. Differences in architecture and grave goods and a two-level settlement hierarchy provide evidence for emerging social ranking and political integration. These coastal villagers were probably speakers of Mixe-Zoquean, not Mayan. They had a mixed subsistence economy based on the cultivation of maize, beans, and squash; root crops such as sweet potato and MANIOC; and the harvesting of coastal and riverine resources.

Toward the end of the Early Preclassic, by about 1200 B.C., the OLMEC civilization had emerged on the Gulf Coast of Mexico. By the Middle Preclassic (1000–400 B.C.), all of Mesoamerica was connected by networks of elite interaction, and through such ties the Olmecs had a strong impact on other societies, including the Maya. These networks were extremely complex, involving multidirectional economic, social, political, and religious interaction, which had a mutual transformational effect on all participating societies. Nevertheless, it is obvious that the Gulf Coast Olmecs, who were predominantly Mixe-Zoquean speakers, played a principal role in these developments. Many of the important forms and themes of Olmec monumental art, such as carved stelae and altars and portraits of named rulers linked with powerful cosmological forces, foreshadow those that appear later among the Maya. Early steps in the development of calendrics, astronomy, and hieroglyphic writing, which would later become intellectual hallmarks of Classic Maya civilization, were taken by the Olmecs and the Olmec-affiliated ZAPOTECS of Oaxaca during the Middle Preclassic.

A population increase occurred throughout the Maya area during the Middle Preclassic, and by about 800 B.C. the highlands and the lowlands were probably dotted with hundreds of agricultural villages, although very few are known archaeologically. While most were simply large villages, some, such as KAMINALJUYÚ in the southern highlands and Nakbe in the central lowlands, were extremely complex, with large temple platforms with elaborate architectural decoration. These sites were the centers of hierarchical chiefdoms with tributary economies.

The trends toward greater social complexity and expanding populations were intensified in the Late Preclassic (400 B.C.–A.D. 100) and the Protoclassic (A.D. 100–250). A number of large chiefly centers developed from their Middle Preclassic antecedents whose rulers vied with one another for economic and political advantage. Ritualized warfare became an important manifestation of elite competition. Widespread homogeneity in ceramics attests to a high level of achievement in craft specialization and strong economic ties throughout the

lowlands and the highlands. Networks of communication between the elites of major centers, such as EL MIRADOR and TIKAL in the central lowlands, Kaminaljuyú and Chalchuapa in the southern highlands, and ABAJ TAKALIK on the Pacific piedmont, served as the crucible for the development of early Maya civilization.

The Classic period (A.D. 250–900) witnessed the emergence of state-level polities in the lowlands. While state formation was truncated in the southern highlands by the cataclysmic eruption of Ilopango volcano in El Salvador about A.D. 250, the lowland centers continued the trends begun earlier. Population increased to as high as ten million during the Late Classic (A.D. 600–900). Stratified, class-based society with a complex division of labor was fully developed by the beginning of the Classic period. About a dozen major centers became the capitals of regional kingdoms whose territories were in constant flux, depending on the successes or failures of their military and political ventures. Each center was ruled by a shamanistic king who traced his royal descent to a founding ancestor. Carved stone monuments recorded the kings' genealogies and commemorated their important deeds and achievements. Maya lords and their wives were obliged to perform blood sacrifice on special occasions to validate their status and perpetuate their royal lineage. Royal courts of the lowlands financed elite arts and crafts, sponsored religious ceremonies, and organized armed expeditions against competing kingdoms.

Classic Lowland Maya civilization collapsed in the ninth century A.D. During the Postclassic period (A.D. 900–1524), the metropolises of the Petén were reclaimed by the jungle. The central and southern lowlands were virtually depopulated, and political organization reverted to the village level. The northern lowlands experienced great growth during this period. CHICHÉN ITZÁ was established in the Early Postclassic (A.D. 900–1200) under the aegis of the TOLTECS as the center of a large tributary state dominating the northern lowlands. This period was marked by the rise of the Putun, or Chontal, Maya. Their homeland was in the Tabasco lowlands of the Gulf Coast region, and their cultural traditions were Mexicanized. They were warriors and merchants, whose movements were motivated by a desire to seize resources and trade routes. Initially concerned with controlling the old riverine and overland routes in the central and southern lowlands, they eventually came to control the coastal routes around the Yucatán Peninsula, and ultimately commerce between Gulf Coast Mexico and Central America. Ports in this network included colonies of resident Putun merchants. Putun expansion culminated in the tenth or eleventh century when they, in alliance with Toltec warriors from Tollan, established a new capital at Chichén Itzá.

According to the chronicles, Chichén hegemony was broken in A.D. 1221. Mayapán rose to power as the new dominant center in Yucatán. There is a great overlap between Chichén Itzá and Mayapán in art style, iconography, architecture, and settlement pattern. The rulers of Mayapán were of the Cocom lineage, descendants of Hunac Ceel, the destroyer of Chichén Itzá. The Cocoms ruled over a fairly unified Yucatán for about 250 years. Shortly before A.D. 1450, Ah Xupan, a noble lord of the Xiu lineage, led a successful revolt against the Cocoms. Mayapán was sacked and looted. On the eve of the Spanish Conquest, northern Yucatán was divided into sixteen autonomous petty states.

In highland Guatemala, the Toltec-influenced Putun ancestors of the ruling lineages of the Quiches (K'ICHE'), the Cakchiquels, and the Tzutujils established themselves in the region in the Late Postclassic (A.D. 1200–1524). They built fortified mountaintop centers at the sites of UTATLAN, IXIMCHÉ, and Atitlán. Other highland Maya groups included the Mams, who built their capital of ZACULEU in the west, and the Pokomams who built MIXCO VIEJO and Chinautla Viejo. The Late Postclassic was a period of intense military competition and political fragmentation in the southern highlands.

This pattern was broken by the appearance of European invaders in the early sixteenth century. Sailing from their New World foothold in Cuba, the Spaniards launched their expedition of conquest under Hernán CORTÉS in 1519, and their first contact with Mesoamerican societies was with the Mayas of Yucatán. With the conquest of the Mexica AZTECS complete in 1523, Cortés dispatched a force from Mexico under the command of Pedro de ALVARADO to Guatemala and El Salvador in 1523–1524. The conquest of Yucatán was led by Francisco de MONTEJO and his son Francisco the Younger from 1527 to 1546.

The conquest of the Maya has been described as a never-ending process of conflict, resistance, accommodation, and integration. Many Maya groups resisted conquest for a long time, and some Maya groups were never conquered by the Spaniards. The Itzás, for example, retained their independence on the island stronghold of TAYASAL until 1697, and the Mopans, the last independent Maya group, were driven to extinction by British loggers in Belize in the late eighteenth century.

The invisible ally of the Spaniards, epidemic disease, had a tremendous impact on Maya (and all native New World) populations. Virulent epidemics preceded the arrival of Spanish troops in 1515 or 1516 in Yucatán and 1519–1521 in highland Guatemala. These scourges probably killed at least one-third of the population. By the end of the sixteenth century, the Maya population in most areas was reduced by as much as 90 percent from their pre-Conquest levels.

During the next two centuries the Maya endured forced resettlement from villages scattered throughout the countryside into centralized villages and towns. Once relocated, they were exploited for labor by the crown, clergy, and colonists and forced to pay tribute to *encomenderos* and the crown.

In the nineteenth century the Maya peoples found themselves caught up in the expansion of the plantation economies of southern Mexico and Central America. Whether it was cotton in Guatemala, coffee in Chiapas, or sugar in Yucatán, high levels of international demand for export crops made large-scale commercial agriculture highly profitable, and plantation owners turned to Maya communities for their labor needs. Contractors would entice Maya men to work with high loans that could only be repaid with plantation wages, and the infamous company store, or *tienda de raya*, trapped many in DEBT PEONAGE. In addition, plantation demands for land and other resources put pressure on Maya holdings, particularly after liberal regimes came to power in the mid- to late nineteenth century and allowed the usurpation of village lands. This dispossession not only forced more Maya to become plantation laborers, but it also seriously disrupted traditional subsistence patterns.

The increasingly desperate economic situation, coupled with repressive local governments, pushed many Mayas into open revolt in the nineteenth century. Perhaps the best-known revolt was the CASTE WAR OF YUCATÁN, which began in 1847. By 1848 the Maya had managed to gain control of most of the peninsula, and they laid waste to the sugar plantations that had been the source of many of their problems. A significant number of Maya rebels retreated into the deep forests of Quintana Roo, where they established autonomous villages with their own military and religious organization.

Despite the temporary success of the Caste War, the plantation became the backbone of the southern Mexican and Central American economies. The agrarian reform carried out after the MEXICAN REVOLUTION broke up many large estates, but it bypassed large areas of CHIAPAS, where debt peonage still exists, and Maya peoples continue to provide the bulk of the labor for the large coffee and cotton plantations of Guatemala. The unequal distribution of land and state repression weigh heavily on the Mayas. Tens of thousands of highland villagers were murdered in the 1970s and 1980s by Guatemalan military and paramilitary forces. On New Year's Day 1994 an armed revolt began in Chiapas, which remains unresolved.

The Mayas have traditionally lived in rural communities, with each community distinguished by a unique style of dress, distinct social conventions, and, in places such as Aguacatán and Sacapulas, their own language. Although most Maya remain rural agriculturists, there is a growing number of Maya teachers, university professors, writers, merchants, engineers, doctors, and other professionals. Rigoberta MENCHÚ, a Maya woman of the northern highlands of Guatemala, won the Nobel Peace Prize in 1992.

MURDO J. MAC LEOD, *Spanish Central America* (1973); TERRENCE KAUFMAN, "Archaeological and Linguistic Correlations in Mayaland and Associated Areas of Meso-America," in *World Archaeology* 8 (1976): 101–118; ROBERT WASSERSTROM, *Class and Society in Central Chiapas* (1983); SANDRA ORELLANA, *The Tzu-*

tujil Mayas (1984); ROBERT M. HILL and JOHN MONAGHAN, *Continuities in Highland Maya Social Organization* (1987); GRANT D. JONES, *Maya Resistance to Spanish Rule* (1989); NANCY M. FARRISS, *Maya Society Under Colonial Rule* (1992); ROBERT M. HILL, *Colonial Cakchiquels* (1992); W. GEORGE LOVELL, *Conquest and Survival in Colonial Guatemala* (1992); MICHAEL D. COE, *The Maya*, 5th ed. (1993); THOMAS C. KELLY, "Preceramic Projectile-Point Typology in Belize," in *Ancient Mesoamerica* 4 (1993): 205–227; ROBERT J. SHARER, *The Ancient Maya*, 5th ed. (1994).

WILLIAM R. FOWLER
JOHN D. MONAGHAN

See also **Forests; Mayan Alphabet and Orthography.**

MAYAN ALPHABET AND ORTHOGRAPHY. Through Government Accord 1046–87, published in the *Diario Oficial* on 30 November 1987, the Guatemalan government made official the Unified Alphabets for the Mayan Languages of Guatemala. This accord invalidated the 1950 decree regarding Mayan alphabets; it also superseded various other alphabets authorized by the Instituto Indigenista Nacional in 1962, 1966, and 1975. The Unified Alphabets were made official to reduce the ambiguities and confusion of multiple written forms.

The Mayan languages of Mesoamerica had an early written tradition. The Classic lowland Maya used a complex writing system based on iconographic and morphophonemic glyphs that survive in stone and ceramics. There is no evidence of a writing system in the Postclassic Guatemalan highlands; bark paper codices from Yucatán are the only record of Maya writing in the Postclassic period.

The Spanish missionaries who came to Guatemala following the Conquest in 1524 propagated Christian doctrine and recorded some Mayan ethnohistoric and cultural accounts, as well as native language vocabularies, in an accommodated Latin alphabet. The POPOL VUH and the *Memorial de Tecpán Atitlán* are two examples of transcribed narratives using Latin characters.

In the eighteenth, nineteenth, and early twentieth centuries, little was written in or about the Mayan languages. Noteworthy works of this period include BRASSEUR DE BOURBOURG's *Dictionnaire, grammaire et chrestomathie de la langue maya* (1862) and Otto Stoll's *Zur Ethnographie der Republik Guatemala* (1884). These early works used an orthography congruent with their authors' own linguistic orientations.

It was not until 1949, at the First Congress of Linguists, that systematic alphabets were first proposed for the four majority Mayan languages of Guatemala. These were made official and published in 1950 as *Alfabeto para los cuatro idiomas indígenas mayoritarios de Guatemala: Quiché, cakchiquel, mam y kekchí.* The 1950 official alphabets, like all those approved by the Instituto Indigenista Nacional during the next several decades, were developed largely by foreign linguists and missionaries. These alphabets imposed conventions of Spanish in order to standardize Mayan orthography and facilitate the transfer of literacy skills from Spanish to the vernacular languages.

Despite the existence of official alphabets since 1950, institutions and individuals working in the Mayan languages tended to develop and disseminate Mayan-language materials in different alphabets. Most adhered to Spanish orthography; only the alphabet of Adrián Chávez to write K'iche' (1967) and that of the Proyecto Lingüístico Francisco Marroquín (1976) made concerted efforts to avoid the overt imposition of Spanish orthographic conventions on the Mayan-language writing systems.

The 1987 Mayan-language alphabet was proposed at

Mayan Language Alphabets:
Summary of Distinguishing Graphemes

Phoneme	*Early*[1] *Missionaries*	*Late*[1] *Missionaries*	*Official 1950*	*Official 1975*	*ALMK*[2]	*PLFM*[3]	*Official 1987*
/ɓ/	b	b	b′	b	ƀ	b′	b′
/k/	c/qu	c/qu	c/q	c/qu	k	k	k
/k′/	ꜭ	q	c′/q′	c/q′u	ɣ	k′	k′
/q/	k	k	k	k	ƛ	q	q
/ʠ/	ɛ	g	k′	k′	ꝋ	q′	q′
/č′/	ꜭh	qh	ch′	ch′	*	ch′	ch′
/t′/	tt	t	t′	t′	đ	t′	t′
/ƈ/	ꜯ	tz	tz′	tz′	ꭓ	tz′	tz′
/š/	x	x	x	x/ẍ	sh	x/xh	x/xh
/w/	v,uh#	v, uh	w	w; u/c_v	w	w	w
/?/	———	———	′	′	`	7	′

[1]Alphabet used by missionaries of the colonial period (1524–1821) for Ki'che' Kaqchikel, and Tz'utujil (Terrence Kaufman, *Proyecto de alfabetos*, p. 42).
[2]Alphabet created by Adrián Inéz Chávez and adopted by the Academia de la Lengua Maya Kí-chè (ALMK).
[3]Alphabet proposed by Terrence Kaufman and modified and adopted by Proyecto Lingüístico Francisco Marroquín (PLFM).

the first seminar of the Academy of Mayan Languages of Guatemala. At this seminar, Mayan-language speakers and linguists moved to adopt a common core alphabet to write the Mayan languages of Guatemala. The criteria were that the alphabets be systematic, phonemic, and accessible, and that they promote Mayan literacy, reduce dialect differences, and affirm the cultural identity of the Maya.

At the seminar, nine graphemes—those at the center of the alphabet controversy—were approved to represent phonemes common to the Mayan languages: *b', k, k', q, q', ch', t', tz', '* (see table). At later regional meetings the remaining graphemes were selected and accommodated to the specific languages.

The phonemic alphabets approved by Government Accord 1046-87 recognize twenty-seven letters shared by the twenty-one Mayan languages of Guatemala, and an additional twenty-six letters used to represent sounds distinctive to specific languages or language groups. Glottalized stops are marked with an apostrophe; no distinctive symbols are used to distinguish whether they are implosive or explosive. Long vowels are represented as digraphs (*vv*) and relaxed vowels are marked with diaeresis (*v̈*).

A comprehensive study of the Mayan glyphs, including an important discussion of the verb morphology and syntax of the Mayan writing system, is in LINDA SCHELE and DAVID FREIDEL, *Forest of Kings* (1990). LYLE CAMPBELL discusses the orthographic conventions employed by the early missionaries in "Quichean Linguistics and Philology" in *Word Anthropology: Approaches to Language,* edited by William C. McCormack and Stephen A. Wurm (1978). For a discussion of the 1949 First Congress of Linguists and the 1950 official Mayan alphabets, see JULIA BECKER RICHARDS, "The First Congress of Mayan Language of Guatemala," in *The Earliest Stage of Language Planning: The "First Congress" Phenomenon,* edited by Joshua Fishman (1992). The general topic of Mayan language alphabets is reviewed by TERRENCE KAUFMAN in *Proyecto de alfabetos y ortografía para escribir las lenguas mayances* (1976); and MARGARITA LÓPEZ RAQUEC, *Acerca de los alfabetos para escribir los idiomas mayas de Guatemala* (1989).

JULIA BECKER RICHARDS

MAYAN ETHNOHISTORY. [Mayan-language orthography is contested. The present essay uses the traditional Hispanic names of nearly 500 years' standing. Other entries adopt a modernized spelling recommended by the Guatemalan government. Such forms appear here as parenthetical variants or as CROSS-REFERENCES. For further information see the article on MAYAN ALPHABET AND ORTHOGRAPHY above. *Ed.*]

Mayan history in the sense of a chronologically placeable text begins with a carved stone monument of A.D. 199 known as the Hauberg Stela. Its provenience is unknown. It is possible that it was anticipated by similar monuments of the Olmec culture, such as Stela 10 from KAMINALJUYÚ, Guatemala (147 B.C.) or even earlier Zapotec and Olmec inscriptions. None of these texts has

been read, and in any case they are not Mayan. The Maya are generally confined to the territories of the states of Yucatán, Quintana Roo, Campeche, and Chiapas in Mexico, the republics of Belize and Guatemala, and the westernmost sections of Honduras and El Salvador.

By the end of the third century we begin to be able to piece together the fragmentary dynastic histories of particular Mayan cities, and after the sixth century these become relatively complete and continuous. The relevant texts are almost entirely inscribed on stone monuments and the surfaces of buildings, though they are supplemented by other "primary sources": hieroglyphic texts on murals or stone and ceramic objects. The latter are historical sources, but unlike the monumental inscriptions, they are not in themselves history. Though the dynastic histories came to an end in the tenth century, when they ceased to be carved in stone, the tradition of hieroglyphic writing continued on less permanent objects of wood and paper, virtually all of which have been destroyed. The sole surviving pre-Conquest paper manuscript is the Dresden Codex, the dating of which is still debated. Three other codices survive from the sixteenth century (Madrid, Paris, and Grolier), and may be copies of pre-Conquest originals. Though they reveal a great deal about Mayan culture, the codices were not intended as history but rather as mythical, ritual, astrological, and astronomical almanacs.

The decipherment and reading of the pre-Spanish history of the Maya is proceeding rapidly and demonstrates that the Maya were the only truly historical people of the Americas from the third to the sixteenth century. The conversion of these thirteen centuries from prehistory into history is the most remarkable recent development in the study of the Maya. This historical tradition was confined to only two of the score or so of the Mayan languages of the time: Yucatec and Chol.

To some extent, the historical gap between the tenth century and the sixteenth can be filled, not by the codices but by histories written by the Maya after the Spanish arrived. Although the Mayan alphabet was adequate for writing two of the Mayan languages, and could even have been used to write Spanish (it was used to write NAHUATL), many of the Mayan peoples, particularly the Chontal and Yucatec of Mexico and the Quiche (K'ICHE') and Cakchiquel (KAQCHIKEL) of Guatemala, rapidly adopted the Latin-based alphabets designed by the Franciscan missionaries. Much of what they wrote was their own history.

Some of the sources for this history may have been hieroglyphic manuscripts since lost, but it is likely that the more important source was oral tradition. Nonetheless, the rigor of the Mayan calendar was such that we may very well accept as historical some rather fragmentarily reported events as early as the ninth century (the occupation of Chichén Itzá by the Itzá Maya in 869–880 and their rule of the city until 1009).

Historiographically the Mayan histories present a

number of distinctive problems. In their present form, none of them are sixteenth-century manuscripts. The dates given below are termini ante quem, indicating the probable dates of the extant copies. All of them were composed over a period of time, sometimes centuries, and by different authors. (The POPOL VUH may be an exception.)

The six fullest and most important of these sixteenth-century Mayan histories are the *Books of Chilam Balam of Tizimin* (1837), *Chumayel* (1837), and *Mani* (1837) in Yucatec; the *Chronicles of Acalan-Tixchel* (1604) in Chontal; the *Popol Vuh* (1704) in Quiche; and the *Annals of the Cakquiquels* (1604) in Cakchiquel. Like the histories of the Classic period (third to tenth century), these works are primarily dynastic. They trace the ruling lineages of their respective areas with varying degrees of historicity and time depth: the Itzá (ninth–eighteenth century) in eastern Yucatán, the Xiu (thirteenth–seventeenth century) in western Yucatán, the Paxbolon (fourteenth–seventeenth century) in western Campeche, the Cavek (thirteenth–sixteenth century) in west-central Guatemala, and the Zotzil (fifteenth–seventeenth century) in east-central Guatemala. In the main they are highly local in reference, though they overlap geographically in some degree, and they refer to places as far afield as southern Veracruz, Cozumel, southeast Chiapas, and the Guatemalan Peten. All of them describe the coming of the Spaniards.

An additional, if problematic, native source is the *Rabinal Achí* (1855), a Quiche drama that appears to refer to fifteenth-century events, preserved in oral and eventually written form, and discovered in the nineteenth century.

The manuscripts have not always been copied in their original order (particularly the *Books of Chilam Balam*), and copyists' errors are frequent. The problems can often be overcome because of the Mayan passion for chronology and accuracy, but it is not always easy. The Mayan cyclical view of time also gets in the way: sometimes the material is both history and prophecy at the same time, on the theory that what happens on a given date will recur on the same date in the next cycle. Dynastic lists are often distorted because of lineage rivalries, and generations may have been added or deleted even in ancient times for political reasons. Mayan history must be attentively and critically read and interpreted.

The historical preoccupations of the Maya that emerge from these sources are unique. Not only are the pre-Conquest histories dynastic, they are also ritualized history. The present owes the past the duty of emulation. Thus the Mayan historian describes the past in terms of its ritual achievements, generalizing it in mythological terms as a basis for the prediction of the future. For the Maya, furthermore, such prophecy was a positive guide to action. Having predicted their future on the basis of the past, they made every effort to make the prediction come true. A famous example is the cycle of 260 *tuns* (ap-

proximately 256 years), the end of which was supposed to occur on a day named 8 Ahau. In Classic times this date was supposed to end dynasties, and it often did. It was a great political advantage to potential usurpers to argue that they had the sun on their side. In colonial times, it was on 8 Ahau 1697 that the Itzá Maya of the Peten surrendered and converted to Christianity, having sent to Mérida for missionaries for the purpose. In social terms, Mayan history is strongly hierarchical; in philosophical terms it is profoundly fatalistic. Always it is religious.

Even after the Spanish conquest, the Maya wrote their own history in a continuous tradition of colonial literacy that lasted in some areas (notably in Yucatec and Quiche) until the nineteenth century. Apart from adding to the early chronicles, they provided the written records, all in Mayan, that are the stuff of history: land documents; wills, *cofradía* ordinances; letters; medical, astrological, and astronomical handbooks; government reports; ritual poetry and drama. These are paralleled by an increasing volume of Catholic materials: catechisms, sermons, missals, church calendars, even occasional translations of secular European narratives.

From many of the Mayan historical sources one may almost gain the impression that the Spanish conquest did not take place. The event itself is described, to be sure, but thereafter the Spanish largely disappear, being fundamentally irrelevant to Mayan history. Mayan resistance to the Europeans was prolonged and stubborn, both overtly and covertly.

Something similar is true for the vast majority of the Spanish chronicles. The Indians existed only as the passive objects of conquest and conversion. In fact, it took the combined efforts of four Franciscans and three Dominicans over a period of three centuries to come close to describing the Maya as well as Bernardino de Sahagún and Alfonso Molina had depicted the Aztecs in central Mexico. The Franciscans are Diego de LANDA, Antonio de Ciudad Real, Diego LÓPEZ DE COGOLLUDO, and Domingo de Vico, all of the sixteenth century. The Dominicans are Bartolomé de LAS CASAS (sixteenth century), Antonio de Remesal (seventeenth century), and Francisco XIMÉNEZ (eighteenth century). In varying ways and to varying degrees these authors were interested in the Maya and endeavored to understand them.

The most important Spanish works relevant to Mayan ethnohistory are Landa's *Relacíon de las cosas de Yucatán*, Ciudad Real's *Diccionario de Motul*, Cogolludo's *Historia de Yucatán*, Vico's *Theologia Indorum*, Las Casas's *Apologética historia*, Remesal's *Historia general de las Indias occidentales* and Ximénez's *Historia de la provincia de San Vicente de Chiapa y Guatemala de la orden de Predicadores*. To these may be added the seventeeth-century secular work of Francisco Antonio FUENTES Y GUZMÁN, *Recordación florida*. Landa, Cogolludo, and Ciudad Real deal with Yucatán; Vico, Las Casas, Remesal, and Fuentes y Guzmán treat Guatemala; Ximénez covers Guatemala and Chiapas. Together they come close to blanketing the territory of the Maya, and they are backed up by an enormous archive of secondary sources and historical materials of all kinds, the most significant of which are the sixteenth-century RELACIONES GEOGRÁFICAS.

The autistic historical traditions of the Maya and the Spanish meet and begin to merge in these early chronicles. Like the Mayan histories, the Spanish ones show a deepening comprehension of the other tradition over time, though only Ciudad Real (Yucatec) and Vico (Quiche) may be said to have had a firm comprehension of a Mayan language. The only Mayan author with a comparably sophisticated command of Spanish was Gaspar Antonio Xiu, credited with the compilation of many of the *Relaciones geográficas* in Yucatán.

By the end of the nineteenth century, the colonial historical tradition had ended in both Yucatec and Quiche. The Latin-based alphabets were replaced by new ones, and although native language historical materials were produced in them, they are relatively minor. Explicit history was not written.

There has been an enormous growth of interest in Mayan ethnohistory in the twentieth century, though this is primarily among "foreign" scholars not resident in Mayan territory. There are, however, some notable exceptions: Alfredo Barrera Vásquez and Alfonso Villa Rojas in Yucatán, and Adrián Recinos and José Antonio Villacorta y Rodas in Guatemala. Nonetheless, the gulf in historical awareness between the Maya and the non-Maya remains almost as formidable as when Landa sat down to write his *Relación* after burning the most valuable sources.

It may be that the most significant development in Yucatán, Chiapas, and Guatemala in the modern period may turn out to be the renascent historical consciousness among the Mayan people themselves. This is particularly evident among the Tzotzil, Yucatecans, Quiche, and Cakchiquel, but is also shared by many of their Mayan neighbors. The modern Maya are increasingly interested in their history and more and more knowledgeable about it. They may even take a hand in shaping their future by writing their past again in their own language.

CHARLES ÉTIENNE BRASSEUR DE BOURBOURG, *Dictionnaire, grammaire et chrestomathie de la langue maya* (1862), which includes *Rabinal Achí*; FRANCISCO XIMÉNEZ, *Historia de la provincia de San Vicente de Chiapa y Guatemala de la Orden de Predicadores*, 3 vols. (1929–1931); ANTONIO DE REMESAL, *Historia general de las India Occidentales*, 2d ed., 2 vols. (1932); JOSÉ ANTONIO VILLACORTA C., *Memorial de Tecpán-Atitlán* (1932); FRANCISCO ANTONIO DE FUENTES Y GUZMÁN, *Recordación florida*, vols. 6–8 (1932–1933); ALFRED M. TOZZER, *Landa's Relación de las Cosas de Yucatán*, Papers of the Peabody Museum of Anthropology, Archaeology and Ethnology, Harvard University, 18 (1941); RALPH L. ROYS, *The Indian Background of Colonial Yucatán* (1943); ALFONSO VILLA ROJAS, *The Maya of East Central Quintana Roo* (1945); ADRIÁN RECINOS, *Memorial de Sololá: Anales de los Cakchiqueles* (1950); DIEGO LÓPEZ DE COGOLLUDO, *Historia de Yucatán*, 5th ed., 2 vols. (1957); NELSON REED, *The Caste War of Yucatán* (1964); FRANCE VINTO SCHOLES and RALPH L. ROYS, *The Maya Chontal Indians of Acalan Tixchel* (1968); MUNRO S. EDMONSON, *The Book of Counsel: The Popol Vuh of the Guatemalan Quiche* (1971); HOWARD F. CLINE, "The Relaciones Geográficas of the Spanish Indies, 1577–1648," in *Handbook of Middle American Indians*, vol. 12 (1972), pp. 183–242; ROBERT M. CARMACK, *Quichean Civilization* (1973); EUGENE R. CRAINE and REGINALD REINDORP, trans. and eds., *The Codex Pérez and the Book of Chilam Balam of Mani* (1979); ALFREDO BARRERA VÁSQUEZ, ed., *Diccionario maya cordemex* (1980), which includes Ciudad Real's *Diccionario*; VICTORIA R. BRICKER, *The Indian Christ, the Indian King* (1981); FRAUKE RIESE, *Indianische Landrechte in Yukatan um die Mitte des 16. Jahrhunderts* (1981); MUNRO S. EDMONSON, *The Ancient Future of the Itza: The Book of Chilam Balam of Tizimin* (1982); RENÉ ACUÑA, "El Popol Vuh, Vico y la Theologia indorum," in *Nuevas perspectivas sobre el Popol Vuh*, edited by Robert M. Carmack and Francisco Morales Santos, (1973); ROBERT M. CARMACK and FRANCISCO MORALES SANTOS, eds., *Nuevas perspectivas sobre el Popol Vuh* (1973); MUNRO S. EDMONSON, *Heaven Born Merida and Its Destiny: The Book of Chilam Balam of Chumayel* (1986); GRANT D. JONES, *Maya Resistance to Spanish Rule: Time and History on a Colonial Frontier* (1989).

MUNRO S. EDMONSON

See also **Annals of the Cakchiquels; Chilam Balam.**

MAYAPAN (meaning "Standard [Banner] of the Maya") is a Late Postclassic Maya site located twenty-four miles southeast of Mérida, YUCATÁN. According to Bishop Diego de Landa, the city was established by a CHICHÉN ITZÁ lord named Kukulcan, who decreed that the native lords of Yucatán should live there. After Kukulcan's departure, Mayapan was ruled by the Cocom, an Itzá lineage who established themselves between 1263 and 1283. Mayapan subsequently was the capital of Yucatan's northern plains until its Cocom rulers were deposed by the rival Tutul Xiu lineage during the Katun 8 Ahau between 1441 and 1461.

Mayapan traditionally was referred to as Ichpa ("within the enclosure"), and archaeology has confirmed that Mayapan was a walled city, containing a population of 11,000 to 12,000. Some 3,500 buildings occupy about 1.6 square miles, including about 100 larger masonry temples or ceremonial structures.

Dominating Mayapan is the centrally located Castillo or Temple of Kukulcan (structure Q-162), a radially symmetrical pyramid temple that is a small, poorly constructed imitation of the Castillo at Chichén Itzá. Nearby is a circular building derived from, but smaller than, Chichén Itzá's Caracol structure. "Colonnaded halls," rectangular-plan buildings with frontal and medial colonnades and benches along the rear walls, front several plazas grouped around the central temples.

Located near Mayapan's center are elite residential buildings with open front rooms and one or more private rear chambers that may contain small "family shrine" altars. These "palaces" have crude block walls, beam-and-mortar roofs, and a thick plaster facing, often modeled into architectural sculpture. Some 2,000 smaller houses, with perishable upper walls and thatch roofs, surrounded the upper-class dwellings.

Mayapan possesses thirteen carved stelae, one of which, Stela 1, features a 10 Ahau glyph probably corresponding to 11.11.0.0.0 (A.D. 1441). Its distinctive polychrome hollow ceramic figurine *incensarios* (Chen Mul Modeled Type) portray both Maya and central Mexican deities.

DIEGO DE LANDA, *Landa's Relación de las cosas de Yucatán*, translated by ALFRED M. TOZZER (1941); H. E. D. POLLOCK, RALPH L. ROYS, TATIANA PROSKOURIAKOFF, and A. LEDYARD SMITH, *Mayapan, Yucatán, Mexico* (1962); ROBERT E. SMITH, *The Pottery of Mayapan: Including Studies of Ceramic Materials from Uxmal, Kabah, and Chichén Itzá* (1970).

JEFF KARL KOWALSKI

MAYORAZGO, a privilege allowing an individual to entail his estate so that his property, real or personal, could be passed on intact to a successor who, following the rule of primogeniture, preferably would be the oldest male son or the nearest relative. The legal basis for such establishments was Castilian law, in particular the 1505 Leyes de Toro. These laws allowed any subject above the rank of peasant to entail his property and thus acquire the privileges of *hidalguía* (nobility), including the title of *don* (gentleman), which forbade his entering any profession attached to commerce or industry on pain of loss of status.

In America rich individuals who could afford to petition the crown or its representatives for the royal decree permitting the establishment, entailed houses, stores, mills, mines, large rural estates, slaves, furniture, and silver and jewelry. The *mayorazgo* became a sought-after privilege of many leading families as a means of preserving the control of property within a kin group and maintaining the lineage and its collective memory. Thus, it became an important institution that perpetuated the elite class.

WILLIAM B. TAYLOR, *Landlord and Peasant in Colonial Oaxaca* (1972); JOSÉ F. DE LA PEÑA, *Oligarquía y propiedad en Nueva España (1550–1624)* (1983).

SUSAN E. RAMÍREZ

MAYORGA, SILVIO (*b.* 1936; *d.* 27 August 1967), Nicaraguan leader and cofounder of the Sandinista National Liberation Front. Mayorga was born in Matagalpa at approximately the same time as Carlos FONSECA. They grew up together and in 1954 entered law school at the National Autonomous University in León. Mayorga immediately became a student leader and joined the Nicaraguan Socialist Party in 1955. Like Fonseca, he soon rejected the passive character of the Socialists and encouraged more aggressive student radicalism. He became active in the Nicaraguan Patriotic Youth organization in the late 1950s and joined Fonseca's New Nicaragua Movement in 1960. In July 1961 Mayorga founded the Sandinista National Liberation Front with Fonseca and Tomás BORGE.

Mayorga was one of the principal commanders of guerrillas based in the village of Walaquistan. There he cooperated closely with Borge in planning the first Sandinista attack at Río Coco in 1963. He was gravely injured in an attack at San Carlos in the same year and spent several months recuperating. He reappeared in 1964 as a student organizer in León and Managua. For the next three years, Mayorga encouraged students and the urban poor to support the Sandinistas. In 1967, he led an expedition to explore Quinagua as an alternative guerrilla base in the mountains of Las Segovias. Mayorga's forces had little military experience, and some of his soldiers were teenagers. This proved disastrous when they attacked Pancasán in August 1967. Mayorga and fifty combatants were killed by the National Guard. His death and the Pancasán fiasco forced the Sandinista leadership to suspend frontal attacks on the Guard and seriously reevaluate its political and military strategy over the next two years. Mayorga was the first original Sandinista to fall in combat.

FRENTE ESTUDIANTIL REVOLUCIONARIO, *Historia del FSLN* (1975); DONALD HODGES, *The Intellectual Foundations of the Nicaraguan Revolution* (1986); U.S. DEPARTMENT OF STATE, BUREAU OF PUBLIC AFFAIRS, *Nicaraguan Biographies: A Resource Book* (1988).

MARK EVERINGHAM

See also **Nicaragua: Political Parties.**

MAZA, MANUEL VICENTE DE (*b.* 1779; *d.* 27 June 1839), Argentine patriot and public official. Maza studied in his native Buenos Aires and in Chile, where he became a lawyer. After being imprisoned at Lima in 1810 as a patriot sympathizer, he returned in 1815 to Buenos Aires, where he held a number of government positions. A friend of Juan Manuel de ROSAS, he was a Federalist, and in 1829 he was deported by the Unitarist regime of Juan LAVALLE, returning the same year. However, he was a moderate who, as acting governor of Buenos Aires in 1834–1835, dismissed some of Rosas's strongest military supporters. He resigned the governorship in the aftermath of the assassination of Juan Facundo QUIROGA, but continued to serve in the legislature and as special judge of those accused of the murder. In 1839, after his son was involved in a plot against Rosas, Maza was assassinated in Buenos Aires.

JACINTO R. YABEN, *Biografías argentinas y sudamericanas*, vol. 3 (1939), pp. 721–723; JOHN LYNCH, *Argentine Dictator: Juan Manuel de Rosas 1829–1852* (1981), pp. 159–162, 171–173, 204.

DAVID BUSHNELL

MAZATLÁN, Mexican port in the state of Sinaloa. A simple landing after 1806, after independence it quickly became the country's leading port on the west coast. At the entrance to the Gulf of California, centrally located on the Pacific coast, Mazatlán steadily expanded its commercial hinterland into the interior, becoming the commercial entrepôt for western Mexico. Foreign merchants quickly came to dominate the port's commerce. Their mercantile rivalry with Culiacán (with its satellite port of Altata) resulted in a forty-year struggle between the two cities for control of the state government and location of the state capital. Mazatlán's relative commercial position declined in the late nineteenth century, as railroads took away its competitive advantage in the interior and San Francisco, California, gradually absorbed the direct trade in Asian commerce. In 1873 the Porfirio DÍAZ–backed political clique led by Francisco CAÑEDO secured the permanent location of the capital in Culiacán but strove to promote the interests of both cities. The port's merchant-capitalists (by then a blend of native and foreign) began diversifying into other economic sectors (especially industry) and captured more and more of the wholesale trade generated by the growing economic activity within the state.

A railroad link with Guadalajara (1912) provided better access to the western interior of the country, but through the twentieth century, the rise of Mazatlán as a major tourist center has been a driving force in the city's continuing growth.

JOHN R. SOUTHWORTH, *El Estado de Sinaloa—sus industrias, comerciales, mineras y manufacturas* (1898); STUART F. VOSS, "Towns and Enterprise in Northwestern Mexico: A History of Urban Elites in Sonora and Sinaloa, 1830–1910" (Ph.D. diss., Harvard University, 1972), and *On the Periphery of Nineteenth Century Mexico: Sonora and Sinaloa, 1810–1877* (1982).

STUART F. VOSS

MAZOMBOS, descendants of settlers from Portugal. These white Brazilians of the colonial period were similar to the *criollos* of New Spain, but they were more likely to have nonwhite ancestors. Their high social position was linked to elite family membership, proprietorship of vast estates (*fazendas* or *engenhos*) with hundreds of slaves, political posts on the SENADO DA CÂMARA, appointment as high-ranking officers in the white militias, or service on the boards of elite white BROTHERHOODS (*irmandades*) of the Catholic church. In spite of their wealth, the Portuguese crown and the REINÓIS limited their role in colonial society, which eventually led to demands for independence from the mother country.

VIANNA MOOG, *Bandeirantes and Pioneers* (1964).

SHEILA L. HOOKER

See also **Race and Ethnicity.**

MAZORCA. Juan Manuel de ROSAS established a repressive dictatorship over the province of Buenos Aires, from 1829 until his overthrow by Justo José de URQUIZA in 1852. In addition to censoring the press and exiling political enemies, Rosas established the *mazorca*, the terrorist arm of his political support group, the Sociedad Popular Restauradora. The term (meaning an ear of corn) symbolized strength through unity. Members tortured and terrorized suspected unitarians, especially during the extremely violent month of October 1840. The terrorists made a slit throat and public display of decapitated heads their trademarks.

JOHN LYNCH, *Argentine Dictator: Juan Manuel de Rosas, 1829–1852* (1981).

RICHARD W. SLATTA

MBAYÁ INDIANS, a people of the Guaycuruan language family that lived in the northern Gran CHACO. At the time of contact with Spaniards in the 1540s, they lived above the Río Pilcomayo. A hunting and gathering group, they called themselves the "people of the palm" because date and coconut trees provided their most important food. Hunting and war were their most prestigious activities, and both were encouraged by their religion. Mbayá hostilities against the Carios of central Paraguay led these GUARANIS to seek an alliance with Spanish explorers in the 1530s. This act made Spaniards the enemies of the Mbayás, who then raided the Europeans for captives, weapons, and tools. Throughout the colonial era, Mbayá chiefs dominated the Guanás, an Arawakian farming people who voluntarily provided the Mbayás with servants and crop foods in return for military protection, an unusual relationship that contributed to the power of the Mbayás.

Mounted Mbayá warriors after 1600 alternately fought and traded with Spaniards and the Guaranis of Paraguay. Despite much nonhostile contact, Paraguayans feared Mbayá hostilities for 300 years. Mbayá attacks after 1670 forced the Paraguayan government to move six Guarani villages from the north of the province toward the center, near Asunción, causing the frontier to contract. Most bands of Mbayás then moved their habitat from the Chaco to the east bank of the Río Paraguay, from which they raided western Brazilian settlements as well. In the 1740s and 1750s, ecological degradation of their habitats by the use of iron tools, overhunting, the grazing of horses and sheep, and increased warfare caused the Mbayás to seek a closer accommodation with the Spaniards.

In the 1750s, Mbayás lived in eight bands and numbered 7,000 to 8,000 people. All bands requested Catholic MISSIONS, but only two missions, Belén and Refugio, were established. Neither flourished, because inadequate Spanish endowments and the insecurity of the Spanish-Portuguese frontier retarded development. Increasing numbers of Mbayás joined Paraguayan and Brazilian society, settling on the outskirts of Concepción, Paraguay, after 1773, and near Cuyabá, Brazil. They provided soldiers and scouts to the antagonistic empires and later to the independent nations. Mbayá bands dwindled as increasing numbers joined the Paraguayan and Brazilian mainstreams. By the 1940s, only a handful of their descendants, the Caduveos, survived in Brazil, where they were studied by such anthropologists as Kalervo Oberg.

JOSÉ SÁNCHEZ LABRADOR, *El Paraguay católico*, 3 vols. (1910–1917); ALFRED MÉTRAUX, "Ethnography of the Chaco," in *Handbook of South American Indians*, vol. 1, edited by Julian H. Steward (1946); KALERVO OBERG, *The Terena and the Caduveo of Southern Mato Grosso, Brazil* (1949); JAMES SCHOFIELD SAEGER, "Eighteenth-Century Guaycuruan Missions in Paraguay," in *Indian-Religious Relations in Colonial Spanish America*, edited by Susan E. Ramírez (1989).

JAMES SCHOFIELD SAEGER

See also **Indians.**

MCLANE–OCAMPO TREATY (1859), an agreement between the United States and Mexico regarding transit rights. Negotiations were conducted during the War of the Reform (1858–1860) by Robert M. McLane (1815–1898), United States ambassador to the Liberal government of Benito JUÁREZ in Veracruz, and Melchor OCAMPO, Minister of Foreign Affairs. The treaty gave U.S. citizens transit rights across the Isthmus of TEHUANTEPEC and also across northern Mexico from the Gulf of California to the vicinity of the lower Rio Grande, and allowed the U.S. government to send in military personnel to protect the route and U.S. citizens in transit. U.S. citizens would not be charged for transit at a rate different from that charged to Mexicans. In exchange for these transit rights, the United States was to pay Mexico $4 million, half upon ratification and the other half to be applied to the claims of citizens of the United States against the government of Mexico. The treaty was rejected by the U.S. Senate in 1860 and a subject of much controversy in Mexico, where some feared the loss of significant territory to the United States. Had it been ratified, it would have given the United States a large measure of control over areas of Mexico that were considered to be crucial to the passage of persons and goods to and from California.

EDWARD J. BERBUSSE, "The Origins of the McLane-Ocampo Treaty of 1859," in *The Americas* 14 (1958): 223–243; AGUSTÍN CUE CÁNOVAS, *El tratado McLane-Ocampo: Juárez, los Estados Unidos y Europa*, 2d ed. (1959); SALVADOR YSUNZA UZETA, *Juárez y el tratado McLane-Ocampo* (1964).

CHARLES R. BERRY

See also **United States–Latin American Relations.**

MEAT INDUSTRY, a major economic activity of the RÍO DE LA PLATA and Brazil since the late eighteenth century.
Río de la Plata. By the mid-seventeenth century, the rich, well-watered grasslands of the PAMPA nourished huge herds of feral horses and cattle. The HIDES INDUSTRY initially dominated colonial LIVESTOCK activity. Trade liberalization during the 1780s made CHARQUI (dried, salted, jerked beef) used to feed slaves in Cuba and Brazil, an important export for Buenos Aires, Montevideo, and other port cities. During the Independence era, Juan Manuel de ROSAS and his cousins, the Anchorenas, built some of the first SALADEROS (meat-salting plants) in riparian locations near Buenos Aires. Salted meat exports from Buenos Aires rose tenfold from about 984 tons in the 1810s and 9,860 tons in the 1830s. Exports more than doubled again during the 1840s. By mid-century, however, the livestock industry began undergoing major changes. Sheep-raising added wool and later mutton to cattle products. Argentina's sheep population jumped to 61 million in 1880. Sheep and farming pushed cattle farther out onto more remote areas of the pampa.

By the 1880s, ranchers of the Río de la Plata began raising hybrid cattle for the European chilled-beef trade. Cereals and chilled beef eclipsed both the traditional hides and salted-beef trades in importance. In 1895, 5,500 Argentines labored in thirty-nine *saladeros*, but salted meat accounted for only about 2 percent of total national exports.

Mataderos (slaughterhouses) in the Río de la Plata became worldwide suppliers of beef. During the first decade of the twentieth century most meat-packing houses (FRIGORÍFICOS) were controlled by the British. By 1914, however, the North American meat-packing industry had taken control of one-half to two-thirds of Argentina's production. Despite worldwide competition and trade barriers, Argentina remains an important meat producer and consumer today.

Brazil. Colonial ranchers of the *sertão*, the dry inland plains of northeastern Brazil, raised cattle for hides, meat on the hoof, and jerky. In 1532 Martim Afonso de SOUSA brought settlers, sugarcane, and cattle to his settlement at São Vicente, near Santos. By the early eighteenth century, the province of Bahia held an estimated 500,000 cattle and Pernambuco 800,000. By the early nineteenth century, the city of Bahia consumed 20,000 head of cattle annually.

Rugged cowboys (VAQUEIROS) herded the animals, assisted by other workers called *fábricas*. The vaqueiro in charge of a ranch (*fazenda*) received one-fourth of the herd's annual increase. Ceará came to dominate dried beef production during the early colonial period. Piauí supplanted Ceará in the late eighteenth century and continued to produce more dried beef than any region until overtaken late in the nineteenth century by Rio Grande do Sul.

The "Great Drought" (1791–1793) decimated northern herds. Thereafter beef production shifted southward to Minas Gerais and Rio Grande do Sul. Minas became the nation's dairying center. Well into the nineteenth century, slave owners in Brazil and Cuba fed tough, stringy dried meat to their slaves.

Beginning in 1535, Jesuits raised livestock on their missions in the interior of South America. In 1793 the captaincy of Rio Grande exported 13,000 arrobas of dried meat. (An arroba is about 25 pounds.) About a decade later the figure jumped to 600,000 arrobas as *charqueadas* (beef-drying plants) multiplied.

As on the northern ranges, ranching techniques remained primitive. Not until the mid-nineteenth century did ranchers in southern Brazil begin furnishing cattle with salt. Some ranchers added wire fencing after about 1880, but southern Brazilian cattle production, work techniques, and social relations changed very little. Ranchers in Rio Grande and northern Uruguay continued to raise cattle for the traditional hides and jerky markets long after ranchers elsewhere diversified into the more lucrative chilled-beef trade.

CAIO PRADO, JR. *The Colonial Background of Modern Brazil*, translated by Suzette Macedo (1967); PETER H. SMITH, *Politics and Beef in Argentina* (1969); JONATHAN C. BROWN, *A Socioeconomic History of Argentina, 1776–1860* (1979).

RICHARD W. SLATTA

MEDEIROS DA FONSECA, ROMY MARTINS (*b.* 30 June 1921), Brazilian women's rights activist. Daughter of José Gomes Leite da Fonseca and Climéria da Fonseca Martins, Medeiros da Fonseca was born in Rio de Janeiro. She married the jurist and law professor Arnoldo Medeiros da Fonseca, with whom she had two children. A graduate of the law school at the Federal University of Rio de Janeiro, Romy Medeiros served as counselor to the State Council on the Rights of Women and has been a leader of the Brazilian Lawyers' Organization (OAB). In addition, she has served as president of the National Council of Brazilian Women (CNMB), an organization founded by Jeronyma Mesquita, a pioneer for women's suffrage.

Medeiros was a coauthor of the Married Woman's Statute, a law that defined social and family rights and supplanted civil code stipulations, which considered married women as "relatively incompetent." In 1972, she organized the First Congress of Women, in which national and international participants debated women's roles in political development. She has served as Brazil's delegate to the Inter-American Commission for Women at the Organization of American States and has been a formal and informal presidential adviser on women's issues since 1947. As a stalwart defender of women's rights, Romy Medeiros has long promoted women's integration into the country's military services and was instrumental in the passage of Brazil's divorce statute.

IÊDA SIQUEIRA WIARDA

MEDELLÍN, the second largest city in Colombia and capital of the department of ANTIOQUIA. In 1985 the city's population was 2,082,000. Medellín is located in the fertile valley of Aburrá in the Central Cordillera at an al-

titude of 5,000 feet. The valley already had some 3,000 inhabitants when the city was formally established in 1675. By 1787 nearly 17,000 people lived in the territory under the city's jurisdiction.

After independence, Medellín became the seat of government for the state (later department) of Antioquia. The continued importance of gold MINING in Antioquia coupled with the subsequent rise of coffee production allowed Medellín to emerge as Colombia's industrial center in the early twentieth century. Even earlier, local foundries were producing machinery for the processing of coffee and other agricultural products. After 1900 Medellín and its environs were home to several modern textile mills, among the most notable of which were the Compañía Antioqueña de Tejidos (1902) and the Compañía Colombiana de Tejidos (1907). Known as Coltejer, the latter became the largest textile enterprise in Colombia, employing 8,500 people in four plants in and around Medellín by 1967.

In the late twentieth century, Medellín gained notoriety as the headquarters of a violent narcotics "cartel." Conflict among drug traffickers and between them and the authorities cost thousands of lives as the number of violent deaths in Medellín rose from 730 in 1980 to 5,300 in 1990.

ANN TWINAM, "Enterprise and Elites in Eighteenth-Century Medellín," in *Hispanic American Historical Review* 59 (1979): 444–475; JORGE RESTREPO URIBE and LUZ POSADA DE GRIEFF, *Medellín: Su origen, progreso y desarrollo* (1981); ALMA GUILLERMOPRIETO, "Letter from Medellín," in *The New Yorker*, 22 April 1991, pp. 96–109.

HELEN DELPAR

See also **Coffee Industry; Drugs and Drug Trade.**

MEDELLÍN CARTEL. *See* **Drugs and Drug Trade.**

MEDIA ANATA, an assessment of a half-year's salary imposed on officials taking posts in the Spanish Indies. In a royal order in council (*cédula*) of 21 July 1625, establishing the impost, PHILIP IV set the assessment initially at one month's salary (*mesada*) but in 1632 raised it to a half-year's stipend, where it remained for the rest of the colonial epoch. As the colonial epoch wore on, revenues from this source began dropping, largely because of the increasing number of exemptions from the assessment, including those for military officers and employees of the tobacco and powder factories. In the 1790s *medias anatas* produced revenues in Mexico of approximately 40,000–50,000 pesos annually, in Peru 8,000–15,000 pesos.

Recopilación de leyes de los Reynos de las Indias, 4 vols. (1681; repr. 1973), libro VIII, título XIX; JOAQUÍN MANIAU, *Compendio de la historia de la Real Hacienda de Nueva España* (1914).

JOHN JAY TEPASKE

MÉDICI, EMÍLIO GARRASTAZÚ (*b.* 4 December 1905; *d.* 9 October 1985), military leader and president of Brazil (1969–1974). Médici was born in Bagé, Brazil, a village in southern cattle country close to the Uruguayan border. He entered a military school in Pôrto Alegre when he was twelve and enlisted in the cavalry nine years later. In 1934 he joined the Command and General Staff School in Rio de Janeiro. He was serving as an intelligence officer in Rio Grande do Sul in 1953 when Artur da COSTA E SILVA, commander of the Third Military Region, named him chief of staff. Eight years later Médici was promoted to brigadier general and appointed commander of the National Military Academy in Agulhas Negras.

Médici was the military attaché at the Brazilian Embassy in Washington, D.C., at the time of the military coup against President João GOULART in 1964. He left the army in 1966 to become civilian head of the National Intelligence Service, returning three years later to take command of the Third Army.

When President Costa e Silva suffered a stroke in August 1969, a three-man junta composed of the military service chiefs assumed control of the government. They bypassed the successor designated in the Constitution of 1967, Vice President Pedro Aleixo, who was perceived as being too much of a politician. After consulting 100 generals, the 10 generals of the Army High Command settled on Médici as the next president. He was then nominated by the government party, the National Renovating Alliance (ARENA), elected by the Brazilian National Congress, and sworn in 30 October 1969.

Médici promised a move toward democracy but instead practiced political repression. He permitted federal elections to Congress in November 1970, but allowed only one opposition party, the Brazilian Democratic Movement (MDB), to compete against ARENA. Before the election, the military carried out a mass crackdown of dissidents and arrested about 5,000 people. According to the Brazilian Amnesty Committee, 170 political opponents were killed during Médici's presidency.

The military considered suppression of dissent necessary for maintaining the stability needed to achieve economic growth. Médici's administration also helped to sustain the "economic miracle" that began in 1968. It attracted foreign loans for large-scale economic development projects and spent heavily on roads, railways, and utility projects—the infrastructure for heavy industry. Government-owned enterprises dominated steel, mining, and petrochemical industries. In 1974, 74 percent of the combined assets of the country's 100 largest firms belonged to state enterprises; state banks accounted for 56 percent of total deposits and 65 percent of loans to the private sector. This created further inequality of wealth among people and regions. Médici attempted to correct this imbalance in 1970 with construction of the Transamazon Highway, which was intended to encourage immigration and development in northeastern Brazil, the nation's poorest region. High government spending, along with the infusion of foreign capital, boosted economic growth rates to between 7 percent and 11 percent during Médici's years in office, but 80 percent of the population remained mired in poverty. Médici died in Rio de Janeiro.

THOMAS E. SKIDMORE, *The Politics of Military Rule in Brazil, 1964–85* (1988); WERNER BAER, *The Brazilian Economy: Growth and Development* (1989).

ROSS WILKINSON

MEDICINAL PLANTS. Upon their arrival in what is today Latin America, European conquerors found an impressive array of healing plants used by the natives. Accompanying the conquerors were missionaries and occasionally a physician, and it is from their chronicles that we know about medicinal plants of pre-Conquest America. Among them, the accounts of Father Bernardino de SAHAGÚN and especially those of the physician Francisco HERNÁNDEZ in Mexico describe a large number of medicinal plants used by the peoples of MESOAMERICA in the sixteenth century. These accounts, however, cover only a fraction of the plants actually used, their applications, and mode of use, since medicine men were understandably reluctant to reveal the secrets of their healing plants to the invaders.

Medicine men and women were involved not only in healing individual patients but also in maintaining the integrity of their community. Their highly sophisticated knowledge of healing plants came from years of apprenticeship in well-established traditions and a lifetime of practice that included familiarity with healing plants, their habitats, their effects and interactions; their remedies almost always used plants in combination. During some healing rituals, medicine men consumed hallucinogenic plants. Considered magical and the quintessential medicine, hallucinogenic plants were used as guides to find the causes of challenging illnesses and to foresee events. Christian missionaries labeled these practices diabolic, and medicine men and women were ruthlessly persecuted.

With the social disintegration of the conquered peoples in the fifteenth and sixteenth centuries and the severe disruption of healing traditions, untold knowledge of medicinal plants was lost. However, because of their highly effective cures, native herbalists were eagerly sought after during colonial and postcolonial times. After the Conquest, missionaries continued using and recording the properties of medicinal plants; the religious orders that followed profited from their trade. Nonetheless, most plants considered magical or sacred by the natives were banished as instruments of the devil. Native classifications of plants such as "male" or "female" were replaced by concepts such as "hot" or "cold," which were then prevalent in European medicine. Healing plants of European, African, and Asian origin were added to the colonial pharmacopoeia; some were readily adopted by native herbalists.

Plants gained or lost favor according to economic and social circumstances. A few examples illustrate this point. In 1569, the writings of the Spanish physician Nicolás Monardes popularized many American medicinal plants in Europe; of these plants, balsam of Peru, the resin from the tree *Myroxylon balsamum,* became a worldwide treatment for wounds, infections, and skin ailments and was used as incense by the Roman Catholic Church (for both ritual and fumigatory purposes). The Pacific coast of El Salvador was the most important producer. Since the advent of antibiotics in the 1930s, the economic importance of this plant diminished considerably.

A different fate befell the forest vines of special species of *Chondrodendron,* used as traditional ingredients of curare, the powerful arrow poison from the Amazon that produces muscle paralysis. One of the active chemicals of curare, tubocuraine, is medically used to reduce convulsions caused by tetanus or electric-shock therapy and as a temporary muscle relaxant in some surgeries and in neuropathological spasms. Similarly, in Mesoamerica, the tubers of wild yams (certain species of *Dioscorea*), used since pre-Columbian times by women to control menstruation and for their soaplike suds, never received wide notice by colonial Europeans. Yet today, thanks to a discovery by a Japanese chemist in 1938, they are very important sources of steroidal sapogenins, from which pharmaceutical companies in Mexico synthesize corticosterol-based anti-inflammatories, androgens, estrogens, progesterones, and oral contraceptives. On the other hand, the barks of several species of CINCHONA trees from the northern Andes, for which there is no evidence of use before the seventeenth century, became extremely important antimalarial drugs from then onward, thereby making European colonial expansion to the world's tropics more feasible. They are today the source of quinine and its derivatives and are also used to treat hemorrhoids, varicose veins, and cardiac arrhythmias.

Mention must be made of two "medicine" plants held in the highest esteem during pre-Columbian times: the first, coca (several species of *Erythroxylon*), cultivated from Bolivia and Brazil to Nicaragua, was almost universally considered a sacred plant. Restricted to men and, among the Incas, to athletes, message runners, and the nobility, the partaking of the leaves for chewing was a highly ritualized social occasion. Its effect was mostly to suppress tiredness and hunger. Some missionaries disapproved of coca, and in the early 1600s the Inquisition bitterly condemned its use. By that time, however, several religious orders were profiting handsomely from coca production and trade, and their members frequently chewed the leaves. After silver was discovered in Peru in the mid-1500s, enormous quantities of coca were brought in to keep the Indian forced laborers in

the mines from feeling tired or hungry. Coca became an important commercial crop in colonial Peru and Ecuador. Cocaine, one of the many alkaloids present in coca, was first isolated in 1858; today, several compounds derived from cocaine are important anesthetics. Cocaine is also used as a recreational drug because of its euphoric and stimulant properties. Unfortunately, cocaine consumption is erroneously confused with traditional coca chewing, a very different activity both socially and physiologically. Recreational cocaine is today an illegal drug; its trade, fueled by a seemingly insatiable demand in the United States and in Europe, has brought grave social and political disruptions to Colombia, Peru, Bolivia, and other Latin American countries.

The second plant, TOBACCO (*Nicotiana tabacum*), was considered a powerful protector of medicine men and warriors, who drank infusions of the leaves, applied them to their bodies, or inhaled smoke from burned leaves. Tobacco was a common component of the hallucinogenic mixtures prepared by medicine men for diagnosis and divination. It also had more mundane uses: to relieve headaches, to cure skin infections, to heal wounds, to kill and repel insects. With the social disruption following the Spanish Conquest, tobacco use was no longer restricted, and the conquered men and women took to inhaling its smoke to soothe their distress. Christian priests at first disapproved of this practice, then took it up themselves; African slaves readily followed.

Tobacco was introduced to Europe in the sixteenth century as a sedative, especially for painful illnesses, but soon its narcotic properties and the novelty of "drinking smoke" or snuffing the powdered leaves turned it into a recreational substance favored by European intellectuals and the colonial elites. Indians, however, continued using tobacco mostly as a medicine; their gardens invariably included a few tobacco plants. Because of the demand, tobacco production was rapidly commercialized, and its preparation and use were standardized. By the seventeenth century, some areas of the colonies, especially in Cuba, Trinidad, and Venezuela, had been selected for production. In those areas, "industrial" cultivation was associated with large-scale hacienda systems and African slave labor; elsewhere, tobacco growing was commonly in the hands of small landholders, poor peasants, and runaway slaves. Eventually, small tobacco growers became important in the popular uprisings that led to independence from Spain. Today, the medicinal properties of tobacco are virtually unknown, and its use is mostly as a legal recreational narcotic.

Advances in chemistry during the late eighteenth century and through the nineteenth century led to the extraction and purification of physiologically active compounds from medicinal plants, allowing medical doctors better control of the effects of their prescriptions and permitting the establishment of a pharmaceutical industry. European countries, interested in learning about plant resources that might yield economic benefits, sponsored systematic searches of the American flora through scientific expeditions. In the late eighteen century, the explorations of Alexander von HUMBOLDT and José Celestino MUTIS enriched knowledge about medicinal plants in the upper Amazon basin and northern Andes, as did Richard Spruce's reports in the nineteenth century. In the twentieth century, scientific explorations intensified, involving universities and government agencies in various countries and resulting in improved botanical and pharmacological information.

In the 1930s, with the advent of antibiotics—called "miracle drugs"—the prestige of skillfully marketed synthetic drugs started to eclipse the importance of medicinal plants, and for several decades the latter were considered less reliable agents of healing; since the 1970s, however, pathogens resistant to antibiotics have evolved, and evidence has accumulated of toxic secondary effects and improper use of pharmaceutical products that cause severe health problems. For these reasons, and also because of the prohibitive cost of synthetic drugs to large segments of the Latin American population, some governments have started programs studying their medicinal herbal lore, especially in countries where large Indian populations have kept the herbal tradition alive. Mexico, for example, has produced several government publications on its medicinal flora, and Bolivia has developed successful programs integrating the biomedical traditions of Western medicine with ethnomedical systems such as those of the highly reputed Kallawaya herbal healers.

Pharmaceutical companies continue to send scientific expeditions to Latin America in search of pharmacologically useful plants. A major debate today concerns whether these European and U.S. companies can have exclusive patent rights—and access to potentially high profits—for synthetic drugs developed from plants found on Latin American soils.

An outstanding source of historical material about Latin American medicinal plants is VICTOR MANUEL PATIÑO, *Plantas cultivadas y animales domésticos en América equinoccial*. Vol. 3, *Fibras, medicinas, misceláneas* (1967). Excellent information about the best-known medicinal plants, including pharmacological and historical aspects of some Latin American natives, is given in JULIA MORTON, *Major Medicinal Plants: Botany, Culture, and Uses* (1977). Regional reference material can be found for Mexico in MAXIMINO MARTÍNEZ, *Las plantas medicinales de México* (1990); and XAVIER LOZOYA L., *Flora medicinal de México* (1982). For the Amazon forest, see RICHARD SCHULTES, *The Healing Forest: Medicinal and Toxic Plants of the Northwest Amazonia* (1990); for Colombia, consult HERNANDO GARCÍA BARRIGA, *Flora medicinal de Colombia* (1974); for the mid-Andean region, especially Bolivia, see JOSEPH BASTIEN, *Healers of the Andes: Kallawaya Herbalists and Their Medicinal Plants* (1987). On specific plants, *Cultural Survival Report* 23, "Coca and Cocaine—Effects on People and Policy in Latin America" (1985).

CARMENZA OLAYA FONSTAD

See also **Drugs and Drug Trade.**

MEDICINE

Colonial Spanish America

Spanish-American medicine in the colonial period is the story of woefully inadequate resources confronting overwhelming crises of public health. Colonial authorities attempted to meet the shortage of trained practitioners by imposing rigorous standards. Reality demanded that these standards be imposed sparingly because any practitioner was better than none.

During the first generation of colonization, tens of thousands of Native Americans succumbed to European DISEASES—smallpox, typhoid, measles, and pneumonia. (Spanish commentators were struck more by the magnitude of the epidemics than by specific symptoms.) Although during the sixteenth century, Native Americans suffered the greatest mortality, periodic epidemics plagued all levels of society throughout the colonial period. Donald Cooper identified at least five major epidemics (most likely smallpox or typhoid) in eighteenth-century Mexico City alone, which cumulatively cost at least 50,000 lives.

The first European physician arrived in the New World with Columbus on his second voyage (1493), a colonizing expedition. Few followed, however; by 1545 there was, for example, only one licensed physician in Mexico City. Self-proclaimed practitioners, or *curanderos*, both indigenous and European, took up the slack. Thus colonial administrators were faced with the irony of a legal tradition that was preoccupied with assuring quality control over the practice of medicine and the stark reality of a population the majority of which had access to virtually no professional medical care whatsoever.

The Royal Protomedicato Since the reign of FERDINAND and ISABELLA, the Spanish monarchy had assumed responsibility for public health. Its concept of public health, however, was restricted to safeguarding the public from unlicensed and unqualified practitioners. Regulation of the medical profession fell to the Royal Protomedicato, a board of physicians appointed by the crown. The Protomedicato licensed all medical practitioners, punished quacks, and provided medical advice to the crown. Hence the corporate society that was late-medieval Spain entrusted the regulation of the practice of medicine to the elite of the medical profession itself. At best this elite endeavored to impose high standards, standards that were completely unrealistic in the New World. At worst, they sought only to preserve the perquisites of the minority of practitioners who possessed licenses.

Quality and standards were a luxury in Spanish America. Western medicine, such as it was, remained restricted to the larger towns and to the European population. Municipal governments competed for practitioners who could serve in public institutions, care for the officials themselves, and assume at least nominal responsibility for public-health standards and the health needs of the poor. Desperate to secure the services of any practitioner, authorities readily overlooked the prohibitions against "foreigners" practicing medicine, and often winked at the dubious credentials applicants presented. The vast majority of the population was served by unlicensed practitioners, some probably as effective as those with proper credentials; others no doubt dangerous quacks. Necessity required that any practitioner be tolerated as long as he maintained a relatively low profile and did not openly resort to magic that would offend the clergy.

Colonial authorities were convinced that the shortage of qualified practitioners was the single most important threat to public health. The solution, they believed, lay in re-creating in America the medical institutions of Spain. Public hospitals, supported by endowments from local authorities or religious orders, were established in major cities. Many were designated for the treatment of the poor; some, such as the Royal Indian Hospital in Mexico City, founded in 1553, were created exclusively for Native Americans. (As in Europe, hospitals were usually a last resort for those who had no one to care for them.)

Universities in Mexico City and Lima had faculties of

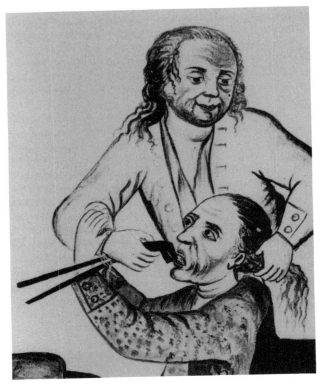

Indian having teeth pulled. Eighteenth-century MS in collection of the Biblioteca del Palacio Real, Madrid. Reproduced from Martínez Compañón, *Trujillo del Perú*. COURTESY OF HARVARD COLLEGE LIBRARY.

medicine with curricula identical to those in Spain. Protomedicatos were established in Mexico City and Lima during the seventeenth century. Unlike the protocol in Spain, members of the university faculties served on the Protomedicato, thereby eliminating the traditional Spanish distinction between the educating and licensing functions that had been designed as a check on both. There were simply too few qualified physicians to go around.

Academic Medicine In both Spain and Spanish America the medical profession was divided into countless categories of practice, each with it own restrictions, privileges, and prerequisites. Physicians (*médicos*), the elite of the profession, possessed a university degree. They had a monopoly on positions in the university, the Protomedicato, and many government posts, all of which carried with them a guaranteed salary as well as the opportunity for private practice. Ironically, the "internal medicine" on which they had a legal monopoly was probably the least effective branch of medicine in practice. Academic medicine, which distinguished the physician from other practitioners and which was the basis of his exalted status, remained deeply rooted in the Aristotelian tradition until the late eighteenth century. "Internal medicine" was an intellectual endeavor, not an empirical one. This medieval tradition looked at the body as a holistic organism; disease resulted from an imbalance of bodily humors. As a result, education consisted of learning the general principles of nature recorded by Hippocrates in the fourth century B.C., Galen in the second century A.D., and Avicenna (Ibn Sīnā) in the eleventh century. Although the formal curriculum remained unchanged throughout the colonial period, academic medicine incorporated contemporary ideas from Europe into its traditional structure. John Tate Lanning's studies have demonstrated that graduates in the late eighteenth century were familiar with such contemporary authors as Hermann Boerhaave and Johannes de Gorter.

In both Spain and Spanish America, medicine had little status within the university. Its faculty was poorly paid, its chairs frequently went unfilled, and few students were attracted to the profession. During the seventeenth century, for example, the University of Mexico granted an average of only three bachelor's degrees in medicine per year. In Guatemala, less a part of the colonial mainstream, only one bachelor's degree was awarded every four years. Medical faculties were hard pressed even to supply enough physicians to educate and administer the profession; law and the church offered far more lucrative opportunities. Indeed, only the universities in Mexico City and Lima were authorized to fill three chairs of medicine, the minimum required by Spanish statutes.

Nonacademic Medicine Nonacademic medicine represented another culture, a culture of experience and practice, not theory. These practitioners—surgeons, bonesetters, bleeders, midwives—learned their craft as informal apprentices, often on a trial-and-error basis. If licensed, they had also passed an examination before the Protomedicato. They provided the untidy everyday procedures of practical medicine—bonesetting, bloodletting, minor surgery. Yet the empirical nature of their training and everyday practice led some to acquire a considerable reputation for the effectiveness of their prescriptions or the swiftness of their surgery. Others, no doubt, had little knowledge of what they were doing, probably causing more harm than good. As a rule, the lower the status of the medical practice, the weaker the efforts to enforce the legal prerequisites for practice. Midwives, the only practice open to women, were seldom subjected to any examination; as in Spain, the profession tended to pass from one generation to the next.

In addition to demonstrating competence, applicants for a license—as well as young men seeking to enter a university—had to prove their *limpieza de sangre* (purity of blood). *Limpieza de sangre,* that is, proof of legitimacy and the absence of any conviction by the Inquisition for three generations, had become common in sixteenth-century Spain as an artifice to exclude non-Christians from universities and the professions.

For the first 200 years of colonization these restrictions, like those prohibiting the practice of foreigners, were generally ignored. Toward the end of the seventeenth century, growing competition for affluent clients in the major cities led to a number of lawsuits designed to force compliance with *limpieza de sangre* standards on both the university and the Protomedicato. In addition, ''legitimate'' practitioners used their influence to prohibit all blacks and mulattoes from entering a university—the first time *limpieza de sangre* was used for purely racial objectives. The controversy over qualifications was apparently also related to the dual culture of medical practice. Physicians, who controlled the enforcement apparatus, both envied the success and scorned the methods of certain mulatto surgeons. Their efforts to restrict the practice of medicine to whites, preferably physicians, were largely unsuccessful, however, due once again to the enduring shortage of any practitioners at all.

Reforms in Medical Education The Enlightenment precipitated significant reforms in medical education in both Spain and Spanish America. On both continents the pattern was similar: the initiative came from individual reformers, well-read and optimistic, who sought the backing of the crown to implement their ideas. In Spain the crown supported new royal colleges because they curbed the traditional autonomy of universities and the Protomedicato. In America, where the medical elite was smaller, reformers were less inclined to meet opposition from entrenched local medical authorities but faced the more serious obstacle of insufficient funds and lack of interest of colonial authorities.

At issue was the purely theoretical nature of academic medicine and the purely practical nature of apprenticeships. Reformers argued the need for hands-on experience in anatomy and clinical studies on the one hand and the need for academic training for surgeons on the other. Chairs of anatomy were established in universities, and public anatomical demonstrations were held in hospitals. Independent colleges of surgery opened in Mexico City (1770) and Lima (1811). Gradually the distinction between pure theory (physicians) and pure practice (surgeons) broke down.

Progressive men of medicine in America were in frequent contact with their colleagues in Spain; indeed, reform in America occurred simultaneously with reform in Spain. Although such prominent physicians as Narciso Esparragosa y Gallardo (a Guatemalan who developed elastic forceps) and José Hipólito UNÁNUE (a Peruvian who established clinical lectures) were in the minority, the best of Spanish-American medicine was in no way behind that of Europe. Inoculation against smallpox was introduced in 1780, and vaccination became fairly widespread after 1800.

Spain addressed many social problems by transferring peninsular institutions to the New World. Spanish America came to possess the hospitals, medical faculties, regulatory agencies, and highly structured profession of Spain. But challenges of public health in colonial Spanish America were too vast for the limited resources of premodern Western medicine. And policies designed to restrict access to a profession that needed more, not fewer, practitioners had limited success.

DONALD B. COOPER, *Epidemic Disease in Mexico City, 1761–1813* (1965); JOHN TATE LANNING, *Pedro de la Torre: Doctor to Conquerors* (1974); MICHAEL E. BURKE, *The Royal College of San Carlos: Surgery and Spanish Medical Reform in the Late Eighteenth Century* (1977); DAVID A. HOWARD, *The Royal Indian Hospital of Mexico City* (1980); JOHN TATE LANNING, *The Royal Protomedicato: The Regulation of the Medical Professions in the Spanish Empire,* edited by John J. TePaske (1985).

MICHAEL E. BURKE

The Modern Era

After the nineteenth-century independence movements in Latin America, liberal governments moved to secularize medical education. They set up government-supported medical schools, eschewing the influence of religious orders and Iberian models, and turning instead to the French model, whose influence in medical education continued into the twentieth century. The standard of instruction in most medical schools was poor. Many of the best creole physicians had been killed in the Wars of Independence. Moreover, the turbulence of CAUDILLO politics from the 1830s to the 1860s caused schools to function irregularly and prevented the formation of a scientific community large enough to generate original medical ideas.

There were, however, instances of original medical contributions in the nineteenth century. In the first half of the century the most interesting works were those published by physicians who, according to the theory of the relation between climate and disease, correlated local diseases with meteorological conditions. Such, for example, were the books by Joseph F. X. Sigaud, a French physician practicing in Brazil, *Du climat et des maladies du Brésil; ou, statistique médicale de cet empire* (1844), and the Peruvian José Hipólito Unanue (1755–1833), *Observaciones sobre el clima de Lima* (1806). Subsequent contributions were made by the German-Portuguese physician Otto Wucherer (1820–1873), who initiated parasitological investigations in Brazil, and Carlos J. FINLAY (1833–1915), a Cuban who hypothesized in 1881 that yellow fever was transmitted by the Aëdes mosquito. The latter's theory was ignored until 1899, when the U.S. army tested Finlay's mosquito hypothesis and proved him correct.

From the 1880s, the medical profession expanded its prestige in several areas. It gained considerable control over medical practice in the urban areas, thereby creating a cleavage between Western medical processes in the cities and the rich traditions of folk medicine in the rural areas of Latin America. Medical schools achieved stability in teaching, more students graduated and went on to practice medicine, and doctors successfully organized themselves into professional associations and began to publish a variety of medical journals. Drawing on the French and English sanitation movements, doctors were at the forefront of campaigns to improve environmental conditions. Their social position was further consolidated when nineteenth-century epidemics, especially of cholera and yellow fever, which threatened the region's ability to make economic progress, spurred governments to expand public-health services and to delegate power to the physicians who served on newly established sanitation boards. The development of bacteriology and advances in knowledge concerning insect vectors highlighted doctors' scientific authority, earned them greater respect, and led governments to support the establishment of research centers.

The rising tide of nationalism and the belief that science could solve the problems of underdevelopment led in the early decades of the twentieth century to one of the most successful periods in the history of Latin America medicine, especially in the overlapping area of public health and medicine. The period is well illustrated by the work of the Brazilian Oswaldo CRUZ (1872–1917), leader of the first Brazilian public health campaign (1903–1909). This effort rid Rio de Janeiro of yellow fever and bubonic plague, although Cruz's attempts to make the smallpox vaccination mandatory were stalled by political opposition. Cruz was also important in promoting experimental research in Brazil by turning the Cruz Institute (established in 1899), originally an organization that imported ideas and techniques from Europe, into a highly regarded microbiological and protozoological research center. Most notable among its researchers was Carlos CHAGAS (1879–1934), who in 1908 discovered that American sleeping sickness (*Trypanosomiasis americana*) is caused by a trypanosome harbored in a Reduviid bug infesting the walls of rural huts.

Another example of successful medical research in this period is the study of biological adaptation to high altitudes. Nineteenth-century high-altitude studies had "proved" that the natives of the highlands were mentally impaired. In an attempt to parry the charges of inferiority, the Peruvian physician Carlos Monge Medrano (1884–1970) led an expedition to Cerro de Pasco in 1927 in which he demonstrated the process of physical adaptation to the oxygen deficiency characteristic of high-altitude environments and discovered the high-altitude disorder—known today as Monge's disease—caused by the loss of tolerance to high altitudes. The discovery led to the establishment of the Instituto de Biología y Patología Andina (1931), which also studied a variety of occupational disorders such as pneumoconiosis. The long collaboration between the Rockefeller Foundation and Latin American countries began in the 1920s, with the foundation's hookworm and yellow fever eradication campaigns in Brazil, Peru, Ecuador, and Mexico.

In the period since World War II, Latin American medicine has been characterized by several processes. First, the influence of the United States eclipsed that of France with Latin Americans flocking to North American universities to study science and medicine. Moreover, U.S. philanthropies deepened their linkages to Latin America by selectively funding research centers at the region's universities and by supporting the establishment of national councils for higher scientific research in order to create a network of complementary investigative work.

Second, the region witnessed major growth in terms of experimental medicine. Argentina, always less interested in the endemic diseases of tropical underdeveloped countries, led the way. The most prominent Argentine researcher of this century was Bernardo A. HOUSSAY (1887–1971), whose work on the physiology of the pituitary gland led to the recognition of the role of the anterior pituitary in carbohydrate metabolism; for this work he won the Nobel Prize in medicine in 1947. His colleague Luis F. LELOIR (1906–1987) expanded Houssay's findings, showing how complex carbohydrates are broken down into simpler sugars; his research earned him the Nobel Prize in chemistry in 1970. Mexico has combined both applied research into tropical disorders and experimental research. Especially prominent in the latter area was Arturo Stearns ROSENBLUETH (1900–1970), a neurophysiologist who, together with the American Walter B. Cannon, deciphered the workings of the sympathetic regulatory action. With the mathematician Norbert Weiner, Rosenblueth helped establish cybernetics as a serious area of inquiry. Other areas of original research are genetic studies with the drosophila in Brazil, and psychoanalysis in Argentina.

Despite Latin America's web of medical research, the political problems and severe economic crises of the 1980s have led to a "brain drain," eroded health-care institutions, and allowed the resurgence of preventable

diseases. Today there is a debate about whether or not the U.S. model of pure research and highly technological and costly medicine is the best one for the region.

GORDON SCHENDEL, *Medicine in Mexico: From Aztec Herbs to Betatrons* (1968); JOHN Z. BOWERS and ELIZABETH F. PURCELL, *Aspects of the History of Medicine in Latin America* (1979); ROSS DANIELSON, *Cuban Medicine* (1979); NANCY STEPAN, *Beginnings of Brazilian Science* (1981); DONALD COOPER, "The New 'Black Death': Cholera in Brazil, 1855–56," in *Social Science History* 10 (1986): 467–488; MARCOS CUETO, "Excellence in the Periphery: Scientific Activities and Biomedical Sciences in Peru" (Ph.D. diss., Columbia University, 1988), and "The Rockefeller Foundation's Medical Policy and Scientific Research in Latin America: The Case of Physiology," in *Social Studies of Science* 20 (1990): 229–254; ILANA LOWY, "Yellow Fever in Rio de Janeiro and the Pasteur Institute Mission (1901–1905): The Transfer of Science to the Periphery," in *Medical History* 34 (1990): 144–163.

JULYAN G. PEARD

MEDINA, HUGO (*b.* 29 January 1897), Uruguayan general and politician, was a key figure in the transition to civilian rule in Uruguay that took place in the mid-1980s. Commander of the Third Military Region in 1984, he was considered a staunch professional soldier who favored following the timetable established by the military for their withdrawal from executive power. Medina was a member of the military's Political Affairs Commission (COMASPO) from 1980 to 1981. On 7 June 1984, with the retirement of General Hugo Arano, he assumed command of the army. His working relationship with Julio Maria SANGUINETTI of the Colorado Party would prove crucial to the talks that resulted in the Naval Club Pact that led to the November 1984 elections. Medina retired from the army in January 1987, after having staunchly defended the armed forces against any trials for human rights violations. Late in 1987, President Sanguinetti appointed Medina minister of defense, a position from which he continued to pressure public opinion against overturning the amnesty law for the military that had been passed in 1986. The referendum on the amnesty law took place in April 1989. The law was upheld, giving Medina excellent credibility with his former military comrades. He continued to serve as minister of defense until the end of the Sanguinetti government.

MARTIN WEINSTEIN

See also **Uruguay.**

MEDINA, JOSÉ TORIBIO (*b.* 21 October 1852; *d.* 11 December 1930), Chilean historian and bibliographer, and the most remarkable Latin American scholar of his time. Although he was offered a seat in Congress and (in 1871) the secretaryship of the National (*Montt-Varista*) party, Medina preferred the life of scholarship. It was interrupted only by two short-term diplomatic jobs, in

Peru (1875–1876) and Spain (1884–1886), and by public service during the WAR OF THE PACIFIC as military adviser and judge. Medina's support for President José Manuel BALMACEDA in the 1891 civil war made it advisable for him to live abroad until 1895. In fact he always enjoyed travel, making five extended journeys to Europe (always with Spain as his most cherished destination) and twice visiting the United States. In 1928, aged nearly seventy-six, he presided at the opening of the Twenty-third International Congress of Americanists in New York. He was honored by a wide variety of learned societies in America and Europe.

Medina was the author or editor of 408 books, essays, and articles. Some 185 of these publications were printed (1888–1919) on his own private presses. His copious writings embrace history, bibliography, biography, literary criticism, geography, cartography, palaeography, numismatics, and many other subjects. Of particular note are the series of books he wrote on the Inquisition in colonial Spanish America (he discovered the Inquisition papers in the Simancas archive in Spain), and the extraordinary sequence of bibliographical studies covering the output of colonial printing presses in more than thirty Spanish-American cities. His devotion to ERCILLA Y ZÚÑIGA yielded the classic modern study of that poet. Both Harvard University and the John Carter Brown Library offered Medina large sums for his magnificent collection of books and manuscripts. He donated it to the Chilean National Library, where it is kept in the beautifully appointed Sala Medina on the upper floor over the main entrance.

GUILLERMO FELIÚ CRUZ, *José Toribio Medina* (1952); SERGIO VILLALOBOS R., *Medina, su vida y sus obras* (1952).

SIMON COLLIER

MEDINA ANGARITA, ISAÍAS (*b.* 6 July 1897; *d.* 15 September 1953), president of Venezuela (1941–1945). In 1941, Medina became the hand-picked successor of President Eleázar LÓPEZ CONTRERAS, whom he had served briefly as minister of war in 1936. Medina, who entered the Military School in 1912, represented the new professional army officers who emerged during the Juan Vicente GÓMEZ era (1908–1935). During his military career he taught at the Military School, served as secretary to the Ministry of War and Marine, and headed military delegations to Ecuador (1930) and the United States (1940).

As president, Medina introduced a number of political reforms. Constitutional revisions instituted direct elections of national deputies and suffrage for women in municipal elections. Medina also introduced the first income tax law. In 1943, a petroleum law gave the government higher revenues through new taxes and royalties, and the petroleum companies gained more security. An agrarian reform law of 1945 addressed some of the nation's basic rural labor problems. Medina had success in negotiating border settlements with Co-

lombia and Great Britain. In 1943 he headed his own party, the Venezuelan Democratic Party (Partido Democrático Venezolano), which advocated moderate reforms. In October 1945, a military-civilian coalition overthrew Medina.

JUDITH EWELL, Venezuela: A Century of Change (1984); NORA BUSTAMENTE, Isaías Medina Angarita (1985); JOSÉ EDUARDO GUZMÁN PÉREZ, Medina Angarita: Democracia y negación (1985); ISAÍAS MEDINA ANGARITA, Gobierno y época del presidente Isaías Medina Angarita, 17 vols. (1987); TULIO CHIOSSONE, El decenio democrático inconcluso (1989).

WINTHROP R. WRIGHT

MEIGGS, HENRY (*b.* 7 July 1821; *d.* 29 September 1877), American entrepreneur who oversaw the construction of RAILROADS in Chile and Peru. Business reverses led the New York–born Meiggs to move to California, where he initially enjoyed great commercial success during the gold rush. Then bad economic times and a willingness to forge documents forced Meiggs, almost a million dollars in debt, to flee his creditors in the United States. In 1854 he arrived in Chile, where he breathed new life into a faltering railroad industry. Beginning in 1861, the informally trained engineer supervised the building of a railroad linking the capital to the south. As promised, he completed the Santiago–Quillota spur in 1863. He later helped construct a rail line between the capital and Chile's principal port, VALPARAÍSO, in less than four years. Meiggs enjoyed enormous success because he paid his workers well and did not maltreat his employees. Apparently well liked, the high-living Meiggs, who built himself a palatial mansion, expanded his activities by trading in GUANO and opening a bank in La Paz, Bolivia.

Meiggs left Chile in the late 1860s for Peru, where he constructed a railroad between Lima and La Oroya, high in the Andes. This task proved to be particularly difficult to complete, since the rail line ran from the coast to the ALTIPLANO, over 14,000 feet above sea level. Although the railroad clearly benefited the Peruvian economy, it hurt Chile's; some twenty-five thousand Chileans in search of work migrated north, never to return to their homeland. Their departure damaged Chilean *hacendados* (landowners) by depriving them of needed agricultural labor. Meiggs's overall contribution proved substantial, however, helping both the Chileans and the Peruvians develop economically by facilitating the export of their raw materials to the United States and Europe.

WATT STEWART, Henry Meiggs: Yankee Pizarro (1946); THOMAS C. WRIGHT, Landowners and Reform in Chile (1981), p. 145.

WILLIAM F. SATER

The Cofa Bridge on the Oroya Railway, Peru, ca. 1908. LIBRARY OF CONGRESS.

MEIRELES, CECÍLIA (*b.* 7 November 1901; *d.* 9 November 1964), Brazilian poet and educator. Born in Rio de Janeiro, Meireles lost her parents at an early age and was raised by her Portuguese Azorian grandmother. She studied in public schools and became a schoolteacher, later completing a graduate degree. In 1919 she published her first book, *Espectros*, sonnets in a Parnassian mold. In 1922, year of the MODERN ART WEEK in São Paulo, she married a Portuguese artist who committed suicide in 1935. From 1930 on, she was a regular contributor to the Rio cultural press, and in 1934 she founded the first library of children's literature in Brazil. An authority on national folklore, she was professor of Luso-Brazilian literature at the University of the Federal District from 1936 to 1938. Following a second marriage, she visited the United States, teaching in one of the earliest programs for Brazilian literature (the University of Texas).

Meireles matured during the modernist period, but her work always maintained a very personal character, influenced above all by symbolism and Portuguese traditions. While thematic and linguistic nationalism became dominant in Brazil, she remained close to the Portuguese lyrical heritage. She published twenty books in her lifetime, the most noted of which, *Romanceiro da inconfidência* (1953), is a cycle of ballads about colonial conspirators for independence. She is one of the outstanding names in Brazilian literary history and is generally considered the nation's most important woman poet. Posthumously, she received the highest prize of the Brazilian Academy of Letters.

JOHN A. NIST, *The Modernist Movement in Brazil* (1967); RAYMOND SAYERS, "The Poetic Universe of Cecília Meireles," in *From Linguistics to Literature: Romance Studies Offered to Francis M. Rogers,* edited by Bernard Bichakjian (1981); MARTA PEIXOTO, "The Absent Body: Female Signature and Poetic Convention in Cecília Meireles," in *Bulletin of Hispanic Studies* 65, no. 1 (1988): 87–100.

CHARLES A. PERRONE

MEIRELES DE LIMA, VÍTOR (*b.* 18 August 1832; *d.* 22 February 1903), Brazilian painter. Along with Pedro AMÉRICO, Meireles is one of Brazil's most important historical painters of the Second Empire. Born in the southern province of Santa Catarina, Meireles commenced his formal artistic formation in 1847 at the Imperial Academy of Fine Arts in Rio de Janeiro. In 1852 he won a travel stipend, the academy's top student honor. During his eight years in Europe, he produced his first important historical painting, and one of his greatest works, *A primeira missa no Brasil.*

Upon his return to Brazil, Meireles devoted his life to painting whether working as the academy's professor of history painting, fulfilling governmental commissions, or readying canvases for presentation in the academy's exhibitions. Between 1866 and 1879, he received three important governmental commissions to produce paintings with military themes. Sought to bolster the Second Empire's image after Brazil's participation in the victorious but draining WAR OF THE TRIPLE ALLIANCE (1864–1870), these military paintings represent his most celebrated works. They include *Combate naval do Riachuelo* and *Passagem de humaitá* (1872), which recreate events from the war, and *Primeira Batalha dos Guararapes* (1879), which documents a 1648 battle in which black, Indian, and Brazilian troops fought against Dutch colonial domination. Beyond these historical compositions, Meireles produced numerous portraits, an Indianist painting, *Moema,* and various landscapes and panoramas.

ARGEU GUIMARÃES, *Auréola de Vítor Meireles* (1977); ANGELO DE PROENÇA ROSA, *Vítor Meireles de Lima (1832–1903)* (1982); QUIRINO CAMPOFIORITO, *História da pintura brasileira no século XIX* (1983); CAREN A. MEGHREBLIAN, "Art, Politics, and Historical Perception in Imperial Brazil, 1854–1884" (Ph.D. diss., UCLA, 1990).

CAREN A. MEGHREBLIAN

MEJÍA, TOMÁS (*b.* 1820; *d.* 19 June 1867), Mexican general. Born in Pinal de Amoles, Querétaro, Mejía became an important military officer while retaining his ethnic ties to the Indian villagers of the Sierra Gorda. An Indian cacique, he led troops from his native region in support of the conservative cause during the Revolution of Ayutla, the War of the REFORM, and in support of MAXIMILIAN's empire.

Mejía began his career in 1841 as a second lieutenant in the militia, engaging migratory Indians in the North in his first campaigns. He fought against the invading U.S. troops in Monterrey, Angostura, and Buena Vista in 1847 and was promoted to squadron commander in 1849. He reached the rank of lieutenant colonel during the Revolution of Ayutla and division general during the Three Years War. Defeated by Jesús GONZÁLEZ ORTEGA in 1860, Mejía later became one of Emperor Maximilian's most trusted generals, and one of the most feared by his republican counterparts. As Maximilian's empire collapsed, Mejía chose to join the emperor in Querétaro, where he was captured, tried, condemned to death, and executed by firing squad alongside Maximilian and Miguel MIRAMÓN.

ALFRED JACKSON HANNA and KATHRYN ABBEY HANNA, *Napoleon III and Mexico: American Triumph over Monarchy* (1971); *Diccionario Porrúa de historia, biografía y geografía de México,* 5th ed. (1986).

D. F. STEVENS

See also **French Intervention; Mexican–American War.**

MEJÍA DEL VALLE Y LLEQUERICA, JOSÉ JOAQUÍN (also Lequerica; *b.* 24 May 1775; *d.* 27 October 1813), spokesperson for the rights of colonial Americans under Spanish imperialism. Mejía, a native of Quito, served as a substitute delegate of the Viceroyalty of New Granada to the CORTES OF CÁDIZ (1810–1814). He ably led the American delegation in their struggle for equal representation in both the congress and the subsequent new constitution. The problem was population: that of Spain at this time was about 10.5 million, whereas that of Spain's overseas holdings totaled about 15–16.9 million. However, only whites enjoyed full citizenship in Spain and its colonies, and the New World had far fewer whites (2.5–3.2 million) than did Spain (10.5 million). Naturally, Spain was utterly unwilling to surrender political control of its empire to overseas whites.

During the Cádiz debates, Mejía advanced a proposal that the New World's free blacks and Indians, if not its slaves, be counted for purposes of proportional representation. The Cortes agreed to include CREOLES, Indians, and MESTIZOS, but not Africans and MULATTOES. Most historians agree that Mejía was the best orator in Cádiz. He died during a yellow fever epidemic in Cádiz.

On events in Spain and at the Cortes of Cádiz, see TIMOTHY E. ANNA, *Spain and the Loss of America* (1983).

RONN F. PINEO

MEJÍA VICTORES, OSCAR HUMBERTO, chief of state of Guatemala (1983–1985). Brigadier General Mejía Victores served as minister of defense under Efraín RÍOS MONTT (1982–1983). After taking part in the 9 August 1983 coup d'état that ousted Ríos Montt from power, Mejía became chief of state, but declined to name himself president of the republic.

571

Guatemala's economy declined precipitously under Mejía's administration. However, Mejía oversaw the "transition to democracy" under which the military permitted the creation and promulgation of a new national constitution and the election of a civilian to the presidency. In 1986, Mejía stepped down to allow Marco Vinicio CEREZO ARÉVALO, a civilian and member of the Christian Democratic Party, to become president of the republic.

BETTINA CORKE, ed., *Who Is Who in Government and Politics in Latin America* (1984); JEAN-MARIE SIMON, *Guatemala: Eternal Spring, Eternal Tyranny* (1987).

VIRGINIA GARRARD-BURNETT

MELÉ, JUAN N. (*b.* 15 October 1923), Argentine painter and sculptor. Born in Buenos Aires, he studied at the Prilidiano PUEYRREDÓN School of Fine Arts. In 1948–1949 he received a grant from the French government and studied at the Louvre under Georges Vantongerloo, Cesar Domela, Robert Delauney, and Constantin Brancusi, among others. Melé has had a distinguished career in abstract painting and sculpture. In Argentina he joined the Asociación Arte Concreto-Invención, a group of nonfigurative artists. His work is a fine example of highly personal abstract art combining purely plastic form and a sensitive treatment of color.

VICENTE GESUALDO, ALDO BIGLIONE, and RODOLFO SANTOS, *Diccionario de artistas plásticos en la Argentina* (1988).

AMALIA CORTINA ARAVENA

MELÉNDEZ CHAVERRI, CARLOS (*b.* 3 June 1926), Costa Rican historian, diplomat, and university professor.

Carlos Meléndez Chaverri is recognized as the most productive and insightful twentieth-century Costa Rican historian. He has focused his research and writing on the colonial period in Costa Rica. His works on the colonial period culminated in the valuable monograph *Conquistadores y pobladores* (1982). He has published general histories of Costa Rica for different educational levels, biographies, a study of blacks in Costa Rica, monographs on other Central American topics, and a scholarly work on the national hero, Juan Santamaría.

Heredia-born Meléndez is a scholar-teacher in the full sense of the term, having taught at two high schools before joining the faculty of the University of Costa Rica (1958). There he served as the director of the School of History and Geography and was responsible for the formation of a more professional generation of Costa Rican historians. In addition to these academic functions, he held other public positions such as head of the anthropology and history section of the National Museum (1953–1966), president of the Academy of History and Geography, and Costa Rican ambassador to Spain.

Among his many honors are national literary awards, election to geographic and historical societies throughout Central America, and an honorary doctorate from Tulane University (1979).

One of the few examples of Meléndez's writings in English, "Land Tenure in Colonial Costa Rica," is contained in MARC EDELMAN and JOANNE KENEN, eds., *The Costa Rica Reader* (1989), pp. 13–28. See also CARLOS MELÉNDEZ CHAVERRI, *Conquistadores y pobladores* (1982); and KENNETH J. GRIEB, ed., *Research Guide to Central America and the Caribbean* (1985).

JOHN PATRICK BELL

MELÉNDEZ FAMILY, a Salvadoran family that held the presidency for three consecutive terms (1913–1927) during the period known as the Meléndez-Quiñónez dynasty era. The Meléndez presidents' fourteen-year occupancy of the nation's highest office is the most obvious example of the restrictive, elitist nature of Salvadoran politics. The Meléndez clan was part of the original Salvadoran landowning oligarchy dating from the early nineteenth century. Originally producers of INDIGO, they were among the first to grow COFFEE on a large scale.

President Carlos Meléndez (*b.* 1 February 1861; *d.* 8 October 1918) took office in 1913 following the assassination of Manuel ARAUJO. He had made many trips to the United States and wished to promote industrialization and the diversification of El Salvador's agrarian economy into HENEQUEN and COTTON. However, his tenure in office is most notable for two policies: his decision to keep El Salvador neutral in World War I, despite heavy pressure from the United States, and his claim to the Gulf of Fonseca as a condominium territory. The latter resulted in the issuing of the so-called Meléndez Doctrine, which challenged Nicaragua's right to grant the United States a naval base in the Gulf of Fonseca as stipulated by the BRYAN–CHAMORRO TREATY of 1913. Meléndez took his case to the Central American Court of Justice in 1914 and won a judgment in his favor.

Carlos Meléndez passed the presidency to his younger brother Jorge (*b.* 15 April 1871; *d.* 22 November 1953) when his health failed in 1918. Jorge ruled for four turbulent years punctuated by military uprisings, urban labor protests, and demonstrations in San Salvador. Of these, the most serious were a February 1922 revolt of students at the Military Polytechnic School and a popular demonstration in December of that same year which was put down by the army and police. Jorge Meléndez continued his brother's program of modernization by opening the first airport, announcing a campaign to eradicate illiteracy, and creating a monetary commission. However, Jorge Meléndez is remembered also for his increased usage of the Liga Roja (Red League), a shadowy paramilitary group designed to thwart labor organization.

The Meléndez's brother-in-law Alfonso QUIÑONES MOLINA was president from 1923 to 1927 and continued the same form of elite-dominated politics as his predecessors. The Meléndez-Quiñónez dynasty governed El Salvador during a crucial period in its modern history. In the 1980s, their descendant, Jorge Antonio Meléndez, fought with the People's Revolutionary Army (ERP) as part of the FMLN–FDR coalition against the government.

MANUEL BELTRAND, ed., *Orientaciones económicas del Señor Presidente Meléndez* (1917); SALVADOR RODRÍGUEZ GONZÁLEZ, *El Golfo de Fonseca y el Tratado, Bryan–Chamorro; La doctrina Meléndez* (1917); CARLOS MELÉNDEZ, *Relations Between the United States of America and El Salvador* (1918); MARÍA LEISTENSCHNEIDER and FREDDY LEISTENSCHNEIDER, *Gobernantes de El Salvador* (1980); TOMMIE SUE MONTGOMERY, *Revolution in El Salvador* (1982).

KAREN RACINE

MELGAREJO, MARIANO (*b.* 15 April 1820; *d.* 23 November 1871), president of Bolivia (1864–1871). Born in Tarata, Cochabamba, General Melgarejo was the archetypical bad CAUDILLO during whose disastrous administration Bolivia gave up large territories to its neighbors, the first systematic assault on the Indian communities occurred, and the public financial system was ransacked. Melgarejo, a MESTIZO who had risen through the ranks of the army, achieved power after overthrowing General José María ACHÁ and later killing former president Manuel Isidoro BELZÚ. Extremely corrupt and with the government always in deficit, Melgarejo and his cronies took advantage of the prosperity of the peripheral regions of Bolivia by selling them to its more powerful neighbors. Thus, in the Chilean treaty of 1866, Melgarejo agreed to all Chilean territorial claims in the NITRATE-rich Mejillones region of the Atacama Desert. In 1868, Melgarejo signed a treaty in which he ceded 40,000 square miles to Brazil in the Amazon region.

In a desperate attempt to gain more revenue, Melgarejo also further debased Bolivian SILVER coinage. The dilution of the silver content in coins, though practiced by virtually every Bolivian administration, was so massive under Melgarejo that it led to difficulties in trade, especially in regions of adjacent countries that heavily used Bolivian coinage for circulation. Melgarejo's sales of Indian community lands in 1866 and 1868 also were tainted by corruption. The terms were exceedingly onerous for the Indians; if they did not purchase their own land within ninety days, it was put on the auction block for the highest bidder. Purchasers bought many lands with government bonds and others were given to friends and relatives, thus depriving the government of needed cash revenue. Most affected by these laws were community lands in the La Paz altiplano and the Cochabamba region.

Although his regime continuously had to combat movements against the government, Melgarejo was ousted in 1870 only when the CREOLE opposition allied itself with the altiplano Indians. A massive Indian revolt

Mariano Melgarejo. Reproduced from Alcides Arguedas, *Los caudillos bárbaros* (Barcelona, 1929). COURTESY OF HARVARD COLLEGE LIBRARY.

forced Melgarejo to flee to Peru, where he died the following year. As a result of the revolt, Indian rebels retook many of their community lands.

There is no adequate biography of Melgarejo. The best is ALBERTO GUTIÉRREZ, *El melgarejismo antes y después de Melgarejo* (1916). An excellent summary of the Melgarejo administration and its context is HERBERT S. KLEIN, *Bolivia: The Evolution of a Multi-Ethnic Society* (1982), pp. 135–141.

ERICK D. LANGER

MELGARES, FACUNDO (*b.* 1775; *d.* ca. 1835), Spanish governor of New Mexico. Born in Villa Carabaca, Murcia, Spain, Melgares, nephew of a judge of the Audiencia of New Spain, entered military service in 1803 as a second lieutenant at the presidio of San Fernando de Carrizal, 75 miles south of El Paso del Norte, New Mexico. When a number of Spanish detachments marched from New Mexico and Texas to intercept American explorers in 1806, Melgares brought reinforcements from Carrizal and led his troops into Pawnee territory. After a party headed by Zebulon Pike, sent by the new governor of the Louisiana Territory to find the sources of the Red and Arkansas rivers, had become lost, a Spanish detachment rescued and arrested the men in 1807. Melgares and his soldiers accompanied Pike from Taos to Santa Fe and then down the Rio Grande to Chihuahua for further interrogation.

During Miguel HIDALGO's revolt of 1810, Melgares led royalist troops from Carrizal against the insurgents at Saltillo, Coahuila. Later he commanded an unsuccessful attack against Ignacio ALLENDE, then participated in Allende's capture near Monclova, Coahuila, on 21 March 1811. By 1817, Melgares was commander of the Santa Fe presidio. In July 1818 he brought troops from Chihuahua to defend New Mexico against Comanche-American attacks, taking over as acting governor. He received permanent appointment to the post one month afterward, and spent the rest of the period of Spanish rule defending the territory against periodic reports of American moves and leading numerous retaliatory campaigns against the NAVAJOS. In August 1819, Melgares successfully concluded a formal peace between Navajos and Spanish.

After Mexico became independent, Melgares refused to allow the colonists in New Mexico to swear allegiance to the new republic until he received a direct order from the commandant general. As a result, he was relieved as governor in April 1822, after citizens of the province brought charges against him on 5 July 1822.

ZEBULON MONTGOMERY PIKE, *The Journals of Zebulon Montgomery Pike*, 2 vols., edited by Donald Jackson (1966); DAVID J. WEBER, *The Spanish Frontier in North America* (1992); ARTHUR GÓMEZ, "Royalist in Transition: Facundo Melgares, the Last Spanish Governor of New Mexico," in *New Mexico Historical Review* 68, no. 4 (1993): 371–387.

                                            ROSS H. FRANK

MELLA, JULIO ANTONIO (*b.* 1905; *d.* 10 January 1929), cofounder and first secretary-general of the Cuban Communist Party. Mella received his early political training in the 1920s as a leader of the movement for university reform. He helped organize the first National Student Congress in 1923, the same year he took part in the famous "Protest of the Thirteen," in which thirteen of Havana's young intellectuals walked out of the Academy of Science when President Alfredo ZAYAS's minister of justice entered the hall.

Mella was also the editor of *Juventud*, a student literary journal, and it was his efforts as a student reformer that brought him in contact with Cuban Marxists, especially Carlos Baliño, a supporter of the Bolshevik Revolution. Along with Baliño, Mella cofounded the Cuban Communist Party in 1925 and was elected the party's first secretary-general. After the founding of the party, Mella gave weekly classes in politics for Havana labor unions, and he also led efforts to organize students in opposition to the Cuban dictator Gerardo MACHADO. Mella was arrested that same year when he led a student strike that shut down the University of Havana. In

prison Mella organized a hunger strike that gained international attention.

In 1927 Mella was deported to Mexico, where he continued his work against the Machado regime and where he also served briefly in 1928 as the secretary-general of the Mexican Communist Party. On 10 January 1929, Mella was assassinated in Mexico City. Fidel Castro's government later claimed that Mella was killed by agents of the Machado government. But it is also possible that internal squabbles may have led to Mella's death, since two weeks before his assassination Mella was expelled from the Mexican Communist Party.

RAMÓN EDUARDO RUIZ, *Cuba: The Making of a Revolution* (1970); SAMUEL FARBER, *Revolution and Reaction in Cuba, 1933–1960* (1976); LOUIS A. PÉREZ, JR., *Cuba: Between Reform and Revolution* (1988).

                                      MICHAEL POWELSON

MELLA, RAMÓN MATÍAS (*b.* 25 February 1816; *d.* 4 July 1864), Dominican revolutionary, active in the nationalist movement that led to the establishment of the Dominican Republic in 1844. In 1822 the island of Hispañola fell under the control of Haitian bureaucrats and soldiers. In 1838 Mella and other Dominican nationalists organized a secret society, La Trinitaria (The Trinitarian), for the purpose of overthrowing the corrupt Haitian dictator, Jean-Pierre BOYER. Mella and the Trinitarians aligned themselves, for tactical reasons, with La Réforme, a Haitian reform movement led by Charles Hérard.

Once Boyer was defeated in 1843, however, Hérard turned on his Dominican allies and had Mella and other Trinitarians arrested and incarcerated at Port-au-Prince. A revolt against Hérard that broke out in 1843 in Port-au-Prince was quelled only with the help of Mella and his Dominican troops. As a reward Mella and his Dominican regiment were released by Hérard. Soon after their arrival in Santo Domingo, the eastern part of the island of Hispañola, Mella and his followers began the process of retaking it and proclaiming independence. On 27 February 1844, Mella and his forces secured the city of Santo Domingo and declared independence from Haiti. Mella was named a member of the new ruling junta that was given the task of organizing the new government. But even after the defeat of the Haitians, Mella's life was not safe, since bitter fighting broke out among the new rulers of the republic. By the summer of 1844, the powerful rancher Pedro SANTANA took over the ruling junta and had Mella imprisoned. In 1848 Mella accepted a general amnesty and was released from prison.

JOHN EDWIN FAGG, *Cuba, Haiti, and the Dominican Republic* (1965); LOUISE L. CRIPPS, *The Spanish Caribbean: From Columbus to Castro* (1979).

                                      MICHAEL POWELSON

MELLO, ZÉLIA MARIA CARDOSO DE (*b.* 20 September 1954), Brazilian minister of economy (1990–1991). The daughter of Emiliano Cardoso de Mello and Auzélia Cardoso de Mello, Mello was born in São Paulo. An economist by training, she was an analyst at the Banco Auxiliar de São Paulo in 1977 and an analyst at the Dumont Assessoria e Planejamento in 1978. She taught at the school of economics and business administration at the University of São Paulo until 1991, when she married television personality and comedian Chico Anísio.

Mello held her first political post in 1983, during the administration of André Franco Montoro, governor of the state of São Paulo. She also served as adviser to the executive board of the Companhia de Desenvolvimento Habitacional do Estado de São Paulo. In 1985, during the administration of President José SARNEY, Mello was invited by Minister of the Treasury Dilson Funaro to work with André Calabi on negotiations regarding the debts owed to the federal government by the states and municipalities. At that time she became acquainted with Fernando COLLOR DE MELLO (no relation), the governor of Alagoas and later president of Brazil (1990).

In 1987, at the time of Minister of Treasury Dilson Funaro's resignation, she left the Sarney administration and founded the firm ZLC-Consultores Associados, which advised public and private enterprises in business negotiations. One of the firm's first major clients was Governor Fernando Collor de Mello. Upon his decision to run for the presidency, Mello joined his campaign. In 1990, she was appointed minister of economy, treasury, and planning, the first woman to hold such a position. She was in charge of implementing economic strategies outlined in the Brasil Novo (New Brazil) plan. Mello's affair with a fellow, married cabinet member led to her resignation, and she left the government on 9 May 1991 to resume her teaching and consulting career.

IÊDA SIQUEIRO WIARDA

MELO, CUSTÓDIO JOSÉ DE (*b.* 9 June 1846; *d.* 15 March 1902), Brazilian veteran of the Paraguayan War and principal figure in a naval revolt during the civil war of 1893. Melo, whose father was a career army officer, distinguished himself in numerous battles during the Paraguayan War. In the Brazilian military he held various positions of command, mostly on ships. Bahian delegate to the Constitutent Assembly of 1890–1891, Melo opposed the dissolution of Congress by President Manoel Deodoro da FONSECA on 3 November 1891 and launched a rebellion of the fleet that produced Fonseca's resignation. Vice President Floriano PEIXOTO took control and named Melo minister of the navy.

A debate over interpretation of the constitution concerning whether Peixoto should have called new elections plus his clash with the Federalists of Rio Grande do Sul brought on the civil war of 1893 and a second revolt of the fleet under Melo. Peixoto resisted and Melo

found himself facing a test of arms. Shore batteries at the military forts challenged the naval ships, some of which escaped, one with Melo aboard, and sailed to Santa Catarina, where they made contact with the Federalist rebels. Agreement between Melo and the rebels proved impossible, and Melo sailed toward Buenos Aires. By March 1894 Vice President Peixoto had acquired warships from Europe and the United States, and his superior naval strength, coupled with the support of five large U.S. naval vessels in the harbor, made the position of the rebel ships in Guanabara Bay untenable. Melo took refuge aboard a Portuguese ship and sailed into exile. He was eventually pardoned and returned to Rio to write his memoirs.

CUSTÓDIO JOSÉ DE MELO, *Apontamentos para a história da revolução de 23 de novembro de 1891*, 2 vols. (1895), and *O governo provisório e a revolução de 1891* (1938); JOSÉ MARIA BELLO, *A Modern History of Brazil*, translated by James L. Taylor (1966); OLINTO LIMA FREIRE DE PILAR, *Os Patronos das Forças Armadas* (1966); JUNE E. HAHNER, *Civilian-Military Relations in Brazil, 1889–1898* (1969), pp. 49–72.

ROBERT A. HAYES

See also **War of the Triple Alliance.**

MELO, JOSÉ MARÍA (*b.* 9 October 1800; *d.* 1 June 1860), Colombian military leader. A consummate professional military officer, Melo revolted in 1854 in defense of a permanent military institution. Born in Ibagué in west-central Colombia, Melo entered the patriot army in 1819 and participated in the battle of AYACUCHO. He served in the Venezuelan military from 1830 to 1835, when he was expelled for his role in the Revolution of the Reforms. Melo served for three years at a Bremen military academy, after which he joined the WAR OF THE SUPREMES (1840–1842) against the Colombian government. President Tomás Cipriano de MOSQUERA restored his military rank in 1849. José María López appointed Melo commanding general of the department of Cundinamarca in 1849. The efforts of the GÓLGOTAS to eliminate the permanent military led Melo to found the promilitary *El Orden* in 1852. Melo's ill-fated 17 April 1854 revolt failed to attract the support of leading Draconian Liberals. In exile, Melo continued his military career in Central America and Mexico, only to be killed in service to Benito JUÁREZ.

ALIRIO GÓMEZ PICÓN, *El golpe militar del 17 de abril de 1854: La dictadura de José María Melo, el enigma de Obando, los secretos de la historia* (1972); DARIO ORTIZ VIDALES, *José María Melo: La razón de un rebelde* (1980).

DAVID SOWELL

MELO, LEOPOLDO (*b.* 15 November 1869; *d.* 6 February 1951), Argentine politician, lawyer, and university professor. Melo was born in Diamante, in the province of Entre Ríos, and graduated from law school in 1891. An expert in maritime and business law, he taught these subjects for over thirty years at the University of Buenos Aires. He served as a national deputy to Congress from Entre Ríos from 1914 to 1916, and as a senator from 1917 to 1930. In the 1928 elections he was the presidential candidate of the conservative wing of the Radical Civic Union (UCR), but he was defeated by Hipólito YRIGOYEN, the candidate of the Personalist faction. Melo served as minister of the interior (the political arm of the executive power in Argentina) under the conservative president Agustín P. JUSTO from 1932 to 1936. He presided over the Argentine delegations to the Inter-American conferences in Panama (1939) and Havana (1940), and wrote extensively on juridical matters. Melo died in Pinamar, in the province of Buenos Aires.

CELSO RODRÍGUEZ

MELO E CASTRO, MARTINHO DE (*b.* 11 November 1716; *d.* 24 March 1795), Portuguese diplomat (1751–1770), overseas minister (1770–1795). Born in Lisbon, Melo e Castro was a younger son of Francisco de Melo e Castro, Governor of Mazagão in North Africa (1705–1713), and Dona Maria Joaquina Xavier da Silva. His older brother, Manuel Bernardo de Melo e Castro, became the first and only viscount of Lourinha in 1777, after having served as governor and CAPTAIN-GENERAL of Grão Pará and Maranhão (1759–1763). In his youth Melo e Castro followed an ecclesiastical career and studied at Évora and Coimbra. At what time he changed careers is not clear. From 1753 to 1755 he served as envoy to the Netherlands. The following year he was transferred to London, where he held the post of envoy extraordinary and minister plenipotentiary from 1756 to 1762. In that latter year he traveled to France, where he represented Portugal as minister plenipotentiary at the peace talks at Fontainebleau (1762) and Paris (1763) that ended the Seven Years' War (1756–1763). Following the signing of the treaties, Melo e Castro briefly visited Portugal before returning to England, where he continued to serve as envoy extraordinary and minister plenipotentiary until 1770.

On 4 January 1770, he was named secretary of state for naval and overseas affairs, a post he held until his death in 1795. His correspondence during that twenty-five-year tenure is of great importance for understanding Brazil during some of the most critical years of its history. Jacome Ratton, the French-born but naturalized Portuguese merchant, industrialist, memoirist, and contemporary of Melo e Castro, described him as honest, though very stubborn and pro-English. He was well aware of the importance of Portuguese America. In 1779 he wrote: "Portugal without Brazil is an insignificant power." A strong opponent of mercantilism, Melo e Castro was in favor of monopoly companies, against "workshops and manufactories" in Brazil, and greatly concerned about the defense of Portuguese America and the extensive illegal trade carried on there. However, he

was outvoted regarding the fate of Brazil's commercial companies, and the Company of Grão Pará and Maranhão lost its monopoly status in 1778, as did the Company of Pernambuco and Paraíba two years later. Melo e Castro was minister during the difficult period of adjustment in Minas Gerais in the aftermath of the gold boom. The Minas conspiracy of 1788–1789 was uncovered while he was in power.

Despite his importance as a statesman, Melo e Castro has not had a biographer. However, he is mentioned frequently in KENNETH R. MAXWELL, *Conflicts and Conspiracies: Brazil and Portugal, 1750–1808* (1973). See also JOSÉ VICENTE-SERRÃO, "Melo e Castro, Martinho de," in *Diccionário ilustrado da história de Portugal,* vol. 1 (1985), p. 459, and JACOME RATTON, *Recordaçoens . . . sobre occurrencias do seu tempo em Portugal . . .* (London, 1813). The second edition of this work is entitled *Recordações de Jacome Ratton sobre ocorrências do seu tempo, de maio de 1747 a setembro de 1810,* 2d rev. ed. (Coimbra, 1920).

FRANCIS DUTRA

See also **Trading Companies.**

MELO FRANCO, AFONSO ARINOS DE (*b.* 27 November 1905; *d.* 27 August 1990), Brazilian constitutional lawyer, politician, writer, and diplomat. The son of diplomat Afrânio de MELO FRANCO, Afonso Arinos was born into a distinguished family of the state of Minas Gerais. A lawyer, he initially devoted himself to legal and historical writing, leaving politics to his father and brother, Virgílio Martins de Melo Franco. At the death of his father in 1943, Afonso Arinos joined the Friends of America to continue his father's opposition to the ESTADO NOVO. He advocated economic and political liberalism and, in 1945, helped found the União Democrática Nacional (UDN), the opposition party to Getúlio VARGAS and later Juscelino KUBITSCHEK. He served as a federal deputy (1947–1959), a senator (1959–1961), and as minister of foreign relations under Jânio QUADROS (1961) and, briefly, João GOULART (1962). Melo Franco was an architect of Brazil's increasingly independent foreign policy vis-à-vis the United States. Under Quadros, he declined to support U.S. pressure on Cuba, advocated seating the People's Republic of China in the United Nations, and sought to restore diplomatic ties with the Soviet Union. However, as Goulart allied with the left, Melo Franco supported the president's overthrow. Only after the military indicated its intention of staying in power did Melo Franco oppose the regime, leading the congressional debate against the Constitution of 1967. When it passed, stripping the Congress of its powers, Melo Franco declined to run again for office, returning to academia (his works on history and law total nearly forty) until asked by President José SARNEY in 1985 to organize the drafting of a new, democratic constitution. He later served again as a senator.

THOMAS E. SKIDMORE, *Politics in Brazil, 1930–1964: An Experiment in Democracy* (1967); PETER FLYNN, *Brazil: A Political Anal-*

ysis (1978); ISRAEL BELOCH and ALZIRA ALVES DE ABREU, eds., *Dicionário Histórico-Biográfico Brasileiro, 1930–1983* (1984); THOMAS E. SKIDMORE, *The Politics of Military Rule in Brazil, 1964–1985* (1988).

ELIZABETH A. COBBS

MELO FRANCO, AFRÂNIO DE (b. 25 February 1870; d. 1 January 1943), Brazilian politician and diplomat.

Afrânio de Melo Franco was born into a prominent family of the state of Minas Gerais. Trained as a lawyer, he joined with other students in 1889 to support Brazil's transition to a republican government dominated by powerful states ("Rule of the Governors"). During the First Republic he served as secretary of the legation to Uruguay, a federal deputy (1906–1929), and eventually as Brazil's representative to the League of Nations (1924–1926). As a leading *mineiro*, Melo Franco benefited from the political power of Minas Gerais and São Paulo, known as the "café com leite" (coffee with milk) alliance. In 1929 Melo Franco threw his support to Getúlio VARGAS in the national contest for power leading to the ESTADO NOVO. Vargas made Melo Franco his first minister of foreign relations (1930–33), giving him a relatively free hand in the running of Itamaraty. Melo Franco reorganized the ministry, emphasizing foreign trade and, in light of growing world tensions, Pan-Americanism. Along with Oswaldo ARANHA, Melo Franco viewed cooperation with the United States as the surest road to national security and the key to Brazil's growing power within Latin America. Melo Franco represented Brazil at the Inter-American Conference of 1938, where he helped induce Argentina to join in the Declaration of Lima. He broke with Vargas in 1933 over a question of political patronage and, just before his death, joined the Friends of America, a group seeking democratization and an end to the Estado Novo.

ALFONSO ARINOS DE MELO FRANCO, *Um estadista da república: Afrânio de Melo Franco e seu tempo*, 3 vols. (1955); STANLEY E. HILTON, *Brazil and the Great Powers, 1930–1939* (1975); PETER FLYNN, *Brazil: A Political Analysis* (1978); ISRAEL BELOCH and ALZIRA ALVES DE ABREU, eds., *Dicionário Histórico-Biográfico Brasileiro, 1930–1983* (1984).

ELIZABETH A. COBBS

MELO NETO, JOÃO CABRAL DE (b. 9 January 1920), Brazilian poet.

Born in Recife, Pernambuco, Melo Neto spent his childhood on a sugarcane plantation and attended Catholic schools. In 1942 he published his first collection of poems and moved to Rio de Janeiro to study for the foreign service. During his long diplomatic career, he resided in England, France, Switzerland, and Senegal, as well as in Spain and Spanish America. From the late 1940s his literary reputation grew steadily, and near the end of the twentieth century he was widely regarded as the most important Brazilian poet of the century's second half.

A unique figure in the cultural sphere, Melo Neto has commanded respect both for pure aesthetic principles and for the social perspectives of his work. He has influenced such diverse genres as concretism, regional verse, literature of commitment, and the poetry of song (MÚSICA POPULAR BRASILEIRA). His is not a conventional lyricism of self-expression but rather a controlled objective discourse, often connected to the actual settings and human realities of the northeastern region. In 1968, he was elected to the Brazilian Academy of Letters. He received the prestigious Camões prize in 1990 for lifetime literary achievement in Portuguese and two years later the Twelfth Neustadt International Prize for Literature (sponsored by *World Literature Today*).

Selected Poetry, 1937–1990 (various translators), edited by Djelal Kadir (1994). See also ANTÔNIO CARLOS SECCHIN, *João Cabral: A poesia do menos* (1985); MARTA PEIXOTO, "João Cabral de Melo Neto," in *Dictionary of Brazilian Literature*, edited by Irwin Stern (1988).

CHARLES A. PERRONE

MELVILLE, THOMAS AND MARGARITA (MARJORIE), U.S. Catholic missionaries in Guatemala who became revolutionaries.

Margarita Bradford (b. 19 August 1929) was born in Irapuato, Mexico, and studied at Loretto Academy in El Paso, Texas. She became Maryknoll Sister Marion Peter and was assigned in 1954 to teach at an upper-class school in Guatemala City. Influenced by the *cursillo de capacitación social* (short course of social empowerment) movement, she began to spend time teaching the urban poor and organizing vacation projects for affluent students in poverty-stricken rural areas. Thomas Melville (b. 5 December 1930), from Newton, Massachusetts, joined the MARYKNOLL ORDER and, after ordination in 1957, was sent to work with Indians in the Guatemalan highlands. He helped them form cooperatives. Later he organized an Indian resettlement program in the Petén.

Both missioners became involved with radical university students, some of whom had contact with guerrillas. Frustrated by what they felt was a lack of commitment to the poor by church leaders, they decided to join the guerrilla movement, in order to give it a "Christian presence." Their plan was discovered, and they were expelled from Guatemala in 1967. Soon both left Maryknoll, and they were married in 1968. They later earned doctoral degrees in anthropology and wrote *Guatemala: The Politics of Land Ownership* (1971).

The Melvilles defend their actions in Guatemala in *Whose Heaven, Whose Earth?* (1971), an autobiography.

EDWARD T. BRETT

MENCHÚ TUM, RIGOBERTA (b. 9 January 1959), recipient of the 1992 Nobel Peace Prize.

Menchú is a Maya-Quiché Indian woman from Guatemala and the

first indigenous Latin American so honored. She is a member of the Coordinating Commission of the Committee of Peasant Unity (CUC) and a founding member of the United Representation of the Guatemalan Opposition (RUOG). She was born in Chimel, near San Miguel de Uspantán, to Vicente Menchú and Juana Tum, Maya peasants and Catholic lay leaders. Self-educated, from the age of eight she accompanied her parents to harvest export crops on south coast plantations, and later worked for two years as a domestic in Guatemala City. She participated with her parents in local pastoral activities.

In the 1970s, expropriation of Indian land in El Quiché threatened Maya subsistence and prompted her family's political activism and involvement with the CUC. In the late 1970s, Menchú organized local self-defense groups, armed with rocks and machetes, in response to the government's escalated counterinsurgency war in the highlands. In January 1980, her father was burned to death in the occupation of the Spanish embassy in Guatemala City by campesinos with the support of trade unionists and students. Menchú continued organizing efforts in local Maya communities until forced to flee in 1981; since then she has lived in Mexico City.

A powerful speaker, Menchú has continued to work for peace and the rights of indigenous people in Guatemala in international forums. She has participated in the U.N. Working Group on Indigenous Populations, the U.N. Subcommission on Prevention of Discrimination and Protection for Minorities, and the U.N. Conference on the Decade of Women. She is a credentialed observer of the U.N. Human Rights Commission and the General Assembly. She serves on the board of the International Indian Treaty Council and was a member of honor at the Second Continental Gathering of the "500 Years of Resistance" Conference. Among other awards, she has received the 1988 Nonino Prize special award, the 1990 Monseñor Proaño Human Rights Prize, the 1990 UNESCO Education for Peace Prize, and the 1991 French Committee for the Defense of Freedoms and Human Rights prize.

ELISABETH BURGOS-DEBRAY, ed., *I, Rigoberta Menchú: An Indian Woman in Guatemala*, translated by Ann Wright (1983).

MARILYN M. MOORS

See also **Human Rights.**

MENDES, GILBERTO (*b.* 13 October 1922), Brazilian composer, teacher, critic. Gilberto Mendes has been associated with experimental movements in Brazilian music, most notably the Música Nova group. The *Manifesto música nova*, published in 1963, expressed a commitment to explore every aspect of contemporary musical language, including concertism, impressionism, polytonalism, atonality, serialism, phono-mechanical sound, and all aspects of electronic media. Composers associated with the Música Nova group included Willy Co-

rreia de OLIVEIRA, Rogério DUPRAT, Damiano Cozzella, and Júlio Medaglia.

Mendes studied composition with Henri Pousseur, Pierre Boulez, and Karlheinz Stockhausen. One of his best-known compositions, "Beba Coca-Cola" (Drink Coca-Cola), is a satire on a Coca-Cola commercial. In 1970 his composition "Blirium a-9" was chosen by the International Council of Composers of UNESCO for broadcast in Europe. In 1974 his composition "Santos Football Music" won an award from the Associação Paulista de Críticos de Artes as the best experimental work. In 1973 "Pausa e Menopausa" (Pause and Menopause), a composition based on a poem of Ronaldo Azeredo, explored the idea of indeterminacy, in which music could be written as poetry without text, music without sound, and visual impressions without sound. In 1978–1979 Mendes accepted an appointment at the University of Wisconsin–Milwaukee. During this period numerous performances of his works were given in the United States.

GÉRARD BÉHAGUE, *Music in Latin America* (1979); DAVID P. APPLEBY, *The Music of Brazil* (1983).

DAVID P. APPLEBY

MENDES FILHO, FRANCISCO "CHICO" ALVES (*b.* 15 December 1944; *d.* 22 December 1988), Brazilian union leader and ecologist. Mendes, from Xapuri, Acre, began his career as a RUBBER tapper at the age of eight, when he assisted his father in gathering rubber. After working twenty-eight years in this profession, Mendes founded the Xapuri Rural Workers' Union in 1977. As its quietly persuasive president, he sponsored education for members and their children, and he helped establish health posts in Acre. Ten years later, Mendes assisted by anthropologist Mary Allegretti, formed the National Council of Rubber Tappers (CNS). Through the CNS, Chico helped organize *Projeto Seringueiro* (Rubber Tapper Project), which promoted cooperatives whose literate members learned to manage their own finances. Mendes also led the Xapuri Rural Workers in their tactic of *empate* (standoff). Large landowners who hired workers to clear the Amazonian rain FOREST were faced with groups of rubber workers who assembled en masse and barricaded the area to be cleared. Although large landowners often removed them at gunpoint, the union achieved success through *empates* about one-third of the time. *Empates* brought worldwide attention to the rubber workers' social and environmental battles. Mendes won international recognition for his efforts and became a consultant to the World Bank and to the U.S. Senate on matters of investments in Amazônia.

Mendes promoted EXTRACTIVE RESERVES, the union's innovative alternative to deforestation, which allows workers to live on and extract products from the rain forest while leaving it intact. In 1988, when the Brazilian government expropriated land from powerful owners for three extractive reserves, Mendes began receiving death threats. He was shot to death on 22 December 1988. News of his death made headlines throughout the world, and he became a martyr in the fight to preserve the Amazonian rain forest. In December 1990, a jury found landowner Darly Alves da Silva and his son, Darci, guilty of Chico's murder.

CHICO MENDES, with additional material by TONY GROSS, *Fight for the Forest: Chico Mendes in His Own Words* (1989); AUGUSTA DWYER, *Into the Amazon: The Struggle for the Rain Forest* (1990); SUSANNA HECHT and ALEXANDER COCKBURN, *The Fate of the Forest: Developers, Destroyers, and Defenders of the Amazon* (1990); ANDREW REVKIN, *The Burning Season* (1990); ALEX SHOUMATOFF, *The World Is Burning: Murder in the Rain Forest* (1990).

CAROLYN JOSTOCK

MENDES MACIEL, ANTÔNIO VICENTE. *See* **Conselheiro, Antônio.**

MÉNDEZ BALLESTER, MANUEL (*b.* 4 August 1909), Puerto Rican dramatist. Born in Aguadilla, Puerto Rico, Méndez Ballester began his career in theater as an actor with the Teatro Rodante (Traveling Theater). His first publications were *Isla cerrera* (Wild island, 1937), a historical novel about the resistance of the Puerto Rican Indians to the Spanish conquest, and *El clamor de los surcos* (1940), a rural drama. In 1939 he studied under a Rockefeller grant in New York, where he penned his famous *Tiempo muerto* (Dead time, 1940), a tragedy about the sugarcane worker during the idle season. His 1958 drama about Puerto Ricans in New York, *Encrucijada* (The crossroads), was staged at the First Puerto Rican Theater Festival. *El milagro* (1957), an avant-garde metaphysical play, debuted the next year in English in New York as *The Miracle*. Two of his well-known satirical works are *Bienvenido, don Goyito* (Welcome, Mr. Goyito, 1966) and *Arriba las mujeres* (Long live women, 1968).

In addition to writing, producing, and directing theatrical productions, Méndez Ballester served as assistant secretary of labor from 1954 to 1962 and subsequently, until 1968, as a member of the House of Representatives, where he initiated environmental reforms. A versatile dramatist, Méndez Ballester has cultivated classical tragedy, historical theater, the theater of the absurd, social satire, farce, and zarzuela (operetta). The conflict of material and spiritual values is an abiding theme in his writing, which in addition to novels and drama includes stories, essays, and a humorous column in *El Nuevo Día*. In 1992 the Institute of Puerto Rican Culture published a two-volume collection of his plays.

ROBERT A. RICCIO, "Studies in Puerto Rican Drama I: *Encrucijada*," *Atenea* (Mayagüez, Puerto Rico) 1, no. 4 (1964): 15–20; FRANCISCO ARRIVÍ, "La generación del treinta: El teatro," *Literatura puertorriqueña: 21 Conferencias* (1969), pp. 387–396.

ESTELLE IRIZARRY

See also **Theater.**

MÉNDEZ FLEITAS, EPIFANIO (*b.* 1917; *d.* 22 November 1985), Paraguayan political leader. An early associate of President Federico CHAVES (1949–1959), Méndez Fleitas first rose to a position of prominence when the latter came to power in 1949. As chief of police, Méndez Fleitas worked to defend Chaves's interests. He was named director of the Agrarian Reform Institute and later president of the Central Bank. At the same time, he rose rapidly within the "leftist" faction of the ruling Colorado Party, in part because of Chaves's patronage but also because of his own exceptional energy and forceful oratorical style.

Wishing to rise still further, Méndez Fleitas organized a plot with the help of General Alfredo STROESSNER, head of the artillery section of the army. In early May 1954, the coup was carried out, but shortly thereafter, Stroessner exiled his fellow conspirator to Buenos Aires and went on to impose a dictatorship that lasted until 1989.

In the Argentine capital, Méndez Fleitas published polemical writings and composed folk music. He also established the Movimiento Popular Colorado (MOPOCO), an emigré group composed of Colorados who had turned against Stroessner. MOPOCO continued to be a major center of opposition to the dictator, though its founder encountered a loss of prestige when it was alleged in the 1970s that he had accepted money from the Central Intelligence Agency. Méndez Fleitas died in Buenos Aires.

CHARLES J. KOLINSKI, *Historical Dictionary of Paraguay* (1973); PAUL H. LEWIS, *Paraguay Under Stroessner* (1980), *passim*.

THOMAS L. WHIGHAM

MÉNDEZ MONTENEGRO, JULIO CÉSAR, (*b.* 23 November 1915), president of Guatemala (1966–1970). Born in Guatemala City, Méndez Montenegro interrupted his legal studies at the University of San Carlos to participate in the 1944 October Revolution. He was the first president of the Frente Popular Libertador (FPL), which supported Juan José ARÉVALO for president in 1945. After receiving his *licenciatura* in 1945, he taught at the National University until 1965, rising to dean of the law school.

After the mysterious death of his brother, two-time Partido Revolucionario (PR) presidential candidate Mario MÉNDEZ MONTENEGRO (1912–1965), he agreed to substitute for him in the 1966 elections. He defeated the military-backed PID (Institutional Democratic Party) candidate by 45,000 votes but, because he did not receive an absolute majority, had to bargain with the military and its legislative supporters to secure the confirmation of the Congress. As a result, Méndez gave the military both a free hand in conducting the war against the guerrillas in the eastern departments of the country and virtual control of the countryside.

The Méndez Montenegro administration is remembered primarily for the "scorched earth" rural pacification campaigns led by Colonel Carlos ARANA OSORIO (his successor in office [1970]), the kidnapping of Archbishop Mario Casariego (1968), and for the emergence of the MANO BLANCA (White Hand) and other right-wing terrorist organizations. However, his government pushed through some reform measures, most notably the nationalization of the railroad owned by the UNITED FRUIT COMPANY. Schools, public hospitals, port facilities, and a major hydroelectric plant were constructed. Some CAMPESINO organizing and limited land distribution were attempted, but the regime was frustrated in its agrarian reform efforts. Attempts to overhaul the tax code were defeated by street demonstrations.

After leaving office, Méndez Montenegro held a law professorship at the University of San Carlos.

THOMAS MELVILLE and MARJORIE MELVILLE, *Guatemala—Another Vietnam?* (1971); WILLIAM E. THOMS, "Civilian President Julio César Méndez Montenegro and His Guatemala" (M.A. thesis, Tulane University, 1977); MICHAEL MC CLINTOCK, *The American Connection*, vol. 2, *State Terror and Popular Resistance in Guatemala* (1985); JAMES DUNKERLEY, *Power in the Isthmus: A Political History of Modern Guatemala* (1988).

ROLAND H. EBEL

MÉNDEZ MONTENEGRO, MARIO (*b.* 30 November 1912; *d.* 31 October 1965), mayor of Guatemala City (1944–1948) and founder of the Partido Revolucionario (PR). Born in Santa Rosa, he interrupted his law studies, which he completed in exile, to participate in the October Revolution (1944). He served as undersecretary of the junta and as secretary general of the presidency under Juan José ARÉVALO (1945–1951). In 1947 he broke with the radicals in the Revolutionary Action Party (PAR) and reconstituted the center-left Popular Liberation Front (Frente Popular Libertador—FPL), which he had helped found in 1944.

In 1957 Méndez Montenegro organized the PR from among the moderate supporters of Arévalo. When the PR was denied legal registration for the elections of 1957, Méndez Montenegro supported the street demonstrations led by General Miguel YDÍGORAS FUENTES (president, 1958–1963) that annulled them. He became the legal PR candidate for the January 1958 electoral rerun and received 28 percent of the vote. Opposed both ideologically and politically to the Ydígoras Fuentes regime, he backed the 1963 military coup that overthrew Fuentes. He died from a gunshot wound in October 1965, shortly before being nominated as the PR presidential candidate for the elections of 1966. Whether Méndez Montenegro was assassinated or committed suicide remains unclear.

FRANCISCO VILLAGRÁN KRAMER, *Biografía política de Guatemala: Los pactos políticos de 1944 a 1970* (1993).

ROLAND H. EBEL

MÉNDEZ PEREIRA, OCTAVIO (*b.* 1887; *d.* 1954), prominent Panamanian educator. He was born in Aguadulce and graduated from the University of Chile in 1913. He taught at and was president of the National Institute, served as minister of education, and became the first president of the University of Panama when it was founded in 1935. Méndez Pereira founded numerous schools and learned journals. He published essays on literature, education, and a variety of historical subjects. He wrote biographies of Vasco Núñez de BALBOA and Justo AROSEMENA, and he founded the Panamanian Academy of Language and the Panamanian Academy of History.

JORGE CONTE PORRAS, *Panameños ilustres* (1978).

JUAN MANUEL PÉREZ

MENDIBURU, MANUEL DE (*b.* 20 October 1805; *d.* 21 January 1885), considered Peru's foremost historian of the early republic and the forerunner to Jorge BASADRE. He was in fact a man of many careers—diplomat, government minister, and military officer. Mendiburu was involved in the highest levels of government for most of his adult life. No doubt the apex of his political accomplishments came when at the height of his political influence as the prefect of Tacna, he vigorously opposed the PERU-BOLIVIA CONFEDERATION of Andrés SANTA CRUZ (1829–1836). He briefly was minister of finance and war in the early years of Ramón CASTILLA's presidency and later was president of the council of state. He served the government of José Rufino ECHENIQUE as minister of finance and then as ambassador to London while the government was negotiating a settlement of the external debt. For the first five months of the WAR OF THE PACIFIC (1879–1883), he served as minister of war. Between these assignments he compiled the invaluable *Diccionario histórico-biográfico del Perú* (8 vols., 1874), a descriptive catalog of colonial Peruvian public figures with heavy emphasis on the sixteenth century. He wrote many other studies, numbers of them unpublished, focusing primarily on diplomatic events of his own era.

TIMOTHY E. ANNA, *The Fall of the Royal Government in Peru* (1979), esp. p. 240; PAUL GOOTENBERG, *Imagining Development: Economic Ideas in Peru's "Fictitious Prosperity" of Guano, 1840–1880* (1993).

VINCENT PELOSO

MENDIETA, SALVADOR (*b.* 24 March 1882; *d.* 28 May 1958), Nicaraguan literary figure and Central American unionist leader. Born in Diriamba to a well-liked, hardworking merchant family, Mendieta grew up to become an ardent Central American unionist. Alejo Mendieta was committed to securing a good education for his sons and, when health problems threatened to intervene, sent young Salvador to Guatemala to finish primary school. He completed his baccalaureate in 1896 with a thesis entitled "The Constituents and the Federal Constituent Assembly of 1824." His doctoral thesis in law, titled "Organization of Executive Power in Central America" (Honduras, 1900) further underscores Mendieta's early commitment to the idea of union.

Mendieta's early activities were not confined to the classroom. In 1895 he organized the Minerva Society, a literary-scientific salon with marked unionist sentiments. In 1899 he cofounded another discussion group, El Derecho, which sponsored a journal of the same name. That same year Mendieta ambitiously declared the existence of the Central American Unionist Party, in response to political upheavals throughout the isthmus. He quickly aroused the animosity of Guatemalan dictator Manuel Estrada Cabrera, his lifelong nemesis, who then expelled Mendieta to Honduras in 1900. Nevertheless, the determined young man refused to be dissuaded and set about extending the Unionist Party to other Central American countries.

Mendieta established a newspaper, *Diario Centroamericano,* in Managua, which led President José Santos Zelaya to imprison Mendieta in 1903. During the first decade of the twentieth century, Mendieta traveled throughout the isthmus and began to write some of his most important works: *Páginas de Unión* (1902), *La nacionalidad y el Partido Unionista Centroamericano* (1905), *Partido Unionista Centroamericano* (1911), and *Cómo estamos y qué debemos hacer* (1911). Mendieta's most famous and enduring work was *La enfermedad de Centro América* (1906–1930), in which he focused on the obstacles to Central American development. Mendieta pointed to the lack of education, poor health and hygiene, unequal distribution of wealth and power, and the generally low level of public consciousness as the roots of the isthmus's infirmities.

Mendieta's ideas of union and social justice did not endear him to the oligarchical political elites of Central America, and he found it difficult to get his masterwork published. He traveled to Europe in search of support and finally reached an agreement with Maucci in Barcelona. Back in Nicaragua, Mendieta served as rector of the Universidad Nacional, but he resigned in protest of his inability to effect needed reforms. Seriously ill with a liver ailment, Mendieta nonetheless continued to head the Unionist Party, for which efforts he was sentenced to jail in 1955 by Anastasio SOMOZA. Fleeing on horseback, the aging Mendieta escaped Somoza's secret police and lived in San Salvador until his death.

JUAN MANUEL MENDOZA, *Salvador Mendieta* (1930); THOMAS KARNES, *The Failure of Union: Central America, 1824–1975* (1976); WARREN H. MORY, *Salvador Mendieta: Escritor y apóstol de la unión centroamericana* (1971).

KAREN RACINE

See also **Central America.**

MENDIETA Y MONTEFUR, CARLOS (*b.* 4 November 1873; *d.* 29 September 1960), president of Cuba (1934–1935). A colonel in the war of independence and afterward a congressman for more than twenty years, Mendieta was also a vice-presidential candidate in 1916. Three years later he became editor of *Heraldo de Cuba,* where he achieved considerable fame as a combative political journalist. He was generally regarded as an honest man, and for a long time he was held by many to be the "hope of the Republic," until army chief Fulgencio BATISTA appointed him Cuba's provisional president on 18 January 1934.

Mendieta proved to be an inept and weak president whose main administrative skill was the ability to organize ephemeral compromises among party leaders. For this reason he was quickly dubbed Batista's puppet. During his brief term in office the revolutionary impetus that had begun the previous year came to an end when a general strike against the government was harshly repressed by the military. Mendieta's administration, however, was not altogether counterrevolutionary, for it confirmed much of the social legislation passed by the preceding revolutionary regime. It was also under Mendieta that women were enfranchised, and the PLATT AMENDMENT (1901), peceived by many Cubans as an infringement on their sovereignty, was finally abrogated by a treaty signed with the United States on 29 May 1934. Mendieta resigned on 10 December 1935.

HERMINIO PORTELL-VILÁ, *Nueva historia de la República de Cuba* (1986): 429–455.

JOSÉ M. HERNÁNDEZ

MENDINUETA Y MÚZQUIZ, PEDRO DE (*b.* 7 June 1736; *d.* 17 February 1825), VICEROY of New Granada (1797–1803). Born near Pamplona, Navarre, Spain, Mendinueta pursued a military career. He served as sub-inspector general of the army of NEW SPAIN (1785–1789), held a successful command during the French War (1793–1795), and had secured promotion to lieutenant general by the time of his assignment to NEW GRANADA. A leader of good ability and sound judgment, Mendinueta ruled during difficult times, facing a plethora of conspiracies inspired by the French Revolution and the threat of invasion during the First British War (1796–1802). Rather than assume personal command on the coast, which was the normal wartime practice for viceroys, he remained in Santa Fe to address questions of domestic security. Mendinueta is well remembered for his strong dedication to public health and the establishment of a school of medicine in Santa Fe. He was replaced by Antonio AMAR Y BORBÓN and returned to Spain, where he assumed a position on the Supreme Council of War and later became councillor of state. He died in Madrid.

JOSÉ MARÍA RESTREPO SÁENZ, *Biografías de los mandatarios y ministros de la Real Audiencia, 1671–1819* (1952), esp. pp. 219–

225; *Historia extensa de Colombia,* vol. 4, *Nuevo reino de Granada: El virreynato* (1970), esp. pt. 2, pp. 393–420; ALLAN J. KUETHE, *Military Reform and Society in New Granada, 1773–1808* (1977).

ALLAN J. KUETHE

MENDOZA, city in western Argentina and capital of Mendoza Province. Mendoza was founded on 2 March 1561 by Captain Pedro del Castillo, by order of the governor of Chile, García Hurtado de Mendoza. Its twenty-one square miles are set on a semiarid plain, about 2,475 feet above sea level at the foot of the Andes. It is surrounded mostly by vineyards and wineries, the principal industry of the province. In colonial times it was an isolated trade center between Buenos Aires, 800 miles to the east, and Chile, across the Andes. In 1861 Mendoza was practically destroyed by an earthquake; it was rebuilt close to the old settlement. In the 1880s the city underwent vast technological change: In 1884 the railway line reached Mendoza, opening a flourishing trade with Córdoba, Buenos Aires, and other provinces of the littoral, but weakening the trade with Chile. In 1885 a streetcar system was established, as well as the first telephone lines. In 1882 Adolfo Calle founded the newspaper *Los Andes,* which continues to serve the city and region. Because of Mendoza's dependence on irrigation, water is of critical importance. The oasis provided by the Mendoza River contributed to the city's continuous growth. From 9,900 inhabitants in 1869, the population of Mendoza reached 58,800 in 1914, 109,000 in 1960, and 126,400 in 1985. While the 1990 estimate saw a decrease in population to 119,600, a phenomenal demographic expansion took place in Mendoza's outlying areas, which today constitute Greater Mendoza (Godoy Cruz, Las Heras, Guaymallén, Maipú, and other adjacent towns). In 1990 this area reached an estimated 800,000 inhabitants, 57 percent of the total population of the province. The arrival of immigrants, especially from Italy and Spain, made an extraordinary commercial, industrial, and cultural contribution to the development of the city. Immigration reached its peak during the pre–World War I years. According to the 1914 census, 31 percent of the population of the capital were Europeans. In 1939 the National University of Cuyo was established (Cuyo is the name given to the region formed by the contiguous provinces of Mendoza, San Luis, and San Juan). Besides this public institution, there are three private universities in the city. The cleanliness of Mendoza is one of its most outstanding characteristics. The irrigation ditches, or *acequias,* open in every street, transform the semidesertic landscape into a charming oasis. The city's wide avenues, plazas, and the attractive General San Martín Park, contribute to the pleasant environment of what constitutes the major urban center in western Argentina.

JORGE M. SCALVINI, *Historia de Mendoza* (1965); MIGUEL MARZO and OSVALDO INCHAUSPE, *Geografía de Mendoza,* 2 vols. (1967); ROSA T. GUAYCOCHEA DE ONOFRI, *Arquitectura de Mendoza* (1978); PEDRO SANTOS MARTÍNEZ, *Historia de Mendoza*

(1979); JAMES R. SCOBIE, *Secondary Cities of Argentina: The Social History of Corrientes, Salta, and Mendoza, 1850–1910* (1988).

CELSO RODRÍGUEZ

MENDOZA, ANTONIO DE (*b.* 1490/94; *d.* 21 July 1552), count of Tendilla, Spain's ambassador to Hungary, and viceroy of Peru (1551–1552). Mendoza, probably born in Granada, was also the first viceroy of Mexico (1535–1549). Chosen to represent the king and the Council of the Indies as well as to provide a check on the personal power of Hernándo CORTÉS, he brought to the office the prestige of the high nobility. Mendoza reached New Spain fourteen years after the military conquest of central Mexico had been completed. Typically, Spanish institutions arrived on the scene as the viability of new colonies became obvious and greater crown control seemed necessary. Yet, once in the colony, Mendoza's direct tie to the crown was relatively loose, considering that fleets containing official letters and orders sailed once a year. Mendoza, like other viceroys, occasionally avoided complying with royal pronouncements, such as his delay in enforcing the New Laws of the Indies that sought to limit ENCOMIENDAS (grants of Indian labor and tribute). (The first viceroy of Peru lost his life in a rebellion following the implementation of the New Laws in that colony.)

Judicial matters and many ecclesiastical ones fell outside Mendoza's domain, but he administered nearly all other social, political, territorial, and economic concerns of the colony. Enhancing revenues through legislation covering taxation, trade, and transportation was probably one of his more pressing goals. Mendoza also supervised matters relating to the indigenous people of the new colony, ironically seeking to protect their rights and to see that they were subjugated and Hispanicized.

ARTHUR SCOTT AITON, *Antonio de Mendoza: First Viceroy of New Spain* (1927; repr. 1967); MICHAEL C. MEYER and WILLIAM L. SHERMAN, *The Course of Mexican History,* 3d ed. (1987), pp. 144–150.

STEPHANIE WOOD

MENDOZA, CARLOS ANTONIO (*b.* 1856; *d.* 1916), Panamanian lawyer and politician and author of Panama's declaration of independence. He headed the radical wing of the Liberal Party. A mulatto, he was very popular with the lower classes. Mendoza served as deputy to the National Assembly and was a member of the Panama City Council. He was also president of the national directorate of the Liberal Party. In 1910 he occupied the presidency for seven months after the death of President José Domingo Obaldía and prior to Pablo AROSEMENA, who completed Obaldía's term.

BALTASAR ISAZA CALDERÓN, *Carlos A. Mendoza y su generación: historia de Panamá: 1821–1916* (1982).

JUAN MANUEL PÉREZ

MENDOZA, PEDRO DE (*b.* 1487; *d.* 23 June 1537), first *adelantado* (frontier military commander) of Río de la Plata (1536–1537). Born in Guadix, Spain, Mendoza probably served in the Italian campaigns of Charles V. As part of an attempt by the Spanish crown to control Portuguese expansion in the New World, he was charged with populating the Río de la Plata area in 1534. Although he fell seriously ill before departing Sanlúcar da Barrameda, he had recovered sufficiently by August 1535 to embark on the expedition, which was composed of eleven ships and more than 2,000 men (and a few women) drawn primarily from the Basque region, Andalusia, and the Low Countries.

In February 1536, Mendoza founded a fortified city on the banks of the Río de la Plata, a city that he christened Santa María del Buen Aire. Within a year he and his men were forced to abandon their settlement because of the hostility of the Querandí Indians and the resultant lack of food. Suffering from hunger, recurring sickness, and Indian attack, Mendoza decided to return to Spain in early 1537; he died at sea. Those who had remained in Buenos Aires were compelled to abandon it in 1541 and to withdraw 1,000 miles upstream to the city of Asunción.

ENRIQUE UDAONDO, *Diccionario biográfico colonial argentino* (1945), pp. 582–587.

SUSAN M. SOCOLOW

MENDOZA CAAMAÑO Y SOTOMAYOR, JOSÉ ANTONIO DE (Marqués de Villagarcía; *b.* ca. March 1668; *d.* 14 December 1746), viceroy of Peru (1736–1745). A grandee of the illustrious Mendoza family who had served Philip V as Spanish ambassador to Venice and as viceroy of Cataluña, Villagarcía took office in Lima on 4 January 1736. Described as a person of limited intelligence and little administrative ability with a certain pious perversity because of his great pleasure in presiding over the *autos de fe* of the Lima inquisition, Villagarcía's overweaning task as viceroy was that of bolstering the Pacific fleet and shoring up coastal defenses against the onslaughts of British naval forces. In 1742 he subdued a serious Indian uprising led by Juan Santos (Apu Inca) in Jauja and Tarma. So great were his military expenditures that Villagarcía ran up a debt of almost 3 million pesos, most of which was unpaid salaries for soldiers, sailors, and militiamen.

In Lima the contentious Villagarcía was constantly at odds with the town council (CABILDO), merchant guild (CONSULADO), royal treasury officials, and the JESUITS, and in the interior, with provincial administrators (CORREGIDORES). Besides his successful defense of Peru during the WAR OF JENKINS' EAR, his other principal achievement was eliminating the practice at the University of San Marcos of awarding university degrees for gifts of money rather than for academic merit. Accused of mismanagement he was summarily relieved of office

on 12 July 1745. He died off Cape Horn on a vessel taking him back to Spain.

MANUEL DE MENDIBURU, *Diccionario histórico-biográfico del Perú*, vol. 7 (1937). See also Villagarcía's report on his tenure in office in *Memorias de los virreyes que han gobernado el Perú* (1859).

JOHN JAY TEPASKE

MENDOZA Y LUNA, JUAN MANUEL DE (marquis of Montesclaros), viceroy of Peru (1608–1615). Facing a sharp decline in state revenues, Montesclaros sought to rejuvenate the silver and mercury mining industries and increase remittances to Spain. His main efforts were directed at increasing Indian tribute and labor. The first viceroy to attempt radical changes in the Toledo resettlement system, Montesclaros proposed that Indian migrants be forced to pay taxes and participate in the state labor system. More important, Montesclaros tried to end the colonial practice of issuing licenses to those who employed YANACONAS, Indians who effectively escaped state demands. Montesclaros also denounced the crown's policy of selling *juros,* annuities that depended on colonial revenues both as security for the purchasers' investments and as the source of interest payments. Although the sale of *juros* was halted in 1615, Montesclaros left office that same year still awaiting crown approval of his policies on Indian labor, which had been bitterly contested by Peru's agricultural and mining elites. His successor, the prince of Esquilache, would reverse most of the Montesclaros program.

KENNETH J. ANDRIEN, *Crisis and Decline: The Viceroyalty of Peru in the Seventeenth Century* (1985), esp. pp. 135–136; and ANN M. WIGHTMAN, *Indigenous Migration and Social Change: The Forasteros of Cuzco, 1570–1720* (1990), esp. pp. 24–27.

ANN M. WIGHTMAN

MENEM, CARLOS SAÚL (*b.* 2 July 1930), president of Argentina (1989–). Menem is the son of Syrian immigrants who settled in the northern province of La Rioja. Active in politics from university days, he was elected to the legislature of his native province on the Peronist ticket in 1955, and subsequently elected and re-elected its governor (1973, 1983, 1987). His career was interrupted by the military regime that deposed President Isabel PERÓN in March 1976, during which time he spent five years in prison. In 1989, defying all predictions, he defeated Antonio Cafiero for the presidential nomination of the Peronist Party, and won a relatively easy victory in the national elections.

Menem's presidency has been a revolutionary one, for Argentina and for Peronism. He reversed a fifty-year-old trend toward statism-populism, opening up the economy by drastically reducing taxes and tariffs, and wiping out huge budgetary deficits by privatizing large state-owned industries. A "convertibility plan" established a stable exchange rate for the Argentine peso in relation to the dollar and permitted the peso's free exchange for foreign currencies. Formerlly politically sensitive areas like oil and hydrocarbons have been opened to foreign investments.

At the same time, Menem has reversed historic trends in Argentine foreign policy, openly aligning the country with the United States and offering cooperation with United Nations efforts at peacekeeping. Though frequently criticized for his rather haphazard style of administration, as well as for the corrupt practices of family members and immediate aides, such has been Menem's popularity that he has been able to convince the opposition Radical Party to support changes in the Argentine Constitution that would allow him to run for another term—for four, rather than six years—in 1995.

MARK FALCOFF

MENÉNDEZ DE AVILÉS, PEDRO (*b.* 1519; *d.* 17 September 1574), Spanish naval officer. Menéndez, a native of Avilés, Asturias, was appointed captain-general of the Indies fleet by PHILIP II in 1560. In a 1565 patent, he was named *adelantado,* governor, and captain-general of FLORIDA; he agreed to settle and pacify the area at his own expense. In return, Menéndez received tax exemptions, a large land grant, and, in addition to those listed above, the title of marqués. At that time, Florida extended from Newfoundland to the Florida Keys; it was enlarged in 1573 to include the Gulf coast. When Philip II learned of the French establishment at Fort Caroline, he furnished royal support for the Menéndez expedition.

Menéndez sailed to Florida and defeated the French, killing many of them. He founded SAINT AUGUSTINE on 8 September 1565, and established garrisons at San Mateo (the renamed Fort Caroline) and elsewhere in the Florida peninsula. In 1566, Menéndez established the city of SANTA ELENA on Parris Island, in present-day South Carolina; he left garrisons there and in GUALE (present-day Georgia). Menéndez planned a line of fort-missions from Santa Elena to present-day Mexico, and sent Captain Juan PARDO on an expedition that reached as far as the Appalachian Mountains. First Jesuit and then Franciscan missionaries went to Florida to evangelize the Native Americans. Despite this and the coming of more than 200 settlers, Menéndez's Florida enterprise failed, largely due to difficulties between the Native Americans and the Spaniards. After the death of Menéndez in Santander, Spain, and the abandonment of Santa Elena, only Saint Augustine remained—the oldest permanent European settlement in the present United States.

EUGENIO RUIDÍAZ Y CARAVÍA, *La Florida: Su conquista y colonización por Pedro Menéndez de Avilés,* 2 vols. (1893); WOODBURY LOWERY, *The Spanish Settlements Within the Present Limits of the United States,* 2 vols. (1901–1905); FÉLIX ZUBILLAGA, *La Florida: La misión jesuítica (1566–1572)* (1941); BARTOLOMÉ BARRIENTOS, *Pedro Menéndez de Avilés, Founder of Florida,* translated by Anthony Kerrigan (1965); EUGENE LYON, *The Enterprise of Florida* (1976).

EUGENE LYON

See also **Explorers.**

MENININHA DO GANTOIS, MÃE (Maria Escolástica da Conceição Nazareth; *b.* 10 February 1894; *d.* 13 August 1986), the fourth priestess of Ilê Iya Omin Axé Iya Massé, known popularly as the Terreiro do Gantois. Born in Salvador, Bahia, Menininha was the great-niece of Maria Julia da Conceição Nazareth, who founded the Terreiro de Gantois in 1849 after a divergence with Engenho Velho, one of the oldest CANDOMBLÉ communities in Bahia. The women of the Conceição Nazareth family, who have led Gantois since its foundation, trace their lineage to the city of Abeokuta in Nigeria and preserve many of their cultural traditions through Candomblé. Menininha was initiated as a devotee of the ORIXÁ Oxum at eight months, and named senior priestess of Gantois at the uncharacteristically young age of twenty-eight; hence, her nickname, which means "little girl." For sixty-four years she was spiritual counselor and inspiration to many well-known politicians, artists, and scholars, including Jorge AMADO, Carybé, Caetano VELOSO, Maria Bethania, and Antonio Carlos Magalhães. Mãe Menininha's openness helped to dispel widespread prejudice against the Afro-Brazilian Candomblé tradition. By the time of her death, she was the most beloved and widely venerated Candomblé priestess in Brazil. Her home in Bahia is now a memorial and museum.

KIM D. BUTLER

See also **African–Latin American Religions.**

MENNONITES, a pacifist, Anabaptist sect that originated in the Low Countries in the early 1540s. Throughout their history, the Mennonites have often been victims of religious persecution because of their beliefs, including their insistence upon separation of church and state, refusal to bear arms, renunciation of participation in secular affairs, refusal to take oaths, and their insistence that their children be educated in religious schools taught in Plattdeutsch, the German spoken by members of the sect.

The Mennonites' desire to remain apart from society at large resulted in frequent mass migrations (*Auswanderungen*) to new lands. A large-scale *Auswanderung* of Mennonites to Latin America took place after World War I and a smaller one after World War II, when the Mennonites' refusal to bear arms and their Germanic ways seemed to call their loyalty into question. In 1922, over two thousand Mennonites migrated from Manitoba, Canada, to CHIHUAHUA, Mexico, where they were joined by Mennonites from Russia fleeing the Bolshevik

Revolution. By 1930, the Chihuahua colony had a population of more than six thousand and had acquired land in Durango. In the mid-1950s, a faction of the Mexican Mennonites, fearful of the government's plans to integrate the sect into the social security system, migrated to British Honduras (Belize), where they established a new colony at Santa Elena, near the Guatemalan border.

Substantial numbers of Mennonites also migrated to other parts of Latin America, most often seeking regions with sizable German populations and land policies that were amenable to the establishment of large agricultural holdings that could be privately owned by the sect. Large numbers of Mennonites emigrated to Paraná, Brazil, and to Paraguay, where, in 1926 and 1927, Canadian and Sommerfelder (South Russian) Mennonites founded the Menno colony in the CHACO REGION, south of Puerto Casado. In the 1930s, German-Russians and Polish Mennonites escaped Nazi persecution and Stalinist purges by immigrating to the Chaco, where they established a colony near Menno, called Colonia Ferheim. During the 1940s, a third wave of German-Russian and Russian Mennonites escaped political turmoil in Europe by moving to the Chaco, where they founded yet another large Mennonite settlement, known as Colonia Neuland. The Paraguayan Chaco is now home to one of the largest Mennonite populations in the world.

JOSEPH WINFIELD FRETZ, *Mennonite Colonization in Mexico* (1952); KARL ILG, *Pioniere in Brasilien: Durch Bergwelt, Urwald und Steppe erwanderte Volkskunde der deutschsprachigen Siedler in Brasilien und Peru* (1972); ANNEMARIE ELIZABETH KRAUSE, *Mennonite Settlement in the Paraguayan Chaco* (Ph.D. diss., University of Chicago, 1952); MOISÉS GONZÁLES NAVARRO, *La colonización en México, 1877–1910* (1960); *The Mennonite Encyclopedia*, 4 vols. (1955–1959); HARRY LEONARD SAWATZKY, *They Sought a Country: Mennonite Colonization in Mexico* (1971).

VIRGINIA GARRARD-BURNETT

See also **Germans.**

MENOCAL, MARIO GARCÍA (*b.* 17 December 1866; *d.* 1941), president of Cuba (1913–1921). Born in Jaguey Granada, Cuba, Menocal attended Cornell University in New York, receiving an engineering degree in 1888. Upon completion of his studies, Menocal went to work with his uncle, Ancieto G. Menocal, a noted canal engineer. Both men worked in Nicaragua, then a proposed trans-isthmian canal route.

Menocal participated in the Cuban WAR OF INDEPENDENCE, he was appointed assistant secretary of war in the revolutionary government (1895), and fought with General Calixto GARCÍA in the Oriente campaign. In 1897, after a strategic success at Tunas he was promoted to general. Menocal cooperated with the U.S. intervention and was named Havana's chief of police. He ran for president on the Conservative Party ticket in 1908 but

was defeated by the Conservative turned Liberal José Miguel GÓMEZ. Renominated in 1912, Menocal won, serving two terms. His presidency was fraught with corruption (including 372 indictments against public officials) and disrespect for the law. Indictments of government officials were rarely taken seriously and convictions were often negated through presidential pardons or congressional declarations of amnesty. Menocal's third attempt for the presidency in 1924 met with failure.

WILLIAM FLETCHER JOHNSON, *The History of Cuba* (1920); LOUIS A. PÉREZ, *Cuba: Betweeen Reform and Revolution* (1988).

ALLAN S. R. SUMNALL

MERCEDARIANS (Order of Our Lady of Mercy for the Ransom of Captives), a Roman Catholic religious order founded in Barcelona by Saint Peter Nolasco in 1218. As indicated in the official title of the order, one of its principal missions was the ransom of captives, specifically Christians taken by Muslims. The order enjoyed rapid growth and sustained support in Spain and Portugal, although it was also successful in France, England, and Germany. The order was instrumental in the Spanish conquest and settlement of the Americas.

Although the FRANCISCANS, DOMINICANS, and AUGUSTINIANS constituted the first important missionary orders in Latin America, in many instances their activities were predated by the Mercedarians. The first Mercedarian in the New World was reputedly Friar Jorge de Sevilla, who sailed on Columbus's second voyage in 1493. The first Mercedarian house in the Americas was not founded, however, until 1514 in Santo Domingo.

Several Mercedarians accompanied the early expeditions. For example, Friar Bartolomé de Olmedo was Hernán CORTÉS's personal chaplain. Friar Francisco de BOBADILLA was active early in Panama and Nicaragua. While Friar Vicente de Valverde, a Dominican, accompanied Francisco PIZARRO to Cajamarca in Peru, the first organized missionary effort was that of the Mercedarians. Under the leadership of Friar Miguel de Orones, five Mercedarians arrived in 1532, prior to the taking of Atahualpa in Cajamarca, and established a house at San Miguel Piura. In 1535 the order founded its first monasteries in Lima and Cuzco.

While the Mercedarians enjoyed early successes in Peru, the order did not become established in Mexico immediately following the Conquest, in spite of Olmedo's participation. They did, however, establish a monastery in León, Nicaragua, in 1527, which was the first step in building what would later become an important Central American base.

The first Mercedarian expedition to Guatemala was organized in 1538 under the leadership of Friar Juan de Zambrana, who, at the invitation of the local bishop, Francisco de Marroquín, arrived with three others to found their house. Although the Franciscans and Dominicans had sent earlier expeditions to the region, it was the Mercedarians who would enjoy the greatest success, especially in the remote parts of the kingdom, which had largely been ignored by earlier missionary efforts.

At the end of the sixteenth century, the Mercedarians finally had established themselves in Mexico, the heart of New Spain, with their foundation in 1594. It was not until 1616 that Mexico became a province independent of Guatemala.

While the order quickly spread out over the American continents, their efforts were still generally controlled from Spain. It was not until 1564–1566 that independent provinces were established in the Americas, when Guatemala, Lima, Cuzco, and Chile were formally recognized as separate provinces, apart from the order in Spain. Other Latin American provinces included Tucumán, Santo Domingo, Mexico, Quito, Colombia, and the vice province of Marañón. Oversight of the provinces was handled by a vicar who served under the master general of the order. Normally the vicar for the Spanish Indies was the provincial of Castile, in keeping with the development of the provinces. From 1587 until 1790, there were two vicars general, one for New Spain, the other for the viceroyalty of Peru. The vice province of Marañón was controlled by the Portuguese province. There were only three Brazilian convents, and in 1787 one of these was suppressed.

Unlike other missionary orders, the Mercedarians initially had cool relationships with the crown. On several occasions the Spanish authorities even threatened to expel the order from the New World. During the colonial period, they were often referred to as "mercenaries" (*mercedarios* versus *mercenarios* in Spanish), an allusion to their acquisition of lands and other rewards for service. A late-seventeenth-century reform ended this tradition, and in 1690 the order was proclaimed a mendicant order by the pope.

By the beginning of the seventeenth century, there were about 250 Mercedarians in Latin America. That number would grow to about 1,200 by 1750. The greatest concentration of the order occurred in Central America, where the order had twenty-nine convents, followed by Peru, with twenty-six, and Mexico, with twenty-two. By 1900, there were fewer than ten convents in all of Latin America.

In spite of the modest size of the order, it made some significant contributions, especially in the colonial period. Friar Diego de Porres was one of the leading Mercedarians in the province of Cuzco. About 1551 Porres arrived in Peru in the company of the newly appointed VICEROY, don Antonio de MENDOZA, and for the next thirty years he engaged himself in missionary work. Near the end of his life he claimed to have baptized 80,000 Indians, married some 30,000, and built no less than 200 churches.

Not all Mercedarians were seen as saintly. Felipe GUAMÁN POMA DE AYALA describes the misadventures of Friar Morúa, a Mercedarian assigned to the village of

Yanaca. According to the Indian chronicler, Morúa forced the natives to weave clothing which he would in turn sell. The natives could seek no assistance from the local magistrate since Morúa served as a judge for him. Moreover Morúa imposed on the Indians his own choice of chief, a man who continued in idolatrous ways, without reprimand from the priest.

The Mercedarians played an important role in the educational life of Latin America. In many cities they established schools for the training of the local elite. The Mercedarian schools had as their principal goal the training of novices for the order. Several Mercedarians came to occupy important positions in the universities of Latin America.

MARIANO CUEVAS, *Historia de la iglesia en México*, 5 vols. (1928); RUBÉN VARGAS UGARTE, *Historia de la iglesia en el Perú*, 3 vols. (1953–1954); PEDRO NOLASCO PÉREZ, *Historia de las misiones mercedarias en América* (1966); ALFONSO MORALES RAMÍREZ, *La Orden de la Merced en la evangelización de América (siglos XVI–XVII)* (1986).

JOHN F. SCHWALLER

See also **Catholic Church.**

MERCEDES, city of 37,200 inhabitants (1985) in Uruguay located at the junction of the RÍO NEGRO and the URUGUAY RIVER and capital of the department of Soriano. Mercedes was founded in 1781, along with other settlements, to discourage Brazilian incursions into the country. Ruling over a vast agrarian hinterland dedicated to grain growing and the raising of livestock, Mercedes competes with FRAY BENTOS on the Uruguay River as the major agricultural center of western Uruguay, also known as Littoral.

ELZEAR GIUFFRA, *La república del Uruguay* (Montevideo, 1935).

CÉSAR N. CAVIEDES

MERCOSUR, the Southern Cone Common Market (*Mercado Común del Sur*). In March 1991, representatives of Argentina, Brazil, Paraguay, and Uruguay signed the Treaty of Asunción, which called for the creation of Mercosur. The four partners agreed that Argentina and Brazil would comply with all provisions of the treaty by 31 December 1994, while the deadline for Paraguay and Uruguay was set for 31 December 1995. The main tenets of the treaty are: (1) an across-the-board tariff reduction intended to eliminate tariffs between Argentina and Brazil by December 1994, and for Paraguay and Uruguay by December 1995; (2) the coordination of macroeconomic policies in accordance with the tariff reduction schedule; (3) the establishment of a common external tariff for third parties outside Mercosur; (4) the development of accords for specific economic sectors; (5) the implementation of an institutional framework to solve trade litigation; (6) the creation of the Council of the

Common Market, Mercosur's highest decision-making institution, made up of ministers of finance and foreign affairs; and (7) the creation of the Common Market Group, in charge of the technical aspects of the negotiation process.

Mercosur is the largest trade bloc of Latin America, comprising 190 million people. In the region it accounts for 55 percent of gross domestic product, 55 percent of industrial trade, and 35 percent of all trade. Since its inception, trade among Mercosur's partners has increased from $5.1 billion in 1991, to $7.5 billion in 1992, and to $8 billion in 1993, fostering more competition, investments, and a broader market.

LUIGI MANZETTI, "The Political Economy of Mercosur," in *Journal of Inter-American Studies and World Affairs* 35, no. 4 (1993–1994):101–141.

LUIGI MANZETTI

MERCURIO, EL Chile's most widely read morning newspaper for most of the twentieth century. Owned for generations by the wealthy, Anglo-Chilean Edwards family, it has played a prominent, and decidedly conservative, role in Chilean politics for most of the twentieth century. It vigorously opposed both the reformist Christian Democratic government of Eduardo FREI MONTALVA (1964–1970) and the Popular Unity government of Marxist Salvador ALLENDE (1970–1973). In an effort to blunt its criticism, Allende withdrew governmental subsidies and support (advertising contracts, etc.), but the paper continued to be published thanks to generous financial support from the U.S government. It hailed the 1973 coup, and during the ensuing sixteen years of military rule, it enthusiastically supported Pinochet's neoliberal economic policies, downplayed the extent of poverty and human rights abuse, and generally sought to discredit the government's civil and religious critics.

GUILLERMO SUNKEL, *El Mercurio: Diez años de educación política-ideológica* (1983); FERNANDO REYES MATTA et al., comps., *Investigación sobre la prensa Chile* (1986); P. SIGMUND, *The United States and Democracy in Chile* (1993)

MICHAEL FLEET

MERCURIO PERUANO, Peruvian periodical of the early 1790s. The *Mercurio Peruano* was a biweekly paper published in Lima, beginning in 1791, by a small group of officials, university faculty members, and other citizens who sought to improve Peru. Articles in the *Mercurio* provided Peruvians with information about the viceroyalty and suggestions for improving their daily lives. For example, they analyzed the viceroyalty's commerce, supported more efficient mining techniques, and recommended ways to improve the health of the citizenry. Supported and encouraged by Viceroy Francisco GIL DE TABOADA Y LEMOS, the *Mercurio* demonstrated that Lima had a number of self-proclaimed adherents of enlightened ideas, including José BAQUÍJANO Y CARRILLO, Ambrosio Cerdán y Pontero, José Rossi y Rubí, and Hipólito UNANUE. Its demise in 1795, however, reflected how small that number was. At no time did the number of subscribers total four hundred.

Mercurio peruano de historia, literatura y noticias públicas que da a luz la Sociedad Académica de Amantes de Lima, 12 vols. (1791–1795; repr. 1964–1966); MARK A. BURKHOLDER, *Politics of a Colonial Career: José Baquíjano and the Audiencia of Lima* (1980), pp. 86–91.

MARK A. BURKHOLDER

See also **Gazetas; Journalism.**

MÉRIDA, capital and principal city of the state of Yucatán in Mexico, located in the northwestern part of the Yucatán peninsula, about 22 miles south of the port of Progreso (and the Gulf of Mexico). Mérida was founded on 6 January 1542 by the conquistador Francisco de MONTEJO on the site of the semideserted Maya town of T'ho. Formerly known as Ichcaazihó (which means Five Mountains in Maya), T'ho was within the Maya city-state of Peches, which allied itself with the conquering Spaniards against rival Maya city-states. It is believed that the conquistadores chose the name Mérida because T'ho's indigenous ruins reminded them of the Roman remains in the city of Badajoz in their native Estremadura.

Since the Spanish lacked the military capability to pacify the entire peninsula, their colonizing strategy hinged on the establishment of garrison towns such as Mérida during the colonial period. Mounted troops were dispatched to trouble spots to maintain peace and subdue Indian uprisings. Mérida's physical layout echoed the classic style of the Spanish Renaissance. Crown authorities had insisted on the traditional grid pattern of wide, straight streets intersecting at right angles to form rectangular blocks and open squares. If the city's architecture replicated the Moorish style in vogue at the time in Spain, its simplicity also reflected the dearth of material wealth found in the province. Throughout the colonial era, Mérida remained the seat of the captaincy-general, a self-governing administrative unit independent of the Viceroyalty of New Spain.

At the beginning of the nineteenth century, Mérida was a small town of 10,000 inhabitants. It grew appreciably during the first twenty years after Independence as the regional economy prospered. An unfortunate result of economic progress, however, was the escalation of tensions between expansionistic sugar planters and Maya peasants on the state's southeastern frontier. Ultimately, the apocalyptic CASTE WAR OF YUCATÁN erupted in 1847, reducing Yucatán's population by more than a third. Ironically, Mérida (and the northwestern portion of the peninsula) benefited economically and demographically from the hostilities, as residents of the southeast fled to escape the attacks of the rebel Mayas.

Political factionalism in Mérida and neighboring

Campeche during the first fifty years following Independence also contributed indirectly to the state capital's growth: when campechanos seceded from Yucatán in 1862, Mérida remained the only viable commercial center in the state. By 1883, the city numbered roughly 40,000, the only state capital to record a sizable increase during the Mexican nation's turbulent first half-century.

By the beginning of Porfirio DÍAZ's dictatorship (1876–1911), Mérida was positioned to assume a dominating role in the rapidly expanding HENEQUEN (hard fiber) industry. The northwest quadrant of the peninsula was converted into large henequen estates, as *hacendados* lived in Mérida and managed their haciendas through overseers. During the henequen boom, a peninsular railway network, built, financed, and managed by indigenous entrepreneurs, was routed through Mérida to transport the monocrop. The combination of henequen monoculture, the railroad, the Caste War, and the secession of Campeche (and later in 1902, the partition of the southeastern territory of Quintana Roo) all contributed to Mérida's steady ascent to the leading city in the region. By 1910, the capital's population had grown to more than 60,000; Valladolid, the second-largest city in the state, had fewer than 12,000 residents.

The late-nineteenth-century henequen boom radically changed the city. During Olegario MOLINA's gubernatorial administration (1902–1909) the most sweeping changes occurred. The Molinista regime taxed the lu-crative monocrop and, with the support of the private sector, transformed housing, transportation, communications, public health and sanitation, education, the arts, and the urban landscape. Mérida soon earned the sobriquets "The White City" and "The Paris of Mexico." It was clean, well lit, paved with asphalt, and increasingly modernized.

Since World War I, henequen monoculture has gradually dissipated, but the state capital has remained the political, economic, and cultural hub of the peninsula. Migration and immigration throughout the twentieth century have swelled the population dramatically. More recently, the city has benefited from TOURISM (as visitors flock to Maya archaeological sites) and as a service sector for the new Caribbean resorts of Cancún and Cozumel. Currently, with a population in excess of a half million, Mérida functions as the unchallenged primary city in the peninsula.

ENRIQUE DULANTO, "Apuntes históricos y anecdóticos sobre Mérida," in *Artes de Mexico* 20, nos. 169–170 (1973): 7–61; RODOLFO RUZ MÉNENDEZ, *Mérida, bosquejo biográfico* (1983); ASAEL T. HANSEN and JUAN R. BASTARRACHEA M., *Mérida: Su transformación de capital colonial a naciente metrópoli en 1935* (1984); ALLEN WELLS and GILBERT M. JOSEPH, "Modernizing Visions, Chilango Blueprints, and Provincial Growing Pains: Mérida at the Turn of the Century," in *Mexican Studies/Estudios mexicanos* 8 (1992): 167–215.

ALLEN WELLS

Izamal Convent at Mérida, Yucatán. ORGANIZATION OF AMERICAN STATES.

MÉRIDA, CARLOS (*b.* 2 December 1891; *d.* 22 December 1984), artist. Although born in Guatemala, Mérida is most often associated with the modern art movement in Mexico. In 1910 he traveled to Paris to study with Kees van Dongen (1877–1968) and Hermen Anglada-Camarasa (1873–1959), becoming closely associated with Pablo Picasso and Amadeo Modigliani. In 1914, Mérida returned to Guatemala to begin experimenting with folkloric themes in his painting. He exhibited his work in the National Academy of Fine Arts in Mexico in 1920, and his uniquely Latin American themes made him one of the pioneers of the Mexican artistic revolution.

The mural renaissance in Mexico in the 1920s greatly influenced his work. He was commissioned in 1921 to do two murals in the Ministry of Education in Mexico City. After a New York exhibition, Mérida again traveled to Europe, where he exhibited his work in Paris (1927). He returned to Mexico in 1929 to continue his work with plastic painting, gradually developing the abstract and plastic-surrealist style for which he is best known. Among his better-known works are mosaic murals in the Benito Juárez housing development in Mexico City (1952) and in the Municipal Building in Guatemala City (1956).

CARLOS MÉRIDA, *Modern Mexican Artists* (1968), pp. 105–113; JEAN CHARLOT, *The Mexican Mural Renaissance, 1920–1925* (1979); CARLOS MÉRIDA, *Carlos Mérida* (1990).

SARA FLEMING

MERINO CASTRO, JOSÉ TORIBIO (*b.* 14 December 1915), Chilean naval officer. Born in La Serena, Merino entered the Chilean Naval Academy in 1931 and graduated as a midshipman in 1936. He specialized in gunnery and fire control. During the last year of World War II he served as an anti-aircraft battery officer on board the U.S. cruiser *Raleigh*. During his career he commanded the corvette *Papudo*, the transport *Angamos*, and the destroyers *Almirante Williams* and *Almirante Riveros*. Between 1956 and 1957 Merino served in the Chilean naval mission to Great Britain.

In 1963 Merino became chief of staff of the fleet. For the next four years he served as the assistant chief of the General Staff and the director of the Bureau of Weapons. In 1970 he became commander in chief and the naval judge of the fleet, the senior naval command afloat, and in 1973 he was named commander in chief and naval judge of the First Naval Zone.

Merino and other naval officers initiated a plot to overthrow the government of Salvador ALLENDE, informing General Augusto PINOCHET, commander of the Chilean army, that the navy would act on 11 September 1973. This forced Pinochet to advance a plot of his own from 14 to 11 September. With the overthrow of the Allende government, Admiral Merino served as a member of the junta and the commander of the navy until his retirement on 8 March 1990.

AUGUSTO PINOCHET, *The Crucial Day* (1982); "Cambio de mando institucional" in *Revista de Marina* (Valparaíso) 2 (1990): 217–220; *El Mercurio* (Valparaíso), 9 March 1990, pp. 1, 12.

ROBERT SCHEINA

MESA DA CONSCIÊNCIA E ORDENS (Board of the King's Conscience and of the Military Orders), a Portuguese court created in 1532 to supervise the administration of religious affairs. Regarding the colonies, its importance as an instrument of royal power was tantamount to that of the Conselho Ultramarino (OVERSEAS COUNCIL). The MILITARY ORDERS' concerns were incorporated into the Mesa da Consciência after 1551, when the king became Grand Master of the Orders of Christ, Aviz, and Santiago. In addition, the board took care of an amazing range of responsibilities, which included the appointment of ecclesiastics to the overseas dominions; the management of the inheritances of all those subjects who had died outside the realm; the surveillance of royal chapels, almshouses, hospices, and hosteleries; and, until 1790, the inspection of Coimbra University. According to the 1603 Statutes, the board was composed of a president, five deputies, and four notaries; it was permitted to summon the King's Confessor, the Chancellor of the Orders, and experts in law and theology for advice. Over the years, the board amassed considerable influence, which was called into question only in the beginnning of the nineteenth century. It was abolished in 1828 (Brazil) and 1833 in Portugal.

ANTÓNIO SÉRGIO et al., eds. "Mesa," in *Grande enciclopédia portuguesa e brasileira*, vol. 17 (1934–1935), pp. 17–18; RUY D'ABREU TORRES, "Mesa da Consciência e Ordens," *Dicionário de história de Portugal*, edited by JOEL SERRÃO, vol. 3 (1968), pp. 42–43; FRANCISCO LUIZ TEIXEIRA VINHOSA, *História administrativa do Brasil*, pt. 2, vol. 8, *Brasil sede da monarquia* (1984), p. 141; ARQUIVO NACIONAL, *Fiscais e meirinhos: a administraçao no Brasil colonial* (1985), pp. 39, 120.

GUILHERME PEREIRA DAS NEVES

MESADA ECLESIÁSTICA, an assessment amounting to one month's stipend that was imposed on all clergy taking posts in the Spanish Indies beginning in 1626. This assessment fell on all ecclesiastics from the august dean and canons of New World cathedrals to priests or regular clergy serving in the most isolated mission posts. All revenues from *mesadas* were allocated to pay the salaries of the COUNCIL OF THE INDIES. In 1777 CHARLES III established an additional assessment of a half-year's stipend (MEDIA ANATA ECLESIÁSTICA) on all clergy having an annual income of more than three hundred pesos—bishops excluded. After 1777 ecclesiastics in this category had to pay both assessments. By 1800 annual income from the two levies combined was approximately 46,000 pesos in Mexico and 30,000 pesos in Peru.

Recopilación de leyes de los Reynos de las Indias, 4 vols. (1681; repr. 1973), libro I, título XVII; GABRIEL MARTÍNEZ REYES, *Finanzas de las 44 Diócesis de Indias, 1515–1816* (1980).

JOHN JAY TePASKE

MESCALA, ISLAND OF. Located in Lake Chapala, to the south of Guadalajara in western central Mexico, the small island was seized and fortified late in 1812 primarily by Indian insurgents from the lakeside villages. Repeated military attacks against the entrenched rebel forces proved unsuccessful. These failures not only embarrassed the Spanish commander José de la Cruz but also drew off royalist forces from more vital antiguerilla action in western Mexico. Eventually weakened by a combination of naval blockade, plague, and offers of amnesty and land, the rebels surrendered in late 1816 after a four-year siege. Subsequently the island served for some years as a high-security penitentiary.

VICENTE RIVA PALACIO, *México a través de los siglos,* vol. 3 (1940); BRIAN R. HAMNETT, *Roots of Insurgency: Mexican Regions, 1750–1824* (1986), esp. pp. 190–192; WILLIAM B. TAYLOR, "Banditry and Insurrection: Rural Unrest in Central Jalisco, 1790–1816," in *Riot, Rebellion, and Revolution: Rural Social Conflict in Mexico,* edited by Friedrich Katz (1988).

ERIC VAN YOUNG

MESILLA, LA. *See* **Gadsden Purchase.**

MESOAMERICA, a cultural and geographical term used to define a vast area embraced by central and southern Mexico, Guatemala, Belize, El Salvador, the westernmost parts of Honduras and Nicaragua, and the Nicoya Peninsula of Costa Rica. At the time of the Spanish conquest, there existed within this area populous, well-adjusted societies capable not merely of meeting basic human needs but also of achieving remarkable results in terms of art and architecture, astronomy, mathematics and the measurement of time, plant domestication, environmental management, written or pictographic communication, and the building of towns and cities. Mesoamerica thus denotes a key area where an advanced culture may be said to have prevailed, distinct from viable but less sophisticated cultures as in such peripheral parts as the Spanish borderlands, the Caribbean littoral, and the Greater and Lesser Antilles.

Elaboration of the term is commonly attributed to the anthropologist Paul Kirchhoff (1900–1972), but the great German scholar Eduard Seler (1849–1992) used the term *Mittel Amerika* to apply to the same conjunction of territory and civilization. The Mesoamerican peoples alive and flourishing at the moment of contact, the Mexicas (AZTECS) foremost of all, are the ones whose accomplishments the historical record has best preserved. These peoples must, however, be seen as but specific expressions of a great cultural tradition that stretches back into the pre-Columbian past and forward, in the cases of Mexico and Guatemala, to our day.

The political and organizational skills characteristic of the Mesoamerican mindset are nowhere better evidenced than in the example of the Aztecs. When Bernal Díaz del Castillo, the conqueror and a chronicler in the making, entered the Aztec capital of TENOCHTITLÁN in 1519, he marveled at the beauty and refinement of the city that met his eyes, later to be even more impressed (as were his fellow countrymen) with the extent and output of the Aztec tribute state, a far-flung dominion whose southern reaches included commercial enclaves in Guatemala and beyond.

Perhaps the single most illuminating measure of the vitality of Mesoamerican culture is the number of people the social system, its structures of privilege and authoritarianism notwithstanding, may have been able to support. Estimates by William T. Sanders place the contact population of the Aztec Empire at between 5 and 6 million, with Mesoamerica as a whole inhabited by between 12 and 15 million. More detailed investigations by Woodrow Borah and Sherburne F. Cook suggest a population for central Mexico alone of 25 million. Even the lower estimates indicate a situation in which the land was worked purposely and fruitfully, to good effect. The Spanish conquest, most notably the destructive aftermath of warfare, disease, enslavement, forced labor, and culture shock, shattered the Mesoamerican order forever.

PAUL KIRCHHOFF's classic "Mesoamérica: Sus límites geográficos, composición étnica y caracteres culturales," in *Acta Americana* 1 (1943): 92–107, has been superseded in English by WILLIAM T. SANDERS and BARBARA J. PRICE, *Mesoamerica: The Evolution of a Civilisation* (1968), which emphasizes ecological adaptation. Sanders's discussion of how many people the social system could support is found in "The Population of the Central Mexican Symbiotic Region, the Basin of Mexico, and the Teotihuacán Valley in the Sixteenth Century," in WILLIAM M. DENEVAN, ed., *The Native Population of the Americas in 1492* (1976): 85–150. A counterview is afforded by WOODROW BORAH and SHERBURNE F. COOK, "Conquest and Population: A Demographic Approach to Mexican History," in *Proceedings of the American Philosophical Society* 113 (1969): 177–183. The eyewitness account by BERNAL DÍAZ DEL CASTILLO, *The Discovery and Conquest of Mexico,* translated by A. P. Maudslay (1956), retains its intoxicating headiness centuries later. And few render the complexity of Mesoamerican culture at contact, or document more powerfully the manner of its change and destruction, than CHARLES GIBSON, *The Aztecs Under Spanish Rule: A History of the Indians of the Valley of Mexico, 1519–1810* (1964). Two recent contributions which afford a Native American, as opposed to a Spanish Colonial, perspective on land and life in Mesoamerica are MIGUEL LEÓN PORTILLA, *The Broken Spears: The Aztec Account of the Conquest of Mexico* (1962, expanded and updated edition 1992) and JAMES LOCKHART, *The Nahuas after the Conquest: A Social and Cultural History of the Indians of Central Mexico, Sixteenth Through Eighteenth Centuries* (1992).

W. GEORGE LOWELL

See also individual countries and regions.

MESOAMERICA: PRE-COLUMBIAN HISTORY. Mesoamerica is the name given to the culture area that includes most of Mexico and Central America. The concept was originally defined by Paul Kirchhoff in 1943 on the basis of the geographical distribution of hundreds of cultural traits shared by the many civilized societies from northern Mexico to western Costa Rica at the time of the Spanish conquest. The traits included virtually all cultural aspects of life, such as AGRICULTURE (the use of the digging stick; cultigens such as MAIZE, BEANS, squash, chili peppers, avocados, and cotton), food preparation (the use of grinding stones and clay griddles; tortillas, tamales), domestic animals (dogs and turkeys), beverages (pulque, chocolate), clothing (cotton tunics for the nobility, loincloths for commoners), architecture (terraced platform temples arranged in plazas, ball courts), economy (regional markets; the use and exchange of obsidian, CACAO, and jade), and religion (pan-Mesoamerican deities such as TLALOC and QUETZALCOATL that were more or less parallel in different societies, ancestor worship, hieroglyphic writing, the Mesoamerican CALENDAR, painted bark paper manuscripts, human sacrifice, and an institutionalized priesthood). Most of these traits were present throughout the Mesoamerican culture area at the time of the Conquest, but they developed gradually in different regions and spread among different societies as a result of interregional contacts from the time the area was first inhabited.

THE PRECERAMIC PERIOD

Biologically modern humans, the ancestors of modern American Indians, first entered the Americas by crossing the Bering Strait from northeast Asia more than 15,000 years ago. At this time a broad landmass, known as Beringia, which was exposed when large amounts of water were locked up in the glaciers, offered passage to these early migrants from eastern Siberia to Alaska. The earliest date of their arrival in the Americas is disputed by specialists, but by the end of the Pleistocene epoch (12,000–9,000 years ago) a very distinctive form of projectile point, known by the type names Clovis and Folsom, was widespread from Alaska and Canada to Tierra del Fuego. These are large, lanceolate points with fluted or channeled bases to facilitate hafting. They were used in hunting big game such as mammoths, mastodons, camelids, and giant sloths, and the remains of such Pleistocene megafauna are often found in association with fluted points at ancient hunting camps and kill sites throughout North, Central, and South America. These sites were the settlements of small social groups of nomadic hunters and gatherers. One such site in Mexico is TLAPACOYA, in the Valley of Mexico, which has yielded evidence suggestive of human presence more than 20,000 years ago.

As the last great ice age came to an end and the large mammals became extinct, the adaptations of the earliest Mesoamericans shifted to a mixed economy emphasiz-

ing hunting of small game and gathering of wild plant foods. These changes characterize the Archaic period (9000–2000 B.C.), during which there was an adaptive shift from hunting and gathering to full-time agriculture supporting sedentary villages. The earliest known evidence of plant domestication occurs in arid highland valleys such as the Tehuacán Valley of Puebla and the Valley of Oaxaca, where a number of excavated sites provide a glimpse of the gradual course of plant domestication in Mesoamerica. Research from these sites has demonstrated that the process was not uniform throughout the area. Different crops were domesticated at different times in widely separated regions.

During the long course of the Archaic period, maize, beans, and squash became the basis of the Mesoamerican diet. Other important cultigens that were domesticated during the period include the bottle gourd, chilies, avocados, and cotton. The evidence from Tehuacán and the Valley of Oaxaca indicates that most of these crops were domesticated between 5000 and 3000 B.C.

Social groupings at this time consisted of small, semisedentary, egalitarian bands that coalesced during times of abundance to form seasonal macrobands. In richer environments, such as the Basin of Mexico and the fertile coastal regions, where fish and shellfish were always available in abundance, sedentism and larger, permanent social groups may have developed earlier. Mesoamerican religious ceremonialism also began to develop during the Archaic. Tehuacán has provided possible evidence of human sacrifice and ritual CANNIBALISM dating to 7000–5000 B.C., and Gheo-Shih, a site in the eastern Valley of Oaxaca dated to about 5000 B.C., has a cleared space lined by stones that may have been a dance ground or possibly a very early ball court.

THE FORMATIVE, OR PRECLASSIC, PERIOD

By about 2000 B.C. almost all of Mesoamerica was inhabited by full-time agriculturalists who lived in small villages of wattle-and-daub houses. These villages were generally small communities, usually containing no more than about a dozen houses with associated cooking sheds and storage pits. Social and political organization was generally egalitarian and kinship-oriented. Status differences were based strictly on age, sex, and personal achievement. Agricultural tasks, craft production, and trading activities were probably organized by extended-family households.

As population increased in most regions during the Early Preclassic, or Formative, period (1500–900 B.C.), some of these small villages grew in size and importance, becoming centers of political, economic, and religious activities. These sites were larger than most contemporary settlements, and they were characterized by nonresidential civic-ceremonial structures. Social inequality, political hierarchies, and tributary economies developed during the latter part of this period. These changes are reflected in differences in grave goods and residential form and construction, and differential dis-

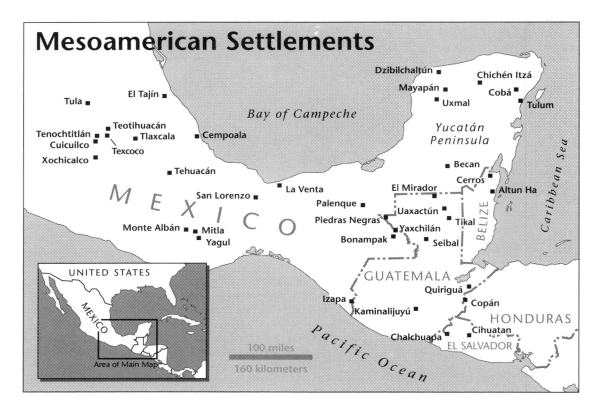

Mesoamerican Settlements

tributions of imported goods (such as ceramics, marine shells, jade, and obsidian).

One of the most complex societies in Formative Mesoamerica was the OLMECS of the Gulf Coast region of Mexico. They emerged during the latter part of the Early Formative, and their power and influence continued into the Middle Formative period (900–400 B.C.). Sometimes considered to be Mesoamerica's first civilization, the Olmecs built sumptuous monumental centers, such as SAN LORENZO, Tenochtitlán (not to be confused with the Aztec capital), and LA VENTA, in the lush tropical lowlands of southern Veracruz and Tabasco. The heartland Olmecs maintained social and economic relations with contemporaneous societies all over Mesoamerica, from CHALCATZINGO, Morelos, in the west, to Chalchuapa, El Salvador, in the southeast. These connections are revealed by the presence of distinctive Olmec iconography, such as the so-called flaming eyebrow and the jaguar paw-wing motifs of the fire serpent and were-jaguar, in ceramics and on stone monuments in these distant centers. The widespread distribution of these symbols reflects interlocking exchange and interaction networks, and probably also the existence of a pan-Mesoamerican belief system.

By the Late Preclassic period (400 B.C.–A.D. 200), Olmec influence had waned in Mesoamerica, but population continued to increase and great centers of a different kind arose throughout the highlands and the lowlands. MONTE ALBÁN, perhaps the earliest urban cen-

ter in the Americas, was established by the Zapotecs on a mountaintop in the center of the Valley of Oaxaca at about 500 B.C. In the highlands of central Mexico, CUICUILCO in the south and TEOTIHUACÁN in the north became prominent centers of political, economic, and ritual activity with populations of approximately 20,000 each at the beginning of the Christian era.

In the Maya lowlands, a population increase on the order of 300 percent from the Middle to the Late Preclassic is suggested by settlement pattern studies. During this time, the distinctive hallmarks that would later characterize Classic Lowland Maya culture (elaborately carved stelae and altars, hieroglyphic writing, masonry structures with corbeled arches, and so on) were developed. Sites such as EL MIRADOR, TIKAL, CERROS, BECAN, and DZIBILCHALTÚN became the centers of complex, hierarchical chiefdoms with very large populations. Large temple platforms and spacious plazas attested to the power and authority of rulers. Ritualized warfare was conducted on a large scale as an aspect of interregional elite competition. Widespread uniformity in Lowland Maya ceramics during the Late Preclassic indicates a high degree of craft specialization and strong interregional economic ties throughout the area that transcended political hostilities. Exchange networks linked the lowland centers with the great Highland Maya capital of KAMINALJUYÚ, on what is now the western edge of Guatemala City, and IZAPA, on the Pacific coast of Chiapas, which shared a common sculptural style.

THE CLASSIC PERIOD

By about A.D. 250–300, major transformations occurred in Mesoamerican culture and society. The Classic period (A.D. 250–900) witnessed the development of macroregional state-level political organization with hierarchical class divisions, an internally stratified ruling class, full-time craft and agricultural specialization, tributary economies, and often large market systems. By A.D. 500, Teotihuacán had become a city of perhaps 200,000 people; most of them were farmers, but a large number were craft specialists. The capital of a hegemonic empire, Teotihuacán had a powerful, centrally organized government. It maintained colonies at distant centers such as MATACAPAN, Veracruz, and Kaminaljuyú for the control of trade in luxury goods such as jade, cacao, animal pelts, and tropical bird feathers. Teotihuacán maintained a special diplomatic relationship with Monte Albán (a group of Oaxacans lived in a special ward of the city), and its influence was felt as far away as Tikal.

The southern Maya lowlands were dominated during the Classic by a number of state-level polities. Major centers included PALENQUE, Piedras Negras, YAXCHILAN, ALTAR DE SACRIFICIOS, SEIBAL, DOS PILAS, Tikal, UAXACTÚN, ALTÚN HA, CARACOL, QUIRIGUÁ, and COPÁN. These city-states claimed a regional territory that included a number of secondary and tertiary centers paying tribute to rulers in the primary centers. These kings erected monuments with hieroglyphic inscriptions legitimizing their authority and glorifying their royal ancestry. The major centers possessed a complex division of labor that included craft specialists such as potters, obsidian and chert knappers, weavers, feather workers, leather workers, basket makers, architects, stonemasons, manuscript painters, and monument carvers. The population in the southern lowlands was very large, at least as high as 10 million in the Late Classic period (A.D. 600–900).

At the end of the Classic the population suffered a precipitous decline. Monument erection and other elite activities ceased in all of the major centers of the southern lowlands between about 800 and 900. Various causes have been suggested for this collapse: ecological deterioration, demographic pressure, endemic warfare, and disease. Whatever the causes, the collapse profoundly altered the balance of power in eastern Mesoamerica. The northern lowlands maintained a large and growing population, and centers such as CHICHÉN ITZÁ and COBÁ experienced florescence rather than decline.

Teotihuacán collapsed as a major economic and political power about 750, an event that undoubtedly had a ripple effect in the decline of Classic Lowland Maya civilization. The population of Teotihuacán had fallen to as low as 30,000 by the end of the Classic. The heart of the civic-ceremonial zone was burned and looted in a massive act of political destruction and desanctification.

Maya bas-relief from Yaxchilán depicting warrior-king Jaguar-Bird with a captive. Late Classic period.
© PHOTO BY JUSTIN KERR / BRITISH MUSEUM, LONDON.

In the wake of the collapse, fortified centers of long-distance trade such as XOCHICALCO and CACAXTLA rose to power, filling the economic vacuum left when the Teotihuacán empire contracted.

THE POSTCLASSIC PERIOD

The Postclassic marks the advent of history in central Mexico. The salient theme is the rise of the Toltec capital, Tollan, founded by the legendary leader Quetzalcoatl at the site of present-day TULA, Hidalgo, in the tenth century. Tollan, which had a strong centralized government, was the center of a multiethnic trading empire within which Nahuatl speakers enjoyed political and probably numerical superiority. The population of Tollan at its peak was around 60,000.

Toltec influence spread throughout Mesoamerica during the Early Postclassic (900–1200). Unmistakable evidence of Toltec art and architecture appears as far away as Chichén Itzá, Yucatán, and CIHUATAN, El Salvador. Nahuatl speakers known as Pipils began to migrate to Central America at this time. Toltecs from both Tollan and Chichén Itzá apparently had close ties with EL TAJÍN, on the north coast of Veracruz.

Toltec dominance ended in the late twelfth century, when Tollan began to experience a long decline caused by drought, famine, rebellion, and CHICHIMEC invasions from the north. After the collapse of Tollan there were no more great centers in central Mexico until the rise of the Mexica AZTECS at TENOCHTITLÁN in 1427. Within less than a century they controlled the greatest empire yet in Mesoamerica, incorporating earlier city-states established in the Valley of Mexico such as TETZCOCO, Atzcapotzalco, and TLATELOLCO, and extending their hegemony from Veracruz to the Pacific Ocean and from central Mexico to southern Chiapas. The population of Tenochtitlán at its peak was 150,000–200,000, and the population of the entire Valley of Mexico in the early sixteenth century was as high as 1 million.

Elsewhere in Postclassic Mesoamerica, the Valley of Oaxaca disintegrated economically and politically with the long decline of Monte Albán, which began around 700. A number of small trading centers, such as LAMBITYECO, arose at this time. MIXTEC warloads from the highland and coastal regions of western Oaxaca began a series of conquests that even took them into the valley. Principal Zapotec centers of the valley at the time of the Conquest included ZAACHILA, YAGUL, and MITLA. In Veracruz, El Tajín collapsed around 1200, and the TOTONACS first encountered the Spaniards at Cempoala in 1519.

In Yucatán, Chichén Itzá, which had been the center of a large tributary state from about 850 to 1224, was overthrown by MAYAPÁN. In the latter, a small, fortified center, a confederation of three elite lineages unified Yucatán from about 1224 to 1441. This unity eventually gave way to an estimated sixteen to twenty-four highly competitive, small city-states. TULUM, a major trading port on the east coast, was sighted in 1517 by Spanish explorers who mistakenly described it as being larger than Seville. In highland Guatemala, the KAQCHIQUELS at IXIMCHÉ, the Quichés (K'ICHE') at UTATLAN, and the ZUTUHILS at Chuitinamit, all of whom were ruled by warrior aristocrats claiming Toltec heritage, were conquered by the Spanish in 1524.

General surveys include RICHARD E. W. ADAMS, *Prehistoric Mesoamerica,* rev. ed. (1991); MICHAEL D. COE, *Mexico,* 4th ed. (1994); and MURIEL PORTER WEAVER, *The Aztecs, Maya, and Their Predecessors,* 3d ed. (1993). More theoretically oriented treatments are RICHARD E. BLANTON, STEPHEN A. KOWALEWSKI, GARY FEINMAN, and JILL APPEL, *Ancient Mesoamerica: A Comparison of Change in Three Regions,* 2d ed. (1993), and WILLIAM T. SANDERS and BARBARA J. PRICE, *Mesoamerica: The Evolution of a Civilization* (1968). The results of the Tehuacán Valley research are summarized by general editor RICHARD S. MAC NEISH in *The Prehistory of the Tehuacán Valley,* vol. 5, *Excavations and Reconnaissance,* by Richard S. MacNeish, Melvin L. Fowler, Angel García Cook, Frederick A. Peterson, Antoinette Nelken-Turner, and James A. Neely (1972). A good overview of the Formative is KENT V. FLANNERY, ed., *The Early Mesoamerican Village* (1976). A detailed settlement history of the pre-Columbian Valley of Mexico is WILLIAM T. SANDERS, JEFFREY R. PARSONS, and ROBERT S. SANTLEY, *The Basin of Mexico: Ecological Processes in the Evolution of a Civilization* (1979). For Oaxaca, see RICHARD E. BLANTON, *Monte Albán: Settlement Patterns at the Ancient Zapotec Capital* (1978); KENT V. FLANNERY and JOYCE MARCUS, eds., *The Cloud People: The Divergent Evolution of the Zapotec and Mixtec Civilizations* (1983); JOHN PADDOCK, ed., *Ancient Oaxaca* (1966); RONALD SPORES, *The Mixtec Kings and Their People* (1967), and *The Mixtecs in Ancient and Colonial Times* (1984); and JOSEPH W.

WHITECOTTON, *The Zapotecs: Princes, Priests, and Peasants* (1977). Several excellent books are available on the pre-Columbian Maya civilization: RICHARD E. W. ADAMS, ed., *The Origins of Maya Civilization* (1977); MICHAEL D. COE, *The Maya,* 5th ed. (1993); ROBERT M. CARMACK, *The Quiche Mayas of Utatlan: The Evolution of a Highland Guatemala Kingdom* (1981); T. PATRICK CULBERT, *The Classic Maya Collapse* (1973); JOHN W. FOX, *Maya Postclassic State Formation* (1987); NORMAN HAMMOND, *Ancient Maya Civilization* (1982); JOHN S. HENDERSON, *the World of the Ancient Maya* (1981); and ROBERT J. SHARER, *The Ancient Maya,* 5th ed. (1994). For the Pipils of Central America, see WILLIAM R. FOWLER, JR., *The Cultural Evolution of Ancient Nahua Civilizations: The Pipil–Nicarao of Central America* (1989). On the Toltecs, see RICHARD A. DIEHL, *Tula: The Toltec Capital of Ancient Mexico* (1983); DAN M. HEALAN, *Tula of the Toltecs* (1989); and NIGEL DAVIES, *The Toltecs: Until the Fall of Tula* (1977), and *The Toltec Heritage: From the Fall of Tula to the Rise of Tenochtitlán* (1980). On the Aztecs, consult FRANCES BERDAN, *The Aztecs of Central Mexico: An Imperial Society* (1982); and ROSS HASSIG, *Trade, Tribute, and Transportation: The Sixteenth-Century Political Economy of the Valley of Mexico* (1985), and *Aztec Warfare: Imperial Expansion and Political Control* (1988); NIGEL DAVIES, *The Aztecs: A History* (1973), and *The Aztec Empire: The Toltec Resurgence* (1987); and SUSAN D. GILLESPIE, *The Aztec Kings: The Construction of Rulership in Mexica History* (1989).

WILLIAM R. FOWLER

MESSÍA DE LA CERDA, PEDRO DE (Messía de la Zerda, Marqués de la Villa de Armijo; *b.* February 1700; *d.* 1783), military figure and viceroy of the New Kingdom of Granada (1761–1772). Born in Córdoba, he pursued a naval career upon completion of his schooling and took part in the Spanish "reconquest" of Sicily and in Mediterranean battles with the English. In 1721 he made his first cruise to the Americas. He was promoted to captain in 1745. He became a knight commander of the Order of Malta. Messía de la Cerda served in the southern Caribbean (1750s). He thus came to his viceregal post with firsthand knowledge of the defense and commercial difficulties that he would face. Important, too, with regard to Messía's qualifications and mandate as viceroy, he was concurrently the commandant general of the Caribbean squadron in charge of the fight against contraband traffic.

In the 1760s the viceroy authorized José Celestino MUTIS to introduce the academic study of mathematics and the sciences at the *colegio mayor* of Nuestra Señora del Rosario in Santa Fe de Bogotá, established the TOBACCO MONOPOLY, and oversaw the expulsion of the Jesuits. By 1767, Messía complained of failing health and sought to return to Spain, which he did in 1772, when Manuel de Guirior (1772–1776) relieved him. He died in Madrid.

For firsthand accounts of the administration of Messía de la Cerda, see his report and that of his confidant, Antonio Moreno y Escandón, in GERMÁN COLMENARES, ed., *Relaciones e informes de los gobernantes de la Nueva Granada,* vol. 1 (1989). See also the discussion in SERGIO ELÍAS ORTIZ, *Nuevo Reino de Granada: El virreynato, 1753–1810* in *Historia extensa de Colombia,* vol. 4 (1970).

LANCE R. GRAHN

MESSIANIC MOVEMENTS

Brazil

Messianism, the expectation of sudden intervention by a divine or superhuman being in human history, has been connected with Brazil since its colonization. The diverse religious movements following apocalyptic prophecies have been so persistent that recent scholars have interpreted the salvific theme to be integral to the Luso-Brazilian cultural identity. Although some groups may have roots in indigenous religions, the most noted messianic movements appeared in the nineteenth century as the outgrowths of popular Catholic emphasis on the approaching cataclysmic end of time, the exclusive redemptive kingdom of the Last Days, and the Second Coming of Jesus.

In the sixteenth century, several religious movements exhibited aspects often associated with messianic groups. Coastal TUPI-GUARANI tribes undertook dramatic migrations under shamanic guidance, seeking a utopian "land without evil." Similarly, Portuguese immigrants, native Brazilians, and biracial colonists in Bahia joined in the *Santidade* ("Holiness") movement; directed by leaders called Pope and Mother of God, the community expected an imminent cosmic disaster and reversals in the power structure. Later rural movements, such as the twentieth-century devotees of the Beato of Caldeirão (Pedro Batista da Silva) and of Padre Cícero, also followed prophetic leaders who articulated contemporary discontent and promised remedies for social and spiritual needs.

Messianic movements interweaving Christian revelations and Portuguese folklore began in the early 1800s in the Northeast, in marginal communities faced with political upheavals. Three movements, the first led by Silvestre José dos Santos at Rodeador, Pernambuco, in 1817, the second by João Antônio dos Santos and João Ferreira at Pedra Bonita in the 1830s, and the third by Antônio "CONSELHEIRO" Maciel in Canudos in the 1890s, drew upon the legends of Portuguese SEBASTIAN-ISMO. Each community awaited the return of King SEBASTIÃO (1557–1578) to overthrow local religious and secular order and establish an earthly paradise with his triumphant angelic army. Armed militia extinguished each of these groups, yet their messianic influence continues in the Northeast, where Antônio CONSELHEIRO himself is now considered a savior.

Messianic movements have also occurred in southern Brazil. In Rio Grande do Sul, a small community formed in the 1870s to follow Jacobina Maurer as the new Christ, and in 1910 a "holy war" was launched in Santa Catarina, aiming military and religious force against the new laws of the republic. Although the latter CONTESTADO REBELLION ended in battle in 1914, its themes persist in regional beliefs.

ABELARDO F. MONTENEGRO, *Antônio Conselheiro* (1954); RENÉ RIBEIRO, "O episódio da Serra do Rodeador 1817–20: Um movimento milenar e sebastianista," in *Revista de Antropologia* 8 (1960): 133–144; DONALD WARREN, JR. "Portuguese Roots of Brazilian Spiritism," in *Luso-Brazilian Review* 5 (1968): 3–34; RALPH DELLA CAVA, *Miracle at Joaseiro* (1970); JOVELINO P. RAMOS, "Interpretando o fenômeno Canudos," in *Luso-Brazilian Review* 11 (1974): 65–83; MARIA ISAURA PEREIA DE QUEIROZ, *O Messianismo, no Brasil e no mundo*, 2d ed. (1976); HÉLÈNE CLASTRES, *Terra sem mal*, translated by Renato Janine Ribeiro (1978); JOSÉ CARLOS DE ATALIBA NOGUEIRA, *Antônio Conselheiro e Canudos: Revisão Histórico*, 2d ed. (1978); CAROLE A. MYSCOFSKI, *When Men Walk Dry: Portuguese Messianism in Brazil* (1988).

CAROLE A. MYSCOFSKI

Spanish America

In Christian belief, the millennium will come when Christ, as He promised, returns and establishes His kingdom of peace and plenty on earth for 1,000 years. Based on the biblical books of Daniel and Revelation, the period is to be ushered in by the Apocalypse, a time of travail and devastation, and end with the Last Judgment, when Satan and his followers shall be forever vanquished. In popular thought, the term is associated with the inauguration of an ideal period, perhaps the return of an imagined golden age of harmony, happiness, and prosperity among all peoples. Many cultures harbor this general belief in messianic movements or millenarianism, with or without the return of their own particular hero.

Such millennial beliefs tend to permeate the ways in which many people understand and practice their daily lives; occasionally, but in no predictable patterns, they can mobilize groups, even masses, for social actions called messianic or millenarian movements. The origins, nature, and outcomes of these disturbances (the state labels them "rebellions," although many millenarians claim to have no quarrel with the government) provoke debate. Most seem to have occurred during periods of social crisis or moral breakdown, but religious belief also can spark movements on its own. Each appears to be based on local concerns and to attract people from all social configurations and classes. Most culminate in a bloodbath, the faithful suppressed by the regime at great cost in men, matériel, and reputation. Nevertheless, Latin Americans continue to yearn for a sanctified and idealized world, and rally around their self-styled prophets for relief. Their leaders, often viewed as messiahs, have received much attention, both in their own times and among more recent scholars. Their charisma derives from their followers, who decide how close the leader is to God and when he or she deserves the title of *santo*. Often the followers are divided, and in the debate that follows, millenarian assemblies may splinter or collapse. People join millenarian groups for reasons other than religious belief; they can include merchants hoping to sell their wares and politicians looking for adherents. Bandits, too, seem to have an affinity for millenarian activities, perhaps because regimes are so quick to label them both "outlaws"—that is, outcasts from society.

Strains of millenarian thought were evident in Latin America prior to the European conquest, have been a vital force in numerous social movements, and continue today. The Aztecs awaited the return of QUETZALCOATL, and the Incas anticipated the restoration of VIRACOCHA, their Creator God. Even the conquistadores came to the New World driven by a millenarian impulse embedded in their heritage, and the promised return of great Christian kings such as San Sebastián and Charlemagne are still awaited with great anticipation by many Latin Americans.

In the aftermath of the Conquest, messianic movements began to appear that are preserved in scholarly works, movies, novels, songs, poetry, comic books, oral traditions, and lore. Just before his execution at the hands of the Spaniards, the God/ruler of the Incas, ATAHUALPA, assured that his father, the sun, would resurrect and return him to his earthly kingdom. According to Spanish accounts, thousands of Indians living in Huamanga, Peru, in the 1560s participated in the Taki Onqoy (dancing sickness), believing that an alliance of gods throughout the Inca empire would defeat the Spanish God and banish the colonizers. The movement manifested itself through "demonic possession," whereby Indians began singing and dancing uncontrollably, renounced their belief in Christianity and obedience to Spanish authority, and reembraced their ancestral gods. Colonial religious authorities in the area launched a thorough anti-idolatry campaign to suppress the movement. Another confrontation occurred among Tzeltal-speaking natives in Chiapas, Mexico, who in 1712 received through their prophets admonitions and guidance from the Virgin Mary that ignited and sustained an armed struggle to oust the colonial presence and to usher in the return of an idealized pre-Hispanic glory. In southern Colombia, the Páez enthusiastically followed the preachings of their new spiritual leader, Undachi.

During much of the second half of the nineteenth century, the Maya in Yucatán worshiped a speaking cross that they believed would defend their homeland against the encroachments of outsiders. And northern Arawaks, who lived in Venezuela, Brazil, and Colombia, followed Venancio Kamiko in messianic-style protest. In the 1890s, at Tomochic in Mexico's Sierra Madre Occidental, followers of a teenage girl named Teresa URREA, whom they declared a *santa*, valiantly defied the bayonets of Porfirio Díaz's dictatorship for the right to practice their religion. More recently, messianism has fueled Jamaica's Rastafarian fervor.

Today the millenarian impulse in Latin America remains strong, with strains in all sorts of religious ideology and practices from LIBERATION THEOLOGY to evangelicalism to *costumbrismo* (traditional native belief). It is embedded in a variety of current social movements, such as that of the Zapatistas, which erupted in CHIAPAS, in southern Mexico, on 1 January 1994, and is bound to appear even more forcefully in many more to come.

EUCLIDES DA CUNHA, *Rebellion in the Backlands,* translated by Samuel Putnam (1944); NELSON REED, *The Caste War of Yucatán* (1964); HERIBERTO FRIAS, *Tomochic* (1968); VICTORIA REIFLER BRICKER, *The Indian Christ, the Indian King: The Historical Substrate of Maya Myth and Ritual* (1981); MARIO VARGAS LLOSA, *Guerra al fin del mundo,* 7th ed. (1984); TODD A. DIACRON, *Millenarian Vision, Capitalist Reality: Brazil's Contestado Revolution, 1912–1916* (1991); KEVIN MARLIN GOZNER, *Soldiers of the Virgin: The Moral Economy of a Colonial Maya Rebellion* (1992); ROBERT M. LEVINE, *Vale of Tears: Revisiting the Canudos Massacre in Northwestern Brazil, 1893–1897* (1992); PAUL J. VANDERWOOD, " 'None but the Justice of God': Tomochich, 1891–1892," in *Patterns of Contention in Mexican History,* edited by Jaime E. Rodríguez O. (1992); STEVEN J. STERN, *Peru's Indian Peoples and the Challenge of Spanish Conquest: Huamanga to 1640,* 2d ed. (1993); PAUL J. VANDERWOOD, "Using the Present to Study the Past: Religious Movements in Mexico and Uganda a Century Apart," in *Mexican Studies/Estudios Mexicanos* 10 (Winter 1994): 99–134.

PAUL J. VANDERWOOD

MESTA, Spanish sheep owners guild. Chartered by Alfonso X in 1273, the *Mesta* was granted important pastoral privileges and protection by the Castilian crown in exchange for financial contributions. It represented the interests of migratory sheepowners, whose flocks moved seasonally between northern and southern parts of Spain in search of pasture. In 1500 the organization came under the control of a royal council, thus giving the crown monopoly control over the WOOL, and in 1501 the *Mesta* received the right to use in perpetuity land it had once leased for a low rent. It was a source of increasing income for FERDINAND II (1452–1516) and ISABELLA I (1451–1504), who extended the traditional tax on herds to a tax on each sheep in the pasture. Frequently the source of hostile pasture disputes, the *Mesta's* privileges came under attack in the eighteenth century and were abolished during the reign of CHARLES III in 1780, when his minister CAMPOMANES became president of the guild. The organization itself was finally destroyed by the liberals in 1836.

In Latin America, a similar institution took root and expanded in New Spain and enabled Spanish authorities some control over pastoral activities. Unlike Spain, the New World adaptation of the institution was designed to benefit all stockmen, not just members of a sheep-raising guild. Liberal opposition brought an end to it in 1812. Although the Spanish crown provided that the Mesta be established elsewhere in Spanish America, in other parts local *cabildos* managed grazing and pastoral affairs.

JULIUS KLEIN, *The Mesta: A Study in Spanish Economic History* (1920); WILLIAM H. DUSENBERRY, *The Mexican Mesta* (1963); NINA MIKUN, *La Mesta au XVIII siècle: Étude d'histoire sociale et économique de l'Espagne au XVIII siècle* (1983); JEAN PAUL LE FLEM, "El Valle de Alcudia en el siglo XVIII," in *Congreso de Historia Rural: Siglo XV al XIX* (1984).

SUZANNE HILES BURKHOLDER